THE FACTS ON FILE
COMPANION TO

AMERICAN DRAMA

Second Edition

EDITED BY JACKSON R. BRYER AND MARY C. HARTIG

Facts On File

An imprint of Infobase Publishing

The Facts On File Companion to American Drama, Second Edition

Copyright © 2010, 2004 by Jackson R. Bryer and Mary C. Hartig

Facts On File, Inc.
An imprint of Infobase Publishing
132 West 31st Street
New York NY 10001

Library of Congress Cataloging-in-Publication Data
The Facts on File companion to American drama / edited by Jackson R. Bryer and Mary C. Hartig.—2nd ed.
    p. cm.
  Includes bibliographical references and index.
  ISBN 978-0-8160-7748-9 (alk. paper)
  1. American drama—Encyclopedias. 2. Dramatists, American—Biography—Encyclopedias. I. Bryer, Jackson R.
II. Hartig, Mary C. III. Facts on File, Inc. IV. Title: Companion to American drama.
  PS330.F33 2010
  812.009'03—dc22   2009021138

Facts On File books are available at special discounts when purchased in bulk quantities for businesses, associations, institutions, or sales promotions. Please call our Special Sales Department in New York at (212) 967-8800 or (800) 322-8755.

You can find Facts On File on the World Wide Web at http://www.factsonfile.com

Text design by James Scotto-Lavino
Composition by Hermitage Publishing Services
Cover printed by Sheridan Books, Ann Arbor, Mich.
Book printed and bound by Sheridan Books, Ann Arbor, Mich.
Date printed: April 2010
Printed in the United States of America

10 9 8 7 6 5 4 3 2 1

This book is printed on acid-free paper.

CONTENTS

PREFACE TO THE SECOND EDITION

Since the publication of the first edition of the *Companion to American Drama,* we have seen the passing of, among other playwrights, three major American dramatists, Arthur Miller, Wendy Wasserstein, and August Wilson, as well as the emergence of new voices in American theater. We have seen American dramatic movements continue to evolve, in some cases, away from movement-specific themes. We have seen established playwrights add to their output and younger playwrights become established. We have seen thematic trends emerge as many playwrights responded to 9/11 and to the consequent political and military realities. These changes in American dramatic literature are reflected in this new edition.

Among the entries new to this edition are three plays that complete August Wilson's "Century Cycle"; *Gem of the Ocean* (2003) and *Radio Golf* (2005) were Wilson's last two plays, the latter premiering at Yale Rep just five months before his death at 60 from cancer. We have also added an entry on his earlier play *Jitney* (1982; revised 1996), which becomes more significant now that the 20th-century cycle is complete. Other new play entries include recent Pulitzer winners *Anna in the Tropics* (2003), *I Am My Own Wife* (2003), *Doubt* (2004), *Rabbit Hole* (2006), *August: Osage County* (2007), and *Ruined* (2008). We have also added, for the sake of completeness, three Pulitzer winners that we omitted last time, *Both Your Houses* (1933), *The Old Maid* (1935), and *Look Homeward, Angel* (1957). In addition, we have included

recent New York Drama Critics' Circle Award winners *Take Me Out* (2002) and *Intimate Apparel* (2003), as well as Obie winners *Small Tragedy* (2003) and *The Intelligent Design of Jenny Chow* (2003). New plays by established playwrights, apart from Wilson, include a farce by David Mamet (*Romance* [2005]) and Wasserstein's final play (*Third* [2005]). Other new play entries are Christopher Shinn's *Dying City* (2006) and Dael Orlandersmith's *Yellowman* (2002), both of which were selected for the *Best Plays* volumes of their years (as is true of many of the aforementioned prizewinners as well).

In this revision are entries on 12 additional playwrights, the significance of whose contribution to American theater has become clearer in the years since the first edition of the *Companion.* These include young playwrights, such as Sarah Ruhl, Christopher Shinn, and Julia Cho, as well as those who have been at work longer but whose more recent plays have brought them greater recognition, such as David Lindsay-Abaire, Stephen Adly Guirgis, Lynn Nottage, Theresa Rebeck, and Craig Wright, among others.

We have, then, supplemented the comprehensive history laid out in the first edition by bringing the reader up to date. Furthermore, we have corrected inadvertent errors and have edited some existing entries for greater clarity or conciseness. The result is a portrait of our country's ever-evolving drama, from the Revolutionary period through 2010.

Kensington, Maryland

INTRODUCTION

American drama has often been regarded as the poor stepchild in the family of American literature, with fiction and poetry receiving more attention and kinder treatment. In her important study, *American Drama: The Bastard Art,* Susan Harris Smith cites a truly remarkable series of critical pronouncements, ranging from playwright Dion Boucicault's 1890 declaration that "there is not, and there never has been, a literary institution, which could be called the American drama" (641), critic and anthologist John Gassner's 1952 assertion that "the literary element was never the strong point of American playwriting" (84), and critic and playwright Eric Bentley's 1954 statement, "[T]here is no American drama" (413), down to director and critic Robert Brustein's provocatively titled 1959 essay, "Why American Plays Are Not Literature," and scholar Morris Freedman's 1971 dismissal of American drama as simply a form of "public entertainment" (1).

Virtually from its inception, American drama has been embattled. What is equally true, however, is that as we write this, there are more than 200 professional theater companies producing plays, many of which are American, in New York City, while the number in Chicago and Washington, D.C., is more than 70 in each city. In fact, pretty much any city of any size in the United States has at least one and often more than one thriving regional theater presenting a full season of plays, many of them American. Similarly, college, university, and community theaters across the country frequently choose their repertories from the Amer-

ican canon. Our drama is also a major export around the world; the works of Tennessee Williams, Arthur Miller, Edward Albee, Eugene O'Neill, and Thornton Wilder are extremely popular overseas—with Miller's reputation in England and Wilder's in Germany and Austria being particularly high. More recent American dramatists like August Wilson, Sam Shepard, David Mamet, Wendy Wasserstein, Neil Simon, and John Guare also are well known and frequently produced overseas. English critic C. W. E. Bigsby speaks for many readers and theatergoers around the world when he maintains that "America has produced some of the very finest drama of the 20th century" ("Why American Drama Is Literature" [11]).

Another way of measuring the popularity and impact of American drama is to look at the number of copies of American plays sold annually. According to publishers' estimates, 200,000 copies of *Death of a Salesman* are sold in a year; 150,000 of *The Crucible;* 75,000 of *The Glass Menagerie;* and 20,000 of *Long Day's Journey into Night*—and these figures do not even include sales of the acting editions of these plays. Clearly, American drama is flourishing; no country in the world has more established and emerging playwrights writing and having their plays produced.

Despite all this activity and the popularity of American plays, students and audiences remain largely unaware of American drama "before O'Neill"; many college courses that purport to be surveys of the subject begin with O'Neill and thus effectively obliterate almost

150 years of American dramatic history. This *Companion* attempts to redress that imbalance and to provide a perspective and sense of history by presenting entries on many playwrights and plays before 1920. While some of these earlier plays may be of uncertain literary and theatrical value, all are part of the story of American drama and are stepping stones to the undeniably greater works that come after them. Our criterion for inclusion has not been an evaluation of America's "best" plays and playwrights; outside of a few obvious choices, that would be a controversial process (this fact is yet further testimony to the richness and diversity of our native drama). Rather, we have included the figures and works that we felt were important, interpreting "important" in as broad a way as possible.

Looking back over the history of American drama, one finds that a number of the reasons for its precarious position in literary studies can be seen right at the beginning. Because some of the first colonizers of this country were members of religious sects fleeing persecution in Europe, there was considerable initial opposition to drama and theater on religious grounds. In 1709, the Governor's Council of New York passed a law forbidding "play-acting and prize-fighting"; in 1750, the Legislature and Council of Boston outlawed stage plays, which, it felt, tended "to increase immorality, impiety and a contempt for religion"; and a 1779 Pennsylvania act forbade all theater performances. During the American Revolution, the Continental Congress prohibited the "exhibition of shews, plays, and other expensive diversions and entertainments" (Meserve 6–7).

Thus, it was established early in the history of drama in America that there was something potentially harmful, dangerous, and possibly even subversive about stage plays; paradoxically, there was also the implication that theater was an inappropriately frivolous art form during times of national crises. Over the years, American drama has been caught between these seemingly contradictory attitudes—that theater is either threatening and immoral or too lightweight—absorbing blows from both sides. Examples of drama being censored or running afoul of the law abound. To cite just three from recent times: In 1993, a production of Terrence McNally's *Lips Together, Teeth Apart* was halted by civic officials in Cobb County, Georgia, because it was thought to promote a homosexual lifestyle (they apparently hadn't read the play). McNally's later play, *Corpus Christi,* was picketed by Catholic organizations at its 1999 New York opening because of its depiction of a group of gay men rehearsing a play about the life of Jesus Christ. In 1963, the advisory board of journalists who had the final say on the awarding of the Pulitzer Prize for drama overruled their own drama jury and withheld the honor from Edward Albee's *Who's Afraid of Virginia Woolf?* because, as one journalist explained, it was "a filthy play" (quoted in Gussow 189). Of course, it is a badge of honor that drama has been regarded for so long as powerful enough to be worthy of this kind of attention.

A second factor in the difficulties faced by American drama was also apparent in its beginnings. Partially because of the lack of a copyright law protecting playwrights and partially because the primarily middle-class individuals who came to the colonies were not particularly interested in theater, there were very few original American plays written. Aside from occasional and ephemeral plays written to commemorate specific occasions or to make political statements, most of what was performed through the 17th and 18th centuries in the New World were English plays—with Shakespeare especially popular. It is therefore not surprising that the first two notable American plays were highly derivative. Thomas Godfrey's *The Prince of Parthia* (published in 1765 and presented in 1767), the first professionally produced play written by an American, is a pastiche of plot ideas and characters lifted from Shakespeare. Royall Tyler's much more successful and influential *The Contrast* (1787), the first professionally produced American comedy and the first American play on an American subject, was similarly quite dependent on the English Restoration comedies Tyler saw in New York in the weeks before he wrote it. This reliance on English and European models—Smith calls it "slavish Anglophilia" (3)—has been yet another handicap American dramatic literature has had to overcome. It took many years, perhaps into the 20th century, for our playwrights to develop a distinctive national voice, uninflected by the culture of Great Britain.

In the 19th century, not very many American plays or playwrights achieved literary distinction, but American drama advanced well beyond its beginnings. Before one dismisses this period as not worthy of scrutiny, as is often the case, it is worth remembering that, in Great Britain, between Richard Brinsley Sheridan in the 18th century and George Bernard Shaw in the early 20th century, there is little of note in dramatic literature. It is not legitimate to compare American drama of this period to 20th-century American drama. What is far more appropriate is to look at the dramatic literature produced in this country during the 19th century and compare it to that written in Great Britain during the same span of years. By this standard, American drama fares quite well.

What we discover is that *The Prince of Parthia* and *The Contrast,* whatever their merits and degree of originality, stand as quite useful points of origin for two distinct strands of American drama. The first of these is romantic tragedy. Some of the best plays of the pre–Civil War period were done in this mode, often in verse and with Shakespeare again the model in genre but decreasingly so with respect to subject matter. While the poets and fiction writers of the period—Nathaniel Hawthorne, Edgar Allan Poe, James Fenimore Cooper, Ralph Waldo Emerson, Henry David Thoreau, Henry Wadsworth Longfellow, and Walt Whitman, to name just the most prominent—tended to write about their own country, albeit often in very romantic and heroic terms, poetic dramatists frequently relied on European settings. John Howard Payne (*Brutus; or, the Fall of Tarquin* [1818]), Robert Montgomery Bird (*The Broker of Bogota* [1834]), and George Henry Boker (*Francesca da Rimini* [1855]) set their plays in exotic locales, while James Nelson Barker (*Superstition* [1824]) and John Augustus Stone (*Metamora* [1829]) used American settings. *Superstition* and *Francesca da Rimini,* especially, present complex and sympathetic characters and situations and deserve recognition as substantial achievements.

If *The Prince of Parthia* led to more sophisticated plays in the romantic, poetic tragedy mode, *The Contrast* prefigured a developing tradition of social comedy. While Tyler's work was essentially an imitation of English Restoration drama, his one innovation was the comically naive Yankee character of Jonathan, the simple man from the "sticks" totally baffled by the sophistication of city life but also a "natural" man among poseurs. This prototypical American comic figure, present in such 20th-century American personalities as Will Rogers and Andy Griffith, not only spawned many subsequent plays with "Jonathan characters" but also inspired the creation of two other native types in drama, the Negro and the Indian. One or more of these types appeared in many social comedies and social dramas before 1865. All three are present in *The Octoroon* (1859), a melodrama by transplanted Irish dramatist Dion Boucicault, which deals with the love of a southern aristocrat for an octoroon slave. Two, the Yankee and the Negro, appear in Anna Cora Mowatt Ritchie's *Fashion* (1845), which is the best of the pre–Civil War American social comedies because, as Arthur Hobson Quinn observes, it is "that rare thing, a social satire based on real knowledge of the life it depicts, . . . without bitterness, without nastiness, and without affectation" (*American Drama from the Beginning* 312).

The post–Civil War period in American drama is closely related to the same period in American fiction in that both are characterized by an emphasis on local color and realism. Alongside such local-color fiction writers as Sarah Orne Jewett (New England), George Washington Cable (the South), Edward Eggleston (the Midwest), and Bret Harte (the West) are playwrights Denman Thompson (New England; *The Old Homestead* [1886]), Bronson Howard (the South; *Shenandoah* [1888]), and Augustin Daly (the West; *Horizon* [1871]).

Concurrent with these geographically specific works were a series of plays that gradually moved American drama in the direction of greater stage realism. Although many of these were melodramas, almost all of them made efforts toward authenticity in settings, characters, and situations. Among the first was Augustin Daly's classic melodrama *Under the Gaslight* (1867); with its sympathetic portrait of a one-armed Civil War veteran and accurate New York settings, it was, despite its preposterous plot, a significant early attempt at realism. So too were Steele MacKaye's *Hazel Kirke* (1880), William Gillette's *Secret*

Service (1895), and William Dean Howells's *The Unexpected Guests* (1893). Interestingly, Howells is the only major American fiction writer of the 19th century who also wrote successfully for the stage; many tried, most notably Henry James and Mark Twain, but failed.

Among the realist playwrights of the last half of the 19th century in America, James A. Herne stands alone as the key figure of this important movement in American drama. Herne was a close friend of such major American realists in fiction as Howells, Stephen Crane, and Hamlin Garland, and he was also acquainted with the advances toward greater realism in world drama made during the last quarter of the century. His article "Art for Truth's Sake in the Drama" (1897) and his play *Margaret Fleming* (1890) brought realism in American drama up to the level it had achieved in fiction and brought American playwriting an important step closer to the level of Henrik Ibsen, August Strindberg, and other innovators from around the world. As Gary A. Richardson has noted, *Margaret Fleming* presented "demonstrably real characters in an emotionally charged but nonmelodramatic action" and focused on an "important issue"—"the dominant patriarchal social and moral codes" (192). The hostile reception the play received from audiences and many critics simply indicated that it was ahead of its time, just as Norwegian audiences had not been ready for Ibsen's *Ghosts* two years earlier. Nevertheless, it is no exaggeration to say that much of serious American drama of the 20th century was foreshadowed and enabled by Herne and *Margaret Fleming*.

Parallel to the rise of realism in American drama was the continued development of social comedy. Bronson Howard (*Saratoga* [1870]), William Dean Howells (in a series of one-act plays about the Roberts and Campbell families [1883–93]), and Clyde Fitch (*The Girl with the Green Eyes* [1902] and *The Truth* [1906]) all advanced the form with witty plays about substantive issues. Just as Herne's *Margaret Fleming* represents the apotheosis of realist drama of the period, so too does Langdon Mitchell's *The New York Idea* (1906) mark the high point of social comedy. Like Herne's play, Mitchell's deals with marriage; in both instances, a marriage that nearly dissolves sur-

vives in the end, but without any assurances that there will be no further problems. Also, as in the case of *Margaret Fleming,* the major advances presented in *The New York Idea* are better (here, wittier) dialogue and more interesting characters facing more complex and challenging situations. What characterizes Mitchell's play, according to Arthur Hobson Quinn, are "rich invention," "consummate theatrical skill," and "a social knowledge so secure that it dares to go to the edge of farce or of the sentimental, knowing it can return at any moment" (*American Drama from the Civil War* 67).

As American drama entered the 20th century, its two major strands—serious social and realistic drama and social comedy—had come a long way from *The Prince of Parthia* and *The Contrast,* or even from *Under the Gaslight* and *Fashion.* The early years of the new century saw Rachel Crothers's *He and She* (1911), a witty and incisive play about the role of women in American society, and Edward Sheldon's more serious realistic dramas about such social issues as racism (*The Nigger* [1909]), poverty (*Salvation Nell* [1908]), and, in his best play, *The Boss* (1911), business and labor conditions and the position of the immigrant. Sheldon and his works are important links between pre-O'Neill American drama and the drama between the world wars, because, while most of his important plays predate 1920, he lived until 1946, knew O'Neill, and even collaborated on plays with Sidney Howard and Charles MacArthur in the 1920s.

It is easy to assume that Eugene O'Neill's emergence in the second decade of the 20th century as an imaginative, innovative, and serious investigator of profound human questions through the medium of theater was an unexplainable phenomenon. Actually, O'Neill came along at exactly the time when American drama was prepared to produce its most important playwright. As has been discussed, American drama had developed from a melodramatic and frivolous imitation of English and continental theater into an art form that, in both its serious and comic manifestations, sought to grapple with consequential matters. Beyond that, the first decade of the century introduced American audiences to the plays and playwrights who were revolutionizing drama in other parts of the world. Not only did O'Neill himself learn a great deal from seeing Ibsen's works and those of the great Irish playwrights performed, but also American theatergoers were gradually and gently familiarized with revolutionary new theatrical methods and daring subject matter. Because, in many instances, these plays were produced in the small art theaters that had arisen around the country for subscription audiences eager to see them, commercial risks were minimized as well.

Also paving the way for O'Neill were developments in science and in politics during the last half of the 19th century that made it obligatory that playwrights write about characters who looked like, talked like, and had the same problems as the members of the audience (rather than kings and queens and exotic figures from history). The political upheavals in Europe and, later, in Russia, produced a more egalitarian society in which all segments now felt that they could be represented on stage, and the scientific theories of Charles Darwin, Carl Jung, and Sigmund Freud meant that dramatists no longer could satisfy audiences with superficial characters but had to be aware of what lay underneath and had to develop theatrical devices to reveal this. The time was ripe for a playwright who could provide this type of drama.

O'Neill brought to the assignment his own background as the son of James O'Neill, one of the country's leading actors of his day. On the one hand, this gave him an innate sense of the theater, having literally been nursed backstage, but, on the other, it instilled in him a fierce determination to innovate and to go beyond the melodramatic and highly commercial theater of his father. The result was that he often wrote very personal plays, full of his own agonies about human existence in a world where he felt himself to be an outsider, that nonetheless were frequently melodramatic and reached too far in their experimentalism. Nurtured by the little theater movement, specifically the Provincetown Players (first on Cape Cod and then in New York), he was able to develop his craft through a series of realistic one-act plays, until, in 1920, he burst upon the Broadway scene with his first full-length work, *Beyond the Horizon.* The American theater was never the same thereafter; through a dazzling series of dramatic experiments, each one slightly different from the last and just about half of which were commercial failures, O'Neill dominated the American theater for the next 13 years. Between 1920 and 1933, 18 different full-length O'Neill plays opened in New York. Illness and depression about a world on the brink of war caused him to stop writing and to halt productions of any of his new plays in the late 1930s. After he died in 1955, his widow released them all, and his career had a glorious renaissance with productions and revivals of the works that many regard as his greatest—*Long Day's Journey into Night, The Iceman Cometh, A Moon for the Misbegotten,* and *A Touch of the Poet.* O'Neill remains the only American playwright to receive the Nobel Prize for literature; it stands as an appropriate recognition of his impact not only on American drama but also on world drama.

O'Neill's work was a major influence on his contemporaries. His utilization of German expressionism in *The Emperor Jones* (1920) and *The Hairy Ape* (1922) undoubtedly stimulated the use of that theatrical device in Elmer Rice's *The Adding Machine* (1923), George S. Kaufman and Marc Connelly's *Beggar on Horseback* (1924), and John Howard Lawson's *Processional* (1925). Likewise, O'Neill's rejection of happy endings and willingness to confront the sadness and unanswerable questions of life certainly created an environment for such plays as Maxwell Anderson and Laurence Stallings's unflinchingly honest portrayal of men at war, *What Price Glory?* (1924); Sidney Howard's *They Knew What They Wanted* (1924), an unsentimental view of a mail-order bride and the two men to whom she is attracted; Elmer Rice's *Street Scene* (1929), a gritty look at life in a tenement; and *The Verge* (1921), Susan Glaspell's unsparing portrait of a woman on the edge of insanity.

While few of O'Neill's plays dealt overtly with social problems of the day, dramatists who did so in his time were now, like O'Neill, required to delve more deeply into the psyches of their characters. Sidney Howard, in *The Silver Cord* (1926), presented a Freudian study of a mother's attempts to control her sons' lives; Owen Davis, in *Icebound* (1923), depicted greed in a New England family; and Paul Green, in *In Abraham's Bosom* (1926), looked at racism and bigotry in the South.

As the Great Depression enveloped the country, drama responded in one of two ways: It confronted the situation graphically and directly, or it escaped from it through witty and romantic satires and comedies. Principal among the plays that met the crisis head-on were the works of Clifford Odets, who, in 1935, had four plays running simultaneously on Broadway. His two best dramas, *Waiting for Lefty* (1935), about taxi drivers preparing to strike, and *Awake and Sing!* (1935), about three generations of a New York Jewish family, endure because they not only are vivid depictions of the times but also transcend them through believable characters and expressive dialogue. Less durable but nonetheless powerful pictures of depression-era America were Sidney Kingsley's *Dead End* (1935), which portrayed life in the New York slums, and *Men in White* (1933), Kingsley's enactment of the personal and professional pressures on a young doctor.

Typical of the more optimistic approach to the stresses of the day were Robert E. Sherwood's *The Petrified Forest* (1935), in which a failed and embittered writer sacrifices his life so that a young woman can realize her dreams; William Saroyan's *The Time of Your Life* (1939), in which a waterfront saloon serves as a haven from life's disappointments and ugliness; and George S. Kaufman and Moss Hart's *You Can't Take It with You* (1936), in which the innocent and fun-loving Vanderhof family wins over the driven and straight-laced Kirbys.

Social comedy, that staple of the American drama tradition, was also prominent during this period, perhaps because it too provided an escape from the unpleasantness of the times. It was present in the witty, sophisticated works of Philip Barry (*Holiday* [1928] and *The Philadelphia Story* [1939]) and S. N. Behrman (*Biography* [1932]). Poetic drama and the attempt to write a modern version of classical tragedy—which O'Neill attempted in *Mourning Becomes Electra* (1931)—were represented also by Maxwell Anderson's *Winterset* (1935), a play about the aftermath of the famous Sacco-Vanzetti trial. Anderson wrote several dramas in verse, some with historical settings (*Valley Forge* [1934] and *Mary of Scotland* [1933]) and some set in contemporary times (*Key*

Largo [1939] and *High Tor* [1937]). Many of these plays deal with the struggle between individual freedom and the need for some government control.

Another venerable strand of the American dramatic tapestry, social drama, was perhaps best represented during the 1930s by one of the two significant female playwrights this country produced in the first half of the century, Lillian Hellman (Susan Glaspell was the other). In *The Children's Hour* (1934) and *The Little Foxes* (1939), Hellman wrote boldly and scathingly about such issues as the destructive effects of public opinion, acquisitive greed, the changing role of women, and the need for social activism.

As the Second World War loomed and then became a reality, American dramatists reacted in different ways, as they had to the depression. Robert E. Sherwood, in *Idiot's Delight* (1936), decried the insanity and irrationality of war, while at the height of the conflict, Thornton Wilder, in *The Skin of Our Teeth* (1942), assured us that, despite all its previous travails and the present crisis, humankind had survived and would continue to do so. Wilder's play, like his earlier *Our Town* (1938), was also noteworthy for its experimental staging; reacting against what he saw as the theater's excessive reliance on superficial realism, he stripped the stage of scenery and violated stage convention by having his characters address the audience directly. These innovations, for which Wilder drew upon his extensive knowledge of European theater, were new to American drama and were to be adapted by many American playwrights of the second half of the century. *Our Town*, of course, became probably the most frequently performed American play; it is estimated that at least one performance of it—and often more than one—is taking place somewhere in the world every day of the year.

American plays written during or just after the war, as noted above, tended to take the same two attitudes toward crisis as had plays during the depression. Lillian Hellman's *Watch on the Rhine* (1941), William W. Haines's *Command Decision* (1945), and Robert E. Sherwood's *There Shall Be No Night* (1940) were serious and patriotic depictions of heroes confronted by an evil totalitarian enemy, while Joshua Logan and Thomas Heggen's *Mr. Roberts* (1948) and John Patrick's *The Hasty Heart* (1945) were more comic and more sentimental, respectively, in their viewpoints on the conflict.

The postwar years saw the emergence of two of the greatest playwrights America has produced, Arthur Miller and Tennessee Williams. Miller fits firmly into the tradition of American social drama, while Williams can easily be situated in the line of dramatists primarily interested in psychological realism. In plays like *All My Sons* (1947), *Death of a Salesman* (1949), *The Crucible* (1953), and *A View from the Bridge* (1956), Miller's major concern was with the individual's relationship to his community (usually an urban one) and with his determination to find his rightful place in it and to have others confirm that judgment. Williams, above all, was a poet of the theater; although he did not write in verse, his dialogue frequently has such characteristics of poetry as metaphor and other figurative language. Setting most of his work in his native South, he depicted the clash between the romantic, fragile, and sensitive dreamers of the world and its practical, down-to-earth, and often cruel realists in plays such as *The Glass Menagerie* (1945), *A Streetcar Named Desire* (1947), *Summer and Smoke* (1948), *Camino Real* (1953), *Cat on a Hot Tin Roof* (1955), and *Orpheus Descending* (1957).

Williams's work certainly influenced William Inge, who had four Broadway successes in succession in the 1950s (*Come Back, Little Sheba* [1950], *Picnic* [1953], *Bus Stop* [1955], and *The Dark at the Top of the Stairs* [1957]); he wrote primarily about lonely people in his native Midwest for whom love seems to provide an answer. Miller's social drama, in turn, can be seen as related to the appearance for the first time of a significant African-American voice in American drama. In plays like Lorraine Hansberry's *A Raisin in the Sun* (1959), Louis Peterson's *Take a Giant Step* (1953), and Alice Childress's *Trouble in Mind* (1955), all written in the early years of the Civil Rights movement, the plight of black people in a racist society was depicted insightfully, compassionately, and even with occasional humor.

A nation emerging from war also needed lighter fare, and Mary Chase's *Harvey* (1944), Jerome Lawrence and Robert E. Lee's *Auntie Mame* (1956), John Patrick's *The Teahouse of the August Moon* (1953), and Garson Kanin's *Born Yesterday* (1946) provided it. The tradition of comedy truly thrived with the arrival, in the early 1960s, of its most important practitioner, Neil Simon. The most commercially successful American playwright in the history of our theater—and by some accounts the most commercially successful in the history of world theater—Simon dominated comic drama during the last 40 years of the century. While all of his plays had generous amounts of gags and humorous situations, many of his later works—especially *Brighton Beach Memoirs* (1983), *Biloxi Blues* (1985), *Broadway Bound* (1986), and *Lost in Yonkers* (1991)—also featured poignantly sympathetic characters.

The 1960s were another watershed decade in the history of American drama, comparable in many ways to the 1920s in that the factors that produced the theater of the 1960s were similar to those that had allowed for Eugene O'Neill. Once again, there had been an explosion of a new kind of drama in Europe, which was beginning to find its way to the United States; in this instance, it was the plays of Samuel Beckett, Eugene Ionesco, and Jean Genet and a movement dubbed the Theatre of the Absurd by critic Martin Esslin. The overriding theme of the movement, according to Esslin, was "its sense of the senselessness of the human condition and the inadequacy of the rational approach" to explain it (6). Paralleling the rise of the little theater movement in the first two decades of the century was the development, in New York, of Off-Broadway and Off-Off-Broadway theaters, smaller houses that were especially hospitable to new plays, and the concurrent burgeoning of the regional theater movement across the country. According to Matthew C. Roudané, between 1960 and 1970, "seventy-four new nonprofit professional theaters" were founded (3). And if O'Neill was the beneficiary of his era's more profound understanding of the human psyche as it had been revealed by science and psychology, the playwrights of the 1960s surely felt the impact of what Roudané calls "the most theatrical of the postwar decades"; as a result, their plays reflected "the strange cluster of values that inevitably contradicted themselves while confronting perceived outer injustices or differences" (15–16).

Just as O'Neill had been the principal figure to emerge from the confluence of factors in the 1920s, so too was Edward Albee the quintessential American playwright of the 1960s. As influenced by the works of Beckett and Ionesco as he was by those of Tennessee Williams and other American dramatists, Albee wrote bitingly funny but nonetheless savage indictments of the complacency of American life, first in one-act plays (*The Zoo Story* [1960], *The American Dream* [1960], and *The Death of Bessie Smith* [1960]) and then in full-length ones (*Who's Afraid of Virginia Woolf?* [1962], *A Delicate Balance* [1966], *All Over* [1971], and *Seascape* [1975]). In assessing Albee's contribution, C. W. E. Bigsby contends that he "has tackled issues of genuine metaphysical seriousness in a way that few American dramatists before him have claimed to do, and done so, for the most part, with a command of wit and controlled humour . . . and created a theatre which at its best is luminous with intelligence and power" (*Critical Introduction* 328).

The anger toward and criticism of American values found in Albee's plays resonated through the African-American community in the plays of Amiri Baraka (*Dutchman* [1964] and *The Slave* [1964]) and James Baldwin (*The Amen Corner* [1964] and *Blues for Mister Charlie* [1964]), while his absurdist satiric tone could be seen in the dramas of Arthur Kopit (*Oh Dad, Poor Dad* [1961] and *Indians* [1968]).

Albee's career was greatly assisted at its outset by the Off-Broadway movement; his one-act plays had all premiered there in 1960 and 1961. Similarly, many of the other playwrights who came to prominence in the 1960s owed their starts to Off-Broadway and Off-Off-Broadway theaters. While Albee went on to have his work done in Broadway houses and new plays by Miller and Williams and other American playwrights were done there as well, an entire new generation of dramatists came out of the much smaller New York venues. Because these houses could afford to take more risks than commercial theaters, the work they produced was often very experimental and diverse in subject matter. Typical of this generation was Sam Shepard, who, heavily influenced by the rock-and-roll and drug culture of his generation, produced serio-comic studies of family life and male-female relationships, set against a satiric examination of such

American myths as the West, Hollywood, patriotism, and celebrity, in, among many other plays, *The Tooth of Crime* (1972), *Curse of the Starving Class* (1976), *Buried Child* (1978), *Fool for Love* (1979), *True West* (1980), and *A Lie of the Mind* (1985). Shepard's cynical view of the shams of American life is also present in the work of David Mamet (*American Buffalo* [1975], *Glengarry Glen Ross* [1983], *Speed-the-Plow* [1989], and *Oleanna* [1992]), who also shares with Shepard an interest in the tenuous male-female relationship and with Albee an interest in language.

Among the playwrights who emerged directly from the Off-Off-Broadway movement were John Guare, whose first works were done at the Caffe Cino and whose later plays include *The House of Blue Leaves* (1971) and *Six Degrees of Separation* (1990), satiric critiques of America's fascination with celebrity, and Lanford Wilson, also first produced at the Caffe Cino, whose plays (*The Hot l Baltimore* [1973], *Talley's Folly* [1979], *5th of July* [1978], *Angels Fall* [1982], *Burn This* [1987], and *Book of Days* [1998]) emphasize the need for community, whether among groups of people or among individuals, in a baffling world.

As American drama diversified, one of the ways it manifested these changes was in the increase of women playwrights, many of whom can also trace their emergence directly to the small theater movement in New York or elsewhere in the country. Megan Terry (*Comings and Goings* [1966] and *Approaching Simone* [1970]) began her career in Seattle and developed her penchant for experimental theater at Off-Off-Broadway's Open Theater. Beth Henley's first depiction of eccentric southern characters, *Crimes of the Heart* (1981), premiered at Louisville's Actors Theatre, which also introduced Marsha Norman's *Getting Out* (1978). Henley went on to write such other important plays as *The Miss Firecracker Contest* (1980), *The Wake of Jamey Foster* (1982), and *Abundance* (1990); Norman is also the author of *'night, Mother* (1983), an unsettling study of a mother-daughter relationship that culminates in the daughter's suicide.

Like Albee, Tina Howe has acknowledged that her "heroes" are absurdists Beckett and Ionesco, and she too began her career Off-Broadway (Barlow 270). In plays like *Painting Churches* (1983), *Coastal Disturbances* (1986), and *Pride's Crossing* (1997), Howe has moved deftly through nonrealistic structures, often to celebrate independent women. The latter have also frequently been the subjects of the plays of Wendy Wasserstein, whose early works premiered Off-Broadway at Playwrights Horizons. Although her plays are considered comedies, Wasserstein had a serious concern for the evolving role of women in American life, an evolution that can be traced from her early portrait of a young woman trying to escape her parents' obsession to see her suitably married (*Isn't It Romantic* [1983]) through her story of Heidi's attempt to decide how to balance a career and romance (*The Heidi Chronicles* [1988]) and her accounts of professional women coping with romance and other distractions of modern life (*The Sisters Rosensweig* [1992] and *An American Daughter* [1997]) to her examination, in her final play, of the possibility that aging feminists may be as capable of stubborn bias as were the men of an earlier generation who once oppressed them (*Third* [2005]).

Another indication of the diversification of American drama is the proliferation of plays written by members of minority groups, including groups with previously little to no representation on stage. African-American drama has flourished, especially through the work of August Wilson, who may have been the best American playwright since Albee. Wilson began his career with the Penumbra Theater in St. Paul, but most of his best plays had extensive pre-Broadway runs in New Haven, Chicago, Washington, and elsewhere before coming to New York. His ambitious cycle, in which he devoted a play apiece to depicting African-American life in each decade of the 20th century, produced 10 richly poetic dramas that celebrate black people's history, not in terms of major events and figures but rather through ordinary people living their lives. Several of his plays, like *Fences* (1985), *The Piano Lesson* (1987), and *Radio Golf* (2005), pose the question of whether African Americans should embrace their past or try to go beyond it; as he remarked, "Without knowing your past, you don't know your present—and you certainly can't plot your future" (quoted in Bigsby, *Modern American Drama*, 293).

Wilson often acknowledged that his work was inspired by that of Ed Bullins, an African-American playwright whose plays, among them *Clara's Ole Man* (1965) and *The Taking of Miss Janie* (1975), were inspi-

rations for the more radical elements of the Civil Rights movement. Wilson was simply the most prominent of a group of African-American playwrights whose works, like his, found acceptance with audiences of all colors. They include Charles Fuller (*A Soldier's Play* [1981]), Ntozake Shange (*For Colored Girls* [1975]), Adrienne Kennedy (*Funnyhouse of a Negro* [1962] and *The Ohio State Murders* [1992]), George C. Wolfe (*The Colored Museum* [1986]), Pearl Cleage (*Flyin' West* [1992] and *Blues for an Alabama Sky* [1999]), and Suzan-Lori Parks (*Topdog/Underdog* [2001]). And just as August Wilson was influenced by the black playwrights who came before him, so too have playwrights like Dael Orlandersmith (*Yellowman* [2002]) and Lynn Nottage (*Intimate Apparel* [2003]) been influenced by the late playwright's poetic depictions of ordinary people.

David Henry Hwang (*M. Butterfly* [1988] and *Golden Child* [1996]) occupies the same prominent position in the ranks of Asian-American playwrights as Wilson does among African-American dramatists; others, such as Elizabeth Wong, Garrett Omata, Amy Hill, Julia Cho and Velina Hasu Houston, are gaining attention in this group, one that is relatively recent in American dramatic history. In Hispanic drama, another vibrant and rapidly expanding group also exists, with Luis Valdéz (*Zoot Suit* [1978]) and Maria Irene Fornés (*Fefu and Her Friends* [1977] and *The Conduct of Life* [1985]) perhaps the most noteworthy, but including also Cherríe Moraga, Eduardo Machado, Nilo Cruz, and Miguel Piñero. Cruz's *Anna in the Tropics* won the 2002 Pulitzer Prize, the first play by a Hispanic dramatist to receive that award.

As with the other minority groups mentioned, gay and lesbian drama has been present on American stages for quite some time; however, overt gay and lesbian drama seems both more abundant and of better quality in recent years. Early gay playwrights Tennessee Williams, William Inge, Lanford Wilson, and Robert Patrick could write only obliquely about the subject or include a gay character or two in a play, but, beginning with Mart Crowley's *The Boys in the Band* (1968), gay drama became more mainstream and accepted. Playwrights such as Harvey Fierstein (*Torch Song Trilogy* [1981]), Terrence McNally (*The Lisbon Traviata* [1989] and *Love! Valour! Compassion!* [1993]),

Tony Kushner (*Angels in America* [1990, 1992]), and Paula Vogel (*Baltimore Waltz* [1992] and *The Mineola Twins* [1996]) are all major contemporary playwrights whose works on gay themes achieved recognition and demonstrated added poignancy and urgency as the AIDS epidemic ravaged the gay community.

Perhaps the best way of discussing these writers, who have been arbitrarily labeled "minority playwrights" in the discussion above, is to hasten to add that it is a mistake to label them so simplistically. August Wilson's plays, while certainly focused on African-American lives, transcend race. Wendy Wasserstein, Tina Howe, and Marsha Norman, while often dealing with women and women's roles, go well beyond gender issues. To call the plays of Terrence McNally, Paula Vogel, or Richard Greenberg "gay plays" is to overlook what they have to tell us about ourselves, regardless of our sexual orientation. Grouping the work of these writers as we have is meant only to testify to the wide variety of communities within our society from which American drama now emerges, not to imply that this writing has limited appeal or significance.

It is undeniable, however, as American drama enters the second decade of the 21st century, that its most salient feature is its diversity—with respect both to the elements of our society from which it is coming and to the forms it takes. Comic satire of various kinds is alive and well, thanks to the talents of Christopher Durang, A. R. Gurney, David Ives, David Mamet, Bruce Norris, Rolin Jones, and David Rabe, among several others. Experimentation flourishes in the unconventional plays of Mac Wellman, Len Jenkin, Elizabeth LeCompte, and others, while solo performers like Holly Hughes, Anna Deavere Smith, and Karen Finley are exploring the relatively new field of performance art. And, of course, what is most exciting is the absolute certainty that playwrights both those included here and those not yet known to us will still be moving American drama in new and exciting directions as the century advances.

BIBLIOGRAPHY

Barlow, Judith E. "Tina Howe." In *Speaking on Stage: Interviews with Contemporary American Playwrights,* edited by Philip C. Kolin and Colby H. Kullman. Tuscaloosa: University of Alabama Press, 1996. 260–276.

Bentley, Eric. "The Drama: An Extinct Species?" *Partisan Review* 21 (1954): 411–417.

Bigsby, C. W. E. *A Critical Introduction to Twentieth-Century American Drama—Volume Two: Williams/Miller/Albee.* Cambridge, England: Cambridge University Press, 1984.

———. *Modern American Drama: 1945–1990.* Cambridge, England: Cambridge University Press, 1992.

———. "Why American Drama Is Literature." In *New Essays on American Drama,* edited by Gilbert Debusscher and Henry I. Schvey. Amsterdam: Rodopi, 1989. 3–12.

Boucicault, Dion. "The Future American Drama." *The Arena* 12 (1890): 641–652.

Brustein, Robert. "Why American Plays Are Not Literature." In *American Drama and Its Critics,* edited by Alan Downer. Chicago: University of Chicago Press, 1965. 245–255.

Esslin, Martin. *The Theatre of the Absurd.* Rev. ed. Garden City, N.Y.: Anchor Books, 1969.

Freedman, Morris. *American Drama in Social Context.* Carbondale: Southern Illinois University Press, 1971.

Gassner, John. "'There Is No American Drama.'" *Theatre Arts* 36, no. 9 (1952): 24–25, 84–86.

Gussow, Mel. *Edward Albee: A Singular Journey.* New York: Simon and Schuster, 1999.

Meserve, Walter J. *An Outline History of American Drama.* New York: Feedback Theatrebooks & Prospero Press, 1994.

Quinn, Arthur Hobson. *A History of American Drama from the Beginning to the Civil War.* 2d ed. New York: Appleton-Century-Crofts, 1951.

———. *A History of the American Drama from the Civil War to the Present Day.* Rev. ed. New York: Appleton-Century-Crofts, 1955.

Richardson, Gary A. *American Drama from the Colonial Period through World War I: A Critical History.* New York: Twayne, 1993.

Roudané, Matthew C. *American Drama since 1960: A Critical History.* New York: Twayne, 1996.

Smith, Susan Harris. *American Drama: The Bastard Art.* Cambridge, England: Cambridge University Press, 1997.

Kensington, Maryland
February 1, 2003
January 5, 2009

ABBOTT, GEORGE (1887–1995) George Abbott enjoyed an 80-year career as actor, director, producer, playwright, play doctor, and librettist. He grew up in southwestern New York. His father was mayor of Salamanca, New York, but became an alcoholic and lost the respect of Abbott's mother. The youngster developed a lifelong aversion to alcohol and tobacco, as well as to excessive familiarity and affection. At age 11, his family moved to post-frontier Cheyenne, Wyoming, where he was a poor student but an avid reader. After graduating from the University of Rochester, he studied playwriting at Harvard University under GEORGE PIERCE BAKER.

Remembered today primarily as a revered, if reserved, director, Abbott spent 12 years as an actor before starting to cowrite plays, later writing libretti for the hit musicals he directed. Abbott rarely initiated writing projects, preferring to collaborate or revise problematic drafts by others. For his first hit, *Broadway* (1926), Abbott reshaped an ill-formed play by Philip Dunning. This backstage story of showgirls, Prohibition gangsters, and murder in a nightclub abounded with now-dated 1920s slang. In *Coquette* (1927; cowritten with Ann Preston Bridgers), a wealthy young woman falls in love with a lower-class man, with tragic results. In the delightful THREE MEN ON A HORSE (1935), Abbott and Cecil Holm concocted a farce about a milquetoast husband with a knack for picking winning horses, who is exploited by dull-witted tinhorns. These early works reflect Abbott's attraction to stories involving questionable behavior (illicit drinking, out-of-wedlock pregnancy, bookmaking) and unpolished characters clashing with high society.

Between 1935 and 1940, Abbott directed five Richard Rodgers and Lorenz Hart musicals, serving as colibrettist for *On Your Toes* (1936) and librettist for *The Boys from Syracuse* (1938). He directed and produced the landmark *Pal Joey* (1940), whose antihero was a lowlife nightclub singer. In 1948, he wrote the book for the Frank Loesser musical comedy *Where's Charley?* Abbott's enduringly popular *Pajama Game* (1954), for which he was cowriter and director, launched the careers of producer Harold Prince, choreographer Bob Fosse, and songwriters Richard Adler and Jerry Ross. The musicals he cowrote and directed during this period continued his exploration of vices and other human foibles: parental alcoholism in *A Tree Grows in Brooklyn* (1951), the devil's temptress in *Damn Yankees* (1955), prostitution in *New Girl in Town* (1957) and *Tenderloin* (1960), and political corruption in the PULITZER PRIZE–winning *Fiorello!* (1959). Abbott's finest solo work is his candid, thoughtful autobiography *Mister Abbott* (1963). At age 92, he wrote a novel, *Tryout* (1979), set in a Broadway environment. He remained active until 1994 when, at age 106, he assisted in the Broadway revival of *Damn Yankees*.

BIBLIOGRAPHY

Abbott, George. *Mister Abbott*. New York: Random House, 1963.

Dunning, Philip, and George Abbott. *Broadway*. New York: George H. Doran, 1927.

Holm, John Cecil, and George Abbott. *Three Men on a Horse*. New York: Dramatists Play Service, 1935.

Smith, Betty, and George Abbott. *A Tree Grows in Brooklyn*. New York: Harper, 1951.

Gary Konas
University of Wisconsin–La Crosse

ABE LINCOLN IN ILLINOIS ROBERT E. SHERWOOD (1938)

Winner of the PULITZER PRIZE, *Abe Lincoln in Illinois* is a portrait of the 16th president of the United States before he took office. The play begins in the 1830s in the cabin of Mentor Graham, the schoolteacher with whom Lincoln, as a young "backwoodsman," discusses grammar and life; it ends in February of 1861 at the train station in Springfield, Illinois, where Lincoln departs for Washington, D.C., to assume the presidency as civil war looms two months hence.

SHERWOOD's play captures the complexity of Lincoln, who is a flawed hero, torn between action and inaction, society and solitude, even life and death. He is articulate and well liked, and he finds the sight of chained slaves "shocking," but he is also gloomy, unambitious, and unwilling to take a public stand against slavery when asked to do so by his law partner. In the early years, he can beat any man in a fight, but he uses his physical prowess—combined with jovial persuasion—to keep peace among others. He is elected to the state legislature, but—as another character observes—is there "for a year without accomplishing a blessed thing." His first love, Ann, dies of "brain sickness," and Abe, having attended her deathbed, wants only to "die and be with her again." Five years later, while practicing law in Springfield, Lincoln meets the socialite Mary Todd, who chooses him among her suitors to marry—much to the dismay of her sister, who declares Lincoln to be "lazy and shiftless." Indeed, Mary Todd's ambition for her fiancé causes him to call off the wedding at the last minute because he does not want to be "ridden and driven"

but "want[s] only to be left alone." After drifting alone for a couple of years, Lincoln experiences an epiphany when an old friend, headed west with his family and a free black companion, tells Lincoln that they will go to Canada or form a new country if his friend and people like him cannot remain free; this inspires Abe to take action for the preservation of the country—though it is years before he runs for public office.

Lincoln returns to Mary Todd and marries her. Years later, in 1858, Lincoln runs for the Senate against Stephen Douglas and loses, and in 1860 he is persuaded to run for the White House. Those of his party who want him to run are certain he is electable and equally certain he will do their bidding once in office (of course, history proves otherwise). He reluctantly leaves Springfield after winning the election; the Civil War is imminent, and there are death threats against him even before his inauguration. His parting words at Springfield's train station inspire admiration among his listeners.

Sherwood's "main source" for this episodic drama was "Carl Sandburg's *Abraham Lincoln: The Prairie Years* (1926). . . . with a lesser debt to works by William H. Herndon, Nathaniel Wright Stephenson, and Albert J. Beveridge, as well as Lincoln's own writings" (Adler 92).

BIBLIOGRAPHY

Adler, Thomas P. *Mirror on the Stage: The Pulitzer Plays as an Approach to American Drama*. West Lafayette, Ind.: Purdue University Press, 1987.

ACTORS STUDIO

In 1947, the Actors Studio was founded as a workshop for actors, directors, and playwrights, a haven where artists could experiment, free from the constraints of commercial theater. Actors Studio founders ELIA KAZAN, Cheryl Crawford, and Robert Lewis were alumni of the GROUP THEATRE, which had developed a realistic style of acting based on the techniques of Russian actor, director, and theorist Constantin Stanislavsky. This style of acting, simply called the "Method," resulted largely from the work of Lee Strasberg, another Group Theatre member, who joined the Actors Studio in 1949 and was its artistic director from 1951 until his death in 1982.

Lee Strasberg adapted the techniques of Stanislavsky, whose methods he had seen at work in the performances of the Moscow Art Theatre (of which Stanislavsky was cofounder in 1897) in New York and under whose disciples he had studied at the American Laboratory Theatre. Stanislavsky essentially believed that the actor's task was to represent life truthfully within the limitations of the stage. He believed this was achieved by drawing on those personal experiences that were equivalent to the character's experience, thus fusing actor and character into an emotionally vital performance.

Strasberg employed and built on Stanislavsky's theories and exercises—though there are ways in which the Strasberg Method and the Stanislavsky System are quite distinct. Method actors employ their "affective memory" to recreate emotion on stage. With the Method, an actor will use emotional—sometimes traumatic—events in his or her own life to convey the emotional life of the character. This is achieved through physical and psychological exercises. Instead of externally building character, the Method actor builds character from within. Lee Strasberg and the Actors Studio have influenced several generations of stage and film actors, including such acting legends as Marlon Brando, James Dean, Eli Wallach, Joanne Woodward, Geraldine Page, Robert De Niro, and Al Pacino.

The work of the Actors Studio brought greater realism and intensity to American theater. Cofounder and Method director Elia Kazan brought this intense and naturalistic style to the stage in the 1940s and the 1950s in his productions of works by ARTHUR MILLER (*DEATH OF A SALESMAN* [1949]) and TENNESSEE WILLIAMS (*A STREETCAR NAMED DESIRE* [1947], *CAT ON A HOT TIN ROOF* [1955], and *SWEET BIRD OF YOUTH* [1959]). Tennessee Williams's work was used more often in workshop than that of any other playwright. Other playwrights to develop works at the Actors Studio include EDWARD ALBEE and JAMES BALDWIN.

BIBLIOGRAPHY

Adams, Cindy Heller. *Lee Strasberg: The Imperfect Genius of the Actors Studio.* New York: Doubleday, 1980.

Hirsch, Foster. *A Method to Their Madness: The History of the Actors Studio.* Boulder, Colo.: Da Capo, 1986.

Strasberg, Lee. *A Dream of Passion: The Development of the Method.* New York: Little, Brown, 1987.

ADDING MACHINE, THE ELMER RICE (1923)

This satirical and expressionistic play by ELMER RICE was an indictment of—as Rice saw it—the conformity, the lack of imagination, and the philistinism of modern life in post–World War I America. EXPRESSIONISM, which is an attempt to interpret rather than to merely represent reality, was novel in American drama at the time, but some American playwrights, EUGENE O'NEILL, for example, in his play *The EMPEROR JONES* (1920), had begun to experiment with this form, which had originated in Germany, starting in about 1911, and flourished into the 1920s.

The play begins in the bedroom of Mr. and Mrs. Zero. Standing before the mirror, Mrs. Zero chatters nonstop throughout the scene, revealing her taste for sentimental movies and gossip and her distaste for Mr. Zero and her life as a housewife. In the next scene, Mr. Zero and his coworker, Daisy Diana Dorothea Devore, add up numbers. Through most of the scene, each, unheard by the other, expresses her or his own thoughts. Daisy contemplates killing herself; Zero contemplates killing his wife. While he considers remarriage, she considers marriage to him. He fantasizes about a promotion after 25 years of faithful service; she fantasizes about a long Hollywood kiss after a lifetime without love. When the whistle blows, Zero runs into his boss, who tells him he will be replaced by an adding machine, but he will get a month's severance pay.

When Mr. Zero returns home late to an irritated and nagging wife, she reminds him that they are expecting guests after dinner. Their guests are six couples named Mr. and Mrs. One, Mr. and Mrs. Two, and so on. All the men are dressed alike, as are all the women. They immediately form two gender-specific circles and discuss stereotypically gender-specific topics: The men tell off-color jokes, call women's suffrage "bunk," and blame bad business on strikes and "foreign agitators"; the women speak of dresses, someone's divorce, someone else's gallstones, and the laziness of men. As in the earlier scene in the office with Miss Devore, this one is a picture of noncommunication between the sexes and the absence of individuality, humanity, and intellectual freedom within them. Eventually the men become so agitated as they consider the foreigners and ethnic groups whom they blame for their problems that they shout, "hang 'em! lynch 'em! burn 'em!" and then rise (in a bit of heavy-handed irony) to sing "My country 'tis of thee/sweet land of liberty." Mr. Zero has remained silent throughout this scene and speaks only when the doorbell rings, revealing a policeman who has come to arrest Zero because, as Zero explains to his wife, he "killed the boss this afternoon."

What follows is Mr. Zero's trial, at which he makes a long speech, trying to justify his actions (he had just been fired after 25 years, he had never been late, he had never missed a day). In the midst of this harangue, he reveals his racism and his tendency to be influenced by others toward violence. When he appeals to the jurors to imagine if they were he, they interrupt his plea with a resounding "Guilty!"

After his offstage execution, Zero emerges from his grave—stiff, with his arms crossed over his chest. Another corpse, also that of a murderer, emerges from a neighboring grave and tells Zero the story of how he was corrupted by reading *Treasure Island,* ran away to have an adventure, and was brought back to his mother with whom he then lived a righteous life working as a proofreader and frequently attending church—until one day, when carving a leg of lamb for Sunday dinner with the minister, he cut his mother's throat instead. This corpse's name is Shrdlu; he is awaiting his torment in hell, believing he will be called there soon. In fact, he and Zero meet next in the Elysian Fields (in Greek mythology, Elysium is the land of the blessed). Shrdlu is mystified by the reality that he is in this paradise and his mother and minister are not. Indeed, he laments that the only ministers he can find are Swift and Rabelais, "who are much admired for some indecent tales which they have written."

Meanwhile, Zero is reunited with Daisy Diana Dorothea Devore, who committed suicide after Zero's execution. They express their affection, enjoy the beauty that surrounds them, and dance to music that Zero is finally able to hear only after he allows himself to appreciate his surroundings and anticipate the prospect of happily staying here with Daisy. His ability to hear the music is short-lived, however; when he understands that most here are engaged in creating works of art—activities that Shrdlu characterizes as "profitless occupations"—Zero decides to leave the Elysian Fields; he does not want to be among "loafers and bums." At his exit, the heartbroken Daisy says, "Without him, I might as well be alive."

In the final scene, we find Mr. Zero in a room using an adding machine. He has been here for the 25 years since his death. Two men come to tell him that it is time for him to be reincarnated. "Charles" explains to Zero that he has been reincarnated many times and with each rebirth he "gets a little worse," until finally he has become "the raw material of slums and war— the ready prey of the first jingo or demagogue or political adventurer who takes the trouble to play upon your ignorance and credulity and provincialism." In order to lure the reluctant Zero from his adding machine toward his bleak new life, Charles tells him he'll send a girl with him for company; Charles turns his head and imitates a female voice, a transparent trick that nevertheless fools Zero. Charles tells him the "girl" is named "Hope," and she'll make him "forget his troubles."

Elmer Rice wrote in 1938, "[T]he dominant concern not only of every human being, but of all of us as we function as members of society should be with the attainment of freedom of the body and of the mind through liberation from political autocracy, economic slavery, religious persecution, hereditary prejudice and herd psychology and the attainment of freedom of the soul through liberation from fear, jealousy, hatred, possessiveness, and self-delusion. . . . [E]verything I have ever written seriously has had in it no other idea than that" (Bigsby 127). Certainly *The Adding Machine* is no exception.

BIBLIOGRAPHY

Bigsby, C. W. E. *A Critical Introduction to Twentieth-Century American Drama: Volume One—1900–1940.* Cambridge, England: Cambridge University Press, 1982.

ADE, GEORGE (1866–1944)

Journalist, novelist, and playwright George Ade was born in Kentland, Indiana. After graduating from Purdue University in 1887, Ade worked in Lafayette, Indiana, for a brief time as a reporter, before moving to Chicago, where he worked at the *Chicago Record.* For the

Record, he wrote an anonymous daily column in collaboration with cartoonist John T. McCutcheon, with whom he had become friends at Purdue. This humorous column, entitled "Stories of the Streets and of the Town," captured the Chicago of the 1890s in all its variety. Ade developed some of the characters from these columns into works of fiction, including the novels *Artie* (1896) and *Doc' Horne* (1899); *Artie* (1907) was later the title of an unsuccessful play. Admired for his ability to write in the American vernacular, Ade is perhaps best known for his satirical pieces, "Fables in Slang"; from 1900 to 1920, he published 10 collections of these pieces, which had originally been written for his syndicated newspaper column. The overwhelming popularity of the fables brought Ade financial security.

As a dramatist, Ade again employed the tone and the character types that had made his prose so commercially successful. Ade's most popular plays were *The County Chairman* (1903), a comedy about small-town politics, and *The College Widow* (1904), a satire of American college life replete with football and a flirtatious president's daughter—the latter earned Ade close to $2 million dollars in royalties. More modest successes were *Just Out of College* (1905), in which a young man turns a profit at his future father-in-law's pickle factory, and *Father and the Boys* (1908), in which a hardworking father finally learns to enjoy himself while his fun-loving sons finally promise to work. Except for *Just Out of College,* these plays toured the country once they had completed their New York runs. Ade's one-act plays include *The Mayor and the Manicure, Nettie,* and *Speaking to Father* (all published in 1923 by Samuel French).

Ade was both admired by and indebted to Mark Twain, whose travel book *Innocents Abroad* (1869) inspired Ade's novel *In Pastures New* (1906), in which a naive Iowan tours Europe and parts of North Africa. Ade continued to write through the 1920s, but turned in the 1930s—by then in his sixties—to politics, fundraising, and his personal affairs.

BIBLIOGRAPHY

Kelly, Fred. *George Ade: Warmhearted Satirist.* Indianapolis, Ind.: Bobbs-Merrill, 1947.

AFRICAN-AMERICAN DRAMA The history of African-American theater and performance has been tied to the social and cultural circumstances of African-American existence. Because of the particular historical conditions of African-American life, the representation of African Americans on stage has contained profound political, social, and cultural meanings, impacts, and effects.

On August 1, 1821, William Brown opened the African Grove Theatre at 51 Mercer Street in New York City. While free Africans and African Americans in New York flocked to his tea-garden theater, Brown found himself in conflict with white authorities, most particularly with Mordecai Manuel Noah, the sheriff of New York City. Noah repeatedly closed productions, made arrests, and even removed actors from the stage of the African Grove Theatre, stating that the theater constituted a public threat. On June 20, 1823, Brown presented his own work *The Drama of King Shotoway,* a no-longer-extant work that commented on Brown's own oppression and imagined black rebellion by recounting the 1795 Garifuna Insurrection against the British on the Caribbean island of Saint Vincent. After the production, the theater closed for good, and Brown disappeared from the public record. Some members of the company went on to found other groups. Two of the more significant were actors James Hewlett and Ira Aldridge. With the African Company, Hewlett undertook key Shakespearean roles, including Richard III. Aldridge, sensing the racism present in American theater, went on to a successful career in Europe, where he acted for more than 30 years, presenting command performances before the crowned heads of Europe.

Among the most durable theatrical images of blackness that have profoundly influenced American racial interactions is that of the "happy-go-lucky darky" in blackface that came onto the American stage during the period of slavery but reverberated through American culture for decades. Through plays such as Harriet Beecher Stowe's *Uncle Tom's Cabin* (1851), as well as through performances on the minstrel stage, this stereotype became ingrained in the American consciousness. As a consequence, black playwrights and theater practitioners have had to confront and contest this historically negative image of blackness perpetuated by the dominant culture. In so doing, black playwrights and performers have had to create alternative images. Black theater practitioners in the late 1800s and early 1900s, like their white counterparts, donned blackface makeup and performed characters that both reinforced and subverted the association of blackness with servility, buffoonery, and inferiority. The first play ever published by a black author in the United States, *The Escape; or, A Leap to Freedom* (1858) by William Wells Brown, confronts these negative stereotypes, most principally through a slave character, Cato, who seems to conform to them. Brown, himself an escaped slave, appeared frequently as an orator at abolitionist meetings, and he wrote *The Escape* not to be staged by a troupe of actors but to be read by himself, in lieu of an oratorical address, at these meetings. The play depicts a series of events on the fictitious Muddy Creek plantation, owned by a Dr. Gaines, that lead three of his slaves, Glen, Melinda, and Cato, as the title suggests, to escape.

The struggle against pejorative black stereotypes continued within the theatrical period after slavery as minstrelsy gave way to a period of black musicals. Through these new black musicals, black performers fought to make audiences aware of their creativity at a time when virtually all avenues of social or economic advancement were closed to African Americans. Nonetheless, demeaning representations of African Americans persisted in these revues with names such as Bert Williams and George Walker's *Two Real Coons* (1896–99), *In Dahomey* (1902–05), and *Bandana Land* (1907–09). Black composer Bob Cole developed an important black musical, *A Trip to Coontown* (1898), starring Sissieretta Jones, better known as "Black Patti." It was the first black musical that worked with a plot that carried from beginning to end rather than the revue-and-sketch formula seen in minstrel shows. That same year, William Marion Cook and Paul Laurence Dunbar created the musical playlet *Clorindy—The Origin of the Cakewalk*. Both of these works resisted negative depictions of blacks as "coons" and "happy darkys," even as they accommodated them. Similarly, the shows of Williams and Walker showed this duality. Walker was an extremely talented light-com-

plected black man who, due to the convention of the time, had to perform in blackface. One of the most significant black musicals, Eubie Blake and Noble Sissle's *Shuffle Along* (1921), unlike other black musicals (save Williams and Walker's *Abyssinia* [1905–07]), featured a black love story. While thin on plot, *Shuffle Along* confronted the pejorative images of African Americans and presented more positive representations. Still, it affirmed notions of an African-American "native" energy in singing and dancing. It was a hit that ran for a year on Broadway at the beginning of the Harlem Renaissance.

Concerned about the representation of Negroes and the power of those representations to transcend the stage, the NAACP in 1915 formed a drama committee under the direction of W. E. B. DuBois. The committee produced *Rachel* by Angelina Weld Grimké in March 1916. Billed as "a race play in three acts," *Rachel* confronts the social and psychological scars of racism as it focuses on the life of a young, middle-class black woman, Rachel Loving, who decided not to marry or have children because of the overt racism faced by black children in America. Some accused the play of promoting racial genocide. Others, such as WILLIS RICHARDSON, felt that the stage should not be the place for propaganda but rather for the promotion of folk themes. The play marked an important moment in black theater history by sparking a critical dialogue about the purposes and responsibilities of black drama, and it also served as an inspiration for other black women interested in the theater.

Frustrated by the portrayals of blacks on the American stage by such white playwrights as EUGENE O'NEILL (*The Emperor Jones* [1920]), PAUL GREEN (*In Abraham's Bosom* [1927]), and MARC CONNELLY (*The Green Pastures* [1930]) in and prior to the 1920s, key African-Americans authors, scholars, and critics called for the independent development of a national black theater and the creation of plays by African Americans that more truthfully reflected black experience. In his well-known 1926 manifesto establishing the Krigwa Little Theatre movement, DuBois stated that "a real Negro theatre" must be "About us, By us, For us, and Near us." Yet, in 1926, few plays satisfied these criteria. Alain Locke published his collection, *Plays of Negro Life,* in 1927. While it included the work of white playwright Eugene O'Neill, it also contained plays by Jean Toomer and GEORGIA DOUGLAS JOHNSON. The anthology, *Plays and Pageants from the Life of the Negro* (1930), edited by playwright Willis Richardson, contained pageants and historical pieces intended for use in schools. As a playwright, Richardson was committed to exploring the Negro experience through folk drama. His one-act play, *The Chip Woman's Fortune* (1923), became the first serious play by an African American to appear on Broadway.

In order to promote black artistic creation and a different representation of the Negro, during the years 1925 through 1927, DuBois, the editor of the NAACP's *Crisis* magazine, and Charles S. Johnson, the editor of the National Urban League's *Opportunity* magazine, held a one-act play contest with the winners receiving cash prizes. Many of the winners of the *Crisis* and *Opportunity* competitions over these years were women. These included ZORA NEALE HURSTON for *Color Struck* (1925), Georgia Douglas Johnson for *Blue Blood* (1925), and Marita Bonner for *The Purple Flower* (1927). Hurston, Johnson, and Bonner were key contributors to an emergent movement of black women playwrights. The work of these women principally concerned social and cultural themes that had an impact on black women's lives. Johnson organized a literary salon at her house on S Street in Washington, D.C., that brought together black writers, poets, and dramatists to read their works.

Another important moment in black theater occurred in 1925 when the bellboy-turned-playwright Garland Anderson's play, *Appearances,* became the first full-length play by a black playwright on Broadway. The protagonist of the play is a black bellhop falsely accused of raping a white woman. During the course of a trial scene, the woman is exposed both as a mulatto and a liar. LANGSTON HUGHES'S *MULATTO* (1935) was significant both for its production history and the complexity with which Hughes examined the much-mined subject of the tragic mulatto. Within this play, Hughes uses the mulatto son, Robert, as a surrogate for black America demanding reparations, here, a blood debt from his white father. In its extant published form, Hughes's play retains this radical mes-

sage. The white director Martin Jones, however, markedly altered Hughes's script for Broadway, adding a rape and changing the ending of the play. Hughes and Jones entered into a protracted confrontation. The play proved successful on Broadway, but Hughes had an extremely difficult time collecting his royalties from Jones. Thus, his own struggle for rights paralleled the efforts of his central figure in *Mulatto.*

Concurrent with the production of *Mulatto,* the depression and the political currents of the times ushered in unique development in African-American theater particularly and American theater more generally. Under the auspices of the Works Progress Administration, HALLIE FLANAGAN directed the FEDERAL THEATRE PROJECT, a national program aimed at putting theater artists back to work. Among the Federal Theatre Project's locally based theaters were 22 Negro Theatre units in cities such as New York, Seattle, Chicago, and Boston. One of the key plays performed by the Chicago unit was Theodore Ward's *Big White Fog* (1938), which examines the struggles and generational conflicts of a black family. The play uses the family drama structure to examine diverse black liberation strategies—Garveyism, Pan-Africanism, capitalism, and, ultimately, socialism. The "big white fog" of the title is not white people nor merely racism but a mindset that leads to both the oppression of blacks and the suppression of class struggle. Perceiving the threat of communist influence, Congress shut down the Federal Theatre Project in 1939 after only four years, and this forced black artists to find other creative venues.

Little theaters sprang up in New York and Chicago and other cities. Langston Hughes helped found the Harlem Suitcase Theatre in 1938. One of the more successful groups was the American Negro Theatre, started in 1941. The group's first production was Abraham Hill's satire on the black middle class, *On Striver's Row* (1941). Also opening in 1941 was the stage adaptation of Richard Wright's acclaimed novel, *Native Son.* The play version resulted from the uneasy collaboration of Wright with white playwright Paul Green. While Wright sought to illuminate the social causes behind the violence of Bigger Thomas, Green was more interested in dramatizing Bigger's complicity in his own fate. Prior to the Broadway opening, producer John Houseman claims to have worked with Hughes to make Green's script conform more to the ending of the novel. However, only the Green adaptation is now extant. *Native Son* ran successfully on Broadway and then went on tour. Still, on the whole, the period of the 1940s was rather quiet for black theater, as America moved into war and the backlash of oppression against African Americans became more apparent.

In the 1950s, the emerging black demand for equality and protest against segregation and second-class citizenship would be reflected in the theater. William Branch's *A Medal For Willie* (1951) concerns a black mother who speaks out against the discrimination her son faced while in school; she refuses the medal he is supposed to be posthumously awarded for his war bravery, citing the hypocrisy of the ceremony. A major breakthrough in the struggle for civil rights came with the 1954 Supreme Court decision declaring separate but equal education unconstitutional. At the end of this decade, LORRAINE HANSBERRY's classic play *A RAISIN IN THE SUN* (1959) came to Broadway. It effectively spoke to its era and beyond as it demonstrated the humanity of a black family on the south side of Chicago struggling to better their lives. The play not only reflected the times but also was a precursor of the more incendiary black theater to follow. It featured a character, Beneatha, in an Afro hairdo for the first time, as well as an intelligent representation of an African character, Joseph Asagai, rather than the stereotypical primitive Africans seen earlier. By focusing on a particular black family and their struggles, pride, and determination, Hansberry established a legacy and created theatrical reverberations that continue to be felt and heard within the black theater.

The 1960s ushered in a period, known as the Black Theatre Movement, in which African-American voices for self-determination and self-articulation rang out. It marked a new black renaissance of sorts as many black theater companies emerged throughout the country and numerous anthologies of black drama were published. The movement, however, did not exhibit simply one ideology nor one style of theatrical practice. LEROI JONES's *DUTCHMAN* (1963) is often credited with initiating the movement. The young middle-class protagonist, Clay, voices the radical directive that only murder of whites by blacks will provide sanity for African Americans; he himself is murdered for his efforts. Soon Jones changed his name to IMAMU AMIRI BARAKA and with like-minded black cultural nationalists founded the Black Arts Repertory School in Harlem in 1965. Baraka became the key figure of the Black Revolutionary Theatre with works such as *Black Mass* (1966), *SLAVE SHIP* (1967), and *The Great Goodness of Life: A Coon Show* (1969). DOUGLAS TURNER WARD's satire *A Day of Absence* (1965), a one-act play that humorously explores what happens to a small southern town when all the black people disappear for a day, helped to establish the Negro Ensemble Company. In this work, black actors play the white townspeople in whiteface. The Negro Ensemble Company, which continues to exist, produced plays not bent on revolution but on showing the prowess and potential of black performers, playwrights, and designers to an integrated audience. ADRIENNE KENNEDY's *FUNNYHOUSE OF A NEGRO* (1965), a nonrealistic avant-garde piece that focuses on the psychological turmoil and ultimate suicide of a young black woman caught between a white world and a black one, evidenced another aspect of the Black Theatre Movement during this period. Kennedy's experimental use of form and language would continue to influence black artists in the 1990s, such as SUZAN-LORI PARKS.

In May 1968, Richard Schechner, editor of the *Drama Review,* the leading journal of avant-garde and cutting-edge theater, invited black playwright ED BULLINS as guest editor; the *Black Theatre Issue,* as it was named, became a critical "collective manifesto" for the Black Theatre Movement. Soon to become cultural minister of the Black Panther Party in Oakland, California, and intensely conscious of the current conditions and the urgent demand for a new black arts practice, Bullins included plays by 14 authors, including two by Baraka (*Home on the Range* [1968] and *Police* [1968]) and one by himself (*CLARA'S OLE MAN* [1965]). The plays contained in this issue purposefully challenged audience expectations and reoriented the separations between spectators, stage performers, and performance as they sought to etch out a distinctly African-American aesthetic practice.

With the 1970s, African-American drama pulled back from the urgency and adamancy expressed in the earlier decade. Playwrights began to focus on other concerns, but the social relationship of black theater to black life in America remained important. In 1975, NTOZAKE SHANGE's *FOR COLORED GIRLS WHO HAVE CONSIDERED SUICIDE/WHEN THE RAINBOW IS ENUF* (1975) created a sensation; in the form of what Shange termed a "choreopoem," this play spoke to the personal and political intersections of black women's lives. It was significant to both the African-American theater and to the burgeoning women's movement in its exploration of a black female communality breaking free of restrictive gender roles and allowing black women to find the god "within themselves" and to love themselves fiercely. Black playwrights continued to go beyond existing definitions of theater and black plays in the decade of the 1970s and into the 1980s.

In 1982, CHARLES FULLER's *A SOLDIER'S PLAY* won the PULITZER PRIZE for Drama and the New York Drama Critics' Circle Award for Best American Play, among other awards. *A Soldier's Play* depicts the debilitating effects of the "madness of race" in America that inhibits and conditions attitudes, perceptions, values, actions, and behavior. In the murder mystery of *A Soldier's Play,* questions of guilt and innocence are not simply black and white but are conflated, confused, and compounded. With this play, Fuller started a trend that would continue to inform black theater of the 1980s and into the 1990s: African-American playwrights explored historic themes and reexamined history to see its impact on the present. Celebrated as a "bold new voice" in black theater, *The Colored Museum* (1986) reverberates with the rage and rhythms of the African-American theatrical past. Playwright GEORGE C. WOLFE "colors" the anger and pain of the African-American experience with an incisive satire that both critiques and revises earlier African-American dramatic texts. He also parodies plays of the African-American theatrical past, even as earlier African-American plays and their playwrights inform *The Colored Museum* in both form and content.

With two Pulitzer Prizes to his credit, the key practitioner of this theatrical return to the past was AUGUST WILSON. Wilson reviewed African-American history in the 20th century by writing a play for each decade. With each work, he recreated and reevaluated the choices that blacks have made in the past by refracting them through the lens of the present. The plays focus on the experiences and daily lives of ordinary black people within particular historical circumstances. Carefully situating each play at critical junctures in African-American history, Wilson explored the pain and perseverance, the determination and dignity in these black lives. Although not written in chronological order, the "Century Cycle" plays, covering the 1900s to the 1990s, advance through the century as follows: *GEM OF THE OCEAN* (2003), *JOE TURNER'S COME AND GONE* (1986), *MA RAINEY'S BLACK BOTTOM* (1984), *The PIANO LESSON* (1987), *SEVEN GUITARS* (1995), *FENCES* (1985), *TWO TRAINS RUNNING* (1990), *JITNEY* (1982), *KING HEDLEY II* (2001) and *RADIO GOLF* (2005). All of Wilson's dramas, except *Ma Rainey,* are set in Wilson's childhood home, the Hill district of Pittsburgh, Pennsylvania. Central to each play in Wilson's historical cycle is the concept that the events of the past can and do have a powerful impact on the present. Wilson's characters' personal stories are inextricably linked to the history of African-American struggle and survival in this country. Wilson's death at age 60 from cancer on October 1, 2005—just two weeks after *Radio Golf,* the 10th and final play of his cycle, ended its run in Los Angeles—will doubtless have a significant impact on the evolution of African-American theater in the new millennium. On October 17, 2005, the Virginia Theater at 245 West 52nd Street in New York City was renamed the August Wilson Theater, making Wilson the first African American to have a Broadway theater named in his honor. Through his work and his words, Wilson has changed the face of American theater and African-American theater more particularly. His plays, his legacy, will endure and will animate the future.

Another important voice of the contemporary African-American theater, Suzan-Lori Parks, has turned to history as well in works such as *The Death of the Last Black Man in the Whole Entire World* (1990), *The American Play* (1993), and *Venus* (1996)—all of which deal in part with historical myths and stereotypes. In these works, through a jazz-like process of repetition and revision, Parks celebrates the elasticity, power, and poetry of black dialect in an original formal structure that offers repetition but does not repeat. Another contemporary voice, Robert O'Hara, irreverently questions the lack of a gay presence in the history of slavery in his play *Insurrection Holding History* (1999), interrogating the African-American past and making space for an alternative narrative. The result of these works is a new experience of history, a new contestatory and contingent engagement with the past that puts into question the historical categorization of race as it probes the meanings of blackness. For Parks, O'Hara, and Wilson, their revisionist historicism has enabled complex renegotiations of blackness.

Suzan-Lori Parks won the Pulitzer Prize for her play TOPDOG/UNDERDOG (2001), about two brothers named Lincoln and Booth. More linear and direct than her earlier work, it marks a new direction for Parks specifically but also for African-American theater more generally. Parks's creative interests lie in developing new dramatic territory beyond the conventional binary of black and white, and she constructs complex interactions among race, sexuality, family, class, and culture. These complexities are exemplary of the current dynamics of American racial politics.

While revivals of Wilson's work have made him the most produced playwright in the first decade of the new millennium, productions of plays by new young African-American playwrights have also further expanded the definitions of black theater. Acclaimed MacArthur Award–winning playwright LYNN NOTTAGE in works such as *Crumbs from the Table* (1995) and INTIMATE APPAREL (2003) has, like Wilson, dealt with historical subjects; yet within this historical frame, Nottage has sought to confront questions of interracial contact and intimacy. In her work, racial identity, personal desire, and the social demands of history collide. Marcus Gardley's haunting and lyrical *Dance of the Holy Ghosts: A Memory Play* shares August Wilson's interest in memory and the blues. It received considerable critical attention when it played at Yale Repertory Theatre and then OFF-BROADWAY in 2006.

Nominated for the 2007 Pulitzer Prize in drama, Eisa Davis's *Bulrusher* offers a unique language of its own as it contests matters of race, violence, and history.

In this same cultural moment, a new genre of theater has emerged, hip-hop theater. Hip-hop artist Danny Hoch founded the Hip-Hop Theater Festival in New York in 2001, and similar events have sprung up across the country featuring artists and playwrights such as Hobo Junction and Kamilah Frobes and Will Power. Will Power's play, *The Seven,* a hip-hop adaptation of Aeschylus's *Seven against Thebes,* played to critical acclaim Off-Broadway at the New York Theater Workshop in 2006. While hip-hop theater is difficult to define, these new plays clearly pick up on the energy and urgency of hip-hop music and purposefully appeal to members of the hip-hop nation. With their celebration of language and rhythm and their diverse forms of theatrical representation, hip-hop theater works speak to racial and cultural hybridity and open new avenues and new audiences for black theater.

In America today, the definitions, implications, and meanings of race have entered "new territory"; consequently, African-American theater continues to evolve, both in form and content, in ways directly related to the changing social contexts of black lives and black politics and the meanings and representations of blackness.

BIBLIOGRAPHY

Abramson, Doris. *Negro Playwrights in the American Theatre, 1925–1959.* New York: Columbia University Press, 1969.

Allen, Carol. *Peculiar Passages: Black Women Playwrights, 1875 to 2000.* New York: Peter Lang, 2005.

Anderson, Lisa M. *Black Feminism in Contemporary Drama.* Urbana: University of Illinois Press, 2008.

———. *Mammies No More: The Changing Image of the Black Woman on Stage and Screen.* New York: Rowman & Littlefield, 1997.

Andrews, Bert, and Paul Carter Harrison. *In the Shadow of the Great White Way: Images from the Black Theatre.* New York: Thunder's Mouth Press, 1989.

Archer, Leonard C. *Black Image in American Theater.* Nashville, Tenn.: Pageant Press, 1973.

Bean, Annemarie, ed. *A Sourcebook on African-American Performance: Plays, People, Movements.* New York: Routledge, 1999.

Bond, Frederick W. *The Negro and the Drama: The Direct and Indirect Contribution Which the American Negro Has Made to Drama and the Legitimate Stage.* Washington, D.C.: Associated Publishers, 1940.

Brown-Guillory, Elizabeth. *Their Place on the Stage: Black Women Playwrights in America.* New York: Greenwood Press, 1988.

Craig, E. Quita. *Black Drama of the Federal Theatre.* Amherst: University of Massachusetts Press, 1980.

Elam, Harry J., Jr., and David Krasner, eds. *African American Performance and Theater History: A Critical Reader.* New York: Oxford University Press, 2001.

Fabre, Genevieve E. *Drumbeats, Masks, and Metaphor: Contemporary Afro-American Theatre.* Trans. Melvin Dixon. Cambridge, Mass.: Harvard University Press, 1983.

Flowers, H. D. *Blacks in American Theatre History.* Edina, Minn.: Burgess International Group Press, 1992.

Fraden, Rena. *Blueprints for a Black Federal Theatre, 1935–1939.* Cambridge, England: Cambridge University Press, 1996.

Gill, Glenda. *White Grease Paint on Black Performers: A Study of the Federal Theatre of 1935–1939.* New York: Peter Lang, 1989.

Hamalian, Leo, and James V. Hatch, eds. *The Roots of African American Drama: An Anthology of Early Plays, 1858–1938.* Detroit, Mich.: Wayne State University Press, 1991.

Harris, Trudier, and Jennifer Larson, eds. *Reading Contemporary African American Drama: Fragments of History, Fragments of Self.* New York: Peter Lang, 2007.

Harrison, Paul Carter. *The Drama of Nommo.* New York: Grove Press, 1972.

Haskins, James. *Black Theater in America.* New York: Thomas Y. Crowell, 1982.

Hatch, James V. *Black Image on the American Stage, 1770–1970.* New York: Drama Book Specialists, 1970.

———. *The Roots of African American Drama.* Detroit: Wayne State University Press, 1991.

———, and Leo Hamalian, eds. *Lost Plays of the Harlem Renaissance, 1920–1940.* Detroit: Wayne State University Press, 1996.

———, Brooks McNamara, and Annemarie Bean, eds. *Inside the Minstrel Mask.* Middletown, Conn.: Wesleyan University Press, 1996.

———, and Ted Shine, eds. *Black Theatre USA: Plays by African Americans, 1847 to Today.* Rev. ed. New York: Free Press, 1996.

Hay, Samuel. *African American Theatre: An Historical and Critical Analysis.* Cambridge, England: Cambridge University Press, 1994.

Hill, Anthony, D. *Pages from the Harlem Renaissance.* New York: Peter Lang, 1996.

Hill, Errol, ed. *The Theatre of Black Americans: A Collection of Critical Essays.* New York: Applause, 1987.

———, and James V. Hatch. *A History of African American Theatre.* Cambridge: Cambridge University Press, 2003.

Hughes, Langston, and Milton Melzer. *Black Magic: A Pictorial History of the African-American in the Performing Arts.* New York: Da Capo Press, 1990.

Isaacs, Edith J. R. *The Negro in the American Theatre.* New York: Theatre Arts, 1947.

Keyssar, Helene. *The Curtain and the Veil: Strategies in Black Drama.* New York: Burt Franklin, 1981.

King, Woodie, Jr. *Black Theatre: Present Condition.* New York: National Black Theatre Touring Circuit, 1981.

Kolin, Philip C., ed. *Contemporary African-American Women Playwights: A Casebook.* London: Routledge, 2007.

Krasner, David. *A Beautiful Pageant: African American Theatre, Drama, and Performance in the Harlem Renaissance, 1910–1927.* New York: Palgrave Macmillan, 2002.

———. *Resistance, Parody, and Double Consciousness in African American Theatre, 1895–1910.* New York: St. Martin's Press, 1997.

Locke, Alain, and Montgomery Gregory, eds. *Plays of Negro Life: A Source-Book of Native American Drama.* 1927. Westport, Conn.: Negro University Press, 1970.

Lott, Eric. *Love and Theft: Blackface Minstrelsy and the American Working Class.* New York: Oxford University Press, 1993.

Marsh-Lockett, Carol P., ed. *Black Women Playwrights: Visions on the American Stage.* New York: Garland, 1999.

Mitchell, Loften. *Black Drama: The Story of the American Negro in Theatre.* New York: Hawthorn, 1967.

———. *Voices of the Black Theatre.* Clifton, N.J.: James T. White, 1975.

Molette, Carlton W., and Barbara J. Molette. *Black Theatre: Premise and Presentation.* Bristol, Ind.: Wyndham Hall Press, 1986.

Nathans, Heather S. *Slavery and Sentiment on the American Stage, 1787–1861: Lifting the Veil of Black.* Cambridge and New York: Cambridge University Press, 2009.

Neal, Larry. *Visions of a Liberated Future: Black Arts Movement Writings.* New York: Thunder's Mouth Press, 1989.

Olaniyan, Tejumola. *Scars of Conquest/Masks of Resistance: The Invention of Cultural Identities in African, African-American, and Caribbean Drama.* New York: Oxford University Press, 1995.

Perkins, Kathy A., ed. *Black Female Playwrights: An Anthology of Plays before 1950.* Bloomington: Indiana University Press, 1989.

Peterson, Bernard L. *The African American Theatre Directory, 1816–1960: A Comprehensive Guide to Early Black Theatre Organizations, Companies, Theatres, and Performing Groups.* Westport, Conn.: Greenwood Press, 1997.

———. *Early Black American Playwrights and Dramatic Writers: A Biographical Directory and Catalog of Plays, Films, and Broadcast Scripts.* Westport, Conn.: Greenwood Press, 1990.

Robinson, Cedric J. *Forgeries of Memory and Meaning: Blacks and the Regimes of Race in American Theater and Film Before World War II.* Chapel Hill: University of North Carolina Press, 2007.

Sanders, Leslie Catherine. *The Development of Black Theater in America: From Shadows to Selves.* Baton Rouge: Louisiana State University Press, 1988.

Sotiropoulos, Karen. *Staging Race: Black Performers in Turn of the Century America.* Cambridge, Mass.: Harvard University Press, 2006.

Southern, Eileen, ed. *African American Theater.* New York: Garland, 1994.

Williams, Dana, A. *Contemporary African American Female Playwrights.* Westport, Conn.: Greenwood Press, 1998.

Williams, Mance, ed. *Black Theatre in the 1960s and 1970s: A Historical-Critical Analysis of the Movement.* Westport, Conn.: Greenwood Press, 1985.

Woll, Allen. *Black Musical Theatre: From "Coontown" to "Dreamgirls."* Baton Rouge: Louisiana State University Press, 1989.

Harry J. Elam Jr.
Stanford University

AFTER THE FALL ARTHUR MILLER (1964)

The action of *After the Fall* takes place in the memory of the protagonist, Quentin, his mind's landscape darkened by the presence of the "blasted stone tower of a German concentration camp." Scenes from Quentin's past are linked together by his direct-address of the "Listener"—an offstage character, perhaps a therapist—as he ponders his relationships with the people, particularly the women, in his life.

Quentin is a lawyer who is no longer practicing law. He has been married twice: His first wife, Louise, resents him because she feels that he behaves as if she does not exist. His second wife is dead, apparently by her own hand. In addition to his wives, Quentin remembers his mother (whom he stopped loving— unable even to mourn her death—after witnessing her cruel contempt for his father when the stock mar-

ket crash of 1929 left him financially ruined); his new lover, Holga; and Felice, a former client for whom he was a pivotal figure but who meant nothing to him. One of the themes of the play is the idea that those we love are merely mirrors in whom we see ourselves reflected. For Felice, Quentin was "a mirror in which she somehow saw herself as . . . glorious"; therefore, she loved him. After years of marriage, when Louise looks at him, she does not seem to exist; therefore, she ceases to love him.

Much of the play is devoted to Quentin's relationship with his second wife, Maggie. He meets Maggie at a bus stop. She remembers him because she has worked as a receptionist in his office building. Quentin is—as all men seem to be—tempted by this sexual beauty but, still married to Louise, he gives her cab fare only to save her from the attentions of two strangers. She mistakes his fear (of taking her to bed) for a respectful "tribute." Here again, love is based on how one person sees herself reflected in another, despite the fact that the reflection is a misinterpretation. Maggie keeps Quentin in mind for four years and eventually seeks him out after she has become a famous singer. Despite her success, she is no less emotionally insecure than she was at their first meeting. As their relationship develops and then deteriorates, Quentin finally refuses to police Maggie's drinking and pill-popping, ceases to be her rescuer any longer, and eventually is left feeling guilty over her death by overdose.

Holga, a German woman with whom Quentin is involved in the present tense of the play, is from a family of German officers. During World War II, she became a "courier for the officers [one of whom was her godfather] who were planning to assassinate Hitler," and she spent two years in a "forced labor" camp. Holga brings Quentin to visit the concentration camp that now dominates his memory. She teaches him that human beings must embrace their lives, despite even the "broken" and "horrible" features of those lives. What *she* has faced and accepted are the war, the countless deaths, and the unspeakable cruelty of which humans are capable. What he must face—and finally does face—is the "death of love."

Love and cruelty are equally human, and we are, each of us, both victim and culprit. Of the concentration camp, Quentin says, "My brothers died here . . . but my brothers built this place." Quentin comes to believe, with Holga's help, that after the death of love, after the death of faith in humankind's goodness, "we meet unblessed, not in . . . Eden, but after, after the Fall." Only then can we "dare to love this world again," and "with a stroke of love—as to an idiot in the house—forgive it; again and again. . . ."

Another of humanity's black eyes brought into the play by Miller is the McCarthyism of the 1950s. Quentin and his law partners were once members of the Communist Party; consequently, they are questioned before the House Un-American Activities Committee. One of the men commits suicide, and the other commits the betrayal of naming the names of men he knew to have been party members in their youth.

C. W. E. Bigsby calls the play "a remarkably sincere, if not wholly successful, attempt to pull together private and public acts of treachery in an effort to understand the terrible facts of modern history and to acknowledge a culpability which links us all" (216). Arthur Miller has expressed dismay at the fact that the play has often simplistically and inaccurately been seen as a portrait of his second wife, Marilyn Monroe. Miller wrote in his memoir: "I was sure that the play would be seen as an attempt to embrace a world of political and ethical dilemmas, with Maggie's agony perhaps the most symbolically apparent but hardly the play's raison d'être. The play was about how we—nations and individuals—destroy ourselves by denying that this is precisely what we are doing" (527).

BIBLIOGRAPHY
Bigsby, C. W. E. *A Critical Introduction to Twentieth-Century American Drama: Volume Two—Williams/Miller/Albee.* Cambridge, England: Cambridge University Press, 1984.
Miller, Arthur. *Timebends.* New York: Grove Press, 1987.

AGITPROP DRAMA

The term *agitprop* is an abbreviation for "agitation and propaganda." Originating in the Soviet Union after the 1917 Revolution, agitprop drama was just one facet of the Department of Agitation and Propaganda, set up by the Soviet Communist Party in 1920. Plays were used as political tools to support the party's ideology.

Agitprop drama spread through Europe and America in the 1920s and 1930s. In America, the GROUP THEATRE produced political theater, which reflected the left-wing politics of its members, during the 1930s. (It should be pointed out that the Group Theatre's major influence, the Moscow Arts Theatre, was founded in 1898 and was not an arm of the Department of Agitation and Propaganda; in fact, MAT's innovative style was constrained under Soviet rule.) In its purest form, agitprop was "a blend of chanted dialogue and mass-movement in which the actors, performing in unison, symbolized the working-class solidarity essential for the overthrow of the bosses. The plots, such as they were, moved ahead so rapidly that the audience had no opportunity to think over the anticapitalist allegations it heard" (Goldstein 32).

Today, the term refers to any drama whose purpose is to convey a political ideology.

BIBLIOGRAPHY
Goldstein, Malcolm. *The Political Stage: American Drama and Theater of the Great Depression.* New York: Oxford University Press, 1974.

AH, WILDERNESS! EUGENE O'NEILL (1933)

In January 1933, EUGENE O'NEILL wrote to his son, Eugene, Jr., that he had just finished "the last play they would ever suspect me of writing" because it was "such a change from the involved and modern and tragic hidden undertones of life I usually go after." He described it as "A Nostalgic Comedy of the Ancient Days when Youth was Young, and Right was Right, and Life was a Wicked Opportunity" (Bogard and Bryer 409).

The only comedy O'Neill ever wrote, *Ah, Wilderness!* takes place in "a large small-town in Connecticut" in 1906 and focuses on the Miller family: Nat, the father who is the editor of the town's newspaper; his wife, Essie, prim and proper and more than a little conservative in her views on parenting and on modern literature; four of their six children—Arthur (19), Richard (16), Mildred (15), and Tommy (11); and Nat's sister Lily, who boards with them. The time, appropriately for a play that its author said depicted "the simple old family life as lived by the typical hardworking American of the average . . . town which is America in miniature" (Bogard and Bryer 412), is July 4th and 5th. In town for the holiday celebrations is Sid Davis, Essie's brother; 16 years ago, Lily broke off her engagement to Sid because of his drinking and womanizing, but they have remained fond of one another.

The play's action centers around Richard Miller's adolescent crush on Muriel McCumber, daughter of a humorless, straitlaced local merchant. Richard is deeply engrossed in the writings of Wilde, Shaw, Swinburne, and Ibsen and quotes them frequently (much to Essie's disapproval and Nat's wry amusement) and derides the Fourth of July as "a stupid farce." Muriel's father angrily confronts Nat with the love letters Richard has written Muriel, as well as with a letter from Muriel to Richard telling him that she doesn't ever want to see him again. Richard hides his devastation at the letter by declaring with false bravado, "There's plenty of other fish in the sea!" When his brother Arthur's college classmate, Wint Selby, asks him to step in for Arthur on a double date with two "swift babes from New Haven," Richard agrees, vowing to show Muriel "she can't treat me the way she's done!" But Richard's encounter with Belle at a local bar, the Pleasant Beach House, ends disastrously: He allows her to ply him with liquor and cigarettes but refuses her offer of sex because he "took an oath [he]'d be faithful"—and he is thrown out of the bar as Belle turns her attention to a traveling salesman. When Richard *"lurches"* into the Miller family parlor that evening, he is promptly designated as "soused" by Sid who has himself earlier returned from the Sachem Club picnic quite drunk, much to Lily's dismay and the rest of the family's amusement.

The next day, Essie is determined that, while Nat must punish Richard severely for his behavior, he must "be careful how [he goes] about it" because Richard is "too sensitive for his own good." Nat vows to have "a straight talk with him—about women and all those things," but he is clearly relieved not to have to do so right away because he has to go to his office before Richard wakes up. When Richard does emerge, his sister Mildred gives him a letter from Muriel in which she explains that her father made her write the earlier letter, that she loves Richard "and always will," and that she is going to sneak out and meet him later

that day. Vowing "I'll see her tonight if it's the last thing I ever do!" Richard ignores his mother's prohibition against leaving the house and goes out the back door to meet Muriel at *"a strip of beach along the harbor."* There he tells her a somewhat embellished version of his visit to the Pleasant Beach House—he knocks down the bartender because the latter insulted "the chorus girl from New York" with whom Richard was drinking—but swears that nothing happened because he loves Muriel. They kiss under the moon and declare their love for one another.

The last scene of the play again finds his parents awaiting Richard's return, but this time they know he has been with Muriel (because Mildred has told them). While Nat still feels he must punish his son, Essie has completely changed her views, explaining that the books Richard reads prove that he has "an exceptional brain." Nat does have his talk with Richard, trying to tell him about the differences between "decent" women and "girls there's something doing with," but he stumbles badly, finally blurting out, "But, hell, . . . you know more about it than I do." Richard assures his parents that he has learned his lesson and will behave in the future because he loves Muriel and will marry her someday; he impulsively kisses his father good-night and leaves his parents gazing romantically at the same moon he and Muriel had kissed under a few minutes earlier.

While O'Neill called *Ah, Wilderness!* "a nostalgia for a youth I never had," depicting "the way I would have *liked* my boyhood to have been" (Bowen 67) and insisted "there is very little actually autobiographical about it" (Bogard and Bryer 408), many critics have noted its similarities to the later and more serious LONG DAY'S JOURNEY INTO NIGHT (1956). The living room/sitting room settings of the two plays are virtually identical, and the themes of excessive drinking, the younger generation reading slightly scandalous writers of the day, a young man introduced to "sin" by an older contemporary, generational conflicts and misunderstandings, and various frustrations of male-female relationships, all of which are treated light-heartedly in *Ah, Wilderness!,* reappear in much darker form in *Long Day's Journey.* And *Ah, Wilderness!* is also an important precursor of O'Neill's later plays in that, as Travis Bogard notes, it is his "first significant step toward openly autobiographical dramas" (Bogard and Bryer 384).

BIBLIOGRAPHY
Bogard, Travis. *Contour in Time: The Plays of Eugene O'Neill.* Rev. ed. New York: Oxford University Press, 1988.
———, and Jackson R. Bryer, eds. *Selected Letters of Eugene O'Neill.* New Haven, Conn.: Yale University Press, 1988.
Bowen, Croswell. "The Black Irishman." In *O'Neill and His Plays: Four Decades of Criticism,* edited by Oscar Cargill, N. Bryllion Fagin, and William J. Fisher. New York: New York University Press, 1961. 64–84.

AIKEN, GEORGE L. (1830–1876)

George L. Aiken is best known for his stage adaptation of Harriet Beecher Stowe's *Uncle Tom's Cabin.* He made his acting debut at 18 and performed in theaters in Rhode Island, Boston, and New York. Legend has it that his cousin, Troy (New York) Museum theater manager George C. Howard, commissioned the 22-year-old Aiken to adapt Stowe's *Uncle Tom's Cabin,* already a phenomenal success, with a part for his daughter, the "infant prodigy" Cordelia. For a bonus of $40 and a gold watch, Aiken worked for a week to shape the play around the character of Little Eva, to be played by Cordelia Howard.

On September 27, 1852, less than seven months after the publication of the novel, the Troy Museum premiered Aiken's adaptation of *Uncle Tom's Cabin,* with Aiken playing the roles of George Harris and George Shelby. Aiken's original version ended with the death of Little Eva and covered only part of the material in the novel. The play was such a success that audiences demanded Aiken create a sequel that showed the rest of the story. Aiken's *The Death of Uncle Tom; or, The Religion of the Lowly,* which opened in November of 1852, was ultimately combined with his original script to create the "complete" version of *Uncle Tom's Cabin.*

Aiken's work as a playwright demonstrates two prevailing influences on American popular culture in the years before the Civil War: the minstrel show and melodrama. To please audiences accustomed to Jim Crow dances and minstrel routines, Aiken exaggerated the character of Topsy, making her perform "break-down" dances and giving her new comic scenes and dialogue. His other strong influence, melodrama, emerges in his treatment of the characters Eva, Tom, and Eliza, all of whom demonstrate the selflessness and virtue of the typical hero or heroine of melodrama.

Aiken transformed one of the most powerful works in American literature into a play that ran all over America for the next 50 years. None of his other literary or dramatic works garnered him the same recognition, though he continued as a successful playwright and author, producing a number of "sensation melodramas," based on stories in the *New York Ledger.* He also wrote a handful of 10-cent novelettes, a popular and generally more lowbrow style of entertainment, including *Chevalier, the French Jack Sheppard* (1868) and *A New York Boy Among the Indians* (1872).

BIBLIOGRAPHY
Birdoff, Harry. *The World's Greatest Hit: "Uncle Tom's Cabin."* New York: Vanni, 1947.

Heather Nathans
University of Maryland

AKINS, ZOË (1886–1958)

Born into wealth in Humansville, Missouri, Zoë Akins became interested in theater as a child when she saw touring productions in St. Louis. The first New York production of an Akins play was of her free verse one-act (an adaptation from the French) *The Magical City,* which was performed in 1915 by the WASHINGTON SQUARE PLAYERS. Over the next two decades, Akins wrote or adapted 15 plays for the New York stage.

Akins's first substantial success was her full-length drama, *Déclassée* (1919), about the reckless behavior of a divorced woman. This success was followed, among others, by *Daddy's Gone a-Hunting* (1921), set in Greenwich Village among the Bohemian set; *The Varying Shore* (1921), the story of a courtesan; *The Moon-Flower* (1924), one of Akins's many adaptations of foreign plays; and *The Greeks Had a Word For It* (1930), a successful comedy in which three beautiful former chorus-girls seek wealthy men to support them.

In 1935, Akins's *The OLD MAID,* her faithful adaptation of Edith Wharton's novel about two women in love with one man, won the PULITZER PRIZE. The decision "was controversial and much maligned, not because the play, old-fashioned and sentimental as it now seems, lacks merit in structure and characterization, but because of the strength of the contenders: *The CHILDREN'S HOUR* by [LILLIAN] HELLMAN and *AWAKE AND SING!* by CLIFFORD ODETS," as well as "ROBERT SHERWOOD'S *The PETRIFIED FOREST* and MAXWELL ANDERSON'S *Valley Forge*" (Adler 28–29). The choice of Akins's play over the others so incensed critics that the New York Drama Critics' Circle Awards were established in response.

Her best work for the stage was considered urbane and witty in its day. In the 1930s, Akins wrote 13 screenplays, often in collaboration with others. She also wrote essays, poetry, and fiction.

BIBLIOGRAPHY

Adler, Thomas P. *Mirror on the Stage: The Pulitzer Plays as an Approach to American Drama.* West Lafayette, Ind.: Purdue University Press, 1987.

Kreizenbeck, Alan. *Zoë Akins: Broadway Playwright.* Westport, Conn.: Praeger, 2004.

ALBEE, EDWARD (1928–)

Edward Franklin Albee III was born in Washington, D.C., only to be abandoned by his natural parents. Edward and Frances Albee of Larchmont, New York, adopted him two weeks later, naming him for his adoptive grandfather. Albee found himself taken in by an enormously wealthy family (the family traveled to Florida in their private train car and the young Albee rode around in a Rolls Royce) with theatrical roots (his grandfather at one time owned one of the most profitable vaudeville theater chains in the country). As a young man, Albee also had the chance to meet such writers as THORNTON WILDER and W. H. Auden. However, Albee did not get along well with his parents, who shipped him off to one boarding school after another. Albee graduated from Choate, a place that nurtured his creative efforts. There, his poems, stories, essays, and one play were published in the school's literary magazine. He attended Trinity College in Connecticut, lasting little more than a year before being asked to leave for not attending certain required classes and chapel.

After working at odd jobs from 1948 to 1958, Albee committed himself to serious playwriting, often revisiting selected issues from his unpleasant family life in many of the plays. There is more than a hint of his ineffectual father in Tobias in *A DELICATE BALANCE* (1966) and his loving grandmother in Grandma in *The Sandbox* (1960) and *The AMERICAN DREAM* (1961). There is the unmistakable presence of his domineering and distant mother in Martha in *WHO'S AFRAID OF VIRGINIA WOOLF?* (1962), Agnes in *Delicate Balance*, the Wife in *All Over* (1971), and, above all, the women in *THREE TALL WOMEN* (1994). Such recurrent themes and motifs as the fear of abandonment, betrayal, the role of truth and illusion, the function of anger, the hope for love, the feeling of not belonging within the family—and, indeed, the universe—refashion themselves in every Albee play. Although his parents inherited $15 million at the start of the Great Depression and provided all the material comforts a child could want, they denied the young Albee the very things he most craved: a sense of love and belonging. Perhaps it is not surprising that, shortly before her death in 1989, his mother suddenly and without explanation disinherited Albee, her final act of betraying the son whom she never really accepted.

As a 30th birthday present to himself, he wrote what would be his first great success, *The ZOO STORY* (1959). The play embodies many of the qualities that have since come to characterize vintage Albee. The necessity of ritualized confrontation enacted by Peter and Jerry, the primacy of communication, the paradoxical mixture of love and hate, the cleverly abrasive dialogue, the ideological implications of his characters' actions, the tragic force of death, the awareness of a gulf between the way things are and the way things could be, and the penalty of consciousness coalesce in *The Zoo Story*, which remains one of the playwright's best works. His other early OFF-BROADWAY works, such as *The DEATH OF BESSIE SMITH* (1960) and *The American Dream*, established Albee as a new, iconoclastic writer, one whose disdain for conformity and love of acerbic repartee quickly made him a key figure in the alternative, and then the mainstream, theater world.

Albee's early reputation was challenged by some critics who noted that, despite the notoriety of his early short plays, he had not staged a full-length play on Broadway, which by the early 1960s was nearing the end of its golden era as the site of original theater in the United States. He was, it seemed, merely another promising young writer staging work in small venues. Albee's response? He wrote an article in the *New York Times Magazine* in which he called Broadway, with its commercial mentality, the true THEATRE OF THE ABSURD and then, eight months later, staged an essentially Off-Broadway play on Broadway. The premiere of *Who's Afraid of Virginia Woolf?* in 1962 astonished theatergoers, for this was one of the first nonmainstream American plays to open on a Broadway stage, with spectacular results. *Who's Afraid of Virginia Woolf?*, which ran for 664 performances and was later made into the highest earning film in 1966 for Warner Brothers, affirmed Albee's place as a serious playwright whose work defined certain public issues as reflected through the private anxieties of the individual. The PULITZER PRIZE drama judges recommended it for the award, but their decision was overturned by the Pulitzer's advisory board of journalists.

Having achieved an epochal Broadway debut with *Virginia Woolf,* Albee baffled theatergoers with his next play, *Tiny Alice* (1964), a flawed examination of the role of truth and illusion and the ways in which they influence one's religious convictions. Two years later, Albee staged *A Delicate Balance,* which restored the theatergoers' faith and which won Albee his first Pulitzer Prize. Beginning with *Box* and *Quotations from Chairman Mao Tse-Tung* in 1968 and continuing with *All Over* in 1971, however, Albee began to lose his audience. His language became increasingly abstract. The plays seemed drained of the witty dialogue and challenging action that had so energized his first compositions. SEASCAPE, which won its author a second Pulitzer Prize in 1975, was his last critical and popular success for nearly 20 years. Albee, considered the heir apparent to EUGENE O'NEILL, LILLIAN HELLMAN, TENNESSEE WILLIAMS, and ARTHUR MILLER, continued to lose his purchase on the theatergoing public. He pressed on, writing numerous plays, but such works as *The Lady from Dubuque* (1980) and *The Man Who Had Three Arms* (1982), despite their theatrical moments, pale when compared to *The Zoo Story, Who's Afraid of Virginia Woolf?* or *A Delicate Balance.* Albee, who always felt that his contentious relationship with

most of the New York critics underscored their misunderstanding of his work, elected to open his plays abroad—in Vienna, London, anywhere but New York City. With the success of *Three Tall Women* in its 1994 American premiere, however, Albee returned to the spotlight. The play's poignant exploration of the playwright's relationship with his mother earned Albee his third Pulitzer Prize.

When at his best, Albee animates his rebellious stages with warring characters enacting their fears and anxieties within a death-saturated world. When Jerry fatally impales himself on the knife in *The Zoo Story,* when Mommy and Daddy recall the ways in which they physically and spiritually dismembered their child in *The American Dream,* and when George and Martha physically and verbally attack each other for nearly four hours in *Who's Afraid of Virginia Woolf?* audiences are taken by the demonic energy of Albee's theater. Not surprisingly, there were a number of critics in the early years who saw the playwright as a nihilistic celebrant of an absurd world. Four decades later, though, most acknowledge that, despite the aggressiveness of Albee's texts, there is ultimately a sense of compassion and even affirmation unifying his work. Such compassion and affirmation underpin plays as different in dramatic conception as *Marriage Play* (1987) and *The Lorca Play* (1992) and *Fragments, A Concerto Grosso* (1993).

Albee experiments with dramatic form and structure and delights in exploring the borders of language itself. The plays range from 14-minute sketches (*Fam and Yam* [1960], *The Sandbox*) to such full-length Broadway productions as *A Delicate Balance* and *Seascape.* Sometimes he presents more overtly social protest plays (*The Death of Bessie Smith, The American Dream, The Man Who Had Three Arms*), but he seems most effective when exploring intimate domestic dramas concerned with psychological imbalances and the various illusions that he thinks too often spiritually anesthetize the individual. The play, for Albee, is an invitation for readers or viewers to immerse themselves in the action, an engagement he animates through language. Indeed, language, for many, stands as the greatest feature of his theater and is perhaps his major contribution to American drama. Just as

Tennessee Williams liberated a generation of playwrights with his poetic language, so, too, Albee liberated a newer group of writers through his clever dialogues. JOHN GUARE, ADRIENNE KENNEDY, MEGAN TERRY, SAM SHEPARD, and PAUL ZINDEL are but a few who felt directly influenced by the originality of Albee's voice. His verbal duels, some of which sound like musical arias, are now a well-known part of American dramatic history. Albee always demonstrates a willingness to take aesthetic and commercial risks. He has adapted works from other writers (*Ballad of the Sad Cafe* [1963], *Lolita* [1981], to name two), only to return to innovative plays whose musical richness complements the textual and visual aspects of his work (*Box* and *Quotations from Chairman Mao Tse-Tung*).

The typical Albee play presents characters who struggle to come to terms with a heightened awareness of their own faults, deceits, achievements, and insecurities. He wants his characters, and the audience, to transcend illusions. Albee never offers any guarantee of order, understanding, or love. Whether each character takes advantage of coming to consciousness varies from play to play, but the thematic and cultural point remains fixed: Albee consistently stages the possibility that his heroes can become more honest with the self, which in turn, as Albee has often said, creates the possibility for better self-government and a more engaged citizenry. His plays are dedicated to cutting through the illusions of his characters' lives, entering what he calls "the marrow" in *Virginia Woolf,* or the essence of human relationships, and creating the opportunity for living with an awakened sense of private responsibility and public commitment.

Albee is no longer the angry young playwright of years ago, but, now in his 80s, is an elder statesman for American theater. Long regarded as a "major" dramatist, Albee clearly has inscribed himself into the cultural history of the American theater. He has written more than 30 plays, including his late plays, *The Play About the Baby* (London, 1998; New York, 2001), a dark and abstract comedy in which a worldly-wise and cynical "Man" and "Woman" introduce a young, passionate, and naïve couple ("Boy" and "Girl") to the bleakness of life; the TONY AWARD–winning *The Goat; or, Who Is Sylvia* (2002), a satire on modern life featuring a family man who is having an offstage love affair with a goat; *Occupant* (2002), in which the late sculptor Louise Nevelson is interviewed; *Peter and Jerry* (2004), a two-act play made up of a new one-act prequel to *The Zoo Story,* titled *Homelife,* and *The Zoo Story* itself (after the New York premiere in 2007, the collective title was changed to *At Home at the Zoo*); and *Me, Myself and I* (2008), a dark comedy about identity, a pair of twins named Otto, and their unsatisfactory mother. In 2005, Albee received a Special Tony Award for Lifetime Achievement in the Theatre. Although he was and, in spirit, remains a decidedly Off-Broadway dramatist, Albee still finds himself at the center of the contemporary American theatrical world.

BIBLIOGRAPHY

Albee, Edward. *At Home at the Zoo.* New York: Dramatists Play Service, 2008.

———. *The Collected Plays of Edward Albee.* 3 vols. New York and Woodstock, N.Y.: Overlook Duckworth, 2004–2005.

———. *Stretching My Mind.* New York: Carroll and Graf, 2005.

———. *Who's Afraid of Virginia Woolf?* Rev. ed. New York: New American Library, 2006.

Amacher, Richard E. *Edward Albee.* Rev. ed. Boston: Twayne, 1982.

Bigsby, C. W. E. *Albee.* Edinburgh: Oliver and Boyd, 1969.

———. "Edward Albee." *A Critical Introduction to Twentieth-Century American Drama: Volume Two—Williams/Miller/Albee.* Cambridge, England: Cambridge University Press, 1984. 249–329.

———. "Edward Albee: Journey to Apocalypse." *Modern American Drama: 1945–1990.* Cambridge, England: Cambridge University Press, 1992. 126–151.

———, ed. *Edward Albee: A Collection of Critical Essays.* Englewood Cliffs, N.J.: Prentice-Hall, 1975.

———, ed. *Twentieth Century Views of Edward Albee.* Englewood Cliffs, N.J.: Prentice-Hall, 1975.

Bottoms, Stephen, ed. *The Cambridge Companion to Edward Albee.* New York: Cambridge University Press, 2005.

Cohn, Ruby. *Edward Albee.* Minneapolis: University of Minnesota Press, 1969.

Debusscher, Gilbert. *Edward Albee: Tradition and Renewal.* Trans. Anne D. Williams. Brussels, Belgium: Center for American Studies, 1967.

De La Fuente, Patricia, ed. *Edward Albee: Planned Wilderness.* Edinburg, Tex.: Pan American University Press, 1980.

Giantvalley, Scott. *Edward Albee: A Reference Guide.* Boston: G. K. Hall, 1987.

Gussow, Mel. *Edward Albee: A Singular Journey.* New York: Simon and Schuster, 1999.

Hayman, Ronald. *Edward Albee.* New York: Ungar, 1971.

Hirsch, Foster. *Who's Afraid of Edward Albee?* Berkeley, Calif.: Creative Arts, 1978.

Horn, Barbara Lee. *Edward Albee: A Research and Production Sourcebook.* New York: Praeger, 2003.

Kolin, Philip C., ed. *Conversations with Edward Albee.* Jackson: University Press of Mississippi, 1988.

———, and J. Madison Davis, eds. *Critical Essays on Edward Albee.* Boston: G. K. Hall, 1986.

McCarthy, Gerald. *Edward Albee.* New York: St. Martin's Press, 1987.

Paolucci, Anne. *From Tension to Tonic: The Plays of Edward Albee.* Carbondale: Southern Illinois University Press, 1972.

Roudané, Matthew. *Understanding Edward Albee.* Columbia: University of South Carolina Press, 1987.

Rutenberg, Michael E. *Edward Albee: Playwright in Protest.* New York: Drama Book Specialists, 1969.

Stenz, Anita Marie. *Edward Albee: The Poet of Loss.* The Hague: Mouton, 1978.

Wasserman, Julian, ed. *Edward Albee: An Interview and Essays.* Syracuse, N.Y.: Syracuse University Press, 1983.

Zinman, Toby. *Edward Albee.* Ann Arbor: University of Michigan Press, 2008.

Matthew Roudané
Georgia State University

ALISON'S HOUSE Susan Glaspell (1930)

Winner of the PULITZER PRIZE, *Alison's House* was inspired by the life of poet Emily Dickinson; in fact, GLASPELL sought the Dickinson estate's permission to use the poet's name and work, and when she was refused, she invented Alison Stanhope. The play deals with a dead poet's family and their decision whether to burn or publish work that reveals her personal life. Glaspell's play considers the immortality of art as well as the relationship between an artist and society.

The play begins 18 years after Alison Stanhope has died. She was an unmarried woman who was very kind and loving to her niece and nephew. As the play begins, her relatives are clearing out the home and examining her belongings. Her home is being sold to some crass people who want to turn it into an inn for tourists. Alison's brother is concerned about her reputation, as he knows that she loved a married man, even though she renounced her love, choosing instead to close herself up in the house and write poetry.

The play is set on the last night of the 19th century and is essentially a struggle between the conservative outlook of the older people and the more open views of the younger generation. The struggle comes to a climax over the discovery of Alison's unpublished poems, which reveal her improper love. Her niece, Elsa, surprises the family by arriving to see the house one more time before it is sold. She is regarded as a disgrace to the family because she did what Alison did not: She ran away with a married man and now lives with him. The family is particularly sensitive to scandal because of her behavior. Elsa and some of the other younger members of the family believe the poems should be published, even if they do reveal Alison's secret love. Elsa's Aunt Agatha is so determined to prevent such a step that she attempts to burn the house and thus destroy the poems.

Alison's brother is the figure who must be persuaded to allow publication of the poems, but he is initially opposed. When Elsa pleads her case, she asks that the dead Alison, who sacrificed her love for propriety, be allowed to give the poems to the people of the 20th century. In the end, she prevails, just as the new century is to begin.

As is true of Glaspell's one-act play TRIFLES (1916), the central figure of the play never appears on stage. *Trifles,* however, is considered a better work, perhaps because Glaspell had such a gift for the distilled form of the one-act play. When the Pulitzer Prize was awarded to *Alison's House,* the choice was called into question by critics, who felt the play's success had been due more to the performance of the lead actress than to the quality of the play itself. Thomas P. Adler suggests that, though it is "unexceptional Pulitzer material," in it, "many of the subjects pursued in the Pulitzer plays over the decades . . . converge: the new woman whose values are a beacon for the future; the artist as quasi-mystical singer for society; and the tempering of harsh paternalism through compassion, often learned from the child" (134).

BIBLIOGRAPHY

Adler, Thomas P. *Mirror on the Stage: The Pulitzer Plays as an Approach to American Drama.* West Lafayette, Ind.: Purdue University Press, 1987.

Yvonne Shafer
St. John's University

ALL GOD'S CHILLUN GOT WINGS

EUGENE O'NEILL (1924) Few other dramas have aroused the social controversy that surrounded the 1924 premiere of EUGENE O'NEILL's *All God's Chillun Got Wings.* The theme of the play—the insidiousness of racism—was lost in the outcry against the stage depiction of an interracial marriage. In many ways, the work, a barometer of the time, was not as compelling a drama as that created by the furor it aroused.

The opening scene of eight interracial children playing together introduces the affection between Jim, who is African American, and Ella, whom he calls "painty face" for her pink cheeks. Life is not kind to either. Jim has a difficult time graduating from high school, although he plans to pursue a law degree. His ambition is undermined by his lack of confidence. Ella fell in love with Mickey, a thug; bore an illegitimate child who died, and has been discarded when she meets Jim again. He is touched by her despair and his youthful feelings reawaken. He proposes marriage and she accepts, grateful to find a safe haven.

Ella cannot, however, conquer her own prejudice and the hostility of society. After their wedding, they exit to a segregated crowd that is united in disapproval. Even in France, where they honeymoon, Ella has increasing difficulty coping with the high visibility of an interracial couple. Upon their return, her Afrocentric sister-in-law, a teacher, brings them a mask from the Congo as a wedding gift. The mask haunts Ella, driving her to the brink of insanity. O'Neill's expressionistic stage directions make Ella's paranoia visual; he instructed the set designer to increase the size of the mask in sequential scenes while narrowing the walls and lowering the ceiling. Jim continues to study but is unable to concentrate. In one scene, Ella attacks him with a knife. He fails the bar exam but vows to care for her right up to the gates of heaven.

The public controversy began months before the May opening with the mayor's office attempting to close the play, white groups insisting Paul Robeson (who played Jim) be replaced by a lighter-skinned African American or Mary Blair (Ella) be replaced by a mulatto. African-American groups condemned the drama as dangerous for race relations, affirming they wanted to work with whites for the betterment of the African-American community. Newspapers like the *New York American* kept the controversy on their front pages in order to sell papers. More moderate groups found the play innocuous and decried the rabble-rousers, but they were ignored.

When the play opened, the critics, who expected pyrotechnics, were disappointed. The mayor's office was reduced to banning the first scene since they had legal control of the child actors. James Light, the director, read it to the audience. Police and private security agents surrounded the theater, but there were no riots, although a Ku Klux Klan booklet was discovered in the theater. Contemporary critics find Jim's passivity and Ella's hostility disquieting. Some also point out that the names O'Neill gave the interracial couple, Jim and Ella, were those of his own parents and that the play is thus a forerunner of LONG DAY'S JOURNEY INTO NIGHT (1956), in which the playwright depicted his parents' struggles more directly. The play is rarely performed today despite its incisive analysis of racism's insidious destruction of a man's confidence and a woman's love. Decades later, similar themes would be addressed in another American play featuring an interracial couple, *The GREAT WHITE HOPE* (1968) by Howard Sackler.

Glenda Frank
New York, New York

ALL MY SONS

ARTHUR MILLER (1947) Written and set immediately after World War II, *All My Sons* expresses a favorite theme of MILLER's: social responsibility. The play pits the capitalist, survival-of-the-fittest mentality of a father against his son's social conscience. It also deals movingly with the simple human theme of a grown child's disillusionment with his parent.

Chris Keller, having returned from service in World War II, works with his father in the family business, a machine shop. He finds himself at odds with his nation's—and, indeed, his own father's—pragmatic view of a war that, for Chris, was an intensely emotional event in which men took responsibility for each other. Chris describes his feelings to his friend, Ann: The men he served with "didn't die; they killed themselves for each other. . . . And [he] got an idea—watching them go down. Everything was being destroyed . . . but it seemed . . . that one new thing was made. A kind of . . . responsibility. Man for man," but then he "came home and . . . there was no meaning in it here; the whole thing to them was a kind of a—bus accident." Chris's brother, Larry, and many of the men who served under Chris did not come home. In order to make palatable his business-as-usual postwar life, Chris wants to marry Ann, his lifelong friend and his dead brother's sweetheart. Chris's mother, Kate Keller, opposes the match because to accept it, for her, is to accept Larry's death. This she will not do.

As the events precipitated by Ann's arrival unfold, Joe Keller's guilt is revealed: During the war Joe knowingly shipped out defective airplane parts to the military. As a result, 21 pilots died. Joe was tried and eventually acquitted of this crime while his partner, Ann's father, remains in prison for it. A confrontation with Chris brings him to admit his guilt to his son. A letter from Larry that Ann possesses reveals that Joe also indirectly caused Larry's death and that Larry held him responsible for the 21 pilots' deaths. Only after hearing Larry's indictment from the grave does Joe admit that his responsibility exceeds meeting the needs of his own family. He says to his wife, "I guess to [Larry] they were all my sons. And I guess they were, I guess they were." Joe exits and moments later a gunshot is heard, a gunshot that causes an earlier line of Joe's—"I'm his father and he's my son, and if there's something bigger than that I'll put a bullet through my head!"—to resonate. There is no ambiguity in Miller's message: There is something bigger than family; there is the community of humans to which we must all be responsible. If we are not, we will be doomed to a "jungle existence . . . no matter how high our buildings soar" (Miller 19).

All My Sons has often been called Ibsenesque, which Miller explains in the introduction to his *Collected Plays* means that it is "a dramatic work [shaped] on strict lines which will elicit a distinct meaning reducible to a sentence"; he adds that this is advocated by some critics and considered "suspect" by others (12). The play is also compared to Ibsen (particularly *The Wild Duck* [1884]) because, as Miller writes, "a great amount of time is taken up with bringing the past into the present." Miller adds, this exposition was not written "in deference to Ibsen," but rather because the play's theme is about "actions and consequences" (20). Joe Keller must face the terrible consequences of his past actions, which he fully understands only when those consequences become personal with the reading of Larry's letter.

All My Sons was Miller's first commercial and critical success, and with it, he began a long professional relationship with director ELIA KAZAN. The play's first production won the New York Drama Critics' Circle Award, and the 1987 New York production won the TONY AWARD for Best Revival.

BIBLIOGRAPHY
Bloom, Harold, ed. *Arthur Miller's "All My Sons."* New York: Chelsea House, 1988.
Miller, Arthur. *Arthur Miller's Collected Plays.* New York: Viking, 1957.

ALL THE WAY HOME TAD MOSEL (1960)

Winner of both the PULITZER PRIZE and the New York Drama Critics' Circle Award, this adaptation of James Agee's 1958 Pulitzer Prize–winning novel, *A Death in the Family,* has been both decried as too lyrical and praised for apt theatricality.

Set in Knoxville, Tennessee, and on nearby country roads and farms during 1915, Mosel's drama depicts both the obvious love and the certified tensions in the marriage of Mary Lynch Follet, who has been raised a prim Roman Catholic, and her more freespirited young lawyer husband Jay—who likes to drive fast and drink booze, and declares himself a sort of agnostic (although he noticeably enjoys singing Negro spirituals). They expect a second child but have not yet shared that news with their boy, Rufus—who, in act 1, bonds with his 104-year-old Great-Great-Granmaw.

The eventual unity of young and old, especially in the mortality that affects each one, is a central theme of Mosel's Ageean adaptation. After all, Great-Great-Granmaw, according to Jay's father, John Henry, should hardly be expected still to have breath. Yet John Henry himself seems threatened with death as act 1 ends, and the even-younger Jay dies, as a result of an offstage auto crash during act 2, while returning to Knoxville from a visit to his now-recovering father's bedside. Mary and Rufus, then, struggle with their shared grief, as well as with Rufus's lack of understanding about death (combined with his confusions about the coming baby's birth, which Mary now announces to him). Mary tries, meanwhile, to make continued sense of her religion and also to adopt into her child-rearing practices some of the late Jay's genial leniency.

In "Knoxville, Summer of 1915," Samuel Barber's musical sequence adapting the same Agee novel, the little-boy narrator reminds his audience of that sense of alienation from others that so regularly accompanies children's realized individuation. The child Rufus, in Mosel's drama, surely also feels this sort of somber alienation within his own growth experiences. Consequently, he briefly even tries to win other boys' favor by bragging that his "daddy's dead!" However, Mosel focuses more on the inevitable alienation of individuated *adults,* especially Jay. Mary cannot fully comprehend Jay's compulsions to drink, to speed in the car, and to share folk wisdom with strangers in all-night lunchrooms; yet she does accept (despite her own relative commitment to standardized Roman Catholic explanations of human duties and fates) that Jay had to live part of his life in personal secrecy. She also takes solace from realizing that he was, nonetheless, not totally separate from his family, and that, indeed, at the moment of his death, he was driving, with fervent desire, "home" (*toward,* but also *beyond,* them).

Jeffrey B. Loomis
Northwest Missouri State University

AMEN CORNER, THE JAMES BALDWIN (1955)

Set in a Harlem storefront church, *The Amen Corner* portrays an evangelical pastor facing her life at a very critical moment: Her husband returns after 10 years, her son repudiates her protective care, and her parish congregation deposes her as leader.

Margaret Alexander, who heard the Lord's call after the stillbirth of her second baby, has been spiritual leader of a neighborhood worship house for 10 years, preaching the need for pure living and unfettered devotion to God. Along with her sister Odessa and her son David, who plays the piano at services, Sister Margaret lives above the church. The three are the physical, as well as spiritual, caretakers of this religious community. The three-act play begins on a Sunday afternoon during a prayer service, where Margaret's preaching is accompanied by the sounds of gospel singing. This first scene introduces BALDWIN's major themes of personal redemption and the power of music. It begins to explore the relationship between the spheres of black music's liberated (jazz and blues) and repressive (church and religious) manifestations, and it demonstrates the characters' responses to lives dominated by the history of white oppression. As the first act ends, Margaret goes off to preach in Philadelphia, leaving her recently returned husband Luke ill and uncared for.

In the second act, Baldwin focuses on the lives of Luke and David—both torn between the individual salvation of music and the search for identity dominated by Margaret. David tells his father of his budding career in music and of the fulfillment playing in a jazz quartet provides him. However, Luke cautions him about the expectations of spiritual fulfillment, telling his son that the music—as potent as it is—is not enough. As the story begins to hint at David's inevitable departure, several members of the congregation, led by Sisters Boxer and Moore and Brother Boxer, begin to sow dissent related to Sister Margaret's improper management of the church. By portraying the fractured reality of this critical black institution, Baldwin integrates into his themes the roles of community and religion in the development of identity.

David decides he must leave home and be honest with himself and with his mother, and, before the final scene, Luke dies after returning to Margaret's arms. Wishing she could start over, Margaret is overwhelmed and now must confront her congregation one last time. In her final address to them, she extols the importance of loving "all [God's] children" with a tolerance and compassion that she for so long was unable to demonstrate to her own husband and son. She has lost everything, but she has gained—as Baldwin himself has written of his character—"the keys to the kingdom. [And] [t]he kingdom is love, and love is selfless" (xvi).

Baldwin's stepfather (whom Baldwin thought was his biological father until he was 18) was a storefront preacher, and like Sister Margaret, he was hard on his son. This experience is the origin of the play. Baldwin explains in his introduction to the published play that "Sister Margaret's dilemma" is "how to treat her husband and son as men and at the same time to protect them from the bloody consequences of trying to be a man in this [racist] society. . . . [H]er love, which is real but which is also at the mercy of her genuine and absolutely justifiable terror, turns her into a tyrannical matriarch" (xvi).

The Amen Corner was first produced at Howard University in 1955. Nearly 10 years later, it was revived in Los Angeles; the Los Angeles production was moved to Broadway in 1965, but in that era of militancy in AFRICAN-AMERICAN DRAMA, it was not enthusiastically received.

BIBLIOGRAPHY

Baldwin, James. *The Amen Corner.* New York: Dial Press, 1968.

Matthew J. Caballero
University of California–Davis

AMERICA HURRAH JEAN-CLAUDE VAN ITALLIE (1966)

JEAN-CLAUDE VAN ITALLIE's *America Hurrah* is a trilogy of plays consisting of *Motel, Interview,* and *TV. Motel,* initially titled *The Savage God* and then later revised as *America Hurrah,* premiered at Ellen Stewart's OFF-OFF-BROADWAY La MaMa Experimental Theatre Club on April 28, 1965, on a twin bill with van Itallie's *Pavane.* Written in 1962, the play tried to shock and surprise bourgeois audiences much like Antonin Artaud's Theatre of Cruelty. *Motel,* inspired by van Itallie's reading of Edward Gordon Craig's productions featuring huge marionettes, depicts two larger than life dolls (A Man and A Woman) who proceed to destroy a motel room run by the matronly Motel-Keeper. As the Motel-Keeper recites a list of junk items that might appear to be antiques purchased from a mail-order catalogue, the Man and Woman rip the bedspreads to shreds, tear apart the bathroom, pull down the curtains, smash the TV and picture frames, write obscenities on the wall, tear pages out of the Bible, throw clothing around the room, and finally tear the arms off the Motel-Keeper. Van Itallie implies that an artificially commercialized civilization concerned more with material possessions than with viable communication among people will see its own destruction. He depicts a sterile, vapid, alienated American society that will ultimately lead to an apocalypse. The myth of the American dream is exposed to reveal underlying violence, alienation, and anomie. *Motel* can be perceived as an archetypal psychodrama that exposes the audience to the nation's nightmares and afflictions and then purges the spectators of this sense of violence and brutality. The audience is led to understand intuitively that they contribute to this national malaise consisting of violence in a society overwhelmed by junk, and unless there is more compassion, the apocalypse will be upon us.

In September 1965, the Open Theater (an experimental improvisational theater troupe) began workshops on *America Hurrah. Interview,* originally titled *Pavane,* was initially staged on April 26, 1965, at the Sheridan Square Playhouse, then was filmed for National Educational Television, and later was performed at Cafe La MaMa with *America Hurrah* (which was later to become *Motel*) before its preparation for OFF-BROADWAY production. *Interview* is structured like a fugue that works by modulations in music. The overall form of the play is derived from the Open Theater's transformation exercises in which performers, without warning, suddenly shift from one character, place, or ideology to another. The play also contains elements of expressionist theater, especially in its loose episodic structure and its stylized set, as well as absurdist drama, which presents images of humanity's alienation and isolation bordering on a grotesque, nightmarish existence. In addition, as in THEATRE OF

THE ABSURD, language is shown in a state of breakdown. Through a series of vignettes that "transform" from one to another, *Interview* conveys humanity's mechanization and depersonalization. The fugue-like refrain—"Can you help me?"—permeates this cold, sterile world. Life is seen as deadening, ritualized into roles that force individuals to conform. Representatives of institutions have lost their individuality; as role players, they lack the feelings to help anyone. As the scenes move from an impersonal interview room to a lifeless and mechanical fitness class to a party in which the guests are oblivious to a story about an accident victim and to the depiction of lack of empathy from representatives of our most powerful institutions (a psychiatrist, a priest, and a politician), van Itallie demonstrates the unfeeling and uncaring nature of contemporary society. As detached role players, individuals have become interchangeable. The result is a society inundated with solitude, loneliness, despair, and insecurity.

Van Itallie wrote *TV,* a one-act play, as the third part of the trilogy to accompany *Interview* and *Motel.* *TV* portrays Hal, Susan, and George as television researchers who spend all day evaluating programs. As the trio discuss their work and gossip about their social lives, a second group of actors whose *"faces are made up with thin horizontal black lines to suggest the way they might appear to a viewer"* play television characters acting in the programs that the evaluators are watching. During the course of the play, the performers playing television personalities begin to occupy more of the stage, slowly invading the viewing room. The action on television eventually encroaches upon the lives of the reviewers (or viewers) watching the programs. *TV* thus depicts synonymy between the illusory world of television and the equally sterile real world. The contrast between what is dramatized on television and the personal lives of the programmers is seen throughout the play, continually reinforcing the concept, made popular by Marshall McLuhan, that the media controls our social perceptions. Television, van Itallie implies, numbs the viewer, anesthetizing the masses into accepting what is advertised by Madison Avenue or Hollywood. It also portrays an American life without transcendent values—a sterile

and impersonal society in which roles have replaced personal identities. Our empty lives become reduced to roles that we see on television daily; personal identities, as reflected in the banal lives and trite dialogue of Hal, Susan, and George, are lost.

Gene A. Plunka
University of Memphis

AMERICAN BUFFALO DAVID MAMET (1976)

American Buffalo premiered at the Goodman Theatre in Chicago, but it later moved to the St. Clement's Theatre in New York City, where it won the New York Drama Critics' Circle Award and quickly established MAMET's reputation as one of America's best young playwrights. A two-act, three-character play, *American Buffalo* is for the most part plotless. The story is mainly exposition, background that serves to intensify and inform the immediate situation: three small-time burglars planning a robbery they never commit. But the play is about much more than petty thievery. It is a scathing attack on American materialism and how the perverse Darwinian business ethic that dominates American culture infects the sanctity of family and friendship.

The action takes place in Don's Resale Shop, where Don, the proprietor, has taken on a fatherly role to Bobby, a drug-addled naif who trusts Don the way a dog might its master. Don and Bobby are planning to steal a buffalo-head nickel back from a man who previously bought it from Don for the improbable price of $90. Skeptical of the man's willingness to pay so much for the coin—he even returned hoping to buy more coins—Don is convinced that he has been swindled and that the man has played him for a fool, and he is determined not to let the man get the better of him. As he explains to Bobby, the planned theft is nothing more than a shrewd business move, a necessary rearguard action to defend his integrity.

The problem with the plan is that Bobby is the one "going in," and it is obvious from the outset that Bobby, a recovering junkie, is not up to the job. Don tries to explain to him the ruling law of business: "People taking care of themselves." If Don is blind to Bobby's ineptitude, the third character, Teach, corrects Don's vision. As soon as he finds out what Don and Bobby are planning, he offers his advice: "[D]on't confuse business with pleasure." Teach, a petty egoist, considers himself not only a good burglar but also a first-rate "businessman," one who knows the meaning of "free enterprise"; he manages to turn Don against Bobby, convincing Don that he should be the one who handles the heist. Don agrees on the condition that they also bring in Fletch, a man he respects for having "skill and talent." This angers Teach, whose relationships with other people are based strictly on cutthroat competition. He calls Fletch a "cheat" and threatens to walk out on the deal. When Bobby tells them that Fletch has been "mugged" and is in the hospital, Teach and Don turn on Bobby, suspicious after he tries to sell Don another buffalo-head nickel; Teach attacks Bobby violently. Bobby, however, is telling the truth, and in a frantic burst of frustration and anger Teach trashes the shop, then goes for his car to take Bobby to the hospital.

American Buffalo is a tale of shifting loyalties and backroom duplicity, a powerful indictment of corporate America. In the world of Don's Resale Shop, a shot at success is purchased at the expense of friendship, and the innocent are sacrificed at the altar of expedience, literally buffaloed—that is, exploited—for the sake of profit and self-vindication. The play details the driving, corrosive, machismo logic inherent in the frantic pursuit of the American Dream. With measured pathos, it illustrates the damage caused by the breakdown of trust and familial bonding as well as the lack of values engendered by dog-eat-dog capitalism.

Jeff Johnson
Brevard Community College

AMERICAN COMPANY, THE See DOUGLASS, DAVID.

AMERICAN DREAM, THE EDWARD ALBEE (1961) In a preface to *The American Dream,* the fifth, longest, and last of his early one-acts, ALBEE describes the play as "an attack on the substitution of artificial for real values in our society, a condemnation of complacency, cruelty, emasculation and vacuity; it is a stand against the fiction that everything in this sleeping land of ours is peachy-keen" (8).

The American Dream illustrates the vapidity and destructive power of American family life through its depiction of a couple who, although childless, call themselves Mommy and Daddy, and Mommy's mother, Grandma, who lives with them. Mommy and Daddy make Grandma do the cooking and housework and continually threaten to put her in a nursing home. Grandma, in turn, claims that her daughter married Daddy only because he was rich. The dynamic between Mommy and Daddy is one in which she constantly belittles him ("You're turning into jelly; you're indecisive; you're a woman."); and they both torment Grandma ("Old people have nothing to say; and if old people *did* have something to say, nobody would listen to them.").

As the play opens, Mommy, Daddy, and Grandma are ostensibly awaiting the arrival of a repairperson to fix their leaking toilet, although Grandma fears they are expecting a van to take her to the nursing home. But when Mrs. Barker comes in, she says she is the "chairman" of Mommy's "woman's club" and "knee-deep" with "this committee and that committee." After Daddy leaves the room to break Grandma's television and "step on" her blind Pekinese and Mommy exits to get Mrs. Barker a drink of water, Grandma reveals that, many years earlier, Mrs. Barker had visited Mommy and Daddy as a volunteer for the Bye-Bye Adoption Agency. In that capacity, she arranged for them to adopt "a bumble of joy" because they couldn't have children of their own. Then, in a passage that perfectly illustrates what Albee has described as the play's portrayal of "the breakdown of language" (Gussow 141), Grandma describes how, subsequently, Mommy and Daddy systematically destroyed their child: Mommy gouged out its eyes when "it only had eyes for its Daddy"; they "cut its hands off at the wrists" and "cut off its you-know-what" when "it began to develop an interest in its you-know-what"; and "they cut its tongue out" when "it called its Mommy a dirty name." When the "bumble" finally "up and died," they "wanted satisfaction; they wanted their money back."

At this point, the doorbell rings again and the Young Man enters. He is, as he describes himself, a "[c]lean cut, midwest farm boy type, almost insultingly good-looking in a typically American way." Grandma, who immediately dubs him "the American Dream," fears that he is the van man, but he tells her he is "looking for work" and will "do almost anything for money" because, as he explains, "I have no talents at all, except what you see." He then reveals to Grandma that he was one of identical twins who were separated at birth and "thrown to opposite ends of the continent"; as a consequence, he explains, "I no longer have the capacity to feel anything. I have no emotions. . . . I let people love me. . . . I can feel nothing." After hearing his story, Grandma, who tells him he looks "familiar," enlists him to pose as the van man and tells Mrs. Barker of her plan.

After Grandma leaves, Mrs. Barker, who has presumably been prompted by Grandma, introduces the Young Man to Mommy and Daddy as a "surprise," and Daddy indicates that the Young Man is the "satisfaction" they demanded of Mrs. Barker when their "bumble" died. Mommy sidles seductively up to the Young Man, remarking that there is "something familiar" about him, suggesting that he is their "bumble's" long-lost twin. Grandma (unseen by the characters onstage except for the Young Man) observes this final scene *stage right, near the footlights* and ends the play by observing, "let's leave things as they are right now . . . while everybody's happy . . . while everybody's got what he wants . . . or everybody's got what he thinks he wants."

According to Albee's biographer, Mel Gussow, *The American Dream* is the play that qualified its author "as a charter member of the Theatre of the Absurd" (141), the movement described by critic Martin Esslin in his 1961 book of that title. Esslin claimed that, with *The American Dream,* Albee translated the THE-ATRE OF THE ABSURD's "sense of metaphysical anguish at the absurdity of the human condition" (5) into "a genuine American idiom" (267). The play also looks forward to Albee's later longer works, especially WHO'S AFRAID OF VIRGINIA WOOLF? (1962), his next play, in that both plays depict an emasculated male and a childless couple, but, more importantly, in their portrayals of what C. W. E. Bigsby calls "a linguistic world constructed to deny the power of reality" (263). As the Young Man cautions after he tells Grandma his story,

"Be careful, be very careful. What I told you may not be true."

BIBLIOGRAPHY
Albee, Edward. *The American Dream.* New York: Coward-McCann, 1961.
Bigsby, C. W. E. *A Critical Introduction to Twentieth-Century American Drama: Volume Two—Williams/Miller/Albee.* Cambridge, England: Cambridge University Press, 1984.
Esslin, Martin. *The Theatre of the Absurd.* Rev. ed. Garden City, N.Y.: Anchor, 1968.
Gussow, Mel. *Edward Albee: A Singular Journey.* New York: Simon and Schuster, 1999.

ANDERSON, LAURIE (1947–)

Born Laura Phillips Anderson in Chicago, Anderson is the epitome of the avant-garde conceptual/performance artist, a *sui generis* multimedia composer and performer who first came to prominence in the early 1970s. She studied violin as a teenager, earned her B.A. in art history from Barnard College in 1969, and received an M.F.A. in sculpture from Columbia University in 1972. A regular participant in SoHo's "Downtown" art scene, she numbered composer Philip Glass among her mentors.

While teaching art history at various New York colleges, she began her public performance career in 1973. Her ambitious work incorporated not just music played on a variety of instruments, many of which she created herself (such as her infamous tape-bow violin, which used magnetic tape as a bow and playback heads in lieu of strings), but also dance, film, mime, and projections. Her work centers upon the mysteries of both written and spoken language, and her wry observations, paradoxically on the theme of alienation caused by a technologically obsessed society, hit nerves with audiences worldwide.

Early works include *O-Range* (1973), whose performers shouted stories through megaphones in City College of New York's empty Lewisohn Stadium, and *Duets on Ice* (1974), in which Anderson played violin on street corners and was accompanied by herself on tape, wearing ice skates embedded in blocks of ice—the performance ended when the ice melted.

Beginning in 1975 and continuing through the 1980s and 1990s, Anderson traveled extensively with numerous shows and installations throughout the United States and abroad, making a name for herself with her eccentric performances and punk persona. Anderson's career reached a pinnacle with the intense media scrutiny accompanying *United States Part 2* in 1980. In 1981, Anderson began recording her compositions, releasing the single *O Superman.* The song, with its electronically altered vocals, became a surprise hit in Great Britain, reaching number two on pop charts and prompting Warner Brothers Records to sign her to a long-term contract. *Big Science,* her first album, was released in 1982.

With newfound fame and increased financial backing, Anderson's pieces became ever more elaborate; her eight-hour opus, *United States I–IV* (1983), secured her position as a premier solo performance artist. A backlash occurred with *Mister Heartbreak* (1984), which was considered to rely too heavily on glossy production without the expected innovative content, despite contributions from romantic partner Peter Gabriel and author William S. Burroughs. In 1985, Anderson released her first full-length film, *Home of the Brave,* culled from various previous performance pieces, which she directed herself. Despite acclaim at the Cannes Film Festival, it was a commercial failure. Anderson also began inroads into the mainstream, with performances on television's *Saturday Night Live* and *The Tonight Show.*

Scaling back, in 1989 Anderson became more overtly political with her *Strange Angels* tour, which also incorporated a more mature singing style, as opposed to her previous "talking" vocals. In 1994, her book *Stories from the Nerve Bible* was published, documenting the first 20 years of her work.

In the past decade, Anderson has continued to collaborate with such artists as composer Brian Eno and rocker Lou Reed, whom she married in 2008, after a 10-year relationship. She has created a number of multimedia presentations, including *Songs and Stories from Moby Dick* (1999), based on the Melville classic. In 2003, an association with NASA inspired her performance piece about space travel, *The End of the Moon.* She also collaborated on the critically acclaimed multimedia ballet *O Zlozony/O Composite* (2004) for the Paris Opera Ballet. In 2005, her exhibition *The Waters Reglitterized,* based on her dream journal, opened in New York City. The journal itself was also published in book form as *Night Life* in 2007. A new performance piece, *Homeland,* was showcased as a work-in-progress in New York throughout 2007, followed by a brief overseas tour.

BIBLIOGRAPHY

Anderson, Laurie. *Stories from the Nerve Bible.* New York: HarperCollins, 1994.

Douglas W. Gordy
Walnut Creek, California

ANDERSON, MAXWELL (1888–1959)

Born in Atlantic, Pennsylvania, Maxwell Anderson was educated at the University of North Dakota from which he graduated in 1911 and at Stanford University where he earned his master's degree in 1914. He taught briefly before becoming a journalist. As a journalist, Anderson worked for the *Grand Forks Herald, San Francisco Chronicle,* and *San Francisco Bulletin.* Later, he was an editorial writer for the *New Republic,* the *New York Globe,* and the *New York World.* Anderson was a prolific playwright, writing or cowriting more than 30 works for the stage; this does not include some 20 completed, but unpublished, plays. Though not all of his plays were written in verse, he was an avid proponent of the use of blank verse in modern drama. Anderson maintained that "prose is the language of information and poetry the language of emotion" (*Off Broadway* 50). His book of dramatic theory, *The Essence of Tragedy,* was published in 1939.

Though Anderson's first play, *White Desert* (1923), a tragedy written in blank verse, failed, he did not give up his hope of writing verse plays for the American stage. His first success, however, was not a verse tragedy but a realistic and irreverent comedy about World War I, WHAT PRICE GLORY? (1924), written in collaboration with LAURENCE STALLINGS. Another success, *Saturday's Children* (1927), dealt with a young couple's marital problems. Though he had returned to tragedy, he had not returned to verse. Not until he chose settings other than contemporary ones did he again attempt verse tragedy; his two historical dramas, *Elizabeth the Queen* (1930) and *Mary of Scotland* (1933), were well received. Once again though, greater recognition came to a prose comedy, BOTH YOUR HOUSES (1933), a satire on the U.S. Congress, which won Anderson the PULITZER PRIZE.

In 1935, WINTERSET, a verse drama set in a contemporary American slum and inspired by the Sacco and Vanzetti case of the 1920s, brought Anderson much success and won the first New York Drama Critics' Circle Award. The play considers the relative guilt of the people involved in sending an innocent man to the electric chair: an eyewitness who withholds the truth to save himself, a judge who believes that to overturn a case that has followed due process is to jeopardize the "common good," and others; events are precipitated by the arrival of the dead man's son who seeks to clear his father's name. The next year, Anderson again won the New York Drama Critics' Circle Award for *High Tor* (1936), a comic fantasy in blank verse, which provides a humorous view of modern civilization. With German composer Kurt Weill, Anderson collaborated on the musicals *Knickerbocker Holiday* (1938), which was based on New York history, and *Lost in the Stars* (1949), based on Alan Paton's novel *Cry, the Beloved Country*. His last play, *The Bad Seed* (1954), about an irredeemably evil little girl, was an adaptation of a novel by William March. Other significant plays include *Night Over Taos* (1932), *Valley Forge* (1934), *Wingless Victory* (1936), *The Star Wagon* (1937), *Key Largo* (1939), *Candle in the Wind* (1941), *Eve of St. Mark* (1942), *Joan of Lorraine* (1946), *Anne of a Thousand Days* (1948), and *Barefoot in Athens* (1951).

BIBLIOGRAPHY

Anderson, Maxwell. *Eleven Verse Plays, 1929–1939*. New York: Harcourt Brace, 1940.
———. *The Essence of Tragedy and Other Footnotes and Papers*. Washington, D.C.: Anderson House, 1939.
———. *Off Broadway: Essays about the Theatre*. New York: William Sloane Associates, 1947.
———, and Laurence Stallings. *Three American Plays*. New York: Harcourt Brace, 1926.
Avery, Laurence G., ed. *Dramatist in America: Letters of Maxwell Anderson, 1912–1958*. Chapel Hill: University of North Carolina Press, 1977.
Horn, Barbara Lee. *Maxwell Anderson: A Research and Production Sourcebook*. Westport, Conn.: Greenwood, 1996.
Shivers, Alfred S. *The Life of Maxwell Anderson*. New York: Stein and Day, 1983.

ANDERSON, ROBERT (1917–2009)

Very much a playwright of the 1950s, Robert Anderson crafted highly literate and well-made, if sometimes melodramatic, works of psychological realism, featuring characters beset by emotional disorders and sexual tribulations. Responding in part to the paranoia rampant during the House Un-American Activities Committee hearings of the McCarthy era, the subtext in his plays of family problems was often the victimized individual's quest for freedom in a repressive society. Consequently, he frequently espoused the need to develop an ethical relativism and a nonjudgmental compassion toward others as an antidote to restrictive social or religious norms.

Born in New York City, educated at Phillips Exeter Academy and Harvard, and a navy lieutenant during World War II, Anderson was introduced to New York audiences with *Come Marching Home* (1946), an Ibsenite play about a returning war hero who enters a political fray in the face of a complacent electorate. Anderson reached a wider audience at Washington's Arena Stage with *All Summer Long* (1953), a philosophically dark Chekhovian mood play about a young boy's rite of passage. Later that year, he arrived on Broadway with what deservedly remains his best-known work, TEA AND SYMPATHY. Set in a New England boarding school, it tells of an artistic and not outwardly manly 18-year-old whose sexuality is questioned by a homophobic father and a housemaster who himself may be a latent homosexual. After failing sexually with a prostitute, the boy's belief in his own heterosexuality is restored when the housemaster's wife tenderly takes him to bed. Anderson's last play of the 1950s, *Silent Night, Lonely Night* (1959), features two people, each married to someone else, who sentimentally come together in a brief encounter sanctioned by a higher morality in rebellion against an inhibiting set of absolute strictures.

The Days Between (1965), produced widely in campus and regional theaters, is told from the viewpoint of a woman who has submerged her own identity in that of her alcoholic writer-teacher husband. Returning to Broadway, Anderson scored his biggest commercial success with YOU KNOW I CAN'T HEAR YOU WHEN THE WATER'S RUNNING (1967), an evening of four one-act plays about the inability to communicate. His last two works are technically somewhat more adventurous. I NEVER SANG FOR MY FATHER (1968) is a cinematically handled, autobiographical memory play, whose narrator berates himself for having failed to love an impossibly demanding father. *Solitaire/ Double Solitaire* (1971) is another evening of long one-acts; the first occurs in a dystopian technocracy where state-sanctioned houses of illusion relieve one's loss of identity, while the more consequential second act employs the form of the morality play artfully blended with multimedia effects to tell about three generations of family relationships founded upon differing attitudes toward the importance of rituals and vows.

Anderson's plays about married sexuality reiterate certain themes: the necessity to set aside traditional moral codes that prevent people from responding openly and unselfishly to the needs of others; the idealization of sexuality that, while warding off mortality and terror of the void, might end by objectifying the other; the tendency of men to confuse manliness with strength and aggression, and thereby fail to foster sensitivity; the propensity of women to sublimate their own identity and fulfillment in the wishes of another. What secures Anderson's position in American dramatic history is his recurrent focus on gender stereotyping and sexual roles, as well as his particular sympathy for those ostracized for being somehow different.

A member of the Playwrights Company, Anderson also wrote radio and television scripts; two novels; and several screenplays, most notably *The Nun's Story* (1959) and *I Never Sang for My Father* (1970), both of which received Academy Award nominations for film adaptation.

BIBLIOGRAPHY
Adler, Thomas P. *Robert Anderson*. Boston: Twayne, 1978.
Anderson, Robert. *All Summer Long*. New York: Samuel French, 1955.
———. *The Days Between*. New York: Samuel French, 1969.
———. *I Never Sang for My Father*. New York: Random House, 1968.
———. *Silent Night, Lonely Night*. New York: Random House, 1960.
———. *Solitaire/Double Solitaire*. New York: Random House, 1972.
———. *Tea and Sympathy*. New York: Random House, 1953.
———. *You Know I Can't Hear You When the Water's Running*. New York: Random House, 1967.

Thomas P. Adler
Purdue University

ANDRÉ WILLIAM DUNLAP (1798)   Perhaps WILLIAM DUNLAP's best-known play, *André* opened to instant furor at New York's Park Theatre on March 30, 1798. Based on the history of Britain's Major John André, the play reopened old wounds in a nation still coming to terms with one of the most controversial incidents of the Revolution. The real André was a romantic figure captured while trying to bribe a group of Americans to help Britain. He was sentenced to execution by hanging. In the late 18th century, the "rules of war" dictated that death by hanging was for common criminals. Yet General Washington, remembering that the British had hanged American officer Nathan Hale, refused to allow André a more dignified death. André was executed on October 2, 1780. Many of Washington's critics considered his handling of André's case a blot on his career.

Thus Dunlap's choice to stage the incident as a blank-verse tragedy struck his audience as potentially disloyal. However, the execution of Major André is, in many ways, not the central focus of the play. Dunlap was writing during a period of high tension between the Federalists and the Republicans, and the play is a metaphor for the dangers of party division and self-interest.

In the play, Dunlap shifts the focus from André to an American soldier, Bland. Bland is a hothead, governed by emotion rather than reason. He learns of André's capture in the first scene of the play and rushes to save him. (André had once saved Bland's life when Bland was a prisoner of war.) Yet as act 2 opens,

André refuses to plead for his life, asking only that he be shot, rather than hanged. In the meantime, the audience learns that Bland's father is a prisoner among the British, one whom the British now threaten to execute in retaliation for the execution of André. The news comes in a letter to Bland's mother, who sets off for Washington's camp to ask him to save her husband.

Even as she journeys to the camp, Bland confronts Washington (referred to only as "The General"). Angrily, Bland tears the American cockade from his hat and throws it underfoot, renouncing his allegiance. (It was this gesture that so inflamed audiences when the play first opened.) In perhaps the most important scene of the play, Bland's friend M'Donald rebukes him for thinking only of himself and how André's death affects him, rather than the thousands of Americans André conspired to betray: "He sav'd thy life, yet strove to damn thy country."

New hope for André comes with his former sweetheart, Honora, who brings offers from the British to save him. She is close to persuading Washington, when news comes that a captured American soldier has been hanged without a trial. Crying, "Why, why my country, did I hesitate," Washington rushes out and André's fate is sealed. As André marches to his death, news comes that Bland's father has been saved. In a scene added after the play's opening, M'Donald returns Bland's cockade, a symbol of his renewed loyalty to America. As the play closes, M'Donald entreats the audience to remember the *true* story of André, and stand together, rather than being divided by party conflict.

There are numerous versions of Major John André's life and death, including various 19th-century plays, poems, songs, novels, and children's stories. Many blend fact and fiction, suggesting that André's history provided romantic fodder for generations of American storytellers. Dunlap, himself, adapted his *André* to a less controversial and more patriotic play entitled *The Glory of Columbia—Her Yeomanry!*, which opened on July 4, 1803.

Heather Nathans
University of Maryland

ANGELS IN AMERICA: A GAY FANTASIA ON NATIONAL THEMES. PART ONE: MILLENNIUM APPROACHES (1990) and PART TWO: PERESTROIKA TONY KUSHNER (1991)

Epic in its sweep, political in its social resonance, fantastic in its drug-induced dream sequences, surreal in its movement between heaven and earth, and apocalyptic in its portrayal of an approaching new world order, *Angels in America: Millennium Approaches* and *Perestroika* is set during the Reagan era at the time of the AIDS epidemic. TONY KUSHNER's epic depicts an America lost and suggests a possible paradise regained.

Moving from downtown New York City to Washington, D.C., to Salt Lake City to the South Bronx to the Kremlin and Antarctica, the audience is transported around the globe and beyond—to heaven. Mormons fall in love with Jews, straights mix with gays, WASPs befriend African Americans, Republicans debate Democrats, ghosts of "Black Jack" (the great plague of an earlier century) interact with AIDS-infected patients at the end of the 20th century—all are a part of Kushner's crowded canvas, which also includes historical characters on stage (Roy Cohn and Ethel Rosenberg) and off (Joseph Smith and Judy Garland, Emma Goldman and Nancy Reagan, Mikhail Gorbachev and Ronald Reagan).

Epic-like, *Angels in America* creates a vast apocalyptic vision at a time when the moral universe seems to have collapsed, when an insensitive political regime appears to be ignoring the needs of the society at large, when the great plague of the AIDS epidemic threatens human existence. Also a morality play, it spotlights the conflict between good and evil in various battles as the protagonist, Prior Walter, fights with Death and the horrifying kiss of Death (lesions); as Mormon and closeted-homosexual Joe Pitt wrestles with the angel in an attempt to discover himself; as the Right attempts to demolish the Left; and as homosexuals and homophobes combat each other while they search for answers.

Central to both the morality play and the epic, the journey motif is also at the soul of Kushner's play: the journey of emigrants from the Old World to the New World, of Jews from the ghettos of Europe to the promised land of America, of Mormons from upstate New York to Salt Lake City, of gays out of their ghettoized closets into daylight. Kushner's epic hero, Prior, embarks on a savagely comic journey that eventually leads him to a heaven that resembles San Francisco. Confronting Prior along the way is the larger-than-death McCarthyite lawyer, Roy Cohn, who denied his own homosexuality until his death in 1968. With sharp wit and demonic grandeur, this saint-of-the-right worships power while celebrating his own heartlessness.

Prior is the chosen one called on by an angel at the end of *Part One: Millennium Approaches* when she crashes through his ceiling to announce that he will lead his people out of their closets, away from their self-absorption and quiet deaths. The time has come for Kushner's spindly, gay, AIDS-infected everyman to accept his role as an epic hero who descends to the underworld by, ironically, ascending to heaven where he finds that God has apparently gone on an extended sabbatical and that the other heavenly forces are not responding to human affairs. The good news he brings back to Earth is the renewed hope in the eternal truths of the heart—love and honor and pity and pride and compassion and sacrifice. These qualities represent a heavy and frightening responsibility, but they are a challenge that Prior—and Kushner—feel humankind can handle. At the end of *Part Two: Perestroika,* a new order is ushered in as Prior proclaims, "The disease will be the end of many of us, but not nearly all. . . . We won't die secret deaths anymore. The world only spins forward. We will be citizens. The time has come. . . . The Great Work Begins."

By the time *Angels in America* was produced in New York, both parts had already been successfully produced in London and Los Angeles. When Kushner's much anticipated work finally opened on Broadway in 1993, *Part One: The Millennium Approaches* was critically acclaimed universally and was awarded the New York Drama Critics' Circle Award, the TONY AWARD, and the PULITZER PRIZE. *Part Two: Perestroika* also won the Tony Award in 1994.

BIBLIOGRAPHY

Geis, Deborah R., and Steven F. Kruger, eds. *Approaching the Millennium: Essays on "Angels in America."* Ann Arbor: University of Michigan Press, 1997.

Nielsen, Ken. *Tony Kushner's "Angels in America."* London and New York: Continuum, 2008.

Colby H. Kullman
University of Mississippi

"ANNA CHRISTIE" EUGENE O'NEILL (1921)

"Anna Christie" opened at Broadway's Vanderbilt Theatre and earned EUGENE O'NEILL a second PULITZER PRIZE. It was the playwright's first full-length play with a female protagonist, a prostitute redeemed by her father's love. It marked the transition from his early male-dominated sea plays to the dramas of the middle period, including *STRANGE INTERLUDE* (1928) and *MOURNING BECOMES ELECTRA* (1931), which are recognizable by their assertive women. *"Anna Christie"* was rewritten twice unsuccessfully with a male protagonist and was originally titled "Chris Christophersen." Only after Anna, "who knows exactly what she wants," as O'Neill wrote to critic George Jean Nathan, had "forced herself on [O'Neill]," did the play come to life (Bogard and Bryer 148). The third act contains one of the strongest feminist assertions of independence in the American canon.

The play opens to a misunderstanding. Chris Christophersen is awaiting the arrival of his daughter, who, according to her letters, has been a nanny. In actuality, she has recently been released from jail, where she was sent for prostitution, and hopes to recuperate on her father's coal barge. He ignores the obvious signs of her profession and takes her aboard. She is still enraged at his abandoning her as a child and at the brutality of the Minnesota farm family hired to care for her, but she begins to heal physically and spiritually on the barge. Chris adores his spirited daughter. One night in response to a call for help, they rescue some sailors whose ship has capsized. One of them, Mat Burke, astonished to find a Scandinavian beauty on a scow, at first believes he is dreaming but soon falls in love with and courts Anna. She too is attracted, but part of her remains skeptical, knowing how he will respond once he knows her past. Chris and Mat, both of whom are possessive and jealous, fight over her. Incensed at their attempt to control her, she confesses her profession and asserts her right to make her own choices: "Nobody owns me, see?—

'cepting myself. I'll do what I please and no man, I don't give a hoot who he is, can tell me what to do! I ain't asking either of you for a living. I can make it myself—one way or other. I'm my own boss." Mat departs, totally dejected. When he returns, he reiterates his proposal of marriage, which Anna accepts, but the men are uneasy and escape their troubles by signing on to the same freighter, leaving Anna alone in New York. O'Neill claimed that there was no happy ending to this drama, just a comma, with the end uncertain. Critics, however, tended to read the story as the tale of a reformed prostitute who finds true love.

As always, O'Neill's thesis was existential, dealing with the relationship between humans and fate. The symbol for fate, the sea, remains an ambiguous force. Chris is sure that "dat ol' davil sea," which drowned so many members of his family and enticed him away from his wife and daughter, sent Mat Burke as a curse upon their lives. But the sea has also rescued Anna from a life of abuse on land, and Mat Burke claims it brings blessings. Although the playwright removed *Anna Christie* from his list of significant works, it remains one of his more popular and often revived plays.

BIBLIOGRAPHY

Bogard, Travis, and Jackson R. Bryer, eds. *Selected Letters of Eugene O'Neill.* New Haven, Conn.: Yale University Press, 1988.

Glenda Frank
New York, New York

ANNA IN THE TROPICS NILO CRUZ (2003)

It was once common practice in Cuban cigar factories for "lectors" to be hired to read aloud to workers. They read from the press and from world literature. Thus, even illiterate workers were kept informed and also became familiar with great literary works. This custom, which ceased in the United States after 1931 (but is, according to the playwright, still practiced in Cuba), is central to NILO CRUZ's play *Anna in the Tropics,* in which the plot and theme hang on the interplay between Leo Tolstoy's novel *Anna Karenina* and those who hear it. Set in a cigar factory in 1929 in Florida among Cuban immigrants, this PULITZER PRIZE win-

ner's themes include the power of literature to influence the human heart and mind and the value of culture and tradition over modernization.

The play opens with alternating scenes in which male and female worlds are juxtaposed. Factory owner Santiago Alcalar and his half brother, Cheché, are drinking and gambling at a raucous and crowded cockfight; this scene alternates with the women— Ofelia Alcalar and her daughters, Marela, 22, and Conchita, 32—"*standing by the seaport. . . . holding white handkerchiefs and . . . waiting for a ship to arrive.*" They await with excitement and romantic notions the arrival from Cuba of the "best lector west of Havana," Juan Julian Rios, 38 and elegantly handsome. The women speak of "love stories" and of the "poetry and tragedy in the novels" that lectors read. Santiago, meanwhile, against the violent background of the cockfight, borrows money from his bitter half brother, putting up a share of the factory as collateral. Cheché, we learn, resents all lectors because his own wife ran off with one. Finally, into the women's scene comes Juan Julian; more a part of their world than of the men's, he will introduce Anna Karenina and her love triangle to all of them and thereby serve as a catalyst for both a synthesis and a collision of these two worlds.

Tolstoy's novel has a powerful influence on all of the play's characters. As Juan Julian reads, the young and inexperienced Marela is too naïve to understand Anna's agony as her sister and mother do; Marela hears only passionate love and yearns for it. Conchita, too, longs for passion but sympathizes with Anna's husband; Conchita tells her own unfaithful and indifferent spouse that she may—under the novel's influence—take a lover herself. Tolstoy has led her to think with clarity about her own situation and has prompted her to speak frankly to her husband about his infidelity as she has not before. The young women's parents, Santiago and Ofelia, angry with each other over the debt to Cheché and its implications, are able to set aside their quarrel to discuss their shared interest in one of the novel's characters, Levin, for whom "there is only one woman"—as there is only Ofelia for Santiago. Having been brought to this remembrance of their love by Tolstoy's words, they are able to temper their own and more calmly discuss their problems.

By act 2, Conchita and Juan Julian have become lovers. Meanwhile, Cheché brings a cigar-rolling machine onto the premises. Claiming it will increase production and revenue, he tries to assert his status as part owner of the factory; but Santiago pays his debt to his brother with borrowed money and stops this encroachment of modernization, with the support of his employees and family (only Conchita's husband, Palomo, sides with Cheché). The machines can "do tobacco stuffing at the speed of light," but over their noise a lector cannot be heard. The workers reject mechanization in favor of the very old tradition of hand-rolling cigars to the music of literature and conversations about literature. Santiago then announces that they will produce a new cigar, "the Anna Karenina," and that Marela, to her delight, will pose for the label in a Russian coat and hat.

Juan Julian's presence reminds Cheché daily of his humiliation at the hands of the lector who seduced his wife. Now his plans for the dismissal of Juan Julian and for modernization have been thwarted. Frustrated and angry, he becomes sexually aggressive with Marela who rejects his advances emphatically, shoving him to the floor and further humiliating him.

Later, during a party to celebrate the new cigar, Palomo is proprietary with his wife Conchita; reconciliation between them, brought on by her affair, has begun. As they drink Palomo compares alcohol to literature: "Literature brings out the best and the worst part of ourselves." As part of the celebration, gunshots are heard offstage, a foreshadowing of the violence to come. When the party is over, Marela—beautiful in her costume—is apparently raped by her uncle Cheché, who on the following day shoots Juan Julian as he reads a passage in which Anna's husband contemplates dueling with Vronsky. At the end of the play, the reading of *Anna Karenina* is taken up by Palomo: He reads that Anna Karenina's husband decides to write to his wife "everything he'd been meaning to tell her"; Palomo looks at Conchita and his similar intentions are clear.

In his afterword to the published play, Cruz writes with admiration of José Martí, "one of Cuba's greatest poets and political leaders" who "read in the cigar factories of Tampa in the late 1800s." Martí "was a firm believer that the purpose of literature was to help humanity" (88). The purpose of literature, the power of literature—these concepts lie at the heart of Cruz's play.

ANNA LUCASTA PHILIP YORDAN (1944)

One of the earliest American plays featuring an all–African-American cast, *Anna Lucasta,* set in early 1941, tells the story of a young woman, cast out by her father, whose opportunity for happiness comes from the love of a man who cares nothing for her past. Yordan's play about a poor Polish-American family gained fame when it was performed by the American Negro Theatre, first at the 135th Street Library Theatre in Harlem and then on Broadway a few weeks later.

Two years before the play begins, Anna has been banished from her family's Pennsylvania home by her father, Joe, because he caught her in a compromising situation with a man. In the opening scene, Joe receives a letter from an old friend in Alabama, saying that Rudolf, the friend's son, is coming to Pennsylvania to find a wife with Joe's help. Joe's wife, Theresa, sees Rudolf's visit as the chance for Anna to marry and escape the life of a prostitute. Theresa's idea does not sit well with Joe, who resists it (partly because of his vaguely implied incestuous feelings for Anna) and gets drunk to avoid the problem. Anna's siblings, Frank and Stella, and Stella's husband, Stanley (all of whom live with Joe and Theresa), assume that Rudolf is a country bumpkin and plot to trick him out of the $800 he is bringing with him, using Anna as bait. They force Joe to travel to New York to bring her back. Joe finds Anna at Noah's Bar in Brooklyn with a boyfriend, Danny, who wants to own his own taxicab and settle down with, though not marry, Anna. She declines his offer because it does not include marriage. After some initial skepticism about why Joe wants her to come home, Anna, unaware of his ulterior motive, accompanies Joe to Pennsylvania.

Shortly after Rudolf's arrival, the schemers discover that he not only has a college degree but is self-assured, at least as sophisticated as they are, and not prone to being swindled. Before Anna and Rudolf meet, she learns the reason she has been brought home but, jaded by her two years in New York, agrees to participate in the scheme. Upon meeting, however, Anna and Rudolf fall instantly in love and agree to marry. To Anna's surprise, Rudolf overlooks her past and sees her true goodness, as Theresa does.

After Anna and Rudolf marry, Danny shows up and finds Anna alone; with renewed fears that Rudolf will reject her in time, Anna returns to New York with Danny, who is now a hardworking cab owner. Once there, Anna, tormented about leaving Rudolf, squanders Danny's small savings on drinking and dancing. Rudolf, meanwhile, comes to Noah's Bar in search of Anna to take her back to Alabama. In Yordan's original play, it is uncertain whether he succeeds, since Anna leaves the bar to find him after learning that he has recently been there looking for her. In the American Negro Theatre production, the resolution was clear and the ending happy: Rudolf returns to the bar one last time to collect his luggage and finds Anna still there.

The play was significant not only for its all-African-American production of a play written for a white cast but also because it was one of the first OFF-BROADWAY productions to receive serious attention, which led to a successful Broadway run.

Joseph E. Gawel
Temple University

ARDREY, ROBERT (1908–1980) Born in Chicago, Illinois, Robert Ardrey was educated at the University of Chicago, where he primarily studied the sciences. He became interested in writing for the theater when he took a course there with playwright THORNTON WILDER. A prolific writer, Ardrey wrote two novels, 12 screenplays—10 of them adaptations—and four books of anthropology, in addition to his plays.

Ardrey's plays include *Star Spangled* (1936), about an escaped prisoner and his thwarted attempt to kill the political boss responsible for his imprisonment; *How to Get Tough about It* (1938), in which a woman manages to rid her life of a thug who seduces, deserts, and returns to her; *Casey Jones* (1938), about an aging railroad man; *Thunder Rock* (1939), in which a disillusioned newspaper man becomes a lighthouse keeper and through the intervention of ghosts comes to the

conclusion that democracy is the world's best hope; *Jeb* (1946), about an African-American soldier who, having lost his leg in service to his country, returns home from the war only to face racial injustice; and *Sing Me No Lullaby* (1954), in which a scientist, who was a leftist in the 1930s, is hounded by the FBI in the 1950s, despite his honorable war record.

Casey Jones and *Thunder Rock* were produced by the GROUP THEATRE and directed by ELIA KAZAN; neither was particularly well received, though *Thunder Rock* got a better reception in Europe than it did in America. Ardrey is actually better known for his somewhat controversial books on the evolutionary underpinnings of human motivation and for his screenwriting than for his plays.

ARIA DA CAPO EDNA ST. VINCENT MILLAY **(1919)** Recognizing the extent of EDNA ST. VINCENT MILLAY's dramatic innovation in *Aria da Capo* is an important step toward understanding the play's impact. As a work written for the PROVINCETOWN PLAYERS, it is filled with their sense of rebellion and their desire to create a new theater that America could call its own. Moving away from the realism dominant in drama at that time, its expressionism and symbolism relate it to the pioneering work of fellow Provincetown playwright EUGENE O'NEILL. Its unusual poetic form, reminiscent of Anglo-Saxon verse, is uniquely Millay's. Just as she adopts a traditional verse form and makes it her own, so too does she adopt the dramatic forms of the harlequinade and the pastoral, which she subverts to her own uses.

The play begins with Pierrot and Columbine idly complaining about their boring lives. Their comic interplay is complicated by the entrance of Cothurnus, a character from classical tragedy. Belonging neither to harlequinade nor to the pastoral saga that follows, he acts as chorus, pointing out the tragic dimensions of both scenes. In the pastoral section, shepherds Thyrsis and Corydon begin as friends, but then argue, become territorial, and after the discovery of treasure, grow deceitfully adversarial. Thyrsis poisons his old friend as he himself is being strangled, and Millay forces her message home as the dying Corydon declares, "This is a very silly game . . . why do we play it?" The play ends with Pierrot and Colum-bine hiding the corpses under the table as they repeat the play's opening dialogue, thus displaying a deci-sion to ignore everything that has taken place.

Harlequin is missing from Millay's harlequinade, possibly because he is the more worldly of the three stock characters. The traditionally innocent Pierrot and Columbine allow Millay to make her point as she upsets their usual characterizations. Their apparent cynicism, worldliness, and apathy destroy any sym-pathy they would normally engender in an audience. Pierrot has lost direction and faith, and his only recourse is to mock and dismiss everything, while Columbine withdraws into a world of opulence, where she hides from the unpleasantness of reality. Although Millay retains the merry harlequinade interior, it becomes ironic given the unloving and dreary life this couple leads.

Thyrsis and Corydon are representatives of ordi-nary, working men. As their scene proceeds, they destroy each other by falling prey to territorialism and pride. As shepherds, they are responsible for the sheep in their care just as leaders are for their people, but we witness how they get caught up in their own petty greed and neglect their responsibilities. Their sheep suffer, and the destructiveness of their actions is thus shown to have repercussions beyond themselves.

Despite its surface simplicity, *Aria Da Capo* is a play constructed on many levels. While offering a veneer of light entertainment, the play mocks its own theatri-cal forms, and through its complex symbolism con-veys serious themes. Millay blends together satirical versions of a harlequinade and a pastoral piece to cre-ate a warning for humanity not to follow what she considered to be common paths toward conflict and war. Her pacifist message, promoting love and com-radeship over territorialism, greed, and intolerance, remains powerful.

Susan C. W. Abbotson
Rhode Island College

ARSENIC AND OLD LACE JOSEPH KESSEL-RING (1941)   In this comic farce, two sweet maiden ladies grant "peace" to lonely old men by poisoning them with arsenic and holding funerals for them in their cellar. It is Joseph Kesselring's only successful play.

When Mortimer Brewster, an excitable theater critic, comes to visit his elderly maiden aunts, Abby and Martha, he discovers that, despite their appear-ance to the contrary, they are insane. The dear ladies take pity on lonely gentlemen who inquire about a room to rent. They give them elderberry wine laced with arsenic so the men may have peaceful deaths and proper funerals. Fortunately for the sisters, the nephew who lives with them, Mortimer's brother, Teddy, is also crazy: He thinks he is Teddy Roosevelt and digs "locks for the Panama Canal" in the cellar; thus, disposal of the bodies is easily accomplished. The ladies simply tell Teddy that another victim has fallen to yellow fever. A horrified Mortimer must find a way both to protect his aunts and to stop the mur-ders. His discovery also gives him second thoughts about his upcoming marriage to Elaine Harper. He warns her, "Insanity runs in my family. It practically gallops."

Complications develop with the arrival of the Brew-ster sisters' other nephew, Jonathan, a murderer, who has escaped from a prison for the criminally insane. Jonathan brings with him his plastic-surgeon accom-plice, Dr. Einstein, as well as the body of his latest vic-tim, which he hopes to dispose of in his aunts' house. In fact, he hopes to intimidate his aunts, who fear and dislike him, into letting him hide out a while. He is surprised to find graves already in the cellar when he takes his victim there for burial. Eventually, Mortimer turns Jonathan over to the bumbling small-town policemen and has Teddy committed to Happy Dale, a home for the insane. To protect his aunts, Mortimer plans to blame the murders on the obviously insane Teddy, but it is not necessary to do so since the police do not believe there *are* bodies buried in the cellar—as Teddy and his aunts insist.

Abby and Martha are delighted to be committed to Happy Dale along with Teddy, from whom they refuse to be separated. Their one concern is that the commit-ment papers might not be valid since Mortimer is not truly their next of kin as he has always believed, but the illegitimate child of a cook they once employed.

Mortimer is elated to find out that he is not a blood relation of the uniformly crazy Brewsters.

When *Arsenic and Old Lace* opened in New York, Brooks Atkinson of the *New York Times* wrote, "Joseph Kesselring has written ['a murder charade'] so funny that none of us will ever forget it. . . . Swift, dry, satirical and exciting, *Arsenic and Old Lace* kept the first-night audience roaring with laughter" (January 11, 1941). When the play was revived in 1986, Frank Rich, also of the *New York Times,* wrote, "The years haven't been kind to Mr. Kesselring's farce, which once provided escapist entertainment for theatergoers who had a real reason to seek escape (World War II) and who had not yet been presented with television, the invention that now permits audiences to watch situation comedies in the privacy of their own homes" (June 27, 1986). Indeed, the play may no longer be the fare of New York's professional theaters, but it remains a favorite among amateur, especially school, groups. This is perhaps because the 1944 Frank Capra film, with Cary Grant and Peter Lorre, keeps it familiar.

AS BEES IN HONEY DROWN Douglas Carter Beane (1997)

BEANE's comedy was proclaimed "A delicious soufflé of a satire . . . [an] extremely entertaining fable for an age that always chooses image over substance" by the *New York Times* (June 20, 1997). Produced by the Drama Dept., it transferred for a long run at OFF-BROADWAY's Lucille Lortel Theatre, where it won the Outer Critics Circle Award.

Alexa Vere de Vere, a fast-talking con woman, hires Evan Wyler, a rising, gay first-novelist, to write the script for a proposed film of her life. She gives him an exorbitant retainer and, as her accountant does not trust her with credit cards, asks him to put her bills on his, so that she will have a receipt. Although he questions some of her farfetched tales, she seduces him into her frantic lifestyle by introducing him to famous people. Alexa tells Evan (born Eric Wollenstein) that they have both created alternative personas to their "real" selves: "You're not the person you were born—who wonderful is? . . . We have art to protect us, even if our greatest creation gets to be ourselves." These lines express the major themes of the play: Art is a means of transcendence over mediocrity, even if the "art" itself is fraudulent, and fame is its own reward. Evan unwittingly falls in love with Alexa, until, in a rude awakening, he discovers that she has vanished, having charged enormous sums to his credit cards.

Evan meets with a producer, Morris Kaden, another of Alexa's victims, who explains that she charms her conquests into willingly sustaining her lavish lifestyle, then moves on before her scam can be discovered. Kaden advises Evan to forget her, but Evan is determined to expose Alexa. He tracks down Mike (her alleged first husband), a gay painter, who tells Evan that Alexa transformed herself from Brenda Gelb, a poor Pennsylvania waitress, through diligent study of the characters Sally Bowles, Holly Golightly, and Auntie Mame. Alexa tries to win Evan back by convincing him that he should join her in her schemes. She almost succeeds, but Evan resists her, begins a romantic relationship with Mike, and publishes his second novel (under his real name), *As Bees in Honey Drown,* which exposes Alexa's con game.

Of the impetus behind the play, Beane has said in an on-line interview with Theron Albis, "As wild as [it] is, it's what I saw happening. A lot of people racing after fame—and nervously so. I'm naive enough that I actually came from a time when fame went somewhat with achievement. . . . Then, suddenly, fame became a goal, and there were these people desperately, nervously, anxiously pursuing it." The play expertly skewers the decade's preoccupation with the pursuit of fame and fortune at any cost, the media's creation of celebrity, and the world's inability to separate pretension from true innovation.

Douglas W. Gordy
Walnut Creek, California

ASIAN-AMERICAN DRAMA

The acknowledged origins of Asian-American drama date to the 1890s and the controversial symbolist plays of Sadakichi Hartmann, including *Christ: A Dramatic Poem in Three Acts* (privately printed, 1893), *Buddha: A Drama in Twelve Scenes* (written, 1891–95; privately printed, 1897), and *Confucius: A Drama in Three Acts* (written,

1894–1916, 1920–22; privately printed, 1923). In the century that followed, the rich and varied contributions of playwrights to the genre have ensured its lasting imprint on American literature. As both artistic and political expressions, Asian-American plays through the years collectively document the assorted concerns—private, public, old, new, and newly constituted—of Asian-American dramatists and the communities they at once represent, interpret, embrace, and critique.

After Hartmann, whose biraciality and close ties to Europe, both psychic and experiential, arguably set him apart from his immediate playwriting descendants, the first wave of Asian-American dramatists from the 1920s through the 1940s wrote plays that largely reflected an inward-turning, monocultural focus (usually Japanese-American or Chinese-American). Given America's exclusionary policies toward Asians and Asian Americans during this era, the playwrights' self-directed, monocultural focus was, perhaps not surprisingly, ambivalently poised against the backdrop of a mainstream America, with whom assimilation was viewed as a mixed blessing—highly desirable yet also a source of cultural disruption, threat, and loss. Thus, the clash of old-world and new-world values, often necessitated by new-world realities, constituted central themes of these early plays. Gladys Li's *The Submission of Rose May* (1924) exemplifies this concern with intracultural and intercultural tensions in its treatment of a young Chinese-American woman's resistance to an arranged marriage. Similarly, Bessie Toishigawa Inouye's *Reunion* (1947) examines issues of self-identity and reassimilation into civilian life for Japanese-American soldiers in the wake of World War II.

Oddly enough, during the 1950s and 1960s, when shifting geopolitical currents yielded enormous Broadway and Hollywood interest in representations of Asia and Asians through Western lenses—for example, JOHN PATRICK's *The TEAHOUSE OF THE AUGUST MOON* (Broadway production, 1953; film, 1956); James Michener's novel-turned-box-office-hit, *Sayonara* (novel, 1954; film, 1957); and PAUL OSBORN's *The World of Suzie Wong* (Broadway production, 1958–60; screenplay by John Patrick, 1961)—Asian-American playwriting entered a period of relative dormancy. This period in fact records only a few plays by Asian Americans, including a short play by Japanese-American playwright Carl Kondo titled *A Dame Did It to Me* (1951), published in *Rafu Shimpo,* a Los Angeles-based newspaper founded by first-generation Japanese Americans in 1903. Reasons for this relative inactivity are multiple, perhaps the most obvious being the need for disenfranchised Japanese Americans to rebuild their disrupted lives and communities after World War II. Moreover, on the heels of World War II and during the decades of acute political turbulence in Korea and Vietnam, many Asian Americans attempted to rewrite their perpetual outsider status through "quiet assimilation" into the mainstream.

This period of sparse activity may also be viewed as a necessary prelude to artistic and political crystallization. In fact, the decades that followed saw an unprecedented flourish of activity. But given the preceding decades' silences, the plays written in the 1970s not surprisingly mirror the concerns of the very early plays in their treatment of largely intracultural concerns or of one Asian-American group's negotiations with the dominant Euro-American mainstream. Two notable plays in this period that fit this description are Momoko Iko's *Gold Watch* (1972) and Frank Chin's *Chickencoop Chinaman* (1973), both first-prize winners of the 1971 playwriting competition sponsored by EAST WEST PLAYERS, the pioneering Asian-American theater company founded in Los Angeles in 1965. *Gold Watch* (1972), notable for being the first professionally produced Asian-American play, examines the effects of Executive Order 9066 on a Japanese-American farming community in Pasco, Washington. Chin's *Chickencoop Chinaman* arguably complicates the notion of cultural binaries (one specific ethnic group versus the Euro-American mainstream) by including a Japanese-American character, Kenji, and an African-American character, Charley Popcorn. Still, these characters function largely as dramatic props in the principal character Tam Lum's struggles both to forge an integrated and self-directed identity as a Chinese-American man and to find his way as a Chinese-American artist. These related threads are memorably brought together in a fantasy scene involving Tam and his childhood television idol, the Lone Ranger, whom Tam in his youth mistook for the ideal "Chinese American boy." Similarly, the widely anthologized play, Wakako Yamauchi's *And the Soul Shall Dance* (1974), focuses on Issei (first-generation Japanese-American) distresses in southern California during the Great Depression: cultural isolation in America, generational and gender challenges arising from relocation in America and exacerbated by acute economic hardships, and conflicted attitudes of Japanese Americans toward America as the land of opportunity and the site of exile.

Later Asian-American dramatists (the second wave) continued this tradition of interrogating the intracultural tensions within a single Asian-American group as well as those resulting from intersections with the Euro-American mainstream. For example, DAVID HENRY HWANG's *FOB* (1979) probes familiar themes of intracultural conflict brought about by cultural displacement—in this case, between an American-born Chinese American named Dale, who, in his assimilationist zeal, shuns any connection to his "fresh off the boat" counterpart, Steve. Like the young girl, Masako, in *And the Soul Shall Dance,* Dale disdains newcomers from the homeland because they remind him of his own tenuous identity in relation to the mainstream Euro-American culture. While the setting of Hwang's play, Torrance, California, in 1980, differs from the setting of the earlier plays, the source of conflict in *FOB* and the earlier plays is rooted in cultural displacement and the fractured identity that such displacement necessarily engenders.

David Henry Hwang's TONY AWARD–winning *M. BUTTERFLY* (1988), perhaps the most widely celebrated of all Asian-American dramas, operates within a similarly dichotomous vision of East versus West. Set in late 1960s Beijing and Paris, the play examines fundamental cultural binaries: Eastern versus Western courtship rituals; Communist China's political and social oppressiveness versus the democratic West's freedoms; gender expectations of the virile Western male seducer versus the submissive Eastern female; Chinese opera versus Western opera. In his "Afterword" to the published play Hwang writes, "*M. Butterfly* has sometimes been regarded as an anti-American play, a diatribe against the stereotyping of the East by the West, of women by men. Quite to the contrary, I consider it a plea to all sides to cut through our respective layers of cultural and sexual misperception, to deal with one another truthfully for our mutual good, from the common and equal ground we share as human beings" (100).

Critics of Hwang's plays, however, accuse the playwright of achieving commercial success by merely reaffirming, not challenging, stereotypes of Asians and Asian Americans. According to this perspective, Hwang seeks validation from the largely Euro-American audience by giving it what it wants to see: in *FOB*, the ridiculous Chinese immigrant with the laughable accent operating in the familiar setting of the Chinese restaurant; in *M. Butterfly,* the simultaneously abject and perversely empowered Song Liling, whom James Moy has described as finally representing "little more than a disfigured transvestite version of the infamous Chinese 'dragon lady' prostitute stereotype" ("David Henry" 54). Moy has included PHILIP KAN GOTANDA, another prolific voice among the second wave of Asian-American playwrights, in his criticism of damaged and damaging reappropriations of Asian-American characters and concerns that echo and thus reinforce established mainstream stereotypes. In his celebrated *Yankee Dawg You Die* (1988), Gotanda draws attention to the ethical dilemma faced by Asian-American actors seeking work in mainstream media: the ethical desire to accept only "real" Asian and Asian-American roles versus economic exigencies that require an actor to take on roles demanded by the mainstream, roles that perpetuate degrading stereotypes. Commenting on *M. Butterfly* and Gotanda's *Yankee Dawg You Die,* Moy claims: "[their characters] provide a good evening's entertainment and then float as exotic Oriental fetishes articulating Anglo-American desire, now doubly displaced into the new order of stereotypical representations created by Asian Americans" ("David Henry" 55). Whether one agrees with Moy's controversial assessment of these plays, what gives many scholars pause is the fact that (as of 2009) Hwang is the only Asian-American playwright to have had a play produced on Broadway. The thorny question of why certain kinds of representations of

Asians and Asian Americans appeal to the mainstream audience while others do not persists.

Despite these serious concerns about artistic complicity and commercial viability, Asian-American playwrights in the last decade of the 20th century continued to struggle for truthful artistic representations and to be more multicultural in their subject material. Elizabeth Wong's *Kimchee and Chitlins* (1993) is based on the real-life organized boycott by African Americans of Korean American–owned businesses in Brooklyn in 1990. Despite the highly charged subject of interracial urban conflict, Wong's play boldly treats the issue with candor, exposing racial misunderstanding and bigotry on both sides. To Wong's credit, the play's potentially explosive charge is defused by its underlying humor and compassionate portrayal of characters of both races. Garrett Omata's *S.A.M. I Am* (1995) also considers the politics of interracial conflict and desire—John Hamabata, a young Japanese-American man, desires the elegant and unattainable Jackie Shibata, who is half Japanese and half white and who is obsessed with the actor and playwright SAM SHEPARD. Both characters consciously and unconsciously desire to elevate their status through associations with whiteness: for John, through a romantic link with a woman who is half-white and who, as a rule, dates only white men; for Jackie, through fantasized associations with Shepard, a popular-culture icon of the white masculine ideal.

The emphasis of the plays written in the 1980s and 1990s on multiethnic and multiracial intersections and the formation of hybrid identities that result from them is in great measure a function of changing demographic realities in Asian-American communities in the 1970s and beyond. Fundamental to these changes was the passage of the 1965 Immigration Act, which removed barriers to Asian immigration to the United States. In time, playwrights of various Asian heritages and interracial identity—Filipino, Indian, Korean, and Vietnamese, to name a few—joined their Chinese-American and Japanese-American predecessors to expand the scope of Asian-American playwriting. Some of these plays, such as Huynh Quang Nhuong's *Dance of the Wandering Souls* (1997), serve to educate America's mainstream audiences about the myths and histories of a specific Asian or Asian-American culture. *Dance of the Wandering Souls* frames China's millennial rule in Vietnam as a story of warring families determined to pass on their long legacy of hostility and aggression to the next generation. The play both informs American audiences about this early phase of Vietnam's history, though in highly mythologized form, and suggests a remedy for war in the promise of the eventual union of the younger generation.

Other playwrights working to broaden the Asian-American dramatic landscape include Jeannine Barroga, Rob Shin, Velina Hasu Houston, and Amy Hill. In *Talk-Story* (1997), Barroga interweaves stories by and about two generations of a Filipino-American family, a father in 1930s rural California and his daughter in 1990s San Francisco. The poignant montage of intergenerational stories, rife with multiracial intersections, reminds audiences of both the advances made toward achieving a racially just society and the obstacles yet to be addressed. Similarly, Shin's *The Art of Waiting* (1991) considers a wide range of multiracial and multiethnic subjects, from white racism to racial animosity between Korean-American and African-American communities. Even largely taboo subjects such as racialized masculine identity and the indictment of all Americans for holding race-based preconceptions and antipathies are broached in this play. Other dimensions of multiraciality in Asian-American plays are brought to the fore in the plays of Velina Hasu Houston, described in 1997 as "easily the most-produced Asian-American woman playwright in the [United States]" (Nelson 73). Derived from her multiracial identity—part Japanese, part African American, and part American Indian—Houston's vision perhaps exemplifies the future not only of Asian-American drama but also of American society in general. Many of Houston's plays, including *Tokyo Valentine* (1992) and *As Sometimes in a Dead Man's Face* (1994), dramatize the complexities of the multiracial experience. Similarly, Amy Hill's humorous *Tokyo Bound* (1991), the first of a trilogy of one-person plays, derives from her childhood and adolescent experiences in South Dakota and Seattle, juggling her Finnish and Japanese heritages.

At the end of the 20th century, Asian-American dramatists, drama critics and scholars, and theater companies reflected an increasingly Pan-Asian vision. Velina Hasu Houston articulates this Pan-Asian emphasis in explaining her selection of plays for an Asian-American drama anthology she edited: "[The anthology] includes a wide spectrum of subject matter and writing styles, some very American, some very Asian, and some a composite of both origins. One thing I can say about all of them is that they are both individualistic and universal in their views of the human condition. Moreover, it is important to note that these are not 'ethnic plays,' but American plays that should not be relegated to the artistic ghetto of Eurocentrism's manufacture" (*But Still, Like Air* xxi). This inclusiveness embraces not only diverse ethnicities and multiethnic and multiracial crisscrossings but also gender perspectives, as the several anthologies devoted to plays by Asian-American women published in the 1990s suggest. In the mid- and late-1990s, dramas examining the intersections of race and sexual orientation also made their way onto the Asian-American stage. Notable among these are Chay Yew's *A Language of Their Own* (1994) and Dwight Okita's *The Rainy Season* (1996).

In the first decade of the 21st century, playwrights have largely continued this trend of probing multicultural intersections. Alice Tuan in *New Culture for a New Country* (1999), for example, examines the history of women's labor on a street corner in Brooklyn, New York, by presenting snapshots of various characters, including a Jewish-American tour guide, a Chinese-American dim sum vendor, and an African-American depression-era "corn girl," who sold both "hot buttered corn" and sex. Karen Shimakawa summarizes Tuan's aim in the play: "[to ask] audiences to consider the operations of capitalism, gender, immigration, and racialization as links connecting these various women across decades and cultures" (162). Another play by Tuan, *Close Encounters of the Third World* (2001), written in response to the anti-immigrant feeling sweeping California at the time, explores the shared and comparative historical subjugation of Asian Americans, Chicanas/os, and Latinas/os. This vision of multicultural solidarity is extended beyond the United States in Gotanda's play *The Wind Cries Mary* (2002), which examines the emergence of an Asian-American identity politics on a college campus in San Francisco in the late 1960s amid the swirl of the black Civil Rights movement and Vietnam War protests. While the play largely focuses on the intergenerational reactions of one ethnic group (Japanese Americans) to the volatile cultural climate, it implies that all ethnic and racial minorities are allied in the struggle for social change and justice and that the struggle reaches beyond the boundaries of the United States to encompass in fact all of the "Third World."

The wide range of dramatic production within Asian-American drama was bolstered, psychically and tangibly, by the emergence of several Asian-American theater companies. With the founding in 1965 of the East West Players in Los Angeles, Asian-American drama enjoyed an unprecedented outlet for creative expression—for performers, production crews, and, finally, in the 1970s, for playwrights when the group's emphasis changed from producing non-Asian plays with all-Asian casts to developing and producing plays written by Asian Americans. Other Asian-American theater companies soon followed suit, most notably the Kumu Kahua, established in 1970 by several University of Hawaii students and Dennis Carroll, a University of Hawaii professor of theater; the Asian American Theater Company (AATC) in San Francisco in 1973; the Northwest Asian American Theatre Company (NWAAT) in Seattle in the mid-1970s; the Pan Asian Repertory in New York City in 1987; and the Ma-Yi (the 14th-century Chinese term for the Philippine Islands) Theater Company in New York City in 1989. The 1990s saw the emergence of smaller theater companies on the West Coast such as Teatro ng Tanan (Theater for the People) and Bindlestiff Studio, both companies founded in the Filipino-American communities in San Francisco. Theater companies committed to the production of Asian-American plays were also formed in the Midwest in the 1990s and 2000s, including Chicago's Angel Island Theatre Company and the Hmong Theatre Project, Rich Shiomi's Theatre Mu, and the Playwrights' Center (all three located in Minneapolis).

One of the most recently formed theater companies, the Silk Road Theatre Project, established in Chicago in 2002 in response to the widespread anti-Arab and anti-Arab-American sentiment in the wake of September 11, 2001, expresses the expanded multicultural vision now shared by many of these theater companies: "Silk Road Theatre Project showcases playwrights of Asian, Middle Eastern, and Mediterranean backgrounds, whose works address themes relevant to the peoples of the Silk Road and their Diaspora communities. Through the creation and presentation of outstanding theater, we aim to promote discourse and dialogue among multicultural audiences . . . and [to] heal rifts through the transformative power of theatre" ("About Us").

The recent interest in Asian-American theater beyond the West Coast promises to offset the charge by some scholars that most anthologies of Asian-American literature advance an almost exclusively California-centric vision. Further, the availability of many fixed venues serves to encourage playwrights, performers, and production staff to engage in and hone their craft. In addition, these theaters as Dorinne Kondo explains, maintain a larger cultural function by providing a "highly significant mediating role . . . as sites for the performance and creation of what it means to be 'Asian American.'" By fostering budding playwrights through competitions, grants, and workshops, and by "training actors and offering them opportunities to perform in plays that would be closed to them in mainstream theatres," these theater companies make "invaluable contributions to American theatre [and] to the continuing creation and re-creation of Asian-American identities and communities" (Nelson x).

BIBLIOGRAPHY

"About Us." Silk Road Theatre Project. Available online. URL: http://www.srtp.org. Accessed August 11, 2008.

Barrios-Leblanc, Joi, ed. *Savage Stage: Plays by Ma-Yi Theater Company.* New York: Ma-Yi Theater Company, 2006.

Berson, Misha, ed. *Between Worlds: Contemporary Asian-American Plays.* New York: Theatre Communications Group, 1990.

Carroll, Dennis, ed. *Kumu Kahua Plays.* Honolulu: University of Hawaii Press, 1983.

Cheung King-Kok, and Stan Yogi. *Asian American Literature: An Annotated Bibliography.* New York: PMLA, 1988.

Chin, Frank. *"The Chickencoop Chinaman" and "The Year of the Dragon": Two Plays.* Seattle: University of Washington Press, 1981.

Ellis, Roger, ed. *Multicultural Theatre II: Contemporary Hispanic, Asian, and African-American Plays.* Colorado Springs: Meriwether, 1998.

Gotanda, Philip Kan. *No More Cherry Blossoms: "Sisters Matsumoto" and Other Plays.* Seattle: University of Washington Press, 2005.

———. *Yankee Dawg You Die.* New York: Dramatists Play Service, 1991.

Houston, Velina Hasu, ed. *But Still, Like Air, I'll Rise: New Asian American Plays.* Philadelphia: Temple University Press, 1997.

———, ed. *The Politics of Life: Four Plays by Asian American Women.* Philadelphia: Temple University Press, 1993.

Hwang, David Henry. *"FOB" and Other Plays.* New York: Plume, 1990.

———. *M. Butterfly.* New York: Plume, 1989.

Kondo, Dorinne K. *About Face: Performing Race in Fashion and Theater.* New York: Routledge, 1997.

Kurahashi, Yuko. *Asian American Culture on Stage: The History of the East West Players.* New York: Garland, 1999.

Lee, Esther Kim. *A History of Asian American Theatre.* Cambridge: Cambridge University Press, 2006.

Lee, Josephine Ding. *Performing Asian America: Race and Ethnicity on the Contemporary Stage.* Philadelphia: Temple University Press, 1997.

Liu, Miles Xian, ed. *Asian American Playwrights: A Bio-Bibliographical Critical Sourcebook.* Westport, Conn.: Greenwood Press, 2002.

Moy, James S. *Marginal Sights: Staging the Chinese in America.* Iowa City: University of Iowa Press, 1993.

———. "David Henry Hwang's *M. Butterfly* and Philip Kan Gotanda's *Yankee Dawg You Die*: Repositioning Chinese American Marginality on the American Stage." *Theatre Journal* 42, no. 1 (1990): 48–56.

Nelson, Brian, ed. *Asian American Drama: 9 Plays from the Multiethnic Landscape.* New York: Applause Theatre Books, 1997.

Perkins, Kathy A., and Roberto Uno, eds. *Contemporary Plays by Women of Color.* London: Routledge, 1996.

Shimakawa, Karen. *National Abjection: The Asian American Body Onstage.* Durham, N.C.: Duke University Press, 2002.

Srikanth, Rajini, and Esther Y. Iwanaga, eds. *Bold Words: A Century of Asian American Writing.* New Brunswick, N.J.: Rutgers University Press, 2001.

Uno, Roberta, ed. *Unbroken Thread: An Anthology of Plays by Asian American Women.* Amherst: University of Massachusetts Press, 1993.

Yamauchi, Wakako. *Songs My Mother Taught Me: Stories, Plays, and Memoir.* New York: Feminist Press at the City University of New York, 1994.

Elizabeth S. Kim
University of Wisconsin–Whitewater

AS IS WILLIAM M. HOFFMAN (1985) Premiering at the Circle Repertory, Hoffman's play transferred to Broadway for a short, unsuccessful run, has been revived several times, and was filmed for cable television. It remains important as the first major play dealing with the AIDS crisis (opening one month prior to LARRY KRAMER's *The Normal Heart,* another influential early AIDS drama). Hoffman won the OBIE AWARD for Distinguished Playwriting. Using a free-form OFF-OFF-BROADWAY style, Hoffman disseminated information about the disease in a nonthreatening manner while it was still a frightening mystery, under the guise of a romantic tragicomedy.

Hoffman's 90-minute, intermissionless play centers on two former lovers: Saul, a photographer, and Rich, a promising writer. The other 37 characters are played by six performers acting as a Greek Chorus (never leaving the stage, bearing witness). An AIDS hospice worker speaks of her patients while the two ex-partners divide the belongings accumulated during their relationship. When Saul expresses his terror because of their many friends who have died or are sick, Rich announces he has also been diagnosed with the new disease. A fluid montage ensues, in which family, friends, doctors, and assorted pick-ups all react with varying degrees of sympathy, wariness, shock, and revulsion. Since Rich has been deserted by his new lover, Saul insists he move back in so that he can take care of him.

They reminisce about the carefree days before AIDS, when drugs and promiscuous sex were rampant, and talk of initial responses to the crisis. Rich attends a support group, where he is in denial about his condition. Two harried Crisis Hotline volunteers provide information to their clients (and hence the audience) while Rich undergoes medical tests. He recalls his painful coming-out process and his relationship with Saul, and he indulges in angry outbursts at his fate, asking Saul to procure sleeping pills so that he can end his life with dignity. Saul initially refuses, but then he does buy pills for both of them; however, he has an epiphany watching a neon sign reflected in a street puddle: While life exists there is still beauty amidst the ugliness. He destroys the pills, telling Rich he will take him "as is." As they pull the hospital curtain closed around themselves, the hospice worker tells of the indomitable spirit of her patients, of whom Rich is now one.

Critic Frank Rich has summed up the play's lasting importance: "The disease forced the theater . . . to portray homosexuals . . . as real people on stage rather than as just figures of either camp farce or bathos. . . . AIDS also brought the American theater back into the social-protest arena" (382). In depicting the fear, anger, and lack of credible information, Hoffman illuminated the beginnings of the AIDS epidemic with compassion and dramatic flair, while applauding the gay community's caring actions and condemning the lack of response by the world at large.

BIBLIOGRAPHY
Rich, Frank. *Hot Seat: Theatre Criticism for the "New York Times," 1980–1993.* New York: Random House, 1998.

Douglas W. Gordy
Walnut Creek, California

AUGUST: OSAGE COUNTY TRACY LETTS (2007) Originally produced by Chicago's Steppenwolf Theatre Company in June 2007, *August: Osage County* opened on Broadway in December 2007 and won the PULITZER PRIZE, the TONY AWARD, and the New York Drama Critics' Circle Award. The play takes place in midsummer in *"Pawhuska, Oklahoma, sixty miles northwest of Tulsa,"* in the *"rambling country house"* of 69-year-old Beverly Weston, a retired college English professor and writer whose only book of poetry was published 40 years previously, and his wife Violet.

The play opens with a Prologue in which Beverly is interviewing Johnna Monevata, a young Native American woman, to be a live-in housekeeper and cook. He explains that because "[m]y wife takes pills and I drink," they can no longer take care of the house. In the midst of the interview, Violet stumbles into the room, speaking incoherently. The Prologue ends as it began: Beverly quotes from T. S. Eliot's "The Hollow Men," giving Johnna the book as he hires her.

As act 1 begins, Beverly has been missing for five days, and the family has gathered to support Violet. Already on the scene are Violet's younger sister Mattie Fae and her husband Charlie Aiken, and Ivy Weston, Beverly and Violet's middle daughter, age 44, who lives nearby. Shortly after the act begins, the oldest Weston daughter, Barbara, 46, and her husband Bill arrive from Colorado with their 14-year-old daughter, Jean. Violet seems very relieved to have her oldest child, Barbara, with her at this time of crisis, a fact not lost on Ivy, on whom the burden of the parents has largely fallen. Violet explains that Beverly simply walked out the door, and she hasn't heard from him since. After three days, she took the precaution of emptying their joint safety deposit box of "an awful lot of cash" and "expensive jewelry" because, she explains, she and Beverly had agreed, "if something were to happen to one of [them]," they should avoid the contents being "rolled into the estate" when the will went to probate. After emptying the box, Violet says, she called the police to report her husband missing.

As act 1 progresses, we begin to see additional conflicts within the family: Violet resents Barbara for living far away, while Barbara resents her mother's addiction. Meanwhile, Barbara's daughter Jean retreats to the attic room of the new housekeeper, Johnna, to smoke marijuana, which she says is all right because her father smokes it too. Jean also reveals that her parents have separated because Bill is having an affair with one of his students. Finally, the sheriff, Deon Gilbeau, who was a high school boyfriend of Barbara's, arrives to tell the family that Beverly's body has been found in a lake; he tells Bill that he suspects it was a suicide. Violet is too far gone on pills to understand what has happened.

Act 2 opens on the afternoon after Beverly's funeral. The Westons' youngest daughter, Karen, who is 40 years old, has arrived from Florida with her fiancé. Violet continues her criticism of Ivy, this time for

wearing a suit to her father's funeral rather than a dress and for not being more attractive to men; the latter causes Ivy to blurt out, "I have a man"—but she refuses to divulge his name. Mattie Fae is similarly critical of her son, whom everyone calls "Little Charles," mocking his plan to move to New York and criticizing him for missing his uncle's funeral because he overslept. Little Charles arrives, in tears over missing the funeral and very aware that his family, especially his mother, consider him odd and unreliable.

As the family starts to sit down for dinner, cousins Ivy and Little Charles meet on the front porch. They embrace and kiss; he is the man in her life, but they vow not to tell anyone. At dinner, Violet informs everyone that she and Beverly had agreed to change their wills so that everything would be left to the surviving spouse but they "never got around to taking care of it legally." Considerable money is involved, and she gets her daughters to agree that their mother will receive all of it. She also reveals to the assembled family that Bill and Barbara are separated; and she scolds her children for complaining about their "rotten childhood," reminding them of her own difficult upbringing and of the fact that Beverly as a child lived with his parents in the family car. Barbara lashes out at her mother, calling her "a drug addict" and trying to wrestle her pills away from her. Pandemonium ensues, and Barbara orders everyone to engage in a "pill raid," announcing, "I'M RUNNING THINGS NOW!"

As act 3 begins, the three sisters are debating how best to cope with their mother. Ivy tells the other two about her relationship with Little Charles and of their plan to move to New York together. She scolds her sisters for moving away and leaving her to care for their parents. Ivy and Little Charles have a moment alone in the living room. They are interrupted by his parents; Mattie Fae chides her son for watching too much TV and for having recently lost his job—causing Charlie to explode at her in their son's defense. Soon afterward, Mattie Fae asks Barbara if "something" is "going on between Ivy and Little Charles." When Barbara confirms the relationship, Mattie Fae exclaims, "That can't happen," explaining that Little Charles is Ivy's brother, the child of an illicit relationship between her and Beverly.

In the next scene, as 14-year-old Jean and her aunt Karen's fiancé, Steve, smoke marijuana together, he makes a crude pass at her, only to be discovered by Johnna brandishing a skillet. Barbara, Bill, and Karen enter, and when Johnna explains what she has seen, Barbara attacks Steve physically and lashes out at Jean verbally, the latter much to Bill's dismay. Karen, still intent on marriage despite Steve's transgression, hurriedly prepares to return to Florida with him; and as Bill and Jean also leave, Bill and Barbara acknowledge that their marriage is over. The divorced sheriff Deon Gilbeau comes by to ask Barbara if they can have lunch together one day and also to tell her that a local motel owner, having seen Beverly's photo in the newspaper, has notified him that Beverly spent two nights there after he left home.

Ivy stops by to tell Barbara that she and Little Charles are leaving for New York the next day. Barbara tries to dissuade her from going and from telling Violet of their plans; but Ivy persists and gets as far as saying to her mother, "Little Charles and I—," when Violet interrupts: "Little Charles and you are brother and sister. I know that." The distraught Ivy rushes away, telling Barbara, "We'll still go away, and you will never see me again." Violet tells Barbara that she has known about Beverly and Mattie Fae for a long time, adding that if she had reached him at the motel she would have told her husband that if his depression was due to guilt over the affair, he should "quit sulking about this ancient history." She also reveals that Beverly left her a note telling her she could call him at the motel but that she waited to call until she had emptied the safety deposit box; when she finally called, he'd already checked out. When Barbara asks if the note indicated her father was contemplating suicide, Violet lashes out at Barbara, saying one reason he killed himself was because Barbara had "abandoned" her parents. She adds that Beverly was "cruel" to make her responsible for his death, to test who was stronger, adding "Nobody's stronger than me, goddamn it." At this point, Barbara leaves the house. Having driven everyone off, Violet stumbles about, *"terrified, disoriented,"* crawls up the stairs to Johnna's room, and *"scrabbles onto Johnna's lap."* Johnna holds her head, smoothes her hair, and *"quietly sings"* Eliot's lines from "The Hollow Men," "This is the way the world ends."

The play's mixture of the comic and the lurid generally captivated audiences and critics. In a frequently quoted and undeniably influential review in the *New York Times,* Charles Isherwood described it as "harrowing" and "hilarious" and called it "the most exciting new American play Broadway has seen in years" (December 5, 2007). Kerry Reid in the *Chicago Reader* deemed it "riotously funny" but also "heartbreaking in its attention to emotional nuance and captivating in its gruff compassion" (July 13, 2007). Among the naysayers was Peter Marks of the *Washington Post,* who complained that "there is nothing close to the kind of shattering payoff that you anticipate from a work of this scale and ambition"; he felt "worn down by the sheer volume of revelation, and . . . by the ordinariness of what's revealed" (December 13, 2007). What are undeniable, however, are TRACY LETTS's ear for dialogue—the play is full of quotable phrases—and his gift for scenes that hold the audience's attention. Typical of the former is Barbara's rejoinder after hearing her mother lament how hard her generation had it: "Why were they 'the Greatest Generation?' Because they were poor and hated Nazis? Who doesn't . . . hate Nazis" or one of Mattie Fae's many put-downs of Little Charles, when her husband compares him to Beverly: "Little Charles isn't complicated. He's just unemployed." And Karen's lines to an incredulous Barbara after Steve has been discovered with Jean—"it's not cut and dried, black and white, good or bad. It lives where everything lives: somewhere in the middle."—serve as a succinct and accurate expression of Letts's nonjudgmental view of the characters and situations in his play.

AUNT DAN AND LEMON WALLACE SHAWN (1985)

Aunt Dan and Lemon explores the motives behind human brutality and the mentality that justifies its existence.

Lemon (whose real name is Leonora), an isolated and sickly 25-year-old, sits in a dark room philosophizing and remembering. In particular, she remembers what she learned from her Aunt Dan (Danielle). The play alternates among short narratives by Lemon, scenes in which Dan lectures Lemon, and short scenes involving Dan's past social circle, which included Lemon's parents. Making an indelible impression on the 11-year-old Lemon are Dan's tales of wild and promiscuous friends—especially the amoral Mindy, who once seduced and killed a man for money—and of Dan's own sexual adventures with married men as well as with the unpredictable Mindy herself. Dan's skewed moral code permits lying to women and sleeping with their husbands, but, she tells Lemon with self-satisfaction, *"I never, ever shout at a waiter"* because, she believes, it is wrong to mistreat someone in a lower position in society: If one does, Dan explains, one will eventually have to provide all the services for oneself; in short, shouting at a waiter would not be in Dan's self-interest, and self-interest is at the core of Aunt Dan's philosophy.

Lemon also remembers Dan's conservative political lessons, which often center on Henry Kissinger, whom Aunt Dan adores, and United States policy in Southeast Asia; Lemon's liberal mother disagrees with Dan, who admires Kissinger's emotional detachment while Lemon's mother would prefer that he weep daily before making policy decisions. The danger of Aunt Dan's reasoning is that it may seem plausible: "If I move into your house and refuse to leave. . . . you just . . . call the police," just as "we . . . get Kissinger to fight" our battles for us.

Framing the play are two monologues, the first a graphic description of the killing of the Jews by the Nazis, the last a rationalization of that killing: People do what they must to "preserve their way of life," Lemon muses—Mindy did this—or they turn a blind eye while others—Kissinger, the Nazis—do the dirty work for them. Lemon says of the Nazis: "They were trying to create a certain way of life," and "the mere fact of killing human beings in order to" do that "is not something that exactly distinguishes the Nazis from everybody else." She compares Nazi action to the way our society deals with criminals because they threaten our "hopes for a desirable future." She compares Nazi action to her own response to "let's say, cockroaches—living in [her] house." Lemon has learned Aunt Dan's lessons well, and Lemon's sickliness is the outward symbol of her intellectual corrup-

tion. Her "education" is Shawn's lesson for the audience in the process of rationalizing human brutality.

AUNTIE MAME Jerome Lawrence and Robert E. Lee (1956)

Based on the popular novel by Patrick Dennis, *Auntie Mame* is a delightful comedy about Dennis's free-spirited aunt, her friends, and her battle against conservative forces for the mind and spirit of her nephew, Patrick.

Upon the death of her brother, Mame Dennis inherits his young son. From the first moment, the affection between them is mutual, but while Mame hopes to open Patrick's mind to the world's possibilities, Mr. Babcock—trustee of Patrick's inheritance at the Knickerbocker Bank—wants to make a conservative stuffed-shirt out of him. Therein lies the central conflict of this episodic comedy, which begins in the late 1920s and ends in the mid-1940s. When Auntie Mame enrolls Patrick in a progressive—sometimes nudist—school in Greenwich Village, Mr. Babcock quickly packs him off to a conservative boarding school.

When the stock-market crash of 1929 leaves Mame with little except her Beekman Place town house and her loyal servants, she tries acting and retail to raise funds. Though she fails at both occupations, while working at Macy's department store during the Christmas season, she meets and falls in love with a wealthy southern oil man, who marries her. Beau (who eventually widows Mame by falling off a mountain) and Mame travel the world as Patrick grows up at prep school and college. Mame has her influence on him during school vacations, but by the time Patrick graduates from college he is more Babcock than free spirit. When Mr. Babcock tries and nearly succeeds in marrying Patrick off to a girl Mame characterizes as having "braces on her brains" from an anti-Semitic, upper-middle-class family, Auntie Mame deftly sabotages the match by throwing a cocktail party to which she invites her avant-garde and endearing friends along with the girl and her parents. The narrow-minded and insipid Upsons are appalled, and Patrick's eyes are opened to the folly of marrying the likes of their Gloria.

The themes of individualism, freedom of thought, and the high cost to one's principles demanded by conformity that are dealt with comically here are also found in the serious dramas of JEROME LAWRENCE and ROBERT E. LEE, *INHERIT THE WIND* (1955) and *The NIGHT THOREAU SPENT IN JAIL* (1970). The play was made into the very successful musical *Mame* (music by Jerry Herman) in 1966.

AUTUMN GARDEN, THE LILLIAN HELLMAN (1951)

Often called Chekhovian for its unhappy and static cast of characters, LILLIAN HELLMAN's *The Autumn Garden* depicts a group of people at a summer guest house whose illusions about themselves and others are stripped away—but little changes.

Constance Tuckerman, the daughter of a rich man who died broke, keeps her home as a summer guest house. As the play opens, the house is full of paying guests on summer holiday: Mrs. Carrie Ellis and her wealthy mother-in-law, as well as her son Fred Ellis, who is engaged to Constance Tuckerman's niece, Sophie; General and Mrs. Griggs; and Edward Crossman, an old friend from Constance's youth. Constance nervously awaits the arrival of her old beau, Nick, whom she has not seen in 23 years, and his wife.

Gradually, the secrets of many of the characters are revealed. Sophie, a European whom Constance brought to live with her after World War II, is not as happy to be in America as her aunt assumes; she longs to go home but cannot afford to. She and Fred Ellis plan to marry for convenience only: She would like a home apart from her aunt and he is willing to help her achieve that. (Implicit in this act of kindness and in his relationship with the opportunistic writer Payson is the idea that Fred may be homosexual; therefore, the marriage, too, would be illusion.) General and Mrs. Griggs are quietly on the verge of divorce after 25 years of marriage; Mrs. Griggs opposes the divorce, but her husband has tired of her girlish behavior even in middle age.

Nick Denery, a painter, arrives with his fashionable wife, Nina, and soon reveals himself to be an insincere opportunist who has exaggerated his artistic success to impress others and take advantage of them. This comes as a surprise to Constance who has deluded herself into thinking that Nick was the love of her life. Ned Crossman, on the other hand, recognizes that Nick has not changed since they were in their teens. Constance also has assumed that Nick's marriage to Nina must be a perfect one; in fact, they too are unhappy.

Because the house is so crowded with the arrival of Nick and Nina, young Sophie has had to sleep in the living room. When Nick comes in late one evening, very drunk, he passes out on Sophie's bed. When Sophie realizes that this annoying, but innocent, incident has scandalized the town and compromised her position in the Ellis family, she blackmails Nina into giving her enough money to return to Europe. Sophie, then, is the only character who takes action and makes a change.

In the end, the others lie to each other and themselves in order to maintain the status quo. Nick convinces Nina not to leave him, saying she needs him to be the target of her contempt. Rose convinces the general to stay, claiming she has health problems. Fred will go to Europe with his mother as originally planned; Fred's grandmother—having dispensed with Payson by informing him that Fred could travel with him but would not bring any money—will continue to control the family by controlling the money.

Finally, Constance, left alone with her old friend Ned Crossman, asks him, "What *have* I built my life on?" This question resonates for all of them: Their lives are built on deception, manipulation, illusion, and self-delusion. Constance believed that bringing Sophie to America was the "right thing," and it turned out to be all wrong for Sophie. She calls herself a "fool" for loving Nick: "All these years of making a shabby man into a kind of hero," she comments to Ned with regret. And Ned who loved her romantically for many years no longer does: This is poor timing since Constance, now free of her infatuation with Nick, can finally see that Ned is the better man. Constance's last line to Ned is also Hellman's last word: "Most of us lie to ourselves, darling, most of us."

Scholar Marvin Felheim in his essay on *The Autumn Garden* points out that while some characters are more deceptive and manipulative than others, none is without fault: "Nick Denery and Rose Griggs are both immoral and selfish people, but their immorality is a matter of degree inasmuch as all of the characters are to some extent tainted (or human)" (51). The absence of heroic behavior contributes to the play's complexity. Lillian Hellman often said that *The Autumn Garden* was her favorite of her own plays; she remarked in an interview in 1975 that she "said more of what [she] felt in *Autumn Garden* than [she] ever said before or afterwards" (Albert 175).

BIBLIOGRAPHY

Albert, Jan. "Sweetest Smelling Baby in New Orleans." In *Conversations with Lillian Hellman,* edited by Jackson R. Bryer. Jackson: University Press of Mississippi, 1986. 165–178.

Felheim, Marvin. "*The Autumn Garden:* Mechanics and Dialectics." In *Critical Essays on Lillian Hellman,* edited by Mark W. Estrin. Boston: G. K. Hall, 1989. 49–53.

AWAKE AND SING! CLIFFORD ODETS (1935)

First produced by the GROUP THEATRE, *Awake and Sing!* is set in the apartment of a Jewish family in the Bronx, New York, and begins with a description: "All of the characters in *Awake and Sing!* share a fundamental activity: a struggle for life amidst petty conditions." ODETS's theme—that it is possible to rise above petty, middle-class concerns—is further suggested by his title, a biblical allusion: "Awake and sing, ye that dwell in dust" (Isaiah 26:19).

Bessie and Myron Berger live in a lower-middle-class two-room apartment with their grown children, Hennie and Ralph, and Bessie's father, Jacob. Myron has been "thirty years a haberdashery clerk." Son Ralph is "a stock clerk in a silk house," but he wants to "be something." Beautiful Hennie hopes to avoid being trapped in a marriage she does not want, and old Jacob hopes for "revolution." Jacob, a man with a social conscience, wants young Ralph to "fix" the world; Ralph just wants to try tap dancing and date his new girl, Blanche. Less central characters include Moe Axelrod, Myron's bookie who lost his leg in World War I and who has a "yen" for Hennie; Mr. Schlosser, who collects the garbage; and Bessie's brother Morty, a successful businessman in the garment industry.

At the end of act 1, Bessie and Myron figure out that Hennie is pregnant; the man has disappeared and left no forwarding address. Bessie casts about for an unsuspecting groom for her daughter. When act 2 begins one year later, Hennie is unhappily married to a recent immigrant, Sam Feinschreiber. Ralph's love life has problems too. He has been dating Blanche for a year and loves her, but Bessie is openly hostile toward her because she has no money. Blanche's aunt and uncle, her guardians, are equally hostile to her involvement with Ralph for the same reason and have made plans to move her to Cleveland.

Jacob is still the spokesman against the petty middle-class values of his sister, Bessie: "In my day, the propaganda was for God. Now it's for success. . . . [A young man] dreams all night of fortunes. . . . But in the morning . . . he can't [even] fix [his] teeth." He reminds his children and grandchildren that strikers have been killed in Kentucky, that people work for starvation wages in the South and in the North.

When Hennie's distraught husband arrives late that evening to ask Bessie if the baby is really not his as Hennie has told him, Bessie and Myron reassure him. However, after Sam leaves, Jacob inadvertently reveals the truth about Hennie's baby to Ralph. Ralph loses what little respect he had left for his parents who, he now knows, trapped Sam. Jacob, having observed all the preceding, goes up to the roof and jumps, sacrificing himself for Ralph to whom he has left an insurance policy. In her final act of acquisitiveness, Bessie plans with her brother to collect the insurance money "for the whole family"; they have no intention of telling Ralph that the money is meant for him until Ralph discovers the truth by chance.

In the end, Hennie deserts her husband and baby to run off to Havana with Moe, finally rejecting her mother's values. Ralph encourages her to do so. He, himself, will stay there in Jacob's room and read Jacob's books and, together with other young men, "fix it so life won't be printed on dollar bills." Ralph's rejection of materialism is his awakening.

There are aspects of melodrama in *Awake and Sing!,* but the villain is an economic system in collapse, capitalism during the depression. All of the characters are victims of it, but only Jacob, the voice of the playwright, condemns it; the others pursue it at their peril. In the end, it is Ralph who is heir to Jacob's anticapitalist views and upon whom—in Odets's view—rests the hope for the future of America. The play proved to be a moderate financial success for the Group Theatre, which capitalized on the publicity surrounding Odets as America's "preeminent revolutionary playwright" (Goldstein 97).

BIBLIOGRAPHY

Goldstein, Malcolm. *The Political Stage: American Drama and Theater of the Great Depression.* New York: Oxford University Press, 1974.

AWARDS In addition to the PULITZER PRIZE and the TONY and OBIE AWARDS, other notable awards given for playwriting include the following:

The New York Drama Critics' Circle Award was established in 1936 in response to a belief among theater critics in New York that the Pulitzer Prize had not been awarded to the worthiest play in 1935 (among the plays losing to ZOË AKINS's *The OLD MAID* were LILLIAN HELLMAN's *The CHILDREN'S HOUR* and CLIFFORD ODETS's *AWAKE AND SING!*). The awards are given annually by critics from all New York City newspapers, magazines, and wire services except the *New York Times*. (Because of the paper's fluctuating policy, from 1988 to 1996 and again from 2002 to the present, *New York Times* critics have been forbidden to be voting members.) Awards are usually given to the Best American Play, the Best Foreign Play, and the Best Musical. For a complete list of American plays that have received the New York Drama Critics' Circle Award, see Appendix I.

The Outer Critics Circle, founded in 1949 under the leadership of John Gassner, annually gives the John Gassner Playwriting Award as well as awards for Outstanding Broadway Play and Outstanding Off-Broadway Play; a single play may be honored with both the play and the playwriting awards. The Outer Critics Circle is made up of critics primarily outside of New York and those of national academic and special-interest periodicals, but the productions under consideration are all in New York. (Like the Tony and Obie Awards, the Outer Critics Circle Awards also include numerous categories for performance and technical excellence.)

The Drama Desk is a theater organization, founded in 1949 to educate the public about issues of concern to the theater community. In 1955, the Drama Desk Awards were established to recognize all theater being produced in New York City, including OFF-BROADWAY and OFF-OFF-BROADWAY shows. The Drama Desk annually gives an award for Outstanding Play. (Drama Desk Awards also include numerous categories for performance and technical excellence.)

The Dramatists Guild is a professional organization for playwrights, composers, and lyricists. The Guild annually gives the Elizabeth Hull–Kate Warriner Award (established 1971), which includes a cash prize and is—in the words of the Guild—"the only award given by playwrights to playwrights." The winner is selected by the Dramatists Guild of America Council, which honors "work or works dealing with social, political, or religious mores of the time."

Notable annual regional theater awards, which include categories honoring outstanding playwriting are as follows: the Helen Hayes Awards' Charles MacArthur Award for the Outstanding New Play produced in the Washington, D.C., metropolitan area; the Los Angeles Drama Critics Circle Award for Writing; and the Joseph Jefferson Award for Best New Work produced in Chicago.

B

BABE, THOMAS (1941–2000) Thomas Babe, a playwright most often associated with Joseph Papp's Public Theater, was born in Buffalo and raised in Rochester, New York. Babe was educated at Harvard and Cambridge Universities and Yale Law School.

In the 1970s and 1980s, Joseph Papp presented many of Babe's plays at the Public Theater. Babe's first success there was *Kid Champion* (1975), a play about the depression and emotional turmoil experienced by a fallen rock star. Other Public Theater productions included *Rebel Women* (1976), about a group of women on a Georgia plantation during the Civil War and their encounter with Yankee general William T. Sherman; *A Prayer for My Daughter* (1978), a psychological play set in a police station; *Fathers and Sons* (1978), about the final days of Wild Bill Hickok; *Taken in Marriage* (1979), in which an impending marriage across social classes brings out hidden frustrations and anxieties; *Salt Lake City Skyline* (1980), a courtroom drama set in 1915 in which a labor organizer is falsely accused of murder; and *Buried Inside Extra* (1983), a farce about a financially failing newspaper and a bomb scare. Many of his later plays, including *Planet Fires* (1985) and *Great Day in the Morning* (1993), were produced in regional theaters. For the musical stage, Babe wrote librettos for *Call the Children Home* (music and lyrics by Mildred Kayden) and *Tesla* (music by Carson Kievman). He was also involved in theater for children, creating works for the 52nd Street Project, as well as *Scared Silly* for the Sundance Children's Theater Festival.

In the *New York Times,* theater critic Mel Gussow wrote at the time of Babe's death, "In his wide ranging plays, Mr. Babe wrote about fathers and daughters, love, individual rights and personal intimacy, and also cultural heroes" (December 15, 2000).

BIBLIOGRAPHY
Babe, Thomas. *Buried Inside Extra.* New York: Dramatists Play Service, 1985.
———. *Fathers and Sons.* New York: Dramatists Play Service, 1980.
———. *Kid Champion.* New York: Dramatists Play Service, 1979.
———. *A Prayer for My Daughter.* New York: Samuel French, 1977.
———. *Rebel Women.* New York: Dramatists Play Service, 1976.
———. *Salt Lake City Skyline.* New York: Dramatists Play Service, 1980.
———. *Taken in Marriage.* New York: Dramatists Play Service, 1979.

BAITZ, JON ROBIN (1961–) Born in Los Angeles, California, Jon Robin Baitz is the son of an executive whose job took him and his family to Brazil and South Africa, among other international locations. These early experiences abroad, particularly the six years in South Africa during the apartheid period, would provide material for some of Baitz's most gripping work. After graduating from high school in Beverly Hills, California, Baitz worked at various jobs, including as an errand-boy for two film producers, an experience that eventually led him to write a comedy about Hollywood.

Baitz's first substantial success, *The Film Society* (1988), set in a conservative school for boys in South Africa in 1970 and based on Baitz's experiences, explores the attitudes of middle-class South African whites toward apartheid. The play was produced in Los Angeles, London, and New York, where it was well received and where Baitz was praised as a promising young playwright. Though his next play, *Dutch Landscape* (1989), was a critical failure, it was followed by the highly successful THE SUBSTANCE OF FIRE (1991), about the decline of a once powerful publishing family, which premiered OFF-BROADWAY to great acclaim. Baitz collaborated on the 1996 screen adaptation of *The Substance of Fire.*

Baitz's *Three Hotels* (1993) is made up of three monologues, each delivered in a different hotel room: the first by a seemingly heartless, hard-drinking American businessman in Morocco; the second by his bitterly unhappy wife, in the Virgin Islands for a conference at which she will give a speech to the other company wives; and the third by the businessman again, after he has been fired because of the speech his wife made (and spoke about in her monologue) in which she gave a frank, cautionary account of her life as a corporate wife stationed in the Third World, a life that included the murder of their son.

Other plays include his first, *Mizlansky/Zilinsky,* a comic portrait of Hollywood, produced in 1985 in Los Angeles, which he revised in 1998 and retitled *Mizlansky/Zilinsky; or, Schmucks, The End of the Day,* about a British psychiatrist whose discovery of family Mafia connections changes his life, produced in Seattle in 1990 and later in New York and London; and *A Fair Country,* a reworking of *Dutch Landscape,* about an American diplomat in South Africa facing a moral dilemma, produced in Chicago in 1997. Baitz has also written an adaptation of Ibsen's *Hedda Gabler,* which opened in New York in 2001. His play *Ten Unknowns* (2001) is set in the world of abstract expressionist art in the 1940s and 1950s.

In 2004, two new plays by Baitz were produced: In *The Paris Letter,* a man who has repressed his homosexuality for most of his adult life has a disastrous affair with an ambitious younger man; and *Chinese Friends,* set in 2030, imagines a dystopic future resulting from the George W. Bush administration's foreign, economic, and environmental policies. In 2006 and 2007, Baitz coproduced and wrote several episodes for the television series *Brothers and Sisters,* which he also created.

BIBLIOGRAPHY

Baitz, Jon Robin. *A Fair Country.* New York: Theatre Communications Group, 1996.
———. *Mizlansky/Zilinsky; or, Schmucks.* New York: Theatre Communications Group, 1998.
———. *The Paris Letter.* New York: Grove Press, 2005.
———. *"The Substance of Fire" and Other Plays.* New York: Theatre Communications Group, 1993.
———. *Ten Unknowns.* New York: Dramatists Play Service, 2001.
———. *"Three Hotels": Plays and Monologues.* New York: Theatre Communications Group, 1994.

BAKER, GEORGE PIERCE (1866–1935)

Baker achieved fame as a teacher of playwriting at Harvard University. Several of his students succeeded as playwrights, most notably EUGENE O'NEILL, who gratefully acknowledged Baker's help. Other students of Baker included the writers PHILIP BARRY, S. N. BEHRMAN, SIDNEY HOWARD, EDWARD SHELDON, and Thomas Wolfe, who later satirized Baker in his novel *Of Time and the River* (1935); the designers Stanley McCandless and Donald Oenslager; the graphic artist Gluyas Williams; and critics Robert Benchley, Heywood Broun, John Mason Brown, and Kenneth Macgowan. Late in his career, Baker moved to Yale and founded the Yale School of Drama, which continues to educate playwrights, actors, directors, and designers.

Often considered the first to teach playwriting at any American university, Baker always acknowledged the contributions of others, especially Brander Matthews at Columbia, Frederick Koch at North Dakota and North Carolina, and Alfred Hennequin at Michigan. Baker believed that educating people who went into theater would improve it. He taught students the principles of the great dramatists and encouraged them to write well about important subjects instead of trivial ones.

Baker was well qualified to lead this change. Born and reared in Providence, Rhode Island, a city with excellent schools and theaters, Baker was familiar with many different plays and actors. In high school, he excelled at public speaking, debating, and acting. Entering Harvard in 1884, he studied hard to become a professor of speech and argument. Harvard appointed him to its faculty immediately after he graduated. Within a few years, he married Christina Hopkinson, the niece of Harvard's president, and published two books on public speaking and debating.

In 1895, Baker began teaching a course about the development of English drama. By 1900, the course's popularity and Baker's friendliness encouraged several students to ask permission to write plays instead of research papers. Baker agreed. Pleased with the results, he persuaded the English department to approve a course in playwriting and called it "English 47."

Naturally, the student-playwrights wanted to see their plays acted before audiences. In 1905, Baker organized the English 47 Workshop. He staged the plays in a lecture hall at Radcliffe College, Harvard's neighbor, but rehearsals and scene-building occurred wherever space could be found. Audiences earned admission to performances by writing comments about the plays on cards. Baker gave the cards to his student-playwrights to help them in revising their work. By 1920, many colleges were teaching playwriting.

However, Harvard's administrators expressed little enthusiasm for the 47 Workshop. Between 1905 and 1924, President Eliot and then President Lowell refused annual requests by Baker to build a proper theater with rehearsal and scene-construction facilities. Meanwhile, many other colleges developed theater programs with modern facilities. In 1922, Northwestern University invited Baker to become dean of its new school of speech. Though strongly tempted, he remained loyal to Harvard.

Then, in 1924, Harvard raised $10 million to build new chemistry laboratories, start a new college of business, and create a special laboratory to train stu-dents to restore paintings and statues in its famous Fogg Museum of Art. President Lowell saw the benefit of practical training in these fields, but he still objected to the "practical" nature of theater education. That year, Yale University, Harvard's greatest rival, started a Department of Drama and invited Baker to lead it. Baker accepted, and his move made front-page news. One headline became famous: "Yale 47, Harvard 0." After eight years at Yale, he retired. His health declined, and two years later he died of pneumonia. Baker's example had convinced many authorities that playwriting and other performing arts deserved to be taught in universities because they were as important in the lives of educated persons as mathematics, the sciences, languages, philosophy, and religion.

BIBLIOGRAPHY
Baker, George Pierce. *Dramatic Technique*. Boston: Houghton Mifflin, 1919.

Clark, Barrett, et al. *George Pierce Baker: A Memorial*. New York: Dramatists Play Service, 1939.

Kinne, Wisner Payne. *George Pierce Baker and the American Theatre*. Cambridge, Mass.: Harvard University Press, 1954.

Arvid F. Sponberg
Valparaiso University

BALDWIN, JAMES (1924–1987)

Novelist, essayist, and playwright James Baldwin had a difficult childhood: An illegitimate child, he never knew his real father. His stepfather, David Baldwin, a storefront Baptist preacher, never accepted James and treated him harshly next to his other children. Baldwin discovered his illegitimacy at 18; the news devastated him but explained his stepfather's behavior. David Baldwin also insisted that all whites were devils, but a series of liberal mentors during James Baldwin's schooling years expanded his political and cultural horizons and belied such assertions. It was as a teen that he also began to reconcile himself to his homosexuality. Asserting the need for racial and sexual equality, Baldwin's work repeatedly exposes the inequities and destruction caused by racism and homophobia in America.

Richard Wright was an early mentor, encouraging Baldwin to concentrate on his stories, essays, and reviews full-time, although they later had artistic disagreements. In 1948, Baldwin traveled to Europe and decided to make Paris his base, there discovering a greater sense of freedom. Much of his subsequent writing displays his central concern with issues of identity and acceptance. Despite a childhood conversion to the Pentecostal Church, in which he became an apprentice minister, he later rejected religion, questioning the acceptance of Christian tenets he saw as being used to enslave. His preoccupation with identity and religion underscore his first play, The AMEN CORNER (1955), set in a storefront Pentecostal church. The play displays the limitations of a narrow religious life, as Sister Margaret struggles to hold onto church and son. She finally discovers a more tolerant faith based on love, which strengthens her for the future. This was followed by a stage adaptation of his own 1956 novel about one man's struggle with his homosexuality, Giovanni's Room (1957).

By the 1960s, Baldwin was viewed as a literary spokesperson for the Civil Rights movement, a burden he took on in BLUES FOR MR. CHARLIE (1964), a tragic tale of one man sacrificing himself for others, based on the racially motivated murder of Emmett Till. The play questions the sincerity of white liberals and asks for a reevaluation of the Civil Rights movement. Influenced by French dramatist Jean Genet's Blacks (1959), the play's characters are mostly allegorical, representing such figures as Malcolm X and Martin Luther King Jr.

Baldwin's plays, like his novels, tend to be parables illustrating the implications of the important statements contained in his essays. His playwriting style relies heavily on the theatrics of a church pulpit and has been criticized for being too preachy. Baldwin also wrote an unproduced screenplay about the life of Malcolm X, One Day, When I Was Lost: A Scenario (published in 1973), which formed the basis for Spike Lee's film Malcolm X (1992). A Deed from the King of Spain (1974), about a disintegrating family in the American Southwest, and "The Welcome Table" (1987), on which he was working at the time of his early death from cancer, remain unpublished and complete his dramatic output.

BIBLIOGRAPHY
Baldwin, James. The Amen Corner. New York: Dial, 1968.
———. Blues for Mr. Charlie. New York: Dial, 1964.
———. One Day, When I Was Lost: A Scenario. New York: Dial, 1973.
Kenan, Randall. James Baldwin. New York: Chelsea House, 1994.
Leeming, David. James Baldwin: A Biography. New York: Holt, 1995.

Susan C. W. Abbotson
Rhode Island College

BALTIMORE WALTZ, THE PAULA VOGEL (1992)

After VOGEL's brother died of AIDS, she wrote The Baltimore Waltz, in which a brother and sister cope with terminal disease and prejudice. An irreverent, comic satire on the treatment of AIDS patients in the late 1980s, this multicharacter play involves only three actors: A single actor plays all roles aside from the brother and sister, Carl and Anna. These other roles include doctors, an airport security guard, a French waiter, "the Little Dutch Boy at Age 50," an announcer who takes Anna through Elisabeth Kübler-Ross's stages of dying, and many others.

Dozing (the "alarm clock" at the end of the penultimate scene suggests sleep) or fantasizing at the deathbed of her brother, Carl, who is dying of AIDS-related pneumonia, Anna dreams of a trip to Europe with him. In the dream, Carl is well and Anna has terminal ATD, "Acquired Toilet Disease." Anna has contracted the illness because she is in a "high-risk category— single elementary schoolteachers." When Anna tells her brother that she does not want anyone to know that she has ATD, he tells her, "It's not a crime. It's an illness," adding "It's your decision. Just don't tell anyone . . . what . . . you do for a living." One reason for their European vacation is to seek cures unavailable in the United States. Carl has heard of a new drug, available only on the black market, and of the 80-year-old Viennese Dr. Todesrochein (German for death rattle), who prescribes urine as a curative drink. As they journey toward these miracle cures and the hope they represent, Anna has many sexual adventures—with a waiter and a bellhop and a radical student activist, among others—cramming as much life into her remaining days as she can.

Eventually, she becomes depressed and remembers with poignant longing the smell of her classroom in the morning. Homesick, she wants to leave, but Carl is still intent on her trying the experimental treatments. When he meets with his shady friend, Harry Lime, about the black market drug, Harry (named after the drug dealer played by ORSON WELLES in the 1949 British film classic, *The Third Man*) confesses that he makes it in his own kitchen and that Anna would be "better off with that quack Todesrocheln." Harry Lime epitomizes the many con artists who took advantage of AIDS patients and their loved ones, especially in the early days of the epidemic: "If you want to be a billionaire, you sell hope," he says. Carl threatens to turn Harry in, and Harry threatens to shoot Carl. Meanwhile, Anna is in the office of the crazy Viennese doctor, whose addiction to urine makes it difficult for him to resist drinking Anna's himself. Anna awakens from her dream to find herself back in the Baltimore hospital where the play began; her brother has died quietly in his sleep.

By inventing a preposterous disease and afflicting a universally inoffensive group—"elementary schoolteachers"—with it, Vogel exposes the prejudices involved in the response to AIDS patients, especially in the disease's early days. The play won the OBIE AWARD for Best New American Play.

BARAKA, AMIRI (LEROI JONES)

(1934–)   Poet, essayist, and playwright Amiri Baraka was born in Newark, New Jersey. Baraka was known as LeRoi Jones until 1968, when he changed his old "slave name" to Amiri Baraka. He attended Rutgers University for one year and Howard University for two before joining the U.S. Air Force for three years. Returning to civilian life in 1957, Jones moved to New York and married white Jewish-American Hettie Cohen. During this period, he was influenced by two connected avant-garde groups of poets, the Black Mountain school and the Beat poets, and wrote essays and music as well as poetry.

In about 1963, his emphasis began to shift from counterculture to Black Nationalism, though it was not until after the assassination of Malcolm X in 1965 that he became fully committed to that cause. Some of his most influential and best-known plays are from the period between 1963 and 1965; three of these plays were produced in 1964: DUTCHMAN, *The Toilet,* and *The Slave.* Of these, the OBIE-AWARD–winning *Dutchman* is the most well known; in it, a white woman is both seductress and tormenter of an African-American man on a subway train. Representing white America, she eventually kills him, but only after he articulates the theory that channeled rage against whites is what black art expresses: "Bird would've played not a note of music if he just walked up to East Sixty-seventh Street and killed the first ten white people he saw. Not a note!"

In Harlem in 1965, Jones established the short-lived Black Arts Repertory Theatre (1965–66), which presented poetry readings, concerts, and plays. After the theater dissolved, he established the Spirit House, a black community theater in Newark. Back in Newark, having divorced Hettie Cohen, Jones married Sylvia Robinson (later called Amina Baraka) and began developing an ideology that would later become known as the BLACK ARTS MOVEMENT, according to which "black" art must speak directly to African Americans about the African-American experience. *Dutchman,* though it was written prior to 1966, certainly embodies some of the doctrines of the Black Arts Movement. The stated purpose of the Black Arts Movement, according to Black Nationalists, was to support the revolutionary movement to form a Black Nation. In his AGITPROP plays, *The Goodness of Life (A Coon Show)* (1967), *Madheart* (1967), SLAVE SHIP (1967), and *Police* (1968), the playwright departed from representational theater to create dramas that were more ritualistic in style and were intended to incite the African-American community to action.

In the mid-1970s, Baraka underwent another ideological shift, this time away from Black Nationalism to Marxist-Leninist philosophy. Two of his plays from this period are *The Motion of History* (1977), which ends with oppressive whites becoming Marxist coworkers, and *What Was the Relationship of the Lone Ranger to the Means of Production?* (1979), in which the Lone Ranger is a capitalist exploiter. Baraka's later plays also include *At the Dim'crack Convention* (1980); *Boy and Tarzan Appear in Clearing* (1981); *Weimar 2* (1981); and *General Hag's Skeezag* (published, 1992; first production, 1996).

Amiri Baraka taught at the New School for Social Research in New York (1961–64), and was a visiting professor at San Francisco State College (1966–67), Yale University (1977–78), and George Washington University (1978–79). He was a permanent faculty member at the State University of New York at Stony Brook from 1980 until he retired from teaching in 2000. He has written some 35 plays and countless essays and poems.

Baraka, who assumed the position of poet laureate of the state of New Jersey in July of 2002, came under pressure from the state and from the Anti-Defamation League to resign after he read his poem "Somebody Blew Up America" at a public event on September 19, 2002. The six-page poem, which he wrote shortly after the terrorist attacks of September 11, 2001, is largely a diatribe against racism, but it offended many, in part because it perpetuated an urban legend that 4,000 Israeli workers were "told" not to come to work that day. In a statement made on October 3, Baraka refused to resign or apologize and went on to accuse U.S. intelligence agencies of knowing the attacks were coming and doing nothing.

Now in his mid-70s, Baraka continues to write poetry and prose that arouse controversy; but his most significant work as a playwright remains that which he produced in the 1960s.

BIBLIOGRAPHY
Baraka, Amiri. *The Autobiography of LeRoi Jones/Amiri Baraka.* New York: Freundlich Books, 1984.

———. *"The Baptism" and "The Toilet."* New York: Grove Press, 1967.

———. *"Dutchman" and "The Slave," Two Plays.* New York: Morrow, 1964.

———. *Four Black Revolutionary Plays, All Praise to the Black Man.* Indianapolis: Bobbs Merrill, 1969.

———. *The LeRoi Jones/Amiri Baraka Reader.* Edited by William J. Harris. New York: Thunder's Mouth Press, 1999.

———. *"The Motion of History" and Other Plays.* New York: Morrow, 1978.

———. *Raise, Race, Rays, Raze: Essays since 1965.* New York: Random House, 1971.

———. *Selected Plays and Prose of Amiri Baraka (LeRoi Jones).* New York: Morrow, 1979.

Benston, Kimberly W. *Baraka: The Renegade and the Mask.* New Haven, Conn.: Yale University Press, 1976.

———, ed. *Imamu Amiri Baraka (LeRoi Jones): A Collection of Critical Essays.* Englewood Cliffs, N.J.: Prentice Hall, 1978.

Brown, Lloyd W. *Amiri Baraka.* Boston: Twayne, 1980.

Effiong, Philip Uko. *In Search of a Model for African-American Drama: A Study of Selected Plays by Lorraine Hansberry, Amiri Baraka and Ntozake Shange.* Lanham, Md.: University Press of America, 2000.

Elam, Harry J., Jr. *Taking It to the Streets: The Social Protest Theater of Amiri Baraka and Luis Valdez.* Ann Arbor: University of Michigan Press, 1997.

Hudson, Theodore R. *From LeRoi Jones to Amiri Baraka: The Literary Works.* Durham, N.C.: Duke University Press, 1973.

Reilly, Charlie, ed. *Conversations with Amiri Baraka.* Jackson: University Press of Mississippi, 1994.

BARKER, JAMES NELSON (1784–1858)

Born to a prominent Philadelphia family, James Nelson Barker enjoyed a successful and varied career as a playwright, politician, and soldier. His father, General John Barker, who had served as mayor of Philadelphia for three terms, ensured his son's political indoctrination at an early age by sending him to the new capital, Washington, D.C., from 1809 to 1810. Like his father, James Nelson Barker was a member of the Democratic Party, and he became a devoted supporter of both Thomas Jefferson and Andrew Jackson.

Though not a professional playwright, James Nelson Barker produced some of the most intriguing plays of the early national period, including *Tears and Smiles* (1807), *The Embargo; or, What News?* (1807), *The Indian Princess; or, La Belle Sauvage* (1808), and *Superstition* (1824). Each of these plays is set in the United States (unusual for the period), and *The Embargo, The Indian Princess,* and *Superstition* treat uniquely "American" topics: the Embargo Act controversy, the story of Pocahontas, and the Puritan persecution of witchcraft, respectively.

A contemporary of James Fenimore Cooper and Nathaniel Hawthorne, Barker's work reflects a growing interest among American writers in claiming and mythologizing the nation's early history. In *The Indian*

Princess, Captain John Smith predicts the rise of a "great, yet virtuous empire" in America, one free from "old licentious Europe." But Barker's work also reflects the struggle that American authors faced in establishing their own "native" voice and the problem that the early national theater encountered in defining an American aesthetic. Even though America had ostensibly thrown off the English yoke, many Americans still looked to Great Britain as the arbiter of culture, convinced that no homegrown American play could compare to sophisticated English fare. The reception of Barker's own play *Marmion* (1812) offers ample proof of the continuing American prejudice against "native" authors. When Philadelphia's Chestnut Street Theatre initially produced *Marmion* (a play based on Sir Walter Scott's poem), the managers advertised the author as an Englishman, Thomas Morton. The play enjoyed considerable success for its first few nights. When audiences learned that the author was in fact American, box office revenue fell sharply. Barker often complained about Americans' unwillingness to support their own artists and writers.

Barker's patriotism sprang from his experiences as a soldier in the War of 1812 and his service as mayor of Philadelphia (elected 1819). From 1829–38, he served as collector of the Port of Philadelphia. He spent the final years of his career as the assistant comptroller of the United States Treasury (1841–58). Theater managers and actors Francis Wemyss, William B. Wood, and WILLIAM DUNLAP all praised Barker's efforts to establish a new American voice in the theater and acknowledged his work as among the finest of America's first generation of playwrights.

Heather Nathans
University of Maryland

BARNES, DJUNA (CHAPPELL) (1892–1982)

From 1914 to 1921, Djuna Barnes was an integral part of Greenwich Village's avant-garde theater scene. In a community of dramaturgical innovators, Barnes stood out as a playwright of genuinely radical vision, pushing boundaries of form and content and expanding perceptions of what is and is not "dramatic."

Undoubtedly Barnes's personal life helped form her anarchistic view of art. She grew up in a radically unconventional household consisting of her free-loving, freethinking father, her similarly free-spirited grandmother, her mother, her father's mistress, and several siblings and half-siblings. The complex currents of antagonisms and attractions that characterized this ménage provided abundant source material for Barnes's novels and plays.

She published nearly 20 plays in Greenwich Village's "little" magazines, and four were produced. These early, short works share a focus on women's experience, especially sexual experience, a disregard for conventional morality and aesthetics, an absurd view of life, and lack of traditional action, relying on verbal acrobatics and revelation of secrets (usually sexual) to build dramatic tension. Her nontraditional structures, cryptically clever verbal sparring, oblique allusions, and non sequiturs prefigure absurdist techniques. Contemporary interpreters, looking for social, or at least, rational comprehension, found her work baffling, yet compelling.

Three from the Earth, produced by the PROVINCETOWN PLAYERS in 1919, is representative. Protagonist Kate Morley is a mature woman with a past. The three "earthy" young men, who visit her to retrieve their late father's love letters, resemble most of Barnes's doltish male characters. The revelation that Kate is in fact the younger son's mother subverts Strindberg's obsession with dubious paternity.

Although Barnes admired playwright John Millington Synge, her Irish dialect play *An Irish Triangle* (1921) parodies Synge's dialogue as well as romantic ideals of feminine beauty: "Sure it's a happy creature I am, and right proud of the glory and beauty of my limbs, and the independent ways of my breasts, and the little canny lights of my two eyes that do be striking fire and blazing this way and that." This play celebrates a peasant couple's plan to gain the manners and attitudes of the aristocracy by sleeping with them. Its heroine Kathleen is, typical of Barnes's younger female characters, eager for illicit sexual experience.

Helena Hucksteppe in *To the Dogs* (1923), who drives men to her cottage with a whip, and Madame Deerfont in *She Tells Her Daughter* (1923), who stabs her lover in a bed of hay, are additional examples of Barnes's mature protagonists. Both Barnes's older and younger heroines appear in *Two Ladies Take Tea* (1923). Young Fanny arrives to announce her love for the Count but finds herself equally fascinated by the Countess's "tall brutality." Lesbian sexuality, suggested in *Two Ladies Take Tea,* is overtly manifested in *The Dove* (1926), a surreal exploration of voyeurism, sexual repression, and sexual violence within a female ménage-à-trois. Rory in *Kurzy of the Sea* (1920), who cannot tell a mermaid from a barmaid, and Gheid Storm in *To the Dogs,* who fails miserably to impress the formidable Helena Hucksteppe, are additional examples of Barnes's hapless male characters.

After a long absence from the theater, during which Barnes produced her literary masterwork, the novel *Nightwood* (1937), she completed her most ambitious play, *The Antiphon.* Published in 1958 and first produced in 1961 at Stockholm's Royal Dramatic Theatre, the play inspired the usual combination of admiration and incomprehension. This complex, poetic, and allusive portrayal of an ill-fated attempt to heal familial wounds is Barnes's most autobiographical work. It is also her most profound indictment of modern values and of modern dramatists' inability "to see things through with the mind." In *The Antiphon,* Barnes abandons the absurd for the tragic vision of life and modern aestheticism for evocations of past traditions, including medieval ritual, Greek tragedy, Senecan closet drama, and Elizabethan and Jacobean tragedy. Probably not destined for wide appeal, *The Antiphon* nevertheless stands as a monumental artistic achievement, explicitly representative of Barnes's distinctive gifts.

BIBLIOGRAPHY

Barnes, Djuna. *The Antiphon.* New York: Farrar, Straus and Cudahy, 1958.

———. *At the Roots of the Stars: The Short Plays.* Los Angeles, Calif.: Sun and Moon Press, 1995.

———. *A Book.* New York: Boni & Liveright, 1923.

Broe, Mary Lynn, ed. *Silence and Power: A Reevaluation of Djuna Barnes.* Carbondale: Southern Illinois University Press, 1991.

Field, Andrew. *Djuna: The Formidable Miss Barnes.* Austin: University of Texas Press, 1985.

Herring, Philip. *Djuna: The Life and Work of Djuna Barnes.* New York: Viking Press, 1995.

Messerli, Douglas. *Djuna Barnes: A Bibliography.* New York: David Lewis, 1975.

Plumb, Cheryl J. *Fancy's Craft: Art and Identity in the Early Works of Djuna Barnes.* Selinsgrove, Penn.: Susquehanna University Press, 1986.

Scott, James B. *Djuna Barnes.* Boston: Twayne, 1976.

Cheryl Black
University of Missouri

BARRY, PHILIP (1896–1949)　A popular playwright of the 1920s and 1930s, Philip Barry was born in Rochester, New York, and educated at Yale University. He interrupted his studies at Yale to serve for the State Department during World War I, working in Washington, D.C., and London. After returning from London, he went back in 1919 to New Haven, where his play *Autonomy,* a one-act satire on President Woodrow Wilson's foreign policy, was performed. After graduating from Yale, Barry signed up for GEORGE PIERCE BAKER's playwriting class, the 47 Workshop at Harvard. Baker was instrumental in the production of at least two of Barry's early plays, *A Punch for Judy* and *You and I,* which were produced in New York in the early 1920s.

After Barry married the daughter of a wealthy lawyer, whose wedding gifts to the young couple included houses in New York and Cannes, he had the financial security to pursue playwriting as a career. In the mid-1920s, several Barry plays were produced in New York, though they enjoyed little success. Not until *Paris Bound* (1927), a popular comedy about infidelity in the upper class, did Barry have a substantial hit. In 1928, he teamed with playwright ELMER RICE to create the murder mystery *Cock Robin,* which achieved moderate success. Later that same year, Barry's very successful HOLIDAY, a comedy of manners in which upper-class conventions—especially the imperative to acquire wealth and property—are pitted against freedom and true love, opened on Broadway.

Living for the most part in Cannes after the stock market crash, Barry continued to write for the New York stage. Two notable successes were *Tomorrow and Tomorrow* (1931) and *The Animal Kingdom* (1932), both dealing with less than ideal marriages. After the death of his infant daughter in 1933, Barry's plays became more serious and were not well received by critics or audiences. These box office failures included *The Joyous Season* (1934), about a Catholic nun and her spiritually bankrupt family; *Bright Star* (1935), in which an egotistical newspaperman marries an heiress, then leaves her shortly thereafter to die in childbirth; and *Here Come the Clowns* (1938), which he adapted from his novel *War in Heaven*.

Barry's next success came as a result of a request from actress Katharine Hepburn, who had starred in a film version of *Holiday*. Hepburn asked Barry to write a play for her. He returned to the satirical comedy of manners at which he had been so successful earlier in his career. The new play was called *The Philadelphia Story* (1939), and it was Barry's most financially successful work. In it, the spoiled, aristocratic Tracy Lord breaks with her fiancé virtually at the altar to return to her first husband who brings out the real woman—as opposed to the unattainable goddess—in her. The play's witty dialogue and comic situations delighted audiences and critics.

In the 1940s, Barry enjoyed moderate successes with *Without Love* (1942), in which a marriage in name only turns into a love match, and *Foolish Notion* (1945), in which a soldier, missing in action for five years, returns just in time for his wife's wedding to another man. Barry's last play, *Second Threshold* (1951), was finished after his death by ROBERT E. SHERWOOD. Over his career, Barry had 21 productions on Broadway.

BIBLIOGRAPHY

Barry, Philip. *States of Grace: Eight Plays.* New York: Harcourt Brace Jovanovich, 1975.

Roppolo, Joseph P. *Philip Barry.* New York: Twayne, 1965.

BASIC TRAINING OF PAVLO HUMMEL, THE DAVID RABE (1971)

Winner of the OBIE AWARD and RABE's first professionally produced play, *The Basic Training of Pavlo Hummel* is the first in Rabe's trilogy of plays about the Vietnam War. The other plays in the trilogy are STICKS AND BONES (1971) and STREAMERS (1976). At a time of great opposition to America's military involvement in Vietnam, Rabe's play exposed some of the war's futility and horror.

The play begins with the fatal wounding of Private Pavlo Hummel in Vietnam. The soon-to-be-dead Pavlo is led, dreamlike, by Ardell, a soldier in a "strangely unreal uniform," through a series of flashbacks. Pavlo revisits basic training in Georgia, where Drill Sergeant Tower berates his men and where the other trainees despise Pavlo for his stupidity and dishonesty. He also revisits his dysfunctional home and his experiences in Vietnam, first as a medic and then as an infantry soldier. By the end of the play, we have a full picture of Pavlo as well as the real story of his ignominious death.

In his author's note to the play, Rabe describes his central character: Pavlo Hummel has "a certain eagerness and wide-eyed spontaneity along with a true, real, and complete inability to grasp the implications of what he does"; he "is, in fact, lost" (31). During basic training, Pavlo is the butt of the other men's jokes (he volunteers for "fireman" duty in the furnace room because he thinks it will involve riding in a red truck). He is the fool of his outfit, but he genuinely does not understand that; he thinks he is the cleverest of them all. He steals from the other men and exaggerates his life as a civilian to them, just as he will exaggerate his life in basic training to those at home. Rabe writes, in his author's note, that, eventually, "[t]oughness and cynicism replace open eagerness, but he will learn only that he is lost, not how, why, or even where." Evidence of this exists in Pavlo's eventual attitude toward killing: after months of infantry duty, he comments, "I'm diggin' it, man. Blowin' people away. Cuttin' 'em down. Got two this afternoon I saw and one I didn't even see."

The device of Ardell serves Rabe's nonlinear plot. Since Pavlo is virtually already dead and Ardell is guiding him through his memories, the play is not bound to a chronological structure. The play begins and ends with Pavlo's death, and the middle consists of the juxtaposition of scenes which illuminate each other. Scenes of Sergeant Tower's advice during basic training are mixed with scenes from the war. Scenes of rifle training and whorehouse exploits suggest a misguided definition of manliness. Furthermore, our knowledge that Pavlo will end up dead influences our perception of the scenes, and Rabe is able to manipulate our response to Pavlo's death: At first we assume it is combat-related, only to find out later that he is killed by a fellow soldier in a dispute over a prostitute.

BIBLIOGRAPHY
Rabe, David. *The Basic Training of Pavlo Hummel.* In *Famous American Plays of the 1970s,* edited by Ted Hoffman. New York: Dell, 1981. 29–116.

BAT, THE AVERY HOPWOOD AND MARY ROBERTS RINEHART (1920)   *The Bat* opened at New York's Morosco Theatre in the late summer of 1920 to lukewarm reviews but to huge popular acclaim. It ran for 878 performances on Broadway, and by the end of 1921, it was playing across the country. Part of the play's appeal lies in the familiarity of its style. *The Bat* is a combination of mystery and melodrama, invoking many of the clichés of each genre.

The story begins on a dark and stormy night in an isolated country house on Long Island. Miss Cornelia Van Gorder has rented the house from Richard Fleming, nephew of banker Courtleigh Fleming, who disappeared (along with a substantial sum of money) just a short time earlier. As the play opens, Courtleigh Fleming has been declared dead, the funds have not been found, and a missing bank clerk named Jack Bailey is the chief suspect.

As act 1 unfolds, Cornelia reveals that she has received threats ordering her to leave the house. She is worried that they may come from "The Bat," a local burglar, also responsible for a string of brutal murders. She suggests that The Bat's target may be Courtleigh Fleming's stolen money, which she believes is hidden in the house. When her maid Lizzie and her Japanese butler Billy urge her to return to the city, Cornelia refuses. She even disdains the advice of Dr. Wells, a local physician and friend to her niece Dale Ogden. Instead, she reveals that she has hired a detective to protect the family and that she expects him that night.

Mysterious strangers begin arriving in rapid succession. First comes a young man who claims to be the new gardener "Brooks," but is in fact Jack Bailey, the missing bank clerk and Dale Ogden's fiancé in disguise. Then comes the Detective. Lastly comes Richard Fleming. Dale has asked him to get her the blueprints of the house to locate a possible hidden room (and the money). Unfortunately, Fleming gets greedy, tries to grab the blueprints, and is shot by an unknown assailant. He falls to the ground, dead.

Act 2 opens as the Detective tries to discover who shot Fleming. While he investigates, a character described only as "The Unknown" creeps in through the window and hides behind the settee. Cornelia, Brooks, and Dale discover The Unknown, who claims to have no memory of who he is. As they question him, the house is plunged into darkness, and when the lights come on again, a black paper bat has been tacked to the door.

As act 3 opens, a masked man appears, opening an alcove to the "Hidden Room." He hides the stolen money there in a duffel bag, and then, hearing Cornelia coming up the stairs, he escapes onto the roof. Initially elated by their discovery of the secret chamber, Cornelia, Dale, and Brooks are disappointed to find it empty. They do, however, discover the body of Courtleigh Fleming, and the plot behind the robbery becomes clearer, as the doctor is revealed as an accomplice. He and Fleming *had* plotted to steal the money and fake Fleming's death, but the plan backfired when The Bat murdered Fleming. Cornelia discovers the money and the others capture the Detective, who is unmasked as The Bat and as the murderer of both Courtleigh and Richard Fleming. The Unknown is revealed as the *real* detective, and Cornelia Van Gorder gets the credit for having solved the mystery.

The play is based on Mary Roberts Rinehart's novel *The Circular Staircase* (1908). Rinehart's three other successful collaborations with Avery Hopwood include an adaptation of a classic Spanish play, *Spanish Love* (1920). Hopwood also enjoyed many commercial successes, usually in collaboration with other writers.

Heather Nathans
University of Maryland

BEANE, DOUGLAS CARTER (1959–)
Beane's reputation rests on a mere handful of plays, which have proved popular for their idiosyncratic blend of quirky characters, elliptical, yet naturalistic

dialogue, and sophisticated, wry humor. The openly gay playwright is also applauded for featuring a non-stereotypical gay character in each of his works. Beane was born in Wilkes-Barre, Pennsylvania, and grew up in the WASP community of Wyomissing, Pennsylvania, which he mercilessly satirized in *The Country Club* (1997). Beane graduated from the American Academy of Dramatic Arts and received additional early training at ASCAP's Musical Theatre Workshop, where he wrote the book and music for *White Lies* (1991), a revue about tabloids.

Beane's first full-length produced play, *Advice from a Caterpillar* (1991), about an artist whose gay confidant sets her up with his bisexual ex-boyfriend, received largely negative reviews in its brief OFF-BROADWAY run, but it was nominated for the Outer Critics Circle Award.

Beane was working as a babysitter when, in seven days, he wrote his first screenplay. His profile rose sharply when Steven Spielberg's company produced that script, the drag comedy *To Wong Foo, Thanks for Everything, Julie Newmar* (released in 1995). Beane worked on several Hollywood projects before returning to the theater; in 1994, he became a founding member and the artistic director of the Drama Dept., a nonprofit Off-Broadway theater collective created to develop and produce new works and neglected classics.

Beane's most successful play, AS BEES IN HONEY DROWN (1997), concerns a female con artist's relationship with the gay writer she employs to ghostwrite her autobiography. It opened to glowing reviews at the Drama Dept. and won the Outer Critics Circle Award. Because of the play's strong leading female character, many prominent actresses were interested in a proposed film version, which Beane abandoned when the studios pressured him to change the writer's sexual orientation.

The Country Club received its initial production at Vermont's Dorset Theatre Festival in 1991. It was largely rewritten, produced by the Long Wharf Theater in New Haven, Connecticut, in 1997, and then by the Drama Dept. in 1999, in a positively reviewed production. The play, chronicling an adulterous affair, takes place in the eponymous setting over the course

of a year, each scene set during a different holiday. A subsequent Los Angeles production won the *Times* Critics' Choice and Dramalogue Awards. *Music from A Sparkling Planet* premiered in a Drama Dept. production in 2001 to mixed notices. The nostalgic comedy concerns three middle-aged men and their search for a minor television celebrity from their youth.

Beane finally achieved Broadway success with the production of his acerbic comedy *The Little Dog Laughed* (2006). The play details the machinations of a ruthless Hollywood agent desperately trying to dissuade her favorite client from announcing his homosexuality, thereby ruining both their careers. Beane returned to his musical roots by writing the librettos for several musical projects: *Lysistrata Jones,* a contemporary gloss on the Greek classic, never progressed beyond the workshop stage. *The Big Time,* set aboard a cruise ship overtaken by terrorists was abandoned as unpalatable after 9/11, but eventually received a full production at the Drama Dept. in 2005. Beane next adapted the camp 1980s film musical *Xanadu* for the stage, which became an unexpected hit on Broadway in 2007–2008; for that show, he won the Drama Desk award for Best Book of a Musical. Beane continues his involvement with the Drama Dept.

BIBLIOGRAPHY

Beane, Douglas Carter. *As Bees in Honey Drown.* New York: Dramatists Play Service, 1998.
———. *The Country Club.* New York: Dramatists Play Service, 2000.
———. *The Little Dog Laughed.* New York: Dramatists Play Service, 2007.
———. *Music from A Sparkling Planet.* New York: Dramatists Play Service, 2002.

Douglas W. Gordy
Walnut Creek, California

BEARD, THE MICHAEL MCCLURE (1965) *The Beard,* a two-character one-act play, is a classic example of post–Beat generation sensibility, couching existential themes in an absurdist context (see also THEATRE OF THE ABSURD). The result is a perverse, iconoclastic critique of a culture in crisis during Vietnam War–era America. The play's reputation was enhanced as much by the scandal it provoked—it climaxes with a scene of graphic oral sex—as for its poetic and dramatic ingenuity. Shortly after its debut at the Actor's Workshop in San Francisco, several performances were secretly tape-recorded by the police, who later arrested the two actors for "lewd and dissolute conduct" in a public place. When the city of Berkeley filed similar charges, the social, political, and legal events outside the play were sensationalized, and *The Beard* became a cause celebre for the American Civil Liberties Union and the emerging free speech movement on the radical University of California at Berkeley campus.

The rather simple surface action of the play centers on a series of circular arguments and repetitive verbal sparring—a sort of weird Socratic dialogue—between two American icons: Jean Harlow and Billy the Kid. The characters, loaded with symbolic significance—the Kid, the rebel outsider and image of the rugged individualist, and Harlow, the paragon of vulnerability and fragile ice princess of desire—struggle to shed the conventional roles into which they have been cast. The play is less a moral fable than a psychodramatic war of the sexes. It is this internal struggle, this dilemma of the will—an exercise in dialectics between titan prototypes of Americana—that allows the characters to move beyond their symbolic status and achieve a convincingly human dimension. The Kid and Harlow wrestle not only to dominate each other but also to establish a transcendental authenticity, what Norman Mailer, in his foreword to *The Beard,* describes as "that electric trip a man and a woman make if they move from the mind to the flesh" (McClure).

At the heart of the play is the symbolic significance of the Kid and Harlow played off against the dueling impulses of the characters trying to locate themselves in "the flesh." The refrain throughout the play, repeated sporadically by each character, reads: "Before you can pry any secrets from me, you must first find the real me! Which one will you pursue?" The implication is that the human exists somewhere between the "divine" and "a bag of flesh." The conflict, masked as a seduction duet, becomes a Platonic struggle between spiritual and material existence. The final desire of Harlow and the Kid is for a descent from their iconographical status into the flesh of real life. McClure suggests that the transcendental vehicle

capable of metaphysically conjoining body and soul is sex.

BIBLIOGRAPHY

McClure, Michael. *"The Beard" and "VKTMS": Two Plays by Michael McClure.* New York: Grove Press, 1985.

Phillips, Rod. *Forest Beatniks and Urban Thoreaus: Gary Snyder, Jack Kerouac, Lew Welch, and Michael McClure.* New York: Peter Lang, 2000.

Jeff Johnson
Brevard Community College

BEGGAR ON HORSEBACK GEORGE S. KAUFMAN AND MARC CONNELLY (1924)

Beggar on Horseback is a transformation of playwright Paul Apel's German expressionist play, *Hans Sonnenstössers Höllenfahrt* (Hans Sunpuncher's trip to hell). The famed 1920s playwriting team of KAUFMAN and CONNELLY fashioned the work into a satire on materialist values in America and employed expressionist techniques, such as a complex dream sequence, nameless characters, and symbolic effects, to contrast materialist Babbitry with an artist's dedication to art.

In *Beggar on Horseback*, Neil McRae is a symphony composer but makes ends meet through hack compositions and teaching. Visiting friend Dr. Albert Rice detects Neil's poor health and compromised lifestyle—made bearable only by his thoughtful and appealing neighbor, Cynthia Mason. On the same day as Albert arrives, Neil's piano student, Gladys Cady, who has set her cap for Neil, has arranged for her family—originally from Neil's hometown, now eastern noveauriche—to scrutinize her intended. The Cadys, satirically written caricatures, dote on sniveling children, gossip about those less fortunate, and brag about golf scores; their musical tastes tend toward church-choir fare or "catchy" tunes. While prescribing sleep medication, Albert advises Neil that a Cady marriage would assure his health and his art. Albert convinces Cynthia of Neil's dire health complications, and she regretfully encourages Neil to marry Gladys, to whom the dejected Neil proposes, as the sedatives take effect.

In Neil's sedative-induced dream/nightmare, the playwrights employ expressionist techniques to dramatize the couple's garish wedding and honeymoon, on which they are accompanied by Gladys's family and her former beaus. In his homelife, Neil's attempts to compose are dashed with endless social engagements and enslavement to the Cady factory with its faceless personnel, meaningless meetings, and persistent paperwork. His life and marriage continue to decline, and Neil's visions and longings for Cynthia torture him. Upset with Neil's insistence on creating music, Gladys shreds his compositions. Still in the dream, Neil murders her along with the Cady family. A bizarre, exaggerated court trial with an obviously stacked jury follows. Murderer Neil is tried by a resurrected Mr. Cady as presiding judge and the other Cadys as prosecuting victims. Neil and Cynthia collaborate on a musical pantomime to show the court his talents. However, the unreceptive jury sentences Neil to work in the Cady Consolidated Art Factory where imprisoned artists are forced to make popular "art" and "catchy" tunes. Finally, Neil awakens from his expressionistic nightmare as Cynthia overhears his disturbed sleep. Gladys's odd request for a "time-out" from their engagement forces the issue; the engagement is broken, and Neil is free for life with Cynthia and his music.

Barrett H. Clark and George Freedley praised the play (even 20-some years after its premiere) as "the first genuinely imaginative satire of its kind" (733). Along with such other plays of the 1920s as EUGENE O'NEILL's *The EMPEROR JONES* (1920) and *The HAIRY APE* (1922), ELMER RICE's *The ADDING MACHINE* (1923), and JOHN HOWARD LAWSON's *PROCESSIONAL* (1925), *Beggar on Horseback* is notable for its introduction of German EXPRESSIONISM into American drama. Unlike O'Neill, Rice, and Lawson, Kaufman and Connelly did so in a comedy, a form not usually associated with expressionism.

BIBLIOGRAPHY

Clark, Barrett H., and George Freedley. *A History of Modern Drama.* New York: Appleton-Century, 1947.

Mary L. Cutler
University of North Dakota

BEHRMAN, S[AMUEL] N[ATHANIEL]

(1893–1973) S. N. Behrman was born in a poor Jewish neighborhood in Worcester, Massachusetts, the son of immigrant parents, but he became famous for his social comedies set in the drawing rooms of the wealthy and privileged. He did not, however, idealize this glamorous milieu but followed his models, Henrik Ibsen, John Galsworthy, and George Bernard Shaw, in using the theater as a vehicle for social criticism. Politically liberal from his youth, he admired Eugene Debs, Emma Goldman, and Chaim Weizmann. As a result, his plays often juxtapose wit and glamour with an awareness of capitalist exploitation, chauvinism, elitism, fascism, and anti-Semitism. This unusual combination often divided both reviewers and audiences on the merits of his work, but he was held in high esteem by many critics, including Joseph Wood Krutch, who called him as preeminent in American comedy as EUGENE O'NEILL was in American tragedy.

Behrman's early efforts remain unperformed and unpublished. Farcical sketches, heavy-handed satires, and shrill melodramas, often written in collaboration, they show few signs of promise. His first Broadway success, *The Second Man* (1927), however, suddenly revealed a mature and thoughtful playwright. The plot is slender, concerning a flapper wooed by a jaded dilettante and an idealistic scientist, but the portrait of the dilettante as a bitter man who is paralyzed by his own intense self-awareness adds a surprisingly dark tone to the otherwise frothy proceedings. *Meteor* (1929) showed Behrman's political concerns more clearly, with its satire of a megalomaniac tycoon who believes he is clairvoyant. Behrman presents evil as single-minded and goodness as doubting and ambivalent, which often gives evil a definite practical advantage. In *Brief Moment* (1931), the wealthy hero reads the works of Russian anarchist/Communist Peter Kropotkin and contemplates moving to the Soviet Union, while his wife is drawn to an egotistical playboy. In *End of Summer* (1936), a generous heiress falls prey to the ruthless ambitions of a manipulative psychiatrist. *No Time for Comedy* (1939) shows a comic playwright suffering impotently over the worsening situation in Europe, while his wife is wooed by a wealthy cynic.

Although Behrman's comedies are structured around romances, they often end with the lovers parting over irreconcilable and often ideological differences. His early notes for *Wine of Choice* (1938) reveal that his model was French dramatist Molière's *The Misanthrope,* and all of the couples in his major plays recall Molière's Alceste and Célimène. In BIOGRAPHY (1932), *Rain from Heaven* (1934), and *Wine of Choice,* Behrman pits intense and politically committed men against relaxed and tolerant women, and each play tests the limits of tolerance and empathy in a violent and unjust world.

With the coming of World War II, Behrman found it more difficult to have his socially critical comedies performed. He worked on dramatic adaptations, contributed to the *New Yorker,* and rarely wrote original plays. His disturbing analysis of American society on the eve of the war, *The Moment Before* (1943), which depicted racism and incipient fascism on an American college campus, did not find a producer, and, after many revisions, appeared on Broadway in 1945 as *Dunnigan's Daughter,* with its setting changed and little of its critique intact. His last play, *But for Whom Charlie* (1964), showed yet another portrait of single-minded evil in a thinly disguised portrait of Eugene O'Neill's third wife, Carlotta Monterey, and her relationship to his children.

BIBLIOGRAPHY

Behrman, S. N. *Four Plays.* New York: Random House, 1952.
———. *Three Plays.* New York: Farrar and Rinehart, 1934.
Gross, Robert F. *S. N. Behrman: A Research and Production Sourcebook.* Westport, Conn.: Greenwood Press, 1992.
Reed, Kenneth. *S. N. Behrman.* Boston: Twayne, 1975.

Robert F. Gross
Hobart and William Smith College

BELASCO, DAVID (1851–1931)

The career of playwright/director David Belasco, in many respects, marks the culmination of 19th-century playwriting ideals. In contrast, as a stage director, his innovations anticipate many important aspects of present-day theatrical production. In his dual roles of playwright and director, Belasco specialized in atmospheric melodramas featuring elaborate realistic sets and dazzling lighting effects written to showcase the talents of his stars.

Belasco was born in San Francisco in 1851 and spent his formative years in the American West, an upbringing reflected in his numerous western-themed melodramas. Early in his career, two actor/playwrights influenced Belasco's ideas about writing: The first was DION BOUCICAULT, author of numerous melodramas, with whom Belasco worked in the silver-mining boomtown of Virginia City, Nevada, and the second was JAMES A. HERNE, a more realistically oriented dramatist, with whom Belasco collaborated in San Francisco. In the 1880s, Belasco moved to New York City, where he stage-managed at the Madison Square Theatre, which was designed by STEELE MAC-KAYE. MacKaye's many innovations—including an elevator stage that allowed for rapid scene changes and a state-of-the-art lighting system designed by Thomas Edison—at this theater clearly impressed Belasco with technology's potential to serve a playwright's imagination.

Belasco's first major breakthrough as a dramatist came with *The Heart of Maryland* (1895), a Civil War play in which the Southern heroine falls in love with a Northern army officer. The melodrama was fashioned for Mrs. Leslie Carter, a divorced Chicago socialite whom Belasco trained as an actor and who would star in three other Belasco-crafted plays. These were *Zaza* (1899), adapted from a French drama dealing with a Parisian dance hall entertainer; *Du Barry* (1901), recounting the life and ultimate death at the guillotine of Louis XV's mistress; and, in collaboration with John Luther Long, *Adrea* (1905), the tragic story of a blind princess betrayed by her lover. During this same period, Belasco was writing or collaborating on plays for other actors whose training he had undertaken and who were destined to become stars in vehicles crafted to showcase their talents. For Blanche Bates he wrote, in collaboration with John Luther Long, *Madame Butterfly* (1900), the story of the fragile Cho-Cho-San, who is betrayed by Pinkerton, the heartless U.S. Navy lieutenant; *The Darling of the Gods* (1902), which unfolded the tale of a Japanese princess and the lover she is trapped into betraying; and a solo effort, *The GIRL OF THE GOLDEN WEST* (1905), a story of California during the gold rush era. Both *The Girl of the Golden West* and *Madame Butterfly* were adapted and scored by Giacomo Puccini for the operatic stage.

His plays, while morally simplistic, were presented with a sumptuous attention to detail and were enhanced, as the subject matter permitted, with music, dance, pageantry, and virtuosic lighting effects. *Madame Butterfly,* for example, featured an extended wordless scene—the heroine's vigil—in which lighting effects carried the viewer from twilight through starry night to the ruddy glow of dawn. Such effects, though standard today, at the time were innovative. In the opening moments of *The Girl of the Golden West,* Belasco employed a massive painted drop on the forestage that could be rolled upward, carrying the viewer from "The Girl's" mountain cabin down a steep pathway to the exterior of the Polka Saloon. The stage was briefly darkened, and when the lights returned the audience was greeted with the building's lavishly detailed interior, alive with the singing, drinking, and gambling of the '49ers. As his career advanced, he focused almost exclusively on staging and directing. In 1927, Constantin Stanislavsky, impressed by Belasco's staging of Shakespeare's *The Merchant of Venice,* made him an honorary member of the Moscow Art Theatre (see ACTORS STUDIO).

Although as a playwright Belasco did little to further dramatic writing in America, he was a pioneering producer/director who coordinated all aspects of production and, together with his innovations in stage lighting and realistic scenic design, established precedents in staging that would serve well the more innovative dramatists of the next generation.

BIBLIOGRAPHY

Belasco, David. *Six Plays.* Boston: Little, Brown, 1928.
———. *The Theatre through Its Stage Door.* New York: Harper, 1928.
Timberlake, Craig. *The Bishop of Broadway: The Life and Work of David Belasco.* New York: Library Publishers, 1954.

Craig Clinton
Reed College

BEYOND THE HORIZON EUGENE O'NEILL

(1920) O'NEILL'S first commercially successful play, his first play to be produced on Broadway, and the play that won him the first of his four PULITZER PRIZES, *Beyond the Horizon* is the story of brothers Robert and Andrew Mayo and of the tragic consequences of not being true to one's nature.

As the play begins, Robert is preparing to leave the family farm to go on a long sea voyage "in quest of the secret which is hidden . . . beyond the horizon." Andrew, *"an opposite type to Robert"* and *"a son of the soil,"* is content to remain on the farm. But when Ruth Atkins, the woman both brothers love, tells Robert that she loves him rather than Andrew, Robert decides to stay with Ruth, who cannot leave her wheelchair-bound mother. Robert announces his change of plans and Andrew, stung by Ruth's rejection, offers to go to sea in his brother's place. When their father angrily accuses him of leaving because Ruth has chosen his brother, Andrew denies it, declaring, "I hate the farm and every inch of ground in it," whereupon his father tells him never to return while "I'm livin'." Andrew admits to Robert that Ruth's choice is the cause of his leaving; reluctantly, Robert accepts his decision, exclaiming, "Why did this have to happen to us? It's damnable."

Three years later, Mr. Mayo has died and Robert has allowed the farm to drift into "rack and ruin." The intervening years have also taken their toll on Ruth, in whose face there is now *"a trace . . . of something hard and spiteful."* Their marriage, which has produced a daughter, is under great stress, and all are looking forward to Andrew's imminent return, which they hope will save the farm. Ruth and Robert have a violent quarrel, during which she blurts out that she hates him and that she loves his brother and always has. Upon his return, Andrew confesses that he hated being at sea but that he plans to go back to Buenos Aires to make his fortune in the grain business. He also tells Robert that he now realizes he never really loved Ruth and intends to tell her so, which he does, much to her disappointment.

Act 3 takes place five years later. The farm has deteriorated further, their child has died, Ruth *"has aged horribly,"* and Robert, *"his face and body emaciated,"* is critically ill. Once again, they are awaiting Andrew's return so that they can leave the farm and start anew in the city, using money they are certain he will loan them from his great success in business. When he arrives, he reveals to Ruth that he has lost all but a small portion of his money and must go back to South America to begin again; but he promises to stay until the farm is running smoothly. Ruth tells Andrew of her quarrel with Robert five years earlier and of telling him that she loved Andrew rather than him (Robert never told his brother of this). Andrew, appalled by her cruelty and insensitivity, urges Ruth to "undo some of all the suffering you've brought on Rob" by telling him now that she never loved Andrew. She leaves to do this, only to discover that Robert has left the house and has crawled outside to die while watching the sunrise. As he tells his wife and brother, "Don't you see I'm happy at last—free—free!—freed from the farm—free to wander on and on—eternally!" He dies and Andrew vows to help Ruth, but she *remains silent, gazing at him dully . . . with the sad humility of exhaustion."*

Beyond the Horizon contains many basic O'Neill characters and themes. Robert, the romantic dreamer described in the stage directions as having *"a touch of the poet about him,"* reappears often in O'Neill's plays, as does the antithetical figure of Andrew, the practical man of business. The bondage of Ruth and Robert's self-destructive marriage is also echoed in his works, as is the theme of death as a welcome release from a cruel and unfair life. But perhaps most significant here to O'Neill's drama are the two characters out of tune with their environments—the poetic would-be traveler who remains on the farm and the farmer driven to roam the seas—who never "belong" (a word that reappears frequently in O'Neill's plays) and are representative of humanity's tragic disharmony with nature.

BILOXI BLUES NEIL SIMON (1985)

The second play of SIMON's coming-of-age trilogy, which also includes BRIGHTON BEACH MEMOIRS (1983) and BROADWAY BOUND (1986), *Biloxi Blues* finds high school graduate Eugene Jerome in Biloxi, Mississippi, for basic training in the United States Army. The year is 1943 and the naive Eugene, expecting to find sanity and logic, must adapt to the reality of army life in general and to his crazy drill sergeant in particular. This mostly comic portrait of army life won the TONY AWARD.

The play begins and ends on a troop train; between the two rides is Eugene's boot camp experience, during which he passes some of the milestones on the way to manhood. It is during this period that he loses his virginity (to a prostitute) and falls in love for the first time (with a convent girl at a USO dance). He also loses innocence of another kind as his naive views of others and of himself change. Along the way he encounters bigotry against Jews and homosexuals, and he learns that life sometimes calls for conscious action over mere observation.

The central conflict is between Arnold Epstein, a sensitive Jew with stomach problems, and the hardened combat veteran, Sergeant Merwin J. Toomey. Epstein confronts Toomey whenever possible, despite the punishment he receives for doing so, because he is philosophically opposed to Toomey's methods. After Epstein undermines one of Toomey's attempts to set the men against each other, Epstein explains his motives to the sergeant: "I don't think it's necessary to dehumanize a man to get him to perform." The irritated Toomey replies: "Men do not face enemy machine guns because they have been treated with kindness. . . . I don't *want* them human. I want them obedient." Eugene is able to see Toomey's point, however distasteful he may find Toomey; he writes in his journal that the boorish Wykowski is "pure animal," but also that his "consistency" and "his earnest belief that he belongs on the battlefield" may eventually earn him the Medal of Honor and certainly make him the most "dependable" soldier of them all.

An avid reader and writer, Eugene is an anomaly in the army barracks. He is most like the intellectual Epstein since they are of the same background, but he stands by when the other men pick on Epstein because he feels the latter brings the abuse on himself. Epstein's objection to Eugene's behavior is that Eugene is a witness only, writing everything in his journal, but never taking a stand against that which he believes is wrong.

At the climax of the play, Sergeant Toomey, drunk and armed with a pistol, harasses Epstein, whom Toomey has called into his room. Toomey reveals that he is going into the veterans' hospital, his active duty "terminated." His wish, he tells Epstein, is to take one "sub-human misfit" and "turn him in to an obedient, disciplined soldier." Toomey orders Epstein to "relieve [him] of [his] loaded weapon" because he is guilty of threatening "the life of an enlisted man." Epstein, fearful and reluctant, disarms Toomey. When the drunken Toomey orders Epstein to escort him to headquarters and turn him in, Epstein refuses, and in an act of poetic justice, orders Toomey to do 200 push-ups in front of the delighted platoon.

As in *Brighton Beach Memoirs,* the audience is privy to both the private and the public Eugene because of the device of the journal kept by this budding young writer. Eugene's candid comments about his fellow recruits and about army life and rules are a major source of the play's comedy. Neil Simon retained this device in his screenplay for the 1988 Mike Nichols film of *Biloxi Blues.*

BIOGRAPHY S. N. BEHRMAN (1932)

Considered by many to be BEHRMAN's best comedy, *Biography* centers around a sophisticated portrait painter who has had many affairs and traveled the world. The play is typical of Behrman's urbane comic style.

Marion Froude has just returned from Europe hoping to get some commissions for paintings. Her old friend Feydak is on his way to a big job in Hollywood and suggests she come along. Nolan, her first lover, now seeking election to the United States Senate, appears on the scene. She is amazed at how proper he seems and laughs at his clear disapproval of her life. Richard Kurt, a radical young magazine editor, wants to publish her memoirs in serial form and offers her $2,000 in advance. Kurt wants her to reveal how she enticed wealthy and famous men to pose for her and to describe her love affairs.

Three weeks later Marion is both painting (a portrait of Nolan) and writing her memoirs. Nolan arrives but will not pose because he is upset by the announcement of Marion's forthcoming book, which may cost him the Senate race. He asks her to give it up, saying that his future father-in-law is a famous publisher who can have Kurt fired from his job, but she refuses to give up her book, and he storms out. Alone with Kurt, she realizes how hard and vindictive he is. At the end of the act, he also reveals that he loves Marion and

hates knowing about her past, especially her affair with Nolan.

As the third act begins, Nolan and his conservative future father-in-law, Kinnicott, arrive, joined shortly by his fiancee, Slade. The argument over the publication of Marion's memoirs continues with Kurt, as Marion acts the gracious hostess to all of the squabbling characters, tolerant and amused by their behavior. Eventually, she rejects both Kurt and Nolan (who breaks his engagement), burns the manuscript, and regains her spirits when a telegram tells her of work in Hollywood. She is on her way to California, Honolulu, and China, saying to the maid, "We travel alone!"

As in other Behrman plays, in *Biography* a "sizable cast of characters revolves loosely around a singularly attractive . . . emancipated woman" (Reed 48). Marion Froude is "the tolerant, civilized, freethinking, experienced, wise woman who champions the liberal way—the *via media* between the unworkable extremes of radicalism on one side and conservatism on the other" (Reed 59). Thus, the play is typical of the high comedies of the period, particularly those by Behrman, which introduced a mix of characters with different outlooks, entertained the audience with witty lines, and challenged them to consider various viewpoints about society and politics.

BIBLIOGRAPHY
Reed, Kenneth T. *S. N. Behrman.* Boston: Twayne, 1975.

Yvonne Shafer
St. John's University

BIRD, ROBERT MONTGOMERY (1806–1854)

During the early 19th century, Philadelphia emerged as a hub of dramatic literature, due in part to its strong theater companies, including the Chestnut Street, Walnut Street, and Arch Street Playhouses, and in part thanks to the efforts of performer Edwin Forrest, who sponsored regular playwriting contests as a means of encouraging new American authors and of creating new star roles for himself. Robert Montgomery Bird first came to fame through Forrest's competitions. Four of his plays, *Pelopidas; or, the Polemarchs* (1830), *The Gladiator* (1831), *Oralloosa, Son of the Incas*

(1832), and *The Broker of Bogota* (1834), won Forrest's annual contests, and *The Gladiator* and *The Broker* gave Forrest two of his best-known acting roles.

Born in New Castle, Delaware, Bird was shaped in his early life by the death of his father when Bird was only four years old. Though his father had been a fairly wealthy man, after his death the family was forced to divide the children. Bird remained in New Castle until he was 16, at which point he moved to Philadelphia to attend the University of Pennsylvania. Although Bird attended medical school there, he vacillated between his medical practice and his love of music, poetry, and sketching. He was often in poor health as a young man, which hindered his abilities to practice as a doctor. He finally abandoned medicine, though he would later return to teaching in the Pennsylvania Medical College from 1841 to 1843. His early ventures into the arts evoke the romantic influence of Byron and the transcendentalist musings of Ralph Waldo Emerson or Henry David Thoreau. Bird worshiped the natural world and was fascinated by the Delaware Water Gap, the Mammoth Cave in Kentucky, and Niagara Falls, which he sketched and which provided inspiration for some of his later writings.

The Gladiator reflects Bird's interest in the romantic tradition and his hope to elevate the American dramatic form, as well as a strong strain of Jacksonian democracy, which advocated the power of the individual against the system. It is also an excellent example of the "blood and thunder" style of theater popular at the time. *The Gladiator* tells the familiar story of Spartacus's slave uprising in Rome, but the play is clearly a metaphor for Jacksonian manliness. Bird's other well-known play, *The Broker of Bogata,* is set in South America and tells the tragic story of Baptista Febro, who sacrifices everything for his children, only to have them betray him. *The Broker* has many of the characteristics of a domestic melodrama, in striking contrast to *The Gladiator.*

A falling out with Edwin Forrest over the profits from his plays (Bird received only $2,000 for providing Forrest with some of his most lucrative roles) prompted Bird to abandon the stage. He continued to write novels, served as a teacher at the Pennsylvania Medical College, dabbled in politics (as a Whig), and worked as a writer for Philadelphia's *North American and United States Gazette.*

BIBLIOGRAPHY

Bird, Robert Montgomery. *Plays.* Edited by Edward H. O'Neill. Bloomington: Indiana University Press, 1965.

Dahl, Curtis. *Robert Montgomery Bird.* New York: Twayne, 1963.

Foust, Clement E. *Life and Dramatic Works of Robert Montgomery Bird.* New York: Knickerbocker, 1913.

Heather Nathans
University of Maryland

BLACK ARTS MOVEMENT   Emerging out of the Civil Rights movement of the 1960s, the Black Arts Movement (BAM) was called the "aesthetic and spiritual sister of the Black Power concept" by Larry Neal in his 1968 essay entitled "The Black Arts Movement." "Black Power," in the 1960s civil rights context, advocated armed self-defense against and separation from racist America, as well as pride in African-American culture. Critics have called the Black Arts Movement racially exclusive; however, even some nonenthusiasts admit that it inspired a great many African Americans to write and paved the way for other ethnic artists to resist assimilation and celebrate their own history and culture. BAM, as such, lasted for about 10 years, from the mid-1960s to the mid-1970s, but its influence on American writing and American dramatic writing in particular is still evident.

BAM officially began after the assassination of Malcolm X in 1965, when AMIRI BARAKA—then and until 1968 known as LeRoi Jones—moved to Harlem and established the Black Arts Repertory Theatre/School (BART/S). At that time, Jones was already a well-known and critically acclaimed poet, music critic, and playwright. His play DUTCHMAN (1964), about an encounter between a seductive white woman and a black intellectual, which ends in the man's death, had won the previous year's OBIE AWARD for best OFF-BROADWAY play. Jones was also a publisher (*Yugen* and *Floating Bear* magazines and Totem Press). A central figure in BAM, Jones helped shape its message and direction. He saw theater as an important element of the movement. The July 1965 issue of *Liberator* contained LeRoi Jones's essay, "The Revolutionary Theatre." In it, he wrote of "political theatre" as "a weapon" (212) and described the purpose of this revolutionary theater with respect to African-American audiences: "Our theatre will show victims so that their brothers in the audience will be better able to understand that they are the brothers of victims, and that they themselves are victims, if they are blood brothers. And what we show must cause the blood to rush, so that pre-revolutionary temperaments will be bathed in this blood, and it will cause their deepest souls to move, and they will find themselves tensed and clenched, even ready to die, at what the soul has been taught. We will scream and cry, murder, run through the streets in agony, if it means some soul will be moved, moved to actual life understanding of what the world is, and what it ought to be" (213).

BART/S lasted only about a year; it was left in some confusion and soon after folded when Jones moved back to his birthplace, Newark, New Jersey. Despite the failure of BART/S, however, the movement survived, in part because of its close association with the growing Black Power movement and also because it had roots in some preexisting groups of writers.

One such group was Umbra (started in 1962), a collective of young African-American writers, based in Manhattan's Lower East Side. The group's focus was poetry and performance. Some members of Umbra joined Jones at BART/S, and some established the "Uptown Writers Movement" in Harlem. Another group of African-American writers at the time was the Harlem Writers Guild, which included Maya Angelou, among others, and was primarily producing prose fiction. New York was not the only major city involved in BAM. San Francisco, Chicago, and Detroit were homes to important periodicals and other publishing ventures, including the *Journal of Black Poetry* and the *Black Scholar* (San Francisco), the *Negro Digest/Black World* and Third World Press (Chicago), and Broadside Press and Lotus Press (Detroit).

The Black Arts Movement focused on developing theater groups and poetry performances and journals, which brought to light the concerns of the African-American community. The theaters not only provided venues for live performance, but they were also used for lectures and meetings important to the community. In addition to Baraka, important artists and thinkers of the "Black Arts" theater included ED BULLINS, Larry Neal, Ben Caldwell, Jimmy Garrett, John O'Neal, Sonia Sanchez, Marvin X, RON MILNER, Woodie King Jr., Bill Gunn, Adam David Miller, Nikki Giovanni, Harold Cruse, Ray Durem, and ADRIENNE KENNEDY. Black Arts theater was active (not only in the literal sense of the word, but also in the sense of activism) around the country.

The Black Arts Movement began to wane in 1974 for two reasons: the decline of the Black Power movement and the internal divide within the movement between Black Nationalists and Marxists. The influences of the movement, however, have been far reaching. Published in 1968, the anthology *Black Fire,* edited by Larry Neal and Amiri Baraka, contains a substantial collection of essays, poetry, prose, and drama, representative of the early period of the Black Arts Movement.

BIBLIOGRAPHY

Baraka, Amiri. "The Black Arts Movement" [1994]. In *The LeRoi Jones/Amiri Baraka Reader,* edited by William J. Harris. New York: Thunder's Mouth Press, 1999. 495–506.

Gayle, Addison. *The Black Aesthetic.* Garden City, N.Y.: Doubleday, 1971.

Jones, LeRoi. "The Revolutionary Theatre." *Home: Social Essays.* New York: William Morrow, 1966. 210–215.

———, and Larry Neal, eds. *Black Fire: An Anthology of Afro-American Writing.* New York: William Morrow, 1968.

BLESSING, LEE (1949–)

Born in Minneapolis, Lee Blessing received a bachelor's degree in English from Reed College and M.F.A. degrees in both poetry and playwriting from the University of Iowa.

As a poet-playwright, Blessing often uses metaphor to focus his work. *Nice People Dancing to Good Country Music* (1982) presents heartbreak-laden guitar ballads as apt accompaniment to average (but also eccentric) lives. *Independence* (1984) sees true freedom, for both parents and offspring, as demanding much stern and lonely silence. In *Riches* (1985), a couple named Rich finds, in a posh hotel room, vast emotional resonance, but only at the point when they finally have admitted their marriage's many deceits. *Oldtimers Game* (1981) richly characterizes multigenerational sandlotters—people who all must compromise, albeit in different ways, with the ultimate "big leagues": transience and mortality.

In *Eleemosynary* (1985), a young orthography champion victoriously spells out the play's title word, realizing how charity—the meaning of the word—describes rare moments in *her* family's life. In *Two Rooms* (1988), while sketching a biologist whose professor husband is abducted and killed by terrorists, Blessing uses animal actions, which the biologist observes, as metaphors for a predatory (though sometimes devotedly fortressed) modern world.

In such a world, impulses toward overzealous competition, intergroup hatred, general social violence, and chauvinistic militarism receive Blessing's chiding in other works: *A Walk in the Woods* (1987), his interpretation of 1980s international arms negotiations; *Chesapeake* (2001) and *Rewrites* (2001), satires of arts fund opponents and "reality" television, respectively; *Cobb* (1989), his acerbic portrait of the infamously virulent and racist Detroit Tigers ballplayer, Ty Cobb; the post-Hamletian (and postmodern) political satire *Fortinbras* (1992); and two plays about the psyches of murderers, *The Authentic Life of Billy the Kid* (1979) and *Down the Road* (1989).

With his diverse choice of subjects, Blessing creates many dialogical debates. *Billy the Kid* questions, as do *Down the Road* and *Fortinbras,* the boundaries between truth and fiction. In *Lake Street Extension* (1992), a pedophilic father confronts his victim son, now a homosexual prostitute, even as the father, having found religion, has been trying no longer to *harm,* but instead to *help,* others. *Thief River* (2002) examines homosexuality from the multiple perspectives of liberals and conservatives, young and old, and sympathetic versus homophobic persons. *Patient A* (1993) contrasts the outlooks upon the AIDS epidemic of a male homosexual suffering from the disease, a girl infected with the disease by her dentist, and a writer-character named Lee.

Blessing's recent output has been varied and inventive. In the comedy *The Scottish Play* (2005), a contemporary American theater company reluctantly produces *Macbeth,* fearing—and experiencing—the play's legendary curse. *A Body of Water* (2007) asks whether marital longevity produces "irremediable failings" or unfathomable "happiness" as a married couple navigates the mystery of their profound memory loss under their grown daughter's care. In *Flag Day* (2007), Blessing asks whether, even in our new millennium, we can hope for much relaxation in American racial tension. *Lonesome Hollow* (2007) is set in a penal colony and looks at civil liberties in America. In *Great Falls* (2008), a 17-year-old girl and her writer stepfather spar verbally as they drive and he attempts to salvage a relationship with her despite having betrayed her mother. In 2009, Blessing's adaptation of the THORNTON WILDER novel *Heaven's My Destination* premiered at the Cleveland Playhouse.

BIBLIOGRAPHY

Blessing, Lee. *The Authentic Life of Billy the Kid.* New York: Samuel French, 1980.

———. *Black Sheep.* New York: Dramatists Play Service, 2003.

———. *A Body of Water.* New York: Dramatists Play Service, 2007.

———. *Chesapeake.* New York: Broadway Play Publishing, 2001.

———. *Cobb.* New York: Dramatists Play Service, 1991.

———. *Flag Day.* New York: Dramatists Play Service, 2007.

———. *Four Plays.* Portsmouth, N.H.: Heinemann, 1991.

———. *Going to St. Ives.* New York: Dramatists Play Service, 2003.

———. *Oldtimers Game.* New York: Dramatists Play Service, 1988.

———. *"Patient A" and Other Plays: Five Plays.* Portsmouth, N.H.: Heinemann, 1995.

———. *Thief River.* New York: Dramatists Play Service, 2002.

———. *A Walk in the Woods.* New York: Penguin Plume, 1988.

Jeffrey B. Loomis
Northwest Missouri State University

BLUES FOR MISTER CHARLIE JAMES BALDWIN (1964)

Written in the context of the Civil Rights movement of the 1950s and 1960s, *Blues for Mister Charlie* is based on the real-life lynching of

Emmett Till, an African-American teenager who in 1955 allegedly flirted with a married white woman and was subsequently murdered by two white men. The men who committed Till's murder were acquitted, but after the trial they confessed to their crime with no remorse. BALDWIN's play investigates the ideological and psychological motivations of racial violence in America. Instead of creating a play where the audience can easily identify with the characters, the play adopts a critical stance and asks the audience to think seriously about how such a crime could be committed and go unpunished in our society.

By employing a dramaturgy reminiscent of the political plays of Bertolt Brecht, Baldwin sets the play during the 1960s in "Plaguesville"—a small town in the Deep South. By virtue of the name of the town and the stark visual segregation of the stage space into "Whitetown" (where the courthouse and American flag are always present) and "Blacktown" (where the church steeple and the cross are the iconic touchstones), Baldwin's sociopolitical message is very clear. The deep aisle running down the center of the stage separating these two playing areas further illuminates the abyss between the two communities.

The play begins in darkness as a gunshot is fired. Lyle, a white storeowner, walks over to the body of the man lying on the ground (Richard), picks him up, and drops him into the aisle upstage. Since the play establishes the murderer and the victim from the very moment that the action begins, the audience is free to expend their energy considering the complex relationships involving race, class, and gender among the characters. These are the central issues that inform the ideological beliefs of each character and affect how they understand their relationship to the community and to this crime. Throughout the rest of act 1, we are introduced to the main characters on both sides of the color line: Meridian, Richard, and Juanita (Blacktown community) and Lyle, his wife Jo, and Parnell (Whitetown community). Act 2, where many of the flashbacks leading up to the murder take place, gives the audience more information about Richard's return to the South from New York. The audience is able to get a sense of his frustration, as well as a very palpable impression of how his return could violently backfire

on both Richard and the community to which he has returned.

Act 3 takes place in the courthouse where the aisle that separated Whitetown and Blacktown in the first two acts is transformed into the aisle down the center of the segregated courtroom. As the witnesses for both the defense and prosecution of Lyle Britten are called to the stand, it is clear that he will not be convicted of the crime. After Lyle is found "not guilty," he confesses to committing the crime and tells Meridian he is not sorry for what he has done. Although there is no justice in the court, the play ends as the members of Blacktown march on City Hall. The play still holds out hope for the power of organized protests and civil rights demonstrations to work in the name of social justice for all.

Kathleen M. Gough
University of California–Berkeley

BOGOSIAN, ERIC (1953–)

Born in Boston and raised in Woburn, Massachusetts, Bogosian first left home to attend the University of Chicago, for which he found he was unprepared. He returned to Woburn, working in retail and living with his parents until he decided to transfer to Oberlin College and study something that was, he believed, completely impractical and useless, but nevertheless interesting: theater. No one was more surprised than he that this decision proved to be a pivotal one. Bogosian became a film, television, and stage actor as well as a writer.

Bogosian's theater pieces examine the modern world, often at its most crude and abusive. He is perhaps best known for his one-man shows. In the late 1970s and the 1980s, Bogosian wrote and starred in several of these, including *Careful Moment* (1977); *Men Inside* (1982); *Fun House* (1983); *Drinking in America* (1986), winner of a Distinguished Playwriting OBIE AWARD; and *Sex, Drugs, and Rock & Roll* (1987), awarded an Obie Special Citation. The most famous of these works is the last, perhaps because of its provocative title. In his introduction to the published *Sex, Drugs, and Rock & Roll,* Bogosian writes, "I could have titled the show *Conflicts and Meditations on My State of Mind in America in 1990.* But then the theater would have remained empty." All of these one-man shows are made up of the monologues of various outrageous, often deliberately offensive, characters. In the 1993–94 season, Bogosian won another Obie Playwriting Award for his one-man show *Pounding Nails in the Floor with My Forehead.*

Bogosian's other monologue sets—these for several actors—include *The New World, Sheer Heaven,* and *Men in Dark Times* (all written between 1977 and 1982). His first play, about an abusive and manipulative radio talk-show host, *Talk Radio* (1987)—which he adapted into the screenplay for the 1988 film—comments on America's voyeuristic appetite for public confession and violence. Other plays include *subUrbia* (1994), in which the main conflict among a group of young people who hang out in the parking lot of a convenience store is whether to leave their suburban hometown; *Griller* (1999), set on the Fourth of July, which portrays a family for whom the American Dream has a rotten center of egotism, addiction, illness, and murder; and *Humpty Dumpty* (2002), about a group of friends on vacation, urban professionals in their thirties, who learn that their dependence on technology and the power of money has left them with few internal assets to draw upon in a crisis.

Eric Bogosian wrote in the 1994 foreword to his collection *The Essential Bogosian,* "I want theater to wake me up, not lull me to sleep. . . . I want my theater to be an event. I want it to push limits, bite the hand that feeds, bang heads. It's about my fears, my ideas, my blind spots, my isolation" (vii).

Since 2002, Bogosian has not added to his output of plays. Instead, he has focused on acting for television, film, and stage—the latter at LAByrinth Theater Company in New York, with which he has had a long association—as well as on writing novels (*Wasted Beauty* [2005] and *Perforated Heart* [2009]).

BIBLIOGRAPHY

Bogosian, Eric. *The Essential Bogosian: "Talk Radio," "Drinking in America" & "Men Inside."* New York: Theatre Communications Group, 1994.
———. *"Humpty Dumpty" and Other Plays.* New York: Theatre Communications Group, 2005.
———. *Pounding Nails into the Floor with My Forehead.* New York: Theatre Communications Group, 1994.
———. *Sex, Drugs, and Rock & Roll.* New York: Theatre Communications Group, 1996.
———. *subUrbia.* New York: Theatre Communications Group, 1995.
———. *Wake Up and Smell the Coffee.* New York: Theatre Communications Group, 2002.

BOKER, GEORGE HENRY (1823–1890)

A poet and playwright, George Henry Boker was born and raised in the colonial tradition of Philadelphia. He was educated at Princeton (then called the College of New Jersey), from which he graduated in 1842. His first play, *Calaynos* (1848), a tragedy in blank verse set in medieval Spain, was staged in London. Its success there encouraged the Walnut Street Theatre of Philadelphia to produce it in 1851. Walnut Street had produced Boker's romantic comedy, *The Betrothal* (1850), a few months earlier. Other noteworthy plays include the social satire *The World a Mask* (1851), the blank verse comedy *The Widow's Marriage* (1852), and *Leonor de Guzman* (1853), which is about the mistress of Alphonse XII of Spain.

Considered one of the great plays of the 19th century and certainly Boker's most frequently anthologized drama, FRANCESCA DA RIMINI was produced in New York in 1855 and more successfully revived in 1882. This tragedy in blank verse is the story of the ill-fated lovers Paolo and Francesca. Francesca is married off to Paolo's brother, Lanciotto—a crippled hunchback—in order to form an alliance between their families. When she falls in love with the handsome younger brother, their tragic fate is sealed.

The success of *Francesca da Rimini* was followed by *The Bankrupt* (1855), considered a mediocre melodrama. In 1856, Boker published *Plays and Poems,* two volumes of his work including more than 70 sonnets and five of his plays. In 1864, he published *Poems of the War,* a collection of the poems he wrote during his Civil War service.

From 1871 to 1878, Boker served, apparently with great success, as a diplomat, first in Turkey and then in Russia. After leaving the diplomatic corps, Boker returned to playwriting, perhaps encouraged by the successful 1882 revival of *Francesca da Rimini.* His next play, *Nydia* (1885), is a tragedy in blank verse based on Edward Bulwer-Lytton's 1834 historical novel, *The Last Days of Pompeii*. The following year, he rewrote the play as *Glaucus*. The latter, certainly considered the better of the two plays, is written in verse that ARTHUR HOBSON QUINN in his *History of the American Drama from the Beginning to the Civil War* calls, "among the best [blank verse] that Boker wrote" (360). After Boker's death in 1890, there was renewed interest in his work, leading to the reprinting of *Poems and Plays* and *Poems of the War*.

BIBLIOGRAPHY
Evans, Oliver H. *George Henry Boker.* Boston: Twayne, 1984.
Quinn, Arthur Hobson. "George Henry Boker and the Later Romantic Tragedy." *A History of the American Drama: From the Beginning to the Civil War.* New York: Harper, 1923. Reprint, New York: Appleton-Century-Crofts, 1951. 337–367.

BOOTH, EDWIN THOMAS (1833–1893)

Edwin Booth was America's greatest tragic actor in the second half of the 19th century, often noted for bringing a more natural style of acting to the stage of his day. Born near Bel Air, Maryland, he was the son of renowned and fiery British star Junius Brutus Booth and was named after the American tragedian Edwin Forrest. Receiving little formal education, young Edwin Booth served as companion and guardian to his often drunk and mentally unstable father on theatrical tours. Booth made his unsuccessful debut in a popular farce, *The Spectre Bridegroom,* in 1847, but his stage career truly began in California in 1852, under the management of his older brother Junius Brutus Jr. In attempting to establish a performance identity distinct from the strenuous, declamatory, and often excessive manner of his father, Edwin Booth developed an acting style based on physical, vocal, and emotional restraint. Booth's thoughtful, intellectual approach and darkly handsome, graceful figure were best suited to intense, melancholy characters. Booth, in what might be called "heightened reality," gave dramatic characters the appearance of truthful and natural human behavior, while consciously selecting gestures and stage pictures that would communicate the poetic and ideal nature of the drama.

Booth rarely performed in American plays (although Julia Ward Howe wrote *Hippolytus* [1858] for him and Charlotte Cushman), preferring the poetic tragedy of Shakespeare and his imitators. His most successful and famous role was Hamlet, which enjoyed an unprecedented 100-night run at the Winter Garden in New York during the 1864–65 season. Only 23 days after the close of this theatrical triumph, his younger brother John Wilkes, another successful and popular actor, assassinated Abraham Lincoln. After this national tragedy, Booth removed himself from the stage for a year but successfully returned, his popularity continuing unabated until near the end of his career in 1891.

Other popular roles included Shylock (*The Merchant of Venice*), Othello and Iago (*Othello*), among other Shakespearean roles, and Brutus in American playwright JOHN HOWARD PAYNE's *Brutus* (1818). Booth performed with many of the great actors of his day, including Henry Irving, Tommaso Salvini, Ellen Terry, Helena Modjeska, and Laura Keene. Joint tours with Lawrence Barrett in the 1880s revived Booth's career and established new standards for production quality.

Booth was a moderately successful theatrical manager. Booth's Theatre (1869), the most impressive yet built in America, featured spectacular sets and revolutionary stage technology, and the productions he mounted were noted for their strong ensemble acting and "historical realism," although Booth was forced to close the theater after mismanagement and the financial panic of 1873. Booth also helped to publish acting versions of several Shakespeare texts, restoring material previously cut, and provided notes for Horace Howard Furness's variorum editions of *Othello* and *The Merchant of Venice*. Booth purchased and founded The Players (1888), a theatrical club in New York City, donating many personal possessions and establishing what is now America's oldest theatrical library, and resided there until his death.

BIBLIOGRAPHY
Oggel, L. Terry. *Edwin Booth: A Bio-Bibliography.* Westport, Conn.: Greenwood Press, 1992.
Ruggles, Eleanor. *Prince of Players: Edwin Booth.* New York: Norton, 1953.

Karl Kippola
American University

BOOTHE (LUCE), CLARE (1903–1987)

Celebrated wit, editor, congresswoman, ambassador, deal-maker, and feminist, Clare Boothe Luce was among the most popular American playwrights of the 1930s. Her plays *The WOMEN* (1936), *Kiss the Boys Good-bye* (1938), and *Margin for Error* (1939) were substantial Broadway successes and vehicles for Hollywood films.

Clare Boothe was born in New York City, the daughter of a former showgirl (Anna Clara Snyder Boothe) and an itinerant musician (William Boothe). Raised in poverty, she was trained by her mother to achieve wealth by marrying a millionaire; she eventually did this twice. As part of this plan, Boothe was educated on scholarship at private schools for girls. Dissatisfied with the shallowness of her education, she embarked on a personal reading plan in literature and philosophy, including the collected works of George Bernard Shaw—her intellectual hero. During the period 1919–21, she wrote five short plays, which varied in style from social comedy to fantasy to poetic drama.

In 1923, she married George Brokaw, an alcoholic millionaire more than twice her age. With an Englishman named Austin Page, she coauthored a farce, *Entirely Irregular,* in 1924, but she was unable to place it with a producer. Physically abused by Brokaw and stifled by the world of Fifth Avenue and Newport society in which she was living, she went to Reno, Nevada, and was granted a divorce in 1929. Though she was awarded alimony that would have maintained her in comfort for the rest of her life, she sought and found a job as a caption writer at *Vogue.* Showing a talent for witty writing and an insider's knowledge of New York high society, she rapidly progressed to become the managing editor at *Vanity Fair.* In 1931, she published a collection of comic short stories about the "upper-crust" under the title *Stuffed Shirts.* She collaborated in 1933 with Paul Gallico (then a sportswriter) on the newspaper comedy *Sacred Cow* (unproduced).

In 1935, she married Henry Luce, founder of *Time* and *Fortune* magazines. In the same year, her play *Abide with Me,* a melodrama about an abusive alcoholic millionaire and his long-suffering wife, was produced on Broadway but closed after a brief run. *The Women* (1936) was Luce's first success, and its production and publication generated national discussion about the psychology and ethics of women, their differences from men, and the role of the woman playwright in American letters. The play is an aggressive satire of wealthy New York women who spend their time playing bridge, buying clothes, being prodded and primped in salons, getting divorces, and destroying the reputations of their "friends." The play was denounced by critics such as Brooks Atkinson, who described it as "a kettle of venom." Many protested that the play was antiwoman. In her preface to the play, Luce denied these assertions, saying that it was an attack upon only a certain set of spoiled upper-class women and not a critique of the sex.

Kiss the Boys Good-bye (1938), a satire of New York intellectuals and the contest to cast the role of Scarlett O'Hara, and *Margin for Error* (1939), one of the earliest anti-Nazi plays to be seen in New York, were both successful Broadway productions and solidified Luce's reputation as a skillful technician and humorist. With the outbreak of war, Luce's life changed irrevocably. She engaged herself in international affairs, traveling widely as a correspondent for *Time* and *Life* magazines. In 1943, she was elected to Congress, where she broke new ground as a female power player, assuming the role of a Republican feminist, progressive on social issues and conservative on foreign affairs and the economy. Shattered by the death of her daughter in an automobile accident in 1944, Luce began a spiritual quest that led her to enter the Roman Catholic Church. She was appointed ambassador to Italy in 1953, serving until 1956. Though Luce attempted play after play during the rest of her life, she seemed to have lost the gift that had touched her work in the 1930s, and only one short play, a reworking of Henrik Ibsen's *A Doll's House,* was produced. In the 1980s, Luce enjoyed a late burst of influence as a policy adviser to President Ronald Reagan, who awarded her the Presidential Medal of Freedom in 1983.

BIBLIOGRAPHY

Fearnow, Mark. *Clare Boothe Luce: A Research and Production Sourcebook.* Westport, Conn.: Greenwood, 1995.

Luce, Clare Boothe. *Kiss the Boys Good-bye.* New York: Random House, 1939.

———. *Margin for Error.* New York: Random House, 1940.

———. *The Women.* New York: Random House, 1937.

Martin, Ralph. *Henry and Clare: An Intimate Portrait of the Luces.* New York: Putnam's, 1991.

Morris, Sylvia Jukes. *Rage for Fame: The Ascent of Clare Boothe Luce.* New York: Random House, 1997.

Shadegg, Stephen. *Clare Boothe Luce: A Biography.* New York: Simon and Schuster, 1970.

Sheed, Wilfrid. *Clare Boothe Luce.* New York: Dutton, 1982.

Mark Fearnow
Hanover College

BORN YESTERDAY GARSON KANIN (1946)

Set in a luxurious "duplex apartment" in a Washington, D.C., hotel immediately after World War II, *Born Yesterday* is a broad comedy whose theme is the serious notion that an educated, informed public is the best remedy for corruption.

Harry Brock, who "[r]an a little junkyard into fifty million bucks" with the help of "World War II," has come to Washington to make a crooked deal with a senator who can be bought. With him is his girlfriend, Billie Dawn, *"breathtakingly beautiful and breathtakingly stupid."* Harry loves Billie, but he also uses her as a front for his fraudulent business practices: On paper, she owns more of Brock's business concerns than he does. Harry wants Billie to make a good impression as they navigate Washington circles; through his lawyer, Ed Devery (formerly "a young man destined for greatness," now an alcoholic with one shady client), Harry hires liberal reporter Paul Verrall to "smooth the rough edges off" of Billie so she will not spoil his deal by saying something inappropriate.

Two months after Paul Verrall is hired, Billie's introduction to reading and learning has opened her eyes to her dissatisfaction with her life and with Brock. One effect of her newfound curiosity is that she refuses to sign any more papers without reading them—until Brock slaps and bullies her into it and then tells her to "get out" until she is "ready to behave." Fed up with Brock and under the influence of Verrall, Billie gives Verrall the evidence of Brock's bribery of Senator Hedges so that he can publish it. When Brock finds out, he tries to bribe and bully Verrall, but Verrall cannot be bought or intimidated; he is dedicated to exposing corruption whenever he can. Billie, grossly underestimated by Brock, reminds him that since she controls much of his business on paper, she controls *him.* She tells him that she will return the business little by little as long as he "behave[s]," and if he does not, she will reveal all of his past criminal activities, including murder.

In the final moment of the play, Ed Devery, former wonderboy, former principled man—corrupted by money—raises his glass in a toast to Billie and Paul (who have left together) and other "dumb chumps [and] crazy broads, past, present, and future—who thirst for knowledge—and search for truth—who fight for justice—and civilize each other—and make it so tough for sons-of-bitches like you—(To HEDGES.)—and you—(To BROCK.)—and me. (*He drinks.*)"

Born Yesterday is the best-known of the plays of GARSON KANIN, who was an actor, director, and writer of fiction, screenplays, documentaries, and television plays, as well as plays for the stage.

BOSS, THE EDWARD SHELDON (1911)

Corrupt business and political practices and their effects are the topic of EDWARD SHELDON's third social problem play, *The Boss.* Sheldon based his portrait of "the Boss" on a real-life Buffalo, New York, political boss, who, like the boss in the play, underpaid his workers, intimidated his competition, and bribed the police. The response to this type of system in the play—as in life—is the formation of labor unions.

Linking Irish-immigrant Boss Regan and an old-money, born-in-America family, the Griswolds, is Emily Griswold, whom Regan marries between acts 1 and 2. Mr. Griswold and his son, Donald, have been pushed to the brink of financial ruin by Michael Regan, whom Donald describes as an "Irish tough of an ex-barkeep" who has "swindled and blackjacked and knifed his way up" to his position of wealth. All three men are engaged in the business of freight and grain handling. Emily Griswold, Donald's sister, is an altruist among the poverty-stricken citizens near the docks in Ward Four, over which Regan has control. He is their employer and also the one who gets them out of trouble with the police. Regan gets back half the meager wages he pays them by firing anyone who does not leave half his paycheck at the bar he owns in their neighborhood.

Regan proposes a merger of the Griswolds' business with his own: He will gain the cover of their legitimacy; they will regain financial security. When the Griswolds refuse, Regan offers to let them run the business honestly if he may marry Emily. Though the Griswold men are outraged, Emily herself accepts the bargain. By showing the Griswolds' outrage and disdain, Sheldon raises the issue of discrimination against immigrants, particularly the Irish who rose to political influence, which was prevalent at the time. Emily brokers a deal that enables her father and brother to keep their own—though reduced—business, entirely independent of Regan. The motivation for her act of self-sacrifice is not to save the family fortune; she agrees to marry Regan only when she finds out that the failure of her father's business will trigger the failure of three banks, and in one of those banks are the meager life savings of people from Ward Four. Privately, she tells Regan that their marriage will be one in name only and that she hopes he will reconsider, but he says he will "take what [he] can get—see? And then . . . get a little more." This is a philosophy that he applies to his business practices as well.

Act 2 begins six months later; Emily is now Mrs. Regan—though the marriage has never been consummated. Emily's brother, Donald, has led Regan's workers in a strike against him and has encouraged them to join the union. The workers demand a wage they can live on and a reduction of their workday to 10 hours. A man sympathetic to the union has been killed on Regan's orders that day.

At the opening of the third act, Regan begins to implement plans to re-create his cheap labor enterprise in Montreal. He hopes to draw all the freight and grain handling business up to Montreal and ruin the Griswolds' hometown. Further, Emily discovers that he has bought up many of the mortgages of the people in her beloved Ward Four and is foreclosing those mortgages. Just as she "married" him to save the people of Ward Four, now she offers herself to him sexually to save those same people. He takes this to mean

she loves him, but she assures him that she "hate[s]" him and that "[i]t's just another bargain!"

When one of Regan's henchmen throws a brick at Donald Griswold, a mob comes for Regan, assuming—falsely this time—that Regan ordered the attack. Emily too believes he is responsible for her brother's possibly fatal injury. Like a child who has misbehaved too often, he begs her to believe him, making bargains: "If you believe me Emily. . . . I'll be good from now on." Within his own criminal universe, Regan has a moral standard, of sorts: He is loyal to his henchman, McCoy, refusing to turn him in for the assault and possible murder of Donald Griswold, though he, himself, will have to face the charges. McCoy has been loyal to him and has a wife and baby.

The ending of the play does not ring true with its sudden resolution. Donald recovers. Emily decides she believes Regan did not order the assault on Donald. McCoy confesses, so Regan is released. Regan is ready to let Emily go. He signs the mortgages over to her, and he decides to forget the move to Montreal. Apparently, these acts, which are an about-face on his path of revenge and further corruption, look like redemption to Emily. Suddenly—and hardest to believe—Emily is ready to be truly married to this man she so recently "hated," and there is a happy ending.

Despite its unlikely resolution, Sheldon's play does work as a social problem play that highlights the plight of the working class's treatment at the hands of corrupt bosses like Regan. Sheldon portrays their miserable living conditions, especially through Emily Griswold's sympathetic view, and their violently thwarted attempts to organize for better wages.

BOTH YOUR HOUSES MAXWELL ANDERSON **(1933)** Critics have called this comic political satire and winner of the 1934 PULITZER PRIZE a propaganda play. MAXWELL ANDERSON himself—also author of the celebrated blank-verse play WINTERSET (1935) and coauthor of the prose indictment of war WHAT PRICE GLORY? (1924)—did not consider *Both Your Houses* one of his best works (Adler 88). The play was written during the Herbert Hoover administration when public confidence in the government was low. Through his main character, Anderson, a former journalist well acquainted with the shortcomings of Washington, appeals for reform among politicians and for an awakening from apathy among citizens.

Set in Washington, D.C., *Both Your Houses* portrays a Congress so full of cynical self-interest that even an idealized man of the people cannot save it. The plot involves a battle over an appropriations bill. The opposing sides are embodied in newcomer Alan McClean, a recently elected Nevada teacher, and veteran congressman Solomon Fitzmaurice; McClean is an "intellectual [who] reads Jefferson," a politician so honest he is "having his own election investigated," while Fitzmaurice is an old-school politician who is hard-drinking, sexist—even by the standards of 1933—and governed by self-interest. Fitzmaurice is surrounded by like-minded cronies.

McClean arrives on Capitol Hill to find his new colleagues padding an appropriations bill with their pet projects. Chairman of the House Appropriations Committee Simeon Gray does his best to cut out the pork so that the bill can pass. Gray appears at first to be almost as honest as McClean; however, McClean later discovers that the older man has been involved in covering up bank fraud in his own district. Indeed, the current appropriations bill if passed will bail out that bank and keep Gray from going to jail.

McClean's investigations into the bill find not only projects to benefit constituents and supporters of various congressmen, but evidence of personal profits for them in the form of kickbacks. As McClean argues for killing the bill altogether, Fitzmaurice reminds the members of the committee that they were all idealistic when they first arrived in Washington, but they quickly learned that until they started to participate in the corrupt system—or, as he puts it, to "play ball"—they were unable to get anything for their districts and were also in danger of losing the next election.

Unswayed and certain that the country is ready for a change from politics as usual, McClean is determined to kill the bill for the good of The People even after he discovers Gray's compromised position in the bank matter and despite his own hopes of gaining the affection of Gray's attractive daughter, whose father

will land in jail if McClean is successful. McClean eventually hatches a plan to so overload the bill with special-interest pork that even the most self-interested congressman, he believes, will balk at passing it. Unfortunately, he gives Congress too much credit in thinking this; in fact, the bill passes with well over the two-thirds majority needed to make it veto proof, despite its astronomical price tag. McClean's plan to beat his new colleagues at their own game backfires.

At the end of the play, a cynical Fitzmaurice speaks for unrestrained capitalism: Since the robber barons built this country by plundering it, why not continue that effective system? McClean argues that the citizens of America, if they understood the extent of their government's corruption, might reconsider their whole form of government. The American people might be ready "to turn from [it] to something else. Anything else but this." He exits, leaving the others to wonder if McClean will ruin their careers when he exposes to the press all that has happened; but Fitzmaurice reassures them that "the natural resources of this country in political apathy and indifference have hardly been touched." He reminds them that the electorate is "just learning how to pay taxes," suggesting that the possibility for profit has only just begun (just 20 years earlier, in 1913, the Sixteenth Amendment had made income tax permanent).

Anderson's play seems to be a warning to the public, whom his character Fitzmaurice calls apathetic and indifferent, to wake up and revolt against government corruption. In McClean's parting speech, he suggests that a second revolution is "fifty years overdue." The play's title comes, of course, from the curse that Mercutio utters after he is fatally wounded in Act III of Shakespeare's *Romeo and Juliet*: "a plague o' both your houses." It is an imperfect analogy, to be sure, but Anderson's point in choosing his title seems simply to be that neither house of Congress should be spared condemnation.

Along with a theme often seen in literature—power corrupts—Anderson conveys a more radical one: A corrupt system may be impervious to change without revolution. Interestingly, in 1939 as World War II and the threat of fascism loomed large, Anderson revised his ending for a production at the Pasadena Playhouse;

he concluded the play with praise for Congress and democracy, indicting only corrupt individuals, not our whole system of government.

BIBLIOGRAPHY
Adler, Thomas P. *Mirror on the Stage: The Pulitzer Plays as an Approach to American Drama.* West Lafayette, Ind.: Purdue University Press, 1987.

BOUCICAULT, DION (1820?–1890)

An actor and a playwright, Boucicault was born in Dublin. He attended the College School (a boys' grammar school) of London University. At about the age of 17, he began acting in provincial theaters in England. *London Assurance,* the second play Boucicault wrote—the first was rejected—was produced at London's Covent Garden in 1841. This play was considered appealing for its freshness, but his subsequent plays were merely imitative of 18th-century English plays. He also adapted many French plays and novels for the London stage.

In 1853, Boucicault sailed to New York and there worked and lived with his second wife, British actress Agnes Robertson (though when he married his third wife, he claimed that he and Agnes were never legally married; his first wife died in France). Boucicault wrote and adapted many works for the stage as acting vehicles for his wife and himself. In 1857, *The Poor of New York,* his adaptation of a French play, was a popular success in New York. He used local scenes and incidents to create this melodrama. He continued to get mileage out of this popular success by adapting his adaptation for the audiences in other cities in *The Streets of Philadelphia, The Rich and Poor of Boston, The Poor of Liverpool,* and *The Streets of London.* Over the course of his career, Boucicault wrote or adapted as many as 125 plays, according to drama critic and historian John Gassner. (This number varies widely from source to source—from as few as 22 to as many as 400—depending on how many of his adaptations and translations are included in the figure.)

One of his greatest successes was a loose adaptation of a novel, *The Quadroon* by Mayne Reid, called *The OCTOROON; OR, LIFE IN LOUISIANA* (1859), which portrayed racial bigotry and southern slavery. He managed—by focusing on the human rather than the political—to maintain a certain ambivalence and hence alienated neither the abolitionists nor their foes. Another success was his adaptation of a famous Washington Irving tale; Boucicault's *Rip van Winkle* (1865) served as a vehicle for actor Joseph Jefferson, to whom this, his signature role, brought fame and wealth.

Boucicault and his wife returned to London in 1860 with a highly successful production of his *The Colleen Bawn,* an adaptation of an Irish play. Boucicault remained abroad until 1872, when he returned to New York and continued to act and write. He died in New York in 1890, while working as an acting teacher making $50 a week.

BIBLIOGRAPHY
Boucicault, Dion. *Forbidden Fruit and Other Plays.* Edited by Allardyce Nicoll and F. Theodore Cloak. Princeton, N.J.: Princeton University Press, 1940.
Fawkes, Richard. *Dion Boucicault: A Biography.* London: Quartet Books, 1979.
Hogan, Robert Goode. *Dion Boucicault.* New York: Twayne, 1969.
Walsh, Townsend. *The Career of Dion Boucicault.* New York: The Dunlap Society, 1915.

BOYS IN THE BAND, THE MART CROWLEY (1968)

One of the earliest commercial plays to depict homosexuals frankly, *The Boys in the Band* is set in pre-AIDS New York City in an apartment where a group of gay men gather for a birthday party. The underlying tension in their lives is brought sharply into focus when the host's college roommate arrives unexpectedly out of his distant—and apparently straight—past.

Michael hosts a birthday party for Harold. Invited are all of their gay friends: Donald "scrub[s] floors . . . to keep alive" and blames his "neurotic compulsion to not succeed" on his mother. Bernard works in the public library. Larry is a fashion photographer who lives with Hank, a public school teacher who left his wife for Larry; Hank is jealous of the promiscuous Larry's many casual-sex partners. Emory, a decorator, is flamboyantly effeminate, and Harold, a former ice skater and the birthday boy, depends on cosmetics and pills to keep his insecurity at bay. Michael himself is "head over heels in debt" from extravagant spending and blames *his* mother for making him "into a girl-friend dash lover," unprepared to face the world. All are between 28 and 33 years of age.

Michael has given up drinking for five weeks until Alan, his old friend from college—and his former roommate—drops by. They have not seen each other since graduation, 12 years earlier. Michael is concerned about his friends being too obviously gay in the presence of Alan. He is grateful for the presence of Hank, who seems as straight as Alan does; but Emory cannot keep from being flamboyant, and finally, in irritation, taunts Alan, who verbally and physically attacks him. This collision of Michael's two worlds so upsets Michael that he begins to drink heavily and soon turns on his friends, belittling them and insisting that they play a game before Alan is allowed to leave: "[W]e all have to call on the telephone the *one person* we truly believe we have loved." Bernard goes first, calling the home of a wealthy woman for whom his mother worked as a laundress for years; the woman's son, the object of Bernard's love, had one drunken sexual encounter with Bernard in their youth (which he never acknowledged) and has since been married three times. Bernard, unable to reach him and speaking to his mother instead, is left feeling depressed and advises Emory not to make his call. But Emory does, with much the same result. Larry and Hank eventually call one another and declare their love. Finally, Michael makes Alan call their college friend, Justin, whom Michael "knows" Alan had an affair with, though Alan denies it. When he seems to be speaking to Justin, Michael grabs the phone only to discover Alan's wife on the line. There is a strong suggestion throughout the play that Alan is a closeted homosexual, who denies his homosexuality in favor of a conventional, acceptable heterosexual marriage; whether this is true or not is left ambiguous, but, in any case, Alan chooses to go home to his wife.

Michael's own self-loathing causes him to lash out at his friends and at Alan. In the end, Harold tells Michael the truth that he does not want to hear: "You're a homosexual and you don't want to be. But there is nothing you can do to change it. Not all your prayers . . . not all the analysis you can buy." Soon after, when Michael and Donald are left alone, Michael acknowledges his self-loathing as the core of his unhappiness: "If we could just *learn* not to hate ourselves quite so very much." However, the truth does not set him free: A Catholic, he goes out for a midnight Mass, suggesting that his guilt over his sexual orientation persists and that Harold's assessment is correct.

The Boys in the Band proved to be a landmark in GAY AND LESBIAN THEATER. Prior to this 1968 play, homosexuality had existed primarily on the edges of American drama, often in plays where a character was falsely accused of being a homosexual (*The CHILDREN'S HOUR* [1934], *TEA AND SYMPATHY* [1953], *CAT ON A HOT TIN ROOF* [1955]). CROWLEY's play sympathetically depicted a variety of homosexual characters (none of whom is marginalized) and was popular among straight as well as gay audiences.

BRACKENRIDGE, HUGH HENRY (1748–1816)

Hugh Henry Brackenridge rose from a poor background to become one of the first playwrights and novelists of the new nation, producing patriotic "dialogues," including *The Battle of Bunkers-Hill* (1776) and *The Death of General Montgomery* (1777), as well as his best-known work, a novel entitled *Modern Chivalry* (1792).

Brackenridge began writing his dialogues (which had a dramatic, blank verse form but were not structured as full-scale theatrical productions) while a student at the College of New Jersey (now Princeton University). Working with classmate Philip Freneau, who would go on to become one of the most famous poets of the Revolutionary and post-Revolutionary period, Brackenridge wrote a poem, "On the Rising Glory of America, being an Exercise delivered at the public Commencement at Nassau-Hall" (1771). At a time of escalating tension between the colonies and England, the poem boldly foretold the day when "freedom shall forever reign."

After his graduation, Brackenridge moved to Philadelphia, where he served as an editor for the *United States Magazine*. He was a teacher and principal at Somerset Academy in Maryland (where he wrote *The Battle of Bunkers-Hill*). He joined the Revolutionary Army as a chaplain in 1777. After the Revolution, he pursued a career as a lawyer, eventually becoming a justice of the supreme court of Pennsylvania in 1800. He continued writing throughout his life, producing numerous editorials and works of fiction (including dramatic dialogues, novels, and poems).

Brackenridge's dramatic dialogues are of particular interest to theater historians because they offer an excellent opportunity to see how Americans translated their political ideology into a popular form. In *The Battle of Bunkers-Hill,* the American officer exhorts his troops, "Fear not, brave soldiers, tho' their infantry / In deep array so far outnumbers us. / The justness of our cause will brace each arm." Interestingly, both of Brackenridge's dramatic dialogues written during the Revolution depict moments of American defeat, rather than triumph; yet, in each play, it is the justness of the American cause that results in the moral victory, even if the battle is lost.

Brackenridge insisted that his dialogues should be considered as "school pieces" only; he made no claim to their being "stage-worthy." However, the dialogues give voice, shape, and personality to the larger debates being played out on the battlefields and in the fledgling American government, and, in each case, they reminded the audience what was at stake in the bloody contest then underway.

BIBLIOGRAPHY

Marder, Daniel. *Hugh Henry Brackenridge.* New York: Twayne, 1967.
——, ed. *A Hugh Henry Brackenridge Reader, 1770–1815.* Pittsburgh: University of Pittsburgh Press, 1970.
Newlin, Claude Milton. *The Life and Writings of Hugh Henry Brackenridge.* Princeton, N.J.: Princeton University Press, 1932.

Heather Nathans
University of Maryland

BREUER, LEE (1937–) Playwright and director Lee Breuer began his career in 1958 with the San Francisco Mime Troupe after dropping out of UCLA. His early influences included the dramatic works of Samuel Beckett and Frank Wedekind and the acting theories of Constantin Stanislavsky (see ACTORS STUDIO), Bertolt Brecht, and Jerzy Grotowski. Breuer's early training in the United States and in

Europe, with the Berliner Ensemble and the Polish Theatre Lab, prepared him for his work with Mabou Mines, the theater company he cofounded in 1970. Over the past 30 years, this ensemble has emerged as one of America's leading experimental companies.

Breuer's first play, *The Red Horse Animation* (1970), is structured as a choral narrative informed by animated film that explores the filmic sequencing of dreams and the fragmentation of character. The play was later published in comic book form. *The Shaggy Dog Animation* (1978) explores the feminist movement through the codependent relationship between Rose, a puppet dog, and her master. Breuer used material from *Shaggy Dog Animation* to create *Prelude to Death in Venice* (1980), an exploration of the midlife crisis through the struggles of an artist and his alter ego—a life-sized doll. *Prelude* won an OBIE AWARD and remained in the Mabou Mines repertoire for 15 years.

In *An Epidog* (1996), Breuer appropriated his research as a Fulbright scholar in India to explore the American resistance to Indian and Japanese cultures. He whimsically fuses Kathakali and Bunraku theatrical traditions to transport the audience through a female dog's journey into Buddhist states of limbo. Such intercultural performance values have been criticized as imperialist. Some critics warn that Breuer merely colonizes cultural traditions for images that must ultimately subject themselves to the dominant culture.

In addition to his work for Mabou Mines, Breuer is also a freelance director. His radical revisions of the classics, including Shakespeare's *The Tempest* and Wedekind's *Lulu,* have included cross-dressed characters and an entrance by helicopter and have balanced classicism with pop culture. His production of *The Gospel at Colonus* (1983) was a deconstruction of Sophocles's second Theban play. The classic tragedy was transformed by a group of blind gospel singers who collectively played Oedipus. This African-American Pentecostal retelling of *Colonus* received the 1984 Obie for Best Musical, made the quantum leap to Broadway, and later aired on PBS.

Breuer continues to question the identity of American theater through the fusion of non-Western arts with American stereotypes, colloquialisms, and performance values. His new works and adaptations are noted for their culturally charged perspectives, which artfully destabilize the boundaries between high art and pop culture.

Breuer's recent work includes *Mabou Mines Dollhouse* (2003), his adaptation of Henrik Ibsen's play, for the production of which Breuer, who also directed, required the actresses to be nearly six feet tall while the actors had to be less than five feet, dimensions that brought additional metaphor to the classic play's social commentary.

BIBLIOGRAPHY

Breuer, Lee. *The Gospel at Colonus.* New York: Theatre Communications Group, 1989.

————. *La Davina Caricatura: A Fiction.* Los Angeles: Green Integer, 2002.

————. "A Prelude to Death in Venice." *New Plays USA.* New York: Theatre Communications Group, 1982. 2–29.

————. "The Red Horse Animation." In *The Theatre of Images,* edited by Bonnie Marranca. New York: Drama Book Specialists, 1977. 111–156.

————. *Sister Suzie Cinema: The Collected Poems and Performances 1976–1986.* New York: Theatre Communications Group, 1987.

————, Bonnie Marranca, and Guatam Dasgupta. *Animations: A Trilogy for Mabou Mines.* New York: Performing Arts Journal, 1979.

Gontarski, S. E. "Lee Breuer and Mabou Mines." In *Contemporary American Theatre,* edited by Bruce King. New York: St. Martin's Press, 1991. 135–148.

Valerie Rae Smith
Messiah College

BRIG, THE KENNETH H. BROWN (1963) Brown

based *The Brig* on his own experiences as a prisoner in a United States Marine Corps stockade. The play depicts one day in such an institution and its consequent dehumanizing effects on 11 prisoners in Japan in 1957. Critics have called Brown's work a "nonplay" for there are neither major events nor resolution of the dramatic action. Brown relies on maddening noise and ritualistic, repetitive actions rather than dialogue to describe the brutality of military life. Minimal language is used throughout, except for the screaming of commands and a steady stream of verbal abuse.

Vicious guards rob the prisoners of their identity and humanity, referring to them by number only. Throughout this exhausting day, the prisoners, forbidden to speak or sit, face verbal and physical abuse from sadistic guards.

The play opens in darkness as guards welcome Number Two, the newest prisoner, with a nighttime beating. He is not yet numbed to the daily brutality, and through his eyes we experience the full horror of the brig. The remaining prisoners are awakened by an assault of bright lights and a barrage of noise. In a frenzy of activity, the hapless soldiers perform a variety of cleaning duties, exercise drills, and generally attempt to avoid the punishing gaze of the guards. In the stage directions, Brown states that a white line divides each exit and entrance to every room. Prisoners are forbidden to cross the white dividing line without requesting permission, regardless of how many times they need to cross ("Sir, prisoner number two requests permission to cross the white line, sir."). This segmentation illustrates the claustrophobic confinement of the prisoners' existence.

The most significant event is the release of Number Five, who receives a final beating before sprinting to freedom. This glimpse of hope proves too much for Number Six, an older man of 34. Breaking from the systematized order, he screams for his own release. Guards eventually lead the anguished prisoner out in a straitjacket. We must assume that rather than freedom, Number Six faces harsher treatment elsewhere. Following this abrupt departure, a new Number Five appears, symbolizing the endless cycle of captivity and violence within the system. The play concludes at bedtime, with some prisoners savoring a brief respite from the brutal regime while others await further violence in the night.

The play was most famously performed by the anarchist collective known as the LIVING THEATRE in New York City in 1963. The controversial production foreshadowed the politicization of the American theater, as theater artists began to respond to the Vietnam War and the polarization of the nation.

Jennifer Madden
Brown University

BRIGHTON BEACH MEMOIRS NEIL SIMON (1983)

The first play in NEIL SIMON's autobiographical coming-of-age trilogy, which also includes *BILOXI BLUES* (1985) and *BROADWAY BOUND* (1986), *Brighton Beach Memoirs* is set in 1937 in a "lower-middle-income," primarily Jewish neighborhood in Brooklyn, New York. Eugene Jerome experiences puberty against the backdrop of the trials and tribulations of his extended family. Intermittently throughout the play, Eugene addresses the audience directly, providing comic commentary on characters and situations.

The Jerome household is made up of Eugene and his older brother, Stanley; their parents, Jack and Kate; Kate's widowed sister, Blanche; and Blanche's two daughters, the asthmatic 13-year-old Laurie and the *"absolutely lovely sixteen-and-a-half-year-old"* Nora, an aspiring chorus girl. Jack holds down two jobs to support everyone, but he loses one of his jobs when the party-favor company he moonlights for goes out of business. As he faces his own worries, his advice is sought at home: Stanley wants his father's counsel about whether to apologize to his boss (for standing up for a coworker) and thereby keep his job. Nora wants her mother's permission to audition for a touring show that may lead to Broadway, but Blanche tells her they will leave it up to Uncle Jack. Meanwhile, Blanche has accepted a dinner date with Mr. Murphy, who lives across the street with his mother; Kate, who is bigoted against the Irish, is disgusted with her sister's choice. Ultimately, the dispute between Blanche and Kate over Mr. Murphy leads the two sisters to express their repressed feelings toward one another. Also preying on Jack's mind is the news from Europe about the plight of Jews in Poland, some of whom are the Jeromes' relatives. As for the pubescent Eugene, when he is not recording his observations about the family in his journal, he is trying to catch a glimpse of bare breasts and thighs, running to the store for his mother, and pumping Stanley for information about bare breasts and thighs.

Finally, all complications are resolved and the family, intact and supportive, settles back into its routine. When word arrives from Europe that Polish relatives—Jack's cousin and his family of six—have "got[ten] out of Poland" and will leave for New York from London

the next day, the family immediately makes plans to embrace these newcomers in their time of need.

Like Tom in TENNESSEE WILLIAMS's *The GLASS MENAGERIE* (1944), Eugene, who will become a writer, speaks directly to the audience to narrate events in his recent past; he is both participant and perceptive observer. However, unlike Tom's, Eugene's observations about the foibles of his family are funny rather than tragic. Eugene's maturation—continued in *Biloxi Blues* and *Broadway Bound*—is evident in his budding sexuality and his growing understanding of his family, both of which he confides to the audience. Neil Simon has suggested that the enduring appeal of this play comes from its "idealization of the family . . . that we all dream about" (Kolin and Kullman 80).

BIBLIOGRAPHY

Kolin, Philip C., and Colby H. Kullman, eds. *Speaking on Stage: Interviews with Contemporary American Playwrights.* Tuscaloosa: University of Alabama Press, 1996.

BROADWAY BOUND NEIL SIMON (1986)

Set in 1949 in Brooklyn, New York, *Broadway Bound* is the third in NEIL SIMON's trilogy (including *BRIGHTON BEACH MEMOIRS* [1983] and *BILOXI BLUES* [1984]) about a young man coming of age in the 1940s.

Eugene Jerome is 23, a stock boy in a music store, who wants to be a comedy writer. Eugene's older brother, Stanley, is manager of a boys' clothing department. The young men live with their parents and grandfather. Their mother, Kate, and their grandfather, as Eugene comments directly to the audience, are naturally funny—though unintentionally so. Kate and her husband, Jack, are having marital problems, and Grandpa is separated from Grandma, who lives with Aunt Blanche.

In *Brighton Beach Memoirs*, Kate's sister, Blanche, along with her two daughters, was completely dependent on Kate and Jack. Now, she is married to a wealthy man, which her old socialist father resents, especially since she arrives at her sister's home in a chauffeur-driven Cadillac wearing a mink coat. Grandpa will not hear of leaving Kate's home to join his wife in Florida at Blanche's expense—in part because he believes Jack is on the verge of leaving Kate.

Soon after the play begins, Stanley comes home excited because he has managed to get himself and his brother an audition to write for CBS. They must write a comedy sketch before 10:00 A.M.; it is now dinnertime. Jack would rather his sons keep their secure jobs in retail since, as he tells his boys, only "[t]en people in this country have a television." Meanwhile, Kate questions Jack about his coolness toward her. He finally admits to having an affair a year before, but he lies about how recently he has seen the woman. When Eugene and Stan write a sketch for a new comedy show, their father is offended by how closely it reflects their family. He feels humiliated. Stan confronts him—knowing it is just his father's guilt over his affair that makes him defensively lash out at his sons.

Kate has a special feeling for her dining room table, left to her by her grandmother with whom she polished it as a child. For her, it signifies family and a connection to past generations. Eugene asks her late one evening as she polishes her table to tell him again the family story about the time she danced with George Raft as a young woman. She tells him that she lied to her parents in order to get out of sitting with the family in mourning over her mother's sister, who had died the day before. She lied so that she could go to a dance hall and see Raft, not because she had a crush on *him*, but because she thought if Raft noticed her it might cause Jack—her future husband—to notice her, too. Eugene convinces her to dance with him as she did with Raft. The scene is about Eugene seeing his mother as a young woman and as an individual who defied her parents to get what she wanted—a young woman who so loved his father that she would defy them. The scene is also about how important family is to Kate, especially poignant because at this time her family is falling apart—her marriage ending, her parents at odds, Grandpa rejecting his daughter Blanche, and Kate's own children growing up and moving out.

Jack leaves Kate the morning after Eugene dances with her, never to return; he tells his father-in-law, who catches him leaving that Sunday morning, that his woman-friend has six months to live and that she is not the whole reason he is leaving. Eugene and Stan get a steady job writing comedy for a popular televi-

sion show and move to a Manhattan apartment. Eugene reports to the audience that his parents never reconciled, though Grandpa did finally join his wife in Florida, where in his late seventies he plays pinochle and donates half his winnings to the Socialist Party.

Of the plays in the trilogy, *Broadway Bound* is the most serious and poignant, and perhaps for that reason received greater praise from critics than the other two very successful comedies. This work and *LOST IN YONKERS* (1991), which won the PULITZER PRIZE, have been the most critically acclaimed of Simon's plays.

BROKEN GLASS ARTHUR MILLER (1994)

Set "in Brooklyn in the last days of November 1938," *Broken Glass* takes place just after the night of terror against German Jews that came to be known as Kristallnacht, the Night of Broken Glass. In this play, ARTHUR MILLER addresses the question: What is in the human soul that allows such events as the Holocaust to take place?

Sylvia Gellburg suddenly loses her ability to walk, but the doctors find nothing physically wrong with her. The onset of her paralysis coincides with the intensification of Jewish persecution in Germany and the reports of Kristallnacht in American newspapers, which Sylvia reads avidly. Phillip Gellburg takes pride in his wife's intelligence ("I don't exaggerate, if Sylvia was a man she could have run the Federal Reserve."), but he cannot understand her obsession with events in Germany. She is upset about the "[f]orcing [of] old men to scrub sidewalks with toothbrushes" in order "to humiliate them," while Gellburg's view is that since these events are "three thousand miles away," why get so upset? "What does it accomplish!" he asks. Sylvia's sister, too, wants to know "what business of [Sylvia's]" it is.

Meanwhile, America is still in the midst of the depression. People—Jewish people—around the Gellburgs are losing their houses every month because of foreclosures. Sylvia's husband, the "only Jew [who] ever worked for Brooklyn Guarantee in their whole history" and head of the Mortgage Department there, is flourishing financially. Gellburg has an odd relationship with his Jewishness: In a sense he rejects his ethnicity by, as another character suggests, trying to blend in with "the Goyim." He becomes extremely irritated when people think his name is Goldberg, when it is Gellburg; he says there is no excuse for what is going on in Germany, "but German Jews can be pretty . . . you know . . .," and he calls Polish and Russian Jews "pushy." He is proud of the fact that his son is at West Point (through his boss's influence) and says he wants to show people "a Jew doesn't have to be a lawyer or a doctor or a businessman." The portrait of Gellburg is of a Jew who collaborates with the anti-Semites by believing in their superiority to Jews.

As Dr. Hyman attempts to treat Sylvia's psychosomatic illness, he talks with the Gellburgs individually and also with Sylvia's sister. Through these discussions, he learns their secrets. Sylvia and Phillip have not had sex in 20 years, though Gellburg's love for his wife is near worship. Gradually, it becomes clear that it is fear that has incapacitated Sylvia, not just fear of the Nazis, but fear of her husband and what he represents. Symbolically, Gellburg's collaboration with the anti-Semites, his belief in their superiority, has emasculated him.

Meanwhile, the stress of his wife's illness takes a toll on Gellburg's work. When he confronts his boss, fearful that the man believes Gellburg has conspired with another Jew to take a piece of property away from him, he becomes so agitated that he collapses from a heart attack. Taken home to recover or die, Gellburg is able to talk to Sylvia honestly. He admits his own fears and his conflicted feelings about his Jewishness: "There are some days I feel like going and sitting in the Schul with the old men . . . and be[ing] a full time Jew for the rest of my life. . . . And other times, . . . yes, I could almost kill them. They infuriate me. I am ashamed of them and that I look like them.— Why must we be different? Why is it? What is it for?" As he has this emotionally charged breakthrough, he begins to have another heart attack; as Sylvia rises from her wheelchair, Phillip dies.

The characters represent American reactions to the rise of Nazi Germany, reactions that range from Sylvia's unusual empathy and consequently paralyzing fear to Gellburg's willful denial. Sylvia's speech in scene 8, as she discusses Germany with Dr. Hyman, is significant: "What is the matter with those people!

Don't you understand . . .? This is an *emergency!* They are beating up little children! What if they kill those children! Where is Roosevelt! Where is England! You've got to do something before they murder us all!" On a more universal level, the play can also be seen to address similar reactions to other more recent tragedies in which nations destroy their own people, citing as grounds nationalism or religion.

The symbolism of the ending suggests that during the rise of Hitler, those—Jews and non-Jews—who collaborated by ignoring events or by buying into anti-Semitism (Gellburg) contributed to the fear among, and the destruction of, European Jews (Sylvia's paralysis). Only when Phillip Gellburg begins to understand his own soul is his wife able to stand again.

BROUGHAM, JOHN (1810–1880) John

Brougham, an Irish-American playwright and actor with a lively and engaging stage presence, is perhaps best remembered for his burlesques of popular American drama, especially those involving Native American or African-American characters. His satires, *Metamora; or, the Last of the Pollywogs* (1847) and *Pocahontas; or, the Gentle Savage* (1855), openly ridicule the genre of "Noble Savage" plays popularized by JAMES NELSON BARKER (*The Indian Princess; or, La Belle Sauvage* [1808]), GEORGE WASHINGTON PARKE CUSTIS (*Pocahontas; or, the Settlers of Virginia* [1830]), and JOHN AUGUSTUS STONE (*Metamora; or, the Last of the Wampanoags* [1829]). Brougham's *Dred; or, the Dismal Swamp* (1856) parodied the abolitionist plays of the pre–Civil War period, with the famous Thomas "Daddy" Rice playing the comic slave role of "Old Tiff" in the first production at New York's Bowery Theatre.

Brougham's satires reveal a keen appreciation for the role of the stage in American popular culture, and his plays form part of a larger dialogue on the development of American theater and society. His burlesques of the "Indian" play were largely responsible for the decline in popularity of that particular style, as his work underscored the hypocrisy of raising Native Americans to saint-like status while the American government was actively campaigning to despoil them of their land and rights. Moreover, his parody of Stone's *Metamora* also poked fun at its famous star, Edwin

Forrest. In one scene, Brougham ridiculed Forrest's propensity for grabbing all the best lines on stage: "It's very probable you'd like to know / The reason why Pollywog don't go / With his red brethren. Pray take notice each / He stays behind to have an exit speech."

Brougham's other significant contribution to the American stage was his collection of "Stage Irish" characters in such plays as *The Irish Emigrant; or, Temptation* (1856), which takes a sympathetic view of Irish Americans and alcoholism. At a point in the nation's history when the Irish were experiencing severe discrimination, Brougham's portraits of likeable Irish characters who retain all the charm traditionally associated with the Stage Irishman but who also demonstrate their ability to integrate into American society, helped to mitigate the irrational prejudice against the influx of new immigrants pouring into the country.

Though a prolific playwright—he created 126 plays throughout his career—Brougham's work is seldom performed in the contemporary American theater, perhaps because it was so intricately connected to its historical moment that few modern audiences can understand the nuances of Brougham's comedy. Yet, his work remains a fascinating source of information about the political and cultural development of the nation, especially during the troubled years before the Civil War.

BIBLIOGRAPHY

Brougham, John. *The Irish Emigrant; or, Temptation.* New York: Feedback Theatrebooks & Prospero Press, 1998.

Heather Nathans
University of Maryland

BULLINS, ED (1935–)

Along with AMIRI BARAKA, Ed Bullins is one of the most important African-American playwrights of the 1960s. His plays, which depict the African-American experience among urban ghetto dwellers as well as among the middle class, consist sometimes of straight realism and sometimes of metaphor. Significant not only as a playwright, Bullins has also been a producer and director, an editor of books and periodicals on African-American theater, and a professor of theater.

In his youth, Bullins lived in Philadelphia, where his transfer to an inner-city junior high school precipitated his joining a street gang; as a teenager, he nearly died as the result of a stab wound to the heart. After dropping out of high school, Bullins joined the United States Navy, and after his military service, moved to Los Angeles, earned his high school equivalency diploma, and attended City College there. He began by writing fiction, essays, and poetry, but he took up drama because he believed that he would reach a larger African-American audience that way. Encouraged by the similar sensibility of Amiri Baraka's work, Bullins was also influenced by Baraka's political activism. He become involved in the cultural wing of the Black Panther Party, until ideological differences alienated him from the group.

His plays were first performed in San Francisco at the Firehouse Repertory Theatre in 1965; three of these plays were *How Do You Do?, Dialect Determinism (or The Rally),* and CLARA'S OLE MAN. For six years beginning in 1967, Bullins was associated with the New Lafayette Theatre in Harlem as resident playwright and as editor of the theater's magazine, *Black Theatre.* During this period, his plays were also produced elsewhere in the New York City area, as well as in Boston. Plays produced during this period included *Goin'a Buffalo* (1968), *In the Wine Time* (1968), *The Corner* (1968), *The Gentleman Caller* (1969), *The Pig Pen* (1970), *The Duplex: A Black Love Fable in Four Movements* (1970), and *The Fabulous Miss Marie* (1971), which won an Obie Distinguished Play Award along with Bullins's other play of that season, *In New England Winter. The* TAKING OF MISS JANIE (1975), perhaps Bullins's best-known work, won the New York Drama Critics' Circle Award and an OBIE AWARD for Playwriting.

Speaking about the theater of the 1960s and 1970s in a 1997 interview with Kim Pearson, Bullins commented on his purpose and audience at that time: "We who began in black theater in the mid-60s into the 70s . . . were lending our energies, voices, artistic minds and everything else to the struggle for physical liberation called the Civil Rights movement, then the Black Power movement. . . . [T]o achieve that, we had to raise the consciousness of the, for lack of a better word, the black masses."

In the 1980s and 1990s, Bullins continued to write, direct, and teach in various locations in the United States, while continuing his own education. In 1989, he completed his B.A. at Antioch University, San Francisco, and in 1994, earned his M.F.A. from San Francisco State University. In 1995, he became a professor of theater at Northeastern University in Boston. For many years, he has been working on the Twentieth-Century Cycle, a group of plays that includes *Home Boy* (1976), *Daddy* (1977), and *Boy X Man* (1995). In 2001, Bullins's revised *City Preacher* (original version, 1984) was produced in Boston. Often one to incorporate music into his plays, Bullins has also collaborated on musicals. In 1977, he wrote the books for *Storyville* and *Sepia Star,* both jazz musicals (music and lyrics by Mildred Kayden).

Now in his 70s, Bullins continues his association with the African-American Studies and Theatre departments at Northeastern University, where he is a Distinguished Artist-in-Residence. In 2008, the one-act *Salaam, Huey Newton, Salaam* (from *New/Lost Plays by Ed Bullins: An Anthology* [1993]) was produced at New York's New Federal Theatre, along with the one-acts *Amarie,* by Hugh L. Fletcher, and *The Toilet,* by Amiri Baraka. In early 2009, a new musical work by Bullins, the late jazz artist Pat Patrick, and Emmett Price, *Ascendance: Movement One,* was showcased at Northeastern University's African-American Institute.

BIBLIOGRAPHY

Bullins, Ed. *Ed Bullins: Twelve Plays and Selected Writings.* Edited by Mike Sell. Ann Arbor: University of Michigan Press, 2006.

———. *New/Lost Plays by Ed Bullins: An Anthology.* Aiea, Hawaii: That New Publishing Co., 1993.

———. *The Theme Is Blackness.* New York: Morrow, 1973.

Hay, Samuel A. *Ed Bullins: A Literary Biography.* Detroit: Wayne State University Press, 1997.

Pearson, Kim. "Interview with Ed Bullins—2/17/97." 2001. Available online: <http://kpearson.faculty.tcnj.edu/Articles/Kp%20interview_with_ed_Bullins.htm>.

BURIED CHILD Sam Shepard (1978)

In this Pulitzer Prize–winning drama, Sam Shepard examines one of his favorite themes: the indelible mark of the family left upon the individual. None can escape the scars left by family secrets, yet there remains hope—however delusional it may be—as each generation takes over from the last.

Dodge and Halie are the elders of the family, the generation that will soon be dead. (Dodge refers humorously to himself as a "corpse," and Halie accuses him later of "decomposing." Furthermore, at two moments during the play, the sons bury their father: Tilden does so with corn husks, and Bradley with Shelly's coat.) Dodge wants only to be left alone on the couch with his blanket and to sneak drinks from his hidden whiskey bottle while he watches television. His nagging, chattering wife, Halie, gives him little peace until she goes out on a social call. Before leaving, she asks that he keep an eye on their son Tilden. Tilden is an emotionally troubled man who has returned to his parents' Illinois farm from New Mexico. The first time he comes on stage, his arms are full of corn, which he says he picked on their land, despite his parents' protests that there has not been corn out there since 1935. (He is the bearer of fertility, new growth, so it is fitting that he is also the father of Vince, the next generation and hope for the—probably doomed—future.) While Tilden is an emotional cripple, his brother Bradley is a physical one, having "chop[ped] his leg off with a chain saw." Dodge and Halie had another son, Ansel, who Halie believes would have been a success; he was a soldier, who died not in action but on his honeymoon. Reference is made to another child, buried outside the house.

Act 2 brings Tilden's son, Vince, and his companion, Shelly. They are on their way to see Vince's father in New Mexico and are surprised to find him here. But neither Dodge nor Tilden recognizes Vince. Tilden—appropriating his father's history—says that he "once had a son, but we buried him." (This is a recurring motif in Shepard: Sons become their fathers—since the mark of the father on the son is indelible for better or for worse.) When Tilden comes into the house in the second act, his arms are full of carrots just picked. When Vince is sent out to get more whiskey for Dodge, he stays out all night, drives a great distance, gets drunk, and nearly leaves for good, but he cannot. While Vince is gone, Tilden tells Shelly the family secret, the secret about the buried child. When

Halie finally returns the next day, she brings with her Father Dewes; they have been drinking. Halie tries to prevent Dodge from recounting in detail the story of the buried child, but he ignores her. A tiny boy—Halie's, but not by Dodge—is buried out back, buried by Dodge, who drowned him.

Vince finally comes back, drunk and disorderly. Dodge recognizes him now and takes a moment to declare his last will and testament: He leaves his tools to Tilden and the house and land to Vince, the rest—himself included—he wants piled high and set ablaze, like the ancients. On Vince's long drive, from which he was tempted never to return, he saw his own reflection in the windshield turn into his father's and grandfather's and "[c]lear on back to faces [he'd] never seen before but still recognized." This he tells to Shelly as he explains that he will stay and live in what is now his house. Dodge, meanwhile, has died. Shelly leaves, and Vince dismisses Bradley by throwing his prosthetic leg out of the house; Bradley crawls after it. Halie is still upstairs, and in the final moments of the play she calls down to Dodge (now a corpse) that she sees from the window, just as Tilden has said, an abundance of corn and carrots, as well as potatoes and peas—a "paradise," a "miracle." As Halie is talking offstage, Tilden passes through holding the muddy and disintegrating "corpse of a small child." The play thus ends with the hope of the next generation—that potential for rebirth—*and* the burdens of the past, both palpably represented.

BURK, JOHN DALY (1770?–1808) John Daly Burk caused quarrels and dissent throughout his career—even with his best-known dramatic work, *Bunker-Hill; or, The Death of General Warren* (1797). His passionate patriotism and his outspokenness on political issues often got him into trouble, both in his native Ireland and in his adopted home, the United States.

Born John Burk in Ireland during the 1770s, Burk entered Dublin's Trinity College at a young age, where he formed connections with various underground organizations struggling to liberate Ireland from the grasp of British authorities. Though little is known of his early life in Ireland, his move to America seems to have been the result of an incident in which he attempted to stop a group of English soldiers from executing an Irish radical. He was recognized and a warrant issued for his arrest. These activities led to his flight from Ireland, with the help of a Miss Daly. She loaned him a dress, and, disguised as a woman, he boarded a ship for America. In gratitude to Miss Daly, he added her name to his own.

Upon his arrival in America, Burk settled in Boston, where he became editor of a new newspaper, *The Polar Star and Boston Daily Advertiser.* The first issue appeared in 1796, but it lasted less than six months before folding. In part, Burk's failure with the *Polar Star* can be linked to his political convictions and the turbulent state of American society in the later part of the 1790s. Burk supported the French Revolution and opposed any form of government that seemed reminiscent of the British monarchy. Yet, for many Americans, their initial enthusiasm for the French Revolution had waned as the struggle grew increasingly bloody and violent. The emerging political parties in America, the Federalists and the Republicans, were sharply divided over how America should be governed. Unfortunately for Burk, his support of the Republicans (or Jacobins, as some called them) struck many Bostonians as little more than a call to open anarchy, and he was forced to flee Boston for New York. One of Burk's most powerful enemies was none other than the arch-Federalist, President John Adams, who prosecuted him under the Alien and Sedition Acts of 1798.

Despite the controversy that dogged his career, Burk remained convinced that America was "a moral, intrepid, and enlightened community, ranged under the banner of equality and justice." His best-known play, *Bunker-Hill,* opened at Boston's Haymarket Theatre in 1797. As the title suggests, it chronicles the brave campaign waged by a handful of poorly armed American soldiers against the powerful British army. The play's hero, General Warren, willingly gives his life for his country: "I die, and swell the glorious list of Patriots, who have died for suffering virtue." The play also offers a romantic subplot between a British soldier (Abercrombie) and an American girl (Elvira), whose conflicting allegiances underscore the pathos of the struggle.

Despite a largely negative response from critics, who labeled it "vile" and "execrable" for its bombastic tone and contrived plot, *Bunker-Hill* enjoyed tremendous popularity both in Boston and in subsequent revivals in cities from Richmond to New York. Some critics of the period suggested that its success had as much to do with the realistic scenery, depicting recognizable locales in Boston, as its patriotic content. None of Burk's other dramatic works ever achieved the same level of renown, though he wrote six other plays during his lifetime: *Female Patriotism; or, the Death of Joan D'Arc* (1798), which was performed at the Park Theatre in New York; *The Death of General Montgomery in the Storming of the City of Quebec* (1807), published but not performed; *Bethlem Gabor, Lord of Transylvania; or, the Man-Hating Palatine* (1807), possibly given one performance by the Richmond Theatre; and three other plays that no longer exist—*The Fortunes of Nigel, The Innkeeper of Abbeville,* and *Which Do You Like Best, the Poor Man or the Lord?*

When political debate again forced Burk to relocate, he settled in Petersburg, Virginia, where he wrote a three-volume *History of Virginia*. Outspoken and argumentative to the last, Burk provoked a quarrel with one Monsieur Coquebert and was killed in a duel on April 11, 1808.

BIBLIOGRAPHY

Campbell, Charles. *Some Materials to Serve for a Brief Memoir of John Daly Burk.* Albany, N.Y.: J. Munsell, 1868.
Wyatt, Edward Avery. "John Daly Burk: Patriot, Playwright, Historian." In *Southern Sketches* 7. Charlottesville, Va.: Historical Publishing Company, 1936. 123–136.

Heather Nathans
University of Maryland

BURN THIS LANFORD WILSON (1987)   *Burn This* is considered by many critics to be WILSON's most intense and mature play. It has many of the recurrent themes and motifs of his earlier works: lonely and displaced people, a sense of isolation, and quirky character traits. However, the primary difference between this play and such previous Wilson works as *Balm in Gilead* (1965), *The HOT L BALTIMORE* (1973), *The Mound Builders* (1975), and *FIFTH OF JULY* (1980) is its deceptively simple style. It has one set and four characters, a straightforward plot with very few diversions, and conversational dialogue; through it, however, Wilson exposes a level of passion between characters that had only been hinted at in his previous plays.

Burn This takes place in a huge loft in Lower Manhattan, which Anna, a dancer and choreographer, shares with Larry, a gay graphic artist, and Robbie, a dancer. In the opening scene, Anna has just returned from Robbie's funeral—he and his lover, Dominic, were killed in a boating accident. Burton, a screenwriter and Anna's boyfriend, has come over to console her and Larry. The second scene begins with the introduction of Pale, Robbie's brother. His real name is Jimmy: Pale is a nickname he picked up from his favorite drink, Very Special Old Pale cognac. Pale, in contrast to the other characters, is brash, loud, and obscene. He immediately alienates Burton and scornfully spurns Larry's half-hearted attempts at seduction, but he sparks a deep-seated attraction in Anna; and, in spite of their wildly different personalities, they end up falling in love.

In many respects, *Burn This* is a continuation of themes Wilson explored in *TALLEY'S FOLLY* (1978): Two vastly different characters find solace and comfort in the failings and apprehensions of each other. Anna's world is art, which Pale sees as all falsehood and fakery. Pale is a married man, father of two, and manages a restaurant in New Jersey. He is clearly not the man for Anna, and yet they find themselves drawn to each other not by their vocations but by their human weaknesses. Where *Burn This* differs from *Talley's Folly* is that Pale and Anna know from the start that their love affair is doomed to fail. Matt Friedman, the Jewish immigrant, and Sally Talley, daughter of a Missouri Baptist, know that they and their love will persevere; after all, the only obstacle to their love is society and Sally's family. In comparison, Pale and Anna's obstacles are their own doubts. Pale's marriage is troubled, and Anna and Burton are not living together, so there is nothing that keeps Anna and Pale from each other except the unknown elements of their own feelings.

Philip Middleton Williams
Miami, Florida

BURY THE DEAD IRWIN SHAW (1936)   This one-act play, SHAW's first, is one of a number of antiwar dramas written between World War I and World

War II. Shaw hoped his nonrealistic play would provoke people to stand up against participation in another war.

Bury the Dead is set "in the second year of the war that is to begin tomorrow night." It is presented on an open stage on two levels, with the action designated by sharp spotlights. There are a few chairs and other props, but they are used sparingly. As the play begins, some soldiers are detailed to bury six soldiers killed several days before. As they smoke cigarettes and dig the grave, they talk about the dead soldiers and the war. They seem hardened to death and complain about the stink of the bodies. After they have dug a mass grave and put the bodies in, they hear groaning and one soldier jumps in to investigate. The six supposedly dead men stand up in the grave with their backs to the audience, and, in a dramatic scene, refuse to be buried because they believe they died for nothing (they had been ordered to try to gain some small piece of land against impossible odds).

The generals running the war are consulted and refuse to believe what they hear. They appear to be indifferent to the fate of the soldiers and only want to avoid problems. The story reaches a newspaper writer who wants to publish it because he believes the people should know what the soldiers feel. The editor calls Washington and finds that he cannot print the story. Although the liberal writer is outraged, the editor says, "In time of war, people have a right to know nothing. If we put it in it'd be censored anyway." The tension in the play builds as the scenes shift from one location to another and the soldiers can still be seen standing in the grave.

Finally, "the women" of the corpses are brought to ask them to succumb to burial. Each woman has a different reaction to the not-dead, dead husband, brother, son, or lover. The last woman to appear, a soldier's wife, conveys the message of the playwright, that the soldier should have stood up earlier. She insists that everyone should stand up against the generals and the warmongers (who make a profit out of war) and refuse to take part. At the end, one general tries to machine-gun the corpses, but they contemptuously move out of the grave and walk past him offstage.

The strength of the original production of the play lay in the theatrical effects of lighting and the continual sound of artillery, as well as its blunt language and antiwar theme. Furthermore, theater critic Barrett H. Clark, writing in 1939 about trends in American drama, suggested that *Bury the Dead* was important, not because it "shows the waste of war"—though it certainly does—but because, like other plays in the 1930s, it demonstrated that its author was compelled to write about a "problem that besets the world today [1939], with the hope that he may persuade his audience to do something about it" (335).

BIBLIOGRAPHY

Clark, Barrett H. "Our Most American Drama: Recent Developments, 1930–39." *English Journal* 28, no. 5 (May 1939): 333–342.

Yvonne Shafer
St. John's University

BUSCH, CHARLES (1954–) The theater of actor and playwright Charles Busch is in many respects a continuation of the gender-bending work of farceur CHARLES LUDLAM and his Ridiculous Theatre Company. For nearly two decades, from the late 1960s until his death from AIDS in 1987, the prolific Ludlam churned out camp dramas in which he would then star. These drag farces, often loosely based on the work of earlier playwrights (Jean-Baptiste Molière, Alexandre Dumas, Émile Zola) or created as send-ups of Hollywood B movies, provided a parodic paradigm that Busch emulated.

A graduate of Northwestern University, Busch launched his career as a dramatist/drag artist in a makeshift theater housed in the scruffy Limbo Lounge in Manhattan's East Village. With a company comprised of friends, he wrote and starred in *Vampire Lesbians of Sodom* (1984), produced on a shoestring budget. Soon a cult sensation, the cleverly conceived, wickedly witty farce eventually transferred to the OFF-BROADWAY Provincetown Playhouse, where it enjoyed an extraordinary five-year run. Busch played the 2,000-year-old vampire lesbian who figures centrally in each of the play's three scenes—Sodom in antiquity, Hollywood in the 1920s, and present-day

Las Vegas. The second production of the company was *Theodora: She-Bitch of Byzantium* (1984), in which Busch, in an homage of sorts to Sarah Bernhardt, took the five-act play that French playwright Victorien Sardou had crafted for Bernhardt and turned it into a 45-minute romp in which he could perform Bernhardt performing Theodora. A subsequent cult hit was the B-film–inspired *Psycho Beach Party* (1987), a wild lampoon in which Busch starred as the ingenue Chicklet, a teenager gravely afflicted with multiple-personality disorder. For the next dozen years, Busch continued to write and star in a profusion of plays and one-person shows that featured his drag persona.

As a playwright (but not as a performer) Busch was to shed his cult status and achieve widespread popular and critical success with *The Tale of the Allergist's Wife* (2000), first produced at the Manhattan Theatre Club, then transferring to Broadway for an extensive run. The play focuses on the midlife crisis of New Yorker Marjorie Taub, rescued from near catatonia by a chance reunion with childhood friend and incorrigible name-dropper Lee, who insinuates herself into Marjorie's life, eventually moving in with Marjorie and her retiring husband Ira. Busch adds to the mix Marjorie's foul-mouthed mother Frieda. Although smacking of television situation-comedy writing, the gag-driven play was nominated for a TONY AWARD and received the Outer Critics Circle John Gassner Award for Playwriting.

In 2003, Busch returned to drag as Lady Sylvia Allington in his farce *Shanghai Moon*. Lady Sylvia is part Mae West, part Barbara Stanwyck, and part debutante, and the play, set in Shanghai, evokes and frequently alludes to Hollywood movies of the 1930s. Also in 2003, Busch starred in a film version of his play *Die Mommy Die,* first produced in Los Angeles in 1999, and in 2007 he resuscitated the work for its New York stage premiere. In this camp homage to mid-century Hollywood film noir, Busch plays aging pop singer Angela Andrew, who, to further a career comeback and her illicit love affair, murders her nefarious film producer husband, Sol Sussman.

In 2005, a documentary film entitled *The Lady in Question Is Charles Busch* (dubbed "A Drag to Riches Story" by the *Village Voice*) was produced. The follow-ing year Busch made his debut as film director with *A Very Serious Person,* which he also cowrote; a gay-themed coming of age story, the film focuses on the relationship between a male nurse (Busch) and the 13-year-old grandson of the terminally ill woman he cares for. Busch wrote, but did not act in, the 2007 Manhattan Theatre Club production of *Our Leading Lady,* a backstage drama centering on actress-manager Laura Keene and events prior to and following the ill-fated performance at Ford's Theatre in Washington the night President Lincoln was assassinated.

BIBLIOGRAPHY

Busch, Charles. *Four Plays.* Garden City, N.Y.: Fireside Theatre, 1988.
————. *Three Plays.* Garden City, N.Y.: Fireside Theatre, 1992.
————. *"Tale of the Allergist's Wife" and Other Plays.* New York: Grove/Atlantic, 2001.

Craig Clinton
Reed College

BUS STOP WILLIAM INGE (1955) *Bus Stop* was INGE's third in a string of four hit plays on Broadway, beginning with COME BACK, LITTLE SHEBA (1950) and PICNIC (1953) and concluding with *The* DARK AT THE TOP OF THE STAIRS (1957). Set in a small Kansas diner where bus travelers are stranded in a prairie snowstorm, the play features an ensemble cast that centers on Bo Decker, a naive and rowdy young cowboy who is away from his Montana ranch for the first time, and Cherie, a second-rate Kansas City nightclub singer whom Bo, in town to perform in a rodeo, has abducted after what Cherie considers a casual overnight tryst. Inge focuses on the humorously stormy progress of the Bo-Cherie love relationship and concludes the play with a predictable resolution for the couple, but it would be a mistake to consider *Bus Stop* merely a mid-1950s romantic comedy.

Inge, a native Kansan who used his life there in almost all his work, expanded *Bus Stop* from *People in the Wind,* a one-act play in which he sought to show the stranded travelers as bewilderingly alone even though they share the warmth of the diner while the blizzard rages outside. This longer version combines popular mid-1950s notions of romantic comedy (Bo and Cherie) with the Chaucerian device of having everyone tell his or her story and put on performances to pass the time. This allows us to see Inge's backdrop of lonely and complicated individuals for whom even the possibility of love seems hopelessly remote. Grace, the proprietor of the diner, prefers to live alone, though she accepts the sexual attentions of Carl, the bus driver. Professor Lyman rides the bus in an alcoholic haze, his eloquence charming the naive young waitress, Elma, who does not see any danger in Lyman's proposal that they meet later in Topeka. Virgil Blessing, Bo's older friend and father figure, tries to help Bo grow up and learn to behave, even though he realizes that success will mean that Bo will separate from him. After Bo is defeated in a fight by Will Masters, the sheriff, he realizes (with Virgil and Will's help) that he must apologize to Cherie and tame his tempestuous ways. That leads to Cherie's agreement to accompany Bo to Montana, but it also leaves everyone else, in Grace's words, "out in the cold," the point Inge intended to make in the shorter play as well.

The roles of Cherie and Bo make *Bus Stop* an enduringly popular play, but audiences and readers also appreciate Inge's complement of supporting characters, whose lives more tellingly reveal the elements of literary naturalism and realism that lie within most of William Inge's plays. As dramatic literature, his plays have a close kinship with poets like Edgar Lee Masters and fiction writers Sherwood Anderson and Sinclair Lewis, whose works show that stereotypically wholesome small-town midwestern life was a facade.

Ralph F. Voss
University of Alabama

C

CAMINO REAL Tennessee Williams (1953)
"More than any other that I have done," Williams observed on the occasion of the Broadway premiere of *Camino Real,* "this play has seemed to me like the construction of another world, a separate existence"; but, he added, "it is nothing more nor less than my conception of the time and world I live in and its people are mostly archetypes of certain basic attitudes and qualities" (viii). It takes place on a plaza in *"a tropical seaport that bears a confusing, but somehow harmonious, resemblance to such widely scattered ports as Tangiers, Havana, Vera Cruz, Casablanca, Shanghai, New Orleans."* On one side of the plaza is the Sieta Mares Hotel, a respectable establishment presided over by Mr. Gutman, *"a lordly fat man wearing a linen suit and a pith helmet"* with *"a white cockatoo on his wrist."* On the other side is Skid Row and the Ritz Men Only, *"a flea-bag hotel or flophouse"* run by A. Ratt. Upstage is a flight of stairs leading to an archway and, through the archway, the "Terra Incognita."

The play begins with the arrival of Don Quixote and Sancho Panza. The latter almost immediately leaves, having recognized the Camino Real as a place in which "the spring of humanity has gone dry . . . there are no birds in this country except wild birds that are tamed and kept in— . . . *Cages!*" Quixote falls asleep and ostensibly "dreams" the rest of the play, which is divided into 16 scenes, called "blocks" on the Camino Real, each one "announced" by Gutman.

Many of the characters who appear are figures from romantic literature or myth—Jacques Casanova, Marguerite Gautier (Camille), Lord Byron, Quixote, and the Baron de Charlus; also present is Kilroy, *"a young American vagrant,"* a Gypsy, and her beautiful daughter Esmerelda. Arrayed against this group of dreamers and romantics are Gutman, a sinister presence who controls the action of the play, is in constant communication with the "Generalissimo," and commands the guards who patrol the plaza; and two street-cleaners who hover about ominously as obvious symbols of death and who occasionally cart off dead bodies. The forbidden word on the Camino Real is *brother,* and all its denizens yearn to escape but are terrified of venturing through the archway into the Terra Incognita.

The "action" of *Camino Real,* such as it is, consists of Casanova's faithful and dogged loyalty to and love of Marguerite, despite her constant betrayals of him with younger men, and the Gypsy's equally tenacious efforts to pair her daughter off with Kilroy. Among the play's more fanciful moments are a "fiesta" in which Kilroy, dressed as a "Patsy" (*"the red fright wig, the big crimson nose that lights up and has horn-rimmed glasses attached, a pair of clown pants that have a huge footprint on the seat"*), is crowned King of the Cuckolds as the Gypsy presides over the re-virginization of Esmerelda by the moon; and a scene in which Kilroy, who appeared to have been disposed of by the street-cleaners, gets dissected by a Medical Instructor and his students but suddenly rises from the table and chases the

90

Instructor through the aisles of the theater, demanding the return of his "heart of gold," which the Instructor has removed.

The play ends when Quixote awakens from his dream and goes to rinse out his mouth in the plaza's fountain, which now flows freely after having previously been dry. He advises the suddenly alive again Kilroy, *"Don't! Pity! Your! Self!"* adding, in words that echo those of many fragile and fractured Williams characters, "The wounds of the vanity, the many offenses our egos have to endure . . . are better accepted with a tolerant smile." Then, he and Kilroy go up the stairs and out through the archway, with Quixote declaring, *"The violets in the mountains have broken the rocks!"* (Earlier in the play, Marguerite had said despairingly to Casanova, "the violets in the mountains—can't break the rocks!" to which he had replied, "The violets in the mountains can break the rocks if you believe in them and allow them to grow!") Gutman acknowledges that "The Curtain Line has been spoken!" and orders that the play end.

Aside from containing some of the most beautifully poetic dialogue Williams ever wrote, especially in the two short scenes between Casanova and Marguerite, *Camino Real* does indeed portray Williams's view of the world. It is one in which its poetic damaged dreamers—Laura in *The GLASS MENAGERIE,* Blanche in *A STREETCAR NAMED DESIRE*—are pitted against its realists—Stanley in *Streetcar,* Jim in *The Glass Menagerie.* Here, Gutman, the street-cleaners, and the guards represent insensitive reality, while Marguerite, Casanova, Quixote, Byron, and Kilroy are the romantic dreamers. As C. W. E. Bigsby points out, these latter characters "are offered the classic Williams dilemma. Either they opt for the momentary but real consolation of love, or they set out into the barren land known as 'Terra Incognita'; love or flight" (78). Williams himself described the play as "a picture of the state of the romantic nonconformist in modern society. It stresses honor and man's own sense of inner dignity which the Bohemian must reachieve after each period of degradation he is bound to run into" (Nelson 178).

BIBLIOGRAPHY
Bigsby, C. W. E. *A Critical Introduction to Twentieth-Century American Drama: Volume Two—Williams/Albee/Miller.* Cambridge, England: Cambridge University Press, 1984.

Nelson, Benjamin. *Tennessee Williams: The Man and His Work.* New York: Ivan Obolensky, 1961.
Williams, Tennessee. *Camino Real.* New York: New Directions, 1953.

CAT ON A HOT TIN ROOF TENNESSEE WILLIAMS (1955)

In this PULITZER PRIZE–winning drama, WILLIAMS examines the love—heterosexual, homosexual, paternal, filial—humans feel and the lies they tell to cope with this love or to get what they want. These feelings within the Pollitt family are brought into intense focus on the occasion of Big Daddy Pollitt's 65th birthday; the Pollitt sons and their wives know from the beginning what is revealed to Big Daddy and Big Mama much later in the play, that Big Daddy is dying of cancer.

Set on a hot summer evening in the bedroom that Brick and Maggie occupy in Big Daddy's plantation house, the play opens as Maggie reports to Brick the ill-mannered supper-table antics of the "no-neck monsters," which is how she refers to the children of her brother-in-law, Gooper. Maggie accuses Gooper and his wife, Mae, of breeding children just to please Big Daddy, from whom they hope to inherit his vast property. Brick stays in the room drinking and nursing a broken ankle, which he injured "jumpin' hurdles" on a "high school athletic field" while drunk late the previous night. Gooper and Mae would like the alcoholic Brick to be shipped off to the "Rainbow Hill" treatment center, not so much for his health but because he is favored by Big Daddy at the expense of Gooper. Since Brick will not go downstairs, the entire family joins him in the bedroom to have birthday cake. Big Daddy soon dismisses everyone but Brick so that he can talk to his favorite son.

Earlier in the day, the family doctor brought Big Daddy and his wife the comforting lie that his cancer was nothing but a "spastic colon." Much relieved, he becomes loquacious with Brick, confiding in his son that he is looking forward—now that he knows he is not dying—to having more women. However, the real reason for this tête-à-tête is Big Daddy's concern about Brick. He wants to leave his property to Brick, but Brick is becoming a drunk; Big Daddy knows Gooper wants it, but he "hate[s] Gooper and Mae." Brick's father questions him about why he drinks so much. Brick claims that he drinks from "disgust"; he is disgusted with "mendacity," to which his father replies, "Hell, you *got* to live with [mendacity]." Big Daddy suggests the real reason for the drinking is something else: He points out that the drinking began when Brick's friend Skipper—with whom Brick played college and pro football—died from "liquor and drugs," and he reveals that he has wondered if Brick and Skipper were homosexuals. Big Daddy is not judgmental as he says this; he tells his son he has been around and knows these things happen, but Brick is angry: "Why can't exceptional friendships . . . between two men be accepted as something clean and decent." He insists that he and Skipper had "a pure an' true thing." Brick tells his father that Maggie put it in Skipper's head that he and Skipper were frustrated homosexuals; Skipper "went to bed with Maggie to prove that wasn't true, and when it didn't work out, he thought it *was* true." Skipper called him to make a "drunken confession," and Brick hung up on him. Big Daddy tells him that his "disgust with mendacity is disgust with [him]self." He tells his son, "*You!* Dug the grave of your friend and kicked him in it!—before you'd face the truth with him!" (Like Blanche DuBois in Williams's *A STREETCAR NAMED DESIRE,* Brick believes that his expressed disgust about another's homosexuality contributed to that person's death. The suicide of Blanche's young husband Allan Grey after she tells him he disgusts her haunts her and is the root of her alcoholism and promiscuity, just as Skipper's death is the root of Brick's alcoholism.) In retaliation for this direct hit and to redirect the conversation, Brick blurts out that Big Daddy does, in fact, have cancer, and adds, "Mendacity is the system that we live in. Liquor is one way out an' death's the other."

Brick and Maggie do what they need to do to survive. Brick needs to drink until he hears the "click" in his head after which he can temporarily forget Skipper. Maggie longs for Brick, whom she loves, but she also needs him for the estate he may inherit. She grew up poor, with an alcoholic father and a mother who tried to make do, and she believes, "You can be young without money, but you can't be old without it." To make sure Big Daddy will leave the estate to Brick, she needs to produce a grandchild. She tells Big Daddy she is already pregnant, and she is determined to make this lie the truth. She has been to a doctor to make sure she is at her fertile time, and as the play ends she hides Brick's liquor with the promise that once they have finished having sex—something they have not done since Skipper's death—he can have it back. She hopes to reignite their love as well as produce a child. When Maggie tells Brick she loves him, he repeats a line his father has said earlier of Big Mama's declaration of love for him: "Wouldn't it be funny if that was true." (This is the last line in Williams's original version.)

There are two versions of act 3 because the director of the 1955 Broadway production, ELIA KAZAN, convinced Williams to make a few changes. The major change was the presence of Big Daddy in act 3; Kazan felt he was too "vivid and important a character to disappear from the play except as an offstage cry after the second act curtain" (Williams 977). Modern revivals often combine elements of both versions.

BIBLIOGRAPHY
Bloom, Harold, ed. *Modern Critical Interpretations: Tennessee Williams's "Cat on a Hot Tin Roof."* Philadelphia, Pa.: Chelsea House, 2001.
Williams, Tennessee. *Plays 1937–1955.* Edited by Mel Gussow and Kenneth Holditch. New York: Library of America, 2000.

CEREMONIES IN DARK OLD MEN LONNIE ELDER III (1969)

First performed in New York by the NEGRO ENSEMBLE COMPANY, *Ceremonies in Dark Old Men* won Outer Critics Circle and Drama Desk Awards. The play offers its audience an accurate, yet nonconfrontational, vision of the African-American experience in America, portraying racial injustice and the economic plight of so many African Americans. A predecessor of AUGUST WILSON, Elder mingles comedy and tragedy to present a lively and positive picture of the vibrant African-American spirit that survives in an inherently racist society.

The play is set in late 1960s Harlem at the failed barbershop of Russell Parker, once a dancer, who passes time playing checkers with his friend William Jenkins. Parker's daughter, Adele, tired of supporting her father and two grown brothers, Theo and Bobby, has told her family to get jobs or leave. While Parker tries unsuccessfully to find a job, the brothers simply refuse: Theo plans to produce and sell bootleg whiskey, and Bobby (unknown to his family) is burglarizing local stores. Theo gets a local thug, Blue Haven, to help him run his bootleg operation, and Parker lets them use the barbershop as a front.

Theo's business thrives, but Parker steals cash to impress a new girlfriend who is obviously using him. Theo argues with Blue; when Blue threatens to kill him, he decides to leave his criminal life behind. We then learn that Bobby has been killed during a robbery. Parker, not knowing this and having been thrown out by his girlfriend, apologizes to Theo and Adele, and the play ends with him asking, "Where's Bobby?"

While we sympathize with Adele, who has allowed her sense of responsibility to burden her, we also sympathize with her less responsible brothers, who seem to have so few options. Their choices are restricted to low-paying, unfulfilling jobs, such as Adele's, or a life of crime. The play implies a preference for the former because Bobby pays the price for the latter. We also see in Blue the underlying violence of the criminal world; despite his political assertions, he is a person out only for himself. Theo is capable of hard work if he sees it as rewarding; he makes a big success of his bootleg business, but he realizes it has no future. He knows that crime is wrong, which is partly why he tries to stop Bobby from stealing, but Bobby will not turn his back on crime while his brother continues to live outside the law.

The play is primarily about survival. Parker survives by indulging in a series of ceremonies, which are not church rituals but human interactions that invest his life with significance—playing checkers with Jenkins, telling stories of his past, and leading his sons in a dance to recall the glories of his past stage career. Although he rarely wins at checkers and many of his stories are fabrications, they allow him to connect with family and friends, build a positive self-identity, and keep spirits alive in a society that seems geared to stripping African Americans of every dignity.

Susan C. W. Abbotson
Rhode Island College

CHARLES THE SECOND; OR, THE MERRY MONARCH JOHN HOWARD PAYNE AND WASHINGTON IRVING (1824)

Considered one of the best early American comedies, *Charles the Second* is based on a French play by Alexandre Duval, *La Jeunesse de Henri V.* PAYNE's first draft is said to have been little more than a translation with the change of character names to those of England's Charles II (1649–85) and his courtier and companion the Earl of Rochester. (According to drama historian ARTHUR HOBSON QUINN, Duval's play was based on Sébastien Mercier's *Charles II, roi d'Angleterre, en un certain lieu* [1789], which may in turn have been based on an English original.) Washington Irving added much to the play, including its most memorable character, Captain Copp, though Irving, who collaborated with Payne on several plays, preferred to keep his collaboration secret.

Lady Clara will marry the Earl of Rochester if that gentleman will reform his wild ways for his own sake and for the sake of the king who, she believes, follows his "licentious example." Rochester promises to reform and contrives a plot, to which the audience is not privy, to effect this change in the king as well.

Meanwhile, Edward, a page and protégé of Rochester, has fallen for Mary, a tavern-keeper's niece, who knows Edward only as Georgini, her music teacher. Knowing this, Rochester takes King Charles to the tavern; they are disguised as sailors. Mary and her uncle, Captain Copp, marvel at the capacity of these "sailors" to consume alcohol, spend money, and make noise. Edward arrives in disguise to give Mary her music lesson and is surprised at the guests he finds there, but he must play along lest Charles recognize him when he should be at the palace. When Charles makes advances to Mary, Edward squirms; to distract Mary, whom he fears he will lose to the charming monarch-in-disguise, he mentions a new song he knows written by the Earl of Rochester. At the mention of the name, Captain Copp declares Rochester to be a "rascally rogue." When pressed for details by the disguised Rochester, Copp reveals that Rochester is also Mary's uncle (Rochester's sister was married to Copp's brother), though he has never helped out the orphaned girl in any way. During these revelations by

Copp, Charles and Rochester find out just how horrible their reputations are.

When the time comes to pay the bill, Rochester and Edward sneak away, taking the king's purse with them. When Charles discovers he has no money to settle the bill, he offers his bejeweled watch and is taken for a thief by Copp, who locks him up and goes to seek the authorities. The king extricates himself from this embarrassing predicament by charming Mary into helping him escape through a window. After sunrise, all parties find themselves together at the palace, all identities are revealed, and all is forgiven. Edward will marry Mary, with the blessings of both her uncles. Rochester will marry Lady Clara and retire to his castle and a life of domesticity, and the king swears everybody to secrecy.

Though he spent 20 years living abroad, Payne's democratic ideals were clearly present in his work. When Mary enters the palace, she says "What a beautiful place this is! But, without content, grandeur is not to be envied. The humble and the good may be as happy in a cottage as in a palace." Equally democratic in sentiment is Washington Irving's creation, Captain Copp, who sees the common behavior of the king for what it is and speaks his mind even to the monarch.

CHASE, MARY COYLE (1907–1981)   Born
and raised in Denver, Colorado, Mary Coyle attended the University of Denver for three years (1921–23), followed by a year at the University of Colorado at Boulder. In 1924, she became a newspaper reporter; she worked for the *Rocky Mountain News* of Denver (1928–31), and later in a freelance capacity for the International News Service and the United Press (1932–36).

Chase's first play, *Me Third* (1936), was written for the FEDERAL THEATRE PROJECT. It was later produced in New York under the title *Now You've Done It* (1937). She is remembered primarily for her PULITZER PRIZE–winning play, HARVEY (1944), a comic fantasy about a man whose constant companion is a six-and-a-half-foot-tall, invisible white rabbit. Of her other plays, only *Mrs. McThing* (1952) was a commercial success. Her other plays include *Too Much Business* (1938), *A Slip of a Girl* (1941), *The Next Half Hour* (1945), *Bernar-*

dine (1952), *Midgie Purvis* (1961), and *Cocktails with Mimi* (1974).

BIBLIOGRAPHY
Westbrook, Perry D. *Mary Ellen Chase*. New York: Twayne, 1965.

CHAYEFSKY, SIDNEY "PADDY" (1923–1981)   A New Yorker, Sidney Chayefsky underwent
a traditional Jewish upbringing, which served as the background for much of his work. After college, during World War II, he served in the military, where he was dubbed "Paddy" (given the Irish nickname for his request to attend Catholic Mass, thereby avoiding KP duty), a name so memorable he decided to retain it professionally. Convalescing in a British hospital after being injured by a landmine, he began to write. He created an army screenplay, *True Glory* (1944), in collaboration with director GARSON KANIN, and a GI musical comedy, *No T. O. for Love* (1945), in which he played the lead role during its services tour.

After the army, Chayefsky worked in his uncle's print shop and wrote *Put Them All Together* on a $500 scholarship from Kanin. Unproduced, it nevertheless won Chayefsky a Hollywood Junior Writers Contract. In Hollywood, he met his wife, but he was otherwise unsuccessful, returning to New York to work as a gag writer, while seeking backing for his plays. Hired to produce radio adaptations for the Theatre Guild of the Air, he also wrote for television shows, which led to an NBC contract, and 11 television plays for the *Philco-Goodyear Playhouse*, including *Marty* (1953), about a lonely butcher and his romance with a mousy schoolteacher; *Printer's Measure* (1953), based on his experiences in the print shop; and *The Mother* (1954), about a widow who fights for independence through employment. All these plays were marked by their realistic concentration on the mundane lives of working-class people.

Moving into live theater, Chayefsky produced *Middle of the Night* (1956), a rewrite of one of his television plays, telling the troubled love story of a middle-aged garment manufacturer and his secretary, who is divorcing her unpleasant husband. Next came *The Tenth Man* (1959), an adaptation of S. Ansky's *The Dybbuk* (1925), in which a young girl appears possessed by an angry spirit;

by moving the story from Eastern Europe to Long Island, Chayefsky explored the changing conditions faced by European Jews who immigrated to America. *Gideon* (1961) retells the Biblical story of Gideon, coerced by God to save his people from invasion. *The Passion of Josef D.* (1964) exposes human injustice surrounding the Russian Revolution, where Russians are exploited by both their old czar and the new Stalinist order. His final play, *The Latent Heterosexual* (1968), is a satire about people's obsession with materialism.

Chayefsky's naturalistic dialogue earned him a reputation as the CLIFFORD ODETS of the 1950s, only without the political agenda. His work insists, in an age of increasing cynicism, that love remains the answer. A sympathetic and good-humored outlook colors his earlier work, filled with ordinary people victimized by a hostile society, but his later writings become more bitingly satiric. Not a prolific dramatist, but one who successfully conquered various media, Chayefsky won his greatest acclaim for his screenplays, including Academy Awards for his adaptation of *Marty* (1955), and for his satires of television, *Network* (1971), and medical care, *The Hospital* (1976).

BIBLIOGRAPHY

Chayefsky, Paddy. *The Screenplays.* New York: Applause Theatre & Cinema Books, 1994.
———. *The Stage Plays.* New York: Applause Theatre & Cinema Books, 1994.
———. *The Television Plays.* New York: Applause Theatre & Cinema Books, 1994.
Clum, John. *Paddy Chayefsky.* Boston: Twayne, 1976.
Considine, Shaun. *Mad As Hell: The Life and Work of Paddy Chayefsky.* New York: Random House, 1994.

Susan C. W. Abbotson
Rhode Island College

CHILDREN OF A LESSER GOD MARK MEDOFF (1979)

Children of a Lesser God illuminates, within a love story, the experience—largely misunderstood by those who can hear—of being deaf in a hearing world. MEDOFF first workshopped the play in 1979 at the New Mexico State University Drama Department, of which he was head; later that year, it was produced in Los Angeles. After the New York production in 1980, the play won the TONY AWARD.

James Leeds, a speech therapist who works with the hearing-impaired, hopes to teach speech and lip-reading to 26-year-old Sarah, who lives and works at the institute for the deaf where Leeds teaches. Sarah has been deaf since birth and has always resisted such instruction, in part because she, a perfectionist, feels she will never do it well and in part because she resents the implication that the language she *does* have (American Sign Language) is inferior to that of a hearing person. This she sees as the arrogance of the hearing world. She resists James's instruction—"I live in a place you can't enter. It's out of reach."—but she does not resist his attention, and they soon become lovers.

Their pasts are revealed to us and to each other: Neither was a happy one. Sarah, estranged from her mother, has been at the institute since she was five. It was at that time that her father abandoned them. We also learn that she was thought to be retarded until she was 12 and that her mother still assumes this is true. James, as a child, pretended to be deaf to avoid his mother's religious fanaticism. When James's father eventually left his mother, James took care of her until her suicide. Sarah and James have in common, then, difficult family circumstances, giving them a bond that offsets their differences.

After James and Sarah marry, he serves as her interpreter to the hearing world. Through him, she reconciles with her mother. He still hopes to teach her a means of communication that can be universally understood; she remains resistant. In one scene, James tries to explain music—beyond vibration and visual cues—to Sarah, but she cannot understand it in the way he does. It is a measure of their inability to communicate fully.

Several supporting characters exist on the edges of the central relationship and put up obstacles to it. Sarah's mother and James's boss, Mr. Franklin, both opposed at first, eventually accept the marriage. Lydia and Orin are hearing-impaired students at the institute: Lydia, who has a crush on James herself, informs Franklin of their affair, and Orin resents Sarah for entering into the world of the hearing and deserting the world of the deaf. Orin wants to file a discrimination suit against the institute and wants Sarah's help.

When Sarah agrees, Orin's lawyer, Mrs. Klein, makes the same mistake most hearing people make with Sarah: She assumes she can speak more effectively for the deaf than they can for themselves. James too has made this mistake, and at the end of the play, it seems that the gap between Sarah's world of silence and James's world of sound may be too profound to bridge, despite their love.

CHILDREN'S HOUR, THE LILLIAN HELLMAN (1934)   *The Children's Hour* is a social drama in which a spiteful and manipulative child's false accusation of lesbianism ruins the lives of two teachers. HELLMAN's inclusion of lesbianism, a sensational plot device for the stage in 1934, for many overshadowed her main theme about the far-reaching consequences of a malicious lie. The play proved to be Hellman's longest-running and one of her most popular.

It is set in the small Wright-Dobie boarding school for 12- to 14-year-old girls. Karen Wright and Martha Dobie, college friends now in their late twenties, have worked tirelessly to establish the school, which has just begun to make money and enjoy a good reputation. Karen is engaged to Dr. Joe Cardin, whose young cousin, Mary Tilford, is the school's most troublesome student. Martha's aunt, Lilly Mortar, a vain and pretentious former actress who is disliked by the younger adults, gives elocution lessons to the girls. In an exchange between Aunt Lilly and her niece, Lilly accuses Martha of having "unnatural" feelings for Karen and an "unnatural" jealousy of Karen's fiancé, Joe. She goes on to say, "You were always like that even as a child. If you had a little girl friend, you always got mad when she liked anybody else." Though this exchange takes place behind closed doors, two students eavesdrop and reluctantly repeat what they have heard to the manipulative Mary who, eager to leave the school where she is frequently in trouble for truancy and other misdeeds, runs away to the home of her grandmother, the wealthy and influential Mrs. Tilford. In order to gain her grandmother's sympathy, she tells her what she has heard and, sensing her grandmother's discomfort, embellishes the tale with details she has gained from a book she is secretly reading, *Mademoiselle de Maupin*. So convinced is Mrs.

Tilford of Mary's story that she phones all of the students' parents, and the school is empty by nightfall. When Joe, Karen, and Martha come to Mrs. Tilford for an explanation, Mary intimidates Rosalie, another student, into backing up her story; Mary knows that Rosalie has stolen another girl's necklace and threatens to reveal that secret, convincing the more naive Rosalie that she will go to prison for the deed.

Between acts 2 and 3, the women sue Mrs. Tilford for libel but lose the case. As act 3 begins, their livelihood is gone, they cannot go into town because shops refuse them service, and the "ladies' club" has printed "circulars" against them; even in their own home, they must suffer the suggestive giggles of a grocery delivery boy. Joe alone remains their faithful friend, but even he has some doubt about the nature of the women's relationship; this doubt causes Karen to break off their engagement, despite Joe's pleas against it. Martha, meanwhile, realizes that she does love Karen romantically and that she is, indeed, a latent lesbian; having come to this realization, she walks out of the room and shoots herself. By the time a contrite Mrs. Tilford comes to see Karen (with dead Martha not yet cold in the next room) to tell her that Mary and Rosalie finally told the truth and that the judge will issue an apology, it is too late—their lives are in ruins.

The play is similar in theme to ARTHUR MILLER's *The CRUCIBLE* (1953); in both dramas, a manipulative child plays upon the fears of a community for self-serving reasons, leaving ruined lives in her wake. Both plays consider the consequences of a community's willingness to believe of others what it most fears.

It was Dashiell Hammett, Hellman's longtime friend and lover, who gave Hellman the idea for the play, after he came across a similar story—involving a Scottish boarding school, a false accusation of lesbianism, and financial ruin—in a book about British court cases. In 1936, Hellman was asked to write a screenplay adaptation of *The Children's Hour*. Since the film censors of the period would not allow the release of a film dealing with lesbianism, Hellman changed the plot device to a heterosexual triangle but maintained her more central theme of the devastating effects of malicious lies. The film, which ended happily, was called *These Three* (1936). A later film version, *The*

Children's Hour (1962) with Audrey Hepburn and Shirley MacLaine, is much more faithful to the play.

CHILDRESS, ALICE (1920–1994)

Born in Charleston, South Carolina, Alice Childress moved to Harlem as a young child to live with her grandmother, a woman who proved to be a great influence. In New York, she was educated in the public school system until she was forced to drop out and take on the task of educating herself, reading as many as two books each day. In 1940, Childress began her career in theater, often working odd jobs to support herself and her daughter while she established herself as an actress, director, and playwright with such notable organizations as the American Negro Theatre in Harlem.

From such humble beginnings emerged the first black female playwright to have a play professionally produced on the New York stage (*Just a Little Simple* [1950]). Childress also holds the often ignored distinction of being the only black woman whose plays have been produced professionally in America over four decades. Her writing is praised for its universality, uncompromising lack of sentimentality, powerful theatricality, realistic dialogue, and strong characters. Certainly, Childress's work had a powerful influence on innovations in both black theater and in feminist drama during the 20th century. Childress worked in a variety of genres, publishing nearly a dozen plays, several novels, a screenplay, an anthology of short stories, and numerous articles and essays in her lifetime.

Childress's first play, *Florence* (1949), is a one-act that depicts a conversation between a white woman and a black woman at a segregated bus station; unfortunately, because of seemingly irreconcilable racial differences, the women are unable to converse on any meaningful level. In future plays, Childress returned to her Charleston roots; WEDDING BAND: A LOVE/HATE STORY IN BLACK AND WHITE (1966) portrays an interracial relationship in a small South Carolina city, doomed to fail because the couple's love cannot overcome the centuries of hate between the white and black people of the South. The dramatization of interracial tensions continues in *Wine in Wilderness* (1969), *String* (1969), and *Mojo, A Black Love Story* (1970), a trilogy of one-acts written by Childress in quick succession and focusing on the sexual and social tensions that grew within black society as a result of the black liberationist movement. Though many of her plays deal with these themes of interracial tensions, the rights of both white and black women, and liberation and revolution, *Gullah* (1977), originally titled *Sea Island Song*, celebrates the racial heritage of the islanders off of the South Carolina coast in a musical collaboration with Childress's husband, Nathan Woodard.

While many of Childress's accomplishments have fallen victim to racial inequities or have simply been swallowed by history, she was the recipient of numerous awards, including the Sojourner Truth Award, the Black Filmmakers first Paul Robeson Medal of Distinction, the Achievement Award from the National Association of Negro Business and Professional Women, and the Radcliffe Alumnae Association Graduate Society Medal for Distinguished Achievement.

BIBLIOGRAPHY

Bower, Martha Gilman. *Color Struck under the Gaze: The Pathology of Being in the Plays of Johnson, Hurston, Childress, Hansberry, and Kennedy.* Westport, Conn.: Greenwood Press, 2003.

Childress, Alice. *String.* New York: Dramatists Play Service, 1969.

———. "Trouble in Mind: A Comedy-Drama in Two Acts." In *Black Theatre: A Twentieth-Century Collection of the Work of Its Best Playwrights,* edited by Lindsay Patterson. New York: Dodd, Mead, 1971. 135–174.

———. *Wedding Band: A Love/Hate Story in Black and White.* New York: Samuel French, 1973.

———. "Wine in the Wilderness: A Comedy-Drama." In *Plays by and about Women,* edited by Victoria Sullivan and James Hatch. New York: Vintage, 1973. 379–421.

Jennings, La Vinia Delois. *Alice Childress.* New York: Twayne, 1995.

Elizabeth A. Osborne
Florida State University

CHO, JULIA (1975?–)

Born in Los Angeles and raised in suburban Phoenix, Arizona, Korean-American playwright Julia Cho often writes about the Asian-American experience. She studied playwriting with CONSTANCE CONGDON at Amherst College, where she earned her B.A. in English. After earning a master's degree in English from the University of California at Berkeley, she earned a second master's, this one in playwriting from New York University. Cho was also a playwriting fellow at Juilliard. She has been commissioned to write plays for Ma-Yi Theatre, New York Theater Workshop, South Coast Repertory, and the Mark Taper Forum, among others.

Cho's most well known works make up what became her trilogy of desert plays, *The Architecture of Loss* (2004), *BFE* (2005), and *Durango* (2006). In all three plays, the Arizona desert is an important presence in the lives of the characters. In *The Architecture of Loss,* a father returns to a family he had abandoned 16 years before and learns from several different perspectives about the subsequent disappearance of his young son. *BFE* is a dark comedy about a 14-year-old girl who is, as the title—an acronym for a slang expression ("Bum Fucking Egypt")—indicates, out in the middle of nowhere; this is true in several senses: she is in desert suburbia; she is between childhood and adulthood; and she is the child of a mother who seems uncomfortable with her own Asian-ness (this mother offers her fine-looking Asian-featured daughter plastic surgery for her birthday). While *Architecture* and *BFE* are from the point of view of female characters, *Durango* focuses on the Asian-American male experience. In it, a recently laid-off widowed Korean-American father takes his two sons—one about to enter medical school and the other a high school swimming champion—on a road trip. Both boys have kept secrets from their father about their seemingly perfect second-generation-immigrant success. The father who has given up so much for his children may never find the fulfillment through them for which he had hoped. Cho's plays are evocative of family memories for nonimmigrant, non-Asian-American audience members as well as those who more closely share her characters' experience.

Cho's other plays include *99 Histories* (2004), in which an unplanned pregnancy causes a young woman to confront the past; *The Winchester House* (2006), in which a young woman's exploration of her past is brought on by contact with a now dying man whom she knew in her childhood; *The Piano Teacher* (2007), about a seemingly harmless retired piano teacher and her reunion with two of her former students who had abruptly quit her lessons years before; and the one-act *Round and Round* (2008), in which a linguist who wonders about dying languages finds himself trying to communicate within his dying marriage. Cho's other one-act plays include *How to Be a Good Son* (2004), which was first produced in Japan; *100 Most Beautiful Names of Todd* (2006); and *First Tree in Antarctica* (2007). Cho also wrote the children's comedy *Bay and the Spectacles of Doom* (2006).

BIBLIOGRAPHY

Cho, Julia. *The Architecture of Loss.* New York: Dramatists Play Service, 2005.
———. *BFE.* New York: Dramatists Play Service, 2006.
———. *Durango.* New York: Dramatists Play Service, 2007.
———. *99 Histories.* New York: Dramatists Play Service, 2005.

CLARA'S OLE MAN ED BULLINS (1965) A one-act play set in the mid-1950s in a "slum kitchen . . . in South Philadelphia," *Clara's Ole Man* is based at least in part on BULLINS's own experience. He was in a gang as a young man and also served in the U.S. military, after which he earned his high school diploma. The play is one of Bullins's earliest.

Jack is out of the service and enrolled in a college preparatory program on the GI Bill when he makes the acquaintance of Clara, an attractive young woman. As the play begins, Jack is at Clara's home visiting with Big Girl, a raucous and foul-mouthed woman of indeterminate age, who would otherwise be at work but who has called in sick today. Also present is Big Girl's retarded younger sister, Baby Girl, and, upstairs, the invalid Aunt Touhy. Big Girl, cursing and coughing and laughing, tells the rather sedate Jack too personal stories of Clara's teen pregnancy and further embarrasses Clara by defending her own practice of teaching Baby Girl curse words. Soon Miss Famie, already drunk, comes by on this rainy weekday afternoon to drink gin with Aunt Touhy. She takes an offered glass of "rotgut" wine as she passes through the kitchen. Jack, Clara, and Big Girl also drink "rotgut" throughout the play. Joining the drinking party are Stoogie, Bama, and Hoss, members of a street gang and friends of Clara and Big Girl; all three boys are under 16. They are trying to avoid the police, having just robbed a man outside a liquor store. The teens are somewhat impressed by Jack's world travels but soon become contemptuous of his Standard English. Jack, quite drunk by now, suggests he and the two women should go out since "Clara's ole man" will be home soon. The teenaged boys snicker as Jack explains that Clara told him to come over in the afternoon while her "ole man" was at work. Big Girl becomes furious because she is, in fact, Clara's lover, the old "man" in question. She asks the now drunken teens to "escort" Jack out, after which the sound of his beating at their hands is audible.

Bullins's work is a harsh portrait of a brutal and alcoholic group, into which Jack has wandered. There is no commentary on the drinking or the violence; Bullins simply presents the events as a slice of life. The subtitle of the play is "A Play of Lost Innocence," and that innocence lost is Jack's: Once a tough street kid himself, he reenters Big Girl's world a naïf, his skills for survival in the ghetto eroded by military service and college preparation.

CLEAGE, PEARL MICHELLE (1948–)

Prolific writer of poetry, plays, fiction, and essays and editor and founder of *Catalyst* magazine (1987), Pearl Cleage was born in Springfield, Massachusetts, and raised on the west side of Detroit. Cleage's commitment to improving the lives of African-American women has its roots in the figure of her father, Jaramogi Abebe Agyemen (also known as Albert Buford Cleage), founder of the Pan African Orthodox Christian Church. After attending Howard University, Spelman College, and Atlanta University, Cleage worked in a variety of media positions and began to earn a reputation as a controversial writer by staging plays dealing with slavery, sexism, economic oppression, racism, politics, and aggression against African-American women.

It was not until the 1980s that she began to achieve recognition as a playwright, first with *puppetplay* (1981), a surrealistic full-length play for two actresses and a marionette, in which two young women are slavishly attentive to a male puppet until they realize it is within their power to break free. *Hospice* (1983) is a one-act domestic drama that focuses on the estranged relationship between a woman dying of cancer and her pregnant daughter, whom she abandoned years before for a Bohemian life in Paris. *Good News* (1984) is a comedy concerning feuding lovers, and *Essentials* (1984) relates the story of a female attorney who becomes the first black elected official in her town.

In both *Chain* (1992) and *Late Bus to Mecca* (1992), Cleage depicts African-American women characters in difficult circumstances. *Chain* is a morality play that portrays the worry of the parents of Rosa Jackson, a 16-year-old drug addict who has been deceived by her drug-user boyfriend. The one-act *Late Bus to Mecca,* set in 1970, focuses on Ava Gardner Johnson, a self-confident and inventive prostitute who hopes to open a beauty parlor someday, and her encounter with a silent, anonymous African-American woman who is physically and psychologically impaired. The silence of one woman brings out the loquaciousness of the other, and Ava's monologue about men, business, makeup, and more is both funny and poignant.

Flyin' West (1992), set in 1898 in Nicodemus, Kansas, a utopian settlement that actually existed, is about the experience of four black women who flee the racism of the South and escape to the West, taking advantage of the land offered through the Homestead Act (as did thousands of other African Americans of the period). In this play, Cleage examines issues of selfhood, individuality, and women's experiences during slavery and in the black pioneer settlements of the West.

Josephine Baker and LANGSTON HUGHES inspired Cleage's drama *Blues for an Alabama Sky* (1997). Set in Harlem in 1930, the play centers on Angel Allen, a blues singer who considers marrying a southern black man she finds dull after the white gangster she has been with. The drama also portrays the relationship between Angel and her neighbors, Guy, a homosexual costume designer, and Delia, who dreams of opening a birth-control clinic to serve the women of Harlem. Cleage masterfully addresses such topics as homosexuality, abortion, interracial sex, conservative religious views, and sexual freedom in Harlem. *Bourbon at the Border* (1997) is the story of a group of ordinary workers who remember when they were young activists in the 1960s attempting—against violent resistance—to help black voters register in Mississippi.

Cleage was closely associated in the 1990s with Atlanta's Just Us Theatre Company, where she was first playwright-in-residence and later artistic director. She has also been playwright-in-residence at Spellman College, as well as a drama and creative writing teacher there. At present, she is a Spellman College Cosby Endowed Professor of Humanities. In recent years, Cleage's creative energy has been focused on the writing of several novels (her first, *What Looks Like Crazy on an Ordinary Day* [1997] was an Oprah Book Club selection and became a best seller). In 2008 a new play, *A Song for Coretta,* was produced in Atlanta; it takes place in 2006 among the mourners in line to pay their respects to Mrs. Martin Luther King as she lies in state at her assassinated husband's church. Cleage has long maintained that the purpose of her writing is to improve the lives of African-American women by endorsing both personal and political activism.

BIBLIOGRAPHY

Cleage, Pearl. *Blues for an Alabama Sky.* New York: Dramatists Play Service, 1999.
———. *"Flyin' West" and Other Plays.* New York: Theatre Communications Group, 1999.
———. *A Song for Coretta.* New York: Dramatists Play Service, 2008.

Estefania Olid-Peña
Georgia State University

CLURMAN, HAROLD (1901–1980)

CLURMAN, HAROLD (1901–1980)   Born in New York, Harold Clurman was first exposed to theater when he went with his parents to see YIDDISH DRAMA with the great Yiddish actor Jacob Adler (Clurman later married his daughter, Stella Adler—actress, member of the GROUP THEATRE, and eventually a famous acting teacher). Clurman, years afterward, called this experience "transforming." Educated at Columbia University and the University of Paris, Clurman first worked in theater as an actor in small parts in Greenwich Village and as a play reader for the THEATRE GUILD. From the very beginning he was interested in what theater could say about society; he

believed that good theater must have purpose and that playwrights should be encouraged to express their political and spiritual visions just as artists in other media were doing at the time.

Clurman was also influenced by the touring Moscow Art Theatre, which, using the acting techniques of Constantin Stanislavsky (see ACTORS STUDIO), had presented a play in which the acting was far more emotional and realistic than anything seen in New York prior to their arrival. In 1931, Clurman, together with Lee Strasberg and Cheryl Crawford, formed the Group Theatre, which, like the Moscow Art Theatre, would be a permanent ensemble of actors working together to achieve emotional realism; they were also committed to conveying a social message. The Group Theatre was considered an experiment, but Clurman was adamant that the Group's work not merely be "experimental"; it must also be (as he wrote on May 7, 1937, in the *New York Times*) "(a) true to the spirit of the play's text; (b) intelligible to the audience it hopes to address; (c) technically as complete and as pleasing as possible; and (d) based on an idea or sentiment it considers vital, inspiriting, fresh and truly entertaining." The Group's most successful productions were those of plays by Group member CLIFFORD ODETS, including *AWAKE AND SING!* (1935), *WAITING FOR LEFTY* (1935), and *GOLDEN BOY* (1937). The Group Theatre lasted only 10 years, but its impact on American theater has endured.

After the Group Theatre folded, Clurman went on to direct plays by some of America's greatest playwrights, EUGENE O'NEILL, LILLIAN HELLMAN, ARTHUR MILLER, and WILLIAM INGE among them. Also a prolific essayist, Clurman was drama critic for the *New Republic* (1949–52), the London *Observer* (1955–63), and the *Nation* (1953–80). He published several books, including a book about the Group Theatre entitled *The Fervent Years* (1945), and three books of essays. He also taught at Hunter College from 1964 until his death in 1980.

Theatrical producer Robert Whitehead, in his introduction to *The Collected Works of Harold Clurman,* writes, "Harold Clurman's ideas and visions . . . have now found their way through the chaos to the center of the working theatre today. Whenever I encounter a strong, clear simple emotional line—and a kind of organic truth in the theatre . . . I think of our debt to Harold" (XIII).

BIBLIOGRAPHY
Clurman, Harold. *The Collected Works of Harold Clurman.* Eds. Marjorie Loggia and Glenn Young. New York: Applause Theatre Books, 1994.
———. *The Fervent Years: The Story of the Group Theatre and the Thirties.* New York: Hill & Wang, 1957.

COASTAL DISTURBANCES Tina Howe (1986)

Set on a north shore Massachusetts beach, *Coastal Disturbances* involves several generations of New Englanders enjoying the end of summer and living out their personal dramas in this fanciful look at love. On the beach, we find a couple of obnoxious and active children, Miranda and Winston; their mothers—former college friends, Faith and Ariel; a young photographer from New York named Holly Dancer; and Leo, the lifeguard who pursues her. Also present are Dr. and Mrs. Hamilton Adams, a retired eye surgeon who collects interesting shells, and his wife, who paints.

Faith's friend Ariel is divorced, is in early menopause, and has tried to kill herself. Happily married Faith is pregnant; this seems miraculous to her since she adopted Miranda, having finally given up trying to conceive. These women represent two extremes of midlife womanhood. Leo and Holly, in their twenties, are both on the rebound from failed three-year relationships. They finally give in to their mutual, physical attraction one night on the beach; Leo's hopes are high until Holly's ex-lover, Andre, arrives. He leads Holly on—as usual—with promises of an exhibition of her work at his gallery. Leo cannot understand Holly's love for this "phony," this "operator"; she admits that Andre "makes her crazy, but [she's] just so alive with him." On her last day, Holly comes to Leo's lifeguard chair to say goodbye, and Leo tries to convince her that *he* is the wiser choice. Holly keeps falling down—it seems that he quite literally makes her weak in the knees—and she must crawl off the beach to avoid further discussion and temptation. During her labored departure, she—almost against her will—gives Leo her address and phone number in New York,

and he begins to hope that eventually she might choose him over the insincere but cosmopolitan Andre. The play ends with the elderly Adamses setting up their annual private wedding-anniversary celebration on the beach. They refer to Mrs. Adams's reluctance to marry Hamilton Adams those many years ago. Here is a marriage that has endured despite rough spots. As Leo "gazes wistfully" at the Adamses, he suddenly pulls Holly's number from his pocket, "breaking into a radiant smile." Howe has described *Coastal Disturbances* as "a love story, more than anything it was a story about a woman falling in love and being torn" (Barlow 268).

In an interview in the *Dramatists Guild Quarterly* in 1994, Howe remarked that in the mid-1980s there was a great deal of "male violence" on stage and that "these weren't the men [she] knew," so she "wrote *Coastal Disturbances* to celebrate the tenderness of men" (McLaughlin 3). These tenderer men are Leo, who is a lifesaver by occupation (smitten with Holly, he tries to save her from the cad, Andre), and Hamilton Adams, who is respectful of the privacy of others on the beach and ever patient with his wife.

The fanciful tone of the play is enhanced at times by the fantastical: Leo suddenly begins to do magic tricks on the sand. Andre describes a clockwork New York skyline—with rising steam and flocks of seagulls—made by his father when he was a child. Faith claims to be knitting a house that she and her husband joke they will move into after the summer.

BIBLIOGRAPHY
Barlow, Judith. "Tina Howe." In *Speaking on Stage: Interviews with Contemporary American Playwrights,* edited by Philip C. Kolin and Colby H. Kullman. Tuscaloosa: University of Alabama Press, 1996. 260–276.
McLaughlin, Buzz. "Conversation with Tina Howe." *Dramatists Guild Quarterly* 31, no. 2 (1994): 2–9.

COCKTAIL HOUR, THE A. R. Gurney (1988)

The Cocktail Hour is a comedy about an angry son who wants his family's permission to produce a play that he has written about them. In this comedy of manners, laughter rises from a bed of pain.

John, a successful but unfulfilled textbook editor, has had two plays produced in New York. Based on family stories, these plays disturbed John's parents. The new play, John warns, "cuts to the bone." Bradley, John's father, a wealthy businessman in his late seventies, vehemently opposes production. He fears that John's play will bring him notoriety and ridicule before his death, an event he believes imminent. He offers John a $20,000 bribe. Anne, John's mother, supports her husband. She fears publicity too, but she realizes that John's future as a writer is at stake; she urges him to forsake theater and rewrite the play as a novel. Nina, John's sister, might support her brother if the part that she inspired were larger. She resents her role in the play and in the family as a "supporting player." Jigger, John and Nina's brother, never appearing but often discussed, earns Bradley's praise at John's expense.

These comparisons reinforce John's secret fear that he may be illegitimate. He knows no better explanation for the lifelong feelings of isolation and insecurity that feed his anger. In spite of his parents' strong objections, he has consulted a psychiatrist who wants John to find out more about the plays that, as a child, he wrote and produced at home. In the process, he finds out much more: Bradley's father, a respected town leader, committed suicide. Anne, as a young mother, stole time from family duties to write a 600-page novel that she abandoned and burned.

The action of the play takes place in the comfortable living room of the family home during the cocktail hour, which Bradley and Anne regard as sacred: "The bishop used to say . . . when he came for dinner that the cocktail hour took the place of evening prayers." John and Nina remember this time differently: "[Y]ou and me . . . stomachs growling, waiting to eat . . . the cocktail hour kept all of life in an amazing state of suspended animation."

GURNEY avoids mere realism. Implied allusions to "Richard Cory" and *Hedda Gabler,* as well as the echo of T. S. Eliot's *The Cocktail Party,* typify Gurney's aim of placing his dramas firmly in the company of other literary and dramatic works. The play comments on and satirizes itself and theater. As John defends his writing, the audience derives double pleasure in realizing that Gurney's play and John's, also titled *The Cocktail Hour,* are identical. Gurney humors audiences

into thinking about the changing rituals of life in a democracy. The characters' maneuvers, challenges, and recriminations expose the crises of our times in family life, sexuality, the theater and criticism, the media, politics, and economics.

Arvid F. Sponberg
Valparaiso University

COME BACK, LITTLE SHEBA WILLIAM INGE (1950)

Come Back, Little Sheba launched INGE's career as one of America's most important playwrights of the 1950s. The play focuses on Doc and Lola Delaney, a childless couple whose longtime marriage is now threatened by their disillusionment and sense of loss. Lola's youthful pregnancy forced their marriage against their parents' wishes, and the subsequent loss of both their child and any hope of having more children adds to Doc's disappointment about having had to drop out of medical school after their marriage to become a chiropractor. Now he is an alcoholic who battles his demons by attending Alcoholics Anonymous (A.A.) and reciting the "serenity prayer" he learned at these meetings. Lola mourns the loss of their child and of her once-youthful beauty, symbolized by her lost dog Sheba, for whom she constantly calls. She spends her days chattering to anyone she sees, listening to escapist radio programs, and snooping into the promiscuous sexual behavior of Marie, a college student who rents their spare room and who serves as a less-than-ideal surrogate daughter for Doc and Lola.

Marie's behavior triggers a traumatic series of scenes wherein Doc gets drunk and luckily passes out after threatening Lola's life with a hatchet. Friends from A.A. come to take him for "drying out," and Lola calls her parents to ask if she can come live with them. Denied refuge by her father, Lola is alone when Marie appears to say she is moving away immediately to be married. Thus, neither Lola nor Doc has any choice: The resolution of their conflict lies in the mutual recognition that they must accept the circumstances of their life together and forge on. Realistic acceptance of life's vicissitudes proved to be a consistent theme in all of Inge's best plays, which include *PICNIC* (1953), *BUS STOP* (1955), and *The DARK AT THE TOP OF THE STAIRS* (1957).

Inge's own psychotherapy and alcoholism are reflected in *Sheba,* which he wrote while undergoing analysis and attending A.A. meetings in St. Louis, where he was working as a teacher before he became a successful playwright. His small-town Kansas background fueled his sharp perceptions about the potentially debilitating effects of small-town life, and the complexities of love in both family and community relationships made his best work lastingly important in American dramatic literature.

Ralph F. Voss
University of Alabama

CONDUCT OF LIFE, THE MARIA IRENE FORNÉS (1985)

In *The Conduct of Life,* Fornés uses the setting of an unnamed Latin American country to explore the violence that results from conflicts between sexual desire and power, as well as the dehumanization caused by life under authoritarian regimes. The play consists of 19 scenes, many of which are cinematically short, a familiar Fornés technique. The play is also a product of the cross-fertilization from her work mentoring young Hispanic playwrights at International Arts Relations (INTAR) Hispanic American Arts Center in New York.

The title provides thematic focus for exploring the ways in which one is expected, is required, or chooses to conduct one's life in a space of political repression. Orlando, an ambitious army officer, afraid that his sexual desire will interfere with his quest for "maximum power," resolves not to allow his wife, Leticia, to get in his way. Unfortunately, his quest for power leads him down the path of emotional and eventually literal destruction. His rise in power puts him in charge of torturing enemies of the state. He does this despite the fact that his prisoners are not necessarily political threats. Orlando refuses to speak about his work, a silence that mirrors the behavior of powerful military figures in several South and Central American countries during the 1970s and 1980s. He brings home one prisoner, Nena, an impoverished 12-year-old girl, to be a slave to his sexual appetites in the hopes of purging his sexual desire and making himself stronger.

Everyone is twisted by this horrific environment. Nena suffers repeated rape and abuse at the hands of Orlando. Leticia, more generous than her husband, chafes under the limitations of the authoritarian environment of a household that mirrors the authoritarian political space outside. Both Leticia and Orlando treat Olimpia, a servant with a speech impediment, harshly. Alejo, a lieutenant commander and friend of the family, asks, "How can one live in a world that festers the way ours does and take any pleasure in life?" Orlando's method of adaptation, corrupting love into something violent and destructive, eventually leads to his destruction, though he believes that his rapes are an act of love. Nena is brought upstairs and becomes a servant in the house. Her attempts to shut away the violence of her situation elicit this speech to Olimpia: "I want to conduct each day of my life in the best possible way. I should value the things I have. And I should value all those who are near me." Though she recognizes that Orlando's violence comes in part from his pain, there is no clear moment of redemption for her or him.

The play closes with Orlando's discovery of Leticia's affair with a colleague. When he stops physically punishing her, she grabs a revolver and kills him, placing the gun in Nena's hand and saying "please." The play deliberately refuses to clarify whether Nena is to take the blame for killing Orlando or whether Leticia wants Nena to shoot her in order to free her, leaving us to grapple with the difficulty of escape from the dehumanizing effects of this repressive environment.

Jon D. Rossini
University of California—Davis

CONGDON, CONSTANCE (1944–)

Initially planning a career as a poet, Constance Congdon turned to playwriting when a friend offered to produce her work. With her first endeavor, *Gilgamesh* (1976), Congdon found drama a much more suitable form than poetry and has since written nearly 30 plays, several opera libretti, and adaptations and has won numerous awards. Congdon earned an M.F.A. at the University of Massachusetts in 1981 and is currently playwright-in-residence at Amherst College.

Congdon's plays are highly theatrical and imaginative in form and style, often juxtaposing tragic and comic, tacky and tasteful, past and present, supernatural and real, and using such devices as cross-casting and multiple stage spaces. While her plays are quite diverse, consistent underlying themes include sexual identity, American identity and culture, and an often epic sense of history. She is particularly fascinated with language, as evident in her intriguing blend of dialogue with poetry and music or in her amusing depiction of characters speaking backwards, like a tape recorder rewinding. In fact, the language of her plays often has absurdist aspects that keep audiences at a distance. Though there are strains of feminism in Congdon's work, they do not derive from traditional feminist theory and agendas; rather, Congdon calls hers "an uneasy feminism" (Hanson).

Congdon's one-act play No Mercy (1986), set simultaneously in 1945 and 1985, explores the first test of the atomic bomb and life in the postnuclear age. In Tales of the Lost Formicans (1989), probably Congdon's best-known work, she humorously views suburban American life from the perspective of a few curious aliens, integrating amusing extraterrestrial behavior with ordinary family conflicts and situations. Casanova (1991) explores themes of love, sexual identity, and transience in a romp though the life of the legendary 18th-century lover, interweaving the youthful Casanova with one now past 70. Losing Father's Body (1993) is a dark farce in which a body is lost en route to the funeral home. Dog Opera (1998), originally produced by GEORGE C. WOLFE's New York Shakespeare Festival, explores the frustrations and futility of love and human connection in gay, lesbian, and heterosexual relationships.

In 1998, the University of Massachusetts Theatre Department commissioned So Far, a play Congdon describes as a dark comedy about a time "after everything bad has happened" (Hanson). In Lips (2000), commissioned by Steven Spielberg's Dreamworks, the first woman president of the United States seeks to focus on issues of gay rights and discrimination by hiring an ex-con to pose as her girlfriend, an outlandish plot that subdues the underlying issues. In 2000, the Profile Theatre of Portland, Oregon, devoted a season to Congdon's works, and their production of No Mercy included a new companion piece, One Day Earlier. Other plays by Congdon, many of which premiered in academic productions, include The Bride (1980), Boarders (1982), Fourteen Brilliant Colors (1982), Native American (1986), Wetlands (1994), and two unproduced plays, Under Lubianka Square and Dark Bridge Mountain, as well as The Automata Pieta (2000), commissioned and produced by the San Francisco American Conservatory Theatre's Young Conservatory, and Moontel Six (2002), cocommissioned by ACT's Young Conservatory and the Royal National Theatre in London.

Congdon's recent work includes a 2006 adaptation of Molière's The Misanthrope. In 2008, she was awarded an Alfred P. Sloan Foundation grant to support her work on her (not yet titled) play-in-progress about water in the western United States.

BIBLIOGRAPHY

Congdon, Constance. Dog Opera. New York: Samuel French, 1998.

———. Lips. New York: Broadway Play Publishing, 2000.

———. "Tales of the Lost Formicans" and Other Plays. New York: Theatre Communications Group, 1994.

Hanson, Jillian. "Her Play's the Thing." UMASS Magazine Online. Fall 1998. Available online. <http://www.umass.edu/umassmag/archives/1998/fall_98/fall98_f_congdon.html>.

Karen C. Blansfield
University of North Carolina–Chapel Hill

CONNECTION, THE JACK GELBER (1959)

Beat-generation writer GELBER's The Connection was met with both condemnation and acclaim when it was first produced in 1959 by the LIVING THEATRE. The 27-year-old playwright had created a brutally realistic portrayal of heroin addiction.

A group of heroin addicts wait in Leach's apartment for the arrival of their "connection," Cowboy, who is expected soon with enough heroin for them all. Into this scene are introduced a producer, a playwright, and a film crew. This device adds greater realism to Gelber's addicts and serves the purpose of bringing the outside world into their isolated sphere: The theatrical conceit is that the playwright, Jaybird, has asked if he can film the junkies in order to mine their conversation for realistic dialogue. Jaybird and the producer, Jim, have also invited jazz musicians to play at Leach's "pad." The producer announces at the opening of the play that though there have been recent works concerned with "this anti-social habit," few are authentic. He promises that at the end of *this* evening there will be no "housewife who will call the police" to come for her husband (a sneering reference to *A Hatful of Rain* [1955], Michael Gazzo's drama about a family faced with addiction).

As the junkies wait for Cowboy, they listen to the music, bicker, and exchange frank stories about their experiences. When Cowboy finally arrives, he is accompanied by a Salvation Army Sister, to whom he has attached himself in order to dodge the police. Each man takes his turn in the bathroom—out of Sister's view—with Cowboy. Jaybird and one of the photographers join the others and for the first time in their lives try heroin. When Jim becomes angry about this, Cowboy tells him that whether they took it or not was "their own responsibility." Leach, meanwhile, complains that he feels nothing; it takes more heroin for him to get high than it once did. Finally, Cowboy gives him more, and he overdoses. The cold self-interest of the men is clear when one of the junkies, Ernie, leaves, not wanting to be involved, and Sam remembers a time when Ernie "threw a kid who took an overdose out the window," not knowing if he was alive or dead.

While this is certainly not a morality play, Gelber is no advocate for the lifestyle of junkies. Jaybird asks Cowboy and the others, "Is that all you know—destruction?" Sam tells Solly, "There ain't nothing gallant about heroin, baby." Leach, the host and a junkie himself, has a painful boil on his neck—a symbol—which bursts shortly before Cowboy arrives with the heroin. When Leach overdoses, he does not die—not this time—but that his life is poisoned is as clear as the boil on his neck.

On the occasion of Gelber's death, Edward Albee told the *New York Times* that he was "so affected and energized" by *The Connection,* adding, "It was exciting, dangerous, instructive and terrifying, all things theater should be" (May 10, 2003). Aside from the realistic treatment of a difficult subject, Gelber was ahead

of his time in another way. The cast was of mixed race, and skin color is unimportant to characterization. Gelber noted in his script that although he pictured certain characters as white and others as African American, in terms of race "there need not be any rigidity is casting." This is one of the first American plays about which this could be said.

In the early 1960s, the Living Theatre toured Europe with *The Connection* and two other plays. The tour was a tremendous success, though at home the play's reception had been mixed, some critics hailing its honesty while others considered it filth. The play won the Obie Award for Best New Play.

CONNELLY, MARC (1890–1980) Born in McKeesport, Pennsylvania, Marcus Cook Connelly was the first son of Patrick Joseph and Mabel Cook Connelly, both actors who had quit the stage after the death of their first child, a girl, to try for a second. The young Marcus enjoyed the kind of idyllic childhood Mark Twain might have appreciated; his parents were leaders in the community and managed the White Hotel, where the young man was exposed to travelers of all stripes, including old acting friends of his parents. He secretly watched Steele MacKaye, Richard Mansfield, Minnie Maddern Fiske, and Robert Mantell practice their gestures before hotel mirrors. When he was seven, his parents took him to see Mansfield in Rostand's *Cyrano de Bergerac,* and he was smitten. By the time he was 11, Connelly had written, produced, and acted in numerous plays performed in a special, nine-seat theater on the second floor of the hotel. He also sang in a church choir and attended Trinity Hall School, but the idyll ended with the death of his father in 1902. He soon left school for Pittsburgh to begin his career as a newspaper writer. Connelly spent the next eight years as a reporter and drama critic before beginning to write for the theater.

His first New York production, *The Amber Princess* (1917), folded after 15 performances. Connelly lacked the funds to return home and so stayed in New York. For the next five years he did odd jobs and freelance writing, and he wrote a number of theatrical failures. Just when life seemed most difficult, Connelly met a fellow newspaperman from Pittsburgh, George S.

KAUFMAN. Their collaboration lasted for the next five years, and during this time the pair wrote several plays. Among the more notable are *Dulcy* (1921), *To the Ladies* (1922), *Merton of the Movies* (1922), and BEGGAR ON HORSEBACK (1924), the last of which is still occasionally revived. Most of Connelly and Kaufman's plays, however, now seem dated to modern audiences. After an amicable breakup of their partnership in 1925, Connelly continued to write in New York and Hollywood. Both men were also members of the Round Table, also known as the Vicious Circle, a group of writers and wits who gathered at the large round table in the Algonquin Hotel in New York. Notable artists such as Alexander Woollcott, Robert Benchley, Ring Lardner, Dorothy Parker, EDNA FERBER, Kaufman, and Connelly regularly met to talk, eat, think, and occasionally to put a theatrical on for their friends. Connelly was also instrumental in helping Harold Ross launch the *New Yorker* magazine and contributed editorial assistance as well as numerous articles.

Ironically, the grandson of Irish immigrants who became one of the most liked and respected writers in New York is largely remembered for his play *The GREEN PASTURES* (1929), a fable about how unsophisticated African Americans of the American South view God. The play was a great success, won the PULITZER PRIZE, ran for more than five years, was made into an equally successful movie, and gave Connelly an international reputation. Connelly wrote several other plays, many of which were made into movies, but he never again achieved the critical or popular success of *The Green Pastures*. He remained an important theatrical presence, notably in the role of the Stage Manager in the New York and London productions of THORNTON WILDER'S *OUR TOWN* and as an engaging and welcomed presence on numerous college campuses.

BIBLIOGRAPHY

Connelly, Marc. *The Green Pastures.* New York: Farrar and Rinehart, 1929.

———. *Voices Offstage: A Book of Memoirs.* New York: Holt, Rinehart and Winston, 1968.

Nolan, Paul T. *Marc Connelly.* New York: Twayne, 1969.

Michael M. O'Hara
Ball State University

CONTRAST, THE ROYAL TYLER (1787)   This first professionally produced American comedy is set, as its prologue declares, not in "foreign climes" but in New York. It is in the prologue of the play that the "contrast" is first articulated between the "genuine sincerity" and "homespun habits" of Americans and the "proud titles" and "hypocrisy" of Europeans. TYLER satirizes the pretentious manners of those who aspire to duplicate British high society in the new United States. In so doing, he writes a dramatic declaration of independence from British influence; after all, as Tyler queries in his play's prologue, "Why should our thoughts to distant countries roam, when each refinement may be found at home?" Ironically, because Tyler's only acquaintance with theater was the English drama he saw in early 1787 in New York, his play is heavily imitative of English Restoration drama. The play's one significant innovation is its introduction of the rustic Yankee character, Jonathan, whose naïveté, though the source of broad comic satire, nevertheless endears him to the audience, which prefers his simplicity to European pretense. This character, a staple in many American plays for a half-century thereafter, is also a precursor to an emblematic figure in American culture, the homespun country philosopher of which later stage and screen personalities such as Will Rogers and Andy Griffith are examples.

As the play opens, Charlotte and Letitia, frivolous, gossipy slaves to fashion, discuss their friend Maria van Rough, who is betrothed to Billy Dimple. Dimple has just returned from England where he has gone to acquire the manners of a gentleman. During his absence, Maria has read widely, and "as her taste improved, her love declined." Further inciting Maria's contempt for her betrothed, England's polish has turned Dimple from a "ruddy youth" to a fop and a cad. Through their asides to the audience, Charlotte and Letitia each reveal a secret attachment to Dimple, who is deceiving not only Maria but also both of these young women.

Meanwhile, Charlotte's brother, the relentlessly grave Colonel Manly, appears. Manly fought in the Revolution and calls his comrades-in-arms his "family." He has none of the European style and none of its small talk, a source of some dismay to his stylish sister. Though Tyler favors the American mentality, his portrayal of the humorless Manly is not without satire. Manly is the perfect match for the serious and sincere Maria; indeed, they are instantly drawn to one another when they meet. In the style of the British drawing room farce, secrets are revealed to characters listening behind doors. Thus, Dimple is revealed for the duplicitous cad that he is, freeing Maria and Colonel Manly to marry.

In a subplot involving the servants of Manly and Dimple, the rustic Yankee servant to Manly (who claims he is not a servant but a "waiter"), Jonathan, is mocked by Dimple's more worldly servant. Dimple's manservant, Jessamy, convinces Jonathan that kisses will be well received by the maid on first acquaintance, which they are not. Jonathan naively describes an evening at the theater: "[T]hey lifted up a great green cloth, and let us look right into the next neighbour's house." Certainly, Tyler is satirizing the naive country bumpkin, along with the notion that in America there are no social classes; however, Jonathan is more affectionately drawn than the contemptuous servants who try to trick him. In the end, it is the essentially American Manly who gets the girl and has the last word: "I have learned that probity, virtue, honour, though they should not have received the polish of Europe, will secure to an honest American the good graces of his fair countrywoman, and, I hope, the applause of THE PUBLIC."

BIBLIOGRAPHY

Kierner, Cynthia, A., ed. *"The Contrast": Manners, Morals, and Authority in the Early American Republic.* New York: New York University Press, 2007.

COOK, GEORGE CRAM "JIG" (1873–1924)

Born in Davenport, Iowa, George Cram "Jig" Cook was educated at Harvard University and the University of Geneva. A novelist, poet, playwright, and director, Cook is best known as the founder, along with his wife, playwright SUSAN GLASPELL, of the PROVINCETOWN PLAYERS.

With Glaspell, Jig Cook collaborated on SUPPRESSED DESIRES (1915), a satire on Freudian analysis, which the couple submitted to the then recently founded WASHINGTON SQUARE PLAYERS. When the play was rejected, Cook and Glaspell staged a reading of it for friends in their Greenwich Village living room; and, in the summer of 1915 in Provincetown, it was informally staged, along with Neith Boyce's *Constancy,* at the seaside home of Boyce and her husband, journalist Hutchins Hapgood. The evening was a success, and Cook decided to present two other one-act plays in a converted fish-house on Lewis Wharf in Provincetown. These plays, presented in early September, were his own *Change Your Style,* a satire on schools of art, and Wilbur Daniel Steele's *Contemporaries.* Thus, the Provincetown Players were born.

Jig Cook was a charismatic figure whose greatest talent lay in inspiring and fostering the talent of others, though he participated in every area of production—writing, acting, directing, scenic and lighting design—as did all members of the Provincetown Players theater collective. It was he who provided the impetus to continue the theater group beyond a summer's passing entertainment. Susan Glaspell quotes her husband in her 1926 memoir *The Road to the Temple* as having said on the subject: "[W]hy not write our own plays and put them on ourselves giving writer, actor, designer, a chance to work together without the commercial thing imposed from without? A whole community working together, developing unsuspected talents" (251–252). Indeed, throughout his tenure with the Provincetown Players, Cook's vision was for an anticommercial theater community for current American playwrights; initially, the Provincetown Players did not even permit reviewers to attend their plays. When others within the group wished to move in the direction of the greater professionalism that would make their theater more commercially successful, Cook broke with the group.

After two summers on Cape Cod, the Provincetown Players established themselves in New York City. In November of 1916, the Players opened at the Playwrights' Theatre on Macdougal Street in Greenwich Village. In that first winter season, they performed four one-act plays by EUGENE O'NEILL and two one-acts by Glaspell, along with several others. In six seasons in New York, the group produced 97 plays by 47 American writers. Most of these plays—even early plays by O'Neill—would probably never have been produced in a theater that depended on commercial success, and Cook was instrumental in keeping the Provincetown a theater in which artistry outweighed commercial considerations.

Cook and Glaspell met O'Neill in the summer of 1916 when he submitted to them the one-act *Bound East for Cardiff,* which was presented in Provincetown that summer, as was another O'Neill one-act, *Thirst.* According to his biographer, Robert Károly Sarlós, Cook's "effect upon the work of O'Neill is both too pervasive and too subtle to be documented point by point" (52). Cook directed the first production of O'Neill's highly successful *The EMPEROR JONES* (1920); he insisted, against the objections of virtually the entire group, on creating an innovative dome set in order to achieve the lighting effects that he and O'Neill envisioned. Ironically, it was the overwhelming success of *The Emperor Jones* that took the group in a direction that Cook vehemently opposed: toward professional, commercial theater, which he found to be at odds with the creative process. In 1921, Cook moved to Greece, where he died in 1924, having disbanded the original Provincetown Players in 1922.

Cook's other plays produced by the Provincetown Players are *The Athenian Women* (1918), a serious treatment of the subject of Aristophanes's comedy *Lysistrata; Spring* (1921), an unsuccessful play about psychic phenomena; and, with Glaspell, *Tickless Time* (1919), a comment on the enslavement of modern man to the clock.

BIBLIOGRAPHY

Cook, George Cram. *Greek Coins.* New York: George H. Doran, 1925.

Glaspell, Susan. *The Road to the Temple.* New York: Frederick A. Stokes, 1927.

Sarlós, Robert Károly. *Jig Cook and the Provincetown Players: Theatre in Ferment.* Amherst: University of Massachusetts Press, 1982.

COUNTRY GIRL, THE CLIFFORD ODETS (1950)

Georgie Elgin, the title character of ODETS's *The Country Girl,* is the self-sacrificing, self-effacing wife of an aging actor, who was once a star. Though she comes close to leaving him several times, Georgie ultimately puts her own needs second to those of her alcoholic husband.

Frank Elgin was once an "important actor," but alcohol and insecurity have ruined his career. Now 50, he is asked to read for a part after the lead actor departs unexpectedly for Hollywood. Bernie Dodd, a young director, remembers Frank from when he was a great actor and convinces him to take the part. In rehearsal, Frank has trouble remembering his lines. To obtain Bernie's sympathy, Frank tells him that after a blissful early marriage, Georgie became a drunk, opposed his career, and tried to slit her wrists. When they lost their only child, he started drinking and she stopped.

The play is to open first in Boston; Frank's dress rehearsal there goes badly. He privately complains to Georgie about his understudy's proximity during rehearsals, about his need for a dresser to achieve some of the rapid scene changes, and about his salary; to Bernie, however, he does not complain, even denying that he is in any way dissatisfied. When Georgie conveys Frank's dissatisfaction to the young director, she reinforces Bernie's low opinion of her. Bernie believes she is out for herself and says to her, "Lady, you ride that man like a broom: you're a bitch!"

The show opens in Boston to good reviews, but Frank has a cold and begins drinking cough syrup that is 20 percent alcohol. Bernie and Georgie are at odds because Bernie believes she hinders Frank's progress toward success; he is completely taken in by Frank's false front. Frank is found sleeping off a drunk the next afternoon in his dressing room. The confrontation that this discovery provokes between Georgie and Bernie reveals that the stories Frank has told about Georgie are either his own frailties projected onto her—she has never attempted suicide, although *he* has—or are lines from a play in which he once starred. In an intense moment of anger on her part and entreaty (for her help with Frank) on Bernie's, Bernie kisses her. She tells him not to get any ideas, but she agrees to stay and help Frank.

Five weeks later in a New York theater, Georgie listens to Frank's opening-night performance as she waits in his dressing room. When Bernie joins her there, he tells her he is in love with her and demands to know if she will leave Frank. Meanwhile, on stage, Frank has gone "wild": In character, he has changed lines and struck his young costar. The audience thinks this is merely exceptional, realistic acting. Frank will make a comeback, and Georgie—though she may love Bernie and, at least, yearns for happiness—will remain with and emotionally support her unstable husband because—as Bernie tells her—she is "steadfast" and "loyal" and "reliable."

The play differs from some of Odets's other works, notably *WAITING FOR LEFTY* and *AWAKE AND SING!*, in that it has no larger social implication. However, it does deal with a theme common to Odets's work: maintaining personal integrity in the face of hardship, in this case posed not by a harsh society but by a deeply flawed spouse.

CRAIG'S WIFE GEORGE KELLY (1925)

The PULITZER PRIZE–winning *Craig's Wife* portrays the emotionally barren, meticulously orderly Harriet Craig and the members of her household, all of whom she ultimately alienates. Harriet Craig has come to represent a type of middle-class American woman, a type criticized elsewhere in American literature. (A more recent example is the exacting perfectionist Beth Jarrett in Judith Guest's 1976 novel, *Ordinary People*.)

Craig's Wife takes place in the Craigs' living room, which "*reflects the very excellent taste and fanatical orderliness of*" Mrs. Craig. Mrs. Craig returns from Albany, New York, where she has been visiting her sister who is seriously ill. With her is her niece, Edith. Harriet Craig's neurotic need to keep her house immaculate soon becomes apparent. She is sure that too much use of the staircase will ruin it; she scolds her husband for leaning "against the piano" as he "might scratch it"; the maids report that she cleans after them; and they fear reprisals if a newspaper is left out. Finding a bouquet of beautiful roses on her piano, Mrs. Craig orders the maid to remove them because "the petals'll be all over the room." The antithesis of Mrs. Craig is her neighbor, Mrs. Frazier, who has brought the roses as a gift for Mr. Craig's aunt, Miss Austen. Mrs. Frazier, a widow, grows masses of roses in honor of her late husband, an avid gardener himself. Harriet Craig is appalled that a neighbor has

even come to visit; she assumes Mrs. Frazier must have ulterior motives since she, herself, makes only calculated moves. But Mrs. Frazier, unlike Mrs. Craig, is a sentimental, friendly, generous woman, whose nature is symbolized by the roses she grows and gives away in abundance.

Miss Austen sees Harriet for what she is and dislikes her. She decides to leave her nephew's unhappy household, but not before she opens his eyes to the damage his wife has done to his social life and his career over their two-year marriage. In warning Walter about her, Miss Austen refers to Harriet's "ridiculous idolatry of house furnishings." She points out to Walter that none of his friends has come to visit him in 18 months; Harriet has scared them off: "Your friends resent being told where they shall sit and how." Miss Austen also reveals to him that Harriet's rudeness to the wife of an influential man cost him a seat on the board of directors of a bank. Walter is reluctant to accept fully his aunt's criticism of his wife.

Meanwhile, in the papers on the day of Mrs. Craig's return from Albany is a news story about a "socially prominent" couple, Mr. and Mrs. Passmore. They have been found dead in their home, an apparent murder. When it comes to Mrs. Craig's attention that her husband was at the Passmore's playing poker the night before, she insists that he say nothing to the police because it will associate their name with a scandal. Walter Craig disagrees with her; he believes the best course is to be open with the police about his recent whereabouts. An argument ensues during which Aunt Austen's view of Harriet is borne out. The police solve the murder before needing to speak to Walter, but not before he has seen his wife as she really is: arrogant enough to think she should control every aspect of every person in her household and selfish enough to exclude those she cannot control. The act ends with Walter asserting himself by smashing a mantlepiece ornament of particular importance to his wife and lighting up a cigarette in her pristine living room, after he has been expressly forbidden to do so.

In the end, Walter, his Aunt Austen, Edith, and even the housekeeper leave Harriet utterly alone amidst the orderliness that has meant so much to her. She receives a telegram with news of her sister's death.

As the curtain falls, she stands "clutching" an armful of white roses, left by the neighbor, "her eyes wide and despairing," with "scattered petals" on the floor.

There is some attempt on KELLY's part to ascribe motivation to Harriet's behavior—a stepmother under whose dominance she lived until she could move in with a married sister—suggesting that given the social position of women at the time, marriage was often the only way to gain any power, if only over a household. However, Harriet does not have any good qualities that might redeem her and make her seem more human and less of a caricature. Thematically, the play is simple and is summed up in Kelly's epigraph from Jane Austen: "People who live to themselves, Harriet, are generally left to themselves" (Adler 11).

BIBLIOGRAPHY
Adler, Thomas P. *Mirror on the Stage: The Pulitzer Plays as an Approach to American Drama.* West Lafayette, Ind.: Purdue University Press, 1987.

CRIMES OF THE HEART BETH HENLEY (1979)

Set in a small town in Mississippi over a two-day period, this funny and touching winner of the PULITZER PRIZE involves three sisters who overcome the past and learn to appreciate the moments of happiness they find in the present.

The play begins on Lenny MaGrath's 30th birthday, but no one remembers, except Lenny's officious and critical cousin Chick, because Babe MaGrath is in jail for shooting her husband, Zachary. Babe, whose real name is Rebecca, is the youngest MaGrath sister and is as childlike as her name would suggest. Babe is soon released on bail and will tell Lenny only that she shot Zachary because she "didn't like the way he looked." Lenny notifies their sister, Meg, an aspiring singer who lives in Hollywood, of the crisis so she can come home.

The three sisters have suffered from the loss of their parents. Their father—"such a bastard," according to Meg—deserted the family, and while the girls were still children, their mother hanged herself in the basement along with her cat. The story got national coverage because of the cat. The MaGrath sisters lived with their grandparents, and Lenny lives with "Old Granddaddy" in his house even now, though he is in the hospital at the moment.

During the course of the two days (or just prior to it, in Babe's case), each sister manages to wrest herself from some controlling influence. Babe breaks free from an unhappy marriage to a domineering husband by having a taboo affair with an African-American teenager and by wounding her husband when he chases the young man away; there is no doubt that Babe's solution to her problem is rash, yet as the character is drawn by Henley, Babe seems less rash than naive and comically endearing. For years, Lenny has been under the thumb of Old Granddaddy and, at the same time, his caretaker, sleeping in the kitchen on a cot so that she can hear him in the night. Old Granddaddy has convinced her that no man will want her because she has a "shrunken ovary." Lenny finally asserts her freedom from family domination when she chases her bossy and condescending cousin Chick from the house. She is then able to call Charlie, the one suitor she has ever had, and ask him if it matters to him that she cannot have children; when he assures her he does not even care for children, they arrange to resume their courtship. Even Meg, who is perceived by the town as having been *too free*—a wild teenager who turned into a loose woman—overcomes what controls her: the vision of her mother hanging from the ceiling. It was Meg who found the body, and it was Meg who, after the suicide, would pore over grotesque pictures in books about disease to toughen herself so that she could "take it." This effort to make herself tough cost her the ability to love and to accept love. When she meets Doc, her old boyfriend (now a married man with children), she wants to run away with him, but this time he does not want to run off with her. She tells her sisters, "I should be humiliated. . . . Maybe these feelings are coming. . . . But for now. . . . I'm happy. I realized I could care for someone. I could want someone."

At the end of the play, as so often in life, there is little definite resolution, only possibilities. Lenny may find happiness with Charlie. Meg may go back to singing. Babe will not go to jail because her lawyer has reached a settlement with Zachary in exchange for keeping certain corruption charges from the papers, but whether she will find romance with the young lawyer, as is implied, is not certain. The final tableau is of the three sisters enjoying a moment of laughter together "over nothing" around Lenny's belated birthday cake.

BETH HENLEY submitted *Crimes of the Heart,* her first full-length play, to the HUMANA FESTIVAL at the Actors Theatre of Louisville; it premiered there in 1979. It premiered in New York OFF-BROADWAY in 1980, later moving to Broadway and winning the New York Drama Critics' Circle Award, as well as the Pulitzer Prize. Henley's eccentric characters have been compared to those of southern authors Eudora Welty and Flannery O'Connor and of playwright LANFORD WILSON. Feminists have praised the play because the sisters—particularly Babe and Lenny who break away from domineering men, Zachary and Old Granddaddy, respectively—are able to find strength and joy in themselves and in each other.

CROTHERS, RACHEL (1878–1958)   Born in Bloomington, Illinois, Rachel Crothers graduated from the New England School of Dramatic Instruction in 1892 and the Stanhope-Wheatcroft School of Acting in New York in 1897. She taught elocution in Illinois and acting in New York until 1901. Her first successful play, *The Three of Us,* was produced in 1906.

Rachel Crothers was the most successful American woman playwright during the first three decades of the 20th century, as well as a highly respected director. Like her contemporaries, EDWARD SHELDON among them, Crothers was influenced by Henrik Ibsen, whose plays about social problems were seen in America in the early 20th century. Her play *A Man's World* (1910) effectively examines the double standard of morality for men and women; it is about a career woman and single mother of an adopted child who rejects her suitor when he refuses to take responsibility for his illegitimate child. Critics at the time compared elements of the play to Ibsen's *A Doll's House.*

Many of Crothers's dramas focus on the choices facing women as more opportunities open to them and as moral standards shift. Very often her solutions were rather traditional, with female characters choosing family over career, rather than somehow combining both, which was virtually unimagined then. However, her examination of problems peculiar to women—the double standard, the career versus fam-

ily struggle, the potential for loneliness in choosing career over marriage and yet the emptiness of many marriages—was in itself progressive.

Crothers wrote more than 30 works for the stage. Her other successes included *HE AND SHE* (1911), *Old Lady 31* (1916), *Expressing Willie* (1924), *Let Us Be Gay* (1929), *As Husbands Go* (1931), *When Ladies Meet* (1932), and *SUSAN AND GOD* (1937). All were treatments of women's lives, which mixed the serious and the comic.

Crothers never married, choosing instead a lifelong career in the theater. In addition to writing, directing, and sometimes producing and designing, she was involved in organizations dedicated to war relief during both world wars and to helping those in need during the depression. In 1939, she was instrumental in founding the American Theatre Wing, which during World War II was primarily a service organization. After the war, the organization began to hold seminars on all facets of theater. In 1947, the American Theatre Wing's TONY AWARDS were established to honor excellence in theater.

BIBLIOGRAPHY
Gottlieb, Lola C. *Rachel Crothers.* New York: Twayne, 1979.
Quinn, Arthur Hobson. "Rachel Crothers and the Feminine Criticism of Life." *A History of the American Drama from the Civil War to the Present Day.* Vol. 2. Rev. ed. New York: Appleton-Century-Crofts, 1955. 50–61.

CROWLEY, MART (1935–   )   Mart Crowley is best known for his 1968 breakout hit *The BOYS IN THE BAND.* The play—which openly portrays gay characters and gay lifestyles on stage with no apology—was the first of its kind to be successfully produced for the American stage. That is, the characters in *The Boys in the Band* (a group of friends at a birthday party that goes terribly wrong) do not function on the periphery of society, constantly moving between public and private worlds, but are the center of their world in ways that were both liberating and challenging to the Broadway audiences of 1968. Crowley went on to be awarded the first Los Angeles Drama Critics Award for *The Boys in the Band* in 1969.

Crowley was born in Vicksburg, Mississippi, where his father owned a tavern and poolroom, while his mother suffered from mental illness and spent much of her later life in and out of institutions. Very little is known of Crowley's early years as an only child growing up in a strict Catholic, middle-class family in the South; what is known, however, can be found in some thinly veiled autobiographical moments in several of his plays, particularly *A Breeze from the Gulf* (1973). The latter is based on his life with his parents in Mississippi and takes the form of a memory play that calls to mind TENNESSEE WILLIAMS's *The GLASS MENAGERIE*. It is an exploration of growing up in an isolated family ruled by a devout Catholic and alcoholic father and an overattentive and micromanaging mother. While the play was not reviewed as favorably as *The Boys in the Band*, it was considered moderately successful in New York.

After *A Breeze from the Gulf*, Crowley continued to work in the theater as a playwright, as well as working as a screenwriter and as the executive producer for the television series *Hart to Hart*. In 1981, he received the Arts and Entertainment Alumni Achievement Award from the Catholic University of America for his work in theater, film, and television. In 1993, his play *For Reasons That Remain Unclear* premiered at the Olney Theater in Olney, Maryland. In the play, the protagonist, Patrick, confronts the priest who sexually molested him when he was a young boy. In the preface to *Three Plays*, Crowley states that the play "was the way I dreamt I'd exorcise my demons. And by finally being able to consider what happened and invent a way to put it down, I think I accomplished that."

While Crowley has worked steadily and successfully in many facets of the entertainment industry, he will always be best known for *The Boys in the Band*. The play not only left a major imprint on the gay liberation movement in drama, but it also presents some of the most honest characters ever to grace the stages of the American theater. In 2002, *The Men from the Boys*, a sequel to Crowley's seminal play, premiered; in it, the *Band* friends meet at Larry's funeral.

BIBLIOGRAPHY

Crowley, Mart. *Three Plays: "The Boys in the Band," "A Breeze from the Gulf," "For Reasons That Remain Unclear."* Los Angeles: Alyson Publications, 1996.

Kathleen M. Gough
University of California–Berkeley

CRUCIBLE, THE ARTHUR MILLER (1953) Set in Salem, Massachusetts, in 1692 during the famous witch trials, MILLER's *The Crucible* examines the effects of a rigid moral system on a community as well as the dangers of self-serving individuals who prey upon the fears of such a community.

Caught dancing in the woods around a boiling kettle outside their Puritan town, a group of girls led by the manipulative Abigail Williams make up stories of witchcraft and coercion in order to avoid punishment. Abigail, who saw "Indians smash [her] dear parents' heads on the pillow next to" hers and who has been the lover of a married man, threatens and intimidates the other more naive girls when they are inclined to be honest with their elders. She begins by accusing marginal members of the community, the slave Tituba and the ragged and raving Sarah Good; she claims that she "saw" them "with the devil" and that Tituba is "always making [her] dream corruptions." Abigail Williams preys upon her Puritan community's greatest fear—the influence of Satan. When Abigail sees that she is believed, she gets caught up in the power she wields and in the attention she receives. Abigail and the girls lead the court, which believes they must be telling the truth since they are children, as they name those they have "seen with the devil." If the accused denies the charge of witchcraft, he is sentenced to hang; if he confesses, he will live.

Greed and vengeance motivate some of the accusers. Thomas Putnam, motivated by greed for the land of his neighbors, implicates others in order to gain their adjacent properties. Abigail names Elizabeth Proctor, for whom she once worked until Mrs. Proctor discovered that Abigail had committed adultery with her husband, John Proctor. When the court comes to arrest Elizabeth Proctor, Proctor protests: "Is the accuser always holy now? Were they born this morning as clean as God's fingers? I'll tell you what's walking Salem—vengeance. . . . the little crazy children are jangling the keys to the kingdom, and common vengeance writes the law!" When his wife is taken, Proctor finally goes to the court to expose Abigail, even though it will mean confessing his own sin of adultery—no small admission in a Puritan society. Ironically, Elizabeth, lying for the first time in her life, denies that her husband is an adulterer in an effort to protect him before she learns that he has already confessed. The efforts of John Proctor and others to speak the truth are seen by the court only as efforts to overthrow it. Both John and Elizabeth are imprisoned.

In the final act of the play, reports of "rotting crops," wandering orphans, and abandoned livestock testify to the chaos left in the wake of the trials. John Proctor is due to hang along with the saintly Rebecca Nurse and the good and frank Martha Corey. Abigail has run off after stealing money from her uncle, the Reverend Parris. The court, thus undermined, encourages John Proctor to confess so that he may live and, for their purposes, lend some credibility to their proceedings. At first, Proctor is persuaded when he sees, for the first time in months, his pregnant wife; however, when the court insists he name others who "conspired with [him] in the Devil's company," he refuses. When they insist that, at the very least, his confession be posted on the church door, he tears it up, refusing to "blacken" his friends' names and his own; he dies at the end of a rope, taking a stand that will finally undo the court.

Thematically, *The Crucible* is about the struggle of an individual against a corrupt system. It is also about the effect of a rigid ideology on the people who are governed by it—those who are victimized by it and those who use it to their advantage, as well as those who simply stand by without protesting. Miller saw his play as parallel to the events in the 1950s surrounding the House Un-American Activities Committee. Indeed, he wrote the play in response to those events. Miller himself refused to cooperate—to "name names" of those who might be connected with the Communist Party—at a time in American history when the word *communist* brought as visceral a response as the word *devil* did in 17th-century Salem.

The play is also about manipulative individuals who prey upon the fears of their communities for their own purposes. In this way, it is similar to LILLIAN HELLMAN's *The* CHILDREN'S HOUR*,* in which a manipulative child ruins the lives of her teachers by falsely accusing them of lesbianism in a homophobic community.

BIBLIOGRAPHY
Bloom, Harold, ed. *Modern Critical Interpretations: Arthur Miller's "The Crucible."* Philadelphia, Pa.: Chelsea House, 1999.
Dukore, Bernard F. *"Death of a Salesman" and "The Crucible": Text and Performance.* Atlantic Highlands, N.J.: Humanities Press International, 1989.
Ferres, John H., ed. *Twentieth-Century Interpretation of "The Crucible": A Collection of Critical Essays.* Englewood Cliffs, N.J.: Prentice-Hall, 1972.
Johnson, Claudia Durst, and Vernon E. Johnson, eds. *Understanding "The Crucible": A Student Casebook to Issues, Sources, and Historical Documents.* Westport, Conn.: Greenwood, 1998.
Martine, James J. *"The Crucible": Politics, Property, and Pretense.* Boston: Twayne, 1993.

CRUZ, NILO (1960–)

Born in Matanzas, Cuba, Nilo (pronounced "knee-low") Cruz left his native country in 1970 with his parents as part of the Cuban airlift that had begun during the Johnson administration in 1965 and was discontinued in 1973. His father, a resolutely anti-Castro shoe salesman, had been a political prisoner in the early 1960s. Cruz spent the second half of his childhood in Miami, and in 1982 at a Miami community college began to take classes with Cuban drama teacher Teresa María Rojas. When Rojas brought in Cuban-American playwright MARIA IRENE FORNÉS to teach a workshop in 1988, Fornés was so impressed by Cruz that she persuaded him to join the INTAR (International Arts Relations) Hispanic Playwrights in Residence Laboratory in New York City. Cruz cites Fornés as a major influence. Despite never having graduated from college, Cruz subsequently attended the graduate playwriting program at Brown University, where he studied with PAULA VOGEL. He has taught at Yale and Brown Universities and at the University of Iowa. Nilo Cruz's work has been developed and performed around the United States.

Cruz wrote his best-known play, ANNA IN THE TROPICS (2002), when he was playwright-in-residence at the New Theatre in Coral Gables, Florida, where the play premiered. When he won the PULITZER PRIZE in 2003 for *Anna,* remarkably, none of the Pulitzer judges had seen a production; it was awarded the prize on the basis of the text alone (the only other play to win the prize without having had a New York production was *The KENTUCKY CYCLE* by ROBERT SCHENKKAN in 1992). Several of the judges praised the play particularly for its ability to take them into a world and culture about which they had been unaware. *Anna in the Tropics* is set in a cigar factory, where a "lector" reads aloud to the workers, as was the custom in cigar factories in Cuba and Florida. The plot centers on the reading of Tolstoy's *Anna Karenina* and the effect it has upon the lives and relationships of the characters. The play's theme—the power of art and the imagination—is found in Cruz's earlier play, *Two Sisters and a Piano* (1998), in which an officer assigned to the case of artistic sisters under house arrest in Cuba becomes interested in one of them through her writing.

Cruz's other early plays include *Night Train to Bolina* (1994); *A Park in Our House* (published 1995; first produced 2000); *Dancing on Her Knees* (1996); *A Bicycle Country* (1999); and *Hortensia and the Museum of Dreams* (2001). *A Very Old Man With Enormous Wings* (2002) is an adaptation for children's theater of Gabriel Garcia Marquez's short story. *Lorca in a Green Dress* (2003), Cruz's first play after *Anna in the Tropics,* premiered in Ashland, Oregon; in it, the Spanish playwright Federico García Lorca, after his murder by fascists, is in Purgatory where he interacts with several versions of himself. In *Beauty of the Father* (2004), a bisexual artist-father and his muse, again the dead poet-playwright Lorca, are visited after years of estrangement by the artist's daughter; the daughter, at first unaware of the sexual complexities of her father's household, becomes involved with his male lover. Certainly, Cruz has a strong connection to Federico García Lorca, having also translated two of his plays, *Doña Rosita the Spinster* and *The House of Bernarda Alba,* prior to winning the Pulitzer Prize. In 2007, Cruz translated and adapted Pedro Calderón de la Barca's 400-year-old play *Life Is a Dream.*

Though his Cuban-American and Latino experience informs all his work, Cruz does not consider himself a political writer. He writes about the human condition rather than anything overtly political. Neither is Cruz compelled to speak from a gay sensibility: "Artists look at the world in a different way than other people—on the outside looking in, observing human behavior. I take that into consideration more than my sexuality or my gender" (Stevenson).

Cruz articulated his artistic aims during interviews after he won the Pulitzer Prize: "I want to document . . . what . . . Cubans and Latinos are trying to provide, our cultural gifts of art to the Anglo world. We have beautiful, powerful traditions. As a writer and a human being, I want to share them" (Anders 35). Cruz may, over his career, give voice to the Cuban-American and Latino experience as AUGUST WILSON gave voice to the African-American experience; these two lyrical playwrights share the ability to create work that is at once specific to a culture and universal.

BIBLIOGRAPHY

Anders, Gigi. "Work and All Play: Nilo Cruz's Play Wins the Pulitzer Prize Despite Great Odds." *Hispanic* (June 2003): 34–35.

Cruz, Nilo. *Anna in the Tropics.* New York: Theatre Communications Group, 2003.

———. *Beauty of the Father.* New York: Dramatists Play Service, 2007.

———. *Night Train to Bolina.* New York: Dramatists Play Service, 2005.

———. *"Two Sisters and a Piano" and Other Plays.* New York: Theatre Communications Group, 2007.

Stevenson, Bill. "Finding Nilo." *The Advocate* 9 (Dec. 2003): 79.

CURSE OF THE STARVING CLASS SAM SHEPARD (1977)

Set in Nevada, the play is one part of SHEPARD's trilogy (also including *BURIED CHILD* [1978] and *TRUE WEST* [1980]) dealing with dysfunctional families who seem doomed to failure from one generation to the next. *Curse of the Starving Class* won an OBIE AWARD.

Weston Tate is an alcoholic husband and father, a World War II veteran, who drinks himself into a stupor on a regular basis. The farm that he and his wife, Ella, live on is in disrepair; Weston is in debt for $15,000 and is hunted by debt collectors who will kill him if he does not pay. Part of his debt comes from being swindled into buying a piece of worthless desert land. Ella Tate, manipulative and slightly crazy (she warns her daughter that swimming during menstruation "can cause you to bleed to death"), secretly plans to sell the farm to Mr. Taylor, a real estate developer she believes will take her to Paris. In fact, Taylor is the same crook who swindled Weston, and he sleeps with Ella only to close the deal. Meanwhile, Weston has sold the farm himself for $15,000 to Ellis, a bar owner, who hopes to make it into a restaurant and perhaps a pitch-and-putt golf course.

In part, the "curse" Shepard refers to is a reference to the credit cards and commercialism that have led Weston into a burden of debt so great it will destroy him. Weston tells his son, "It's all plastic shuffling back and forth. . . . Why not go into debt for a few grand if all it is is numbers? . . . So I just went along with it, that's all." This consumerism, as well as the commercialism of people like Ellis and Taylor, has led the Tates away from a healthier existence connected to their land.

The "curse" is also, as Ella Tate puts it, something "in the cells and genes" and "tiny little swimming things making up their minds without us. Plotting in the womb." Ella says, "We inherit [the curse] and pass it on." Certainly, her children suffer from being raised in this chaotic household—whether that chaos is attributable to genetics or environment. Son Wesley is crude and insensitive enough to urinate in the kitchen on his sister's 4-H poster. Daughter Emma, after Ellis the bar owner buys the farm for a fraction of its worth, rides her horse through his bar and riddles the place with rifle bullets. Shepard's choice of the names Wesley and Emma, which are so close to the parents' names Weston and Ella, suggests that the children will be more like their parents than unlike them.

Weston asks his son if he recognizes his (the father's) poison, and when the son says yes the father is glad; he was not able to recognize his own father's poison until he was much older and only then "because he saw himself infected with it." At the end of the play, this poisoning of the next generation is evident when Wesley puts on Weston's filthy, discarded clothes and literally becomes his father— Shepard's pessimistic view of the inevitability of our embodiment of our parents' flaws.

While Ella visits Emma in jail, after Emma has shot up the bar, Weston is redeemed by reconnecting with his land. When he awakens from a drunken stupor, he walks his land; in his present condition—filthy, hungover—he does not "feel like the owner of a piece a' property as nice as this." Therefore, he goes back to the house and takes a piping hot and then an ice cold bath, shaves, and puts on clean clothes (having thrown out what he was wearing). Thus "reborn," Weston makes himself breakfast and gets to work on repairing the back door and doing the laundry. Weston may feel like "a whole new person now," but his renewal comes too late; the debt collectors are after him, and the $15,000 that could have paid off his debts has reverted back to Ellis for damages to his bar. Weston must flee to Mexico. His redemption is also too late to be of any use to his teenaged children. Young Wesley retrieves Weston's dirty clothes—"old bum's clothes" that have been "thrown-up in, pissed in"—from the trash barrel where Weston deposited them during his rebirth, puts them on, and thus becomes a symbol of how indelibly damaging his upbringing—genetic and environmental— has been. Wesley tells his sister, "I can feel him coming in and me going out." The boy is cursed to become like his father just because he "grew up here," but his sister will not stay. Having made "sexual overtures to the sergeant," she gets out of jail and comes back to the house; she tells her brother she is "going into crime" and leaves for good. There is a good chance, however, that she is blown up moments later in a car explosion meant for her father.

In addition to the destruction of children by their parents, Shepard's other theme deals with the American Dream and the irony in the fact that there are two competing forms of that dream that might be as easily distinguished as east from west. The reborn Tate wishes to reclaim perhaps the oldest form: making a living off one's own land out west. Taylor, the land developer, speaks of "building up this great land"—a refrain straight out of the American Dream—but his eastern, commercial land development schemes (and those of Ellis) are diametrically opposed to the western American Dream of working land of one's own. Before he becomes the degenerate version of his father, young Wesley says of the real estate developer's plan to buy his family farm: "[I]t means more than losing a house. It means losing a country."

CUSTIS, GEORGE WASHINGTON PARKE

(1781–1857) Since he was the adopted son of George Washington, raised at Mount Vernon after his father's death at Yorktown, it is hardly surprising that George Washington Parke Custis's work should sound a patriotic note. Though he wrote only a handful of plays and dramatic dialogues, Custis constantly returned to the theme of America's "destiny," creating historical plays that seemed to foretell America's greatness and thus lend legitimacy to the efforts of the fledgling nation. His first play, *The Indian Prophecy,* performed at the Chestnut Street Theatre in Philadelphia in 1827, recounts an episode from George Washington's life, in which an Indian reveals that he is fated to become the leader of a free and mighty nation. His *Pocahontas; or, the Settlers of Virginia,* first staged at the Walnut Street Theatre in Philadelphia in 1830, echoes the theme of America's inevitable triumph over an untamed land. The Indian chief Powhatan predicts in the play's final scene that "Looking thro' a long vista of futurity," there will come a "time when these wild regions shall become an honor'd part of a great and glorious American Empire." Indeed, the greatness of the "American Empire" echoes as a constant theme through Custis's other less well-known dramas, including *The Eighth of January; or, Hurrah for the Boys of the West* (1828), which celebrated Andrew Jackson's military triumphs and his candidacy for president; and *The Rail Road* (1830), which commemorated the opening of the Baltimore and Ohio Railroad Company.

Custis's writings appeared at an interesting moment in American theatrical history, when the stage was becoming an increasingly important political vehicle. The powerful performer Edwin Forrest was rapidly popularizing a new kind of hero—a rough and rugged self-made man, who embodied the democratic values of the Jacksonian era. His heroes offered a contrast to the more genteel models of masculinity that had dominated the American stage since ROYALL TYLER'S *The CONTRAST.* While Custis seems to have been a wholehearted supporter of Jackson's presidency, his plays represent an interesting middle ground in this transitional period. While they incorporate elements of national history to create uniquely "American" characters, they also present a more moderate (and more refined) hero than the ones beginning to dominate the stage with the advent of Edwin Forrest. Custis represents a point of view that is patriotic but perhaps ultimately hesitant to place the fate of the nation in the hands of the people, preferring instead to entrust it, as Powhatan says in *Pocahontas,* to those elite, "gifted with rare talents and the most exalted patriotism."

Heather Nathans
University of Maryland

D

DALY, (JOHN) AUGUSTIN (1838–1899)

Augustin Daly is credited with writing about six original plays and adapting more than 90 from Shakespeare, English comedies (the majority from the 18th century), and popular French and German plays of his day. The nebulous nature of Daly's sources and collaborations (most notably with his brother Joseph) makes it difficult to determine a more exact count of his work. Daly is best known for his sensational melodramas and contributions to social comedy, but his work is also significant for its modified realism, marking the transition in American drama from romanticism to the realism of the late 19th century.

A fortuitous move to New York City by his widowed mother in 1849 gave the young Daly the opportunity to learn about playwriting and theater management by seeing the works of the most prominent playwrights and producers on the New York stage. He frequently attended plays while a business clerk, and by 1859 had moved from being an audience member to writing articles, frequently on the theater, for the *New York Sunday Courier*. By 1869, he was the drama critic for five newspapers, including the *New York Sun* and the *New York Times*. During this period as a journalist and critic, Daly developed ideas that would later influence his dramatic writings: an attraction to romantic realism, a reliance on complicated plot structure and action rather than dialogue, and an appreciation for local settings and details.

Daly had his first success as a dramatist with *Leah the Forsaken* (1862), an adaptation of S. H. von Mosenthal's *Deborah*. This play, set in an 18th-century Austrian village, deals with the persecution of Jews, as Leah, a Jewish girl, learns to forgive her Christian lover, Rudolf, years after he has abandoned her to the law that drove her and other Jews out of Austria. Much of the play's effectiveness lies in the theatricality of the role of Leah and in Daly's use of melodramatic tableaux. *UNDER THE GASLIGHT* (1867) was the first original play by Daly to achieve a long run. A prime example of sensational melodrama, the complicated plot revolves around the obscure origins of the virtuous heroine Laura Courtland and the efforts by the scheming Byke to extort money from her family. While the plot stretches its believability too thin at times and the dialogue is stilted, this play is rich in its depiction of the New York underworld at the Tombs Police Court, set against the polite middle-class society of the Courtlands' Cottage at Long Branch. The play's most sensational scene demonstrates Daly's mastery of theatrical suspense and thrills: Laura has to smash her way out of a locked station building to save the helpful Snorkey, tied to the tracks by Byke, from the wheels of an oncoming train. The frontier drama *HORIZON* (1871) is perhaps Daly's best literary effort; in it, he sets the love interest of Captain Alleyn Van Dorp against the rough western backdrop of outcasts, a Vigilance Committee, and the threat of Indian raids. Its literary significance lies in Daly's treatment of the West as a subject for American national drama and his creation of Captain Van Dorp as a heroic national character.

Since his theatrical career was dominated by his role as a theater manager, it is no surprise that Augustin Daly's dramatic writings were created for performance. He was not a literary innovator, but he was a playwright/adapter who created works with topical audience appeal by mixing a moral, romantic atmosphere with exciting action and realistically detailed theatrical moments.

BIBLIOGRAPHY

Daly, Augustin. *"Man and Wife" and Other Plays by Augustin Daly*. Edited by Catherine Sturtevant. Bloomington: Indiana University Press, 1940.

———. *Plays by Augustin Daly*. Edited by Don B. Wilmeth and Rosemary Cullens. New York: Cambridge University Press, 1984.

Daly, Joseph Francis. *The Life of Augustin Daly*. New York: Macmillan, 1917.

Felheim, Marvin. *The Theater of Augustin Daly*. 1956. New York: Greenwood Press, 1969.

Jennifer Stiles
Boston College

DARK AT THE TOP OF THE STAIRS, THE WILLIAM INGE (1957)

Set in the 1920s in a tiny Oklahoma oil-boom town modeled after Independence, Kansas, INGE's hometown, *The Dark at the Top of the Stairs* focuses on the Floods, a family that bears a striking resemblance to Inge's own. Derived from personal psychoanalysis and a reworking of the first dramatic work he ever wrote, the play follows the four principal Floods as they confront their most fundamental fears. Like the young Inge, 10-year-old Sonny Flood is a piece-reciting "mama's boy" scorned by his male peers. Like his mother, Maude Inge, Cora Flood holds her son too closely, creating an Oedipal bond that negatively influences his social development. Like his father, Luther Inge, Rubin Flood is a traveling salesman who philanders on the road and worries that the changing times will leave him behind and unable to provide for his family. Like his sister, Helene Inge, Reenie Flood is a desperately shy wallflower. Indeed, all the Floods have fears deeply rooted in their sexual and family roles, fears symbolized by the dark Sonny sees at the top of the stairway leading to the Floods' bedrooms.

Inge's well-crafted plot features the resolution of these fears. For Cora, learning that her sister's apparently happy marriage is far from what it appears makes her more receptive to Rubin's apology when he returns after they have had a quarrel over money. For Rubin, whose viability as a traditional male breadwinner is crucial to his self-esteem, a willingness to apologize and admit his fears both to himself and to Cora brings a new dimension to their relationship. Her fight with Rubin and subsequent realization that she must find her own strengths cause Cora to tell Sonny that she cannot continually draw him close to her and always protect him from the taunts of his contemporaries. At the play's end, Sonny confronts his tormentors and accepts that he can no longer retreat to his mother's arms. For Reenie, whose need for a new party dress provoked Cora and Rubin's fight, the suicide of her blind date for the party causes her to realize that she must not feel sorry for herself and shrink away from others.

These neat resolutions in Inge's fourth consecutive successful play, which affirm conventional ideas about marriage and family relationships in small-town midwestern settings, caused some critics to suggest that his range was limited. Such criticism stung Inge, whose emotional equilibrium had long been fragile because prevailing 1950s attitudes about homosexuality forced him to conceal his sexuality from public scrutiny. Harsh criticism continued to haunt him and precipitated the decline of his career and his eventual suicide. *The Dark at the Top of the Stairs* features good dramatic roles and a tightly crafted plot. Aside from *My Son Is a Splendid Driver* (1971), a novel Inge published near the end of his life, it is his most autobiographical work.

Ralph F. Voss
University of Alabama

DARKNESS AT NOON SIDNEY KINGSLEY (1951)

KINGSLEY's most successful adaptation, *Darkness at Noon* is based on the 1941 novel by Arthur Koestler. The play won the New York Drama Critics'

Circle Award. In choosing to dramatize *Darkness at Noon,* Kingsley set himself a task unlike anything else that he had attempted in his other professional work—adapting what would seem to be the unpromising stage material of a novel based in thought and memory to create a play requiring stage action. His previous works had not prepared him for this task: multiple simultaneous storylines in DETECTIVE STORY (1949) requiring precise stage movement, boys jumping off a pier into a river built into the theater for DEAD END (1935), and the minutely choreographed surgical operation in MEN IN WHITE (1933) are examples of the physicality Kingsley built into other plays. *Darkness at Noon* did not lend itself to this physical approach; nevertheless, Kingsley found a way to dramatize the novel through the tapping the prisoners used to communicate from cell to cell. In fact, Kingsley limited himself more rigidly than did Koestler—in the play, scenes taking place outside the prison are rendered in memory only, unlike the novel. Another difference is in Rubashov's communications with the other prisoners: Allowed, for example, to talk in an exercise yard by Koestler, Rubashov is confined by Kingsley to tapping on the cell walls with the exception of two scenes, an inquisition and when a prisoner is dragged past his cell. Kingsley felt strongly about the novel's theme and saw in it a clear relationship to the concerns he expressed in some of his works, including *Detective Story,* which cautions against the rise of a police state.

Darkness at Noon is the story of N. S. Rubashov, a member of the Old Guard Bolsheviks, who finds himself out of step with the Leader (who never appears in the play) and the new generation of Soviets, represented by Gletkin. Imprisoned for his "political divergencies," Rubashov faces the ghosts of his past through flashbacks, acknowledges the debt he owes to many who suffered because of the way he served the Communist Party, and realizes that his inquisitor/torturer Gletkin and the younger generation of Soviets are in fact the natural offspring of Rubashov's own cruel ideology. The outcome is inevitable: Rubashov knows that he will be executed. What remains in question is the way in which he will go to that execution—remaining silent, recanting publicly whatever confession he has made under torture, or making a complete though false confession to serve the needs of the Party to which he has dedicated his entire life.

As with Kingsley's other plays, *Darkness at Noon* and its clear anticommunist sentiment had an impact beyond the theater. The play was broadcast on Voice of America to listeners in Eastern Europe, the Soviet Union, Latin America, and the Far East. Arthur Koestler benefited personally from the adaptation: Because of his Communist activities, he had been barred from residing in the United States; however, a bill was passed in Congress allowing him to take up permanent residency, in part on the strength of Kingsley's dramatic version of *Darkness at Noon.*

Nena Couch
Ohio State University

DAVIS, OWEN (1874–1956)

Born in Portland, Maine, playwright Owen Davis moved with his family to southern Kentucky in 1888. In 1889, he entered Harvard, where he studied science, played sports, and wrote a few plays in his spare time. He left Harvard without graduating and, after working briefly as a mining engineer in Kentucky, moved to New York, where he hoped to get his plays produced.

His first attempts to find a producer failed, and he worked for a while as an actor and backstage-hand on tour. Eventually, he began to write formulaic melodramas in order to earn money. When Davis was 25, his *Through the Breakers* (1899), the first of his lucrative thrillers, was produced. Over the next 20 years, Davis wrote scores of popular melodramas and became wealthy doing so. Typical of these thrillers was *Nellie: The Beautiful Cloak Model* (1906), in which Nellie is tied to the railroad tracks by the villain as the train approaches. The plays all contain life-threatening, visually exciting predicaments out of which the good emerge at the ultimate expense of the villains who put them there. Davis at times had so many productions touring simultaneously that he used several pseudonyms, including John Oliver, Arthur J. Lamb, Walter Lawrence, Martin Hurley, and Robert Wayne. Davis himself had no illusions that these popular potboilers were art; he described in his autobiography his plot formula and the emphasis on the visual over the written word that enabled him to churn these plays out with such speed.

Davis's reputation as a lowbrow writer made his transition to the legitimate Broadway stage difficult. Critics did not take him seriously, and his first attempts at more thoughtful drama failed. However, critical acclaim finally came with *The Detour* (1921), a social melodrama about a farm wife who dreams of helping her daughter to a better life in the city, a dream she, herself, had to abandon, and ICEBOUND (1923), for which Davis won the PULITZER PRIZE. In *Icebound,* the greedy Jordan family is aghast when their dying matriarch leaves the family money to her nursemaid and distant cousin Jane, in the hope that Jane will be able to reform Mrs. Jordan's problematic and favorite son through love.

After winning the Pulitzer Prize, Davis became the first president of the Dramatists Guild in 1923. He continued to write plays—more than 100 more, including comedies, dramas, and adaptations. These adaptations include *The Great Gatsby* (1926), based on F. Scott Fitzgerald's novel; *The Good Earth* (1932), based on Pearl S. Buck's novel; and *Ethan Frome* (1936), based on Edith Wharton's novel. He also wrote for the screen, turning his unsuccessful play *Jezebel* (1933) into the very successful film *Jezebel* (1938), starring Bette Davis.

Even if one sets aside the first 20 years of formulaic, moneymaking melodrama, there can be little doubt that Owen Davis was one of the most prolific stage writers in the history of American theater. Davis also wrote two autobiographies: *I'd Like to Do It Again* (1931) and *My First Fifty Years in the Theatre: The Plays, the Players, the Theatrical Managers and the Theatre Itself as One Man Saw Them in the Fifty Years between 1897 and 1947* (1950).

BIBLIOGRAPHY

Davis, Owen. *The Detour: A Play.* Boston: Little, Brown, 1922.
———. *Icebound: A Play.* Boston: Little, Brown, 1923.
———. *I'd Like to Do It Again.* New York: Farrar and Rinehart, 1931.
———. *My First Fifty Years in the Theatre: The Plays, the Players, the Theatrical Managers and the Theatre Itself as One Man Saw Them in the Fifty Years between 1897 and 1947.* Boston: Walter H. Baker, 1950.

DEAD END SIDNEY KINGSLEY (1935) The day after MEN IN WHITE (1933) closed on Broadway, KINGSLEY walked to a New York City wharf and watched children playing in the East River; the scene was juxtaposed against a luxury club, and the idea for his next play was born. With *Dead End,* Kingsley followed what had already become his trademark way of writing—exhaustively researching his subject. Again, Kingsley wrote a painfully realistic play, exploring the ways in which poverty and hopelessness can maim and twist people. He immersed himself in a study of slum neighborhoods and built his play with what he found: malnourished, mistreated, and uneducated children; juvenile delinquents; criminals, such as "Pretty Boy" Floyd and "Baby Face" Nelson; the gang mentality; the issues of raising children in a hostile environment; and questions about the efficacy of reformatories and prisons.

Dead End is set at the *"Dead End of a New York street, ending in a wharf over the East River."* At left is *"the back of* [an] *exclusive"* apartment building and *"filing up the street are . . . squalid tenement houses."* A gang of boys from the tenements, Tommy, Spit, Angel, Dippy, and T. B., contrast with Philip Griswald, who lives in the East River Terrace Apartments. Gangster "Baby Face" Martin, an eight-time murderer on the run from the police, represents the future for most of these boys, the ones who survive a childhood of malnourishment, mistreatment, and disease. Gimpty, whose childhood diseases included crippling rickets, grew up in the same environment, but he and his mother worked hard to support his studies. Nevertheless, he finds himself back in his old neighborhood, as an unemployed architect. He has fallen in love with Kay, the beautiful and kind mistress of wealthy Jack in the Terrace. Drina, also from the neighborhood, fights to keep her brother Tommy under control and for better working conditions. Gimpty emerges from his romantic dream to realize that "Baby Face" Martin will corrupt the boys beyond redemption. In the end, he turns Martin in to the authorities, intending to use the reward to help Tommy and Drina build a new life.

In his realistic approach to his subject, Kingsley incorporated profanity and graphic language into the boys' dialogue, which shocked some critics even though many accepted the need to adhere to reality. The main problem that critics found in the play was the weak romantic subplot between Gimpty and Kay. Yet, the impact of Kingsley's statement overwhelmed such minor considerations: The play was not only a Broadway success but also became a byword of many in society and government concerned with housing inadequacies and related problems as well as with societal inequalities. *Dead End* was cited by Eleanor Roosevelt when discussing housing issues and by journalists and legislators in print and in discussions that preceded the passage of the Wagner Housing Bill (S. 4424) by the United States Congress in 1936. The bill proposed the elimination of poor and unsafe housing in favor of safer and more sanitary dwellings for low-income families and also addressed unemployment issues.

Nena Couch
Ohio State University

DEATH OF A SALESMAN ARTHUR MILLER (1949)   Although it did not receive a universally positive response from New York reviewers when it opened on February 10, 1949, *Death of a Salesman* went on to win the PULITZER PRIZE, the New York Drama Critics' Circle Award, and the TONY AWARD. In the more than 50 years since its premiere, it has continued to elicit debate and controversy, but it also has become perhaps the best-known and most popular American play worldwide; and two very successful Broadway revivals within the past 25 years (in 1984, with Dustin Hoffman and John Malkovich, and in 1998, with Brian Dennehy and Elizabeth Franz), in addition to a much-publicized 1983 production in Beijing, among many others, have proven its enduring power to affect audiences.

On the surface, the play depicts the last two days in the life of Willy Loman, a 60-year-old over-the-hill traveling salesman, and his family—his wife Linda and their two sons Biff and Happy. But Miller has said that his first image in conceiving the play was "an enormous face the height of the proscenium arch which would appear and then open up, and we would see the inside of a man's head" (in fact, his first title for the play was "The Inside of His Head"); the concepts behind the play's structure are that "nothing in life comes 'next' but that everything exists together and at the same time within us" and that a human being "is his past at every moment" (Weales 155–156). Thus, while Willy and his family proceed through these final days, we also see scenes from their past, scenes that the playwright insists are not flashbacks but rather "a mobile concurrency of past and present" (Weales 158–159) and, as such, are representations of Willy's confusions, contradictions, and disorientations and of his inability to distinguish between "then and now."

The play opens as Willy returns to his Brooklyn home from a sales trip, which he had to cut short because "[t]he car kept going off onto the shoulder." When Linda tells him he should ask his boss to take him off the road and give him a job in New York, he replies, "I'm the New England man. I'm vital in New England." Their older son Biff has returned home after drifting around the country from job to job for the past 10 years; their younger son Happy, meanwhile, has a steady job, a car, an apartment, and all the girls he wants. On this day, they are back in the bedroom they shared growing up, worried about their father and admitting to one another that they would both like to find a nice girl and settle down. Biff decides to go the next day and ask businessman Bill Oliver, for whom he once worked, for a job. At this point, Willy's mind drifts back to a time when Biff was a high school football star promising to score a touchdown for his father in the big game, but, as that scene plays out, we also see Bernard, Biff's brainy classmate, trying unsuccessfully to get Biff to study. Willy tells his sons that, although Bernard gets "the best marks in school," the "man who makes an appearance in the business world, the man who creates personal interest, is the man who gets ahead. Be liked and you will never want." Willy has "knocked them dead" in New England because he is "well liked," and, as his family reassures him of this, he fleetingly thinks of The Woman he has seduced on the road because he was lonely. When his mind returns to Biff's senior year in high school, it turns out that Biff has stolen a football and is driving a car without a license; but Willy maintains, "There's nothing the matter with him! . . . He's got spirit, personality."

Back in the present, Willy's friend and next-door neighbor and Bernard's father, Charley, who is a successful businessman, enters and, hearing of Willy's aborted trip, offers him a job—to which Willy replies, "Don't insult me. I got a good job." During this scene, Willy thinks of his older brother Ben, who has recently died and who made a fortune in African diamond mines, and of their father, a flute-maker who took his family all over the country before abandoning them when Willy was very young. In the present, while Willy goes out for a walk, Linda chastises her sons for not being more attentive to their father, especially Biff, who always seems to quarrel with Willy: "He's not the finest character that ever lived. But he's a human being, and a terrible thing is happening to him. So attention must be paid." She tells them that Willy has been trying to kill himself by deliberately crashing his car and by attaching a rubber hose to the gas pipe. When Willy returns, Biff tells him that he's going to see Bill Oliver about a job; Willy, in turn, says he will see his boss about getting off the road.

Act 2 begins the next day with Willy and Linda full of hope for Biff's new start with Bill Oliver and for Willy's meeting with his boss, Howard. Linda tells him that his sons want to take him to dinner to celebrate after the two meetings. But when he goes to see Howard, the latter fires him, explaining, "there just is no spot here for you." Willy thinks of a moment in the past when he refused Ben's offer of a job in Alaska by saying, "The whole wealth of Alaska passes over the lunch table at the Commodore Hotel, and that's the wonder . . . of this country, that a man can end with diamonds here on the basis of being liked." In the present, Willy wanders into Charley's office, where he meets Bernard, now a successful lawyer, who asks Willy why Biff didn't go to summer school after he flunked math so that he could attend the University of Virginia on the football scholarship they had offered him. He recalls that Biff was ready to do this, but after Biff got back from visiting Willy in Boston, he burned his sneakers and, as Bernard explains, "I knew he'd

given up his life." He asks Willy what happened in Boston; Willy replies, "Nothing." When Charley again offers Willy a job, he again refuses: "I just can't work for you."

Happy and Biff arrive at the restaurant, and Biff tells his brother that, after waiting six hours to see Bill Oliver, the latter did not remember him, saw him for one minute, and had no job for him. "I realized," Biff says, "what a ridiculous lie my whole life has been!" He admits that, after Oliver left, he stole a fountain pen from his desk. Happy begs Biff not to tell Willy what happened, but when their father arrives, he tries to tell him the truth. Simultaneously, we see a scene from the past in which Bernard tells Willy that Biff has flunked math and then a scene in a Boston hotel room where Biff has gone to get his father to intercede with his teacher—"Because if he saw the kind of man you are, and you talked to him in your way, I'm sure he'd come through for me"—only to find Willy with The Woman. Back in the restaurant, Biff and Happy leave Willy to go off with two women Happy has found for them.

When Biff and Happy return home, Linda is furious with them for abandoning their father in the restaurant and kicks them both out of the house. Biff insists on one last conversation with his father, who is planting seeds in his backyard and having an imaginary conversation with Ben about killing himself so that Biff can collect his $20,000 life insurance policy. When Ben says that suicide would be cowardly, Willy replies, "Does it take more guts to stand here the rest of my life ringing up a zero?" and promises to give Biff "something and not have him hate me." Biff enters, puts the rubber hose he has detached from the gas pipe on the table, and tells his father, "I never got anywhere because you blew me so full of hot air I could never stand taking orders from anybody" and "I'm a dime a dozen and so are you!" When Willy responds, "I am not a dime a dozen! I am Willy Loman and you are Biff Loman!" Biff breaks down in tears and Willy says to Linda, "isn't that remarkable? Biff—he likes me. . . . that boy is going to be magnificent." Happy and Linda assure him that he's right; after they go to bed, Willy drives off in his car.

The play ends with a brief "Requiem," as Charley, Bernard, Linda, Biff, and Happy gather at Willy's grave. Biff says, "He had the wrong dreams." Happy declares that he's going to show everyone that Willy "had a great dream . . . to come out number one man" and that he's "gonna win it for him"; Linda can't understand why Willy killed himself just as she made the last payment on the house: "We're free."

A good deal of the critical wrangling about *Death of a Salesman* has centered on whether or not Willy Loman is a tragic figure or merely a pitiful man with the wrong dreams. He has been called a "loud-mouthed dolt and emotional babe-in-the-woods," a "poor, flashy, self-deceiving little man," and a schizophrenic (Weales xvi). Miller, in his essay "Tragedy and the Common Man," published shortly after the play opened and clearly intended as a statement about his intention in writing it, provided his own definition of tragedy, a definition that certainly does fit Willy: "I think the tragic feeling is evoked in us when we are in the presence of a character who is ready to lay down his life, if need be, to secure . . . his sense of personal dignity" (*Theater Essays 4*). By this standard, Willy surely is tragic; he gives up his life to maintain his sense of himself as a provider for a son who can be "magnificent."

The play has also been seen by many as an indictment of American capitalism and materialism. C. W. E. Bigsby articulates this view when he calls Willy "an ageing [sic] salesman, baffled by a lifetime of failure in a society which apparently values only success" and a distillation of "the anxieties of a culture which had exchanged an existential world of physical and moral possibility for the determinisms of modern commercial and industrial life" (174). We can find added support for this perspective in Willy's continual raging against the towering apartment buildings that surround his small house and against the lack of fresh air and of grass, as well as in the figure of Ben, who obviously represents the triumph of capitalism. Seen this way, *Death of a Salesman* belongs in the American dramatic tradition of EUGENE O'NEILL's *THE HAIRY APE* (1922), ELMER RICE's *The ADDING MACHINE* (1923), CLIFFORD ODETS's *AWAKE AND SING!* (1935), and other plays that criticize the dehumanization of American life.

But, ultimately, *Death of a Salesman* resists such easy categorization: Willy's problem is both personal and social. If his were simply a social and economic quandary, he would take the job Charley offers him; he cannot because to do so would be to falsify his own view of himself. On the other hand, to maintain that Willy's predicament is in no way related to the capitalist system in which the salesman epitomizes the American Dream of success (significantly, we never learn what Willy sells, because, in American culture, the salesman sells himself, not the product—hence Willy's reliance on being "well liked") is equally wrong. But that viewpoint is also complicated, as Miller and others have pointed out, by the fact that Charley, "the most decent man in the play," is also a capitalist "whose aims are not different from Willy's." But key here is Miller's explanation of what distinguishes Willy from Charley: Charley "is not a fanatic. . . . [H]e has learned to live without that frenzy, that ecstasy of spirit which Willy chases to his end" (*Theater Essays* 150).

It is that fanaticism, that frenzy, which, in Miller's eyes, makes Willy a tragic figure. Unlike Biff, whom many critics see as a classically tragic figure because he seems to have a moment of recognition about himself at the end of the play, Willy cannot have such a moment, because it would be antithetical to the playwright's perception of what makes him tragic. As Miller asserted in the introduction to his *Collected Plays* (1957), "the less capable a man is of walking away from the central conflict of the play, the closer he approaches a tragic existence. In turn, this implies that the closer a man approaches tragedy . . . the closer he approaches what in life we call fanaticism" (*Theater Essays* 118). Thus, when Bernard says to Willy, "sometimes . . . it's better just to walk away," Willy's reply, "But if you can't walk away?" makes him worthy of tragic stature.

BIBLIOGRAPHY

Bigsby, C. W. E. *A Critical Introduction to Twentieth-Century American Drama: Volume Two—Williams/Miller/Albee.* Cambridge, England: Cambridge University Press, 1984.

Bloom, Harold, ed. *Arthur Miller's "Death of a Salesman": Updated Edition.* New York: Chelsea House, 2007.

Dukore, Bernard F. *"Death of a Salesman" and "The Crucible": Text and Performance.* Atlantic Highlands, N.J.: Humanities Press International, 1989.

Harshbarger, Karl. *The Burning Jungle: An Analysis of Arthur Miller's "Death of a Salesman."* Washington, D.C.: University Press of America, 1978.

Hays, Peter L., with Kent Nicholson. *Arthur Miller's "Death of a Salesman."* New York: Continuum, 2008.

Hurrell, John D., ed. *Two Modern American Tragedies: Reviews and Criticisms of "Death of a Salesman" and "Streetcar Named Desire."* New York: Scribners, 1961.

Koon, Helene Wickham, ed. *Twentieth Century Interpretations of "Death of a Salesman": A Collection of Critical Essays.* Englewood Cliffs, N.J.: Prentice-Hall, 1983.

Marino, Stephen A., ed. *The Salesman Has a Birthday: Essays Celebrating the Fiftieth Anniversary of Arthur Miller's "Death of a Salesman."* Lanham, Md.: University Press of America, 2000.

Miller, Arthur. *"Salesman" in Beijing.* New York: Viking Press, 1984.

———. *The Theater Essays of Arthur Miller.* Rev. ed. Edited by Robert A. Martin and Steven R. Centola. New York: Da Capo, 1996.

Murphy, Brenda. *Miller: "Death of a Salesman."* Cambridge, England: Cambridge University Press, 1995.

Roudané, Matthew C., ed. *Approaches to Teaching "Death of a Salesman."* New York: Modern Language Association, 1995.

Sterling, Eric J., ed. *Arthur Miller's "Death of a Salesman."* Amsterdam/New York: Rodopi, 2008.

Weales, Gerald, ed. *Arthur Miller: "Death of a Salesman": Text and Criticism.* New York: Viking Press, 1967.

DEATH OF BESSIE SMITH, THE EDWARD ALBEE (1960)

The second of ALBEE's early one-act plays to be produced professionally, *The Death of Bessie Smith,* like its predecessor, *The ZOO STORY* (1959), was first presented in Berlin, Germany. It opened at the Schlosspark Theater on April 21, 1960; its New York premiere was not until January 24, 1961, at the York Playhouse. The play, according to Albee, originated when he was listening to a Bessie Smith record and read on the album cover how the legendary black blues singer had died: "the automobile accident outside of Memphis, her arm outside the window of the car, her arm almost cut off, how she was taken to a white hospital and was refused admission and died on the way to a second hospital" (Gussow 99). For his play, Albee invented the second hospital and the three central characters who work there. None are given names; two are white—the Nurse, who presides over the admissions room (where most of the play takes place), and her boyfriend, the Intern—while the third, the Orderly, is a "light-skinned Negro."

The play, which takes place in and around Memphis on September 26, 1937 (the day Bessie Smith died), unfolds in eight short scenes, three of which are very brief vignettes. We first meet the Nurse as she is bickering with her Father (also unnamed) while preparing to leave home for work. He complains about the "goddam nigger records" she plays at full volume, and she mocks him for hanging out at the local Democratic Club with "a bunch of loafers" and for bragging about his supposed friendship with the mayor. This scene is flanked by two others that introduce us to the only characters in the play who are named; significantly, and ironically, they are all black. We meet Jack, Bessie Smith's manager, who, in scene 3, is trying to rouse his unseen sleeping client so that they can drive to New York to cut a record. Jack tells Bessie that his friend Bernie, whom he has just met in a bar (the beginning of their encounter constitutes the first scene of the play), asked, "Whatever *happened* to Bessie?" If she doesn't get out of bed and on the road to New York to make the record, Jack tells her, "people are gonna stop askin' where you been." Scene 3 ends with the sounds of a car starting and *"moving off."*

Scene 4 finds the Nurse on duty in the admissions room with the Orderly, whom she contemptuously accuses of bleaching his skin. He denies this, but he tells her that he does not intend "to stay here carrying crap pans and washing out the operating theatre until I have . . . a long beard . . . I'm going beyond that"— and his vocabulary indicates that he is better educated than she is. The Nurse tells him he should consider himself lucky and "keep this good job you've got . . . just shut your ears . . . and keep that mouth closed tight, too."

A brief scene 5 shows a Second Nurse at another hospital bantering vapidly on the telephone with the Nurse we've already met. Their conversation is interrupted by the offstage sounds of a car crash and Jack's anguished cries and then resumes, only to be concluded when the Intern enters and the Nurse gets off the phone. In scene 6, the Intern flirts with the Nurse, and, clearly, she delights in keeping him interested while at the same time tormenting and teasing him by withholding sex. He asks her to marry him, but she refuses, noting that he makes only $46 a month: "You can't afford marriage. . . . Best you can afford is lust." The Intern admits that he longs "to get away from here," to help in the Spanish civil war. Their masochistic relationship is revealed further when she tells him that she still wants him to drive her home, and he bitterly complains of the "fifteen minutes or so" of "tantalizing preliminary love play ending in an infuriating and inconclusive wrestling match." When he blurts out that he is "probably the only white man under sixty in two counties" who has not had sex with her, she calls him a "no-account mother-grabbing son of a nigger" and vows to get him fired from the hospital. Meanwhile, though, she tells him, he will drive her home "*tonight* . . . and *tomorrow* night . . . you will *court* me, boy, and you will do it *right!*" To this, he can only reply, "You impress me. No matter what else, I've got to admit that."

In the brief scene 7, we see Jack rush into the other hospital (ironically named Mercy) and tell the Second Nurse that he has a badly injured Bessie Smith outside in the car, only to have her respond, "I DON'T CARE WHO YOU GOT OUT THERE. NIGGER. YOU COOL YOUR HEELS." The final scene returns us to the original hospital, where the Nurse is flirting with and tormenting both the Intern and the Orderly, ordering the former to get her some strong hot coffee with cream and sugar and telling the latter, "You and I are practically engaged." At that, the Orderly responds, "Really . . . you go much too far," and the Nurse suddenly bursts into the play's most important piece of dialogue, which begins, "I am sick of everything in this hot, stupid fly-ridden world." It includes a sentiment that many a later Albee character would echo: "I am tired of the truth . . . and I am tired of lying about the truth." At this moment, Jack "*plunges into the room,*" barely able to speak, but manages to say, "I've got someone outside." Both the Nurse and, significantly, the Orderly try to get him to leave, but when the Intern returns with the Nurse's coffee, he agrees to help and rushes out to the car—despite the Nurse's command, "DON'T GO OUT THERE!" When Jack

disjointedly tells her about the accident and the identity of the injured woman, her response is to tell him she will report him to the police for leaving the scene of an accident. The Intern returns and asks Jack, "when you brought this woman *here*. . . . DID YOU KNOW SHE WAS DEAD?" Jack replies that he did and exits, as the Intern asks him, "WHAT WAS I SUPPOSED TO DO?" Continuing her sarcastic taunts, the Nurse suggests that perhaps Jack expected "the great white doctor" to "bring her back to life," adding that she can sing just as well as the "dead nigger lady" and begins to sing and laugh simultaneously, although "*the laughter is almost crying.*" The Intern asks her to stop, and when she can't, he slaps her in the face and backs toward the door.

It is easy to see *The Death of Bessie Smith* as Albee's plea for racial justice and as a denunciation of racism in the South in the late 1950s, but the playwright has said that it is about "people trapped in the skin of their environment and people trapped in the environment of their skin" (Gussow 133). With this in mind, one can see that all three main characters are conflicted and yearn to escape their current existences. Although said in spiteful anger, there is considerable truth in what the Nurse says to the Orderly: "[Y]ou are now an inhabitant of no-man's land, on the one hand shunned and disowned by your brethren, and on the other an object of contempt and derision to your betters." The Nurse and the Intern are locked in a love-hate relationship that prefigures George and Martha's marriage in Albee's *WHO'S AFRAID OF VIRGINIA WOOLF?* (1962), as well as many of Albee's portrayals of male-female relationships. He feels "stranded" and would "like to get away from here," while she complains of the "disparity between things as they are, and as they should be" and utters a sentence that speaks for all three of them: "I WANT OUT!" As C. W. E. Bigsby observes, the play is best seen as "about individuals trapped in their own myths, condemned to act out their fictions to the point at which they are forced to deny their own humanity and desires" (260–261).

BIBLIOGRAPHY

Bigsby, C. W. E. *A Critical Introduction to Twentieth-Century American Drama: Volume Two—Williams/Miller/Albee.* Cambridge, England: Cambridge University Press, 1984.

Gussow, Mel. *Edward Albee: A Singular Journey.* New York: Simon and Schuster, 1999.

DELICATE BALANCE, A EDWARD ALBEE

(1966) *A Delicate Balance* won for ALBEE the PULIT-ZER PRIZE (the first of his three) that he had been denied four years earlier when the trustees of Columbia University reversed the decision made by the drama jury to give the award to WHO'S AFRAID OF VIR-GINIA WOOLF? (1962).

The play depicts a couple in their late fifties or early sixties, Agnes and Tobias, and Agnes's younger sister, Claire, an unreformed and unapologetic alcoholic who lives with them and who probably once had a relationship with Tobias that Agnes terminated. Some years before the action of the play, Agnes and Tobias's son, Teddy, died; their daughter, Julia, at 36, has had three unsuccessful marriages and has returned home after each. Agnes and Claire constantly snipe at one another, while Tobias tries to keep the peace and even serves drinks to Claire when Agnes is out of the room. Amidst all this, Agnes insists that "There are no mountains in my life . . . no chasms. It is a rolling pleasant land," and she and Tobias have adopted as their motto, "We do what we can." Early in the play, they learn that Julia's fourth marriage has collapsed and that she is coming home. Agnes urges Tobias to speak with Julia's husband and with Julia herself—to show her that "her father cares." Tobias says that he "might" do so, if he "saw some point to it" or if he thought he might "break through to her," but he does not know what he would say.

At this point, Tobias tells the story of his relationship with a cat he had as a young man. Through no fault of his that he could see, the cat withdrew her affection from him, and he began unsuccessfully to try to force the cat to like him again. When, in return, the cat bit him, Tobias hit her, feeling hatred because he had been "*betrayed*" and was being "judged." Ultimately, he has the cat "killed" by the vet; now he wonders whether he should have "tried longer . . . worn a hair shirt, locked myself in the house with her, done penance." This story, which recalls the very similar tale of Jerry and the dog from Albee's earlier play *The Zoo Story* (1960), foreshadows the action of the rest of

the play. As soon as Tobias finishes telling it, the door-bell rings, and Harry and Edna, Agnes and Tobias's best friends, enter and ask to stay. They explain that they were home alone and suddenly "were scared. It was like being lost: very young again, with the dark." After some initial consternation and confusion, Agnes and Tobias agree to let them spend the night in Julia's room.

Early the next evening, Julia has returned and is very upset that her room has been taken over by Harry and Edna, who have spent the entire day there without emerging (they've had their meals brought up by the maid). When they finally do come downstairs, they announce that they are going home—to get their things—and will be back shortly. The next evening, Julia chides her mother for her autocratic behavior at dinner, and Agnes replies, "I shall keep . . . this family in shape. I shall maintain it; hold it," adding, "There is a balance to be maintained, after all, though the rest of you teeter, unconcerned, or uncaring, *assuming* you're on level ground." When Harry and Edna return with their belongings, they begin to act very territorially, with Edna suggesting that Agnes have one of her chairs redecorated and scolding Julia for her marital "shenanigans." This simply makes Julia even more furious, and she screams, "I WANT WHAT IS MINE!!"—to which her mother replies, "Well, then, my dear, you will have to decide what that is, will you not." With that, Julia goes to her room, throws all of Harry and Edna's things on the floor, and returns with a pistol, which Tobias calmly takes from her. She demands that her father make Harry and Edna leave, but he will not. Edna tells them, "Friendship is something like a marriage; is it not . . .? For better and for worse?"—and she and Harry go up to bed.

The next morning, Agnes tells Tobias that it was "nice" to have him in her room for the night (they have not slept together for many years)—Julia having moved into his room—and that she could "get used" to his "unfamiliar presence" again. After first telling Tobias that it is an "illusion" that she makes all the decisions and that he must decide what to do, Agnes explains—in some of the play's most important dialogue—that they have been worrying about the "patient," rather than the "illness." She explains, "It is not Harry and Edna who have come to us," it is "a disease," the "plague," that they have brought with them. "If you are immune" to the disease, she says, "you treat the patient," but "if you are not immune, you risk infection." The implication is that they are not immune, that Harry and Edna in fact are their mirror images, and that Agnes and Tobias cannot "risk infection."

Harry asks to speak with Tobias alone. After Tobias assures him that "we can make it . . . if you want us to," Harry tells him that he and Edna have decided to leave because they've realized that, if the situation were reversed, they wouldn't have let Agnes and Tobias stay. In a rambling and sometimes almost hysterical response, which Albee's stage directions describe as *"an aria,"* Tobias concedes that, while "I DON'T WANT YOU HERE!" and "I DON'T LOVE YOU!," "BY CHRIST YOU'RE GOING TO STAY HERE! YOU'VE GOT THE RIGHT!"—and he pleads, "Stay? Please? Stay?" But Harry and Edna do leave, as Agnes says the lines that Albee regards as the most "crucial" in the play (Gussow 256): "Time happens, I suppose. To people. Everything becomes . . . too late finally."

Albee has said that *A Delicate Balance* is "concerned with the isolation of people who have turned their back on participating fully in their own lives and therefore cannot participate fully in anyone else's life" (Gussow 257); it is also about people who have lost the ability to make choices that would effect change in their lives (Bigsby 299; Kolin 92, 180). The title, he explains, refers to the "delicate balance" separating "what we should be doing and what we ultimately decide we need to do to protect ourselves" (Gussow 257).

The portrait of Agnes resembles Albee's mother (whom he would depict far more fully and directly in *THREE TALL WOMEN* [1994]), and Teddy is one of several absent, silent, or nonexistent sons in Albee's plays. However, the ending of *A Delicate Balance* is in marked contrast to that of *Who's Afraid of Virginia Woolf?*. In the latter, George and Martha at least have the hope that, with their illusory son destroyed, they may be able to face the next day changed for the better; here, Tobias's taking a stand occurs, significantly, only after Harry has told him of their decision to leave. Agnes

has already made it clear *why* they must leave—because her family, with the exception of Claire, who, as "walking wounded," probably is immune, is decidedly not immune to the terror Harry and Edna have brought. Ironically, their leaving robs Tobias of his final opportunity to act and to be effectual, and his realization of that fact accounts for the manic nature of his long speech at the end of the play.

BIBLIOGRAPHY

Bigsby, C. W. E. *A Critical Introduction to Twentieth-Century American Drama: Volume Two—Williams/Miller/Albee.* Cambridge, England: Cambridge University Press, 1984.

Gussow, Mel. *Edward Albee: A Singular Journey.* New York: Simon and Schuster, 1999.

Kolin, Philip C., ed. *Conversations with Edward Albee.* Jackson: University Press of Mississippi, 1988.

DESIRE UNDER THE ELMS EUGENE O'NEILL (1924)

O'NEILL'S early plays were largely realistic depictions of essentially simple and, in some cases, not very articulate sailors, farmers, prostitutes, and other characters of humble origins. In the early 1920s, with plays like *The EMPEROR JONES* (1920) and *The HAIRY APE* (1922), he began to experiment with dramatic form in order to delve more deeply into the backgrounds and psyches of his characters, using such innovative theatrical techniques as EXPRESSIONISM. In *Desire under the Elms,* he combined the realistic surface and superficially simple characters of his early plays with the more ambitious aims of his late work to produce a folk drama about a family on a run-down mid-19th-century New England farm, with echoes of classical myth, Greek tragedy, Nietzschean philosophy, and Freudian psychology. These elements considerably increase the power of the work.

Desire under the Elms takes place "in, and immediately outside of" the Cabot farmhouse, over which two large elm trees "brood oppressively." They are, according to O'Neill's stage directions, "like exhausted women resting their sagging breasts and hands and hair" on the house's roof. As the play begins, Ephraim Cabot, the farm's 75-year-old owner, has been gone for two months and his three sons—Simon and Peter, by his first wife, and Eben, by his second—are speculating on his whereabouts. The last time he left was 30 years ago to marry Eben's mother; this time, Eben blurts out, much to his half brothers' surprise, "I pray he's dead." Eben has never forgiven his father for working his mother to death and his half-brothers for doing nothing to save her; Simon and Peter feel that Ephraim is working them all too hard, and they yearn to go to California, where "they'd be lumps o'gold" in the ground. Eben tells them they'll never go to California because, if they did, they would forfeit their rights to inherit two-thirds of the farm; he believes that the farm belonged to his mother, whom he thinks still haunts it, and should be his after Ephraim's death.

Eben returns after visiting Min, the town prostitute, with the news that Ephraim has married a 35-year-old woman, and he offers to buy their share of the farm with money he will steal from his father's secret hiding place—which he has heard about from his mother. After some hesitation, Simon and Peter, who assume that, with this new woman in the picture, they will never inherit anything, agree to Eben's offer and leave for California as Ephraim arrives with his new bride.

Abbie Putnam is *"buxom"* and *"full of vitality"* and has *"about her whole personality the same unsettled, untamed, desperate quality which is so apparent in Eben."* She immediately begins speaking of the farm as hers, but Ephraim makes clear that it's "our'n" and cautions her not to assert her ownership to Eben, who, while *"physically attracted"* to her, is outraged that his father has bartered away the farm for her youth and beauty— and she freely admits to him that the farm was the only reason she married Ephraim.

Two months later, Abbie seductively tells Eben that, despite his hostility to her, they both know that he has been attracted to her ever since she arrived. He vehemently denies this and defiantly goes off to visit Min, who, he tells Abbie, is "better 'n yew" because she "owns up fa'r 'n' squar' t' her doins's." When Ephraim informs her that he's not leaving the farm to Eben or her or anyone, she asks him, if "the Lord" gave them a son, "Would ye will the farm . . . t' me an' it"—to which he responds that, in that event, "I'd do anythin' ye axed." Later that night, Abbie promises Ephraim that they will have a son, but she repulses

his advances and he retreats to the barn, where "I kin talk t' the cows. They know the farm and me."

Abbie then goes into Eben's room and kisses him; at first submitting, he then tells her he hates her. She brazenly tells him, "I on'y wanted yew for a purpose o' my own—an' I'll have ye fur it yet 'cause I'm stronger'n yew be!" and invites him to "court" her in the parlor, which has been closed since his mother's death. In the parlor, Eben tells Abbie that the farm was really his mother's, and she asks him to kiss her, "Same's if I was a Maw t' ye," assuring him that his mother wants him to love her. Declaring that "It's her vengeance on him—so she kin rest quiet in her grave," Eben admits he's been "dyin' fur want o' ye!"—and they embrace passionately. After they've made love, Abbie claims the parlor as their room now, and Eben, asserting that "Maw's gone back t' her grave," makes peace with his father, telling him that Eben's mother now is "quits with ye."

A year later, the baby has been born, and everyone but Ephraim knows that Eben is the father. Ephraim tells Eben that the farm will now go to the child and Abbie and that Abbie had wanted Eben cut out of the inheritance. Furious with Abbie, Eben decides he will go to California and get rich so that he can come back and fight them all for the farm they stole from him. He tells Abbie that he wishes the child had never been born—"I wish he'd die this minit!"—and that, although he did love her "like a dumb ox," now he hates her for tricking him. When she asks him if he would love her again if she could make things as they were before the baby, he replies that he might but "ye ain't God, be ye?"

That morning, Abbie tells Eben, who is packed to leave, that "I killed him." Eben assumes she means Ephraim, and when she tells him that it was the baby, she realizes that she *should* have killed Ephraim instead. Eben is horrified and goes off to tell the Sheriff, ignoring Abbie's explanation that she loved him more than her son. When Ephraim finds the baby dead, Abbie tells him she hates him and that the child was Eben's— and Ephraim praises Eben for turning her in to the law. But Eben begs Abbie to forgive him because he has realized that he does love her and says that they should run off together before the Sheriff arrives. She refuses, asserting that she must "pay fur my sin"—whereupon Eben insists on sharing the blame with her. Ephraim says he hates them both, wishes them hanged, and will destroy the farm and go to California, only to find that Eben has stolen his money. "God's hard, not easy!" is his only comment. The Sheriff enters and after Eben tells his story, he leads them off hand in hand, proclaiming their love, leaving the Sheriff to say the play's ironic final line: "It's a jim-dandy farm, no denyin'. Wished I owned it!"

O'Neill, in a 1925 letter, described *Desire under the Elms* as "a tragedy of the possessive—the pitiful longing of man to build his own heaven here on earth by glutting his sense of power with ownership of land, people, money—but principally the land and other people's lives" (Bogard and Bryer 194). The overriding desire of everyone to own the Cabot farm is something like the frenzy over Big Daddy's land that dominates TENNESSEE WILLIAMS's *CAT ON A HOT TIN ROOF* (1955); and the situation of the young wife of an older man coming to the latter's farm, where she is seduced and becomes pregnant by a younger man, also invites comparison with a much lighter play, SIDNEY HOWARD's *THEY KNEW WHAT THEY WANTED* (1924), the manuscript of which, Travis Bogard suggests, O'Neill may have seen before he wrote *Desire under the Elms* (201–203). But other forces are at work in the play: There is surely something of the Oedipus myth in Eben's lovemaking with Abbie as a symbol of his mother, and Abbie's killing of her child certainly suggests Medea. But these echoes of myth are not imposed on the play, as they are in later O'Neill plays like *MOURNING BECOMES ELECTRA* (1931); instead, they lie behind it, giving it depth and scope and justifying Bogard's labeling it "the first important tragedy to be written in America" (200).

BIBLIOGRAPHY

Bogard, Travis. *Contour in Time: The Plays of Eugene O'Neill.* Rev. ed. New York: Oxford University Press, 1988.

———, and Jackson R. Bryer, eds. *Selected Letters of Eugene O'Neill.* New Haven, Conn.: Yale University Press, 1988.

DETECTIVE STORY SIDNEY KINGSLEY (1949)

In *Detective Story,* KINGSLEY followed his established pattern of extensive research, this time immersing himself in the activities of a New York City police precinct, where he observed the many types of people with whom he filled the play. As with almost all of Kingsley's work, *Detective Story* conveys a strong message to society; in this play, the message is about the dangers of a police state, a concern of Kingsley's since he heard speeches by General George C. Marshall in 1947 in which Marshall referred to such a state. In naming his police station the Twenty-first Precinct, Kingsley was looking toward the 21st century and wondering whether our future society would be free.

Thinking that ultimately there would be a single world government, Kingsley was concerned about the nature of that government and the need for human rights guarantees. He approached this concern by creating Jim McLeod, a detective who is unable to accept personal weakness or failure, who sees only absolutes of right and wrong. Kingsley wrote in his introduction to the play: "Men like McLeod constitute a serious threat, for such men may well rule the world state of the future" (242). With untiring passion, McLeod pursues Kurt Schneider, an illegal abortionist, some of whose patients have died. In the course of the investigation, McLeod is confronted with the devastating news that, prior to meeting and marrying McLeod, his own wife Mary had had an abortion at the hands of Schneider. Unable to accept her past and equally unable to stop loving her, McLeod is faced with a dilemma that he cannot solve. After a failed attempt at reconciliation, Mary sees that he will never be able to forget what he regards as her shame, so she leaves him. Also faced with McLeod's strident justice is Arthur, a much-decorated veteran and first offender who stole from his employer in order to hold on to his wartime girlfriend. Though Arthur's boss agrees to drop the charges against the contrite Arthur, the unyielding McLeod will not hear of it. In the end, McLeod is shot in the squad room while foiling an escape attempt by a hardened criminal who has grabbed an officer's gun. Only as McLeod is dying is he able to understand what his lack of compassion has cost him personally. McLeod's last act is to do for Arthur what he cannot do for Mary: to give him a second chance as he allows the charges against him to be dropped.

Interwoven with the McLeods' personal drama are the stories of the numerous people who come through the police station: burglars Charley and his not-too-bright partner Lewis, a pickpocket's victim, a shoplifter, a paranoid neighborhood crackpot, the police-beat reporter, the lieutenant, detectives, patrolmen, station janitor, and others. Written for a single set, each story dovetails intricately with the next, creating an action-packed script that requires split-second timing and choreography in performance.

While Kingsley's portrayal of McLeod is very black-and-white, for once the primary message of the play is somewhat understated in comparison to his other works. The realistic, action-packed drama and the sympathy generated for McLeod obscure Kingsley's deeply felt concern about the police state.

BIBLIOGRAPHY
Kingsley, Sidney. *Sidney Kingsley: Five Prizewinning Plays.* Ed. Nena Couch. Columbus: Ohio State University Press, 1995.

Nena Couch
Ohio State University

DIARY OF ANNE FRANK, THE FRANCES GOODRICH AND ALBERT HACKETT (1955) This
PULITZER PRIZE–winning play is based on *Anne Frank: Diary of a Young Girl* (1952), the firsthand record of an adolescent girl's experience hiding from the Nazis with her family in Amsterdam during World War II. A mixture of the mundane and the terrifying, the play remains a moving account of a horrifying chapter in 20th-century history.

The play is framed by first and final scenes set in November of 1945 when Otto Frank, Anne's father and the only surviving member of the family, returns to the hiding place after the war is over. Mr. Frank finds Anne's diary at the end of the first scene. As he begins to read the diary, Anne's voice overtakes his and serves as a bridge into the action of the play. Excerpts from the diary read by Anne in voice-over also serve as a transition between the scenes, and such an excerpt finally returns us to Mr. Frank in the final scene as he finishes reading the diary. By structuring the play in this way, Goodrich and Hackett anchor the play firmly in the actual diary, thus effectively retaining that document's poignant first-person point of view.

Mr. and Mrs. Frank, their daughters Anne and Margot, and Mr. and Mrs. Van Daan and their son Peter, go into hiding in Nazi-occupied Amsterdam as life there becomes increasingly dangerous for Jews. The time is the summer of 1942; Anne is 13 years old. By the time the two families are joined by the dentist, Mr. Dussel, life on the outside has become even more perilous for Jews, hundreds of whom are disappearing every day, deported to the "death camps." The even-tempered Otto Frank holds the group together, acting as teacher to the teenagers and mediator in the many conflicts that flare up because of generational differences or close quarters. Their lifeline is the courageous Dutch gentile, Miep, who brings them news, food, and friendship regularly.

During the two years that the group resides in the attic hiding place, Anne reaches puberty and is filled with all the confusion and longing of adolescence. Anne's adolescence is typical—the conflict with her mother ("We have nothing in common. She doesn't understand me."), the budding sexuality (*"For a second* ANNE *stands looking up at* PETER, *longing for him to kiss her."*)—but it is played out against the backdrop of the horrifying Nazi threat. Anne finds a kindred spirit in Peter, and their meetings in his "room" for talk and affection become the highlight of her day. By the time the Nazis come for them, Anne has grown from an enthusiastic child to *"a woman with courage."* As they hear the door breaking, Anne looks *"over at her father and mother with a soft, reassuring smile."* The sad irony is that the Franks, the Van Daans, and Mr. Dussel are found by the Nazis just weeks after Miep brings news of the D-day invasion and with it renewed hope for liberation.

A line of Anne's has become the most famous of the play: "In spite of everything, I still believe that people are really good at heart." The emphasis on this line—placed as it is at the end of the play, giving it greater significance than it has in the diary, where it appears in the context of Anne's discussion of "horrible truth" and "shattered" hopes (Frank 263)—has angered some critics who maintain that the 1955 play presents a sweetened version of Anne's diary. A less sentimental version of the play, an adaptation by Wendy Kesselman, was produced in 1997. Kesselman's adaptation, though still wedded to the Goodrich and Hackett version, was closer to the unexpurgated diary that was published after Otto Frank's death. Novelist and essayist Cynthia Ozick has criticized film and stage adaptations of Anne Frank's diary for their "false optimism" (101); she maintains that Anne's story over the last 50 years "has been infantilized, Americanized, homogenized, sentimentalized; . . . and arrogantly denied" (77). Regardless of the controversy over the historical accuracy of its tone and content, Goodrich and Hackett's play will always be a story of hope in the midst of evil.

BIBLIOGRAPHY

Frank, Anne. *The Diary of a Young Girl*. 1952. New York: Bantam, 1993.

Ozick, Cynthia. *Quarrel & Quandary*. New York: Knopf, 2000.

DIETZ, STEVEN JOHN (1958–)

One of the most prolific, versatile, and widely produced playwrights of his generation, Steven Dietz was born in Denver, Colorado. After receiving a B.A. in theater arts in 1980 from the University of Northern Colorado, Dietz moved to Minneapolis and worked at the Playwrights' Center from 1980–91, developing both his playwriting and directing skills. Since relocating to Seattle in 1991, Dietz has continued to work steadily, fashioning close relationships with several regional repertory companies, notably Seattle's A Contemporary Theatre (ACT), Tucson's Arizona Theatre Company, the Milwaukee Repertory Theatre, and EMILY MANN's McCarter Theatre (Princeton, N.J.).

Melding the socially engaged dramaturgy of German playwright Bertolt Brecht, the fragmented narrative structures and fascination with historical subjects of English playwright Tom Stoppard, and the absurdist perspective of EDWARD ALBEE, Dietz is noteworthy on the contemporary American scene for an ear finely attuned to contemporary vernacular and a willingness to grapple with the "big" issues—both political and philosophical. His plays are almost always leavened by humor and a pervasive sympathy for the humanity of his characters.

Dietz's early successful plays, including *More Fun than Bowling* (1985), *Painting It Red* (1986), and *Ten November* (1987), reveal a penchant for formal experimentation that has remained a hallmark of his work. The late 1980s marked the emergence of a more overtly political turn in Dietz's playwriting. He excoriates the radical right in one of his most produced plays, *God's Country* (1988), a docudrama about Denver talk-show host Alan Berg's assassination and the racial hatred that motivated it. Quick-paced and hard-hitting, the play's multirole casting provides a theatrical challenge that can undermine the play's themes. In *Foolin' around with Infinity* (1988) and *Halcyon Days* (1991), Dietz provides scathing indictments of Reagan-era nonchalance about prospective nuclear weapons use and the public relations effort to justify the 1983 Grenada invasion. The early 1990s ushered in Dietz's renewed interest in the private. In *Trust* (1992) and *Private Eyes* (1996), he again focused on the minefields of romantic relationships. He poignantly argues for embracing the joys and demands of friendship in a world complicated by AIDS in *Lonely Planet* (1993), another of his most popular plays. In *Rocket Man* (1998), his most metaphysical and challenging play, Dietz tellingly weaves together a midlife crisis of faith with an examination of our common understanding of time and place. Transmuting the techniques of painting to dramatic structure, Dietz investigates inspiration, artistic beauty, and authenticity in *Inventing Van Gogh* (2001). *Fiction* (2003), which uses exchanged diaries to suggest the melding of facts and fabrications at the core of human relationships, won Dietz a second Kennedy Center "Fund for New American Plays" award in 2002. His *Last of the Boys* (2004), first produced in the wake of the U.S. incursion into Iraq, examines the psychological, political, and emotional legacy of the Vietnam war as it affects two Vietnam-era veterans. Dietz's strengths as a writer/director led to his appointment to the University of Texas at Austin faculty in 2006 as a professor of playwriting. Despite his new duties, he has remained extremely productive. 2008–09 saw the premieres of three new plays, *Becky's New Car* (2008 in Seattle), *Shooting Star* (2009 in Austin), and *Yankee Tavern* (2009 in Manalapan, Florida).

Dietz has also penned adaptations of novels by Goethe, Bram Stoker, and Shusaku Endo; reworkings of Gillette, Chekhov, and Ibsen; and award-winning children's theater, including *The Rememberer* (1994), winner of a Lila Wallace/Readers Digest Award, and *Still Life with Iris* (1997), the first play for young people to win the Kennedy Center's "Fund for New American Plays" award.

BIBLIOGRAPHY

Dietz, Steven. *Dracula.* New York: Dramatists Play Service, 1996.

———. *Fiction.* New York: Samuel French, 2005.

———. *Foolin' around with Infinity.* New York: Samuel French, 1989.

———. *Force of Nature.* New York: Dramatists Play Service, 2003.

———. *God's Country.* New York: Samuel French, 1989.

———. *Halcyon Days.* New York: Dramatists Play Service, 1995.

———. *Last of the Boys.* New York: Dramatists Play Service, 2008.

———. *Lonely Planet.* New York: Dramatists Play Service, 1994.

———. *More Fun than Bowling.* New York: Samuel French, 1985.

———. *Nina Variations.* New York: Dramatists Play Service, 2003.

———. *Painting It Red.* New York: Samuel French, 1986.

———. *Private Eyes.* New York: Dramatists Play Service, 1997.

———. *Rocket Man.* New York: Dramatists Play Service, 2003.

———. *Sherlock Holmes: The Final Adventure.* New York: Dramatists Play Service, 2007.

———. *Still Life with Iris.* Woodstock, Ill.: Dramatic Publishing Company, 1998.

———. *Ten November.* New York: Samuel French, 1987.

———. *Trust.* New York: Dramatists Play Service, 1995.

Gary A. Richardson
Mercer University

DINING ROOM, THE A. R. GURNEY (1982)

A play about the changing values of prosperous white Americans in the 20th century, *The Dining Room* laments the yielding of elegance, ceremony, sacrifice, and commitment in private and public life to shabbiness, laxity, and self-centeredness. But it also ridicules the infidelities, exploitations, and prejudices sustained and masked by genteel rituals. Equally, it satirizes late-20th-century trends, like pursuing sexual freedom without regard to consequences for children and regarding education only as a path to social prestige. The play approves the growth in tolerance for homosexuals and opportunities for women, and it empathizes with grown children distressed by the needs of caring for aging parents.

Around a *"lovely burnished, shining"* dining room table that commands the set in every scene, characters of different decades gather, some to suffer and others to celebrate. The play concerns no single hero or family. In a span of slightly less than two hours, it presents 60 characters in 18 crisply written scenes; yet, the script calls for only six actors (three men and three women) to play persons ranging in age from six to more than 80. GURNEY adroitly links the scenes by overlapping their ends and beginnings. Thus, the audience frequently sees characters from two different times seated at the table, the contrasts of act and word developing the play's emotions, ironies, and humor. Gurney's acute insight into American behavior keeps each moment in focus without losing momentum or sacrificing unity.

Two other features strengthen the play's coherence. Though the play covers the period from the 1930s to the 1980s, the audience perceives the events as if they occur throughout a single day. The first scene—a real estate agent showing the dining room to a client—occurs in the optimistic light of a new day; the final scene—a dinner party around the beautifully set dining room table—unfolds as the melancholy light of sunset shades into night. Second, the table's location is never specified. It exists in a limbo that, in the audience's imaginations, becomes the tables of their own lives, and the characters, by association, become more like people they have known.

Arvid F. Sponberg
Valparaiso University

DINNER AT EIGHT GEORGE S. KAUFMAN AND EDNA FERBER (1932)

The third play written by KAUFMAN and FERBER, *Dinner at Eight* was enormously successful. Although it contains comic dialogue and situations, the play is quite dark. Nevertheless, the elegant New York City settings and high-fashion costumes delighted audiences in the depth of the depression.

The play is set in action by a silly, egotistical social climber, Mrs. Oliver Jordan. She has invited an English lord and his wife to dinner. Absorbed by what she considers enormously important invitations and preparations, she ignores the serious problems of her husband and daughter. Oliver Jordan knows from Dr. Talbot, one of the guests, that he may have a heart attack at any time. He is about to lose his shipping business through the crooked machinations of another guest, the nouveau riche Dan Packard.

The Jordans' daughter, Paula, is engaged to a suitable young man, but she has fallen in love with another invitee, the alcoholic, penniless, egocentric, aging actor Larry Renault. Visiting him in his first-class hotel, where they carry on their affair, she tells him she loves him and wants to break her engagement. He knows their relationship is hopeless and decides to commit suicide when he is turned down for a role and can no longer pay his hotel costs.

Another guest in the hotel is Carlotta Vance, a formerly beautiful actress, now fat and nearly broke, who is forced to sell her Jordan stock to Packard. The latter is married to a beautiful, but selfish, woman who is having an affair with Dr. Talbot. In an argument with Packard, she taunts him with the fact that she is having an affair but will not tell him with whom. Her maid, who knows the truth, begins to blackmail her.

On the evening of the party, tragedy strikes for Mrs. Jordan. The servants have a fight in the kitchen and the lobster aspic falls on the floor. Worse yet, the English lord and lady leave for Florida, so she has to invite her sister and ill-tempered brother-in-law to fill their places. All the guests arrive, and the interaction among them is revealed in double entendres and secret looks. Jordan, aware that Packard has bought all his stock, is facing death. Mrs. Jordan tries to carry on with the party, blithely unaware that it is useless to wait for Renault, as he is dead.

This behind-the-scenes satire on the lives of the rich and famous was one of the most effective of Kaufman and Ferber's collaborations. When the play was revived in 1966, Ferber told a reporter, "When George and I wrote that play, we wrote it not just as a high swift comedy, but as a comment on our world in that critical and really dreadful period just before we went over the cliff." The play, which is expensive to produce, has rarely been revived (though it did receive a limited-run Broadway production in 2002), but it was made into a 1933 film directed by George Cukor.

BIBLIOGRAPHY
Dudar, Helen. "Woman in the News: Edna Ferber." *New York Post,* 1 Oct. 1966, 25.

Yvonne Shafer
St. John's University

DINNER WITH FRIENDS DONALD MARGULIES (1999)   When half of a pair of inseparable couples ends its marriage, the other couple's sense of security—and sense of themselves—is shaken. The action takes place through a series of shared meals and meal preparations. Originally commissioned by the Actors Theatre of Louisville, *Dinner with Friends* premiered at the HUMANA FESTIVAL in 1998. Revised twice before its New York premiere in late 1999, the play won the 2000 PULITZER PRIZE.

Gabe and Karen and Tom and Beth have been a foursome for 12 years; they frequently dine together, regularly vacation together, and have simultaneously experienced the joys and rigors of parenthood. Gabe and Tom were college friends, and Gabe and Karen first introduced Tom, a lawyer, to Beth, "a painter." It is a great shock, then, to Gabe and Karen, who thought they knew their friends well and thought their friends were as happy as they, when Beth announces at dinner that Tom has left her for another woman. After Beth and her children go home, Gabe and Karen discuss the news. Karen sides completely with Beth and tells Gabe that she would never tolerate unfaithfulness in *him*. Gabe is less strident, calling Tom's affair a "transgression." However differently they may perceive the details, both are shaken by the news. As Karen says, "You think you're . . . on solid ground, then all of a sudden the earth cracks open."

In a subsequent scene between the separating couple, Tom accuses Beth of turning their oldest friends against him. During the ensuing argument, he reveals that he has never believed she had any talent for painting, and he calls "perpetuating this myth of talent" exhausting. Later, Tom makes a late night visit to Gabe and Karen to give his side of the story. Karen's reception is cold, but Gabe listens. According to Tom, Beth has been hypercritical of him for years and is not affectionate. By this he does not mean sexually distant, and Gabe is amazed that despite the situation they still have sex—made more intense because of the anger they feel. By contrast, Nancy, Tom's new girlfriend, is "a *delightful* woman who made [him] feel worthwhile." When Gabe begins to suggest that perhaps Tom is making an irresponsible choice, Tom leaves.

A flashback to 12 years before reveals that Tom and Beth were never very well suited to one another. Even at their first real meeting (they met prior to that briefly at Karen and Gabe's wedding), Beth is mildly critical and nitpicking. They seem attracted beyond the physical, but perhaps only because they are both ready to be married.

Five months after the breakup, Karen and Beth lunch together. Beth has stopped painting, admitting she was never good at it, and, she tells Karen, she is "seeing someone" named David, whom she plans to marry. When Karen advises her to go slowly, Beth's resentment of what she perceives as Karen's perfectionism and feelings of superiority becomes evident. Meanwhile at a bar in Manhattan, the two men meet for what Gabe knows will be the last time. Tom is ecstatic, full of tales of great sex and the excitement of a new relationship. He says he was dying, and Nancy saved his life. He never really wanted to settle down; he did it because it was "expected" of him. Gabe is not sympathetic and takes the failure of Tom's marriage very personally. At the end of the scene, Tom mentions without rancor that David and Beth had an affair years before; in fact, Tom likes David and has no objection to his marrying Beth now.

In the end, little in Tom and Beth's marriage is what it seemed to Karen and Gabe. This rocks their world. For them it is like a death—the death of their past. They fear the implications the breakup may have for their own marriage. They acknowledge that after chil-

dren and mortgages and "practical matters," growing less passionately in love may be "inevitable," since "practical matters begin to outweigh . . . abandon." They try to avoid getting "lost" to each other: In the final moments of the last scene, they play an "intimate game" from the early days of their relationship.

When asked in an interview after winning the Pulitzer Prize if the play contains "an affirmation of long-term marriage," MARGULIES responded, "I think it's a hopeful play . . . [but not] a sentimental or a simplistic view of marriage. . . . [T]here aren't simple solutions to any of the issues that arise in the play, as there are not in life." In the same interview, Margulies made it clear that the play is about more than just marriage and divorce: "It's really about the aftershocks that we all experience when certain constants in our lives, things that we perceive to be constant, suddenly shatter and are no longer dependable."

BIBLIOGRAPHY
Farnsworth, Elizabeth. "Donald Margulies Interview." *Online Newshour.* 13 Apr. 2000. 8 Oct. 2002 (accessed). Available online. <http://www.pbs.org/newshour/gergen/jan-june00/Margulies_4-13.html>

DODSON, OWEN (1914–1983) Playwright, director, poet, novelist, and educator, Owen Dodson was born in Brooklyn, New York. The son of a journalist who was also the director of the National Negro Press Association, Dodson came in contact as a child with some of the most significant African-American minds of the early 20th century, including Booker T. Washington, W. E. B. DuBois, and James Weldon Johnson. Dodson was educated at Bates College in Maine (B.A., 1936) and Yale University (M.F.A., 1939). He interrupted his career as an academic to serve in the United States Navy during World War II. His distinguished college teaching career included work in the drama departments of Spelman College, Atlanta University, and Howard University, where he was professor of drama from 1947 to 1969, also serving as drama department chair at Howard for his last nine years there. While at Howard, Dodson directed numerous productions, including the premiere of JAMES BALDWIN's *AMEN CORNER* in 1953, as well as productions of European classics. In 1949, the Howard

University Players performed throughout Europe, under Dodson's direction and with the sponsorship of the United States State Department.

When Dodson retired from Howard in 1969, he was in his mid-fifties. In the 1970s, his traditional, humanist approach was at odds with the militancy among many African-American educators and artists; however, he did continue to lecture and conduct seminars at such institutions as Vassar College, Kenyon College, and Cornell University and worked as director and consultant to various theater groups, while continuing to write his own works. Because Dodson was too young to be a part of the Harlem Renaissance and was much more traditional than the militant playwrights of the 1960s and 1970s—one of the most famous of whom, AMIRI BARAKA, was his student at Howard—his work is often overlooked.

He began writing sonnets in college, publishing some by the time he graduated in 1936. While at Yale, Dodson saw produced his *Divine Comedy* (1938), a verse drama that exposes a type of evangelical con man; the play was revived in New York City at the New Federal Theatre in 1977. Also first produced at Yale was *Garden of Time* (1939), a reworking of *Medea* set in Greece and in post–Civil War North Carolina, which deals with race relations; *Garden of Time* was revised for a 1945 American Negro Theatre production. Dodson's play *Amistad* (1939) was performed at the dedication of Alabama's Talladega College Savary Library, a building that features murals of the historic Amistad incident. During Dodson's naval service, he was asked to write a series of plays to raise morale among African-American sailors; of these plays, two were subsequently published in *Theatre Arts* magazine: *The Ballad of Dorie Miller* (published 1943), which depicts the heroic African-American sailors who shot down Japanese planes during the attack on Pearl Harbor, and *Everybody Join Hands* (published 1943), which deals with the resistance of the Chinese people against their Japanese oppressors. *New World A-Coming: An Original Pageant of Hope* (1944), first produced in New York City at Madison Square Garden, recognizes the contributions of African Americans to the war effort. Dodson's other plays include *The Shining Town* (1937); *Doomsday Tale* (1941); *Gonna Tear Them Pillars Down* (1942); *The Third Fourth of July* (1946),

written with Countee Cullen; *Bayou Legend* (1946), an adaptation of *Peer Gynt; The Decision* (1947); *Medea in Africa* (1963), written with Countee Cullen; and *Freedom, the Banner* (1984).

Among Dodson's most notable published works in other genres are two poetry collections, *Powerful Long Ladder* (1946) and *The Confession Stone* (1970), and two novels, *Boy at the Window* (1951) and *Come Home Early, Child* (1977).

BIBLIOGRAPHY

Dodson, Owen. "The Ballad of Dorie Miller." *Theatre Arts* 27 (1943): 436.
———. "Bayou Legend." In *Black Drama in America: An Anthology,* edited by Darwin T. Turner. Greenwich, Conn.: Fawcett, 1971. 205–295.
———. "Divine Comedy." In *Black Theatre, USA,* edited by James V. Hatch and Ted Shine. New York: Free Press, 1974. 322–349.
———. "Everybody Join Hands." *Theatre Arts* 27 (1943): 555–565.
———. "The Shining Town." In *The Roots of African American Drama,* edited by Leo Hamalian and James V. Hatch. Detroit: Wayne State University Press, 1991. 332–352.
———, and Countee Cullen. "The Third Fourth of July." *Theatre Arts* 30 (1946): 488–493.
Hatch, James V. *Sorrow Is the Only Faithful One: The Life of Owen Dodson.* Urbana: University of Illinois Press, 1993.

DOUBT JOHN PATRICK SHANLEY (2004) The premise of JOHN PATRICK SHANLEY'S PULITZER PRIZE–winning play, *Doubt,* is this: In 1964, the principal of a Catholic school, a nun, suspects and accuses the parish priest of having molested an eighth-grade boy; the priest emphatically denies it. Shanley's theme surrounds the concept of doubt—how it can be an agent for safety, for growth, or, at the very least, for genuine discussion. By the end of the play there is no real answer to the priest's innocence or guilt. (This, at any rate, was the playwright's intention, though some productions may seem to take sides.) The audience is meant to struggle with the question "Whom should I believe?"—taking its own doubt out of the theater and beginning its own discussions.

The middle-aged principal Sister Aloysius is traditional in her approach to education. She is pre–Vatican II, meaning she adheres to the belief that there should be clear boundaries and a strict code of conduct between adults and their pupils; the Second Vatican Council in the early 1960s began a more informal, familiar approach by the clergy toward Catholic parishioners and schoolchildren. The characterization of Sister Aloysius begins to take shape as she points out the inadequacies to the young nun Sister James of Sister James's teaching; we see that Sister Aloysius has some very old-fashioned (and entertaining) ideas indeed—regarding F.D.R.: "I do not approve of making heroes of lay historical figures"; regarding ballpoint pens: "Students really should only be learning script with true fountain pens. . . . Ballpoints make them press down, and . . . they write like monkeys"; regarding "Frosty the Snowman": the popular Christmas song "espouses a pagan belief in magic." But lest we think she is just a foolish throwback to outmoded orthodoxy, we also know that Sister Aloysius is of this world; she was married until her husband died "in the war against Adolph Hitler." She has a great deal of experience with children and has keen powers of observation and intuition, and she, as Shanley said in an interview, "is a real defender of good against evil, and she knows which is which" (*Charley Rose*). She will do whatever it takes to protect children.

Her adversary is the young priest Father Flynn, who subscribes to the more relaxed post–Vatican II philosophy. We see him coaching basketball and witness his good rapport with the boys; he seems sensible as well, as he advises them in a friendly way about hygiene. He preaches sermons on such topics as tolerance and the destructiveness of gossip. We don't see a villain here, but we, the audience, do begin to suspect him along with Sister Aloysius when she finds out that he has taken one of the boys under his wing, that this same boy has been alone with him in the rectory and has returned to Sister James's class with alcohol on his breath. We are also prone to suspect him because at the time this play was written the newspapers were full of the scandals involving Catholic priests and the schoolboys some of them took advantage of over the course of decades. But Father Flynn denies any wrongdoing, explains that the boy was caught stealing altar wine and that he kept it quiet so

that this boy—the first black child at the school—might remain an altar boy. Father Flynn would rather exempt the child from so public a punishment than feed into the racial stereotypes held by some in the congregation. This is a feasible explanation, one accepted with relief by Sister James, but Sister Aloysius does not believe him.

Sister Aloysius is absolutely certain she is right; she has no doubt even as Father Flynn flatly and credibly denies her accusations. The context of the confrontations between them is the patriarchal hierarchy of the Catholic Church. Father Flynn is her superior, and above him is an "otherworldly" and innocent monsignor. Sister cannot, she feels, go to the monsignor because he would simply ask Flynn, who would deny all, and that would be the end of the matter. Since the Church's rigid male hierarchy does not permit her to go outside the chain of command to the bishop, she believes she must take care of the matter herself in order to protect the child.

Sister Aloysius calls in the mother of the boy, Mrs. Muller, who—stunningly—is less troubled by the possibility of the molestation of her son Donald than is the nun. Donald's father, she reveals, does not like him, and he beats him for being "that way" (Donald was also assaulted by students at the public school for apparently being gay), and Mrs. Muller is just glad that there is an educated man who is taking an interest in him. She wants her son to make it through eighth grade at this school so that he can go to a good high school and have a better chance at college. She is looking at the big picture; she is black and lives in the reality of 1964 civil rights. She tells Sister Aloysius, "Let [Donald] take the good and leave the rest when he leaves this place in June. He knows how to do that. I taught him how to do that." Whatever the priest's motives may be, Donald's mother sees his kindness and wants to take from it what can be gained for her son.

Father Flynn begins to avoid Donald Muller for fear of being misunderstood. He has an ally in Sister James, who, like he does, believes in treating children with warmth and kindness rather than rigid formality. Despite Mrs. Muller's pragmatic wishes, Sister Aloysius will not be stopped. In her final confrontation with Father Flynn, she claims to have called his previous parish; she claims to have knowledge that he has "a history." She feels his reaction to these statements proves his guilt with Donald. Her relentless pursuit of the truth as she sees it forces him out of the parish; but he simply moves to another parish—where he becomes the pastor, a promotion—because the monsignor, just as she predicted, did not believe Sister Aloysius's accusations. Meanwhile, Sister James reports that Donald is "heartbroken."

The play contains great ambivalence: Whom shall we believe? Is he guilty? If so, *how* guilty and, perhaps, *when*? Were Sister's actions justified? Were Mrs. Muller's attitudes legitimate?

The fact is that a bit of doubt in the authority of the priesthood would have helped the young people who were actually molested by some members of that insulated group. There was a period when this "men's club" carried on unquestioned, shielding its own from prosecution and publicity, moving offenders from parish to parish, at the expense of young victims. This is something Sister Aloysius, who came to the convent with some real-world experience, can see for what it is and rail against. Shanley has indicated that he disapproves of the male dominance of the Church because it leads to the oppression of women—and that is certainly evident in his play; Sister Aloysius "has to be ruthless," according to Shanley, because she is powerless in this system (*Charley Rose*). Shanley writes in his preface to the published play, "When trust is the order of the day, predators are free to plunder. And plunder they did. As the ever widening Church scandals reveal, the hunters had a field day" (ix). So we must doubt the infallibility of institutions and their partisans—it is safer to do so. Following this line of reasoning, one might think that maybe Flynn is guilty.

However, we must also doubt our own stridently held positions—therein lies the potential for growth (maybe he's not guilty). This brings us to the flip side: What if in this case Sister Aloysius is wrong? She is so sure of her vision, so utterly without doubt that she is perhaps incapable of seeing possibilities outside her own perception. In fact it was Shanley's observation of this type of refusal to doubt that was the impetus for his play. Shanley feels that we are living in an age—a polemical age in public discourse—when people are so *certain* of their views that there is no real discussion: "Discussion has given way to debate. Communication has become a contest of wills" (Shanley vii). He has suggested that in the world of politics, both sides are "so busy holding a position" that neither steps back and *thinks* (*Charley Rose*).

Therefore, while Father Flynn *may be* guilty of molestation (and deserving of our doubt), Sister Aloysius may be guilty of "holding a position" to the exclusion of really thinking (and deserving of our doubt.) Shanley does not give us the answer and he does not stack the cards against either; "I believe in a fair fight," he said (*Charlie Rose*).

In addition to the Pulitzer Prize, *Doubt* also won the TONY AWARD, the New York Drama Critics' Circle Award, and for its original OFF-BROADWAY run, an OBIE for Playwriting.

BIBLIOGRAPHY
Shanley, John Patrick. *Doubt*. New York: Theatre Communications Group, 2005.
———. Interview with Charley Rose. *Charley Rose*. PBS. WNET, New York. 14 Mar. 2005.

DOUGLASS, DAVID (?–1786)

Actor/manager David Douglass and his American Company were responsible for the expansion of professional theater in the colonies prior to the Revolutionary War. The company toured extensively for a decade and a half, from 1758 to 1774, with a repertoire that included Shakespeare and the plays of the contemporary English theater. The troupe adopted the name "The American Company" as early as 1763 to counter anti-British sentiment.

Douglass's career in the theater began in 1754 in the British colony of Jamaica, where a large English population attempted to re-create in the tropics the social life and entertainments of their homeland. Wealthy planters, merchants, and government officials provided a clientele for professional theater. Douglass and his company, fresh from England, joined forces with the English acting company of Lewis Hallam Sr., who came to Jamaica after performing for a period of time in the American colonies. (Hallam's Company—himself, his wife, his children, and 10 other actors—toured the colonies from September 1752 until they went to Jamaica in January 1755.) After Lewis Hallam's death, his wife married Douglass, and in 1758 the newly formed company, with Lewis Hallam Jr. and the new Mrs. Douglass as the leading actors, set out for New York City to try their fortunes.

For the next eight years The American Company toured, with Douglass constructing temporary theaters in many of the cities in which they performed. These theaters were built in a matter of weeks, with scant attention paid to audience safety or comfort. They are thought to have contained a pit, gallery, and boxes with a capacity of up to 300 persons. While varying in size, they might have been roughly 40 feet wide and 100 feet deep and were, of course, devoid of amenities such as plumbing. In these temporary theaters, The American Company would generally perform on Mondays, Wednesdays, and Fridays. To offset the antitheatrical prejudices of religious and civic authorities in many of the communities in which the company temporarily settled, Douglass would have to resort to billing his plays as "moral dialogues" or "dissertations" on morally instructive topics and erect his theaters beyond the city limits. In northern cities such as Newport, Providence, and New York, the Puritan heritage created a tradition of strong opposition to theatrical entertainments, whereas The American Company's reception in the South was inevitably friendlier.

In 1766, Douglass was largely responsible for organizing the financing and construction of the Southwark Theatre in Philadelphia, the first permanent theater to be built in colonial America. Larger than Douglass's temporary theaters, the Southwark was also of much sturdier construction, being built of brick and timber. It was here that Douglass staged Thomas Godfrey's tragedy The PRINCE OF PARTHIA (1767), the first play by an American author to be given a professional production in the colonies. From Philadelphia, Douglass went to New York City, where he was responsible for the construction of another permanent playhouse, the John Street Theatre. Neither New York nor Philadelphia could support a company on a permanent basis, and The American

Company continued to tour to such cities as Annapolis, Williamsburg, and Charleston. It was in the latter city, in Church Street, that Douglass oversaw the construction of yet another permanent theater, regarded as the most stylish and attractive in the colonies.

In October of 1774, the Continental Congress, on the eve of the Revolution, passed an edict to encourage frugality and discourage extravagant entertainments, including stage plays. With their means of livelihood officially curtailed, Douglass and his wife retired to Jamaica, where Douglass died in 1786.

BIBLIOGRAPHY
Seilhamer, George O. *History of the American Theatre Before the Revolution.* Philadelphia: Globe Printing House, 1888.

Craig Clinton
Reed College

DRAMATIC THEORY Dramatic theory, explains Marvin Carlson, is a set of "statements of general principles regarding the methods, aims, functions and characteristics of this particular art form" (9). While sometimes such statements are used to prescribe how a play "should" be written, interpreted, or made artistically and socially useful, it is more often the case that dramatic theories are speculative, offering possible avenues that lead to sources of pleasure and knowledge when a play is read or viewed. Thus, dramatic theories (unlike, say, scientific theories) do not develop from naive to sophisticated or even from incorrect to more correct; rather, a culture's expression of its "general principles . . . of this particular art form" tends to represent the prevailing attitudes of a given period (or in some cases opinions that strongly conflict with mainstream values).

American dramatic theory is no exception, and it has developed amid changing social, educational, and cultural contexts. During the Revolutionary War, prohibitions banned any form of professional acting. "Dramatic theory" during such times consisted exclusively of attacks against drama, stating general principles (religious, political, moral) upon which the argument forbidding theater could be supported.

After the war, between 1794 and 1815, these attitudes changed quickly, and a lively theater scene developed along the east coast in New York, Boston, Philadelphia, and Charleston. There was, however, little need to theorize about this drama, because it consisted almost wholly of imported plays from England and France (or imitations of them) that already had been championed by various literary critics abroad. Theoretical statements that exist before the late 19th century in America tend therefore to express traditional European beliefs in the aims, methods, and purpose of drama that might be called "belletristic" (from the French *belle lettres,* meaning all nontechnical forms of writing, but implying as well a humanist belief that the appreciation of literature is crucial to the development of a well-rounded individual). The two great pillars of belletristic literary theory are classicism and romanticism, and although these differ markedly from one another, they share the foundational idea that the form and content of literature directly affect the sensibilities of the reader and elevate one's morality, intellect, and emotions. A cultured person thus need not—in fact, should not—require special knowledge or training (let alone a theory) to respond to a work of dramatic art. Rather, belletristic dramatic theory largely serves to explain why some works are better able to arouse certain responses than others (that is, why tragedy stimulates noble passions and deep pathos, while comedy provokes satire and laughter).

Although the belletristic tradition remains strong today in American dramatic theory, around the end of the 19th century, new approaches to reading and understanding plays emerged. About the same time that a uniquely American drama was beginning to appear as an alternative to European traditions, an important shift in the country's social fabric and in educational institutions began to affect dramatic theory and the way in which students were taught to read and appreciate dramas. As an effect of the Industrial Revolution, class differences in America became more sharply defined. An educated middle class marked its distance from a mostly illiterate working class by maintaining connections to "cultured" leisure activities, such as drama. The word *drama,* in fact, came to mean almost exclusively a form of writing that contained meanings and pleasures that only an educated

and cultured reader might enjoy (as opposed to mass or "low" theatrical entertainments like vaudeville, minstrel shows, stand-up comedy, burlesque, and so on). One manner of distinguishing and ranking these various theatrical modes was to enshrine the noblest of them within institutions of higher education, thereby suggesting that proper appreciation of such cultural objects required professional training and intellectual refinement. Thus, a prominent critic such as George Jean Nathan could proclaim that tragedy could never become meaningful for the masses but could move only a minority of educated and cultivated minds (32).

However, once enshrined in educational institutions, American dramatic theory also sought to make the understanding and appreciation of drama more democratic and available to anyone with a standard education. Influenced by German models and an emerging American technocracy that valued scientific rigor and practical application of learning, institutions of higher education began early in the 20th century to promote the study of drama through the dual lenses of form and technique—the elements that give the proper structure to a play and render it emotionally and intellectually satisfying. Brander Matthews, the first professor of dramatic literature in America, taught courses at Columbia University that drew upon European theories of proper dramatic form to argue that the only test of a good play was whether its shape (the arrangement of action, the development of conflict, and so on) excited the sensibilities of the audience when it was performed. By mid-century, the arrival of New Criticism (under the influence of literary critics such as Cleanth Brooks and I. A. Richards), with its focus on analyzing with great rigor the formal elements of literature, further drove American dramatic theory to consider plays as freestanding artifacts whose meanings could best be understood through "practical criticism" based in a close reading of the linguistic structures (clusters of imagery, metaphor, irony, and other literary devices) that produced emotional and intellectual effects. In its most extreme forms, called sometimes "dramatism," "archetypal criticism," or "structuralism," different genres of drama were said to exhibit the same structures at a deep level across widely different time periods, providing evidence for drama's ability to mimic the dynamics of the social order (Burke) or even the very structures of human thought (Fergusson).

More recently, in the wake of further social upheavals (such as the Civil Rights movement and feminism) and demographic changes in American educational institutions, attention has shifted from the dramatic text as a self-contained artifact of meaning and toward consideration of the historical and social effects produced when plays are read in different cultural contexts or performed in varied social settings. As part of larger movements (multiculturalism, postmodernism, poststructuralism, and New Historicism, among others) that cast doubt on the very idea of "general principles" to explain any artistic form, the canon of Western drama has come under sharp scrutiny and has been challenged by playwrights, readers, and theorists to represent formerly marginalized styles of writing from women (Case; Dolan; Austin) and from minorities who combine Western styles with indigenous forms from Mexico, Latin America, Africa, Asia, and other locations (BARAKA; Elam). Recent dramatic theory has thus focused more intently on the wider cultural sphere in which dramas are read and performed.

BIBLIOGRAPHY

Austin, Gayle. *Feminist Theories for Dramatic Research.* Ann Arbor: University of Michigan Press, 1990.

Baraka, Amiri (LeRoi Jones). "The Revolutionary Theater." *Selected Plays and Prose of Amiri Baraka.* New York: Morrow, 1979. 130–133.

Burke, Kenneth. *A Philosophy of Literary Form: Studies in Symbolic Action.* Berkeley: University of California Press, 1974.

Carlson, Marvin. *Theories of the Theatre: A Historical and Critical Survey, from the Greeks to the Present.* Ithaca, N.Y.: Cornell University Press, 1993.

Case, Sue-Ellen. *Feminism and Theater.* New York: Routledge, 1988.

Dolan, Jill. *The Feminist Spectator as Critic.* Ann Arbor, Mich.: UMI Research Press, 1988.

Elam, Harry, Jr. *Taking It to the Streets: The Social Protest Theater of Luis Valdéz and Amiri Baraka.* Ann Arbor: University of Michigan Press, 1997.

Fergusson, Francis. *The Idea of a Theatre: The Art of Drama in Changing Perspective.* Princeton, N.J.: Princeton University Press, 1949.

Matthews, Brander. *The Principles of Playmaking, and Other Discussions of the Drama.* 1919. Freeport, N.Y.: Books for Libraries Press, 1970.

Nathan, George Jean. *The Critic and Drama.* New York: Classic Books, 1922.

Michael Vanden Heuvel
University of Wisconsin–Madison

DREXLER, ROSALYN (JULIA SOREL)

(1926–) Born in the Bronx, New York, Rosalyn Drexler is a playwright, painter, and novelist who occasionally writes under the pseudonym of Julia Sorel. Although her plays have been compared to the films of the Marx Brothers because of their anarchic wit and humor, Drexler has also been strongly influenced by Czech-born writer Milan Kundera, Irish-born French playwright Samuel Beckett, French novelist Colette, and American writer Elizabeth Hardwick. In her OFF-OFF-BROADWAY avant-garde plays, she intermingles fantasy and reality and explores violence, incest, domestic life, and sex. Her controversial subjects have not prevented her from winning OBIE AWARDS: She won for her musical *Home Movies* (1964), for her play *The Writer's Opera* (1979), and for her trilogy of one-act plays *Transients Welcome* (1985).

Despite her use of comedy, Drexler's plays often end with the death of the central character. In *The Investigation* (1967), a rapist commits suicide; in *The Writer's Opera* (1979), we witness the life and death of Susan, an artist who perishes as an old woman; in the unpublished "camp comedy" *Starburn: The Story of Jenni Love* (1979), a father commits suicide; in *Graven Image* (1980), Amy provokes her husband to kill her; and in *The Green River Murders* (1985), a serial murderer threatens his own mother with a knife and chokes a prostitute to death. Drexler often shows the empty lives of characters whose longings guide them to a tragic death.

In addition to the deaths she so often portrays, Drexler also animates her stage with such disturbing subjects as rape, physical and verbal violence, and incest. Based on her own experience as a wrestler, *Delicate Feelings* (1984) recounts a heartrending story of two lesbian mud wrestlers. In *Bad Guy* (1982), a psychotherapist treats a teenage assassin and rapist whose role models have been characters on television. *She Who Was He* (1974) is the feminist history of Hatshepsut, an Egyptian queen who was killed by Thutmose, her husband, in order to become pharaoh of Upper and Lower Egypt. By raping and killing his wife, Drexler suggests, Thutmose not only commits a brutal act against a human being but also brutalizes Egypt itself, which is represented by the figure of the queen.

In most of her plays, Drexler includes her feminist political view of the world. These attitudes are seen in such works as *Hot Buttered Roll* (1966), *The Line of Least Existence* (1967), *Cosmopolitan Girl* (1974), *Cara Piña* (1992), and *Dear* (1997). Drexler's most recent work is a novel, *Vulgar Lives* (2007), about incest and art.

BIBLIOGRAPHY
Drexler, Rosalyn. *Bad Guy.* New York: Dutton, 1982.
———. *Dear.* New York: Applause Theatre Books, 1997.
———. *"The Line of Least Existence" and Other Plays.* New York: Random House, 1967.
———. *Transients Welcome.* New York: Broadway Play Publishing, 1984.

Estefania Olid-Peña
Georgia State University

DRIVING MISS DAISY ALFRED UHRY (1987)

Set in Atlanta, Georgia, from 1948 until 1973, *Driving Miss Daisy* primarily depicts the relationship between a wealthy, elderly, Jewish southern widow and her aging African-American chauffeur in a racist South. UHRY does not focus on racism, though it is certainly present—even in the title character—but he focuses instead on the human bonds that can undermine that racism. The play won the PULITZER PRIZE.

Following an opening, offstage automobile crash, Daisy Werthan's son, Boolie (the prosperous head of an inherited business), insists on hiring a driver for his very independent 72-year-old mother. Thus begins the 25-year relationship between Miss Daisy and Hoke Coleburn, a widower 12 years her junior. Initially, Miss Daisy refuses to allow Hoke to drive her anywhere, though he is present and being paid. She is proud and stubborn and fond of saying that she was raised without money and is not rich now (though, in fact, she is). Her resistance to having a chauffeur

comes in part from her fear that others—especially the women at her temple—will think she is "put[ting] on airs." Hoke threatens not only her independence but also her sense of privacy; she believes that Hoke and her housekeeper, Idella, discuss her "behind [her] back in [her] own house." After these early days of misunderstanding and mistrust (she also falsely accuses Hoke of stealing from her), Miss Daisy moves into a kind of irritable acceptance. When she discovers that Hoke cannot read, she—a former teacher—begins to instruct him, without sentimentality. Hoke learns to understand and appreciate her frank, even abrasive, ways.

It takes Miss Daisy somewhat longer to understand and appreciate Hoke as an individual. After years of service, Hoke must sometimes insist on being treated like a man. When he drives Miss Daisy to a family birthday party and they get lost in Alabama, Hoke must insist on stopping the car to urinate when she forbids him to do so: "I ain't no dog and I ain' no chile and I ain' jes the back of the neck you look at while you goin' wherever you want to go. I'm a man nearly seventy-two years old." Later, when Miss Daisy is in her nineties and has become an admirer of Martin Luther King, she asks Hoke in an offhanded manner just as they reach the auditorium if he wants to accompany her to hear Dr. King speak. (Boolie has declined his mother's invitation for fear that attending will adversely affect his business.) Much to her surprise, Hoke declines, knowing that the invitation came a month before and she has inconsiderately waited until moments before the event to invite him; he tells her, "[N]ext time you ask me someplace, ask me regular." When Miss Daisy's temple is bombed, Hoke sympathetically relates the story of a lynching he witnessed as a child; Miss Daisy's own racism does not allow her to see the connection between these two hate crimes ("Ridiculous! The temple has nothing to do with that!"). Uhry subtly depicts the heart of racism, indeed, of all intolerance: viewing another only in terms of oneself.

When her mind begins to fail, it is Hoke who is there to help her and to telephone her son. When this first moment of confusion passes, she tells Hoke, "You're my best friend." Finally, living in a nursing home, Miss Daisy does not often see Hoke, who, too old to drive himself, must rely on his granddaughter—a college professor—for transportation. On Thanksgiving, when Miss Daisy is 97 and Hoke is 85, Hoke and Boolie make the trip together. She is having one of her "good days," and the two old friends talk while Hoke feeds her some pumpkin pie.

The play is a portrait of friendship and growing understanding. Daisy Werthan and Hoke Coleburn seem so different—their religions, their races, their financial situations, their personalities (he is kind while she is feisty and critical)—but both are members of groups who are the targets of hate, both are aging humans who must increasingly rely upon their children, and both are proud and private individuals. They learn they have more in common than they have differences.

DUNLAP, WILLIAM (1766–1839) Born in Perth Amboy, New Jersey, William Dunlap, the son of an Irish immigrant father, showed early promise as a painter and passionate patriot, but he gave little indication that he would become the most prolific playwright of the early national period. Often called the "father of American drama," Dunlap produced a staggering volume of plays during his career in the early national theater, writing, translating, and adapting more than 50 during his lifetime; yet, he was more than just a playwright. He served as the manager of New York's Park Theatre (1798–1805), and he wrote the first *History of the American Theatre* (1832), as well as a biography of well-known British actor George Frederick Cooke (*Life of George Frederick Cooke* [1813]). He was also an enthusiastic supporter of all the arts in America, not just the theater. Initially trained as a painter, he created a number of his own works, based on religious or national themes. He was also one of the directors of the American Academy of Fine Arts (1817) and a founder of the National Academy of Design (1826). In his *History of the Arts of Design* (1834), he claimed "industry, virtue, and talent" as the only true patrons of the arts, drawing a sharp contrast with the traditional European system of patronage, through which artists became the servants of wealthy aristocrats.

Indeed, this nationalistic strain runs through much of Dunlap's writings on both art and the theater. In his *History of the American Theatre,* he suggested that the time had come to "take the mighty engine into the hands of the people" and to create an American theater that would teach lessons of "patriotism, virtue, morality, [and] religion." He urged the government to create a national theater as a nursery for the dramatic arts. He feared that the American theater would fall under the influence of wealthy citizens who would control its content (fears based on his own experience at the Park Theatre). Though Dunlap's wish for a nationally funded theater did not materialize during his lifetime, he did much to legitimize theatrical entertainments in the new nation. His *History of the American Theatre* represents the first effort to define and understand the role of theater in American society. It has also become an invaluable source for contemporary theater scholars in mapping the play of politics and personality that shaped our early national theater.

A number of Dunlap's most successful plays, including *The Father; or, American Shandyism* (1789), *Darby's Return* (1789), ANDRÉ (1798), *The Glory of Columbia* (1803), and *A Trip to Niagara* (1828), tried to define the "American" character for the national audience. One of Dunlap's best-known and most controversial plays, *André,* contrasts the claims of self-interest and republican virtue on the national conscience. Based on actual events, *André* follows the story of a British soldier, Major John André, who was captured as a spy, and executed under George Washington's orders. In Dunlap's play, Bland, a young American soldier and a former friend of André's, pleads for his life, but Washington ("The General") refuses to relent, for the good of the nation. Bland learns that the welfare of the nation is more important than one man's wishes. Though on the surface *André* seems to echo familiar patriotic notions, it appeared at the height of the Federalist/Republican acrimony of the 1790s, when party loyalties had begun to strain the new nation. For many, *André* opened both old and new wounds of partisan conflict.

Dunlap also translated numerous plays, many by the prolific German author August von Kotzebue, including *The Stranger* (1798), *False Shame* (1799), and

Pizarro in Peru (1800). Kotzebue's work reflected the sentimental themes gaining popularity in early 19th-century American literature, elevating the power of emotion and feeling over intellect and reason.

In addition to his passion for the arts, Dunlap also demonstrated a strong interest in political and humanitarian causes—especially that of the abolitionists. Dunlap grew up surrounded by slave-owning families, including his own; this experience led him to join the New York Abolition Society, serving as its secretary for a number of years. He was also a trustee of the African School in New York. Upon his father's death, he freed his family's slaves.

Dunlap's life and career were marked by a series of highs and lows. His partner in the Park Theatre, John Hodgkinson, deserted him, leaving him to cope with the theater's staggering debts. The playhouse had cost more than $130,000, yet political and economic troubles meant that neither Dunlap nor the theater's investors were likely to reap any kind of profit from its activity. Though a skilled playwright and artist, Dunlap was ill-equipped to handle such a perilous financial venture. His sojourn as manager of the Park Theatre left him bankrupt, with his property confiscated. Yet, he knew many of the most distinguished writers, thinkers, and artists of his day, and he was instrumental in creating some of the country's most important cultural organizations, as well as in providing the nation with some of its most influential and entertaining drama.

BIBLIOGRAPHY

Canary, Robert H. *William Dunlap.* New York: Twayne, 1970.

Coad, Oral Sumner. *William Dunlap: A Study of His Life and Works and His Place in Contemporary Culture.* New York: Russell and Russell, 1962.

Dunlap, William. *Diary.* 3 vols. Edited by Dorothy C. Barck. New York: New-York Historical Society, 1930.

———. *History of the American Theatre.* 1832. New York: Burt Franklin, 1963.

———. *A History of the Rise and Progress of the Arts of Design in the United States.* 1834. 3 vols. New York: Benjamin Blom, 1963.

Heather Nathans
University of Maryland

DURANG, CHRISTOPHER (1949–   )

The wit and erudition behind much of Christopher Durang's drama reflects his solid educational background. He studied English at Harvard and earned a master's degree in playwriting at the Yale School of Drama, where he performed at the Yale Repertory Theatre. Before beginning graduate work, Durang had written a number of short absurdist plays, such as *The Nature and Purpose of the Universe* (1971), which explores the title concept through the life of a Job-like protagonist, and *'dentity Crisis* (1971), about a malfunctioning family who refuse to admit their insanity. While attending Yale, Durang continued to write one-acts and cabaret shows.

Durang's first professional production, *The Idiots Karamazov* (1974), a satiric comedy, was coauthored with his Yale classmate ALBERT INNAURATO. This musical play mocks classic literature, as an overwhelmed student relates a garbled version of Dostoevsky's novel, which includes the seduction of Alyosha by Anais Pnin and Mrs. Karamazov portrayed as Mary Tyrone. In 1976, Durang presented *Titanic,* an outrageous tale of sex and seduction aboard the titular ship, starring another Yale classmate, Sigourney Weaver. Opening at the Direct Theatre in 1976, it transferred to OFF-BROADWAY, along with a satiric mock Brecht-Weill–style cabaret, *Das Lusitania Songspiel,* coauthored by Durang and Weaver, and featuring them both.

In 1975, Durang had won a CBS playwriting grant, with which he would teach at Yale Drama School and write a new play for the Yale Rep. *The Vietnamization of New Jersey* (1977) satirizes the overearnestness of the period's antiwar plays, particularly those of DAVID RABE. Durang was at the same time working on another musical, *A History of the American Film* (1977), inspired by the 1933 movie *A Man's Castle.* The play deals with a romantic relationship set against a history of American movie archetypes. The following year, Durang lost his mother to cancer and moved to Washington, D.C., to rest and to get over the writer's block he had experienced during her final illness.

Moving away from dramatic parody in his longer pieces, Durang instead began to explore his own life and family, creating SISTER MARY IGNATIUS EXPLAINS IT ALL FOR YOU (1979), which won him an OBIE AWARD, and *Beyond Therapy* (1981), which is his work closest to mainstream comedy and his most often produced play. In *Sister Mary Ignatius,* an enormous critical success despite censorship difficulties, Durang exposes what he sees as the dogma and limitation of the Catholic Church of the 1950s, as Sister's ex-students confront her, and she sanctimoniously turns on them. *Beyond Therapy* questions psychiatry by presenting therapists who are crazier than their patients, as it also explores complex issues of bisexuality.

Baby with the Bathwater (1983) is a throwback to an earlier absurdist style, from which Durang had been moving away. We follow the troubled growth of Daisy, a male character with abusive parents, who learns to transcend the usual cycle in order to become a caring adult. While in Washington, Durang had begun another play about a dysfunctional family, *The MARRIAGE OF BETTE AND BOO* (1985). This won him a second Obie and is based directly on his own experience as a child and on his parents' sad marriage and eventual breakup. He followed this with the highly experimental *Laughing Wild* (1987), two stream-of-consciousness monologues in which a woman and man individually search for meaning in a bewildering "New Age," with a third act creating dreamlike interactions between them.

Between 1988 and 1993, despairing of satisfying the critics, Durang produced no new plays in New York and wrote very little, aside from the short piece *Naomi in the Living Room.* Instead, he formed a lounge act with two backup singers; calling themselves Chris Durang and Dawne, they successfully went on tour, eventually winning a 1996 Bistro Award and performing at the Rainbow Room and Caroline's Comedy Club. Durang also appeared in minor roles in several feature films and turned his hand to screenplays and television writing, but the theater appears to be his natural medium. His play *Media Amok* (1992) satirizes the flagrant and inflammatory characters who appear on television talk shows along with the obsession of those who watch; it premiered at the American Repertory Theatre in Cambridge, Massachusetts. His return to the New York theater was a program of one-act plays (mostly parodies) called *Durang/Durang* (1994). Since then we have seen the dark, mock-epic *Sex and*

Longing (1996) and *Betty's Summer Vacation* (1999), another Obie winner, which satirizes America's tabloid culture and mocks the audience's own complicity in its appetite for such things.

In 2002, inspired to skewer that annual feel-good American indulgence of satisfying one's moral complacency with seasonal viewings of such classics as *A Christmas Carol* and *It's a Wonderful Life,* Durang wrote a crazy Christmas play called *Mrs. Bob Cratchit's Wild Christmas Binge.* His most recent works continue to display the two prongs of his attack: outrageous parody and dramatic satire. *Adrift in Macao* (2005) is a musical parody of film noir and America's celluloid racism, and *Miss Witherspoon* (2005) exposes the inequities of a world so terrible that a person would rather stay dead than be reincarnated. *Why Torture Is Wrong, and the People Who Love Them* (2009) is about a woman who wakes up to find herself married to a seemingly violent stranger.

With an inventive imagination, Durang embraces his subjects with great audacity and originality. Allied closely to an absurdist tradition in earlier work, his plays have become more realistic, though not without comic exaggerations and intriguing innovations. Durang uses laughter as a response to the grave and inherently tragic in order to contain and control such forces. Common targets for Durang are the myth of the happy American family and such institutions as psychiatry and organized religion. He is concerned about people's fears of engagement in a world full of dangers, the strangulating nature of family ties, the pain of sexual disorientation, and social intolerance. His scrambling of genders within plays often exposes people's unacknowledged homophobia.

Frequently toying with and mocking stage conventions, Durang shows audiences the absurdity of theater itself in its inescapable artifice; yet, he is deadly serious as a theater practitioner, aware that the success of his plays depends on *how* they are played. He is wary of performers who overact in his plays in a misguided attempt to match his exaggerated style. He prefers them, instead, to uncover the truthful, psychological underpinnings of his characters so that they can play them beyond a single dimension. It is through this that his comedy gains its more serious undercurrents. Although critics have not always been able to agree on Durang's talent, his is a welcome anarchic spirit. His battles against theatrical convention, his experimentation with form, and his disregard for taboos have done much to stretch the possibilities of American drama.

In 2008, Durang was honored by the William Inge Festival and was given the Festival's Award for Distinguished Achievement in the American Theatre.

BIBLIOGRAPHY
Durang, Christopher. *Betty's Summer Vacation.* New York: Grove Press, 2000.
———. *Christopher Durang: 27 Short Plays.* Lyme, N.H.: Smith and Kraus, 1995.
———. *Christopher Durang Explains It All For You: Six Plays.* New York: Avon, 1983.
———. *Complete Full Length Plays 1975–1995.* Lyme, N.H.: Smith and Kraus, 1997.
———. *Durang/Durang.* New York: Dramatists Play Service, 1996.
———. *"Miss Witherspoon" and "Mrs. Bob Cratchit's Wild Christmas Binge."* New York: Grove Press, 2007.
———. *"Naomi in the Living Room" and Other Short Plays.* New York: Dramatists Play Service, 1998.

Susan C. W. Abbotson
Rhode Island College

DUTCHMAN Amiri Baraka/Leroi Jones (1964)

At the time of the first production of *Dutchman,* Jones had not yet changed his name to Amiri Baraka (he did so in 1968, leaving behind his "slave name"), nor had he begun to articulate the philosophy of the Black Arts Movement. However, *Dutchman* was a stunning seminal work in that movement. Recognized immediately for its dramatic value, the play won an Obie Award, even as its unflinching political statement raised controversy.

Lulu, a sexy, young white woman, catches the eye of Clay, a conservatively dressed, young African-American man, and sits next to him on a New York subway train. Eve-like, she offers him apples and begins her seduction. She is sexually provocative, irritable, and mocking by turns. Clay is attracted and repelled and confused by her erratic behavior. Eventually, she gets louder and begins to dance suggestively, trying to force him to join her, taunting him with loud mockery ("Uncle Tom. Thomas Woolly-Head."). Clay loses his temper, forcing her into her seat, slapping "her as hard as he can," demanding that she "let [him] talk." He feels a murderous rage ("I could murder you now"), but he does not kill her.

What follows this moment of arrested violence is a speech in which Clay articulates his rage, first attacking Lulu's misguided belief that she has any understanding of African Americans and then turning to white people's belief—delusion, in his view—that they have any real appreciation of jazz: "They say, 'I love Bessie Smith.' And don't even understand that Bessie Smith is saying, 'Kiss my ass, kiss my black unruly ass.'" Of great jazz musician Charlie "Yardbird" Parker, Clay says, "Bird would've played not a note of music if he just walked up to East Sixty-seventh Street and killed the first ten white people he saw. Not a note!" He goes on to tell Lulu that if he were to shed some of her blood, he would produce one less poem. African-American art, the play asserts, is born of repressed rage against white America, but, Clay continues, "Let them sing curses at you in code," because if the white man succeeds too well in converting "these blues people" to "Western rationalism," there will be "no more blues," and they will "murder you, and have very rational explanations." Having had his say, Clay bends to get his belongings and is stabbed by Lulu. His body is thrown off the train by the other passengers. At the next stop another young, African-American man boards the train, and Lulu "gives him a long slow look."

The play may be read as a fable about the destruction of African Americans by white society. It may also be read as a statement about the folly of choosing words over action: If Clay had acted—or had continued to act after slapping Lulu—rather than expressing his rage in words, he could have saved himself.

DYING CITY Christopher Shinn (2006)

Dying City employs a device that Christopher Shinn used in another of his plays, *The Coming World* (2001), that of a single actor playing temperamentally dissimilar identical twin brothers. *Dying City* is set against the backdrop of the Iraq War, during which one of the brothers, Craig, has died a year prior to the opening scene. In seven scenes that alternate between an evening in July 2005—the play's present tense—and 18 months earlier, just before Craig was deployed, we learn of the secrets and complex relationships of the brothers and Craig's wife, Kelly. Assumptions made by the audience are again and again proved wrong or, at least, not as simple as they at first seem. Shinn gets at the folly of believing that life is unambiguous.

As the play begins, Peter, Craig's gay brother who is an actor, arrives unannounced at Kelly's New York apartment. Peter is disappointed that his friendship with Kelly ended with his brother's funeral. Despite his efforts to keep in touch with her, she has been unreachable. He is interested in talking about Craig and about his (Peter's) skepticism over the official army report that Craig died in an accident during target practice. Peter assures his sister-in-law that both he and Craig were well trained as boys by their father in the careful use of guns. He speaks also of his boyfriend, Tim, a teacher, who, he says, has returned to California to prepare for the coming school year. Peter is in New York because he has a part in a revival of EUGENE O'NEILL's LONG DAY'S JOURNEY INTO NIGHT. He reveals to Kelly that he has walked out on the performance because the actor playing James Tyrone to his Edmond Tyrone beckoned to Peter in the wings and then made a pointed and hostile reference to Peter's sexual orientation.

In this first scene alone we draw all sorts of inferences: Kelly and Craig must have been happily married. Peter and Tim must have a stable relationship. The actor playing James Tyrone must simply be a bigot whose remarks were provoked only by his own hatred of homosexuals. Every one of these assumptions turns out to be either false or at least more complicated than we have inferred. Only the mystery surrounding Craig's death makes us correctly consider the possibility that he might have committed suicide.

In subsequent scenes, we learn that Craig went to Harvard on an ROTC scholarship and served four years in a noncombat capacity before being called up from the reserves while in graduate school, where he was working on a dissertation on Faulkner. He "believes in the war." We learn that Peter and Craig's

father was a Vietnam veteran who suffered from post-traumatic stress disorder and from whose violent flashbacks their mother tried to keep them as far away as possible. All of this exposition comes out very gradually in naturalistic dialogue. In fact, in his review of the 2007 New York production (the play premiered in London in 2006), *New York Times* theater critic Ben Brantley commented, "Few young dramatists are better than Mr. Shinn at writing clumsy naturalistic dialogue crippled by the weight of the unspoken" (March 5, 2007).

Kelly is a therapist; one of her clients is a misogynist who spends his time recounting his sexual exploits; Craig believes the man is "manipulating" her and wants to "torture" her with the vivid and hostile descriptions of what he does to women and how they respond. We realize only much later that Craig understands this man so well because he is like him. Is that what we expect of a Faulkner-loving, Harvard-educated graduate student? Again, our assumptions prove simplistic in the face of the ambiguities of real life.

Peter has brought with him e-mails from Craig that he wants to share with Kelly. She has no e-mails from her husband. (She tells Peter this is because she preferred the greater intimacy of the telephone, but we learn in the final scene that actually Craig severed contact with her and effectively ended their marriage before he went to Iraq.) Kelly is surprised to learn from the e-mail that Peter reads aloud that her husband had turned against the war. Furthermore, in this e-mail Craig equates the power he feels in post–Abu Ghraib Iraq (Abu Ghraib refers to a prison, the site of a notorious incident in which American forces tortured Iraqi captives by sexually demeaning them) to the power he witnessed as a child when his father broke the car windshield with his fist during a PTSD flashback. He writes to his brother that the war has changed him: "The horror I feel here is not just a consequence of the war, but is a horror of the core of me, of who I have always been." And then comes a revelation—stunning to his wife—that one of the changes he has undergone is that he "ha[s]n't felt the overwhelming need to sexually demean women that has haunted [him] [his] entire life." Previous scenes suddenly take on new meaning as we reassess his views about his wife's client; this is just one example of several such reassessments the audience must make.

Writing from Iraq, Craig refers to Baghdad as the city that is dying and cannot, he now believes, be resuscitated by the American forces. That is the overt reference to the title; however, Baghdad is also a "dying city" in the sense that it is a city for dying in—men are dying in Baghdad in the perpetual give-and-take of the war's violence, and Craig has died in Baghdad—as both Peter and Kelly become convinced—by his own hand. The title also takes in the idea that New York, too, is a city for dying: 9/11 is recent history (Craig and Kelly remember the "*cloud of death*" they witnessed from their own couch that day); the police-murder drama *Law and Order* plays in the background on Kelly's television; all of the relationships among the principal characters and the significant people they mention die or have died; and, finally, remaining illusions die.

E

EAST WEST PLAYERS Founded in Los Angeles in 1965 and born out of the frustration of Asian-American artists who could not get work in the then almost exclusively white world of theater and film, the East West Players is an Asian-American theater group, which began by producing non-Asian plays with all-Asian casts. In the mid-1970s, under the leadership of actor/director Mako (Makoto Iwamatsu), the group's primary mission became the development and presentation of the works of Asian-American playwrights who focus on Asian-American themes. East West Players alumni include such notable playwrights as DAVID HENRY HWANG, PHILIP KAN GOTANDA, and R. A. Shiomi.

EWP was the first theater group of its kind and has been the model for other groups in the United States and Canada dedicated to Asian Pacific drama. Committed to the support of Asian-American actors and writers, EWP has premiered scores of plays and musicals that focus on the Asian Pacific-American experience and has held hundreds of readings and workshops through its educational and artistic programs. According to founding artistic director Mako, the goals of the group are "to help break down stereotypes of Asians, to preserve stories of our immigrant histories, to share the unique experiences of being Asian and American, and to make visible the significant achievements of Asian Americans on the landscape of America" (www. eastwestplayers.com). When Mako left the group in 1988, he was succeeded by actress Nobu McCarthy, who in turn was succeeded by actor/director/producer Tim Dang in 1993. In 1996, EWP moved into a new space, the David Henry Hwang Theater in the Union Center for the Arts in downtown Los Angeles.

BIBLIOGRAPHY

Kurahashi, Yuko. *Asian American Culture on Stage: The History of the East West Players.* New York: Garland, 1999.

EDSON, MARGARET (1961–) See WIT.

EFFECT OF GAMMA RAYS ON MAN-IN-THE-MOON MARIGOLDS, THE PAUL ZINDEL (1970) In the former vegetable store that is their home, a widow and her two daughters live a chaotic existence. The disorder of the home and the abusive and erratic behavior of the mother have taken their toll on the teenaged girls, but despite their harsh environment, at least one of the girls maintains a sense of her own worth. ZINDEL's optimistic testament to human resiliency won the PULITZER PRIZE.

As the play begins, Tillie's science teacher, Mr. Goodman, telephones to encourage Tillie's mother, Beatrice, to allow her to attend school every day, because she is so bright. Beatrice is an unhappy woman who is verbally and psychologically abusive to her daughters. She has tended a series of elderly and terminally ill people for $50 a week and is also unkind to them. Beatrice resents that she has two teenagers—the elder of whom, Ruth, has a seizure disorder—and an ancient lady boarder on her hands. Worse than neglect-

148

ful, she does damage to her girls: keeping Tillie out of school, encouraging Ruth to smoke, making cynical and threatening gestures behind Nanny—the woman she is being paid to care for—for the girls to see. She tells Tillie that her marriage was "one mistake" that led to "two stones around [her] neck for the rest of [her] life" (referring to her daughters). Soon after this remark, she threatens to kill her daughter's pet rabbit for making "manure." The portrait of Beatrice is not entirely one-dimensional, however. In a scene that serves to humanize her somewhat, we learn that her own mother died when she was a child. She loved her father, who on his deathbed begged her to marry, which she did in haste and unhappily. She tells this to Ruth, to whom she shows some affection, and weeps.

Tillie conducts an experiment for the science fair on the effects of varying degrees of radiation on marigold plants. When Tillie is named a finalist, Beatrice at first refuses to participate; but when the evening arrives, she feels proud and is willing to sit on the stage with the other parents. Ruth, too, is excited, but when Beatrice tells her she must stay with Nanny, Ruth—having been taught cruelty by a master—lashes out at her mother by repeating the gossip about Beatrice she has heard among the teachers. Beatrice stays home and gets drunk. When the girls return from the science fair finals with the news that Tillie has won, Beatrice tells Ruth to shut up and reveals that she has killed the rabbit in their absence. This news sends Ruth into a seizure. Once the seizure is over, Beatrice comments to Tillie that she "hate[s] the world."

Tillie's science fair experiment is the central metaphor of the play. The girl finds that the more intense the radiation, the worse the effects on the growth and development of the marigolds. Similarly, the two sisters are damaged by the toxic presence of Beatrice, but Ruth, who is older and closer to her mother, has suffered the worse for it while Tillie will probably emerge relatively unscathed. As in her experiment where the plants subjected to moderate radiation mutated into sometimes beautiful variations—"double blooms," for example—Tillie, in response to her harsh environment, has withdrawn into a love of science that will be her salvation.

Zindel's most successful play, *The Effect of Gamma Rays on Man-in-the-Moon Marigolds* won the OBIE AWARD and the New York Drama Critics' Circle Award, in addition to the Pulitzer Prize.

ELDER, LONNE, III (1931–1996)

Born in Georgia, Lonne Elder was orphaned as an adolescent and raised by relations. He became interested in writing poetry and short stories under the guidance of poet/teacher Robert Hayden, whom he met when Elder found himself stationed near Fisk University on military service. Later, sharing a room with DOUGLAS TURNER WARD, he was inspired by how easily Ward seemed to create *Day of Absence* (1965) and, attracted to the immediacy of the theater, decided to write plays.

As a struggling playwright, he worked a variety of low-paid jobs, which gained him access to many walks of life he could later use in his drama. While taking acting lessons, he was approached by LORRAINE HANSBERRY to audition for *A RAISIN IN THE SUN* (1959); he played the part of Walter's friend Bobo for two years, in New York and on tour, during which period he had time to write. Although he dismisses his early one-acts, such as *A Hysterical Turtle in a Rabbit Race* (1961) and *Kissing Rattlesnakes Can Be Fun* (1966), as unpolished and as demeaning subjects he had intended to elevate, they were a training ground for *CEREMONIES IN DARK OLD MEN* (1969), which won Outer Critics Circle and Drama Desk Awards. This was the first play produced by the Negro Ensemble Company that took place entirely in Harlem, and its depiction of the Parker family offers its audience a realistic picture of the African-American experience in America, illustrating racial injustice, economic instability, and the threat and appeal of crime.

Elder also wrote for television while in New York, but, feeling a sense of closure after the success of *Ceremonies* and tired of New York, he moved to Hollywood. He continued to write theatrical pieces, such as *Charades on East Fourth Street* (1972), about a policeman who is kidnapped and forced to confess to a rape of which he is innocent, but Elder's main concentration was on television and film. His biggest screenplay success was his adaptation of William H. Armstrong's

Sounder (1972). Returning to New York, he wrote a television sequel, *Sounder, Part 2* (1976), and the award-winning biography of Harriet Tubman, *A Woman Called Moses* (1978). Meanwhile, for the theater, he created the monodrama *Splendid Mummer* (1988), based on the life of the black tragedian Ira Frederick Aldridge, who left America in the 1820s to become a successful Shakespearean actor in Europe, and *King* (1990), a musical about the life of Martin Luther King Jr., which was produced in London. Both highlight Elder's continued commitment to celebrate and disseminate African-American culture on stage.

His plays aimed to humanize African Americans, offering them alternative identities to those stereotypes that frequently were depicted by mainstream culture. Aside from his earlier shorter plays, which are more political statements than art, Elder's dramatic output was minimal, and his reputation rests on *Ceremonies in Dark Old Men*. Little of his dramatic writing has been published.

BIBLIOGRAPHY
Elder, Lonne, III. *Ceremonies in Dark Old Men*. New York: Farrar, Straus and Giroux, 1969.
———. "Charades on East Fourth Street." In *Black Drama Anthology,* edited by Woodie King and Ron Milner. New York: Columbia University Press, 1972. 147–166.

Susan C. W. Abbotson
Rhode Island College

ELEPHANT MAN, THE BERNARD POMERANCE (1979)

A moving 21-scene drama by New York-born playwright Pomerance, *The Elephant Man* was suggested by events in the life of Joseph Merrick (1862?–90), a 19th-century Englishman afflicted with a genetic disorder that grotesquely distorted his head and body (with the exception of one perfectly formed arm). In the play, Merrick, who is billed in carnival sideshows as "The Elephant Man," suffers brutalizing treatment by his exploitative manager. Merrick, whose unhappy life has brought him little affection or intellectual stimulation, comes to the attention of Dr. Frederick Treves, a progressive London doctor who manages to wrest control of Merrick from his manager, liberating him from the abject misery of his freak-show existence. Treves introduces Merrick to a life of dignity, seeing to it that he is treated with kindness at the hospital where Treves works. Although Treves encounters difficulty with hospital administrators for his plan to house Merrick indefinitely, and although some nurses and hospital employees are either frightened by Merrick or mock him as a curiosity, Treves is able to bring to Merrick more positive human experiences than he has ever known. The doctor even provides Merrick with acquaintances among the leading figures of British society.

Merrick becomes especially friendly with the celebrated actress Mrs. Kendal, who is intrigued by the depth of Merrick's emotions and his intellectual and artistic pursuits—Merrick proves to be a gifted sculptor (he is seen making an elaborate model of a cathedral) and is a thoughtful and stimulating conversationalist. Some attempts to normalize Merrick's life fail—for example, he is unable to get a good night's rest, for lying down will cause his breathing to be choked off by the excessive weight of his head, and he longs to know the tenderness of a woman. Mrs. Kendal is profoundly moved by Merrick's expression of desire for the opposite sex and disrobes so that he may see her body. Treves interrupts this encounter, which he feels cruelly exposes Merrick to something he can never fully experience. This episode underscores the play's strength—its poignant depiction of a man striving to live a full and normal life despite overwhelming obstacles.

Pomerance based *The Elephant Man* on a 1973 book by Ashley Montagu chronicling Merrick's life. The play, which was initially performed in London, moved to an OFF-BROADWAY stage in New York, where it won an OBIE AWARD. The Broadway production won the TONY AWARD for Best Play and the New York Drama Critics' Circle Award for Best Play. The play's Brechtian structure and universal themes of human striving have made *The Elephant Man* a frequently produced work on both professional and amateur stages.

BIBLIOGRAPHY
Graham, Peter W. *Articulating the Elephant Man: Joseph Merrick and His Interpreters*. Baltimore, Md.: Johns Hopkins University Press, 1992.

Howell, Michael, and Peter Ford. *The True History of the Elephant Man.* New York: Penguin, 1993.

Montagu, Ashley. *The Elephant Man: A Study in Human Dignity.* New York: Ballantine Books, 1973.

James Fisher
University of North Carolina at Greensboro

EMPEROR JONES, THE Eugene O'Neill (1920)

The first American play to feature an African-American actor in a serious role, *The Emperor Jones* also marked O'Neill's departure from the realistic style of his earlier work in its use of imaginative theatrical devices to depict the inner workings of its protagonist's mind.

Consisting of eight brief scenes, *The Emperor Jones* is the story of Brutus Jones, an African-American Pullman car porter who has killed two men, escaped from prison, and fled to a West Indian island, where he has exploited the ignorant natives' superstitions, amassed a fortune, and established himself as an emperor who can be killed—he tells the natives—only with a silver bullet.

When the play opens, Jones is informed by Smithers, a cynical white cockney trader who has helped him become Emperor, in one of the drama's only two entirely realistic scenes, that the natives have fled to the hills and are planning a rebellion against him, led by a man named Lem. Jones responds by announcing to Smithers that he "resigns de job of Emperor right dis minute," that he will escape through the forest—which he knows "high an' low like a book"—and that he will sail away to safety with all the money he has stolen from his "subjects" and hidden away on the island. But, just in case, he reveals, he has had a silver bullet made; he has five lead bullets in his gun "good enuff' fo' common bush niggers and . . . de silver bullet left to cheat 'em out o' gittin' me." As the sound of the natives' tom-tom marking the beginning of their war ceremony beats ominously in the background, Jones *"saunters"* out the front door of his palace.

The five scenes that follow exist on two levels simultaneously. Realistically, they depict Jones's increasing panic as he cannot find his hidden treasure and loses his way in the woods; the only dialogue consists of his often frantic monologues. More sym-bolically, O'Neill was the first American to use the theatrical style of EXPRESSIONISM (first introduced in the modern German theater), in this case, to demonstrate through Jones the Swiss psychiatrist Carl Jung's theory of the collective unconscious. In Jung's words, "the contents of the collective unconscious . . . have never been individually acquired but owe their existence exclusively to heredity" (60). Thus, as the beat of the tom-tom increases in frequency and volume, at once indicating both the closer approach of the natives and the heightening of their blood-lust, as well as Jones's quickening heartbeat and increased frenzy, the scenes move from the present through Jones's past to the past of his race. As he flees, he first hallucinates real people from his recent past—the fellow Pullman car porter and prison guard he killed—but then sees visions of events from the history of the American black—a slave auction, a slave ship, and a Congo witch doctor. Jones is stripped almost naked, losing his Emperor's uniform, as he flees; he uses all his lead bullets shooting at the ghosts from his and his race's past. In scene 7, he fires the silver bullet at a crocodile who has been summoned by the witch doctor to kill Jones as a sacrifice. The play's final scene, also rendered realistically, takes place back at the palace, where Jones is killed by Lem and his followers, who have superstitiously made silver bullets by melting down some of the coins Jones has been hoarding. Jones, having lost his way—literally and symbolically—in the forest, has ended up where he started—both literally and symbolically.

Brutus Jones is typical of other O'Neill protagonists in his inability to "belong" in an essentially hostile universe. Also typical are his means of dealing with his predicament—the assumption of a false identity or mask in an effort to fit in—and his ultimate failure to escape his true self. But, in this play, O'Neill went beyond his depiction of this isolated figure. As C. W. E. Bigsby observes, *The Emperor Jones* is more than "a study of a paranoid individual"; it is also "an observation about the psychopathology of a group" (57). Beyond this expansion of a familiar O'Neill theme, stylistically, *The Emperor Jones* was "startlingly innovative" in its use of expressionism, which introduced a new "plasticity" to the American stage (Bigsby 57).

BIBLIOGRAPHY
Bigsby, C. W. E. *A Critical Introduction to Twentieth-Century American Drama: Volume One—1900–1940.* Cambridge, England: Cambridge University Press, 1982.
Jung, Karl Gustav. *The Portable Jung.* New York: Viking, 1971.

ENSLER, EVE (1953–)

Eve Ensler was born and raised in Scarsdale, New York, the daughter of a food company executive and a homemaker. After attending Middlebury College in Vermont, she moved to New York City in the late 1970s and started writing. At the Neighborhood Playhouse, she began an association with actress/director Joanne Woodward, who encouraged her to write plays. Since then, Ensler has focused her work on social criticism, especially issues that affect women worldwide. Her plays are often controversial for their blunt language about sexuality and the body.

Her early work in the 1980s followed traditional dramaturgical patterns in the formation of plot and character. *Conviction* (1981) tells the story of two sisters, one of whom has been in prison. *Lemonade* (1982) is about a man who murders his family and takes on a new identity. *The Depot* (1985), a one-woman play about nuclear disarmament, toured the country for two years and included a performance at a nuclear test site in Nevada. *Scooncat* (1989) tells the tale of a man ruled by technology. *Extraordinary Measures* (1991) was inspired by the death from AIDS of a friend, acting teacher Paul Walker. *Floating Rhoda and the Glue Man* (1990) is a short comedy about a woman having a hard time loving a good man.

Her most famous works, however, use a more experimental form of dramaturgy. By the late 1980s, Ensler was experimenting with using interviews to construct her plays. Her first experiment with this form, *Ladies* (1989), a play about homeless women, was based on Ensler's interviews as a shelter volunteer. Her most well-known work, *The Vagina Monologues* (1996), is composed of soliloquies from interviews with more than 200 women about their sexuality. It is both a celebration of female sexuality and a condemnation of its violation; the play is presented in a staged-reading format. Winner of an OBIE AWARD, *The Vagina Monologues* has been translated into 26 languages and has become a worldwide phenomenon, with productions in London, Stockholm, Athens, Zagreb, and Jerusalem. The New York production finally closed in early 2003, and the play was made into a feature film for HBO. The play's popularity among female audiences inspired Ensler to offer it free of charge to universities for use in a benefit performance to call attention to violence against women. The event, V-Day, has been held on college campuses all over the country during February since 1998.

In *Necessary Targets* (2001), Ensler tells the story of two American trauma counselors and their reactions to the women of a Bosnian refugee camp. The play assesses the impact of such a process on both the questioners and the questioned. While Ensler returns to traditional narrative structure in this play, it is still based on interviews conducted by her during the war in Bosnia.

From October 2005 to April 2006, Ensler toured 20 North American cities with her play *The Good Body,* following engagements on Broadway, at ACT in San Francisco, and in a workshop production at the Seattle Repertory Theatre. *The Good Body* addresses why women of many cultures and backgrounds perceive pressure to change the way they look in order to be accepted in the eyes of society. *The Treatment* (2006) explores moral and psychological trauma as a result of participation in military conflicts. Her latest work is the book *Insecure at Last* (2006), which explores the measures people take to keep themselves safe, and how people can experience freedom by letting go of the deceptive notion of "protection."

Ensler continues to be a prominent antiviolence activist. In 2008, more than 4,000 V-Day events took place in 1,250 locations in the United States and around the world. To date, the V-Day movement has raised more than $60 million and educated millions about the issue of violence against women and the efforts to end it.

BIBLIOGRAPHY
Ensler, Eve. *Insecure at Last: Losing It in Our Security-Obsessed World.* New York: Villard, 2006.
———. *Ladies: A Play with Music.* New York: Central Park Editions, 1989.

———. *Necessary Targets: A Story of Women and War.* New York: Villard, 2001.

———. *The Vagina Monologues.* New York: Villard, 1998.

———, and Joyce Tenneson (photographs). *Vagina Warriors.* New York: Bulfinch, 2005.

Helen Huff
City University of New York—
Borough of Manhattan Community College

EXECUTION OF JUSTICE Emily Mann (1984)

In 1982, then 30-year-old playwright Mann was commissioned by San Francisco's Eureka Theatre Company to write a play about the 1978 assassination of that city's mayor, George Moscone, and its first openly gay supervisor, Harvey Milk, by fellow supervisor Dan White. Adopting a docudrama approach that incorporates verbatim sections from the resultant trial's transcripts, as well as firsthand interviews (as in the subsequent works of Anna Deavere Smith and in Moises Kaufman's *The Laramie Project* [2000]), Mann developed her play with the company's members for 18 months. The script was the cowinner of the 1983 Great American Play Contest sponsored by the Actors Theatre of Louisville, where the play received its premiere in March 1984. The Broadway production of 1986, directed by the playwright (and featuring then relatively unknown actors Wesley Snipes, Stanley Tucci, John Spencer, and Mary McDonnell), received respectful notices, but it closed within a week. As Richard Hummler predicted in *Variety:* "This non-profit-spawned play, precisely the kind of material the nonprofit theatres should be doing, may prove too unpleasant a dose of reality for today's increasingly escape-oriented Broadway public" (March 19, 1986). However, the play proved extremely popular in regional productions nationwide, with major productions at Baltimore's Center Stage, Seattle's The Empty Space, Arena Stage in Washington, D.C., Houston's Alley Theatre, Berkeley (Calif.) Rep, and Minneapolis's Guthrie Theater, among many others.

The play begins with the actual videotaped announcement by Supervisor Dianne Feinstein of the deaths of Moscone and Milk. It then intersperses the White trial testimony with a kaleidoscopic array of "uncalled witnesses," epitomized by an uptight right-wing cop and his polar opposite, Sister Boom Boom, a member of a group of drag faux nuns. The testimony incorporates the controversial so-called Twinkie defense, a ploy by defense lawyers to excuse White's actions due to his overconsumption of junk foods and sugar, causing temporary insanity. Although the playwright judiciously balances the testimony of both sides, the play pointedly derides the injustice of the jury verdict of voluntary manslaughter rather than murder, as exemplified by the title's double meaning. The play also concludes that the inequity of the verdict was predicated on society's continued discomfort with homosexuality and implies that had White killed only Moscone rather than the more easily dismissed Milk, the outcome would have been much different.

Mann updated the play after the initial productions, in order to include the eventual suicide of White in October of 1985, following his five-year incarceration for the double homicide. A film version of the play was produced for the Showtime cable network in November 1999.

Douglas W. Gordy
Walnut Creek, California

EXPRESSIONISM

Though realism was still considered a new style in early-20th-century theater, by the 1920s, American playwrights had begun to look beyond realistic surfaces toward their characters' inward, often tortured lives. Shaped initially by German playwrights and directors in the era just before World War I, expressionism tried to convey inner psychological and emotional states through boldly distorted sets and stylized dialogue. Its nightmarish distortions, strange angles, jarring sounds, staccato speech, and briskly episodic plots may be found in works by such leading American dramatists as Eugene O'Neill, Elmer Rice, John Howard Lawson, and Sophie Treadwell. Despite its relatively brief heyday during the 1920s, American theatrical expressionism generated a desire for alternatives to realistic theater that is still very evident among artists and audiences today.

Though lacking a manifesto or a central proponent, expressionism was driven by the same need to explore the human psyche found in painters like Vincent van

Gogh and Edvard Munch and theorists like Carl Jung and Sigmund Freud. Besides the more traditional media, expressionism was especially potent in cinema, with its new art of visual montage, as in *The Cabinet of Doctor Caligari,* a 1919 German film cited by several American playwrights as an influence. Such German playwrights as Walter Hasenclever, Ernst Toller, and Georg Kaiser produced a body of plays between 1914 and 1922 that established expressionism not only as a bold theatrical style but also as a mode of political and cultural criticism. Expressionism attempted to give voice to anxieties created by an increasing sense that life had become inhumanely fast, mechanized, and impersonal, dominated by the very technology that was supposed to liberate humanity.

The origin of expressionism in theater is usually traced to the later plays of Swedish playwright August Strindberg, especially his radically nonrealistic *A Dream Play* (1902) and *The Ghost Sonata* (1907). As Strindberg explains in his preface to the latter work, the dream is a heightened reality in which a single consciousness is fractured, liberated from everyday realities and logic, but tormented by its own hidden anxieties. These expressionistic plays offered an alternative to the social realism of Ibsen and his admirers, appealing especially to those who wished to explore what Nietzsche had called the Dionysian forces in art and life.

By the time Eugene O'Neill began to write his most expressionistic works in the early 1920s, much of the ferment in European theater had reached America, but O'Neill took his lessons not so much from the German expressionists as from Strindberg. Several American plays had already featured elements akin to expressionism, including Alice Gerstenberg's *Overtones* (1915), but O'Neill's The EMPEROR JONES (1920) and *The HAIRY APE* (1922) established expressionism as an important theatrical style in America, with his later works—ALL GOD'S CHILLUN GOT WINGS (1924), DESIRE UNDER THE ELMS (1924), *The Great God Brown* (1926), and *Days without End* (1933)—showing the lingering influence of expressionism in a more realistic mode. Notably Strindbergian in their portrayal of a single consciousness becoming increasingly alienated and divided, *The Emperor Jones* and *The Hairy Ape* also relied on a series of scenes (a technique called "station drama," suggesting the Stations of the Cross) that lead their protagonists toward destruction. Jones, a black convict, and Yank, a steamship hand, are powerful individuals crushed by forces beyond their control. Yank's cramped engine room and the "sky-dome" under which Jones confronts his destiny are also important landmarks in American stagecraft. In 1932, O'Neill wrote the brief "Memoranda on Masks," a key text in the theory of expressionistic staging.

Its leading American practitioner, O'Neill was by no means alone in his use of expressionism on Broadway. Elmer Rice's The ADDING MACHINE (1923), with its broader caricatures of modern life, is revived frequently on college and regional stages. Rice's Mr. Zero, like the play generally, is drawn more whimsically than are O'Neill's Jones or Yank, more like a generic modern everyman than a tragic hero. A bookkeeper whose firing prompts him to murder his boss, Mr. Zero is first shown in a confining room lined with the foolscap sheets used in his trade, suggesting a life without joy or escape. A full range of visual, aural, and mechanical effects are deployed to convey the disorder of Mr. Zero's psyche, including loud music, distorted scenery, swirling lights, and, in the original THEATRE GUILD production, a spinning platform built into the office floor. Rice's subsequent expressionist play, *The Subway* (1925), enjoyed far less success than did *The Adding Machine.*

The American expressionist play with perhaps the most overt social message is Sophie Treadwell's MACHINAL (1928), loosely based on a well-known case of a wife who murders her husband. Treadwell uses the expressionist techniques of staccato dialogue and generic characters to depict the powerlessness of the Young Woman, trapped first in a numbing job and then in a senseless marriage. The trial and execution scenes emphasize her lack of any significant voice in her world, a feminist theme that has been emphasized in more recent productions of the play.

Other plays from the 1920s that show expressionist features include John Howard Lawson's *Roger Bloomer* (1923) and PROCESSIONAL (1925), which combine often grotesque characterizations with a critique of capitalism, and E.E. Cummings's *HIM* (1928), which resembles O'Neill's *The Great God Brown* in its stylized alter egos and pointed contrast between the worlds of business and art. *BEGGAR ON HORSEBACK,* by GEORGE S. KAUFMAN and MARC CONNELLY (1924), likewise uses exaggerated dream imagery to attack the degradation of art by the demands of business.

After the 1920s, the more surreal technical innovation that marked expressionist drama began to wane, but its influence may be seen in works by THORNTON WILDER, TENNESSEE WILLIAMS, ARTHUR MILLER, EDWARD ALBEE, ADRIENNE KENNEDY, SAM SHEPARD, MEGAN TERRY, TONY KUSHNER, and many other later playwrights, along with theater companies like the FEDERAL THE-ATRE PROJECT, the LIVING THEATRE, Café La Mama, and the Wooster Group (see LECOMPTE).

BIBLIOGRAPHY

Grace, Sherrill. *Regression and Apocalypse: Studies in North American Literary Expressionism.* Toronto: University of Toronto Press, 1989.

Valgamae, Mardi. *Accelerated Grimace: Expressionism in the American Drama of the 1920s.* Carbondale: Southern Illinois University Press, 1972.

Walker, Julia A. *Expressionism and Modernism in the American Theatre: Bodies, Voices, Words.* New York: Cambridge University Press, 2005.

Kurt Eisen
Tennessee Tech University

F

FAITH HEALER, THE WILLIAM VAUGHN MOODY (1909)

One of MOODY's two prose plays, *The Faith Healer* examines the struggle between spiritual faith and human sexual love and reaches the conclusion that they are not mutually exclusive.

As the play begins, Ulrich Michaelis, a man who has had visions of Christ and who has "raised [a boy] from the dead," has been at the Beelers' home for three days. He brings hope to Mrs. Beeler, who has been confined to a wheelchair for five years from a stroke. Mr. Beeler, however, is skeptical, as is his sister, Martha; he favors science over religion, as his scientific books and conspicuously hung pictures of Charles Darwin and social scientist Herbert Spencer testify. Living with the Beelers is Rhoda, Mrs. Beller's niece, whose attraction to Michaelis, and his for her, is clear. By the end of the first act, Michaelis has cured Mrs. Beeler; at his bidding, she rises and walks. The Beelers' house is soon surrounded by others looking for a cure. Michaelis seems almost fearful of the supplicants but is resigned to help them.

The one time in the play that the Indian boy who was "raised from the dead" is named, he is called Lazarus. It is no coincidence then that the Beeler women, sisters-in-law, are named Mary and Martha, the names of the sisters of Lazarus. The biblical Mary sat at the feet of Christ and listened to him while her sister Martha did all of the housework. Similarly, Mary Beeler listens with rapt hope and attention to the Christ-figure, Michaelis, while her sister-in-law, Martha, cooks and cleans and cares for the family.

The temptation of the Christ-figure is passion for Rhoda, who has had a wild and passionate youth. In fact, her former lover, the cynical physician Dr. George Littlefield, seeks her out and takes the job of family doctor in this small midwestern town in order to persuade Rhoda to resume their affair. The Littlefield character serves two purposes in the play: He, in contrast to Michaelis, represents human, sexual love that is cynical and devoid of all spirituality. He is also an additional, authoritative voice of science as opposed to Michaelis, the man of faith. Littlefield explains to Mr. Beeler that Mrs. Beeler's walking is simply a case of mind over matter.

As the sick congregate outside the Beelers' farmhouse, Michaelis proclaims his love to Rhoda. When a young woman rushes into the house with a critically ill infant, Michaelis is unable to cure the baby and believes that his feelings for Rhoda have made him weak. Furthermore, upon hearing that the infant is "dead," Mrs. Beeler relapses into paralysis. Michaelis goes out to tell the crowd that God "has smitten" him as He would "His enemies."

Michaelis is convinced that his religious calling has deserted him because he is passionate about Rhoda, whom he loves "more than the visions that came to [him] in desert places, more than the powers that fell upon" him. Rhoda, unable to bear the responsibility of diminishing his faith and power, reveals her "wicked" past to him, and by doing so, hopes to "give [him] back [his] mission." At this point, the cynical Dr. Littlefield comes in to say that the baby who was in a coma is beyond help and to claim Rhoda as his lover—or as his bride, if she insists. But she rejects him, and Michaelis backs her up with sympathy and understanding—and with contempt for the ruthless Littlefield.

Michaelis is finally able to resume his spiritual life when he realizes that he can have human love too because "God does not deny love to any of His children, but gives it as a beautiful and simple gift to them all." This was a truth he hadn't seen when he first felt love for Rhoda, and "in that blind hour [his] life sank in ruin." With the realization that human love and spirituality can exist in harmony, he is able to heal Mary Beeler and the baby and meet the crowds outside the house.

Unlike Moody's other prose play, the highly regarded *The* GREAT DIVIDE (1906), *The Faith Healer* was not a popular or commercial success, closing after only 12 performances. However, it remains recognized as an early 20th-century play made interesting by its portrayals of the conflict between science and faith and of the synthesis of human sexual love and faith. The play also contains poet Moody's characteristically lyrical style.

FASHION; OR, LIFE IN NEW YORK ANNA CORA OGDEN MOWATT (1845) This comedy of manners has seen more revivals than many other 19th-century American comedies. In *Fashion,* MOWATT satirizes the foolishness of adopting European fashions and customs over more honest and forthright American ones. The play is similar in theme to *The* CONTRAST by ROYALL TYLER, which draws the same distinction. The frivolous Mrs. Tiffany, for the sake of fashion, brings her family to the brink of financial ruin. Fortunately, the family is saved by the homespun wisdom of the levelheaded Mr. Trueman, who agrees to bail them out financially if they move to the country and there "learn economy, true independence, and home virtues, instead of foreign follies."

Mrs. Tiffany, a silly, pretentious woman who speaks a comic, butchered French, spends her husband's money with abandon in order to maintain a fashion-able household. Her advice on European etiquette and fashion comes from her French maid, Millinette. Mrs. Tiffany hopes to acquire the fashionable Count di Jolimaitre as a husband for her daughter, Seraphina. What she does not know is that the count is no count at all, but a cook and con man who is well aware of the propensity of some Americans to "pay homage to titles where [they] profess to scorn them." The count, however, is not the only one who is not what he seems; Mrs. Tiffany, herself, was once a humble milliner, a fact she takes pains to conceal. Mr. Tiffany's wealth is mere illusion; he has, in fact, been reduced to bankruptcy by his wife's extravagant spending. Mr. Tiffany has promised the hand of Seraphina to his associate, Mr. Snobson, because Mr. Snobson, having witnessed Mr. Tiffany's dubious business practices, has blackmailed him. Trueman, the forthright, rural all-American character, tells his old friend Mr. Tiffany, "Deception is your household ideal."

Colonel Howard, an honest, stalwart United States Army officer, is drawn to Gertrude, Seraphina's governess, who came from Geneva to New York because her "mania" as she says "is a love of independence." Colonel Howard and Gertrude, together with Trueman, embody the American ideal.

The fraudulent count wants the apparently wealthy Seraphina for his wife and Gertrude for his mistress. His attempt to seduce the truehearted Gertrude is rebuffed, while his attempt to elope with Seraphina is thwarted when she returns to her parents' house for her jewels. It is then that Millenette, who has known the "count" for years and hopes to marry him herself, discloses the count's true identity to the family. Trueman reveals that Gertrude is his granddaughter and the heiress to his fortune. Trueman has waited to reveal himself to her until she has found a husband who loves her for herself and not her money. This she has found in the good Colonel Howard.

After rescuing the Tiffanys from financial ruin on the condition that they reform, the good-natured, honest, and wealthy Trueman reforms even the count—whose real name is Gustave Treadmill—by promising to set him up in honest business as a cook. In the end, fashion is exposed for what it is, and Trueman's view of the folly of fashion prevails, a view he has articulated early in the play: "Fashion! . . . An agreement between certain persons to live without using their souls! To substitute etiquette for virtue—decorum for purity—manners for morals! To affect a shame for the works of their Creator! And expend all their rapture upon the works of their tailors and dressmakers!"

FEDERAL THEATRE PROJECT (1935–1939)

1939)   The New York Stock Exchange crash of October 1929 turned what had been an economic recession into an economic nightmare. Widespread unemployment and the inability of the economy to recover forced the federal government to contend with unprecedented human need. Financial and business institutions failed daily, investment losses affected vast numbers of people, and unemployment lines grew longer with each week. By 1933, about 16 million American workers were unemployed; among these were thousands of artists, musicians, writers, and theater workers. Unable to compete with film and radio, thousands of theater artists were without work. As the numbers of unemployed rose, musicians and actors found themselves competing with unskilled laborers for manual jobs.

The Emergency Relief Appropriation Act of 1935 gave President Franklin D. Roosevelt the authority to create the Works Progress Administration (WPA). The WPA was a temporary work-relief agency that hired only those who were both employable and unemployed in work situations that matched their skills and training. Thousands of welders, engineers, machine operators, and others were put back to work on hundreds of projects that built bridges, dams, roads, and public buildings all across the country. Workers not only earned a paycheck, they also gained a measure of self-respect and pride in themselves and their country. Among the thousands of workers the federal government employed were hundreds of artists, musicians, and actors.

President Roosevelt appointed HALLIE FLANAGAN, a little known professor of drama at Vassar College, to direct the Federal Theatre Project (FTP). Though the FTP was neither the first nor the only theater relief organization of the 1930s, it was and remains the only national theater effort supported by the United States government. Flanagan intended that the FTP be more than a relief program; she hoped that it would become a broadly based, noncommercial uniquely American expression of culture. The FTP not only succeeded in providing relief work but also brought performances to one-third of the nation before Congress ended its funding in 1939. At its peak, the FTP employed more than 12,000 actors, stagehands, painters, playwrights, and others in 158 theaters in 28 states and was America's largest single producer of theater. The FTP also published a nationally distributed theater magazine and operated a play and research bureau that not only served the project's own theaters but also helped tens of thousands of schools, churches, and community groups to produce theater throughout the United States.

Despite the problems and limitations inherent in being a governmental relief agency, the FTP managed to mount several notable and important plays. The vast majority of all productions done by the FTP, however, were free performances of circus, vaudeville, and children's productions. One of the most noteworthy innovations developed by the FTP was the LIVING NEWSPAPER—plays developed collaboratively by actors, writers, and journalists that were essentially theatrical documentaries. Among the most successful was Arthur Arent's *One Third of a Nation* (1938), which addressed the needs and passions of the one-third of the country that was ill-housed, ill-clad, and ill-nourished. Another notable accomplishment of the FTP was the unusual relationships it had with authors such as George Bernard Shaw, EUGENE O'NEILL, MAXWELL ANDERSON, and ELMER RICE. Led by the example of Shaw, several American playwrights offered the bulk of their work to the FTP at very low royalty rates, thus allowing the FTP unprecedented access to a large body of high-quality plays. The project could thus claim several important firsts for theater: the simultaneous opening of Sinclair Lewis's *It Can't Happen Here* in 21 cities across the nation; regional productions, such as PAUL GREEN's *The Lost Colony* (1937), which is still performed annually on Manteo Island in North Carolina; and the American premiere of Shaw's *On the Rocks* (1938).

Despite a promise by the administration to allow a free, adult, and uncensored theater, the FTP faced trouble on numerous occasions. ORSON WELLES and John Houseman's production of *The Cradle Will Rock* (1938), a blatantly left-wing musical, had to be moved to a new theater to circumvent governmental efforts to prevent its opening. Some within Congress opposed several black theater projects in Harlem, Los Angeles, Seattle, and elsewhere, while Jewish and Catholic theater projects angered others. In the attempt to be a socially aware, democratic theater, the FTP managed to anger many conservatives. In 1939, after a heated debate, Congress abolished the theater project a year before they ended funding for the art, music, and writers' projects. Nevertheless, the FTP remains notable as America's only officially supported, national theater that played to a national audience.

BIBLIOGRAPHY

Buttitta, Anthony, and Barry Witham. *Uncle Sam Presents: A Memoir of the Federal Theatre, 1935–1939.* Philadelphia: University of Pennsylvania Press, 1982.

Flanagan, Hallie. *Arena.* New York: Duell, Sloan, and Pearce, 1940.

Goldstein, Malcolm. *The Political Stage: American Drama and the Theatre of the Great Depression.* New York: Oxford University Press, 1974.

Mathews, Jane DeHart. *The Federal Theatre, 1935–1939: Plays, Relief, and Politics.* Princeton, N.J.: Princeton University Press, 1967.

O'Connor, John, and Lorraine Brown, eds. *Free, Adult, Uncensored: The Living History of the Federal Theatre Project.* Washington, D.C.: New Republic Books, 1978.

Schwartz, Bonnie Nelson, ed. *Voices from the Federal Theatre.* Madison: University of Wisconsin Press, 2003.

Witham, Barry B. *The Federal Theatre Project.* Cambridge: Cambridge University Press, 2003.

Michael M. O'Hara
Ball State University

FEFU AND HER FRIENDS MARIA IRENE FORNÉS (1977)

FORNÉS won an OBIE AWARD for Playwriting (as well as one for her stage direction of the American Place Theatre premiere of the play) for *Fefu and Her Friends*. The play features, in part 2, four simultaneous scenes placed in four different rooms, so that all audience members, while walking through these sets, must closely experience the interplay of multiple character voices.

The play represents a women's group gathering in Fefu's New England country home during 1935. Eight women plan to rehearse an educational piece of creative dramatics—yet, the emphasis generally falls not on their specific written speeches, but instead on the costuming, flair, and sincere zeal of their theatrical performance (which becomes a model for their participation in all of life).

Among the women, flamboyant and confident feminist theoretician Emma Blake declares herself "happy." She also utters the one lengthy visionary speech in the group's play-within-a-play. Her words derive, however, from a namesake of hers: one Emma Sheridan Fry, a turn-of-the-20th-century New York City children's acting instructor. The speech-paired Emmas together urge the others to "seize all," as part of a "great" feminist "quest."

Others in the group experience both more inner and more interpersonal tensions than any we sense in Emma. Cindy is sometimes an apparently giddy tippler, but she also reports nightmares about males oppressing her. Christina is easily perplexed, indeed shocked, by others' iconoclasm against social norms, yet she eventually admits to being "all shreds inside." Troubled lesbian couple Paula and Cecilia often draw spiritually back toward each other, but then veer apart again. Sue, who seems to be the group's treasurer, may be overly preoccupied with that position's duties, but she has a contrasting propensity to serve as a caregiver.

Wheelchair-bound, hallucinatory, perhaps shamanistic, Julia lengthily recounts male victimization of women. She constantly, bleakly, ponders inevitable death—such as that which evidently comes to her at the play's final curtain, with a gunshot wound to her head. Fefu, the apparent shooter, has earlier taunted Julia to "fight" (perhaps because she believed that she had seen Julia actually once rise from her wheelchair and walk). However, Fefu was not obviously shooting at Julia, so it is uncertain whether she (who often shoots blanks from her gun, in an ongoing Strindbergian marital "game" with her husband, Philip) was a deliberate aggressor against Julia.

This play honors women's efforts to establish what Cecilia deems their necessary "community." The drama definitely senses in womankind much diversity and unexplored darkness (to Fefu, something like the underside to "stone[s]" in "damp soil"), as well as many variegated styles (especially Julia's hyper-meditativeness matched against Fefu's daring and impulsive active exploration).

Jeffrey B. Loomis
Northwest Missouri State University

FEIFFER, JULES (RALPH) (1929–)

Jules Feiffer was born in the Bronx, New York. He attended New York's Art Students League (1946), Pratt Institute (1947–48 and 1949–51), and served with the United States Army Signal Corps (1951–53), working in an animation unit. This early association with graphic art has continued throughout his life and has earned him a high degree of public attention. In 1986, he was awarded a PULITZER PRIZE for editorial cartooning.

Feiffer's singular point of view, dark humor, and interest in using humor as a reflection of the confusion and disturbance of urban and collegiate America served him well as he began to write for the stage. His willingness to deal with sexual life as it really was, his ability, according to Clive Barnes writing in the *New York Times,* to face "a world full of the perils of rejection, the dangers of acceptance, the wild and perpetual struggles of ego for id, the dire discomfort of parenthood [and] the unceasing wars between men and women" (January 24, 1977), enabled him to people his plays with sharply drawn characters speaking in words that accurately capture urban anxieties.

In LITTLE MURDERS (1967), perhaps the most successful of Feiffer's plays, we are presented with a family comedy set against an urban background that has gone literally mad. As Feiffer makes us watch ordinary characters adjust to a deranged world of rampant and random gunfire in the streets, we are forced, in spite of ourselves, to laugh at the grotesqueness of this worst of all possible worlds. Feiffer was named the most promising playwright of the 1966–67 season by the New York Drama Critics and received the London Theatre Critics Award in 1967; *Little Murders* received the OBIE AWARD in 1969 and the Outer Critics Circle Award, which also went to Feiffer for *The White House Murder Case* (1970) the following year.

The White House Murder Case is an incisive satire aimed at the war posture of a United States of the future. In the play, this year's target is Brazil, where an American gas attack backfires. As the president and his cabinet are attempting to concoct a cock-and-bull story, the president's independent-minded, radical wife is murdered; the outcome suggests that Jules Feiffer has about as dark a view of American society and human possibility as can be found in contemporary theater.

Knock Knock (1976) is an uncharacteristic fantasy about two old Jewish bachelor recluses who have lived together for 20 years, are bored with each other, and constantly squabble. When one of them wishes for intelligent company, enter Wiseman—part Mephistopheles, part Groucho Marx—followed by Joan of Arc, who is recruiting for a spaceship trip to heaven. Antic hell breaks loose in what can be described as a laugh-saturated miracle play in the absurdist tradition. Alan Rich, in *New York* magazine, noted that the reason the play is often "screamingly funny is the incredible accuracy of [Feiffer's] language and his use of it to paint urban neurosis in exact colors" (February 2, 1976).

Among Feiffer's other plays are *Hubble* (1963), *The Unexpurgated Memoirs of Bernard Mergendeiler* (1968), *God Bless* (1968), *Dick and Jane* (one-act)—produced as part of *Oh! Calcutta!* (1969), *Grownups* (1981), *Elliot Loves* (1989), *Anthony Rose* (1990), and *A Bad Friend* (2003). He wrote the screen adaptation of his play *Carnal Knowledge* (1971). Feiffer was a faculty member at Yale School of Drama (1973–74) and a senior fellow, National Arts Journalism program, Columbia University (1997–98).

In mid-2006, Disney announced that its next stage musical would be an adaptation of Feiffer's 1993 children's book, *The Man in the Ceiling,* and that Feiffer himself would write the libretto; no timetable was given. Feiffer also continues his award-winning work as illustrator and editorial cartoonist.

BIBLIOGRAPHY
Feiffer, Jules. *Anthony Rose.* New York: Dramatists Play Service, 1990.
———. *Elliot Loves.* New York: Grove Press, 1989.

————. *Hold Me!* New York: Random House, 1963.

————. *Knock Knock.* New York: Hill & Wang, 1976.

————. *Little Murders.* New York: Random House, 1968.

————. *The Unexpurgated Memoirs of Bernard Mergendeiler.* New York: Random House, 1965.

————. *The White House Murder Case.* New York: Grove Press, 1970.

Philip M. Isaacs
New York, New York

FENCES AUGUST WILSON (1985) Set in 1957, *Fences* is WILSON's 1950s play in his cycle of plays representing the African-American experience in each of the decades of the 20th century. A family drama set on the eve of the Civil Rights movement, the play is one of Wilson's most universal in theme.

Troy Maxson, 53 and a garbage collector, was once a baseball star in the Negro League. Too old to play by the time the major leagues were integrated, he is bitter. Now his son, Cory, a high school senior and a football player, is being recruited to play college football. Troy is convinced that "the white man ain't gonna let him get nowhere with that football" and refuses to sign the recruiter's papers. Though Troy's wife, Rose, and friend, Bono, try to convince him that times have changed since he played baseball and that this is Cory's one opportunity to go to college, Troy is certain of his vision of the world. Troy's world view is shaped by his own difficult experiences, including—aside from discrimination—prison time and a brutal father who, though he did not teach Troy love, taught him responsibility. Troy tells Cory to forget about football, to learn instead to "fix cars or build houses," so he will not have to haul garbage. He tells Rose, "I want him to move as far away from my life as he can get."

Complicating Troy's feelings about the world and about himself is his younger brother Gabriel, who suffered a head injury during World War II. It is only because of the compensation money Gabe received from the government that Troy could afford to buy his house, where Gabe has lived too, on and off. Troy tells Rose, "If my brother didn't have that metal plate in his head . . . I wouldn't have a pot to piss in or a window to throw it out of. And I'm fifty-three years old." During the action of the play, Gabe is renting a room from Miss Pearl because he wants some measure of independence, though he is so simpleminded as a result of his injury that he does not eat enough when left to his own care. Rose worries about him and believes he would be better off living in the mental hospital where he would eat more regularly, but Troy insists he should be free. This belief is based more on his own experience of imprisonment (15 years for killing a man during a robbery) than on an understanding of what is best for his brother. Yet, he means well, just as he does in his choices for Cory.

Like so many of Wilson's major female characters, Rose is strong and independent. Troy loves her and appreciates her strength and candor, but this does not stop him from having an affair with a younger woman, Alberta, who makes him "laugh out loud" and helps him temporarily "get away from the pressures and problems" of his life. When Alberta becomes pregnant, he confesses his affair to Rose, who does not accept his justification, asking "Don't you think I had dreams and hopes? . . . That I wanted to lay up somewhere and forget about my responsibilities? That I wanted someone to make me laugh so that I could feel good?" When Alberta dies in childbirth, Troy asks Rose to raise the child. Rose accepts Troy's infant daughter, but she makes clear that while the baby is no longer motherless, Troy is now a "womanless man."

Life becomes cold for Troy. Rose is raising baby Raynell, but her relationship with Troy does not go beyond cooking his meals. Cory, angry about his father's treatment of his mother and about the loss of his football scholarship, is contemptuous of Troy. Father and son have a final confrontation, in which Troy insists on Cory's respectful behavior in *Troy's* house and in *Troy's* yard—earned by *Troy's* sweat. When Cory reminds him that the house and yard were bought with Uncle Gabe's injury money, tempers flare. Cory threatens Troy with a bat, and Troy, disarming him and holding back from striking his son, tells him to "get out."

The final scene of the play is on the day of Troy's funeral in 1965. Raynell is seven. Cory has been a marine for six years and has not seen his father since their fight, but he returns for Troy's funeral at Rose's request. Lyons (Troy's son by his first wife) is on leave from the "workhouse" where he is serving time for some kind of check fraud. Rose tells Cory that Troy tried to give him "the best of what [was] in" him. He could not do better than that. In the play's final scene, Raynell and Cory sing a song about an old dog, "Old Blue"—it is a song that Troy learned from his own father.

What is good in us and what is bad—the sins of the fathers—come to the children, inevitably. In a 1987 interview, August Wilson said, "Cory's . . . going to arrive at the same place as Troy. I think one of the most important lines in the play is when Troy is talking about his father: 'I got to the place where I could feel him kicking in my blood and knew that the only thing that separated us was the matter of a few years.' Hopefully, Cory will do things a bit differently with his son. . . . I suspect with Cory it will repeat with some differences and maybe, after five or six generations, they'll find a different way to do it" (Savran 300–301).

First produced at the Yale Repertory Theatre, *Fences* won the 1987 PULITZER PRIZE, New York Drama Critics' Circle Award, and TONY AWARD after Lloyd Richards's Yale Rep production (with a few cast changes) moved to New York. Troy Maxson, complex and contradictory, remains one of Wilson's most enduring characters.

BIBLIOGRAPHY

Menson-Furr, Ladrica. *August Wilson's "Fences."* New York: Continuum, 2009.

Savran, David. *In Their Own Words: Contemporary American Playwrights.* New York: Theatre Communications Group, 1988.

Shannon, Sandra. *August Wilson's "Fences": A Reference Guide.* Westport, Conn.: Greenwood Press, 2003.

FERBER, EDNA (1885–1968)

A prolific writer of novels and short stories, Edna Ferber is also known in the world of drama for her collaborations with GEORGE S. KAUFMAN. Born in Kalamazoo, Michigan, Ferber began her writing career as a journalist when she became a reporter in Appleton, Wisconsin, after graduating from high school there. Two years later, she moved to the *Milwaukee Journal,* where she stayed for three years. Most of her writing, however, is fiction. She sold her first short story in 1910 and published her first novel in 1911. During her long career, she wrote several collections of short stories and more than a dozen novels, dealing with American life in the 19th and 20th centuries. She also wrote two autobiographies, *A Peculiar Treasure* (1939) and *A Kind of Magic* (1963).

Ferber's first work in the theater was in collaboration with George V. Hobart, with whom she adapted her own Mrs. McChesney, a character from a series of short stories; *Our Mrs. McChesney,* a comic vehicle for Ethel Barrymore, opened in 1915. Ferber wrote only one play alone; this was *The Eldest* (1920), which was produced by the PROVINCETOWN PLAYERS. Her real success in the theater came when she teamed with George S. Kaufman, with whom she first wrote *Minick* (1924), an adaptation of her story about an old man determined to remain independent of his grown children. This first endeavor with Kaufman, though not a commercial success in New York, enjoyed a long life within the LITTLE THEATER MOVEMENT. The most successful Ferber-Kaufman plays were *The ROYAL FAMILY* (1927), a comedy about the irregular life of a theater family based on the Drew-Barrymore clan; *DINNER AT EIGHT* (1932), a dark comedy about depression-era New York high society; and the less critically acclaimed *Stage Door* (1936), about young actresses living in a New York boardinghouse. Their two other collaborations, *The Land Is Bright* (1941) and *Bravo!* (1948), were critical and commercial failures. The landmark musical *Show Boat* (1927) is based on Ferber's novel.

BIBLIOGRAPHY

Ferber, Edna. *A Kind of Magic.* Garden City, N.Y.: Doubleday, 1963.

———. *A Peculiar Treasure.* Garden City, N.Y.: Doubleday, 1939.

———, and George S. Kaufman. *Three Comedies by Kaufman and Ferber: "The Royal Family," "Dinner at Eight," and "Stage Door."* New York: Applause Theatre Books, 1999.

Gilbert, Julie Goldsmith. *Edna Ferber: A Biography.* Garden City, N.Y.: Doubleday, 1978.

Shaughnessy, Mary Rose. *Women and Success in American Society in the Works of Edna Ferber.* New York: Gordon Press, 1977.

FIERSTEIN, HARVEY (1954–) Playwright and actor Harvey Fierstein was born in New York and educated at Pratt Institute (B.F.A., 1973). While still in his teens, Fierstein appeared as a female impersonator in New York and was cast in the lead role in Andy Warhol's *Pork* (1971), playing a lesbian maid. Fierstein first began to write for the stage in order to create acting vehicles for himself.

His plays include *In Search of the Cobra Jewels* (1972), a musical based on his efforts to clean playwright Harry Koutoukas's apartment; *Freaky Pussy* (1973), about cross-dressing prostitutes who live in a public men's room; *Flatbush Tosca* (1975), based on Puccini's opera, *Tosca; Spookhouse* (1982), about a Coney Island fortune-teller and her three children (one of whom is a drug addict and a rapist) and the naive, gay social worker who tries to help them; *La Cage aux Folles* (1983)—music and lyrics by Jerry Herman, adapted from Jean Poiret's play—about a night club owner and his drag-queen "spouse" and their attempts to help their son win over his fiancée's conservative father; *Safe Sex* (1987), a trilogy of one-act plays—all dealing with responses to AIDS—made up of *Manny and Jake, Safe Sex,* and *On Tidy Endings; Forget Him* (1988), a one-act about a man looking for someone better, even when he has found an almost "perfect" love; and, in collaboration with Charles Suppon, the musical *Legs Diamond*—music and lyrics by Peter Allen (1988).

The most well known of Fierstein's stage plays are the one-acts *The International Stud* (1978), *Fugue in a Nursery* (1979), and *Widows and Children First!* (1979), which together constitute TORCH SONG TRILOGY, produced together for the first time in 1981. In *The International Stud,* Arnold Beckoff loses his bisexual lover, Ed, to a woman. The play is a series of monologues by the two men, who only appear together in the last scene. In *Fugue in a Nursery,* Ed and his girlfriend invite Arnold and his new boyfriend, Alan, to Ed's summerhouse one year after the end of *International Stud.* In the guest bedroom that Arnold occupies, various combinations of the four characters pair and unpair. In the final *Widows and Children First!,* five years have passed. Alan has died—the victim of a hate crime; Ed—still confused about his sexuality—and Arnold are together again; and Arnold mothers a 15-year-old foster son while working on his relationship with his own homophobic mother.

Both *La Cage aux Folles* and *Torch Song Trilogy* won TONY AWARDS. Fierstein is generally credited with being one of the first to bring universal human themes—family love and conflict, the need for commitment and intimacy—into the gay context. He is an AIDS and gay rights activist and continues to act and write. In 2002, he played the heroine's mother in the hit musical *Hairspray,* a role for which he won another Tony Award. In 2008, Fierstein both starred in and wrote the book for the musical *A Catered Affair,* based on the 1955 television play and 1956 film.

BIBLIOGRAPHY
Fierstein, Harvey. *La Cage aux Folles.* New York: Samuel French, 1993.
———. *Safe Sex.* New York: Samuel French, 1993.
———. *Torch Song Trilogy.* New York: Gay Presses, 1990.

5TH OF JULY (1978) (FIFTH OF JULY [1980]) LANFORD WILSON *5th of July* is the first of the three "Talley" plays written by WILSON. Directed by Marshall W. Mason, it was first presented in 1978 at the Circle Rep Theatre in New York. It sets the stage for the two plays, *Talley's Folly* and *Talley & Son,* that come after and give a fairly full accounting of the fictional Talley family of Lebanon, Missouri.

Set in *"the large sun porch/family room of a prosperous southern Missouri farmhouse built around 1860,"* 5th of July brings together the last of the Talley family: Ken Talley; his sister, June; June's daughter, Shirley; and Sally Talley Friedman, Ken and June's aunt. Joining them is Jed Jenkins, Ken's lover; John Landis, a childhood friend of the Talleys; John's wife, Gwen, an aspiring country-western singer; and Wes Hurley, a musician friend of Gwen's. It is the Fourth of July weekend of 1977, and they have gathered ostensibly to be with Sally for the purpose of scattering the ashes of her late husband, Matt Friedman. Ken, who lost both legs in the Vietnam War, has signed a contract to teach English at the local high school. He is having second thoughts about his career choice and has made overtures to John and Gwen to sell them the house to use as a recording studio. This decision, when revealed, meets with considerable resistance from

June. She has her own reasons for not wanting to sell the house to John and Gwen, one of them being that John is the father of Shirley, although he has never acknowledged this formally.

The themes of *5th of July* can be summarized in the idea that the past can foretell the future. Ten years after their antiwar and antiestablishment protests, done mostly for fun, these old friends find themselves a part of the society against which they rebelled. Ken, who contemplated dodging the draft, ended up joining the army. John and Gwen, who protested against corporate greed, now have become engaged in the wheeling and dealing that they once firebombed. June tearfully defends her marching in protests, even though she now admits, "It was all a crock." This Fourth of July weekend finds all of them facing their future and making decisions that will change it and them. Even Sally decides that moving to a California retirement community at the urging of her family is not what she wants to do; she has other plans. In the end, the various important plot lines are resolved. Ken will stay in Lebanon to teach, Gwen receives an offer to make records, and Sally scatters the ashes in the formal garden that Jed is creating on the grounds of the family home. These resolutions do not come easily or tidily, but, as Wilson himself has noted, it is rare in life that they do.

The play got mixed reviews when it opened in 1978. Most of the criticism of the play was that it was disconnected—the characters and situations, while charming and interesting in and of themselves, did not add up to a workable play. In most cases, that would be the end of the life of the play, but one of Mason's directing techniques is to ask the actors to examine thoroughly the characters they are playing. The actress playing Sally asked Wilson for more information about Sally's husband, Matt Friedman. What began as an acting exercise evolved into the two-character play TALLEY'S FOLLY (1979).

After the success of *Talley's Folly,* Wilson rewrote *5th of July* (and also changed the spelling of the title to *Fifth of July*). Based on what Wilson saw in the first production and ideas he received from director Mason, the beginning of the play was changed to focus more on establishing the relationship between Ken Talley and his lover Jed. Rather than beginning the play with the entrance of John and Gwen, Wilson firmly establishes that Ken and Jed are lovers (they exchange a kiss) and that Jed is a substantial character in the story. Wilson also revised the end of the play to give Gwen a much stronger and more multidimensional impact on the resolution of the story. In the 1978 version, she provides little more than ditzy comic relief. In the 1980 version, Gwen, while still ditzy, shows a strength of character and an awareness of her relationship with her husband that was missing in the first play.

Philip Middleton Williams
Miami, Florida

FINLEY, KAREN (1956–) Perhaps best known in the popular media as "the chocolate-smeared woman," Karen Finley was born in Chicago, where she participated in the Chicago Art Institute's Young Artist Studio program from the age of 12. Her mother was a political activist, and her father, a jazz musician and practicing Buddhist, committed suicide when Finley was 21. Finley studied painting at the San Francisco Art Institute, where she grew increasingly weary of what she felt was a male-dominated art world. Influenced by performance artists such as Chris Burden and Vito Acconci, she began performing with the Kipper Kids, a group whose performances relied heavily on physicality, focusing much more on bodies than on language. Touring with the Kipper Kids in 1981, she and her then-husband Harry Kipper created a riot in Germany in response to their explicit performance that depicted Hitler and featured sausages, whips, and human feces.

Setting out on her own, Finley began performing in American nightclubs, for many years avoiding galleries, theaters, and the art circuit. Soon, Finley began to attract the attention of avant-garde performance critics, inspiring admiration as much as shocked outrage. Her pieces, such as *The Constant State of Desire* (1986) and *We Keep Our Victims Ready* (1987), were performed in established art venues such as The Kitchen in New York and the Walker Art Center in Minneapolis. Both works unearth repressed violent desires in often hard-hitting explicit language. Telling stories of child molestation and violence against women from the point of view of multiple characters, Finley uses her versatile voice and body to perform both victim and perpetrator. To develop a performance piece, she researches a topic (varying from the murder of a young African-American woman for *We Keep Our Victims Ready,* to an early 20th-century outbreak of tree disease for *American Chestnut* [1995], to the AIDS epidemic for *A Certain Level of Denial* [1992]) and works from a memorized script, as in the tradition of theater. During her performances, however, she often departs from the script to talk to the audience about the making of the performance, joking and chatting with them in a way that is more characteristic of performance art than theater. Finley explains that she works in a trance state, and indeed her scripted moments have the look and sound of someone possessed. When she snaps out of this state to speak nonchalantly to her audience, the result is a performance that seems at once polished and improvised.

Finley's mode of revealing deep-seated hatred and abuse is often expressed using her own body—spreading chocolate, raw eggs, or other gooey substances on her seminude body to symbolize the degradation of women's bodies. It was this practice that earned her the moniker "chocolate-smeared woman," given to her pejoratively by the *Washington Post* in response to a performance of *We Keep Our Victims Ready* in 1990. That same year, the National Endowment for the Arts announced that it was rescinding a grant they had promised Finley, calling her "obscene." This decision, which also affected three other artists (HOLLY HUGHES, John Fleck, and Tim Miller), inaugurated eight years of trials, appeals, and public debate, ultimately reaching the Supreme Court. Out of the ensuing debates, slander, and de-funding, Finley developed a performance piece called *The Return of the Chocolate Smeared Woman* (1998) in which she challenged the attempts to censor her work by accusing Senator Jesse Helms, a leader of the complaints against her, of having an uncontrollable need to dominate her sexually.

Finley's *Shut Up and Love Me* (1999) finds her smeared with honey and inviting audience participation. Here again she addresses themes of sexual dysfunction, but she also resolutely presents a woman who is not a victim of hatred or violence, preferring unapologetically to emphasize eroticism in her performance.

Always controversial, in 2006 Finley published a book based on her own short play of 2004, in which a couple named George and Martha carry on their illicit affair in a seedy hotel room; there are allusions to EDWARD ALBEE's George and Martha, from his *WHO'S AFRAID OF VIRGINIA WOOLF?* but Finley's George and Martha are none other than then-sitting president George W. Bush and home-decorating diva and ex-convict Martha Stewart.

BIBLIOGRAPHY

Finley, Karen. *A Different Kind of Intimacy: The Collected Writings of Karen Finley.* New York: Thunder's Mouth Press, 2000.

Maria Ghira Renu Cappelli
University of California–Berkeley

FITCH, CLYDE (1865–1909)

Born in Elmira, New York, Clyde Fitch attended Amherst College, where he was involved in many aspects of the dramatic arts—acting, directing, painting scenery, and designing costumes, as well as writing. He moved to New York City in 1886 and there attended a great deal of theater. His first play, *Beau Brummell,* was commissioned by the actor Richard Mansfield. The play was finally performed in 1890 and enjoyed some success, but it was overlooked by those critics of the early 1890s who preferred action (having enjoyed the likes of STEELE MACKAYE's *HAZEL KIRKE* in 1880 and BRONSON HOWARD's *SHENANDOAH* in 1888) over witty dialogue. Fitch was a prolific playwright. He wrote more than 40 plays, including comedies, melodramas, and histories. He was so popular in his day that in 1904, in New York, four of his plays ran simultaneously. He was a keen observer of human behavior, particularly human social behavior, and many of his plays reflect American social life of the period.

Among his most noteworthy plays are *Nathan Hale* (1898), an enthusiastically received drama about the Revolutionary War hero in which Fitch includes a fictitious love story; *The Climbers* (1901), a social drama about a social-climbing woman and her daughters who learn upon his death that their husband and father died broke; *The Girl with the Green Eyes* (1902), a portrayal of a family flawed by nearly pathological jealousy; *The TRUTH* (1907), a comedy of manners about a young socialite who tells so many lies she gets herself into trouble with her very easygoing husband; and *The City* (1909), which shocked audiences with an onstage morphine injection and an unconsummated incestuous marriage.

BIBLIOGRAPHY

Fitch, Clyde. *The Girl with the Green Eyes.* Edited by Walter J. Meserve and Mollie Ann Meserve. 1905. New York: Feedback Theatrebooks & Prospero Press, 2001.

Moses, Montrose J., and Virginia Gerson. *Clyde Fitch and His Letters.* Boston: Little, Brown, 1924.

FLANAGAN, HALLIE (1890–1969)

Educator, director, playwright, theater historian, and director of the FEDERAL THEATRE PROJECT (FTP), Hallie Mae Ferguson was born in Redfield, South Dakota, at the end of the homesteading rush, and lived a nomadic childhood. Her parents, Fred and Louisa Ferguson, moved frequently during the depression of the 1890s, spending time in Omaha, Chicago, St. Louis, and Iowa. While the family struggled, Hallie nurtured an active imagination in spite of difficult circumstances. She was an unusually mature and confident young lady, drawing on her mother's poise and her father's conviviality. When she was 10, prosperity returned and her family moved to the utopian community of Grinnell, Iowa.

In 1911, Hallie graduated from Grinnell College, where the school's focus on social idealism and public service influenced her and her classmates. There, she met her first husband, Murray Flanagan, whom she married in 1912, but after the birth of two boys, John in 1915 and Frederic in 1917, Murray fell ill and never recovered. After his death, Hallie taught at a local high school and then at Grinnell College. She slowly built a drama program, and her one-act play, *The Curtain* (1920), won a playwriting contest. She also earned an invitation to study with GEORGE PIERCE BAKER at Harvard, but these successes were overshadowed by the tragic death of her oldest son. She decided to attend Baker's class nevertheless, and she earned a master's degree and had her satirical comedy *Incense* (1924) produced by Baker as his first show when he went to Yale University. Although encouraged to continue writing, financial demands forced her to return to Grinnell College (1924–25). There, she created the Grinnell Experimental Theatre, which attracted nationwide attention and prompted an offer from Vassar College to establish an experimental theater there. Soon after her return east, she became the first woman to win a Guggenheim Foundation grant, and she spent the spring of 1926 in Europe undertaking a comparative study of continental drama.

She brought back to Vassar many of the techniques and ideas she saw in Europe. Her book *Shifting Scenes of the Modern European Theatre* (1928) detailed her experiences. Vassar's theater program soon earned national recognition; even Broadway critics journeyed north to Poughkeepsie for major productions. Flanagan's most famous work, *Can You Hear Their Voices?* (1931), was an experimental one, depicting the Arkansas drought and the suffering of the farmers there; it was a forerunner to the famous LIVING NEWSPAPERS of the Federal Theatre Project. The show gained her international attention.

In 1934, she married a Vassar professor of Greek, Philip H. Davis, who was a widower with three small children, and combined a honeymoon with directing and studying theater throughout Europe. Upon her return, she took up an even greater challenge when her old school friend from Grinnell, Harry Hopkins (an adviser to President Franklin D. Roosevelt), asked her to direct the Works Progress Administration's Federal Theatre Project.

Her tenure (1935–39) as director of America's largest and only government-sponsored theater project was an extraordinary adventure she later detailed in *Arena* (1940). Flanagan envisioned a theater that was socially relevant, exciting, and capable of living on after the government subsidies had ended. Her leadership and dedication enabled more than 800 shows to be produced before an audience of one-third of the American population. Despite the FTP's many successes, conservative politicians ensured that the project would end, and in 1939 Congress simply withheld funding. Flanagan returned to Vassar, but in the same year her husband died. In 1942, she accepted a position as dean and professor of theater at Smith College, a post she held until 1946, after which she continued solely as professor of theater until 1955, when Parkinson's disease forced her to retire.

BIBLIOGRAPHY

Bentley, Joanne. *Hallie Flanagan: A Life in the American Theatre.* New York: Knopf, 1988.

Flanagan, Hallie. *Arena.* New York: Duell, Sloan and Pearce, 1940.

———. *The Curtain.* New York: Samuel French, 1932.

———. *Dynamo.* New York: Duell, Sloan and Pearce, 1943.

———. *E=mc²: A Living Newspaper about the Atomic Age.* New York: Samuel French, 1948.

———. *Shifting Scenes of the Modern European Theatre.* New York: Coward-McCann, 1928.

———, and Margaret Ellen Clifford. *Can You Hear Their Voices?* Poughkeepsie, N.Y.: The Experimental Theatre of Vassar College, 1931.

Mathews, Jane DeHart. *The Federal Theatre, 1935–1939: Plays, Relief, and Politics.* Princeton, N.J.: Princeton University Press, 1967.

Michael M. O'Hara
Ball State University

FOOL FOR LOVE Sam Shepard (1983)

Fool for Love, which premiered, like many of SHEPARD's plays, at the Magic Theatre in San Francisco, signals a turn in Shepard's writing away from the antirealism of his earlier, more expressionistic work toward an almost hyper-realism that zooms in on the idiosyncratic lives of ordinary people struggling with extraordinary conflicts. Many critics described *Fool for Love,* along with *TRUE WEST,* as the first of Shepard's mature work, which for the most part meant that it was accessible to a larger audience. Other critics complained, however, that this shift in emphasis from the bizarre to the banal created less interesting plays. Nevertheless, *Fool for Love* was a success, winning an OBIE AWARD and spawning a film version directed by Robert Altman and released in 1985.

Ostensibly a four-character play, the focus of the action is on the fiery love-hate relationship between Eddie, a rugged, dust-bitten, "broken down" cowboy, and May, a tough but vulnerable young woman; they are tangled in a passion they cannot control. The other characters—the Old Man and Martin—act as foils for the two lovers. The Old Man, the only nonrealistic element in the play, perched on a downstage platform, speaks the voice of memory, uniting Eddie and May in a contiguous past, echoing their behavior, suggesting, in the mode of classical Greek tragedy, that the sins of the fathers are visited upon the children. Martin, May's current beau, is an earnest local man in his mid-thirties who serves as a counterimage to Eddie's unbridled machismo.

Eddie has returned from one of his many desertions to find May living in a *"low rent motel room on the edge of the Mojave desert."* Dispirited by his sudden appearance and desperate to maintain her life independent of him, she tries to resist, but it is the fatal flaw of her nature to be simultaneously repulsed and attracted to him, a dilemma that underscores the central conflict in the play: the dangerous charm of destructive desires. She is suffering an existential crisis, caught in an all-consuming affair that threatens to "erase" her identity. Eddie too shares her flaw, torn by the same contradictions: He both needs May and fears her, attracted to her animal sexuality but driven to conquer and control her the way he might a wild horse he wants to capture. Locked in a dance of dueling desires, their urge is to create and destroy, each fighting for self-preservation while flirting with total abandon.

In a *Paris Review* interview, Shepard calls the play "a quasi-realistic melodrama" that "came out of falling in love." But the love depicted between Eddie and May—as well as between the Old Man and the women in his life (supposedly both Eddie and May's mothers, reinforcing the blood-ties of their destructive passion)—amounts to a brutal game of violence and intimidation, dominance and survival, fueled by a need beyond reason. Yet, Eddie and May seem to have no choice but to reject the tamer protocol of more predictable romances as they endure the instability of their volatile passions.

Jeff Johnson
Brevard Community College

FOOTE, HORTON (1916–2009)

Horton Foote's distinctive authorial voice begins, as critics frequently note, with his carefully nuanced evocation of place—southeast coastal Texas. It was country he knew in his very marrow, having spent his childhood in the small town of Wharton, a fifth-generation Texan and descendant of two of the oldest and best-known families in the state. Like many southern writers, his gift for narrative can be traced to a tradition of family storytelling. He recalled listening with fascination to local and family tales being told and retold, noting how the story changed from speaker to speaker.

Foote began his career as an actor, not a writer, studying at the Pasadena Playhouse in California for two years in his late teens and training for two more at the Tamara Daykarhanova School for Acting in New York City (1937–39), where he was introduced to "Method" acting (see ACTORS STUDIO) by protégées of Stanislavsky. This approach, which emphasized psychological honesty, inner truthfulness, and natural movement, was to have a lasting effect on Foote's style. While a student in New York, he met Mary Hunter, who, along with Foote, Agnes de Mille, Jerome Robbins, Mildred Dunnock, and Valerie Bettis, founded the American Actors Company, whose mission was to produce authentic American drama as an alternative to the commercial fare of Broadway. His first play, a one-act entitled *Wharton Dance* (1940), came out of an improvisational exercise done for this group. Following it with *Texas Town* (1941), his first full-length play, he found writing so satisfying he stopped acting. *Only the Heart,* his next play, was produced on Broadway in 1944. After the war, he experimented briefly with a less realistic style, writing dance plays choreographed by the great dancers Valerie Bettis and Martha Graham.

Most of his energy in the 1950s was devoted to writing for television in an era when shows like *Studio One, Playhouse 90,* and the *U.S. Steel Hour* featured live dramas by talented writers like Foote, Gore Vidal, and PADDY CHAYEFSKY. Foote used the new medium of television to hone his craft, writing teleplays such as *The Tears of My Sister, The Dancers, The Night of the Storm,* and *A Young Lady of Property,* many of which he would later rework and develop for the stage. Three new plays received Broadway productions at this time as well: *The Chase* (1952), *The TRIP TO BOUNTIFUL* (1953), and *Traveling Lady* (1954).

During the 1960s, with its radical rhetoric, guerrilla theater, and onstage nudity, Foote's subtle style

and realistic, character-driven dramas fell out of favor, and he moved his family to New Hampshire. With the exception of two OFF-BROADWAY productions, a revival of *Bountiful,* and an adaptation of William Faulkner's short story "Tomorrow," Foote left the New York stage scene and began to write screenplays, most notably his acclaimed adaptation of Harper Lee's novel, *To Kill a Mockingbird* (1962), for which he won an Academy Award. He continued writing screenplays throughout his career, including those for such films as *Tender Mercies* (1983) (for which he received a second Academy Award) and *The Trip to Bountiful* (1985).

During the 1970s, after losing both his parents within two years, Foote wrote what most critics consider his masterpiece, nine plays entitled *The ORPHANS' HOME CYCLE,* set in Harrison (a fictionalized Wharton), Texas, from 1902 to 1928, and based on his parents' courtship and marriage. An ambitious undertaking, unparalleled in American dramatic literature (with the possible exception of EUGENE O'NEILL's unfinished 11-play historical cycle and AUGUST WILSON's decade-by-decade depiction of African-American life in the 20th century), each play stands alone, yet also functions as part of a longer narrative. *Cycle* traces the story of Horace Robedaux (based on Foote's father) from the time he is orphaned at 12 (*Roots in a Parched Ground* [1976]), through his courting of Elizabeth Vaughn (*Courtship* [1978]) and their early marriage (*Valentine's Day* [1980] and *1918* [1981]), to his middle age and the appearance of 10-year-old Horace Jr. (a fictional Horton Foote), a sensitive boy and writer in the making (*The Death of Papa* [1997]). Innovative in its use of dramatic form, the cycle employs strategies that are more typical of the novel than drama: symbolic motifs, parallel characters, parallel and inverted episodes, and even paired plays. Not necessarily meant to be played in sequence, individual plays were produced in Off-Broadway and regional venues through the 1980s and 1990s. In 1984–85, Foote and his wife Lillian began producing films of the cycle plays.

During the 1980s, Foote's plays continued to explore mysteries within the lives of ordinary people who sometimes display extraordinary courage. Drawing always upon his memories of Wharton, which appears as the fictitious Harrison throughout all but his earliest plays, Foote said that if there is a theme to his work, it is the ultimate mystery of human experience. Ranging from early 20th-century to contemporary settings and from small-town Harrison to urban Houston, some of his other plays include *In a Coffin in Egypt* (1980), *The Roads to Home* (1982), and *The Habitation of Dragons* (1982), along with many one-acts. In 1994–95, the Off-Broadway Signature Theatre devoted its entire season to his work, producing four of his plays, the last of which, *The YOUNG MAN FROM ATLANTA,* won him the PULITZER PRIZE in 1995. It was restaged on Broadway two years later. Until his death at 92, Foote continued to write and direct new plays, including *The Last of the Thorntons* (2000), *The Carpetbaggers' Children* (2001), which received the American Theatre Critics/Steinberg New Play Award, and *The Actor* (2003). Recent major revivals of Foote plays include, in 2005, *The Trip to Bountiful,* which won the Lucille Lortel Award for Outstanding Revival, and, in 2007, *Dividing the Estate,* which won both an OBIE AWARD and an Outer Critics Circle Award. Foote also completed two volumes of his memoirs, *Farewell: A Memoir of a Texas Childhood* (1999) and *Beginnings: A Memoir* (2001).

Foote's intimate knowledge of the world of which he wrote provides a depth that allows his characters to escape regional quaintness. His control of language and texture is also key, with much of the meaning communicated in what the characters *don't* say. Their speech is limited almost entirely to everyday speech patterns and prosaic diction. His plots, likewise, are understated and seem uneventful. Often compared to Chekhov, Foote eschewed the usual conventions of dramatic action—conflicting ideas or characters, suspense, and intrigue—opting instead for what critic Gerald C. Wood calls "dedramatization." A final characteristic is his preference for endings that lack a sense of finality or closure, as if to insist that life's mysteries cannot be definitively solved. A southerner, his themes and style are akin to those of writers like William Faulkner, Flannery O'Connor, and Katherine Anne Porter. Like these southern writers, he was obsessed with stories of death and resurrection, of leaving home and finding it. Often wrongly accused of being sentimental, he wrote with clear-eyed honesty—and sometimes grim candor—of the place and people he

knew so well, transcending regionalism and taking his place among the best and certainly the most prolific of 20th-century American playwrights. At this writing, more than 85 of his dramas have been produced for theater, television, and film.

BIBLIOGRAPHY

Briley, Rebecca. *You Can Go Home Again: The Focus on Family in the Works of Horton Foote.* New York: Peter Lang, 1993.

Foote, Horton. *Beginnings: A Memoir.* New York: Scribner, 2001.

———. *"The Carpetbagger's Children" & "The Actor": 2 Plays.* Woodstock, N.Y.: Sewanee Writers' Series/The Overlook Press, 2003.

———. *Farewell: A Memoir of a Texas Childhood.* New York: Scribners, 1999.

———. *"Getting Frankie Married—And Afterwards" and Other Plays.* Lyme, N.H.: Smith and Kraus, 1998.

———. *Horton Foote: Collected Plays: Volume II.* Lyme, N.H.: Smith and Kraus, 1996.

———. *Horton Foote: Four New Plays.* Newbury, Vt.: Smith and Kraus, 1993.

———. *Horton Foote: Genesis of an American Playwright.* Edited by Marion Castleberry. Waco, Tex.: Baylor University Press, 2004.

———. *The Orphans' Home Cycle.* New York: Grove Press/Stage & Screen, 2000.

———. *Selected One-Act Plays of Horton Foote.* Edited by Gerald C. Wood. Dallas: Southern Methodist University Press, 1989.

———. *Three Plays: "Dividing the Estate," "The Trip to Bountiful," and "The Young Man from Atlanta."* Evanston, Ill.: Northwestern University Press, 2009.

Porter, Laurin. *Orphans' Home: The Voice and Vision of Horton Foote.* Baton Rouge: Louisiana State University Press, 2003.

Watson, Charles S. *Horton Foote: A Literary Biography.* Austin: University of Texas Press, 2003.

Wood, Gerald C., ed. *Horton Foote: A Casebook.* New York: Garland, 1998.

———. *Horton Foote and the Theater of Intimacy.* Baton Rouge: Louisiana State University Press, 1999.

Laurin R. Porter
University of Texas–Arlington

FOR COLORED GIRLS WHO HAVE CONSIDERED SUICIDE/WHEN THE RAINBOW IS ENUF NTOZAKE SHANGE (1976) This first performance piece produced by SHANGE is a

strong and original feminist voice within AFRICAN-AMERICAN DRAMA. Taking an idea from Judy Grahn's book of poems, *The Common Woman* (1973), which explores different kinds of women, and developing a series of poems she had written while in a women's studies program, Shange introduces a group of African-American women. Identified only by the colors of their garments and relating stories of fear, pain, loss, and joy, the women forge a triumphant collective African-American female voice by the play's close. Her emotive mix of poetry, prose, music, and dance creates a theatrical expression closely related to African performance, but her text is informed by the conditions faced by African-American women in a racist and patriarchal American society.

For Colored Girls shows a variety of possibilities faced by African-American women, many of whom seem to have abusive lovers who will not allow them to be themselves. Starting with a mélange of voices naming a series of American cities and female adolescent concerns, the play then separates into individual characterizations. The first presents a defiant dance-hall girl who sees herself as an Egyptian goddess despite the negative opinions of others. The second depicts a young dreamer who runs away from home with Haitian rebel Toussaint Louverture as her imaginary companion. Upon meeting a real-life Toussaint, she decides to return home. Next is a woman, "[t]he lady in red," who lures men to her bed only to throw them out vengefully the next morning. She is followed by a lady who comforts women who are victims of harassment and then three more women who set aside their rivalry over one man to bond together like sisters. For the play's climax, "the lady in red" relates how beau willie brown tries to persuade his children's mother to marry him by holding those children out of a five-story window, but, before she can answer, he drops them. Despite such a horrifying event, the women refuse to despair; instead, inspired by images of nature around them, they discover in the strength of their community the power to transcend the difficulties of their lives.

While some of the monologue-poems in the play come out of Shange's own experiences, others are drawn from her studies in the mythology of women.

Somewhat idealistic in its suggestion that female empowerment rests in women's ability to form a community, the play is unified thematically rather than by an extended line of action. Shange simultaneously illustrates the unjust patriarchal past and the possibility of an improved nonhierarchical future. Balancing images of dirty, lonely cities and the technological circumstances that oppress African-American women against images of natural beauty accompanied by song and dance, through which women can become free of oppression and gain equality, Shange creates a world filled with ugliness and beauty and asks that we choose which we would prefer.

Susan C. W. Abbotson
Rhode Island College

FOREIGNER, THE LARRY SHUE (1983) *The Foreigner* is a delightful comedy set in the rural southeastern United States. Although the play tackles such serious matters as stereotypes, xenophobia, and white supremacy, it does so in a humorous manner—exposing the hypocrisies and inanities of these prejudices and the individuals who hold them. Predictably, by the end of *The Foreigner,* order is restored and a romance blossoms.

Charlie, a shy and often-cuckolded Englishman, comes to a remote Georgia guest house accompanied by his military friend Froggy LeSueur. While he conducts some out-of-town business, Froggy places the heartsick Charlie at a lodge operated by Betty Meeks—a chatty, good-hearted southern widow. Rather than interact with the backwoods residents of Tilghman County, Georgia, Charlie feigns an ignorance of the English language, thus becoming a "foreigner" in an extremely provincial, sheltered household. Much of the play's comedy arises out of the beleaguered Betty's attempts to communicate with Charlie. Often, she resorts to shouting in the poor man's face while carefully enunciating her words. Charlie is subsequently befriended by the simpleton Ellard who takes it upon himself to teach the "fawer-rain-err" how to "talk good Eeenglish." Meanwhile, Ellard's sister, Catherine, slowly falls in love with Charlie, attracted by his good listening skills.

Because Charlie pretends not to understand the native tongue, he gradually becomes privy to the evil intentions of Catherine's fiancé, Reverend David, and his lackey, Owen Musser. The two are members of a Ku Klux Klan chapter seeking to relocate from the Atlanta area. Burned out of their previous headquarters, the Reverend David and Owen seek to swindle Betty Meeks out of her estate. Aided by Ellard, Charlie outwits the Klan's nefarious intentions, while also managing to raise Ellard's self-esteem. By the end of the play, Catherine is placed in charge of the guest house, and Charlie obtains divorce papers from his adulterous wife. Newly single, Charlie opts to remain at the guest house, presumably to marry Catherine.

The Foreigner had its world premiere in January 1983 at the Milwaukee Repertory Theatre, a company with which LARRY SHUE had enjoyed a long association as both an actor and a playwright. In November 1984, the play opened at New York's Astor Place Theatre and became one of OFF-BROADWAY's longest-running plays. For the New York staging, Shue played Froggy LeSueur. Later in the run, the playwright played the role of Charlie. An audience-pleasing comedy, *The Foreigner* is frequently revived by academic institutions and community theaters.

Mark Cosdon
Allegheny College

FOREMAN, RICHARD (1937–   ) Born in
Staten Island and raised in Scarsdale, New York, Richard Foreman has directed his own Ontological-Hysteric Theater (OHT) in SoHo since 1968. After attending Brown (B.A., 1959) and Yale (M.F.A. in playwriting, 1962), followed by several unsuccessful years trying to write mainstream plays, Foreman founded the OHT as a venue to direct his own avant-garde work. Academic, enigmatic, metatheatrical, and unabashedly self-referential, Foreman's ouevre reflects his own erudition and the tastes of the experimental artistic communities of Lower Manhattan and Paris, where a branch of his theater operated from 1979 to 1985. As Foreman himself realized early in his career, his work is far too intellectual for Broadway, but he has become an icon of the theatrical avant-garde. In three decades, he has written 50 plays, four of which won OBIE AWARDS (*Rhoda in Potatoland* [1975], *The Cure* [1986], *Film Is Evil, Radio Is Good* [1987], and *Pearls for*

Pigs [1997]). Foreman has also won Obie Awards for Sustained Achievement (in 1988) and Direction (in 1986). He has received the PEN/Laura Pels Master American Playwright Award, the literature prize from the American Academy of Arts and Letters, and a Lifetime Achievement Award from the National Endowment for the Arts.

Foreman follows in the modernist lyric poetic tradition of GERTRUDE STEIN, not writing so much as choreographing words and things in space. As in the surrealist and absurdist theaters (see THEATRE OF THE ABSURD), Foreman's stage world is an abstract experiment that frames humans as performing objects. The drama of this theater arises from the "hysterical" conflict of human interaction at the level of "ontological," rather than mundanely social, existence. By "ontology," Foreman refers to philosophical questions regarding what is real, that is, what exists in the world; his notion of ontology is evident in the abstract, mechanistic environments of his plays, evocative not of any real time or place so much as the scene of some absurd divine experiment. He situates his theater at the intersection of dramatic social conflict and a philosophically skeptical perception of reality.

Foreman has claimed that he considers his writing "material" rather than "plays," each production merely a distillation of his current meditation on the same abiding problems. The performers in his first play, *Angelface* (1968), interact without any normal patterns of small talk, and an angel with comically exaggerated wings gets stuck in a door. In another play of his early career, *Rhoda in Potatoland (Her Fall-Starts)* (1975), large potatoes walk onstage as farcical metaphors of sexual "tumescence." In *The Cure* (1986), the performers meditate in a secret chamber on occult sources of an unspecified human "interiority." *Film Is Evil, Radio Is Good* (1987), perhaps Foreman's clearest work, invokes the golden age of radio in a meditation on the artifice of film. Having achieved an international reputation by the 1990s, Foreman took a new production, ironically titled *Pearls for Pigs*, on tour in 1997. The play attacks American audiences and the banal mainstream theaters that pander to them. As Foreman had expected, the play did poorly at professional theaters but well at universities. In *Panic! (How to be*

Happy!) (2003), the interior of the human mind is represented in a dreamlike comedy in which people are always misfits and the world will always frustrate and confuse. In the visually rich and highly theatrical *King Cowboy Rufus Rules the Universe* (2004), Foreman takes aim at the politics of George W. Bush, here represented as a power-hungry fop with an English accent. In *The Gods Are Pounding My Head (AKA Lumberjack Messiah)* (2005), Foreman conveys disgust for a modern world without substance. With *Zomboid* (2006) and *Wake Up Mr Sleepy! Your Unconscious Mind Is Dead!* (2007), Foreman began combining film and stage performance in his productions. *Deep Trance Behavior in Potatoland* (2008) again mixed film and live performance and is set, in part, in England and Japan (on screen).

Over the course of his career, Foreman has also directed operas and classic plays as well as contemporary plays by other playwrights in the United States and in Europe.

BIBLIOGRAPHY

Davy, Kate. *Richard Foreman and the Ontological-Hysteric Theatre.* Ann Arbor, Mich.: UMI Research Press, 1981.

———, ed. *Richard Foreman: Plays and Manifestos.* New York: New York University Press, 1976.

Foreman, Richard. *My Head Was a Sledgehammer: Six Plays.* Woodstock, N.Y.: Overlook Press, 1995.

———. *"Paradise Hotel" and Other Plays.* Woodstock, N.Y.: Overlook Press, 2001.

———. *Reverberation Machines: The Later Plays and Essays.* Barrytown, N.Y.: Station Hill Press, 1985.

———. *Unbalancing Acts: Foundations for a Theater.* Edited by Ken Jordan. New York: Pantheon, 1992.

Rabkin, Gerald, ed. *Richard Foreman.* New York: Performing Arts Journal Books, 1999.

Evan D. Winet
Cornell University

FORNÉS, MARIA IRENE (1930–) Maria
Irene Fornés was born in Havana, Cuba, into a family of modest means. Not long after her father's death in 1945, she immigrated to New York City with her mother and a sister. During the 1950s, she traveled in Europe and pursued work as a painter and textile designer before settling in Greenwich Village and joining its bohemian counterculture. In 1960, she wrote her first play, *Tango Palace* (originally titled *There! You Died*), on a lark, and its production in San Francisco in 1963 inspired her to continue playwriting. Over the next four decades, she wrote or adapted 50 works for the stage, including comic sketches, long and short one-acts, full-length dramas, and translations of modern classics. Most of these are composed in a series of brief, often enigmatic scenes, some only a few lines long, in which characters are caught in the midst of troubling thoughts or unsettling emotions. Many of her characters move from a state of innocence to experience, a process that often includes an emerging consciousness of self and an overwhelming passion that is both sexual and spiritual. Even when her characters suffer, Fornés's plays evince a joy in the wonder of life itself.

Fornés's early work helped to define the OFF-OFF-BROADWAY movement of the 1960s, which centered around such venues as Caffe Cino, Judson Poets Theatre, and Café La MaMa. Manic and absurdist in spirit, these plays are full of language and logic games, zany transformations, fanciful incongruities, and characters with unbridled libidos and devil-may-care attitudes. The most important of these, *Promenade,* was first performed in 1965 and became Fornés's one true commercial hit when it was produced OFF-BROADWAY in 1969. With a bright and eccentric musical score by Al Carmines, *Promenade* traces the peripatetic journey of two escaped prisoners, known only as 105 and 106, as they search for evil in a world of hedonistic high-society types.

Fornés's 1970s plays suggest a search for a more personal style, which she achieved in *FEFU AND HER FRIENDS* (1977), her single most important play. It depicts a casual afternoon gathering of eight women to plan a fundraising event, during which psychological forces of patriarchy threaten members of the group in mysterious ways. A landmark in feminist drama, the play is also remarkable for its environmental second act, which divides the audience into four groups and leads them to different locations for each of its four scenes.

In the 1980s, her most prolific period, Fornés wrote a series of plays that achieve a balance of lyricism, emotionalism, and formalism. Even as they depict characters in the throes of a passionate ordeal, they present themselves as several precise and reserved stage images that ask to be contemplated as if at a distance. Set in Budapest, *The Danube* (1982) uses Hungarian-language tapes to frame a series of tableaux that reveal a gentle world overtaken by a gradual holocaust. *Mud* (1983) depicts an odd and tragic sexual triangle of backwoods illiterates, one of whom, Mae, makes a heroic effort to learn how to read as the first step toward self-realization. The oppression of women and the mastery of language also surface as themes in *The Conduct of Life* (1985), which takes place in the household of a sadistic military officer in an unnamed Latin American country. Set in New York City before World War I, *Abingdon Square* (1987) tells the story of Marion, a child-bride whose marriage and identity are in jeopardy when her imaginary lover comes to life.

Fornés's plays of the 1990s exhibited signs of a more personal reflection on her life as an artist. *Enter the Night* (1993), *The Summer at Gossensass* (1997), and *Letters from Cuba* (2000) all include characters who are performers or writers. Fornés's body of work cannot be understood independently of her career as a director and a playwriting teacher. She has taught workshops at colleges, theaters, and writing centers all over America and around the world. Since 1968, she has directed the original productions of all her plays except for one. After an early affiliation with the Judson Poets Theatre, Fornés has had longstanding associations with INTAR (International Arts Relations) Hispanic American Arts Center, Padua Hills Playwrights Festival, and Theatre for the New City. The 1999–2000 season of New York's Signature Theatre was devoted to her work.

Of Fornés's many prizes and commendations, perhaps the most telling are her nine Obie Awards, five of them for writing, over 35 years. For her sustained achievement, her unique maturation of the Off-Off-Broadway aesthetic, her pioneering work in site-specific theater, her inspiration to many, her celebration of the power of the imagination, and the uncompromising precision of her plays, Fornés is one of the most important American woman playwrights of the 20th century.

BIBLIOGRAPHY

Delgado, Maria M., and Caridad Svich, eds. *Conducting a Life: Reflections on the Theatre of Maria Irene Fornés.* Lyme, N.H.: Smith and Kraus, 1999.

Fornés, Maria Irene. *Fefu and Her Friends.* New York: PAJ Publications, 1978.

———. *"Letters from Cuba" and Other Plays.* New York: PAJ Publications, 2007.

———. *Plays.* New York: PAJ Publications, 1986.

———. *"Promenade" and Other Plays.* New York: PAJ Publications, 1987.

———. *What of the Night?: Selected Plays.* New York: PAJ Publications, 2008.

Kent, Assunta Bartolomucci. *Maria Irene Fornés and Her Critics.* Westport, Conn.: Greenwood Press, 1996.

Moroff, Diane Lynn. *Fornés: Theater in the Present Tense.* Ann Arbor: University of Michigan Press, 1996.

Robinson, Marc, ed. *The Theater of Maria Irene Fornés.* Baltimore: Johns Hopkins University Press, 1999.

Scott T. Cummings
Boston College

FRANCESCA DA RIMINI George Henry Boker (1855)

Francesca da Rimini is a romantic tragedy in blank verse, set in medieval Italy and based on one of the episodes in Dante's *Inferno*. While in Dante's version the lovers are innocent, in Boker's version they are not. Furthermore, Boker's portrait of the ugly husband is not that of a mere villain, but rather that of a complex, sympathetic character. This ambiguity is an aspect of the play that contributes to its reputation as one of the best American plays of the 19th century.

Malatesta and his sons, Lanciotto and Paolo, of Rimini are the enemies of Guido, Lord of Ravenna. Much blood has been spilled on both sides. Malatesta seeks an alliance through marriage—his son Lanciotto to Guido's daughter Francesca. Lanciotto, a crippled hunchback, is loath to "bear / The sidelong shuddering glances of a wife," especially one as beautiful as Francesca. Like that other famous hunchback, Shakespeare's Richard III, Lanciotto feels most at home in battle and leaves romance to his handsome brother; the similarity with Richard III ends there, however, as Lanciotto—though not without his dark moods—is well loved for his courtesy and his courage.

Lanciotto sends Paolo to fetch his bride and asks him to prepare her realistically to meet her deformed husband. Francesca's father has gone to great lengths to keep Lanciotto's looks a secret from her; as a result, she momentarily mistakes the handsome Paolo for her betrothed until her maid, Ritta, sets her straight. Paolo dutifully prepares Francesca to meet her groom. He describes his brother's character with much praise but also includes Lanciotto's self-doubt and bouts of gloominess; Paolo even reports that Lanciotto's enemies think him rash. However, out of loyalty to his brother, he omits Lanciotto's physical description, fearing that it will turn Francesca toward him and away from Lanciotto. He, keenly aware of his own rising passion for her, distrusts his own motives.

When Paolo brings Francesca to his brother, Lanciotto sees her recoil and offers to release her from the engagement if she so chooses. Pressured by her father, Francesca insists that the bargain be kept and feigns love, though not very convincingly. Moments after the marriage takes place, Guido's army attacks, and the bridegroom departs for the battlefield.

Meanwhile, in the garden Paolo reads the story of Lancelot and Guinevere aloud to Francesca. Overcome with passion, they kiss for the first time and seal their doom. The Count's fool, Pepe, who has been spying on them from the bushes, dashes off gleefully to report their love to Lanciotto on the battlefield and is slain for his message. When Lanciotto returns from the battlefield to confront the lovers, he begs them to deny what Pepe has told him. When they will not, he kills them both and dies himself, his heart broken, not by his wife so much as by the brother he loved more than honor and by his own deed in slaying him.

Pepe, the Count's fool, is a noteworthy invention of Boker's. He is in part a stock character—the wise fool who provides acerbic commentary and comic relief—but he is also a mouthpiece for some American ideals. He makes a speech about the value of finding status based on merit rather than on birth and on the evils of the law of primogeniture. He extols the virtues of "a simple commonwealth . . . / In which aspiring merit takes the lead, / And birth goes begging." If anyone is a villain in the play, it is Pepe, for his tale-telling and

deception, yet even his behavior must be weighed against his position of subjugation within an aristocratic system.

The complexity of Lanciotto's character and, indeed, of all the characters is what sets *Francesca da Rimini* apart from the American plays that precede it. No one is utterly villainous nor utterly heroic; instead, they are human. This was a departure for a national drama that had previously offered far more melodrama than drama.

FRANKEN, ROSE (1895–1988) Born in Gainesville, Texas, playwright, novelist, short story writer, director, and producer Rose Franken (née Lewin) moved, after her parents' divorce, to New York City, where she attended the Ethical Culture School. She did not go on to college as her mother had hoped, but instead she married oral surgeon Sigmund Franken in 1913. Encouraged by her husband, she wrote short stories for their own entertainment and eventually for publication in magazines. Her first novel, *Pattern,* was published in 1925, the same year that the second of her three sons was born.

Franken's first play, *Another Language* (1932), was a great success. It is a portrait of the Hallams, a middle-class family with a domineering matriarch at its head. When the unconventional protagonist, Stella, having miscarried a baby, considers taking up sculpture or getting a job instead of pursuing the art of homemaking, she finds herself at odds with her mother-in-law, her catty sisters-in-law, and their materialistic husbands. The relationship between Stella and her in-laws does not warm when she falls for her husband's nephew, and he for her.

After Franken's first husband's death from tuberculosis, she moved to California and there collaborated with other writers on film scripts; one of these collaborators was W. B. Meloney, whom she married in 1937. During this period, she invented the character "Claudia," who would become the heroine of eight of Franken's novels, all featuring this woman who married too young; the last of these was published in 1952. Back in New York, she adapted the first two Claudia novels into a stage play called *Claudia* (1941), which was a critical and box office success. Franken's next play, *Outrageous Fortune* (1943), was controversial for its day because it tackles the themes of homosexuality and anti-Semitism. A few critics admired the play as courageous and intelligent, but many seemed to find the subject matter off-putting. Franken directed her *Doctors Disagree* (1943), in which a woman surgeon saves a boy that a male doctor has decided cannot be saved, and in so doing convinces her fiancé that she should not give up her work when they marry, as he had previously demanded. In *Soldier's Wife* (1944), Franken explores the postwar adjustments faced by wives who have become independent while their husbands were away. Her final play, *The Hallams* (1948), is a sequel to *Another Language* and ran only 12 performances.

After 1948, Franken retired from the theater but continued to write novels and short stories. Her autobiography, *When All Is Said and Done,* was first published in London in 1962 and in New York the following year.

BIBLIOGRAPHY
Franken, Rose. *Another Language*. New York: Samuel French, 1932.
———. *Claudia*. New York: Farrar and Rinehart, 1941.
———. *The Hallams*. New York: Samuel French, 1948.
———. *Outrageous Fortune*. New York: Samuel French, 1944.
———. *Soldier's Wife*. New York: Samuel French, 1945.
———. *When All Is Said and Done: An Autobiography*. Garden City, N.Y.: Doubleday, 1963.

FRANKIE AND JOHNNY IN THE CLAIR DE LUNE TERRENCE MCNALLY (1987)

A two-character play set in a one-room tenement apartment in New York City, *Frankie and Johnny in the Clair de Lune* is the portrait of two lonely, middle-aged, working-class people as they reveal themselves to each other and finally choose connection over isolation.

The play begins as Frankie and Johnny, acquaintances from the restaurant where he is a cook and she a waitress, finish having sex for the first time. Johnny is a talker who is very interested in every detail of Frankie; she is put off by his intensity. She would prefer that he leave soon, but Johnny wants to "connect" with her. He characterizes himself as "nervy and per-

sistent" and "courageous. I want you and I'm coming after you." Johnny talks about himself and his ideas and feelings. They find they have in common places (both are from Allentown, Pennsylvania), people (he knew her cousin there), experiences (both, as children, had absent mothers). Frankie gradually begins to open up too, though her enthusiasm is never as great as his. Johnny is determined not to miss this opportunity: "My life was happening to me. Now I'm making it happen." By the end of act 1, they are making love again to the sound of Debussy's "Clair de Lune," which is playing on the radio at the request of Johnny, who called the radio station and asked that the "most beautiful music ever written" be played and "dedicate[d]" to them.

Act 2 reveals that the second attempt at sex has failed and that Johnny, after this episode of impotence, is not quite as enthusiastic about Frankie as he was earlier. As Johnny cooks Frankie some western eggs, they share their dreams and secrets. Frankie, a high school dropout, dreams of becoming a teacher. Johnny has been married, has two children, used to have a drinking problem, and has spent time in jail for forgery. Johnny continues to push too hard, and Frankie continues to pull back when he does, but by dawn they are still together. As the sun rises, they are engaged in the most mundane of tasks: teeth-brushing. The radio station is playing an encore of Debussy's music for "Frankie and Johnny," "whoever, wherever you are." In this final moment of the play, we see a tableau of ordinary life, which is made up mostly of the mundane and sometimes of the beautiful. Contentment may be found when either is experienced with another human being, one with whom a connection has been made.

TERRENCE MCNALLY has said of the play, "*Frankie and Johnny* examines intimacy and what people who are over forty do about having a relationship. . . . It's not about people who meet and in one night say, 'I'm going to love you forever.' It's about love among the ashes" (Bryer 191). He has also commented that the play is about the human tendency—embodied in Frankie—to dwell on "what separates us" because "we're so frightened of what connects us" (Kolin and Kullman 341).

BIBLIOGRAPHY
Bryer, Jackson R., ed. *The Playwright's Art: Conversations with Contemporary American Dramatists.* New Brunswick, N.J.: Rutgers University Press, 1995.
Kolin, Philip C., and Colby H. Kullman, eds. *Speaking on Stage: Interviews with Contemporary American Playwrights.* Tuscaloosa: University of Alabama Press, 1996.

FRIEDMAN, BRUCE JAY (1930–)

FRIEDMAN, BRUCE JAY (1930–) Novelist, short story writer, essayist, and playwright, Bruce Jay Friedman was born in New York City and educated at the University of Missouri–Columbia, where he majored in journalism, graduating in 1951. After college, Friedman served in the United States Air Force until 1953. He worked briefly in publishing in the mid-1950s but has spent most of his career as a fiction writer. In addition to eight novels and five collections of short stories, Friedman has written screenplays and stage plays. Friedman's Jewish-American protagonists are often shallow, materialistic, and disconnected from their Jewish heritage.

His plays for the stage include *23 Pat O'Brien Movies* (1966), a one-act, adapted from his eponymous short story; *Scuba Duba: A Tense Comedy* (1967), winner of an OBIE AWARD, about a billboard-copy writer who loses his wife to another man while renting a chateau in the south of France (the jilted husband considers himself a "liberal," but his wife's choice of a black lover exposes his prejudices); the musical *A Mother's Kisses* (1968)—music by Richard Adler—adapted from Friedman's novel about a Jewish man and his overbearing mother; *Steambath* (1970), in which the protagonist realizes that he and his fellow bathers are dead, that this is the afterlife, and that God is a Puerto Rican steambath attendant; and *Have You Spoken to Any Jews Lately?* (1995), a commercial and critical failure about anti-Semitism and paranoia. Friedman was also a contributor to the erotic musical revue, *Oh! Calcutta!* (1969).

His most successful screenplay, *Splash!* (1985), was written with Lowell Ganz and Babaloo Mandel.

BIBLIOGRAPHY
Friedman, Bruce Jay. *Scuba Duba: A Tense Comedy.* New York: Simon and Schuster, 1968.
———. *Steambath.* New York: Knopf, 1971.
Schultz, Max F. *Bruce Jay Friedman.* New York: Twayne, 1975.

FRONT PAGE, THE

FRONT PAGE, THE BEN HECHT AND CHARLES MACARTHUR (1928) Former newspapermen HECHT and MACARTHUR drew on their experience as journalists to write this farce set in the world of journalism and corrupt politics. The brisk-paced comedy takes place in the pressroom of the Criminal Courts Building in Chicago.

The play opens as a group of disheveled reporters play poker and await the hanging of Earl Williams, an anarchist convicted of shooting an African-American policeman "in a town where the [African-American] vote is important." The sheriff and the mayor, running on a "law-and-order ticket" in an election to be held three days hence, need the execution to secure that vote; in fact, they have postponed the hanging twice in order to keep it fresh in the minds of the voters. The reporters occasionally interrupt their card game to phone their papers and update the story. Sometimes pure fabrication, the stories are never flattering to the politicians ("Sheriff Hartman has just put two hundred more relatives on the payroll to protect the city"; "The governor's gone fishing and can't be found"). During the early scenes, several people are looking for reporter Hildy Johnson, who is described by the playwrights as *"a vanishing type—the lusty, hoodlumesque, half-drunken caballero that was the newspaperman of our youth."* When Hildy finally arrives in the pressroom, he confirms a rumor that he is getting married and leaving journalism to take a lucrative job in advertising with his fiancée's father. The other reporters cheerfully deride him for choosing a future in which he will be "punching a clock" and talking like a "stuffed shirt." Hildy says goodbye to his cohorts and assures his fiancée by telephone that he will be with her in 15 minutes—"Really this time"—but as he walks through the door, shots ring out from the courtyard below. Earl Williams has escaped, and Hildy, who cannot resist the lure of a good story, calls his editor and is back on the job.

Earl Williams suddenly comes in through the window of the pressroom, and Hildy hides him in a rolltop desk and phones his editor, the gruff and ruthless

Walter Burns. Eventually, in a farcical scene, the sheriff and the reporters discover Williams, and he is recaptured; Hildy and Burns are arrested, but a message from the governor arrives just in time to turn the tables on the corrupt sheriff.

Hildy's paper will expose the corrupt politicians, Earl Williams will go free, and Peggy, having forgiven Hildy, will marry him. As the engaged couple take their leave, Burns becomes uncharacteristically sentimental and gives his engraved watch to Hildy as a parting gift; true to form, however, as soon as Hildy and Peggy depart, he arranges for Hildy to be arrested on the train for the theft of his watch.

The Front Page mocks corrupt local politics and captures the irreverent and cynical tone of the all-male pressroom of the time. Its original production, directed by George S. Kaufman, was praised for its authenticity. It has proved to be an enduring American comedy, revived twice on Broadway, in 1970 and in 1986, and frequently performed in regional and college theaters.

FULLER, CHARLES H., JR. (1939–)

Born in Philadelphia, Charles H. Fuller Jr. had a traditional middle-class upbringing, including college and military service. His plays are thoughtful and poignant, exploring human relationships, often between black and white characters in realistic settings and without any strong bias, and attempting to rectify common literary and stage portrayals that distort blacks. He first came to critical attention as a playwright with *The Village: A Party* (1968), which was later retitled *The Perfect Party* (1969), about a village of racially mixed couples. The black leader falls for a black woman and gets murdered to preserve the status quo, while his white widow takes on a new black husband—an allegory suggesting integration will not eradicate racial tension.

Throughout the 1960s and early 1970s, Fuller produced a series of plays that explore themes of racism and discrimination from various angles, such as the uneven *In the Deepest Part of Sleep* (1974), about a black youth coping with a mentally disturbed mother. He also founded and codirected the Afro-American Arts Theatre in Philadelphia. Fuller gained national recognition for *Brownsville Raid* (1975), based upon a 1906 incident in which an entire United States Army regiment was dishonorably discharged because none of its black soldiers would confess to inciting a riot in Brownsville, Texas. The decision was a gross injustice, for there was no evidence against the men, but it took the Army 66 years to clear the men's records.

Zooman and the Sign (1980), a call for community spirit and justice, won an Obie Award and more critical acclaim. In a decaying Philadelphia neighborhood, an innocent girl is shot and killed by a psychotic black teen named Zooman. The neighbors are fearful of naming the murderer, but the girl's father hangs a sign decrying their reticence; when Zooman tries to remove the sign, the father obtains justice by killing him.

Fuller became the second African-American playwright to win a Pulitzer Prize for drama with *A Soldier's Play* (1981). Influenced by Herman Melville's *Billy Budd* (1924), it focuses on a black company in a Louisiana army camp in 1944 as an officer tries to uncover who murdered a sergeant—his fellow men, a white officer, or the Klan—and in the process uncovers racism in everyone involved. Fuller wrote the screenplays for both the 1984 film *A Soldier's Story* and the 1995 film version of *Zooman*.

Fuller's plays have continued to depict the plight of blacks in a racially biased society and include an ambitious series, known as the "We" plays, based on the United States Civil War and postbellum race relations, produced by the Negro Ensemble Company. Presented in the style of Brechtian epic drama, the plays interrelate with crossover characters. The first two parts, *Sally* and *Prince*, were produced in 1988, with *Jonquil* in 1989 and *Burner's Frolic* in 1990. Fuller's most recent work for the stage, *Life, Death (a Dance)* (1999), is about a group of men in a hospital cardiac ward learning how to face life again after the trauma of a heart attack, an experience through which Fuller himself has gone.

Fuller wants to reach the largest possible audience with his stereotype-challenging depictions of African Americans; believing that theater is sadly losing its reach, he now writes predominantly for television and film. Noteworthy among these endeavors is *Love Songs,* a trilogy of interlocking contemporary love stories, which he both wrote and produced for the cable network Showtime in 1999.

BIBLIOGRAPHY

Anadolu-Okur, Nilgun. *Contemporary African-American Theater: Afrocentricity in the Works of Larry Neal, Amiri Baraka, and Charles Fuller.* New York: Garland, 1997.

Fuller, Charles H., Jr. *A Soldier's Play.* New York: Hill & Wang, 1982.

———. *Zooman and the Sign.* New York: Samuel French, 1982.

Susan C. W. Abbotson
Rhode Island College

FUNNYHOUSE OF A NEGRO ADRIENNE KENNEDY (1962)

While several plays before and during the 1960s examined the experiences of African Americans, *Funnyhouse of a Negro,* written on the eve of the Black Power movement, was one of the first plays to lay bare the myth of racial purity, examine the question of racial identity, and highlight the legacy of colonial oppression. A nonnaturalistic play, *Funnyhouse of a Negro* refuses to accept the fallacy of "pure" (and thus more "authentic") racial origins and presents this idea through the use of mixed-race characters and by drawing on the multiple colonial histories that continue to inform the creation of America. The play is also a powerful feminist indictment of white, patriarchal America.

KENNEDY sets the play in the room of the protagonist, the Negro Sarah. At first glance, the room appears to be quite naturalistic. Almost immediately, however, the audience realizes that the room is also a place where the characters in Sarah's psyche (Duchess of Hapsburg, Queen Victoria Regina, Jesus, and Patrice Lumumba) materialize into human flesh and act out her psychological confusion on the stage around her. This is the story of an African-American woman trying, literally, to escape being trapped in her own skin. She is unable to make her many divided selves into a unified whole, and, in her madness, can think of no alternative except suicide.

The plot follows a nonlinear progression. It is divided into 10 sections of monologues and dialogues that are repeated by different characters in different scenes; this repetition of the language is one of the

powerful forces behind Kennedy's play. The play begins in darkness. A woman (an apparition of Sarah's mother) crosses the stage wearing a white nightgown and carrying a bald head in her hands. In the next scene, we are transported to the chambers of Queen Victoria and the Duchess of Hapsburg, who talk of the father who has returned. As the light fades to black, Sarah's mother crosses the stage again and shouts that she should not have allowed the black man to rape her. When the lights come back up, Negro Sarah is on the stage with a noose around her neck, red blood on her face, and a patch of hair missing from her head. In this way, she foreshadows her own death.

During a monologue, Sarah discusses her New York apartment, her white boyfriend, and the love of her light-skinned mother. The scene ends with the appearance of the white Landlady, and the following scene introduces the only other white character, Sarah's boyfriend, Raymond. Both the Landlady and Raymond think that they can more accurately portray the "truth" of Sarah's life than Sarah can. It is left to the audience to decide whom to believe.

When the lights come up on the next scene, the audience sees the figure of Patrice Lumumba carrying an ebony mask while he repeats Sarah's monologue from an earlier scene. After he is finished, Sarah appears downstage and tells the audience how her father's mother wanted him to be Christ and how Sarah's mother became pregnant with her after being raped by her father in Africa. Afterward, Jesus and the Duchess of Hapsburg comb each other's hair as it falls to the ground. After several short scenes that indicate Sarah's ultimate spiral into madness, Sarah appears on stage in her room. We hear knocking, the figure of her father comes rushing at her, and there is a quick blackout. When the lights come back up, the Landlady is on stage and we see *"the hanging figure of the Negro [Sarah]."* In the last moments of the play, Raymond tells the Landlady how Sarah's father did not kill himself (as Sarah tells us), but is a doctor married to a white whore living in New York.

During the era of Civil Rights and Black Power, where slogans such as "black is beautiful" were touchstones for a generation of young African Americans, Kennedy's play was a cautious reminder that internalized self-hatred and internalized racism continued to complicate race relations in this country. It is not enough to replace white power with black power in an exterior way; African-American race pride must come from a deep, introspective place that may take some time to integrate with the institutionalized changes taking place in the world outside.

Kathleen M. Gough
University of California–Berkeley

FUTZ ROCHELLE OWENS (1965) *Futz* was first performed in October 1965, by the Tyrone Guthrie Workshop at the Minnesota Theatre Company. Its fame resonates most, however, from its OFF-OFF-BROADWAY New York run at the La MaMa Experimental Theatre Club in March 1967. Recognized as an important American avant-garde work, the play was made into a movie in 1969 and immediately attained cult status.

A minimalist piece of absurdism (see THEATRE OF THE ABSURD) with a strong moral spine, its comedic irreverence is enhanced by its cartoonish characters, and its poetic density is made more palpable by Owens's use of dialect, bizarre language, and extravagant imagery. The bestiality at the center of the play— the main character, Cy Futz, has sex with a pig he calls Amanda and claims to love—scandalized many critics and viewers; however, the play's levity and its overt didacticism elevate it from any perceived perversity to its current status as a scintillating parable of a man's search for innocence in a world corrupted by conformity.

Presented in 13 loosely connected scenes, the action involves a farmer, Cy, who loves his animals more than people. The girl, Majorie, whom he spurns for the pig, is enraged at this unthinkable act of betrayal, and she incites the town against Cy. Another man confesses that he murdered a young girl because he witnessed Cy copulating with his pig, and in a comical turn the town blames Cy for the girl's death more than the actual killer. In the end, Cy is stabbed to death by Majorie's brother who, with the blessing of the town, must avenge his sister's humiliation and rid the community of its most shameful citizen.

Cy, according to most standards of decency and civilization, and in any conventional context, should be seen as a truly despicable character. Even though he claims to love his pig—speaking of it as if it were his wife—his outrageous behavior should qualify him not only as a criminal but as an incorrigibly debased human. But his intentions, no matter how degrading, are pure: He tells Majorie, "I have faith for my love of the animals. . . . They laugh more real than the mayor and your mother." Ironically, Cy is accused of being an "unnatural man" when, in fact, his desire is to transcend the petty, self-centered world of the townspeople and return to an animal simplicity. Essentially, his crime is a longing for Eden, a natural world of right motives and unconditional love.

Futz is finally a scalpel by which Owens strips away the veneer of civilization to expose the bigotry, fear, and jealousy operating at the core of conventional morality. Against the venality of the other people in his village, Cy's outrageous behavior looks saintly, his sacrifice that of a martyr. But the eeriest implication is that in a world rife with hypocrisy and violence, true love may be possible only at some base, physical level, without the noise and ambiguity—the artificiality— of language.

BIBLIOGRAPHY
Nash, Susan Smith. *Apocalyptic Enactments in the Work of Rochelle Owens*. Norman, Okla.: Texture Press, 1994.

Jeff Johnson
Brevard Community College

G

GALE, ZONA (1874–1938) Predominantly a novelist, Zona Gale also worked as a dramatist, achieving her greatest success with the PULITZER PRIZE–winning theatrical adaptation of her novel *Miss Lulu Bett.*

Gale was born in Portage, Wisconsin, a small midwestern town, and was educated at the University of Wisconsin. Inspiration for much of her writing came from her detailed recollections of life in Portage during her childhood. Gale's short stories and novels have typically been appreciated for their rich and realistic local-color depictions of the incidents and characters of late-19th-century American life.

Aside from her novels, short stories, poetry, and narratives, Gale also dabbled in playwriting and, prior to World War II, was one of a small group of pioneering women dramatists, including SUSAN GLASPELL, ZOË AKINS, Frances Hodgson Burnett, RACHEL CROTHERS, Alice Gerstenberg, ZORA NEALE HURSTON, Anne Nichols, SOPHIE TREADWELL, and LILLIAN HELLMAN. *The Neighbors* (1917), a one-act play taken from Gale's *Friendship Village* short-story collection, was produced by the prestigious WASHINGTON SQUARE PLAYERS, but her most celebrated dramatic work, *Miss Lulu Bett* (1921), is her only important play.

The play closely follows Gale's novel in recounting the barren life of frumpy Lulu Bett, who lives with her sister, Ina, and her brother-in-law, Dwight, in a small Wisconsin town. The dull placidity of Lulu's existence is disturbed when Ninian, Dwight's brother, arrives for a visit. After Ninian casually (and somewhat mockingly) flirts with the repressed Lulu, Dwight adds to the cruel merriment by reading the civil marriage ceremony over them before realizing he has actually married Lulu to Ninian. In spite of the absurdity of their wedding, Lulu and Ninian leave for a honeymoon, but she quickly returns, having learned that Ninian is already married. In Gale's original ending, after her return to Ina and Dwight's home, Lulu turns down the marriage proposal of another suitor, to go off on her own—liberated by her brief "marriage" to Ninian—and find herself rather than return to the position of servitude she, as a spinster, held in her sister's home. However, giving in to public opinion, soon after the play opened, Gale changed the ending to a more conventional one: Ninian finds out his wife has been dead for years, as he suspected; he returns to Lulu, who resumes her marriage to him, and they live happily ever after.

Critics applauded the play for its sensitive details of small-town midwestern life and its witty tone. *Miss Lulu Bett* (with the second ending) won the Pulitzer Prize for drama, encouraging Gale to dramatize some of her other novels and stories, including *Mr. Pitt* (1924, from her novel *Birth*) and *Faint Perfume* (1934). Prior to World War II, Gale's plays were popular and frequently produced, especially by amateur groups, but her theatrical work is rarely seen today.

Among Gale's nondramatic achievements, her short-story collections, *Friendship Village* (1908), *Yellow Gentians and Blue* (1927), and *Bridal Pond* (1930), vied with her novels, *Birth* (1918), *Miss Lulu Bett* (1920), *Faint Perfume* (1923), *Preface to a Life* (1926), *Borgia* (1929), and *Papa La Fleur* (1933), for popularity with readers. Gale also published a volume of poetry, *The Secret Way* (1921), as well as two autobiographical narratives, *When I Was a Little Girl* (1913) and *Portage, Wisconsin* (1928), which provide background that enriches appreciation of her fictional works.

BIBLIOGRAPHY

Derleth, August. *Still Small Voice: The Biography of Zona Gale.* New York: D. Appleton-Century, 1940.
Simonson, Harold Peter. *Zona Gale.* New York: Twayne, 1962.

James Fisher
University of North Carolina at Greensboro

GARDNER, HERB (1934–2003)

Despite having written just a handful of plays, Herb Gardner was one of the most popular playwrights of the late-20th-century American theater. Brooklyn-born and reared, Gardner set his plays in familiar, iconic New York settings and populated them with a quintessentially American collection of Jews, African Americans, Russian émigrés, Irish toughs, dope dealers, and Italian mafioso. Revered for his gently comic pathos and insights into urban life, Gardner was the recipient of the 2000 Lifetime Achievement Award from the Writers Guild of America.

Gardner achieved fame in the early 1950s when his cartoon "The Nebbishes" was nationally syndicated to more than 40 metropolitan newspapers. Gradually, Gardner found that the drawings in his comics were being outsized by his characters' dialogue, and he turned to writing plays.

A THOUSAND CLOWNS (1962) was Gardner's first Broadway success. The eccentric Murray Burns has recently left a high-paying job as a writer for a children's television show in order to find himself. Entrusted with the care of his impressionable and doting nephew Nick, Burns is urged by his well-meaning brother and his new girlfriend to get back onto a career path. For the film version's screenplay (1965), Gardner received an Academy Award nomination.

In 1968, Gardner directed his play *The Goodbye People*. Bucking wisdom and his dwindling finances, a determined elderly man opens a Coney Island hot dog stand in the middle of the winter. Despite the casting of Milton Berle in the lead role, *The Goodbye People* received mixed reviews. Gardner's play *Thieves* opened on Broadway in 1974. A portrait of two schoolteachers' troubled marriage, the piece comically depicts the suspicions, jealousies, and insecurities of love.

After a long absence, Gardner triumphantly returned to Broadway in 1985 with *I'M NOT RAPPAPORT*. A touching study of aging, the play is set on a Central Park bench where two elderly men named Nat and Midge meet daily to spar affectionately with words. The Jewish Nat fondly recalls his younger days as a labor organizer. When a dispute jeopardizes Midge's job and home, Nat's solutions threaten to do more harm than good. The play was an unqualified Broadway success, running for nearly three years. Gardner won the 1986 TONY AWARD for the play. A 2002 Broadway revival saw Judd Hirsch reprise his role of Nat.

Like *I'm Not Rappaport*, *Conversations with My Father* (1992) began at the Seattle Rep, once again under the direction of Daniel Sullivan and starring Judd Hirsch. Set in a Lower East Side barroom, it is a moving, bittersweet memory play, documenting a Jewish family's attempts to assimilate into America's proverbial melting pot.

Teeming with some of the late-20th-century stage's most vibrant misfits, outsiders, and dreamers, Gardner's plays successfully capture the angst of New Yorkers attempting to hold onto their dignity and passion in the face of seemingly overwhelming odds. Herb Gardner was that rare dramatist who managed to package deep sociological and political observations into touchingly familiar situations that are rife with comic banter.

BIBLIOGRAPHY

Gardner, Herb. *The Collected Plays.* New York: Applause Theatre Books, 2000.

Mark Cosdon
Allegheny College

GARLAND, HAMLIN (1860–1940)

Primarily a critic and writer of fiction, Hamlin Garland was well known in the 1890s for his short stories about the hard life of farmers on the western frontier and for his critical writing about literary realism, which he called "Veritism." His connection to the theater began in 1889 with his friendship with JAMES A. HERNE, who had similar ideas about the potential of dramatic realism to express the Progressive politics that the two shared. Garland began to write drama criticism that advanced the cause of realism in the theater and praised the work that Herne was doing in such groundbreaking plays as MARGARET FLEMING (1891).

Garland also wrote plays of his own, which were intended to be realistic in their reflection of the lives of the people he chose to write about and didactic in their obvious social and political statements. Garland's plays were not produced. The best known of them is *Under the Wheel* (1890), a drama that was published in the Progressive magazine *Arena* and intended to support tax reform that would alleviate poverty, particularly for the small farmer. The play begins in Boston, where the Edwards family has been driven out of their home by rising rents and falling wages, and they prepare to go west and take up farming as a solution to their poverty. The rest of the play takes place in the West, as the Edwards' dreams of independence and prosperity are destroyed by a combination of nature—three bad seasons, a drought, and a hailstorm—and capitalism—a foreclosure on their mortgage. Garland wrote in his preface to the play that he believed most of America's social problems could be cured by the levy of a single tax on land.

A second play, *A Member of the Third House* (1890), which concerned a scandal in the Massachusetts legislature involving a railway monopoly, was given a staged reading in Boston, but it was not published because of its potential for libel. Garland later turned it into a novel. He wrote several other unproduced plays and motion picture scenarios.

BIBLIOGRAPHY

Arvidson, Lloyd A., ed. *Hamlin Garland: Centennial Tributes and a Checklist of the Hamlin Garland Papers in the University of Southern California Library.* Los Angeles: University of Southern California, 1962.

Bryer, Jackson R., and Eugene Harding, with the assistance of Robert A. Rees. *Hamlin Garland and the Critics: An Annotated Bibliography.* Troy, N.Y.: Whitston, 1973.

Garland, Hamlin. *Selected Letters of Hamlin Garland.* Edited by Keith Newlin and Joseph B. McCullough. Lincoln: University of Nebraska Press, 1998.

———. "Under the Wheel: A Modern Play in Six Scenes." *Arena* 2 (1890): 182–228.

Holloway, Jean. *Hamlin Garland, A Biography.* 1960. Freeport. N.Y.: Books for Libraries, 1971.

Newlin, Keith. *Hamlin Garland: A Bibliography.* Troy, N.Y.: Whitston, 1998.

Brenda Murphy
University of Connecticut

GAY AND LESBIAN THEATER

The definition of what exactly constitutes "gay and lesbian theater" determines where one begins an examination of its place in American drama. Gay and lesbian drama is generally regarded as a contemporary phenomenon, denoting those plays specifically written or performed by homosexuals for a largely homosexual audience and therefore concerned with the social, political, and personal ramifications of being a member of the sexual minority; as such, it is deemed to have come into fruition as a specific genre in the late 1960s as a result of the increasing freedom derived from the gay liberation movement. However, if one counts those plays and characterizations depicting any aspect of homosexual life, one needs to look back as far as the late 1800s. Once the concept itself developed through the work of early psychologists such as Richard Krafft-Ebing, Havelock Ellis, and Sigmund Freud and became part of public consciousness, homosexuality began appearing onstage, albeit usually covertly.

Initial depictions necessarily considered homosexuality an exotic and somewhat frightening mental illness, whose cause was unknown, but whose effect was shameful and destructive. The first known instance of an American stage portrayal of "inversion," as it was then known, occurs in Henry Blake Fuller's *At Saint Judas's* (1896), a brief play meant to be read rather than staged, in which a Best Man reveals his jealous love for the Groom upon his wedding day and commits suicide because of his shame. In 1922, the YIDDISH DRAMA staple *God of Vengeance* by Sholem Asch, the story of a brothel owner's daughter's love for one of his prostitutes, introduced lesbianism to the New York stage in a truncated English-language PROVINCETOWN PLAYERS production. DJUNA BARNES, a playwright connected with the Provincetown Players, also touched upon the theme of lesbianism in some of her plays. Edouard Bourdet's French melodrama, *The Captive* (1926), about a married woman falling under the spell of a mannish society lady, was a scandalous hit in New York. The play was closed by police after a three-month run; the resulting court battles prompted the Wales Padlock Act, which prohibited depictions of any form of "sexual deviancy" upon the New York stage and technically remained in effect until its repeal in 1967.

Savvy producers found ways to circumvent the law, however. Mae West simply flouted it altogether in her blackmail drama *The Drag* (1927), and a backstage melodrama, *The Pleasure Man,* the following year, derived added publicity from her legal skirmishes. Although the portrayals in both plays of effete and effeminate male homosexuality would be considered offensive today, they were among the most enlightened and sympathetic of the time. Building upon the popularity of such transvestite vaudeville/burlesque performers as Bert Savoy and Julian Eltinge, a veritable "pansy craze" hit the early 1930s, with Harlem drag balls also becoming popular sources of underground entertainment for sophisticated New Yorkers.

But most of the homosexual characters from this era, usually in imports from abroad such as Noël Coward's *The Vortex* (1925) and Mordaunt Shairp's *The Green Bay Tree* (1933) (featuring Laurence Olivier in his American debut), or homegrown characters such as EUGENE O'NEILL's Charles Marsden in *STRANGE INTERLUDE* (1928), were so heavily codified as to escape detection from the authorities and sometimes even the audiences. Such telltale signs as effeminacy, preoccupation with dress, use of witty language, and interest in interior décor, mother fixations, and heightened, often hysterical emotionalism became longstanding stereotypical indications of male homosexuality; while masculine attire, self-determination, misogyny, and even an affection for violets (in Bourdet's *The Captive*) became identifiable hallmarks of lesbianism.

LILLIAN HELLMAN's *The CHILDREN'S HOUR* (1934) brought its lesbian theme to the foreground, remaining the most successful gay-themed play until 1981. However, that play and other mid-century successes such as *TEA AND SYMPATHY* (1953) and *A VIEW FROM THE BRIDGE* (1955) were the work of heterosexual playwrights whose plots usually depended upon suspected rather than actual homosexual orientations. Gay playwright TENNESSEE WILLIAMS was among the first to use his own experience, dramatizing the fears other characters had of closeted characters that were typically already dead (Allan Gray in *A STREETCAR NAMED DESIRE* [1947], Skipper in *CAT ON A HOT TIN ROOF* [1955]), or otherwise kept conveniently offstage. Although EDWARD ALBEE resisted discussing his sexual orientation through his work, critics insisted on detecting its presence in his plays *The ZOO STORY* (1960) and *WHO'S AFRAID OF VIRGINIA WOOLF?* (1962). WILLIAM INGE was more open about placing his personal struggles onstage in such early 1960s plays as *Tiny Closet* (1962) and *The Boy in the Basement* (1962), which were never as popular as his more mainstream fare. Most gay-themed plays from the 1950s and early 1960s still focused on the shameful aspects of homosexuality and abysmal attempts to fit into heterosexual society, with homosexuality either having to be disavowed or disposed of through suicide.

The rise of small avant-garde theaters OFF-OFF-BROADWAY in the 1960s, as well as the sexual revolution itself, led to the proliferation of overt, somewhat more favorable, and ostensibly more honest portrayals of homosexuals by openly gay playwrights. In such tiny venues as the Caffe Cino, Judson Poets' Theatre, and La MaMa, rising talents such as Doric Wilson, Robert Patrick, and William Hoffman found acceptance for their innovative work. LANFORD WILSON's landmark 1964 play *The Madness of Lady Bright,* a bitter portrayal of a suicidal drag queen, was among the most successful of these offerings.

Gay drag and "camp" were also emerging as popular subgenres through the work of New York's Playhouse of the Ridiculous and its various offspring: CHARLES LUDLAM's Ridiculous Theatrical Company, CHARLES BUSCH's Theatre in Limbo, New York's Hot Peaches collective, and its San Francisco counterpart,

The Cockettes, all of which specialized in outrageous excess and genre parody. Many of these groups were largely improvisational, and their shows varied widely from performance to performance.

Gay theater reached a turning point with the critical and commercial success of MART CROWLEY's *The Boys in the Band* (1968), which became the first gay play to attract a large crossover audience with its bold language, humor, and frank, though downbeat, portrayal of contemporary gay lifestyles. The concurrent emergence of a visible gay subculture following the 1969 Stonewall Riots in New York City, as well as the repeal of the Wales Act, opened the floodgates to the depiction of homosexuality on stage, in plays geared to both gay and straight audiences. While gay playwrights tended to place their homosexual characters centerstage and focus on myriad aspects of the gay experience, straight playwrights more often relegated gays to the sideline as colorful, witty, or bitchy supporting characters. Many of the plays that flourished during this period, however, still dealt with internalized homophobia, the coming-out process, ongoing persecution by the heterosexual majority, and the struggle for acceptance and equality.

The proliferation of work by gay playwrights led to the establishment of numerous theater companies devoted exclusively to work by, for, and about homosexuals. Led by Doric Wilson's TOSOS (The Other Side of Silence) Theatre Company in New York in 1973, soon every major metropolitan city had at least one gay theater (including Theatre Rhino in San Francisco, Lionheart in Chicago). The national Gay Theatre Alliance was founded in 1978 to help promote and develop gay theater.

Because of the dearth of female playwrights and perhaps because of the perception that lesbianism was neither as controversial nor as commercially viable, plays about lesbians remained few. Starting in the 1970s, several lesbian playwrights did get their work produced; these included Susan Miller and Jane Chambers, whose popular *Last Summer at Bluefish Cove* (1982) is considered a distaff version of *Boys in the Band*. Others, such as MARIA IRENE FORNÉS and MEGAN TERRY, tended to write more feminist than overtly lesbian dramas.

As the gay community made gains in the 1970s and 1980s, the focus of gay theater broadened its concerns. Several plays are considered historical milestones in the struggle: Along with numerous plays about such pivotal figures as Oscar Wilde and Edward Carpenter came Jonathan Katz's examination of gay American history, *Coming Out!* (1975); Doric Wilson's reenactment of Stonewall, *Street Theater* (1982); *Bent* (1979), Martin Sherman's treatment of the Nazi persecution of homosexuals; and EMILY MANN's *EXECUTION OF JUSTICE* (1983), about the assassination of San Francisco's first gay supervisor, Harvey Milk. Genres other than drama or historical docudrama were also broached, including domestic comedy (Doric Wilson's *A Perfect Relationship* [1979]), farce (TERRENCE MCNALLY's *The Ritz* [1975]), and even musicals (Al Carmines's *The Faggot* [1973], Bill Solly's *Boy Meets Boy* [1975]). Sexual promiscuity and male prostitution were perennially popular subjects, and nudity also became commonplace.

The apotheosis of gay theater undoubtedly came in 1981 with the international success of HARVEY FIERSTEIN's four-and-a-half-hour epic, *TORCH SONG TRILOGY*. Originally staged as three separate one-acts at La MaMa, Fierstein's semiautobiographical story of a drag queen's search for love ran for more than two years on Broadway, winning Fierstein TONY AWARDS for Best Play and Best Actor. However, some gay radicals excoriated the play's promulgation of heterosexual values and grudging acceptance as the pinnacle of gay achievement.

An indication of how far gay theater had made inroads into the mainstream by the early 1980s was the increasing number of plays in which homosexuality was an accepted given that did not define a character's entire existence or in which a gay person's struggles were seen against the larger landscape of the society. Such plays as Lanford Wilson's *FIFTH OF JULY* (1980), whose protagonist's gay relationship is neither an issue nor even commented upon, and Kathleen Tolan's *A Weekend near Madison* (1983), in which a lesbian couple search for an appropriate sperm donor among their blasé chums, provide evidence that homosexuality was no longer a shameful or shocking subject.

The advent of the AIDS crisis in the early 1980s changed the face of gay theater forever, as it changed the sexual landscape as a whole. The fear, confusion, and lack of appropriate governmental response to the epidemic was documented in a rush of angry AGITPROP plays, beginning with William M. Hoffman's domestic tragedy *As Is* and LARRY KRAMER's *The Normal Heart,* the playwright's personal account of the creation of the Gay Men's Health Crisis organization, both of which appeared in 1985. Although the latter became the New York Shakespeare Festival's longest-running nonmusical play, Kramer was vilified by many for what was seen as an antisex diatribe. Because AIDS remained the defining issue for the gay community, virtually every gay play of the next decade focused on some aspect of the disease and its toll. By the mid-1990s, however, a second generation of AIDS plays that no longer focused specifically on the disease reflected its entrenched position in society.

A few successful lesbian playwrights emerged in the late 1980s and 1990s, such as PAULA VOGEL and Claire Chafee, with New York's WOW Theatre Café providing a venue for experimental work by women. HOLLY HUGHES, whose "dyke-noir" parodies include *Dress Suits for Hire* (1987) and *The Lady Dick* (1985), was one of the few to achieve widespread recognition, primarily through the notoriety of having her NEA grants rescinded. Several women's ensembles also sprang up, notably Split Britches and The Five Lesbian Brothers, who created their work collectively.

TONY KUSHNER's mammoth two-part ANGELS IN AMERICA, an ambitious work subtitled a "gay fantasia on national themes," became, in 1993, one of the most highly praised and award-winning gay plays ever. A sprawling, politically dense, theatrically innovative, angry, and comic epic portrait of America's failures, it proved the ability of gay theater to transcend its limitations as a ghettoized genre.

At the beginning of the 21st century, gay theater continues to push the boundaries. An exciting trend is the amalgamation of homosexual concerns with those of other marginalized minority groups in the work of African Americans such as Pomo Afro Homos, Cheryl L. West, and Shay Youngblood; Asians Chay Yew and Diana Son; and Latina CHERRIÉ MORAGA and Latino Guillermo Reyes. Individual performance artists such as Tim Miller, Marga Gomez, and John Fleck also extend the parameters of gay theater in their largely autobiographical solo pieces. While many gay theater companies find it difficult to survive in the harsh economic climate, mainstream theaters are increasingly more open to producing gay-themed work that, in the past, would have been considered of limited commercial appeal.

While no individual play has had the same impact as *Angels in America* (1990 and 1991), the proliferation of gay and lesbian themes and characters in more mainstream writing continues. Even such an unlikely candidate as DAVID MAMET has included gay/lesbian characters in his three most recent works (*Boston Marriage* [1999], ROMANCE [2005], and *November* [2008]). Although the majority of new work continues to premiere in, and often does not travel beyond, regional productions, Broadway welcomes commercial productions centering on gay issues, such as the recent productions of DOUGLAS CARTER BEANE's *The Little Dog Laughed* (2006) and a 2006 revival of Simon Gray's *Butley* (1971). OFF-BROADWAY, some stalwart gay playwrights of previous decades continue to produce successful new work (PAUL RUDNICK's *Regrets Only* [2006] and *The New Century* [2008]; Terrence McNally's *Some Men* [2007]), while such exciting young playwrights as CHRISTOPHER SHINN (*Four* [revival, 2002] and *The DYING CITY* [2007]) and Roberto Aguirre-Sacasa (*Based on a Totally True Story* [2006] and *Good Boys and True* [2008]) are taking gay theater to imaginative new heights.

A challenge for many gay and lesbian theater companies has, ironically, been the increasing proliferation of images of homosexuality within other media (including print, film, and television), which has obviated one of its previous primary functions of providing positive gay portrayals not obtainable elsewhere. As social acceptance, if still not full equality, becomes more commonplace, many playgoers no longer feel the need to seek out theatrical representations of homosexuality. The very diversity within the community also presents an obstacle, since no individual issue (such as marriage equality or the military's "don't ask, don't tell" policy) can be relied upon to interest all segments of the gay population. The imbalance between representations of lesbianism and male homosexuality, as well as the schism between lesbian and gay theater companies, also unfortunately continues, as does an underrepresentation of the bisexual and transgendered communities.

BIBLIOGRAPHY

Brecht, Stefan. *Queer Theatre.* Frankfurt am Main, Germany: Suhrkamp, 1978.

Clum, John M. *Still Acting Gay.* New York: St. Martin's Press, 2000.

Curtin, Kaier. *"We Can Always Call Them Bulgarians": The Emergence of Lesbians and Gay Men on the American Stage.* Boston: Alyson, 1987.

De Jongh, Nicholas. *Not in Front of the Audience.* London: Routledge, 1992.

Fisher, James. *"We Will Be Citizens": New Essays on Gay and Lesbian Theatre.* Jefferson, N.C.: McFarland, 2008.

Harbin, Billy J., Kim Marra, and Robert A. Schanke, eds. *The Gay and Lesbian Theatrical Legacy: A Biographical Dictionary in the Pre-Stonewall Era.* Ann Arbor: University of Michigan Press, 2007.

Hoffman, William M., ed. *Gay Plays: The First Collection.* New York: Avon, 1979.

Sinfield, Alan. *Out on Stage: Lesbian and Gay Theatre in the Twentieth Century.* New Haven, Conn.: Yale University Press, 1999.

Douglas W. Gordy
Walnut Creek, California

GEIOGAMAH, HANAY (1945–) See NATIVE-AMERICAN DRAMA.

GELBART, LARRY (1928–2009) During his long career, Larry Gelbart became—through his writing for radio, television, film, and stage—one of America's sharpest satirists. Born to Polish-Jewish immigrants in Chicago, the young Gelbart moved to Los Angeles with his family; the barber's son began writing comedy for Danny Thomas and the radio series *Duffy's Tavern* while still in high school. He graduated to the television writing staff of the legendary Sid Caesar, joining such comedy luminaries as Carl Reiner, NEIL SIMON, and Mel Brooks.

After two early stage failures, Gelbart wrote the book for the musical *A Funny Thing Happened on the Way to the Forum* (1962) with Burt Shevelove. From 26 extant plays of the Roman playwright Plautus, the librettists selected situations and character types (such as the senile husband Senex, bullying wife Domina, and conniving slave Pseudolus) to create one of Broadway's funniest musicals. Stephen Sondheim's first solo score skillfully complemented the book's farce.

Throughout the 1970s and 1980s, Gelbart flourished as principal creator/writer for the television series *M*A*S*H*, as well as screenwriter for *Oh, God!* and *Tootsie.* He returned to the theater with *Sly Fox* (1978), an updating of Ben Jonson's *Volpone* by way of a 1924 Austrian adaptation. In Gelbart's version, Foxwell Sly swindles gold from various San Francisco residents by promising to make each his sole heir. The play satirizes human avarice and gullibility, but while Jonson's vulpine protagonist is ultimately jailed, the foxy Sly escapes with his gold.

Mastergate (1989), a parody of the Iran-contra affair, depicts a Senate hearing investigating the covert funneling of movie-studio funds into a Central American revolution. As in other Gelbart works, this play features appropriately named characters, including CIA chief Slaughter, Congressmen Byers and Sellars, and Major Battles. The text lampoons rhetorical obfuscation, selective amnesia, and media complicity through puns, neologisms, malapropisms, circumlocution, double entendre, and general nonsense. Gelbart's relentless wordplay challenges the audience's ability to endure nonstop political lies—no doubt his intention. His next work, *Power Failure* (1990), explores various institutional and personal forms of power, including capital punishment, corporate espionage, medical and priestly malfeasance, adultery, and blackmail. The play consists of successive two-character scenes in which a new character interacts with a holdover from the previous scene. Power ebbs and flows with each new pairing; in the end, deception and greed win, while justice loses.

Gelbart's book for the musical *City of Angels* (1990), like that for *Forum,* sparkles with one-line humor. His smart, complex send-up of 1940s film noir reveals a love-hate relationship with Hollywood as it alternates between two parallel stories: novelist/screenwriter

Stine dealing with an egotistical studio boss, and Stine's detective character Stone investigating a missing-persons case. Cy Coleman's jazzy score perfectly matched the playwright's sophisticated dialogue. Although this musical demonstrates Gelbart's ability to make audiences laugh, his comedy of the past quarter century shows an increasing disgust with hypocrisy, corruption, and injustice. He employs satire to battle what he fears may be an unbeatable foe.

In the last two decades, Gelbart wrote little for the stage. In 2008, he received the PEN USA (the West Coast branch of International PEN) Lifetime Achievement Award for his 60-year career as a writer working in multiple genres.

BIBLIOGRAPHY

Gelbart, Larry. *City of Angels.* New York: Applause Theatre & Cinema Books, 1990.

———. *"Mastergate" and "Power Failure": Two Political Satires for the Stage.* New York: Applause Theatre Books, 1994.

———. *Sly Fox.* New York: Samuel French, 1978.

Malarcher, Jay. *The Classically American Comedy of Larry Gelbart.* Lanham, Md.: Scarecrow Press, 2003.

Shevelove, Burt, and Larry Gelbart. *A Funny Thing Happened on the Way to the Forum.* New York: Dodd, Mead, 1963.

Gary Konas
University of Wisconsin–La Crosse

GELBER, JACK (1932–2003) Jack Gelber is best known for his work with the LIVING THEATRE, particularly his landmark play within a play, *The CONNECTION* (1959), which won OBIE and Vernon Rice Awards. Gelber was an active participant in the experimental New York theater scene of the 1960s and 1970s, which consistently challenged the commercialism of Broadway. Always innovative, Gelber continued to write but found it increasingly hard to get his work produced. He gained some recognition as a director, notably of works by SAM SHEPARD and Robert Coover, and developed a successful college teaching career.

Born in Chicago, Illinois, Gelber had no formal training in the theater. Through an association with a small collaborative New York theater company that allowed him to use their space for jazz concerts, he decided to try to write a play. Emulating the sponta-neity of jazz improvisation in its presentation, *The Connection* riffs on the lives of drug users and the mainstream society they avoid, simultaneously exploring these two worlds and the complex connection between fiction and reality. Through actor/audience interaction and its continuous challenges against theatrical convention, the play makes the addict's experience an intensely personal one for the audience. Gelber was named most promising playwright of 1960 by the New York Critics' Poll. At the time of Gelber's death, ARTHUR KOPIT called *The Connection* a "seminal work that had a visceral effect on the audience" (*New York Times,* May 10, 2003).

Gelber's next play was *The Apple* (1961), which he based on an incident from the rehearsal period of *The Connection. The Apple* depicts an acting group rehearsing in a coffee shop. The first and third acts present events from the point of view of the actors, as their performance is wrecked by one of their number who becomes mad. The second act offers the madman's perspective in the form of surreal dream sequences. Through this juxtaposition, Gelber attempts to convey the chaotic senselessness of life. The less successful *Square in the Eye* (1965), with its chronological shifts and use of multimedia, conveys a domestic tragicomedy about the sudden death of a frustrated artist's first wife and his speedy remarriage. The artistic merits of *The Cuban Thing* (1969), an examination of the effects of the Cuban revolution on a middle-class Cuban family, became overshadowed by its politicized reception. During the previews, objecting to what was seen as the play's pro-Castro agenda, five powder bombs were set off. Nervous producers closed the play after only one performance.

Gelber continued to explore theatrical boundaries with such plays as *Sleep* (1972), in which a sleep subject interacts with both his researchers and his dreams, which are played out on stage. *Jack Gelber's New Play: Rehearsal* (1976) returns to the play-within-a-play format in its depiction of a group of ex-convicts vainly attempting to put on a play, and *Starters* (1980) deals with a 1950s activist dealing with advancing age. However, Gelber is best remembered for his plays from the 1960s, which helped fire New York's alternative theater, while his later work rarely found publication.

BIBLIOGRAPHY

Gelber, Jack. *"The Apple" and "Square in the Eye."* New York: Viking, 1974.

———. *The Connection.* New York: Grove Press, 1960.

———. *The Cuban Thing.* New York: Grove Press, 1969.

———. *Sleep.* New York: Hill & Wang, 1972.

Susan C. W. Abbotson
Rhode Island College

GEMINI Albert Innaurato (1977)   Set in the backyards of adjoining houses in a working-class neighborhood in South Philadelphia, *Gemini* is a comedy about a confused young man, Francis Geminiani, as he turns 21, surrounded by well-meaning and eccentric neighbors, family, and friends.

A student on summer vacation from Harvard, Francis receives an unexpected visit from two rich, WASP college friends, Judith and Randy. He tries to discourage them from staying by telling them that his father is in the Mafia, nearly succeeding in scaring them off when his warm and welcoming father, Fran, arrives and dispels his son's lies. At the heart of Francis's cold reception of his friends is his confusion about his sexuality. He has had a fling with the beautiful Judith but has since developed a crush on her younger brother, Randy. Fran, who has begun to suspect that his son is homosexual, welcomes Judith and her brother heartily, delighted at the prospect that Francis may have a girlfriend.

Innaurato creates a group of hilarious characters: Bunny Weinberger lives next door to the Geminianis with her fat and asthmatic son, 16-year-old Herschel, who she claims is a genius, citing his IQ frequently. Obsessed with public transportation, Herschel is so socially backward that he seems more retarded than bright. Bunny herself, often vulgar and a heavy drinker, fluctuates between warmth and abuse and between reasonably good sense and suicidal lunacy. Lucille Pompi is Fran's "lady friend"; skinny and prim, she is the opposite of the voluptuous, mouthy, bleach-blonde Bunny. In a comic dinner scene in the Geminiani's backyard, Lucille steadfastly refuses a plate of her own on the grounds that she is not hungry, only to eat off the plates of everyone else at the table. Fran has had a relationship with Bunny, which Bunny would like to rekindle; since Lucille can cook Italian while Bunny cooks only Irish, Fran stays put.

The college set is riddled with identity crises. In addition to his confused sexuality, Francis worries that he could never attract anyone because he is overweight. Stunning Judith wants to be perceived as having the depth to love someone for his inner qualities. She explains this to Francis, to whom she is still attracted, but Francis cannot believe someone as beautiful as she could love someone as fat as he. Meanwhile, brother Randy believes he is too skinny and is forever trying to gain weight. Randy is also exceedingly accommodating, amiably agreeing to accompany Herschel on transportation-system outings and to view transportation-related artifacts whenever asked—though he has no real interest. When he finally refuses Herschel, it is to volunteer to help Francis determine his sexual preference once and for all inside his tent—though he has no real interest there either, as it turns out.

When Fran, Lucille, and Bunny bring on Francis's birthday cake, he grabs it by the handful and flings it at his tormentors. The scene ends when Herschel arrives with rat poison all over his mouth; this is not the first time he has attempted suicide. Herschel recovers, and the guests leave for the train station. When Francis decides he should join them after all, the band of misfits who love him spring into action: Herschel is dispatched to bring Judith and Randy back; Bunny offers her house money for a train ticket since Fran has no cash; and Lucille runs to grab Francis's big bag of dirty laundry from his room. They are, as they say to each other often—in the affectionate tone of the play— "good people," despite their flaws. Francis's sexuality is left ambiguous, though he does embrace Judith after she and her brother are retrieved by Herschel.

Albert Innaurato was awarded an Obie for Playwriting in the 1976–77 season for both *Gemini* and *The Transfiguration of Benno Blimpie,* a play that was produced earlier in the season. Moving to Broadway, *Gemini* became one of the longest-running (nonmusical) plays in its history.

GEM OF THE OCEAN August Wilson (2003)   Written ninth of the 10 plays in August Wilson's cycle dramatizing the African-American experience in the 20th century, *Gem of the Ocean*—set in 1904—is the first chronologically. The play examines the hardships faced by former slaves and the children of former slaves trying to make lives for themselves—trying to find the freedom they have been granted—in America amid persecution and exploitation at the turn of the century. Just 40 years after emancipation, the wounds of slavery are still fresh, and whites are loath to relinquish the power they once had. Thematically, Wilson once again suggests that it is essential for African Americans to remember the past and honor the sacrifices of their ancestors in order to make it possible to lead a meaningful life.

The play is set in the Hill District of Pittsburgh in the house of Aunt Ester Tyler, the *"very old, yet vital spiritual advisor for the community."* Aunt Ester is a character Wilson introduced as an offstage presence in *TWO TRAINS RUNNING* (1990) and who is an offstage character again in *KING HEDLEY II* (2001). In *Gem of the Ocean,* Aunt Ester lives with Eli, a former conductor on the Underground Railroad, and Black Mary, who is a laundress and the sister of Caesar, the constable. The other characters are Solly, Eli's friend and once his partner on the Underground Railroad, and Selig, the white traveling pot-and-pan salesman, who in *JOE TURNER'S COME AND GONE* (1986)—set in 1911—is also a "people finder" of and for dislocated black refugees from the South.

The play opens with two related events, one we witness and one we are told about: A troubled young man recently arrived from Alabama named Citizen Barlow seeks the counsel of Aunt Ester, having been referred to her by "the people"; and another man, Garret Brown, has drowned in the river rather than surrender to the constable for a crime he did not commit—stealing a bucket of nails.

Citizen Barlow testifies to the terrible treatment blacks are enduring in both the South (in Alabama "the roads [are] closed to the colored people") and the North, where black workers are being exploited. Citizen gets a job at the tin mill in Pittsburgh, and within a matter of days he owes more money to the company for room and board (the latter he never receives) than he makes. Aunt Ester listens to him with sympathy, offering him food and a bed and a bit of her Christian philosophy. Citizen eventually confesses to her that he is responsible for the death of Garret Brown; it was Citizen who stole the nails out of desperation, but he remained silent while Brown drowned. Citizen has come to Aunt Ester "to get [his] soul washed," even after Black Mary tells him that Aunt Ester has "no magic power." Aunt Ester advises him to "find something [besides the stolen bucket of nails] to be the center of [his] life." She sends him upriver to find two pennies, but this is just "to give him something to do," she says after he leaves. He will think the pennies have "power" and that "his trouble will be over." She tells Black Mary, "He need to think that before he can come face to face with himself." She tells Mary (who is in a sense her apprentice) that most of the time the people that will come to tell her their problems are "looking for love and don't know what it is. . . . You got to show them how to find it for themselves."

It is in this play that the mythical Aunt Ester is made real. In both *Two Trains Running* and *King Hedley II,* the character Aunt Ester is said to be over 300 years old, and, as Wilson himself has explained in discussing *Hedley,* she represents the connection to the past, to 1619 when Africans first were brought in slavery to America. In *Gem of the Ocean* lies the explanation for how Aunt Ester can be so old and yet be real: She is not just one woman. When the Ester Tyler in this play was nine years old, she was sent to live with a woman named Ester Tyler. She stayed with her until her death, when the younger woman took on the elder's name and the collective memory she had carried of African-American history, including the searingly painful memories of the Middle Passage. She tells Black Mary that she is carrying memories "for a lot of folk. All the old-timey folks"—in other words, all those who were sold into or born into slavery. By the time of *Gem,* the Aunt Esters are, collectively, 285 years old. The present Aunt Ester would like to pass this necessary burden to Black Mary if she will accept it. Otherwise, the old woman will have to find someone else before she dies. The memories she speaks of in this play are a mixture of her own personal memories and the collective African-American memory of which she is custodian. Certainly she herself was a slave, but she did not come over during the Middle Passage, yet she speaks of these experiences with equal authenticity. It is this comprehensive recognition of the past that is the source of Aunt Ester's wisdom.

When Citizen comes back with the two pennies, Aunt Ester, with the assistance of Black Mary, Eli, and Solly, takes him on a symbolic journey—a pantomime with narration by Ester and singing and acting in masks by the others—to "The City of Bones," a beautiful afterlife in the middle of the Atlantic Ocean built of the bones of all the Africans who died on their way across the ocean. Black Mary brings out a quilted map and Ester folds her own "Bill of Sale" into a paper "magic boat" called *Gem of the Ocean.* The journey promises to enable Citizen to wash his soul clean. On this symbolic journey, Citizen faces Garret Brown in the afterworld and admits his own culpability in Brown's death; he also connects with the past, since part of the journey is a reenactment of the Middle Passage. These events represent two recurring themes in Wilson's work: getting "right with" oneself and keeping one's connection to African-American history (as in *Hedley,* there is salvation in connecting with black history—in recognizing its connection to oneself). It is only after Citizen has been through this journey that he can offer himself to and be accepted by Black Mary and also find his true calling, which is to become the next Solly, helping as many of those who suffer because of their race as he can.

Solly is one who knows his connection to the past and knows who he is. He carries a piece of the chain that bound him as a slave. When Solly reached freedom in Canada in 1857 by way of the Underground Railroad, he couldn't stay because of his "mama and all the other people still in bondage." So he became a conductor on the Underground Railway; he and Eli worked together. In the present tense of the play, Solly plans to go back to Alabama and get his sister because she writes that the "white peoples is gone crazy and won't let anybody leave" for the North. Solly knows what Caesar the constable cannot understand, which is that the mistreatment that has persisted since the end of slavery has brought many people to the point where they feel they have nothing to lose and that level of despair can make men dangerous.

While Solly is a Wilson hero, Caesar is a man who betrays his race. Caesar's position as constable was given to him after he, during his own imprisonment, caught some black escapees for the white guards. He has contempt for many of his fellow African Americans, saying some were "better off in slavery" because "they don't know how to act otherwise." Caesar exploits his own people, charging too much for bread from his bakery and evicting people from rooms he rents. Black Mary stopped working for her brother and came to work for Aunt Ester three years ago, after Caesar killed a boy for stealing a loaf of bread. Caesar believes the law is everything.

Halfway through the play, the mill is set on fire. The fire and the general unrest surrounding the drowned man has white people discussing the reinstatement of slavery. Rumor has it that someone saw who set the blaze, and Caesar is determined to find the arsonist, who we eventually learn was Solly. When Citizen's magical journey is over, Caesar arrives to arrest Solly, who declares that he burnt down the mill because "freedom got a high price. You got to pay." He goes on to say, "I didn't mind settling up the difference after the war. But I didn't know they was gonna settle like this. I got older I see where I'm gonna die and everything gonna be the same. I say well at least goddamn it they gonna know I was here!" Solly, himself, then, is one of the dangerous men of whom he speaks earlier in the play—those who are driven to violent action when there seems to be nothing left to lose.

Solly escapes temporarily, but Caesar also has a warrant for the arrest of Ester for aiding him. She goes peacefully but not before she explains that the warrant is analogous to her Bill of Sale—just because it is the law "don't make it right." Eventually Solly is shot by Caesar, who vows to hunt down Citizen, as well, for helping Solly escape. At this point Black Mary irrevocably denies her traitorous brother. In the end, Citizen, becoming the new Solly, takes the dead man's coat, hat, stick, and sister's letter. He is now a man who will unfailingly bring relief to others no matter what the personal cost, just as Black Mary will become the next Aunt Ester, keeper of African-American history.

GETTING OUT MARSHA NORMAN (1977)   In *Getting Out,* NORMAN portrays a woman's struggle for self-determination, a theme that she came to explore in subsequent plays. Arlene, an ex-convict, wants to be free of prison and free of the life that led her there, but there are forces she must overcome in order to gain control over her own life.

The staging of the play symbolizes Arlene's imprisonment in her past. In the center of the stage is the *"dingy one-room"* apartment to which Arlene moves once she is released from prison. Surrounding the apartment is her prison cell on one side, a catwalk overhead, and areas for the playing out of other scenes from the past; Norman's stage directions indicate that *"[t]he apartment must seem imprisoned."* Making Arlene's past and its inescapability even more palpable is the presence of Arlie, Arlene's younger self and a separate character. Scenes of the recently released Arlene are juxtaposed with scenes of young, violent Arlie committing crimes, in her jail cell, and in disturbing childhood scenes.

Arlene Holsclaw, paroled after serving eight years for second degree murder (a crime she committed after escaping from prison, where she was serving time for prostitution and forgery), arrives at her apartment with her former guard, Bennie, who has befriended her and driven her to Louisville from the Alabama prison. When Bennie leaves the apartment to get carryout, Arlene's mother arrives. During this scene, it becomes clear that Arlie suffered sexual abuse at the hands of her father and that her relationship with her mother is beyond repair. When Arlene expresses her hope of getting custody of her son, her mother is quick to point out that her son does not know who she is. When Arlene speaks of having changed for the better, her mother responds dismissively, "I'm your mother. I know what you'll do."

Her sexually abusive father is not the only man to have victimized Arlie. Carl, her former pimp, soon makes an appearance. A drug addict and escaped convict, Carl assumes Arlene will return to work for him. When she insists she can get "real work," he demeans and harasses her. When she remains unreceptive, he tries to convince her that a few hours of prostitution at $450 per week is more likely to buy gifts for her son than a 48-hour week of dishwashing at $75. He is persuasive and Arlene is discouraged, though she does not return to him. Even Bennie, the ex-guard who seems to want to help her, very nearly rapes her in his enthusiasm to have her for his girlfriend.

The women in the play do not offer much hope either. Arlene's mother is hostile and highly critical. The women in prison were often violent—or kind in return for sexual favors. Arlene's sister, a prostitute named Candy, whose apartment Arlene has taken over, has gone back to her own pimp; in fact, Arlene's new neighbor, Ruby, warns her that Candy's customers may come by looking for her. Only Ruby offers any real sympathy, yet her life presents a discouraging lesson. Ruby, too, is an ex-convict living a clean life, but with little income she lives it in a slum.

In the end, Arlene rejects both Carl and Bennie while accepting the friendship of Ruby. Arlene also seems to forgive her younger self, Arlie, when at the end of the play the two characters simultaneously remember with fondness and humor a childhood prank performed at their mother's expense. Finally, a more integrated Arlene/Arlie, having chosen Ruby's company and lifestyle over those determined by men, makes progress toward self-determination.

Getting Out was first produced at the HUMANA FESTIVAL OF NEW AMERICAN PLAYS at the Actors Theatre of Louisville, where it won the prize for best festival play. It was produced in Los Angeles and New York the following year. In this, her first play, Norman establishes her focus on women struggling in a world dominated by men.

GIBSON, WILLIAM (1914–2008)   Born in New York City, William Gibson studied at City College of New York but left without getting his degree. He published poetry, novels, and nonfiction, but he is best known for his two highly successful plays, *Two for the Seesaw* (1958) and *The MIRACLE WORKER* (1959).

Commercially successful and critically acclaimed, *Two for the Seesaw* (1958) is a tart portrait of tender but problematic love between Jerry—a would-be Manhattan lawyer, who is separated from his wife in Nebraska—and Gittel, a feisty, but emotionally insecure, lifelong urbanite. Eventually, Jerry returns to his wife, but not before he has learned from Gittel how to be a more loving human being. Gibson's play was later adapted as the musical *Seesaw* (1973) by Michael Bennett, with music by Cy Coleman and lyrics by Dorothy Fields.

Even in his lesser-known plays, Gibson evoked characters of emotional authenticity. He depicts the Virgin Mary as a girl abused by her child-hating thug brothers in *The Butterfingers Angel, Mary & Joseph, Herod the Nut, & the Slaughter of 12 Hit Carols in a Pear Tree* (1975). Later, he pointedly sketches fractiousness between a conservative judge and a liberal nun in *Handy Dandy: a comedy but* (1984).

Gibson's greatest fame came via historical dramas—through his combining of "happenings [that are] factual enough" with "characterization[al] acts of the imagination," as he noted while introducing the published version of his play *Monday after the Miracle* (1983). Always acutely psychological, Gibson shows, in that play, how marital failure, for Annie Sullivan and her husband John Macy, unfortunately resulted from the noble workaholism of Sullivan, as she painstakingly taught Helen Keller.

Gibson enshrines Sullivan's work, as Keller's beloved "Teacher," in *The Miracle Worker* (1959), his acclaimed play about Sullivan's first encounters with the deaf and blind child Keller (and, simultaneously, with her intrusive family). One of Gibson's other historical-biographical works, *Golda* (1977), focuses on another resolute woman, Golda Meir, and her twin ambitions for mothering both a new Jewish nation and a world full of safe children. In 2002, Gibson reworked the play into a one-woman show, which he called *Golda's Balcony*.

Gibson's *A Cry for Players* (1969) envisions young Will Shakespeare as a desperate iconoclast, struggling against the still feudally oriented village of Avon and its many constricting bonds—even, indeed, against his marriage to a wise but older Anne Hathaway. Gibson's other historical drama, *American Primitive* (1971), evokes a more fully contented marriage—although John and Abigail Adams still suffer the burdensome separations enforced by his political career.

Gibson served as librettist for Joe Raposo's *Raggedy Ann and Andy* (1984–86) and for Norman Dello Joio's *The Ruby* (1955). In 1964, he adapted (into the dramatized milieu of African-American boxing, as a stage vehicle for Sammy Davis Jr.) the most famous play, GOLDEN BOY (1937), of Gibson's own mentor, CLIFFORD ODETS. Gibson's *Dinny and the Witches* (1959) interpolates songs into a Faustian fable about a jazz musician's encounters in Central Park with the supernatural.

Winner of the Harriet Monroe Memorial Prize (for poetry) and the Sylvania Prize and WILLIAM INGE Award (for drama), William Gibson also cofounded the Berkshire Theatre Festival.

BIBLIOGRAPHY

Gibson, William. *American Primitive*. New York: Atheneum, 1972.

———. *A Cry of Players*. New York: Atheneum, 1969.

———. *The Butterfingers Angel, Mary & Joseph, Herod the Nut, & the Slaughter of 12 Hit Carols in a Pear Tree*. New York: Dramatists Play Service, 1975.

———. *Golda*. New York: Dramatists Play Service, 1978.

———. *Golda's Balcony*. New York: Applause, 2003.

———. *Handy Dandy: a comedy but*. New York: Dramatists Play Service, 1986.

———. *Monday after The Miracle*. New York: Atheneum, 1983.

———. *The Seesaw Log: A Chronicle of the Stage Production, with the Text of "Two for the Seesaw."* New York: Knopf, 1959.

———. *Two Plays and a Preface: "The Miracle Worker" and "Dinny and the Witches."* New York: Atheneum, 1960.

Jeffrey B. Loomis
Northwest Missouri State University

GILLETTE, WILLIAM (HOOKER) (1853–1937)

Born and raised in Hartford, Connecticut, William Gillette was the son of a United States senator and a descendant on his mother's side from the Puritan leader Reverend Thomas Hooker (who came to Massachusetts from England in 1633 and who, along with his congregation, founded Hartford in 1636). Gillette showed early interest in acting and oratory; he left college to pursue a career on the stage. In 1875, he appeared in a walk-on role in New Orleans in a production of *Across the Continent; or, Scenes from New York Life and the Pacific Railroad*; that same year in New York he had a small part—obtained for him by his

Hartford neighbor Mark Twain—in *Colonel Sellers* (coauthored by Twain and later titled *The Gilded Age*).

Gillette began writing his own plays in 1881. Eventually becoming an actor of some acclaim, he appeared in as many as 28 productions, many of them his own plays and adaptations. He became known as a playwright for *Held by the Enemy* (1886) and Secret Service (1895), both Civil War melodramas. *Secret Service,* the more famous of the two, is both a thriller, which portrays the dangers and heroism of the life of a spy during the Civil War, and a love story in which love supersedes political loyalties.

Gillette was a pioneer of realism in American drama; this is made evident by his lengthy and specific stage directions describing sets, characters, and situations. His early descriptions of sets are meticulous and detailed, but in later plays, he went beyond mere verisimilitude of place to illuminate character and conflict through realistic setting. In his *Electricity* (1913), for example, the contrast between a Manhattan townhouse and a Bronx flat serves to underscore character motivation.

BIBLIOGRAPHY

Cook, Doris E. *Sherlock Holmes and Much More; or, Some of the Facts about William Gillette.* Hartford: Connecticut Historical Society, 1970.

Gillette, William. *Plays by William Gillette.* Edited by Rosemary Cullen and Don B. Wilmeth. New York: Cambridge University Press, 1983.

GILMAN, REBECCA (CLAIRE) (1964–)

One of the most intriguing American playwrights to emerge in the last decade, Rebecca Gilman was born in Birmingham, Alabama. Growing up in the small town of Trussville, Alabama, Gilman discovered drama at an early age and became fascinated with the problem plays of George Bernard Shaw and the social comedies of George S. Kaufman and his collaborators. She began writing plays in her youth and wrote during her college years at Middlebury College (1982–85) and Birmingham Southern College, from which she graduated with a B.A. in English in 1987. She subsequently received an M.A. in English from the University of Virginia (1988) and an M.F.A. in playwriting from the University of Iowa (1991).

Early efforts such as *My Sin and Nothing More* (published, 1997) and *The Land of Little Horses* (1997) reveal a wry vision of the incongruities of American life and families that find fuller expression in her later, better-known plays. *The Glory of Living* (1996), her breakthrough play, examines a teenage girl who, in the wake of her mother's neglect and her older husband's psychological and physical abuse, becomes a multiple murderer. Her best-known play to date, *Spinning into Butter* (1999), is a disquieting exploration, set in an exclusive New England college, of American racism's persistence. The abiding chasm separating blacks and whites is revealed, ironically enough, not by overt bigotry but by a liberal dean's alienation from the very minority students she is intent upon helping. Also premiering in 1999, *The Crime of the Century* poignantly examines violence's cost by giving voice to the eight student nurses murdered in Chicago by Richard Speck. *Boy Gets Girl* (2000) is a suspenseful and terrifying look at stalking in which American society's penchant for objectifying women is the basis of a new understanding of the plot formula alluded to in the play's title. The protagonist's carefully drawn resistance, anguish, and eventual pyrrhic victory are tellingly rendered in brisk scenes leavened with grim humor. The summer of 2001 saw the premieres of two plays, *The American in Me* and *Blue Surge.* The former combines a biting satire on American materialism with a tale of a couple confronting the desire to have a child. The latter uses the interwoven lives of two midwestern policemen and two local prostitutes to examine the still-pervasive American assumption that goodwill and decency can redeem the American dream of upward mobility from the countervailing forces of ignorance and indolence.

The year 2004 saw the production of *The Sweetest Swing in Baseball* in which a painter's mental breakdown and subsequent appropriation of Darryl Strawberry's identity proves the means to explore the relationships among creativity, celebrity, and commercialism in art using the metaphor of baseball. The next year Gilman provided two stage adaptations, a reworking of Carson McCuller's *The Heart Is a Lonely Hunter* for Atlanta's Alliance Theatre and an updated version of the Ibsen classic *A Doll's House* titled *The*

Dollhouse for Chicago's Goodman Theatre. Gilman explored new territory in *The Crowd You're in With* (2007), in which easy American middle-class assumptions concerning love, marriage, and the reproductive imperative are carefully anatomized by three couples over the course of a Fourth of July Chicago cookout.

While collectively her plays are noteworthy for their wrestling with social problems, they are also consistently marked by strong portrayals of often edgy characters, by unflinching honesty, and by a wry humor. They resist sensationalism and sentimentality even as they provoke audiences to question the genesis and implications of the situations they detail. Often produced in Chicago, Gilman's works have won three of the city's Joseph Jefferson Awards for Best New Play and two for Best New Adaptation.

BIBLIOGRAPHY
Gilman, Rebecca. *Blue Surge*. New York: Faber and Faber, 2001.
———. *Boy Gets Girl*. New York: Faber and Faber, 2000.
———. *The Glory of Living*. New York: Faber and Faber, 1998.
———. *The Land of Little Horses*. Woodstock, Ill.: Dramatic Publishing Company, 1998.
———. *My Sin and Nothing More*. Woodstock, Ill.: Dramatic Publishing Company, 1997.
———. *Spinning into Butter*. New York: Faber and Faber, 2000.

Gary A. Richardson
Mercer University

GILROY, FRANK D[ANIEL] (1925–)

Frank D. Gilroy was born in the Bronx, New York. He served in the United States Army (1943–46) and fought for 18 months with the 89th Infantry Division in Europe during World War II. Gilroy graduated from Dartmouth College in 1950 and studied for a year at the Yale School of Drama before leaving to pursue his writing career.

After serving a long apprenticeship writing for various television programs, Gilroy achieved his first major success with *Who'll Save the Plowboy?* (1962), which won the OBIE AWARD for Best American Play. *Plowboy* deals with the reunion of two veterans, Albert and Larry, 15 years after the end of World War II.

Larry, who saved Albert's life in combat, is now dying of a terminal illness and visits Albert to reassure himself that Albert is leading a fulfilling life. Over the years, Albert has been writing Larry about his son and wife without revealing that the boy is mentally handicapped and his marriage is in serious trouble. When Albert has to leave the house, his wife reveals the truth to Larry, but when Albert returns accompanied by a boy he has hired to act as his son, Larry chooses to accept the ruse, thus saving Albert a second time by sparing his dignity.

With his next play, *The SUBJECT WAS ROSES* (1964), Gilroy achieved even greater success, winning the New York Drama Critics' Circle Award followed by the TONY AWARD and the PULITZER PRIZE in 1965. About another failing marriage, *The Subject Was Roses* portrays a husband and wife and their tenuous relationship with their only son as he returns from service in World War II. At the end of the play, the son extricates himself from a war he cannot win to begin his own quest to become a writer. This play eloquently describes three people who love each other but flounder in their inabilities to communicate.

In his commentary in the *Complete Full-Length Plays* (2000), Gilroy wryly discusses the negative aspects of so much success so early. Searching hard for new subject matter, he lit on the Greek legend of Hippolytus and Phaedra and wrote *That Summer, That Fall* (1967). This play, set in contemporary New York, seemed forced, lacking the believability that had characterized his earlier work. He next turned to a subject he knew well, gambling, and wrote *The Only Game in Town* (1968), a romantic comedy set in Las Vegas about a relationship between a hooked gambler desperate to escape the town and a dancer. Both are so determined to maintain their own autonomy that they almost fail to recognize the depth of their attachment. Gilroy wrote the screen adaptation of *The Only Game in Town* as he had done for *The Subject Was Roses* the previous year.

Eleven years passed before a play by Frank Gilroy was seen again on Broadway. In *Last Licks* (1979), he returned to the theme of familial conflict. Here, the struggle is between a father and son. The father, newly widowed, is guilt-ridden by his lifelong habit of infidelity but determined to maintain his hold on his dutiful son by feigning physical debilitation. The son, about to leave town for a new job, is tormented by his father's seeming helplessness and the apparent need to put him in a nursing home. When an applicant for the job of housekeeper turns out to be his father's former lover, the truth is out and a stalemate is reached.

Last Licks was not well received critically, and Gilroy turned his creative attention to the shorter play form, producing several one-acts at New York's Ensemble Studio Theatre, and to his ongoing work in film. He has written, directed, and produced several independent films, including *Desperate Characters* (1971), adapted from the novel by Paula Fox; *From Noon till Three* (1976), adapted from his novel; *Once in Paris* (1978); *The Gig* (1985); and *The Luckiest Man in the World* (1993). He marked his return to Broadway, after a 14-year absence this time, with *Any Given Day* (1993), in which he revisited characters first introduced in *The Subject Was Roses*. In his next play, *Contact with the Enemy* (1999), he again used his wartime experience for subject matter.

In 2006, *The Subject Was Roses* had a major revival in Washington and New York; Gilroy conjectured at the time that the renewed interest was related to the fact that young men were returning to their families from the American wars in Iraq and Afghanistan. Gilroy's recent work includes *The Lake* (2006), a play about a lake community's development and gradual decline from the late 1920s to the post–World War II period, which has been presented as a reading at Ensemble Studio Theatre in New York, and *Piscary* (2008), a one-act play in which a couple bets its future on a game of Scrabble.

BIBLIOGRAPHY
Gilroy, Frank D. *Complete Full-Length Plays, 1962–1994.* Hanover, N.H.: Smith and Kraus, 2000.
———. *15 One-Act Plays.* Hanover, N.H.: Smith and Kraus, 2000.

Philip M. Isaacs
New York, New York

GIN GAME, THE D. L. COBURN (1976) In part a portrait of the conditions endured by the aged, *The Gin Game* is more centrally about the human tendency to blame chance for one's failures rather than to accept one's own responsibility for those failures. By clinging to the concept of our own blamelessness, we alienate those who might give us comfort. The play won the PULITZER PRIZE.

On the dilapidated, *"unused sunporch of a home for the aged,"* Weller Martin meets Fonsia Dorsey. Both are unhappy with the home and its residents, and neither receives any visitors. Weller's invitation to play a game of cards and Fonsia's reluctant acceptance begin a volatile friendship between the two.

Over many hands of gin, Weller and Fonsia exchange personal information. Both divorced young and have children by that early marriage. Fonsia explains her lack of visitors to Weller, saying her son, Larry, lives in Denver and her sister, in Ottawa. Weller has two sons and a daughter, with whom he lost touch years ago after his divorce. When he mentions that his wife moved with their children to another city and remarried, Fonsia is sympathetic but adds that some men "deserve" that—men like her husband; Weller says no one deserves it. He tells her about the business he owned, which he lost because of his "bad luck" with partners. He speaks with admiration of his father who owned his own company and went into his office until the day he died at 83. As singing comes from the day room, Weller expresses his annoyance at the do-gooders who come there. During the course of this conversation, Fonsia, claiming ignorance of the game, has won every hand.

One week later—on another Visitors' Day—they speak of the indignities they and other elderly residents endure: Visitors speak too loudly to residents or, worse, as if they were not there; "the help" speak to them as if they were children; their few belongings are stolen and the police do nothing. They lament the lack of good conversationalists among their fellow residents, of whom they do comic impersonations. They play gin again, and again Fonsia wins every time. Weller's irritation at her for winning, slight at first, grows into frustration and anger. She threatens to stop playing if he will not stop yelling at her. They resume; she wins, and he knocks the table over.

The next evening he apologizes and convinces her to play again by reminding her that the alternative is to go back inside the "warehouse for the intellectually and emotionally dead." When Weller finally wins a hand, he accuses her of letting him win. When she wins the next hand, Weller's angry response is well out of proportion to the event. He calls her a "bitch," and she slaps him for it. Again apologetic, he begs her to play one more hand. They play, but he is cursing and sputtering, and she is upset. She wins again.

The following Sunday, after she has reported his behavior to the staff, he criticizes her since the complaint could get him committed to the state mental institution. When she gets sanctimonious, he suggests that mothers like her are the world's problem and guesses correctly that her son actually lives here in town—not in Denver at all—and that he does not visit her because he "hates" her. She admits that when Larry tried to look up his father, she left her house to the Presbyterian Church just to spite him. She further admits that she, like Weller, is now on welfare. He comforts her. When she's feeling better, he insists on a game of cards. She refuses at first, even tries to leave, but he physically pulls her back and accuses her of "manipulating" him. As they play, Fonsia accuses him of calling the failure of his business "bad luck," so that he doesn't have to admit he had bad judgment. When she slips and says she has had "bad luck" with men, Weller in turn accuses her of being unwilling to admit that she is "rigid, self-righteous [and] vicious." She, who frowns upon the use of vulgar language, calls him a "Fuck." When she wins *again,* he strikes the table violently and repeatedly with his cane and then silently walks out. Fonsia is left alone, and as the lights fade, she utters the words, "Oh, no."

Coburn's sympathy seems to lie more fully with Weller than with Fonsia; indeed, Thomas P. Adler, in his book about Pulitzer Prize–winning plays, calls Fonsia one of the "virulent portraits of women as emasculators" along with Harriet Craig in CRAIG'S WIFE (1925), who is also left to herself in the end (9). Of Weller, Adler writes, "[T]he game was his assertion to himself of his value as a human being. If he is a sore loser who overreacts like a petulant child, it is a symptom of his terror at being treated as if he were dead and useless before he really is. . . . [H]e has resorted to something external to himself—winning—as his chosen means for establishing self-respect" (15).

Whichever character one finds more sympathetic, it is clear that through his or her own behavior, each has alienated those who might provide comfort in their desolation.

BIBLIOGRAPHY
Adler, Thomas P. *Mirror on the Stage: The Pulitzer Plays as an Approach to American Drama.* West Lafayette, Ind.: Purdue University Press, 1987.

GIRL OF THE GOLDEN WEST, THE

DAVID BELASCO (1905)   One of BELASCO's most popular western-themed melodramas, *The Girl of the Golden West* played for nearly three years on Broadway and found a second life in 1910 when Puccini's operatic version, directed by Belasco and starring Enrico Caruso, debuted at New York's Metropolitan Opera House.

The play, set in a mining camp during the California gold rush, develops a triangular love story involving the virtuous Minnie Falconer, known to the miners who worship her simply as "The Girl"; Jack Rance, the camp's sheriff; and Dick Johnson, a newly arrived stranger. The Girl runs an orderly saloon, the Polka, located at the base of Cloudy Mountain; she dispenses whiskey to the miners but also keeps their gold safely under lock and key and acts as their teacher, using her dance hall as a classroom during off-hours. Rance is enamored of Minnie, but she spurns him, realizing that he has a wife living elsewhere. With the arrival of the gentlemanly Dick Johnson, The Girl's world is turned upside down. Charmed by his manner, she invites him to visit her mountain cabin. A blizzard prevents his leaving and when a posse appears at The Girl's door she learns that Dick Johnson is in fact the notorious outlaw Ramerrez. She has fallen for Johnson—in fact, given him her first kiss—and does not turn him in. Ultimately, events overwhelm the outlaw, and he is captured and sentenced to be hanged. The tender final words between The Girl and Johnson convince the miners that, under her influence, the outlaw's innate nobility has come to the fore. They determine that Johnson should be given another chance, and in the play's epilogue, we find the couple heading across the prairie, intent on making a new life for themselves.

Belasco both wrote and directed *The Girl of the Golden West,* and the play's significance is in large measure related to the realism of his staging. The sets were replete with all manner of authentic properties (including a stuffed bear holding a parasol), while the howling blizzard offered further opportunity for realistic detail. In a most unusual touch at the play's opening—perhaps Belasco's attempt to rival the increasingly popular moving pictures—canvas scenery on rollers moved upward, carrying the viewer from the painted image of The Girl's cabin high in the mountains, down a long and winding pathway, to the exterior of the Polka Saloon. This picture and accompanying music faded, and the play proper began as the saloon's interior was revealed, alive with miners and the music of a concertina. Belasco's justly famed lighting effects were featured in the play's epilogue, which moved from darkest night to the ruddy hues of the rising sun. Despite the surface realism, the play is sentimental and formulaic, but in bringing to the stage the image of actual life, Belasco paved the way for a new generation of dramatists who were to reject, as Belasco did not, the clichés of melodrama.

Craig Clinton
Reed College

GLASPELL, SUSAN (KEATING) (1876–1948)

Neglected for decades after her death, Susan Glaspell is now widely recognized as one of the most influential playwrights in the development of American drama as an indigenous art. Between 1915 and 1945 she wrote 14 plays, including the widely anthologized one-act TRIFLES (1916) and the PULITZER PRIZE–winning ALISON'S HOUSE (1930). During her most productive era (1915–22), she vied with EUGENE O'NEILL as the leading playwright of the PROVINCE-TOWN PLAYERS.

Born in Davenport, Iowa, Glaspell resisted the genteel, domestic existence of middle-class, midwestern womanhood, but retained an affinity for the region, frequently setting her plays in the Midwest and tempering her social criticism with the idealism of her pioneer ancestors. After graduation from Drake University, Glaspell quickly made a name for herself as a journalist, covering the 1900 murder trial that inspired *Trifles.* During the next decade, she became a best-selling novelist. In 1913, Glaspell married GEORGE CRAM COOK, and they became an integral part of the Greenwich Village/Provincetown community that created the Provincetown Players. Glaspell was especially instrumental in formulating and maintaining the company's policy of developing new American playwrights, and she contributed four full-length and seven one-act plays to the Provincetown repertory.

She collaborated with Cook on SUPPRESSED DESIRES (1915), inspired by the Village's faddish obsession with Sigmund Freud, and *Tickless Time* (1918), inspired by Cook's fascination with the sundial as a symbolic escape from the modern age. Glaspell's *Close the Book* (1917), in which a free-spirited young rebel discovers a respectable past, and *Chains of Dew* (1922), in which a "radical" poet reveals his personal conservatism, similarly satirize self-conscious nonconformity. In her modern morality plays, *The People* (1917) and *Woman's Honor* (1918), Glaspell distances topical concerns (the workings of a radical journal and sexual stereotyping) with witty, symbolic characterizations: Earnest Approach, Firebrand, the Scorned One, and the Shielded One. *Trifles,* in which two women suppress evidence that would convict their neighbor of killing her husband, is a more serious examination of domestic and social relations.

Glaspell was an inventive stylist, frequently employing nontraditional structures and combining realistic dialogue and domestic interiors with symbolic, expressionistic, or surreal undercurrents. One of her most striking innovations, introduced in *Trifles* and repeated in *Bernice* (1919) and *Alison's House,* is the centering of attention on an unseen protagonist, a device that works to increase the universality of the absent characters. *The Outside* (1917), one of her early philosophical dramas, includes expressionistic elements and the hesitant and oblique dialogue used to even greater effect in later plays, such as *Bernice* and *The Verge* (1921). Several critics suggested that the thoughtful, hesitant speech in *Bernice* enhanced the play's truthfulness and heightened its emotional appeal. Glaspell's most radical experiments in language, however, are manifested in her expressionistic *The Verge,* which features the erratic rhythms, hesitancies, and inventions now associated with *écriture féminine. The Verge* is also Glaspell's most reflexive and most radically feminist work. Its protagonist, metaphorically engaged in creating a new plant species, is actually seeking a different way to be human, especially woman, and her horticultural experiments parallel Glaspell's experiments in life and art.

Glaspell was an uncompromising social critic who challenged conventional sexual relations and political and moral hypocrisy, but her criticism was grounded in idealism, and she wrote from a firm faith in a human capacity for positive action. Both *The People,* in which a midwestern woman renews a jaded editor's liberal vision, and *Inheritors* (1921), in which a young woman sacrifices her own freedom to defend that of others, manifest a profoundly moving idealism that might be identified today as "Capraesque," although Glaspell's "Woman from Idaho" predated film writer/director Frank Capra's "Mr. Smith" by several decades.

The dissolution of the Provincetown Players in 1922 and the death of Cook in 1924 nearly ended Glaspell's playwriting career. In 1928, she coauthored, with her second husband, Norman Matson, *The Comic Artist,* a melodramatic meditation on "male lust and female loyalty." In 1930, her *Alison's House,* inspired by the life of Emily Dickinson, premiered at Eva LeGallienne's Civic Repertory and, after winning the Pulitzer Prize, enjoyed a brief commercial run. From 1936–38, Glaspell served as director of the Midwest Play Bureau of the FEDERAL THEATRE PROJECT, promoting such projects as Theodore Ward's *Big White Fog* (1938) and Arnold Sundgaard's *Spirochete* (1938).

Occasionally faulted by contemporary critics for a lack of traditional action and a tendency toward propaganda, Glaspell's plays nevertheless established for her a national and international reputation as a sensitive observer of human nature, a "dramatist of ideas" with gifts comparable to Henrik Ibsen, Anton Chekhov, and George Bernard Shaw. In 1945, she completed her last play, "Springs Eternal," which has never been published or produced.

BIBLIOGRAPHY

Ben-Zvi, Linda, ed. *Susan Glaspell: Essays on Her Theater and Fiction.* Ann Arbor: University of Michigan Press, 1995.

———. *Susan Glaspell: Her Life and Times.* New York: Oxford University Press, 2005.

Carpentier, Martha C., ed. *Susan Glaspell: New Directions in Critical Inquiry.* Newcastle, England: Cambridge Scholars Press, 2006.

———, and Barbara Ozieblo, eds. *Disclosing Intertextualities: The Stories, Plays, and Novels of Susan Glaspell.* Amsterdam: Rodopi, 2006.

Gainor, J. Ellen. *Susan Glaspell in Context: American Theater, Culture, and Politics, 1915–48.* Ann Arbor: University of Michigan Press, 2001.

Glaspell, Susan. *Susan Glaspell: Plays.* Edited by C. W. E. Bigsby. Cambridge, England: Cambridge University Press, 1987.

Hinz-Bode, Kristina. *Susan Glaspell and the Anxiety of Expression: Language and Isolation in the Plays.* Jefferson, N.C.: McFarland, 2006.

Noe, Marcia. *Susan Glaspell: Voice from the Heartland.* Macomb: Western Illinois University, 1983.

Ozieblo, Barbara. *Susan Glaspell: A Critical Biography.* Chapel Hill: University of North Carolina Press, 2000.

———. *Susan Glaspell and Sophie Treadwell.* New York: Routledge, 2008.

Papke, Mary. *Susan Glaspell: A Research and Production Sourcebook.* Westport, Conn.: Greenwood Press, 1993.

Waterman, Arthur. *Susan Glaspell.* New York: Twayne, 1966.

Cheryl Black
University of Missouri

GLASS MENAGERIE, THE TENNESSEE WIL-LIAMS (1945)

The Glass Menagerie is a classic modern American drama. The play, largely autobiographical, began as a film scenario, which was rejected by MGM when WILLIAMS was under contract to that studio in Hollywood. With the lapse of his contract, Williams left Hollywood armed with material for a play that would run for more than 550 performances on Broadway and earn its author a New York Drama Critics' Circle Award.

Williams describes *The Glass Menagerie* as a "memory" play; the events are the recollections of the play's protagonist, Tom. In an opening monologue, which occurs in present time, Tom sets the scene, while at the play's end, once again in the present, he undergoes a wrenching emotional catharsis, the result of his confrontation with the subject matter of his narrative. The play is set in the 1930s, and Tom, as narrator, quickly locates his story in the context of the Great Depression. He also remarks on his proclivity, as both poet and storyteller, to use symbols, thus encouraging us to regard the play as other than strictly realistic.

The play proper begins with the introduction of the three main characters as they share a meal in their dingy St. Louis apartment. The mother, Amanda, who romanticizes her southern upbringing, is a woman of social aspirations living in less-than-genteel poverty. Her son, Tom, struggling to find himself as a writer, suffers with a dead-end job in a shoe factory, while Laura, Tom's sister, lame and terribly shy, finds solace in her phonograph records and collection of glass animals. Silent but ever present through his portrait on the wall is the father who, long ago, abandoned the family.

Amanda hopes desperately to find a suitor for her daughter and prevails on Tom to bring a young man from the shoe factory home for dinner. The fatal evening arrives, and Laura is shocked to discover that Jim, the "gentleman caller," is a boy she distantly knew and admired in high school. The lights in the apartment go out—Tom has failed to pay the electric bill—and Amanda conspires to leave Laura and Jim alone together. Jim's friendly and optimistic demeanor encourages Laura to open up. Shyly, in the candlelight, she dances with him to music coming from a dance hall across the alley. As they dance, they bump against Laura's glass animals and her unicorn falls to the floor, breaking the horn from the body. Attaching a poetic significance to the event, Laura tells Jim that the animal is now more normal, less freakish. Amanda interrupts the two with lemonade, but, after impulsively kissing Laura, Jim apologizes and hastily departs to meet his returning fiancée at the train station. Amanda is dumbstruck, feeling she has been tricked into entertaining a boy who is "spoken for"; in the ensuing argument, Tom flees the apartment, never to return.

In the monologue that closes the play, Tom, clothed as a merchant marine, confesses that Laura is forever on his mind; he cannot escape her memory, and in a moment that fuses past and present, he steps toward her, begging her to blow out the candles illuminating the scene. Separate from him, in her own moment in time, she does so, thus extinguishing, momentarily, Tom's anguished feelings of bereavement, self-recrimination, and guilt.

The Glass Menagerie develops thematic concerns and qualities of character Williams would go on to explore in subsequent plays. The quintessential Williams protagonist is torn by opposing desires: Sensual appetites conflict with spiritual longing—the need to discover and embrace a higher purpose. Tom, in his drinking and escapist film-going, offers a restrained view of the one extreme, while Amanda, despite being depicted as a comic fantasist, provides a glimpse of the other. In later dramas, Williams locates this opposition—desires of the flesh in conflict with spiritual aspiration—in a single individual, but this thematic obsession is clearly embedded in the divisiveness that pits Tom against Amanda. Williams's other recurring themes are also observable in the play: The isolation of the artist, or more universally, the solitary nature of human existence is one, while the implacable nature of time, which carries us relentlessly to an unknown future of terrifying possibility, is another. And in *The Glass Menagerie,* as in virtually all his plays, Williams explores the dilemma of human existence in which, so often, the fragile and emotionally vulnerable are overwhelmed by the crass and insensitive forces of a materialistic and spiritually impoverished society.

BIBLIOGRAPHY

Bloom, Harold, ed. *Modern Critical Interpretations: Tennessee Williams's "The Glass Menagerie."* New York: Chelsea House, 1988.

Parker, R. B., ed. *"The Glass Menagerie": A Collection of Critical Essays.* Englewood Cliffs, N.J.: Prentice-Hall, 1983.

Presley, Delma E. *"The Glass Menagerie": An American Memory.* Boston: Twayne, 1990.

Craig Clinton
Reed College

GLENGARRY GLEN ROSS DAVID MAMET (1984)

Produced first at London's National Theatre in 1983 on the recommendation of Harold Pinter, *Glengarry Glen Ross* came in 1984 to New York where it won both the PULITZER PRIZE and the New York Drama Critics' Circle Award. The play is set in a real estate office and a nearby restaurant, where a group of middle-aged businessmen ruthlessly compete for sales.

As we eavesdrop on conversations between pairs of men in the restaurant, we come to understand that the salesmen are attempting to unload some Florida real estate known as Glengarry Highlands ("Glen Ross Farms" was a land development years before). The top sellers are being given the "premium leads" (the names of prospective buyers) by Williamson, the boss. One of the older salesmen, Shelley Levene, complains to Williamson, who agrees to give him one good lead for a percentage of his profit and $50 cash. Moss and Aaronow are angry about the way Williamson is now running the office, and Moss suggests that they break into the office at night, "trashing it," making it look "like robbery, and tak[ing] the [five thousand premium] leads out of the files." Moss has already arranged to sell the list to Williamson's competitor and tries to blackmail Aaronow into committing the actual robbery. In another part of the restaurant, Roma makes a sale: He starts out philosophically, speaking to a man, Mr. Lingk, of the beauty of moral relativism and necessity of exploiting one's opportunities, and ends by closing a shady land deal with Lingk.

By the beginning of act 2, the robbery (committed, we later find out, by Levene doing the dirty work for Moss) has taken place, and the police are inspecting the ransacked office. The leads, the phones, and some of the contracts are gone. Roma is irate because he has to go out and "reclose" deals. Levene comes in happy that he has just sold "eight units" and "[b]roke a bad losing streak." Meanwhile, police detective Baylen is questioning all of the salesmen. Levene tells the other men the story—"Listen to this, I actually said this."—of his cynical taking advantage of "Bruce and Harriet Nyborg." (Eventually, he is informed that the Nyborgs are notorious for making deals that fall through since they are just a dotty couple who like to talk to salesmen.) When Roma's Mr. Lingk comes into the office, having reconsidered his purchase, Roma and Levene launch into a well-practiced routine in which Levene (in this case) poses as a satisfied and wealthy customer whom Roma is in a hurry to take to the airport. Despite this act, Lingk insists he wants out of the deal

and knows his legal rights because his wife has checked with the "attorney general" and "some consumer office." Roma gives him assurances, which are blatant lies, as he attempts to buy enough time to make it legally impossible for the man to withdraw his commitment. When Williamson, "the company man," enters and inadvertently exposes one of Roma's lies, finally killing the deal, Roma questions Williamson's manhood. The way Levene backed him up, impersonating a client and saving his crooked deal, was manly, but Williamson's blunder causes Roma to lament to Levene: "[I]t's not a world of men [anymore]. . . . We are a dying breed." At the end of the play, Levene is questioned by the police about the burglary, and, as is typical in MAMET's world, this desperate loser takes the heat, while the man who put him up to it goes free; indeed, the higher up one is in the hierarchy, the greater is one's freedom to engage in corrupt practices.

Mamet's play is a searing indictment of a type of American "manhood" that calls for competitive, ruthless self-service and of a type of American business in which those who are prepared to be ruthless on a large scale succeed—without remorse—at the expense of their more timid colleagues and of the public. Mamet has said when speaking of this play, "[America's] national culture is founded very much on the idea of strive and succeed. Instead of rising with the masses, one should rise from the masses. Your extremity is my opportunity. . . . [T]his also affects the spirit of the individual. It's very divisive. One feels one can only succeed at the cost of someone else." *Glengarry Glen Ross,* says Mamet, "concerns . . . how the hierarchical business system tends to corrupt. It becomes legitimate for those in power in the business world to act unethically" (Kolin and Kullman 178–179).

BIBLIOGRAPHY

Kane, Leslie. *David Mamet's "Glengarry Glen Ross": Text and Performance.* New York: Garland, 1996.

Kolin, Philip C., and Colby H. Kullman, eds. *Speaking on Stage: Interviews with Contemporary American Playwrights.* Tuscaloosa: University of Alabama Press, 1996.

GODFREY, THOMAS (1736–1763)　See PRINCE OF PARTHIA, The.

GOLDEN BOY CLIFFORD ODETS (1937)

In this depression-era drama by ODETS, a young man gives up his art, which yields little money, in favor of the lucrative and ruthless world of professional boxing. Joe Bonaparte is a violinist-turned-boxer who eventually kills a man in the boxing ring and realizes too late what is really important to him.

Tom Moody, a boxing manager, has not had a winner in years. If he can find one, he can divorce his wife and marry his girlfriend Lorna. Into Moody's life comes Joe Bonaparte—sure of his talent and begging for a chance to fight. Joe's Italian immigrant father does not approve of boxing as a career for Joe, who is a talented violinist. When Joe first begins to fight, he holds back, much to the dissatisfaction of his handlers, for whom he is a moneymaking property. When they find out from Joe's father that Joe is "'besta violin' in New York," they realize Joe has been protecting his hands from injury. When Joe admits he is not sure whether he wants to be a fighter or a musician, Moody sees his "mealticket," his "last chance for a decent life, for getting married" to Lorna, disappearing, but Lorna promises that she will "make [Joe] fight." Moody asks, "How?" and she answers "I'm 'a tramp from Newark'. . . . I know a dozen ways."

Lorna does convince Joe to fight, and he begins to fall in love with her. Rejecting his father's gift of a fine violin, Joe leaves on a boxing tour. When he returns six months later, he has had some victories but is still not fully committed to boxing. He and Lorna have by now fallen in love, but she, reluctant to hurt Moody, plans to go through with the marriage to him.

By the time Joe is ready to face his toughest opponent, the Baltimore Chocolate Drop, in a bout that may put him in contention for the championship, he has already broken his hands, thus permanently leaving his old life behind him; he is now firmly in the world of fast cars and expensive suits and possesses an arrogance that has the sports writers waiting gleefully for Joe Bonaparte's "Waterloo." The night of the big fight is also the night before Lorna's wedding. Upset about Lorna, Joe fights "like a bum" and is nearly "slaughtered," but with a final punch, into which Joe puts "the fury of a lifetime," the Chocolate Drop is knocked out and killed.

Horrified that he has killed another man, Joe begins to realize that he has also "murdered [him]self": "I was a real sparrow, and I wanted to be a fake eagle." When Lorna suggests they run away together, Joe's fevered response is that they will speed through the night. His desperation combined with his yearning for speed foreshadow his and Lorna's death in a crash that night. The fast car, which boxing prize money enabled Joe to buy, is associated with the self-destructive course he is on and is therefore a fitting instrument of his death. Thematically, then, Odets suggests that to abandon art for the sake of financial success or fame is folly; it is destructive of the self—if not literally, as is the case for Joe, then figuratively.

Golden Boy was the most popular play ever produced by the GROUP THEATRE, which was temporarily kept afloat by its revenues. The play's structure was influenced by Odets's work on films, in that it is made up of 12 short scenes, which easily facilitate shifts in tone. Ironically, members of the Group Theatre saw Odets's defection from left-wing political theater to commercial Hollywood (prior to writing the play) as the same kind of sellout and abandonment of art for money that he condemns in Joe Bonaparte.

GORDON, CHARLES F.   See OYAMO.

GORDONE, CHARLES (1925–1995)

Playwright, director, and actor Charles Gordone was born in Cleveland, Ohio, and went to college in California, where he earned his B.A. in drama from California State University in Los Angeles. After graduation, he moved to New York City where he became a waiter and an actor. (He won the Best Actor OBIE AWARD in 1953 for his performance in *OF MICE AND MEN.*) His experience as a waiter in a barroom inspired him to write his only successful play, *NO PLACE TO BE SOMEBODY,* which was first staged OFF-BROADWAY in 1969; in 1970, the play moved to Broadway, where it won the PULITZER PRIZE, making Gordone the first African-American playwright to win the award.

In the 1950s and 1960s, Gordone spent much of his time directing both classics and contemporary plays. During this period, he also became socially active, cofounding in 1962 the Committee for the

Employment of Negro Performers. His first play, *Little More Light around the Place,* written with Sidney Easton, was produced in New York at the Off-Broadway Sheridan Square Playhouse in 1964.

Gordone's short-lived triumph as a playwright came with *No Place to Be Somebody,* a barroom drama about a group of social outcasts—both black and white—who try to help the barkeep and pimp Johnny Williams outwit the Mafia. Williams loses in the end, but during the course of the action the characters' lives are revealed. Critics compared the play to EUGENE O'NEILL's barroom classic *The ICEMAN COMETH* (1946), and Gordone was hailed as a new and promising voice in American drama.

That promise, however, remained unfulfilled. Though he produced other plays in the 1970s—*Willy Bignigga* and *Chumpanzee* in 1970, *Baba-Chops* in 1975, and *The Last Chord* in 1977—none was successful with audiences or critics. The reasons are probably both philosophical and personal. In a time of radical black theater, Gordone believed in multicultural rather than ethnically specific theater, which alienated him from the more militant black theater movement (*No Place to Be Somebody* had been rejected by the NEGRO ENSEMBLE COMPANY). Furthermore, *No Place to Be Somebody* had taken Gordone seven years to write, and his already heavy drinking became even heavier after the success of the play.

Gordone continued his social work in 1975, when he began using theater in the rehabilitation of inmates in New Jersey at the Cell Block Theatre in Yardville and Bordentown Youth Correctional Institution. In the early 1980s, Gordone, by then a recovering alcoholic, moved to California and directed plays at a community theater there. From 1986 until his death from cancer in 1995, Gordone was on the faculty of Texas A&M University, teaching theater and English. In this last decade of his life, he became interested in the Native American, specifically the Elko, and the cowboy culture of the American West.

GOTANDA, PHILIP KAN (1951–) Philip

Kan Gotanda grew up in Stockton, California, within an active Japanese-American community, the experience of which deeply informs his work. His father, a second-generation Japanese American (nisei), came to the mainland from Hawaii to become a doctor and was interred in a camp for Japanese Americans during World War II. In 1969, Gotanda visited Japan, where he discovered major differences between the Japanese he saw there and the Japanese Americans he had known in America. Returning to an America he now recognized as his country, he became more involved in Asian-American culture, realizing the uniqueness of its identity. While pursuing a singing career, he met playwright DAVID HENRY HWANG, whose influence drew Gotanda toward theater. Hwang would direct several of Gotanda's early plays and codirect, with him, the Asian American Theater in San Francisco.

Recognizing the limited power of single songs, Gotanda wrote a musical, *The Avocado Kid; or, Zen in the Art of Guacamole* (1978), recasting a Japanese children's tale to depict a group of outcasts who discover the power of community against a backdrop of images from American popular culture. Gotanda acknowledges SAM SHEPARD's influence on his early work; like Shepard, he uses music for dramatic punctuation and plays with American iconography. In 1979, Gotanda began writing directly for Asian-American theater companies. His work evolved from musicals to straight drama, including the family trilogy *A Song for a Nisei Fisherman* (1980), *The Wash* (1987), and *Fish Head Soup* (1991). *A Song for a Nisei Fisherman* is based on his father's experiences, difficulties, and dreams, while *The Wash* is a study of male/female relationships within Japanese-American culture. *Fish Head Soup* is a violent and negative portrayal of the generational conflicts that tear a Japanese-American family apart. All three deal with the dynamics of racism and the resilience of the human spirit. An earlier play, *Yankee Dawg You Die* (1988), explores the hard choices made by Asian-American actors of different generations, further exposing racist attitudes. After *Fish Head Soup,* Gotanda stopped writing in order to reevaluate what he hoped to accomplish as an artist. On his return to theater, he wrote *Day Standing on Its Head* (1994), about an Asian-American professor grappling with middle age, and *Ballad of Yachiyo* (1996), about the troubled life and loves of a teenage girl, based upon stories he had uncovered about his own aunt, who had committed suicide. *Sisters Matsumoto* (1999) is about three well-to-do Japanese-American sisters trying to reconstruct their lives after internment, and *Yohen* (1999) recounts the story of an interracial marriage between an African American and his Japanese war bride.

Gotanda has produced many works for the stage since the new century began. His *floating weeds* (2001) is a raw but humorous portrait of young urban adults dealing with mental and emotional problems. The two one-acts that make up *Under the Rainbow* (2002) deal with the white male obsession with female "orientalism" and the toxic relationship between an aging actress and her daughter. In 2002, Gotanda also loosely adapted Henrik Ibsen's *Hedda Gabler,* retitling it *The Wind Cries Mary.* In recent years Gotanda has experimented with several collaborative works, including *a fist of roses* (2004), an amalgam of sound, movement, and image, depicting male violence against women, and *Manzanar: An American Story* (2005), a multimedia, orchestral, and spoken-word reenvisioning of the internment experience. Gotanda returned to a more linear format with the epic *After the War* (2007) and its intertwined love stories occurring across race and culture in San Francisco during the 1940s. His latest project is a parody of the children's book *The Five Chinese Brothers* for the Asian American Theater Company that he has titled *4 Chinks and a Dyke.*

Gotanda's plays recreate on stage the changing reality of Asian-American life, with all of its frustration, contradiction, and glory. He is concerned with generational and gender expectations and the role of racism within the dynamics of the Asian-American experience. His texts are filled with Japanese-American references and Japanese words, which give them authenticity and make them partly inaccessible to non-Japanese-American audiences. Instead of pandering to the majority, Gotanda forces them to understand his culture on its own terms. Strongly committed to ASIAN-AMERICAN DRAMA and to the forward motion of Asian-American culture, Gotanda places that culture in a humane spotlight, which encourages a recognition of the Asian-American experience as an important aspect of the whole American story.

BIBLIOGRAPHY

Cheung, King-Kok, ed. *Words Matter: Conversations with Asian American Writers.* Honolulu: University of Hawaii Press, 2000.

Gotanda, Philip Kan. *Ballad of Yachiyo.* New York: Theater Communications Group, 1996.

———. *Day Standing on Its Head.* New York: Dramatists Play Service, 1994.

———. *"Fish Head Soup" and Other Plays.* Seattle: University of Washington Press, 1995.

———. *No More Cherry Blossoms: "Sisters Matsumoto" and Other Plays.* Seattle: University of Washington Press, 2005.

———. *"The Wind Cries Mary": Loosely Adapted from Ibsen's "Hedda Gabler."* New York: Dramatists Play Service, 2004.

Susan C. W. Abbotson
Rhode Island College

GREAT DIVIDE, THE WILLIAM VAUGHN MOODY (1906)   One of MOODY's two prose plays, *The Great Divide* looks at the dichotomy within the American soul: On the one side, there is the Puritan tradition, which dictates that we must suffer for our sins and defer pleasure. On the other, there is the notion that we can "go west" and re-create ourselves, redeem ourselves in action, and make something out of rock and desert, literally and figuratively.

Philip Jordan, his wife Polly, and his sister Ruth have gone west to Arizona to save the family fortune by investing in a venture involving cactus fiber. The West's untamed beauty appeals to Ruth, who early in the play exclaims to her sister-in-law that she will "be punished for being so happy." Polly responds that Ruth is a "Simon-pure New Englander"—a Puritan. Hence, in the first moments of the play, the central conflict between East and West is foreshadowed. Young Dr. Winthrop Newbury, also a New Englander and a childhood friend of the Jordans, wants to marry Ruth, but she is looking for a man who is "a sublime abstraction—of the glorious unfulfilled—of the West." Winthrop is too much "a completed product" for her.

When Ruth is left alone at the ranch one night, three drunken men break into the cabin and threaten to rape her. She makes a bargain with one of the men, Steve Ghent, that if he will protect her from the others she will marry him. Ghent pays off one man with gold nuggets and shoots (but does not kill) the other. When left alone with Ghent, Ruth hopes she will not have to keep her bargain, and when Ghent offers to leave, she begs him to do so. He retracts his offer, but then, this man who in his own words has gone "to the bad," is touched by Ruth's kindness in binding his wounded arm. He asks that she give him a chance to "make good" and "to make a queen" of her. She goes with him—not willingly, but she goes. There is ambivalence in this scene: She is both drawn to and repulsed by Ghent.

Act 2 begins eight months later. Ruth and Ghent are married. His mine is prospering, and he has become a wealthy man, but Ruth is miserable and haggard. She is dressed in the same clothes as the night of her ordeal. She has steadfastly refused to use any of Ghent's money, though he has been generous. She cannot rid her mind of the images of the night Ghent broke into her cabin, drunk and lust-filled, and bought her like "an animal from the market" or "a woman of the street." All of her husband's money and all of his gifts represent to Ruth just an increase in her price.

She weaves rugs and baskets and sells them at a hotel near Ghent's mine to earn money of her own in order to buy back the chain of gold nuggets from the man whom Ghent paid off that night. It is at this hotel that Ruth's brother and his wife and their friend Dr. Newbury catch a glimpse of her and follow her home. In front of her family, Ruth pretends to be happy, but when they leave for the hotel, she presents Ghent with the chain of gold nuggets she has redeemed and that she hopes will redeem her. She tells Ghent that she "know[s] it is only a symbol," but she begs him to "take [them] and tell [her she is] free," not only for her sake, but for his and for the sake of their unborn child. Ghent refuses, saying that her price has risen and that she is his. Just as Ruth was repulsed and attracted to Ghent, so Ghent is first generous, then possessive, first tender, then emotionally brutal. Here again, Moody creates a character with complex and ambivalent motives and feelings—unlike the stock melodramatic characters of the period.

Ruth returns with her brother Philip to New England. When act 3 begins, months have passed, and she is distracted and preoccupied, even when caring for her infant son. She does not know that Ghent has come to the financial rescue of her mother and brother, that he has seen the baby, and that he is staying in Massachusetts. (Ghent has even taken over Philip and Ruth's failed cactus fiber business and made it a financial success—as if further proof were needed that he can make something from nothing.) Eventually, all is revealed to Ruth. During their final confrontation, Ghent dismisses Ruth's Puritan ancestors whose portraits hang on the walls around them: "It's they who keep your head set on the wages of sin, and all that rubbish. That may be the law for some. . . . [b]ut our law is joy and selfishness; the curve of your shoulder and the light on your hair as you sit there says that as plain as preaching." Ruth tells him that though she loved him, she tried to "cleanse" herself and him of their base beginning before "an angry Heaven" in the only way she and her "fathers" knew— "by wretchedness, by self-torture." Finally, as she is placing the chain that has come to symbolize so much for her around his neck, she says, "You have taken the good of our life and grown strong. I have taken the evil and grown weak, weak unto death. Teach me to live as you do!"

Moody's play was a milestone in American drama, moving it in the direction of a psychological realism that went beyond mere realistic sets and dialogue. Dead at the age of 41, Moody was not able to develop fully this type of realism in his work. That task was left to another American playwright, EUGENE O'NEILL.

GREAT WHITE HOPE, THE HOWARD SACKLER (1968)

Based on the life of African-American heavyweight champion Jack Johnson, who won the title in 1908 and lost it in 1915, *The Great White Hope* examines a life and career destroyed by racism. The play's complex view of race in the period before World War I resonated with the civil rights–era audiences of the late 1960s. Sackler's play won the PULITZER PRIZE and the New York Drama Critics' Circle Award.

When Jack Jefferson—the son of a slave, like so many others of his generation—wins the heavyweight title from a white man, the white boxing establishment and white fans feel threatened and "beat the bushes for another white hope," a white boxer who can dethrone him. Meanwhile, members of Jack's own race perceive him as *their* champion (in both senses of the word), while he prefers to see his victory as an individual accomplishment. He further alienates both races when his romance with a white woman is revealed. Whites want his "head on a platter." The authorities attempt to get him through his girlfriend, but she refuses to be used. Ellie Bachman, a divorcée, is very frank about her love and sexual attraction for Jack Jefferson and defies all attempts to portray their relationship as rape or abduction. Undeterred, a federal marshal arrests Jack when he and Ellie take a vacation at Jack's cabin in Wisconsin: Jack is accused of being in violation of the Mann Act, since he "drove Miss Eleanor Bachman across the . . . state line" and had sex with her. While out of jail on bail, Jefferson, accompanied by Ellie, escapes to Canada and from there to England. He travels Europe looking for boxing opponents; he finds few, and after turning down a lucrative offer to throw a fight, he is reduced to playing the part of Uncle Tom to Ellie's Little Eva in a Budapest cabaret.

The offer to take a bribe comes from the same group who set him up to be arrested, including the federal agent, Dixon, who resents Jefferson for making the law look foolish: "We cannot allow the image of this man to go on impressing and exciting [other African Americans]." Boxing promoters have found their new White Hope but fear his defeat at Jefferson's hands; together, the promoters and the feds decide to offer money and a reduced sentence to Jefferson if he throws the fight. Jefferson's refusal prompts the men to consider extreme measures like drugging him in the middle of a "fair" fight, but instead they dry up his small income and pay off his sparring partners so that he cannot train. He is reduced to living in a "flophouse" and training in a barn on the border of Mexico and Texas. Under great stress, Jack tells a now sickly Ellie to get out. When his old enemies reappear to force him at gunpoint to accept a fixed fight, he refuses until Ellie's dead body is brought in; she has committed suicide. Filled with remorse, Jack finally gives in and loses the title to the White Hope.

Minor characters give voice to points of view on race relations. Scipio, a "bizarre-looking colored man," sug-gests in one of his monologues that the root of Jefferson's problem is his desire to be immersed in the white world: "[H]e's swimming half-drowned in the whitewash." Later, at Jack's mother's funeral, Scipio indicts Christianity. He views it as a way in which whites appease African Americans through African-American preachers: "White man keep pullin' de teeth outa you head an preacher here giving you de laughin-gas—." Furthermore, Scipio condemns the self-loathing that "Goodie-Book thumper[s]"—in his view—promote in their own race. Scipio's voice is silenced when he is dragged off by police and beaten or perhaps killed. In sharp contrast to Scipio is Mrs. Bachman, Ellie's mother, who, addressing the audience, admits her racism and confronts the audience with its own: "Tell yourselves . . . that I'm a half-mad woman . . . making far too much of it. . . . Wait until it touches your own flesh and blood." Another female point of view comes from Jefferson's former common-law wife, Clara, who expresses bitterness at being rejected in favor of a white woman. She addresses the absent Ellie, inviting her to "drag him on down," to destroy Jefferson as a lesson to every other black man who is "dreamin him a piece a what HE got." At the end of her monologue, she holds out a garment—"a nightgown, stiff with blood and excrement"—which foreshadows the bad end of the doomed couple.

GREEN, PAUL (1894–1981)

Born on his family's farm in Harnett County, North Carolina, Paul Green spent his first 22 years in that rural community along the Cape Fear River in the southeastern part of the state. In 1916, he enrolled at the state university in Chapel Hill and the next summer enlisted for a two-year stint in the army, the second year of which found him in France for the final months of World War I and the first several months following the armistice. Returning to Chapel Hill in the fall of 1919, he graduated in 1921, remained for a year of graduate work and writing, then went to Cornell University for a second year of study and writing. In the fall of 1923, he returned to Chapel Hill and joined the university faculty.

Best known as a playwright, Green was also an influential crusader for human rights. As a child, he quietly revolted against the racist attitudes dominant in his society and, in the 1920s, began to speak out forcefully for the rights of African-American people. During the 1920s and 1930s, he devoted much time to prison reform, aid for textile workers in southern mills, and the abolition of capital punishment. After World War II, he was an effective supporter of school desegregation during the turmoil following the 1954 Supreme Court ruling in *Brown v. Board of Education*. In the 1960s, he was an outspoken opponent of the Vietnam War. Through the 1970s, he argued vigorously for disarmament and against the arms race between the nuclear superpowers. When he died on May 4, 1981, it was clear that his life had made a difference in developments toward a new order in the South.

Green began writing plays in the stimulating environment of the Carolina Playmakers under the direction of Frederick Koch at the University of North Carolina. In the 1920s, his plays about African-American life were among the early attempts in American theater to take seriously the experience of African-American people, and one of the plays, IN ABRAHAM'S BOSOM, won a PULITZER PRIZE in 1927. Production of *The House of Connelly* in 1931 launched the GROUP THEATRE on its career through the 1930s. *Hymn to the Rising Sun* (1935), produced widely by the FEDERAL THEATRE PROJECT, is a powerful work that contributed to the abolition of chain gangs in the South. In *Johnny Johnson* (1936), with his collaborator, the composer Kurt Weill, Green created a poignant musical drama on the imperative of world peace. In 1941, he dramatized Richard Wright's *Native Son,* which ORSON WELLES brought to the stage in a powerful Broadway production. Of Green's numerous plays, 11 had Broadway or other professional productions.

In France during World War I, Green was struck by the hierarchical nature of European societies, where people's scope of action and even "worth" were related to the class into which they were born. In the late 1920s, he returned to Europe on a Guggenheim Fellowship to study theatrical developments and came home with an enhanced appreciation of the role of movement, music, and light onstage. Both experiences stand behind *The Lost Colony,* the piece of OUTDOOR HISTORICAL DRAMA first performed on Roanoke Island in 1937. Played at the site of the earliest English colony in North America, *The Lost Colony* espouses an egalitarian social structure by showing how frontier conditions broke down European class distinctions between serf, peasant, and noble (as well as social distinctions between men and women) and placed everyone on a level playing field in the game of life. The play makes lavish use of music, dance, song, and special lighting and sound effects, and it has an acting style commensurate with the script, both of which rely on large gestures. These presentational elements are useful in a play designed for performance before a large audience in an outdoor theater. Intended at first for one summer, *The Lost Colony* still plays each summer on Roanoke Island. It was the earliest of Green's 17 outdoor historical plays, and it can be fairly said to have inspired a national movement, which now numbers dozens of such plays every summer from Alaska to Florida.

BIBLIOGRAPHY

Avery, Laurence G., ed. *A Southern Life: Letters of Paul Green, 1916–1981.* Chapel Hill: University of North Carolina Press, 1994.

Clark, Barrett. *Paul Green.* New York: Robert M. McBride, 1928.

Green, Elizabeth Lay. *The Paul Green I Know.* Chapel Hill: North Carolinian Society, 1978.

Green, Paul. *Five Plays of the South.* Edited by John Gassner. New York: Hill & Wang, 1963.

———. *"The House of Connelly" and Other Plays.* New York: Samuel French, 1931.

———, with Kurt Weill. *Johnny Johnson.* New York: Samuel French, 1937.

———. *The Lost Colony.* Edited by Laurence G. Avery. Chapel Hill: University. of North Carolina Press, 2001.

———. *Out of the South.* New York: Harper, 1939.

———. *A Paul Green Reader.* Edited by Laurence G. Avery. Chapel Hill: University of North Carolina Press, 1998.

———. *Texas.* New York: Samuel French, 1967.

———. *This Body the Earth.* New York: Harper, 1935.

———. *Wilderness Road.* New York: Samuel French, 1956.

Kenny, Vincent S. *Paul Green.* New York: Twayne, 1972.

Lazenby, Walter S., Jr. *Paul Green.* Austin, Tex.: Steck-Vaughn, 1970.

Roper, John Herbert. *Paul Green: Playwright of the Real South.* Athens: University of Georgia Press, 2003.

Laurence G. Avery
University of North Carolina–Chapel Hill

GREENBERG, RICHARD (1958–)

Playwright Richard Greenberg was born in East Meadow, New Jersey, and educated at Princeton University (B. A., 1980) and Yale University School of Drama (M. F.A., 1985). Greenberg usually writes about New Yorkers—at home and on vacation—who are well-educated, well-off WASPs. Full of language play and allusion, Greenberg's plays feature the articulate and mock the nonverbal.

Greenberg first gained attention when he won a George Oppenheimer Award (given to the best New York debut by an American playwright for a nonmusical play) for *The Bloodletters* (1984), an odd comedy about a teen who has a malady that makes him smell of feces. This success was followed by several one-acts, of which perhaps the most notable was *The Maderati* (1987), a satire about self-absorbed artists in New York—the "mad literati," as they call themselves—and their response when a poet among them disappears. Other early one-acts include *Life under Water* (1985), *Vanishing Act* (1986), and *The Author's Voice* (1987).

Greenberg's full-length plays include *Eastern Standard* (1988), in which a group of privileged young urban professionals mix with a homeless woman to assuage their guilt over social inequity; *The American Plan* (1990), about a woman in 1960 whose bitter mother—a German-Jewish refugee—interferes with her daughter's summer love affair with a gentile in the Catskills; *The Extra Man* (1991), in which a blocked writer manipulates the lives of his friends as if they were characters, with unhappy consequences; *Jenny Keeps Talking* (1992), a play made up of three monologues—delivered by two sisters and their grandmother who find themselves at odds when their plans for a family cottage in Maine conflict; *Night and Her Stars* (1997), about the quiz show scandal of the 1950s; *Three Days of Rain* (1997), which travels from 1995 back to 1960 to reveal what a son and daughter can never fully understand about their enigmatic father after his death (the title is the sole journal entry made by this cold and noncommunicative man during the most significant week in his life); *Everett Beekin* (2001), a comedy about an immigrant family over two generations; *The Dazzle* (2001), a fictionalized account of the obsessive/compulsive Collyer brothers; *TAKE ME OUT* (2002), a play about baseball and homosexuality in which a superstar ballplayer decides to declare publicly that he is gay (it won the TONY AWARD and New York Drama Critics' Circle Award); and *The Violet Hour* (2003), a post–World War I drama about a novice independent publisher faced with choosing between the work of his best friend or the work of his lover.

The Naked Girl on the Apprian Way (2005) is a comedy about the machinations of a liberal upper-middle-class multiracial (through adoption) New York family at their summer house in the Hamptons. *The Well-Appointed Room* (2006), a much darker play, premiered at Chicago's Steppenwolf Theatre; it is made up of two one-acts, *Nostalgia,* about an insecure playwright and his caustic wife, and *Prolepsis,* in which another couple's happiness is jeopardized by an uncertain world. The two short plays are connected by their setting, a New York condo occupied by the two couples in different years. *The House in Town* (2006) is set in 1929 in the home of a wealthy New York couple, whose lives are shadowed by the stock market crash to come—though that event is not dealt with overtly. Greenberg also wrote a new book for the revival of the Rodgers and Hart musical *Pal Joey* (2008). Greenberg often writes for film and television.

BIBLIOGRAPHY

Greenberg, Richard. *"The Dazzle" and "Everett Beekin."* New York: Faber and Faber, 2003.
———. *Eastern Standard.* New York: Grove Press, 1989.
———. *Jenny Keeps Talking.* New York: Dramatists Play Service, 1995.
———. *Life under Water.* New York: Dramatists Play Service, 1985.
———. *The Maderati.* New York: Dramatists Play Service, 1987.
———. *Night and Her Stars.* New York: Dramatists Play Service, 1997.
———. *Take Me Out.* New York: Faber and Faber, 2003.
———. *"Three Days of Rain" and Other Plays.* New York: Grove Press, 1999.
———. *Vanishing Act.* New York: Dramatists Play Service, 1987.
———. *The Violet Hour.* New York: Dramatists Play Service, 2005.

GREEN PASTURES, THE Marc Connelly (1930)

This folk drama is very loosely based on a group of short stories by Roark Bradford (1896–1948) entitled *Ol' Man Adam an' His Chillun* (1918). These were Bible stories in an early-20th-century southern African-American dialect—Connelly acknowledged his debt to Bradford for that idea—but the play's sources are, to a greater extent, the Old Testament and Connelly's research and experience in Louisiana. The play won the Pulitzer Prize, even though adaptations are ineligible, because it was deemed sufficiently original to qualify. *The Green Pastures* was tremendously successful both in the United States and in Europe and made a fortune for Connelly. In its day, it was a breakthrough play for two reasons: The cast was entirely African American, and the theme was religious: Both initially scared off producers who believed such a project was doomed to commercial failure. (Indeed, a revival in 1954 did fail, not surprisingly, as the Civil Rights movement began. Today's audiences might well find the play offensive for its racial stereotypes.)

The play begins in a Louisiana Sunday school class in a "Negro church." Mr. Deshee, the preacher, teaches the children some Old Testament stories and answers their naive questions. The children want to know if, before God created the Earth, the angels had picnics; Deshee tells them, "Dey probably had fish frys, wid b'iled custard and ten cent seegars." This imagery leads us into scene 2, in which "pre-Creation Heaven" is depicted as "a company of happy Negroes at a fish fry"; they are angels "with wings protruding from their backs." The "Lawd" creates the Earth at the celestial fish fry because He needs a place to "dreen" off the extra firmament He has made. (When He decrees, "Let it be a whole mess of firmament," the cherubs get "soaked to de skin." Since God "don't want de chillun to ketch cold," He makes the Earth as a receptacle for the extra moisture.)

God visits the Earth, and the play moves through the ups and downs of human existence as depicted in the Old Testament stories: Adam's fall, Cain and Abel, Noah and the ark, Moses freeing the Hebrews from Egypt, and the Babylonian captivity. A few times, the frame of Mr. Deshee and his class returns to comment on the misbehavior of humankind, and sometimes God and His angels offer further comment on the action. However, all of the characters, celestial and earthbound alike, resemble, in appearance and speech, Louisiana African Americans of the period. Therefore, Adam and Moses are dressed as "*fieldhands*"; God's office has the "*general atmosphere . . . of the office of a Negro lawyer in a Louisiana town*"; the throne room of the Pharaoh "*suggests a Negro lodge room*"; and the Babylonian setting is "*a room vaguely resembling a Negro night club in New Orleans.*" Within these settings, the plotlines are biblical, but the behaviors of the characters are often racial stereotypes, obvious to the modern reader.

Eventually, God becomes fed up with humans, who are unable to stay out of trouble, and He abandons them for a time, until He learns from Hezdrel and Hosea that they believe in a merciful God and have themselves found "mercy. . . . through suffering." The play ends with a "voice," a witness, exclaiming over the suffering of Jesus at Calvary.

GRIMKÉ, ANGELINA WELD (1880–1958)
See *Rachel*.

GROUP THEATRE, THE

Founded in 1931 by Harold Clurman, Cheryl Crawford, and Lee Strasberg, the Group Theatre was an ensemble theater formed as a response to the old-fashioned theater of light entertainment that prevailed in the late 1920s. During its 10-year existence, the Group mounted some 20 productions of original contemporary plays by American playwrights. Members included Elia Kazan, Stella Adler, John Garfield, Luther Adler, Will Geer, Howard Da Silva, Franchot Tone, John Randolph, Joseph Bromberg, Michael Gordon, Paul Green, Clifford Odets, Paul Strand, Kurt Weill, and Lee J. Cobb. Though short-lived, the Group Theatre had a substantial impact on American theater, as it embraced naturalistic acting, ensemble production, and socially conscious drama.

It was originally at the Group Theatre that Lee Strasberg, basing his work on the innovative techniques of the Russian actor and director Constantin Stanislavsky, developed "Method" acting (see Actors

STUDIO). Actors in the ensemble used physical and psychological exercises to bring honest emotion to their acting. The results were more natural and more intense performances.

The philosophy of the Group was not unlike its politics; individual glory was less important than the good of the Group. Many hoped to produce plays that exposed social problems. Through Clifford Odets's work, the Group expressed the plight and feelings of the working class. Most held political views that were called "left-wing." During the 1950s, many members of the Group Theatre were investigated by the House Un-American Activities Committee. While some, such as Kazan and Odets, cooperated with the committee and implicated others, most members refused to "name names" and were consequently blacklisted for years in Hollywood.

Late in the 1930s, persistent financial problems and disagreements among the members led to the dissolution of the Group. When several of the ensemble's members went to Hollywood hoping to ease their financial problems, some did not return, and Strasberg and Crawford both resigned. The success of Odets's GOLDEN BOY (1937) was not enough to save the Group Theatre, and it folded in 1941. The Group's influence on American theater, though, was far-reaching. Many Group members became influential acting teachers and directors. Kazan, Crawford, and Robert Lewis founded the Actors Studio, of which Strasberg served as artistic director for three decades and which has served as the training ground for three generations of America's finest actors.

Among the Group Theatre productions were Paul Green's The HOUSE OF CONNELLY (1931), JOHN HOWARD LAWSON's Success Story (1932) and Gentle Woman (1933), Marc Blitzstein's Condemned (1932) and The Cradle Will Rock (1937), Albert Maltz's The Black Pit (1933), SIDNEY KINGSLEY's MEN IN WHITE (1933), Clifford Odets's AWAKE AND SING! and WAITING FOR LEFTY (1935), WILLIAM SAROYAN's MY HEART'S IN THE HIGHLANDS (1939), and Native Son (1941) by Richard Wright and Paul Green.

BIBLIOGRAPHY

Clurman, Harold. The Fervent Years: The Story of the Group Theatre and the Thirties. New York: Hill & Wang, 1957.

Smith, Wendy. Real Life Drama: The Group Theatre and America, 1931–40. New York: Grove Press, 1992.

GUARE, JOHN (1938–   )

Largely due to the universal appeal of his best-known plays, The HOUSE OF BLUE LEAVES (1971) and SIX DEGREES OF SEPARATION (1989), and for the screenplay of the film Atlantic City (1981), John Guare has been one of the playwrights to give renewed life to the contemporary American theater by examining the fraudulence of modern society.

Guare was born in Manhattan, the son of Irish Catholic parents, and he attended two Catholic schools—St. Joan of Arc Elementary School in Queens and St. John's Preparatory School in Brooklyn. Guare continued his Jesuit education at Georgetown University, where he wrote a new play each year, and graduated with a B.A. in English in 1960. He received his M.F.A. in playwriting at Yale University in 1963. Selected in 1965 by the O'Neill Theatre Center in Waterford, Connecticut, as a promising young playwright, Guare was commissioned to write a new play. He wrote the first act of The House of Blue Leaves, but, unable to write the second act, he returned to Yale under an ABC Television grant to study film writing. While at Yale, Guare wrote two short one-act dramas: Something I'll Tell You Tuesday and The Loveliest Afternoon of the Year, which were first performed in 1966 at OFF-OFF-BROADWAY's Caffe Cino.

While Guare was at Yale studying film writing, he wrote Muzeeka, which opened in 1968 at the Provincetown Playhouse in New York; it won Guare an OBIE AWARD—his first major theater prize. Structured in six short scenes, the play traces Jack Argue's travails from domesticity to his involvement in the Vietnam War. Guare examines the issue of whether one can establish an identity or find inner peace within a society that turns us into conformists. His next play, Cop-out, was presented in 1969, on a double bill with Guare's Home Fires at the Cort Theatre, his first Broadway production. Cop-out, structured as a series of vignettes, is similar to film montage. There are four realistic documentary-type "scenes" revealing the relationship between the Policeman and a cute peacenik attracted to him. These scenes alternate with three vignettes, staged with the stylized flair of a "Universal/MGM film," that trace super sleuth Brett Arrow's search for a murderer. The play depicts the madness of contemporary society in which myths, fabricated and embellished by the media, tend to overshadow reality. *Home Fires,* written as the curtain raiser for *Cop-out,* is a compact one-act play that occurs in Catchpole's New England funeral parlor the day after the signing of the armistice ending World War I. Catchpole is the owner of a posh establishment and therefore must be solicitous about his image and what his clients might say about him. The play explores the idea that, in modern America, class matters and an individual's worth is determined by class or celebrity status, not by inner qualities.

The House of Blue Leaves opened at OFF-BROADWAY's Truck and Warehouse Theater in 1971 and was a huge success. The play demythologizes the American Dream; it is concerned with how we try to avoid humiliation when we realize that our dreams cannot be realized. It became Guare's first major breakthrough in the theater: The drama was voted Best American Play of the 1970–71 season by the New York Drama Critics' Circle, received an Obie Award (Guare's second), the Los Angeles Drama Critics Circle Award, and an Outer Critics Circle Award.

Marco Polo Sings a Solo, which had its New York debut at Joseph Papp's Public Theater in 1977, is ostensibly concerned with a utopian society, where the characters are all rich and famous and therefore have no limits to their dreams and aspirations. Each character in the play yearns for a greater beauty, a greater glory, and a greater power, and this quest to create a legacy leads to a dependence on self. Guare's next play, *Rich and Famous,* written in only three days, is one of his best. The definitive version of the play was initially staged at Papp's Public Theater in 1976 and concerns Bing Ringling, the protagonist of the play, who is a confused young man with a consuming desire to be rich and famous. Bing can be compared to Artie Shaughnessy in *The House of Blue Leaves,* another dreamer who wants to make it "big" in show business but cannot seem to escape the reality of his lack of talent. The play takes us through a series of vignettes, each suggesting Bing's increasing alienation and his inability to learn about himself.

In 1977, Guare's LANDSCAPE OF THE BODY opened at the Public Theater. The play looks at the inability of those without imagination and without the power to reflect to connect with others in meaningful relationships. His next play, *Bosoms and Neglect,* had its New York premiere in 1979, at Broadway's Longacre Theatre, closing after only four performances. *Bosoms and Neglect* is primarily concerned with whether individuals in contemporary American society can connect with each other in some meaningful or spiritual way, despite the fact that neglect, indifference, and alienation reflect the norm in human relationships. The play examines how we seek refuge from reality and from our guilt by immersing ourselves in self-centered fantasy lives.

In the late 1970s, Guare began writing the Lydie Breeze tetralogy, which traces the history of the founders of a once-prosperous commune named Aipotu (*utopia* spelled backwards), beginning with its founding near the end of the Civil War and concluding near the end of the 19th century. The tetralogy, written as realism and melodrama, attempts to trace the loss of spirituality in modern society to the greed and self-interest of the Gilded Age. *Lydie Breeze* (1982), chronologically the last in the cycle, opened first, and, two months later, *Gardenia* (1982), chronologically the second, opened. While in London later in 1982, Guare wrote *Women and Water,* which is chronologically the first play in the cycle, occurring in 1861 and 1864. The revised version of the play was given a major production at Arena Stage in Washington, D.C., in 1985. Guare has been working for years on the last play in the tetralogy, *Bulfinch's Mythology,* which is to take place a year after the events of *Gardenia;* the play currently remains unfinished.

Six Degrees of Separation (1989) opened to enthusiastic reviews and won the 1990–91 New York Drama Critics' Circle Award for Best Play, an Obie Award, and a Hull-Warriner Award. Based on a real event, the play is about a young African-American man who cons a wealthy New York couple by pretending to be Sidney Poitier's son; the play satirizes materialism and superficiality among wealthy Americans—especially "liberals."

Guare's *Four Baboons Adoring the Sun* (1992) begins in Sicily, where recently married Philip and Penny

McKenzie are awaiting the arrival of their children (he has four, she five) flying in from New York. Penny and Philip, who are archaeologists working on a dig at La Muculufa, have divorced their former spouses in order to avoid the neuroticism of modern urban life and thus tap into their imaginative selves through their love of the classical art of ancient civilizations. As is typical in Guare's dramas, however, the utopian dreams and fantasies of an idyllic life free from the anomie of modern civilization that creates alienation and leaves individuals unable to connect soon degenerate into failure. At the end of the play, Philip returns to the university with the children, but Penny stays in Sicily; she remains an idealist who pursues the fantasy, the mythology of the imagination, until the bitter end.

In 1995, the revised version of *Moon under Miami* premiered in Chicago. *Moon under Miami* is a parody of the ABSCAM scandal that began in February 1978 and ran through the early 1980s as a result of the FBI secretly taping meetings with public officials, including congressmen, who accepted bribes from undercover agents posing as Arab sheiks. In the play, Miami replaces New York as a microcosm of greed, fraudulence, and corruption—a lawless East Coast frontier town that epitomizes the decadence of modern American society.

In the 1990s, Guare also continued to write one-act plays. *New York Actor* (1993) takes place in Joe Allen's theater bar in Manhattan where stage performers Nat, Barry, and Eileen have gathered to welcome Craig, one of their own, back to New York. Ego forces these actors to wear the mask of big-time celebrities seeking fame and fortune. Guare's latest projects include a musical adaptation of the film classic, *The Sweet Smell of Success,* and productions of his most recent plays, *Lake Hollywood* (1999) and *Chaucer in Rome* (2001). The latter is a sequel to *The House of Blue Leaves* and satirizes the warped hunger for fame, the worship of celebrities, and the betrayal involved in the creation of art. *A Few Stout Individuals,* a play about Ulysses S. Grant trying to write his memoirs despite all kinds of distractions, opened Off-Broadway in 2002. Guare's *Blue Monologue,* part of an evening's entertainment consisting of seven new short plays and monologues

about the places we call home, was produced by the 13th Street Repertory Company in New York City during March 2007.

BIBLIOGRAPHY

Curry, Jane Kathleen. *John Guare: A Research and Production Sourcebook.* Westport, Conn.: Greenwood Press, 2002.

Guare, John. *Chaucer in Rome.* New York: Dramatists Play Service, 2002.

———. *A Few Stout Individuals.* New York: Grove/Atlantic, 2003.

———. *Four Baboons Adoring the Sun and Other Plays.* New York: Vintage, 1993.

———. *Gardenia.* New York: Dramatists Play Service, 1982.

———. *"The General of Hot Desire" and Other Plays.* New York: Dramatists Play Service, 1999.

———. *"The House of Blue Leaves" and Two Other Plays: "Landscape of the Body" and "Bosoms and Neglect."* New York: Plume, 1987.

———. *Lydie Breeze.* New York: Dramatists Play Service, 1982.

———. *Six Degrees of Separation.* 2d ed. New York: Vintage, 1994.

———. *Three Plays by John Guare: "Cop-out," "Muzeeka," "Home Fires."* New York: Grove Press, 1970.

———. *The War against the Kitchen Sink.* Lyme, N.H.: Smith and Kraus, 1996.

———. *Women and Water.* New York: Dramatists Play Service, 1990.

Plunka, Gene A. *The Black Comedy of John Guare.* Newark: University of Delaware Press, 2001.

Gene A. Plunka
University of Memphis

GUIRGIS, STEPHEN ADLY (1965?–)

Born in New York and raised on the city's Upper West Side, Stephen Adly Guirgis writes about a New York inhabited by those who are not fortunate or affluent. In 2003 when he was 38, a profile in the *New York Times Magazine* suggested that Guirgis might "be the best playwright in America under 40" (B. Weber 40).

Guirgis received his early education at a Catholic school, and later at the Rhodes School, a private academy to which he received a scholarship. By his own admission he squandered much of his time there. It was at the State University of New York at Albany—where he earned his bachelor of arts degree over a period of seven and a half years—that Guirgis met fellow actor John Ortiz, at whose urging he, in 1994, joined LAB (which stood for Latino Actors Base, though Guirgis himself is not Latino but the son of an American mother and an Egyptian father). LAB soon became LAByrinth, an ethnically diverse acting and producing company in which Guirgis became an important member, not as an actor but as a writer. Besides Ortiz and Guirgis, LAByrinth's membership also includes such well-known contemporary theater figures as playwrights ERIC BOGOSIAN, JOHN PATRICK SHANLEY, and JOSÉ RIVERA, as well as actor and director Philip Seymour Hoffman, who frequently directs Guirgis's plays.

It was Ortiz who encouraged Guirgis to write. His first play was the one-act *Francisco and Benny* (1994) in which two neighborhood youths debate the merits of partying versus planning for the future. His other early plays for LAByrinth include *Moonlight Mile* (1996), a working-class romantic comedy; *Race, Religion, Politics* (1997), which looks at relationships and social philosophy among blue collar workers in a bar; *Den of Thieves* (1997), a comedy about petty criminals; *Boom, Boom, Boom, Boom* (1997), a farce about a depressed loser who finds love on a cruise ship; and *In Arabia We'd All Be Kings* (1998), set in a seedy bar (within a newly glittering Giuliani-era Times Square) and peopled with the kind of social outcasts—hookers and addicts among them—about whom EUGENE O'NEILL also wrote with realism and some sympathy decades earlier.

The play that brought Guirgis and LAByrinth to the attention of the international theater community was *Jesus Hopped the 'A' Train* (2000). Set at New York's Riker's Island prison, the play involves two mishandled prisoners, one a young man who has shot a religious cult leader in the behind for converting his best friend, the other a serial killer who has found God. In 2001, LAByrinth took the production to the Edinburgh Festival, where it won the Fringe First Award. When the production moved to London in 2002, the *Daily Telegraph* review called it "stunningly well written" (March 15, 2002). Guirgis, who describes himself as a "lost" Catholic has said that *Jesus Hopped the 'A' Train* is about his "struggle" with the idea of submitting "to the care

of God" and all "the responsibilities that go with that" submission (B. Weber 43). Because of the great success *Jesus Hopped the 'A' Train* had had in London, *In Arabia We'd All Be Kings* was also produced there in 2003.

Guirgis's plays continue to be influenced by his Catholic upbringing. In *Our Lady of 121st Street* (2002), a group of Catholic school graduates gather for the funeral of Sister Rose, a well-loved childhood influence, and rage against the bleak reality of their lives. *The Last Days of Judas Iscariot* (2005) is a serio-comic and irreverent reexamination of the case of the infamous betrayer of Jesus, which mixes historical periods and levels of language and is set in a purgatorial courtroom. In an interview in the *Catholic Digest,* Guirgis said that he began to think about the plight of Judas in the fourth grade when he learned of Judas's despair, suicide, and condemnation to hell; he wondered how God could be so unforgiving. Guirgis continued, "The idea in the play that's borrowed from a lot of Christian philosophers is true: that we're responsible for our own salvation" (K. Weber). In the wake of the success of these two plays, Guirgis won the 2006 PEN/Laura Pels Foundation Award given to a midcareer playwright.

More recent works include the two one-acts *The Sissy Letters: Numbers 14, 29, and 47* (2006) and *Yelba, Princess of 10th Avenue* (2007), as well as the full-length play *The Little Flower of East Orange* (2008). The latter is set primarily in a charity hospital in the Bronx at the bedside of the narrator's mother. She is visited there by her sometimes angry, sometimes ambivalent son and daughter *and* by the apparition of her own dead alcoholic father among other remembered figures from her past. Ben Brantley in his review in the *New York Times* remarked that the mother, Therese Marie, "emerges as a convincing study in the contradictions born of a life of denial" (April 7, 2008).

Guirgis's characters are typically frustrated and often enraged to be faced with situations and forces over which they have no control. He cares deeply about such people: "Whatever I'm writing about, it better be something that really matters to me. . . . And for me it's stories about people in pain in New York" (B. Weber 42).

BIBLIOGRAPHY

Guirgis, Stephen Adly. *Den of Thieves.* New York: Dramatists Play Service, 2004.

———. *The Last Days of Judas Iscariot.* New York: Faber and Faber, 2005.

———. *The Little Flower of East Orange.* New York: Faber and Faber, 2009.

———. *Our Lady of 121st Street; Jesus Hopped the 'A' Train;* [and] *In Arabia We'd All Be Kings.* New York: Faber and Faber, 2003.

Weber, Bruce. "The Sound of Fury." *New York Times Magazine* 2 Mar. 2003: 40–43.

Weber, Kerry. "Stephen Adly Guirgis, Playwright." *Catholic Digest* (Jan. 2008). Available online. URL: http://catholic-digest.com/article/print/stephen-adly-guirgis-play.

GURNEY, A[LBERT] R[AMSDELL]

(1930–)   Born in Buffalo, New York, in an extended family that still operates a real estate business, A. R. Gurney attended the Nichols School in Buffalo, St. Paul's in Concord, New Hampshire, and Williams College in Williamstown, Massachusetts. After serving in the United States Navy, he earned a master of fine arts degree at the Yale University School of Drama.

Gurney's grandmother often took him to Buffalo's Erlanger Theater to see musicals. At Williams, he cowrote two college shows with Stephen Sondheim. Encouraged by his teacher, Nikos Psacharopolous, he wrote Yale's first original musical, "Love in Buffalo," which interested Richard Halliday, Mary Martin's husband, who was a producer. Gurney might have succeeded in musical theater. However, the needs of his growing family turned him to teaching, and in 1960 he joined the humanities faculty of MIT.

Between 1956 and 1968, he wrote one-act plays distinguished by lively characters and humorous dialogue. Most notable as a sign of plays-to-be is *The Comeback* (1964), in which Odysseus returns to a suburban cocktail party. The braiding of classical subject and modern idiom became a hallmark of Gurney's style in *The David Show* (1966), *Another Antigone* (1987), and *Overtime* (1995). *The Love Course* (1970) satirizes academic life, also a target for Gurney in *The Old One-Two* (1971), *The Wayside Motor Inn* (1977), *The Perfect Party* (1986), *Another Antigone, The Old Boy* (1991), and *The Fourth Wall* (1992; revised version, 2002).

In 1970, with a National Endowment for the Humanities fellowship and encouraged by Boston drama critic Elliot Norton, Gurney went to the Tanglewood Festival and created a full-length drama, *Scenes from American Life.* This play, often performed in the years since its premiere, staked out Gurney's artistic territory: the dreams and fears of prosperous Americans in our time. It dramatizes the effects of losing prestige and power on the Americans who were most accustomed to it. It drew its inspiration from Gurney's youth in Buffalo, as did *The Middle Ages* (1977). His plays have most often been premiered either at Off-Broadway or Off-Off-Broadway theaters in New York City or at such regional theaters as the Long Wharf in New Haven or the Old Globe in San Diego.

In addition to *The Dining Room* (1982), *Love Letters* (1988), *The Cocktail Hour* (1988), and *Sylvia* (1995), theater audiences have found greatest interest in *The Middle Ages, Later Life* (1993), *Overtime,* and *Far East* (1999). The first three and the last owe some of their spirit to John Cheever, whose fiction Gurney admires and to whom he has paid tribute in *A Cheever Evening* (1994). Henry James's fiction has also inspired Gurney: *Later Life* grew out of Gurney's esteem for "The Real Thing," and "The Aspern Papers" led him to write *The Golden Age* (1981). Edwin Arlington Robinson's poem "Richard Cory" also became a play, *Who Killed Richard Cory?* (1976).

The Fourth Wall satirizes the pretentiousness of academic theorizing about theater while honoring Congreve and Ibsen and the aspirations of American women for more power in public life. *Overtime,* a modern sequel to *The Merchant of Venice,* looks comically at the orthodoxies of politically correct multiculturalism. *Labor Day* (1998), a sequel to *The Cocktail Hour,* dramatizes the agonies a playwright's calling inflicts on his family. *Later Life* is akin to *The Golden Age* in evoking the spirit of Henry James. *Ancestral Voices* shares the form of *Love Letters* but shows the pain of divorce. *Far East* criticizes the "rules" separating a young American naval officer from his Japanese lover.

Gurney is often labeled a WASP writer, but a better understanding of his artistry may be gained by attending to his themes, his innovativeness, and his complexity. At MIT, he taught major works of world civilization. His theatrical imagination is rooted in the popular drama of the Greeks and Romans, of Restoration England, especially William Congreve, and of late Victorian England, particularly Oscar Wilde and George Bernard Shaw. His overarching concern is the fate of democratic society. Parties, meetings, and dinners abound in the plays because they reflect the democratic ideal of intelligent citizens behaving justly and humanely. References to singing and the use of music in almost every play underscore his characters' yearning for personal and social harmony.

He writes plays that challenge actors with double and triple roles or double characters (as in *Sweet Sue* [1986], his only Broadway play). By mingling ancient and modern stories, staging multiple scenes in the same space (as in *The Dining Room* and *The Wayside Motor Inn* [1977]), imagining the fantastic (as in *Sylvia*), drawing the audience into reflection on the nature of theater itself (as in *The Cocktail Hour* and *The Fourth Wall*), or trying to escape the limitations of theater altogether (as in *Love Letters* and *Ancestral Voices* [2000]), Gurney gives shape to his restless imagination, his desire to tell stories in interesting ways, and his lifelong quest to sustain drama's relevance to the lives of American audiences.

Since 2000, Gurney has adapted his novel, *Entertaining Strangers,* for the stage under the title, *Human Events* (2001); written a libretto for an operatic version of Edith Wharton's *The House of Mirth;* and paired two one-act plays, *The Problem* and *The Guest Lecturer,* under the title *Strictly Academic* (2003).

He has also written nine new full-length plays. *Big Bill* (2003) traces the career of tennis star Bill Tilden. *O Jerusalem* (2003) deals with the conflict between Israel and Palestine. In a departure from his previous stance as a playwright, some of Gurney's new work has aggressively attacked the policies of the George W. Bush administration. Gurney's disgust with Bush appeared first in a 2004 revision of *The Fourth Wall.* Then, in the guise of a play about a creative writing class, Gurney deploys the title character of *Mrs. Farnsworth* (2004), who threatens to write a story exposing the indiscretions of a sitting U.S. president whose New England family strongly resembles that of President Bush. *Screen Play* (2005), riffing on the movie *Casablanca,* imagines a future United States from which, because of Bush's policies, U.S. citizens are prevented from escaping to Canada via Gurney's hometown of Buffalo. *Post Mortem* (2006) is set in a world taken over by the Christian right where censorship takes hold. Once again mining the playwright's own past, *Indian Blood* (2006) and *Crazy Mary* (2007) add to the group of plays drawing on Gurney's experiences growing up in northwestern New York during the 1930s and 1940s. In the summer of 2008, a revised *Buffalo Gal,* which invokes the themes and spirit of Chekhov's *The Cherry Orchard,* opened a six-week New York run to strongly positive reviews. With 49 plays to his credit, Gurney shows no sign of slacking his pace. As of late 2008 he has two new plays in progress. Gurney's most recent play, *Light Lunch,* which premiered in December 2008, again takes aim at the Bush administration; in it, a playwright named Gurney and his new play are discussed over lunch by his agent and a Texas lawyer who represents powerful opponents to the play.

BIBLIOGRAPHY

Gurney, A. R. *Ancestral Voices.* New York: Broadway Play Publishing, 2000.

———. *A. R. Gurney: Collected Plays.* 5 vols. Portsmouth, N.H.: Smith and Kraus, 1995–2001.

———. *Big Bill.* New York: Broadway Play Publishing, 2004.

———. *Buffalo Gal.* New York: Broadway Play Publishing, 2002.

———. *Crazy Mary.* New York: Broadway Play Publishing, 2007.

———. *Human Events.* New York: Broadway Play Publishing, 2001.

———. *Indian Blood.* New York: Broadway Play Publishing, 2006.

———. *Mrs. Farnsworth.* New York: Broadway Play Publishing, 2004.

———. *O Jerusalem.* New York: Broadway Play Publishing, 2003.

———. *Post Mortem.* New York: Broadway Play Publishing, 2006.

———. *Screen Play.* New York: Broadway Play Publishing, 2005.

Sponberg, Arvid F., ed. *A. R. Gurney: A Casebook.* New York: Routledge, 2003.

Arvid F. Sponberg
Valparaiso University

HAIRY APE, THE EUGENE O'NEILL (1922)

HAIRY APE, THE EUGENE O'NEILL **(1922)** In a November 16, 1924, letter to the *New York Herald Tribune,* O'NEILL described the subject of *The Hairy Ape* as "the same ancient one that always was and always will be the one subject for drama, . . . man and his struggle with his own fate. The struggle used to be with the gods, but is now with himself, his own past, his attempt 'to belong.'" One of O'Neill's two early experimental plays, *The Hairy Ape,* like its predecessor, *The EMPEROR JONES* (1920), is divided into a series of short scenes rather than acts; is presented in a style that, according to the playwright's own stage directions, *"should by no means be naturalistic"*; and "concentrates on its hero's run through a kind of wilderness to his eventual destruction by a primitive force" (Bogard 242).

The play begins in *"[t]he firemen's forecastle of a transatlantic liner."* This area of the ship *"is a cramped space, . . . imprisoned by white steel,"* in which the men found there *"cannot stand upright"* and thus *"resemble those pictures in which the appearance of Neanderthal Man is guessed at."* Their leader is Yank, *"broader, fiercer, more truculent, more powerful, more sure of himself than the rest,"* who boasts of their superiority over "dem slobs in de foist cabin": "Who makes dis old tub run? Ain't it us guys? Well den, we belong, don't we? We belong and dey don't." Only old Paddy disagrees and yearns for the bygone days of the clipper ships, when "a ship was part of the sea, and a man was part of a ship, and the sea joined all together and made it one."

The play's second scene takes place on the ship's promenade deck, where we find Mildred Douglas, a young woman *"with a pale, pretty face marred by a self-conscious expression of disdainful superiority . . . dressed all in white,"* who is the daughter of the president of Nazareth Steel. Fresh from "social service work on New York's East Side" and chaperoned by her aunt, the two *"artificial figures, inert and disharmonious,"* contrast sharply with *"the beautiful vivid life of the sea all about."* Mildred has received the captain's permission to visit the stokehold to "investigate how the other half lives and works on a ship." When she appears, Yank, who, along with his men, is feeding coal into the vessel's furnace, *"whirls defensively with a snarling, murderous growl, crouching to spring, his lips drawn back over his teeth, his small eyes gleaming ferociously."* Mildred, *"paralyzed with terror,"* stares at his *"gorilla face,"* screams, "Oh, the filthy beast!" and faints.

As scene 4 opens, Yank sits *"in the exact attitude of Rodin's 'The Thinker,'"* refusing to eat or wash the dirt off his body. When Paddy tells him that Mildred looked at Yank "as if she'd seen a great hairy ape escaped from the Zoo," he replies, "Hairy ape, huh? I'll show her I'm better'n her, if she on'y knew it. I belong and she don't, see!" He vows to get even with her, to "show her who's a ape!" Three weeks later, in scene 5, it is Sunday morning on New York's Fifth Avenue, where the beautiful sunny day is in *"tawdry disharmony"* with the harsh commercialism of a

215

jewelry store and a furrier's establishment. Yank enters, unshaven and in dirty dungarees; he unsuccessfully taunts the worshipers who emerge from church, "*a procession of gaudy marionettes, yet with something of the relentless horror of Frankensteins in their detached, mechanical unawareness.*" They ignore his insults and his insistence that he "belongs" and they do not; when he punches one of them, the latter is totally unaffected, and the police arrive to arrest Yank.

In jail in scene 6, Yank is bloodied but unrepentant, still determined to have revenge on Mildred, much to the amusement of his fellow inmates, who urge him to join the International Workers of the World. Hearing that the IWW "blow up tings" and "turn tings round," Yank bends the bars of his cell and escapes. Almost a month later, scene 7 finds Yank at an IWW local where he tells the members he wants to join so that he can blow up the steel factory run by Mildred's father. Horrified by his violent plan, the members, suspicious that he is a spy from the Secret Service trying to frame them, throw him out, calling him "a brainless ape." Finally discouraged, he urges a passing policeman to "Lock me up! Put me in a cage!" When the policeman asks what his crime is, Yank answers, "Enuf to gimme life for! I was born, see?"

The play's final scene is in the zoo's monkey house, where a gorilla squats in the same pose of Rodin's *The Thinker* that Yank has assumed earlier. When Yank enters, he asks the gorilla, "Ain't we both members of de same club—de Hairy Apes?" He explains that the difference between them is that, while the gorilla "don't belong wit" humankind because he "can't tink" and "can't talk," he, Yank, "kin make a bluff at talkin' and tinkin'—a'most git away with it," adding, in the play's most important lines, "I ain't on oith and I ain't in heaven. . . . I'm in de middle, tryin' to separate 'em, takin' all de woist punches from bot' of 'em." He opens the cage and extends his hand, whereupon the gorilla grabs him and crushes him to death. O'Neill's final stage direction reads, "*And, perhaps, the Hairy Ape at last belongs.*"

While generally considered, along with *The Emperor Jones,* an example of O'Neill's experiments with Ger-

man EXPRESSIONISM, Bogard and others have pointed out that *The Hairy Ape* contains only one nonrealistic scene (on Fifth Avenue, where we see everything through Yank's eyes after the worshipers emerge from church), and O'Neill told his first biographer, Barrett H. Clark, that he wrote both plays before he'd seen or read any expressionist plays (Clark 84). Perhaps more useful as a touchstone to the play is O'Neill's description of Yank, in a 1921 letter to his friend Kenneth Macgowan, as "a man bewildered by the disharmony of his primitive pride and individualism at war with the mechanistic development of society" (Bryer 32). Viewed in this way, *The Hairy Ape* presents a classic theme of modern American drama: "[M]aterialistic America distorts and destroys the individual's spirit, destroying man's creative potential by divorcing him from those qualities of humanity which give him dignity and the sense of manhood" (Bogard 249)—a theme found in such other plays as ELMER RICE's *The ADDING MACHINE* (1923), JOHN HOWARD LAWSON's *PROCESSIONAL* (1925), CLIFFORD ODETS's *AWAKE AND SING!* (1935), and ARTHUR MILLER's *DEATH OF A SALESMAN* (1949). And, as C. W. E. Bigsby has noted, Yank can also be seen as an early absurdist figure, "suddenly dimly aware of the unbridgeable gulf between his simply conceived aspirations for harmony and order and the refusal of the world to manifest it. He is stranded in a world to which he cannot relate. He finds himself in a present which lacks any causal relation to the past" (62).

BIBLIOGRAPHY

Bigsby, C. W. E. *A Critical Introduction to Twentieth-Century American Drama: Volume One—1900–1940.* Cambridge, England: Cambridge University Press, 1982.

Bogard, Travis. *Contour in Time: The Plays of Eugene O'Neill.* Rev. ed. New York: Oxford University Press, 1988.

Bryer, Jackson R., ed. "*The Theatre We Worked For*": The Letters of Eugene O'Neill to Kenneth Macgowan. New Haven, Conn.: Yale University Press, 1982.

Clark, Barrett H. *Eugene O'Neill: The Man and His Plays.* Rev. ed. New York: Dover, 1947.

HANLEY, WILLIAM (1931–) See *SLOW DANCE ON THE KILLING GROUND*.

HANSBERRY,   LORRAINE   (1930–1965)

African-American dramatist and the first woman of color to have a play successfully produced on Broadway, Lorraine Hansberry was born on Chicago's South Side. She was the youngest of four children whose parents were well-educated, middle-class activists centrally engaged in the fight against racial discrimination. Early figures in the Civil Rights movement, including such luminaries as LANGSTON HUGHES, Paul Robeson, Duke Ellington, and W. E. B. DuBois were frequent visitors to the Hansberry home. Educated in Chicago schools prior to entering the University of Wisconsin in 1948, Hansberry spent two years studying drama there before leaving for New York City in 1950. Having spent her earliest years in Chicago's economically depressed black community, Hansberry had the unique experience of viewing American life from both sides of the economic and racial divide. Her family had lived in middle-class comfort and was one of the first black families to move into a white neighborhood, inspiring a court battle her father fought successfully all the way to the United States Supreme Court.

After she worked for a time as a reporter for a black newspaper, the experiences of her early life inspired the outstanding achievement of Hansberry's career, *A RAISIN IN THE SUN* (1959). Directed by Lloyd Richards and produced on Broadway with a large percent of its financing coming from the black community, *A Raisin in the Sun* opened on March 11, 1959, at New York's Ethel Barrymore Theatre, winning the New York Drama Critics' Circle Award (the first awarded to an African American) and running for an impressive 530 performances. The play's title is taken from Langston Hughes's poem "A Dream Deferred," which reflects on the shriveling of hopes among the American black population, a focus of the play. The Younger family—Lena, the matriarch, her grown daughter Beneatha, and her grown son Walter Lee, his wife Ruth, and their son Travis—share a cramped apartment in a poor, predominantly black Chicago neighborhood. The recent death of Lena's husband provides a ray of hope in the form of a $10,000 life insurance policy, arousing dreams in all of the members of the family: Lena wants to move to a nice suburban home where she can have a garden (a dream shared by Ruth), Beneatha wants to go to college to become a doctor and perhaps return to the family's roots in Africa, and Walter Lee wants to invest the money in a dubious partnership in a liquor store. Lena finds a house in an all-white neighborhood, but when the residents learn that a black family is moving in, they send an emissary, Lindner, to offer the Youngers money to keep them out. The family's response to the offer brings the climax and the resolution of the play. Critics were uniformly enthusiastic, and several of the stage actors reprised their roles in the well-received 1961 screen version, which, like the play, demonstrated Hansberry's skill at characterization and language, while also examining themes of contemporary significance. The play's greatest achievement may be that it educated a largely white Broadway audience about the realities of the lives of African Americans and the obstacles caused by prejudice and segregation.

Hansberry followed *A Raisin in the Sun* with *The Sign in Sidney Brustein's Window* (1964), which dealt with the turbulent lives of Greenwich Village intellectuals. It failed to attain the success of *A Raisin in the Sun,* and during its preparations Hansberry learned she was suffering from cancer. She died at the age of 34, a tragically premature death that robbed the American theater of an original voice, a significant pioneer in African-American drama, and a political activist. Following her death, Hansberry's white husband (and literary executor), writer and producer Robert Nemiroff, whom she had married in 1953, pieced together Hansberry's unfinished writings, *To Be Young, Gifted, and Black* (produced 1969) and *Les Blancs* (produced 1970), and he encouraged frequent revivals of *A Raisin in the Sun.* Ultimately, other pieces of previously unproduced (except as excerpts in *To Be Young, Gifted, and Black*) Hansberry works emerged, including a script commissioned in 1959 (but rejected as being too controversial) by NBC-TV for the 100th anniversary of the Civil War, *The Drinking Gourd.* It deals with the harsh conditions of slavery and its effects on a young black couple; Nemiroff published *The Drinking Gourd* and *What Use Are Flowers?* in 1972. In 1973, he and Charlotte Zaltzberg adapted *A Raisin in the Sun* into a musical, *Raisin,* which won the TONY AWARD for Best Musical and was revived successfully in 1981. There have also been several other significant revivals of *A Raisin in the Sun,* including 25th and 30th anniversary productions, and one acclaimed television film version starring Esther Rolle and Danny Glover in 1989.

BIBLIOGRAPHY

Bower, Martha Gilman. *Color Struck under the Gaze: The Pathology of Being in the Plays of Johnson, Hurston, Childress, Hansberry, and Kennedy.* Westport, Conn.: Greenwood Press, 2003.

Carter, Steven R. *Hansberry's Drama: Commitment amid Complexity.* Urbana: University of Illinois Press, 1991.

Cheney, Anne. *Lorraine Hansberry.* Boston: Twayne, 1984.

Effiong, Philip Uko. *In Search of a Model for African-American Drama: A Study of Selected Plays by Lorraine Hansberry, Amiri Baraka and Ntozake Shange.* Lanham, Md.: University Press of America, 2000.

Hansberry, Lorraine. *Les Blancs: The Collected Last Plays.* Edited by Robert Nemiroff. New York: Random House, 1994.

———. *A Raisin in the Sun/The Sign in Sidney Brustein's Window.* New York: Random House, 1995.

Leeson, Richard M. *Lorraine Hansberry: A Research and Production Sourcebook.* Westport, Conn.: Greenwood Press, 1997.

Nemiroff, Robert, ed. *To Be Young, Gifted, and Black: Lorraine Hansberry in Her Own Words.* Englewood Cliffs, N.J.: Prentice-Hall, 1969.

James Fisher
University of North Carolina at Greensboro

HARRIGAN, EDWARD (1844–1911)

Although he was born on New York's Lower East Side, Edward Harrigan's theatrical career began in San Francisco, where he joined the company of the well-known comedienne Lotta in 1867. After traveling the country, performing in a variety of roles in both theater and vaudeville, Harrigan's major success began when he met Tony Hart (Anthony Cannon) in Chicago and the two formed the vaudeville team Harrigan and Hart. Harrigan's comic writing skills were honed in more than 80 vaudeville sketches between 1870 and 1879, in which he wrote about such topics as politics, baseball, life insurance, the cakewalk, the army, and the militia. In the more than 40 full-length plays after that, mostly comedies based on the relations between competing ethnic groups in New York—the Irish, German, Italian, and Jewish immigrants, and African Americans who had come north to New York—during the enormous wave of immigration between 1848 and the turn of the century, Harrigan was given credit for advancing the realism of the American stage by such significant critics as WILLIAM DEAN HOWELLS, who praised him for creating local-color work in which he dramatized "the actual life of this city" at a time when the American stage was dominated by melodrama and farce.

Harrigan is best known for his cycle of plays based on the Mulligan family and their various ethnic neighbors. He wrote that in constructing a plot, he strove for the simple and natural, "just like what happens around us everyday," and he was commended for writing realistically and sympathetically about the city's "low life"—street cleaners, contractors, grocers, shysters, politicians, washerwomen, tradespeople, servant girls, teamsters, policemen, idlers, and gamesters—that made up the life of the city.

In the Mulligan plays, Harrigan played Dan Mulligan, a New York corner grocer who is the head of his clan and in whom Harrigan developed a complex character out of the traditional stage Irishman. Critic ARTHUR HOBSON QUINN described Dan as honest, courageous, loyal, impulsive, irrational, likely to become drunk and disorderly at slight provocation, and while also irascible and quarrelsome, forgiving and generous, even to his enemies. Tony Hart played female characters in the plays, most notably Rebecca Allup, the African-American cook who works for the Mulligans. Other ethnic types include the German butcher who is Mulligan's arch rival, the Jewish tailor, the African-American barber, and the Italian landlord. The first of the cycle was *The Mulligan Guard* (1873), which was followed by *The Mulligan Guard Picnic* (1878), *The Mulligan Guard Ball* (1879), *The Mulligan Guard Chowder* (1879), and *The Mulligan Guard Christmas* (1879), all of which feature clashes between ethnic groups that end in reconciliation. In *Cordelia's Aspirations* (1883) and *Dan's Tribulations* (1884), Harrigan attacked the subject of social climbing, creating a moral tale in which the social aspirations of Dan's wife Cordelia destroy the Mulligans' hard-won prosperity, and their happy life is restored only when they lose all their money and are forced to return to the old neighborhood and the simple life.

BIBLIOGRAPHY

Kahn, E. J. *The Merry Partners: The Age and Stage of Harrigan and Hart.* New York: Random House, 1955.

Moody, Richard. *Ned Harrigan: From Corlear's Hook to Herald Square.* Chicago: Nelson-Hall, 1980.

Brenda Murphy
University of Connecticut

HART, MOSS (1904–1961)

Born into poverty in the Bronx, playwright Moss Hart was introduced to the theater early in his life by an aunt who took him to two matinees a week. Hart dropped out of school after the seventh grade in order to go to work to help support the family. After holding several odd jobs, he came to work for theatrical manager Augustus Pitou, first as an errand boy and typist. Before long, he was asked to read some scripts and select one for a touring company; he found nothing good so he wrote his own, *The Hold-Up Man.* Pitou produced the play in two cities, where it flopped, causing Pitou to fire the 19-year-old Hart. However, he continued to work at jobs connected to theater, including acting and directing. He did not stop writing, but his plays—all of them serious—were rejected time and time again. When he finally turned to comedy, teaming with already established playwright GEORGE S. KAUFMAN, his career took off. Their first venture was *Once in a Lifetime* (1930), a satire on Hollywood at the time that sound films were developed.

With Kaufman, he won the 1937 PULITZER PRIZE for the comedy *YOU CAN'T TAKE IT WITH YOU* (1936), a farce about a household in which every occupant does exactly as he pleases. His other collaborations with Kaufman include *Merrily We Roll Along* (1934), a serious play about a playwright who sells out his ideals on the way to commercial success (Stephen Sondheim's 1981 musical of the same name is an updated version of this Kaufman and Hart play); *The Fabulous Invalid* (1938), about a New York theater haunted by the ghosts of a pair of actors who observe 38 years of successes and failures there; *The American Way* (1939), about a German immigrant family's loyalty to their new country; *The MAN WHO CAME TO DINNER* (1939), a comic farce about an impossibly self-centered houseguest (a character based in jest on writer and drama critic Alexander Woollcott) who turns a household upside-down; *George Washington Slept Here* (1940), a comedy about an urbanite who, longing for a place in the country, purchases a ramshackle farmhouse on the basis of its alleged historical significance; and the book for the Richard Rodgers and Lorenz Hart musical *I'd Rather Be Right* (1937), which satirizes Franklin D. Roosevelt and his New Deal policies.

Moss Hart collaborated on two musicals with Irving Berlin, *Face the Music* (1932) and *As Thousands Cheer* (1933). He also collaborated on musicals with Cole Porter—*Jubilee* (1935)—and with Kurt Weill—*Lady in the Dark* (1941). *Lady in the Dark,* about an insecure magazine editor and her psychiatric treatment, was Hart's biggest musical commercial success. His solo plays include *Winged Victory* (1943), about the United States Air Force's role in World War II; *Christopher Blake* (1946), about the psychological effects of divorce on a child; and *Light Up the Sky* (1948), a comedy about a playwright and all those connected with his play—whose support for him is, to say the least, fickle—waiting for opening night notices in a hotel suite.

Hart also wrote a dozen or so screenplays, including the classics *Gentleman's Agreement* (1947) and *A Star Is Born* (1954). In 1957, he won a TONY AWARD for his direction of the Lerner and Loewe musical *My Fair Lady.*

BIBLIOGRAPHY

Bach, Stephen. *The Life and Times of Moss Hart.* New York: Knopf, 2001.

Hart, Moss. *Act One: An Autobiography.* 1959. New York: St. Martin's Press, 1989.

———. *Christopher Blake.* New York: Random House, 1947.

———. *Light Up the Sky.* New York: Dramatists Play Service, 1950.

Kaufman, George S., and Moss Hart. *Six Plays by Kaufman and Hart.* New York: Random House, 1942.

HARVEY Mary Chase (1944) Chase is best
remembered for this Pulitzer Prize–winning comic
fantasy about a lovable drinker and his invisible companion, a six-and-a-half-foot white rabbit named
Harvey.

Veta Simmons and her daughter Myrtle Mae live
with Veta's brother, Elwood P. Dowd. Elwood has as
his constant companion—or so he claims—Harvey, a
"Pooka" or "fairy spirit in animal form . . . a wise and
mysterious creature. Very fond of rumpots [and]
crackpots." Veta and Myrtle Mae are mortified by
Elwood's behavior, especially because Veta is trying to
introduce young Myrtle Mae into the town's proper
and pretentious social set. Veta decides it is time to
have Elwood committed to a sanitarium for the
insane.

Shortly thereafter, while Elwood is escorted from a
taxi to a hydrotherapy tank, Veta explains her brother's condition to a young psychiatrist, Dr. Sanderson.
She admits confidentially that she sees Harvey herself
"once in a while," at which point Dr. Sanderson
becomes convinced that Veta is the patient and that
he has accidentally committed a sane man. Elwood is
sent for, so that apologies may ensue, while Veta,
kicking and screaming, is admitted to the sanitarium.
Comic scenes follow, and by the time the doctors figure out that Elwood is the patient, he has gone downtown, and Veta, having suffered many indignities, is
ready to sue "Chumley's Rest."

Dr. Chumley searches for Elwood, and when he
finds him, they go out drinking. This scene is not
played but is reported by Elwood to Dr. Sanderson
and his assistant Miss Kelly, when Elwood returns to
the sanitarium to pick them up for an evening out
they had arranged when Elwood was mistaken for a
sane man. He reports to them that when he and Dr.
Chumley *and Harvey* went out, the doctor and Harvey had much to talk about and that the last he saw
of them they were arguing about which bar to go to
next. Dr. Sanderson is more convinced than ever
that Elwood is insane and takes him "upstairs." After
they leave the room, Dr. Chumley arrives; following
his entrance, the door opens and closes again as if by
an unseen hand. It seems Harvey is following Dr.
Chumley.

Though Dr. Chumley now believes in Harvey, he
goes along with his younger colleague's plan to give
Elwood a shot that will rid him of his delusion. Finally,
it is Veta who puts a stop to Elwood's treatment when
the cab driver tells her that "after [the shot] he'll be a
perfectly normal human being and you know what
bastards they are!" Elwood's approach to life—always
kind, pleasant, considerate—seems saner than the
approach of those who are "responsibly" engaged in
the rat race. When Dr. Sanderson tells Elwood that he
must "face reality," Elwood answers, "I wrestled with
reality for forty years, and I am happy to state that I
finally won out over it."

Thomas P. Adler suggests that the play makes the
point "that surface reality tells only a part of the story,
and those who accept only experiential, empirical
knowledge, who attempt to remove all mystery and
magic in life, become fools rather than wise" (25).
Adler also writes that in a year when Tennessee Williams's *The Glass Menagerie* premiered, the fact that
Harvey won the Pulitzer Prize instead of Williams's
classic is a testament to the "escapist mood of the war
years that favored entertainment and forgetfulness
above all else" (24). Even if Adler is right, *Harvey* continues to delight audiences.

BIBLIOGRAPHY
Adler, Thomas P. *Mirror on the Stage: The Pulitzer Plays as an
Approach to American Drama.* West Lafayette, Ind.: Purdue
University Press, 1987.

HASTY HEART, THE John Patrick (1945)
Patrick's first major success, *The Hasty Heart* was
inspired by the playwright's experiences in military
field hospitals during World War II. He served in
Egypt, India, Burma, and Syria as a captain and an
ambulance driver with the American Field Service
and the British Army. Adding to his military hospital
experience was the fact that, while in the service, he
contracted malaria twice.

The play consists of three acts set in a British con-
valescent ward along the Burma front. Through teasing and friendly banter, Patrick establishes the
camaraderie shared by the patients and their nurse,
Margaret. The patients reflect the diversity of the British Empire: Digger, the Australian; Kiwi, the New

Zealander; Tommy, the Brit; and an African who neither speaks nor understands English. An American nicknamed Yank, who speaks often of his overbearing Scottish grandfather, completes the group.

In the first act, the Colonel who oversees the hospital approaches Margaret and the men to tell them about a dying Scotsman; Lachlen McLachlen, who lost a kidney after being wounded and whose remaining kidney is defective, will die within a few weeks. The Colonel asks the men to befriend "Lachie" in order to make his final weeks more comfortable; however, the Scot remains ignorant of his fate, and when he enters the ward, he immediately alienates the others with his brusque, isolated demeanor. Still, Margaret reaches out to Lachie and urges her patients to do the same.

In act 2, Margaret reveals her plan to surprise Lachie on his birthday with a full regimental ensemble, including a kilt. The Scot, deeply touched, then makes tentative friendly overtures toward the others. Within a few days, Lachie is transformed and engages in unending conversation. He reveals his affection for and desire to help his new friends. Margaret encourages him, and, as the act closes, she kisses him.

Lachie dons his kilt in act 3 for group photographs taken in honor of Yank's pending departure. The two men discuss Margaret's kiss, and Lachie decides to propose to her. She accepts, but when the Colonel reveals Lachie's prognosis to him, the Scot returns to angry isolation. Thus, when army leaders offer to ship Lachie back to Scotland as a well-publicized hero, he accepts. At the last moment, however, Lachie recognizes his mistake and opts to remain among his friends. His decision emphasizes Patrick's theme that people cannot live in isolation but are interdependent, needing love, friendship, and encouragement.

The Hasty Heart is one of many postwar plays depicting the experience and effects of World War II. Others include Arthur Miller's *All My Sons* (1947) and Arthur Laurents's *Home of the Brave* (1945); comedies include Thomas Heggen and Joshua Logan's *Mister Roberts* (1948) and Patrick's own Pulitzer Prize–winning *The Teahouse of the August Moon* (1953).

Sarah Reuning and Robin Seaton Brown
University of North Carolina–Chapel Hill

HATFUL OF RAIN, A Michael Gazzo (1955)

A Hatful of Rain deals with the devastating impact of drug addiction on a family. Johnny, a married veteran holding down a job and hoping to use the GI Bill to get an education, is the favorite son of his visiting father. Polo, Johnny's brother, lives with Johnny and his pregnant wife, Celia. Their father blames Polo for the loss of the $2,500 he hoped to invest in his business, but Polo alone knows the truth: Johnny is a junkie, and all the money went to support his habit. Furthermore, Johnny is in debt to drug dealers for an additional $700 and has lost his job for making too many mistakes.

Johnny's problem began in a veteran's hospital, where he became addicted to morphine; he kicked the habit once with the help of his brother, but he is hooked again and now has a $40-a-day habit. Unaware of her husband's addiction, Celia believes that he must have another woman since he has withdrawn from her. Indeed, so unfulfilled are her sexual needs that she is tempted by her brother-in-law Polo, who is in love with her.

The two brothers have a strained relationship with their father even under the best of circumstances. When their mother died during their childhood, he put them in a home and later placed them with various aunts, uncles, and foster parents. Polo, loyal to his brother, tells neither Celia nor his father about Johnny's addiction, though he angrily urges Johnny to tell them himself.

Meanwhile, the police are sweeping the city looking for pushers, leaving Johnny desperate for a fix. He finally reveals his addiction to his wife and father and vows to quit if his brother will help him again, but Celia insists that the illness cannot be conquered that way and calls the police, hoping to get Johnny placed in a facility for addicts in Kentucky. Celia's phone call ends the play.

In addition to the theme of drug addiction and its devastating effects is another theme, not fully developed but given voice by Celia and her father-in-law; this secondary theme involves the state of mind of Americans in the cold war era of the mid-1950s. Johnny's father feels no one believes in anything anymore and that they live in the "age of the vacuum." He says,

"People look lost to me. All I see is movement." Celia argues that such talk and mention of the "white light" of nuclear war make her "blood boil." Expecting a child herself, she feels that it is enough to live for one's children and laments the pessimism of her era, which she fears will keep people from wanting children.

HAZEL KIRKE Steele Mackaye (1880)
Set in England, this drama about a young woman who marries for love despite her father's wishes is considered a milestone in the early development of American dramatic realism. By today's standards, *Hazel Kirke* is a very conventional melodrama, but taken in the context of its day, it represents a departure from the convention of personifying evil in a single character, the Villain.

The title character is the beautiful and charming miller's daughter. When Hazel was 14, a bargain was struck between her father and the local land owner, Squire Rodney—then in his forties—that in return for rescuing the mill from financial ruin, Rodney would have Hazel for his wife when she comes of age. Hazel was sent away to school at Rodney's expense. When the play opens, Hazel has been home for six months and for one month now has been nursing back to health a handsome young man, Arthur Carringford, who is, unbeknownst to the Kirkes, a lord. Arthur was rescued from drowning by Hazel's father. Hazel and Arthur have fallen in love, though they have not yet declared their love to one another; this is a dilemma for the good and already betrothed Hazel.

Enter the lively and eccentric Pittacus "Pitty" Green, inventor of silly puns, who provides the comic relief in the play. Pitty recognizes Carringford as Lord Travers. He confides in Dolly, Hazel's cousin, with whom he quickly forms an attachment. The two interfere by revealing the young couple's feelings to Squire Rodney and to Hazel's mother, Mercy. Both are understanding, and Rodney releases Hazel from her promise to him; however, both Rodney and Mercy fear the "iron will" of Hazel's father, who would rather "bury her wi' [his] own hands than have her faithless to her word." The interference of Pitty and Dolly forces the young couple to admit their love. Hazel's father discovers the situation and commands Hazel to throw out Arthur Carringford. When she refuses, he curses and disowns her.

Act 2 begins a year later; Hazel is married to Arthur Carringford, Lord Travers. They are happy, though estranged from their families. Soon, Squire Rodney and Pitty Green (now engaged to Dolly) come independently of one another in outrage to confront Carringford. It seems he and Hazel are not really married because the "Scottish marriage" took place on the English side of the border and was therefore illegal. This is news to the innocent Carringford, whose servant, Barney, made the arrangements for the marriage and assumed his master could only mean for him to arrange a mock marriage since the bride was a mere peasant. Carringford immediately runs off (without telling Hazel) to fetch a curate to perform a legal ceremony and restore his wife's honor.

Meanwhile, Lady Travers, Carringford's mother, arrives. She tells Hazel to leave Arthur and tells her about the invalid marriage. Hazel is shocked: "He, Arthur, my brave, gentle Arthur, has deceived me, betrayed me, and I trusted him as though he were a god. Oh, my heart is breaking. *She sobs.*" Lady Travers explains that Arthur was promised by his father to Lady Maud, whom he must marry for the sake of family honor and financial security. (Arthur's father lost Maud's father's fortune, and now that Maud is old enough, the way out for both families is marriage.) Hazel departs, declaring, "I go to cover up his infamy with my shame—and may heaven forgive you all!"— at which point Lady Travers, who has been ill for years, drops dead.

Act 3 begins one month later. Everyone shows up at the mill looking for Hazel, who has been missing since her encounter with Lady Travers. Hazel eventually arrives after dark, unseen by anyone except Rodney who is, as ever, kind and generous to her. Her father, now blind, denounces her again to Rodney within her hearing, and she flees to the river to drown herself.

In act 4, we learn that Hazel has been saved from drowning by a faithful servant and by her husband, who—it turns out—is indeed her husband. It seems Barney was bad at geography: The inn was in Scotland and the ceremony, legal. Carringford reports that on his mother's death he instructed his lawyers to restore all lost family money to Lady Maud; this leaves him penniless, except for "the endless wealth of [his] love for [Hazel]." In the end, the "iron willed" Mr. Kirke (who has been blind—figuratively and literally) sees his way to forgive and accept his only child.

Certainly, this play sounds like a conventional and rather silly melodrama by today's standards, yet *Hazel Kirke* is recognized as a significant step in the development of American drama toward realism. Brenda Murphy, in her *American Realism and American Drama, 1880–1940,* explains that despite its sensational and convoluted plot and its melodramatic conventions, *Hazel Kirke* is a precursor of realism because "[i]t is not a single evil force [i.e., the stock villain in a melodrama] in a community of good people that is at fault here but the evil of character that places the human heart at the mercy of the human will, . . . or the evil of social conventions that allow parents to barter away their children in order to meet their pecuniary obligations and then believe they must hold to the bargain because of a perversely inflated ideal of honor" (7).

BIBLIOGRAPHY

Murphy, Brenda. *American Realism and American Drama, 1880–1940.* New York: Cambridge University Press, 1987.

HE AND SHE RACHEL CROTHERS (1920)

One of the most commercially successful playwrights of her day, CROTHERS initially wrote *He and She* in 1912 (originally produced in Boston as *The Herfords*), later revising it and performing the leading role herself in the New York production. In the play, Crothers analyzes a woman's decision to give up her career to devote herself to being a housewife and mother.

Ann and Tom Herford are both sculptors, and their marriage seems successful and happy. Tom is proud of being enlightened and liberal, but when they both compete for a $100,000 prize and the possibility of executing a large frieze and Ann wins, she is shocked and hurt by her husband's conservative response. He tells her—actually, he orders her—to give up the commission and says he will never touch a penny of her money. Her relatives and friends, with the exception of another career woman, tell her she has behaved deplorably. Ann accuses her father of always condemning her for working and never believing in her ability. Now that she has proven herself, she thinks he should be proud of her, but he continues to say that a woman should devote herself to her husband and children and that nothing else is important. Her father also tells her that no man could take the blow that her husband has been given.

Ann is determined to go forward with her work when her daughter suddenly runs away from boarding school. Sixteen-year-old Millicent feels her mother has ignored her, and she wants to run off and marry the school chauffeur. When the other girls went home for a vacation, she had to stay at school, and it was then that she began the inappropriate relationship. Ann resolves to give up her career and care for her child. She says she knows how unhappy she will be and speaks of her aspirations and how proud she would have been to create the frieze. She knows she has to do her duty and asks Tom to create the sculpture.

Paralleling her situation is that of her friend Ruth who has a successful career but is engaged to a man who will not let her work after they marry. Ruth does not want to have children and thinks she and Keith could be happy if he would only be more liberal in his views. Finally, she realizes he will not change and breaks off their engagement. Tom's sister, Daisy, is a woman with conventional views who works only because she has to support herself. At the end of the play, Keith decides he will marry Daisy because her views about the role of a wife are more acceptable than Ruth's.

The play came at a time when many women were moving into careers. Despite the contrived and conventional ending, Crothers's exploration of the problems facing a mother with a career and the problem of the double standard faced by all women was compelling.

Yvonne Shafer
St. John's University

HECHT, BEN (1894–1964)

A prolific writer of nonfiction, fiction, plays, and films, Ben Hecht is best known in the theater world for *The FRONT PAGE* (1928), one of several plays he wrote in collaboration with Charles MacArthur.

Born in New York City and raised in Racine, Wisconsin, Hecht never attended college but was an avid reader. Soon after high school, he became a reporter in Chicago, first for the *Chicago Journal* (1910–14) and then as foreign correspondent and columnist as well as reporter for the *Chicago Daily News* (1914–23). In Chicago, he eventually became associated with a literary circle that included Sherwood Anderson, Theodore Dreiser, Carl Sandburg, and Margaret Anderson, who, as editor of the *Little Review,* published some of Hecht's early stories.

Hecht began to write one-act plays in Chicago in collaboration with Kenneth S. Goodman. Their play *The Wonder Hat* (1916) was produced in Detroit, and *The Hero of Santa Maria* (1917) was performed in New York. Hecht wrote his first full-length play alone: *The Egotist* (1922), about a playwright who fancies himself a great lover, was produced in New York to negative reviews. His other solo plays include *To Quito and Back* (1937), *Christmas Eve* (1939), *Lily of the Valley* (1942), *We Will Never Die* (1943) *A Flag Is Born* (1946), *Hazel Flagg* (1953)—a musical—and *Winkelberg* (1958), none of which was received with much critical acclaim.

Though he collaborated with others, it was Hecht's partnership with Charles MacArthur, a fellow Chicago journalist, that brought him his biggest theatrical success. Based on their shared experience as newspaper reporters, *The Front Page* is a comedy that satirizes politicians and law enforcement as well as the cynical inhabitants of the newsroom. The reviews this time were favorable. The partnership with MacArthur produced five other works. Together, they wrote *Twentieth Century* (1932), a satire about theater people; *Jumbo* (1935), a Rodgers and Hart musical set in a circus; *Ladies and Gentlemen* (1939), adapted from a work by Ladislaus Bus-Fekete and centering around a murder trial and jury deliberations; *Fun to Be Free* (1941), which features conversations with historical American leaders; and the very unsuccessful *Swan Song* (1946), adapted from Ramon Romero and Harriett Hinsdale's *Crescendo,* about a pianist who is murdered by her jealous brother.

Hecht wrote 11 novels, but his nonfiction collections of newspaper columns, *1001 Afternoons in Chicago* (1922) and *1001 Afternoons in New York* (1941), were among his most popular works. (The line between fiction and nonfiction, however, was not absolute for Hecht, who confessed in his autobiography, *A Child of the Century* [1954], that much of his human interest "reporting" was made up.) Other notable nonfiction includes *A Guide for the Bedevilled* (1944), an analysis of anti-Semitism, and *Charlie: The Improbable Life and Times of Charles MacArthur* (1957).

Hecht was also a prolific screenwriter, with 60 films to his credit. He received Academy Awards for *Underworld* (1927) and *The Scoundrel* (1934)—the latter coauthored by Charles MacArthur—and Academy Award nominations for four other screenplays.

BIBLIOGRAPHY
Fetherling, Doug. *The Five Lives of Ben Hecht.* Toronto: Lester & Orpen, 1977.
Hecht, Ben. *1001 Afternoons in Chicago.* 1922. Chicago: University of Chicago Press, 1992.
———. *1001 Afternoons in New York.* New York: Viking, 1941.
———. *Charlie: The Improbable Life and Times of Charles MacArthur.* New York: Harper, 1957.
———. *A Child of the Century.* New York: Simon and Schuster, 1954.
———, and Kenneth S. Goodman. *"The Wonder Hat" and Other One-Act Plays.* New York: Appleton, 1925.
Hecht, Ben, and Charles MacArthur. *The Front Page.* New York: Covici-Friede, 1928.
MacAdams, William. *Ben Hecht: The Man behind the Legend.* New York: Scribners, 1990.

HEIDI CHRONICLES, THE WENDY WASSERSTEIN (1988)

Winner of the PULITZER PRIZE and the TONY AWARD, WASSERSTEIN'S play chronicles the experiences, from high school to midlife, of Heidi Holland, a baby boomer who struggles with expectations for women before, during, and after the women's movement of the 1970s.

The play begins in 1989 as Heidi Holland, an art historian, gives a slide lecture on neglected women painters. A painting from 1869, *We Both Must Fade,* "a meditation on the brevity of youth, beauty and life," reminds her of herself in high school, and so begins a series of scenes spanning her life. The awkwardness of a Chicago high school dance in 1965, attended with her outgoing friend Susan, is made less excruciating by her first encounter with witty Peter Patrone, who will become her lifelong soulmate. Next, Heidi, a college student in 1968, campaigns for liberal presidential candidate Eugene McCarthy and meets her first lover, Scoop Rosenbaum; charming and unfaithful, Scoop is the editor of a radical newspaper, *The Liberated Earth News.* Heidi spends the summer following college seeing old movies with Peter, who is about to enter medical school as she is about to enter a Yale graduate program. Her affair with Scoop continues at Yale, where he is in law school.

In 1970, when Heidi visits her old friend, Susan, in Ann Arbor, she attends her first women's group meeting. At first reluctant to join in, she finally admits that Scoop is not good for her: "I keep allowing this guy to account for so much of what I think of myself. . . . And . . . I know that's wrong." Heidi expresses her longing for change in the way women view themselves as she turns to another woman at the meeting—one who serves her boyfriend slavishly and is made to feel as if she is inadequate: "I hope our daughters never feel like us. I hope our daughters feel so . . . worthwhile."

In 1974, Heidi is demonstrating for equal representation of women artists at the Museum of Fine Arts in Chicago. Peter, now a pediatrician, comes to meet her at the demonstration. They talk of Scoop, with whom she is still involved, on and off. Peter's big revelation, not easy for him to tell or for Heidi to hear, is that he is gay. Heidi feels some anger at Peter "for not being desperately and hopelessly in love with" her. Aside from the personal revelations, also important to the scene is the fact that Heidi finds irritating the position of some members of the women's movement that the movement should be exclusively female. When one of her fellow demonstrators makes clear that Peter cannot march for women's art because his maleness disqualifies him, Heidi says, "I thought our point was that this is *our* cultural institution. 'Our' meaning everybody's. Men and women."

At his 1977 wedding to Lisa, Scoop tells Heidi that he could not marry Heidi because she wants "to go out into the world each day and attempt to get an 'A'" and because she wants "self-fulfillment" and "self-determination"; in other words, she wants exactly what he wants, and his position is that they cannot both have that. This is one of the dilemmas that Wasserstein articulates in the play: The women's movement enabled women to break into a world previously held by men, but men had not changed enough to see them as equal partners *in life.* Scoop could not marry Heidi because they would be in competition with one another; he needed a woman who would devote her life to him.

In the later 1980s, the women-can-have-it-all myth takes hold so firmly that if a woman does not have it all, she feels "worthless," despite whatever accomplishments she has to her credit. Heidi is not happy, and when she goes to tell her woes to Peter, he tells her that "a sadness like [hers] seems a luxury" compared to the AIDS epidemic, which surrounds him and has claimed so many of his friends and is about to claim his lover. Again, Wasserstein addresses the complex realities of the period instead of taking a simplistic feminist approach.

In the end, Heidi adopts a baby. Feminists took aim at this resolution to the play and its suggestion that only in the conventional female role of mother can a woman find true happiness and fulfillment. However, as we recall Heidi's words at the feminist meeting in Chicago early in the play—"I hope our daughters never feel like us. I hope our daughters feel so . . . worthwhile."—it seems quite possible that the meaning of the ending is that it is the daughters raised by women of Heidi's generation who will truly reap the benefits of the women's movement. Wasserstein herself had this to say about the adoption of the baby at the end of the play in an interview at the Smithsonian Institution on October 9, 1991: "That was the right choice for Heidi, for her as a person" (Bryer 267). Wasserstein's character, then, does not, and was never intended to, represent *all* women.

BIBLIOGRAPHY
Bryer, Jackson R., ed. *The Playwright's Art: Conversations with Contemporary American Dramatists.* New Brunswick, N.J.: Rutgers University Press, 1995.

HEIFNER, JACK (1946–) Playwright Jack Heifner was born in Texas and earned a B.F.A. at Southern Methodist University. He is best known for his very successful play *Vanities* (1976), which was the longest-running OFF-BROADWAY play (nonmusical) in history; it ran for five years. Set in Texas, *Vanities* is a comedy/drama about three high school cheerleaders growing apart through college and into adulthood. When they reunite several years after college, their lives filled with disillusionment, they can no longer connect. *Patio/Porch* (1978), two one-act plays performed together, involves two pairs of unhappy southern women—two sisters with little in common and a miserable mother and daughter; while *Vanities* was still running, this play closed in its third week. Heifner's one-act *Bargains* appeared in *The Best Short Plays of 1988*.

Since 1999, Heifner has developed more than a dozen plays at the Playwright Project, a summer program in Healing Springs, North Carolina; these include *Blessed Unrest, Brilliants, China Dolls, Comfort and Joy, Dwarf Tossing, Earth to Bucky, The Gulf, Hate Mail, Heartbreak, Here She Is, Jumping for Joy*, and *The Lemon Cookie*—some of which have been produced around the country.

In 2007, Heifner created a musical adaptation of his most successful play, *Vanities*. In the musical version, the playwright imagines what becomes of the three protagonists—women who come of age during the upheaval and change of the 1960s and the women's movement—as they enter their 40s. Heifner calls the new ending in which the women come to value their friendship less cynical than his original ending.

Heifner has also collaborated on six other musicals, including *Leader of the Pack* (1985), and has written for television and film. He teaches in the Department of Theatre at Stephen F. Austin State University in Texas.

HEIRESS, THE RUTH AND AUGUSTUS GOETZ (1947)

Based on Henry James's 1880 novel *Washington Square, The Heiress* is set in New York City in the 1850s. Catherine Sloper, shy and plain, lives with her exacting father and her widowed aunt when a charming idler enters her life, hoping to win her fortune through marriage.

To her father, who lost his beloved, beautiful, and charming wife in childbirth, Catherine is "an entirely mediocre and defenseless creature with not a shred of poise." When Morris Townsend, a dashing young man of no means and little ambition, is introduced into the household, Dr. Sloper is certain that his interest in Catherine is purely mercenary. Within days, Catherine has agreed to marry Townsend. Dr. Sloper interviews Townsend's sister, who is protective and forgiving of her charming younger brother's faults, which include his failure to help her, a widow with many children. She refuses to disparage him, but neither can she dispute his apparent idleness and selfishness.

Catherine has inherited a very comfortable income ($10,000 a year) from her mother, but it is her father's money that enables them to live in tasteful luxury. Reminding Catherine that if she marries against his wishes he will disinherit her, Dr. Sloper takes her to Europe for six months so that she will forget Morris Townsend. However, Morris has a powerful ally in Catherine's romantic Aunt Penniman, and he keeps his connection with the household during Catherine's absence—enjoying the doctor's excellent cigars and brandy, as well as his exquisitely appointed drawing room. Together, Morris and the silly old woman have plotted an elopement to take place as soon as Catherine returns.

When Catherine is still determined to marry Morris upon their return, her father sarcastically remarks that her "gaiety and brilliance will have to make up the difference between the ten thousand a year [she] will have and the thirty thousand [Morris] expects." He tries to dissuade her by bluntly telling her that there is only one reason a handsome young man could have for wishing to marry her since "a hundred [girls] are prettier, and a thousand more clever." Devastated by her father's opinion of her, Catherine decides to break irrevocably from him. She begs Morris to marry her that night, explaining that she wishes to have nothing more to do with her father. Morris agrees to return at half past midnight, but knowing that Catherine's value is now only ten thousand a year, he does not return. An inconsolable Catherine is sure now that no one has or ever will love her.

When act 2 begins, two years have passed and Dr. Sloper has died. Morris returns; having failed at his endeavors in New Orleans and California, he hopes to marry Catherine now that the full fortune is securely hers. She lets him think she is willing, only to leave him knocking and calling her name at the front door as she climbs the stairs to bed. She has—as she tells her Aunt Penniman—been "taught" this kind of cruelty "by masters."

The Goetzes' adaptation of Henry James's classic tale of psychological cruelty and revenge was the most commercially and critically successful of their dramatizations of novels, which include adaptations of André Gide's *The Immoralist* in 1954 and Storm Jameson's *The Hidden River* in 1957.

HELL-BENT FER HEAVEN HATCHER HUGHES (1924)

Set in the Appalachian Mountain region of western North Carolina, *Hell-Bent fer Heaven* centers on Rufe Pryor, a religious zealot who uses pious platitudes to try to win the hand of Jude Lowry, while using violence to manipulate others who threaten his plan.

Sid Hunt has returned home from World War I a hero. He sets his sights on Jude Lowery, whom he had wooed before leaving for Europe. Rufe Pryor, who earned an "edzemption" from the war and took a job as a clerk in Matt Hunt's store in Sid's absence, uses Andy Lowry, Jude's weak-minded, violent-tempered brother, as a pawn to rekindle an old feud between the Lowrys and the Hunts. Rufe hopes Andy will murder Sid and clear a path to Jude for Rufe. Although several characters in the play suspect Rufe of hypocrisy and point out his inherited traits of cowardice and laziness, Rufe manages to keep his machinations secret. Rufe also appeals to the base religious convictions of Meg Hunt (Sid's mother) and Jude, often inspiring these women by making emotional speeches about the will of God, which enable him to continue his plot without arousing their suspicion.

Andy does in fact attempt to shoot Sid offstage, and the appearance of the latter's horse without its rider arouses the anger of the Hunts, who go looking for Andy, leaving Rufe alone to face Sid when he returns. Sid discovers Rufe's plot and announces he will use the phone underneath the dam, which protects the residents of the region from the river, to alert Andy's family of Rufe's actions. Claiming the will of God is at work, Rufe uses dynamite to destroy the dam, hoping to kill Sid. The explosion does not kill Sid, although it does release the water from the dam. This, coupled with a raging storm, brings the river to a life-threatening level. Rufe's actions are ultimately exposed by Sid, who manages to get him to admit his schemes, finally convincing Meg to turn against the hypocrite. Ultimately, the Hunts escape sure death and leave Rufe alone to die in the flood. Astonishingly, Rufe attempts to trick God into performing a miracle that will enable him to live, then curses his creator when death is imminent.

Winner of the 1924 PULITZER PRIZE, Hughes's drama is a classic example of folk drama, a subset of the realistic melodrama that dominated the period. The play has virtually disappeared in contemporary academia because its intense melodrama and its Appalachian speech patterns do not appeal to modern audiences, nor is it particularly distinguishable from the countless other melodramatic works of the time. Still, it is interesting to note that the lives of Rufe Pryor and people like him were considered worthy of stage examination and taken seriously by the New York critics at the time of its production.

Christopher Brooks Bell
Georgia Military College

HELLMAN, LILLIAN (1905–1984)

Lillian Hellman came to detest the collaborative demands and tensions of the theater, but 32 of her 50 unusually public years in American life were devoted primarily to dramatic writing. In addition to eight original plays and four adaptations for Broadway, she wrote screenplays for Hollywood studios, directed three Broadway productions of her work, reported for newspapers and magazines on a broad range of topics, edited the letters of playwright Anton Chekhov and the stories of mystery writer Dashiell Hammett, and, in her plays and memoirs, provided the source material for another five films and an opera.

The only child of Julia Newhouse and Max Hellman, she lived in New Orleans until age six, when business failure precipitated the family's move to New York City. For the next decade, Hellman spent half the year in New York and the other half in a New Orleans boardinghouse run by two paternal aunts, attending school in both cities. She studied for two years at New York University without completing a degree. In 1925, she married press agent Arthur Kober and, in 1930, accompanied him to Hollywood where she read scripts for Metro-Goldwyn-Mayer Studios and met novelist Dashiell Hammett, author of *The Thin Man* (in which the character of Nora Charles is loosely based on Hellman) and *The Maltese Falcon*. Hammett remained the central figure in her life in what Hellman identified as "thirty-one on and off years" of a volatile relationship. She and Kober divorced in 1932, and she never remarried.

Hellman invited—many would say she thrived upon—controversy. She was thrust into the limelight at age 29 by fierce attempts to censor *The CHILDREN'S HOUR*, which opened on Broadway in 1934 but was banned in other American cities, including Boston and Chicago. The furor surrounding Hellman's inclusion of lesbianism as a thematic issue almost certainly deprived *The Children's Hour* of its anticipated PULITZER PRIZE for drama, and, more significantly, it obscured the play's principal subjects: the destructive power of gossip and (as the Hellman-directed 1952 Broadway revival made explicit) the political ends to which such gossip can be put.

Hellman shifted from the Ibsen-influenced structure and topicality of her most familiar plays (*The Children's Hour* [1934], *The LITTLE FOXES* [1939], *Watch on the Rhine* [1941] and *Another Part of the Forest* [1946]) to Chekhovian character analysis (*The AUTUMN GARDEN* [1951] and *TOYS IN THE ATTIC* [1960]) and experimentation with dramatic form in her stage adaptations (*Montserrat* [1949], *The Lark* [1955], the Leonard Bernstein operetta *Candide* [1956], for which she cowrote the libretto, and *My Mother, My Father and Me* [1963]). Money—the awfulness of not having it, its corrupting influence when you get it—is a prominent subject in her plays, notably *The Little Foxes, The Autumn Garden,* and *Toys in the Attic.*

With few exceptions, Hellman's plays enjoyed substantial Broadway runs and international attention. In *Watch on the Rhine,* she expressed her characteristic loathing for those who (as a character in *The Little Foxes* puts it) "stand around and watch" while others "eat the earth." Arguing for United States intervention in World War II, *Watch on the Rhine* opened on Broadway just eight months before the bombing of Pearl Harbor, thus ensuring its place as one of the most prescient plays in the history of the American theater. It was given a Washington, D.C., command performance in honor of President Franklin D. Roosevelt's birthday in 1942 and became a rallying cry for the war effort. *Watch on the Rhine* won the New York Drama Critics' Circle Award as Best American Play. (Hellman won this award a second time, for *Toys in the Attic,* two decades later.)

Hellman coproduced (with Ernest Hemingway and others) the documentary film *The Spanish Earth* (1937). Her screenplays include *The Dark Angel* (1935), *Dead End* (1937), *The Chase* (1966), and several film adaptations of her own plays, notably *The Little Foxes* (1941) and the first, substantially censored, version of *The Children's Hour,* entitled *These Three* (1936). (Hellman did not write the screenplay for the accurately plotted and titled remake, *The Children's Hour* [1962], which starred Audrey Hepburn and Shirley MacLaine as the two schoolteachers.)

In the 1960s and 1970s, her reputation soared. Hellman received numerous honorary degrees, taught writing seminars at Harvard and other universities, and won major awards, including the Gold Medal for Drama from the National Institute of Arts and Letters (1964) and the National Book Award (1970) for her memoir *An Unfinished Woman.* Hellman detested the "woman playwright" label frequently attached to her, but, characteristically, she denied that her memoirs certified her as a feminist. Those memoirs, *An Unfinished Woman* (1969) and *Pentimento* (1973), were nevertheless embraced by the women's movement, contributing to her reemergence as a cultural heroine 20 years after her blacklisting in Hollywood for alleged pro-Communist sympathies.

Hellman had been subpoenaed to appear before the House Committee on Un-American Activities in 1952. In a highly publicized letter employing a metaphor with which she became permanently identified, she expressed a willingness to discuss herself but refused to answer questions regarding others: "I cannot and will not cut my conscience to fit this year's fashions [of naming names]," she wrote. *Scoundrel Time* (1976), her third memoir, portrayed events surrounding her courageous stand before the House Committee on Un-American Activities, but it reopened unhealed cold war wounds, provoking attacks on Hellman by intellectuals she criticized in the book. Her belligerent response in *Three* (1979), the collected edition of her memoirs, escalated the level of rancor and led to charges in the early 1980s by writers Mary McCarthy (whom Hellman sued for libel) and Martha Gellhorn (whom she did not) that Hellman was a liar who had misrepresented herself in her memoir self-portraits, particularly in the "Julia" chapter of *Pentimento.* Hellman died before her libel suit against McCarthy came to trial.

Lillian Hellman's work includes two of the most enduring, frequently performed plays in American dramatic literature: *The Children's Hour* and *The Little Foxes.* Her politically charged subjects are driven by suspenseful plots and pungent dialogue, rich in caustic humor. In Hellman's universe, diabolical behavior is exposed to moral condemnation—but not before her characters' skullduggery is also revealed to be uncommonly entertaining.

BIBLIOGRAPHY

Bryer, Jackson R., ed. *Conversations with Lillian Hellman.* Jackson: University Press of Mississippi, 1986.
Estrin, Mark W., ed. *Critical Essays on Lillian Hellman.* Boston: G. K. Hall, 1989.
———. *Lillian Hellman: Plays, Films, Memoirs. A Reference Guide.* Boston: G. K. Hall, 1980.
Feibleman, Peter. *Lilly: Reminiscences of Lillian Hellman.* New York: William Morrow, 1988.
Hellman, Lillian. *The Collected Plays.* Boston: Little, Brown, 1972.
———. *Six Plays.* New York: Vintage, 1979.
———. *Three: "An Unfinished Woman," "Pentimento," "Scoundrel Time."* Boston: Little, Brown, 1979.
Horn, Barbara Lee. *Lillian Hellman: A Research and Production Sourcebook.* Westport, Conn.: Greenwood, 1998.
Mahoney, Rosemary. *A Likely Story: One Summer with Lillian Hellman.* New York: Doubleday, 1998.
Mellen, Joan. *Hellman and Hammett: The Legendary Passion of Lillian Hellman and Dashiell Hammett.* New York: Harper-Collins, 1996.
Rollyson, Carl. *Lillian Hellman: Her Legend and Her Legacy.* New York: St. Martin's, 1988.
Wright, William. *Lillian Hellman: The Image, the Woman.* New York: Simon and Schuster, 1986.

Mark W. Estrin
Rhode Island College

HENLEY, BETH (1952–)

Beth Henley was born in Jackson, Mississippi, earned her B.F.A. in 1974 from Southern Methodist University (SMU), and did graduate work at the University of Illinois in 1975 and 1976. While an acting major at SMU, she discovered the works of Anton Chekhov, Samuel Beckett, George Bernard Shaw, and William Shakespeare as live theater.

The dramatic world of Beth Henley is a mixture of bizarre tragedy and pathetic comedy, with most of her plays deeply rooted in the southern oral tradition. A strong sense of family, the ability to make the improbable real, a grotesque mixture of humor and horror, the laying on of gothic overtones, the appreciation of eccentricity no matter how bizarre, the use of southern vernacular in a particular setting are all hallmarks of Henley's scripts for stage and screen. Critics frequently celebrate her work by praising the complexity of her characters, the preciseness of her dialogue, the weird humor of her southern grotesqueries, the subtlety of her exposition, and the richness of small details.

Am I Blue (1974) is the story of a 16-year-old, dreamy urchin, Ashbe Williams, who meets 18-year-old fraternity boy John Polk Richards in the squalid section of New Orleans, where they confess their insecurities and loneliness to each other and form a tentative bond of affection. CRIMES OF THE HEART (1979) celebrates the MaGrath sisters gathered together in Hazlehurst, Mississippi: Babe, the youngest, has just shot her powerful and abusive husband in the stomach because, as she so bluntly explains, "I didn't like his stinking looks"; Meg, the middle sister, has just returned from her failure to launch a singing career in Hollywood; and Lenny, the eldest, is celebrating her

30th birthday, very much aware that there is no man waiting in the wings for her. Henley's first successful play, *Crimes of the Heart* won the PULITZER PRIZE and the New York Drama Critics' Circle Award. Filled with southern madness, grotesque humor, and comic despair, *The MISS FIRECRACKER CONTEST* (1980) takes place in the small town of Brookhaven, Mississippi, when the town is preparing for its annual July Fourth Miss Firecracker beauty contest. Determined to emulate her beautiful cousin Elain by winning the contest and leaving Brookhaven "in a crimson blaze of glory," Carnelle Scott attempts to put together an act consisting of tap-dancing, sparklers, the American flag, and rifle-twirling—all to the tune of the "The Star Spangled Banner." She is one of three women in the play desperately trying to find who they really are and to come to terms with what they may reasonably expect out of life.

In *The Wake of Jamey Foster* (1981), Jamey Foster, a failed poet and would-be historian (who left his wife for a twice-divorced, yellow-haired sweetshop baker) has died, and his family and friends have gathered for his wake. The occasion of *The Debutante Ball* (1985) is Teddy Parker's autumn coming-out party in Hattiesburg, Mississippi, at her stepfather's nouveau riche mansion. Like so many of Henley's crippled characters, what Teddy wants most is just to stand in the rain and the thunder holding onto somebody and having that somebody hold onto her. In *The Lucky Spot* (1987), Henley takes her audience back in time to Pigeon, Louisiana, on Christmas Eve in 1934 (the heart of the Great Depression), where she introduces Reed Hooker, a former bootlegger trying to create a new life for himself by making a big success of his rural dance hall, the Lucky Spot. It is essentially the story of a dreamer trying to rebuild his life from a past filled with only fragmented images and a woman struggling to revive love betrayed by making her past seem right.

With *Abundance* (1989), Henley moved out of her southern landscape and into the Wyoming Territory to observe mail-order brides. Beginning in the 1860s, the play covers a friendship between two vastly different women that spans more than 25 years. In this play, she explores the conflict between our need for security and love as it is set up against our desire for rapture and danger.

Henley's *L-Play* (1995) is perhaps her most bizarre drama. As a fragmented, THEATRE OF THE ABSURD pastiche of scenes, it moves from Pitt's Diner in South Louisiana to a cheap apartment in Los Angeles to a street scene to suburbia to a college campus to an asylum to a decayed boudoir to a garret apartment to Earth at the dawn of humans to a college campus in the present. The title of each of the 12 scenes begins with the letter "L"—"Loneliness," "Linked," "Loser," "Lunatic," "Learner," "Lost," and so on. Connections gradually appear as Learner, in love with Lucheea, falls sick from the trail of her smell as he dedicates himself to the "eternal search of the word, the letter, the breath that would please her." Set in Savannah, Georgia, and focusing on two sisters, *Impossible Marriage* (1998) unfolds around the marriage of the younger sister to a much older man. Supposedly having the perfect marriage, the older sister disapproves. Realizing she cannot play innocent all her life, one of the sisters embraces passionate love. *Sisters of the Winter Madrigal* (2001), a one-act set in medieval times, is another play about sisters—one a whore, the other a cowherd to one cow. First produced in 2001, the play was actually written before *Crimes of the Heart*. *The Exposed* (2003) is a comedy set during the Christmas season in Los Angeles.

Ever present in Henley's plays is her ability to entice and excite the audience's imagination. Operating on many different levels, the whimsical humor and diverse surprises of her plots often cover up underlying tragic themes. Her characters have failings that are real; and much like Bliss in *The Debutante Ball,* they "just have this hole inside them" as they desperately long to love and be loved. Often, their compassion, understanding, forgiveness, and love know no boundaries as some kind of awakening and bonding usually takes place at the end of each drama.

Just such a play is Henley's latest, *Ridiculous Fraud* (2006), which premiered at Princeton's McCarter Center; it is set, as Charles Isherwood wrote in the *New York Times,* "in the whimsical world of Ms. Henley, where the lonely and the lost are prey to strange urges and violent changes of heart" (May 16, 2006). Also a teacher, Henley is Distinguished Professor of Theatre Arts at Loyola Marymount University in Los Angeles.

BIBLIOGRAPHY

Fesmire, Julia A., ed. *Beth Henley: A Casebook.* New York: Routledge, 2002.

Henley, Beth. *Beth Henley: Collected Plays, 1980–1989 and 1990–1999.* 2 vols. Lyme, N.H.: Smith and Kraus, 2000.

———. *Revelers.* New York: Dramatists Play Service, 2002.

———. *Ridiculous Fraud.* New York: Dramatists Play Service, 2007.

———. *Signature.* New York: Dramatists Play Service, 2002.

———. *Three Plays: "Control Freaks," "L-Play," "Sisters of the Winter Madrigal."* New York: Dramatists Play Service, 2002.

Plunka, Gene A. *Plays of Beth Henley: A Critical Study.* Jefferson, N.C.: McFarland, 2005.

Colby H. Kullman
University of Mississippi

HERNE, JAMES A. (1839–1901) The career of actor and playwright James A. Herne reflects a deep commitment to advancing the role of theater in the intellectual life of the community. Herne believed that theater, as an institution, should aspire to social consequence, as opposed to being mere diversion, and that drama, through the relevancy of its subject matter, should provide guidance or instruction. He laid forth his ideas in an article for *The Arena* in 1897 entitled "Art for Truth's Sake." Aligning himself with those who, in all facets of the arts, sought through realism to shed the light of truth on moral and social issues, he established himself in the vanguard of modern American playwriting.

Herne was born in Cohoes, New York, in 1839 and, at age 20, began his career in theater as an actor, settling in the mid-1870s in San Francisco. It was here that he began his association with writer/director DAVID BELASCO, an association that culminated in 1879 with the jointly written *Hearts of Oak,* in which Herne acted with his wife and lifetime costar Katherine Corcoran. Although Herne discovered at a later date that the play's plot was taken by Belasco from an English melodrama, he eventually became sole owner,

buying Belasco's interest in the play. Though the play failed in New York, Herne and his wife toured successfully with it for the next several years. Its realistic detail, the product of Herne's text and Belasco's staging, proved extremely popular with audiences, a fact that no doubt made a significant impression on the playwright.

With his drama *Drifting Apart* (1888), the story of an alcoholic's reformation, Herne came to the attention of several Boston literary figures who championed the realism of his writing; with their encouragement, he wrote and produced MARGARET FLEMING (1891). This drama dealt with marital infidelity, an unsavory topic made worse by the play's focus on society's double standard, whereby adulterous behavior in men was tolerated, if not condoned, while women who so offended were damned. After its failure in Boston, Herne revised the play, but its subject matter and moral perspective proved unacceptable to New York audiences when it was produced there in 1894 with the Hernes in leading roles. The original manuscripts of *Margaret Fleming* were destroyed in the flames that leveled the Hernes' estate in 1909, and the present version of the play is a 1914 reconstruction from memory made by Katherine Corcoran Herne. *Margaret Fleming* is now regarded as the most important precursor of dramatic social realism in 20th-century American theater.

The success of SHORE ACRES (1892) revived Herne's fortunes as a dramatist. The play, set on a farm on the coast of Maine, relates the story of two brothers of opposing temperament, one married and one single, who, at midlife, are divided by the married brother's intention to sell the family farm for commercial development and his related desire to see his daughter marry his business associate in this venture. The play abounds in realistic details of domestic activity and eschews intricacies of plot in favor of the development of strong and believable characters. The Hernes performed the play to great acclaim in Boston and New York and then toured with it for five years, earning more than $1 million in the process.

Herne completed two more plays; his last, the successful *Sag Harbor,* is a reworking of *Hearts of Oak.* Although not a playwright of the first rank, his reformist view of theater and his dedication to a drama of moral and social consequence in the tradition of Norwegian playwright Henrik Ibsen establishes his secure place in the history of American theater.

BIBLIOGRAPHY

Edwards, Herbert J., and Julie A. Herne. *James A. Herne: The Rise of Realism in the American Drama*. Orono: University of Maine Press, 1965.

Perry, John. *James A. Herne: The American Ibsen*. Chicago: Nelson-Hall, 1978.

Craig Clinton
Reed College

HEYWARD, DOROTHY (HARTZELL KUHNS) (1890–1961) and (EDWIN) DUBOSE (1885–1940)

The husband-and-wife team of Dorothy and DuBose Heyward is known primarily for its contribution to the classic George and Ira Gershwin opera *Porgy and Bess* (1935). They also collaborated on several other plays adapted from DuBose Heyward's novels, including PORGY (1927) and *Mamba's Daughters* (1939). Individually, playwright Dorothy Heyward's works were consistently produced in New York, while DuBose Heyward's essays, poems, plays, novels, and lectures helped revive national respect for the southern writer.

Born in Ohio, Dorothy Kuhns was determined to be a successful playwright. She first toured the country acting in small companies, then attended GEORGE PIERCE BAKER's famous "47 Workshop" at Harvard University. By the time she married DuBose Heyward, one of her plays, *Nancy Ann* (1924), about a society girl who flees the restrictions of family and position to work in the theater, was in the early stages of a Broadway production.

DuBose Heyward was born in Charleston, not long after the Civil War's Reconstruction period, to a poor, formerly aristocratic family (their fortunes resided in plantations devastated by the war). After his father's death, he quit school and went to work, eventually finding employment on the waterfront checking cotton alongside local African Americans, an experience that provided the observations he later used in the novel *Porgy* (1925). His other important novels include

Angel (1926), *Mamba's Daughters* (1929), and *Peter Ashley* (1932), each of which reveals a progressively more liberal social critic in its author. In addition to his own writings, Heyward championed the writing of the South; he cofounded the Poetry Society of South Carolina in Charleston (1920) to help bring about a southern cultural renaissance.

Porgy was the first major novel written by a southerner that went beyond stereotypes in its portrayal of African Americans. To accomplish this, Heyward took care to write in the local dialect and portray passionate and sympathetic characters. While the novel swept the country, DuBose and Dorothy Heyward cowrote the play *Porgy*, a piece that helped revolutionize the portrayal of African Americans in American theater. Like the novel, the play presented an authentic portrayal of a particular sector of southern African Americans, using black actors (as opposed to white actors in blackface) and spirituals to provide a forum for the representation of African Americans on the legitimate American stage. There were, however, objections raised in the African-American community against the play because it contained no acknowledgment of the existence of a black professional class. The George Gershwin opera, *Porgy and Bess* (1935), with lyrics by Dubose Heyward and Ira Gershwin and libretto by DuBose Heyward, received mixed reviews initially—though these stemmed largely from the debate about whether or not it was an "opera." It has since been successfully revived repeatedly and was chosen as part of a goodwill tour representing the United States during the height of the cold war. The Heywards frequently returned to themes of racial discrimination, the glory of the South, and the changing relationship between blacks and whites in their other works.

BIBLIOGRAPHY

Durham, Frank. *DuBose Heyward: The Man who Wrote "Porgy."* Columbia: University of South Carolina Press, 1954.

Heyward, DuBose. *Brass Ankle: A Play in Three Acts*. New York: Farrar and Rinehart, 1931.

———, and Dorothy Hartzell Heyward. *Mamba's Daughters: A Play*. New York: Farrar and Rinehart, 1939.

———. *Porgy: A Play in Four Acts*. Garden City, N.Y.: Doubleday, 1927.

Hutchisson, James M. *A Charleston Gentleman and the World of "Porgy and Bess."* Jackson: University Press of Mississippi, 2000.

———, ed. *A DuBose Heyward Reader.* Athens: University of Georgia Press, 2003.

Slavick, William H. *DuBose Heyward.* Boston: Twayne, 1981.

Elizabeth A. Osborne
Florida State University

HIM E. E. CUMMINGS (1928)

The poet Cummings's only full-length play, *Him,* is an amalgamation of expressionist, surrealist, Dadaist, and realist styles, which also prefigured the aesthetics of the THEATRE OF THE ABSURD (especially Samuel Beckett). Following its 1927 publication, it premiered at New York's famous Provincetown Playhouse, creating a firestorm of controversy. Vilified by critics, the production, budgeted at three times the normal cost and using 30 actors in 105 parts, lasted only 27 performances. Popular among academics, the philosophically dense, lengthy, and difficult-to-stage piece is rarely performed; racist and homophobic stereotypes and topical allusions also present problems for contemporary audiences.

The play begins with three identically masked, robed "Weird Sisters" (possibly meant as representations of the Fates) rocking in chairs and knitting while spouting nonsensical conversation about pet hippopotami. Upstage is a cutout depicting a female patient (the character Me) being etherized by a Doctor, setting the entire play as a hallucination dreamed by Me, who is undergoing either childbirth or an abortion (depending on one's interpretation). Me is married to Him, a frustrated, failed playwright who is "patiently squeezing fourdimensional ideas into a twodimensional stage." He obsesses over the larger questions of identity, human connection, love, and language, couching his ideas in elaborate poetic metaphors, non sequiturs, and images of the circus. Me is convinced Him cannot love her, as she finds his ideas impossible to comprehend. Their discussions take place in a room that rotates between each scene, so that the invisible fourth wall keeps shifting.

Act 2 is Me's imagined nightmarish staging of Him's current work-in-progress. The Doctor, Me, and Him appear as various characters in the play-within-a-play, which is conveyed in various styles: vaudeville/burlesque, medicine show, gangster film, minstrel show, and parodies of EUGENE O'NEILL and George Bernard Shaw. Me investigates her relationship with Him, her own identity, and various American ideologies through the distorted, bizarre sequences. The newly fashionable notions of Sigmund Freud are prevalent, as when a proper Englishman carries a trunk containing his unconscious.

In act 3, Him's quest for transcendence of the self leads him to Paris (a venomous satire of expatriatism). Upon his return, as a final effort to break through Him's existential isolationism, Me imagines a sideshow filled with freaks, the last of which is herself as mother with newborn child, the sight of which fills Him with terror. In the final scene, Me annihilates Him's philosophical house of cards by pointing out the invisible fourth wall, the audience, and the separation between reality and dramatic fiction, thereby summoning up the fortitude to leave Him.

Undeniably difficult to decipher, Cummings's play is nevertheless rife with humor, intellectual profundity, and imaginative use of language. The playwright himself printed a "Warning" in the program for the original production: "[R]elax, stop wondering what it is all 'about'—like many strange and familiar things, Life included, this Play isn't 'about,' it simply is. . . . DON'T TRY TO UNDERSTAND IT, LET IT TRY TO UNDERSTAND YOU" (Kennedy 295).

BIBLIOGRAPHY

Kennedy, Richard S. *Dreams in the Mirror: A Biography of E. E. Cummings.* New York: Liveright, 1980.

Douglas W. Gordy
Walnut Creek, California

HISPANIC DRAMA

The history of Hispanic drama in what is now the United States begins in 1598 in present-day New Mexico with a theatrical recreation of Cortés's conquest of Mexico staged by Juan Oñate and his followers entitled *Los Moros y los cristianos.* This early use of theater was also accompanied by a tradition of staging *pastorelas,* pastoral dramas that explore the lives of humorous shepherds in relationship to the birth of Christ, primarily staged in New Mexico and Texas. This tradition of folk drama, which continues to the present day, emerged from various forms of religious drama including the Spanish *auto sacramentales* of the 15th and 16th centuries.

The first documented professional drama performed in Spanish in California may have taken place as early as 1789. However, it was not until the middle of the 19th century that Spanish-language, professional theater was significantly documented in California. These works by Spanish authors were primarily melodramas with broad audience appeal. Performances centered in Los Angeles, although there are records of performances in San Francisco and in Tucson. The development of Spanish-language theater in Texas occurred somewhat later, and there was significant growth in the last two decades of the 19th century, primarily in San Antonio and Laredo. In addition to the performances of melodramas and other plays in established theater buildings or marketplaces, there are also records of *carpas* (tent shows) and other forms of popular Spanish-language performance that would influence some of the acting styles of the later Chicano theater.

The late 19th and 20th centuries saw a tremendous growth in Hispanic theater in Los Angeles, New York, San Antonio, and Tampa. Much of the work was in the tradition of the Spanish *zarzuela* (comic operetta) and was in many ways an expression of both community ideals and community formation within the immigrant and ethnic Spanish-speaking populations in these cities. Like other forms of ethnic theater during this period, the appeal tended to be relatively insular since they were monolingual performances.

The history of contemporary Hispanic drama reflects a shift from Mexican, Cuban, and Spanish traditions (such as performance of the *zarzuela*) to a greater investment in the experiences of Mexican Americans, Cuban Americans, and Nuyoricans (Puerto Ricans in New York). The plays reflecting this shift articulate the realities of an ethnic existence lived in an emerging space between cultures. The first examples of this work addressed the socioeconomic and cultural difficulties of adjusting to life in the mainland United States for those who had recently arrived and also documented and combated the racial and economic discrimination that continued to plague groups that had been present here for generations. As these conflicts became more focused on the interpersonal, the attention often shifted to the realities of linguistic codeswitching (moving back and forth between English and Spanish) and other negotiations of Hispanic identity in the United States.

During the 1960s and 1970s, the most visible Hispanic drama was Chicano drama. The word *Chicano* is used in this context to refer to individuals of Mexican descent in the United States who acknowledge their indigenous roots that emerged out of the civil rights struggles of the 1960s. In 1965, in conjunction with the Delano, California, grape strikes and the organizing work of Cesar Chavez, El Teatro Campesino (the Farmworkers' Theater) was born. Under the organizational leadership of Luis Valdéz, this collaborative ensemble composed of migrant farm workers began staging short political AGITPROP skits they labeled *actos*. Drawing upon Mexican popular performance traditions and the acting experience of some of the workers, as well as Valdéz's experience with the Bread and Puppet Theater of New York, they developed a style of acting and performance related to Italian *commedia dell'arte* as well as the *carpa* tradition. Popular *actos* include works like *Los Vendidos* (The sellouts, or Those who are sold [1967]), which explore contemporary Chicano stereotypes, as well as pieces that explore more explicitly the lived realities of the striking farm workers. The understanding of Chicano theater aesthetics during the 1960s and early 1970s was that it should be by, for, and about Chicanos. There was no sense that the work was a part of mainstream culture, and Chicano artists positioned themselves in opposition to mainstream values.

El Teatro Campesino, along with the Chicano movement itself, led to the formation of a number of collaborative troupes based on this model, such as Teatro de la Esperanza (founded in Santa Barbara, California, in 1971). These *teatros* performed highly politicized works following the aesthetics of Chicano nationalism, which argued symbolically for a new Chicano nation, Aztlán, to separate from the United

States. The growth of *teatros* during the early 1970s led to the formation of TENAZ, El Teatro Nacional de Aztlán (The National Theater of Aztlán), an umbrella organization for Chicano theater. Along with Luis Valdéz, important early playwrights include Estela Portillo-Trambley, whose *Day of the Swallows* (1971) is the first published play by a Chicana (the female counterpart of Chicano), and Carlos Morton, who has transformed myths and biblical accounts into comedies with a Chicano sensibility. Morton's best play, *The Many Deaths of Danny Rosales* (1977), is a docudrama that recounts the attempted cover-up of the murder of a Chicano by a Texas sheriff.

The most famous Chicano play, Luis Valdéz's ZOOT SUIT (1978), centers on the Sleepy Lagoon Murder Trial in 1940s Los Angeles and serves an important historical function within the history of Chicano theater. *Zoot Suit* is notable not only for its success in Los Angeles but also for the fact that it was the first Chicano play on Broadway. In this production, El Teatro Campesino used professional actors (rather than migrant workers and other amateurs) for the first time, marking a clear shift toward professionalization. Since this watershed moment, focus in Chicano drama has shifted from the *teatro* to the individual playwright and from the *barrio* audience to more mainstream regional venues.

CHERRÍE MORAGA is the most prominent representative of a second generation of Chicana and Chicano playwrights and a leader in the emergence of drama by Hispanic women in the mid-1980s. Moraga's numerous plays deal not only with economic and political issues but also with questions of sexual identity. Her first play, *Giving Up the Ghost* (1986), uses two manifestations of the protagonist to dramatize the negotiations of coming to understand a lesbian identity. *Heroes and Saints* (1992), her most celebrated work, returns to many issues raised by El Teatro Campesino in exploring the difficult lives of agricultural workers in California. Other important Chicana playwrights include Edit Villareal, Josefina López, Elaine Romero, and Evelina Fernandez.

In Cuban theater in the United States, a distinction is often made between Cuban-American drama and Cuban exilic drama. Cuban exilic drama is produced by those artists who left after the 1959 revolution, who focus on island experiences, and who understand themselves as participating in a specifically Cuban aesthetic. For some scholars, this group includes playwrights such as René Ariza, Matías Montes Huidobro, and Leopoldo Hernandez. Cuban-American drama, on the other hand, may deal with the realities of the situation in Cuba but also address issues of being Cuban in America. The most prominent Cuban-American playwrights include MARIA IRENE FORNÉS, EDUARDO MACHADO, and Dolores Prida. Fornés's early work demonstrated an investment in the avant-garde, but her mentoring and teaching of new Hispanic playwrights during the 1980s at INTAR (International Arts Relations) Hispanic American Arts Center in New York City has led to an increased focus on Hispanic subjects and themes. In *Sarita* (1984) and *The CONDUCT OF LIFE* (1985), she addresses the problems of masculine power within Hispanic culture. Dolores Prida's bilingual and Spanish works, such as *Beautiful Señoritas* (1977) and *Botánica* (1990), address questions of the representation of Hispanic women, the gentrification of neighborhood communities, and generational negotiation. Eduardo Machado, who was himself influenced by working with Fornés, is best known for *The Floating Island Plays* (1991), a quartet that spans the lives of two Cuban families from their 1920s existence on the island to a wedding in exile in the 1980s. As a teacher, he has also worked with emerging playwrights such as Rogelio Martinez, whose work, *Illuminating Veronica* (1999), about a bourgeois woman who stays behind when the rest of her family leaves Cuba after the revolution, critiques the residual gender bias of a supposedly transformed revolutionary society. Another important Cuban-American playwright is NILO CRUZ, whose play *Night Train to Bolina* (1994), about the experiences of two young Latin American runaways, explores the power of the imagination and the difficulty of youthful intimacy. In 2003, Cruz's ANNA IN THE TROPICS (2002), set in 1929 in a Spanish-Cuban section of Tampa, Florida, became the first play by a Hispanic dramatist to win the PULITZER PRIZE.

Puerto Rican theater on the island and Puerto Rican theater in the mainland United States are two very different things. The most important transition in sensibility—the gap that eventually led to the development of the term *Nuyorican*—is exemplified by René Marqués's play, *La Carreta* (The ox-cart [1953]), which emerged out of his awareness of the realities of the Puerto Rican experience in New York, an awareness gained during his 1940 stay in New York to study playwriting. *La Carreta* recounts the journey of one family from rural Puerto Rico to the urban space of San Juan and eventually to New York City in the hopes of economic improvement. They eventually return to San Juan after the father is killed. This play so effectively captured the difficult transitions in Puerto Rican migration that, according to John Antush (an important scholar of Puerto Rican theater in New York), "Miriam Colón and others founded the Puerto Rican Traveling Theater (PRTT) primarily to bring this play, free of charge, to the people of New York" (*Nuestro* xiii). MIGUEL PIÑERO's work follows up on this transition by articulating the realities of life on the streets. Emerging out of his experiences on the street and in prison, Piñero's plays provide commentary on the position of Puerto Ricans in New York as well as explore the difficulties of expressing masculinity in various communities. His most famous work, SHORT EYES (1974), provides a glimpse into the power dynamics and the difficulties of retaining any sense of self-integrity in prison. Celebrated for its gritty realism and accurate portrayal of prison life, *Short Eyes* was produced on Broadway and was eventually filmed. Reynaldo Povod's *Cuba and His Teddy Bear* (1986) was also successfully produced on Broadway, though many attribute its success more to the choice of celebrity actors (such as Robert De Niro and Ralph Macchio) than to the play itself. Edward Gallardo, in plays such as *Simpson Street* (1979), shifts the conflicts from the streets to the family and demonstrates to some critics a shift away from a nostalgic privileging of Puerto Rico and toward a focus on life in New York. Other important contemporary Puerto Rican playwrights in the United States include Cándido Tirado, Juan Shamsul Alám, and Edwin Sánchez.

Hispanic drama's transition from the 1980s to the 1990s is marked by a shift from very localized concerns with issues of Hispanic identity to broader concerns about negotiating identity in a variety of spaces. This transition can be clearly seen in the work of two Puerto Rican–American playwrights: Migdalia Cruz and JOSÉ RIVERA. Migdalia Cruz, whose earlier pieces, such as *The Have-Little* (1991) and *Miriam's Flowers* (1990), give accounts of growing up amid the commonplace violence of the Bronx, moves later to works such as *Fur* (1995), in which difference and the ability to love, two of her crucial themes, are explored in a love triangle experienced in the future on the outskirts of Los Angeles. Her most recent work is *Grito: A Cry for the Bronx* (2008). Beginning in the 1980s with works such as *The House of Ramon Iglesia* (1983) and *The Promise* (1988), set in domestic Puerto Rican spaces in New York, Rivera has moved into much more expansive plays of ideas, such as *Marisol* (1992), which explores the entire space of New York City, and *Sonnets for an Old Century* (2000), which takes place in limbo. Rivera was nominated for an Oscar for his 2004 screenplay for *The Motorcycle Diaries*.

As the 1990s progressed into the 21st century, several playwrights began testing the limits of Hispanic drama, acknowledging the expanding heterogeneity of Hispanic and Latino identity in the United States (a number of playwrights prefer the term *Latino* to *Hispanic* because they see the latter as a term created by government as opposed to a self-selected identity; many individuals also distinguish between these terms based on political affiliation). This expanding heterogeneity is characterized by more explicit references to issues of sexuality and by recognition of "new" forms of identity (Colombian American, Chilean American, and so on). In his powerful play *Deporting the Divas* (1996), Guillermo Reyes explores the identity crisis of a bisexual Mexican-American INS agent and includes new Latino characters, such as a blonde Argentinian of German descent. Luis Alfaro goes even further in *Straight as a Line* (1997), which has neither the expected themes nor characters of Hispanic drama, focusing instead on a British mother and son dealing with the realities of the physical devastation of AIDS while living in Las Vegas, forcing critics and audiences to rethink the definition of Hispanic drama. Other important playwrights emerging in the 1990s include Oliver Mayer, best known for

Blade to the Heat (1994), about a young boxer accused of being homosexual; Octavio Solis, best known for *Santos and Santos* (1993), about the burdens of family responsibility and ethics; and Caridad Svich, a prolific writer also heavily engaged in thinking about Hispanic drama.

Another development in the 1990s was the emergence of comedic performance, blending stand-up comedy and theater, by a range of groups, such as Culture Clash and Latins Anonymous, and individuals, such as Marga Gomez, Monica Palacios, Luis Alfaro, and Carmelita Tropicana. The most widely recognized mainstream example of this is John Leguizamo, whose one-man shows such as *Mambo Mouth* (1990) and *Freak* (1997) have been both published and televised.

The 21st century has seen a substantial change in the mainstream attention given to Hispanic drama. Following Nilo Cruz's Pulitzer Prize, his works, such as *Hortensia and the Museum of Dreams, Lorca in a Green Dress, Beauty of the Father,* and many others, have been widely produced, and other playwrights have seen increasingly wide dissemination of their work, including Luis Alfaro's *Electricidad* (2004), a retelling of *Electra,* and Eduardo Machado's *The Cook* (2003). Recently, Octavio Solis's *Lydia* (2008), about a family in the 1970s negotiating personal loss and secrets, has attracted wide critical attention.

While writers like José Rivera and Eduardo Machado continue to create important work for the theater, new playwrights have emerged onto the scene, including Jorge Ignacio Cortiñas and Karen Zacarías. Perhaps the most successful young writer is Quiara Alegria Hudes, whose *Elliot, A Soldier's Fugue* (2006), about the Iraq war, was a finalist for the 2007 Pulitzer Prize. She also wrote the book for the musical *In the Heights* about the primarily Dominican-American Washington Heights neighborhood, which received the 2008 TONY AWARD for Best Musical.

The transformations of Hispanic theater from a politically specific collaborative aesthetic in the 1960s to a broader place in mainstream culture during the 1980s to its increasing proliferation and diversity in the 1990s and into the 21st century, serve as evidence that this important area of American drama will continue to grow and develop while still exploring politically important ideas that reflect the diversity of our culture.

BIBLIOGRAPHY

Antush, John V., ed. *Recent Puerto Rican Theater: Five Plays from New York.* Houston, Tex.: Arte Público Press, 1991.

———, ed. *Nuestro New York: An Anthology of Puerto Rican Plays.* New York: Mentor, 1994.

Arrizón, Alicia. *Latina Performance: Traversing the Stage.* Bloomington: Indiana University Press, 1999.

———, and Lillian Manzor, eds. *Latinas on Stage.* Berkeley, Calif.: Third Woman Press, 2000.

Broyles-González, Yolanda. *El Teatro Campesino: Theater in the Chicano Movement.* Austin: University of Texas Press, 1994.

Cortina, Rodolfo J., ed. *Cuban American Theater.* Houston, Tex.: Arte Público Press, 1991.

Culture Clash. *Culture Clash: Life, Death and Revolutionary Comedy.* New York: Theatre Communications Group, 1998.

Feyder, Linda, ed. *Shattering the Myth: Plays by Hispanic Women.* Houston, Tex.: Arte Público Press, 1992.

Flores, Richard. *Los Pastores: History and Performance in the Mexican Shepherd's Play of South Texas.* Washington, D.C.: Smithsonian Institution Press, 1995.

González-Cruz, Luiz F., and Francesca M. Colecchia, eds. *Cuban Theater in the United States: A Critical Anthology.* Tempe, Ariz.: Bilingual Press/Editorial Bilingüe, 1992.

Huerta, Jorge. *Chicano Drama: Themes and Forms.* Ypsilanti, Mich.: Bilingual Press, 1982.

———. *Chicano Drama: Performance, Society, and Myth.* Cambridge, England: Cambridge University Press, 2000.

———, ed. *Necessary Theater: Six Plays about the Chicano Experience.* Houston, Tex.: Arte Público Press, 1989.

———, and Nicolás Kanellos, eds. *Nuevos Pasos: Chicano and Puerto Rican Drama.* Houston, Tex.: Arte Público Press, 1989.

Kanellos, Nicolás. *A History of Hispanic Theatre in the United States: Origins to 1940.* Austin: University of Texas Press, 1990.

———, ed. *Mexican American Theatre: Then and Now.* Houston, Tex.: Arte Público Press, 1989.

———, ed. *Mexican American Theatre: Legacy and Reality.* Pittsburgh, Penn.: Latin American Literary Review Press, 1987.

Latino Plays from South Coast Repertory: Hispanic Playwrights Project Anthology. New York: Broadway Play Publishing, 2000.

Osborn, M. Elizabeth, ed. *On New Ground: Contemporary Hispanic-American Plays.* New York: Theatre Communications Group, 1987.

Pérez Firmat, Gustavo. *Life on the Hyphen: The Cuban-American Way.* Austin: University of Texas Press, 1994.

Pottlitzer, Joanne. *Hispanic Theater in the United States and Puerto Rico.* New York: Ford Foundation, 1988.

Ramos-García, Luis A. *The State of Latino Theater in the United States: Hybridity, Transculturation and Identity.* New York: Routledge, 2002.

Rossini, Jon D. *Contemporary Latina/o Theater: Wrighting Ethnicity.* Carbondale: Southern Illinois University Press, 2008.

Sandoval-Sánchez, Alberto. *José Can You See? Latinos On and Off Broadway.* Madison: University of Wisconsin Press, 1999.

———, and Nancy Saporta Sternbach. *Stages of Life: Transcultural Performance and Identity in U.S. Latina Theater.* Tucson: University of Arizona Press, 2001.

———, eds. *Puro Teatro: A Latina Anthology.* Tucson: University of Arizona Press, 2000.

Svich, Caridad, and Marma Teresa Marrero, eds. *Out of the Fringe: Contemporary Latina/Latino Theatre and Performance.* New York: Theatre Communications Group, 2000.

Jon D. Rossini
University of California—Davis

HOGAN'S GOAT William Alfred (1965)

Hogan's Goat is a study of how single-minded devotion to a goal may ultimately destroy everyone involved. Though written in verse, the language is eminently stage-worthy and re-creates the ambiance of the raw ethnic nature of an immigrant neighborhood, complete with its religious mores and superstitions. Anger alternates with warm sensitivity against a background of corruption and power.

Matthew Stanton, an Irish immigrant (in his late thirties) and sixth-ward leader in 1890, has received his party's back room–negotiated nomination for mayor of Brooklyn. Edward Quinn, the 70-year-old incumbent from the same party, simply needs to be persuaded to step aside to make way for the Young Turk. Matthew married Kathleen, a devout Catholic woman, in a civil ceremony in London three years ago. Now, she begs him for an immediate church ceremony, so that they may stop "living in sin," and

reminds him that she left country, family, and God for him. In the ensuing argument, he verbally abuses her and tells her a church wedding is not possible now because the Irish Catholic voters simply will not tolerate a candidate living outside the church's rules. However, as soon as he is elected, she may have as big and public a church wedding as she would like.

Meanwhile, Quinn has no intention of meekly vacating his office and sets about to ruin Matthew's chances, in part to "keep his office" and in part to settle an old score. Years back, Agnes Hogan threw over Quinn in order to take up with Matthew. She, once a well-off woman, "kept" and cultivated the much younger Matthew, thus making him "Hogan's goat." The fact that Matthew had found Agnes Hogan and Quinn in bed together only intensifies the animosity between the two men. Agnes is now suffering an agonizingly consumptive death. At Agnes's wake, Quinn and Matthew fight, and Kathleen begins to learn about the sordid affair.

Quinn, ordered by the party bosses in Albany to step aside, is determined to hold onto power at any cost. He is not satisfied with the trouble he has already caused and seeks revenge. He blackmails an acquaintance to gain access to Agnes Hogan's strongbox and a document it contains. Two days later, Quinn informs Kathleen that Matthew had in fact married Agnes and shows her the marriage certificate to prove it. Later, at their flat, Matthew finds Kathleen packing to leave him, an action he simply will not allow. In his rage, he throws her down the stairs and kills her.

While it may appear at first that it is Quinn who is single-minded about his goals, actually both Quinn and Matthew are obsessed with achieving and holding onto power. The play contrasts the failures in Matthew's personal life and the failures in his political life as both are falling apart around him. The progressive peeling away of layers reveals that at his core Matthew is every bit as corrupt and morally bankrupt as Quinn and that both men merely used other human beings as commodities to purchase their own desires. This evil within was emblematic of the literary and social unease of the 1960s in which the play was written.

Though the play aspired to tragedy, it remains a melodrama. However, its charm was its historic atmosphere and emotional sensitivity. Alfred's musical adaptation, *Cry for Us All* (1970), was unsuccessful, but he won the 1966 Drama Desk-Vernon Rice Award for *Hogan's Goat*.

Robert Lewis Smith
Kutztown University of Pennsylvania

HOLIDAY Philip Barry (1928) A comedy of manners, *Holiday* wittily pits conventional upper-class values of the period against freedom and true love. As in Barry's other famous play, *The Philadelphia Story* (1939), those who thwart convention are the heroes of the piece.

A wealthy heiress, Julia Seton, meets and becomes engaged—after only 10 days—to a lawyer with a promising career, Johnny Case, while on holiday in Lake Placid. Home again, Julia must break the news of her engagement to her family. Her sister Linda and brother Ned hope for the best but are sure Father will be a hard sell, since Johnny has no wealth, no "blood," and no connections. Father, resistant at first, comes enthusiastically around when a shrewd investment on Case's part proves him to be a "comer" and, indeed, a man not unlike Grandfather himself (now just a portrait on the living room wall), who came from nothing to become a millionaire. However, John Case has a different idea; rather than accumulating money and possessions within a restrictive conventional society, he wants to use the money he has earned to explore the world and *all* classes of people while he is still young. When he runs out of money, he'll go back to work. This plan comes as something of a shock to his beautiful, but thoroughly conventional and self-satisfied, fiancée; it is Julia's sister, Linda, who really understands Johnny.

Linda finds the life of a wealthy woman stifling and useless: Women like her have "nothing left to do or need or want," and some she knows have ended their lives in suicide, others in a sanitarium. Her brother, Ned, whom she longs to save from his alcoholism, is another casualty of her class, stuck as he is in his father's business, though he has no interest in it. Linda's dissatisfaction has so far been expressed in sarcasm and small acts of rebellion. On New Year's Eve,

she boycotts her sister's extravagant and stuffy engagement party and asks some friends, who happen also to be friends of Johnny's, for an intimate late supper in the childhood "playroom" (chosen by Linda because it is the only room in the house where anyone ever had fun). The fun-loving Potters, Johnny, Linda, and Ned have a grand time up in the playroom until Father and Julia come in to insist that everyone join the party downstairs. Linda refuses, and Johnny stays with her for a moment, dancing with her and kissing her at midnight, before going downstairs himself. Linda tells Ned that she loves Case just minutes before Father publicly announces Julia's engagement to him.

Because of Johnny's unconventional plan, Julia postpones the marriage, and Johnny disappears. Linda is anxious to see them reunited because she wants to see her sister rescued from staid convention; what she does not realize is that Julia is not like her at all. Julia is, in fact, very happy with her father's conventional life and his views. Father thinks Johnny's ideas against piling up money are un-American, and he and Julia both hope this bright and able young man will come around to their way of thinking. But in the end Johnny boards a ship for Europe with the Potters. Once Linda is assured that her sister does not truly love Johnny, she runs to join him on his adventure—with Ned's blessing.

The play has been seen variously as a satire on high society, a justification for the hedonism of the 1920s, and a study of the machinations of society insiders (Father and Julia and their camp) as contrasted to outsiders (John Case). *Holiday* is still successfully revived around the country. Perhaps its endurance comes from the fact that the two American myths it focuses on remain a part of our national psychology: Wealth, particularly self-made wealth, is nearly a religion to us, but equally compelling is our search for self through exploration.

HOME OF THE BRAVE Arthur Laurents (1945) Written in the final year of World War II and set in the Pacific during that war, *Home of the Brave* deals with the physical and psychological price of war: death, amputation, posttraumatic stress syndrome, and survivor's guilt; marriages broken because they could not withstand the long years of separation; and the young and inexperienced men who have to deal directly and indirectly with these traumas. Though LAURENTS includes the anti-Semitism faced by his Jewish protagonist, he focuses on the similarities among soldiers, particularly the commonly experienced relief and subsequent guilt of the survivor.

As the play begins, Private Peter Coen is suffering from post-traumatic stress. Under physician Captain Bitterger's guidance and with the help of sodium pentothol, "Coney" reveals the trauma that led to his amnesia and paralysis. In a flashback, Coney takes us to the Japanese-occupied island that was the site of a dangerous mission he and four other men—Finch, T. J., Mingo, and Major Robinson—recently undertook. Their mission was to survey and map one side of the island for an imminent American invasion. (While they are on the island, T. J.'s anti-Semitism toward Coen is revealed; T. J. calls Finch, Coney's best friend, a "little kike lover.") When the Japanese come into the area, the men are forced to relocate as they wait for their rescue plane. Finch is wounded by rifle fire and insists that Coney take the completed maps and clear out with the others; the mission, Finch insists, is more important than his safety. Coney leaves him and finds the others; later, they hear Finch's tortured screams as the Japanese attempt to lure the other Americans to their deaths. Coney is racked with guilt for leaving his wounded friend. Mingo tries to distract him from the screams with small talk and by reciting a fragment of a poem written by his wife: "We are only two and yet our howling / Can encircle the world's end. / Frightened, / you are my only friend. / And frightened, we are everyone. / Someone must take a stand. / Coward, take my coward's hand." Later, when Coney is left in a clearing to guard the gear, Finch—near death—crawls to him and dies in his arms. As the Japanese taunt Coney from the surrounding jungle, Coney tries irrationally to bury his dead friend. When the Major and Mingo return to collect the maps and Coney, they find Coney physically unwounded but unable to walk.

Through his work with Doctor Bitterger. Coney comes to believe his paralysis results from the guilt he feels for having felt a moment of gladness when Finch

was shot; he felt glad, he believes, because Finch, his one true friend—a gentile with whom Coney planned to open a bar after the war, a gentile who hoped Coney would marry his sister—had almost called him a "lousy yellow Jew" before he caught himself and ended the phrase with "jerk" instead. The doctor insists, however, that Coney's is not "some special kind of guilt." He is "the same as anybody else. . . . no different . . . no different at all." The moment of gladness and the consequent guilt is common among "*every soldier in this world.* . . . Because deep underneath he thinks: I'm glad it wasn't me. I'm glad I'm still alive." Coney remains skeptical until, in the final scene of the play, the doctor's theory is verified by Mingo who has had the same experience in battle.

Mingo has received a regretful letter from his poet-wife informing him that she has fallen in love with another man in her husband's years-long absence. Mingo is headed back to the United States with a Purple Heart, an empty sleeve, and no home to return to. Coney and Mingo decide to come back together, partners in a business, the bar that Finch and Coney would have opened. The play ends as Coney, recalling Mingo's wife's poem, invites him, "Hey, coward," to "take [his] coward's hand." The two veterans, one Jew and one gentile, one an amputee and one psychologically traumatized, yet more similar than dissimilar, face a postwar future together.

Arthur Laurents's first play, *Home of the Brave* received mixed reviews, some critics predicting it would win all the big awards (it did not) and others finding it tedious. It was one of several postwar plays, both dramas (JOHN PATRICK's *The HASTY HEART* [1945] and ARTHUR MILLER's *ALL MY SONS* [1947]) and comedies (Thomas Heggen and Joshua Logan's *MISTER ROBERTS* [1948] and John Patrick's PULITZER PRIZE–winning *The TEAHOUSE OF THE AUGUST MOON* [1953]), to depict the fighting man's experience of World War II and the war's effects on him. Raising the issues of survivor guilt and posttraumatic stress disorder as Laurents does became more commonplace in the Vietnam period than it was in the post–World War II era.

HORIZON AUGUSTIN DALY (1871) Staged three years after Bret Harte's short story about the West,

"The Luck of Roaring Camp," was published, *Horizon* initiated a theatrical vogue for frontier plays that lasted into the next century. The first major post–Civil War melodrama on a western theme, *Horizon* charts the love that develops between a brave young army officer and his adopted mother's long-lost daughter on the rough-and-ready frontier.

Newly commissioned Captain Alleyn Van Dorp returns to his adopted mother's New York mansion to discover that she has been very ill and still pines for her daughter, spirited away 14 years previously by her estranged husband. Van Dorp announces his imminent departure for a fictional Fort Jackson, where he is to subdue the local Indians. He will be accompanied on this trek by Sundown Rowse, a political operative who has secured a major congressional frontier land grant and wishes to survey his holdings; Rowse's daughter, Columbia; and the Honorable Arthur Smith, a younger son of a British earl. The adventures begin when the play shifts to Rogue's Rest, a town 60 miles from Fort Jackson. Here, a Vigilance Committee is contemplating the fates of several local ne'er-do-wells, including John Loder (alias White Panther), a gambler; the drunkard Wolf Van Dorp (Alleyn's mother's estranged husband); a "Heathen Chinee"; and Wannemucka, an ignoble savage who lusts after Wolf Van Dorp's innocent daughter, Meddie (who is, of course, Mrs. Van Dorp's long-lost child). Captivated by Meddie—but at that point unaware of her identity—Alleyn quickly falls in love but must depart to fulfill his duties at Fort Jackson, promising to visit her as soon as he is able. Meddie's father initially defies the Vigilance Committee but later decides to flee. Before he can do so, however, he is murdered by Wannemucka. The remainder of the play charts Wannemucka's efforts to capture Meddie, her attempts to elude him, and finally her rescue. Loder, who quietly loves her, finally sacrifices his love for the young girl so that Alleyn can return her to the East, a more appropriate environment for the delicate Meddie.

Augustin Daly's melodrama continues several themes associated with earlier frontier plays such as James Kirke Paulding's *The Lion of the West* (1830) and W. R. Derr's *Kit Carson* (1850): the contrast between an East characterized by propriety, restraint, and legal order and a West marked by informality, exuberance, and legal instability; the attempt to bend native populations to the will of white society; the challenges and privations of frontier life; and the rugged individualism of pioneers. At the same time, *Horizon's* introduction of new characters such as the "gambler-with-a-heart-of-gold" and the frontier land speculator opened the West to new thematic interpretation. The West as moral crucible and, simultaneously, as commodity suggested new dramatic avenues that subsequent playwrights followed. Similarly, characters such as "the heathen Chinee" and the Englishman, the "Honorable Smith," suggested the changing face of the frontier. Nevertheless, the play's romantic aura and moral universe are the surest signs of its melodramatic core.

Gary A. Richardson
Mercer University

HOROVITZ, ISRAEL ARTHUR (1939–)

Born poor in the blue-collar Massachusetts town of Wakefield, Horovitz has mined his New England origins to write plays of social consciousness, critiquing American capitalist competition and urban violence. Ironically, his fame is greater abroad than at home, where his own ambition led him into the dishonesty his dramas so often condemn. Author of more than 50 plays that range from absurdism to realism, fantasy, and parable, his work has been translated into 30 languages. Perhaps the most popular American playwright in France and Germany today, Horovitz, as writer, actor, producer, and director, is less celebrated in the United States.

Born into a small Jewish community north of Boston, Horovitz experienced anti-Semitism and social isolation growing up. He escaped into literature as a teenager when he stopped to read the books he was tearing up for recycling at his uncle's junk shop. He wrote his first novel at 13 and his first play at 19.

Trained at the London Royal Academy (1961–63) and resident playwright with the Royal Shakespeare Company (1965), Horovitz had his big break in 1968 with four of his plays running Off-Broadway simultaneously to critical raves. It began with *Line,* an allegory of four men and a woman trading insults and sexual favors as they struggle for first place in a line that goes nowhere. *It's Called a Sugar Plum* led a double bill with his now classic *The Indian Wants the Bronx,* which won a Distinguished Play OBIE AWARD, in which two punks, out of boredom and ignorance, torment an Indian man who is lost and unable to speak English. Street toughs Murph and Joey are psychically lost, unable to communicate in their native English beyond obscene taunts and macho insults. *Rats,* featuring talking rodents invading a baby's Harlem crib, opened the month of Martin Luther King's assassination.

Line (1969) became not only one of the longest running plays Off-Broadway but also the longest running American play in France, where it won the Critics Prize. Samuel Beckett sought his friendship in Paris, and City College of New York appointed him playwright-in-residence. But when his publisher put an old résumé on the back of his novel, *Capella* (1973), a keen-eyed *Harvard Crimson* reporter and later *New York Times* drama critic, Frank Rich, discovered Horovitz had claimed an unearned Harvard diploma. Disgrace was sudden but brief as Horovitz was quickly hired at New York University and, later, Brandeis.

Horovitz returned to his roots for material and his *Alfred Trilogy* (*Alfred the Great* [1972], *Our Father's Failings* [1976], and *Alfred Dies* [1977]) and *Quannapowitt Quartet* (1976) make up *The Wakefield Plays,* dark comedies of sex, guilt, and revenge, comparable in their complexity and themes to the *Oresteia.* A 1979 move to Gloucester, Massachusetts, where he founded the Gloucester Stage Company, which went on to premiere most of his subsequent plays, allowed him to blend concretely his own experiences with working-class life on the model of THORNTON WILDER's OUR TOWN. These *Gloucester Plays* (*The Widow's Blind Date* [1979], *The Mackerel* [1979], *Park Your Car in Harvard Yard* [1984], *Henry Lumper* [1985], *North Shore Fish* [1987], and *Fighting over Beverly* [1992]), continue Horovitz's painful examination of America's dark side. His recent plays include *3 Weeks after Paradise* (2002); *My Old Lady* (2002); one-acts *Sins of the Mother* (2004) and *North Shore Fish* (2004), both set in Gloucester, Massachusetts, among the working

class; and the one-act *Beirut Rocks* (2007), which involves students caught up in military conflict in Lebanon in 2006.

BIBLIOGRAPHY
Horovitz, Israel. *Collected Works: Volume I—16 Short Plays.* Lyme, N.H.: Smith and Kraus, 1994.
———. *Collected Works: Volume II—New England Blue.* Lyme, N.H.: Smith and Kraus, 1995.
———. *Collected Works: Volume III—"The Primary English Class" and Six New Plays.* Lyme, N.H.: Smith and Kraus, 1997.
———. *Collected Works: Volume IV—Two Trilogies.* Lyme, N.H.: Smith and Kraus, 1998.
Kane, Leslie, ed. *Israel Horovitz: A Collection of Critical Essays.* Westport, Conn.: Greenwood Press, 1994.

Philip Zwerling
Ursinus College

HOT L BALTIMORE, THE LANFORD WILSON (1973)

The Hot l Baltimore was the first commercially successful play staged by the Circle Repertory Theatre Company. The production served as the springboard for the company to become one of the most successful and influential OFF-BROADWAY theater companies in New York.

Set in a dilapidated railroad hotel in Baltimore (the missing "e" from the title signifies the burned-out neon sign over the door), the play follows the lives and stories of the residents of the hotel on a "recent" Memorial Day. The residents include three prostitutes, April, Suzy, and Girl (she hasn't decided what to call herself yet); Millie, a retired waitress; Mr. Morse, a slightly addled old man; and Jackie and Jamie, a sister and brother who have been making plans to seek their fortunes out west. The hotel staff, which includes Bill Lewis, the night clerk, Mrs. Oxenham, the day clerk, and Mr. Katz, the manager, keep an eye on the place—and on the residents. Also in the mix is a young man, Paul Granger, who is searching for his grandfather; the hotel was his last known address. The hotel, located next to a dying passenger railroad station, has been sold and is marked for demolition. The residents have different reactions to this news: Girl is devastated—the railroad still holds a romantic sway over her. She knows the schedule of every train that passes by, and to her the end of the hotel is the end of an era. April, the worldly, wise, and pragmatic hooker, takes the news in stride—enjoy life while you can and then move on.

LANFORD WILSON credits Arlo Guthrie's 1972 hit song "City of New Orleans" as his partial inspiration for the play. He had wanted to write a play about an old hotel and its residents—at one time, he had worked as a night clerk in a New York hotel—and he wanted to write about prostitutes and their lives. He had previously touched on the seedier side of a city's nightlife in *Balm in Gilead* (1965), but thematically *The Hot l Baltimore* reflects a vision of people and their lives that had not been seen in Wilson's previous works. Coming on the heels of such dark and disturbing Wilson scripts as *Serenading Louie* (1970) and *The Gingham Dog* (1968), this play marks a noticeable change in his approach to character and writing style. *The Hot l Baltimore* took a much more lighthearted and farcical approach. Its characters are not desperate, despondent, or violent. They are loving and caring, even if they are unsavory or unattractive. They all have dreams of a better future for themselves, and even if their world—a rotting, old building—is about to be destroyed, they know that they have the courage and the passion to go on and make the best of it.

Part of this change in style was due to Wilson's close relationship with the actors at Circle Rep who would play the parts. Until 1969, most of his plays had reflected a dark world of lonely and displaced characters, unable to free themselves from their own demons or to find a way out of their sadness. However, after working continually with the same Circle Rep performers, Wilson began to see them as fitting into characters he had in mind for his writing. While the characters were still lonely and displaced, they took on the full dimensions of the actors who created them. Under the direction of Marshall W. Mason, the play achieved an ensemble effect that critic HAROLD CLURMAN noted was so well done that it was impossible to tell where the writing left off and the acting began. Instead of ending in despair, the play ends on a hopeful note for the people who live there: Even if the hotel is to be torn down, there are better things waiting for them afterwards. *The Hot l Baltimore* won the New York Drama Critics' Circle Award and a Best American Play OBIE AWARD.

Philip Middleton Williams
Miami, Florida

HOUSE OF BLUE LEAVES, THE JOHN GUARE (1971)

In February 1970, GUARE finished *The House of Blue Leaves*, after nearly five years and nine drafts of work on the second act. It became Guare's first major breakthrough in the theater and was voted Best American Play of the 1970–71 season by the New York Drama Critics' Circle. It also received an OBIE AWARD, the Los Angeles Drama Critics Circle Award, and an Outer Critics Circle Award.

The House of Blue Leaves centers on the life of Artie Shaughnessy, a zookeeper by day and an aspiring songwriter by night. Guare set the play where he grew up, in Queens. Artie's family life in Queens is a big disappointment, a bitter pill to swallow for someone who has great aspirations. In the zookeeper's domestic menagerie, he cares for his mentally ill wife, Bananas. At the same time, he is saddled with an alienated and rebellious 18-year-old son named Ronnie who is AWOL from the United States Army. Bananas's insanity and Ronnie's deeply rooted insecurity indicate that the Shaughnessy household is highly dysfunctional. In hopes of fulfilling his dreams of making it "big" in Hollywood one day, Artie plays the piano on amateur nights at the El Dorado Bar. Dissatisfied with his drab domestic life, Artie forms a relationship with his downstairs neighbor, Bunny Flingus, whose goal is to have Bananas committed to a mental institution so that she can escape with Artie to Hollywood, where fantasies are fulfilled and stars are born.

Artie and Bunny view Pope Paul's visit to New York to deliver a speech about peace to the United Nations as a chance to get close to a well-known celebrity; their hope is that His Holiness will bless Artie's songs, providing Artie with the impetus to make his own luck in Hollywood with a little help from Artie's old friend, big-shot Hollywood director Billy Einhorn. Meanwhile, Ronnie makes plans to kill the pope with a homemade bomb in order to obtain celebrity status through this infamous act. In Guare's black comedy, however, things go awry. Ronnie's bomb misses the target and instead kills two nuns and Billy Einhorn's girlfriend, starlet Corrinna Stroller. Bunny flees to Australia with Billy to help him make movies there, leaving Artie in Queens with his deranged wife and felonious son. Artie, desperate in the realization that his existence has been based on an elusive fantasy and now faced with the grim reality of a life of hopeless dreams, kisses his wife one last time and then strangles her to death.

The House of Blue Leaves demythologizes the American Dream, and it is concerned with how we try to avoid humiliation when we realize that our dreams cannot be realized. The reality of our failed dreams is always painful, and thus we perceive it as a blessing when our religious institutions and our popular culture embellish the notion that being rich and famous is within our grasp. Guare demonstrates how our individual goals are subsumed by a more powerful, glamorized media conception of celebrity. This infatuation with celebrities allows us to dream of fame and fortune while we ignore the reality around us, including what may be meaningful relationships with family and friends, as well as spiritual connections. However, once the superficial and self-deceptive dreams are exposed and we are left with a real world that does not measure up to our fantasies, we are reduced to violent behavior in trying to cope. Guare's play touches an American conscience that dreams of a more perfect life yet refuses to recognize the intrinsic value of relationships based on shared experiences.

Gene A. Plunka
University of Memphis

HOUSE OF CONNELLY, THE PAUL GREEN
(1931) *The House of Connelly* is the last of GREEN's plays focused on the South. Conceived in 1926, it is the earliest work of imaginative literature to forge that picture of the South later used in one version or another by William Faulkner, LILLIAN HELLMAN, Margaret Mitchell, TENNESSEE WILLIAMS, and others: a South whose aristocrats go back in memory to a time when social power and enlightened values coincided

in their family but who lack the ability to act and find themselves threatened with extinction in the present. It is also the play that launched the GROUP THEATRE on its historically significant career through the 1930s when Group leaders chose it for their first production in the fall of 1931.

In the play Will Connelly (William Byrd Connelly), scion of a prominent North Carolina family, is incapacitated by guilt. On one hand, he is sickened by family members back through the generations whose behavior showed that they did not accept the humanity of African Americans. On the other, he is guilt-ridden about his own behavior—a dutiful son driven to renounce his family and its past: "There's something to search for," he believes, "a way to act right and know it's right. [But] Father and Grandfather didn't [find] it, and we're paying for it. All the old Connellys have doomed us to die. Our character is gone." Last of the family line, his plantation in decay, and he himself incapable of action, Will is correct at that point in his prophecy of doom. But to the plantation has come a tenant girl whose character is *not* gone. Unburdened by the past, Patsy Tate is full of energy, common sense, and decency. Although Will cannot undo the injustices of the past, with Patsy's support he gains the strength to expose and free himself from them. And his marriage to her, in the version produced by the Group Theatre, signals his salvation and a hopeful outlook for the family and the region. "The dead and the proud have to give way to us—to us the living," Patsy says for the two of them: "We have our life to live and we'll fight for it to the end."

The House of Connelly exists in two versions. In the second (the earliest written, but not produced professionally), Patsy is not allowed to revitalize the Connelly line. Two African-American maids, lifelong members of the Connelly household and sympathetic to Will's widowed mother and old-maid sisters, cannot accept the changes implied by Will's marriage to Patsy. This bleak version of the play ends with the maids smothering Patsy to death before the wedding day. Both versions are in print. The bleak version is found in Gassner's edition, *Five Plays of the South*; the hopeful version is in *"The House of Connelly" and Other Plays*. In a 1975 letter to Group Theatre cofounder

Cheryl Crawford, Green expressed his belief that "[t]he original tragic ending of the play was the right one. It came out of the nature of the material, out of the author's seeing and feeling, and it should have been kept" (Avery 682). Crawford and HAROLD CLURMAN of the Group Theatre had convinced Green to make the change.

BIBLIOGRAPHY

Avery, Laurence G., ed. *A Southern Life: Letters of Paul Green, 1916–1981.* Chapel Hill: University of North Carolina Press, 1994.

Green, Paul. *Five Plays of the South.* Edited by John Gassner. New York: Hill & Wang, 1963.

———. *"The House of Connelly" and Other Plays.* New York: Samuel French, 1931.

Laurence G. Avery
University of North Carolina–Chapel Hill

HOWARD, BRONSON (1842–1908)

Bronson Howard is known as the first American playwright to make his living by writing plays and was among the first in America to write about the process of writing drama. Howard began his association with drama as the theater critic for the *Free Press* in the city of his birth, Detroit, Michigan. His first produced play, an adaptation of episodes from Victor Hugo's *Les Miserables,* entitled *Fantine,* was performed in 1864 in Detroit.

In 1865, Howard moved to New York, where he continued writing for newspapers for several more years as he simultaneously wrote plays. Howard's play, *Saratoga* (1870), a comedy about a man who is engaged to four women at once, was very successfully produced in New York. Following this were the comedy of manners *Diamonds* (1872) and *Moorcroft; or, the Double Wedding* (1874), which, based on a short story by John Hay, is about a man who sells his half-brother into slavery. In his book *The Autobiography of a Play* (1886), Howard chronicles the development of one of his plays, first called *Lillian's Last Love* (1873), then revised into *The Banker's Daughter* (1878). It is about a woman who marries a wealthy man she does not love for her father's sake. It was the success of *The Banker's Daughter* that finally prompted Howard to give up

newspaper work entirely, convinced at last that he could make his living through playwriting alone.

Other Bronson Howard plays include *Old Love Letters* (1878), a one-act play; *Hurricanes* (1878) and *Fun in the Green Room* (1882), both comedies of little note; and *Wives* (1879), a comedy adapted from Molière's *École des Femmes* and *École des Maris.* In *Young Mrs. Winthrop* (1882), a couple, estranged because of the husband's preoccupation with his work, are reconciled through their child. *One of Our Girls* (1885), a comedy, compares American and French customs and women. This was followed by an unsuccessful romantic comedy, set in part in the Adirondacks, entitled *Met by Chance* (1887). This failure, however, was followed by the enormous success of *The Henrietta* (1887), a satire of life on Wall Street. *Aristocracy* (1892) is a comedy about upper-class Americans and Europeans. *Peter Stuyvesant* (1899), an historical comedy, was the last Bronson Howard play to be performed. He wrote two others, *Knave and Queen* and *Kate,* before his death in New Jersey in 1908.

The most popular of Bronson Howard's plays was the Civil War melodrama, SHENANDOAH (1888). The play begins and ends with a united nation, starting as it does with the firing on Fort Sumter and ending after Lee's surrender. During the course of the play—that is, the course of the war—young couples in love find themselves on opposite sides of the conflict. Ultimately, they, like the nation, are united as love conquers all. *Shenandoah* was not acclaimed by the critics, but it was loved by audiences, who seemed, 22 years after the end of the war, to connect with Howard's themes of unified patriotism and the supremacy of romantic love.

Bronson Howard is significant for having brought to the stage distinctly American themes. *The Banker's Daughter,* which—like Howard's other serious plays—is a very conventional melodrama, is also distinctly American. Westbrook, the banker, is a recognizably *American* banker; indeed, Howard was the first playwright to feature the American businessman in his plays. Howard also dealt with contemporary issues; Brenda Murphy, in her *American Realism and American Drama, 1880–1940,* writes: "Although it does so in a sentimental and conventional way, [*The Banker's*

Daughter] discusses current problems in current social institutions. Howard was using his drama to discuss a much debated issue in taking on the Victorian dilemma of duty or honor versus love as a basis for marriage. Although the play's moving force is as far from the artistic impulse of realism as it could be, these less central aspects [of American characters grappling with American social issues] are precisely what the realists would be concerned with in building a realistic theory of drama" (16–17). Though his plays were in many ways steeped in convention, he broke new ground by introducing distinctly American themes and characters.

BIBLIOGRAPHY

Howard, Bronson. *Autobiography of a Play*. 1886. New York: Dramatic Museum of Columbia University, 1914.

———. *The Banker's Daughter and Other Plays by Bronson Howard*. Edited by Alan Halline. 1940. Bloomington: Indiana University Press, 1963.

Murphy, Brenda. *American Realism and American Drama: 1880–1940*. Cambridge, England: Cambridge University Press, 1987.

HOWARD, SIDNEY (1891–1939)

Sidney Howard rose to fame as a playwright in the 1920s with his innovative and boldly realistic dramas of American life. Born into a well-to-do Oakland, California, family with wide-ranging cultural interests, he graduated from the University of California–Berkeley in 1915 and then enrolled in the first university-sponsored class devoted to teaching the practical aspects of playwriting, GEORGE PIERCE BAKER's "47 Workshop" at Harvard. World War I interrupted Howard's studies; following his service in the war, he worked as a journalist and investigative reporter in New York City.

His breakthrough as a dramatist came in 1924 when THEY KNEW WHAT THEY WANTED was produced by the prestigious THEATRE GUILD. The play develops a bittersweet triangle involving 60-year-old Tony, a warm-hearted Italian immigrant now the owner of a fine California vineyard, his mail-order bride Amy, and Joe, Tony's trusted employee. Joe and Amy are attracted to each other; they have a brief affair, which, repenting, they confess to Tony. At the play's resolution, Tony and Amy are reconciled, even though he realizes she is pregnant with Joe's child, and Joe goes off to organize farm workers, realizing that this calling is what matters most to him. Howard's play, which became the basis for the 1956 musical *The Most Happy Fella,* survived an attempt by New York City officials to close it for purported immorality, going on to win the author a PULITZER PRIZE in 1925.

The playwright's next major success was another Theatre Guild production, *The Silver Cord* (1926), which develops the story of a possessive mother's attempt to drive a wedge between her sons and the women in their lives. Mrs. Phelps is successful in the case of her son, Robert, driving his fiancée to suicide, but in Christina, David's wife and a skilled scientist, she meets her match. With his wife's support, the son is able to break with his pathological mother.

In 1929, Howard began a new phase of his career, signing with Hollywood's Samuel Goldwyn to write screenplays at a time when the film industry was making the transition to "talkies." Howard did not believe that screenplays should be patterned on writing for the stage, yet he was convinced that his theater training had forged skills that would enable him to elevate the quality of film writing. Although his screenplays, all adaptations of novels, were nominated for Academy Awards on three occasions—he received an Oscar for *Gone with the Wind* in 1939—he never abandoned the theater. His most noteworthy plays of the 1930s were *Dodsworth* and *Yellow Jack* in 1934 and *Paths of Glory* in 1935, each adapted from an existing text. Although not a success, the antiwar *Paths of Glory* was a remarkable departure from Howard's traditional realism; it was performed on a stage virtually bare of scenery and employed light and sound to establish and direct the mood.

In 1935, Howard was elected president of the Dramatists Guild; here, he was instrumental in establishing a play service, a major innovation at the time, which allowed nonprofessional theaters to apply for performance rights to Guild members' works, thus opening a vast new market for dramatists and expanding their right to reap the profits of their own work.

Howard's career was cut short by a fatal accident on his Massachusetts farm in 1939. His legacy of challenging and morally probing dramas, which often focus on issues involving the newly emancipated woman, places him securely in the forefront of those American dramatists who, in the early decades of the 20th century, sought to make of the theater something more than mere diversion.

BIBLIOGRAPHY

Howard, Sidney. *The Silver Cord.* New York: Scribners, 1927.
———. *They Knew What They Wanted.* Garden City, N.Y.: Doubleday, 1925.
———. *Yellow Jack.* New York: Harcourt, Brace, 1934.
White, Sidney Howard. *Sidney Howard.* Boston: G. K. Hall, 1977.

Craig Clinton
Reed College

HOWE, TINA (1937–   )   Playwright and teacher Tina Howe was educated at Sarah Lawrence College (B.A., 1959) as well as Columbia University and Chicago Teacher's College, where she did graduate work. Howe won a Distinguished Playwriting OBIE AWARD in 1983.

Although her plays generally seem to feature recognizable surfaces of contemporary life, Howe officially spurns pure psychological realism for an absurdist focus on decentered human motivations, on gaffes in human communication, and on behavioral giddiness and pratfalls. Hence, art gallery visitors, in *Museum* (1976), bizarrely rob from, and then deface and demolish, esteemed art objects. In *The Art of Dining* (1979), gourmet restaurant patrons abrasively try to seize others' menu choices by falsely claiming those orders as their own.

Ever since her early play *The Nest* (1969), much of Howe's work has considered patriarchal constraints upon society, especially upon women. However, Howe often has also shown a somewhat patient empathy with even the foibles of harried modern males. Her feminist dialectic is, in general, never simple. *One Shoe Off* (1993) has received some feminist critics' scorn for including male characters' comments disparaging professional women, and yet the play also surely implies that domesticity holds its own dangers (a house trailer may careen, with murderous results, down a highway; a house closet may mysteriously transform itself into a weird garden of fetid vegetation). Howe's *Birth and after Birth* (1973) demonstrates, in the character of Sandy Apple, the needless caging of some contemporary women within mere housewifery; yet, the same play also shows, in the character of professional anthropologist Mia Freed, a pathological fear of motherhood. Photographer Holly Dancer, in COASTAL DISTURBANCES (1986), feels ardor both for the rambunctious and forthright lifeguard Leo Hart and for her urbane and insincere professional associate, art gallery owner André Sor. Gourmet chef Ellen, in *The Art of Dining,* continually strives to achieve personal feats of gastronomic delight, but she also wants effectively to share the restaurant duties with her perplexing (often doltish) husband. Fanny Church, the Boston Brahmin matriarch of PAINTING CHURCHES (1983), taunts her painter daughter Mags for never having married, but she also sadly misses her own long-past artistic experiences.

Art and other stellar human achievements always fascinate Howe. Nonetheless, while the main artist figure whose psyche is explored in Howe's *Approaching Zanzibar* (1989) is the inspiration-impoverished male composer Wally Blossom, the play—authored by a conscious but compassionate feminist—more dominantly examines the varied struggles of its multigenerational women: the death-fearing child Pony Blossom, her menopause-tormented mother Charlotte, and their cancer-ridden, but spiritually defiant, octogenarian crone relative Aunt Olivia Childs. This play about the power of the "Life-Force," as it is encountered from "A to Z," resembles both PRIDE'S CROSSING (1997), which celebrates Mabel's, another dying old woman's, continued celebration of existence, and *Museum,* wherein all true artists and true art are sensed as "*Noisy* with life!"

Howe's chief theme seems to remain the supremacy of loving deeds over any artistic brushstroke. The eponymous Dutch artist of *Rembrandt's Gift* (2002) returns from the dead and then prods a modern actor to revive (albeit imperfectly) the ardency of his marital relationship. *Such Small Hands* (2003) contrasts a renowned painter's two daughters (one intellectually gifted and physically beautiful; the other plain, but much more loving). The painter Catherine Sargent, in

Chasing Manet (2009), at first proves a surly nursing home recluse. Yet she eventually, and affectionately, "adopts," as a colleague in adventure, her dementia-suffering roommate.

Howe's Ionesco translations were performed in 2004 at the Atlantic Theater Company, where her revision of *Birth and after Birth* appeared in 2006. She is now writing a play under a Sloan Science Foundation grant.

BIBLIOGRAPHY
Howe, Tina. *"Approaching Zanzibar" and Other Plays.* New York: Theatre Communications Group, 1995.
———. *Coastal Disturbances: Four Plays.* New York: Theatre Communications Group, 1987.
———. *Pride's Crossing.* New York: Theatre Communications Group, 1998.
———. *"Rembrandt's Gift." Humana Festival 2002: The Complete Plays.* Edited by Tanya Palmer and Amy Wegener. Hanover, N.H.: Smith and Kraus, 2002, pp. 80–125.
Ionesco, Eugène. *"The Bald Soprano" and "The Lesson."* Translated by Tina Howe. New York: Grove Press, 2006.

Jeffrey B. Loomis
Northwest Missouri State University

HOWELLS, WILLIAM DEAN (1837–1920)

Novelist, critic, essayist, playwright, poet, and editor, William Dean Howells was one of the major American literary figures of the late 19th and early 20th centuries. His primary significance now is as a realistic novelist and the leading critical voice for the realist movement in the United States between 1880 and 1900. Amazingly prolific, Howells produced some 35 novels, nine volumes of short fiction, eight volumes of criticism (in addition to his 30 years of regular monthly columns in various issues of *Harper's Magazine*), 36 plays, 10 travel books, five volumes of autobiography, and four volumes of poetry. Among his many critical reviews and essays are 60 pieces of drama criticism that champion the groundbreaking work of playwrights like Henrik Ibsen and George Bernard Shaw and articulate a realistic approach to drama, praising American playwrights, such as JAMES A. HERNE, BRONSON HOWARD, EDWARD HARRIGAN, and CLYDE FITCH, for the advances each made toward creating a more fully realized realistic drama, both in the text and in the theater.

As a critic, Howells had a straightforward and consistent message: Playwrights should strive to present a direct reflection of life on the stage—in character, dialogue, and setting—with as little artificiality, convention, and arbitrariness in the action as possible. He was an early and avid champion of the problem play, defending the right of Europeans to write about the less savory aspects of life, but he also praised contemporary Americans for foregoing sensationalism in favor of dramatizing simple, everyday life. His own plays have been praised for realizing his convictions in their natural, "nonliterary" dialogue that still manages to be witty and clever, their psychological characterization, their detailed and carefully described settings that were typical of the middle-class life he wrote about, and their discussion of significant and timely social issues.

The best known of Howells's plays are a series of 12 one-act society farces that he wrote during the 1880s and 1890s and published in magazines. The plays are based on a close-knit circle of upper-middle-class Back Bay Boston friends, particularly two couples, the Robertses, based on Howells and his wife Elinor, and the Campbells, based on close friends of the Howellses, Livy and Sam Clemens (Mark Twain). They revolve around incidents in the characters' daily lives that are suggested in the titles—*The Sleeping Car* (1882), *The Elevator* (1884), *The Mouse Trap* (1886), *Five O'Clock Tea* (1887), *The Albany Depot* (1889), *A Letter of Introduction* (1892), *Evening Dress* (1892), and *The Unexpected Guests* (1893). In these plays, Howells used the deceptively innocent form of the farce to assault some of the basic assumptions of this society, particularly its anomalous moral position as a social group that professes to believe in truth, but actually could not function without constant falsehood and deceit. Howells also made use of the traditional comic types of fool and knave to attack the fundamental corruption of this social order: Through Roberts, Howells demonstrates the social structure that necessarily excludes the innocent from its deceitful workings, and through Campbell, he shows the fragility of the social order when confronted by an outsider who is intent on deceiving the deceivers. While these one-act plays did not receive many professional productions, they were widely read and often produced by amateur theater groups well into the 20th century.

Howells never achieved great financial success in the professional theater, but he had some in collaboration with actor-manager Lawrence Barrett, who toured with *A Counterfeit Presentment* (1877). This play was ahead of its time in taking a stock comic device, mistaken identity, and making it into a serious problem. With its depth of characterization, its treatment of a psychological dilemma, and its straightforward presentation of a problem, it had much more in common with the newly emerging realistic drama in Europe than with anything in the American theater in the 1870s. The most advanced of Howells's plays, however, was *Out of the Question* (1877), which foreshadowed what Shaw was to define in 1891 as the "drama of discussion." In contrast to the "well-made play," which dominated serious drama in 19th-century America, this drama about the pervasive effect of social class in America is centered in the discussion of an issue rather than the construction of the plot. While Howells concentrated on his social farces during the next decades, he returned to the discussion play toward the end of his career, to point out the hypocrisy and commercialism of Christmas in *The Night before Christmas* (1910) and to attack one of his perennial targets, romantic self-sacrifice, in *True Hero: Melodrama* (1909).

BIBLIOGRAPHY

Brenni, Vito J. *William Dean Howells: A Bibliography.* Metuchen, N.J.: Scarecrow Press, 1973.
Howells, William Dean. *Complete Plays.* Edited by Walter J. Meserve. New York: New York University Press, 1960.
———. *A Realist in the American Theatre: Selected Drama Criticism of William Dean Howells.* Edited by Brenda Murphy. Athens: Ohio University Press, 1992.
Lynn, Kenneth Schuyler. *William Dean Howells: An American Life.* New York: Harcourt Brace Jovanovich, 1971.

Brenda Murphy
University of Connecticut

HOW I LEARNED TO DRIVE PAULA VOGEL **(1997)**   A dark comedy about pedophilia, *How I Learned to Drive* won the New York Drama Critics' Circle Award, the PULITZER PRIZE, and an OBIE AWARD for Playwriting.

The main character, Li'l Bit, ranges in age from 35 to 11, but she is played by a single actress. Uncle Peck, VOGEL advises in the published play, is an "attractive man in his forties" who, "despite [his] problems, . . . should be played by an actor one might cast in the role of Atticus in *To Kill a Mockingbird*"—in other words, the most-trusted and well-loved character one can imagine. All other characters are played by the three members of the "Greek Chorus." These include Grandfather, Grandmother, Mother, Aunt Mary, high-school boys and girls, and a waiter. In production, there is a "neutral voice (the type that driver education films employ)" used to read such scene titles as "You and the Reverse Gear" and "Defensive driving involves defending yourself from hazardous and sudden changes."

The play opens with a 17-year-old Li'l Bit in a parked car with a married man who feels her breasts and who turns out to be her Uncle Peck. (Peck's oblivious wife, Aunt Mary, says in a later scene, "Peck's so good with [kids] when they get to be this age.") An adult Li'l Bit comments: "I was sixteen or so before I realized that pedophilia did not mean men who loved to bicycle." Despite the subject matter, it is clear from the first scene that *How I Learned to Drive* is comic as well as serious.

As we move through her adolescence and finally back to her first abusive encounter at age 11 with Uncle Peck, we gain an appreciation of how much she has had to tolerate and how resilient she must be to have survived. Uncle Peck teaches her much more than how to drive a car. It is Uncle Peck, an alcoholic, who introduces her to alcohol before she is of age, and Uncle Peck who starts to take *Playboy* magazine–style photographs of her when she is 13. By the time Li'l Bit is old enough to escape to college, she is also damaged enough to drink a fifth of liquor a day and flunk out. Uncle Peck writes to her and sends her packages obsessively, until she agrees to see him on her 18th birthday: Her plan is finally to sever their relationship, while his is to propose marriage. When she rejects him, he proceeds to drink himself to death—succeeding seven years later.

The women in her life do not offer much guidance. As a teenager, Li'l Bit is teased mercilessly by members of her family about her large breasts, but her mother's response is "[S]he's so sensitive. You can't say boo." When Aunt Mary is not in complete denial, she is blaming Li'l Bit for manipulating a "good man," her husband. Her mother's lengthiest advice pertains to drinking in the company of any man: When doing so, she urges, one should wear a girdle "so tight that only a surgical knife or acetylene torch can get it off you." Furthermore, all of her life, the girl has witnessed the dynamic between her oversexed grandfather and his fed up wife, her grandmother, who proclaims in disgust, "Men are bulls! Big bulls!"

Her peers are no help either. The voluptuous teenager is the object of both lust and ridicule in her high school. The girls think she is weird, and the boys long to touch her breasts. She comments to another girl at a dance, who says that Li'l Bit "should take it as a compliment that the guys want to watch you jiggle": "[S]ometimes I feel like these alien life forces, these two mounds of flesh have grafted themselves onto my chest, and they're using me until they can 'propagate' and take over the world."

Ultimately, she comes to the conclusion that Peck was probably himself molested as a child. Her abuse began with her first driving lesson, when Uncle Peck invited Li'l Bit, age 11, to drive from his lap and then proceeded to take gross advantage of her position and her trust. In the final scene, long after Uncle Peck's death, she sees his image in her rearview mirror. She will never be completely without him.

Vogel explained her play's theme in an interview with Arthur Holmberg in 1998: "Many people stay rooted in anger against transgressions that occurred in childhood, and this rage will be directed to other people in their adult lives and toward themselves. Whether we call it forgiveness or understanding, there comes a moment when the past has to be processed, and we have to find some control. There are two for-givenesses in the play. One forgiveness for Peck, but the most crucial forgiveness would be Li'l Bit's forgiving Li'l Bit."

BIBLIOGRAPHY

Holmberg, Arthur. "Through the Eyes of Lolita: Pulitzer Prize–Winning Playwright Paula Vogel Is Interviewed." *American Repertory Theatre.* Available online. URL: http://www.amrep.org/past/drive/drive1.html. Downloaded October 7, 2002.

HOYT, CHARLES HALE (1860–1900)

Playwright Charles Hale Hoyt began his career as a journalist, serving as sports editor and drama critic for the *Boston Post,* as well as becoming one of the nation's first newspaper columnists. He also became a successful producer of his own plays, amassing a fortune in his relatively short career. Hoyt is best known for his broadly satirical comedies, which poke fun at various aspects of American life, particularly the prejudices, self-righteousness, and hypocrisy of small-town "leading citizens." His most popular play, *A Trip to Chinatown* (1891), ran for 650 performances in New York, the longest consecutive run of an American play up to that time.

Hoyt achieved his first success in the theater with *A Bunch of Keys; or, Where There's a Will, There's a Play* (1883), a good example of his early farcical bent. The play is essentially an extended joke about three sisters, one of whom is left a hotel in their uncle's will on the condition that she be declared the homeliest of the three by a traveling salesman staying in the hotel. Subsequent farces exercise a more satirical sensibility, although Hoyt declared that his first priority was always to amuse his audience. *A Parlor Match* (1884) satirizes the contemporary fad of spiritualism. *A Rag Baby* (1884) makes fun of the intrigues of small-town life. One critic suggested that *A Hole in the Ground* (1887), which takes place in a railroad station, portrays nearly every event that happens to traveling and suffering humanity while waiting for delayed trains. Hoyt described the targets of *The Brass Monkey* (1888) as superstition, obtrusive grief, and the "guerillas of journalism" who have created prejudice against their profession by their violation of truth and decency.

The Midnight Bell (1889), which Hoyt described as "a legitimate comedy," has more of a plot than his earlier plays, but the melodrama of its self-sacrificing hero and its obvious villain was already outdated in 1889. Two of Hoyt's strongest plays followed this effort: *A Texas Steer* (1890) brings a newly elected congressman, Maverick Brander, and his family to Washington, where they become entangled in intrigue and blackmail, and *A Trip to Chinatown* (1891) uses a flimsy plot about a masked ball to caricature several society types. In *A Temperance Town* (1893), the town drunk and the saloon-keeper turn out to be the only honest and kindhearted men in a town where alcohol is prohibited. In *A Runaway Colt* (1895), Hoyt called on his experience as a former sports editor to write an early treatment of a baseball player, Captain Adrian Anson of the Chicago Colts, who is shown to be morally superior to clergymen and bank cashiers. Hoyt took on two of his favorite targets in *The Contented Woman* (1897), his play about a husband and wife who run against each other for office, poking fun at their gender differences as well as the American political system.

BIBLIOGRAPHY

Hunt, Douglas L. *The Life and Work of Charles H. Hoyt.* Nashville, Tenn.: Joint University Libraries, 1945.
———, ed. *American's Lost Plays Vol. IX: Charles Hoyt.* Princeton, N.J.: Princeton University Press, 1941.

Brenda Murphy
University of Connecticut

HUGHES, HOLLY (1955–   )

Born in Saginaw, Michigan, Holly Hughes grew up with her younger sister, her stay-at-home mother, and her father, who worked at General Motors and who Hughes felt was perpetually absent from her life. She earned a B.A. in painting from Kalamazoo College and moved to New York City in 1979 to continue painting at the Feminist Art Institute. In her published artist's statement, Hughes explains that this move was motivated not only by her desire to develop a painting career but also by a growing need to find a community of lesbian and feminist women, sorely lacking from her midwestern, small-town upbringing.

Working as a waitress to pay the rent, Hughes soon found that the financial demands of living in New York impinged on her ability to develop her painting; furthermore, she had difficulty finding a feminist community comfortable with her lesbianism (the Feminist Art Institute broke up because of ideological conflicts).

In 1982, Hughes attended the WOW (Women's One World) Festival, an event that featured many women performance artists. She then began volunteering at the WOW Café, a lesbian/feminist performance space and bar. It was at the WOW Café that Hughes wrote and performed her first plays: *The Well of Horniness* (1983) and *The Lady Dick* (1985), approximating the style of 1940s film noir and featuring detectives and femmes fatales, but also significantly departing from that classic genre by explicitly and positively depicting lesbian sexual desire. By 1986, Hughes had moved her work to other New York City performance art venues such as Performance Space 122, where Lois Weaver and Peggy Shaw of the troupe Split Britches performed Hughes's third play, *Dress Suits to Hire* (1988), and where she performed her solo piece, *World without End* (1989). Although Hughes's early plays feature multiple parts for actors, like performance art in general, their meaning derived from the specific places in which they were performed for a particular audience who was as much a part of the show as the actors themselves. *World without End* signaled a departure from Hughes's earlier plays, not only because it is a solo performance but also because its content was mainly autobiographical, interweaving stories about Hughes's family, her childhood, and her sexuality.

Only four blocks from the WOW Café, the move to Performance Space 122 also meant a move into the public eye: P.S. 122 attracted a larger audience and was more readily attended by theater and art critics. Public controversy and debate followed the move, as Hughes, along with performance artists KAREN FINLEY, John Fleck, and Tim Miller, later known as "the NEA four," had their grant funding rescinded by the National Endowment for the Arts. In 1990, the public announcement of the NEA's decision began an eight-year process of trials, Supreme Court appeals, and public debates centered on censorship and on standards for distinguishing between "art" and "obscenity." As much as it was emotionally and physically taxing, this controversy also catapulted Hughes into a much broader spotlight than she had previously enjoyed, and she developed performances that directly address issues of censorship and public funding for the arts. Her 1999 piece, *Preaching to the Perverted,* restages the federal funding debates, emphasizing the constitution of "queer" community not only by those who would define it from within its folds but also by those who attack it from without.

At the boundaries between theater and performance art, Hughes continues to employ her small-town, midwestern upbringing to address complex political issues. Hughes has lectured at colleges and universities across the United States and is now a tenured professor at the University of Michigan, where she teaches in both the School of Art and Design and the Department of Theatre and Drama. Her newest performance piece, "The Dog and Pony Show (Bring Your Own Pony)," is still a work-in-progress, though she has performed parts of it, as she did in 2006 at a benefit for Highways Performance Space in Santa Monica, California. She is also in the process of coediting, with Alina Troyano, the book *Memories of the Revolution: The First Ten Years of the WOW Café,* which will be published by University of Michigan Press.

BIBLIOGRAPHY

Hughes, Holly, and David Román, eds. *O Solo Homo: The New Queer Performance.* New York: Grove Press, 1998.

Maria Ghira Renu Cappelli
University of California–Berkeley

HUGHES, LANGSTON (1902–1967)

Although he is known primarily as a poet, Langston Hughes had a lifelong interest in the theater. He wrote more than 60 plays, 23 in collaboration with others and 40 as sole author. Hughes worked in many genres throughout his career, including traditional tragedy and comedy, folk comedy, AGITPROP, opera, the gospel play, and the historical pageant. He brought originality and a spirit of innovation to the drama, conscious always of creating plays that were authentic expressions of what he characterized in his famous essay, "The Negro Artist and the Racial Mountain," as "our individual dark-skinned selves" (*The Nation,* June 23, 1926).

As a high-school student in Cleveland, Hughes became involved with Karamu House, the home of the Gilpin Players, the most distinguished black theater company of the early 20th century, which was eventually to produce his first one-act play, *A Gold Piece* (1921). Hughes's greatest success in the theater came with his first full-length play, written during his residence at Jasper Deeter's Hedgerow Theatre near Philadelphia in 1930. MULATTO is a tragedy about a southern family whose father is the white owner of a plantation and whose mother is his black housekeeper. After their son Robert returns from school in the North, he refuses to behave like a servant in the house any longer, and his escalating rebellion against his father ends in a confrontation in which Robert kills his father. The play ends with Robert's suicide to escape a lynch mob. Hughes objected strongly to the addition of a rape scene in Martin Jones's 1935 New York production, but it was his greatest financial success in the theater, running for 373 performances.

The 1930s was the most intense period of work in the theater for Hughes. After writing *Mulatto,* he collaborated with ZORA NEALE HURSTON on the folk comedy *Mule Bone,* an experience that ended their friendship when Hurston claimed sole authorship. The play was finally produced under both names by New York's Lincoln Center in 1991. Hughes's acquaintance with the work of the great Russian directors during his extended trip to the Soviet Union (1932–33) opened his eyes to new possibilities for his own drama, and a period as playwright-in-residence with the Gilpin Players gave him the opportunity to put these into practice. Besides *Mulatto* as originally written, the Gilpin Players produced two other serious plays—Hughes's drama about the career of Jean-Jacques Dessalines in Haiti, *Troubled Island* (1936), and *Front Porch* (1938), a play that concerns color prejudice, class, and labor politics within the black middle class. They also produced three comedies, *Little Ham* (1936), an urban folk comedy with a mild moral about the exploitation of the black community by the numbers racket; *When the Jack Hollers* (1936), a comedy about black sharecroppers and their white neighbors; and *Joy to My Soul* (1937), a farcical treatment of sharp urbanites preying on a newly arrived and rich country bumpkin.

A committed leftist, Hughes also wrote plays with a straightforward political purpose. The best known of these, *Scottsboro, Limited* (1931), is an agitprop play that was written to support the cause of the "Scottsboro boys," nine young black men falsely convicted of rape in Alabama. The play was intended and used as a portable production that was performed at rallies in the United States and abroad. Also in the agitprop tradition is *Don't You Want to Be Free?* (1938), which Hughes described in a program note as an "emotional history" of African Americans. It was produced by the Harlem Suitcase Theatre (1938–39), an offshoot of the John Reed Club of New York and the first theater of which Hughes was a founder, followed by later productions at the New Negro Theatre in Los Angeles (1939) and the Skyloft Theatre in Chicago (1942). Hughes's unproduced political plays include *Harvest,* a collaborative effort about the 1933 farm workers' strike in California's San Joaquin Valley, and *Angelo Herndon Jones,* about a Communist organizer imprisoned in Georgia.

In 1942, the Skyloft Players produced *The Sun Do Move,* a historical play about a family's slavery and escape to freedom, which foreshadowed a series of plays by Hughes featuring gospel music that were produced in New York, including *Black Nativity* (1961), *Tambourines to Glory* (1963), *Jericho-Jim Crow* (1964), and, the most successful, *The Prodigal Son* (1965), based on the biblical parable. Hughes also wrote a number of operas and musicals, including *The Barrier* (1950), based on *Mulatto; Simply Heavenly* (1957), based on his character Jesse B. Simple; and the libretto for ELMER RICE and Kurt Weill's opera version of Rice's *STREET SCENE* (1947).

BIBLIOGRAPHY

Dickinson, Donald, *A Bio-bibliography of Langston Hughes 1902–1967.* Hamden, Conn.: Archon, 1967.

Hughes, Langston. *The Collected Works of Langston Hughes, Volume 5: The Plays to 1942: "Mulatto" to "The Sun Do Move."* Edited by Nancy Johnston and Leslie Catherine Sanders. Columbia: University of Missouri Press, 2001.

———. *The Collected Works of Langston Hughes, Volume 6: Gospel Plays, Operas, and Later Dramatic Works.* Edited by Leslie Catherine Sanders. Columbia: University of Missouri Press, 2003.

———. *Five Plays.* Edited by Webster Smalley. Bloomington: Indiana University Press, 1963.

———. *The Political Plays of Langston Hughes.* Edited by Susan Duffy. Carbondale: Southern Illinois University Press, 2000.

Rampersad, Arnold. *The Life of Langston Hughes.* 2 vols. New York: Oxford University Press, 1986, 1988.

Brenda Murphy
University of Connecticut

HUGHIE EUGENE O'NEILL (1941)   This one-act play was originally conceived by O'NEILL as one of eight plays in a series to be called "By Way of Orbit." Set in a third-class New York hotel late one night in 1928, it portrays the down and out "Erie" Smith ("born in Erie, PA"), just days after the funeral of Hughie, the hotel's former night clerk.

As the play begins, Erie is returning to the hotel after several days' absence, during which he has been "on a drunk." He returns to find a new night clerk, Hughie's replacement. Though it is a two-character play, most of the lines are Erie's. As he tells the new night clerk about himself and about Hughie, we learn that Erie lives by gambling and running shady errands for gangsters, that his time is spent on horses and dice, drinking and women, and that his luck ran out when Hughie was taken to the hospital.

Erie grieves for the loss of Hughie because Hughie fed Erie's fantasies about himself: "He saw me as some kind of dream guy. The bigger I made myself, the more he lapped it up." Because Hughie believed in his exaggerated tales of women, gambling, and gangster connections, Erie feigns contempt for Hughie, whom he calls "a sap" and "a sucker"; in reality, he is devastated by Hughie's death because with Hughie went Erie's confidence. He tells the new desk clerk, "I'd get to seein' myself like he seen me."

Throughout Erie's long monologues, the new night clerk, Charlie, tunes him out, preoccupied by his own thoughts of the more exciting—even violent—life he craves. His lines until the final quarter of the play are few and are disconnected from what Erie says. When the garbage men pass, he imagines being a garbage man and making enough noise with the cans to "wake up the whole damned city." When the police pass, he imagines a shoot-out, and when fire engines pass, a fire that will burn down the entire city. These impulses are in sharp contrast to his silent, indifferent exterior.

Finally, the two men turn to each other to find what they need. When Charlie realizes that listening to Erie can bring his life vicarious excitement, he begins to question him about gambling and gangsters; in turn, Erie soon realizes he has found a replacement for Hughie, someone who can bring the pretense of significance to his dismal, lonely life. As in O'Neill's full-length The ICEMAN COMETH, a character with little to live for is sustained by a "pipe dream"—a delusion of hope—and someone to believe in that pipe dream.

HUMANA FESTIVAL OF NEW AMERICAN PLAYS

An internationally recognized drama festival, the Humana Festival of New American Plays was started in 1976 by the then producing director of the Actors Theatre of Louisville (ATL), Jon Jory (who remained in the position through 2000). The festival, held annually at ATL, showcases new dramatic works by American playwrights. These works include full-length and one-act plays, as well as other innovative works of drama (for example, at the 2001 festival, seven short "phone plays" could be heard only on dummy pay phones in the lobby of one of the theaters). The festival lasts six weeks, but those critics, agents, artistic directors, and others who come from outside Louisville usually arrive in the middle of the festival when all the plays are running and may be seen within two or three days. Since its founding in 1976, tens of thousands of scripts have been submitted to the New Play Program at ATL.

The list of plays that have premiered at the Humana Festival includes many that have gone on to great success: the PULITZER PRIZE–winning plays The GIN GAME (1977) by D. L. Coburn, CRIMES OF THE HEART (1979) by BETH HENLEY, and DINNER WITH FRIENDS (1998) by DONALD MARGULIES; as well as GETTING OUT (1978) by MARSHA NORMAN, Agnes of God (1980) by John Pielmeier, Extremities (1981) by WILLIAM MASTROSIMONE, Courtship (1984) by HORTON FOOTE, Danny and the Deep Blue Sea (1984) by JOHN PATRICK SHANLEY, Tales of the Lost Formicans (1989) by CONSTANCE CONGDON, In the Eye of the Hurricane (1990) by EDUARDO MACHADO, Marisol (1992) by JOSÉ RIVERA, Slavs! (1994) by TONY KUSHNER, Y2K (1999) by ARTHUR KOPIT, Omnium-Gatherum (2003) by THERESA REBECK and Alexandra Gersten-Vassilaros, and The Unseen (2007) by CRAIG WRIGHT. (All dates are Humana Festival production dates.)

BIBLIOGRAPHY

Actors Theater of Louisville. Available online. URL: www. actorstheateroflouisville. com.

Dixon, Michael Bigelow, and Liz Engelman, eds. Humana Festival '96: The Complete Plays. Lyme, N.H.: Smith and Kraus, 1996.

———, eds. Humana Festival '97: The Complete Plays. Lyme, N.H.: Smith and Kraus, 1997.

Dixon, Michael Bigelow, and Amy Wegener, eds. Humana Festival '98: The Complete Plays. Lyme, N.H.: Smith and Kraus, 1998.

———, eds. Humana Festival '99: The Complete Plays. Lyme, N.H.: Smith and Kraus, 1999.

———, eds. Humana Festival 2000: The Complete Plays. Lyme, N.H.: Smith and Kraus, 2000.

Hansel, Adrien-Alice, and Julie Felise Dubiner, eds. Plays from Actors Theatre of Louisville: Humana Festival 2005. New York: Broadway Play Publishing, 2007.

———, eds. Humana Festival 2006: The Complete Plays. New York: Playscripts, Inc., 2007.

———, eds. Humana Festival 2007: The Complete Plays. New York: Playscripts, Inc., 2008.

Palmer, Tanya, and Adrien-Alice Hansel, eds. Humana Festival 2004: The Complete Plays. Lyme, N.H.: Smith and Kraus, 2005.

Smith, Marisa, ed. Humana Festival '93: The Complete Plays. Lyme, N.H.: Smith and Kraus, 1993.

———, ed. Humana Festival '94: The Complete Plays. Lyme, N.H.: Smith and Kraus, 1994.

———, ed. Humana Festival '95: The Complete Plays. Lyme, N.H.: Smith and Kraus, 1995.

Volansky, Michele, and Michael Bigelow Dixon, eds. Humana Festival: 20 One-Act Plays from Twenty Years of the Humana Festival. Lyme, N.H.: Smith and Kraus, 1995.

Wegener, Amy, and Tanya Palmer, eds. *Humana Festival 2001: The Complete Plays*. Lyme, N.H.: Smith and Kraus, 2002.

———, eds. *Humana Festival 2002: The Complete Plays*. Lyme, N.H.: Smith and Kraus, 2002.

———, eds. *Humana Festival 2003: The Complete Plays*. Lyme, N.H.: Smith and Kraus, 2003.

HURLYBURLY DAVID RABE (1984)

Set on the edge of Hollywood over the course of one year in a turbulent world of drugs, alcohol, self-destruction, and abuse, *Hurlyburly* is a play about men behaving badly and male bonding gone awry.

Eddie awakens hungover and half-dressed on his couch when his friend, Phil, an actor, arrives and describes his latest fight with his wife: Phil admits that he came home "ripped," that he was "demented and totally ranting" and woke her up, but he resents her intolerance, and Eddie concurs that she is "perverse." Phil eventually confesses that he hit her and that he fears this time she will not take him back. By the end of the first act, it is just "eight forty-five in the morning" and Eddie and Phil have already had marijuana, bourbon, and cocaine. Mickey, Eddie's roommate, awakened by their noise, resents Eddie's early morning drug and alcohol consumption because they are expected at a business meeting. Mickey's irritation prompts Eddie to mention Darlene, a woman Eddie brought home but Mickey dined with and took to bed on the grounds that there was an irresistible "vibe" between them. Now it is clear that the union meant little to Mickey, while to Eddie, the woman represented the "possibility of happiness." Soon Artie—a "slick" California type, *"a mixture of toughness and arrogance"*—stops by with Donna, a 15-year-old street girl he has found in the elevator of his building; he has had sex with her and now "gives" her to Eddie and Mickey "[l]ike a care package" for their sexual pleasure. As Mickey begins to take Donna, Eddie, still irate at the loss of Darlene, removes Donna, *"a little stoned and scared,"* to his bedroom, inviting Phil to join them. He sarcastically dismisses Mickey, reminding him that he has "a serious relationship" with Darlene. When Darlene comes to the house at the beginning of the following scene, the cynical Mickey, with false

sincerity, bows out of their "relationship" in favor of Eddie. (Although Darlene and Eddie become involved, the "possibility for happiness" that he saw in her never materializes.)

Phil's instability and tendencies toward anger and violence increase as the play develops. He butts Donna in the head, throws an exotic dancer from a moving car, and knocks a stranger unconscious. Artie accuses Eddie of investing time and energy in the crazy, violent, loser Phil because "no matter how far [Eddie] manage[s] to fall, Phil will be lower . . . looking up in wide-eyed admiration." At the end of the play, Phil commits suicide by driving "a hundred MPH" in an "attempt to land in a tree on the side of a cliff-like incline." Returning from Phil's funeral, Eddie finds in his mail Phil's cryptic suicide note, a "fortune cookie" kind of message, in which Eddie wants desperately to find meaning. Soon, he is *"grabbing for his box of dope and coke,"* alone with the television and his own desperation until Donna—absent for a year—comes in quietly. Despite her life on the streets, Donna is an innocent. Without cynicism, she listens to Eddie's emotional description of the funeral and then falls asleep next to him as *"he holds her"* on the couch and the play ends.

Like many of the characters in RABE's Vietnam trilogy (*The BASIC TRAINING OF PAVLO HUMMEL* [1971], *STICKS AND BONES* [1971], and *STREAMERS* [1976]), "Eddie and Mickey, and, indeed, all the characters in *Hurlyburly*, are 'streamers,' desperately refusing to acknowledge their downward plunge towards oblivion, generating fantasies for themselves as they do for others, blotting out the world whose threat they wish to deny" (Bigsby 281).

BIBLIOGRAPHY

Bigsby, Christopher. "David Rabe." In *Contemporary American Playwrights*. Cambridge, England: Cambridge University Press, 1999. 252–288.

HURSTON, ZORA NEALE (1891–1960)

Zora Neale Hurston was born in Notasulga, Alabama. Her parents, Lucy Potts and John Hurston (a carpenter, mayor, and preacher), moved to Eatonville, Florida, where Hurston spent her infancy and youth. In 1904, Lucy died and young Zora was devastated. Her father remarried a woman who had no affection for Zora, and he sent her away to boarding school in Jacksonville. In 1917, she earned her high school diploma and attended Howard University for the next four years. Although known for her fiction, Hurston wrote many plays and musicals, most of which were never published or performed. She entered her dramas *Spears* and *Color Struck* in the *Opportunity* magazine contest (1925) and won second place for the latter; *Spears* won honorable mention. This award launched her career as a major Harlem Renaissance writer.

In *Color Struck* (1925), a group of blacks travel by train to a cakewalk contest. Hurston, who was a mulatta, depicts a psychotic Emmaline (Emma), a dark "Negro," who is jealous of her light-skinned beau (John) and the light-skinned women who flirt with him. Emma rejects John a second time when he returns 20 years later. After all her railing against mulattoes, she has had an affair with a white man (we assume). John returns to find Emma alone and poor but with a very sick child. She delays going for the doctor, and when she finally does, she returns to find John in the girl's room. Emma accuses John of molesting her. The "almost white" child dies before the doctor arrives. Emma rejects John's proposal and throws him out. The doctor leaves her a box of pills, and the play ends with Emma sobbing and rocking in her chair. One way to interpret Emma's action is that she is so guilty about her white child and her affair that she deliberately delays going for the doctor—causing the child's death—and finds an excuse to reject John. Color is at the center of another published play, *The First One* (1927), a satire on the Noah/Ham Bible story, in which a drunken Noah turns the skin of his son Ham and his wife black and exiles them. The unpublished "Spunk" tells the story of a black youth who falls in love with and steals another man's wife. He kills the man while defending himself and goes to prison, but he is set free. Written in 1935, when Hurston was involved in voodoo research, this powerful play is laced with spirituals, blues, and voodoo. Hurston's obsession with skin color surfaces again in the many unpublished revues, plays, and skits she penned, housed in the NAACP collection at the Library of Congress.

Hurston attended Barnard College during 1925–28 to study anthropology with the famous Franz Boas, who sent her to Haiti and Jamaica to study folklore. Her musical revue *The Great Day* (1932) was produced on Broadway but closed abruptly. She was awarded a Guggenheim Fellowship (1936) for doctoral research in anthropology at Columbia and in 1938 published her findings on voodoo in *Tell My Horse*. In 1939, Hurston published her autobiography, *Dust Tracks on a Road*. After failing to mount "Polk County" on Broadway, Hurston returned to fiction in 1947. She is best known for her novel, *Their Eyes Were Watching God* (1937).

Hurston's final decades were fraught with problems, financial, political (she was against desegregation), and social. Although she was exonerated, she never recovered from the accusation that she molested a 10-year-old boy in 1948. Hurston died in poverty in a welfare home in Fort Pierce, Florida, in 1960. Alice Walker marked her grave in 1973 and was responsible for the Hurston revival when her article "In Search of Zora Neale Hurston" was published by *Ms.* Magazine in 1975.

BIBLIOGRAPHY

Bower, Martha Gilman. *Color Struck under the Gaze: The Pathology of Being in the Plays of Johnson, Hurston, Childress, Hansberry, and Kennedy.* Westport, Conn.: Greenwood Press, 2003.

Boyd, Valerie. *Wrapped in Rainbows: The Life of Zora Neale Hurston.* New York: Scribners, 2002.

Hemenway, Robert E. *Zora Neale Hurston.* Urbana: University of Illinois Press, 1980.

Hurston, Zora Neale. *Dust Tracks on a Road.* New York: Harper, 1991.

———. "Spunk" and other plays and revues. C-299, NAACP Collection. Library of Congress, Washington, D.C.

Kaplan, Carla, ed. *Zora Neale Hurston: A Life in Letters.* New York: Doubleday, 2002.

Martha Gilman Bower
Indiana University of Pennsylvania

HWANG, DAVID HENRY (1957–) Born in Los Angeles to immigrant Chinese parents, David Henry Hwang, at the age of 12, wrote down his grand-

mother's family stories to preserve them. Initially seeing himself as a prose writer, he felt more drawn to plays by the time he enrolled at Stanford University. He enjoyed what he felt was the more immediate connection he had with an audience through writing in direct speech. In 1978, during his summer vacation, he signed up for a playwriting workshop at the Padua Hills Playwrights Festival with SAM SHEPARD, whom he credits as an inspiration. A year later, he wrote his first play, *FOB* (1979), which won an OBIE for Best Play. Modeled on Shepard's *Angel City* in structure, *FOB* tells of a Chinese immigrant, "fresh-off-the-boat," meeting two Chinese-American students and exploring issues of assimilation as opposed to preserving cultural heritage; it uses Chinese theater techniques to present the characters as figures from Chinese myth. It was followed by two plays, *The Dance and the Railroad* (1981) and *Family Devotions* (1981), which complete a trilogy describing Hwang's vision of the Chinese-American experience. *The Dance and the Railroad* explores the past and potential future of two 19th-century Chinese immigrants working on the transcontinental railroad, while *Family Devotions,* set in the 20th century, farcically satirizes a wealthy Chinese-American family as it exposes a complicated East-West relationship.

Attempting to move away from Asian chronicles and not willing to be limited by popular expectation, Hwang next wrote a series of experimental one-acts, including *The House of Sleeping Beauties* (1983), in which an aging writer and a brothel owner find companionship and sadly reassess their past lives; *The Sound of a Voice* (1983), which explores Japanese gender psychology in the developing relationship between a samurai and a female hermit; and *As the Crow Flies* (1986), which looks at the multicultural connection between two women, a Chinese American and an African American. In the full-length *Rich Relations* (1986), the dysfunctional family portrayed is non-Asian, and Hwang uses these characters to satirize upper-middle-class attitudes toward religion and wealth. His collaboration with composer Philip Glass, *1000 Airplanes on the Roof* (1988), is science fiction and explores a character's need to discuss her alien abduction.

Hwang became the first Chinese-American dramatist to win a TONY AWARD with *M. BUTTERFLY* (1988), his play about the love affair between a French diplomat and a Chinese opera actor and spy, which explores issues of gender expectation, imperialism, identity, and relationships. In a quest for new artistic direction, Hwang then wrote the libretto for Philip Glass's opera, *The Voyage* (1992), an allegory about Columbus coming to America. Other libretti include *The Silver River* (1997), set in Central America, and *Aida* (2000), the latter with Linda Woolverton and Robert Falls.

The 1990s saw a series of further investigations into the social construction of race and gender first explored in *M. Butterfly* and include *Bondage* (1992), set in an S&M parlor; *Face Value* (1993), based on the casting controversy over *Miss Saigon;* and *Trying to Find Chinatown* (1996), about a white man coming to terms with his adoption by an Asian couple. *Golden Child* (1996), though considered a flop on its initial OFF-BROADWAY production, still won an Obie for playwriting. After extensive rewriting, it gained a more positive reception when it reopened on Broadway in 1998. It explores the disruption of Chinese feudal traditions in a multigenerational saga that stretches almost a century. Hwang has also written a pop-culture translation of Ibsen's *Peer Gynt* (1998), with Stephan Müller, and a new version of Rodgers and Hammerstein's 1958 musical *Flower Drum Song* (2002), which was extensively rewritten from the original and was nominated for a Tony Award for Best Book of a Musical. Another collaboration with Philip Glass in 2003 produced the libretti for two theatrical operas, *The Sound of a Voice* (based on his earlier play) and *Hotel of Dreams,* set in a mysterious brothel catering to old men who cannot sleep and need a way to relive the dreams of their youth. Hwang continues to work steadily in the world of opera and musical theater; this work includes the book for the 2006 Broadway musical of *Tarzan,* the libretto for an operatic version of *Alice in Wonderland* (with Unsuk Chin) in 2007, and the libretto of a new opera for Plácido Domingo, based on the movie *The Fly.* He has also written texts for several dance pieces.

For the screen, in addition to the screenplay for *M. Butterfly* in 1993, Hwang wrote *Golden Gate* (1994) for

American Playhouse, about an FBI agent's prejudice against a Chinese laundryman and his subsequent redemption through the man's daughter; the 2001 television miniseries *The Lost Empire,* based on Chinese myths; and a film adaptation of A. S. Byatt's novel *Possession* (with NEIL LABUTE and Laura Jones), about a pair of literary sleuths and the secret lives of two Victorian poets.

In 2004, the Seattle Children's Theatre offered the premiere of Hwang's *Tibet Through the Red Box,* based on the book by Czechoslovakian Peter Sis. More recently, Hwang developed his early play, *Face Value* (1993), into the PULITZER-nominated *Yellow Face* (2007), a semiautobiographical comedy about racial identity.

Hwang's passion for mingling historical detail, pure fantasy, and naturalistic elements has produced plays that explore race, culture, and gender beyond the Asian-American experience. However, his interest in Chinese and Japanese literature and Asian theatrical forms remains evident in much of his work—through its form, sense of cultural connection, and philosophy. Like his early mentor, Sam Shepard, Hwang likes to explore the mythical states that underlie reality, a thematic concern that often dictates an expressionistic format. Hwang is interested in how people of different cultures and genders perceive and react to each other; therefore, the fluidity of identity is a theme common to most of his work.

He has codirected, with PHILIP KAN GOTANDA, the Asian-American Theatre Company in San Francisco since 1987 and is cofounder of the Stanford Asian-American Theater Project. In 1998, the Los Angeles–based Asian-Pacific-American theater group, EAST WEST PLAYERS, named their theater space, the David Henry Hwang Theater.

BIBLIOGRAPHY

Hwang, David Henry. *Flower Drum Song.* New York: Theatre Communications Group, 2003.
———. *"FOB" and Other Plays.* New York: Plume, 1990.
———. *Golden Child.* New York: Theater Communications Group, 1998.
———. *M. Butterfly.* New York: Penguin, 1988.
———. *Peer Gynt.* New York: Playscripts, Inc., 2006.
———. *Rich Relations.* New York: Playscripts, Inc., 2002.
———. *Tibet Through the Red Box.* New York: Playscripts, Inc., 2006.
———. *Trying to Find Chinatown.* New York: Theater Communications Group, 1999.
———. *Yellow Face.* New York: Theatre Communications Group, 2009.
Street, Douglas, *David Henry Hwang.* Boise, Idaho: Boise State University Press, 1989.

Susan C. W. Abbotson
Rhode Island College

I

I AM MY OWN WIFE DOUG WRIGHT
(2003) This PULITZER PRIZE– and TONY AWARD–winning play is based on three years of interviews by
DOUG WRIGHT with an East German transvestite who
lived openly under two repressive regimes, the Nazis
and the communists—most of "her" adult life under
the latter. _I Am My Own Wife_ is the story of Charlotte
von Mahlsdorf, born Lothar Berfelde, and the playwright's friendship with her. Wright developed the
play for a single actor who plays all 35 characters
while remaining in Charlotte's simple black dress,
sensible shoes, and pearls. The primary characters are
the playwright "Doug" and Charlotte; the 33 other
characters include relatives and friends of Charlotte,
Charlotte herself as a young boy, various officials,
members of the German media, American military
personnel, and others. For Jefferson Mays, the actor
who originated the role, the part was a tour de force.

At the beginning of the play, we meet Charlotte
when Doug meets her. "She" is clearly a man yet in
demeanor, a woman—an understated, unflamboyant
hausfrau. Charlotte lives in a 19th-century mansion
filled with beloved objects. She shows Doug her house,
a museum in which she has collected and preserved
the artifacts of an era—the late 19th-century _Gründer-
zeit_—often by rescuing the furnishings of buildings
about to be destroyed. Her basement holds the most
remarkable treasure of all: the entire contents of a
Weimar cabaret—every piece of furniture, every
glass—that she rescued when the building was slated

for demolition by the East German regime. She
explains that after the Wall went up between East and
West Berlin, gay life was forced underground; officially, it did not exist. The reconstructed basement
cabaret served as a weekly gathering place for homosexuals for 30 years under the repressive East German
regime.

Charlotte's marvelous story is revealed through her
monologues. Sometimes we wonder if these tales can
be true: She reports that as a teen during World War
II, she beat her abusive Nazi father to death with a
rolling pin in order to prevent him from killing the
family, as he had threatened; that she escaped from
her subsequent imprisonment when the bombs of the
Russian liberators hit the prison; that an SS commander allowed young Lothar, dressed as a girl but
admitting to being a boy, to walk away from the wall
where he awaited the bullets of an "execution squad."
Is Charlotte a reliable narrator?

Wright explains in his introduction to the published play that because Charlotte had preserved the
cabaret and had kept her singular identity despite two
repressive regimes he expected a story of complete
heroism, but the release of her Stasi (the East German
secret police) file revealed that she had to some extent
collaborated with the authorities in exchange for
maintaining her lifestyle and pursuing her collecting
obsession (xi–xvi).

When the character Doug—disappointed in his
heroine—questions her about the Stasi connection,

she says she was coerced into signing up as an informant and that she was simply being "as smart as the snakes"; but the German tabloid press gets hold of a copy of her Stasi file and reports that she—among other things—informed on a gay friend and fellow collector, who was arrested as a result. Charlotte reluctantly admits to this, but justifies her actions by saying that her friend encouraged her to cooperate so that she could save herself and her collection. We are left to wonder if she is conveniently whitewashing her own incriminating actions. We are never sure how reliable Charlotte is; she is at once endearing and suspect; she is an enigma.

Wright leaves us with affection for Charlotte and with unanswered questions about her guilt and about ourselves. How would we have behaved in her situation? Near the end of the play, Charlotte defensively asks a reporter who questions her veracity, "You are from the West, yes? Did the Stasi ever come to your door?" She might be asking any of us.

In an interview with Charlie Rose in 2004, Doug Wright said, "I love her because she experienced all of 20th-century European history through the most marginal lens imaginable and still makes her stories as thrillingly universal as they could be. I wanted to write a paean to someone I thought was a hero, and she stunned me because instead she turned out to be a human being."

Once Wright decided to work on the play *not* as an objective biographical piece—since Charlotte's truth was elusive—but as a play constructed largely of the interviews themselves, he signed up director Moisés Kaufman, whose play *The Laramie Project* (2000) is made up of interviews, to help him shape the hours of recordings. The use of only one actor started with Wright's desire to limit cost just in the initial workshop phase; at that time he signed on Jefferson Mays, who stayed with the play from workshop development to Pulitzer Prize and beyond, and decided he needed no larger cast.

In a departure from Wright's original concept, *I Am My Own Wife* was presented in 2005 with a two-person cast at the Wilma Theatre in Philadelphia, a theater with which Wright has a long relationship. With the playwright's permission, director Blanka Zizka, seeing the play as a meeting of two political systems and a meeting between "a seeker of truth and a guardian of myth" (Zizka), decided that Charlotte and all the people in her stories would be played by one actor, and that Doug and all the other outsiders who question Charlotte's life would be played by a second.

BIBLIOGRAPHY
Wright, Doug. Interview with Charlie Rose. *Charlie Rose.* PBS WNET, New York 30 July 2004.
———. *I Am My Own Wife.* New York: Faber and Faber, 2004.
Zizka, Blanka. "Reimagining Wright: Blanka Zizka on Her Approach to *I Am My Own Wife*" *Open Stages* Sep./Oct. 2005: 2.

ICEBOUND Owen Davis (1923) Set in the frozen landscape of a New England winter, *Icebound* is a drama about selfishness, frigidity, and redemption. Like the environment that surrounds them, the Jordans are icebound.

As the play opens, the unemotional Jordans are awaiting the death of their elderly mother, and, more important to them, waiting to hear how she wishes her money to be divided among them. Mrs. Jordan is never onstage, but the references to her by other characters suggest that she is as incapable of expressing and receiving love as are her offspring. Outside the room, winter has begun, and inside the room the atmosphere is equally bleak: DAVIS describes the room as having *"the cleanliness that is next to godliness, but no sign of either comfort or beauty, both of which are looked upon with suspicion as being signposts on the road to perdition."* Davis's setting is symbolic of the interior lives of his characters.

Mrs. Jordan's favorite son, Ben, is in trouble with the law for burning down a barn while drunk. Though Ben is not expected to show up, he does arrive; before he can see his mother, though, she dies. Ben and his mother share an affection for animals, which suggests the potential for greater humanity in these two than in the rest of the family. The others have feared that Ben will inherit the money and are stunned when they hear that Mrs. Jordan has left everything to Jane, a distant cousin who has been caring for her. It eventually becomes evident that Jane has sent for Ben at the request of Mrs. Jordan and that Ben will indirectly inherit if he reforms. Jane pays his bail and arranges for him to stay on the farm to help rebuild it. The community gossips about the two living together, calling Ben, her "white slave." Their relationship is turbulent; Ben does not treat Jane well. He eventually reads his mother's letter to Jane in which Mrs. Jordan instructs Jane that Ben's redemption will come "through a woman who will hold out her heart to him and let him trample on it as he has on mine." Ben finally—though not without hesitation—decides that he will reject the "hard, mean life" that is his Jordan birthright in favor of a life with Jane, whom he marries.

When Owen Davis won the PULITZER PRIZE for *Icebound,* his transition from creator of sensational, moneymaking, lowbrow melodramas to playwright for the legitimate stage was complete. However, some critics at the time objected that there were better plays that season, one that included the now classic *The ADDING MACHINE* by ELMER RICE.

ICEMAN COMETH, THE EUGENE O'NEILL (1946)

Although O'NEILL completed *The Iceman Cometh* in 1940, the four-hour play was not produced until 1946, after World War II had ended. Immediately after finishing the play, O'Neill did not feel quite up to the physical and emotional strain of a production (Bogard and Bryer 501), and once the United States entered the war, he feared that the New York audience would find "[t]he pity and tragedy of defensive pipe dreams . . . downright unpatriotic," though, as he wrote in a letter to critic and writer Dudley Nichols, "[a]fter the war . . . American audiences [would] understand a lot of *The Iceman Cometh* only too well" (Bogard and Bryer 537).

The play is set in the "backroom" of Harry Hope's "saloon and boarding house," a dive hospitable to those who have hit rock bottom. As act 1 begins, a group of drunken has-beens await the arrival of Hickey, a hardware salesman, beloved for his propensity to buy drinks and tell jokes; the men, including the gruff but soft-hearted Harry, sleep in their chairs, afraid that if they go to their beds upstairs they will miss Hickey's arrival.

O'Neill's lengthy character descriptions are more like those of a novel than a play; he details features—Hugo's head is *"much too big for his body"*; Harry Hope *"has badly fitting store teeth, which click like castanets"*—that any production would find nearly impossible to replicate, but which give readers O'Neill's ideal vision of the play's characters. In fact, O'Neill wrote to critic and editor George Jean Nathan in 1940, "I hate to think of it being produced—of having to watch a lot of actors muscle in their personalities to make strange for me these characters of the play that interest me so much—now, as *I* have made them live!" (Bogard and Bryer 501).

As each wretched man reveals his story, he also reveals his "pipe dream," the illusion that sustains him. Rocky, the night bartender, maintains that he is not a pimp and that the young women, Margie and Pearl, who turn their money over to him are only "tarts," not whores. The two women share in this delusion. Cora, the third whore, and her bartender boyfriend Chuck say they will marry and buy a farm in Jersey one day. Several of the men—Mosher, McGloin, Mott, Jimmy Tomorrow—remember their careers as successes and fool themselves into thinking that they can get their jobs back any time, when in reality they lost those jobs for various reasons ranging from lack of ambition and alcoholism to corruption. Willie Oban, a graduate of Harvard Law School and the son of a man who was convicted of fraud and died in prison, emerges from his stupor to claim that he can practice law again if he so chooses. Captain Cecil Lewis and General Piet Wetjoen fought on opposing sides of the Boer War and talk of earning enough money for their passages home to England and South Africa, respectively. Hugo Kalamar and Larry Slade were both a part of the anarchist movement; while Hugo awaits the revolution, Larry claims he now rejects the movement utterly—that the movement was the pipe dream from which he awakened, and now all he wants is death. Larry believes that he alone has no pipe dream. Harry Hope himself was once a politician. He has not "set foot out of" the bar in the 20 years since his wife died. He is sentimental about his late wife, who in reality "nagged the hell out of him." His pipe dream is that he will walk around the ward and again become a man with friends in high places.

When Hickey finally arrives, he is uncharacteristically sober and talks about "sav[ing them] from pipe dreams." He wants everyone at Harry's to be honest with himself. The "tarts" should admit they are whores. Rocky should admit he is a pimp. Each man who plans to change should do it now or admit that he cannot. All are resentful of Hickey's insistence that they be honest with themselves, and they become defensive and belligerent. They lash out at Hickey, asking him if this time his wife really did have an affair—with the iceman as he has so often joked—to cause such a change in him. Hickey reveals that his wife is dead, but that he is glad she is at peace. She loved him and he, by cheating and drinking, only caused her pain.

Driven to do so by Hickey, Harry begins his walk around the ward. He gets only as far as halfway across the street before he runs back in the door, lying that a car nearly ran him over. When witnesses force him to admit there was no such car, Harry—bitterly complaining of his nagging late wife and complaining that the "booze" has "no kick"—wants only to pass out. The others have similar experiences, and by the beginning of act 4 all have returned to the bar, their pipe dreams exploded. They are irritable, sullen, hopeless, and at each other's throats. In the midst of this despair and self-loathing, Hickey confesses that he has shot his wife in order to save her from the heartbreak of loving him, a scoundrel. He had considered suicide but knew that that would break her heart. When Hickey remarks that he must have been "insane" to call his wife, whom he loved, a "damned bitch" after he shot her, Harry and the others begin to *grasp at some dawning hope.* After Hickey is taken away by the police (whom Hickey himself has called), they decide that he was insane during his visit, which invalidates everything that happened. They pretend to themselves that they followed Hickey's suggestions only to humor him in his insanity. They return to their pipe dreams and are able to live as they had been—sustained by illusion—hopeful, despite their squalid, alcoholic circumstances.

Parallel to Hickey's story is that of Don Parritt, a young man who comes to Harry Hope's to find Larry, the former anarchist. Parritt's mother had been Larry's lover for a time, and Larry had been kind to the boy Parritt, who resented his mother's single-minded devotion to the movement. Gradually over the course of the play, Parritt's story and finally his guilt are revealed. He committed the unforgivable sin: He turned his mother in to the police and he has come in search of Larry because only Larry can forgive or condemn him. As Parritt hears Hickey's confession, his guilt overwhelms him, and Larry tells him that he (Parritt) knows what he must do. Larry waits to hear the thud of Parritt's body hit the ground as he throws himself from the fire escape, an action Larry himself could not take, despite all his talk of welcoming death. Now as he thinks of the "Poor devil" Parritt and hopes he has found peace, Larry hopes death will "come soon." As the others blissfully kid themselves and drown reality in the oblivion of alcohol, only Larry sits apart, "the only real convert to death Hickey made."

The title refers to the old off-color joke about a wife's infidelity with the ice delivery man, but it also refers to the ultimate iceman, death. O'Neill wrote of the title, "I love [it] because it characteristically expresses so much of the outer and the inner spirit of the play" (Bogard and Bryer 501). In 1940, O'Neill commented about *The Iceman Cometh,* "[T]here are moments in it that suddenly strip the secret soul of a man stark naked, not in cruelty or moral superiority, but with an understanding compassion which sees him as a victim of the ironies of life and of himself. Those moments are for me the depth of tragedy" (Bogard and Bryer 511). O'Neill's vision of *The Iceman Cometh* was not fully realized in the original 1946 production, which was weak; not until the now legendary 1956 revival with Jason Robards Jr. and later, the equally fine 1998 revival in London with Kevin Spacey, did this masterwork by one of America's master playwrights come wholly to life.

BIBLIOGRAPHY

Bloom, Harold, ed. *Modern Critical Interpretations: Eugene O'Neill's "The Iceman Cometh."* New York: Chelsea House, 1987.

Bogard, Travis, and Jackson R. Bryer, eds. *Selected Letters of Eugene O'Neill.* New Haven, Conn.: Yale University Press, 1988.

Frazer, Winifred D. *E. G. and E. G. O.: Emma Goldman and "The Iceman Cometh."* Gainesville: University Presses of Florida, 1974.

———. *Love as Death in "The Iceman Cometh": A Modern Treatment of an Ancient Theme.* Gainesville: University of Florida Press, 1967.

Raleigh, John Henry, ed. *Twentieth Century Interpretations of "The Iceman Cometh": A Collection of Critical Essays.* Englewood Cliffs, N.J.: Prentice-Hall, 1968.

Vena, Gary. *O'Neill's "The Iceman Cometh": Reconstructing the Premiere.* Ann Arbor, Mich.: UMI Research Press, 1988.

IDIOT'S DELIGHT ROBERT E. SHERWOOD

(1936)   Set at the crossroads of Europe on the brink of world war, SHERWOOD's prophetic antiwar play portrays the outbreak of a second world war as fascism takes hold in Germany and in Italy. In this PULITZER PRIZE–winning play, Sherwood indicts both nationalism and the weapons industry that exploits it.

From the picture window of a cocktail lounge, the itinerant guests of an Alpine hotel look out over four nations: Italy, Austria, Switzerland, and Bavaria. The group assembled is comprised of Europeans and Americans who are thrown together when the borders close as war seems imminent. The German scientist, Dr. Waldersee, is on the verge of finding a cure for cancer and fears his lab rats will die if he is not allowed to continue his journey. Mr. and Mrs. Cherry, the British honeymooners, are secure in their belief in British superiority and good sense: "[T]hey can't start any real war without England . . . [and] our people simply won't stand for it." The Marxist worker Quillery, who was born in France but claims no citizenship, works in a factory that makes artificial limbs, "an industry that has been prosperous in the last twenty years." Quillery believes that war cannot break out because the world has learned too much since the last war: Because the ideas of Lenin and others have taken hold, he believes the fascists will be exposed for what they are. Achille Weber is a French arms dealer, for whom war—anybody's war, for any cause—represents financial gain. Achille is travelling with the mysterious Russian, Irene ("*pronounced 'EAR-RAY-*

NA'*"), who claims to be the niece of the late Russian czar. There is something about her that makes Harry Van, an American vaudevillian touring with six blonde chorus girls, think that he has met her before (he will eventually recognize her as a fellow vaudevillian and former lover he knew briefly in Omaha). By the end of act 1, an Italian officer, Captain Locicero, who frequents the hotel, brings the rumor that war has been declared between France and Italy. The assembled guests drink and dance to the orchestra's "*spirited but frail performance of 'Valencia'*" as they await confirmation.

Weber, the arms dealer, knows that planes have been dispatched from Italy to bomb Paris and that a response from France is inevitable. Since the planes have gone out from the air base within sight of the hotel, this place will be a certain target when the retaliation occurs. Weber plans to leave as soon as he can. It is at this point that the playwright's most overt antiwar speech is delivered by Irene as she addresses Achille. Irene has just characterized the antics of humankind as "a game that never means anything, and never ends," as God playing "Idiot's Delight" or solitaire. Her tone is not impassioned, which makes Sherwood's imagery all the more haunting. She pictures Mr. Cherry, who is at present in the next room "holding hands" with his bride, in uniform "shooting a little pistol at a huge tank," which rolls over him and leaves his "fine strong body" with its "capacity for ecstacy . . . a mass of mashed flesh and bones." She goes on to say that at the "moment before his death," he will console himself by thinking that his pregnant wife is safe in England, when, in fact, she will be "lying in a cellar that has been wrecked by an air raid, and her firm young breasts are all mixed up with the bowels of a dismembered policeman, and the embryo from her womb is splattered against the face of a dead bishop." She ends by remarking dryly to Achille that it makes her "proud" to be so close to him, "who make[s] all this possible." But Weber justifies his business by asking who is worse: Those who sell or those who buy? Those who furnish or those who require the "illusion of power" that arms provide? He refers not only to dictators but to all national governments.

When word arrives that Paris has been bombed, even the internationalist and pacifist Quillery is filled with nationalism and shouts, *"Vive la France!"* He allies himself with Mr. Cherry—a man for whom he had only contempt earlier in the day—against the Italians. In response, Captain Locicero, usually charming and mild, becomes "white with rage." Quillery, in a demonstration of the transformative power of nationalism, is led away and eventually shot. The German doctor decides to abort his promising cancer-cure research in favor of returning to his homeland in case he is "needed" there.

Captain Locicero arranges for all the guests to cross the border. Weber is in a hurry to get to France and increase production of weapons there so that the French can counterattack Italy, which, of course, Weber has also supplied with weapons. He arranges for Irene to be detained because she knows too much about his work and has of late hinted at her disapproval of it.

It is Harry Van who comes to Irene's rescue. He invites her to join his act, for which he will train her as a mind reader. An air-raid siren is heard and bombs begin to fall, but Harry and Irene decline to go to the cellar. Instead, they drink champagne and watch the spectacle through the picture window. As the bombs get closer and louder, the window breaks. The curtain falls on the two of them seated at the piano, singing "Onward, Christian Soldiers."

Sherwood's satirical *Idiot's Delight* is considered one of the best antiwar plays written by an American playwright. In that same year, during the period between the world wars, IRWIN SHAW's one-act *BURY THE DEAD* offered a more nightmarish antiwar message, as dead soldiers refuse to be buried because they have died in vain.

I'M NOT RAPPAPORT HERB GARDNER (1984)

Set on a bench in Central Park, *I'm Not Rappaport* is a poignant comedy about two elderly New Yorkers who reluctantly become friends. GARDNER highlights some of the difficulties and truths of old age while creating characters with great humanity, particularly Nat, who never stops believing in his youthful ideal of social activism.

The two men, Midge and Nat, are both about 80, and both are partially blind from cataracts and glaucoma; *"Midge is black and Nat is white."* Midge is still employed as the night superintendent of an apartment building. Despite his advanced age and poor vision, he has kept his job because he remains "invisible," working at night and not having asked for a raise since he passed retirement age. The park bench had been Midge's spot for six months until a week ago when Nat showed up. Nat is a talker, whose tall stories Midge calls "lies" and Nat himself calls "alterations," preferring them to the grim reality of bypass surgery, doctor bills, and yesterday's club rolls from the Plaza Hotel.

When Mr. Danforth of the Tenants' Committee jogs by looking for Midge to discuss his retirement, Nat, old socialist and defender of the persecuted worker, jumps in and pretends to be Midge's union's legal representative. He convincingly threatens the committee and Mr. Danforth with legal action if Midge is not retained. Mr. Danforth, sufficiently worried, agrees to talk to the Tenants' Committee about the matter. Nat gives Danforth a phone number that will connect him to Nat's daughter's office (she is used to taking bizarre messages for her father and does not give him away). Buoyed by this victory, Nat is determined to take on the young thug to whom Midge pays protection money ($3). This battle, however, ends with Nat getting mugged and knocked unconscious.

As act 2 begins, Nat, his head bandaged, returns to the park, using a walker but singing "Puttin' on the Ritz." Midge will not speak to him for the trouble he has caused. Soon Clara, Nat's daughter, appears. She is tired of fielding calls for her eccentric father at her office. This morning, she tells him, she took a message from the unsuspecting Danforth that "the [Midge] Carter matter is settled." Clara is alarmed to see that her father has been mugged and attempts to force him to choose among living with her family, going into a retirement home, or staying in his apartment but reporting daily to the senior center. Nat says to her, "I'm afraid of what you'll do out of what you think is love." When he rejects all of her options, she threatens to take him to court for a competency hearing. In order to divert her, he makes up a story about an illegitimate Israeli daughter who has come to find him and will take him back to Israel and care for him there.

Soon after Clara leaves, the two men witness an encounter between a pusher and a junkie who owes him money. Once again determined to help the downtrodden, Nat poses as a Mafia boss in order to scare off the pusher, but the pusher is not as easily fooled as Danforth and Clara. Nat is hurt badly enough this time to send him to the hospital for 12 days. When he returns to the park, he is a defeated man. He tells Midge that he has just come by on his way to the senior center and that, truthfully, his working life was spent as a waiter and nothing more. With some prodding, Midge gets him to "admit" that he was more than just a waiter: He was "for a brief time" a movie "mogul." And with that, he is off again.

Gardner's Nat is a powerful spokesman for the elderly. In his encounter with Danforth, he tells the young man: "[Y]ou *will* get old; I hate to break the news. And if you're frightened now, you will be terrified then. The problem's *not* that life is short but that it's very long." He says of the elderly themselves, "The old people, they're the *survivors,* they *know* something, they haven't just stayed late to ruin your party." Other notable comedies that address, in part, the theme of aging include NEIL SIMON's The SUNSHINE BOYS and PAUL OSBORN's MORNING'S AT SEVEN.

Unlike Gardner's earlier plays, *I'm Not Rappaport* was workshopped at the Seattle Repertory Theatre under the guidance of Daniel Sullivan. Subsequently, Sullivan oversaw the play's transfer to New York, where it ran for nearly three years and won for Gardner the 1986 TONY AWARD.

IN ABRAHAM'S BOSOM PAUL GREEN (1926)

Green first gained national attention with *In Abraham's Bosom,* which was produced by the PROVINCETOWN PLAYERS in their 1926–27 season and which won the PULITZER PRIZE. The play ends with the death of the central character, who is shot by his Ku Klux Klan–like neighbors, and Green's achievement was that the work is not a simplistic protest play but a complex folk tragedy. Green accomplished this by concentrating on the character of his protagonist.

Abraham McCranie, a mulatto raised on a farm in the North Carolina of the late 19th century, has a thirst for learning. As a young man, intelligent and ambitious, he struggles with borrowed books to educate himself. Then his vision expands, and he dreams of building a school for the African-American children of the area and inspiring them with hope and ambition. Practicing a speech, he develops a theme that resonates with the ideas of W. E. B. DuBois and numerous others of the era: "Looking over the country, ladies and gentlemen, we see eight million souls striving in slavery, yea, slavery, brethren, the slavery of ignorance. And ignorance means being oppressed, both by yourselves and by others. . . . We want our children and our grandchildren to march on towards full lives and noble chareckters, and that has got to come, I say, by education. We have no other way."

Two forces contend against the realization of that inspiring dream. One is the racism at the heart of Abe's society. The play is set during the most repressive era for African Americans in post–Civil War history, when the Jim Crow laws and customs that began to unravel only in the 1950s were being established, and it depicts racist behavior ranging from the subtle (lack of concern among whites for the education of African Americans) to the blatantly violent (lynching). The powerful opening scene includes a highly charged episode in which his white father beats Abe with a bullwhip to save him from worse treatment for hitting a white man.

The other force undermining Abe's educational endeavor is his own "chareckter." He comes to see himself as the savior of the African-American race, and in his messianic fervor he can be overbearing and physically violent. During the course of the play, he alienates even those closest to him: first, his maternal aunt; most painfully, his talented son (whom he named for Frederick Douglass); the other African-American people of the community; and, finally, his wife. With the death of his father, Abe is left with no support in the community. In a rage of frustration at both whites and blacks for failing to support his school, he kills his bigoted, white half-brother, and for this he is gunned down by a mob. But by then he is a leader with no following, a visionary who failed, and that is the tragic realization with which he meets his death: Black folk are "asleep, asleep, and I can't wake 'em!. . . . But they'll wake up, they'll wake—a crack of thunder and deep divided from deep—a light! A light, and it will be!"

Like so many early-20th-century treatments of race that seemed progressive at the time, *In Abraham's Bosom* by today's standards is more racist than progressive. Historically, however, it is noteworthy since it is the first play that dealt with the African-American experience to receive the Pulitzer Prize. This was not to be the case again until the prize went to *The GREAT WHITE HOPE* (1969), by white playwright Howard Sackler, followed immediately by *No PLACE TO BE SOMEBODY* (1970), by African-American playwright CHARLES GORDONE.

Laurence G. Avery
University of North Carolina–Chapel Hill

INDIANS ARTHUR KOPIT (1969) Among the few commercial American plays to focus on Native Americans (see NATIVE AMERICAN DRAMA), *Indians* portrays and indicts the treatment of the native tribes of North America by whites in general and by the United States government in particular. KOPIT's absurdist, comic play also deals with the American tendency to mythologize and distort the past, especially when the events are painful or incriminating. The play, which has a large cast (26 specific characters and unspecified numbers of reporters, soldiers, and Indians) and therefore has rarely been done, was produced first in London by the Royal Shakespeare Company in 1968, then opened in Washington, D.C., and later in New York in 1969.

The play begins and ends with three glass showcases on a bare stage: One contains an effigy of Buffalo Bill Cody, grandly costumed; a second, Sitting Bull, modestly costumed; and the last, artifacts of the West. Framing the play is also Buffalo Bill's Wild West Show, in which Buffalo Bill and Sitting Bull worked for years, mythologizing the American West.

A defensive Buffalo Bill attempts to help the Indians whose buffalo herds he and others wiped out. He has promised Sitting Bull a meeting with the presi-

dent of the United States; the president refuses, sending a small Senate committee in his place. The scenes of the meetings between Sitting Bull and the Senate committee alternate with scenes that illustrate, variously, the absurdity of American policy, the tragic plight of the Indians, and the self-deception of the guilty. Sitting Bull tells the senators that he wants only what "the Great father" promised his people. Explicit in that name for the U.S. president is the paternal attitude of the white government toward the Indians; the government, the senators report, is holding the money owed to Sitting Bull's people in trust until the Indians are sufficiently capable, in the white man's view, of handling it themselves. In one of the meeting scenes, Buffalo Bill explains to the senators—and, ironically, he *does* understand this, despite his own culpability in killing off the buffalo essential to their culture—the Indian perspective in such areas as farming (plowing the sacred earth is sacrilege) and land sales (a practice as foolish as paying for a piece of sky or ocean). The talks with the senators come to nothing in the end, and Sitting Bull and his hungry, defeated people are slaughtered at Wounded Knee in December of 1890. The Wounded Knee massacre is not staged; instead, two army officers, some reporters, and Buffalo Bill visit the site, by then a burial ground, after the massacre. The army is self-satisfied, while a regretful Buffalo Bill stays behind and talks to the ghost of Sitting Bull. After Sitting Bull leaves and before the ghosts of all of those buried there rise up and surround him, Buffalo Bill makes a ludicrous defense of U.S. Indian policy: The Cherokee were resettled in the "lovely" Mohave desert after the state of Georgia acquired "certain valuable mineral rights" from them; the "shipment of smallpox-infested blankets" has "worked wonders, and the Mandan [Indians] are no more"; and the extinction of the buffalo will force the Indians, who will be motivated by hunger, to farm.

The buffalo and the Indians are inextricably linked in the play; like the buffalo around which their lives centered, the Indians, too, were wiped out by Cody and other whites. To emphasize the point, Kopit portrays the visit of a European Grand Duke, who tours the West with Buffalo Bill as his guide. Buffalo Bill shoots buffalo at night, showing off before the Duke. The Duke, impressed by Bill's exaggerated tales of killing Comanche, is anxious to shoot one himself. He fires his rifle indiscriminately into the dark and accidentally shoots an old acquaintance of Bill's, an Indian who is not a Comanche. Believing he has bagged his "Comanche" trophy, the Duke is overjoyed, and Bill—though stunned—does not disabuse him of his belief. Buffalo Bill is like the nation—a participant in the destruction, but one not without occasional feelings of regret; the regret, however, is never so great that it cannot be rationalized, as when he makes his ludicrous defense of policy. In contrast to such justifications, Kopit includes some of the documented speeches of Native American chiefs. The final words of the play are those of Chief Joseph of the Nez Percé. The speech of a brokenhearted man speaking for a defeated people, it ends with the famously poignant words: "I will fight no more forever." Kopit's intention was also to comment—albeit obliquely—on United States policy governing the war in Vietnam, believing there were parallels between that policy and the historic treatment of Native Americans.

I NEVER SANG FOR MY FATHER ROBERT ANDERSON (1968)

This autobiographical memory play, like other works of its kind, such as TENNESSEE WILLIAMS's *The GLASS MENAGERIE* (1945), takes the form of a guilt play, an examination of conscience by a narrator seeking reassurance that he has not failed in his obligation to love. Anderson's narrator, the middle-aged Gene Garrison, himself recently a widower, recalls the death of both his mother and father, but it is the father's death that obsesses him and cries out for some resolution.

Tom Garrison was a difficult man to love. Crotchety and cranky in his old age, he had always been authoritarian, opinionated, and insensitive to the feelings of others; long neglectful of his wife Margaret's emotional needs, he also ostracized his daughter Alice for marrying a Jew. Perhaps sensing the emptiness of his old age, he becomes fixated on remembering his youth. Tom's father had deserted his mother, and, when she died, Tom had pushed him from the funeral coach; he still maudlinly nurtures his grief over his mother's death, crying more for her than for his own wife. In the Oedipal pattern that plays itself out through the closeness of both Tom and Gene to their mothers, Anderson's play approaches the level of archetype and myth.

If the form of *I Never Sang for My Father*—with its cinematically fluid dissolves between past and present effected through narrative passages (Anderson originally conceived of it as a film)—recalls *The Glass Menagerie,* the content and rhetoric—with its father/son conflict and its almost stereotypical rendition of Tom's rags-to-riches reworking of the Horatio Alger myth—echo MILLER's *DEATH OF A SALESMAN* (1949). Tom's values are part and parcel of the American Dream of success through self-reliance; however, his never-say-quit attitude, accompanied by a daily regimen for self-advancement, left him materially satisfied but emotionally shallow.

Now Tom seems jealous of his son's youth and sensitivity and of the satisfaction he finds in writing and teaching, and so he casts Gene in an adversarial role; he even wants to deny Gene another chance to succeed as husband by standing in the way of Gene's remarrying. Despite his sister Alice's insistence that he not put duty to a father who is trying to emasculate him over responsibility to himself, Gene asks Tom to come live with his new wife and stepchildren, but the petulant old man refuses, demanding things on his terms or not at all. Though Gene leaves, he still feels that he has failed in his moral responsibility to love unquestioningly and cannot forgive himself for being less than the perfect son. The narrative passage that closes the play precisely repeats the self-laceration and recrimination of its opening: "Death ends a life . . . but it does not end a relationship, which struggles on in the survivor's mind . . . toward some resolution, which it never finds."

Thomas P. Adler
Purdue University

INGE, WILLIAM (1913–1973)

William Inge's best works are his plays *COME BACK, LITTLE SHEBA* (1950), *PICNIC* (1953), *BUS STOP* (1955), and *The DARK AT THE TOP OF THE STAIRS* (1957), as well as the screenplay for *Splendor in the Grass* (1961). All four of the plays were made into highly successful films, adding to his celebrity. His work reflects his upbringing in tiny Independence, Kansas, particularly *Picnic,* which won a PULITZER PRIZE, and *Splendor in the Grass,* for which he won an Academy Award. He portrays conflicts within families and in small-town, midwestern communities. Inge brought the people of heartland villages to the stages of New York City without heavily romanticizing them, and his work continues to be produced. He is the only significant playwright among those writers, including Sherwood Anderson, Sinclair Lewis, and Edgar Lee Masters, whose work about the people of midwestern, small towns is often referred to by American literary historians as "the revolt from the village." Furthermore, Inge wrote compellingly about the complexity of love within heterosexual and familial relationships while, like other homosexual artists of the era, carefully concealing his own sexuality.

Come Back, Little Sheba, for which Inge was named "most promising" playwright of 1950, reflects Inge's psychotherapy and alcoholism. The play features Doc and Lola Delaney, a childless couple in midlife crisis. Doc's alcoholism adds to his deep disappointment in life; Lola daydreams about escape and calls for her lost little dog Sheba, the symbol of her lost youth. Events build to an eruption of Doc's repressed frustration, forcing both Doc and Lola to recognize their desperate need to accept and cope with their situation. Accepting life and coping with its disappointments are recurring themes in all of Inge's work.

Picnic, Inge's most enduring work, is the story of how Hal Carter, a lonely and handsome young drifter, affects the lives of several lonely women in a small Kansas town. Principal among these women is Madge Owens, the local beauty queen. The play's well-crafted plot involves an ensemble of interesting supporting characters whose lives change during Hal's brief visit on the day of the town's annual Labor Day picnic. Though Inge wanted *Picnic* to end with Hal leaving alone after romancing Madge, director Joshua Logan convinced him that audiences would want Madge to leave with Hal, and Inge reluctantly agreed, probably assuring the play's commercial success.

Inge was classically suited to expose the wholesome image of rural, small-town life as largely mythical. He discovered his homosexuality in an era and an environment that considered it anathema, and he spent most of his adulthood trying to balance his sexuality with the other elements of his life. He was the last child of Luther and Maude Inge, the former a philandering traveling salesman and the latter a nervous, overprotective housewife who coddled the young Inge and encouraged his "sissy" pursuits of reciting pieces and charming teachers and local society ladies. He often performed in high school and college plays and dreamed of an acting career but settled for teaching after graduating from college. He taught and directed plays in small Kansas and Missouri towns, where his necessarily closeted sexuality doubtless contributed to what would become lifelong battles with alcoholism and depression. On a break from teaching in 1944, Inge met TENNESSEE WILLIAMS, who encouraged him to write plays. Inge began writing while returning to teaching, and after two of his plays appeared in Dallas and St. Louis, a third, *Come Back, Little Sheba,* was produced in New York.

Inge's third play on Broadway was *Bus Stop,* and it also features an ensemble cast in a Kansas setting: Grace's Diner, where bus travelers are stranded during a snowstorm. The play presents the comic courtship of Bo Decker, a brash and naive Montana cowboy, and Cherie, a nightclub singer he has abducted to take to Montana and wed. Though this central romance is resolved in a *Picnic*-style audience-pleasing way, Inge does not let love conquer all. Bo's older friend and father figure, Virgil Blessing, remains behind when Cherie and Bo reboard the bus, and Grace tells him he has to wait outside in the cold.

Inge's fourth consecutive success, *The Dark at the Top of the Stairs,* is his most autobiographical. It centers on the Flood family in a small oil-boom town during the 1920s, a family and town closely modeled after Inge's own when he was a boy. Each member of the family, which includes 10-year-old Sonny, a piece-reciting "sissy," must face complicated individual fears of inadequacy, loss, and sexuality, symbolized by the darkness at the head of the staircase leading to their bedrooms. Inge's psychoanalysis is clearly evident in this play, and the Floods' fortuitous resolution of their fears perhaps betrays Inge's own desire to affirm family values for the sake of the box office. After this play's success, Inge's career seemed golden, though some critics began to question his creative range. Inge's fifth Broadway play, *A Loss of Roses* (1959), failed, but his disappointment was softened by the success of *Splendor in the Grass,* for which his screenplay received the Academy Award. Showing how idealistic young love can be thwarted by hypocritical parents in a small town, the film, directed by ELIA KAZAN, starred Warren Beatty and Natalie Wood. It was Inge's last triumph. Influential theater critics now faulted him for his limited small-town material, but when he presented urbanites in two more unsuccessful plays, *Natural Affection* (1963) and *Where's Daddy?* (1966), they faulted him for trying to be too violent in the former and trying to be too hip in the latter. Inge tried screenwriting again, but his original story, *Bus Riley's Back in Town* (1965), was changed so much by the studio that he removed his name from the credits. He continued to write but could not interest producers. Deeply depressed, Inge published two novels, the second, *My Son Is a Splendid Driver* (1971), highly autobiographical, but neither attracted serious attention. Disconsolate and convinced he was a failure, Inge took his own life on June 10, 1973.

BIBLIOGRAPHY

Inge, William *Four Plays.* New York: Random House, 1958.
———. *"Summer Brave" and Eleven Short Plays.* New York: Random House, 1962.
Johnson, Jeff. *William Inge and the Subversion of Gender.* Jefferson, N.C.: McFarland, 2005.
McClure, Arthur F., and C. David Rice, eds. *A Bibliographical Guide to the Works of William Inge (1913–1973).* Lewiston, N.Y.: Edwin Mellen Press, 1991.
Shuman, Robert Baird. *William Inge.* Rev. ed. New York: Twayne, 1989.
Voss, Ralph F. *The Strains of Triumph: A Life of William Inge.* Lawrence: University Press of Kansas, 1989.

Ralph F. Voss
University of Alabama

INHERIT THE WIND JEROME LAWRENCE AND ROBERT E. LEE (1955)

Loosely based on the famous Scopes "monkey trial" of 1925, *Inherit the Wind* is a courtroom drama in which a young teacher is tried for teaching Darwin's theory of evolution in a community that believes strongly in creationism. The play's theme is clear: Freedom of thought and expression—regardless of what one believes—are rights worth fighting for.

The schoolteacher, Bert Cates, is on trial for exposing his sophomore biology class to Darwinism—in violation of the law of Tennessee. Defending Cates is a famous lawyer from Chicago, Henry Drummond (based on Clarence Darrow); arguing for the prosecution is three-time presidential candidate and "the champion of ordinary people," Matthew Harrison Brady (based on William Jennings Bryan). Following the trial and acting as a kind of chorus (indeed, he speaks in blank verse) throughout the play is the cynical newspaper reporter from the *Baltimore Herald,* E. K. Hornbeck (based on H. L. Mencken). Hornbeck views Brady, who believes he speaks for small-town, rural America, as hopelessly outdated and laughable; as Hornbeck points out, Brady fails to appreciate the effects of modern communication and travel on once isolated regions of the country: "Brady's virginal small-towner / Has been *had*— / By Marconi and Montgomery Ward." Hornbeck, as an urban outsider (emphasized by his being the only character who speaks in verse), is allied with Drummond, but his cynicism sets him apart from the lawyer, who is at heart benevolent.

During the trial, Brady seems to have the upper hand, with the crowd and the judge on his side. However, when Brady himself is put on the stand, in a clever move by Drummond, the tables turn. Brady and his position of blind acceptance of the Bible—and blind rejection of science—are made to look foolish when Drummond gets him to admit that not everything in the Bible can be taken literally, including the length of the "day" described in Genesis. Nevertheless, the jury returns a "guilty" verdict; though the judge's sentence is light, Drummond plans to appeal on principle. Ridiculed by the crowd, Brady collapses and dies (as, symbolically, he must, so tied to the past is he). When Hornbeck expresses his contempt for Brady, it is Drummond who objects: "Brady has the same right as Cates: the right to be wrong."

Representing those less certain of their own vision is Rachel Brown, daughter of the town's fire-and-brimstone minister and friend and colleague of Bert Cates. Rachel is compelled by her father to testify against Cates, whom she loves. Eventually, she reads Darwin's *On the Origin of Species,* and she tells Bert after the trial is over, "I don't understand it. What I do understand, I don't like. . . . But I think that's beside the point." She wins Drummond's admiration by being open-minded enough to read and consider Darwin, despite pressure from her father. Rachel articulates the theme of the play when she realizes that "[b]ad or good, it doesn't make any difference. The ideas have to come out." Rachel learns that what was at stake in the trial was the freedom to think.

Though *Inherit the Wind* is based on historical events, it is not history; it is a piece of theater in which the playwrights have invented characters and dialogue and courtroom confrontations. LAWRENCE and LEE wrote it as they did others of their plays, "to 'rough up' the individual conscience and 'scrape the moss off young minds.' *Inherit the Wind* was subsequently translated into thirty-four languages" (Kolin and Kullman 10). With its themes so central to democratic thinking, it remains a frequently revived and powerful drama.

BIBLIOGRAPHY

Kolin, Philip C., and Colby H. Kullman, eds. *Speaking on Stage: Interviews with Contemporary American Playwrights.* Tuscaloosa: University of Alabama Press, 1996.

INNAURATO, ALBERT (1948[47?]–)

Albert Innaurato was born in Philadelphia and was educated there at Temple University (B.A.), before he went on to receive a B.F.A. from the California Institute of the Arts and an M.F.A. at the Yale University School of Drama. He has since taught at both Columbia and Princeton, while also publishing analytical criticism of opera and classical music in newspapers, magazines, and scholarly journals.

Innaurato began, even as a teenager, to create both music and libretti for his own ambitious operas. Eventually, however, he came to believe himself too derivative as a composer. In contrast, while his dramatic works all can be shown to demonstrate links with earlier literature, they are markedly original at the same time—and often quite dissimilar, at least in style, one from the other.

Indeed, given that Innaurato's later plays can at times pay fairly reverent homage to antecedent literary materials, it is intriguing that he most noticeably began his career by coauthoring, in 1974, with his Yale classmate CHRISTOPHER DURANG, *The Idiots Karamazov.* This farce spoofs pedantic literati (like the play's cartoonish main character, an uproarious caricature of Constance Garnett, the famed early translator of Russian novels and plays). As the play also skewers Dostoevsky's saintly character, Father Zossima, envisioning him as an addled pedophilic homosexual, *The Idiots Karamazov* also seems thematically quite distant from the mood we find in most of Innaurato's later plays. These subsequent works demonstrate a deft sensitivity to "queer" characters, and yet *The Idiots Karamazov*—like Innaurato's other plays of the same period, *Urlicht* (1971), *Earth Worms* (1974), and *Wisdom Amok* (1974)—mostly treats sexual inversion as an indicator of inner debasement.

On the other hand, Innaurato, in *Earth Worms,* does portray with some sympathy an elderly intellectual transvestite character named Bernard. The playwright thus prefigures what will prove to be one very sensitive response to "otherness": his achingly somber portrait of the overweight, pariah-like protagonist in *The Transfiguration of Benno Blimpie* (1977). Benno's tale of deep-set human alienation ends with him ready to maim or even kill himself; yet, he has meanwhile also shown aesthetic and spiritual aspirations far superior to the attitudes of any other character in the play.

Innaurato's *Ulysses in Traction* (1977) quite directly castigates selfish theater professionals—who, in this play, lock themselves into an auditorium, despite major social protests that are occurring in neighboring streets. In Innaurato's most popular drama, GEMINI (1977), an academically bright South Philadelphia boy must deal both with his sense of social class inferiority and his sexual confusion (he is sexually attracted to "Gemini" brother and sister characters, both of whom are his Harvard classmates).

The tolerance of "difference," for which *Gemini* repeatedly calls, is also a theme of other Innaurato dramas. *Passione* (1981) especially honors unusual women, like a circus "fat lady" and two Amazonian farm girls. In *Coming of Age in SoHo* (1985), a bisexual writer, Bartholomew "Beatrice" Dante, while he is surely sketched as especially eccentric, also seems valorous when he affirms his physical and spiritual fatherhood of the boy known as Puer—though "Beatrice" does so only after first conquering his dangerous lust for another boy, the lost teenage runaway Odysseus MacDowell.

In *Gus and Al* (1989), a stage character called Al Innaurato travels by time machine back to 1901 Vienna, where he receives much needed spiritual mentoring from composer Gustav Mahler (whose artistic efforts, like Al's own, endured many misunderstandings by his contemporary audiences). Al also meets a young gardener named Camillo, finds him sexually striking, but then he realizes that this same fellow will in later history become his own grandfather: a man with whom he sadly never shared the words "I love you." Innaurato thus rather subtly and tenderly declares that homosexual love, like that which Al briefly starts to feel for Camillo, is part of the total fabric constituting *human* love.

Gus and Al also celebrates Mahler's lesson to Innaurato that "[C]onsciousness is everywhere in the universe!" As his playwriting developed, Innaurato increasingly paid a more-than-parodistic attention to previous literature. He recalls Aeschylus's *Agamemnon* when the farm woman Aggy returns, in *Passione,* to visit (and successfully reunite with) her ex-husband Berto. In *Coming of Age in SoHo,* "Beatrice" seems especially to affirm Dantesque themes of spiritual love, asserting such love to be more truly vital than "soldier of fortune" renegadism, like that which drove the play's troubled boy character Odysseus (and his Homeric namesake before him). *Gemini,* meanwhile, appears clearly to recall WILLIAM INGE's PICNIC—especially as Bunny, a blowsy older woman (like Inge's similar character Rosemary), tries to seduce a young boy at a picnic dance. Also, the young lover characters of *Gemini,* like those of *Picnic,* dash away, at the final curtain, toward their dreams. All these examples do show that Innaurato (who continues to produce new plays in regional theater, like *Magda and Callas* in 1988 and *Dreading Thekla* in 1997) eventually arrives at a point of rather deep reverence for the collective human consciousness that unites all great art—and all people.

BIBLIOGRAPHY

Innaurato, Albert. *Best Plays.* New York: Gay Presses of New York, 1987.
————. *Bizarre Behavior: Six Plays.* New York: Avon, 1980.
————. *Coming of Age in SoHo.* New York: Dramatists Play Service, 1985.
————. *Gus and Al.* New York: Dramatists Play Service, 1989.
————. *Magda and Callas.* New York: Theatre Communications Group, 1989.
————, with Christopher Durang. *The Idiots Karamazov.* New York: Dramatists Play Service, 1981.

Jeffrey B. Loomis
Northwest Missouri State University

INTELLIGENT DESIGN OF JENNY CHOW: AN INSTANT MESSAGE WITH EXCITABLE MUSIC, THE ROLIN JONES (2003)

First produced at South Coast Repertory in Costa Mesa, California, *The Intelligent Design of Jenny Chow* won Rolin Jones a 2006 OBIE AWARD for Playwriting with its New York production. This fantastical, often hilarious, and very 21st-century comedy is part satire of computer geek shut-ins, part poignant family drama.

The play is framed as an "instant message" (IM) to a "freelance bounty hunter" whom Jennifer Marcus—22, adopted, obsessive-compulsive, and a genius—wants to hire to find Jenny Chow, who has been gone for three days. We do not at first know who Jenny Chow is, but eventually understand that she is a rocket-propelled robotic version of Jennifer Marcus herself, constructed by the obsessive-compulsive genius to fly to China to find Jennifer's birth mother, Su Yang Chow. Jennifer Marcus is prevented from going herself because she has recently developed agoraphobia. Jennifer sends the IM from her cluttered bedroom in a her parents' suburban California home; within the IM are a couple of flashback "attachments" giving the background of the Jenny Chow project and how it came about. As the play opens, we find Jennifer

Marcus at her computer. She has a silk scarf around her neck, which is the only artifact that comes from the Chinese birth mother who gave her up for adoption. As Jennifer tells her story, she speaks, at times, over her computer to the audience as she types, and, at times, participates in scenes from the recent past.

Jennifer IMs the bounty hunter that, through her former mentor, Dr. Yakunin, she "got a job reengineering missile components after [she] lost [her] job at the mall." In exchange for this work for the Defense Department, she receives parts from Raytheon so that she can construct the robot. Thus, we get a sense very early just how outlandish the plot is. When Jennifer decided to find her biological mother, she enlisted the help of a young Mormon missionary in China, whom she met online and who helps her in exchange for cybersex. The Mormon finds Su Yang Chow, and as soon as Jennifer finishes building Jenny, she sends the robot to meet with her birth mother and find out the circumstances of her adoption.

Jennifer's adoptive mother is a hard-edged and critical businesswoman who has no patience for the mental illness that accompanies her daughter's brilliance. From Adele Marcus's perspective, Jennifer needs to get over it, get out of the house, and get something tangible accomplished. The cruelty—in the name of help—Adele is capable of showing her daughter goes beyond criticism; at one point she shoves her agoraphobic daughter out the door in an effort to cure her, shouting, "I WILL NOT LIVE IN CHAOS, JENNIFER." However, Adele is not entirely a caricatured villain, as we discover when Jennifer's kind-hearted father explains how much she loved their "perfect girl" when she was first put into her arms; unfortunately, it is Adele's need for perfection that makes it impossible for her to accept unconditionally the flawed daughter whom she does not begin to understand.

Jennifer assumes she was abandoned in China because she was a girl; so there is irony in the fact that her intelligence is of the type most often associated with males—missile propulsion and robotics, computers and mathematics. Furthermore, the playwright has reversed the traditional gender roles in Jennifer's adoptive parents: Adele is a take-no-prisoner busi-

nesswoman, as we see from her abusive calls to her assistant; she is an intense, often angry, and very critical workaholic. Her husband is the stay-at-home parent (a fireman retired on disability), offering sympathy and food to their odd daughter, accepting her with all her idiosyncrasies and mental quirks. He lets Jennifer *be,* partly out of obliviousness (he spends a great deal of time up on the roof looking for fires and listening to a police scanner), but also out of genuine affection.

Aside from her parents (and the robot), the only other character Jennifer interacts with in the flesh is Todd, her high school friend—her only friend—a pizza delivery guy. Todd likes Jennifer in all her eccentricity, and he too is eccentric (in one exchange, Todd *"[Alien like]"* says to Jennifer, "Greetings, gestures." She replies "*[Alien like]* Greetings received.") For the most part, Jennifer lives in cyberspace. One actor plays five characters with whom Jennifer has comic computer interactions. Perhaps the most memorable of these is Dr. Yakunin. He is disappointed in Jennifer because though she had, even as early as high school, made news in the field of "cognitive artificial intelligence," her mental illness got in the way of his dreams for her. Yakunin is a very funny character, particularly in his vehement broken-English disdain for certain universities' robotics departments. He has left MIT, and now at Yale he tells Jennifer about first being shown his inadequate lab there: "I say why don't you throw some straw on the floor and GET SOME GOATS IN HERE!" Of his Yale students he says, "I tell them first day, you should all be RIVERBOAT CAPTAINS!"

Ultimately, Jennifer finds out nothing helpful or significant from Jenny Chow's encounter with her birth mother, and her adoptive mother's conduct toward her intensifies her illness. The words and actions that cause the loss of the robot are Jennifer's, but they poignantly echo Adele's treatment of Jennifer, as Jennifer becomes verbally and physically abusive toward Jenny. At the end of the play, we are back where we started as Jennifer wraps up her instant message to the bounty hunter she hopes will be able to retrieve Jenny Chow; she very much regrets the loss of her own "perfect girl."

Rolin Jones said in an interview with *American Theatre* magazine that after sitting in the audience many times he knows that those who are "under 35" are more sympathetic to Jennifer Marcus than older members of the audience. Furthermore, Jones said of the play, "I was testing out how dramatic can you go, and then how broad can you go in the very next scene, and what happens when you slam those two scenes up together, so that [the audience] go[es] on a little bit of a ride. . . . [The play is] set up to be a kind of suburban comedy—with some fantastical elements to it—and it ends up in a pretty grim place" (66).

BIBLIOGRAPHY

Jones, Rolin. Interview. *American Theatre* (Sept. 2006): 66–67.

INTIMATE APPAREL LYNN NOTTAGE (2003)

Winner of the New York Drama Critics' Circle Award and the American Theatre Critics Association/Steinberg New Play Award, *Intimate Apparel* imagines the life of an African-American seamstress living in lower Manhattan in 1905. In this lyrical and touching play, LYNN NOTTAGE has created and transports audiences into a world too often overlooked by historians, into what John Lahr in his *New Yorker* review of the play called "the fine emotional filigree of an ordinary black life." The main character, he continued, "is neither a victim nor a champion of her race; she is just a plain, hardworking Christian woman with talent and a sense of beauty" (April 19, 2004).

As the play begins, virginal Esther Mills, 35, sews lace on another woman's honeymoon camisole while the wedding reception goes on in the parlor of the rooming house where she lives. Though disappointed that there has yet been no wedding for her, Esther continues to dismiss Mrs. Dickson's suggestion that she consider the well-dressed, overweight bellman who enjoys Esther's bread pudding. Mrs. Dickson, the boardinghouse owner, encourages Esther to be less "particular" ("When I met the late Mr. Dickson he was nearly 60 and I forgave his infatuation with the opiates.").

Each scene reveals Esther sewing or fitting a garment or examining a piece of fabric. One of Esther's faithful clients is a wealthy and unhappy white woman, Mrs. Van Buren, who attempts to keep her husband's growing contempt for her childlessness at bay by means of Esther's stunning corsets and camisoles. Another client is the beautiful African-American prostitute, Mayme. These two women, and to a lesser extent Mrs. Dickson, are Esther's confidantes, and she theirs. To Mayme in particular she confides her dreams of opening a beauty parlor with the money she has saved over many years and keeps sewn in her "crazy quilt."

The tedium of Esther's days is interrupted when a Barbadian man of about her age begins a correspondence with her to relieve his own loneliness as he works on the Panama Canal. The dejected socialite Mrs. Van Buren helps the illiterate Esther respond to the letters of George Armstrong, assuaging her own need for romance in the process. They write to him of buying fabric and listening to the hymns at church; he writes to Esther of the "near impossible mission of digging" the canal, of the deaths of fellow laborers, and of the importance of her letters. Back at the boardinghouse, Mrs. Dickson disapproves of the correspondence, even ripping up one of George's letters. Mayme, however, joins in the conspiracy, and she, too, writes a letter for Esther to George; this one is sensual and contains some fantasy. As the letters grow in intimacy and affection, George declares his love and eventually asks Esther to marry him.

Throughout the play, Esther buys her fabric from an orthodox Jew, Mr. Marks, who more than anyone else appreciates Esther's great talent. He enjoys showing her beautiful fabric because he knows she alone among his clients can discern the difference in quality among the pieces. Their relationship is one of mutual respect, but there is also an unspoken sexual attraction between them; however, Mr. Marks is forbidden by his faith even casually to touch a woman who is not a member of his own family. Like Esther he longs for love and physical affection; he is betrothed to a woman he has never met and who still lives in his native Romania. When Esther tells him that she is to marry, Mr. Marks gives "Miss Mills" the gift of an exquisite piece of fabric for her wedding gown.

Act 1 ends with a wedding tableau looking like a sepia-tone photograph of the wedding couple: George Armstrong—Panama Canal laborer and letter writer with a fine hand—and Esther Mills—fine-garment seamstress, confidante of Mrs. Van Buren and Mayme and Mrs. Dickson, dearest client of Mr. Marks. Above George and Esther is the projection: "Unidentified Negro Couple ca. 1905." One of the themes that Nottage addresses here is that millions of African Americans toiled in anonymity and lived and died in obscurity, their personal histories lost with them. Someone needs to tell their stories. Indeed, Nottage's own great-grandmother was a seamstress of undergarments who arrived in New York in 1902. The play is very loosely based on her story; she too corresponded with and married a Barbadian laborer who worked on the Panama Canal (Gener 145). These few facts and a box of silent old family photographs were the inspiration for the play.

After the wedding, Esther's hopes quickly begin to evaporate: George's English is coarser than the graceful, gentlemanly voice in the letters, and it soon becomes clear that he too employed a letter writer, an old man whom he paid "ten cents extra for the fancy writing." George, who is handsome, is disappointed in the plainness of his new wife. He is most interested in the nest egg sewn in her quilt and eventually is able to cajole and pressure her into giving him all of this money to invest in a business venture. Instead of making that investment, he drinks and gambles Esther's savings away in one night. George has also become a regular customer of Mayme's, though Mayme does not realize that he is Esther's new husband. Esther understands the truth of George's frequent absences when Mayme shows her a lovely silk smoking jacket, a gift from her special new client; Esther recognizes it as the one she made for George as a wedding present.

Mayme returns the jacket to Esther, who gives it to Mr. Marks in a scene of tension and real intimacy. They share a moment of forbidden closeness, eyes locked, when, having tried it on, he allows her to smooth lightly the jacket's shoulders and lapels. Then she returns to her old room at Mrs. Dickson's and starts a new quilt. The play ends with another sepia photograph tableau and projection. This one reads, "Unidentified Negro Seamstress ca. 1905." But the audience knows better; Nottage has revealed the life behind another anonymous and silent photograph.

BIBLIOGRAPHY
Gener, Randy. "Conjurer of Words." *American Theatre* (Oct. 2005): 22–24, 144–145.

ITALLIE, JEAN-CLAUDE VAN See VAN ITALLIE, JEAN-CLAUDE.

IVES, DAVID (1950–) David Ives originally wanted to be a priest but decided on playwriting as a career after seeing EDWARD ALBEE's *A DELICATE BALANCE* on Broadway as a high school student. As an undergraduate student at Northwestern University, he started writing plays. After completing his studies, Ives moved to New York City, where he became associated with the Circle Repertory Theatre when they produced one of his early works, *Canvas*. He also became editor of *Foreign Affairs,* a periodical focusing on political policy on the world stage. Ives enrolled at Yale Drama School in 1981 and received an M.F.A. in playwriting. His one-act plays were first staged at the Manhattan Punch Line's festival of one-act comedies.

Ives specializes in the one-act play form. His full-length plays, such as *Red Address* (1997), have not been successful. Most of his one-acts were originally performed in such venues as benefit performances and one-act play festivals. Outlandish 10-to-15-minute comedies, which several critics have called little gems, Ives's one-act plays examine the romantic, fantastical, and hopelessly optimistic aspects of the human condition. They do not contain complex plots or psychological depth of character, but rather brilliant words and ideas and much theatrical excitement. Inherently theatrical, Ives makes reference to famous and infamous plays and playwrights and frequently parodies identifying elements. The language of his plays is often described as linguistic pyrotechnics, and he sets out deliberately to disorient the audience. Ives frequently collaborates with director John Rando and with a stable ensemble of actors.

In *The Sure Thing* (1995), chance meetings and romantic beginnings are highlighted as two people meet in a café and find their way through a conversational minefield while an offstage bell interrupts their false starts, gaffes, and faux pas on the way to falling in love. *Variations on the Death of Trotsky*

(1995) takes a look at the Russian revolutionary's last few confused hours as he desperately tries to cope with the mountain-climber's axe he has discovered in his head. *Words, Words, Words* (1995) examines three chimps to see if an old adage about Shakespeare and typewriters is true and asks, "[W]hat would the monkeys talk about?" In *The Universal Language* (1995), two lonely types find comfort in a goofy language and their own eccentricity. Dawn, a young woman with a stutter, and Don, the creator and teacher of Unamunda, a wildly comic language, fall in love amid a dazzling display of verbal fireworks. *Philip Glass Buys a Loaf of Bread* (1995) is a parodic musical vignette about the new age theater composer Philip Glass as he has a moment of existential crisis in a bakery. In *The Philadelphia* (1995), a young man in a restaurant falls into a "philadelphia," a Twilight Zone–like state in which he cannot get anything he asks for. His only way out is to ask for the opposite of what he wants.

Time Flies (1997) is a tale of two mayflies on a date who examine their mortality as they near the end of their one-day lifespan. *Babel's in Arms* (1997) is the tale of two Babylonian blue-collar workers who have to build the Tower of Babel—or else. *Soap Opera* (1997) concerns a washing machine repairman who falls in love with the appliance. *Mere Mortals* (1998) explores the lives of Frank, Joe, and Charlie, three construction workers seeking the meaning of their (past) lives. *Degas, C'est Moi* (1998) is the story of an unemployed drifter who decides to spend his day being painter Edgar Degas. *Dr. Fritz; or, The Forces of Light* (1998) is a metaphysical examination of God and Sigmund Freud, based on a story Ives read in the *New York Times* about a South American mechanic turned healer who performed gruesome medical operations without anesthesia while under the spiritual influence of a dead German doctor. *Speed-the-Play* (1998) is a parody of DAVID MAMET, a playwright known for big thoughts wrapped in short sentences. Ives's full-length plays up to 2005 are collected in *"Polish Joke" and Other Plays.* The title play, *Polish Joke,* is a surrealistic but humorous glimpse into Ives's Polish-American background.

Ives is a regular adapter for New York's celebrated "Encores!" series of classic American musicals done in concert, producing two or three a year. His "Encores!" adaptation of *Wonderful Town* moved to Broadway's Al Hirschfeld Theatre in 2003. He also cowrote the book for the musical *Irving Berlin's White Christmas,* which premiered in San Francisco in 2004 and has since toured the country. His new translation of Georges Feydeau's classic farce *A Flea in Her Ear* premiered in Chicago in 2006. In 2007–08, he had two plays produced in New York: *Is He Dead?,* a comedy adapted from a short story by Mark Twain, opened on Broadway in December 2007; and *New Jerusalem,* about the excommunication of Baruch Spinoza, was produced OFF-BROADWAY in early 2008. Ives teaches at Columbia University in New York City.

BIBLIOGRAPHY

Ives, David. *All in the Timing: Fourteen Plays.* New York: Vintage Books, 1995.

———. *"The Other Woman" and Other Pieces.* New York: Dramatists Play Service, 2008.

———. *"Polish Joke" and Other Plays.* New York: Grove Press, 2004.

———. *"Time Flies" and Other Short Plays.* New York: Grove Press, 2001.

Helen Huff
City University of New York—
Borough of Manhattan Community College

J

J. B. **ARCHIBALD MACLEISH (1958)** Winner of the PULITZER PRIZE, *J. B.* is without question the most significant verse drama, as well as one of the most astute considerations of religious belief, in the history of the American theater. Employing elements of medieval drama in his staging, MacLeish recasts the Book of Job for the postnuclear age of anxiety.

Set in a circus tent strewn with worn-out sacred vestments, the play is framed by a contest between two out-of-work-actors turned vendors, the confident Mr. Zuss and the cynical Mr. Nickles. Once they assume, respectively, the masks of God and Satan, they do battle for the soul of J. B., a wealthy banker and modern everyman first seen celebrating Thanksgiving Day, the American feast that expresses most forcibly the connection between spiritual election and material prosperity. J. B., less impious and arrogant than his biblical original, is a staunch Calvinist, certain that, though he has done nothing to deserve or earn election, God is on his side, showering down grace and blessings as a pure gift. In return, J. B. thanks his creator by immersing himself with childlike exuberance in the simple things of life, worshipping God through his creation.

In contrast, his wife Sarah is less complacent and more uneasy; a believer in strict reciprocity, she feels that they owe something in return and fears that they could as easily be punished as rewarded. As loss after horrendous loss befalls them—the death of a son in war, the loss of another son and daughter in an auto accident, the sexual assault and murder of yet another daughter, the death of their youngest child, an explosion that reduces J. B.'s business empire to rubble, a physical malady that leaves him near naked and covered with sores—she concludes that all God does is take from them and kill for some unknown wrong they did, and so she is brought close to despair.

J. B., for his part, desperately holds onto a conviction that the presence of evil does not mean that no good exists; he believes that the reason for their suffering is simply hidden from them. Certain that God would not punish without cause, that God's actions would be capricious if humankind were innocent, J. B. concludes that he himself must be guilty. Although J. B. can never understand, he still abhors his actions and repents—which seems at least partially to vindicate Nickles and to annoy Zuss, who is resentful that J. B. thinks man's acceptance rather than God's will justifies suffering. Yet, as in the biblical story, the last scene is one of restoration, with Sarah returning to a physically healed J. B. and bearing a sprig of forsythia blossoms that almost miraculously sprang up out of the ashes as a promise of renewal. It is left to Sarah to experience a secular epiphany.

In this Beckettian world of ash heap and dunghill, in which religion no longer suffices and from which an, at best, indifferent deity seems to be absent, no justice can be expected, and so the only wonder remaining is human love. The ultimate value becomes, then, feelings of the heart, a sentimental deification of affective emotions. The play's final image is one of a paradise regained, of a modern Adam and Eve in a new, humanistic age setting to work optimistically to reinvigorate the American ideal of self-reliance.

Thomas P. Adler
Purdue University

JEFFERS, ROBINSON (1887–1973)   Robinson Jeffers was the son of a minister and a professor of Old Testament literature. Born in Pittsburgh, Jeffers spent extensive periods in Europe as a child. His family later moved to California, where he earned a B.A. at Occidental College in Los Angeles and later attended graduate school at the University of Southern California (studying medicine) and the University of Washington (majoring in forestry). In 1912, he published his first book of poetry, beginning what would eventually become a lucrative career as a serious poet. The height of his fame peaked in the mid-1920s.

Interestingly, Jeffers turned to writing plays in the 1940s, a decade after his reputation with literary critics, along with his popularity among the American public, began to suffer. With an adaptation of *Medea* (1947), Jeffers regained a measure of fame (although it should be noted he never embraced his popularity), as the play had a successful run on Broadway. Some theater critics, however, were not so taken with the play, which Jeffers himself called a "free adaptation." Although the play follows Euripides's plot closely, the general mood is more misanthropic than tragic. Furthermore, many critics balked at Jeffers's modern verse, feeling it took too much away from Euripides's own voice.

Jeffers followed *Medea* with two other verse plays. The first, *The Tower beyond Tragedy* (1950), adapted from the poet's own narrative poem, is again steeped in Greek legend, this time that of Electra. This play received less acclaim from theater critics and was virtually ignored in literary circles. With an adaptation of the Phaedra legend entitled *The Cretan Woman* (1954), Jeffers offered his third and final play. Although it was performed in Washington, D.C., at Arena Stage

and OFF-BROADWAY, this play received even less attention than *The Tower beyond Tragedy* from playgoers and literary critics.

It is perhaps easy to conclude that Jeffers is a minor footnote in the history of American drama. Yet, his presence is noteworthy because his plays show how the ancient Greeks continue to influence modern artists and appeal to their audience. Furthermore, Jeffers is one of the few serious poets of the 20th century who achieved a measure of success as a playwright and as a poet.

BIBLIOGRAPHY
Gelpi, Albert, ed. *The Wild God of the World: An Anthology of Robinson Jeffers*. Palo Alto, Calif.: Stanford University Press, 2003.
Jeffers, Robinson. *Medea: Freely Adapted from the "Medea" of Euripides*. New York: Random House, 1946.

Christopher Brooks Bell
Georgia Military College

JEFFERSON, JOSEPH, III (1829–1905)   Born into an acting family that traced its history back to the earliest days of American theater, Joseph Jefferson III made his stage debut while still an infant. In a career that spanned almost 75 years, he played hundreds of roles, though his most popular was that of Rip Van Winkle, the loveable ne'er-do-well who sleeps away 20 years of his life and wakes to a world transformed around him. In many ways, Rip was the antithesis of Jefferson, who toured and performed continuously across America and around the world, never seeming to rest. His travels took him from the most lavishly appointed theaters in cities like New York and London to hovels with ramshackle scenery on the frontiers of America and the border towns of Australia.

In an age in which declamatory performance styles were the norm and actors counted the "points" or moments of applause they could garner each night, Jefferson's acting style seemed strikingly natural by comparison. Though he was equally committed to winning the audience's favor, he infused his characters with a kind of individuality that was unusual in the days when characters were "expected" to be played in certain ways. Audiences applauded his comic gift and his ability to bring personality and pathos to even the most seemingly shallow characters. Rip Van Winkle was the perfect example of Jefferson's dedication to the art of creating a character. The 1865 script that Jefferson made famous was the result of his collaboration with the Irish-born playwright, DION BOUCICAULT (with whom Jefferson had also worked on Boucicault's well-known play, *The OCTOROON,* in 1859). Though temperance plays were the norm by the mid-19th century, Jefferson managed to portray Rip as a sympathetic drunkard who acknowledged his faults and accepted the consequences of his actions, without ever preaching to the audience. The play was so successful that Jefferson continued to play the role for the next 30 years, earning hundreds of thousands of dollars in the process.

Though he is primarily associated with the character of Rip, Jefferson put his stamp on a range of other popular roles, including Asa Trenchard in *Our American Cousin* (the play best remembered as the one President Lincoln was watching at the time of his assassination), Bob Acres in Richard Brinsley Sheridan's *The Rivals,* and Newman Noggs in *Nicholas Nickleby.* Jefferson was clever enough to know the limits of his skills, and he never attempted serious tragedy or classical theater (except for parodies of Shakespeare).

Throughout his life, Jefferson was associated with the most prominent performers and playwrights of his day, including actress and manager Laura Keene, playwright Dion Boucicault, actor and manager William Warren, and the best-known tragedian of the 19th century, EDWIN BOOTH. Royalty and presidents attended his plays, and he was often called the "dean of the American Theatre." Countless images, from photographs to portraits by American master John Singer Sargent, depict Jefferson in the roles that he made famous and testify to his influence and importance in the history of American theater.

BIBLIOGRAPHY

Bloom, Arthur W. *Joseph Jefferson: Dean of the American Theatre.* Savannah, Ga.: Frederic C. Beil, 2000.

Heather Nathans
University of Maryland

JENKIN, LEN (1941–   )   Playwright, director, and author Len Jenkin was born in New York City and educated at Columbia University, where he received a Ph.D. in English in 1972. As a playwright, Jenkin emerged in the 1970s, part of a new breed of American dramatist, unconcerned with traditional linear narration. Jenkin's texts display gritty, uniquely American situations and landscapes via poetically surreal mood pieces, rather than through conventional storytelling. Plays such as *Dark Ride* (1981), one of his most well-known works, and *Careless Love* (1993) present the existential human condition through random occurrence, repetition, and seemingly unrelated events and characters. Jenkin plumbs the depths of the American experience and its tawdry underpinnings with nonnaturalistic settings, imagistic language, and dark humor. Most notable is Jenkin's ability to create evocative images and locations through language. His characters, derived from popular culture, include strippers, gangsters, lounge singers, Babe Ruth, and singing tumbleweeds. A constant motif in Jenkin's work is the exploration of the American vernacular, which expands the limits and possibilities of both language and theater. His plays are as much about the magic of theater as they are about the human experience. Jenkin's works are often metatheatrical, with characters directly communicating with the audience, commenting on and critiquing both the experience of spectatorship and the performance.

Jenkin defies easy categorization for he writes modernist pieces for the stage, creates plays for children's theater, freely adapts from classic texts, composes libretti for musical compositions (including *Madrigal Opera,* [1985]), writes for film and television, directs his own plays, and also works collaboratively with other playwrights such as MAC WELLMAN (to whom he is often compared for his imaginative use of language and imagery) and his daughter, writer Emily Jenkins. In 1992, he adapted the stage play *Ramona Quimby* from children's author Beverly Cleary's beloved Ramona series, which concerns the antics of a rambunctious eight-year-old girl. Also for children's theater, he adapted H. G. Wells's *The Invisible Man* (1993) and wrote the children's book *The Secret Life of Billie's Uncle Myron* (1996) with Emily Jenkins. While the merging of the avant-garde and children's theater may seem incongruous, Jenkin's sense of wonder and love of stage magic is ideally suited for creating work for young audiences.

A sampling of his adaptations includes *The Birds* by Aristophanes (2001), Voltaire's *Candide* (1982), *A Country Doctor* (1983, from the short story by Franz Kafka), and *Tallahassee,* written with Mac Wellman (based on Ovid's *Metamorphosis* and first produced in 1991).

Jenkin won OBIE AWARDS for *Five of Us* (1981) and *Limbo Tales* (1980). His other plays include *The Death and Life of Jesse James* (1974), *Gogol: A Mystery Play* (1976), *Kid Twist* (1977), *My Uncle Sam* (1983), *American Notes* (1986), and *Poor Folk's Pleasure* (1987). Jenkin is professor of dramatic writing and cohead of graduate studies at New York University's Tisch School of the Arts.

BIBLIOGRAPHY

Jenkin, Len. *"Dark Ride" and Other Plays.* Los Angeles: Sun and Moon, 1993.
———. *Plays by Len Jenkin.* New York: Broadway Play Publishing, 1999.

Jennifer Madden
Brown University

JITNEY AUGUST WILSON (1996) The original version of *Jitney* premiered in 1982 at the Allegheny Repertory Theater in Pittsburgh; that version, which predates MA RAINEY'S BLACK BOTTOM (1984), was much shorter and lacked the character development now present in the play. It was not until 1996 that the revised version of the play was performed for the first time at the Pittsburgh Public Theater; this was after several of the other plays in AUGUST WILSON's 10-play cycle chronicling the 20th-century African-American experience had already appeared. The New York production of *Jitney* in 2000 won for Wilson his seventh New York Drama Critics' Circle Award.

Jitney is set in 1977 at a *"gypsy cab station"* or "jitney station" in the Hill District of Pittsburgh. The men who make their living driving their own cars to shuttle people to the airport or the grocery store are a group of African-American men. The station's boss is Becker, a man who retired from the mill and collects a pension; Becker is a hardworking man who has always been responsible and played by the rules—white rules. When the play begins Becker's son is about to be released from prison after serving 20 years for murder. Becker's friend and longtime associate is Doub, a retired railroad man, also collecting his pension. The other drivers of the older generation are Fielding, a former tailor whose drinking problem brought an end to that career and threatens the job he has now, and Turnbo, a busybody whose love of gossip constantly causes trouble. The younger generation is represented by Youngblood, a Vietnam veteran who is impatient with the uphill struggle he faces to get ahead, but who is ultimately willing to work two or three jobs if necessary to support his girlfriend and their child. He is using the GI Bill to help him buy a house. He has great respect for Becker and seems by the end of the play to be headed down a similarly responsible path. In contrast, there are frequent references in the men's talk to young men who have taken the other path, the one that leads to the penitentiary. This talk coupled with Turnbo's gossip provides tension: We are unsure until well into the play which direction Youngblood has taken.

The most important conflict in the play is between Becker and his son, Booster. By the emotional end of act 1, we have learned the story of Booster's crime. A brilliant science student, Booster went to college and was the pride and joy of his parents. In college he became involved with a rich white girl. When her father caught them making love in her car, the girl accused Booster of rape in order to avoid her father's rage. Certain that they would be able to fight the lie, Becker hired a lawyer and got Booster out on bail; Booster went straight to the girl's house and shot her. He was first given the death penalty, and before it was commuted his mother took to her bed and died, unable to face a world without her son.

In the climax of the play, the drivers argue about Booster's motives. Booster describes the moment of disillusionment in his childhood when he witnessed his father quietly listening to their landlord berate him and threaten to put them out on the street if Becker did not pay the rent (Becker was uncharacteristically behind in his payment because he had had to pay for a funeral). The boy waited for his father to be the "big" man he admired who could "fill up" a room, but Becker passively took the abuse. Booster decided he was not ever going to let anyone make him that "small"; so when Susan McKnight "shout[ed] out that lie" many years later, it was his "chance to make the Beckers big again." He describes his action as that of a "warrior. . . . dealing with the world in ways that [his father] didn't or couldn't or wouldn't." Becker is appalled that his son sees his crime in these terms and with frenzied emotion speaks to him about being a man with responsibilities and with the hope that life will be better for his son ("Becker's taking this ass whipping so his boy can stride through this shit like Daniel in the lion's den! Watch out for Becker's boy! [. . . *now near tears*] And what I get, huh? You tell me. What I get?"). Becker cannot forgive his son for throwing his life away and will never understand his son's motivation. Furthermore, each man blames the other for the death of Booster's mother.

As the play nears its conclusion, Becker moves away from passivity in the face of an unfair system, as he makes plans to fight, through legal action, the city's plan to board up the buildings on the block. He and the other men know that the slated demolition and new construction will probably never occur and that his and other businesses will be destroyed for nothing. His efforts are cut short by his accidental death at the mill where he has gone to fill in temporarily when the foreman finds himself shorthanded. After his funeral, his son is sad that his father didn't get "out of life what he put in," but he is finally, once again, "proud to be Becker's boy."

In an interview in 1999, Wilson said that the setting of a jitney station provided "an opportunity to use this group of men to expose the culture, to get at some of the ways that this particular community of people solved its problems [and] abused itself" during the "urban renewal" period of the 1970s (Heard 225).

BIBLIOGRAPHY

Heard, Elisabeth, J. "August Wilson on Playwriting: An Interview." *Conversations with August Wilson.* Edited by Jackson R. Bryer and Mary C. Hartig. Jackson: University Press of Mississippi, 2006, 223–234.

JOE TURNER'S COME AND GONE

AUGUST WILSON (1986)   Set in 1911 in a Pittsburgh boardinghouse, *Joe Turner's Come and Gone* deals with the effects of slavery—lingering into the 20th century—on the black community. WILSON wrote in his explanation preceding the published play that he was writing of the "sons and daughters" of "freed African slaves" who came from the South to the city. Strangers, "they carry as part and parcel of their baggage a long line of separation and dispersement which informs their sensibilities and marks their conduct as they search for ways to reconnect, to reassemble." This disconnection from family and history was brought about both by slavery itself and by other racist forces. Such a force specific to this play is the historic figure Joe Turner, the white brother of the governor of Tennessee, who abducted black men from the road and forced them to labor for years at a time on chain gangs. A pivotal character in Wilson's play is such an abducted man, Herald Loomis, who, once released, begins his search for his wife, hoping to find a starting place from which to "make [his] own world."

A variety of African Americans come through Bertha and Seth's boardinghouse. Seth is in his early fifties, the son of "Northern free parents." He makes pots and pans for a man who sells him the materials and buys what he makes to sell on the road. Rutherford Selig is the salesman, and he is also a "people finder" because he writes down the names and addresses of his customers. A white man, Selig is the great-grandson of a slave trader and the son of a man who found runaway slaves; once the slaves were freed, Selig's family began finding "Nigras for Nigras." Bynum is a "conjure man," who uses powders and pigeon blood to "bind" people together. Jeremy is a young man from the country, a musician who is working on a road gang temporarily and who, Seth says, is like many southern blacks "coming up . . . carrying Bibles and guitars looking for freedom. They got a rude awakening." Jeremy soon finds out he will be cheated up North because of his race, and, when first we meet him, he has spent the night in jail—arrested without cause. The talk among the male characters about Jeremy's experiences with unjust law officers is reminiscent of similar complaints by male characters in other Wilson plays, including *FENCES* (1985) and *SEVEN GUITARS* (1995). The women, too, are typical Wilson characters: Mattie has been abandoned by her man and becomes involved with Jeremy for company; Molly, like Ruby in *Seven Guitars* and the offstage Alberta in *Fences,* is irresistible to men and knows how to use her sexuality to get what she wants. Jeremy drops Mattie to run off with Molly. Bertha, like Rose in *Fences,* is the salt of the earth, the loyal, nurturing, self-sacrificing wife and mother figure.

Bynum speaks of people's "songs": A man must find his song. Bynum's is the binding song; he binds people together—hence his name—in this time of great wandering. In the play, a man's "song" is a metaphor for his roots or identity—familial and historical. Because African Americans were dispersed by slavery and by the likes of Joe Turner, each needs to relocate his identity, his connection to the past. When Herald Loomis's wife Martha is found by Selig, the people finder, Martha thanks Bynum, whom she hired to bind her to her young daughter, Zonia, who has been traveling with Loomis in search of Martha for four years. Loomis has been searching for his wife, not to reunite with her, but to "say [his] goodbye and make [his] own world." He returns Zonia to her mother. Martha wants Herald Loomis—a deacon before he was snatched by Joe Turner—to return to the church, but Herald rejects Christianity ("Great big old white man . . . your Mr. Jesus Christ. Standing there with a whip in one hand and tote board in another, and them niggers swimming in a sea of cotton"; "I done been baptized with blood of the lamb and the fire of the Holy Ghost. But what I got, huh?"). In the highly charged final moment of the play, Loomis slices his own chest with a knife and cleanses himself with his own blood and then, as Wilson notes in his final stage directions, *"comes to a realization"* that he has *"found his song, the song of self-sufficiency."*

There was some criticism that without Wilson's illuminating stage note the meaning of Loomis's final action, though stunningly theatrical, is unclear. Despite this criticism, the play won the New York Drama Critics' Circle Award. *Joe Turner* is one of the plays in Wilson's cycle—one play set in each decade— depicting the African-American experience in the 20th century.

BIBLIOGRAPHY
Wilson, August. *Joe Turner's Come and Gone.* New York: Plume, 1988.

JOHNSON, GEORGIA DOUGLAS (1877–1966)

Georgia Douglas Johnson was known primarily for her poetry, but she wrote many plays and musicals that were never produced. She was 60 years old before she earned a well-deserved place among the best poets and dramatists of the Harlem Renaissance. Johnson published four volumes of poetry and five plays, although she wrote more than 30. Born in Marietta, Georgia, to George and Laura Jackson Camp, Johnson was educated in the public schools and attended Atlanta University, Howard University, and Oberlin School of Music. She married Henry Lincoln Johnson (Recorder of Deeds under President Taft) in 1900. He died of a stroke in 1925. A charter member of the "New Negro" movement, she hosted a discussion group at her home in Washington, D.C., for celebrities such as Jean Toomer, Alain Locke, Countee Cullen, and LANGSTON HUGHES.

As a playwright, Johnson concentrated on the controversial subject of lynching. One exception to this was her play *Plumes* (1928), in which a mother chooses to spend her savings on a lavish funeral for her dying daughter rather than on the appendectomy that might have saved her life. This play won first place in the 1927 *Opportunity* magazine contest. Three of her most compelling works, *Safe* (1929), *Sunday Morning in the South* (1925), and *Blue-eyed Black Boy* (1926), focus on black men wrongly accused of rape and minor offenses such as "brushing up against a white woman." In *Safe,* a young mother strangles her newborn baby boy rather than subject him to the torture of a lynch mob. Between 1935 and 1938, Johnson was commissioned by the NAACP under the FEDERAL THEATRE PROJECT to write plays that would aid the passage of an antilynching bill that was before Congress. These plays were recently discovered among the NAACP papers in the Manuscript Division of the Library of Congress: "A

Bill to Be Passed" and "Yet They Paused" juxtapose the settings of the United States Congress in Washington, D.C., and a congregation in Mississippi who prays for the passage of the bill as they witness a brutal lynching. Executives at the NAACP rejected Johnson's plays because of their graphic depictions of torture, thick dialect spoken by the black characters, and negative references to President Franklin D. Roosevelt, who remained silent during the debates. Johnson wrote two other plays during this period, *Frederick Douglass* (1940) and *William and Ellen Craft* (1935).

Much of Johnson's work reflects her mulatto heritage—her father was part white and Native American—and her own ambivalence about race. In her play *Blue Blood* (1927), two mothers, before the wedding of their children, brag about the children's white blood lines, until they discover that they (the mothers) were raped by the same white banker. The marriage is cancelled in the nick of time. Much of Johnson's poetry and drama resound with references to miscegenation and the complications that stem from being a mulatto. In her later years, Johnson, surrounded by mounds of notes, unfinished manuscripts, and a menagerie of cats and dogs, lived an eccentric, lonely, and abject existence until her death in 1966.

BIBLIOGRAPHY

Bower, Martha Gilman. *Color Struck under the Gaze: The Pathology of Being in the Plays of Johnson, Hurston, Childress, Hansberry, and Kennedy.* Westport, Conn.: Greenwood Press, 2003.

Gates, Henry Louis, Jr., ed. *Selected Works of Georgia Johnson.* New York: G. K. Hall, 1997.

Hull, Gloria T. *Color, Sex and Poetry: Three Women Writers of the Harlem Renaissance.* Bloomington: Indiana University Press, 1987.

Johnson, Georgia. "Lynching Plays." C-299, NAACP Collection, Library of Congress, Washington, D.C.

Stephens, Judith L., ed. *The Plays of Georgia Douglas Johnson: From the New Negro Renaissance to the Civil Rights Movement.* Urbana: University of Illinois Press, 2006.

Martha Gilman Bower
Indiana University of Pennsylvania

JONES, LEROI   See BARAKA, AMIRI.

JONES, PRESTON (1936–1979)   Preston St. Wain Jones, a theater professional identified primarily with the Dallas Theater Center, became a playwright so that he could recreate everyday life in the rural Southwest on the stage. By design a regional writer, Jones at his best transcended his Texas and New Mexico settings to reveal a larger vision of a racist, sexist, materialistic society clinging to self-serving myths as it disregards religious values and a viable work ethic. Born in Albuquerque, New Mexico, he was the youngest of five children. After attending Catholic schools, he graduated from the University of New Mexico.

Jones began as an actor with the Dallas Theater Center, later directing plays as well. In the early 1970s, Jones began writing plays since he had a professional's knowledge of the theater and a personal gift for storytelling. He began a draft of *Lu Ann Hampton Laverty Oberlander,* the first of the three plays, known as *A TEXAS TRILOGY,* on which his reputation largely depends; but the second play of the trilogy, *The Last Meeting of the Knights of the White Magnolia,* was actually performed first, in the Down Center Stage at the Theater Center in December 1973. A few months later, in February 1974, *Lu Ann* was performed in the same theater. Finally, in November 1974, *The Oldest Living Graduate* opened in the upstairs Kalita Humphreys Theater. The first two plays of the trilogy were revised and alternated in the repertory. In the final week of the trilogy's production, it was possible for audiences to see all three during a six-and-a-half-hour period each night. The project was so successful that it established Jones as the most popular playwright at the Theater Center and spawned regional productions of his works in Chicago, Washington, and Seattle. New York, however, was not so receptive. Although the scheduling of the trilogy was generously heralded by the popular press, Broadway critics were skeptical. Reviewers in the *New York Times, The New Yorker,* and the *New Republic* found Jones's work derivative, sentimental, and insignificant. Stunned by this negative reception, Jones retreated to the Dallas Theater Center, with which he had been associated for 19 years and where he remained a celebrity.

Juneteenth (1978) was the last of Jones's dramas to have a specific Texas locale. It described an annual celebration of emancipation by Texas African Americans, known as "Juneteenth." Jones's next two plays were set in his native New Mexico. They are less ambitious works than *A Texas Trilogy,* with its large cast of characters and complex use of time. *A Place on the Magdalena Flats* (1979) has a deterministic quality and resonances of the work of EUGENE O'NEILL and SAM SHEPARD. *Santa Fe Sunshine* (1977) was written between the first version of *Magdalena Flats* (1975) and its revision (1979). It is a satire of semitalented American artists whose work primarily interests well-to-do philistines of a liberal persuasion. In his last and most autobiographical play, *Remember* (1979), produced at the Dallas Theater Center a few months before his death, Jones created the part of an actor named Adrian, whose life paralleled Jones's.

Jones's heavy drinking and the late-night schedule of constant theater productions caught up with him, and he began to experience continuing difficulties with a stomach ulcer. Following an attack of bleeding ulcers, he underwent surgery and died in an intensive care unit on September 19, 1979, in Dallas, Texas.

BIBLIOGRAPHY

Busby, Mark. *Preston Jones.* Boise, Idaho: Boise State University, 1983.

Jones, Preston. *A Place on the Magdalena Flats.* New York: Dramatists Play Service, 1984.

——. *Santa Fe Sunshine.* New York: Dramatists Play Service, 1977.

——. *A Texas Trilogy.* New York: Hill & Wang, 1976.

Kimball King
University of North Carolina–Chapel Hill

JONES, ROBERT EDMOND (1887–1954)

Having studied "the New Stagecraft" in Europe, particularly with Max Reinhardt, Robert Edmond Jones introduced his interpretation of it to the American theater in his first professional design, for the 1915 production of Anatole France's *The Man Who Married a Dumb Wife.* Jones pursued the goal of aesthetic unity in all elements of production throughout his career. He thought of a drama as a living organism with an inner rhythm, which he sought to embody in the scenic composition, the lighting, the costuming, and the realization of the setting with the overarching goal of realizing the dramatist's vision on stage and intensifying the audience's experience of the play. Jones combined the imagination and vision of the artist with the many skills of a fine craftsman and a unique willingness to attend to detail in executing a design. He wrote that a designer is forced to think in a hundred different ways—as architect, housepainter, electrician, dressmaker, sculptor, and jeweler—but that he or she must be constantly aware of the "high original intention of the dramatist," and follow it.

Jones's many design credits range from opera and ballet to Shakespeare and Molière to Henrik Ibsen and EUGENE O'NEILL to Clare Kummer and PHILIP BARRY. For producer Arthur Hopkins, he created a series of extraordinary modernist designs for Shakespeare's plays, particularly his expressionistic *Macbeth* (1921), which made startlingly effective use of intense beams of light and enormous abstract masks, and his 1937 and 1944 productions of *Othello,* his *Hamlet* (1922), and his *Richard III* (1920). Beginning with *"ANNA CHRISTIE"* in 1922, Jones was the major scenic designer for O'Neill's plays, and along with O'Neill and Kenneth Macgowan, became a director of the PROVINCETOWN PLAYERS when it reorganized in 1923. For the Provincetown, Jones collaborated with O'Neill on *Welded, The Ancient Mariner, The EMPEROR JONES,* and *ALL GOD'S CHILLUN GOT WINGS* in 1923–24 and *S.S. Glencairn, Diff'rent,* and *DESIRE UNDER THE ELMS,* creating the latter's well-known, innovative simultaneous setting, the following season. In the next season, he designed O'Neill's *The Fountain* and *The Great God Brown.*

He also directed productions for the Provincetown, including its experimental production of August Strindberg's *Spook Sonata* (1924) and an imaginative production of ANNA CORA MOWATT'S *FASHION* (1924), in which his versatile talents were called on for scene and costume design as well as for direction. This production, which negotiated a fine line between historical reproduction and travesty, ran for more than 150 performances and started a new vogue for revivals in New York. After the Provincetown period, he designed the THEATRE GUILD productions of O'Neill's major plays, *MOURNING BECOMES ELECTRA* (1931), *AH, WILDERNESS!* (1933), *The ICEMAN COMETH* (1946), and *A MOON FOR THE MISBEGOTTEN* (1947).

Jones's ideas had an important influence on the 20th-century American theater through a generation of designers whom he mentored, including Jo MIEL-ZINER, Donald Oenslager, Lee Simonson, and Cleon Throckmorton, as well as through his seminal work on scenic design, *The Dramatic Imagination* (1941), and other writing on the theater.

BIBLIOGRAPHY

Jones, Robert Edmond. *The Dramatic Imagination: Reflections and Speculations on the Art of the Theatre.* New York: Theatre Arts Books, 1941.

———. *Drawings for the Theatre.* Edited by Donald Oenslager. New York: Theatre Arts Books, 1970.

Macgowan, Kenneth, and Robert Edmond Jones. *Continental Stagecraft.* New York: Harcourt, Brace, 1922.

Pendleton, Ralph, ed. *The Theatre of Robert Edmond Jones.* 2d ed. Middletown, Conn.: Wesleyan University Press, 1977.

Brenda Murphy
University of Connecticut

K

KANIN, GARSON (1912–1999) Playwright, screenwriter, and director Garson Kanin was born in Rochester, New York. He attended the American Academy of Dramatic Arts for two years before beginning a career in theater, which included acting in many Broadway productions in the 1930s; he also began his career as a director, at first in collaboration with GEORGE ABBOTT and then on his own. Kanin directed such American classics as THREE MEN ON A HORSE (1935) (codirected with Abbott) and The DIARY OF ANNE FRANK (1955). While in the army during World War II, Kanin served in various capacities, including as film director in the Office of War Information; a film from this period, The True Glory (1945), directed by Kanin and Carol Reed, won the Academy Award for feature documentary. After the war, Kanin wrote his first and most famous play, BORN YESTERDAY (1946).

Born Yesterday is a comedy that questions the dangers of political lobbying through its portrait of the brashly corrupt businessman Harry Brock and his attempts to influence congressional legislation. Unfortunately for Brock, investigative reporter Paul Verrall awakens the moral responsibility in Brock's mistress, Billie Dawn, so that she helps expose Brock's proposed crimes. Billy's transformation from breathtaking stupidity to an astuteness that brings with it power conveys Kanin's view of the importance to a democracy of an informed electorate.

In his next play, The Smile of the World (1949), Kanin returned to a Washington, D.C., setting to portray Reuben Boulting, a Supreme Court justice whose current narrow-minded, stuffy persona is far from the young idealist his wife first loved and then wed. Boulting's icy behavior, while serving the politics of the Court, eventually kills all the former warmth of— and thus by play's end the very viability of—his marriage.

Kanin often captured the ambience of a special show business milieu. He centered The Rat Race (1949) around tango dancing and jazz music; Helen is the disillusioned dancer and Gus is the naive young saxophone player from the Midwest newly arrived in a merciless New York. The musical Do Re Mi (1960), based on Kanin's own short novel, centers around a mobster's neglect of his marriage in favor of his involvement in the jukebox industry. Come on Strong (1962) depicts the approach-and-retreat parrying, conducted over several years, by an actress and her photographer beau. In Peccadillo (1985), an especially histrionic symphony conductor and his opera-singer wife endure various marital strains and adulterous temptations, and then they negotiate an evidently jubilant divorce.

Kanin's 1962 dramatic adaptation, A Gift of Time, depicts Lael Wertenbaker's poignant memoir (Death of a Man) of her husband's last months as he succumbed to cancer. Another Kanin adaptation, Dreyfus in

Rehearsal (1974), translates a Jean-Claude Grumberg script about Jews in 1930s Poland. As they prepare to dramatize the malicious 1890s French trial of the Jewish soldier Alfred Dreyfus, they encounter, in their own locale, gentile neighbors' hatred and violence against them—along with the Communists' contrasting, but equally delusive, promises of a nebulous societal salvation.

Kanin adapted Johann Strauss's *Die Fledermaus* (1950), Felicien Marceau's *The Good Soup* (1960), and his own book, *Remembering Mr. Maugham* (1969). He also wrote, besides the plays already noted, *The Live Wire* (1950) and *Happy Ending* (1989). For the body of his work as a playwright, Garson Kanin received several prizes, including those named for playwrights SIDNEY HOWARD and WILLIAM INGE. A prolific writer in other genres as well, his output includes nine novels, six nonfiction books, a volume of short stories, and 16 screenplays.

BIBLIOGRAPHY

Kanin, Garson. *Born Yesterday.* New York: Viking Press, 1946.

———. *Come on Strong.* New York: Dramatists Play Service, 1964.

———. *Do Re Mi.* Boston: Little, Brown, 1955.

———. *Dreyfus in Rehearsal.* New York: Dramatists Play Service, 1983.

———. *A Gift of Time.* New York: Random House, 1962.

———. *The Live Wire.* New York: Dramatists Play Service, 1951.

———. *The Rat Race.* New York: Dramatists Play Service, 1950.

———. *The Smile of the World.* New York: Dramatists Play Service, 1949.

Jeffrey B. Loomis
Northwest Missouri State University

KAUFMAN, GEORGE S. (1889–1961)

Born in Pittsburgh, Pennsylvania, George S. Kaufman was stagestruck by the time he graduated from Pittsburgh Central High School in 1907. In 1909, he began sending humorous items to Franklin Pierce Adams, already famous for his New York newspaper column. In 1912, Adams recommended Kaufman to a Washington, D.C., publisher who needed a staff humorist. Kaufman

lasted a year, until the publisher realized he was Jewish and fired him.

Returning to New York, Kaufman began writing reviews and became the drama critic for the *New York Times* in 1917, a post he held until 1930. He simultaneously made himself a playwright. He studied playwriting privately and at Columbia University. In 1918, the Broadway producer George C. Tyler hired him to rewrite a comedy, *Someone in the House.* Tyler produced five more shows of a total of eight cowritten by Kaufman and MARC CONNELLY. Kaufman made collaboration his style of working.

Between *Dulcy,* his first play with Connelly in 1921, and *Amicable Parting,* written with his second wife, Leueen McGrath, in 1957, Kaufman collaborated on 41 plays with 14 different writers. Of that number, 27 resulted from partnerships with Connelly, EDNA FERBER (six shows), Morrie Ryskind (five), and MOSS HART (eight). From the latter three partnerships came plays that audiences around the world love to see revived: With Ferber, *The ROYAL FAMILY* (1927), *Stage Door* (1936), and *DINNER AT EIGHT* (1932) became standards in the repertoire.

With Ryskind, Kaufman helped launch the career of the Marx Brothers. In a rare solo effort, Kaufman had written the first Marx Brothers musical, *Coconuts,* in 1925; in 1928, he teamed with Ryskind on *Animal Crackers.* Those two shows made the Marx Brothers famous and led to the film versions for which Kaufman and Ryskind wrote the screenplays. They repeated their success with an original film for the Marx Brothers in 1935, *A Night at the Opera.* Their musical satire on presidential campaigns, *Of Thee I Sing* (with lyrics by Ira Gershwin and music by George Gershwin), won the PULITZER PRIZE for 1932.

Two plays Kaufman wrote with Moss Hart, however, remain the peak achievements of his career as a playwright. *YOU CAN'T TAKE IT WITH YOU* won the Pulitzer Prize in 1937. In 1939, the two collaborated on *The MAN WHO CAME TO DINNER.* These two plays are revived more often than any other of Kaufman's works.

Kaufman's marriage to Beatrice Bakrow lasted from 1917 until her death in 1945. The shared unhappiness of a stillborn child led them to adopt tolerant views toward each other's love affairs, one of which, between

Kaufman and film star Mary Astor, caused Astor's infamous divorce trial in 1936. The Kaufmans' marriage, and their devotion to the daughter they adopted in 1925, survived that crisis and many others. After Beatrice's death, Kaufman produced only one more original comedy that has lasted, *The Solid Gold Cadillac* (1953), cowritten with Howard Teichmann. His later years were distinguished, however, by his award-winning direction of musicals, particularly *Guys and Dolls* (1950) and *Silk Stockings* (1955).

As an artist, Kaufman brought to all of his collaborations great talent for plotting and dialogue. He passed on to younger writers the example of how to pace comic action so that laughs build upon one another without losing their link to characters' personalities and motives. His dialogue channeled into the plays his widely feared and well-documented power in private life to attack foolish people and absurd situations with memorable wisecracks. However, he earned the respect and affection of his collaborators for his forbearance, patience, deference, and kindness. These qualities also helped him become the leading stage director of his era.

His influence can be seen most fully today in television and motion picture comedy, rather than in theater. At about the time that Kaufman's career drew to a close, television invaded American homes. One comedy program, *Your Show of Shows*, satirized popular theatrical and motion picture entertainment and the behavior of America's middle and upper classes, as did many of Kaufman's plays. The writers for that show included NEIL SIMON, Mel Brooks, Carl Reiner, and Woody Allen. All have acknowledged their debt to George S. Kaufman.

BIBLIOGRAPHY

Goldstein, Malcolm. *George S. Kaufman: His Life, His Theater.* New York: Oxford University Press, 1979.

Kaufman, George S., and Edna Ferber. *Three Comedies: "The Royal Family," "Dinner at Eight," "Stage Door."* New York: Applause Theatre Books, 1999.

———, and Moss Hart. *Six Plays by Kaufman and Hart.* New York: Modern Library, 1942.

———, Ring W. Lardner, and Edna Ferber. *George S. Kaufman and His Collaborators: Three Plays.* New York: Performing Arts Journal Publications, 1984.

Meredith, Scott. *George S. Kaufman and His Friends.* Garden City, N.Y.: Doubleday, 1974.

Pollack, Rhoda-Gale. *George S. Kaufman.* Boston: Twayne, 1988.

Teichmann, Howard. *George S. Kaufman: An Intimate Portrait.* New York: Atheneum, 1972.

Arvid F. Sponberg
Valparaiso University

KAZAN, ELIA (1909–2003)

Elia Kazan was born Elia Kazanjoglou in Constantinople (now Istanbul), Turkey. His parents brought the family to New York City in 1913. Kazan's immigrant experience and that of his family have formed the core of a good deal of his autobiographical writing, including his first novel, *America America* (1962), and its film version about his uncle's emigration as a boy, and another novel, *The Anatolian* (1982), about the family's adaptation to American culture. While Kazan's father expected him to join him in the carpet business, his mother supported his desire to go to college. Kazan eventually worked his way through Williams College and, having found his vocation, went on to the Yale School of Drama, where he gained the technical expertise that gave him his enduring theatrical nickname, "Gadget," but where he primarily concentrated on his real interest, which was directing.

In 1933, Kazan joined the GROUP THEATRE, the innovative theater collective and producing organization run by HAROLD CLURMAN, Lee Strasberg, and Cheryl Crawford, which adapted the ideas of Constantin Stanislavsky to develop the acting and directing technique known as the "Method" (see ACTORS STUDIO). With the Group, Kazan served as stage manager, actor, and, finally, director. When the Group dissolved in 1941, Kazan directed a series of successful plays on Broadway, including THORNTON WILDER's philosophical farce *The SKIN OF OUR TEETH* (1942), the comedies *One Touch of Venus* (1943) and *Jacobowsky and the Colonel* (1944), and *Deep Are the Roots* (1945), a significant postwar treatment of American racism.

In 1947, Kazan's career as a director entered a new phase, with his premiere productions of ARTHUR MILLER's *ALL MY SONS* and TENNESSEE WILLIAMS's *A STREETCAR NAMED DESIRE*. In these two plays and in Miller's

DEATH OF A SALESMAN (1949), Kazan, along with designer JO MIELZINER and an extraordinary group of largely Method-trained actors, established a new form of theater that came to be known as "the American style," or "subjective realism." It combined the emotional authenticity of the Method's approach to character with staging that departed from traditional realism to suggest a subjective perception of reality through the use of music, lighting, transparent and disappearing walls, partially constructed buildings, and minimal furniture and props.

Kazan's direction became known for its synthesis of his two absorbing interests: the effect of economic and social forces on individuals within American society and the explosive dynamics of the family that result from it. Although he, the founder with Cheryl Crawford and Robert Lewis of the Actors Studio, taught the technique of the Method and used it effectively, his unique quality as a director was his ability to connect with each actor individually, to help actors find the performances they were capable of in their own way, and to synthesize these performances into a unified, often emotionally explosive production.

Kazan's direction of the highly successful films *A Tree Grows in Brooklyn* (1945), *Gentleman's Agreement* (1947), and *A Streetcar Named Desire* (1951), among others, established him as a major film director at the same time that he reached his peak as a Broadway director. In 1952, Kazan testified in congressional hearings about his brief membership in the Communist Party in 1933–34 and, in order to avoid being blacklisted from future film work, named other former members of the Group Theatre who had also been members, alienating himself from many in the Hollywood film industry. This antipathy continued throughout Kazan's life, erupting in a storm of protest when, at the age of 89, he was awarded an Academy Award for lifetime achievement in 1999.

Kazan worked with extraordinary energy in both film and theater during the 1950s, directing the films *Viva Zapata!* (1952), *On the Waterfront* (1954), *East of Eden* (1955), *Baby Doll* (1956), *A Face in the Crowd* (1957), *Wild River* (1960), and *Splendor in the Grass* (1961). In the theater, his best work was done in the context of his relationships with playwrights of sig-nificant literary stature: Tennessee Williams, WILLIAM INGE, ROBERT ANDERSON, Archibald MacLeish, and Arthur Miller. With Williams especially, he worked in an increasingly close creative collaboration. Williams followed Kazan's suggestions for major cuts and revisions in CAMINO REAL (1953), his existential fantasy about the repressive social and political atmosphere of the 1950s. Williams also followed Kazan's advice for major changes in his most successful Broadway play, CAT ON A HOT TIN ROOF (1955), but resented the changes enough to include his original version of the altered third act in his published version of the play. Their next collaboration, on SWEET BIRD OF YOUTH (1959), was to be their last. Meanwhile, Kazan had directed Anderson's TEA AND SYMPATHY (1953) and Inge's The DARK AT THE TOP OF THE STAIRS (1957), two successful examples of the psychological focus of the Broadway theater of the 1950s and of Kazan's subjective realism.

In 1961, weary of the commercialism of the Broadway theater, Kazan agreed to codirect the repertory theater that was to be developed in New York's newly created Lincoln Center. With the exception of Arthur Miller's autobiographical AFTER THE FALL (1964), in which the character Mickey is not too flatteringly modeled on Kazan, his direction there was disappointing. For various reasons, Kazan left this venture and began a career as a successful novelist. He directed only four films after 1961, including *America, America* (1963), the film version of his bestselling *The Arrangement* (1969), and an adaptation of F. Scott Fitzgerald's *The Last Tycoon* (1976). In the plays and films of his prolific period from 1945 to 1961, however, Kazan created an unparalleled body of work.

BIBLIOGRAPHY

Baer, William, ed. *Elia Kazan Interviews*. Jackson: University Press of Mississippi, 2000.

Ciment, Michel. *Kazan on Kazan*. New York: Viking, 1974.

Kazan, Elia. *Elia Kazan: A Life*. New York: Knopf, 1988.

Murphy, Brenda. *Congressional Theatre: Dramatizing McCarthyism on Stage, Film, and Television*. Cambridge, England: Cambridge University Press, 1999.

———. *Tennessee Williams and Elia Kazan: A Collaboration in the Theater*. Cambridge, England: Cambridge University Press, 1992.

Pauly, Thomas H. *An American Odyssey: Elia Kazan and American Culture.* Philadelphia: Temple University Press, 1983.

Brenda Murphy
University of Connecticut

KELLY, GEORGE E[DWARD] (1887–1974)

George E. Kelly was born to an established and respected Philadelphia family—the second youngest of 10 siblings. His brothers included Walter, a vaudeville star ("Virginia Judge"), and John, an Olympic medalist in rowing and father of film star (later princess) Grace. Kelly entered the theater in about 1912 as an actor. After a brief stint in the army in World War I, Kelly returned to the United States, where he became a vaudeville star performing skits and one-acts he wrote for himself, including "Mrs. Ritter Appears" and "Poor Aubrey." Kelly's early plays were noted for their realism, satire, and single-minded characters. His later, less comedic plays were not as popular; disappointed with the Broadway theater and critics, Kelly moved to Hollywood in the 1930s, where he worked as a script consultant but wrote only one credited film script (*Old Hutch* [1935]).

Kelly's focus as a writer was always on individual character flaws, which he presented in a clearly (some would say "heavy-handed") moralistic fashion. *The Torch-Bearers* (1922) was Kelly's first full-length play and first Broadway success. It is a satire of the burgeoning LITTLE THEATRE MOVEMENT in the United States. Kelly's next Broadway play was *The Show-Off* (1924), an expanded version of his vaudeville staple, "Poor Aubrey." Aubrey Piper is the show-off of the title, a man of little means and perhaps less wit who insists on believing in and attempting to live up to his own sense of self-importance. A major commercial success, *The Show-Off* was also reportedly considered for the PULITZER PRIZE. That award, however, was not forthcoming until Kelly's next work, CRAIG'S WIFE (1925). While the humor and satire of his first two plays was aimed at unquestionably foolish but well-meaning characters, the center of *Craig's Wife* is the imperious Harriet Craig. Harriet's goal is complete control over the events, objects, and people in her life. The cost of her domination, however, is isolation and, ultimately, abandonment by husband and friends. Harriet achieves control but at an absurdly high price. Kelly's other plays include *Daisy Mayme* (1926), *Behold, the Bridegroom* (1927), *Maggie the Magnificent* (1929), *Philip Goes Forth* (1931), *Reflected Glory* (1936), *The Deep Mrs. Sykes* (1945), and *The Fatal Weakness* (1946). Kelly's plays often feature female protagonists who are portrayed as foolish (*The Torch-Bearers*), overbearing (*Craig's Wife*), and jealous (*The Deep Mrs. Sykes*). These extremes are balanced—often within the same play—by female characters who are intelligent, compassionate and clear-thinking.

Kelly believed in the educational possibilities of the theater. He saw himself as a moralist and used his plays to present his uncompromising view that we bear personal responsibility for our actions and choices. Kelly did not accept the easy solutions offered by popular psychology and its reliance on heredity and environment as the primary social determinants. It was his insistence on portraying these values in his later works that led audiences and critics to turn away.

BIBLIOGRAPHY

Graves, Mark A. *George Kelly: A Research and Production Sourcebook.* Westport, Conn.: Greenwood Press, 1999.
Hirsch, Foster. *George Kelly.* New York: Twayne, 1975.
Kelly, George E. *Behold, the Bridegroom.* Boston: Little, Brown, 1928.
———. *Daisy Mayme.* New York: Samuel French, 1927.
———. *The Deep Mrs. Sykes.* New York: Samuel French, 1946.
———. *The Fatal Weakness.* New York: Samuel French, 1947.
———. *"The Flattering Word" and Other One-Act Plays.* Boston: Little, Brown, 1927.
———. *Philip Goes Forth.* New York: Samuel French, 1931.
———. *Reflected Glory.* New York: Samuel French, 1937.
———. *Three Plays: "The Torch-Bearers," "The Show-Off," "Craig's Wife."* New York: Limelight Editions, 1999.

Timothy D. Connors
Central Michigan University

KENNEDY (HAWKINS), ADRIENNE (1931–)

Adrienne Kennedy saw *The GLASS MENAGERIE* when she was 16, read *OUR TOWN* in college, and was inspired to write dramas about her own life. After completing her first (and, to date, unpublished) play, "The Pale Blue Flowers" (1954), she realized that the tradition of TENNESSEE WILLIAMS and THORNTON WILDER did not suit her, and she began to explore other styles. A trip to Ghana led her to write FUNNYHOUSE OF A NEGRO (1964), a violent, poetic play about a young woman on the verge of death. Upon her return to the United States, she was selected to join a playwrights workshop with EDWARD ALBEE, and she toned down the play's language for a reading. Albee, however, urged her to revert to the original version, explaining that a playwright should "put his guts on that stage." She has taken this advice to heart for more than 30 years.

Born in Pittsburgh and raised in Cleveland, Kennedy learned to read when she was three and had devoured every book in her school library by fifth grade. Her parents had grown up in Georgia, and her mother constantly told stories of life in the rural South—stories that became the prototype for the monologues in Kennedy's plays. She attended Ohio State University, an environment she found far more racist than her integrated neighborhood in Cleveland, and her anger at this experience has surfaced throughout her drama (most notably in *The Ohio State Murders* [1992]). After graduation, she moved to New York, started a family, and began to write plays. She has won two prestigious OBIE AWARDS (one in 1964 for *Funnyhouse* and one in 1996 for the paired plays, *June and Jean in Concert* and *Sleep Deprivation Chamber*), and New York's OFF-BROADWAY Signature Theatre Company devoted its 1996 season to her work. Her autobiography, *People Who Led to My Plays* (1987), is a scrapbook-style collection of memories and photographs in which she includes such diverse examples as Jane Eyre, the Wolf Man, and Patrice Lumumba as influences on her writing.

Although Kennedy calls all her work autobiographical, she does not necessarily adhere to the facts of her life when writing her plays. Her characters frequently share her concerns and her oppressions, but they are fictionalized and often symbolical. Her three most famous plays, *Funnyhouse, The Owl Answers* (1965), and *A Movie Star Has to Star in Black and White* (1976), present young African-American women whose con-flicting desires literally tear them apart, fragmenting them into divided selves who are visually realized onstage. In *Funnyhouse,* four historical figures appear, pathetic and maimed, to recite Sarah's lines; in *A Movie Star,* Clara's monologues are voiced by leading ladies enacting scenes from classic films. In these early plays, African-American characters often long to be white, mothers wish their children were never conceived, and characters of both races and genders are treated with mixed sympathy and hatred. As a result of such complexity, Kennedy was not at first embraced by communities of African-American or feminist writers.

Kennedy's later plays include a constant main character named Suzanne Alexander, a middle-aged playwright from Cleveland who not only shares much of Kennedy's past but who also claims to have written her plays. Suzanne inhabits a more racially polarized world than Kennedy's earlier protagonists, and her plays tend to be more linear in their story lines: In *The Ohio State Murders,* Suzanne remembers how her white professor fathered and then murdered her twin daughters; in *Sleep Deprivation Chamber* (1996), cowritten with Adam P. Kennedy, she tells the story of her son's brutal beating and arrest by a white policeman.

Kennedy's relatives have always inhabited her writing, first as veiled influences, later as identifiable characters, and most recently as partners in creation, so that, as Philip C. Kolin writes, "To understand Kennedy's plays is to understand her family" (Kolin 5). *Mom How Did You Meet the Beatles?: A True Story of London in the 1960s* (2006), subtitled *Adam P. Kennedy talks to Adrienne Kennedy,* looks like an interview in book form (in fact, it won the 2007 PEN Oakland National Book Award), but on the stage it fits perfectly into Kennedy's mysteriously autobiographical dramatic oeuvre. "Kennedy aficionados familiar with the writer's mimetic networks in which new plays are cross-wired with earlier ones and dark things condense into multivalent images may be lured into thinking that *Mom How Did You Meet the Beatles?* will offer a truly 'true story,' the Ur-experience from which her post-1960s creative work springs," wrote Elin Diamond in her review of the play's first production at New York's Public Theatre in 2007 (666). And perhaps it does offer a truly true story, but perhaps, as all Kennedy's work suggests, truth does not exist in any consistent, irrefutable form.

Constant in all of Kennedy's drama is her trademark use of nightmare imagery and incantatory repetition. Each of her plays is a pastiche of symbols and a chorus of voices; the stories she tells, while based on her life, are not merely her own. Kennedy won the OBIE Lifetime Achievement Award in 2008.

BIBLIOGRAPHY

Bower, Martha Gilman. *Color Struck under the Gaze: The Pathology of Being in the Plays of Johnson, Hurston, Childress, Hansberry, and Kennedy.* Westport, Conn.: Greenwood Press, 2003.

Bryant-Jackson, Paul K., and Lois More Overbeck, eds. *Intersecting Boundaries: The Theatre of Adrienne Kennedy.* Minneapolis: University of Minnesota Press, 1992.

Diamond, Elin. *Unmaking Mimesis.* New York: Routledge, 1997.

————. Rev. of *Mom How Did You Meet the Beatles?: A True Story of London in the 1960's. Theatre Journal* 59 (2007): 666–667.

Kennedy, Adam P., and Adrienne Kennedy. *Mom How Did You Meet the Beatles? A True Story of London in the 1960's: Adam P. Kennedy talks to Adrienne Kennedy.* Williamsburg, Va.: Kennedy Publishing, 2006.

————. *Sleep Deprivation Chamber.* New York: Theatre Communications Group, 1996.

Kennedy, Adrienne. *The Alexander Plays.* Minneapolis: University of Minnesota Press, 1992.

————. *Deadly Triplets: A Theatre Mystery and Journal.* Minneapolis: University of Minnesota Press, 1990.

————. *In One Act.* Minneapolis: University of Minnesota Press, 1988.

————. "Motherhood 2000." In *Plays for the End of the Century,* edited by Bonnie Marranca. Baltimore: Johns Hopkins University Press, 1996. 1–8.

————. *People Who Led to My Plays.* New York: Theatre Communications Group, 1987.

Kolin, Philip C. *Understanding Adrienne Kennedy.* Columbia: University of South Carolina Press, 2005.

Claudia Barnett
Middle Tennessee State University

KENNEDY'S CHILDREN ROBERT PATRICK (1975)

Originally performed in an unnoticed OFF-BROADWAY production in 1973, *Kennedy's Children* became a West End hit in London in 1975 and then transferred to a long run on Broadway. Patrick's dirge for the failed idealism of the 1960s "Love Generation" was unusual in its innovative format, bringing an "underground" OFF-OFF-BROADWAY aesthetic to a mainstream audience.

The play takes place in a seedy bar on New York's Lower East Side on Valentine's Day, 1974. The five speaking characters (there is also a silent bartender) never talk to or even acknowledge each other's presence. While anesthetizing their pain with alcohol, they present what are essentially ongoing, rambling monologues that resonate with each other thematically. The play examines how the altruistic ideals (social justice, racial equality, and so on) that were hallmarks of President Kennedy's administration died with the assassination that ended his life.

Wanda is a lonely single woman who tells of the life-changing shock of the assassination and her nostalgia for the glamour of "Camelot." Although Kennedy's death impelled her to pursue her teaching degree, her altruistic work with "subnormal" children is a dispiriting dead end. Sparger, a flamboyant, middle-aged gay actor, discusses his avant-garde theater career as a means of assuaging his sense of disenfranchisement from the norm. Based largely on Patrick's own history with the Caffe Cino, Sparger's tale relates how his colleagues all either sold out by going legitimate or burned out from drugs.

Rona is a lost young woman who tells of her days as a typical "flower child," living on a commune and demonstrating against various social ills, until disillusionment, hallucinogens, and violence destroyed her dreams for unity and a thriving counterculture. Mark, a Vietnam veteran, reads from his journal and his letters home, trying to explain the horrors he witnessed. Now an emotionally stunted, pill-popping pothead, Mark examines how his escalating paranoia led him to kill his best army buddy, a suspected traitor.

Carla is a 26-year-old blonde bombshell, whose defining moment was not the death of Kennedy, but the suicide of Marilyn Monroe. Her inability to parlay her own limited talents into a career as a film goddess, the dehumanizing jobs for which she has had to settle, and the realization that millions pursue the same dream as she lead her to emulate her idol by overdosing on barbiturates. The play ends with her slumped and unconscious on the bar, none of the others noticing her demise.

In giving voice to these marginalized characters, Patrick brought a fresh approach to his dramatic, though ultimately depressing, view of the 1970s zeitgeist. Infrequently revived because of its topical nature, the play managed to capture the political spirit of the post–Kennedy era for its contemporary audience.

Douglas W. Gordy
Walnut Creek, California

KENTUCKY CYCLE, THE ROBERT SCHENKKAN (1991)

A tragic depiction of seven generations of Appalachian farmers and coal miners. *The Kentucky Cycle* came to national attention as the first play to win the PULITZER PRIZE (1992) before being produced in New York. SCHENKKAN's play had its 1991 premiere in Seattle and went on to receive the 1992 Los Angeles Drama Critics Circle Award for Best Play. It was subsequently produced at the Kennedy Center in Washington, D.C., and on Broadway, where its unique demands (20 actors and a running time of six and a half hours) made it the most expensive dramatic production mounted in New York to date.

The Kentucky Cycle is comprised of nine one-act plays presented in two parts. The first part begins in 1775 with an Irish immigrant's purchase of Appalachian land. In paying the Cherokees with smallpox-ridden blankets, Michael Rowen establishes a pattern of merciless greed from which few of his descendants can free themselves. Michael's son Patrick kills his father largely to get what he believes to be prime farmland. When the land proves unprofitable, he loses it to Jeremiah Talbert, who keeps Patrick on as a sharecropper. Patrick's son Jed later reclaims the land by killing Jeremiah's son while serving under him in the Civil War; he then returns to destroy the Talbert home and most of its inhabitants.

"Tall Tales," which opens the second part, is the most richly developed of the plays. J. T. Wells, a min-

ing company representative, convinces Jed Talbert to sell the mineral rights to his land for a dollar an acre. J. T. finally confesses to Jed's daughter that the land holds thousands of tons of coal and the mining company will spare none of the natural habitat to get it out. Despite this information, Jed remains convinced he got the best end of the bargain. In the seventh play, set in 1920, Jed's daughter Mary Anne is spurred on to lead a labor movement by a northerner who has come to organize a union. The cycle of betrayal and revenge continues as Mary Anne's husband turns the union organizer over to his enemies, resulting in his execution. Thirty-four years later, the United Mine Workers local is an established part of the community, and Mary Anne's son Joshua heads it. Joshua's compromises on safety perpetuate the curse of his ancestors, and his own son dies in a mine explosion. The cycle concludes with a 65-year-old Joshua hunting on his ancestral property, now ravaged by years of strip mining. Joshua discovers the corpse of a baby girl, oddly preserved in a Cherokee buckskin. While unaware that he is holding a child Michael Rowen left to die in 1776, Joshua is nonetheless overcome by reverence for what he has found. He returns the baby to the earth, thus symbolically putting an end to the curse of his ancestors.

Schenkkan's play has been criticized for its negative portrayals of Appalachian people. However, the author sees the mentality that leads to environmental ruin as a national rather than regional issue: "Ultimately, I realized the play was about American mythology." At the core of such mythology, according to Schenkkan, lies the "Myth of the Frontier," which suggests that America's resources are endless and that one can always move to new territory and leave the past behind (Schenkkan 336). *The Kentucky Cycle* attempts to expose the dark side of such mythology.

BIBLIOGRAPHY

Billings, Dwight W., Gurney Norman, and Katherine Ledford, eds. *Confronting Appalachian Stereotypes: Back Talk from an American Region*. Lexington: University Press of Kentucky, 1999.

Mason, Bobbie Ann. "Recycling Kentucky." *New Yorker* (November 1, 1993): 50–62.

Schenkkan, Robert. *The Kentucky Cycle.* New York: Plume, 1993.

John Paul Middlesworth
University of North Carolina–Chapel Hill

KING HEDLEY II August Wilson (2001)

WILSON's cycle of plays documenting the African-American experience in the 20th century includes one play for each decade. *King Hedley II,* one of the plays in this cycle, is set in 1985 in the backyards of two run-down houses in the Hill District of Pittsburgh. In the play, Wilson examines the terrible cost and far-reaching implications of the violent urban environment in which many African Americans lived during the Reagan years; indeed, in Wilson's view, the Reagan administration's economic policy left this segment of the population so few choices that it bears some responsibility for the violence of the period.

King Hedley II is the sequel to *SEVEN GUITARS* (1995), which is set in the same Pittsburgh Hill District neighborhood and which chronicles the lives of King Hedley's parents' generation in the 1940s. Ruby, a young pregnant woman in *Seven Guitars,* is King's mother. Ruby marries Hedley, also a character in *Seven Guitars,* and names her child King Hedley II, telling the child that Hedley is his father. The opening of *King Hedley II* follows by two months the death from leukemia of Ruby's Aunt Louise, the woman with whom Ruby comes to stay in *Seven Guitars* and whom King calls Mama Louise because she raised him. Canewell and Elmore are also characters from *Seven Guitars.* Mentioned in yet another Wilson play, *TWO TRAINS RUNNING* (1990), is the character Aunt Ester; in both *Hedley* and *Two Trains,* she is offstage and reputed to be more than 300 years old. Aunt Ester reappears in *GEM OF THE OCEAN* (2003), set in 1904, as an onstage character. In that play's sequel, *RADIO GOLF* (2005), set in 1997, she is referred to and her house is an important symbol.

When *King Hedley II* begins, King has recently been released from prison for killing a man who knifed him in the face. King is trying to raise enough money to open a video store with his friend, Mister. Their current "business" is selling stolen refrigerators, and when this does not prove profitable enough, they rob a jewelry store. King is passionate about growing something in his harsh environment: He wants a business and he wants a child, but his pregnant wife, Tonya, would rather have an abortion than bring another child into a family where the child's father will likely return to prison. Perhaps the most poignant and beautiful speech in the play is spoken by Tonya (35 and a grandmother), in which she articulates the heartbreak of mothers who too often lose their children to violent death or imprisonment. Symbolic of King's hunger to produce something in his life is the tiny garden he plants behind Mama Louise's house. He is able to cultivate some seeds there and fiercely protects this square of urban dirt with barbed wire. His attempts to save his tiny plants among the broken glass and garbage seem doomed, as indeed do his attempts to sustain other forms of life in this cruel environment.

Ruby's old boyfriend, Elmore, a charming gambler, turns up and courts her as he once did in the 1940s, but Elmore's health is failing and he wants to make peace with himself before he dies. Elmore confesses to King that he killed King's real father, who was not Hedley, as Ruby has said, but another man. It is this revelation that upsets both King and Ruby, leading to the violent accidental death of King at the hands of his mother.

The African-American community's relationship to its own history is an important element in the play. Stool Pigeon (known as Canewell in *Seven Guitars*) lives next door to King, Tonya, and Ruby. His house is filled from floor to ceiling with newspapers, from which he reads aloud headlines, most about violence in the city; when he reads a headline, he says, "you got to know that!" Neighborhood thugs burn some of Stool Pigeon's newspapers, an act that, according to Wilson in an interview at the Smithsonian Institution in Washington, D.C., on March 1, 2001, represents "the destruction of history." Aunt Ester, the more than 300-year-old woman, represents, Wilson says, the connection to the past, the connection to 1619 when Africans first set foot in North America. Her death in the play is representative of the fact that in the 1980s people lost track of their connection to the past: "Therefore," said Wilson, "we need a Messiah—the play presents one: King Hedley II." Aunt Ester's "death creates the necessity for being saved." At the end of the play, King's accidental death is referred to in biblical terms by Stool Pigeon. King is seen as a worthy sacrifice by Stool Pigeon, who refers to King as "the fatted calf" and as "Isaac"; King's blood resurrects the cat, which is the reincarnation of Aunt Ester, that is, the reincarnation of the connection to the past. Viewed this way, Wilson sees the play not as depressing but as "uplifting." King, the messiah, will save the lost young African-American men who have no connection to history and who are motivated only by impulse.

In his *New York Times* review of the 2001 New York production, Ben Brantley compared the play to ARTHUR MILLER's classic modern tragedy, DEATH OF A SALESMAN: "Tragedy and the common man is a phrase famously associated with 'Death of a Salesman,' Arthur Miller's epochal indictment of the American dream factory. In 'Hedley,' Mr. Wilson seems to be directly invoking Mr. Miller's masterpiece and pointing out with renewed vigor how an affluent, success-driven society maims those who fall by its standards" (May 2, 2001).

KINGSLEY, SIDNEY (KIRSHNER) (1906–1995)

Sidney Kingsley (né Kirshner) was born in New York City to Robert and Sophie Kirshner. While New York City was the locale of several of his most important plays, childhood experiences of a tonsillectomy and adenoidectomy in Philadelphia and living in what Kingsley referred to as a "haunted house" in Schenectady provided material for his play MEN IN WHITE (1933). Kingsley attended Townsend Harris High School in New York City and went on to Cornell University, where he studied with Alexander Drummond, who had a tremendous and lifelong influence on Kingsley's career as a playwright. At Cornell, Kingsley was a member of the dramatic club and debate team, receiving the 94 Memorial Stage Prize in debate. His one-act play *Wonder-Dark Epilogue* was produced by the Cornell Dramatic Club in 1928 and published in *Cornell University Plays,* edited by Drummond (1932).

Following graduation from Cornell, Kingsley acted, first in the Tremont Stock Company in the Bronx, New York, and then in *Subway Express* on Broadway, while continuing to pursue his deep interest in playwriting. Success came with *Men in White,* which won the PULITZER PRIZE, closely followed by DEAD END (1935). Kingsley's third Broadway play was *Ten Million Ghosts* (1936), set during World War I and dealing with the hypocrisy of French and German branches of a family of munitions manufacturers. Kingsley based *The World We Make* (1939) on Millen Brand's novel, *The Outward Room.* In *The World We Make,* Kingsley tells the story of a young woman trying to make a normal life for herself in a blue-collar environment after slipping away from the mental hospital where she was undergoing treatment.

In 1939, Kingsley married actress Madge Evans. He served in the United States Army during World War II, managing to continue his writing. *The Patriots* (1943) won the New York Drama Critics' Circle Award. Concerned about political and societal dissension, Kingsley set the play, about the building of a democracy, immediately following the American Revolution, a period of instability. Kingsley returned to Broadway with DETECTIVE STORY (1949) and DARKNESS AT NOON (1951), adapted from the novel by Arthur Koestler. The latter won the New York Drama Critics' Circle Award. In 1954, Kingsley wrote *Lunatics and Lovers,* which, as a farcical tour de force, stands as the most atypical play in the Kingsley oeuvre. Kingsley's final Broadway play was *Night Life* (1962), a naturalistic study of the clientele of a New York key club. In his final play, *Falling Man* (1981), Kingsley, an avocational visual artist himself, returned to the topics of artists and death that he had first explored in *Wonder-Dark Epilogue* at Cornell. (He worked on *Falling Man* for years and never finished it to his satisfaction; it was finally produced in 1981 at Florida State University.)

While he devoted most of his energy to writing for the stage, Kingsley also wrote occasionally for the movies and maintained a lifelong interest in film. From 1976 to 1980, he served as chair of the New Jersey Motion Picture and Television Development Commission.

Kingsley's writing style has been referred to as realistic or naturalistic. His commitment to presenting major American social problems on the stage is the hallmark of his work. The issues Kingsley addressed in his plays were, and continue to be, serious human concerns: the need for adequate health care, housing, and education; the need for freedom of thought and expression; and the need for protection from abuse of power. His works, especially *Men in White, Dead End,* and *Detective Story,* had a long-term influence on film and television; his settings, such as the hospital and the police station, have become commonplace to modern television audiences. While Kingsley's style of writing may now be considered dated, the topics he wrote about are not.

The Academy of Arts and Letters awarded Kingsley the Medal of Merit in 1951 and the Gold Medal for drama in 1986. In 1988, Kingsley received the WILLIAM INGE Award for Distinguished Achievement in the American Theatre.

BIBLIOGRAPHY

Kingsley, Sidney. *Sidney Kingsley: Five Prizewinning Plays.* Edited by Nena Couch. Columbus: Ohio State University Press, 1995.

Nena Couch
Ohio State University

KOPIT, ARTHUR (1937–)

Born in New York City, playwright Arthur Kopit was educated at Harvard (B.A., 1959) and has taught playwriting at Yale and New York Universities, among others. Kopit's initial reputation came out of his absurdist Harvard plays, which included OH DAD, POOR DAD, MAMA'S HUNG YOU IN THE CLOSET AND I'M FEELIN' SO SAD: A Pseudoclassical Tragifarce in a Bastard French Tradition, his most widely seen work, first produced at Harvard in 1960, then in London in 1961, and finally in New York in 1962. *Oh Dad* is characterized by the same type of comic absurdism in its approach to serious subjects as is Kopit's most ambitious—and perhaps his best—play, INDIANS (first produced in London, 1968; New York, 1969).

Several of Kopit's plays involve adolescent or preadolescent boys interacting with a confusing adult world. *The Questioning of Nick* (first produced at Harvard, 1957; New York, 1973) is about an arrogant teenaged athlete who is questioned and finally humiliated by the police; *Sing to Me through Open Windows* (first produced at Harvard, 1959; revised version produced in New York, 1965) is about a boy in search of a father figure in a circus setting. In *Oh Dad* (1960), a crazy and controlling mother emotionally damages her son.

Other early plays, all produced only at Harvard, are *Gemini* (1957), *Don Juan in Texas* (written with Wally Lawrence, 1957), *On the Runway of Life, You Never Know What's Coming Off Next* (1958), *Across the River and into the Jungle* (1958), and *Aubade* (1959).

Many of Kopit's post-Harvard plays take on larger themes. *The Hero* (1964) is a two-character, one-act pantomine about the meaninglessness of human existence. In the one-act, metaphoric *The Conquest of Everest* (1964), a generic man and woman, oblivious to the dangers of their endeavor, climb Mount Everest. In *The Day the Whores Came Out to Play Tennis* (1965), a group of prostitutes invades the tennis courts of an exclusive country club and cause upheaval in the social order. *Indians* (1968) is an indictment of the United States government's treatment of the American Indian as well as an oblique commentary on United States policy during the Vietnam War. While all of these plays have absurdist characteristics, WINGS (first broadcast on National Public Radio, 1978; produced in New Haven and New York, 1978) is a departure from absurdism (see THEATRE OF THE ABSURD). It takes a poignant look at a woman's partial recovery from a stroke, from the woman's fragmented point of view.

Kopit's work in the last two decades of the 20th century includes *End of the World* (1984), a funny and ultimately pessimistic play about nuclear armament, and *The Road to Nirvana* (1991), a ruthless parody of DAVID MAMET's SPEED-THE-PLOW, originally entitled *Bone-the-Fish* and produced under that name at the HUMANA FESTIVAL at the Actors Theatre of Louisville. Kopit's play *Y2K* (1999) was also first produced at the Humana Festival; for a 2006 production, Kopit changed the title to *Because He Can*. In it, a vengeful former student destroys a man's life by hacking into his computer and depleting his bank account and planting child pornography, among other effronteries. Kopit has collaborated with Maury Yeston on two musicals, *Nine* (1981) and *Phantom* (1991), and adapted Henrik Ibsen's *Ghosts* for Broadway in 1982.

Kopit is developing another musical, *Lewis and Clark* (a version of which was produced in 2002 at the Lark Theatre) in collaboration with Donald Siegal. Arthur Kopit is currently playwright-in-residence and Playwrights' Workshop Director at New York's Lark Play Development Center.

BIBLIOGRAPHY

Auerbach, Doris. *Sam Shepard, Arthur Kopit, and the Off Broadway Theater.* Boston: Twayne, 1982.

Kopit, Arthur. *"The Day the Whores Came Out to Play Tennis" and Other Plays.* New York: Hill & Wang, 1965.

———. *End of the World.* New York: Hill & Wang, 1984.

———. *Good Help Is Hard to Find: A Play in One Act.* New York: Samuel French, 1982.

———. *Nine: The Musical.* New York: Samuel French, 1983.

———. *Road to Nirvana.* New York: Samuel French, 1991.

———. *Three Plays.* New York: Hill & Wang, 1997.

———. *Y2K.* Woodstock, N.Y.: Overlook Press, 2000.

KRAMER, LARRY (1935–)

Larry Kramer's plays have had a major impact on 20th-century GAY AND LESBIAN THEATER. Born in Connecticut, Larry Kramer and his family moved to Maryland when he was eight, allowing him regularly to visit Washington's National Theatre as a young teen. Although this caused his father to label him a "sissy," his mother encouraged his theatrical interest. Pressured by his father to attend Yale, Kramer did so, studying English and getting involved in dramatics, but he also attempted suicide and entered psychiatric treatment. Soon after, a male professor seduced him, prompting him to acknowledge his homosexuality, a "condition" for which his family insisted on further therapy.

After graduating, he eventually became involved with the movie industry. The peak of his involvement and success in films was his purchase of the rights to D. H. Lawrence's controversial novel *Women in Love* (1921), for which he wrote the screenplay. The resulting 1969 movie won him awards and fame.

His first attempt to write for the stage, "A Minor Dark Age," was neither published nor produced. This was followed by *Sissie's Scrapbook* (1973), about the relationships between a gay man and his three straight college friends. This was revised into *Four Friends* (1974), but neither version was well received. With the onset of AIDS in America, Kramer turned his attention to social activism, much of which is semiautobiographically depicted in his best-known play, *The Normal Heart* (1985). This play is an historical account of the early days of AIDS as well as an examination of gay life in general and the impact on it of this epidemic. Kramer followed this with an uncomfortable sex farce about how he felt AIDS was allowed to reach plague proportions during the Reagan administration, *Just Say No* (1988).

Unnatural Acts, based on excerpts from Kramer's book *Reports from the Holocaust* (1989), about his experiences as an AIDS activist, was adapted for the stage by Jeffrey Storer and Ed Hunt in 1990. Kramer then wrote a sequel to *The Normal Heart,* which began as *Furniture of Home,* was retitled *The Tyranny of Blood,* and ended up as *The Destiny of Me* (1992); it takes us, in a series of flashbacks, to the formative periods of the protagonist's childhood, as he lies in the hospital with full-blown AIDS. Kramer himself has developed AIDS, but he continues to write.

Reports of his death in 2001 proved unfounded as Kramer received a last-minute liver transplant. That same year, his brother Arthur, on whom Kramer had based the homophobic character Ben Weeks in *The Normal Heart,* gave Yale University a $1 million grant to establish the Larry Kramer Initiative for Lesbian and Gay Studies, a program focusing on gay history. Kramer agreed to leave his papers to Yale's Beinecke Library. The program ran for five years. In 2004, upset by the reelection of George W. Bush, Kramer gave a speech and call to arms for continued action against AIDS, which he subsequently published as *The Tragedy of Today's Gays.* For the past two decades, Kramer has also been at work on a manuscript called *The American People,* a historical work that begins in the Stone Age and continues into the present. The year 2007 saw Kramer celebrating the 20th anniversary of ACT UP, the AIDS coalition he cofounded.

Combined with his poems and novels, Kramer's drama has helped to rewrite what is allowable in the arts regarding depictions of homosexuality. Although he has clashed with some in the homosexual community, partly because of his criticism of homosexual promiscuity, the force of his influence may be best proven by the title of David Drake and Michelangelo Signorile's play about gay activism, *The Night Larry Kramer Kissed Me* (1993); Kramer does not appear in the play as a character, but his name has become synonymous with the gay-rights movement and AIDS activism.

BIBLIOGRAPHY
Kramer, Larry. *Just Say No.* New York: St. Martin's Press, 1989.
———. *"The Normal Heart" and "The Destiny of Me."* New York: Grove Press, 2000.
———. *Reports from the Holocaust: The Story of an AIDS Activist.* New York: St. Martin's Press, 1994.
———. *The Tragedy of Today's Gays.* New York: Tarcher, 2005.
———. *"Women in Love" and Other Dramatic Writings.* New York: Grove Press, 2002.
Mass, Lawrence D., ed. *We Must Love One Another or Die: The Life and Legacy of Larry Kramer.* New York: St. Martin's Press, 1997.

Susan C. W. Abbotson
Rhode Island College

KRASNA, NORMAN (1909–1984)

Playwright, screenwriter, director, and producer Norman Krasna was born in Corona, Queens, New York, and completed his education with degrees at New York University, Columbia University, and Brooklyn Law School before beginning his career writing for various newspapers and doing publicity work for Warner Brothers, one of the major Hollywood studios of the era.

Krasna began writing plays in his early twenties, and his first Broadway production, *Louder, Please* (1931), won a mostly approving response from critics and audiences. *Louder, Please* was followed by another moderate success, *Small Miracle* (1934), which he adapted into a melodramatic screenplay, *Four Hours to Kill* (1935). The success of this film led to an opportunity to write for the celebrated German director Fritz Lang. Krasna crafted the story for the Lang-directed dramas, *Fury* (1936), which brought him an Academy Award nomination, and *You and Me* (1938). Krasna struck a happy balance writing for both stage and screen, often adapting his plays for the movies. (Krasna's other early films include, among many others, *The Richest Girl in the World* [1934] and *The Devil and Miss Jones* [1941], both of which were nominated for Academy Awards for Best Screenplay.) Krasna frequently returned to the stage, and in 1941 he directed his play *The Man with Blonde Hair,* which was a moderate success. Two years later, he scripted and directed the film *Princess O'Rourke* (1943), for which he won an Academy Award for Best Original Screenplay.

Krasna continued to write numerous plays and screenplays after World War II, achieving his greatest stage successes with *Dear Ruth* (1944), a wartime comedy about a teenager who writes letters to a lonely soldier using her older sister's name and photo, and *John Loves Mary* (1947), another lighthearted wartime comedy about a soldier marrying his best friend's English girlfriend in order to bring her to the United States, with the resultant romantic complications. Another Krasna stage success, *Kind Sir* (1953), provided a rare nonmusical vehicle for singer Mary Martin, who played an actress romantically involved with a staid banker. Krasna adapted *Kind Sir* into the hit film *Indiscreet* (1958), which starred Ingrid Bergman and Cary Grant.

Krasna's last significant success came with *Sunday in New York* (1961), a pioneering "sex comedy" in which a much-desired 22-year-old virgin finds true love in a play that foreshadows the films of Woody Allen and others who viewed New York City as the perfect backdrop for romantic stories. Krasna also had modest stage successes with *Time for Elizabeth* (1948), a lighthearted vehicle for comedian Groucho Marx, which failed on Broadway but found great popularity in summer theaters; *Love in E Flat* (1967), another sex comedy; and the melodrama *We Interrupt This Program* (1975). Among Krasna's later film successes were *The Big Hangover* (1950), Irving Berlin's *White Christmas* (1954), and *Let's Make Love* (1960), which starred Marilyn Monroe.

BIBLIOGRAPHY
Krasna, Norman. *Dear Ruth.* New York: Dramatists Play Service, 1998.
———. *John Loves Mary.* New York: Dramatists Play Service, 1947, 1998.

————. *Kind Sir.* New York: Dramatists Play Service, 1954.

————. *Louder, Please.* New York: Samuel French, 1932.

————. *Love in E-Flat.* New York: Dramatists Play Service, 1967.

————. *Small Miracle.* New York: Samuel French, 1935.

————. *Sunday in New York.* New York: Dramatists Play Service, 1998.

————. *Time for Elizabeth.* New York: Dramatists Play Service, 1949.

————. *Who Was That Lady I Saw You With?* New York: Dramatists Play Service, 1959.

James Fisher
University of North Carolina at Greensboro

KUSHNER, TONY (1956–)   Born in Manhattan, Tony Kushner grew up in Lake Charles, Louisiana. In 1974, he returned to New York, where he was educated at Columbia University (B.A., 1978) and at New York University (M.F.A. in directing, 1984). As a graduate student at NYU, Kushner cofounded a theater company called 3P—for poetry, politics, and popcorn—Productions, later known as the Heat and Light Company. By the time his first play, *A Bright Room Called Day* (1987), was produced by the Heat and Light Company, Kushner had left NYU. The play, which is set in Europe, considers the relationship of history to the present, the idea being that historical events are cautionary tales.

Kushner's most well-known play, the seven-hour, two-part ANGELS IN AMERICA: A GAY FANTASIA ON NATIONAL THEMES, won many honors, including, for the first part, the PULITZER PRIZE, TONY AWARD, and the New York Drama Critics' Circle Award. The second part also won the Tony Award. The two parts of the play—two plays really—are entitled *Millennium Approaches* (1990) and *Perestroika* (1992). They focus on three overlapping sets of characters: a gay couple, one of whom is dying of AIDS; a closeted homosexual and his neurotic wife; and the infamous lawyer Roy Cohn, a historical figure who worked with Senator Joseph McCarthy and who died of AIDS in 1986, denying his homosexuality to the very end of his life. It is a play "about a community under pressure, the gay community, but also the community that is America" (Bigsby 113).

Kushner's next play, *Slavs!* (1994) was first presented at the HUMANA FESTIVAL and later won an OBIE AWARD for Playwriting. *Slavs!,* which is composed of material cut from *Perestroika,* contemplates history and the collapse of communism. Kushner has also written adaptations, including *Stella. A Play for Lovers* (1987), adapted from the play by Goethe; *The Good Person of Setzuan* (1994), adapted from the play by Bertolt Brecht; *The Dybbuk; or, Between Two Worlds* (1995), adapted from the play by S. Ansky, as well as a new translation of Brecht's *Mother Courage and Her Children* (2006). In the 1980s, Kushner directed productions of his own plays of that period at various theaters around the country: *The Age of Assassins* (1982), *La Fin de la Baleine* (1983), *Last Gasp at the Cataract* (1984), *Hydriotaphia; or, The Death of Dr. Browne* (1987), *In Great Eliza's Golden Time* (1987), and *In That Day (Lives of the Prophets)* (1989).

Kushner's *Homebody/Kabul* (2001) is set in London and Kabul just before and after the 1998 American bombing of suspected terrorist training camps in Khost, Afghanistan; it won Kushner another Obie Award for Playwriting. For the musical *Caroline, or Change* (2003), he wrote both the lyrics and the book (music by Jeanine Tesori); it won a Lucille Lortel Award for Oustanding Musical; the work deals with the relationship between a black housekeepr and the white motherless boy she cares for against the backdrop of the civil rights changes of the 1960s.

Kushner, who lives in Hollywood and New York, has been writing more screenplays than stage plays recently, but he hopes soon to shift his focus back to the stage since winning the Steinberg Distinguished Playwright Award in the autumn of 2008, with its generous cash prize of $200,000 (a Pulitzer comes with a comparatively modest $10,000). Kushner, who is not only a significant American playwright but also an important and serious American intellectual, admits that it is difficult to make a living by writing for the stage alone.

BIBLIOGRAPHY
Bigsby, Christopher. "Tony Kushner." In *Contemporary American Playwrights.* Cambridge, England: Cambridge University Press, 1999, 86–131.

Fisher, James. *The Theater of Tony Kushner: Living Past Hope*. New York: Routledge, 2002.

———. *Understanding Tony Kushner*. Columbia: University of South Carolina Press, 2008.

Kushner, Tony. *Angels in America. Part One: Millennium Approaches*. New York: Theatre Communications Group, 1993.

———. *Angels in America. Part Two: Perestroika*. New York: Theatre Communications Group, 1994.

———. *A Bright Room Called Day*. New York: Theatre Communications Group, 1994.

———. *Death & Taxes: "Hydriotaphia" and Other Plays*. New York: Theatre Communications Group, 2000.

———. *"A Dybbuk" and Other Tales of the Supernatural*. New York: Theatre Communications Group, 1998.

———. *Homebody/Kabul*. New York: Theatre Communications Group, 2002.

———. *Slavs!* New York: Broadway Play Publishing, 1996.

———. *Thinking about the Longstanding Problems of Virtue and Happiness: Essays, a Play, Two Poems, and a Prayer*. New York: Theatre Communications Group, 1995.

Vorlicky, Robert, ed. *Tony Kushner in Conversation*. Ann Arbor: University of Michigan Press, 1998.

L

LABUTE, NEIL (1963–) Like DAVID MAMET, one of his major influences, Neil LaBute moves easily between stage and screen. LaBute first achieved notoriety for his controversial film *In the Company of Men* (1997), in which two businessmen devastatingly toy with a deaf woman's emotions; the film's brutal examination of gender relationships and of the strong preying on the weak are also major components of his plays. LaBute presents his characters' cruelties, but he does not judge them; instead, he forces the audience into the uncomfortable position of having to reconcile their own emotional and moral responses with those of the characters.

LaBute began his study of theater and film at Brigham Young University. While there, he converted to Mormonism. He then received an M.F.A. in dramatic writing from New York University. His first OFF-BROADWAY play, *Filthy Talk for Troubled Times* (1992), featured a series of profane monologues. Disturbed by one character's homophobic sentiments, an audience member cried out "Kill the playwright." The reaction inspired LaBute's creative mission: to provoke the audience and confound their expectations. With this idea in mind, he returned to Brigham Young for his Ph.D. in theater and wrote the play *Lepers,* which he used as the basis for *In the Company of Men.*

While LaBute had written a number of plays, his first major mark on the American theater scene was *bash: latterday plays* (1999). Comprised of three short plays, two of which are monologues, *bash* is heavily influenced by Greek drama as well as the Mormon Church; all of the characters are Mormons. In *Iphigenia in Orem,* a father tells a stranger about the horrifying death of his daughter. In *Medea Redux,* a young woman explains to the police the situation surrounding the murder of her son. In *A Gaggle of Saints,* a young couple, attired in evening wear, talk about their weekend travails in the city. As the female describes the social occasions they attended, the male reveals that he and his friends beat up a homosexual in a public park bathroom. LaBute received criticism for the play's depiction of Mormons, but the playwright defended his characterization by arguing that because someone is religious does not mean that he or she is necessarily good.

In his next play, *The Shape of Things* (2001), LaBute continued his examination of the gender wars, but this time he created the mirror image of *In the Company of Men* with a Pygmalion twist: A female M.F.A. student in art manipulates an insecure, unattractive undergraduate to help her complete her thesis, with devastating emotional consequences. In the play, LaBute raises questions about ethics, about the nature of art, and about the emphasis placed on the superficial within American culture. *The Distance from Here* (2002), which has strong structural, emotional, and theatrical ties to English playwright Edward Bond's *Saved* (1965), focuses on high-school youths and finds a world of cruelty, brutality, deception, and animalistic actions. The piece ends with a horrifyingly disturbing murder of a baby and was LaBute's darkest play to date.

LaBute's searing *The Mercy Seat* (2002) joined a number of emotionally timely plays, such as Anne Nelson's *The Guys* (2002) and CHRISTOPHER SHINN's *Where Do We Live* (2002), that emerged in the months after September 11. Unlike these two plays, which look at finding equilibrium after the disaster, *The Mercy Seat* focuses on an adulterous couple, Ben and his boss, Abby, who see the terrorist attack as an opportunity to be presumed dead, so they can run away and begin a new life together. While all of LaBute's plays are driven by his innate ear for picking up nuances of American dialogue, this play features a recurring harrowing sound effect, perhaps the only play of his to use such a theatrical element so effectively, of Ben's cell phone continually ringing as his distraught wife keeps calling, hoping to discover that her husband is still alive.

After the publication of a collection of short stories, *Seconds of Pleasure* (2004), and the production of *autobahn* (2005), which features a number of one-acts that all take place in cars, LaBute returned to full-length plays with *Fat Pig* (2004). In the play's preface, LaBute admits to a boost in his self-esteem after losing 60 pounds, and he uses this obsession with weight in *Fat Pig* as he examines society's prejudices toward the obese through a romantic relationship between Tom, a physically normal male, and Helen, an overweight librarian. Tom struggles to reconcile his personal attraction to Helen with the societal repulsion to her looks as represented by comments made by a cruel male coworker and Tom's ex-girlfriend.

While LaBute's plays have always challenged audiences with uncomfortable topics, *This Is How It Goes* (2005) is his first piece to address race. Using an unnamed and highly likeable narrator, who continually blurs and questions the accuracy of his narrative, LaBute introduces us to a love triangle involving the narrator, a former lawyer, Cody, a successful black businessman, and Belinda, Cody's stay-at-home wife. Throughout the play, LaBute cunningly challenges the audience's prejudices about race through the narrator's murky and manipulative recollections about

Cody and his abusive treatment of Belinda. Ultimately, the ambiguity of the story and the characters' motives can only be answered through the lens of each audience member's preconception about race.

Interested in creating a contemporary Candide figure as well as crafting strong female roles, LaBute wrote *Some Girl(s)* (2005) about a teacher and newly successful author, who, on the verge of matrimony, revisits four of his past loves to resolve old wounds. Through these meetings, LaBute not only reveals how the male's selfish behavior led to the breakups, but also builds upon each visit, so by the final scene a disturbing motive for his wanting to see these women is suddenly revealed. *Wrecks* (2006), like *bash*, relies upon monologue and Greek drama. A mourning, chain-smoking husband Edward details his personal and business successes and failures with his spouse, Mary Jo, and reveals that, like Oedipus before him, he married his own mother. However, in the final moments of his monologue Edward reveals he was not as inculpable as Sophocles' protagonist was.

Inspired by LaBute's experience of growing up with an abusive father, *In a Dark Dark House* (2007) features two estranged brothers, Drew and Terry, who are forced to confront not only the brutal physical and psychological abuse of their father but also the experience of being abused by a male drifter and how these two aspects of their childhood influenced their current positions in life. Unlike his other plays, this one turns on family dynamics, featuring two strongly written scenes between the brothers that confront the secrets of their past and reveal a violent act of revenge for one of them.

Considered by critics to complete LaBute's trilogy dealing with the power of appearance (the first two plays being *The Shape of things* and *Fat Pig*), *reasons to be pretty* (2008) opens with a volatile fight between a couple concerning a comment made by Greg about the average appearance of his live-in girlfriend's face. This one comment, made to a male buddy, ripples through Greg and Steph's future relationships and affects their friends' marriage. LaBute calls the play his first coming-of-age piece as, over the course of the story, Greg grows up and takes responsibility for his actions and words. The play is also a coming-of-age play for LaBute. By putting away narrative tricks, he finally acknowledges that his unrivaled depiction of the raw, unfettered, and explosive nature of male and female relationships in America can stand firmly on its own.

BIBLIOGRAPHY

Bigsby, Christopher. *Neil LaBute: Stage and Cinema.* Cambridge and New York: Cambridge University Press, 2007.

LaBute, Neil. *bash: latterday plays.* Woodstock, N.Y.: Overlook Press, 1999.

———. *The Distance from Here.* Woodstock, N.Y.: Overlook Press, 2003.

———. *Fat Pig.* New York: Faber and Faber, 2005.

———. *In a Dark Dark House.* New York: Faber and Faber, 2007.

———. *The Mercy Seat.* New York: Faber and Faber, 2003.

———. *reasons to be pretty.* New York: Faber and Faber, 2008.

———. *The Shape of Things.* New York: Faber and Faber, 2001.

———. *Some Girl(s).* New York: Faber and Faber, 2005.

———. *This Is How It Goes.* New York: Faber and Faber, 2005.

———. *"Wrecks" and Other Plays.* New York: Faber and Faber, 2007.

William C. Boles
Rollins College

LANDSCAPE OF THE BODY John Guare (1977)

Guare's *Landscape of the Body* opened in October 1977 at the Public Theater in New York. Guare had written the play in two days while trying to get over his depression brought on by the closing of his previously unsuccessful play, *Marco Polo Sings a Solo,* in March 1977. *Landscape of the Body,* divided into two acts, includes fade-ins and fade-outs that move us from one interlude to another, similar to the way montage works in film. The play is narrated by the now-deceased Rosalie, sister of Betty Yearn (the protagonist); she traces Betty's history from the time she left New England to the unsolved mystery of Betty's son Bert's death.

After Betty leaves Maine to visit her sister in New York City, attempting to bring her sibling back to the safe haven of New England, she decides to stay when Rosalie is killed in a bicycle accident. Betty and 14-year-old Bert remain in Greenwich Village; in order to pay the bills, Betty becomes a pornographic film star in Mafia-made movies and also takes a job selling honeymoon holidays in a travel agency run by a suave Latino named Raulito, a con man who wears 1940s Rita Hayworth evening gowns over his business suit because they make him feel wealthy. Meanwhile, Bert is hanging out with a depraved group of teenagers. Bert and his friend Donny bring gay men back to their apartment, rob them, roll them out the door, urinate on them, and then spill wine on the victims to make them appear to be drunk. When Betty receives a better offer and goes off to live with a new beau named Durwood Peach in South Carolina, she leaves Bert with a thousand dollars and tells him to fend for himself. Betty eventually learns that Durwood is not the wealthy landowner he claimed to be but was instead briefly vacationing in New York because the doctors at the mental asylum thought a trip might do him some good. Unfortunately, while Betty is away, Donny, upset because Bert hugged him out of desperation from being abandoned, picked up a monkey wrench and accidentally killed him. Then his friend Joanne helped him decapitate Bert and dump the body by the docks. The price of Betty's aimless meanderings is now clear: Her son is decapitated, and she is now the chief murder suspect. Guare told theater reviewer Holly Hill, "The play is about a decapitation, a loss of head, about people living life without any reflective powers, without their reason, without their imagination." In short, Betty, without a strong sense of identity—a person who fails to know herself—is unable to connect with others or to nurture her family.

Betty's chance to connect with others comes in the form of Captain Marvin Holahan, who has known her for the past five months, since his investigation of her son's death began. While uncovering Betty's past and during his one-on-one conversations with her, Holahan feels as if he has made a contact with her that has otherwise been absent in his life. Holahan, in his role as a police officer, views daily the underlying violence and rage of contemporary urban life; Betty has also witnessed its repercussions firsthand. The key to their survival will be how they can connect with each other emotionally and search for a passion that they can celebrate together. In essence, *Landscape of the Body* explores the way in which people who have nothing, who lack dreams and imaginative vision, try to connect in a society that is onerous, violent, and destructive.

BIBLIOGRAPHY

Hill, Holly. "John Guare Talks About Landscape. . . ." *New York Theatre Review,* December 21, 1977, 21.

Gene A. Plunka
University of Memphis

LAST NIGHT OF BALLYHOO, THE

ALFRED UHRY (1997)   A comedy set in Atlanta, Georgia, in 1939, *The Last Night of Ballyhoo* portrays a family of southern, secular Jews who are more concerned with the upcoming country club dance—called Ballyhoo—than with Adolf Hitler's invasion of Poland. Into their midst comes a Jew from Brooklyn, who reminds them of their Jewish heritage and makes them aware of the discrimination against other Jews of which they themselves are guilty.

As the play begins, the flighty Lala Levy is decorating a Christmas tree, which her mother, Boo, calls a "festive decoration like a Halloween pumpkin"; Boo draws the line at putting a star on top since she does not want anyone to think they are pretending to be Christians. Lala and the widowed Boo live with Boo's brother Adolph Freitag, a businessman and a bachelor; also a part of Adolph's household is the sweet but dizzy Reba, his brother's widow. Reba's daughter Sunny is away at college.

Adolph, lacking male company and substantive conversation (he alone in his family is worried about Hitler's invasion), brings home Joe Farkas, a young man he has recently hired at the Dixie Bedding Company. Joe is from Brooklyn and has an Eastern European background. He finds these Christmas tree–loving, southern Jewish women curious. He is what Boo and Lala call the "other kind" of Jew, but since Lala has not yet found a date for Ballyhoo, she thinks Joe might serve. Lala tries to get Joe to come downtown with her and gawk at the celebrities who have gathered for the premiere of *Gone with the Wind,* but Joe makes an excuse and departs.

Later, on a train from Baltimore, Joe meets Sunny, Lala's cousin. Sunny is everything Lala is not: intellectual, sensible, a junior at Wellesley (Lala, as her mother puts it, "snuck home in disgrace from the University of Michigan in the middle of her first term"). Sunny's intelligence and greater substance make her Adolph's favorite. Lala resents Sunny for Sunny's more loved father (his funeral was bigger than Lala's father's funeral) and for her non-Jewish features, complaining, "You've always gotten all the attention. Even from God." When, finally, the self-important Peachy Weil, whom Boo characterizes as "the finest escort in the South," comes to call on Lala and asks her to the dance, she feels triumphant.

When Joe tells Sunny that she seems not to want to be Jewish, she responds that religion does not matter; when Joe says that it certainly matters to Adolf Hitler, Sunny dismisses Hitler as an "aberration." She has experienced discrimination, herself, as a child at a gentiles-only country club, yet she is unable to see the discrimination of which her own social set is guilty. When the two young couples attend the country club dance together, Peachy mentions to Joe that this club is for German Jews only, that the "Russian" Jews and the "Orthodox" Jews—the "Other Kind"—go to their own club, but that Joe need not worry since he is with Sunny. When asked, Peachy tells Joe that Sunny knows all about the restrictions, which disappoints and offends Joe, who leaves.

The ending of this comedy with serious undertones is one of happiness and reconciliation. Peachy decides to marry Lala and go into Adolph's business; such a marriage elates Boo as well as Lala. Joe seeks Sunny out on another train, and Sunny admits her ignorance of her heritage. In a final scene, the entire group—Sunny, Joe, Reba, Peachy, Lala, Boo, and Adolph—observe the Sabbath together in the Freitag home.

In *The Last Night of Ballyhoo,* ALFRED UHRY portrays with humor the end of an era of relative innocence: Hitler's invasion of Poland and the events that followed brought into sharp focus the self-defeating nature of intraracial prejudice. The play won a TONY AWARD for Best Play. Uhry's other nonmusical play, the PULITZER PRIZE–winning *DRIVING MISS DAISY* (1987), also features southern Jews and, in part, the conflict between those who would assimilate into the mainstream Christian culture of the South and those who would not.

LAURENTS, ARTHUR (1918–)   As a playwright, Arthur Laurents shows an affinity with the psychological realists of the post–World War II period, in his case, focusing on emotionally distraught characters, oftentimes women beset by anxiety and self-doubt. The son of Jewish parents—his father was a Times Square lawyer whose secretary introduced the young Arthur to Broadway theater—Laurents attended Cornell University, then wrote radio dramas and, later, army training films, before heading to Hollywood as a screenwriter on *The Snake Pit* (1948). Because of his liberal politics, he was eventually blacklisted and experienced passport difficulties during the McCarthy era. As both a Jew and a homosexual, Laurents was doubly the outsider. Always intolerant of anything he considered bigotry, he judged informers—those who named names during the House Un-American Activities Committee hearings—harshly for their failure in character.

In his autobiography, *Original Story By* (2000), Laurents delineates the themes that pervade his plays: first, discovery and acceptance of self; second, prejudice and betrayal. Elsewhere, he has traced the source of his characters' misery and loneliness to their inability to accept themselves as flawed; they will never be able to give of themselves or to arrive at a sense of completion and fulfillment until they first accept themselves and begin to *feel* sufficiently. The personal psychological pain they experience within themselves, which causes them to lash out at others, is further exacerbated by social forces, such as prejudicial attitudes, the drive to conformity, and the continued hold of traditional sexual mores and conventions.

Although he wrote an early play, *The Knife* (1945), about racial discrimination in the army, his first work to gain the attention of audiences and critics was the somewhat expressionistic HOME OF THE BRAVE (1945), about anti-Semitism among a group of soldiers and the psychosomatic trauma experienced by one who is stigmatized for being a Jew. Three plays during the next decade turn their focus to women, including

Laurents's best-known drama, *The* TIME OF THE CUCKOO (1952), the source of the popular film *Summertime,* starring Katharine Hepburn, and the musical *Do I Hear a Waltz?* (1965), for which Laurents wrote the book. In it, a lonely, inhibited American spinster travels to Venice hoping to find happiness; her fleeting romance with an Italian shopkeeper is curtailed when she cannot break free from a repressive sexual morality into an acceptance of a more instinctual lust for life. In the theatrically intricate, stream-of-consciousness play, *A Clearing in the Woods* (1957), a woman and her three younger selves all appear on stage to act out past experiences with various men. Only when the woman, who always wanted to be extraordinary and so imposed destructive expectations upon others, becomes content with her self can she accommodate and integrate her former selves and move into the future. In the whimsical, fairy tale–like *Invitation to a March* (1960), which echoes Cinderella and Sleeping Beauty, a young bride-to-be keeps falling asleep as her way of quietly rebelling against a confining and regimented existence. Only by rejecting conformity to ideals of social class and economic security and by choosing to dance to a different drummer can she break free and assert her difference.

Although none of his post-1960s plays—*The Radical Mystique* (1995), *My Good Name* (1997), *Jolson Sings Again* (1999), *Claudio Lazlo* (2001), *The Vibrator* (2002), and *2 Lives* (2003)—have achieved success, Laurents has gone on to attain continued recognition as a screenwriter of several notable films, including *The Turning Point* (1977) and *The Way We Were* (1973)—based on his 1972 novel of the same name; as the author of the books for such memorable musicals as *West Side Story* (1957), *Gypsy* (1959), and *Anyone Can Whistle* (1964); and as the director of the hit Broadway musical, *La Cage Aux Folles* (1984).

Laurents's 2003 play, *Attacks on the Heart,* explores how the romantic relationship between an American man and a Turkish woman is complicated by the events of 9/11. In 2008—his 90th year—Laurents was nominated for a TONY AWARD for best director of a musical for the highly acclaimed revival of *Gypsy;* and he directed a new bilingual production of *West Side Story,* which premiered in December in Washington, D.C.

BIBLIOGRAPHY

Laurents, Arthur. *A Clearing in the Woods*. New York: Random House, 1957.

———. *Invitation to a March*. New York: Random House, 1961.

———. *Original Story By: A Memoir of Broadway and Hollywood*. New York: Knopf, 2000.

———. *The Radical Mystique*. New York: Samuel French, 1996.

———. *Selected Plays of Arthur Laurents*. New York: Back Stage Books, 2004.

———. *The Time of the Cuckoo*. New York: Random House, 1953.

Thomas P. Adler
Purdue University

LAWRENCE, JEROME (1915–2004), and ROBERT E. LEE (1918–1994)

Jerome Lawrence and Robert E. Lee, writing partners for 52 years, are best known for their dramas INHERIT THE WIND (1955) and The NIGHT THOREAU SPENT IN JAIL (1970) and for their comedy AUNTIE MAME (1956). Both men were born and educated in Ohio. Lawrence attended Ohio State University, and Lee, Ohio Wesleyan. They both started out in radio, but they did not meet and work together until 1942, when they collaborated on the radio piece "Inside a Kid's Head." Their partnership continued during World War II—when the pair worked for Armed Forces Radio, writing and producing programs—and beyond, when they continued to write and direct for civilian radio.

Their first experience in the Broadway theater came when they wrote the book for the musical *Look, Ma, I'm Dancin'!* (1948), a show that was only moderately successful despite the involvement of Jerome Robbins and GEORGE ABBOTT. They resumed their successful radio careers until television transformed radio into a medium with little interest in comedy and drama series. In the mid-1950s, Lawrence and Lee returned to the stage and, this time, had tremendous success. Based on the Scopes "monkey trial" of 1925, *Inherit the Wind* is a fictionalized account of the case of a Tennessee schoolteacher who is tried for teaching evolution to his science class in a community that believes strongly in creationism. The play raises the issues of

freedom of speech and religion, and, most importantly, it advocates the freedom to think for oneself regardless of prevailing public opinion.

Inherit the Wind was produced first at a regional theater in Dallas, Texas. Though this is not uncommon now, at that time it was virtually unheard of for a play to start in a regional theater, rather than having pre-Broadway runs in such East Coast cities as Boston, Philadelphia, and New Haven. Having had a good experience with this procedure themselves, Lawrence and Lee hoped to create a similar working atmosphere for other playwrights when they created in 1963 the American Playwrights Theatre (APT). During its peak, APT had 160 member theaters to whom the APT selection committee would recommend unproduced plays by professional playwrights; if enough of these theaters around the country were interested, commercial success was possible without ever producing the play in New York. One such success was Lawrence and Lee's own *The Night Thoreau Spent in Jail*, the themes of which—nonviolent resistance, opposition to war, and nonconformity—spoke to audiences during the Vietnam era.

A lighter approach to themes of nonconformity and freethinking is embodied in Lawrence and Lee's popular comedy *Auntie Mame*, based on Patrick Dennis's best-selling novel. The team later adapted the play as the musical *Mame* (1966), with music and lyrics by Jerry Herman. They collaborated on other musicals as well, including *Shangri-La* (1956), adapted from James Hilton's novel *Lost Horizon* (music by Harry Warren), and *Dear World* (1969), based on Jean Giraudoux's play *La Folle de Chaillot* (The Madwoman of Chaillot) (with music and lyrics by Jerry Herman).

Other Lawrence and Lee plays include *The Gang's All Here* (1959); *Only in America* (1959), adapted from Harry Golden's work; *A Call on Kuprin* (1961), adapted from Maurice Edelman's novel; *Diamond Orchid* (1965), revised into *Sparks Fly Upward* (1967); *The Incomparable Max* (1971); *Jabberwock: Improbabilities Lived and Imagined by James Thurber in the Fictional City of Columbus, Ohio* (1972); and *First Monday in October* (1975), later revised for a New York production (1978). Their final collaboration was *Whisper in the Mind* (1990; revised 1994). The partnership ended with

Robert E. Lee's death in 1994. Individually, the two men each produced a significant amount of work, but their most successful and best-known endeavors are those that they produced together.

BIBLIOGRAPHY

Lawrence, Jerome, and Robert E. Lee. *Selected Plays of Jerome Lawrence and Robert E. Lee.* Edited by Alan Woods. Columbus: Ohio State University Press, 1995.

LAWSON, JOHN HOWARD (1894–1977)

Born in New York City, John Howard Lawson was, in the years between the world wars, frequently hailed as one of the most "promising" young American playwrights. After graduating from Williams College in 1914, two of his scripts (*Standards* and *Servant-Master-Lover*) were produced regionally in the mid-1910s. The tepid critical and popular reception of both was a primary motive behind Lawson's choice to enlist as a volunteer in the Norton-Harjes Ambulance Corps, serving on the French front. En route to Europe in the spring of 1917, he met John Dos Passos, who would prove highly influential in Lawson's development as an avant-garde artist and eventual political revolutionary. It was through Dos Passos that Lawson began an in-depth study of nonrealistic forms of artistic expression and radical politics.

Following the war, Lawson lived as an expatriate in Paris from 1920 to 1922, composing the first drafts of what would become his first two major plays: *Roger Bloomer* (1923) and PROCESSIONAL (1925). In *Roger Bloomer,* the title character, a restless youth, leaves his home in Iowa for New York. By way of an expressionist-inspired method (character as type, telegraphic language, and episodic structure), Lawson significantly advanced the expressionistic mode as it existed in the United States in the first years of the 1920s. He moved it away from the pessimistic mysticism of EUGENE O'NEILL and ELMER RICE, wherein the protagonist is defeated by the world, toward optimistic activism, wherein this figure triumphs. *Roger Bloomer,* first produced in New York in 1923, received many favorable reviews. With *Processional,* often considered his most remarkable script, Lawson fused formal elements from jazz music,

vaudeville, and dadaism to tell the story of a labor dispute in a West Virginia coal-mining town. It was produced by the THEATRE GUILD in 1925 and received glowing reviews. Not as successful was *Nirvana* (1926), in which Lawson sought to address the limiting nature of monotheistic creeds in the modern world through a conventional play structure mixed with surrealism.

In 1927, Lawson was one of the founding members of the New Playwrights' Theatre. Dedicated to producing pieces for and about the working class, via a method Lawson termed "the new showmanship," the New Playwrights—who also included notables Dos Passos and Mike Gold—struggled through three seasons of commercial and critical failures. Along the way, two of Lawson's scripts were written and produced: *Loudspeaker* (1927), a farcical lampooning of American politics and big business, borrowing heavily from Russian director Vsevolod Meyerhold's notions of constructivism, and *The International* (1928), an epic musical that juxtaposes scenes of stark realism against choral odes that echo Greek tragic form in an endeavor to tell the story of a future war in which the forces of capitalism, communism, and fascism destroy one another.

Following the dissolution of the New Playwrights' Theatre, Lawson spent the next four years living in Hollywood, writing screenplays and rereading Marx under the tutelage of noted Marxist critic Edmund Wilson. In the autumn of 1932, Lawson returned to New York and the theater with his play, *Success Story,* which tells of the spectacular rise and fall of Sol Ginsberg, a one-time radical who betrays his ideals for material success in corporate America. Following the GROUP THEATRE's lauded production of *Success Story* in the fall of 1932, Lawson returned to Hollywood, where he became involved in the newly formed Screenwriters Guild, eventually serving as its first president (1933–34). In the spring of 1934, Lawson refused renomination to his post with the SWG and once again returned to New York and the theater with simultaneous productions of *The Pure in Heart,* which draws on many of the nonrealistic modes of expression central to the playwright's work in the 1920s, and *Gentlewoman,* which relies on a realistic conventional play structure. Both plays deal with modern people's recognizing and responding to the degradation of spiritual and emotional life in the United States. Significantly, the productions of both were severely castigated by leftwing critics, who accused Lawson of ideological confusion.

In late 1934, Lawson joined the Communist Party. He spent the next two years participating in various "united front" causes and preparing the manuscript for his book-length study, *The Theory and Technique of Playwriting* (1936), which espouses the view that dramatic conflict is, in fact, social conflict. Lawson's next play, *Marching Song* (1937), the story of a sit-down strike in an automotive plant in Michigan, was a modest critical and commercial success. However, unsatisfied with his abilities to find a balance between his revolutionary political convictions and his notions regarding the theater, in late 1937, Lawson returned to Hollywood.

Making his living as a screenwriter, Lawson spent the next 10 years serving as a leading member of the Hollywood branch of the Communist Party. Correspondingly, in 1947, he was one of the infamous Hollywood Ten, called before the House Un-American Activities Committee. Cited for contempt of Congress, Lawson spent two years in federal prison, from 1950 to 1952. His principal writings that followed were Marxist critical studies of American culture.

BIBLIOGRAPHY

Chambers, Jonathan L. *Messiah of the New Technique: John Howard Lawson, Communism, and American Theatre, 1923–1937.* Carbondale: Southern Illinois University Press, 2006.

Lawson, John Howard. *The Hidden Heritage.* New York: Citadel, 1950.

———. *The International.* New York: Macaulay, 1927.

———. *Loud Speaker.* New York: Macaulay, 1927.

———. *Marching Song.* New York: Dramatists Play Service, 1937.

———. *Processional.* New York: Thomas Seltzer, 1925.

———. *Roger Bloomer.* New York: Thomas Seltzer, 1923.

———. *Success Story.* New York: Farrar and Rinehart, 1932.

———. *Theory and Technique of Playwriting.* New York: Putnam's, 1936.

———. *Theory and Technique of Playwriting and Screenwriting.* Rev. ed. New York: Putnam's, 1949.

———. *With a Reckless Preface: Two Plays—"The Pure of Heart" and "Gentlewoman."* New York: Farrar and Rinehart, 1934.

Jonathan L. Chambers
Bowling Green State University

LECOMPTE, ELIZABETH (1944–)

Elizabeth LeCompte became famous for her radical and ironic deconstructions of plays, which critique American as well as European theater and culture. In 1974, she started directing in Richard Schechner's Performance Group (1967–80), which in 1968 acquired the space that is now known as the Performing Garage at 33 Wooster Street in New York City's SoHo district. In 1975, she became a founding member of the Wooster Group, a permanent theater company housed in the Performing Garage. Other founding members include the actors Willem Dafoe, Kate Valk, Peyton Smith, and Ron Vawter and the set designer Jim Clayburgh. The Group has toured the United States and Europe, as well as Asia, Australia, Canada, and South America.

The Wooster Group productions are assemblages of juxtaposed elements. LeCompte usually works with sections of diverse texts by a range of authors and playwrights, and these are set against excerpts from movies, comedy routines, biographies of the actors, and elements of improvisation. These create a critical counterpoint to the texts. The approach sometimes becomes controversial, as was the case in the Group's work with excerpts from THORNTON WILDER'S *OUR TOWN* (*Route 1 & 9* [1981]), which were juxtaposed against Pigmeat Markham comedy routines, and, adding to the controversy, the actors played in blackface. Further stagings loosely based on dramas include *L.S.D (. . . Just the High Points . . .)* (1984), using excerpts from ARTHUR MILLER'S *The CRUCIBLE*. These were juxtaposed with, among other elements, random selections of a speech by Timothy Leary, the drug guru of the 1960s, from his record album *LSD.* A legal entanglement developed with Arthur Miller over the use of excerpts of four scenes from his play; this part of the production had to be withdrawn in 1985. Anton

Chekhov's *Three Sisters* was adapted in *Brace Up!* (1991). Here, elements of Japanese Noh and Kyogen theater were woven into the Russian author's play; a narrator/television moderator was also added. Other productions drew on EUGENE O'NEILL's *The HAIRY APE* (*The Hairy Ape* [1995]) and *The EMPEROR JONES* (*The Emperor Jones* [1993]). The Group's *The Emperor Jones* was inspired by the performance of Paul Robeson (played by Kate Valk, in the title role). With the Group's *House/Lights* (1999), GERTRUDE STEIN's *Doctor Faustus Lights the Lights* was set against Joseph Mawra's 1960s cult movie, *In Olga's House of Shame*. And *To You, the Birdie!* (2002) was loosely based on Racine's *Phèdre*.

Recent Wooster Group productions include *Poor Theater* (2004), an homage to the director Jerzy Grotowski, the choreographer William Forsythe, and the artist Max Ernst; *La Didone* (2007), after the opera by Francesco Cavalli and Gian Francesco Busenello; and *Hamlet* (2007), inspired by Richard Burton's 1964 performance in the Shakespeare play.

Born in Summit, New Jersey, LeCompte has a background in film and painting, having earned a degree in 1967 at Skidmore College. This major influence enriches her sensibility as a director and helps her to shed a new, ironic, and humorous light on dramatic texts. LeCompte was impressed by John Cage and the dada artist Kurt Schwitters; these and other influences as varied as William S. Burroughs, American musicals, and television cartoons also figure in her sensibility. From the theater world itself, she has been influenced by the work of Jerzy Grotowski, the LIVING THEATRE, RICHARD FOREMAN, and Robert Wilson.

In all Wooster Group productions, the text is no more important than the use made of video images, choreography, or sound space. In fact, the work on a show usually starts by creating a set design, blocking choreography, and working with video technology. The text is often added at a later stage, and live performances are set against video images to generate a mixed-media collage. This approach questions the very basis of theater, with technology challenging traditional practices, such as those of the actors learning lines or speaking in audible voices. The Group's actors actually wear small headphones that prompt them

with their lines, which they then vocalize into microphones. Theatrical illusion per se is not rejected; it is used in an ironic and playful way, but it is undermined by distancing devices, such as dances and campy, comic interludes. The text is therefore only one of several means of expression used in transcending conventions and taboos. In so doing, LeCompte and the Wooster Group give new life to classics and reinterpret them for modern audiences.

BIBLIOGRAPHY
Callens, Johan, ed. *The Wooster Group and Its Traditions.* Brussels: Peter Lang, 2004.
Quick, Andrew, ed. *The Wooster Group Work Book.* New York/London: Routledge, 2007.
Savran, David. *Breaking the Rules: The Wooster Group.* New York: Theater Communications Group, 1988.

Claire Leich-Galland
City University of New York

LEE, ROBERT E.   See LAWRENCE, JEROME.

LETTS, TRACY (1965–)   The PULITZER PRIZE–winning playwright Tracy Letts was born in Tulsa, Oklahoma, the son of novelist Billie Letts and actor Dennis Letts. He grew up in Durant, a college town, where his parents were both professors. Letts, having acted as a teenager with his father, dropped out of Southeastern Oklahoma State after one semester to move to Dallas, Texas, to become an actor himself. Finding Dallas unsatisfactory both professionally and personally, he tried Chicago and Los Angeles and eventually settled in Chicago permanently, becoming a part of its vibrant theater scene as both actor and playwright.

His first play, *Killer Joe,* a gory, dark—and darkly funny—piece about idiotic trailer dwellers behaving badly, takes place in Texas. To avoid being killed by his suppliers, drug dealer and user Chris Smith conspires with other members of his family—and a policeman-hitman named Killer Joe Cooper—to kill his mother for an insurance payoff. *Killer Joe* was first given a reading at Next Lab in Evanston, Illinois, in 1991, and finally produced there by Letts himself and his friends in 1993. Despite being disparaged by some critics for its unabashed vulgarity and extreme violence and despite accusations of misogyny even from some of Letts's own friends, the play became a cult hit. The Chicago cast took it to the Edinburgh Festival, where it won the Fringe First Award. In the wake of that success, the play was produced to enthusiastic reviews both OFF-BROADWAY and in London. In London, *Killer Joe* was seen by Irish playwright Martin McDonagh, who "found in [the play] the liberation he needed to write" his own extravagantly gory black comedies (Nance). Letts's skewed vision of the world was evident early in his life. He told Patrick Healy of the *New York Times* in 2008 of a "first grade" assignment for which he was asked to write a "little book"; his was called "'The Psychopath.' The cover showed a man hanging in the closet," who "had also shot himself in the head" (July 20, 2008).

Letts's second play, *Bug* (1996), premiered in London. Set in Oklahoma, it is a tale of paranoia and violence, in which a luckless middle-aged addict hopes for love from a man who believes the government has infused his blood with tiny bugs as a means of control. At the time of the American premiere in Washington, D.C., in 2000, Letts told the *Washington Post*, "A lot of the play has to do with the accommodations people make" in unhealthy relationships (March 28, 2000). In 2004 when *Bug* was produced in New York, Hilton Als, in his *New Yorker* review, wrote that the violence in the second half of the play reminded him of such "groundbreaking" theater groups as the LIVING THEATER, which "forced the spectator to confront his own worst fear: that by watching the performance he was somehow complicit in the violence that was unfolding before him" (May 17, 2004). *Bug* was also made into a film in 2007.

In 2002, Letts became an ensemble member of Chicago's Steppenwolf Theatre, where his next three plays premiered. *Man from Nebraska* (2003) is a departure from the confrontational disposition of his first two plays. The play opens nearly silently as we see Ken and Nancy go through the routine of their relationship. We learn that Ken has lost his faith in God. When his spiritual adviser suggests a restorative trip, he heads for London, where he becomes involved in the life of a young bartender and her roommate; mean-

while, Nancy assuages her loneliness with the spiritual adviser's father. Letts's gift for dialogue is evident here; the play was a finalist for the Pulitzer Prize in 2004.

Letts's third play, *AUGUST: OSAGE COUNTY* (2007), is a hilarious and sometimes poignant portrait of a sprawling and dysfunctional family—one that seems to embrace every malady ever discussed on confessional television—brought together by the suicide of its patriarch, a retired English professor and poet. The play is to some extent based on Letts's maternal grandparents' story: His grandfather committed suicide and his grandmother is the model for the play's drug-addled matriarch Violet. *August* won the Pulitzer Prize, the TONY AWARD, and the New York Drama Critics' Circle Award. In the original Steppenwolf production, the playwright's father, Dennis Letts, played the role of the suicidal Beverly Weston; the senior Letts died during the run, leaving his son with a painful loss at the center of his most successful year as a playwright.

Far less ambitious than *August: Osage County* is *Superior Donuts* (2008), another dark comedy, this one set in a Chicago neighborhood in the initial stages of the transition from poverty to gentrification. The play is filled with Chicago references and is as much about the city as it is about the interaction between its main characters, a disgruntled Vietnam War–era draft dodger who owns an independent donut shop and his new assistant, a bright 21-year-old African-American man from the neighborhood.

BIBLIOGRAPHY
Nance, Kevin. "Tracy Letts: No Place Like Home." *American Theatre* 24.6 (July–August 2007): 42 (4).

LEVIN, IRA (1929–2007)   Ira Levin grew up reading Edgar Allan Poe, Agatha Christie, and Ellery Queen; he subsequently redefined the landscape of the horror-fantasy genre for the novel, the stage, and film. Prior to graduation from New York University with a B.A. in English in 1950, Levin wrote "The Old Woman" (1950), runner-up for a CBS-sponsored script contest for college seniors; it was eventually produced in December of that year by NBC.

Consequently, Levin's parents supported his writing for two years, during which time he wrote more television scripts and a first novel, *A Kiss before Dying* (1953), that won the Edgar Allan Poe Award for the best first mystery novel. In this thriller, Bud Corliss, a charming but evil gold digger, woos and kills two wealthy sisters, potential heirs to the Kingship copper fortune, before trying to marry the third. The intricate plotting that Levin used became a signature for much of his later work. As with many of Levin's novels and stage plays, the work was adapted for film.

Following military service, in 1958, Levin adapted for the stage Mac Hyman's novel, *No Time for Sergeants,* which dealt with a country bumpkin whose naive actions point out the absurdities of military regulations. Following that successful adaptation, Levin wrote a string of original Broadway shows over the next 12 years. *Interlock* (1958) shows a budding ménage à trois going horribly awry. *Critic's Choice* (1960) examines what happens when a theater critic's wife writes a Broadway play. In *General Seeger* (1962), the title character investigates the circumstances of his son's heroic military bravery and death. The musical *Drat! The Cat!* (1965) depicts a bumbling detective falling in love with and trying to reform a pretty cat burglar in turn-of-the-century New York. In *Dr. Cook's Garden* (1967), a visiting doctor investigates the local, kindly physician's practice of eliminating disagreeable people from his small idyllic Vermont community. Of the original scripts, only *Critic's Choice* was a modest success and became a 1963 film. The poor reception of the other shows, particularly the musical, caused Levin to return to novel writing, where he achieved considerable success with *Rosemary's Baby* (1967), *The Stepford Wives* (1972), and *The Boys from Brazil* (1976), all of which became hit movies.

Levin returned to the Broadway stage with the moderately successful *Veronica's Room* (1973). In it, Cissie's incestuous relationship with her brother is discovered by their sister, Veronica, resulting in Veronica's murder. Years later, the incestuous couple invites Veronica look-alikes to their home to relive the original murder. In Levin's next play, *Deathtrap* (1978), Sidney Bruhl is facing a dry period as a playwright when he "discovers" a surefire hit by one of his male students. The two conspire to murder Sidney's wife and then set up house as lovers. Complications develop as the lovers' falling-out over the script leads to their own murders. *Deathtrap* was a huge success, running for 1,793 performances, before being made into an equally successful 1982 film. *Break a Leg* (1979) shows the lengths to which a theatrical producer goes to confound a critic who panned the producer's previous shows. In *Cantorial* (1989)—Levin's final work for the stage—after a yuppie couple moves into a haunted condominium in a former synagogue, the husband becomes obsessed with the building's restoration as a synagogue.

BIBLIOGRAPHY

Fowler, Douglas. *Ira Levin.* Mercer Island, Wash.: Starmont House/Borgo Press, 1988.

Levin, Ira. *Critic's Choice.* New York: Dramatists Play Service, 1962.

———. *Deathtrap.* New York: Random House, 1979.

———. *Dr. Cook's Garden.* New York: Dramatists Play Service, 1968.

———. *General Seeger.* New York: Dramatists Play Service, 1962.

———. *No Time for Sergeants.* New York: Dramatists Play Service, 1958.

Robert Lewis Smith
Kutztown University of Pennsylvania

LIE OF THE MIND, A SAM SHEPARD (1985)

Tracing the aftermath of a violent beating that ruptures a marriage, *A Lie of the Mind* examines the dangers of too rigidly defining gender. SHEPARD shows a particular disdain towards macho posing and an apparently deepened sensitivity to the needs and strengths of women. The play won the New York Drama Critics' Circle Award, the Outer Critics Circle Award, and the Drama Desk Award.

The play begins when Oklahoman Jake telephones his brother Frankie, reporting that he (Jake) has probably killed his wife, Beth, before fleeing the scene. Montanan Beth, in the next dramatic episode, awakens, babbling with sounds hinting at brain damage, in a hospital room where her brother, Mike, sits with her. Frankie, followed eventually by a humiliated Jake, soon goes to Montana seeking news of Beth. The first stage directions of the play describe the vast "distance" that these characters must travel—a distance between people that, the play suggests, can be narrowed but probably never closed.

As the drama develops, we meet more and more of both Jake's Oklahoman and Beth's Montanan relatives—learning, as we do, that Shepard recognizes various sorts of mental "lies" (both falsehoods and mental states or topographies). Mental falsehoods can result from injury (like Beth's brain-battering) or from disease (like the Alzheimerian forgetfulness sometimes afflicting Beth's mother Meg), yet neither Beth nor Meg is truly mendacious—unlike those given over to obsessions, who often *are*. Such people may too narrowly define human genders: Beth's father, Baylor, acts (until the play's very last minute) mostly as an animalistic hunter, while Jake's mother, Lorraine, is an emotionally overwrought and smothering maternal figure. Unlike this pair, Meg is proud of her daughter Beth's androgynous "male[ness]." Beth also champions Frankie's relatively feminine androgyny, trying to wrap and shield him with the male shirt that she wears.

When Jake rebels and leaves her home, Lorraine takes to lying on his bed—one of several mythological hints in this often primitivistic Ibsenesque/Sophoclean symbol-drama. Jake, by trying to outrun and then outdrink his father in a Mexican border town, years before, evidently caused his death in a vehicle-pedestrian accident, much as Oedipus killed *his* father, Laius, on another open roadway. Jake's sister Sally may have experienced her father's (or brother's) incestuous lust. And Lorraine deems all Jake's problems primordial ones: "Had nothin' to do with his upbringing."

However, Lorraine's behavior, as an almost sexually predatory mother, counters her denials of psychosocial influence in the world. *A Lie of the Mind,* after all, does realistically delineate common behaviors resulting from bad child-rearing and spousal abuse. By the play's symbol-rich end (where "fire" and "snow" seem melded together), Beth's ultimate spurning of Jake allows (although tentatively) for a spiritually emergent cooperation between the better-matched Beth and Frankie.

Jeffrey B. Loomis
Northwest Missouri State University

LIFE WITH FATHER HOWARD LINDSAY AND RUSSEL CROUSE (1939) Based on Clarence Day's stories about his youth in New York in the 1880s, *Life with Father* is a fondly drawn portrait of the Day household: the opinionated, irreverent, and eccentric—but loving—Clarence Sr.; his affectionate and dizzy wife, Vinnie; and their four sons, Clarence Jr., John, Whitney, and Harlan. As Father tries to run their lives, his offspring and wife try to get what they want—and usually succeed.

As the play begins, Vinnie Day is training a new maid in the idiosyncrasies of working for Mr. Day. Since Father's irascible behavior scares off maids routinely, Vinnie is forever breaking in new ones; indeed, there is a new maid in each scene of the play. It is not just the household staff to whom Clarence Day Sr. makes his opinions known. A Wall Street broker, he insists that his wife account for every penny she spends on the household. Vinnie's grasp of things financial is anything but precise. (She actually believes that when a charged purchase is exchanged for something else, her husband will pay nothing.) Despite her husband's firm beliefs, Vinnie usually manages to manipulate him to her satisfaction. When Father reveals by chance that he was never baptized—his parents being "free-thinkers"—Vinnie is appalled and questions the legitimacy of her marriage and children. However, Father will not be moved on the subject and steadfastly refuses to be baptized.

So powerful is Father's personality that when Clarence Jr. must wear an old suit of Father's that has been cut down to fit him, he finds he is infused with Father's demeanor, making it impossible to court a visiting 16-year-old named Mary. When she sits on his lap—that is, on "Father's trousers"—he jumps up, which deeply offends the girl. At church, he finds he cannot kneel since Father never does. In order to buy a new suit, Clarence joins John in taking a job selling patent medicine, with which the boys—in an effort to help their mother recover from a cold—poison Vinnie. When she becomes gravely ill, Dr. Lloyd suggests that it would ease her mind and perhaps cure her if her husband were to be baptized. Father at first refuses, but finally—so upset is he at the thought of losing his wife—promises her he will be baptized. He is immediately "aghast" at his own promise, and as the play ends, Father *"stalks out"* of the house ("I'm going to be baptized, damn it!") as Clarence Jr. kneels before Mary in his new suit.

This nostalgic domestic comedy broke the record for the longest-running play on Broadway, opening in November of 1939 and closing in July of 1947.

LINDSAY-ABAIRE, DAVID (1969–)

Born David Abaire and raised in blue collar South Boston, this PULITZER PRIZE–winning playwright received a scholarship at age 12 to the Milton Academy, a Massachusetts prep school (class of 1988). From Milton, he went to Sarah Lawrence College, where he majored in theater. After marrying Chris Lindsay, whom he met at Sarah Lawrence, he became David Lindsay-Abaire. While working in New York in arts administration and getting his plays produced OFF-OFF-BROADWAY, Lindsay-Abaire entered and completed Julliard's playwriting program from 1996 to 1998, where he studied with MARSHA NORMAN and CHRISTOPHER DURANG.

Words like *zany, wacky, quirky, freewheeling, absurdist, dark,* and *hilarious* are used time and again in reviews of much of Lindsay-Abaire's work. A review in the *Los Angeles Times* of *A Devil Inside* (1997) suggested that readers "imagine JULES FEIFFER channeling Lewis Carroll" (June 10, 1999); John Simon in his review of *Fuddy Meers* (1999) in *New York Magazine* declared that Lindsay-Abaire was Ionesco's "true heir" (November 8, 1999). But while much of his work is zanily comic, and it was the dark comedy *Fuddy Meers* that brought Lindsay-Abaire to national attention, it was his quite conventional and realistic drama about parental grief following the death of a child, *RABBIT HOLE* (2006), that earned him the Pulitzer Prize.

Rabbit Hole is about a husband and wife who, eight months after their four-year-old son has been struck and killed by a car, are trying to navigate the tricky emotional waters of this indelible grief. By the end of the play, they have begun to move closer to the point at which they will be able to carry the grief while not being completely sunk by it. When Lindsay-Abaire was at Julliard, Marsha Norman suggested he write about something that frightened him; it was not until he became a parent himself that he found an answer to her suggestion in the subject he tackles in *Rabbit Hole.*

In an interview that appeared in his prep school alumni magazine in 2003, Lindsay-Abaire commented, "I think theater has an obligation to be theatrical. It's not real. Don't pretend it's real. I'm not a realist. For some, the game is how real can you make it? That's silly to me. It's a play" (Hughes). *Rabbit Hole* is a departure from this philosophy and indeed, though it won the Pulitzer, was not as universally applauded by critics as some of his less realistic and more theatrical works.

His full-length plays include *A Devil Inside* (1997), a comedy in which a 21-year-old is asked by his mother to avenge his long-dead father's murder and in which the complex plot satirizes classic Russian novels; *Wonder of the World* (2000), a picaresque farce in which two women, one abandoned by and the other abandoning a husband, light out for Niagara Falls, that great North American symbol of romance and thrill-seeking. Lindsay-Abaire's breakthrough play, *Fuddy Meers,* is an absurdist comedy about a woman whose memory is erased whenever she goes to sleep and who must try to make sense of a world peopled by characters with various communication difficulties, including a mother whose recent stroke has affected the clarity of her speech and a stranger who often speaks through a sock puppet. When Lindsay-Abaire heard about a real case of a woman with this type of amnesia, he recalls thinking, "What a convenient device to get out of exposition" (Marks). *Kimberly Akimbo* (2001), another dark comedy, calls for a 60ish actress to play a teenager with a rare condition that causes her to age rapidly; she must cope with her self-absorbed parents as well as with her own fears. Ben Brantley, in his review in the *New York Times,* called the play "at once a shrewd satire, a black comedy and a heartbreaking study of how time wounds everyone" (February 5, 2003). The play won the Los Angeles Drama Critics Circle Award for playwriting.

Lindsay-Abaire's early short plays, ranging from a few minutes to more traditionally lengthed one-acts, include *The Kitchen Sink Drama* (1995), a one-act in which a soap opera actor is stranded in the desert home of a lonely woman and her preoccupied husband; *The Li'l Plays* (1997–1999), a collection of five 10–15-minute comedies; *Snow Angel* (1998), a one-act favorite among high school drama groups, about a mysterious stranger who emerges from the banks of a blizzard and into the lives of a group of Vermont teenagers, whose journal entries provide the narrative; and *How We Talk in South Boston* (1999), a very brief comedy, the title of which is descriptive of the piece. Since 2000, Lindsay-Abaire has contributed to festivals and showcases of short plays, including the HUMANA FESTIVAL of New Plays at the Actors Theatre of Louisville (*Snapshot* [2002], a multi-playwright anthology of scenes); the "24 Hour Plays" (*Baby Food* [2004], *That Other Person* [2005], and *Wakey Wakey* [2007]); and the New School of Drama's "Random Acts!" showcase of short plays (*Crazy Eights* [2007]).

Lindsay-Abaire also wrote the books for the musicals *High Fidelity* (2006) and *Shrek, the Musical* (2008); for the latter he wrote the lyrics as well as the book. The film version of *Rabbit Hole* is currently in production; the playwright himself wrote the screen adaptation.

BIBLIOGRAPHY

Hughes, Evan. "Truthful, Honest—But Funny." *Milton Magazine* (online) (Winter 2003).

Lindsay-Abaire, David. *A Devil Inside*. New York: Dramatists Play Service, 2000.

———. *Fuddy Meers*. New York: Dramatists Play Service, 2000.

———. *Kimberly Akimbo*. New York: Dramatists Play Service, 2003.

———. *Rabbit Hole*. New York: Theatre Communications Group, 2006.

———. *Three One-Acts: "Crazy Eights," Baby Food," and "That Other Person."* New York: Dramatists Play Service, 2007.

———. *Wonder of the World*. New York: Dramatists Play Service, 2004.

Marks, Peter. "Finding the Humor and the Hope in Fractured Lives." *New York Times* (March 12, 2000).

LINNEY, ROMULUS (ZACHARIAH, IV) (1930–)

Romulus Linney was born in Philadelphia but spent his first four years in Boone, North Carolina. He later spent many summers there "hearing the voices of Appalachia," the inspiration for three novels and a number of his more than 40 long and short plays. He studied acting and directing at Yale before turning to writing. His first novel, *Heathen Valley* (1962), based on the Episcopal mission established in Valle Crucis, North Carolina, during the 1840s, was dramatized by Linney in 1986.

Linney returned to his North Carolina roots in his other novels, *Slowly, By Thy Hand Unfurled* (1966), dramatized as *A Woman without a Name* (1986), and *Jesus Tales* (1980), dramatized in the two short plays *Old Man Joseph and His Family* (1978) and *Why the Lord Came to Sand Mountain* (1985). Another popular one-act play based on an Appalachian legend is *Tennessee* (1980). Perhaps the best known and most often produced of the southern plays is *Holy Ghosts* (1989), which portrays a snake-handling religious sect in a poignant and often humorous manner. Linney writes with respect, affection, and understanding of the hardy and independent people of the region.

Linney's first produced play is a historical drama, a type for which he has received considerable acclaim. *The Sorrows of Frederick* (1967) is about Frederick the Great and his difficult relationship with his father. Other historical plays include *Childe Byron* (1982), about an imaginary conversation between Lord Byron's daughter and her dead father, and *2: Goering at Nuremberg* (1991), about the trial of Hermann Goering. Linney is an avid reader and researcher, and his love of language is reflected in his plays.

There are also dramas of contemporary life that Linney calls personal plays, such as *The Love Suicide at Schofield Barracks* (1985), based on his time in the army when he was stationed in Hawaii. Other modern plays include a number of one-acts like *F. M.* and *Goodbye, Howard,* which appear together under the title *Laughing Stock* (1984). Another collection of six short pieces is *Pops* (1987), all based on different aspects of love.

Linney has also written dramatizations of other writers' works, such as an adaptation of Ernest J. Gaines's novel *A Lesson Before Dying* (2000), the story of a young black man falsely convicted of murder who can only hope to learn to die like a man.

Music plays a prominent part in most of Linney's plays. Regional folk music and songs are included in the Appalachian plays, and each of the six plays in *Pops* is titled by a different piece of music appropriate to the theme of the play and integrated into the action. The transition to writing for opera in 2005 was a natural progression for Linney when the Washington National Opera presented *Democracy,* music by Scott Wheeler and libretto by Linney based on Linney's play *Democracy* (1974), which was in turn based on two Henry Adams novels about Ulysses S. Grant.

Frequently performed in regional theaters and schools and OFF-BROADWAY, Linney was selected in 1991 for a season devoted to a single American playwright by the Signature Theatre in New York. His plays are spare, literate, and written to be staged simply, with the focus maintained on language and character. They may be more important to the American theater than many Broadway successes because they reflect the lives of people who are familiar to audiences.

Linney has received two OBIE AWARDS, the first in 1980 for *Tennessee* and the second in 1992 for Sustained Excellence in Playwriting. He has also received the EDWARD ALBEE Last Frontier Playwrights Award, the WILLIAM INGE Award, and a North Carolina Award for Literature. Linney continues to write one-act plays and has written another long play about historical figures. The latter, *Klonsky and Schwartz* (2005), is an exploration of the fiery relationship between poet Delmore Schwartz and his young protégé and lifelong partner Milton Klonsky.

BIBLIOGRAPHY

Fleming, John. *Romulus Linney: Maverick of the American Theatre.* Hanover, N.H.: Smith and Kraus, 2008.

Linney, Romulus. *Klonsky and Schwartz.* New York: Dramatists Play Service, 2006.

———. *Nine Adaptations for the American Stage.* Hanover, N.H.: Smith and Kraus, 2000.

———. *Seventeen Short Plays.* Newbury, Vt.: Smith and Kraus, 1992.

———. *Six Plays.* New York: Theatre Communications Group, 1993.

Susan S. Cole
Appalachian State University

LION IN WINTER, THE JAMES GOLDMAN (1966)

Set in 1183, *The Lion in Winter* portrays a 50-year-old King Henry II of England and his queen, 61-year-old Eleanor of Aquitaine, engaging in a war of words and wit as each promotes a favorite son for heir apparent.

Henry has a very young mistress, Alais, the sister of the king of France, and a wife, whom he has kept locked up for 10 years. It is Christmastime, and he has let her out for the holidays. Their eldest son died young, and now Henry must decide whom he will name heir to the throne. His choice is John, 16 and stupid but fondly regarded by his father. Eleanor's choice is Richard, at 26 the eldest surviving son and a great warrior. (Indeed, history shows that Richard will succeed his father, but not for long.) The middle son, Geoffrey, keenly intelligent, cannot "remember anything from [Mother] or Father warmer than indifference." The politics within this royal family of five is filled with duplicity and hostility, eavesdropping and shifting alliances; their exchanges—except those of John—are filled with wit.

When it eventually becomes clear to Henry that his sons are plotting against him with the young King Philip of France, he disowns them all, telling Eleanor that what he really wants is to marry Alais and have a son by her. Richard, Geoffrey, and John, he declares, are like "warts and goiters—and I'm having them removed." When Eleanor refuses to agree to an annulment, Henry vows to go to Rome and get one despite her objections. Eleanor declares that she and her sons will take over the kingdom in his absence, giving Henry reason to lock the boys up, which he does.

The three princes, now imprisoned in the wine cellar, contemplate killing their father with the weapons their mother smuggles in to them for their escape. Eleanor tries to dissuade them and finally betrays their intentions to Henry when he arrives. When Henry invites them to go ahead, however, they cannot bring themselves to kill him, nor can he bring himself to kill them. He says to Eleanor "[t]hey're all we have" and bids them go.

Henry sends Eleanor off on her barge to resume her imprisonment until Easter when, presumably, they will all get together for another skirmish. Despite a long history of infidelity and power struggle, there may be some love left between Henry and Eleanor, but one is never sure if apparent intimations of love are simply more ammunition in the unending battle between them.

Despite the historical setting of the play and its royal characters, the play's themes as they relate to family dynamics are surprisingly universal. The family Goldman portrays is—though certainly extreme in its tactics—one in which the relationships are complex, and one in which blame is not easily assigned. Furthermore, the play has endured in regional and repertory theaters because it provides, in the sharp-tongued Henry and Eleanor, fine vehicles for middle-aged actors.

LIPS TOGETHER, TEETH APART Terrence McNally (1991)

Frank Rich observed that McNally's play is as much about what homosexuals "have in common in an infected, diminished civilization as it is about what sets them apart" (*New York Times,* June 26, 1991), an apt description of this three-act play in which no homosexual characters appear but in which the gay world and the AIDS epidemic are major presences nonetheless.

Two straight couples are spending the Fourth of July weekend in a gay community on New York's Fire Island. They are there because one of the women, Sally, has recently inherited the house from her brother David, who died of AIDS. Sally's husband Sam is a New Jersey contractor and the brother of Chloe, married to John, a smug and aristocratic admissions officer at a New England prep school. Chloe talks incessantly and constantly provides food and drink for the group. Sally is painting an ocean scene and is worried about a swimmer who waved to her before going in the water and who seems not to have returned. There is obvious tension between John and Sam, who seems to resent what he perceives to be his brother-in-law's air of superiority. John and Chloe have three children who are spending the weekend with their grandparents; Sam and Sally are childless (Sally has had several unsuccessful pregnancies). Both couples are aware that they seem to be the only heterosexuals in a homosexual enclave and are not very comfortable with it; although Chloe waves and talks to the neighbors, the loud music and friendly men in bikini briefs distress Sam and, especially, John, who calls them "[g]oddamn fairies."

It is a convention of the play that the characters occasionally address the audience rather than one another. The tone and subject matter of these brief asides is set at the outset when Chloe, trying unsuccessfully to get everyone's attention to determine what they want for breakfast, says, "Sometimes I wonder who we're talking to." In two other such passages, Sam asserts, "No one wants to listen to who we really are" and "Put two people together and truth doesn't stand a chance." On another occasion, John tells Sally, with whom he is having an affair but who isn't listening to him, that he has cancer.

As the day proceeds, tensions increase. Sam tells Sally that he knows that she has slept with John. Sally denies it, but she says in an interior monologue, "It's gone, that moment to speak the truth. . . . The truth is, I don't want him to know." John is exasperated by his wife's nonstop chatter; Chloe explains, "I talk too much probably because it's too horrible to think about what's really going on." Chloe confides to Sam that she knows their spouses are having an affair but that John has told her it's over and she believes him, because she wants to believe it is so. As Chloe begins to practice for her role as Adelaide in a community theater production of *Guys and Dolls,* Sally spots a body on the beach, confirming her fears about the swimmer she saw earlier.

That evening, noisy parties fill both neighboring houses, but Sally is still upset and guilty about the drowned man: "He wanted to die and I helped him." She chides them all for not wanting to swim in the house's pool for fear that it has been contaminated by David and his black lover Aaron; she drinks from the pool and kisses Sam, who recoils and admits that she's right. Left alone in what is perhaps the play's most important scene, Sally tells John that she made love to him because "I wanted the parts you don't give to anyone else. Your secrets, your fears. Not the parts that connect us, the parts that separate us." He replies, "No one gets them. . . . I respect the distance between people," explaining, "To know me is not necessarily to like me."

As the fireworks begin, Sam is watching two men openly and lustily having sex next door, and Sally is thinking about when she visited her dying brother in the hospital. Chloe tells Sally and Sam that John has cancer and the doctors don't think they can operate, but "we're going to fight and hope." Both wives complain that their husbands grind their teeth in their sleep; Sally reports that Sam's doctor has recommended that he fall asleep saying, "lips together, teeth apart," but he won't do it, so she has to say it to him. As Sam and Chloe begin to dance to the music from next door and the ultraviolet bug light "zaps" the mosquitoes, Sam confesses to Chloe that he doesn't want children because he's afraid they wouldn't love him and that he wouldn't have anything to give them because he's "empty."

It is clear that McNally uses the interior monologues, reminiscent of the asides in EUGENE O'NEILL's STRANGE INTERLUDE (1928) and of the oblique dialogue in the plays of Russian dramatist Anton Chekhov, to emphasize the loneliness and isolation of these characters and their inability to communicate on anything but a superficial level. As Steven Drukman has noted, one of the prevalent motifs in McNally's work is the idea that, despite our "yearning for intimacy, human beings have myriad ways of building barriers between one another, denying and evading emotion and keeping their distance" (333).

The comparison the play suggests between the gay and straight communities, however, is a bit more complicated and ambivalent. On the one hand, there is surely a contrast depicted in the music-at-full-blast partying and open, exuberant coupling of the residents of Fire Island and the uptight and to some extent sexually dysfunctional straight couples. On the other hand, David is dead from AIDS, the swimmer has drowned, John is dying, Sally may well be unable to have children, and Sam is "empty." John M. Clum thus may be correct in suggesting that the real "sadness of the play is built on the heterosexuals' refusal to see their commonality with the gay men surrounding them; that their fears, particularly of mortality, are the same" (105).

BIBLIOGRAPHY

Clum, John M. "Where We Are Now: Love! Valour! Compassion! and Contemporary Gay Drama." In Terrence McNally: A Casebook, edited by Toby Silverman Zinman. New York: Garland, 1997. 95–116.

Drukman, Steven. "Terrence McNally." In Speaking on Stage: Interviews with Contemporary American Playwrights, edited by Philip C. Kolin and Colby H. Kullman. Tuscaloosa: University of Alabama Press, 1996. 332–345.

LISBON TRAVIATA, THE TERRENCE MCNALLY (1989)

The Lisbon Traviata has been called "pivotal" in MCNALLY's "transformation into a mature and contemplative theatrical voice" in that it is the first of his full-length plays to deal with "complex relationships among . . . fully-developed characters who are . . . desperate, damaged people" (Zinman xiii). The play was initially done in a noncommercial showcase presentation in June 1985 at New York's Theatre Off Park. In the summer of 1989, after the success of McNally's FRANKIE AND JOHNNY IN THE CLAIR DE LUNE (1987), it received its first commercial production at the Manhattan Theatre Club and was moved to another New York theater in the fall. McNally revised the play each time and did so again when it was released for production around the country.

The first act takes place in the "warm, romantic" West Village (New York) apartment of Mendy, a flamboyant, lonely, middle-aged gay man, whose huge collection of opera cassettes, phonograph records, and reel-to-reel tapes are "strewn all over the place." His friend Stephen, also gay, who is younger than Mendy and works in publishing, is visiting; the two share an encyclopedic knowledge and love of opera—conversing in lines from operas and debating the relative merits of singers and recordings, each knowing who recorded which opera when. They also share what can only be described as an obsession with the late Greek soprano Maria Callas. Mendy becomes frantic when Stephen tells him that he owns a recording Mendy didn't even know existed—of Callas singing Verdi's opera La Traviata in Lisbon, Portugal, in March 1958.

After first trying unsuccessfully—and hilariously—to order it at a local record store, Mendy suggests that they go to Stephen's apartment to listen to it, but Stephen tells him that he has a date later that evening. Then Mendy asks if he can go over to Stephen's apartment and get it himself; Stephen says that Mike, a doctor who has been his partner for the last eight years, is there entertaining a friend. Mike and Stephen's relationship is apparently at a moment of crisis: Although Stephen insists they have "an agreement about this sort of thing," he is obviously upset that Mike is with another man. Mendy calls Mike to ask if he can stop by to pick up the recording, and when Mike refuses, explaining that he and his friend Paul are going out to a movie, Mendy explodes in anger at him, exclaiming, "[A]t this particular moment in my not-so-terrific life," listening to the Lisbon *Traviata* "is probably the most goddamn important thing in the world to me." When Stephen gets on the phone to explain Mendy's outburst, he and Mike chat amiably about their respective plans for the evening; Stephen assures his partner that, as soon as his evening is arranged, he will call and let him know whether he will be coming home—so that Paul can stay overnight.

At that point, Stephen's friend calls and breaks their date; almost simultaneously, Mike appears with the recording for Mendy. It's clear that he is anxious to know whether or not he and Paul will have the apartment to themselves; Stephen says he will call and leave a message as soon as his plans are finalized. As soon as Mike leaves, Stephen calls their machine: "My date just called. We're on. Have fun. We sure plan to." Mendy is exasperated to discover that Mike, who doesn't like opera and knows little about it, has brought the wrong recording, but he convinces Stephen to let him make up a bed for him, and they settle down to listen to the PBS documentary on Callas.

As act 2 begins, Stephen is returning early in the morning to his and Mike's apartment, which is "lean and modern," with all the tapes and recordings "alphabetically arranged." Clearly, Mike and Paul are not prepared for his arrival; Stephen cannot resist taunting Mike about Paul, especially when Mike concedes, "I really like him." Similarly, Stephen baits Paul about his lowbrow taste in music, shows Paul pornographic Polaroid pictures he and Mike took of each other during their first year together, and turns the opera music up to full volume. Mike cannot contain himself and punches Stephen twice, drawing blood the second time; this fracas causes Paul to flee, bumping into Mendy as he opens the door. Mendy has come to return the recording but beats a hasty retreat when he sees that he's come at "a bad time."

Mike tends to Stephen's wounds and apologizes but at the same time tells him that Paul wants to live with him. When Stephen asks if he is in love with Paul, Mike responds that he's not sure but that he is certain that "[t]his arrangement isn't working for either" him

or Stephen. As Mike begins to collect his things to go stay with his brother for a while, Stephen becomes increasingly agitated, putting the Lisbon *Traviata* on the record player and confessing that, with the threat of AIDS, he feels safer alone listening to Callas—to which Mike replies, "You live in some opera no one's ever heard of. It's hard loving someone like that." Crying out, "It's hard loving someone like me!," Stephen picks up a pair of scissors and blocks Mike from leaving; when Mike takes off the ring Stephen gave him and throws it down, Stephen kills him. The phone rings and Mendy leaves a message that a friend has just brought over a copy of the Lisbon *Traviata* and "it's to die."

The changes McNally made in the play primarily had to do with the ending. In both the 1985 version and the first 1989 production at the Manhattan Theatre Club, Stephen killed Mike; but in the second 1989 New York production and in the text published in *Three Plays by Terrence McNally* (1990), Stephen threatened Mike but let him leave unharmed. In the text released around the country thereafter and currently available in the acting edition, he returned to the more violent ending. Neither ending pleased critics, who were troubled by what they perceived to be a disjunction and incompatibility between the witty repartee of the first act and the much darker domestic drama of the second act. Acknowledging that "[i]t is clearly not a well-made play in which the first act prepares us for everything that happens in the second," McNally has observed, "Yesterday did not prepare me for what happened today. Life is a lousy playwright that way" (*Three Plays* xii).

Actually, a good deal of what happens in Stephen's apartment is foreshadowed in act 1 (one of many examples is Mendy's offhand assessment of Stephen—"Have it your way. You usually do," which becomes Mike's much more consequential "I'm tired of being told what opera to like, what book to read, what movie to go to" in act 2). And while the very end is perhaps a bit too imitative of the last scene of Bizet's opera *Carmen* (even some lines are identical), Stephen and Mendy, as act 1 makes obvious, are men who live their lives at the highly emotional and melodramatic pitch of opera (as Mendy says, "Opera doesn't reject me. The real world does."). If act 1 shows us the comic results and possibilities of that type of existence, act 2 shows us the tragic consequences of it. Another way of putting this is that Stephen operates far more successfully in the isolated, protected, and safe world of opera that he and Mendy share, but when he moves into Mike and Paul's real world, he cannot adjust and must cling to his operatic view of life rather than deal with reality. Like TENNESSEE WILLIAMS's Blanche DuBois in *A STREETCAR NAMED DESIRE* (1947), he might well say "I don't want realism. . . . I want magic!"

BIBLIOGRAPHY

McNally, Terrence. *Three Plays by Terrence McNally: "The Lisbon Traviata," "Frankie and Johnny in the Clair de Lune," "It's Only a Play."* New York: Plume, 1990.
Zinman, Toby Silverman, ed. *Terrence McNally: A Casebook.* New York: Garland, 1997.

LITTLE FOXES, THE LILLIAN HELLMAN (1939)

Set in a small town in the South just 35 years after the Civil War, *The Little Foxes* portrays the Hubbard family, whose ruthlessness puts them in the category of "people who eat the earth" while the rest of the world stands by and watches.

As the play begins, the Hubbards are entertaining Mr. Marshall from Chicago, with whom they hope to form a partnership and build a lucrative cotton mill. Before the Civil War, the Hubbards were a family of tradesmen; Ben, the eldest, now 55, was 20 when the war ended. He has always resented the southern aristocracy and gleefully tells Marshall that it is the Hubbards' class that has inherited the South: "Twenty years ago, we took over their land, their cotton, and their daughter." The "daughter" he refers to is his younger brother Oscar's unhappy wife, Birdie, whom Oscar married—on behalf of the family—for purely mercenary reasons. The family is rich now, but moderately so. The youngest Hubbard is Regina Hubbard Giddens, an attractive woman of 40, who is giddy at the prospect of wealth on a scale that will enable her to live extravagantly in Chicago and Europe. Her share of the investment, however, must come from her estranged husband, Horace, whom she turned from her bed 10 years earlier. Horace can well afford it but is at present gravely ill and hospitalized in Baltimore, where he has been for five months. Regina convinces her brothers that Horace

is holding out for a larger share of the profits before he transfers any money to them; Ben, whose shrewdness is equaled only by Regina's, understands that Regina is the one who is holding out. Amused, he promises her a larger share, to be deducted from Oscar's. In order to placate the outraged Oscar, Ben suggests that Leo, Oscar's son, and Zan, Regina's daughter, marry; this will ensure that all of the money remains in the family. While Zan is a lovely, kind young woman, Leo is as despicable (dishonest with people, brutal to animals) as his father and uncle, but he is without even their superficial charm. Birdie, who favors Zan over her own son, warns her of this plan and begs her to reject such an offer. When Oscar overhears his wife, he strikes her— probably not for the first time.

When Horace returns from Baltimore—still seriously ill—he declines to invest in the mill because he does not respect the Hubbards' business practices, "their dirty tricks to make a dime." Now that he is dying and has had five months to think back on his life, he does not want to participate in anything that will "mak[e] the world any worse." Without Horace's investment, the Hubbard brothers would need to go outside the family, but the unethical Leo, who works at the bank, has looked in Horace's safe deposit box. When he reveals to his father that there are enough bonds there to cover their needs, they hatch a plan to take the bonds and return them before Horace makes his biannual visit to his box. But two weeks later, in sorting out his affairs, Horace discovers the theft and guesses the truth. He tells Regina that he will change his will in order to protect Zan from her and from her brothers and nephew. Everything will go to Zan, except the preinvestment value of the stolen bonds, which will be the extent of the greedy Regina's inheritance; he will take the position that he loaned the bonds to Ben, preferring to shortchange Regina even if it means making his brothers-in-law richer. During the ensuing argument, he has an attack and, dropping his bottle of medicine, asks for Regina's help. She ignores him, and he dies. Regina and her brothers then continue—unstopped—to "eat the earth," but Zan, washing her hands of her mother, decides she is "not going to stand around and watch them do it."

LILLIAN HELLMAN was disappointed in the frequent reception of Regina and her brothers as simple villains in a melodrama: She wrote, "I had meant the audience to recognize some part of themselves in the money-dominated Hubbards; I had not meant people to think of them as villains to whom they had no connection" (180). Hellman would write more of the Hubbards' story in *Another Part of the Forest* (1946), set 20 years before *The Little Foxes,* in which Ben Hubbard blackmails his unscrupulous father and young Regina transfers her allegiance from her father to Ben just as soon as she realizes there has been a transfer of power. There was to have been a third play, set in "1920 or 1925, [with Regina] in Europe" and Zan "maybe a spinsterish social worker, disappointed, a rather angry woman," but Hellman never wrote it because, as she admitted to an interviewer in 1964, "I'm tired of the people in *The Little Foxes*" (Bryer 56). *The Little Foxes* was commercially successful as well as critically acclaimed, winning the New York Drama Critics' Circle Award. The opera *Regina* (1949), by Marc Blitzstein, is based on Hellman's play.

BIBLIOGRAPHY

Bryer, Jackson R., ed. *Conversations with Lillian Hellman.*
   Jackson: University Press of Mississippi, 1986.
Hellman, Lillian. *Pentimento.* Boston: Little, Brown, 1973.

LITTLE MURDERS Jules Feiffer (1967)

Set on the Upper West Side of New York City, *Little Murders* is an absurdist drama depicting urban life (characterized by more than 300 unsolved murders, obscene phone callers, and a family's indifference to it all) in the 1960s.

Patsy Newquist brings Alfred home to meet her family and to announce their engagement. Although Carol, Patsy's father, is mortified by his daughter's plan to marry this photographer, who readily admits that he allows unprovoked attackers to beat him up while he merely hums, there is nothing that can stop Patsy's desire. Intermittent power failures and periodic phone calls from a heavy breather contribute to the play's offbeat tone, as does Patsy's younger brother Kenny, who incessantly wanders offstage and back onstage, often preceded by the flush of a toilet, carrying such books as *Harlots of Venus*. The sound of gunshots is a source of curiosity for the characters, and Feiffer reveals that Carol and his wife Marjorie have lost their oldest child in the rash of murders that plague the city.

After the wedding is announced, Feiffer carefully constructs the remainder of the play around three monologues that show the lack of effectiveness traditional institutions have in these characters' lives. The first is given by a judge whom Carol has commissioned to convince Patsy and Alfred to allow God's name to be used in their wedding. The judge, however, simply offends Patsy and Alfred by dismissing their generation as one that does not respect authority. The second monologue is given by Reverend Dupas of the First Existential Church, whose sign reads, "Christ died for our sins. Dare we make his martyrdom meaningless by not committing them?" Dupas's speech offends virtually everyone present at the wedding with its mockery of the ceremony and leads to a riot, effectively creating chaos within the Newquist household equal to that going on outside of it, where the murders continue. Lieutenant Practice gives the final monologue, in which he defends the fact that his police department has been unable to solve 345 murders in the city, one of which now includes Patsy (killed by a random gunshot on her wedding day). After Practice's speech, Kenny produces a rifle, and Carol and Alfred join him in taking turns shooting out the window at innocent victims; they laugh and congratulate each other on their kills, the last of which is Lieutenant Practice. Marjorie, while serving refreshments, ends the play happily proclaiming, "It's so nice to have my family laughing again. You know, for a while I was really worried."

Little Murders exemplifies Philip Roth's claim that the contemporary writer is virtually defenseless against reality, which has contributed to the absurdity of much postmodern writing. Feiffer, perhaps most renowned as a cartoonist, certainly is practiced at creating exaggerated characters and scenarios, both of which are present in this play. Although the playwright creates the kind of caricatures that lead to easy satire, his play remains effective in its criticism of contemporary society, as America remains a country confronted with daily acts of violence that are dismissed routinely as "little murders."

Christopher Brooks Bell
Georgia Military College

LITTLE THEATER MOVEMENT   The rise of the "little theater" movement was a reaction to the traditional practices of the American stage prior to 1910. Although the smallest towns had theater buildings and vaudeville houses in which well-worn plays and players kept up a lively brand of theatrical entertainment, new works came out of New York's theaters. Little theaters were a first important step toward moving the American theater away from the exclusivity of the New York stage. In most cases, little theaters made it their mission vigorously to encourage new playwrights, designers experimenting with innovative staging and scenic techniques, and actors and directors testing new theories of their art. What emerged was a community-based theater responsive to the needs and interests of the audience within its immediate region. By the mid-20th century, most of the smaller, largely amateur little theaters, in their purest sense, were gone, but in their place—and very much indebted to their forebears—sprang up professional regional theaters, usually operating a repertory system.

Eighteenth- and 19th-century America's vital, but largely superficial, plays slowly gave way to a more serious drama as the little theater movement emerged, producing a generation of dramatists, actors, and designers who would lead American theater into the middle of the 20th century. Little theaters produced writers at all levels of achievement, including EUGENE O'NEILL, America's first internationally significant dramatist, and SUSAN GLASPELL, an early feminist playwright, as well as a generation of young actors. Critics and scholars recognized the importance of the little theater movement from its very beginning, debating and analyzing ways in which the various theaters defined their missions. Typically, a little theater sought either to elevate the art form or to create a drama attuned to matters of social, political, and moral import, sometimes both.

The true beginnings of this movement, which flourished in the years just prior to World War I and into the 1920s, are difficult to pinpoint, as its roots reach back to the beginnings of theater in North America. To some extent, the little theater movement grew out of the 19th-century tradition of local dramatic societies and drawing room theatrical and literary entertainments. However, something new was introduced in the early 1910s as little theaters were established by a new generation of intellectuals, writers, and artists, many of whom were amateurs in theatrical work but on the cutting edge of new ideas drawn from Sigmund Freud, Friedrich Nietzsche, Charles Darwin, and Henrik Ibsen, among others. These stages provided an opportunity not only to experiment with technique and try out new plays with little financial risk but also to offer a platform for cultural debate, an element missing from much pre-1910 American drama.

Several elements conjoined at the beginning of the 20th century to inspire this sudden expansion of theaters largely run by a mix of amateurs and theater professionals, who stressed the new forms and concepts emerging from the art theaters of Europe since the 1880s. Social reformers Jane Addams and Laura Dainty Pelham established the Hull House Players in Chicago in 1900 on the principle that good amateur theater could provide a positive influence in a community. Their idea did not catch on immediately, but following the triumphant American tour of the Irish Players (a troupe that functioned as many little theaters would) led by Lady Gregory in 1911 and a clarion call from playwright and critic PERCY MACKAYE for the encouragement of "constructive leisure," the movement began. MacKaye called for a stage divorced from commercialism in his books *The Playhouse and the Play* (1909) and *The Civic Theatre* (1912), at the time a novel notion, but one that many artists recognized as necessary. The founding of the Drama League in 1909 and the creation of GEORGE PIERCE BAKER's "47 Workshop" at Harvard University, which gave academic legitimacy to the making of theater, were significant first responses to MacKaye's challenge. At the same time, the influence of such European stage reformers as Edward Gordon Craig and Adolphe Appia and several books and essays on the evolution of the modern theater in Europe fueled an enthusiasm for "art" theaters aimed at elevating the quality and purpose of theater in the United States. Other diverse influences encouraged the rise of little theaters: *Theatre Arts* magazine began publication in 1916 (continuing into the 1960s) and gave considerable coverage to the rise of little theaters; and designer Sam Hume, who had studied for a time with Edward Gordon Craig at Craig's short-lived theater school in Florence, Italy, presented a New York exhibition on the new European movements in theatrical practice, causing a minor sensation among American theatrical artists, inspiring little theater workers. Craig himself published widely on the art of the stage in numerous books and in his periodical, *The Mask,* which he published from 1908 to 1929, articulating many of the concepts inherent in what is often referred to as the "New Stagecraft," which featured techniques explored by many little theaters.

Each little theater identified its own particular mission, often creating a manifesto spelling out its goals. Many experimented with new stage techniques, exploring the nonrealistic scenic and lighting practices that Craig, Appia, and other European reformers proposed, despite the fact that the typical little theater had fewer than 100 seats and usually a small stage with a proscenium opening of less than 20 feet. Some little theaters chose to focus on promoting the works of new and promising young American writers. Others presented the plays of the modernist European stage, performing dramas by Henrik Ibsen, George Bernard Shaw, August Strindberg, and other iconoclasts. Most importantly, the small size of these theaters and the amateur status of most of the personnel involved meant small budgets, which made it easier for the little theaters to take a chance with a play or director whose work was untried. Removing the financial risk encouraged the vital experimentation evident in the work of most little theaters.

In 1909, the establishment of The Players in Providence, Rhode Island, followed in 1911 by Thomas H. Dickinson's Wisconsin Dramatic Society in Madison and Milwaukee, seemed to start a chain reaction, leading to the founding of similar organizations in a number of locations: The Boston Toy Theatre, founded by Mrs. Lyman Gale in 1912; the Little Country Theatre in Fargo, North Dakota, led by Alfred Arvold in 1912; and Maurice Browne's Chicago Little Theatre in 1912 led the way for many others. The influence on young writers was profound—in Chicago, several little theater groups presented plays by BEN HECHT, who went on to a long and prolific writing career that produced

such popular plays as *The FRONT PAGE* (written in collaboration with CHARLES MACARTHUR) and many classic screenplays, and Kenneth Sawyer Goodman, whose death in the influenza epidemic of 1918 ended a promising playwriting career. In the years just prior to America's entry into World War I, the appearance of more little theaters underscored the need for stages of experimentation. In 1915, the Little Theatre of Indianapolis was founded by Samuel Eliot, followed by the 1916 establishment of the Arts and Crafts Theatre in Detroit, led by Sam Hume, Craig's former disciple. That same year, the Cleveland Play House was founded by Frederick McConnell, and many other little theaters appeared before United States involvement in World War I slightly hampered operation of some of the theaters. In terms of influence on the development of drama in America, no little theater became as influential as the PROVINCETOWN PLAYERS, founded on Cape Cod in 1915, and the WASHINGTON SQUARE PLAYERS, established in New York City the following year. Eugene O'Neill produced his earliest plays with the Provincetown Players, as did Susan Glaspell and other dramatists of less significance, and such prominent theater technicians as ROBERT EDMOND JONES worked there. There is little doubt that if Eugene O'Neill, arguably America's greatest playwright, had attempted to produce his earliest experimental one-act plays on a Broadway stage, he would have failed. Instead, by working with a little theater, he was able to learn his craft through trial and error, without risking vast sums of money and therefore without risking the theater's survival.

As O'Neill rose to prominence on the international stage at the end of World War I, other little theaters continued the tradition that had helped to develop him, although no other dramatist of O'Neill's stature (or, for that matter, Glaspell's) would emerge from the movement. Among the more important little theaters emerging after World War I were the Pasadena Playhouse, established in 1918 by Gilmore Brown; Le Petit Théâtre du Vieux Carré, which opened in 1919 in New Orleans; Theatre Memphis, which opened its doors in 1920; the Dallas Little Theatre, set up in 1920 by Oliver Hinsdell; and the Omaha Community Playhouse, founded in 1925, which produced a remarkable number of successful actors (most of whom quickly turned their attentions to Broadway and Hollywood), including Henry Fonda, Dorothy McGuire, and Margaret Sullavan. Despite the obvious success of many little theaters, some had doubts about the value and quality of the work being done in these largely amateur theaters, doubts that were amusingly satirized in GEORGE E. KELLY's popular comedy *The Torch-Bearers* (1922).

A number of these theaters maintained their little theater status for decades, while others evolved into larger scale regional and repertory theaters as that movement took hold in the late 1950s. As the 21st century advances, the vigor of these regional and repertory theaters acknowledges the significance of the little theater movement both in encouraging experimentation and in creating theaters of merit in virtually every major city in the United States.

BIBLIOGRAPHY

Chansky, Dorothy. *"Composing Ourselves": The Little Theatre Movement and the American Audience.* Carbondale: Southern Illinois University Press, 2004.

Cheney, Sheldon. *The Art Theatre.* New York: Knopf, 1917.

Crowley, Alice Lewisohn. *The Neighborhood Playhouse: Leaves from a Theatre Scrapbook.* New York: Theatre Arts Books, 1959.

Dickinson, Thomas H. *The Insurgent Theatre.* 1917. North Stratford, N.H.: Ayer, 1972.

Houghton, Norris. *Advance from Broadway: 19,000 Miles of American Theatre.* New York: Harcourt, Brace, 1941.

Koenig, Linda Lee. *Vagabonds: America's Oldest Little Theatre.* Madison, N.J.: Fairleigh Dickinson University Press, 1983.

Macgowan, Kenneth. *Footlights across America: Towards a National Theater.* 1929. New York: Kraus, 1969.

Mackay, Constance D'Arcy. *The Little Theatre in the United States.* New York: Henry Holt, 1917.

MacKaye, Percy. *The Civic Theatre.* New York: Kennerley, 1912.

Poggi, Jack. *Theater in America: The Impact of Economic Forces, 1870–1967.* Ithaca, N.Y.: Cornell University Press, 1968.

Taylor, Karen Malpede. *People's Theatre in Amerika.* New York: Drama Books, 1973.

Wainscott, Ronald. *The Emergence of the Modern American Theater, 1914–1929.* New Haven, Conn.: Yale University Press, 1997.

James Fisher
University of North Carolina at Greensboro

LIVING NEWSPAPERS　By the time the "living newspaper" production style was introduced in the United States as part of the Works Progress Administration's (WPA) FEDERAL THEATRE PROJECT (FTP), the form had already run its course in Europe, where it had been particularly popular for a short period in Germany and Russia.

Under the supervision of HALLIE FLANAGAN, the FTP was formed to put unemployed theater artists—actors, writers, and technicians—back to work in much the same way that other areas of the WPA sought useful employment for blue-collar workers. The FTP was national in scope, with offices in more than 30 states and myriad producing units, including vaudeville, Yiddish theater, theater for the blind, puppet theater, classical repertory, experimental theater, "Negro" theater, and the "living newspaper."

The Living Newspaper Unit was formed in 1935 when Flanagan suggested to ELMER RICE that they "could dramatize the news without expensive scenery—just living actors, light, music, movement" (Flanagan 65). It was agreed that the living newspaper would be a vehicle to reemploy a large number of people at a fairly low cost; their job would be to produce socially relevant material in a timely manner. Rice enthusiastically agreed, took control of the Living Newspaper Unit, and announced that the first production was to be *Ethiopia* (1935–36), a look at the recent invasion of that country. The production was virtually ready for performance when government officials, fearful of offending Italian dictator Benito Mussolini, ordered that no real persons could be quoted or represented on the stage without prior approval of the State Department. Although Flanagan thought the request was not out of line, Rice objected to this intrusion into his artistic vision, held a public dress rehearsal of the uncut play, and then cancelled its performance rather than submit to censorship.

The FTP presented nine living newspapers: *The Living Newspaper* (1936), written by a staff of writers and produced in Cleveland; *Triple-A Plowed Under* (1936), credited to the Living Newspaper Staff and presented in New York and four other cities (a "history" of the plight of America's farmers from pre–World War I through the creation in 1934 of the Agricultural

Adjustment Administration—the "Triple-A" of the title—and the consequent losses for small farmers); *Highlights of 1935* (1936), credited to the Living Newspaper Staff and produced in New York (an essentially plotless overview of major events of 1935, including scenes dealing with Bruno Hauptmann, Dutch Schultz, John L. Lewis, Huey Long, Barbara Hutton, and Nazi Germany); *Living Newspaper, First Edition* (1936) and *Living Newspaper, Second Edition* (1936), both written by Cleveland Bronner and presented in Norwalk, Connecticut; *Injunction Granted* (1936), credited to the Living Newspaper Staff and produced in New York (a sweeping "historical" survey of labor movements and strife in the United States); *Power* (1937), written by Arthur Arent and produced in New York and four other cities (a look at the commercialization of electrical power in the United States and a call for support of the TVA and similar programs); *One-Third of a Nation* (1938), written by Arthur Arent and produced in New York and nine other cities (using Franklin Delano Roosevelt's second inaugural speech—"one-third of a nation is ill-housed, ill-clad, and ill-nourished"—as its basis, the play presents another historical survey of housing conditions in New York from colonial times to the present; when produced in other cities, statistics and examples from that locale were interpolated into the text); and *Spirochete* (1938), written by Arnold Sundgaard and produced in Chicago and four other cities (a look at the history of the spread of syphilis, how it affected the people, and how medical research was finding ways to prevent and cure it).

The living newspaper varied in form and content but always focused on current issues and events, sometimes using a sweeping historical approach to an issue (as in *Injunction Granted*) and sometimes a more time-delineated approach (as in *Highlights of 1935*). The best of the living newspapers used a central character that represented the common people ("Mr. Average Consumer" in *Power* or "Little Man" in *One-Third of a Nation*) who is guided through a series of vignettes designed to give him (and the audience) the "facts" surrounding the issue at hand. The texts of the plays, often written by groups of writers, used government statistics, newspaper headlines and stories, anecdotal evidence, and fictive characters and events to educate, entertain, and inspire action. The living newspapers were written in an epic style, contained many short, noncausally related scenes, and used live action, projected scenery, and film clips to follow the central character through his journey to enlightenment.

BIBLIOGRAPHY
Arent, Arthur. *One-Third of a Nation.* Brooklyn, N.Y.: Program for Multimedia Studies in American Drama, Humanities Institute, Brooklyn College, 1984.
———, Vera Jiji, and Mark Mannucci. *One-Third of a Nation: A Living Newspaper.* Princeton, N.J.: Films for the Humanities, 1984.
Buttitta, Tony, and Barry Witham. *Uncle Sam Presents: A Memoir of the Federal Theatre, 1935–1939.* Philadelphia: University of Pennsylvania Press, 1982.
de Rohan, Pierre, ed. *Federal Theatre Plays.* New York: Da Capo, 1973.
Flanagan, Hallie. *Arena: The History of the Federal Theatre.* New York: Duell, Sloan and Pearce, 1940.
Fraden, Rena. *Blueprints for a Black Federal Theatre, 1935–1939.* Cambridge, Eng.: Cambridge University Press, 1994.
O'Connor, John, and Lorraine Brown, eds. *Free, Adult, Uncensored: The Living History of the Federal Theatre Project.* Washington: New Republic Books, 1978.

Timothy D. Connors
Central Michigan University

LIVING THEATRE, THE   Founded in 1947 by Julian Beck and Judith Malina, the Living Theatre started inauspiciously in the Becks' living room, seating not more than 20 spectators. In these early years, the company produced experimental work by Paul Goodman, GERTRUDE STEIN, Bertolt Brecht, and Federico García Lorca. As a literary theater specializing in modern verse drama, they mainly appealed to a select group of New York literati. From the beginning, the company defined itself in opposition to Broadway, opting to become a repertory theater where actors could collaborate closely for extended periods on a limited number of plays. Free from state interference and surviving on little money in the margins of the commercial circuit in New York, they set an example for other OFF-BROADWAY companies.

From 1951 to 1964, the company looked for bigger audiences, establishing themselves in three successive

New York locations. Each site led to evictions because of failures to comply with fire and safety regulations or to pay tax arrears. Because these laws unfairly targeted small, noncommercial companies, the Becks contested them as insidious forms of censorship. The Living Theatre took its protest against an oppressive establishment into the street, at the height of the cold war, organizing three successive general strikes and urging citizens not to comply with mandatory civil defense drills. Thus was formed a tradition of activism and civil disobedience that would cost the company fines, beatings, and jail terms but that would guarantee its visibility in the years to come.

In the 1950s and early 1960s, the Living Theatre mounted a challenging and diverse repertoire that included T. S. Eliot's *Sweeney Agonistes,* Kenneth Rexroth's *Beyond the Mountains,* Pablo Picasso's *Desire Trapped by the Tail,* W. H. Auden's *The Age of Anxiety,* and William Carlos Williams's *Many Loves.* In 1958, they scored their first critical success with JACK GELBER's *The CONNECTION,* a jazz play about heroin addicts waiting for their fix, reminiscent of Samuel Beckett's *Waiting for Godot.* With this play, the company made its European debut in 1961, receiving the Paris Theatre Critics' Circle Award for best acting and the Grand Prix of the Théâtre des Nations at the international theater festival in Paris. In 1963, the Living Theatre produced its landmark production of Kenneth Brown's *The BRIG,* a nightmarish depiction of the debasement of military prisoners. The Becks turned this play into a harrowing visual and auditory spectacle, having recognized in Antonin Artaud's concept of a "theatre of cruelty" their own vision of a theater that would pierce through layers of cliché and conditioning to alter radically the perceptions of actors and spectators.

Evicted from their last theater and pursued by creditors, the company toured Europe between 1964 and 1968. As a collective heeding Artaud's advice to end the theater's enslavement to text, they experimented with collaborative creation, improvisation, and audience participation. This resulted in a series of original performance pieces inspired by the company's protest against the Vietnam War: *Mysteries and Smaller Pieces* (1964), *Frankenstein* (1965), and *Paradise Now* (1968). *Paradise Now* included a scene in which the audience was invited to join a pile of writhing and groping actors in various states of undress that ended with a march out of the theater into the streets in search of paradise. All too often, however, actors and enthusiastic spectators found not paradise but the police with charges of public indecency.

After 1968, the Living Theatre was slowly left behind by new political and artistic developments. In France, the "Happenings" staged by the Living Theatre had almost naturally merged with *les évènements,* the 1968 student rebellion in Paris. Back in the United States, the Living Theatre found itself surpassed by other radical companies, such as Richard Schechner's "guerrilla theater" (political, avant-garde, street theater) and Peter Schuman's Bread and Puppet Theatre. To many who, after the assassination of Martin Luther King Jr., sympathized with the violent militancy of Black Panthers and Weathermen, the Living Theatre's blend of pacifism and anarchism sounded increasingly naive. In 1969, internal dissension caused the Living Theatre to split into a number of "action cells," each with a distinct political philosophy.

By 1970, the Living Theatre had played out its role as an innovator. Once more, though, they would hold the world's attention when the Becks' action cell was imprisoned for two months during its Brazilian tour, where it had presented its ever-expanding cycle of plays on the nature of violence, *The Legacy of Cain.* In the 1980s, they returned to the theater with a string of original works, including *Prometheus at the Winter Palace* and *The Archaeology of Sleep.*

Julian Beck died in 1985. From then until 2005, the company was led by Judith Malina and Hanon Reznikov, a longtime member of the group who became Malina's husband. After the theater's premises on Third Street in Manhattan were closed by the Buildings Department in 1993, the company continued to tour in the United States and Europe. Since Reznikov's death in 2005, Malina has continued to direct productions in the company's current performance space on Clinton Street in New York.

BIBLIOGRAPHY
Beck, Julian. *The Life of the Theatre: The Relation of the Artist to the Struggle of the People.* San Francisco: City Lights, 1972.

————, and Judith Malina. *Paradise Now: Collective Creation of the Living Theatre.* New York: Random House, 1971.

Biner, Pierre. *The Living Theatre.* New York: Horizon Press, 1972.

Malina, Judith. *The Diaries of Judith Malina: 1947–1957.* New York: Grove Press, 1984.

————. *The Enormous Despair: Diaries 1968–1969.* New York: Random House, 1972.

Rostagno, Aldo, and Gianfranco Mantegna. *We The Living Theatre.* New York: Ballantine, 1969.

Silvestro, Carlo. *The Living Book of The Living Theatre.* New York: Greenwich Art Press, 1971.

Tytell, John. *The Living Theatre: Art, Exile, and Outrage.* New York: Grove Press, 1995.

Luc Gilleman
Smith College

LONERGAN, KENNETH (1962–)

Kenneth Lonergan was born in the Bronx but grew up in Manhattan, the child of privileged upper-class parents. He started writing plays while in college; one of these, *The Children,* won the first Young Playwrights Festival Award in 1982. After college, he graduated from New York University's Playwriting Program.

Lonergan's dramas are character driven, and these characters are full of ambiguities, imperfections, humor, loneliness, warmth, and rage. He has freely admitted that his plays contain autobiographical elements. His characters are pressured from without and within as they deal with emotional tensions imposed on them by an element of the plot. Lonergan's focus is on the characters' personalities. The plays are naturalistic and the style is conversational. This naturalistic style is especially apparent in Lonergan's use of overlapping dialogue between characters. His plays frequently have a "loser" character, someone struggling in a seemingly hopeless situation. Yet, he draws this character in such a way that the audience cares about him or her. His characters struggle with situations bigger than they are and that are not always resolvable by the end of the play.

His first major play, *This Is Our Youth* (1996), is built around the small crises in the lives of three young people, Warren, Jessica, and Dennis. A tale of overgrown slackers and stoners, it is a character study of aimless young Manhattanites and their amoral, self-abrasive, patternless lives. Lonergan follows these children of the privileged elite as they deal in drugs, scam their uninterested parents, and re-create their broken homes in dysfunctional friendships.

The Waverly Gallery (2000) portrays the decline of a partly deaf octogenarian, Gladys Green, as she slides into the incoherence of Alzheimer's disease. Lonergan has acknowledged the strong autobiographical slant of this play. His grandmother owned an art gallery in Greenwich Village and developed dementia in the final years before her death. The drama is a memory play, like TENNESSEE WILLIAMS's *The GLASS MENAGERIE* (1945), in that it has a narrator who frames the evening's scenes with lyrical retrospective monologues; yet, it is also a play about memory and how it fails us. The other family members—Gladys's daughter Ellen, Ellen's husband, and Gladys's grandson Daniel—demonstrate the harmful effects of stress on memory as they "disremember" events. Critics commented that, in this play, Lonergan is not simply writing a play about Alzheimer's but is more interested in the fact that we recognize that it will happen not only to those we love but also to ourselves. Lonergan uses his signature stylistic device of overlapping dialogue as a way of capturing the startling language patterns of senility, as other characters' conversations are carried around and over the mumbled soliloquies of Gladys.

Lobby Hero (2001) charts the bruising relationships of two New York City police officers and two uniformed doormen as they experience the corrosive effects of sexual jealousy, police corruption, racial defensiveness, and a clumsy yearning for human contact. The plot concerns Dawn, the principal character, a female police officer trying to fit into a male-dominated world, and Jeff, the "lobby hero loser," or doorman, of the title. Their struggle to succeed and to connect with others, despite being judged by unfair standards, is a principal theme in the play. Critics remarked that this play had more melodramatic elements than Lonergan's early work.

Lonergan lives in New York City and is a member of New York's Naked Angels Theatre Company. Both a playwright and a screenwriter, he wrote and directed the 2001 film *You Can Count on Me,* about a brother and sister in crisis; the film won a number of prizes, including awards from the Los Angeles Film Critics, the Writers Guild, and the American Film Institute. Lonergan's film career continued with *Gangs of New York* (2002). He also wrote and directed the 2007 film *Margaret*, starring Anna Paquin, Matt Damon, Matthew Broderick, and Lonergan's wife, J. Smith-Cameron.

BIBLIOGRAPHY
Lonergan, Kenneth. *Lobby Hero.* New York: Grove Press, 2002.
———. *This Is Our Youth.* Woodstock, N.Y.: Overlook Press, 2000.
———. *The Waverly Gallery.* New York: Grove Press, 2000.
———. *You Can Count on Me: A Screenplay.* New York: Vintage Books, 2002.

Helen Huff
City University of New York—
Borough of Manhattan Community College

LONG CHRISTMAS DINNER, THE THORNTON WILDER (1930)

The setting of this poignant one-act play is the dining room of the Bayard home on a series of Christmas Days starting in about 1850 and carrying through intermittently until about 1940. Each Christmas dinner flows into the next, the change in time marked by aging, death, and birth. WILDER's experimental technique, which strips away the realistic trappings of the traditional stage performance in favor of the greater truth of human life, later seen in his famous full-length play, *OUR TOWN* (1938), is in evidence here. The experience of all American families is telescoped into one act—the births of babies with their attendant hope, the expected deaths of the elderly and the unexpected deaths of the young, the estrangement of children from their parents, the expressions that are repeated one generation after another, the impact of war and business. The theme of this short play and of many other Wilder dramas is the preciousness of human existence, even the simplest and most mundane moments of it.

LONG DAY'S JOURNEY INTO NIGHT EUGENE O'NEILL (1956)

Brooks Atkinson, the respected theater critic of the *New York Times,* concluded his opening night review of *Long Day's Journey into Night* by asserting that the play "restores the drama to literature and the theatre to art" (November 8, 1956).

Twenty years later, Jack Kroll, in *Newsweek,* declared, "*Long Day's Journey into Night* is not just the greatest American play, it is the only really great American play" (February 9, 1976). While some might quarrel with the second half of Kroll's statement, most agree that the play, if not the greatest American play, is among the two or three best. It was completed in 1940, but debilitated by illness, depressed by World War II, and concerned that its autobiographical revelations might embarrass surviving family members, O'NEILL in 1945 gave the script to Bennett Cerf, his longtime publisher, with instructions that it not be published until 25 years after his death. In early 1956, less than three years after he died, his widow, Carlotta Monterey O'Neill, gave permission to Sweden's Royal Dramatic Theatre to produce the play, which they did in February, and to Yale University Press to publish it in the same month (Cerf refused to violate his agreement with O'Neill when he was offered the opportunity to publish the play); in November 1956, it opened on Broadway and won for O'Neill a posthumous fourth PULITZER PRIZE.

The play portrays a day in August 1912 in the life of the Tyrone family, closely modeled on O'Neill's own, and the events replicate circumstances that occurred in the playwright's life in the fall of 1912. It begins early in the morning as James Tyrone Sr., an actor, his wife, Mary, and their two sons, Edmund and James Jr. (Jamie), are emerging from breakfast. Everyone seems in good humor, though there are hints of trouble and discord. James Sr. is disturbed that Jamie seems unable to make his own way in the world; both parents are concerned about Edmund's health. The sons and their father all watch Mary very carefully for signs of nervousness and inability to sleep at night. Jamie chides his father for sending Edmund to a cheap doctor, claiming also that Mary's at-this-point unspecified "curse" began with the "cheap quack" James found to treat her when Edmund was born; James taunts Jamie for throwing his money away on "whores and whiskey." Fearing that Edmund has consumption, the illness she says killed her father, and resentful that she has to endure the constant suspicions of her family, Mary goes upstairs to take a nap, explaining that she could not sleep the night before because of the foghorn and James's snoring.

At midday, as Edmund and Jamie are sneaking a drink, Mary comes downstairs, her eyes *"brighter"* and *"a peculiar detachment in her voice and manner,"* confirming their fear that she has relapsed into her drug addiction. Alternately complaining about her husband's penny-pinching ways and defending him against his sons' accusations, Mary observes, "None of us can help the things life has done to us. They're done before you realize it, and once they're done they make you do other things until at last everything comes between you and what you'd like to be, and you've lost your true self forever." The family goes in to lunch, with James distressed and angry about his wife's relapse.

After lunch, there is a telephone call from the doctor, who wants to see Edmund later that afternoon, which causes Mary to go upstairs "to fix [her] hair" and "find [her] glasses" (which she looks for throughout the play but never finds, a symbol, according to Travis Bogard, of her inability to "see what she is" [434]). After Edmund leaves to comfort his mother, James tells Jamie that his brother does indeed have consumption and will have to be sent to a sanitorium; Jamie, who urges his father not to put Edmund in a "cheap dump," says he will go to the doctor with Edmund to keep him company. As all three leave the house, Mary, who has reminded her husband that when she married an actor, many of her convent friends dropped her (especially after James's former mistress sued him), and that they lost their son Eugene when Jamie deliberately exposed him to the measles he had contracted, is glad to be left alone. But then, she laments, "Mother of God, why do I feel so lonely?"

Early in the evening, with the foghorn sounds in the background, indicating that the fog (literal as well as symbolic) is rolling in, Mary and the maid Cathleen have just returned from the drugstore, where Cathleen has had some difficulty getting the pharmacist to fill Mary's prescription for rheumatism medicine. Avowing, "Only the past when you were happy is real," Mary tells Cathleen of her childhood dream of becoming a nun, of her happy days in the convent where she was a promising pianist, and about how all that ended when she met matinee idol James Tyrone and fell in love. But, after Cathleen leaves, Mary calls

herself "a sentimental fool" and tries to regain "the faith I lost" by praying to "the Blessed Virgin," only to admit that she's only "a lying dope fiend reciting words." When James and Edward return, Mary reminds her husband that he got drunk on their honeymoon and on many evenings thereafter, leaving her in "ugly hotel rooms" to wait for him, but then says she forgives him and wonders where her wedding gown is. As James leaves briefly, Edmund tries unsuccessfully to make his mother understand that he has consumption and must go to a sanitorium; when her husband returns, she breaks down, sobbing that Edmund is going to die and that it would have been better if he'd not been born and "wouldn't have had to know his mother was a dope fiend."

The play's final act takes place at midnight as Edmund and James wait for Jamie to come home, nervously listening to Mary moving around upstairs. James criticizes his son's taste in literature—Oscar Wilde, Emile Zola, Henrik Ibsen, Charles Baudelaire, Edgar Allan Poe, whom he calls "whoremongers and degenerates"—and recommends that he substitute Shakespeare for them. He also corrects Mary's account of her childhood and convent days, telling Edmund that her father became an alcoholic on champagne at 40 and that she was neither a very good pianist ("That was put in her head by the nuns flattering her.") nor a very promising nun ("She was never made to renounce the world."). When Edmund attacks his father for not giving Mary a real home and for his stinginess, revealing that he has discovered that he intends to send him to a state sanitorium, James responds by telling him of his childhood. When he was 10, his father deserted the family and he had to go to work in a machine shop for 50 cents a week to help support his mother and his three siblings, and it "was in those days I learned to be a miser." He also describes how he gave up a promising career as a classical actor to buy a play and act the same part year after year for "thirty-five to forty thousand dollars net profit a season."

His father's reminiscences cause Edmund to recount some of the "high spots" in his life, all of which have to do with being at sea, where "I became drunk with the beauty and singing rhythm of it, and for a moment I lost myself—actually lost my life." He concludes his memories with a declaration that, in many ways, is characteristic of many an O'Neill protagonist: "It was a great mistake, my being born a man; I would have been much more successful as a sea gull or a fish. As it is, I will always be a stranger who never feels at home, who does not really want and is not really wanted, who can never belong, who must always be a little in love with death!"

Jamie then stumbles in, exceedingly drunk, and vacillates between telling his brother, "I love your guts" and resentfully calling him "Mama's baby and Papa's pet"; he informs Edmund that he deliberately made a "bum" of him: "Never wanted you to succeed and make me look even worse by comparison." He ends by declaring, "I can't help hating your guts," but "I love you more than I hate you." As the three men sit in silence, they hear someone playing the piano in the parlor like *"an awkward schoolgirl"* and then Mary appears, her face *"a marble mask of girlish innocence"* and her hair braided in pigtails, dragging her wedding gown. She has regressed to her convent days and regrets losing "something I miss terribly," presumably her faith; she recalls going to Mother Elizabeth, who told her to leave the convent "for a year or two" and test her devotion to becoming a nun by living in the world. If she "still felt sure, [she] could come back to see her and [they] would talk it over again." But then, she remembers, "in the spring something happened to me. . . . I fell in love with James Tyrone and was so happy for a time."

In a June 1940 letter, just after he finished writing *Long Day's Journey into Night,* O'Neill called it "deeply tragic" and described the four Tyrones at the end of the play as still "trapped within each other by the past, each guilty and at the same time innocent, scorning, loving, pitying each other, understanding and yet not understanding at all, forgiving but still doomed never to be able to forget" (Bogard and Bryer 506–507). In his experimental plays of the 1920s and 1930s, such as *The Great God Brown* (1926) and *STRANGE INTERLUDE* (1928), O'Neill had often used theatrical devices such as masks and asides to reveal the hidden recesses of his characters' psyches; but in *Long Day's Journey,* one of his greatest achievements is that he exposes this complexity, ambivalence, and uncer-

tainty naturally and realistically through dialogue and character interaction. And by deliberately not assigning blame, O'Neill allows us to see each of the four Tyrones as tragic figures, simultaneously victims and victimizers, bound together, for better and for worse, by a love that literally prevents them from walking away from one another. Although their long day literally leads to darkness, in another sense, it leads the characters and the audience to considerable understanding, enlightenment, sympathy, and empathy. Different viewers and readers of the play will inevitably come to different conclusions about each character, but no one leaves it feeling unacquainted with these four fascinating human beings.

BIBLIOGRAPHY

Bloom, Harold, ed. *Modern Critical Interpretations: Eugene O'Neill's "Long Day's Journey into Night."* New York: Chelsea House, 1988.

Bogard, Travis. *Contour in Time: The Plays of Eugene O'Neill.* Rev. ed. New York: Oxford University Press, 1988.

———, and Jackson R. Bryer, eds. *Selected Letters of Eugene O'Neill.* New Haven, Conn.: Yale University Press, 1988.

Hindin, Michael. *"Long Day's Journey into Night": Native Eloquence.* Boston: G. K. Hall, 1990.

Murphy, Brenda. *O'Neill: "Long Day's Journey into Night."* Cambridge: Cambridge University Press, 2001.

LOOK HOMEWARD, ANGEL Ketti Frings (1957)

A "comedy-drama," this adaptation of a portion of Thomas Wolfe's massive novel of the same title won both the PULITZER PRIZE for drama and the New York Drama Critics' Circle Award. The play opened in late 1957 with sets and lighting by the legendary designer Jo Mielziner.

Set in Altamont, North Carolina, in 1916 at a deteriorating boardinghouse with a dubious reputation, the play spans three weeks in autumn during which 17-year-old Eugene Gant falls in love for the first time and must endure not only the end of this affair with a boarder but also the death of his brother, Ben, his *"hero protector."* The backdrop for Eugene's coming of age is the bitter marriage of his parents, the money-grubbing and nagging Eliza and the alcoholic, philandering, and abusive W. O. Gant, a stone carver who has never been able to realize his artistic dream of replicating the beauty of the "*lustrous white Carrara marble*" angel he keeps in his shop. The stone angel stands as a symbol of an artistic ideal in contrast to Eliza's obsession with money and property.

Early in the play we discover that Ben is disgusted with his mother for keeping Eugene from college, and, instead, confining him to the seedy Dixieland Boardinghouse, where she uses him—in too-small clothes and uncut hair—to drum up business at the train station. Ben, himself a 30-year-old newspaper writer, wants to escape into the Canadian army and World War I but is too frail and sickly to get a medical clearance. Though it is impossible for Ben to flee the toxic Gant household, he encourages his young brother to do so, telling Eugene to steal the money for college from their parents if necessary. Ben finds some solace in the company of his confidante, Mrs. Fatty Pert, a kind and barely respectable boarder, of whom Eliza disapproves.

Both of Eliza's sons, perhaps because they are deprived of a nurturing mother, find comfort in the arms of older women. Unlike Ben's public friendship with Mrs. Pert, Eugene's love affair with the 23-year-old—and, unbeknownst to him, engaged—Laura James develops in secret. Eugene, who is in love with trains and the distant places trains have seen, finds in Laura James a link to the world beyond the horizon. When Laura first appears at Dixieland, Eugene inundates her with questions about Richmond—its people and parks, its buildings and thoroughfares, its theaters and library. The longing he develops for her is inextricably linked to his longing to see the world. Eugene himself is not fully aware of this since he is willing by the end of the play to take a job in Altamont with his uncle in order to marry, as he eventually discovers, the unavailable Miss James.

Meanwhile, the conflict between the bitter senior Gants rages on—over money and property and each other's shortcomings. The death of Ben from pneumonia brings grief to both parents but no unity between them. Two weeks later Laura deserts Eugene to return to her fiancé, leaving him for his own good as well as her own. This experience and some money left to him by Ben give Eugene the push he needs finally to leave the troubled and destructive Gants behind to seek his own future, something his brother Ben was never able to do. In the play's brief epilogue, the spirit of the dead Ben returns to give Eugene his blessing and a message of self-reliance: "*You* are your world" is Ben's and the play's last line.

Eugene and Ben are somewhat reminiscent of the brothers Edmund and Jamie in EUGENE O'NEILL's *LONG DAY'S JOURNEY INTO NIGHT*. Both younger brothers, Eugene Gant and Edmund Tyrone, long for distant places; and their older brothers, Ben and Jamie—both wise to the worlds of women and alcohol—give advice and some protection; but while Jamie Tyrone by his own admission harbors some animosity toward the brother he loves, Ben Gant is wholly benevolent,

Look Homeward, Angel is based on the climax of Wolfe's novel—the death of Ben and Eugene's departure from the family. However, there are significant differences from the novel in sequence and emphasis; to name just one, in the novel, Eugene has already been to college by the time Ben dies. Regardless of those differences, Wolfe's theme remains: the American struggle to break free of the limitations of one's family and hometown to take the individual path.

Frings wrote the book for a musical version of *Look Homeward, Angel,* entitled *Angel* (1978), which closed after only five performances. Her other two plays are *The Long Dream* (1960), based on a novel by Richard Wright, and *Mr. Sycamore* (1942), based on a story by Robert Ayre.

LOOMER, LISA (1955?–)

Raised in New York and in Guanajuato, Mexico, playwright Lisa Loomer was educated at Brandeis University and New York University's Tisch School of the Arts, where she studied theater. Loomer began her career as an actress, eventually writing monologues for herself. In the early 1980s, she created the one-woman show *All by Herself,* which was produced at Westside Arts Theatre in New York. In 1985, her playwriting career began in earnest when she was writer-in-residence at INTAR (International Arts Relations) Hispanic American Arts Center in New York, where she worked with MARIA IRENE FORNÉS.

Loomer's first play, *Birds,* premiered during the 1986–87 season at South Coast Repertory in Costa

Mesa, California. It is about a Mexican-American family who return to Mexico. Another early work of note is *¡Bocón!* (1989), a play with songs, written for young audiences and set in an unspecified war-torn Central American country. The title means "Big Mouth" and refers to the garrulous 12-year-old Miguel, a storyteller who loses his voice when his parents are arrested by the military. In a mixture of magical legend and coming-of-age tale, the refugee Miguel sets out to find his voice, literally and figuratively.

One of Loomer's most often produced and most popular plays is *The Waiting Room* (1994). In it, an 18th-century Chinese woman with bound feet who has lost a toe, a 19th-century English woman in a tight corset that is causing some rearrangement of her internal organs, and a contemporary American woman with enormous breast implants that have caused cancer find themselves together in a doctor's waiting room. Loomer's play not only addresses abuse for the sake of "beauty"—as defined by male-dominated societies—but also the medical and pharmaceutical industries' shortcomings. Loomer told Mel Gussow in 1994, "The play addresses the literal waiting room and the state in which we all wait for things to change." The play won for Loomer the Susan Smith Blackburn Prize, awarded each year to a woman for an outstanding work written for the English-speaking theater, as well as the Jane Chambers Award, which recognizes feminist plays.

Expecting Isabel (1998) is a comedy about an infertile couple seeking a child. When the natural course of action fails to bring about pregnancy, Miranda and Nick begin a journey that leads them through the perilous emotional landscapes of fertility treatments and adoption—and of each other's families. Other plays from the 1990s include *Chain of Life, Accelerando,* and *Maria! Maria, Maria, Maria!*

Living Out (2003) is a comedy-drama about an American woman, a lawyer, who goes back to work after the birth of her baby—albeit with some ambivalence—and her Salvadoran nanny. In some ways they are alike (the nanny, Ana, would be a professional had she not been forced to leave dental school by war; both are working mothers whose husbands leave the details of childrearing to them), but race and circumstance have cast them in very different roles, roles that often make each uncomfortable. A chorus made up of two other Latina nannies and their white employers comment on the strange habits of the group that is not their own. Loomer said in an interview that with this story of two women she "could explore larger issues of race, power, and citizenship that impact Anglo/Latino relations in general in [the United States]."

Another comedy, *Distracted* (2007), looks at parenthood in contemporary America. The mother of an extremely unruly nine-year-old boy is faced with balancing necessary discipline and restraint with equally necessary room for freedom and growth, while also taking into account a diagnosis of attention deficit disorder (ADD). The world the family inhabits is filled with the distractions of the 21st century—the screens and machines that produce a constant barrage of information and interruption. As the parents consider various solutions or treatments for their boy, including everything from drugs to discipline, Loomer, as she said in an interview during the play's second production, in Ashland, Oregon, asks "What is ADD in an ADD world? . . . We are bombarded with computers, cell phones, call waiting. It's likely none of us has gotten through a conversation without an interruption. Is all the technology that's supposed to help us do things faster getting in the way of real communication? . . . The play asks if we are forgetting to pay attention to what's . . . important" ("Revels").

Loomer has also written for the cinema, most notably the 1999 film adaptation of the memoir *Girl, Interrupted* by Susanna Kaysen.

BIBLIOGRAPHY

Gussow, Mel. "Playwright's Tough Subject Draws Funny Offers." *New York Times* (Nov. 2, 1994). Available online. URL: http://query.nytimes.com. Accessed June 11, 2008.

Loomer, Lisa. Interview with Carlo Botero. *Revolutionary Worker* #1227 (Feb. 1, 2004). Available online. URL: http://rwor.org/a/1227/lisainterview.htm. Accessed Sept. 26, 2008.

"Revels: 'Distracted.'" *Ashland Daily Tidings* (July 5, 2007). Available online. URL: http://www.dailytidings.com/2007/0705/stories/adt5uly_distracted.php. Accessed Sept. 27, 2008.

LOST IN YONKERS NEIL SIMON (1991)

Winner of the PULITZER PRIZE and the TONY AWARD, *Lost in Yonkers* is considered one of NEIL SIMON's finest works. The play is both funny and heart-wrenching as Simon portrays a family that has survived—though not without scars—despite an absence of expressed love from its matriarch.

When, in 1942, widower Eddie Kurnitz must go on the road to make a living as a salesman, he is forced to leave his young sons Arty and Jay with his mother and sister. The boys' new home is above a candy store, owned and run by their grandmother; this might be good news if she were not a tyrant. Grandma, bitter and in chronic pain, lives with her grown but mildly retarded daughter, Bella, whom she both relies on and constantly belittles.

We eventually learn about Grandma's treatment of her other children (Bella says of her two siblings who died as children: "Aaron and Rose are the lucky ones"). The boys' father, Eddie, learned to be very "careful" in order to avoid punishment—"He'd tie himself to the radiator" to avoid being locked in a closet; Uncle Louie, now a gangster, was locked in a closet for two or three hours at a time if he broke a dish; and her daughter Gert was so terrified as a child that she still has trouble speaking, though she is now middle-aged. Louie, who ran away 12 times as a kid, admits some grudging admiration for his mother: She's got "moxie." Louie explains to the boys, "she was no harder on us than she was on herself." When she was 12 and at a political rally in Berlin, a horse crushed her foot: "It hurts every day of her life but I never once seen her take even an aspirin. . . . She coulda had an operation, but she used the money she saved to get to this country with her husband and six kids." Though Grandma's coldness may be rooted in her own suffering, the effect on her children is nonetheless damaging.

When Bella finds love with a mildly retarded 40-year-old movie house usher, she hopes to marry and have children. The usher, unwilling to leave the security of his parents' home, gets cold feet, but the experience gives Bella the nerve to stand up to her mother. In a poignant monologue at the end of act 2 and in the final scenes of the play, Bella reveals—to her stunned mother—her secrets and her longings, as well as her insights into her mother's loneliness. In the end, the boys are rescued by their father, and Bella and her immutable mother are alone once more, but Bella's need—so unlike her mother's—to seek and *express* love will not be extinguished.

A balance of the humorous and the poignant, *Lost in Yonkers* achieves a depth that Simon approached earlier in *BROADWAY BOUND* (1986). In *Lost in Yonkers*, Grandma Kurnitz's abuse of her children—stemming from her own difficult childhood in Germany and the loss of a husband and two children in America—continues profoundly to affect their lives even as adults. Such weighty subject matter, particularly as it is seen in the damaged Bella, cannot be overwhelmed by the play's comedy, but neither does it overwhelm. Simon said in an interview in 1994 that he disagreed with playwright LILLIAN HELLMAN who advised him never to mix comedy and drama; on the contrary, Simon says, "we're laughing and having a great time and the telephone rings and there is tragedy on the other end of the phone. If that can happen in life, why can't it happen in the theatre?" (Konas 221).

BIBLIOGRAPHY
Konas, Gary, ed. *Neil Simon: A Casebook.* New York: Garland, 1997.

LOVE LETTERS A. R. GURNEY (1988)

A standard in the repertoire of American theaters, *Love Letters*, as its author notes, needs "no theater, no lengthy rehearsal, no special set, no memorization of lines, and no commitment from the actors beyond the night of performance. . . . [It should be] read aloud by an actor and an actress . . . sitting side by side at a table, in front of a group of people of any size."

Almost without a plot, the play reveals the relationship between Andrew Makepeace Ladd III and Melissa Gardner, who meet as schoolchildren and begin writing letters to each other. They write for more than 40 years. The audience experiences the stages of their lives—childhood, education, love, careers, marriages, families, death. Andy and Melissa take us into the world of privileged Americans between the 1930s and the 1980s. Both attend private boarding schools and colleges. Andy becomes a naval officer, a Harvard-trained lawyer, and then a United States senator. Melissa becomes a painter, a good one. Andy marries once, and his family life seems happy. Melissa marries three times, unhappily. Apparently destined for romance, they miss falling in love with each other. Alcohol separates Melissa from her family, from her friends, and, at last, from her art. A sense of duty bordering on self-righteousness separates Andy from Melissa. She is flashy, flippant, and fast. He is plain, planned, and plodding. Late in life, when she is at her most psychologically fragile, they have an affair. Andy breaks it off, from obligation to his family and constituents.

Andy loves to write letters; Melissa hates to, preferring the drawings that she adds in the margins. She begs him to use the phone; he hates to call. Andy likes to write letters because he "feel[s] most alive when [he's] holed up somewhere writing things down." Melissa protests his letters' inauthenticity: "I know you more from your LETTERS than I do in person. . . . [Y]ou're not quite the same when I see you."

The play's universal quality reminds some of THORNTON WILDER'S *OUR TOWN* (1938), with which it shares both a New England background and a minimalist artistic philosophy. *Love Letters* also contributes to postmodern debates about the ways in which artistic and social forms alter identities. Andy and Melissa struggle to find a form for their relationship, as GURNEY pays tribute to the oldest form of personal writing. Gurney asks, who are we when we write? Do we create identities different from our "real" selves, or do we disclose aspects of our selves that, without writing, remain not only unexpressed but also inexpressible?

Arvid F. Sponberg
Valparaiso University

LOVE! VALOUR! COMPASSION! TERRENCE McNALLY (1994)

While many of McNALLY's previous plays had included homosexual characters, none so directly depicted the gay community in the time of AIDS as *Love! Valour! Compassion!* Drawing his title from an entry in the journal of bisexual American novelist and short story writer John Cheever, McNally, who is gay, has disclosed that, in the play, he "wanted to tell everyone else who we are when they aren't around," and he added, "I wanted to reach out and let

more people into those places in my heart where I don't ordinarily welcome strangers" (xii).

The three-act play takes place at a Dutchess County country house, two hours north of New York City, belonging to Gregory, a respected dancer-choreographer in his early forties. Each act depicts the same group of house guests over a different holiday weekend—in succession, Memorial Day, Fourth of July, and Labor Day. Assembled are Bobby, Greg's boyfriend, in his early twenties and blind; Arthur and Perry, both in their late thirties or early forties and a couple for 14 years (Perry is a lawyer who does pro bono work for Greg's dance company; Arthur is an accountant); Buzz, in his mid-thirties and the designer of costumes for Greg's company (he is also a musical theater fanatic and has AIDS); John, in his late forties and Greg's rehearsal pianist (he is English and a not-very-successful composer); and Ramon, in his early twenties and reveling in his own sexuality (he is a very talented dancer born in Puerto Rico).

Memorial Day weekend, John, who a number of years ago was Buzz's lover for six months and who now is disliked by some members of the group, particularly Perry, for his caustic tongue and his devious ways (his last name is Jeckyll), has brought Ramon as his date. Ramon, immediately attracted to Bobby, sneaks out of their room and accosts Bobby in the kitchen, where they kiss and embrace passionately. The characters frequently interrupt the action to narrate what happens directly to the audience; the convention is that the events of the play have already taken place, and we are being told about and shown them. Greg has signed them all up to dance the *Dance of the Swans* from *Swan Lake* for an AIDS benefit at Carnegie Hall later in the year, something they protest they will not do. As act 1 ends, John is playing the piano offstage; Greg is dancing *Swan Lake* alone.

By July Fourth weekend, John's twin brother James (the two characters are played by the same actor), a seamster for the National Theatre who has AIDS, has come to the United States to visit. James is at Greg's, along with Ramon, who ostensibly is there again with John but is really there to be with Bobby, with whom he's been having an affair, unbeknownst to Greg. Ramon swims to the raft on the lake to wait seductively for Bobby; just as the latter gets there, Greg hurts his leg playing tennis, and Bobby is summoned to help him. Bobby learns by phone that his sister, two years older than he, has been killed in a freak accident in India; devastated, he tells Greg that he and Ramon have made love. Although Bobby assures him that it will not happen again, Greg says he should leave that evening for his sister's funeral—but they hug as he does so. Buzz and James, both suffering from AIDS, hit it off very well. Arthur swims to the raft and is briefly tempted by Ramon; as the act ends, Arthur and Perry celebrate their anniversary with a cake and a dance— in which they are joined by Buzz and James.

Labor Day weekend, Buzz and James are now a couple, and Greg and Bobby's relationship is still strained because of Ramon, who is present again and still interested in Bobby—although Bobby seems resistant. After Greg scuffles with Ramon, the latter tells him that their fight wasn't due to his affair with Bobby: "You're old and you're scared and you don't know what to do about it." Arthur and Perry talk about AIDS and about the fact that they feel both guilty and grateful that they have escaped the disease. Greg finishes a dance he has been struggling with for a long time and, realizing that he will be physically unable to perform it, asks Ramon, who accepts gratefully. Greg has finally convinced everyone but Perry to do the *Swan Lake* piece, but as they begin to rehearse in tutus and toe shoes, James, whose illness has worsened, collapses. John, who has earlier told us of a conversation with his brother in which James forgave John "all the wrongs [he] had done him," goes to help his brother. When the rehearsal resumes, each character comes forward and tells us how and when they will die; then the lights suddenly go out. The play ends as the entire group decides to go skinny-dipping together in the moonlight (the nudity in this case is less about arousal than it is about innocence and vulnerability).

Love! Valour! Compassion! is a celebration of the gay community as a family, which, despite disputes, stresses, acrimony, jealousy, and even occasional physical clashes, remains together, bound, ultimately, by affection, understanding, and respect. As such, it can be compared with such other depictions of the complex ambivalences of the American family as EUGENE O'NEILL'S *LONG DAY'S JOURNEY INTO NIGHT* (1956) and NEIL SIMON'S *BRIGHTON BEACH MEMOIRS* (1983).

McNally's play has been compared to an earlier drama about a gathering of gay men, MART CROWLEY'S *THE BOYS IN THE BAND* (1968); however, as John M. Clum has pointed out, the major difference is that, in Crowley's play, the characters are defined by their homosexuality—they appear to have no reason to be together except that they all are gay. The men in *Love! Valour! Compassion!* are functioning and respected members of society who are together because they genuinely care for, support, and understand one another (108–110).

BIBLIOGRAPHY

Clum, John M. "Where We Are Now: *Love! Valour! Compassion!* and Contemporary Gay Drama." In *Terrence McNally: A Casebook,* edited by Toby Silverman Zinman. New York: Garland, 1997. 95–116.

McNally, Terrence. *"Love! Valour! Compassion!" and "A Perfect Ganesh": Two Plays.* New York: Plume, 1995.

LOWELL, ROBERT (1917–1977)

The period in which Robert Lowell wrote has been called "The Age of Lowell," a testament to his genius as a poet, but Lowell also wrote for the theater. Robert Traill Spence Lowell was born in Boston, Massachusetts, a city with which his distinguished family had long been associated. He attended Harvard but left after two years. Lowell eventually took his degree in classics from Kenyon College in Ohio in 1940. During this time, he studied with poets Allen Tate, John Crowe Ransom, and Robert Penn Warren and with critic Cleanth Brooks. Much of the influence on Lowell's poetry comes from work with his contemporaries, but Lowell also positioned himself within a deeper tradition of American literary history extending as far back as Nathaniel Hawthorne and Herman Melville. He was interested in the history of American government and politics, especially the founding of the first colonies in Massachusetts, and these interests are manifest in his work. Lowell's appropriation of early American history and his various literary influences extend from his poetry into his relatively modest output as a dramatist.

With the publication of his poetry collection *The Mills of the Kavanaughs* (1951), Lowell began experimenting with dramatic monologues in his poetry. His first play was an adaptation of Jean Racine's *Phèdre.* Lowell wrote with a detached irony and a personal, confessional voice, set against images of Christian symbolism, political history, and ancient mythology, all in a formal meter and style. Lowell's *Phaedra* (1961), written in heroic couplets, was considered for Broadway in 1962 but was not produced until 1967 in Philadelphia. The production itself was criticized, but Lowell's script garnered positive reviews. Lowell adapted Aeschylus's *Oresteia* in 1965 and *Prometheus Bound* in 1967. The *Oresteia* went unfinished and unperformed at the time, and it was not published until 1979. *Prometheus Bound* premiered at Yale in 1967 where it was praised for its extravagant language and strong performances but criticized for its failure to maintain dramatic conflict. The adaptations from Aeschylus focus on the human struggle with unseen forces, with the temptations of power, and with the suffering that comes with knowledge, while also commenting indirectly on the political situation in America in the 1960s.

During World War II, Lowell was imprisoned as a conscientious objector; his liberal impulses also found expression in his drama. Guided by his methods of adaptation, what he called "imitation," and his politics, Lowell published his greatest contribution to American theater: *The Old Glory* (1965). A trilogy made up of *Endecott and the Red Cross* and *My Kinsman, Major Molineux,* based on stories by Hawthorne, and *Benito Cereno,* based on the story by Melville, *The Old Glory* deals with issues of nonconformity, violence, and enslavement during America's colonial beginnings. *Endecott* dramatizes the founding of Merry Mount and the struggle between Puritanism and Dionysiac libertinism, a struggle Lowell considered relevant to his time. *My Kinsman* was dismissed by many as a cartoonish satire with little dramatic value, but *Benito Cereno,* a savage telling of two ships that meet at sea, was a success. Delano, the captain of an American ship, stops to help a troubled vessel captained by the ailing Benito Cereno, but secretly controlled by his slaves. Delano represents the contradictions inherent in democracy and imperialism while Benito represents the fallen ideals of absolute power that inevitably lead to an explosion of violence. While all of Lowell's theater has been criticized for lacking dramatic action and for its repetitive dialogue, *The Old Glory* was generally successful.

BIBLIOGRAPHY

Axelrod, Steven Gould. *Robert Lowell: Life and Art.* Princeton, N.J.: Princeton University Press, 1978.

Hamilton, Ian. *Robert Lowell: A Biography.* New York: Random House, 1982.

Lowell, Robert. *The Old Glory.* Rev. ed. New York: Farrar, Straus and Giroux, 1968.

———, trans. *The Oresteia.* By Aeschylus. New York: Farrar, Straus and Giroux, 1979.

———, trans. *Phaedra.* In *"Phaedra" and "Figaro,"* by Jean Baptiste Racine. New York: Farrar, Straus and Cudahy, 1961. 5–90.

———. *Prometheus Bound.* New York: Farrar, Straus and Giroux, 1969.

Williamson, Alan. *Pity the Monsters: The Political Vision of Robert Lowell.* New Haven, Conn.: Yale University Press, 1974.

Paul N. Calvert
Georgia State University

LUCAS, (CHARLES) CRAIG (1951–)

Born in Atlanta, Georgia, Craig Lucas was abandoned by his birth parents and subsequently adopted by an FBI agent and his wife in Pennsylvania. Upon graduation from Boston University, Lucas moved to New York, working as a singing waiter and actor. His first Broadway credit was as a chorus boy in the musical *Shenandoah* in 1974, and subsequent work in the musicals *Rex, On the Twentieth Century,* and *Sweeney Todd* allowed him the time and financial security to pursue writing.

Frequent collaborator Norman René directed Lucas's first effort, *Missing Persons* (1981), at Off-Off-Broadway's Production Co., after they first worked together on a Sondheim song cycle, *Marry Me a Little,* in which Lucas starred. *Missing Persons,* a whimsical play about a professor's memories, bore the hallmarks of Lucas's later work: fantastical situations, fluid theatricality, and witty characters who examine their foibles with philosophical sophistication.

Reckless (1983), about a naive middle-aged woman whose husband hires a hitman to kill her, was originally presented by the Production Co. and was revived by Circle Repertory Theatre Company in 1988. *Blue Window* (1987) won the first Marton Award for Playwriting and was filmed for PBS; it examines the troubled lives of a disparate group of New Yorkers seen before, during, and after a cocktail party, using a musical motif to examine their ultimate inability truly to know each other. The musical *Three Postcards* (1987), written with composer Craig Carnelia, premiered at South Coast Repertory in Costa Mesa, California, and centers on a reunion of three girlhood friends, each of whose public presentation differs from her true character.

South Coast Repertory also commissioned Lucas's most successful play to date, PRELUDE TO A KISS (1988). The New York production at Circle Repertory Theatre Company transferred to Broadway, winning Lucas numerous awards. This fairy tale, concerning a bride whose personality magically switches with that of a dying old man, was seen as a metaphor for the ravages wrought by AIDS, which had taken a personal and professional toll on Lucas; several of his partners, as well as René, succumbed to the disease.

God's Heart (1993), an overtly political drama about drugs and racism whose elaborate multimedia staging overwhelmed the bleak material, was critically savaged. More successful was *The Dying Gaul,* presented at Lucas's artistic home at that time, OFF-BROADWAY's Vineyard Theatre, in 1998. A modern "revenge tragedy," the play concerns an AIDS widower/playwright and the wife of his bisexual producer/new boyfriend, who impersonates his dead lover over Internet chatlines when she discovers their affair. *Stranger,* a dark play that examines a secret past shared by two people seated together on a plane, premiered at the Vineyard in 2000 to mixed reviews.

Among Lucas's other works are the libretti for composer Gerald Busby's operas *Breedlove* and *Orpheus in Love* and numerous short plays and essays, often on gay topics. Lucas has also branched out into directing, working primarily with fellow playwright Sarah Schulman on several projects.

In 2001, with a production of *The Dying Gaul,* Lucas found a new artistic home at Seattle's Intiman The-atre, where he is currently associate artistic director. He wrote the book for and also directed the initial 2005 Intiman production of the musical *The Light in the Piazza,* which successfully transferred to Lincoln Center in New York. Lucas's drama *The Singing Forest* (2004), a muddled three-hour Stoppardesque opus about psychoanalysis, set simultaneously in the 1930s and the present day, premiered at Intiman, as did *Prayer for My Enemy* (2007), about an Iraq-bound soldier reconnecting with his boyhood friend. Lucas has adapted new English translations of Chekhov's *Three Sisters* and *Uncle Vanya* (produced at Intiman in 2005 and 2007, respectively), and Strindberg's *Miss Julie.*

SMALL TRAGEDY (2003), which did not premiere at Intiman but in Minneapolis, won the OBIE AWARD for Best New American Play after its 2004 New York production. The play examines the human tendency to overlook—indeed, become blind to—inconvenient truths. It is set within a theater group's rehearsal period for a production of *Oedipus Rex,* and features interplay between Lucas's dialogue and Sophocles' lines.

Lucas made a smooth transition into film directing with the movie adaptation of *The Dying Gaul* in 2005; it was nominated for the Sundance Film Festival's Grand Jury Prize; he has written several other screenplays, including *The Secret Lives of Dentists* (2002)—based on a novella by Jane Smiley—which won the New York Film Critics Award for Best Screenplay.

BIBLIOGRAPHY

Lucas, Craig. *Small Tragedy.* New York: Samuel French, 2005.
———. *What I Meant Was: New Plays and Selected One-Acts.* New York: Theatre Communications Group, 1999.
———, and David Schulner. *This Thing of Darkness.* New York: Dramatists Play Service, 2003.

Douglas W. Gordy
Walnut Creek, California

LUCE, CLARE BOOTHE   See BOOTHE (LUCE), CLARE.

LUDLAM, CHARLES (1943–1987)   Actor, playwright, and director Charles Ludlam was born in New York City and raised in Northport, Long Island.

Ludlam received a degree in dramatic literature from Hofstra University in 1964. When he became a member of John Vaccaro's Play-House of the Ridiculous, a small OFF-OFF-BROADWAY company, Ludlam found his unique theatrical style. With Vaccaro's company, Ludlam saw his earliest plays, *Big Hotel* (1967) and *Conquest of the Universe* (1967), produced, introducing the theatrical flamboyance, outrageous camp humor, gay-themed travesties, and popular culture satires that made him a fixture of New York's OFF-BROADWAY theater scene. Despite his initial successes with Vaccaro, artistic differences led Ludlam to form his own troupe, the Ridiculous Theatre Company. Under this banner, and for the remainder of his career, Ludlam perfected his style as both a playwright and an actor, combining elements of high camp, high art, Grand Guignol, melodrama, and the movies with often shocking humor in a range of plays inspired by opera, classic literature, and mainstream American theatrical and cinematic forms. A particularly characteristic touch was Ludlam's use of female impersonation, as he usually took on the leading role in his own plays, portraying such diverse fictional characters as Marguerite Gautier and Hedda Gabler, as well as genuine icons, including Greta Garbo and Maria Callas.

From among his canon of more than 20 plays, the most critically appreciated are *Bluebeard* (1970), *Camille* (1973; revived, 1990), *Stageblood* (1975), *Professor Bedlam's Punch and Judy Show* (1975), *Der Ring Gott Farblonjet* (1977), *Le Bourgeois Avant-Garde* (1982), and *The Mystery of Irma Vep* (1984), the last being perhaps the most enduring of his numerous stage works. Ludlam was also an important theatrical theorist; five years after his death, the publication of his diverse essays on theatrical art, *Ridiculous Theatre: Scourge of Human Folly—The Essays and Opinions of Charles Ludlam,* brought a fuller appreciation of his achievement as an actor and playwright. At the time of Ludlam's death, he was preparing a play called *A Piece of Pure Escapism* in which he intended to portray the legendary early 20th-century magician Harry Houdini.

The Ridiculous Theatre Company dealt openly with homosexuality well before the subject became commonplace in American drama, a fact that gained particular poignancy when Ludlam died from complications of AIDS in New York in 1987. Aside from his own works, Ludlam's legacy continues in the plays of his one-time protégé, CHARLES BUSCH, and in a growing appreciation (or revival) of interest in the bold theatricality, camp, and grotesquerie Ludlam pioneered on late 20th-century American stages.

BIBLIOGRAPHY

Kaufman, David. *Ridiculous!: The Theatrical Life and Times of Charles Ludlam.* New York: Applause Theatre Books, 2002.

Ludlam, Charles. *The Complete Plays of Charles Ludlam.* New York: HarperCollins, 1989.

———. *The Mystery of Irma Vep and Other Plays.* New York: Consortium, 2001.

———. *Ridiculous Theatre: Scourge of Human Folly—The Essays and Opinions of Charles Ludlam.* Edited by S. Samuels. New York: Theatre Communications Group, 1992.

Roemer, Rick. *Charles Ludlam and the Ridiculous Theatrical Company: Critical Analyses of 29 Plays.* Jefferson, N.C.: McFarland, 1998.

James Fisher
University of North Carolina at Greensboro

M

MACARTHUR, CHARLES (1895–1956) See HECHT, BEN.

MACBIRD! BARBARA GARSON (1967) *MacBird!* controversially applied Shakespearean paraphrases (from *Macbeth* and other plays), along with wildly crude invective tones, to the lambasting of Washington politics.

The play's plot begins when three witches (a beatnik Berkeley protestor, a black Los Angeles Watts-district rioter, and an aging American socialist) tell Texas politician MacBird (a mock-LBJ) that he will be not only a Senate leader (as he is already) but also a United States vice president and then president. When the Ken O'Dunc (Kennedyesque) brothers Bobby and Ted soon afterwards offer MacBird a vice-presidential nomination as part of their brother John's presidential contest ticket, one witch prophecy has come true. Not much later, when President Ken O'Dunc is assassinated during a motorcade in MacBird's home state, MacBird, ascending to the presidency, has the almost-fulfilled prophecy in his grasp.

Gleeful in his new prominence, MacBird plans to create a "Smooth Society": "For each, a house, a car, a family, / A private psychoanalyst, a dog." For a time, he faces no critics. Lord Stevenson, the humpty-dumpty-like Egg of Head, "fear[s] to break," and so stays silent; eventually, a heart attack (or perhaps a "poison dart") fells him. The Earl of Warren, when investigating the John Ken O'Dunc assassination, deems his job to be "bury[ing] doubt," not "set[ting] things right." But Bobby Ken O'Dunc, who literally has steel where his heart should be, proves, indeed, to be MacBird's ultimate nemesis, as predicted by the witches; he is aided by opponents of "Viet Land" warfare, like the Wayne of Morse, and, especially, by African-American insurgents marching against MacBird while they burn Washington, D.C., cherry trees. A desperate MacBird has a heart attack, placing Bobby Ken O'Dunc in office.

Barbara Garson first intended *MacBird!* only as a University of California–Berkeley protest rally skit, but she soon received New York performance financing and box office rewards. The play also faced much opposition—from one OFF-BROADWAY playhouse, one potential director, and one potential printer of the performance program, besides the FBI's J. Edgar Hoover and such incensed theater critics as Anthony West of *Vogue,* Walter Kerr of the *New York Times,* and Edith Oliver of *The New Yorker.* However, Robert Brustein of the *New Republic* and Jack Kroll of *Newsweek* declared the play highly effective, with Brustein judging it similar, both in purpose and technique, to Bertolt Brecht's *Arturo Ui.*

The text was soon translated and performed in other countries. Its sheer dependency on its moment in time, though, was decisively (and somberly) proved during the next year, when the real Bobby Kennedy was himself assassinated while campaigning (and with some apparent success) against the policies of the real Lyndon Baines Johnson.

Jeffrey B. Loomis
Northwest Missouri State University

MACHADO, EDUARDO (1953–   )   Eduardo Machado was born in Havana, and his early years were significantly shaped by Fidel Castro's revolution in Cuba. At the age of eight, he was sent to live with relatives in Miami through Operation Pedro Pan and was joined by his parents a year later. Experiencing difficulty with the cultural and linguistic adjustment, Machado found solace in the works of Shakespeare. Working with MARIA IRENE FORNÉS on a production of *FEFU AND HER FRIENDS,* as well as in technical and production capacities on a number of other shows, aided significantly in his development as a writer. His investment in the larger cultural history of Cuba and its diaspora is reflected in the fact that three-quarters of his more than 40 plays deal with Cuba or his family.

His most recognized work is the quartet entitled *The Floating Island Plays,* published in 1991 but first performed together in 1994. The collection narrates the lives of two interrelated Cuban families from the 1920s to the late 1970s. The first play, *The Modern Ladies of Guanabacoa* (1983), details the adulterous and ambitious lives of bourgeois Cubans in the late 1920s and 1930s. The matriarch of the family, Maria Josefa, attempts to maintain her own domestic space in the face of a number of familial and cultural changes. The first play's glimpse of prerevolutionary Cuba, with its problems and successes, sets the stage for *Fabiola* (1985), in which the revolution occurs. The title of this play comes from a dead woman whose passing haunts the family in this play, much as the historical and political transformation of Cuba before, during, and after the revolution changes their lives. *In the Eye of the Hurricane* (1994) spans only two days in 1960 and recounts the nationalization of a bus company despite the best efforts of the owners to keep it. The final play, *Broken Eggs* (1984), translated into Spanish as *Revoltillo* (1989) and actually performed in Cuba, is set in Los Angeles in 1979 and recounts the familial conflicts on the edges of a wedding celebration involving the second and third generations of the family.

Havana Is Waiting (2001), originally titled *When the Sea Drowns in Sand,* explores the question of returning to Cuba. Federico, who left the island 38 years before, returns to find his childhood home and undergoes a period of self-discovery. This journey echoes the real concerns of life lived between cultures and in which it is difficult to find a place called home. The change in the title reflects the waiting that Cubans undergo on the island as well as the island's own waiting for the return of its people. Machado's most widely produced recent work is *The Cook* (2003), about a servant who attempts to preserve the home in which she worked, after her mistress has fled the revolution; the servant eventually realizes her misguided folly when the woman's daughter returns for a visit.

Other works include *Once Removed* (1992), which concerns Machado's arrival from Cuba on Halloween day; *Crocodile Eyes* (1999), which focuses on some of the men from Federico García Lorca's *The House of Bernarda Alba* (1999); *A Burning Beach* (1989), which reflects on the impending political changes in 1895 Cuba; and *Kissing Fidel* (2005), about a man planning to return to Cuba to kiss and forgive Fidel Castro.

Machado is also important for his work as a teacher and artistic director. He was head of the Columbia University graduate playwriting program for many years, and a number of his Columbia students, including Rogelio Martinez and Jorge Gonzales, have been making important contributions to the theater world. He is currently a professor of playwriting at New York University and since 2004 has been the artistic director of INTAR.

BIBLIOGRAPHY

Machado, Eduardo. *The Cook.* New York: Samuel French, 2004.

———. *The Floating Island Plays.* New York: Theatre Communications Group, 1991.

———. *Havana Is Waiting.* New York: Samuel French, 2008.

———. *Kissing Fidel.* New York: Samuel French, 2006.

———. *Once Removed.* New York: Samuel French, 2008.

Jon D. Rossini
University of California—Davis

MACHINAL SOPHIE TREADWELL (1928)   *Machinal* (the title is French for "mechanical" or "automatic") is the most famous work of dramatist and journalist TREADWELL. She based the play on the sensational case of Ruth Snyder and Judd Gray, who were convicted of murdering Snyder's husband.

Machinal tells the story of "an ordinary young woman" (only late in the play do we learn that her name is Helen) who finds herself stifling in an urban office. The young woman—at her mother's urging— weds her boss, a well-meaning but smug man proud of his latest "possession." Unhappy in marriage and oppressed by new motherhood, Helen takes a lover, an adventurer whose freewheeling lifestyle contrasts sharply with her domestic entrapment. When her lover leaves to seek new adventures, Helen kills her husband in a frenzied attempt to gain her own freedom. She is tried by an all-male jury and sentenced to death in the electric chair, the ultimate victory of society and the machine. The plot is deliberately clichéd, and Treadwell even summarizes it at the beginning of the published text. She wants audiences to focus not on *what* happens but on *why*.

Treadwell chose the expressionist style for her play. This early 20th-century reaction against realism attempts to objectify inner experience by employing symbolic rather than individualized characters as well as by using monologues in which characters express their thoughts aloud. The dialogue in *Machinal,* as in most expressionist plays, is repetitive and banal, and most scenes are accompanied by the harsh sounds of machinery. With its nightmarish distortion, EXPRESSIONISM is the perfect medium for presenting the life of a young woman who asks an indifferent society: "Is nothing mine?"

In *Machinal,* Treadwell attacks capitalism for putting even intimate relationships on an economic footing, but her critique extends to technology, medicine, law, motherhood, the press, romance, and even religion. Helen is caught in a patriarchal society: Throughout the play, Treadwell depicts her confronting male characters with the power to determine her life. Again and again, Helen complains of claustrophobia, a motif of entrapment that runs as a common thread through the plays of such Treadwell contemporaries as SUSAN GLASPELL, ZONA GALE, GEORGIA DOUGLAS JOHNSON, and LILLIAN HELLMAN.

A *New York Times* reviewer prophesied accurately that *Machinal* "should still be vital and vivid" a hundred years later. The last decades of the 20th century saw numerous revivals in theaters around the world, and its popularity continues to grow. Not only an outstanding expressionist drama, *Machinal* is also a remarkably contemporary picture of what happens to a sensitive individual in our increasingly standardized, impersonal world.

Judith E. Barlow
State University of New York–Albany

MACKAYE, PERCY WALLACE (1875–1956)

Percy MacKaye was the son of Mary Keith Medberry and noted 19th-century American playwright STEELE MACKAYE. Born in New York City, MacKaye was educated primarily at home until he entered Harvard, from which he graduated in 1897. Influenced primarily by his father, MacKaye's career is marked by abiding interests both in verse as a dramatic medium and in the prospects of large communal dramatic enterprises. These two predominant aspects of his career precluded the kind of financial success that his father enjoyed but compensated him with a reputation for artistic and civic commitment.

MacKaye began writing plays before becoming an undergraduate, and his early efforts reveal a writer searching for a voice. The SCARECROW (1909), his first and best major play, is a romantic fantasy in which a witch and demon magically conjure a scarecrow who serves to satirize the vices and foibles of Massachusetts's colonists (as well as early-20th-century society) even as he evolves to possess true humanity. The play was widely praised and produced in Europe by Max Reinhardt and CONSTANTIN STANISLAVSKY. *Anti-Matrimony* (1910) is a satire of the popularity of the plays of Henrik Ibsen played out in the contrasting attitudes about marriage of two young Americans. Drawing upon his personal familiarity with Italian playwright Carlo Gozzi's work with improvisational drama, MacKaye wrote *A Thousand Years Ago* (1913), a romantic intrigue set in China that involves a group of touring Italian actors who must constantly improvise—both onstage and offstage. His last major work was *The Mystery of Hamlet, King of Denmark; or, What We Will* (1949), a series of four plays on the theme of Shakespeare's *Hamlet*.

MacKaye explored an alternative vision of theater in a series of civic masques and community dramas, works that in large measure overshadow his more conventional plays. Having derived an interest in large-scale drama from his father, MacKaye's work in this arena reflected his belief that drama could serve an educative, democratic, and progressive cultural function. He detailed his thoughts in three books: *The Playhouse and the Play* (1909), *The Civic Theatre* (1912), and *Community Drama* (1917). By using local people in every element of the event's production, including a greatly expanded cast of characters, MacKaye enlarged the scope of his works and produced a series of spectacular dramas designed for outdoor performance. *Saint Louis: A Civic Masque,* which conveyed the history of St. Louis, was produced from May 28 to June 1, 1914. It employed more than 7,000 performers to reach an audience estimated at 500,000. For a commemoration of the tercentenary of Shakespeare's death, MacKaye staged *Caliban, by the Yellow Sands* (May 25 to June 5, 1916) in New York City. Aided by designers such as Robert Edmond Jones, actors such as John Drew, and composer Arthur Farwell, MacKaye's production included more than 2,500 actors and reached an audience of thousands.

In his efforts at poetic drama, MacKaye prefigures Eugene O'Neill. In his emphasis on drama as civic art, he helped lay the foundation of the Little Theater Movement and regional American drama.

BIBLIOGRAPHY

Ege, Arvia MacKaye. *The Power of the Impossible: The Life Story of Percy and Marion MacKaye.* Falmouth, Me.: Kennebec River Press, 1992.

MacKaye, Percy. *The Civic Theatre in Relation to the Redemption of Leisure.* New York: Mitchell Kennerly, 1912.

———. *Community Drama: Its Motive and Method of Neighborliness.* Boston: Houghton Mifflin, 1917.

———. *The Playhouse and the Play and Other Addresses concerning the Theatre and Democracy in America.* New York: Macmillan, 1909.

———. *The Scarecrow.* New York: Macmillan, 1908.

———. *Saint Louis: A Masque of American Civilization.* New York: Doubleday, 1914.

Gary A. Richardson
Mercer University

MACKAYE, STEELE (1842–1894)

MACKAYE, STEELE (1842–1894) Steele MacKaye ranks among the most influential theater artists of the second half of the 19th century, profoundly affecting American theater through wide-ranging and innovative undertakings, which included playwriting, training actors, and designing playhouses. Throughout his extraordinary career, MacKaye was dedicated to expanding the social relevancy and moral reach of American theater.

Born near Buffalo, New York, MacKaye studied with François Delsarte in Paris in 1869 and introduced the Delsarte system of actor training to America two years later. Delsarte sought to analyze the body in its various physical conditions in order to evoke precisely, through outward expression, specific emotional and mental states of being. Through schools MacKaye established, he introduced Delsarte-inspired precision and method to actor training. The most successful of these schools was the Lyceum Theatre School (1884), the forerunner of the present American Academy of Dramatic Art.

MacKaye was also an accomplished playwright, producing in the course of his career 19 dramas—original works and adaptations—the most successful of which was *Hazel Kirke* (1880). While essentially a melodrama, the play was notable for the absence of a traditional "villain," developing, in realistic terms, the story of a young woman rejected by her father for refusing to marry the man he has chosen for her. After running for more than a year in New York, the show toured widely; at its peak, there were 10 "combination companies"—shows with full casts and scenery—simultaneously "on the road." MacKaye's lack of business acumen—a characteristic that marked his entire career—resulted in his earning virtually nothing from his play.

Theaters designed by MacKaye featured extraordinary innovations. His Madison Square Theatre (1880) contained a two-level elevator stage. While a scene was unfolding before an audience, a new set was installed on the companion stage. In a matter of minutes, this stage could be raised from the basement or lowered from the flies into position. At the Lyceum Theatre (1884), MacKaye's innovations, most of them commonplace today, were directed chiefly toward audience comfort and safety. An elaborate system of ducts brought fresh air to the audience; a fireproof safety curtain would lower automatically to seal the stage from the house in the event of fire, while trap-doors above the rigging loft acted as chimneys to carry off deadly smoke and fumes; and patented seats would fold in seconds to turn the auditorium into a series of aisles for emergency exits.

The most innovative of MacKaye's theaters was his Spectatorium, designed for the Chicago World's Fair but never completed. It was conceived as a showcase for spectacular theatricals that would incorporate pageantry, pantomime, music, choral chanting, and grandiose technical effects. MacKaye wanted lighting to replace painted scenery, and he tried to re-create electrically the hues of the natural world—rainbows, meteor showers, and the tint and glow of the various hours of the day. The economic downturn of the 1890s brought the project to an end, and the emotional and physical strain of the aborted endeavor contributed to MacKaye's death in 1894.

BIBLIOGRAPHY

MacKaye, Percy. *Epoch: The Life of Steele MacKaye.* New York: Boni & Liveright, 1927.

Sokalski, J. A. *Pictorial Illusionism: The Theatre of Steele Mac-Kaye.* Montreal: McGill-Queen's University Press, 2007.

Craig Clinton
Reed College

MACLEISH, ARCHIBALD (1892–1982) See *J. B.*

MALE ANIMAL, THE JAMES THURBER AND ELLIOTT NUGENT (1940)

Set at a fictitious midwestern university on the weekend of a big football game, *The Male Animal* takes a comic look at the ongoing struggle at a university between the intellectuals and the "stadium builders."

A young and slightly absentminded English professor, Thomas Turner, and his pretty and charming wife, Ellen, live in their comfortable but modest home with Ellen's younger sister, Patricia, a student at the university. Pat has two boyfriends, the handsome and hearty football player, Wally, and the earnest intellectual editor of a student publication, Mike. On this football weekend, Ellen's old boyfriend and Thomas's former rival, Joe Ferguson, arrives. In college, Joe was a football star, and Thomas, an earnest intellectual. Joe and his wife have separated, and he freely shows his enduring interest in Ellen, remembering her birthday with flowers and dancing with her—attentions that Thomas does not show her. Meanwhile, as the two sisters make their choices between brawn and brains, a controversy rages at the university: The board of trustees, to whom the football program is precious, is firing humanities professors for being "Reds" (one of them vacationed in the Soviet Union to attend a "Drama Festival" there). Mike writes a "fiery" editorial in which he calls the trustees "fascists" and praises "Professor Thomas Turner" for being "courageous" enough "to bring up even the Sacco-Vanzetti case" in class. Now Thomas's job is in jeopardy, though he was only *considering* using a Vanzetti letter as an illustration of eloquent writing by nonprofessional writers. When the trustee, Ed Keller, tells Thomas he must *never* read the letter, Thomas is determined to read it on principle. By the end of act 1, Pat and Ellen are inclined to choose their football players over Mike and Thomas, who complicate life with their principles.

While the women are at the football game with their Neanderthal rivals, Mike and Thomas get drunk and rethink Thomas's sober advice to Mike that he must "suppress the male animal in [him]" and "be swayed by Reason." Their attempt to fight their rivals leaves Mike on the floor and Thomas unconscious. The next day, Mike is suspended for his editorial, and Joe brings Ed Keller over to convince Thomas to denounce Mike so that he may keep his job. Thomas refuses, and as he answers Keller, he articulates the serious message of this comedy: "You can't suppress ideas because you don't like them—not in this country—not yet. . . . This is a university! It's our business to bring what light we can into this muddled world—to try to follow truth!" Thomas reads the controversial Vanzetti letter aloud to the assembled interested parties. Ellen is moved by it, and Joe has to admit "it's not so bad," but Keller is adamant: He will not have his "authority" defied, even when Mike arrives with a petition to keep Professor Turner, signed by some of the football stars. Thomas has probably won the battle for his job, but the war over intellectual freedom is ongoing. In the end, he wins his private battle for Ellen as well: Both Ellen and Patricia finally choose the men with the courage of their convictions.

According to Malcolm Goldstein, in this play, Thurber and Nugent presented a theme new to the American stage, namely "the intimidation of liberals by ultraconservatives flaunting the shibboleth 'Americanism'" (410). Young Professor Turner "was a fitting representative of the democratic tradition at the moment in time when the European democracies were suffering under threat of totalitarian onslaught" (411–412). Furthermore, Goldstein contends, "the play was also prophetic" since, starting in 1947, "it was as though the [House Un-American Activities] Committee wished to wipe out the theatrical achievement of an entire decade, along with the livelihood of those who had created it" (412).

BIBLIOGRAPHY

Goldstein, Malcolm. *The Political Stage*. New York: Oxford University Press, 1974.

MAMET, DAVID (1947–)

MAMET, DAVID (1947–) David Alan Mamet was born in Chicago and grew up with a father, a lawyer and an amateur semanticist, who demanded that his children always find the exact word when expressing themselves, training that helped form the power and precision of the language in his son's plays. He later moved with his mother to a "model suburb," where the oppression of middle-class values and lifestyles provided Mamet with his major dramatic themes. Rather than pursuing sports, Mamet was drawn to the energy and liberation of the theater and attended Francis Parker High School, which had an outstanding theater program. He was also a voracious reader and found escape in the world of the mind; later, he became attached to theaters in Chicago, where he received his early training. He attended Goddard College in Vermont, which allowed him to spend a year in New York City studying at the Neighborhood Playhouse. After college, he worked in a number of blue-collar jobs—taxi driver, boatman, and carpet salesman—and in the theater as a dancer and actor, all of which provided material for his plays.

The early 1970s found Mamet teaching at Goddard, where he formed a theater group that put on early versions of his first works. By the fall of 1972, some of his early work was performed in a small Chicago theater and later by the more established theater companies in Chicago. By 1975, Mamet decided to try his luck in New York, where his first major success was AMERICAN BUFFALO (1976).

Mamet's main dramatic power comes from his language, similar in some ways to that of Harold Pinter— spare, oblique, inferential, and catching the everyday cadences and vocabulary of desperate people. Typically, the interactions of his characters are formed by a sort of "teacher-student" relationship, even when the "teacher" is incapable and unaware of the needs of the "student." The majority of his plays deal with the male ego, male relationships, and the shallowness of the lives and activities of his male characters; the underlying cause of this shallowness is the corrupting power of material values and the American obsession with money.

Sexual Perversity in Chicago (1974) was first produced in Chicago and won the Joseph Jefferson Award there. A sad, comic, despairing commentary on modern male sexuality presented through a series of 34 brief scenes, it mainly involves Bernie, who does not know what he is talking about, trying to teach Dan how things work between men and women; it is set against the city and the singles bar scene.

American Buffalo (1975) also won the Joseph Jefferson Award before moving from Chicago to New York, where it won the Outer Critics Circle Award. In 1978, it became the first American play to be produced in England's new National Theatre. The action takes places in Don's Resale Shop, an old junk store, and revolves around the fact that Don believes that someone has swindled him out of a buffalo-head nickel. The play is about "social interaction" among three men and the moral degeneracy of their lives brought about by the corrupting power of American material values and symbolized in the idea that the mythic grandeur of the Old West has been reduced to the image of a buffalo on a coin.

A Life in the Theatre (1977) depicts Robert, an older actor who is lonely, and John, a younger actor who has a life outside the theater, rehearsing, preparing, changing before or after a performance, and playing in actual scenes in which the older actor is, ironically, "educating" the younger one.

In *The Water Engine* (1977), Charles Lang has invented an engine that runs on water, an invention that will clearly eliminate modern society's need for oil and ultimately destroy the power of the gigantic oil companies. Mamet, through the mysterious murder of Lang, renders a devastating indictment of the total degeneracy of the power of money.

In *Edmond* (1982), the title character, who is disdainful of women, blacks, and homosexuals, leaves his wife and goes on a journey through the lower depths of society. On his journey, he encounters the very types for whom he has contempt. After a series of shocks to his identity, Edmond ends up in jail where, with a black cellmate, he seems to move toward better understanding.

GLENGARRY GLEN ROSS (1983) premiered in London and opened in Chicago and New York the following year. Winner of the PULITZER PRIZE and the New York Drama Critics' Circle Award, it involves a group of salesmen who sell worthless swampland in Florida to naive clients. Theirs is a cutthroat enterprise that exposes the dehumanizing relationship among the men in a value system where a "sale" is sought at any cost. This play employs a style of dialogue that emphasizes the egocentric, vapid mentality of people who have been brutalized by material values.

SPEED-THE-PLOW (1988) is set in Hollywood and revolves around Bob Gould, who is torn between "greenlighting" a script, which is a piece of trash but has potential as a moneymaker and which is sponsored by Charlie Fox, a long-time movie-business associate, or an "artsy" book about the effects of radiation, supported by Karen, a temporary secretary. Fox eventually manages to expose Karen as a devious, power-hungry "broad" and wins out in the end. Mamet's treatment of Hollywood reveals a deep-seated discomfort with the values that decide what movies are made and, once again, makes a frontal assault on the American obsession with money; the play is all the more ironic given his involvement during the nineties in the moviemaking industry. In 1997, the character

Bobby Gould returned to the stage in Mamet's trilogy of one-act plays, *The Old Neighborhood,* in which a middle-aged Gould goes back to his childhood neighborhood and encounters an old friend, his sister, and his estranged wife as he searches for his life's meaning.

In OLEANNA (1992), Carol, a student, has come to her professor's office for the purpose of trying to find out how she can do better in his class. In her next visit in act 2, Carol accuses her professor, John, of having made sexual advances toward her, which she has reported to her "committee." By the third act, John has been denied tenure because of Carol's accusations. The play leaves open the question of whether John did in fact sexually harass Carol, but it clearly deals with several vital issues: the power of language, perception as reality, arrogance, insensitivity, and the difficulty of human relationships.

In 1994, *The Cryptogram* was first produced in London and premiered in America in 1995. A young boy, John, is getting ready to go on a camping trip with his father while his mother, Donny, is visited by her old friend Del. Donny soon discovers by means of a letter that her husband has left his family. The play focuses on the boy John, who has trouble sleeping, and with the fact that his home life is falling apart.

Boston Marriage (1999), which received productions in Cambridge, Massachusetts, and London before its Broadway opening in 2002, is a response to those who have criticized Mamet for not creating meaty roles for women. It is set in Victorian-era New England and centers on Anna, who is being kept by a married man but prefers the company of women, especially Claire, her former lover, who is now in love with a younger woman. The only other character in the play is Catherine, Anna's hapless maid. Reviewing the Broadway premiere, *New York Times* critic Ben Brantley saw it as "the flip side of *American Buffalo*" in that both feature "three desperate, logorrheic characters" (November 21, 2002).

Although Mamet wrote several screenplays while focusing primarily on playwriting earlier in his career, as time goes on he has become even more involved in filmmaking—writing, directing, and producing—as well as writing in other literary forms such as essays and longer nonfiction work, novels, and poetry, while still continuing to write some plays. In 2004, Mamet published a lauded adaptation of the Faust story, *Faustus,* which when it was staged in San Francisco that same year was soundly criticized by reviewers. In 2005, he wrote the comedy ROMANCE, a courtroom farce that skewers both political correctness and intolerance; and in 2008, he returned to the stage with another comedy, *November,* a broad satire of the George W. Bush administration, and a comic musical "fable" entitled *A Waitress in Yellowstone,* for which Mamet himself wrote the music, lyrics, and book.

BIBLIOGRAPHY

Bigsby, Christopher, ed. *The Cambridge Companion to David Mamet.* New York: Cambridge University Press, 2004.

———. *David Mamet.* London, New York: Methuen, 1985.

Carroll, Dennis. *David Mamet.* New York: St. Martin's Press, 1987.

Dean, Anne. *David Mamet: Language as Dramatic Action.* Rutherford, N.J.: Fairleigh Dickinson University Press, 1990.

Hudgins, Christopher, and Leslie Kane, eds. *Gender and Genre: Essays on David Mamet.* New York: Palgrave, 2001.

Kane, Leslie, ed. *David Mamet: A Casebook.* New York: Garland, 1992.

———. *David Mamet in Conversation.* Ann Arbor: University of Michigan Press, 2001.

———. *Weasels and Wisemen: Ethics and Ethnicity in the Work of David Mamet.* New York: St. Martin's Press, 1999.

Mamet, David. *American Buffalo: A Play.* New York: Grove Press, 1977.

———. *The Cryptogram.* New York: Vintage Books, 1995.

———. *Edmond: A Play.* New York: Grove Press, 1983.

———. *Glengarry Glen Ross: A Play.* New York: Grove Press, 1984.

———. *A Life in the Theatre: A Play.* New York: Grove Press, 1977.

———. *November.* New York: Vintage, 2008.

———. *The Old Neighborhood.* New York: Vintage Books, 1998.

———. *The Old Religion.* New York: Free Press, 1997.

———. *Oleanna.* New York: Pantheon Books, 1993.

———. *Romance.* New York: Vintage, 2005.

———. *"Sexual Perversity in Chicago" and "The Duck Variations": Two Plays.* New York: Grove Press, 1978.

———. *Speed-the-Plow: A Play.* New York: Grove Press, 1987.

———. *Three Children's Plays.* New York: Grove Press, 1986.

———. *"The Water Engine: An American Fable" and "Mr. Happiness": Two Plays.* New York: Grove Press, 1978.

Nadel, Ira. *David Mamet: A Life in the Theatre.* New York: Palgrave Macmillan, 2008.

Price, Steven. *The Plays, Screenplays and Films of David Mamet.* New York: Palgrave Macmillan, 2008.

Sauer, David K. *David Mamet's "Oleanna."* New York: Continuum, 2009.

———, and Janice A. Sauer. *David Mamet: A Research and Production Sourcebook.* Westport, Conn.: Praeger, 2003.

Tony J. Stafford
University of Texas–El Paso

MANN, EMILY (1952–)

Acclaimed as both a playwright and a director, Emily Mann grew up in Northampton, Massachusetts, where her father, Arthur Mann, was a professor of history at Smith College. One of her earliest theatrical experiences was seeing the musical *Fiorello!,* based on the life of New York City mayor Fiorello LaGuardia, about whom Mann's father had written a biography. From an early age, she was attracted to and experimented with various forms of art, including fiction, dance, and sculpture, ultimately recognizing theater as a way to combine and focus those interests. After receiving her undergraduate degree from Harvard, Mann earned an M.F.A. at the University of Minnesota. Since 1990, she has served as artistic director of the McCarter Theatre in Princeton, New Jersey, which received the 1994 TONY AWARD for Outstanding Regional Theatre. She is also McCarter Theatre's resident playwright. In 2002, Princeton awarded Mann an Honorary Doctorate of Arts.

Mann's plays are rooted in historical events, found texts, oral interviews, and other materials; she considers her work to be documentary theater, or "theatre of testimony" ("Sources" 33). She feels the need "to preserve the unheard voices in our society," interweaving her creativity with thorough research to create reality-based theater that confronts social issues and justice but is never polemic (Tolkoff 3). Her first play, *Annulla, An Autobiography* (1977), was inspired by her father's project on Holocaust survivors and based more specifically on extensive interviews with a friend's aunt in Poland; those transcripts generated the play and, says Mann, "every subsequent play has followed from that play" ("Sources" 33). *Still Life* (1980) addresses the Vietnam War—and, by extension, American violence—from several viewpoints. With EXECUTION OF JUSTICE (1984), Mann not only made her Broadway debut as a playwright but also became the first woman to direct her own play on Broadway. *Execution of Justice* is based on the 1978 murders of San Francisco mayor George Moscone and city supervisor Harvey Milk, the first openly gay official elected in the United States, chronicling the trial of the killer, former city supervisor Dan White.

Probably Mann's most well-known play is *Having Our Say: The Delany Sisters' First 100 Years* (1995). Adapted with Amy Hill Hearth from a book of the same title by two black centenarians, Sarah and Bessie Delany, the play reflects on life before and after the Civil Rights movement through the eyes of the two sisters, their own professional accomplishments, and their maintenance of strong family ties amid generations of upheaval. *Greensboro (A Requiem)* (1996) is Mann's response to an anti–Ku Klux Klan march that took place November 3, 1979, in Greensboro, North Carolina, in which five demonstrators were killed by klansmen. *Meshugah: A Comic Tragedy* (1998), an adaptation of Isaac Bashevis Singer's novel, focuses on a trio of Holocaust survivors living in New York City in the 1950s.

Mann's numerous directorial credits include the world premiere of ANNA DEAVERE SMITH's *Twilight: Los Angeles, 1992* (1993); EDWARD ALBEE's *All Over* (2002), for which Mann won an OBIE AWARD; NILO CRUZ's ANNA IN THE TROPICS (2003); as well as revivals of such classics as *The* GLASS MENAGERIE (1945) and CAT ON A HOT TIN ROOF (1955), and she has served as resident director at the Guthrie Theater and the Brooklyn Academy of Music Theatre Company.

Mann's most recent play, *A Seagull in the Hamptons* (2007), is "freely" adapted from Chekhov's *The Seagull*.

BIBLIOGRAPHY

Mann, Emily. *Having Our Say: The Delany Sisters' First 100 Years*. New York: Dramatists Play Service, 1996.
———. *Testimonies: Four Plays*. New York: Theatre Communications Group, 1997.
———, and Roy Harris, eds. *Eight Women of the American Stage: Talking about Acting*. New York: Heinemann, 1997.
———, and David Roessel, eds. *Political Stages: Plays That Shaped a Century*. New York: Applause Theatre & Cinema Books, 2002.
———, et al. "Sources of Inspiration." *American Theatre* 17, no. 2 (September 1998): 32–33, 81–83.
Tolkoff, Esther. "From Textbook to Stage Test: The Tricks of Dramatizing History." *Back Stage* (23 May 1997): 3–4.

Karen C. Blansfield
University of North Carolina–Chapel Hill

MAN WHO CAME TO DINNER, THE
GEORGE S. KAUFMAN AND MOSS HART (1939)   A comic farce about an impossibly self-centered houseguest, *The Man Who Came to Dinner* was based in friendly jest on the personality of writer and drama critic Alexander Woollcott, to whom KAUFMAN and HART dedicated the play.

Mr. and Mrs. Stanley, their children, Richard and June (21 and 20, respectively), and Mr. Stanley's odd sister, Harriet, are coping with their guest, Sheridan Whiteside—"critic, lecturer, wit, radio orator"—who has been bedridden for two weeks because of an injury he suffered from slipping on the Stanleys' icy Ohio doorstep. The play begins as Mr. Whiteside is about to emerge from bed for the first time since the accident. In a wheelchair, he takes over the Stanleys' living room, rudely banishing the family from the ground floor. He appropriates the servants and the telephone, to the outrage of Mr. Stanley, and is soon ordering lunch from the cook for himself and his guests: two convicts and a guard from his favorite charitable organization, "The Crockfield Home for Paroled Convicts." He also befriends the local newspaper editor, a bright young man named Bert Jefferson. Also staying with the Stanleys is Whiteside's indispensable assistant, Maggie Cutler. In a week, Maggie falls in love with Jefferson, a development that Whiteside cannot tolerate since it would be too inconvenient for him to train a new assistant. He therefore cooks up a plan, involving a beautiful and conniving actress, to sabotage Maggie's budding relationship. When Whiteside eventually realizes Maggie's love for Jefferson is no passing fancy—and since he is not really such a bad fellow—he and a member of his entourage ship the actress, Lorraine Sheldon, off in a mummy case—literally.

Whiteside also meddles in the Stanley family's personal affairs. He offers jobs to their excellent cook and butler. He takes a liking to the Stanley children and they to him, and he encourages them to follow their dreams: Richard, to become a photographer, and June, to marry the union organizer she met at her father's factory. Both run away until Mr. Stanley, outraged again, has them retrieved. When Whiteside—a true-crime enthusiast—realizes that Miss Harriet Stanley is the Lizzie Borden of her town, having killed her parents with an axe 25 years before, he blackmails Mr. Stanley into letting his children do as they please with their lives. When he *finally* walks out of the Stanley home, Whiteside falls again on the steps, shouts for his nurse, and threatens to sue Mr. Stanley as the curtain falls.

After Moss Hart had entertained Alexander Woollcott at his home, Woollcott wrote in Hart's guest book: "This is to certify that I had one of the most unpleasant times I ever spent." When Hart reported this to George S. Kaufman and quipped that he was glad Woollcott hadn't broken his leg and been with them all summer, the idea for the play was born (Meredith 551). One of several highly successful plays by the Kaufman-and-Hart writing team, this enduring American comedy is frequently revived around the country.

BIBLIOGRAPHY

Meredith, Scott. *George S. Kaufman and His Friends*. Garden City, N.Y.: Doubleday, 1974.

MA RAINEY'S BLACK BOTTOM AUGUST WILSON (1984)

Winner of the New York Drama Critics' Circle Award and WILSON's first commercial success, *Ma Rainey's Black Bottom* depicts the historical figure Gertrude "Ma" Rainey within a cast of fictional characters. Set in a Chicago recording studio in 1927, the play, as Wilson writes in his descriptive preface, deals with people who frequent the "bars and juke joints" of Chicago: "It is with these negroes that our concern lies most heavily: their values, their attitudes, and particularly their music"—the blues (xv–xvi).

The men in Ma's band are Cutler, middle-aged and practical, the leader of the band who believes in Ma Rainey's right to run her own band her own way; Toledo, an intellectual and the voice of Black Nationalism, who maintains that if "every living colored man" works together, their lives will improve and that it is a mistake to look for the white man's approval; Slow Drag, whose philosophy is that "good times makes life worth living" and who says that he does not worry about "the colored man," who "got through slavery," and "[wi]ll get through whatever else the white man put on him"; and Levee, who is younger than the other men, more personally ambitious, and quicker to anger. For much of the first act of this two-act play, the band is alone in the band room of the studio talking, bickering, telling stories, and rehearsing.

Slow Drag tells a story about a poor man who sold his soul to the devil and then became rich and got away with murder. While the older men still believe in the wrath of God, Levee is ready to sell his soul because he figures God "done went to sleep." He scoffs at Cutler's warning that such talk will bring him bad luck, saying, "I ain't knowed nothing but bad luck all my life."

Toledo speaks of "the colored man" as being the "left-overs" of history, and "the colored man" does not know that he "[d]one went and filled the white man's belly and now . . . [the white man] want you to get out the way and let him be by himself." Indeed, Irvin, Ma's agent, and Mr. Sturdyvant, the recording company owner—both white—are out to take their fill of Ma and the musicians for their own profit. Ma Rainey does not let them railroad *her*, however: She chooses the songs and how to sing them, and so she has got the leverage—at least until they get her voice recorded.

At the end of act 1, Levee, provoked by the others' response to his deferential demeanor toward Mr. Sturdyvant (with whom Levee hopes to get a recording contract), tells his heartbreaking story: Levee's mother was gang-raped by white men, and eight-year-old Levee, attempting to save her, was knifed in the chest. Levee's father, restraining his rage, smiled in the face of one of the rapists in order to sell his land and move his family away, knowing that he would return alone and kill that man and the others for the attack on his family. ("He got four [of 'eight or nine'] before they got him.") Perhaps the best definition of the blues comes out of the juxtaposition of Levee's story and Slow Drag's oblique and sorrowful response to it, which ends the act: Slow Drag sings, "If I had my way / If I had my way / If I had my way / I would tear this old building down."

In act 2, Ma elaborates on the blues: "White folks don't understand about the blues. They hear it come out, but they don't know how it got there. They don't understand that's life's way of talking. You don't sing to feel better. You sing 'cause that's a way of understanding life."

To the recording session, Ma brings along her nephew, Sylvester, who has a pronounced stutter, but Ma insists that he will speak an introduction to her song, "Ma Rainey's Black Bottom." Ma keeps the upper hand as long as she can with these white men for whom she makes a great deal of money. She insists that Sylvester repeat the introduction until he gets it right (which he eventually does) despite complaints from the aptly named "control booth" that the retakes are costing money; she refuses to proceed until Coca Colas are sent for when she finds that Irvin has failed to provide her customary beverage. She complains about Irvin and Sturdyvant to Cutler: "Wanna take my voice . . . and then too cheap to buy me a Coca Cola. . . . They don't care nothing about me. . . . As soon as they get my voice down on them recording machines, then it's just like if I'd be some whore and they roll over and put their pants on." After the recording has been completed, Sturdyvant tries to cheat Ma out of Sylvester's pay; however, Ma has not signed the release form yet. When the two men realize this, they hasten to pay Sylvester. Ma has a measure of power within this white-controlled world only as long as she can withhold her song or her signature.

In the final scene of the play, Sturdyvant rejects Levee as a potential recording artist and dismissively offers him "five dollars apiece" for the songs he has written at Sturdyvant's request. When the band is alone again, Toledo accidentally steps on Levee's shoe. Levee becomes enraged and stabs Toledo to death. His disproportionate reaction to Toledo is really, of course,

his response to Sturdyvant, who has cheated him and whom he cannot touch. Through Levee's final act of misdirected violence, the Black Nationalist Toledo is silenced and the artistic potential of Levee is extinguished by inevitable imprisonment or death.

The exploitation of black musicians and the violence that resulted from it is a theme in *Ma Rainey* that Wilson also explores, though less centrally, in SEVEN GUITARS (1995), which is set in the 1940s. It was with the success of *Ma Rainey* (he had already written JITNEY [1982], set in the 1970s) that Wilson conceived of the idea of writing a cycle of 10 plays depicting the African-American experience in each decade of the 20th century. Indeed, the success of *Ma Rainey* "secured Wilson's future as a playwright" and also provided "the first full-blown public demonstration of his newly formulated artistic agenda" (Shannon 75).

BIBLIOGRAPHY
Shannon, Sandra. *The Dramatic Vision of August Wilson.* Washington, D.C.: Howard University Press, 1995.
Wilson, August. *Ma Rainey's Black Bottom.* New York: Plume, 1985.

MARGARET FLEMING JAMES A. HERNE (1890)

Margaret Fleming stands as a harbinger of an American theater intent on exploring serious social and moral issues. The play's lack of success with Boston audiences, and after revision, its failure in New York, suggest that the public was not yet willing to accept drama of an overtly confrontational nature. Decades would pass before a serious social drama would emerge in American theater; however, *Margaret Fleming* indicates the direction this more mature drama would take.

The play focuses on Philip Fleming, a successful industrialist, and his wife Margaret. Early in the play, Margaret learns that her husband has fathered an illegitimate child. Shortly after giving birth, the young mother dies, and Margaret prepares to take in the child and raise it as her own. With his wife's discovery of his infidelity, Philip, true to his dissolute nature, goes on a drinking binge. He returns home, seeking forgiveness, only to discover that the shock of his adultery has aggravated a chronic infirmity in Margaret, leaving her blind. The play ends with a confrontation between the two in which Margaret tells Philip that her "wife-love" is gone and that "the old Margaret is dead. The truth killed her."

Complicating an appreciation of the play for readers of today is the fact that all manuscripts were destroyed by fire in 1909; the present text is a reconstruction from memory made in 1914 by JAMES A. HERNE's wife, Katherine Corcoran Herne, who acted the role of Margaret in all of the productions of the 1890s.

As originally produced, *Margaret Fleming* affronted the public for various reasons; the topic of adultery was but one. It was thought that, if this matter were to arise at all in the serious theater, it should be treated as a sin, not as something to be discussed or examined as a domestic problem. Also, there was the conclusion of the third act, in which Margaret, hearing the whimper of the illegitimate baby, *"unbuttons her dress to give nourishment to the child,"* thereby revealing her underclothing, a manifest shock to an audience of the 1890s. Most disturbing of all, however, was Margaret's refusal, in all of the play's early versions, to forgive her husband for his lapse. Margaret's determination not to accept a double standard, whereby a man's adulterous behavior might be forgiven but never a woman's, resulted in her being condemned as a moral monster for rejecting her husband. In the 1914 "reconstructed" version, however, Margaret's stance has been softened; the door to reconciliation is left open.

Margaret Fleming points the way to the serious American drama of the next generation. The text is abundant with the realistic detail of daily life, imparting truthfulness to storytelling, and on those occasions when Herne employs symbolism, it is unforced, cohering easily within the play's realistic aesthetic. In demanding that the drama deal with "unmentionable" but very real social issues, Herne, in *Margaret Fleming,* made a major advance in a maturing American theater.

Craig Clinton
Reed College

MARGULIES, DONALD (1954–)   Donald
Margulies was born in Brooklyn, New York. Although he was initially interested in the visual arts and studied graphic design at Pratt Institute, he later turned his attention to playwriting at the State University of New York at Purchase, where he received a B.F.A. degree in 1977. His work has been seen primarily in regional theaters and OFF-BROADWAY, with the South Coast Repertory Theatre in Costa Mesa, California, and New York's Manhattan Theatre Club each producing four of his seven major full-length plays to date.

Margulies's work reflects his identity both as a Jew and an artist. In five of his plays, the issue of Jewish identity is central. As Michael Feingold has written in his introduction to *"Sight Unseen" and Other Plays:* "[T]he real beauty of Margulies's work is that he's managed to create an ethnic theatre without the tubthumping self-consciousness that often mars ethnic-minority art. In art the things you assert are your identity; the questions you raise are your way of transcending it" (xi).

Margulies's first major work, *Found a Peanut* (1984), is set in the author's native Brooklyn in 1962. The characters are children ranging in age from four to 12. When one of them finds a paper bag filled with money, the discovery has a profound impact on their relationship to one another. The play explores the nature of friendship, as well as the racial animosity that surfaces when tougher gentile boys attempt to wrest the cash from the more fragile Jewish children. In *What's Wrong with This Picture?* (1985), a middle-class Brooklyn Jewish family is mourning the sudden death of the adolescent hero's mother, who choked to death on pork at a Chinese restaurant. As the family contemplates their loss and a future without her, she mysteriously returns to Earth and begins tidying up the messy apartment. While much of the play is wildly comic, this picture of a grieving, but bewildered, family is a sensitive and touching treatment of love and loss.

The Model Apartment (1995) takes place in a Florida condominium where Lola and Max, Holocaust survivors from Eastern Europe, attempt to escape from their mentally disturbed daughter and from memories of her half-sister who perished in a death camp. Their efforts are thwarted when the surviving daughter and her African-American lover, a mildly retarded 15-year-old, follow them down from Brooklyn.

A middle-class Brooklyn Jewish family are the main characters in *The Loman Family Picnic* (1989). A self-described "black comedy," the play focuses on the upcoming bar mitzvah of the family's older son. The title of the play refers to a musical version of ARTHUR MILLER's *DEATH OF A SALESMAN* written by the younger brother; in his version, the Lomans have a family picnic in Prospect Park, something the two boys have never experienced.

The next two Margulies plays deal with artists. A painter, struggling with his Jewish identity and his sense of integrity, is the main character in *SIGHT UNSEEN* (1991). *Collected Stories* (1996) covers six years in the lives of a well-known Greenwich Village short story writer and her protégé, who uses her mentor's experiences in her own work. *DINNER WITH FRIENDS* (1999) looks at two married couples and the impact of the breakup of one marriage on the other. The play, which earned the writer the PULITZER PRIZE, also examines the nature of friendship, a theme frequently reflected in other Margulies works.

God of Vengeance (2000), adapted from the Yiddish-language drama by Polish writer Sholem Asch, was originally set in 1906, but is here transferred to New York's Lower East Side in 1923. The basic narrative of Asch's play is retained, but Margulies has shifted focus to the American scene, particularly to the experience of Jewish immigrants in the New World. The "hero" Jack Chapman (formerly Yankel Tshaptshovitsh) manages a brothel on the ground floor of his tenement building. His "business" has made him wealthy, but in an ultimately futile attempt to reclaim his piety, he seeks to have his daughter, Rivkele, marry an upright scholar. Unlike earlier Margulies plays, *God of Vengeance* is written on a large canvas with a cast of more than 20 characters. At the same time, it deals with familiar Margulies subjects—how we deal with our heritage and history.

In the semiautobiographical *Brooklyn Boy* (2002), the protagonist Eric Weiss has written a commercially successful novel about his early life in Brooklyn, but nevertheless struggles to escape his Jewish past, his religion, and those who helped create his identity. In a series of sharply written episodes, Weiss confronts his dying father, a childhood friend whom Eric initially rejects, an estranged wife, a young fan in a Los Angeles hotel room, a tough movie producer who desires a less ethnic screenplay, and an actor being considered to play Weiss's alter ego in a projected film version of the novel. Weiss's visit to his hospitalized father is both comic and poignant as Eric tries to explain to his befuddled parent the difference between what is true and what is fictional in the novel. Yet when Eric learns during his visit to Hollywood that the screen version will bear little resemblance to his own fictionalized experiences, he, in effect, returns to his roots and turns down the film.

Shipwrecked! An Entertainment—the Amazing Adventures of Louis de Rougement (As Told by Himself) was commissioned and produced by South Coast Repertory in 2007 and seen at both the Ahmanson Theatre and the Long Wharf Theatre in 2008. Using only three actors, the play chronicles the fictional adventures of de Rougement, whose fabulous tales of living with Australian aborigines and other astonishing adventures made lively reading in Victorian England before his lies were ultimately exposed. Another new work, *Time Stands Still*, commissioned by the Geffen Playhouse in Los Angeles, had its world premiere in 2009.

BIBLIOGRAPHY

Margulies, Donald. *Brooklyn Boy.* New York: Theatre Communications Group, 2005.

———. *Collected Stories.* New York: Theatre Communications Group, 1998.

———. *Dinner with Friends.* New York: Theatre Communications Group, 2000.

———. *God of Vengeance.* New York: Theatre Communications Group, 2004.

———. *July 7, 1994: Short Plays and Monologues.* New York: Dramatists Play Service, 1997.

———. *Luna Park: Short Plays and Monologues.* New York: Theatre Communications Group, 2002.

———. *"Pitching to the Star" and Other Short Plays.* New York: Dramatists Play Service, 1993.

———. *"Sight Unseen" and Other Plays.* New York: Theatre Communications Group, 1995.

———. *Two Days: Two Short Plays.* New York: Dramatists Play Service, 2004.

Leonard Fleischer
Brooklyn, New York

MARRIAGE OF BETTE AND BOO, THE

CHRISTOPHER DURANG (1985) An acerbic combination of slapstick and satire, *The Marriage of Bette and Boo* is a memory play of 33 scenes in two acts, framed by the narration of Matt ("Skippy"), the son of Bette and Boo. Matt remembers family stories he has heard as well as events he has himself witnessed. He tries to understand the past, hoping he will be different from his relatives.

The events in the life of this family are universal: a wedding, a honeymoon, the births of children, holidays with in-laws, divorce; but the Brennans and Hudlockes are a grotesque—albeit hilarious—parody of a typical family. The simpleminded Bette (who takes her inspiration almost exclusively from the writings of A. A. Milne) wants to have many children. Only her first child survives; the rest are stillborn (killed by Rh incompatibility), tossed to the floor each time by the doctor, whose gesture is as senseless as Bette's insistence on conceiving them time after time against medical advice. Boo, whose father calls him "Bore," becomes an alcoholic like his father, Karl. Emotionally abusive, Karl calls his submissive and ever cheerful wife, "Soot." Bette's family is not much better off: Her neurotic sister, Emily, is forever apologizing for small faults, real or imagined; Margaret, Bette's mother, seems unable to provide any useful guidance to her daughters; and Bette's father, Paul, has had a stroke, which has rendered his speech unintelligible. This satiric device, aimed here at family communication, is used again later when a divorce lawyer, equally unintelligible, is played by the same actor in the same way to skewer the legal profession. Once again, as in his *SISTER MARY IGNATIUS EXPLAINS IT ALL FOR YOU* (1979), DURANG takes aim at the Catholic Church in the character of Father Donnally, whose inept advice only makes matters worse.

Durang's irreverent, fast-paced satire exposes the stupidity and cruelty of emotionally defective family relationships and articulates (in Matt's line to his grandfather Karl) the apprehension of offspring everywhere: "[M]y fear is that I can see all of you but not see myself, and maybe I'm doing something similar, but I just can't see it." Based on Durang's own childhood, *The Marriage of Bette and Boo* won an OBIE Playwriting Award.

MASTER CLASS TERRENCE MCNALLY (1995)

Winner of the TONY AWARD for Best Play, *Master Class* is a portrait of real-life opera diva Maria Callas as she conducts master classes for young opera singers. She is occasionally transported back into the past and remembers events in her life, including her unhappy childhood and her ill-fated relationship with Greek billionaire Aristotle Onassis.

Late in her career, when she was past singing herself, legendary soprano Maria Callas gave a series of master classes at Juilliard. In MCNALLY's play, we are the audience for such classes. The portrait of the singer that emerges is of a demanding, egotistical, opinionated—at times, catty—talent who expects her nervous young students to sacrifice as much for their art as she did for hers. She complains about the lights and the temperature of the hall, teases the accompanist, and jokes about her next "victim." When the first young soprano arrives on stage, Callas torments her: "You should be nervous. . . . All these people looking at you. . . . I'd be terrified." When the young woman takes the bait and admits that she *is* nervous, Callas tells her to "stop it. You can't sing if you're nervous." She demands her footstool and her water and her pillow. However, McNally's portrait is not a caricature, but one full of humanity and wit.

As important to Callas as voice is authenticity—of feeling and of acting. She chastises the young singers for their lack of detailed preparation (the tenor does not know the name of the church in which he, as Cavaradossi, is painting a portrait in the opening scene of *Tosca*) and their inattention to acting (the soprano makes no attempt to *act* the part of Lady Macbeth as she reads the letter that will make her both murderer and queen). It was such authenticity and depth of feeling that set Callas apart from her "rivals."

In each of the two acts, there is a scene in which the voice of Callas in her prime overtakes a student-soprano's voice, and she is transported back into memory. She remembers her childhood in which she was "the fat ugly greasy one with thick glasses and bad skin." She remembers secretly gloating, once she became famous, to think that her "enemies"—including her own mother—must see she was by then "the center of the universe." She remembers her early, passionless marriage to Battista Meneghini, many years her senior, which she ended after her transformation into a thin and sophisticated diva. She remembers her lover, Aristotle Onassis, "crude," "vulgar," and the object of her adoration. Most poignant of these memories is that of her only pregnancy, terminated at the insistence of Onassis, whose child she longed to have. (The story of this abortion is based on Callas's often-repeated version of events; others contend that the child was not aborted, but stillborn. However, that is real life and not McNally's play.) In *Master Class,* McNally has resurrected the Maria Callas of legend—talented and vulnerable and larger than life.

Cary M. Mazer has observed that McNally's play combines two genres. It is the autobiographical one-person show (though, of course, *Master Class* involves some peripheral characters), "in which the historical figure, through some theatrical pretense (Emily Dickinson inviting us in as neighbors to share her recipes, Truman Capote speaking into a tape recorder for the benefit of a journalist) retells and relives formative events from his or her life"; but it is also in the American dramatic tradition of what Mazer calls the "psychotherapeutic whodunit," plays in which "a protagonist's tragic agony or a family's crippling dysfunction can be traced . . . to a . . . traumatic event, real or imagined" (176). Mazer includes among such plays EUGENE O'NEILL's LONG DAY'S JOURNEY INTO NIGHT (1956), ARTHUR MILLER's DEATH OF A SALESMAN (1949), EDWARD ALBEE's WHO'S AFRAID OF VIRGINIA WOOLF? (1962), and SAM SHEPARD's BURIED CHILD (1978).

BIBLIOGRAPHY

Mazer, Cary M. "*Master Class* and the Paradox of the Diva." In *Terrence McNally: A Casebook,* edited by Toby Silverman Zinman. New York: Garland, 1997. 165–179.

MASTROSIMONE, WILLIAM (1947–)

Author of more than 20 plays, William Mastrosimone is renowned for his gritty, realistic confrontations between men and women and for his unflinching studies of violence. Born in New Jersey, Mastrosimone was educated at Rider College and Rutgers University, where he received his M.F.A. in 1976. He returns to both institutions with some frequency for workshops and readings of his in-progress plays. Like a growing number of American playwrights, Mastrosimone frequently also writes for television and movies; many of his TV and film scripts have been adapted from his plays.

His early play *The Woolgatherer* (1979) suggests that men and women are compelled to misunderstand each other. A tough-talking truck driver meets a salesgirl who invites him to return to her home. However, instead of the expected sexual encounter, the two soliloquize about life on the road, loneliness, and the cultivating of a sweater collection from ex-partners. Mastrosimone presents some of the same themes of misunderstanding in *Shivaree* (1983), in which a housebound hemophiliac falls in love with a belly dancer, despite his mother's protests.

Mastrosimone is best known for plays that depict violence, power, and the cruelties that humans inflict upon one another. His most widely produced play is *Extremities* (1980). In a series of harrowing scenes, a young woman named Marjorie brutally tortures her would-be rapist. Subsequently, she decides to kill the man. When Marjorie's housemates return home, they are unable to understand why she would have acted with such rage and sadism. In an ever-shifting study of power, *Extremities* questions the roles of victim and victimizer, a theme to which the playwright returned in his 1986 play *Cat's-Paw.* Here, he presents an American ecoterrorist spewing a rant of hate-filled justifications for the murder of those who spoil the environment. After the atrocities of September 2001, many of the terrorist's fictive ideas seem prescient.

More recently, Mastrosimone's plays have examined the culture of violence and its effects on young adults. In *Like Totally Weird* (1998), a pair of skate punks has ceased to understand the differences between reality and movie mayhem. Subsequently, they break into the mansion of a Hollywood mogul whose violent films they admire. Taking the producer and his starlet hostage, the two intruders proceed to terrorize the couple. In response to a slew of tragic school shootings, Mastrosimone composed *Bang Bang You're Dead* in 1998. The play imagines the aftermath of a school shooting, as seen through the eyes of Josh, the young, rampaging murderer. In a series of tense scenes, Josh is confronted by the victims of his crime.

Mastrosimone has made the play available to school groups through a free download on the Internet, for which he charges no fee (www.bangbangyouredead.com). The play is enormously popular with school groups and has been produced thousands of times in recent years. Mastrosimone continues to explore themes of teen angst and disconnection in his play *Sleepwalk* (2004).

BIBLIOGRAPHY

Mastrosimone, William. *Collected Plays*. Newbury, Vt.: Smith and Kraus, 1993.

———. *Collected Plays, Volume II*. Lyme, N.H.: Smith and Kraus, 2001.

Mark Cosdon
Allegheny College

MATCHMAKER, THE THORNTON WILDER (1955)

A revision of WILDER's 1938 play *The Merchant of Yonkers*, *The Matchmaker* was first produced in Scotland in 1954 and then in Philadelphia and New York in 1955. Set in the 1880s, this comedy, which Wilder acknowledged was an adaptation of Austrian Johann Nestroy's 1842 play, *Einen Jux will er sich Machen* (itself based on *A Day Well Spent* [1835] by Englishman John Oxenham), concerns the adventures of a group from Yonkers who are in New York City for the day, trying to put some joy in their lives. It was made into the musical *Hello, Dolly!* in 1964.

Horace Vandergelder, *"sixty, choleric, vain and sly,"* wants to marry again. Dolly Levi is helping him find a wife. To that end, she will take him to New York City to meet Mrs. Molloy, an attractive young widow who runs a millinery shop. Horace leaves his prosperous Yonkers store in the hands of his clerks, Cornelius and Barnaby. Before leaving Yonkers, Mr. Vandergelder forbids his niece Ermegarde to marry her sweetheart, the artist Ambrose Kemper. Vandergelder's certainty that he is in charge of everyone and everything he surveys is misguided, however. Cornelius, 33, and Barnaby, 17, heat and explode some jars of tomatoes to give them an excuse to leave the store and go to New York City themselves; they vow not to return "until [they]'ve kissed a girl." Mrs. Levi, "a woman who arranges things," decides to help Ermegarde and Ambrose marry without eloping as Ambrose proposes.

Once in New York, Cornelius and Barnaby meet Mrs. Molloy by chance and, also by chance, ruin her chances to marry the wealthy Horace Vandergelder. Mrs. Molloy insists that Cornelius, whom Dolly Levi has led her to believe is rich, and Barnaby take her and her assistant to dinner at the Harmonia Gardens Restaurant. Smitten with the two women, they agree.

All the principal characters—Cornelius's party, Ermegarde and Ambrose, and Mrs. Levi and Mr. Vandergelder—converge on the Harmonia Gardens. When Mr. Vandergelder loses his purse, it falls into the hands of Cornelius, enabling him to pay for the lavish dinner Mrs. Molloy has ordered and emboldening him to tell her the truth about himself. When Mr. Vandergelder discovers Cornelius and Barnaby at the next table on the other side of a screen, he fires them both; in fact, he fires everybody, even people he does not employ. He threatens Ermegarde and Ambrose, who run from him, and Vandergelder himself runs from Mrs. Levi, who is trying to manipulate him into marrying her.

The final scene takes place at the home of Ermegarde's bewildered "Aunt Flora," who has been awaiting the young woman's arrival all day. There is much mistaken identity, much forgiveness, and much falling in love. And finally, Horace Vandergelder asks Dolly Levi to marry him (an idea that she put in his head). She will marry him "for his money" because "we're all fools and we're all in danger of destroying the world with our folly. But the surest way to keep us out of harm is to give us the four or five human pleasures that are our right in the world,—and that takes a little *money!*"

Rex J. Burbank writes that Wilder called the play a parody of "'the stock-company plays'" he saw as a boy in California in the early 20th century: "Much of its humor arises from the use of such old comic stage devices as mistaken identity, quick leaps from hiding places under tables, characters dressed in clothes of the opposite sex, and people caught in folding screens." It is a farce featuring "stock characters and absurd situations that develop into a conventional complicated plot" (Burbank 84).

BIBLIOGRAPHY
Burbank, Rex J. *Thornton Wilder.* 2d ed. Boston: Twayne, 1978.

M. BUTTERFLY DAVID HENRY HWANG (1988)

Loosely based on a true story, *M. Butterfly* is the tale of an insecure French diplomat, Rene Gallimard, and his relationship with a Chinese opera diva; after a 20-year affair, Gallimard finds out the woman he has loved with such consuming passion is actually a man and a Chinese spy. DAVID HENRY HWANG's TONY AWARD–winning play challenges cultural and gender stereotypes and exposes what Hwang calls the "rape mentality" of imperialism.

The play begins in the 1980s with Rene Gallimard in a French prison for treason; this is the frame in which the play exists. From his prison cell, Gallimard remembers his ecstasy and his humiliation. As a married diplomat stationed in Beijing, Gallimard meets Song Liling, a performer—apparently a woman—with the Chinese opera, when she sings an aria from Puccini's *Madame Butterfly* at a reception. When Gallimard compliments her on her performance, she is not surprised that he admires the opera since, as she tells him, *Madame Butterfly* is a favorite fantasy—"the submissive Oriental woman and the cruel white man"—among Westerners. One of the great ironies of the play is that this fantasy is turned on its head. Gallimard believes that he is acting out this fantasy after their initial meetings; once she seems interested in him, he withholds his attention from her for weeks until she seems to be a butterfly "turning on [his] needle." Then he feels sick for abusing the power he has gained over her. The irony, of course, is that Song Liling is the one with all of the power, and—as is made clear in the second act when Song testifies as himself, a man, in court—quite the cruel one, while the French diplomat unwittingly submits to the power Song Liling has over him.

It is after his promotion to vice consul in charge of intelligence that Gallimard begins a sexual affair with Song Liling. Pretending to be a woman, Song tells Gallimard that while he is inexperienced and modest, he is not ignorant of what will please a man. In all the years of their affair, he remains covered and in charge. Song tells the court during the trial scenes in act 3, "It was my job to make him think I was a woman." He explains, "It wasn't all that hard. See, my mother was a prostitute. . . . [S]he learned a few things about Western men. So I borrowed her knowledge. In service to my country." Song explains further, "The West has a sort of an international rape mentality towards the East. . . . The West thinks of itself as masculine . . . so the East is feminine. . . . [W]hen he finally met his fantasy woman, he wanted more than anything to believe that she was, in fact, a woman . . . [a]nd . . . I'm an Oriental. And being an Oriental, I could never be totally a man" to him.

In addition to cultural stereotypes, Hwang addresses gender stereotypes as well. During his affair with Song, Gallimard is unfaithful when he has an affair for several months with a Danish college student. He finds her willingness and lack of modesty and inhibition "exciting" but "too masculine." In fact, what most excites him when he is with the Danish girl are the imagined silence and tears of his Butterfly; the dominance over, the infliction of pain on the more "feminine" Song Liling is what he likes. Once again, the rape mentality of the Western male is an important theme, whether applied to his approach to women or to Asia.

During the eight years of their affair in China, Song Liling gathers information for Mao's government on French and American activities in Vietnam as well as these governments' positions vis-à-vis China. Finally, Gallimard is sent back to France just as the Cultural Revolution in China is getting started. Song Liling suffers during this movement for having engaged in homosexual acts with Gallimard in the process of gaining information from him. Song is sent to France and told to don his disguise again and resume spying for China using Gallimard.

Once in France, Gallimard divorces his wife, and he and Song Liling resume their affair. Song encourages him to become a diplomatic courier so that Song can also resume spying for China. Eventually, Gallimard is found out and tried for treason. In a final irony, Gallimard takes on the role of Puccini's Butterfly—better death than dishonor—and commits suicide as she did.

In his "Afterword" to the 1989 Plume edition of the play, David Henry Hwang wrote, "*M. Butterfly* has sometimes been regarded as an anti-American play, a diatribe against the stereotyping of the East by the West, of women by men. Quite the contrary, I consider it a plea to all sides to cut through our respective layers of cultural and sexual misperceptions, to deal with one another truthfully for our mutual good, from the common and equal ground we share as human beings" (100).

BIBLIOGRAPHY
Hwang, David Henry. *M. Butterfly*. New York: Plume, 1989.

MCCULLERS, CARSON (1917–1967) See *MEMBER OF THE WEDDING, THE*.

MCNALLY, TERRENCE (1939–) Terrence McNally is probably the most consistently successful—both commercially and artistically—of the several contemporary American playwrights who have written about this country's gay community as it faced the scourge of AIDS during the last two decades of the 20th century. He was born in St. Petersburg, Florida, but grew up in Corpus Christi, Texas. Two of his most vivid childhood memories are of his parents taking him to New York when he was six years old to see Ethel Merman in *Annie Get Your Gun* and four or five years later to see Yul Brynner and Gertrude Lawrence in *The King and I*. He was also a faithful listener to the Saturday afternoon radio broadcasts of the Metropolitan Opera; classical music, especially opera, has been one of the abiding passions of his life, and it is prominent in many of his plays.

After getting his B.A. (1960) at Columbia University and attending the New York theater regularly, he worked for two years as a stage manager at the ACTORS STUDIO, where he met and saw the work of, among many others, playwrights EDWARD ALBEE, ARTHUR KOPIT, and TENNESSEE WILLIAMS and director ELIA KAZAN, and where he wrote his first professionally produced play, *And Things That Go Bump in the Night* (1965). An absurdist comedy about a family who have chosen to live in their basement, it received negative reviews and ran only two weeks, devastating McNally,

who gave up the theater and returned to journalism, his original career choice.

In 1966, he applied for and won a Guggenheim Fellowship and resumed writing plays, producing a number of one-acts, mostly focused on political and social issues of the day. These included *Sweet Eros* (1968), about a man, twice unsuccessful in love, who kidnaps a young woman and binds her, naked, to a chair; *Witness* (1968), evocative of John F. Kennedy's assassination; *¡Cuba Si!* (1968), a critique of America's involvement in Vietnam; *Noon* (1968), a sex farce; and *Next* (1969), which satirizes American bureaucracy through its depiction of a physical exam being given to an overweight middle-aged man who has obviously been mistakenly drafted into the army.

Returning to the longer play form, McNally's next two efforts were *Where Has Tommy Flowers Gone?* (1971), which focuses on an unemployed actor who plots to blow up Lincoln Center, and *Bad Habits* (1974), which deals farcically with two sanitariums with very different approaches to treating the mentally ill and for which McNally won a Distinguished Play OBIE AWARD. *The Ritz* (1975), another farce, about a group of mobsters creating havoc in a gay bathhouse, was McNally's first major commercial success and was made into a successful film in 1977.

Following the failure of *Broadway, Broadway* (1979), a comedy about the theater, McNally stopped writing for five years. In 1984, he wrote the book for *The Rink*, a musical by John Kander and Fred Ebb, the first of what were to be several successful side trips into musical theater. His next production, *It's Only a Play*, a revision of *Broadway, Broadway*, opened at the Manhattan Theatre Club in January 1986 and began McNally's very fruitful relationship with that OFF-BROADWAY theater, which has since premiered most of his plays. It is also the work that the playwright regards as the "turning point play" in his career, in that it is "part satiric and part heartfelt" in its portrayal of a Broadway company awaiting opening night reviews (Drukman 342).

The adjective "heartfelt" certainly describes McNally's *FRANKIE AND JOHNNY IN THE CLAIR DE LUNE* (1987), a funny and affectionate portrait of two middle-aged "not beautiful" people, a waitress and a short-order cook, who, after spending the night together, grapple with the risks of a more serious and committed relationship. McNally adapted the play for a film version in 1991. *The LISBON TRAVIATA* (1989) continued his exploration of the difficulties of intimacy in the time of AIDS, this time in the gay community, and this play demonstrates his first overt emphasis on classical music. Mendy and Stephen find themselves much more comfortable in the world of opera than in the far more dangerous, real world of a domestic triangle that involves Stephen, his long-time partner Mike, and the latter's new lover Paul.

LIPS TOGETHER, TEETH APART (1991) deals with two straight couples in the gay environment of New York's Fire Island and demonstrates that the two worlds are equally susceptible to death and fear. After writing the book for Kander and Ebb's musical *The Kiss of the Spider Woman* (1993), for which he won his first TONY AWARD, McNally next wrote *A Perfect Ganesh* (1993), about two very different older women on a trip to India; both are fleeing decaying marriages, both have lost children, and both are seeking some sort of redemption from the Indian god Ganesha (who appears as a character).

LOVE! VALOUR! COMPASSION! (1993) won both the Tony and the New York Drama Critics' Circle Awards (both in 1995) and represents McNally's most personal and intimate representation of the gay community; focusing on a group of eight men who gather on three successive holiday weekends, it explores such universal topics as friendship, jealousy, envy, fear, death, and commitment against the background of the AIDS epidemic. *MASTER CLASS* (1995), which also won the Tony Award, portrays opera star Maria Callas as she conducts a class for aspiring singers; at times chilling and at other times thrilling, it expresses its author's personal admiration for Callas and for the persistence and sacrifices great artists make in order to inspire us with their talent.

McNally won another Tony Award for his book of the musical *Ragtime* (1998), but his next play, *Corpus Christi* (1998), engendered controversy and elicited outrage and protests from Catholic organizations for its portrayal of a group of gay men in Corpus Christi, Texas, putting on a play depicting the life of Jesus Christ. The Manhattan Theatre Club first cancelled its production but then reinstated it after a vigorous response from the artistic community, led by American playwright TONY KUSHNER and South African dramatist Athol Fugard. In 2008, *Corpus Christi* was revived in New York without incident.

McNally wrote the libretto for the opera *Dead Man Walking* (2000) and books for the musicals *The Full Monty* (2000), *The Visit* (2002), and *A Man of No Importance* (2002). His most recent works include *The Stendhal Syndrome* (2004), comprising two one-acts: *Full Frontal Nudity,* about the contrast between great art and ordinary human existence, and *Prelude and Liebestod,* about an orchestra conductor who, despite his egotistical personality, remains the conduit for the composer's genius; *Dedication; or, the Stuff of Dreams* (2005) is about a life spent in the theater; *Deuce* (2007) involves two aging female tennis greats who are reunited at the U.S. Open in order to be honored for their contributions to the game; and *Some Men* (2007), which in a series of scenes chronicles the changing culture of gay relationships over nearly a century.

McNally's plays, both those that focus directly on the gay community and those that do so indirectly, go well beyond the stereotypes to be found in such earlier works of GAY AND LESBIAN THEATER as MART CROWLEY'S *The BOYS IN THE BAND* (1968), as well as beyond the more nuanced portrayals in such later works as LARRY KRAMER'S *The Normal Heart* (1985) and William M. Hoffman's *As Is* (1985), and even Tony Kushner's *ANGELS IN AMERICA* (1990, 1991). The characters in these last three plays are pretty much defined by the AIDS crisis, while McNally's characters are human beings who happen to be gay or straights who confront their own humanity in the gay community. As a result, they serve to increase the much-needed communication between those two communities, and they remind us that being human transcends superficial labels.

BIBLIOGRAPHY

Drukman, Steven. "Terrence McNally." In *Speaking on Stage: Interviews with Contemporary American Playwrights,* edited by Philip C. Kolin and Colby H. Kullman. Tuscaloosa: University of Alabama Press, 1996. 332–345.

McNally, Terrence. *Corpus Christi.* New York: Grove Press, 1998.

————. *Dedication; or, The Stuff of Dreams.* New York: Grove Press, 2006.

————. *15 Short Plays.* Lyme, N.H.: Smith and Kraus, 1994.

————. *Lips Together, Teeth Apart.* New York: Plume, 1992.

————. *The Lisbon Traviata.* Rev. ed. New York: Dramatists Play Service, 1990.

————. *"Love! Valour! Compassion!" and "A Perfect Ganesh."* New York: Plume, 1995.

————. *Master Class.* New York: Plume, 1995.

————. *"The Ritz" and Other Plays by Terrence McNally.* New York: Dodd, Mead, 1976.

————. *Some Men.* New York: Dramatists Play Service, 2008.

————. *The Stendhal Syndrome: "Full Frontal Nudity" and "Prelude and Liebestod."* New York: Grove Press, 2004.

————. *Three Plays by Terrence McNally: "The Lisbon Traviata," "Frankie and Johnny in the Clair de Lune," "It's Only a Play."* New York: Plume, 1990.

Zinman, Toby Silverman, ed. *Terrence McNally: A Casebook.* New York: Garland, 1997.

MEDEA ROBINSON JEFFERS (1947)

Freely adapted from Euripides' ancient Greek play, JEFFERS's *Medea* retells the traditional story of the violence and destruction wrought by a vengeful woman. Written originally for actress Judith Anderson, Jeffers's *Medea* was critically acclaimed during its 1947–48 Broadway run.

The story centers around Medea's revenge against her husband, Jason, who has abandoned her to marry a younger woman, the daughter of the King of Corinth, in order to establish social and political security. Medea is outraged by this betrayal, since she had assisted Jason years earlier in his quest for the Golden Fleece, owned and jealously guarded by her father, the King of Colchis. Medea, a sorceress, had fallen in love with Jason, and in helping him secure the prize, she deceived her father and killed her brother. Since fleeing her homeland with Jason to live in exile, she has borne him two sons. As the play begins, King Creon has banished Medea and her children from Corinth, fearful that she will avenge Jason's marriage to his daughter Creusa. Medea does indeed exact a bloody and fiery retribution, killing both Creusa and Creon, then slaughtering her own children to leave Jason completely bereft. She subsequently departs with the boys' corpses to Athens, where King Aegeus has promised her refuge in return for her magical powers in ensuring him offspring.

While Jeffers's adaptation of *Medea* retains the theme of vengeance, it modernizes and streamlines the language, making it more direct, less lyrical, and more fraught with vicious animal imagery than that of Euripides. Jeffers also downplays the role of the gods as well as that of the Chorus, identifying them as Three Women and having them often speak individually; whereas, Euripides' Chorus always chants as a group and is more clearly sympathetic to Medea. Dramatically, Jeffers develops the imagery of light and dark more fully. Less effective is his division of the play into two acts. The first act ends as Medea summons Jason to announce her reconciliation with him and his new wife; breaking the action at this point weakens the tension of the play, thus defusing the grip of this powerful piece of psychology. Furthermore, Jeffers's *Medea* implies more emphatically than Euripides' version that Aegeus's childlessness inspires Medea's murder of her sons, and the play's ending has Medea walking from the house with the children's bodies rather than departing deus ex machina style in an overhead chariot as in the original.

Jeffers found a contemporary relevance in *Medea,* perceiving parallels between the disillusionment of the Euripidean age and that of postwar America, as well as a correspondence between Medea's emotional struggle and his own ambiguities toward his country and his art. While Jeffers was best known as a poet, often epic in style, his rendition of *Medea* was intended directly for the stage, exposing him to audiences who may not have been familiar with his work; however, his *Medea* did not spark any movement towards verse drama in American theater. Jeffers has dramatized other Greek myths as well, including Euripides' *Hippolytus,* and much of his poetry is infused with the themes and mood of Greek tragedy, including "Solstice," a retelling of the Medea story in a California setting.

Karen C. Blansfield
University of North Carolina–Chapel Hill

MEDOFF, MARK (1940–)

Playwright, director, actor, and educator, Mark Medoff was born in

Mount Carmel, Illinois, and educated at the University of Miami (B.A., 1962) and Stanford University (M.A., 1966). Medoff's long teaching career has been spent primarily at New Mexico State University–Las Cruces, where he has also served as head of the department of theater arts. Medoff was artistic director of the American Southwest Theatre Company from 1982 to 1987. His plays have been produced in Los Angeles, San Francisco, and New York, as well as in regional theaters around the country.

Medoff's first successful play was *When You Comin' Back, Red Ryder?* (1973), for which he received an OBIE AWARD for Distinguished Playwriting. The play concerns a violent, disaffected young man who terrorizes the patrons and workers at a diner in New Mexico. The following year, Medoff offered a comic drama set in academia, *The Wager* (1974), in which a graduate student bets his roommate that the roommate cannot seduce the wife of a young professor within a two-day period. (*The Wager* was, in fact, a reworking of Medoff's first play—a one-act that he rewrote many times over a period of eight years.)

Medoff's best-known play, *CHILDREN OF A LESSER GOD* (1980), is about the relationship between a deaf woman, Sarah, and a speech therapist, John. Believing Sarah would be better off if she could communicate directly with the hearing world, John hopes to teach her to read lips and to speak. Sarah resists his "help" and resents his notion that her language (American Sign Language) is inferior to his. Despite falling in love and marrying, the two continue to face fundamental difficulties in understanding each other's world. An early version of the play was produced at New Mexico State University. Medoff revised the play, and it opened in New York in 1980. Despite mixed reviews, it won the TONY AWARD for Best Play of the year.

Other Medoff plays published by the Dramatists Play Service include *The Kramer* (1976), *The Majestic Kid* (1986)—a musical, *The Hands of Its Enemy* (1987), *Big Mary* (1989), *The Heart Outright* (1990), *Stefanie Hero* (1994), *Kringle's Window* (1994), *Stumps* (1995), and *The Homage That Follows* (1995). Medoff has also written screenplay adaptations of his own and others' works. Because of his extensive work in film, Medoff's teaching has shifted focus in recent years from theater arts to film arts.

In 2004, Medoff returned to Broadway with the critical failure *Prymates,* about a gorilla named Graham.

BIBLIOGRAPHY

Medoff, Mark. *Children of a Lesser God.* Clifton, N.J.: J. T. White, 1981.

———. *Gunfighter: A Gulf War Chronicle.* New York: Dramatists Play Service, 2003.

———. *The Wager.* New York: Dramatists Play Service, 1975.

———. *When You Comin' Back, Red Ryder?* New York: Dramatists Play Service, 1974.

MEE, CHARLES L. (1938–)

Born and raised outside of Chicago, Charles L. Mee began writing plays while a student at Harvard. After graduating in 1960, he moved to New York to pursue his interest in theater, but personal, professional, and political events led him into a career as an historian and an editor. He is the author of a dozen books of history, on such subjects as the origins of the cold war, summit diplomacy, the Constitutional Convention, and Rembrandt. In the mid-1980s, he resumed playwriting, initially by providing texts for Martha Clarke's dance-theater piece, *Vienna: Lusthaus* (1986). By the early 1990s, Mee's work was being staged in experimental venues by such innovative American directors as Anne Bogart, Robert Woodruff, Tina Landau, and David Schweizer. In the late 1990s, he moved into the theatrical mainstream, with productions at important, institutional theaters such as Steppenwolf Theatre in Chicago, Magic Theatre in San Francisco, American Repertory Theatre in Cambridge, Actors Theatre of Louisville, and New York Theatre Workshop.

The abiding themes of Mee's work are love, violence, and the commingling of the two in various forms, from Sigmund Freud's concepts of primeval Eros and Thanatos to the conflicting emotions that often define intimate interpersonal relationships. Inspired by the collage techniques of such 20th-century artists as Max Ernst and Robert Rauschenberg, Mee's plays frequently feature a jumble of edgy characters and fragmentary scenes juxtaposed in odd, amusing, and sometimes disconcerting ways. Mee eschews character psychology, a unified narrative, and a single point of view in favor of an openness of form, an endless and surprising variety, and a multiplicity of perspectives—male and female, tragic and comic, authoritarian and anarchic. Mee bolsters this heterogeneity by culling passages from literary sources—as wide-ranging as *The Pillow Book of Sei Shonagon,* Valerie Solanus's *SCUM Manifesto,* newsstand magazines from *Vogue* to *Soap Opera Digest,* Klaus Thewelt's *Male Fantasies,* the Menendez Brothers trial transcripts, on-line chat room conversations, and his own students' writing—and incorporating them verbatim into the dialogue of his characters.

This cut-and-paste strategy manifests an aesthetic of appropriation, which stems from Mee's conviction that culture is caught up in a perpetual process of remaking itself, of tearing down and building up, of recycling ideas, values, and practices from the past as a way of creating the future. In fact, many of Mee's plays are radical revisions of classical dramas, particularly Greek tragedies, which he pulls apart and sifts through for appealing situations, images, and themes. *Trojan Women: A Love Story* (1996) refracts Euripides and the composer Hector Berlioz through contemporary political events and cultural preoccupations. *Full Circle* (1998) ponders the new Europe by resituating Bertolt Brecht's *Caucasian Chalk Circle* in East Berlin in 1989, with Grusha as a student revolutionary and a dissolute, self-critical Heiner Müller in the Azdak role. *Big Love* (2000) stages an archetypal, visceral, and ironic battle of the sexes that picks up where Aeschylus's *The Suppliants* leaves off. Written for Anne Bogart and the SITI Company, *bobrauschenbergamerica* (2001) combines borrowed texts from Walt Whitman, William S. Burroughs, and others with Mee's own writing to generate a kaleidoscopic portrait of America in the second half of the 20th century.

In the first decade of the new century, Mee's plays were ubiquitous, both in New York and around the United States. The 2007–2008 season of the Signature Theatre was devoted to his work and included three world premieres, *Iphigenia 2.0* (2007), *Queens Boulevard (the musical)* (2007), and *Paradise Park* (2008). With Shakespeare scholar Stephen Greenblatt, he coauthored a romantic comedy based on the lost Shakespeare play *Cardenio* (2008). His collaboration with Bogart and SITI Company extended to include two more plays inspired by American artists: *Hotel Cassiopeia* (2006), an elegiacal collage play inspired by the box constructions of Joseph Cornell, and *Under Construction* (2009), a purposefully unfinished, then-and-now collision of Norman Rockwell and installation artist Jason Rhoades.

Mee's plays can be found at www.charlesmee.org, a Web site that encourages any and all comers to take the texts, cut them up, rearrange them, add and subtract material, and make new works. Those interested in an account of Mee's experience as a teenager with polio in the 1950s may want to consult his memoir, *A Nearly Normal Life* (1999).

BIBLIOGRAPHY

Cummings, Scott T. *Remaking American Theater: Charles Mee, Anne Bogart and the SITI Company.* Cambridge: Cambridge University Press, 2006.
Mee, Charles L. *History Plays.* Baltimore: Johns Hopkins University Press, 1998.
———. *A Nearly Normal Life.* Boston: Little, Brown, 1999.

Scott T. Cummings
Boston College

MEMBER OF THE WEDDING, THE CARSON McCULLERS (1950)

Adapted by McCullers from her 1946 novel of the same name, *The Member of the Wedding* is a coming-of-age play set in the American South in the summer of 1945. Frankie Addams, nearly 13, becomes infatuated with the idea of her brother's wedding, indeed, with the engaged couple themselves. Only after the ceremony, when the couple insists on leaving without her does Frankie accept that their "we" does not include her, that her dreams were "child plans." This experience, together with the deaths of people close to her, initiate Frankie into the "sudden place" that is the adult world.

As the play begins, Frankie is at loose ends and on the brink of adolescence. Her best friend has moved away; the older girls in her neighborhood exclude her from their club; and even her cat has run off. Her summer companion has been her seven-year-old cousin, John Henry. Caring for the two children that summer is Berenice, the Addams's middle-aged African-American housekeeper. Frankie's mother died shortly after Frankie's birth, so Berenice has long been her mother figure. Berenice immediately spots Frankie's "crush on the *wedding*" and understands that Frankie is feeling "lonely and left out." Frankie is determined to leave with her brother and his wife after the ceremony, telling Berenice, "I know [now] that the bride and my brother are the 'we' of me."

This summer, Frankie is, for the first time, considering and commenting on some of the mystifying and disturbing aspects of life: "No power on earth could bring [the present moment] back again" once it has passed; "this new atom bomb is worth twenty thousand tons of T.N.T." She sees security in joining the married couple: "[A]fter the wedding I won't have to worry about things anymore." But, of course, she is left behind after the ceremony with promises that once they are settled, she can "come for a nice visit." Frankie runs away, but in the morning she returns home, after "running around the dark scary streets" and considering suicide by means of her father's pistol, which she has packed in her suitcase. Little time is spent dwelling on Frankie's internal drama, however, because John Henry has come down with meningitis and Honey Camden, Berenice's "foster brother," is running from the law.

Honey Camden, a talented musician and an angry victim of racism, has used a razor on a white man who refused to serve him. Though he is a fugitive from the law, he feels liberated; Honey tells Berenice, "No more 'boy this—and boy that' . . . I'm free," but Berenice can "[a]lready feel that rope," the rope of a lynch mob. Early in the play, Berenice sees a parallel between the behavior of Frankie and that of Honey Camden when both take out their frustration on little John Henry—Frankie after the club girls exclude her, and Honey Camden after a racist encounter with a white military policeman. Berenice observes, "When people are lonely and left out, they turn so mean." But while Frankie is able to move into adulthood, the tragedy of Honey Camden's life—that of an African-American man in the pre–Civil Rights era South—is that he is kept in a condition of restriction akin to childhood from which he cannot break free, except

in ways that will bring him into conflict with the law. Berenice, the black woman of the southern tradition, disapproves of and grieves over Honey Camden's rebellion because she believes it will lead to his death, as indeed it does. Ironically, some of her disapproval comes as a result of the significant role she plays in raising and protecting the white children. McCullers, then, touches on the complex and difficult interdependent relationship between black and white in the Jim Crow South.

The final scene takes place months later. John Henry and Honey Camden are both dead. Frankie has a new best friend. Berenice is saying goodbye to Frankie because Frankie and her father are going to move in with John Henry's parents now.

Much of the action in the play—Frankie's rejection by the bride and groom, Frankie's frightening night, the razor fight, the deaths—takes place offstage; what takes place onstage are the conversations about these events, conversations usually among Berenice and the two children. The play won the New York Drama Critics' Circle Award for Best Play of 1950. McCullers, primarily a novelist and short-story writer, wrote only one other play, *The Square Root of Wonderful* (1957), which was not well received.

MEN IN WHITE SIDNEY KINGSLEY (1933) The hospital drama and Broadway success *Men in White* demonstrates the methodology that KINGSLEY followed for the remainder of his long career: he did meticulous research on his subjects and immersed himself in the environment about which he would write. In this case, he familiarized himself with hospital life by accompanying an intern friend on his rounds. He reaped the rewards of this careful work when *Men in White* was embraced by the medical communities in the United States and abroad. Following its Broadway opening, *Men in White* was produced to great acclaim in Budapest, Hungary (in Hungarian), and in London, England, somewhat revised by Kingsley with the help of British doctors. It has also been translated into Spanish, German, and Russian. *Men in White* won the PULITZER PRIZE (though the manner of its selection created controversy: The jury proposed MAXWELL ANDERSON's *Mary of Scotland* but was overridden by

the Pulitzer advisory committee, which selected *Men in White*).

Men in White is about the demands of medical life and their impact on personal relationships, the need for medical research, and the consequences of illegal abortion, all told through the story of a young and talented physician, George Ferguson. George is caught between his desire to work in medical research with the highly respected Dr. Hochberg and his fiancée Laura Hudson's intention that he set up a lucrative practice. During a critical rift in their relationship, George has a one-time affair with a sympathetic young nurse, Barbara Dennin, which results in pregnancy. Later, as George and Laura, having reconciled, prepare for their wedding, Barbara is brought into the hospital for emergency surgery following a botched illegal abortion. George, who was unaware of Barbara's pregnancy, is horrified and intends to shoulder what he considers to be his responsibility to marry Barbara by giving up his beloved Laura, his study in Vienna, and the opportunity to work with Hochberg. Barbara survives the surgery but not a postoperative embolism, for which adequate treatment had not yet been found. With a greater understanding of each other and the life of a dedicated doctor, Laura and George part while leaving open the small possibility of a future relationship.

Men in White, entitled "Crisis" in early versions, was inspired and formed in part by several medical experiences: Kingsley's own tonsillectomy, his exploration of hospital life with his intern friend, and his observation of an autopsy on a young woman who died from an illegal abortion. While not the main storyline of the play, Kingsley's early advocacy of legalized abortion is articulated by his character Dr. Hochberg. Kingsley revisited the horrors of illegal abortion in *Detective Story* (1949).

Kingsley went to great pains to create a work in *Men in White* that was filled with realistic details of hospital life and portrayals of the doctors, nurses, orderlies, and patients and their families that he encountered in his on-site research, an effort that was appreciated by many viewers, though not all critics.

Nena Couch
Ohio State University

METAMORA; OR, THE LAST OF THE WAMPANOAGS John Augustus Stone (1829)

This sweeping, five-act "Indian tragedy" by Stone was written in response to a widely advertised playwriting contest sponsored by the celebrated early American actor, Edwin Forrest (1806–72), who wished to add an original American play about the lives of Native Americans to his stage repertory.

Metamora is a drama that explores the unlikely possibility of reconciliation between Native Americans and white settlers in a fictionalized drama based on King Philip's War (1675–76), in which Metacomet, chief of the Wampanoag Indians (and known to colonists as "King Philip"), led raids on settlers. Despite some battlefield successes, Metacomet was killed by another Indian, and his tribe was essentially wiped out by hostile colonists. The historical sources for Stone's play are many, and harsh depictions of Metacomet are found in Increase Mather's *Brief History of the War with the Indians* (1676) and William Hubbard's *Narrative of the Troubles with the Indians* (1677). More sympathetic treatments, both historical and fictional, appear in a Washington Irving essay on the subject published in *The Sketch Book,* James Fenimore Cooper's *The Wept of Wish-ton-Wish,* D. P. Thompson's *The Doomed Chief,* and Esther Forbes's *Paradise,* among others.

Stone's similarly sympathetic account, which was first performed at New York's Park Theatre on December 15, 1829, depicts Wampanoag chief Metamora (played by Forrest), a noble Indian in the manner of Native American depictions in Cooper's *Leather-Stocking Tales.* Metamora grapples with his determination to hold onto the lands of his forefathers despite his realistic assessment of a situation that will lead to the eventual extermination of his tribe. In one powerful sequence, Metamora confesses to his wife, Nahmeokee: "[T]he power of dreams has been on me, and the shadows of things that are to be have passed before me. . . . [W]hen our fires are no longer red, on the high places of our fathers; when the bones of our kindred make fruitful the fields of the stranger . . . then will the stranger spare, for we will be too small for his eye to see." Despite Metamora's anger at the settlers, this profoundly conflicted man of deep conscience saves the life of Oceana, a white woman in love with

Horatio (named Walter in some versions of the play). Metamora assists the lovers, but the fortunes of the Wampanoag tribe decline, and Metamora fights to the bitter end, cursing "the stranger" as he dies.

Despite its occasional Eurocentric stereotyping of Indians (or perhaps because of it), *Metamora* became one of Forrest's most popular productions (even more popular in a slightly revised version by ROBERT MONTGOMERY BIRD in 1836), and the play remained in his repertory throughout the remainder of his career. *Metamora* popularized "Indian plays" on the American stage and inspired many to be written, including JOHN BROUGHAM's 1847 burlesque parody, *Metamora; or, The Last of the Pollywogs*. Like much 19th-century American drama, *Metamora* has rarely been performed in the last 100 years.

James Fisher
University of North Carolina at Greensboro

MIELZINER, JO[SEPH] (1901–1976)   Jo Mielziner, the preeminent 20th-century Broadway stage designer, was born in Paris but received early art training at the Pennsylvania Academy of Art in Philadelphia and the National School of Design in New York. He also studied in Europe, traveling on two school scholarships. At the urging of his brother, actor Kenneth MacKenna (born Leo Mielziner Jr.), Mielziner began to consider a career in stage design. On his second scholarship, he decided to focus on scenic art, studying with Oskar Strnad in Vienna but devoting the rest of his time to observing the scenic trends at experimental theaters in Paris, Vienna, and Berlin. Before returning to America, he managed to obtain an audience with English director and designer Gordon Craig in Rappalo, Italy, an event that helped to shape his ideas about stage design.

Mielziner's total practical preparation for his new profession was a brief apprenticeship at Joseph Urban's Scenic Studio, his study with Strnad, and part of a season at a summer stock company as a backstage jack-of-all-trades. His brother introduced him to Lee Simonson at the THEATRE GUILD, which eventually led to an apprenticeship with ROBERT EDMOND JONES and an opportunity to design for the company. Jo Mielziner's design for the Guild production of Ferenc Mol-

nar's *The Guardsman* (1925) earned him critical plaudits and helped solidify his goal of finding a niche in the theater. In the next years, Mielziner established a reputation as an inventive and innovative designer, following the precepts of the New Stagecraft as promulgated and practiced by Jones, Simonson, and Norman Bel Geddes, who saw the scenic designer as "an indispensable collaborator in the interpretation of a script" (Henderson 24), rather than as simply the provider of a backdrop against which the play took place. To their theories, he added his own: to find the emotional nuance of the play and make it the inspiration for his design. Although many of the plays were based in realism, he found a scenic expression for them, which lifted them out of the ordinary and into the poetic. His accompanying lighting was so blended into his scenery that it became an inextricable part of the design.

During the 1930s and 1940s, he was offered design assignments on Broadway for the leading playwrights of the time: EUGENE O'NEILL (STRANGE INTERLUDE [1928]), MAXWELL ANDERSON (a dozen plays and one musical), ROBERT E. SHERWOOD (notably *ABE LINCOLN IN ILLINOIS* [1938]), PHILIP BARRY (notably *Foolish Notion* [1945]), S. N. BEHRMAN (seven comedies), LILLIAN HELLMAN (three plays, including *The Lark* [1955]), SIDNEY HOWARD (four plays, including *Yellow Jack* [1934]), PAUL OSBORN (five plays, including *MORNING'S AT SEVEN* [1939]), ELMER RICE (*Dream Girl* [1945] and *STREET SCENE* [1929]), ARTHUR MILLER (notably *DEATH OF A SALESMAN* [1949]), TENNESSEE WILLIAMS (*The GLASS MENAGERIE* [1945] and *A STREETCAR NAMED DESIRE* [1947], among others), ROBERT ANDERSON (*TEA AND SYMPATHY* [1953]), and WILLIAM INGE (*PICNIC* [1953]), as well as for dozens of lesser-known plays written by now-forgotten contemporary dramatists. His design for Maxwell Anderson's *WINTERSET* (1935) marked a turning point in his career. Because of his strong affinity for the play, he was able to persuade Anderson to let him depict the soaring Brooklyn Bridge in the background, as a way of providing an emotional focus, instead of setting the play in the earthbound scene that the playwright had specified. The setting broke new ground for Mielziner and established his reputation.

After service in World War II, he returned to find a different Broadway. Always using stage technology that was at hand, he devised a setting for Miller's *Death of a Salesman* that remained an icon for the play for many years. Lifting the play out of the commonplace, Mielziner designed the set as an X-ray by revealing the "bones" of the house and by slicing away half of the structure, just as the playwright sliced through the psyches of the characters. For Williams's *A Streetcar Named Desire,* Mielziner created a low-ceilinged and windowless set that he stretched across the stage to compress the action of the play within its narrow and airless confines. It had the effect of trapping the characters within its walls and entangling them in a tragic web.

Mielziner designed almost 270 productions, most of them original plays and musicals, with an occasional assignment to create scenery for plays by Shakespeare, George Bernard Shaw, Luigi Pirandello, and many continental playwrights.

BIBLIOGRAPHY

Henderson, Mary C. *Mielziner, Master of Modern Stage Design.* New York: Watson Guptill, 2001.

Mielziner, Jo. *Designing for the Theatre.* New York: Atheneum, 1965.

———. *The Shapes of Our Theatres.* New York: Clarkson Potter, 1970.

Mary C. Henderson
Congers, New York

MILLAY, EDNA ST. VINCENT (1892–1950)

Complementing her fame as a poet, Edna St. Vincent Millay, throughout her life, had close ties to theater. After college, she worked as an actress; much of her famed verse was dramatic in content, and during her life, she completed six plays.

Raised in Rockland, Maine, Millay, in high school, played roles in class plays and took parts with local amateur theatrical groups and stock companies traveling through the town. At Vassar College, she acted in college productions and took a playwriting course, which resulted in three pieces. The first, begun earlier but completed during the course, was *The Princess Marries the Page* (1916), a short play in blank verse. It was performed at the college, and Millay took the lead

in this light, romantic story about love and sacrifice between the title characters. Her next play, *Two Slatterns and a King* (1917), has similar fairy-tale elements and was written in four-beat (tetrameter) couplets in the manner of a moral Renaissance interlude, telling the story of a foolish king who is deceived into picking the wrong bride. The third piece written at Vassar was "The Wall of Dominoes," Millay's only prose play; it was neither produced nor published. With a contemporary setting, it traces the hedonistic, empty lifestyle of a young female sophisticate. Its mixture of comedy and an underlying seriousness and its promotion of honor and integrity make it typical of Millay's work.

Upon graduating in 1917, Millay went to New York to become an actress and lived in Greenwich Village. It was a location suited to her growing sense of the avant-garde, her social conscience, and her free-thinking. She worked with the THEATRE GUILD and the PROVINCETOWN PLAYERS; for the latter, she wrote and directed the innovative and highly popular *ARIA DA CAPO* (1919). Adopting a poetic form reminiscent of Anglo-Saxon verse, the play mixes the harlequinade with the pastoral to create an insightful and entertaining commentary on the combative nature of humankind.

Although she wrote up to her death, Millay would produce only two more plays. *The Lamp and the Bell* (1921) was commissioned by Vassar Alumnae for its 50th anniversary celebration and was based on a fairy tale, "Rose White and Rose Red." Much longer than her previous plays, its five acts relate the tortuous love triangles created around two stepsisters and is reminiscent of Elizabethan drama. Her final play was *The King's Henchman* (1927), commissioned as a libretto by the Metropolitan Opera to accompany music by Deems Taylor. It is a powerful story of divided loyalties, which pitches love against honor and ends tragically for those who have acted selfishly.

Millay's experimental *Aria da Capo,* which foreshadows the expressionistic, symbolic drama of THORNTON WILDER, is an important and lasting contribution to American poetic drama.

BIBLIOGRAPHY

Atkins, Elizabeth. *Edna St. Vincent Millay and Her Times.* Chicago: University of Chicago Press, 1936.

Brittin, Norman A. *Edna St. Vincent Millay.* New York: Twayne, 1982.

Freedman, Diane P., ed. *Millay at 100: A Critical Reappraisal.* Carbondale: Southern Illinois University Press, 1995.

MacDougall, Allan Ross, ed. *Letters of Edna St. Vincent Millay.* New York: Harper, 1952.

Milford, Nancy. *Savage Beauty: The Life of Edna St. Vincent Millay.* New York: Random House, 2001.

Millay, Edna St. Vincent. *The King's Henchman.* New York: Harper, 1927.

———. *The Princess Marries the Page.* New York: Harper, 1932.

———. *Three Plays.* New York: Harper, 1926.

Nierman, Judith. *Edna St. Vincent Millay: A Reference Guide.* Boston: G. K. Hall, 1977.

Sheean, Vincent. *The Indigo Bunting: A Memoir of Edna St. Vincent Millay.* New York: Schocken, 1973.

Thesing, William B., ed. *Critical Essays on Edna St. Vincent Millay.* New York: G. K. Hall, 1993.

Susan C. W. Abbotson
Rhode Island College

MILLER, ARTHUR (1915–2005)

Arthur Asher Miller was born in New York City into comfortable circumstances; however, in 1929 his father's garment manufacturing business failed, and the Millers eventually lost their home. Miller's experiences as a young person during the depression shaped his ideology. His sympathy for the individual faced with circumstances beyond her or his control stems from this early period. Witnessing the collapse of an economy based on capitalism led him to favor socialism.

After high school, Miller worked to save up money to pay for college and in 1934 entered the University of Michigan. While at Michigan, he wrote his first plays. He twice won the Avery Hopwood Award (an undergraduate playwriting award), which gave him both prize money and encouragement. After graduating from Michigan with a degree in English in 1938, he briefly worked for the FEDERAL THEATRE PROJECT. He did not serve in the military during World War II because of a physical deferment.

Miller's first New York play, *The Man Who Had All the Luck* (1944), was neither a critical nor a box office success, and in 1945 he published *Focus,* a novel in which an anti-Semite is mistaken for a Jew. But two years later, *ALL MY SONS* (1947), a postwar drama about the individual's responsibility to the common good of society, opened and won for Miller his first New York Drama Critics' Circle Award. This success was followed by the greater success of *DEATH OF A SALESMAN* (1949), for which he won the TONY AWARD, the PULITZER PRIZE, and another New York Drama Critics' Circle Award and which established his reputation. Considered an American classic, *Death of a Salesman* examines the tragic final days of Willy Loman, a salesman for whom the world no longer has use, but who retains his heroic stature by, in Miller's words, laying down his life "to secure . . . his sense of personal dignity" (*Theatre Essays* 4).

The CRUCIBLE (1953), set during the Salem witch trials of 1692, examines the overpowering of the individual by the institution, against all logic. Miller meant the play to be seen as analogous to the events of the McCarthy era; however, it also stands apart from that parallel as a powerful piece of human drama. *A VIEW FROM THE BRIDGE* (1955), set on the waterfront of Brooklyn, won the New York Drama Critics' Circle Award. Originally a one-act play, *A View from the Bridge* was first produced with another one-act entitled *A Memory of Two Mondays,* set in a Manhattan warehouse. Both plays continued Miller's examination of the often tragic circumstances of the common man.

After the failure of his first marriage, Miller married film actress Marilyn Monroe in 1955. During this time, he wrote the screenplay for *The Misfits* (1961), based on a story he had written for *Esquire* magazine in 1957; the movie starred Monroe, Clark Gable, and Montgomery Clift. Miller divorced Monroe in 1961; his play *AFTER THE FALL* (1964), which portrays a man between his second and third marriages—the second to a beautiful but insecure entertainer—has autobiographical elements, but Miller objected to how those elements overshadowed the reception of the play. Its theme suggests that a man is not so much a product of his past as he is a product of the choices he makes as he emerges from the past. The same year, *Incident at Vichy* (1964), a treatment of the conflict between the Nazis and Jews, was produced. *The PRICE* (1968), about the conflict and resentment between two brothers as they come to terms with their father's life and death and their own choices, was a popular success. Miller's next two plays, *The Creation of the World and Other Business* (1972) and *The American Clock* (1980), failed.

In recent decades, Miller's work has been well received in London, more so than in New York. *The Archbishop's Ceiling* (1986) was produced in London by the Royal Shakespeare Company and has not yet been seen in New York. Also, Miller's two one-acts, *I Can't Remember Anything* and *Clara,* collected as *Danger: Memory!* (1987), were more successful in London than in their New York production, and *The Ride down Mount Morgan* (1991) opened in London and was popular there.

BROKEN GLASS (1994) deals with the toll that social injustice—in the form of the Nazi persecution of the Jews—takes on an individual. The play takes place shortly after Kristallnacht, the night of broken glass; the characters represent the various American reactions to the news of the persecution of Jews abroad. *Mr. Peters' Connection* (2000), set in an abandoned nightclub, mixes fantasy with confession.

Miller's penultimate play, *Resurrection Blues,* premiered at the Guthrie Theater in Minneapolis in August of 2002. It takes place in a fictional South American country, where 2 percent of the country's population own 98 percent of its wealth, ruled by a ruthless dictator who, to solidify his power, plans to execute a rebel leader by crucifying him. An American film company pays $25 million for the exclusive rights to film the crucifixion. As Bruce Weber pointed out in his *New York Times* review, the play decries such Reagan-era legacies as "greed, powermongering, the unfair distribution of wealth, [and] political hypocrisy" (August 15, 2002). Miller's final play, *Finishing the Picture,* premiered at the Goodman in 2004 and is about the making of *The Misfits.*

Arthur Miller's essays on theater are an enduring contribution to the understanding of playwriting and of modern tragedy. These essays were first published in 1971 as *The Theatre Essays of Arthur Miller* (edited by Robert A. Martin); a second collection, *Echoes down the Corridor* (edited by Steven Centola), appeared in 2000.

British scholar C. W. E. Bigsby has written that Arthur Miller "touched a nerve of the [American] national consciousness" in a way that other American dramatists have not, "engag[ing] the anxieties and fears, the myths and dreams, of a people desperate to believe in a freedom for which they see ever less evidence" ("Arthur Miller" 248). However, his themes are by no means exclusively American; Miller's work is also embraced by the international community. When *The Crucible* was performed in China, it was seen as "relevant to a Cultural Revolution in which youth had exacted its revenge on an adult world. [And] *Death of a Salesman* has been hailed in countries where the profession itself is unknown" (Bigsby, "Arthur Miller," 248).

At the time of Miller's death, the theater critic Charles Isherwood wrote in the *New York Times,* "By now, the American dream has been thoroughly dissected, but American values continue to be touted by politicians as the country's most fruitful export. And so Mr. Miller's greatest plays, in which he used both his conscience and his compassion to question the prerogatives of American society, remain . . . as necessary as ever." Furthermore, Isherwood wrote, Miller's "greatest concerns, in the handful of major plays on which his reputation will last, were with the moral corruption brought on by bending one's ideals to society's dictates, buying into the values of a group when they conflict with the voice of personal conscience" (February 12, 2005).

BIBLIOGRAPHY

Abbotson, Susan C. W. *A Critical Companion to Arthur Miller.* New York: Facts On File, 2007.

———. *Student Companion to Arthur Miller.* Westport, Conn.: Greenwood Press, 2000.

Ali, Syed Mashkoor, ed. *Arthur Miller: Twentieth Century Legend.* Jaipur, India: Surabhi, 2006.

Bigsby, C. W. E. "Arthur Miller." *A Critical Introduction to Twentieth-Century American Drama: Volume Two—Williams/Miller/Albee.* Cambridge, England: Cambridge University Press, 1984. 135–248.

———. *Arthur Miller: A Critical Study.* Cambridge: Cambridge University Press, 2005.

———, ed. *Arthur Miller and Company: Arthur Miller Talks about His Work in the Company of Actors, Designers, Directors, Reviewers and Writers.* London: Methuen, 1990.

———. *Arthur Miller: 1915–1962.* London: Weidenfeld and Nicolson, 2008.

———. *The Cambridge Companion to Arthur Miller.* Cambridge, England: Cambridge University Press, 1997.

———, ed. *Remembering Arthur Miller.* London: Methuen, 2005.

Brater, Enoch. *Arthur Miller: A Playwright's Life and Work.* New York: Thames and Hudson, 2005.

———, ed. *Arthur Miller's America: Theater and Culture in a Time of Change.* Ann Arbor: University of Michigan Press, 2005.

———, ed. *Arthur Miller's Global Theatre.* Ann Arbor: University of Michigan Press, 2007.

Carson, Neil. *Arthur Miller.* 2nd ed. New York: Palgrave Macmillan, 2008.

Centola, Steven, ed. *The Achievement of Arthur Miller: New Essays.* Dallas: Contemporary Research, 1995.

———. *Arthur Miller in Conversation.* Dallas: Northouse & Northouse, 1993.

———, and Michelle Cirulli, eds. *The Critical Response to Arthur Miller.* Westport, Conn.: Praeger, 2006.

Ferres, John H. *Arthur Miller: A Reference Guide.* Boston: G. K. Hall, 1979.

Gottfried, Martin. *Arthur Miller: His Life and Work.* New York: Da Capo, 2003.

Griffin, Alice. *Understanding Arthur Miller.* Columbia: University of South Carolina Press, 1996.

Gussow, Mel. *Conversations with Arthur Miller.* New York: Applause, 2002.

Koorey, Stefani. *Arthur Miller's Life and Literature.* Lanham, Md.: Scarecrow Press, 2000.

Langteau, Paula, ed. *Miller and Middle America.* Lanham, Md.: University Press of America, 2007.

Marino, Stephen. *A Language Study of Arthur Miller's Plays: The Poetic in the Colloquial.* New York: Mellen, 2002.

Martin, Robert A., ed. *Arthur Miller: New Perspectives.* Englewood Cliffs, N.J.: Prentice-Hall, 1982.

Mason, Jeffrey D. *Stone Tower: The Political Theater of Arthur Miller.* Ann Arbor: University of Michigan Press, 2008.

Miller, Arthur. *"The American Clock" and "The Archbishop's Ceiling": Two Plays.* New York: Grove Press, 1989.

———. *Arthur Miller: Collected Plays 1944–1961.* Edited by Tony Kushner. New York: Library of America, 2006.

———. *Arthur Miller's Collected Plays.* Vol. 2. New York: Viking Press, 1981.

———. *Broken Glass.* New York: Penguin, 1994.

———. *Danger: Memory!* New York: Grove Press, 1986.

———. *Echoes down the Corridor: Collected Essays—1944–2000.* Edited by Steven R. Centola. New York: Viking Press, 2000.

———. *Everybody Wins.* New York: Grove Press, 1990.

———. *"The Golden Years" and "The Man Who Had All the Luck."* London: Methuen, 1989.

———. *The Last Yankee.* New York: Penguin, 1994.

———. *Mr. Peters' Connection.* New York: Penguin, 1999.

———. *On Politics and the Art of Acting.* New York: Viking Press, 2001.

———. *The Portable Arthur Miller.* Rev. ed. Edited by Christopher Bigsby. New York: Penguin, 1995.

———. *Resurrection Blues.* New York: Penguin, 2006.

———. *The Ride down Mount Morgan.* New York: Penguin, 1992.

———. *The Theatre Essays of Arthur Miller.* Rev. ed. Edited by Robert A. Martin and Steven R. Centola. New York: Da Capo, 1996.

———. *Timebends: A Life.* New York: Grove Press, 1987.

———. *Two-Way Mirror: A Double Bill.* London: Methuen, 1984.

———. *Up from Paradise.* New York: Samuel French, 1984.

Moss, Leonard. *Arthur Miller.* Rev. ed. Boston: Twayne, 1980.

Nelson, Benjamin. *Arthur Miller: Portrait of a Playwright.* New York: David McKay, 1970.

Otten, Terry. *The Temptation of Innocence in the Dramas of Arthur Miller.* Columbia: University of Missouri Press, 2002.

Roudané, Matthew C., ed. *Conversations with Arthur Miller.* Jackson: University Press of Mississippi, 1987.

Savran, David. *Communists, Cowboys, and Queers: The Politics of Masculinity in the Work of Arthur Miller and Tennessee Williams.* Minneapolis: University of Minnesota Press, 1992.

Viswamohan, Aysha. *Arthur Miller: The Dramatist and His Universe.* Chennai, India: T.R. Publications, 2005.

Welland, Dennis. *Miller the Playwright.* London: Methuen, 1979.

MILLER, JASON (1939–2001) See THAT CHAMPIONSHIP SEASON.

MILNER, RONALD (1938–2004) Playwright Ron Milner was an important figure in the BLACK ARTS MOVEMENT of the late 1960s and early 1970s and continued to write plays through the end of the 20th century. Along with Woodie King Jr., he edited the *Black Drama Anthology* (which includes his own play *Who's Got His Own* [1966]). Over the course of his long career as a playwright, he continued to write about the African-American experience and to promote his strong belief in the importance of theater to the black community.

Born and raised in Detroit, Michigan (where most of his plays are set), Milner became involved in 1964 with Woodie King and the Concept East Theater in Detroit. Both men eventually went to New York; Milner did so in order to attend novelist Harvey Swados's writing workshop at Columbia University. In New York, Milner once again joined King, this time at the American Place Theatre, which was then forming. His first play, *Who's Got His Own,* was produced there.

The play deals with a family at the time of the father's death; the widow's revelations to her children—particularly her angry son—cause them to see their father's tyranny in the context of his personal history. Milner's next play, *The Warning—A Theme for Linda* (1969), is a one-act about a 17-year-old who has in her family only broken and bitter women from whom to learn about men; their views sharply contrast with the girl's fantasies. The play was first produced in New York with three other plays as *A Black Quartet* at the Chelsea Theatre Center of the Brooklyn Academy of Music (BAM).

One of Milner's most critically acclaimed plays, *What the Wine Sellers Buy* (1973), also deals with the choices faced by black youth with disastrous role models. The play is about an innocent young man's seduction by a persuasive pimp who tries to convince him to put his girlfriend to work on the streets in order to solve his family's significant financial and medical problems. Besides being a portrait of the challenges faced by young, poor African Americans, Milner said that the play is also an indictment of American big business, which makes many of the same arguments as Rico, the pimp.

In the mid-1970s, Milner returned to Detroit and focused on the teenage audience. Three musicals aimed at black youth and first produced in Detroit were *Season's Reasons* (1976), at Langston Hughes Theatre; *Work* (1978), first produced for the Detroit public schools; and *Crack Steppin'* (1981), at Detroit's Music Hall. Many young musicians and choreographers collaborated on these works.

Milner returned to the adult stage with *Checkmates* (1987), about two African-American couples: an educated upwardly mobile pair in their thirties and their older, unsophisticated landlords. The older couple—and presumably their whole generation—has always lived with an eye toward building a better future, while the younger couple, for all their advantages, is not sure what they stand for—except themselves. This contrast in values exposes the younger couple as less well-equipped to deal with life's and marriage's difficulties.

Other works include *The Monster* (1969), a one-act satire set on a black college campus; *M(ego) and the Green Ball of Freedom* (1971), a one-act first produced in Detroit at Shango Theatre; *Jazz-set* (1980), first produced in Los Angeles at the Mark Taper Forum, then in New York in 1982, about the lives of a jazz group (with music by Max Roach); *Roads of the Mountaintop* (1986); and *Don't Get God Started* (1987)—music and lyrics by Marvin Winans.

Milner's late work includes *Defending the Light* (2000), first produced in New York at the TriBeCa Performing Arts Center, a courtroom drama set in 1846, in which a black man is treated savagely by the justice system. The play is based on Earl Conrad's historical novel *Mr. Seward for the Defense.*

Milner was founding director of both the Spirit of Shango Theater Company and the Langston Hughes Theatre in Detroit.

BIBLIOGRAPHY

Caldwell, Ben, et al. *A Black Quartet: Four New Black Plays.* New York: New American Library, 1970.
Milner, Ron. *What the Wine Sellers Buy.* New York: Samuel French, 1974.
———, and Woodie King Jr., eds. *Black Drama Anthology.* New York: New American Library, 1971.

MIRACLE WORKER, THE WILLIAM GIBSON (1959)

As much about Annie Sullivan as it is about her famous pupil, Helen Keller, *The Miracle Worker* portrays the miraculous transformation of six-and-a-half-year-old Helen Keller from savage child, isolated within her deaf, mute, and blind body, into a child with civil manners and—far more importantly—language.

Set in the 1880s, the play begins when Helen, aged 18 months, is left blind and deaf by a fever. Five years later, her parents have tried every "cure" and taken her to many specialists, but to no avail. Their love takes the only form they believe it can, indulgence. Helen has been allowed to roam the Kellers' Alabama homestead completely undisciplined. When she overturns her infant sister's cradle, the Kellers decide to try yet another doctor and through him are led to a young teacher from Boston's Perkins Institute for the Blind. Annie Sullivan, whose own blindness has been cured through surgery, is hired to teach the unruly child. Their first encounter leaves Annie locked by Helen in her bedroom with a bloody lip and a missing tooth. At her first meal with the Kellers, Annie is shocked to see Helen helping herself to handfuls of food from the plates of her parents and her much older brother. When she attempts to do the same to Annie's plate, Annie stops her, asks the family to leave the room, and embarks on a battle with Helen that will last for hours and end with Helen using a spoon and folding her napkin—the room around her in a shambles.

Based on this modest success, the Kellers reluctantly allow Annie to take Helen to live for two weeks in a garden house on their property so that she can have complete control over her pupil. (A long buggy ride leads Helen to believe she is far from home.) Annie teaches Helen civilized manners and the alphabet for the blind. At the end of their time alone together, the child can sign many words, but she does not connect the hand motions to their meaning; for her it is simply a game. In the climax of the play, Helen's breakthrough comes when at the water pump her infant word for water, "wah wah," long buried, resurfaces, and she makes the essential cognitive connection between meaning and signing. Her teacher has saved her from isolation by giving her language.

Annie is motivated by her own experience. Her childhood is revealed through a series of audio flashbacks. Now just 20, she spent her childhood in a "state asylum," where rats, disease, death, and insanity were a way of life. Annie is haunted by the loss of her brother, Jimmy, whom she vowed never to desert but was helpless to save from death in the asylum. In Helen, Annie finds her lost brother, whom she could not save, and herself, who was not spared—as she can spare Helen—the asylum's horrors. By saving Helen from darkness and desertion, Annie is able to put to rest the voices that have haunted her since her brother's death.

Of GIBSON's historical plays, *The Miracle Worker* is his best known and, along with *Two for the Seesaw,* is one of his most commercially and critically successful plays. The portrayals in it of Sullivan and Keller have become inextricably mixed with the public perception of these two real people—though Gibson telescoped time and invented elements of their characterizations—particularly after a 1962 film adaptation brought the portraits to a wider audience. His stage sequel, *Monday after the Miracle* (1983), was less successful.

MISS FIRECRACKER CONTEST, THE
BETH HENLEY (1984)   *The Miss Firecracker Contest,* first produced in 1984 at the Manhattan Theatre Club in New York, is HENLEY's quintessential American comedy about a small-town beauty contest, an underdog, and southern stereotypes. It was her third full-length play, and it is in many ways complementary to CRIMES OF THE HEART (1981) and a fine example of southern gothic humor on stage.

When the play opens, Carnelle Scott, 24, dressed in a purple leotard, her hair dyed bright red, is practicing her talent routine for the Fourth of July beauty contest. Her tune is "The Star Spangled Banner." She has substituted knives, wooden spoons, and shouts of "Pow" for the Roman rockets and sparklers she plans to use. She is a bizarre figure but no odder than Popeye, the seamstress who arrives to sew the red, silver, and blue costume Carnelle has designed. As the women snack on saltine crackers, they share their stories. Both are life's losers. Neglected by her father, then orphaned, Carnelle was reared by her aunt. Needing affirmation, she became promiscuous and was dubbed Miss Hot Tamale by the town of Brookhaven, Mississippi. She has resolved to remake her life by attending church, volunteering at the cancer drive, and becoming a Big Sister. Popeye received her nickname after a childhood accident left her half-blind. They become a team.

In the second act, set on the carnival grounds, the disasters—and laughter—snowball. The red dress Carnelle borrows from her cousin Elain is too small, so she inserts a wedge of pink and tries to hide the patch with a Mardi Gras mask. She reenters bedraggled: Onstage, she trips over the gown, rises, and is bombarded with insults, peanuts, and trash by a former boyfriend. Ironically, the setback increases Carnelle's resolve, and she receives admiration and applause for her star-spangled routine. Still, she finishes fifth, even though she entered the contest a likely second. She accepts defeat with grace. Ignoring her cousins' advice to drop out, she is resolved to walk behind the float in the parade. The theme of a woman's battle to become a winner is as American as the holiday the play celebrates.

Carnelle's older cousins, Elain and Delmount, are parodies. Elain is the southern belle, a former Miss Firecracker, who has been invited to deliver a speech—"My Life as a Beauty"—at this year's contest. She has parlayed her charm into a remunerative marriage but feels no love for her husband and two sons. Delmount has just been released from a mental institution for "dueling" with broken beer bottles over a woman. He becomes obsessed with beautiful features and stalks his fantasy figure, writing a love poem, which he then burns. The play is marked by a comedic playfulness and dramaturgical skill.

Glenda Frank
New York, New York

MISS LULU BETT Zona Gale (1920) See Gale, Zona.

MISTER ROBERTS Thomas Heggen and Joshua Logan (1948) Based on Heggen's collection of short stories, the comedy *Mister Roberts* is set on a cargo ship in the Pacific during World War II. The play is a tribute to the men who served in support of the combat ships of the United States Navy, but who did not themselves see combat. The subordinate officers and crew—ordinary American sailors—are affectionately drawn, especially Mister Roberts, who—in sharp contrast to the captain—is honest, loyal, reasonable, and self-sacrificing.

The play begins just prior to V-E day. A navy cargo ship operating in the Pacific is suffering from low morale. The captain is an unreasonable and petty tyrant, who thinks more of his potted palm tree—an "award" for "working cargo"—than he does his crew.

The second in command, Lieutenant (junior grade) Douglas Roberts, requests a transfer to a battleship weekly and is denied weekly. The conflict between Mister Roberts and the captain comes in part from the captain's belief that the younger, college-educated man feels superior to him; despite his animosity toward Roberts, the captain persistently refuses his transfer request because he needs Roberts—an excellent cargo officer—to help him get one more promotion before he retires. Within Roberts, there is another conflict: He wants to fight for the cause he believes in and to test his mettle in combat, but his job is to supply the ships that see action, and he can find no value in that.

The crew has not had liberty in a year, and tension is high. Roberts makes a deal with the captain: He agrees to stop requesting a transfer and to stop contradicting the captain in front of the men in return for their long overdue liberty. Further, Roberts must agree not to disclose this deal to the men. A raucous liberty follows, so raucous, indeed, that the ship is ordered from the harbor the next day. Roberts keeps his bargain with the captain, which puts him at odds with the crew.

Perhaps the most memorable and comic character in the play is Ensign Frank Pulver, the "Laundry and Morale Officer." Pulver does so little work and keeps such a low profile that the captain, when he chances to see him, does not know who he is. Pulver's idea of placing a homemade firecracker under the captain's bunk to celebrate V-E day cheers Roberts, but when Pulver tests the "firecracker," which he has foolishly made from a powerful explosive, he destroys the laundry room and the materials necessary to make another such "firecracker." (This is the closest Pulver has come to following through on a scheme to irritate the insufferable captain.) Roberts is disappointed, but inspired later by a radio broadcast encouraging listeners to destroy "the forces of ambition, cruelty, arrogance and stupidity," he marches to the captain's potted palm tree, uproots it, and throws it overboard. The ensuing argument between Roberts and the captain is overheard by the crew, who then fully understand how much Mister Roberts has sacrificed for them. In appreciation, they write another request for his transfer and forge the captain's signature on the letter. Roberts finally gets his transfer, to a destroyer.

More than a month later, Pulver is now second in command and does little to agitate in the crew's favor against the captain. The mailbag brings a letter—written three weeks before—from Roberts to Pulver; Roberts is satisfied with his new assignment, but he is now appreciative of the strength it takes for the men on "that bucket—all the guys everywhere who sail from Tedium to Apathy and back again"—to do their necessary, inglorious work. Another, more recent letter brings the sad news of Mister Roberts's death: A "suicide plane" hit his destroyer and killed Roberts and another officer as they drank coffee together in the boardroom. In the final moments of the play, Ensign Pulver finds his backbone, flings overboard the captain's *two* replacement palm trees, and confronts the captain in order to improve conditions for the men—as Mister Roberts would have done.

One of several post–World War II plays, the comic *Mister Roberts* honors the sacrifices of the ordinary sailor; it also presents such memorable characterizations as those of Pulver and the captain and captures the senselessness of war in the irony of Roberts meeting his death while engaged in an activity as mundane as a coffee break. Other plays depicting the experiences and effects of the war include JOHN PATRICK's comedy *The TEAHOUSE OF THE AUGUST MOON* (1953), ARTHUR LAURENTS's drama *HOME OF THE BRAVE* (1945), and ARTHUR MILLER's drama *ALL MY SONS* (1947), among others.

MITCHELL, LANGDON ELWYN (1862–1935)

Born in Philadelphia, Langdon Mitchell studied law at Harvard and Columbia, though he never practiced law after he was admitted to the New York bar in 1886. His earliest poems and plays appear under the pen name John Philip Varley. He is best known for the comedy *The NEW YORK IDEA* (1906), a satire about frivolous divorce and marriage habits among wealthy Americans. The play is considered by many to be the best American social comedy of the early 20th century. His other noteworthy plays include *Becky Sharpe* (1899) and *Major Pendennis* (1916), adaptations of William Thackeray's novels *Vanity Fair* and *Pendennis,* respectively; *The Kreutzer Sonata* (1906), an adaptation of the Yiddish play of the same name by Jacob Gordin; and *The New Marriage* (1911), another—though much less successful than *The New York Idea*—portrayal of two dissatisfied couples.

Mitchell taught English literature at George Washington University from 1918–20. He became the University of Pennsylvania's first professor of playwriting in 1928, a post he held for two years. Mitchell's nondramatic works include *Poems* (1894); *Love in the Backwoods* (1897), a collection of stories; and *Understanding America* (1927), a collection of essays written for various magazines.

BIBLIOGRAPHY
Mitchell, Langdon. *The New York Idea.* Boston: W. H. Baker, 1908.
———. *Understanding America.* New York: George H. Doran, 1927.
———, et. al. *The Art of Playwriting.* Philadelphia: University of Pennsylvania Press, 1928.

MITCHELL, LOFTEN (1919–2001)

Playwright, theater historian, and educator, Loften Mitchell is known for his contributions to the chronicling of the history of African Americans, particularly in American theater, through his plays and musicals as well as through his essays and scholarship. Mitchell was born in Columbus, North Carolina, but grew up in Harlem, where, in the 1930s, he visited vaudeville houses and saw some of the great black performers of the period. He tried acting but found opportunities for black actors limited. He attended City College briefly (1937–38) after high school, and during this period his antiwar play *Shattered Dreams* (1938) was produced in New York. Granted a scholarship, he left New York for Alabama's Talladega College (B.A., 1943). It was at Talladega that Mitchell wrote his first musical, *Prelude to the Blues* (1940).

After serving in the United States Navy during World War II, Mitchell returned to New York and studied playwriting at Columbia University (M.A., 1951), where one of his mentors was critic and anthologist John Gassner. He encouraged Mitchell to continue producing work on the history of African-American theater, a subject Mitchell had first begun to write about as an undergraduate.

The result, in part, was Mitchell's important work, *Black Drama: The Story of the American Negro in the Theatre,* which was published in 1967.

Mitchell's plays further chronicle the African-American experience. Sometimes they deal with that experience in theater: The musical *Star of the Morning: Scenes in the Life of Bert Williams* (1965) is a portrayal of the legendary comedian and his struggle to perform with some dignity in America's theaters (music by Louis D. Mitchell, lyrics by Romare Bearden and Clyde Fox). Another musical, *Bubbling Brown Sugar* (1975), takes a contemporary black couple on a journey back to Harlem in its heyday (the original concept for the piece came from actress Rosetta LeNoire and the music and lyrics are by various artists). *Miss Ethel Waters: To You* (1983) portrays the famous actress and singer. Sometimes Mitchell's works chronicle the African-American experience outside of theater: *A Land beyond the River* (1957) is about the battle for desegregation of schools in the South, featuring Dr. Joseph Armstrong DeLaine, and is Mitchell's best-known play. His concert drama, *Tell Pharaoh* (1967), is a series of scenes with music surveying the history and experience of African Americans (*Tell Pharaoh* was originally written for television in 1963).

Other plays include *Blood in the Night* (1946), *The Bancroft Dynasty* (1948), *The Cellar* (1952), *The Phonograph* (1961), the pageant *Ballad of the Winter Soldiers* (1964)—written with John Oliver Killens, and *The Final Solution to the Black Problem in the United States; or, The Fall of the American Empire* (1970). Other musical works include *Ballad for Bimshire* (1963; revised version, 1964), with Irving Burgie, and the opera *And the Walls Came Tumbling Down* (1976), music by Willard Roosevelt.

In the 1950s and early 1960s, Mitchell also wrote regularly for radio in New York City. He was professor of theater and African-American studies at State University of New York at Binghamton from 1971 until 1985, when he became professor emeritus.

BIBLIOGRAPHY

Mitchell, Loften. *Black Drama: The Story of the American Negro in the Theatre.* New York: Hawthorn, 1967.

———. *Bubbling Brown Sugar.* New York: Broadway Play Publishing, 1984.

———. *A Land beyond the River.* Cody, Wyo.: Pioneer Drama Service, 1963.

———. *Star of the Morning: Scenes in the Life of Bert Williams.* New York: Free Press, 1965.

———. *Tell Pharaoh.* Rev. ed. New York: Broadway Play Publishing, 1987.

———, ed. *Voices of the Black Theatre.* Clifton, N.J.: James T. White, 1975.

MOODY, WILLIAM VAUGHN (1869–1910)

Born and raised in Indiana, William Vaughn Moody was influenced by his mother's love of literature, art, and music. In high school, he was editor of the school newspaper and valedictorian of his class. He entered Harvard University on a partial scholarship, which he supplemented by working. While still an undergraduate, he published poems and short stories, and he finished his bachelor's degree in three years. Moody received his master's degree from Harvard in 1894 and subsequently worked as an instructor there. He later taught English at the University of Chicago. Eventually, the financial security he gained from the sale of the English literature textbooks he wrote with Robert M. Lovett freed him from the necessity of teaching.

Moody's poems are more often anthologized than his plays; indeed, during his lifetime, he was regarded as a major American poet. He wrote only five plays, one of them unfinished. His trilogy of verse dramas, *The Masque of Judgement* (1900), *The Fire-Bringer* (1904), and *The Death of Eve* (unfinished), draw from the Bible and mythology for their subjects and were never staged. His prose dramas, *The GREAT DIVIDE* (1906) and *The FAITH HEALER* (1910), established his reputation as a modern American dramatist. Both plays are early examples of what drama historian ARTHUR HOBSON QUINN called "the drama of revolt," plays in which the "struggle of the individual against some opposing force" (5)—often social custom or law—results in the "growth of spiritual life through the evolution of character" (7).

The Great Divide is considered one of the finest plays of its time, a milestone in American drama. The title refers to the gulf between the American West and the American East—freedom versus Puritanism—and the ideals of each, which are embodied in the main characters. The realism of the play emerges from Moody's complex characters and conflicts—conflicts not simply or tidily resolved. *The Faith Healer* examines the struggle between spiritual faith and human sexual love and reaches the conclusion that they are not mutually exclusive.

Dead at the age of 41 of a brain tumor, William Vaughn Moody is considered a minor playwright and an important poet. Had he lived longer, he might well have attained the status of one of the great modern American playwrights.

BIBLIOGRAPHY

Brown, Maurice F. *Estranging Dawn: The Life and Works of William Vaughn Moody.* Carbondale: Southern Illinois University Press, 1973.

Halpern, Martin. *William Vaughn Moody.* New York: Twayne, 1964.

Moody, William Vaughn. *The Plays and Poems of William Vaughn Moody.* 2 vols. Edited by John M. Manly. Boston: Houghton Mifflin, 1912.

Quinn, Arthur Hobson. "William Vaughn Moody and the Drama of Revolt." *A History of the American Drama from the Civil War to the Present Day.* Rev. ed. Vol. 2. New York: Appleton-Century-Crofts, 1955. 1–26.

MOON FOR THE MISBEGOTTEN, A

EUGENE O'NEILL (1947) O'NEILL's last completed play, *A Moon for the Misbegotten* was produced by the THEATRE GUILD in 1947 but closed out of town. It did not premiere in New York until 1957 and did not receive a successful Broadway production until 1974, when José Quintero directed Jason Robards Jr., Colleen Dewhurst, and Edward Flanders in what is regarded as the definitive production of the work. A companion piece and sequel to LONG DAY'S JOURNEY INTO NIGHT (1956), it picks up the story of James Tyrone Jr., closely modeled on O'Neill's brother, 11 years later.

Set in 1923, the play centers on the relationship between Tyrone, called Jim here, and the Hogans—father Phil, a feisty and devious Irish immigrant, and his daughter, Josie, *"so oversize for a woman that she is almost a freak"* but nonetheless feminine and charming. The action begins as Josie is helping her one remaining sibling Mike to follow his brothers and escape the ramshackle Connecticut farm and their tyrannical father. Before he leaves with money Josie has stolen from Phil, Mike taunts his sister for being "the scandal of the neighborhood," a designation she readily accepts, and advises her to marry in order to "stop your shameless ways with men." When she says she will never marry, because she does not want to be "tied down to any man," he asks if that includes Jim Tyrone, who is about to inherit his recently deceased mother's estate—and on whose land the Hogans are tenants. He also suggests that Phil and Josie probably already have a scheme to trick Jim into marrying Josie by getting him to seduce her and then having witnesses catch them in bed together. Josie angrily denies this.

After Mike leaves, Josie derisively tells her father about her brother's scheme, but Phil, who also thinks that Josie is "the scandal of the countryside," likes the idea because he thinks that Josie and Jim are "two of a kind, both great disgraces," and also because he is afraid that once Jim's mother's estate is settled, he will sell the Hogans' farm. Josie protests so much and defends Jim so fervently ("He only acts like he's hard and shameless to get back at life when it's tormenting him.") that her feelings for him are obvious. Jim enters and banters good-naturedly with Phil but chastises Josie for her rough talk and pose as a loose woman, telling her he's no longer interested in "dainty tarts" but instead in women who are "tall and strong and voluptuous . . . with beautiful big breasts." He also reveals to them that their neighbor, Standard Oil man T. Stedman Harder, has made him a generous offer for their farm, an offer that he is seriously considering—despite his promise to Phil that he would have the right of first refusal.

Late that same evening, as Josie waits for Jim, who is two hours late for a promised "moonlight date" with her, Phil arrives from the local inn to report that Jim has accepted a $10,000 offer from Harder. He also tells her that Jim thinks she's a virgin and will not see her anymore because he loves her and "it'd be a sin on his conscience if he was to seduce you." Hearing this, Josie proposes putting Mike's scheme into effect, promising her father that she will not let Jim actually seduce her but will blackmail him into signing the farm over to her nonetheless. When Jim unexpectedly appears, Phil pretends he is too drunk to remember anything that happened at the inn, and Josie of course pretends that she knows nothing. Jim professes his love for her, and when she accuses him of just wanting to get her into bed, he denies it, saying, "I'd like tonight to be different." Josie, torn between her affection for him and her determination not to let him sell the farm, pours drink after drink for both of them. They kiss, and he tells her the true story of what happened at the inn; he told Phil that he had no intention of selling to Harder and that Phil would be the only person he would sell to. Assuring Josie, "you and I belong to the same club," he explains: "We can kid the world but we can't fool ourselves, like most people, no matter what we do—nor escape ourselves no matter where we run away." He also tells her that both he and Phil are wise to her "brazen-trollop act." After Josie confesses that she is indeed a virgin and offers herself to him, he at first drunkenly makes a pass at her but then apologizes and starts to leave.

Josie prevails on him to stay and maternally lays his head on her bosom: "[I]f there's one thing I owe you tonight, after all my lying and scheming, it's to give you the love you need, and it'll be my pride and my joy." He tells her that ever since his mother's death, he has lost all interest in living: He had stopped drinking "for her sake" for two years but had been so distraught over her illness that he had started again, and she had seen him drunk just before she died. Then, bringing his mother's body back east—she died in California—on the train, he got drunk again and spent much of the trip with a prostitute he hired for $50 a day to make him forget "what was in the baggage car ahead"—and was too drunk to attend her funeral. Josie assures him that his mother forgives him and tells him to sleep in peace—as he falls asleep on her breast.

Early the next morning, Josie and Jim are still in the same positions when Phil returns, and Josie castigates him for lying to her—to which he responds that he was only trying to bring her some happiness. Jim wakes up and finds himself strangely "at peace with myself and this lousy life—as if all my sins had been forgiven" and assures Josie that "I'll never forget it—here with you." She replies that she wants him "to remember my love for you which gave you peace for a while" and wishes him "good-bye and God bless you," knowing he will die soon and that she will never see him again. After Jim leaves, Phil and Josie reconcile, and as the play ends, Josie looks down the road and says, "May you rest forever in forgiveness and peace."

In reality, James O'Neill Jr. never recovered from his mother's death and died a horrible death less than a year later at age 45, carted off in a straitjacket to a sanitarium, virtually blind and his hair turned prematurely white. *A Moon for the Misbegotten* is thus in many ways O'Neill's attempt to give his brother, who had lived a dissolute and loveless existence, what Travis Bogard calls "a gentler fate," almost "a blessing for a damned soul" (451). As such, it is the one truly romantic play he wrote, his one love story, albeit—and significantly—devoid of sex and of the ambivalences and difficulties of marriage. It is also an elegy, but an elegy for a man whose life had little apparent value, but who at last, in this telling of his story, can find refuge in the love, understanding, and acceptance of another human being. As Josie's last line—possibly the last line O'Neill ever wrote—indicates and as the endings of several O'Neill plays, from BEYOND THE HORIZON (1920) and *The* HAIRY APE (1922) to *The* ICE-MAN COMETH (1946), make clear, for Eugene O'Neill, the peace of death was the only hope and the only answer to humankind's tortured existence.

BIBLIOGRAPHY
Bogard, Travis. *Contour in Time: The Plays of Eugene O'Neill.* Rev. ed. New York: Oxford University Press, 1988.

MORAGA, CHERRÍE (1952–)

Cherríe Moraga's work in American drama reflects her clear identification as a Chicana lesbian feminist. Initially feeling outside of the Chicano movement, both because of its sexism and her own mestizo (mixed) heritage (her father was "Anglo"), Moraga realized that she would have to work to create a space for her unique and powerful artistic voice. The most important early examples of this are her book of critical writings and poetry entitled *Loving in the War Years/lo que nunca pasó por sus labios* (1983) and, coedited with Gloria Anzaldúa, *This Bridge Called My Back: Writings by Radical Women of Color* (1981), the first anthology of feminists of color. Her theatrical output is invested not only in questions of feminism and sexuality but also other forms of social justice and Chicana identity.

Her first play, *Giving Up the Ghost* (1986), reflected her expertise in poetry in its early forms. An exploration of Chicana identity and sexuality, the play has three characters: Marisa; a younger version of herself named Corky; and Amalia, an older artist and sometime lover of Marisa. *Giving Up the Ghost* is organized into three *retratos,* portraits that provide a glimpse into the characters' senses of identity and the nature of love, sex, and violence. *Shadow of a Man* (1990) charts the psychological development of Lupe, a girl whose father, Manuel, knows that she is the product of an adulterous encounter between his wife, Hortensia, and his *compadre,* Conrado. The play explores the patriarchal shadow cast by Conrado and by Manuel's decision to sanction the encounter. *Heroes and Saints* (1992) returns to many of the issues of the early El Teatro Campesino *actos* (see LUIS VALDÉZ) and explores the effects of pesticides on a California community, including a cancer cluster among children of the workers. A victim of birth defects, the central character, Cerezita, is essentially a talking head, the result of pesticide poisoning during her mother's pregnancy. She functions as a symbol for the emerging voice of the people, and the play charts her movement into the public sphere to help organize resistance to the destructive practices of agribusiness. The play ends with a cry to burn the fields and a call to action for the audience.

Watsonville: Some Place Not Here (1995), set eight years later, explores a cannery strike in Watsonville, California, using some of the characters from *Heroes and Saints.* Clearer in this production are the politics of organizing and the complex relationship between marxism and Catholicism, demonstrated by union politics and liberation theology. In this work, Dolores, Cerezita's mother, becomes a central figure of religiously inflected activism. *Circle in the Dirt: El Pueblo de East Palo Alto* (1995) continues this sense of localized activism within particular communities of color, exploring the reinvocation of the indigenous inhabitants; the play attempts to imagine a different future for an impoverished community suffering from the displacement caused by development and gentrification. *Heart of the Earth: A Popul Vuh Story* (1994), a work of puppet theater, uses indigenous mythology to retell the story of creation. *The Hungry Woman: A Mexican Medea* (1995) is set in a future based on an alternative past and combines the cultural influence of Mexico, Mayan mythology, and Greek myth to explore questions of sexuality and politics. All of Moraga's work for the theater implicitly or explicitly demands social justice in the face of oppression based on class, gender, sexuality, and ethnicity. This advocacy increases its power because of Moraga's unique and compelling imagery and the richness of her poetic language.

BIBLIOGRAPHY

Anzaldúa, Gloria, and Cherríe Moraga, eds. *This Bridge Called My Back: Writing by Radical Women of Color.* Watertown, Mass.: Persephone Press, 1981.

Moraga, Cherríe. *"Heroes and Saints" and Other Plays.* Albuquerque, N.Mex.: West End Press, 1994.

———. *The Hungry Woman.* Albuquerque, N.Mex.: West End Press, 2001.

———. *The Last Generation: Poetry and Prose.* Boston: South End Press, 1993.

———. *Loving in the War Years/lo que nunca pasó por sus labios.* Boston: South End Press, 1983.

———. *Watsonville/Circle in the Dirt.* Albuquerque, N.Mex.: West End Press, 2002.

Rossini, Jon D. *Contemporary Latina/o Theater: Wrighting Ethnicity.* Carbondale: Southern Illinois University Press, 2008.

Yarbro-Bejarano, Yvonne. *The Wounded Heart: Writing on Cherríe Moraga.* Austin: University of Texas Press, 2001.

Jon D. Rossini
University of California–Davis

MORNING'S AT SEVEN PAUL OSBORN (1939)

Set in a small town in the Midwest, *Morning's at Seven* has the distinction of being one of the few American plays ever written in which the characters are for the most part elderly. The seven main characters are in their late sixties and early seventies; there are two younger people, a couple, aged 39 and 40. The play takes place in the backyards of neighboring houses. In one house live Theodore and Cora Swanson and

Cora's sister, Arry. Next door live Ida (sister to Cora and Arry) and Carl Bolton and their 40-year-old son, Homer. Homer has been engaged for seven years but is reluctant to leave his mother. In the same town are Esther (a fourth sister) and her husband David Crampton.

This is a family with its fair share of eccentricity. Carl has what his family calls "dentist spells," which spiral into "where am I spells" and then into those most dreaded by his wife and son, "fork spells." It eventually becomes clear to the audience—though it mystifies his family—that Carl has moments of regret at not becoming a dentist, which often lead him to ask himself how he came to be at the particular place in his life where he is and to wonder where he missed important opportunities in his life—that is, where he went wrong at some past "fork" in the road. The eccentricity, then, is less a trait of Carl's than of the others. The one member of the family who understands Carl is his brother-in-law, David, a former college professor. But David is odd in his own way: He forbids his wife to visit her sisters and their families because he thinks they are "morons." David tells Esther that if she goes to see them again, she will have to "live on the second floor" of their home, and he will live downstairs. And then there is Homer, who is so attached to his mother that he cannot bring himself to marry his girlfriend of 12 years, to whom he has been engaged for seven. In fact, five years ago, Carl built the couple a house, which stands empty, waiting for the reluctant Homer and the patient Myrtle.

The action of the play develops around the arrival of Myrtle, who in all these years has never met Homer's family. Her arrival instigates several events: Carl has a recurrence of his "spells" of introspection about his life and its meaning; Esther secretly comes to visit in order to meet Homer's girlfriend and as a result is banished by her husband to the second floor (ultimately she realizes she prefers the greater freedom of banishment to obedience); David invites Carl to live with him on the first floor so they can figure out the meaning of Carl's life together; Homer decides not to marry Myrtle because his father's "spells" seem worse to him (though Homer changes his mind when he finds out she's pregnant); and Cora wants to lease

Homer's house from Carl for herself and her husband. It seems she has resented the presence of her sister, Arry, all these years (and, indeed, it is revealed that years ago Theodore and Arry had a brief affair while Cora was in a hospital).

In the play's title, OSBORN alludes to a song in Robert Browning's poetic drama *Pippa Passes*: "The year's at the spring / And day's at the morn; / Morning's at seven; . . . God's in his heaven— / All's right with the world!" The title is meant somewhat ironically in this play, where in fact the characters are not in the early morning of their lives, but in the twilight, although there are new beginnings for them all in this warm-hearted comedy. As is true of this play in other respects, the characters' new beginnings are not radical or earth-shattering but understated and wryly humorous.

MOURNING BECOMES ELECTRA EUGENE O'NEILL (1931)

The second of O'NEILL's two very long plays—*STRANGE INTERLUDE* (1928) was the first at approximately four and a half hours in nine acts—*Mourning Becomes Electra*, in its original production, started at 5:30 P.M., broke for a one-hour dinner intermission after the first play, and ended just before 11 P.M.; it was a surprisingly big hit, however, with a run of 150 performances. Today, revivals—and they are quite frequent—usually make cuts in the text and condense the play into a consecutive, approximately four-hour playing time, with two or three brief intermissions. O'Neill based the play on the tragic Greek myth of Agamemnon, Clytemnestra, Electra, Orestes, and the House of Atreus, substituting for the Greek sense of Fate what he called "a modern psychological approximation" (Bogard 347) and setting it in a New England seaport at the end of the Civil War.

Mourning Becomes Electra is actually a trilogy, with two of the plays divided into four acts each and one into five. The first play, *Homecoming*, begins, as the other two do, with a group of townspeople who act as a Greek chorus. Here they fill us in on the history of the Mannon family. Abe Mannon, prosperous in the shipping business, had two sons. David married a "French Canuck nurse girl" named Marie Brantome, whom he had gotten pregnant, and was disinherited by his father. In his rage, Abe also tore down the Mannon house and built the present dwelling, in and around which the action of the trilogy, with the exception of one scene, takes place. In this house, his other son, Ezra, a West Point graduate and much-respected former mayor of the town who is about to return from the war a general and a hero, lives with his wife Christine, his daughter Lavinia, and his son Orin—who has also been in the war. Lavinia and Christine look very much alike, as do Orin and Ezra.

Lavinia is being courted by Peter Niles, whose sister Hazel is romantically interested in Orin. Peter, jealous of Adam Brant, a ship captain who has been attentive to Lavinia and who is coming to visit that evening, proposes marriage to her. She refuses, saying her father needs her, but insists she has no interest in Brant. After Peter and Hazel leave, Seth Beckwith, the Mannons' 75-year-old gardener who, throughout the trilogy, is heard singing "Shenandoah," reveals to Lavinia his suspicion that Brant is the child of David Mannon and Marie Brantome. When Brant, who looks very much like Ezra, arrives, Lavinia confronts him, and he admits that it is so, telling her that Ezra refused to help Marie Brantome when she was dying, and he swore on her body that "I'd revenge her death on him."

Lavinia believes that her mother and Brant are having an affair, and when she asks Christine about this, the latter explains that, while she loved Ezra at first, "marriage soon turned his romance—into disgust" and that she has always held it against Lavinia that she was the product of this loveless union. Orin, on the other hand, was born while his father was away at the Mexican War, and "he seemed my child, only mine, and I loved him for that!" In her loneliness for Orin when he went off to war—which Lavinia suggested he do out of duty (further building up the animosity between mother and daughter)—she turned to Brant, who said he loved her. Lavinia indicates that she will say nothing to her father if Christine gives up Adam Brant, pointing out that Ezra would never divorce her and that their affair could ruin Brant's career. Christine agrees, but she later tells Brant to get poison, which she will then administer to her husband and which will cause everyone to think he has had a heart attack. At first, Brant is reluctant, but

when Christine reminds him that Ezra is coming back to her bed, he gives in to her.

When Ezra returns, he asks about Brant, whom Christine calls Lavinia's "latest beau," but Lavinia assures her father, "You're the only man I'll ever love! I'm going to stay with you!" Christine rebuffs Ezra's attempts to kiss her, but when he tells her that he wants to remove the emotional wall that he has built up between them for so long—"I came home to surrender to you—what's inside me"—she tells him she loves him, and they go up to their bedroom together, leaving Lavinia to exclaim, "I hate you! You steal even Father's love from me again!" After Christine allows Ezra to make love to her, in the hope that it will bring on a heart attack, she reveals her affair with Adam Brant to him—whereupon Ezra does have an attack, and she gives him the poison to ensure that he will die. Lavinia enters, and Christine faints, dropping the box of poison as she does so; Lavinia, realizing what has happened, vows to prevent her mother from marrying Brant.

The second play, *The Hunted,* begins as Orin returns for his father's funeral. When he arrives, Lavinia tells him of his mother's affair with Brant; knowing how much Orin loves Christine, she warns him not to be taken in by her. Christine tells her son that Lavinia's accusations are untrue and are caused by his sister's own love for Adam, and she suggests that if they can get Lavinia to marry Peter, "there will be just you and I." Even after Lavinia shows him the box of poison, Orin remains unconvinced; she strikes him in what she knows is a vulnerable spot, however, when she acknowledges that while he might not care that his mother murdered his father (whom he hated), she hopes that he is "not such a coward that [he's] willing to let her lover escape!"—and she reveals that Christine and Brant are planning to run off and get married. Enraged by this, he agrees to Lavinia's plan that they follow Christine when she goes to Brant, to verify that they are having an affair.

On board Brant's ship in Boston Harbor, Christine arrives to tell Brant that although Lavinia knows the truth, she believes that Orin still thinks her innocent; together they go below, where Lavinia and Orin overhear them planning to leave soon for the East. After

Christine leaves, Orin shoots Brant and smashes up the cabin to make it look as if a burglary has occurred. Returning home, they disclose to their mother what has happened; Orin tries to console Christine by telling her that the two of them can now "go away on a long voyage" together, but Christine goes into the house and shoots herself. Lavinia's response is "It is your justice, Father!" but Orin laments, "How can I ever get her to forgive me now?"

The third play, *The Haunted,* represents O'Neill's major addition to the Greek legend. As he explained in a 1931 letter, in the Greek version, the Electra figure "fades out into a vague and undramatic future," in one version even marrying Pylades (Peter in his play), but he felt that in "our modern psychological chain of fate certainly we can't let her exit like that," and we must give her "an end tragically worthy of herself" (Bogard and Bryer 389–390). As *The Haunted* begins, Hazel and Peter are awaiting the return of Orin and Lavinia, who have been on a long voyage to the East, punctuated by a month in the "Blessed Isles" that Orin has always dreamed of visiting—and that Adam Brant had spoken of romantically as well. Orin has grown a beard and mustache and looks more like Ezra than ever, and Lavinia has filled out, making her resemblance to Christine even more apparent (she is even wearing her mother's favorite color, green). Orin remains grief-stricken and guilt-ridden over his mother's death, but Lavinia tells him that they have come home to rid themselves of their ghosts and must go on with their lives. Peter assures Lavinia that he still wants to marry her, and she reports that being in the Blessed Isles has freed her to feel love for him, and they will wed as soon as Orin is free of his guilt and can return to normal.

A month later, Orin is writing a history of the Mannon family, which will trace all their crimes, and he tells Lavinia that there is no way either of them can escape being punished for what they have done: "Can't you see I'm now in Father's place and you're Mother! That's the evil destiny out of the past I haven't dared to predict! I'm the Mannon you're chained to!" When she breaks down in tears, exclaiming, "[I] would give my life to bring you peace," he admonishes her, "Don't cry. The damned don't cry." He begs her to go to the

authorities with him, confess, and "pay the penalty for Mother's murder," but she turns on him and blurts out, "You'd kill yourself if you weren't such a coward!" Heeding her advice, Orin goes in the house and shoots himself, and Lavinia hides his manuscript from Peter and Hazel. She announces her intention to marry Peter and leave the house: "I'll close it up and leave it in the sun and rain to die. . . . And the Mannons will be forgotten. I'm the last and I won't be one long. I'll be Mrs. Peter Niles."

Hazel begs Lavinia not to marry Peter and bring the Mannon curse on him, and she says that Orin told her that she must show his manuscript to Peter before he marries Lavinia. But when Peter comes in, Lavinia throws herself into his arms and urges him to consummate their relationship right now—"Want me! Take me, Adam!"—but she is shocked and appalled by her inadvertent use of her mother's lover's name and realizes that she cannot escape her destiny. She sends Peter away, and as Seth sings "Shenandoah" and gets to the line "I'm bound away," she accepts her fate: "I'm bound here—to the Mannon dead!" and adds, "Living alone here with the dead is a worse act of justice than death or prison." She retreats into the house, ordering Seth to "close the shutters and nail them tight."

O'Neill believed that, at the end, Lavinia is "broken and not broken" in that by "yielding to her Mannon fate she overcomes it" and is therefore "tragic." He did not mean "tragic" in the Greek sense of the word; as he explained, no modern audience "was ever purged by pity and terror by witnessing a Greek tragedy," because, unlike the Greeks, modern audiences have no "Gods or a God," "Faith," or other "healing subterfuge by which to conquer Death. . . . [O]ur tragedy," he contended, "is just that we have only ourselves, that there is nothing to be purged into except a belief in the guts of man, good or evil, who faces unflinchingly the black mystery of his own soul!" (Bogard and Bryer 390).

That the Mannons are trapped forever in their fate is suggested not only by the word "bound" in "Shenandoah" but also by the chorus of gossiping townspeople who constantly report the family's transgressions, by the portraits of the family members on the walls of the house, by the similarities of appearance within the family, and by the recurrence of the "Blessed Isles" as the symbol of an escape that all the Mannons yearn for but none can permanently achieve. As in so many O'Neill plays, these characters cannot escape their own humanity—who they are—and the introduction of Oedipal feelings between Orin and his mother and of the Electra complex, which ties Lavinia to her father and to Brant, merely provide more reasons for their entrapment.

In many ways, *Mourning Becomes Electra* stands as an important transitional play between O'Neill's experimental works and his later great autobiographical dramas (*The Iceman Cometh* [1946], *A Moon for the Misbegotten* [1947], and *Long Day's Journey into Night* [1956]). At different points in its composition, he considered using masks and asides—as he had done in *The Great God Brown* (1926) and *Strange Interlude* (1928), respectively—but, ultimately, decided against it because, as he explained in a 1931 interview, "these people are intense, people with lots of will power. You see what they want from their actions" (Estrin 110). As a result, as C. W. E. Bigsby puts it, with this play, "he was moving towards a psychological drama in which character would have to carry a weight which had previously been borne by a theatricality which had . . . been on occasion distorting and distracting" (78).

BIBLIOGRAPHY

Bigsby, C. W. E. *A Critical Introduction to Twentieth-Century American Drama: Volume One—1900–1940.* Cambridge, England: Cambridge University Press, 1982.

Bogard, Travis. *Contour in Time: The Plays of Eugene O'Neill.* Rev. ed. New York: Oxford University Press, 1988.

———, and Jackson R. Bryer, eds. *Selected Letters of Eugene O'Neill.* New Haven, Conn.: Yale University Press, 1988.

Estrin, Mark W., ed. *Conversations with Eugene O'Neill.* Jackson: University Press of Mississippi, 1990.

MOWATT, ANNA CORA OGDEN (1819–1870)

Born in France to American parents, Anna Ogden was educated at private schools in New York and through extensive reading at home. She is said to have read all of Shakespeare before age 10. At 15, she married James Mowatt, a wealthy New York lawyer.

When her husband lost his fortune, she began to give dramatic readings in order to earn money for her family; her first public reading was in late 1841. She supplemented these earnings by writing articles for magazines under the pseudonym Helen Berkley, as well as books of fiction and nonfiction, including a biography of the German poet, Goethe, under the pseudonym Henry C. Brown.

She was among the first American women to become a successful playwright and is best known for her comedy of manners, *Fashion* (1845), in which she satirizes the foolishness of adopting European fashions and customs over more honest and forthright American ones. This play has the distinction of being one of the most frequently revived 19th-century American comedies. Mowatt's other plays, *Gulzara; or, The Persian Slave* (1840) and *Armand; or, The Peer and the Peasant* (1847), were popular at the time but are not particularly remembered now.

While still in her twenties, Mowatt embarked on a successful acting career in America and in Britain. She retired from acting when she remarried in 1854 (to William Foushee Ritchie; her first husband died in 1851). She wrote an autobiography entitled *Autobiography of an Actress; or, Eight Years on the Stage* (1854), as well as other narratives of life in the theater. She lived in Richmond, Virginia, with her husband until the outbreak of the Civil War, at which time she left the country. She lived abroad after 1861 and wrote romantic novels. She died in England in 1870.

BIBLIOGRAPHY

Barnes, Eric Wollencott. *The Lady of Fashion: The Life and the Theatre of Anna Cora Mowatt.* New York: Scribners, 1954.

Mowatt, Anna Cora. *Mimic Life; or, Before and Behind the Curtain.* 1856. Edited by Jeffrey H. Richards. Acton, Mass.: Copley Publishing, 2001.

MULATTO Langston Hughes (1935)

Hughes's first full-length play is an exploration of the problems caused by miscegenation. The play ran a year on Broadway and later toured, despite only sporadic interest at that time in African-American drama. A typical melodrama of the period, its impact is increased by a forthright approach to what was, at the time, an inflammatory issue.

In the South during the post–World War I era, Cora, an African-American housekeeper, has lived with white plantation owner Colonel Thomas Norwood for years, bearing him several children. Cora persuades the Colonel to educate their "mulatto" children so they might get good jobs up North, but he refuses to acknowledge them as his legitimate offspring. When Bert, their youngest child, was seven, the Colonel severely beat him for calling him "Papa" in front of whites. Bert has grown up angry and rebellious, refusing to accept his identity as an African-American man, seeing himself as white. Cora worries that Bert's behavior will ruin their relatively comfortable situation. The Colonel worries about how improved racial tolerance in the North might affect his plantation, making the African Americans who work for him rebellious and desirous of better conditions. He finds Bert's attitude so offensive that he threatens to kill him. Bert and his father try unsuccessfully to reconcile, but they end up fighting, and Bert kills the Colonel. Trying to escape, Bert is cut off by a mob, and he returns to the house where, to the mob's annoyance, he shoots himself rather than be caught.

The play comes out of the dilemma Hughes expressed in an early poem, "Cross," which illustrates the mulatto's inner conflicts regarding "being neither white nor black." The injustices suffered by Bert and Cora, indeed suffered by all African Americans in the rural South, are forcefully presented, but with Bert and Cora's development, the play goes beyond mere polemical drama. It is Bert's stubborn pride (ironically inherited from his father) that brings about his downfall and death, more so than his unhappy, untenable situation. Cora, in contrast, shows patience and dignity as she waits for Bert to realize the totality of his tragic situation. Bert's suicide indicates a new understanding of his heritage and can be seen as a final act of courage and self-determination.

However, Hughes also allows us to sympathize with the Colonel as he too struggles against his own prejudices. He wants his children to be educated and is proud of their success, but he does not want African Americans in general to be so. Although Bert looks nearly white, neither his father nor the town can see him as anything but African American, so they cannot acknowledge the kinship Bert desires. Bert is almost lynched, just for complaining to a white female post office clerk about a damaged parcel. Bert is caught in a dilemma: He cannot be white, but he does not want to be black, so he ends up hating both—and himself. Cora provides the voice of reason: She understands the necessary compromises of life for African Americans in the South and sees the future belonging to mixed children like hers; her words of hope continue to ring, despite the tragedy enacted through her son.

Susan C. W. Abbotson
Rhode Island College

MUSICAL THEATER

MUSICAL THEATER   Although the Broadway musical traces its roots to European opera and operetta, it evolved during the 20th century into an indigenously American art form. However, only during the second half of the century did the musical adopt, to any degree, the seriousness of purpose common to the best nonmusical drama.

Experts generally cite the opening of *The Black Crook* (1866) as the birth of the American musical. This extravaganza had songs, a melodramatic story, scantily clad dancing girls, and various stage effects designed to keep its audience engaged for five hours. Soon, shows—such as EDWARD HARRIGAN and Tony Hart's *Mulligan Guard* musical plays (1877–85), which depicted newly arrived immigrants in New York— moved toward showing the local color of America.

The 20th-century American musical began with a British import, *Florodora* (1900), which enjoyed great popularity. Victor Herbert's *Babes in Toyland* (1903) yielded the hit songs "March of the Toys" and "Toyland." George M. Cohan, one of the most popular performers of his day, wrote the book and score for *Little Johnny Jones* (1904), which gave America "The Yankee Doodle Boy" and "Give My Regards to Broadway."

As musical comedy and European-style operetta developed, so did another form of musical. *The Passing Show* (1894) is considered the first American revue. Producer Florenz Ziegfeld further developed the genre in 1907 with the first of his annual *Follies*. Revues told no linear story; instead, they presented a succession of production numbers, comedy skits, and vaudeville acts. Ziegfeld patterned his shows on the French revue, with its emphasis on topical satire. His shows also featured top American performers, as well as new scores by such songwriters as Irving Berlin.

The American musical comedy as we know it today—an entertaining mix of dialogue, song, and dance, all of which tells a story—arguably began with composer Jerome Kern and his "Princess" musicals. These shows, including *Very Good Eddie* (1915) and *Leave It to Jane* (1917), did not rely on large casts or gaudy effects. Instead, Kern employed character-driven humor and charming songs.

As 1920 approached, a new songwriting voice emerged: George Gershwin. A musical genius whose output ran the gamut from musical comedy and jazz to symphonic music and opera, Gershwin was influenced by Kern's musical sophistication. He teamed with his lyricist brother Ira to create a string of great musical comedy scores, such as *Lady, Be Good* (1924), *Oh, Kay!* (1926), *Strike Up the Band* (1927), and *Of Thee I Sing* (1931), the first musical to win the PULITZER PRIZE for drama. With Ira Gershwin and playwright DUBOSE HEYWARD, George Gershwin created the immortal American opera *Porgy and Bess* (1935). While the plots of Gershwin's musicals were often silly and forgettable, the scores included a bounty of songs that became "standards": *Girl Crazy* (1930) alone yielded "Embraceable You," "Bidin' My Time," "But Not for Me," and "I Got Rhythm."

Another songwriting team, Richard Rodgers and Lorenz Hart, also distinguished itself during the 1920s. After contributing songs to successful revues like *The Garrick Gaieties* (1925), which featured their initial hit "Manhattan," they went on to write the scores for *A Connecticut Yankee* (1927), *Babes in Arms* (1937), and *The Boys from Syracuse* (1938). Going beyond the pop idiom of the day, Rodgers frequently underpinned great melody with complex harmonies, and Hart's lyrics were often cynical, antiromantic, or melancholy. Rodgers and Hart's *On Your Toes* (1936) is recognized as the first modern musical to incorporate ballet as an integral component. Their last great show, *Pal Joey* (1940), was considered unsavory because of its amoral, sexist protagonist. An antihero who might have been accepted in a play by EUGENE O'NEILL seemed more disturbing when singing and dancing.

Revues continued to be a Broadway staple throughout the first half of the century. *The Ziegfeld Follies* spawned imitators, including *George White's Scandals* (1919–29, 1931, 1936, 1939). The zenith of the genre came in the early 1930s with *The Band Wagon* (1931), with a score by revue specialists Arthur Schwartz and Howard Dietz. Other notable examples included Irving Berlin's *Music Box Revue* (1921) and Harold Rome's *Pins and Needles* (1937), which was performed by actual garment-union members. Several other 1930s revues included the sort of pointed commentary on conditions in depression-era America found in the plays of CLIFFORD ODETS.

While revues and musical comedies with contemporary American settings were Broadway staples, operettas—generally featuring romance, exotic settings, and lush scores—were also popular. Victor Herbert composed several memorable "comic operas," including *Naughty Marietta* (1910). Lyricist Oscar Hammerstein wrote such popular operettas as *Rose-Marie* (1924) with Rudolf Friml, while Sigmund Romberg wrote the equally beloved *Student Prince* (1924). But in 1927, a fourth type of musical was born: Kern teamed with Hammerstein to create the landmark *Show Boat*. It featured a hit-filled score, including "Ol' Man River," "Make Believe," "Bill," and "Can't Help Lovin' Dat Man." Hammerstein's libretto, however, transcended comedy and operetta to make the show a true musical drama. Because of its seriousness of purpose, epic sweep, memorable characters, and brilliant score, *Show Boat* stands as the first great Broadway musical.

Like Irving Berlin, Cole Porter wrote both words and music. Whereas Berlin was a nearly uneducated, all-American songwriter of popular shows like *Annie Get Your Gun* (1946), which gave America "There's No Business Like Show Business," the rich, ivy-league Porter was a world traveler whose witty, sophisticated scores for such shows as *Fifty Million Frenchmen* (1929) reflected his cosmopolitan character. *Anything Goes* (1934) and *Leave It to Me* (1938) also enjoyed great success. Porter's finest musical, *Kiss Me, Kate* (1948), featured a string of hits.

In 1943, Richard Rodgers and Oscar Hammerstein began a partnership that would last the remainder of Hammerstein's life when they wrote *Oklahoma!* Set in the heartland in a more innocent time, this musical struck a chord with wartime America and ran nearly 3,000 performances. A string of hits followed, including *Carousel* (1945), *South Pacific* (1949; Pulitzer Prize), *The King and I* (1951), *Flower Drum Song* (1958), and *The Sound of Music* (1959). Drawing from a variety of literary sources, these musical dramas told stories of romance, but they also dealt with racism, spousal abuse, cultural and political clashes, and war. These serious issues were made palatable, even appealing, by Hammerstein's generous spirit and Rodgers's gift for melody.

The team of Lerner and Loewe became nearly as famous as Rodgers and Hammerstein, thanks largely to the enormous success of *My Fair Lady* (1956). This adaptation of *Pygmalion* borrowed freely, and profitably, from George Bernard Shaw's 1914 play. The ambitious lyricist Alan Jay Lerner had worked well with composer Frederick Loewe before (*Brigadoon* [1947] and *Paint Your Wagon* [1951]) and would do so again with *Camelot* (1960).

Kurt Weill was primarily a classical composer in his native Germany, but once he immigrated to this country, he became thoroughly American, writing music for *Lady in the Dark* (1941), *One Touch of Venus* (1943), and *Street Scene* (1947). Another distinctive songwriter, Harold Arlen, carved a niche for himself as a writer of blues. Although his shows, including *Bloomer Girl* (1944), *St. Louis Woman* (1946), and *Jamaica* (1957), were not big hits, several of the songs he wrote, especially with lyricist E. Y. "Yip" Harburg, were. Harburg would, however, have his biggest hit show with Burton Lane in *Finian's Rainbow* (1947), which showcased Harburg's humanity and social conscience, as it lampooned southern racism.

Although Frank Loesser is not always ranked alongside Rodgers, Porter, and Gershwin as a theatrical composer, his lyrics are universally admired, and he wrote two of Broadway's most beloved musicals, *Guys and Dolls* (1950) and *How to Succeed in Business without Really Trying* (1961; Pulitzer Prize). Loesser also nurtured the talents of several songwriters who would write their own enduring musicals under his guidance: Robert Wright and George Forrest (*Kismet* [1953]), Richard Adler and Jerry Ross (*The Pajama Game* [1954] and *Damn Yankees* [1955]), and Meredith Willson (*The Music Man* [1957]).

Jerry Herman, a hit-making composer-lyricist, albeit in the more sincere Berlin tradition, wrote the blockbuster *Hello, Dolly!* (1964), which ran six years, thanks in part to promotion by super producer David Merrick, who seemed to produce half of the successful musicals staged between 1954 (Harold Rome's hit *Fanny*) and 1980 (a stage adaptation of *42nd Street*). Herman also wrote *La Cage aux Folles* (1983), a show about gay men that appealed to "straight" audiences too.

As the 1960s brought rapid, radical cultural changes, the traditional musical typified by Herman may have seemed to some passé and irrelevant. The "tribal love-rock" musical *Hair* (1967), with energetic music by Galt MacDermot, certainly tried to appeal to a new audience. It delivered an antiwar message and tapped into the hippie zeitgeist, yet it hardly signaled the death of the traditional musical. Indeed, few rock musicals were able to duplicate *Hair*'s success. Although not really part of this genre, Stephen Schwartz's *Godspell* (1971) and *Pippin* (1972) have youthful, rock-inflected scores that still sound fresh. Most recently, Schwartz's *Wicked* (2003), which tells the Oz story from the witches' point of view became a hit.

Meanwhile, more mainstream songwriters flourished throughout the 1960s and 1970s. Charles Strouse and Lee Adams scored with their first show, *Bye Bye Birdie* (1960). In 1977, Strouse teamed up with lyricist-director Martin Charnin to write the megahit *Annie*. Other songwriting duos produced traditional, skillful work during these decades. Tom Jones and Harvey Schmidt's *The Fantasticks* opened OFF-BROADWAY in 1960 and ran for 42 years, only to be revived in 2006.

John Kander and Fred Ebb worked together for nearly 40 years, beginning with their 1966 hit *Cabaret*. Like Rodgers and Hammerstein, they sometimes tackled serious subjects, such as Weimar Germany in *Cabaret*, murdering wives in *Chicago* (1975), and South American prisons in *Kiss of the Spider Woman* (1993). After Ebb's death in 2004, Kander worked to complete several of their works in progress, including *Curtains* (2007), a musical murder mystery. Jerry Bock and Sheldon Harnick struck literary gold when they adapted the stories of Sholem Aleichem into *Fiddler on the Roof* (1964). They preceded this with their Pulitzer Prize–winning *Fiorello!* (1959) and *She Loves Me* (1963), both of which feature memorable scores.

In terms of longevity, however, librettist-lyricists Betty Comden and Adolph Green were the champions, having worked together exclusively from the late 1930s until Green's death in 2002. They began on Broadway in 1944 with Leonard Bernstein's *On the Town,* and duplicated their success with him in 1953 for *Wonderful Town.* They wrote several shows with composer Jule Styne, including *Bells Are Ringing* (1956) and *Do Re Mi* (1960). More recently they wrote *On the Twentieth Century* (1978) and *The Will Rogers Follies* (1991) with Cy Coleman. Coleman combined his pop style in successful collaboration with several other lyricists, including Carolyn Leigh (*Wildcat* [1960] and *Little Me* [1962]), Dorothy Fields (*Sweet Charity* [1966] and *Seesaw* [1973]), and Michael Stewart (*Barnum* [1980]).

Jule Styne also collaborated with various other lyricists on hit shows, including *High Button Shoes* (1947), *Gentlemen Prefer Blondes* (1949), *Peter Pan* (1953), and *Funny Girl* (1964). Styne's finest work came with *Gypsy* (1959), which was conceived by choreographer Jerome Robbins.

Styne's lyricist on *Gypsy* was Stephen Sondheim, who had already written the lyrics for the songs in *West Side Story* (1957) with composer Bernstein. Sondheim's mentor as a youngster was Oscar Hammerstein; as America's preeminent composer-lyricist, Sondheim continues to exhibit a songwriting genius comparable to that of George Gershwin. Sondheim has written several of musical theater's finest works: *Company* (1970), *Follies* (1971), *A Little Night Music* (1973), *Sweeney Todd* (1979), and *Sunday in the Park with George* (1984; Pulitzer Prize). Several of Sondheim's shows have been labeled "concept musicals," shows built around an idea rather than a linear plot (such as *Company*'s exploration of commitment and marriage). Sondheim's newest musical, the much-revised *Road Trip* (2008), finally arrived in New York after unsuccessful versions in Chicago and Washington, D.C.

Although the success of a musical is often driven by its musical score, directors and choreographers increasingly have become key figures. GEORGE ABBOTT was the guiding force behind many musicals, beginning in 1935 when he directed Rodgers and Hart's *Jumbo* and continuing until, at age 106, he helped stage the 1994 revival of his 1955 hit *Damn Yankees.* Director-choreographer Jerome Robbins guided a dozen musicals in the two decades between *On the Town* and *Fiddler on the Roof. Jerome Robbins' Broadway* (1989) celebrated the work of this genius. Other influential choreographers include Agnes DeMille (*Oklahoma!* and *Brigadoon*), Jack Cole (*Kismet* and *A Funny Thing Happened on the Way to the Forum* [1962]), Michael Kidd (*Guys and Dolls, Can-Can* [1953], and *Li'l Abner* [1956]), and Gower Champion (*Bye, Bye, Birdie; Hello, Dolly!; Carnival* [1960]; and *42nd Street* [1980]). With a number of successful musicals, principally *Contact* (1999) and *The Producers* (2001), Susan Stroman has quickly become one of the most successful current director-choreographers.

As a choreographer (and later as director), Bob Fosse left an indelible stamp on musicals such as *Pajama Game, Red Head* (1959), *How to Succeed, Sweet Charity, Pippin,* and *Chicago.* Two long-running dance revues, *Dancin'* (1978) and *Fosse* (1999), have showcased his distinctive style. After codirecting and choreographing *Follies,* Michael Bennett became a musical auteur with *A Chorus Line* (1975). With a score by Marvin Hamlisch and Edward Kleban, the show, which had evolved from conversations that Bennett had had with dancers, won the Pulitzer Prize and ran for 15 years. Bennett followed this success with *Dreamgirls* (1981).

Like Kleban, several other people who primarily achieved success away from Broadway have managed to write one hit show that ran for at least 1,000 performances: Mitch Leigh and Joe Darion, *Man of La Mancha* (1965); Burt Bacharach and Hal David, *Promises, Promises* (1968); Sherman Edwards and Peter Stone, *1776* (1969); Jim Jacobs and Warren Casey, *Grease* (1972); Charlie Smalls, *The Wiz* (1975); Carol Hall, *The Best Little Whorehouse in Texas* (1978); Roger

Miller, *Big River* (1985); and Jonathan Larson, *Rent* (1996; Pulitzer Prize).

Starting in the late 1970s and continuing well into the 1990s, a new trend was evident: rewriting older shows in order to recycle great songs. *My One and Only* (1983) and *Crazy for You* (1992) were successful reworkings of the Gershwins' *Funny Face* (1927) and *Girl Crazy* (1930), respectively. The very successful *42nd Street* included many Harry Warren/Al Dubin songs to supplement the ones originally used in their 1933 film of the same title. Another popular type of musical might be called the "compilation revue," an assemblage of songs associated with one songwriter. The most notable examples include *Ain't Misbehavin'* (Fats Waller [1978]), *Sophisticated Ladies* (Duke Ellington [1981]), and *Smokey Joe's Café* (Jerry Lieber and Mike Stoller [1995]). *Mamma Mia!* (2001), a musical drawing upon the ABBA song catalog, became an enduring hit. Unfortunately, a string of flop "jukebox musicals" followed, each filled with songs of writers ranging from the Beach Boys (*Good Vibrations*) to John Lennon (*Imagine*). However, *Jersey Boys* (2005) transcended the formula by telling the story of Frankie Valli and the Four Seasons while giving authentic renditions of the group's hits.

During the 1970s, 1980s, and 1990s, the most successful musicals were imports, primarily from England. By the end of the century, it appeared that the European invasion had subsided, at least temporarily. In 2001, the traditional American musical had a new and most unlikely champion in Mel Brooks, who adapted his 1968 film *The Producers* into the new millennium's blockbuster, thanks in part to Susan Stroman's inventive direction and choreography. Brooks's infectiously hummable score reminded listeners of what they liked best in the old musicals, though Brooks's *Young Frankenstein* (2007) did not duplicate the movie-adaptation formula that worked with *The Producers*.

Nonetheless, more and more musicals based on films have opened in New York. The best was *Hairspray* (2002), with an electrifying *faux*-1962 rock score ("Welcome to the '60s," "You Can't Stop the Beat") by Marc Shaiman and Scott Wittman. Others included *The Color Purple* (2005; originally an Alice Walker novel), *Monty Python's Spamalot* (2005), *Mary Poppins* (2006), *Legally Blonde* (2007), *Xanadu on Broadway* (2007), *The Little Mermaid* (2008), *Billy Elliot* (2008), *Shrek The Musical* (2008), and Dolly Parton's *9 to 5: The Musical* (2009).

This dominance of film adaptations made such original musicals as *The Drowsy Chaperone* (2006) seem all the more refreshing. This "musical within a comedy" spoofed mindless 1920s musicals. *Avenue Q* (2003) was both entertaining and smartly insightful, with delightful Robert Lopez/Jeff Marx songs ("It Sucks to Be Me," "The Internet Is for Porn") mostly "sung" by large hand puppets.

When *Rent* (1996), the rock update of Puccini's *La Bohème,* finally closed in September 2008, two other musicals carried on *Rent*'s ability to transcend the traditional Broadway musical to excite younger audiences. *Spring Awakening* (2006), based on an 1891 Frank Wedekind play, showed teenagers discovering their sexuality in a repressive adult world. The score by Steven Sater and rock composer Duncan Sheik might signal a new direction for musical theater. Similarly, Lin-Manuel Miranda's *In the Heights* shows a modern slice of life in the Latino community of Washington Heights. The show won the 2008 Tony Award for Best Musical, with its appealing salsa-inflected score.

Several younger songwriters have followed Sondheim's model of thought-provoking musicals, including Stephen Flaherty and Lynn Ahrens (*Ragtime*, 1998), Michael John LaChiusa (*The Wild Party,* 2000), and Adam Guettel (*Light in the Piazza,* 2005). It appears that theatergoes will continue to get the eye-poppingly entertaining Broadway musicals they demand in abundance, along with the occasional work of intelligence and originality—often presented Off-Broadway—they did not realize they wanted.

BIBLIOGRAPHY

Alpert, Hollis. *Broadway! 125 Years of Musical Theatre.* New York: Arcade, 1991.

Block, Geoffrey. *Enchanted Evenings: The Broadway Musical from "Show Boat" to Sondheim.* New York: Oxford University Press, 2004.

Bordman, Gerald Martin. *American Musical Theatre: A Chronicle.* 3d ed. New York: Oxford University Press, 2001.

Coleman, Bud, and Judith A. Sebesta, eds. *Women in American Musical Theatre.* Jefferson, N.C.: McFarland, 2008.

Engel, Lehman. *American Musical Theater: A Consideration.* New York: Macmillan, 1975.

Everett, William A., and Paul R. Laird, eds. *The Cambridge Companion to the Musical.* 2nd ed. Cambridge and New York: Cambridge University Press, 2008.

Ewen, David. *Complete Book of the American Musical Theater.* Rev. ed. New York: Holt, 1959.

————. *The Story of America's Musical Theater.* Rev. ed. Philadelphia: Chilton, 1968.

Flinn, Denny Martin. *Musical! A Grand Tour.* New York: Schirmer Books, 1997.

Gottfried, Martin. *Broadway Musicals.* New York: H. N. Abrams, 1979.

————. *More Broadway Musicals.* New York: H. N. Abrams, 1991.

Green, Stanley. *Broadway Musicals, Show by Show.* 3d ed. Milwaukee, Wisc.: Hal Leonard, 1990.

Hischak, Thomas S. *Boy Loses Girl: Broadways Librettists.* Lanham, Md.: Scarecrow Press, 2002.

Jones, John Bush. *Our Musicals, Ourselves: A Social History of the American Musical Theatre.* Hanover, N.H.: Brandeis University Press, 2004.

Kenrick, John. *Musical Theatre: A History.* New York: Continuum, 2008.

Kirle, Bruce. *Unfinished Show Business: Broadway Musicals as Works-in-Progress.* Carbondale: Southern Illinois University Press, 2005.

Kislan, Richard. *The Musical: A Look at the American Musical Theater.* Rev. ed. New York: Applause Theatre Books, 1995.

Knapp, Raymond. *The American Musical and the Performance of Personal Identity.* Princeton, N.J.: Princeton University Press, 2006.

McMillin, Scott. *The Musical as Drama.* Princeton, N.J.: Princeton University Press, 2006.

Miller, Scott. *Strike Up the Band: A New History of Musical Theatre.* Portsmouth, N.H.: Heinemann, 2007.

Most, Andrea. *Making Americans: Jews and the Broadway Musical.* Cambridge, Mass.: Harvard University Press, 2004.

Sennett, Ted. *Song and Dance: The Musicals of Broadway.* New York: Metro Books, 1998.

Smith, Cecil, and Glenn Litton. *Musical Comedy in America.* New York: Theatre Arts Books, 1981.

Sternfeld, Jessica. *The Megamusical.* Bloomington: Indiana University Press, 2006.

Swain, Joseph P. *The Broadway Musical: A Critical and Musical Survey.* New York: Oxford University Press, 1990.

Walsh, David, and Len Platt. *Musical Theater and American Culture.* Westport, Conn.: Praeger, 2003.

Wolf, Stacy. *A Problem Like Maria: Gender and Sexuality in the American Musical.* Ann Arbor: University of Michigan Press, 2002.

Woll, Allen. *Black Musical Theatre: From "Coontown" to "Dreamgirls."* Baton Rouge: Louisiana State University Press, 1989.

Wollman, Elizabeth. *The Theater Will Rock: A History of the Rock Musical, from "Hair" to "Hedwig."* Ann Arbor: University of Michigan Press, 2006.

Gary Konas
University of Wisconsin–La Crosse

MY HEART'S IN THE HIGHLANDS WILLIAM SAROYAN (1939)

A one-act dramatization of SAROYAN's short story, "The Man with the Heart in the Highlands," *My Heart's in the Highlands* first appeared in *One Act Play* magazine in 1938. Saroyan expanded the play into a longer one-act for its GROUP THEATRE production in 1939. It was produced later that same year by the THEATRE GUILD.

This simple, nearly plotless play is set in Fresno, California, in 1914, as war breaks out in Europe. It centers around a penniless and unknown poet, Ben Alexander, and his charming, faithful, and hopeful young son, Johnny. The two befriend an old Scottish actor, Jasper MacGregor, who has a gift for playing the bugle. During the opening moments of the play, he plays "My Heart's in the Highlands," *"the loveliest and most amazing music in the world: a solo on a bugle."* MacGregor has walked out of an "Old People's Home" and first comes to the Alexander house in search of a glass of water. Ben, though he has no food and no money (they've been living on popcorn), cordially invites MacGregor in for a meal, sending Johnny down to Mr. Kosak's store to ask for bread and cheese on credit.

Using various tactics, none of them particularly devious, Johnny tries to charm the storekeeper into extending his father more credit. Mr. Kosak suggests that Johnny and his father should get jobs, but he finally gives the boy the food. Back at the house, the meager meal is shared among Johnny, Ben, MacGregor, and Johnny's Armenian grandmother. After dinner, MacGregor, still hungry, plays his bugle so beautifully that it draws a crowd. He barters his next song for an abundance of food, asking each listener to go back to his house for "some morsel"; when they return, he plays. MacGregor stays with the Alexanders until an attendant from the "Old People's Home" comes to collect him; the residents are going to put on *King Lear* and need him to play the lead.

Johnny then meets an orphaned newsboy who has a gift for whistling. The boy presents him with the morning paper. In it, Ben reads of war and proclaims, "They've gone crazy again." The postman brings word that the *Atlantic Monthly* has rejected Ben's poems, and the discouraged poet roars, "Why do they destroy themselves running after things of death, and thrust aside all things of life?" The real estate agent brings word that they must vacate the house since they have not paid rent in three months. When Ben goes to say good-bye to Mr. Kosak, he gives him his rejected poems because "poetry must be *read* to be poetry."

MacGregor arrives, wanting to be with Ben and Johnny when he dies. Upon his return, the neighbors again bring food for him in hopes of hearing him play his bugle. By the end of the play, MacGregor dies, and Johnny and his father are homeless. As they leave the house to make room for its new occupants, Ben says, "Never mind, Johnny. You just follow me," to which Johnny delivers the curtain line: "I'm not mentioning any names, Pa, but something's wrong somewhere."

Johnny's last line is Saroyan's suggestion that there is something wrong in a world where artists go hungry and war is financed. Saroyan's tone is not virulent, however; whoever is guilty is not specifically represented in the play—the real estate agent who evicts them and the shopkeeper who declines them further credit are both kind. The guilty party is an unnamed "system" that starts wars and does not fund art. MacGregor represents the ideal: He is an artist who is supported by the community in return for the beauty he creates. Group Theatre founder HAROLD CLURMAN, who encouraged William Saroyan to submit a play to the Group, described *My Heart's in the Highlands* years later as "a folk tale—humorous, tender, with a loosely articulated ideological point." Some of the other Group members were reluctant to produce it, Clurman wrote, "because in those days young folk felt that plays had to be 'dynamite!'" (466).

BIBLIOGRAPHY
Clurman, Harold. *The Collected Works of Harold Clurman.* Edited by Marjorie Loggia and Glenn Young. New York: Applause Theatre Books, 1994.

N

NATIVE AMERICAN DRAMA Though Native American cultures often place a great value on performance, public ceremony, symbolic dance, and ritual, drama per se was relatively rare until the last quarter of the 20th century. This is perhaps particularly noteworthy since the figure of the Native American has been present in American drama since Ann J. Kemble Hatton's *Tammany* (1794) and has been a staple, even an obsession, of Euro-American playwrights since Edwin Forrest organized a national competition for an "Indian" play in 1828. The winner, JOHN AUGUSTUS STONE'S *METAMORA; OR, THE LAST OF THE WAMPANOAGS*, was performed around the country by Forrest's troupe for 40 years.

One significant Native American playwright from the first half of the 20th century was R. LYNN RIGGS, whose work was presented on established New York stages in the 1930s. His most memorable play may well be *The Cherokee Night* (1932), a compelling and unconventional portrait of mixed-blood Cherokee in eastern Oklahoma. He also wrote *Green Grow the Lilacs* (1931), a play that was the source of Rodgers and Hammerstein's musical, *Oklahoma!*, produced a dozen years later.

Native American drama has experienced a new birth since the production of Hanay Geiogamah's plays in the 1970s. *Body Indian* (1972) presents the grotesque fate of an alcoholic Native American with an artificial leg who passes out on the floor of a small apartment. The play is composed of five repeated scenes in which the protagonist is dispossessed by friends, relatives, and acquaintances. *Foghorn* (1973) is a collection of scenes that rewrite several Euro-American accounts, from John Smith's encounter with Pocahontas to a scene from a Wild West show to a radically revisionary episode of "The Lone Ranger." This deconstruction of popular images of Native Americans is superimposed on a presentation of the 1969 occupation of Alcatraz Island, during which federal authorities used foghorns to weaken the resolve of the protesters. Geiogamah's play *49,* first produced in 1975, has a dual temporal setting that juxtaposes a contemporary extemporaneous celebration with a traditional ritualistic practice from a hundred years before. The two periods are connected by the presence of Night Walker, an ageless ceremonial figure. Since 1975, Geiogamah has written several plays and had them produced in a variety of venues; they have not yet appeared in print, however. One of his plays, *Land Sale* (1985), has been adapted for television.

Together, these works embody a number of the most important themes and practices of contemporary Native American theater: brutally realistic portrayals of the impoverished living conditions of Native Americans, the creation of a discourse meant to attack stereotypical images, and the presentation of Native American community, values, and sensibility. These plays are also representative in other ways: their use of new theatrical forms to reuse and refresh older modes of performance (especially the rite of storytelling) and to refashion traditional beliefs (the trickster figure is one favorite). Another important feature is their concern with issues of identity, including who is or is not a Native; in this area, virtually all playwrights argue for inclusive definitions and a pan-tribal approach. Stylistically, Native American dialectical forms and expressions (sometimes called "Red English") are preserved, and selections from indigenous languages are remembered. Throughout, Native American drama stresses survival—of their cultures, their history, their identity, and even themselves as distinct peoples. They are, in the words of playwright Diane Glancy, "voices speaking against the darkness."

Several female playwrights have recently gained prominence in Native American performance circles, including Monique Mojica, Elvira and Hortensia Colorado, Diane Glancy, and performance artist Murielle Borst. Glancy's short play, *The Truth Teller* (1991), set in an Indian village on the Upper Mississippi around 1800, reveals the interaction of two figures, an Indian woman and a man of mixed blood, who meet several times over the years to discuss the effects of the coming of the whites. It eloquently weaves the themes of history and memory, performance and narrative, and theater and ceremony into a moving call for cultural preservation. The most celebrated female group is probably the Spiderwoman Theater collective, which for 25 years has been producing stimulating and provocative theater pieces. Often, these begin with a partially improvised storytelling situation that then is enacted on stage and enhanced with other media, testifying to the continued significance of the oral tradition and at the same time drawing on its inherent theatricality.

This body of work has been added to substantially by the plays of Tomson Highway and William Yellow Robe Jr. In Highway's *The Rez Sisters* (1988), seven sisters from a reservation attempt to go to Toronto for the world's biggest bingo game; these plans are complicated by the playful interventions of Nanabush, a trickster figure. Yellow Robe has written a number of powerful dramas that unflinchingly portray daily struggles and indignities faced by Native Americans; in *The Body Guards* (1997), he takes up the subject of the Native American body, raised earlier by Geiogamah, and stages his own perspective as two Natives in a remote area in winter guard the corpse of a friend

and relative from dogs and other scavengers. Yellow Robe has also mentored promising new Native playwrights like Terry Gomez and Bunky Yellow Hawk.

The early 21st century has seen exciting and impressive growth in Native American theater. The playwrights active in the 1980s and 1990s have gone on to develop new works, and many other Native American playwrights have emerged or become known to a wider audience, including Daniel David Moses, Yvette Nolan, Floyd Favel, Drew Hayden Taylor, and Annette Arkeketa. The plays exhibit a wide array of styles, including naturalistic, Brechtian, poetic, nonlinear, supernatural, and postmodern.

Very important is the proliferation of new anthologies and related resources. Hanay Geiogamah and Jaye Darby have put together anthologies of Native American plays and performance studies; Darby and Stephanie Fitzgerald have assembled a volume of plays by Native American women; and Monique Mojica and Ric Knowles have edited an impressive anthology of First Nations drama. Though institutional funding is still inadequate and general audience demand unpredictable, the current state of Native American drama is strong, and its future promising.

BIBLIOGRAPHY

Brask, Per, and William Morgan, eds. *Aboriginal Voices: Amerindian, Inuit, and Sami Theater.* Baltimore: Johns Hopkins University Press, 1992.

D'Aponte, Mimi Gisolfi, ed. *Seventh Generation: An Anthology of Native American Plays.* New York: Theatre Communications Group, 1999.

Darby, Jaye T., and Stephanie Fitzgerald, eds. *Keepers of the Morning Star: An Anthology of Native Women's Theater.* Los Angeles: UCLA Native American Studies Press, 2003.

Geiogamah, Hanay. *New Native American Drama: Three Plays.* Norman: University of Oklahoma Press, 1980.

———, and Jaye T. Darby, eds. *American Indian Theater in Performance.* Los Angeles: UCLA American Indian Studies Center Press, 2000.

———, eds. *Stories of Our Way: An Anthology of American Indian Plays.* Los Angeles: UCLA Native American Studies Center Press, 1999.

Glancy, Diane. *War Cries.* Duluth, Minn.: Holy Cow Press, 1997.

Highway, Tomson. *The Rez Sisters.* Saskatoon, Saskatchewan: Fifth House, 1988.

Mojica, Monique, and Ric Knowles, eds. *Staging Coyote's Dream: An Anthology of First Nations Drama in English.* Toronto: Playwrights Canada Press, 2003.

Perkins, Kathy A., and Roberta Uno, eds. *Contemporary Plays by Women of Color.* London, New York: Routledge, 1996.

Yellow Robe, William S., Jr. *Where the Pavement Ends: Five Native American Plays.* Norman: University of Oklahoma Press, 2000.

Brian Richardson
University of Maryland

NEGRO ENSEMBLE COMPANY See WARD, DOUGLAS TURNER.

NELSON, RICHARD (1950–) Richard Nelson was born in Chicago and graduated from Hamilton College, in upstate New York, in 1972. He has had a prolific career as playwright, literary manager, dramaturge, translator, adapter, and director. His work has been produced almost solely in nonprofit theaters throughout the United States and in England, with a number of them, beginning with *Some Americans Abroad* (1989), commissioned and produced by Great Britain's Royal Shakespeare Company.

Despite an output that numbers more than 40 plays and adaptations, as well as radio and television dramas, a screenplay (*Ethan Frome* [1992]), and the revised book for the musical *Chess* (1988), his work is not well known and has attracted little scholarly examination. Although Nelson's plays have been produced by many of this country's major regional and OFF-BROADWAY theaters, they have rarely been seen on Broadway. It was not until his award-winning musical adaptation of James Joyce's *The Dead* was commercially mounted and toured nationally after a successful Off-Broadway run in 2000 that he reached anything like a mass audience.

The range of Nelson's work is impressive—historical epics, Brechtian political satire (he frequently uses titles for ironic comments on the action onstage), farce, domestic drama, and fable. Several of Nelson's early works have been labeled "reporter" plays, since they deal with aspects of the profession of journalism. His first full-length play, *The Killing of Yablonski* (1978),

examines a reporter's involvement—both as observer and as would-be protagonist—in the assassination of Jock Yablonski, a leader of the United Mine Workers, whose cold-blooded murder by a rival faction shocked the nation. *Conjuring an Event* (1978) is a fable about an ego-driven schizophrenic reporter quite literally attempting to "create" an event to write about. *Jungle Coup* (1978), a work set in an African jungle and reminiscent of EUGENE O'NEILL's *The EMPEROR JONES,* deals with a reporter concocting false stories about a revolution.

Many of his plays deal with clashes between cultures. Two Czech exiles, a director and his actress wife, try to cope with life in New York in *Between East and West* (1985). In *The Vienna Notes* (1979), an American politician facing an ugly hostage situation while in Austria rewrites the truth and simultaneously polishes his own image to the world. These clashes often involve historical and literary figures and actual events. *The Return of Pinocchio* (1983) brings the ex-puppet-turned-American-movie-star back to his native Italy, a nation still suffering the ravages of World War II. *Rip Van Winkle; or, "The Works"* (1981) dramatizes the famous Washington Irving tale (as adapted for the stage in the 19th century by actor JOSEPH JEFFERSON), treating the story as a conflict between the rural idealism of an earlier America and the rapacious materialism of a technologically driven nation. *Two Shakespearean Actors* (1990) documents the rivalry between British actor William Macready and the American Edwin Forrest, whose rival New York productions of *Macbeth* in 1849 provoked a riot that killed 34 people. *The General from America* (1996) deals sympathetically with the traitorous Benedict Arnold as a man who loses his place in two nations.

Writers, artists, and academics also figure prominently in Nelson's plays. *An American Comedy* (1983), a farcical work set on an ocean liner in the 1930s, dramatizes what happens when one-half of a successful playwriting team (see GEORGE S. KAUFMAN and MOSS HART) decides to eschew Broadway for a newly discovered Marxism. *Principia Scriptoriae* (1986), a political drama set in an unnamed Latin American nation, is about two writers, an innocent American and his friend, a native of that country, who are both imprisoned and tortured by the local government. The oddly poignant *Some Americans Abroad* (1989) skewers a group of American college teachers and students on a theater tour in London and Stratford. Its insights into academic politics and cultural consumerism are understated but deftly made. *Sensibility and Sense,* produced on television in 1990 under that title but later published as *Left,* examines the personal sources of political ideology. Moving back and forth in time from the 1930s to the 1980s, it focuses on a dying former college president devastated by the published memoirs of an old friend. In *Columbus and the Discovery of Japan* (1992), Nelson views the prevaricating explorer as a selfish and sometimes bumbling con artist whose triumphant journey gets him across an ocean but not to where he intended to go.

Later Nelson plays—*New England* (1994), *Goodnight Children Everywhere* (1997), *James Joyce's The Dead* (2000), and *Madame Melville* (2000)—are less overtly political in focus; instead, they are quietly domestic in a manner more Chekhovian than Brechtian. These dramatize emotional and sexual tensions—between long-separated siblings, between husband and wife, between teacher and student. Nelson wrote the book and lyrics for the musical *My Life with Albertine* (2003)—music by Ricky Ian Gordon; he also directed this work based on parts of Marcel Proust's *Remembrance of Things Past.*

In recent years, Richard Nelson has continued to write (and often direct) small-scale "family" plays that reach beyond domestic drama and deal with such larger themes as incest, art, and politics. *Rodney's Wife,* produced by the Williamstown Theatre Festival and Playwrights Horizons in 2004, is set in a small villa on the edge of Rome where Rodney is acting in a film about the American West. With him are his second wife, an alcoholic former actress; his sister; his daughter by his first wife; her fiancé; and Rodney's current manager. Although the play seems to be about Rodney's professional career, it is really about the sexual tensions among the family members. In *Frank's Home,* produced by the Goodman Theatre in 2006 and Playwrights Horizons in 2007, the family of the great architect Frank Lloyd Wright is torn by anger over Wright's many (heterosexual) love affairs, as well as the shared disappointment over his professional failures. At age 55, he has come back to the United States and has moved to California looking for work. Although much of the play focuses on Wright's relationship with his alcoholic mistress and his children, it is his enduring bond with another great architect, Louis Sullivan, also down on his luck, and their devotion to finding beauty and making art, that forms the spine of the play.

Nelson's most recent "family play," *Conversations in Tusculum,* produced by the Public Theatre in 2008, takes place in 45 B.C. in various villas in the town of Tusculum outside Rome. A somewhat static and cerebral drama, it includes in its small cast of characters—most tied by blood and marriage—such familiar historical figures as Brutus, his brother-in-law Cassius, and close friend Cicero, as well as Brutus's wife and mother. Never seen but important to the play are two other Romans—Julius Caesar and Cato, Brutus's uncle and father-in-law—who are the off-stage subjects of many of the "conversations." According to Nelson's "Note" in the program for the Public Theatre production, Cato's suicide in the face of Caesar's advancing army was "the singular principled act in an age of compromise and expediency." The play examines the last days of the Roman Republic and, more specifically, the painful decision by Brutus and the others to assassinate Caesar the following year.

BIBLIOGRAPHY

Nelson, Richard. *Conversations in Tusculum.* London: Faber and Faber, 2008.

———. *Frank's Home.* New York: Broadway Play Publishing, 2008.

———. *Franny's Way.* New York: Broadway Play Publishing, 2003.

———. *Plays by Richard Nelson: Early Plays—Vols. 1–3.* New York: Broadway Play Publishing, 1998–99.

———. *Richard Nelson: Plays Vol. 1.* London: Faber and Faber, 1999.

———. *Rodney's Wife.* New York: Theatre Communications Group, 2006.

———, and David Jones. *Making Plays: The Writer Director Relationship in the Theatre Today.* London: Faber and Faber, 1995.

Leonard Fleischer
Brooklyn, New York

NEW YORK IDEA, THE LANGDON MITCH-ELL (1906) This social satire is set among wealthy New Yorkers in the first decade of the 20th century. The New York "idea" of the title is that one should "marry for whim and leave the rest to the divorce court." MITCHELL's play is a vehicle for comic commentary on the marriage and divorce habits—that is, the ease and frequency with which these took place—of upper-class Americans in his day. It portrays many of the same situations and character types later seen in PHILIP BARRY's far superior play, *The PHILADELPHIA STORY* (1939).

Cynthia (an irresistible, dynamic, spoiled, rich woman) and John (the handsome and charming ex-husband who never quite got over her) Karslake and Philip (stodgy, boring) and Vida ("empty-headed, pleasure-loving, and fashionable") Phillimore are divorced couples in New York. On the eve of the marriage of Cynthia Karslake and Philip Phillimore, their ex-spouses arrive at the Phillimore family home. Cynthia still shares her ex-husband's love of horseracing and excitement and finds her soon-to-be in-laws exceedingly boring; they, in turn, find her behavior somewhat shocking. Through the interference of Vida and a British visitor and horseman, Sir Wilfred Cates-Darby, Cynthia balks at the marriage, running off to the races with Sir Wilfred just hours before the wedding. Cynthia returns to the house close to midnight, insisting that the wedding is still on; however, when the ex-spouses, who are in attendance, leave together moments before the ceremony is to begin, Cynthia once again deserts Philip and runs off to stop John from marrying Vida.

When she arrives at her ex-husband's home, it is Sir Wilfred and Vida who have married. Furthermore, a letter comes from John's lawyer informing him that the Karslake divorce decree was not valid. This convenient device serves to reunite the couple, and in the end John and Cynthia Karslake admit that they want nothing more than to resume their marriage, which they then do.

Mitchell satirizes marriage and divorce habits among the well-to-do in America. Sir Wilfred Cates-Darby and Vida Phillimore represent those opportunistic matches between British peers who brought a title and American heiresses who brought wealth to the marriage. Mitchell also mocks the frivolous American attitude toward marriage, which prompts many to marry or divorce at the drop of a hat. Cynthia left John after seven months of wedded bliss simply because he would not drop what he was doing—legal work, his profession—to take her to the races that instant; soon afterward, she is, as the play begins, on the brink of marriage to a man she does not love.

While in the earliest American dramas (ROYALL TYLER's *The CONTRAST* [1787] and ANNA CORA MOWATT's *FASHION* [1845]) the guileless American proves truer than the more sophisticated European, in the early 20th century, the comic contrast was more often between the old-fashioned elders and their less conventionally moral offspring. Often cited as the best American social comedy of the early 20th century, *The New York Idea* seems dated and contrived by today's standards.

NIGGER, THE EDWARD SHELDON (1909) SHELDON's deliberately provocatively titled play is a story of race prejudice and its corrosive effect on the post-Reconstruction South. While appallingly racist by current standards, *The Nigger* represents a sincere Progressive-era attempt to focus attention on the festering racial antipathies that characterized turn-of-the-20th-century America.

Successful farmer and local sheriff Philip Morrow is the bigoted scion in a nameless southern state. Although personally committed to treating both blacks and whites with dignity. Morrow, adhering to the pervasive prejudices of his place and time, believes that African Americans are inferior to whites intellectually and morally. He is supported in these attitudes by his cousin, Clifton Noyes, owner of a local distillery, and Georgiana (Georgie) Byrd, who becomes Morrow's fiancée early in the play. Morrow's racial attitudes are sufficiently orthodox that his cousin asks him to stand for governor in the next election in an attempt to defeat Senator Long, a champion of a progressive racial policy, who also wishes to institute a prohibition on alcohol as a means of saving the state's blacks from squandering their wages and debasing themselves in drunkenness. Whatever his attitudes about alcohol, Morrow is a firm believer in the law, a character trait that is sorely tested when an African-American rapist and murderer seeks the sheriff's help to prevent himself from being lynched. Morrow initially stands down the mob, but when he tries to spirit the confessed criminal to jail, Noyes restrains him, and the mob seizes the murderer and satisfies its thirst for vengeance.

Untainted by his attempted intervention, Morrow is elected governor. Soon thereafter, racial tensions resurface when a race riot breaks out. Over the course of the insurrection, Governor Morrow becomes convinced that prohibition is necessary in order to prevent a recurrence of the violence he is trying to suppress. Noyes, seeing financial ruin ahead, confronts Morrow with evidence that the latter is the product of an illicit relationship between Morrow's grandfather and a quadroon slave. When that reality is confirmed by his "Mammy," Jinny, Morrow refuses to rescind his order to close all the bars, and Noyes says that he will give Morrow three days to rethink his position. Morrow reveals his racial status to Georgie who is at first horrified but later asserts that her love can ignore his racial heritage. Having explored at length with Senator Long the means by which racial reconciliation might ultimately be achieved and having once again refused to bow to Noyes's blackmail, Morrow determines to reveal his heritage, resign the governorship, break with Georgie, and work for the betterment of African Americans.

The Nigger seeks to turn a progressive spotlight on a range of related racial themes: The moral, social, and legal legacy of slavery; the erosion of law by lynching; the debasement of African Americans by the liquor industry; the inequities of racially discriminatory labor practices; and, finally, the essential inhumanity of racial bigotry all find expression in the play.

Gary A. Richardson
Mercer University

'NIGHT MOTHER MARSHA NORMAN (1983)

Winner of the PULITZER PRIZE, NORMAN's *'night Mother* is a grim, heart-wrenching drama about a widowed mother and her divorced daughter in the hour or so before the daughter's suicide (the play runs 90 min-

utes with no intermission). The troubled Jessie asserts her choice to leave her life; by doing so, ironically, she takes charge of it. The struggle in the play is between the neurotic mother, who tries to stop her daughter by expressing her love and her guilt and her fear of being left alone, and the disturbed, unstoppable daughter, who expresses her loneliness and despair and who assures her mother that her suicide is not her mother's fault. During this struggle, they achieve a greater closeness than ever before.

Jessie is making preparations to do something in her bedroom. She asks her mother if she has any towels she does not want, a large sheet of plastic, and her late father's gun. When her mother presses her for an explanation, Jessie tells her simply, matter-of-factly, that she is going to shoot herself in an hour—and so begins an hour in their lives that is filled with more honesty than any other they've spent together. Through their final discussion, the facts of their lives are revealed to the audience: Jessie's husband left her a year ago; since then, she has lived with her mother. Jessie has a delinquent son who is a thief and probably a drug addict, and she has a seizure disorder for which she takes medication. Her father is dead. Beyond this exposition are the secrets the two women reveal to each other: Jessie's mother, Thelma, did not love Jessie's father ("He wanted a plain country woman and that's what he married, and then held it against me."). Jessie's epilepsy started in childhood, not after a horseback riding accident as she has always been told; instead, she apparently inherited it from her father, who had a mild seizure disorder and whom her mother blames for passing it to their child. Jessie's husband left her for another woman: "He had a girl, Jessie. I walked right in on them in the toolshed." For her part, Jessie reveals her unhappiness: "I'm tired. I'm hurt. I'm sad. I feel used." She also tells her mother that she, herself, wrote the tender good-bye note from her husband Cecil, not he: "I said I'll always love me, not Cecil. But that's how he felt."

Jessie makes sure that Thelma has all the information she will need: the location of the laundry soap, the words she will say to Jessie's brother, to the police, and to Jessie's son. As the time for the suicide draws near, no suggested alternative, no argument, no hysterical pleading from Thelma can alter Jessie's determination. Moments after the gunshot is heard from the locked bedroom, the play ends as Thelma begins to go through the motions that Jessie has planned for her.

Feminist criticism of the play has been harsh because, some feminists argue, it depicts women who have failed at the stereotypical female roles of marriage and motherhood and who, therefore, find that their lives are meaningless. Those who disagree with this assessment argue that such a reading fails to consider the complexity of the characters, not to mention the fact that a play about two women is not necessarily about all women.

NIGHT OF THE IGUANA, THE TENNESSEE WILLIAMS (1961)

Set in a seedy resort hotel on the west coast of Mexico in 1940, *The Night of the Iguana* was the last critically acclaimed and commercially successful Broadway offering of WILLIAMS's career.

On the hotel's verandah, two strangers find themselves conversing long into the night as they struggle with their "devils"—the dark aspects of their personalities—which threaten to overwhelm and plunge each of them into the abyss of emotional breakdown. One of these is T. Lawrence Shannon, an alcoholic ex-cleric currently employed as a tour guide, and the other is Hannah Jelkes, a portrait artist who travels the world with her aged grandfather Nonno, a poet struggling to finish his last poem before he dies.

The resort is operated by Maxine Faulk, an affable woman possessed of an uncomplicated sensual nature and well aware of Shannon's history of emotional instability. On those occasions in the past when psychic collapse threatened, Shannon had found consolation with his longtime friend, Faulk's recently deceased husband. On this occasion, though, unaware of his friend's death, Shannon seeks aid where none is available. Indeed, Maxine pounces on the distraught man, intent on making him her new business partner and lover.

Shannon's immediate emotional difficulties stem from his seduction of a teenage member of his tour group and the outrage of the rest of his party when their affair is discovered, while Hannah Jelkes is contending with what she knows is the imminent death

of her grandfather. When Shannon, drinking heavily, threatens suicide, Maxine has him tied in a hammock on the verandah. Here the ex-cleric and Hannah, who is maintaining a vigil for the dying Nonno, begin to converse, ultimately sharing their innermost selves; in so doing, they discover a life-affirming resiliency that offsets their emotional disarray.

Their conversation is bluntly honest in its self-revelation: Hannah discloses her emotional isolation and fear of intimacy, while Shannon reveals the psychic conflict that perpetually torments him—a spiritual longing confounded by unappeasable carnal appetites. In the play's closing moments, Shannon symbolically releases an iguana leashed beneath the verandah where it is being fattened for slaughter; Hannah discovers that her grandfather, having completed his poem, has died. She realizes that both she and Shannon have struggled to get through a night as difficult as any they have ever experienced. Both have endured and will go on—alone perhaps—but with courage inspired by knowing that in their night they shared one of life's most precious gifts, a union brought about through compassionate understanding.

Williams's recurring themes—the desires of the flesh in conflict with spiritual yearning, the escape from life's torments into alcohol, the lonely isolation of the individual, and the need for compassion and stoic endurance—are mingled in a play that shows the playwright at the peak of his powers. His skillful characterization, the poetic cadence of dialogue that combines coarse humor with philosophic rumination, and the symbolism that transforms the play's literal framework, enriching its emotional texture, make *The Night of the Iguana* one of Williams's finest achievements.

Craig Clinton
Reed College

NIGHT THOREAU SPENT IN JAIL, THE JEROME LAWRENCE AND ROBERT E. LEE (1970)

During his well-documented residence on Walden Pond near Concord, Massachusetts, in the mid-1800s, Henry David Thoreau was jailed for failing to pay his poll tax. It was an act of civil disobedience about which he later wrote in his essay "Civil Disobedience." LAWRENCE and LEE use that brief stay in jail as the focal point from which their episodic memory play, *The Night Thoreau Spent in Jail,* portrays the famous thinker.

In the play—as in reality—Thoreau refuses to pay the tax on principle: Taxes fund the war against Mexico; if he were to pay for a foot soldier's rifle, Thoreau tells his jailer at the end of act 1, he would be "as much a killer as the foot soldier who crashes across the border in faraway Mexico, charges into his neighbor's house, sets fire to it and kills his children."

Central to the set is the jail cell, surrounded by areas in which scenes from the past are played out. The cell is a metaphor for the imprisonment of convention—the convention of the church and of the schoolhouse. In a series of flashbacks, Thoreau is portrayed, first as a recent graduate of Harvard, for whose "academic droning and snorting" he has little respect; next as a son whose "peculiar" irreverence and nonconformity worry his mother; then as an affectionate brother to John Thoreau—a kindred spirit who dies as a young man from lockjaw; then as an inspiring teacher who eventually loses all of his pupils because their parents are offended by his views and methods; and, finally, as a disciple of transcendentalist Ralph Waldo Emerson, for whom he works as handyman and tutor to his son and on whose land he carries out his famous experiment in simplified living.

Emerson's lectures at Harvard inspired Thoreau; eventually, though, Thoreau's unqualified admiration of Emerson falters when an escaped slave—on his way to Canada—is shot in Concord. Thoreau has met the former slave and, without pretense, has treated him as an equal. When the man is killed, Thoreau cannot get Emerson to appreciate his outrage. After Emerson declines to speak out against this act of violence as well as against those committed in Mexico—all in the name of the United States government—to a crowd Thoreau has assembled, Thoreau becomes disillusioned with his "God," Emerson. In a subsequent dream sequence, a Mexican soldier and the fleeing slave become one in an explicit equating of these victims of government policy.

In his jail cell, Thoreau awakens from the dream to find that his Aunt Louise has paid his tax bill; he then refuses to leave the cell until his cellmate, Bailey, is promised an immediate trial. He uses what he has—civil disobedience—to hasten justice. Having accomplished this, he leaves the cell determined to quit Walden Pond and rejoin the world. The playwrights see Thoreau's journey during the course of the night as one moving away from "hermitizing to social justice" (Lawrence and Lee 103). The historic Thoreau was nothing like a hermit during his stay on Walden Pond—he often visited and entertained friends—but the Thoreau "imprisoned" in the play, the playwrights write, "belongs more to the 1970s than to the age in which he lived" (vii).

The play spoke to its Vietnam War–era audience. Its themes echoed those of the counterculture movement of the period: nonconformity, opposition to war, and nonviolent resistance against a government acting unjustly. The environmentalism and anticommercialism of Thoreau's philosophy also made him a fitting icon for the time.

BIBLIOGRAPHY
Lawrence, Jerome, and Robert E. Lee. *The Night Thoreau Spent in Jail.* New York: Hill & Wang, 1971.

NOONAN, JOHN FORD (1943–) Play-
wright John Ford Noonan was born in New York City and educated at Brown University (B.A., 1964) and Carnegie Institute of Technology (M.A., 1966). After graduate school, Noonan taught briefly, first high school Latin, English, and history in the late 1960s, then drama at Villanova University in the early 1970s. For most of his career, he has been a writer for stage, film, and television, as well as an actor.

The Year Boston Won the Pennant (1969), one of Noonan's best-known works, is the story of a baseball pitcher, Marcus Sykowski, and his efforts to earn enough money to buy an artificial arm to replace the one he lost in an unexplained accident. Through a series of episodes, including a fraudulent kidnapping plot and involvement with an underworld figure, Sykowski finally does obtain a prosthetic limb, but things still turn out badly for the revitalized athlete. After his return to baseball, he suffers a nervous breakdown, and his comeback is abbreviated by assassination. Many critics found the play confusing. *Variety* described it as "a surrealistic, satirical, symbol-crammed attempt to illuminate subconscious strains in American life, which the author represents as cruel, ugly, exploitative—in short, inhuman" (May 28, 1969). With *Older People* (1972) came more negative reaction. In several unrelated sketches, Noonan explores the frustrations encountered by the elderly. Despite severe criticism, some critics predicted that Noonan's wild imagination promised interesting future work.

Some of this promise was fulfilled in *A Coupla White Chicks Sitting around Talking* (1981) and *Some Men Need Help* (1983). Both of these two-character plays have a suburban setting in which two oddly matched people vie for supremacy in situations fraught with the tensions of trying to cope with the demands of modern life. In *A Coupla White Chicks Sitting around Talking,* a garrulous, eccentric woman from Texas forces herself into the kitchen (and life) of her new neighbor, a buttoned-up, in-control neurotic, with ultimately mutually beneficial results. In *Some Men Need Help,* the interloping neighbor is named Gaetano Altobelli, and the one in need of help is Hudley T. Singleton III. Here Noonan refrains from stressing obvious ethnic differences in finding a solution to Hudley's problems.

Noonan's notable more recent works include *Talking Things over with Chekhov* (1991), a comedy about an aspiring, off-the-wall playwright and his ex-girlfriend, who insists on starring in his first production; her performance is lauded by critics while his play, to his despair, is dismissed as "an insignificant vehicle unworthy of her gifts." In *Music from down the Hill* (1995), Margot, a middle-aged hysteric with a big heart hiding in a frightened body, finds release after moving in with Claire, a young schizophrenic who loves Bruce Springsteen—at top volume. *A Critic and His Wife* (1997) is about a self-centered married pair who become rival writers.

Noonan's work is sometimes revived, as was *All She Cares about Is the Yankees* (published in 1988) in Washington, D.C., in 2002. Noonan continues to act in films.

BIBLIOGRAPHY

Noonan, John Ford. *A Coupla White Chicks Sitting around Talking.* New York: Samuel French, 1981.

———. *A Critic and His Wife.* New York: Applause Theatre Books, 1997.

———. *Music from down the Hill.* New York: Samuel French, 1995.

———. *Some Men Need Help.* New York: Samuel French, 1983.

———. *Talking Things over with Chekhov.* New York: Samuel French, 1991.

———. *The Year Boston Won the Pennant.* New York: Grove Press, 1970.

Philip M. Isaacs
New York, New York

NO PLACE TO BE SOMEBODY CHARLES GORDONE (1969)

The first play by an African American to win the PULITZER PRIZE, *No Place to Be Somebody* is less militant than other plays of the period dealing with the African-American experience of the late 1960s. (See, for example, *DUTCHMAN* by AMIRI BARAKA.) Indeed, the play's central character, "the fair-skinned Negro," Gabe, "a black playwright," tells the audience that he is not "hung up on crap like persecution an' hatred," nor is his a play "about Negro self-pity"; he will, he tells the audience, "leave that social protest jive" to others. Gabe's direct address to the audience provides a framework, which suggests that the play is nonrealistic, occurring only in his mind.

The interracial cast of characters includes Johnny, in whose bar the play is set; Dee, a prostitute and Johnny's girlfriend; Evie, another prostitute; Shanty, the bartender; and Cora, his girlfriend and also a prostitute (although she insists she is a practical nurse); Melvin, a short-order cook and dancer; Sweets Crane, an elderly ex-convict; Mary Lou Bolton, college graduate, daughter of a judge, civil rights activist, and eventual girlfriend of Johnny; Mike Maffucci, a childhood friend of Johnny's and a member of the Italian mob; and various other minor characters. All of the sexual relationships in the play are interracial.

Johnny, a small-time pimp and petty criminal, has been waiting 10 years for his mentor in crime, Sweets Crane, to be released from prison so he can become a big-time criminal like Sweets. But by the time Sweets shows up, he looks like an old wino and has only six months to live; furthermore, he has found religion while in prison and hopes that young Johnny will reform himself too. Instead, Johnny comes to a bad end after betraying both of his white girlfriends—the prostitute *and* the college graduate—as well as his old friend Sweets.

In part, the play is about dreams that do not materialize: Johnny's dream of Sweets and the big time, Sweets's dream of Johnny's reformation, Melvin's dream of being a dancer, Shanty's dream of being a drummer, Cora's dream of Shanty, Dee's dream of Johnny, and Mary Lou's dream of being an activist who—though white—makes an authentic sacrifice for the cause of African-American rights. None of these dreams comes true: sometimes because people—regardless of color—use and abuse others for their own gain (this is certainly true of Johnny and Maffucci); sometimes because the dreamers are deluded (like Melvin, Dee, and Shanty). As a play about dreamers in a bar, it is reminiscent of EUGENE O'NEILL's The ICEMAN COMETH (1946).

Thematically, then, there is much in the play that is simply human and not racial, but GORDONE is also making a statement about the plight of inner-city African Americans in the volatile late 1960s. What has made Johnny the way he is? What has made him a user and a betrayer and a man who will die by violence? Sweets Crane says it is "Charlie fever" ("Charlie" being the "White Man"), and Sweets admits that he is the one who taught it to Johnny as he had been taught by his "daddy and his daddy before him." He elaborates: "Couldn't copy Charlie's good points an' live like men. So we copied his bad points. We just pissed our lives away to be like bad Charlie. . . . With all our fine clothes an' big cars. All it did was make us hate him all the more an' ourselves, too."

In the end, it is the formerly nonviolent Gabe who kills Johnny. Thomas P. Adler writes, "The rather cluttered melodramatic action, reminiscent of a B-grade gangster movie . . . is important mainly for the effect that it—real or imagined or both—has upon the light-skinned Gabe and, by extension, the black race in general, in the change from non-violence to violence" (79). Finally, in an epilogue, Gabe, *dressed as a woman in mourning,* addresses the audience and speaks of his intentional provocation of them; he wants them to wake up to the weeping of the "Black Lady in Mourning," she who "mourns the death of a people dying."

Other elements in the play include the character Machine Dog—a figment of Johnny's imagination who seems to indict Gabe's nonviolence as collaboration in the killings of "innusunt cherbs'a the ghetto"—and the three long poems Gabe recites during the course of the play, which together suggest an evolution from nonviolence to violence among African Americans.

BIBLIOGRAPHY

Adler, Thomas P. *Mirror on the Stage: The Pulitzer Plays as an Approach to American Drama.* West Lafayette, Ind.: Purdue University Press, 1987.

NORMAN, MARSHA (1947–)   In a lecture delivered in 1988, Marsha Norman defined the role of the author as "[n]othing more than getting things straight. That is the job of the writer—to get things straight—things that people say, things that people think, things that people feel," and so the writer must produce a work that is authentic in its depiction of the human condition. Norman's success as a playwright stems from her ability to do just that. She creates characters that are at once unique and universal. Her plays explore the intricacy of social and familial relationships, elevating the seemingly unremarkable to the unforgettable. Though Norman demonstrates an astounding mastery of language, her most significant contribution to American drama is a body of literature that examines female experience. In presenting psychologically complex women, she expresses the concerns of a community too long ignored by the theater. Norman does not write exclusively about women, however; her goal to make visible those who are rarely noticed extends to anyone overlooked by society.

Growing up in Louisville, Kentucky, Norman felt the burden of invisibility. Her parents, strict fundamentalists, never tolerated expressions of anger or skepticism. Norman was not allowed to watch television or play with the neighborhood children, and despite having three younger sisters, her childhood was a lonely one. To entertain herself, she turned to reading, playing the piano, and confiding in an imaginary friend. Always a diligent student, Norman won a scholarship to Agnes Scott, a women's college in Decatur, Georgia. She graduated with a B.A. in philosophy and then earned a master's degree from the University of Louisville.

Norman first received recognition as a major playwright with GETTING OUT (1977), the story of Arlene Holsclaw's parole after an eight-year prison term. As Arlene establishes a new life for herself, she must confront the ghosts of her past: her emotionally distant mother, her former pimp, and a threatening prison guard. However, Arlene's most significant visitor is the memory of Arlie, the abused and abusive girl Arlene once was. Norman based Arlie on a violent teenager she had encountered years earlier while working at the Kentucky Central State Hospital.

In 1978, *Third and Oak: The Pool Hall* and *Third and Oak: The Laundromat* premiered at the Actors Theatre of Louisville, where Norman had earlier been named playwright-in-residence. Although these one-act plays were generally well received, directors found them difficult to stage. The next year, *Circus Valentine* (1979) premiered in Louisville; it was a work that, Norman laments, "people hated more than they ever imagined they would hate anything." Disheartened, she abandoned playwriting for nearly three years.

Ironically, the anger and humiliation Norman experienced with *Circus Valentine* proved indispensable. From this failure grew 'NIGHT, MOTHER (1983), Norman's most stunning success and winner of the PULITZER PRIZE. *'night, Mother* unflinchingly dissects the thought processes that culminate in suicide. When Jessie Cates, a middle-aged divorcée, announces her intent to kill herself, Thelma, Jessie's mother, must convince her to live. Thelma ultimately loses her daughter, yet the final shot, which signals Jessie's death, has divided critics: Does Jessie demonstrate control in choosing to act rather than be acted upon? Or has she surrendered to the forces that would destroy her? Whether triumphant or tragic, *'night, Mother* is an undisputed tour de force.

Norman has been a screenwriter for television and film and published a novel *The Fortune Teller* (1987), but theater remains her forte. In 1983, she wrote *The Holdup,* based on stories her grandfather told about his youth in New Mexico. One year later came *Traveler in the Dark,* a philosophical look at death. *Sarah and Abraham,* a modern version of the biblical story, pre-

miered in 1988. In 1992, Norman's musical adaptation of Frances Hodgson Burnett's *The Secret Garden* won a TONY AWARD. That same year, *Loving Daniel Boone* appeared, followed by *The Red Shoes* (1993) and *Trudy Blue* (1995). Her most recent play, *Last Dance* (2003), is about an American poet who lives in the south of France. Norman also wrote the book for the musical version (2005) of Alice Walker's *The Color Purple.* Since 1994, she has served on the faculty of the Juilliard School, where she is currently codirector of the Playwrights Program.

BIBLIOGRAPHY
Brown, Linda Ginter, ed. *Marsha Norman: A Casebook.* New York: Garland, 1996.
Norman, Marsha. *Collected Plays.* Lyme, N.H.: Smith and Kraus, 1998.
———. *The Secret Garden.* New York: Theatre Communications Group, 1992.

Sarah Reuning
University of North Carolina–Chapel Hill

NORRIS, BRUCE (1960–)

Raised in Houston, Texas, playwright Bruce Norris was trained as an actor at Northwestern University in Evanston, Illinois (B.A., 1982). He has had a long association with Chicago's Steppenwolf Theatre, both as an actor and as a playwright. While continuing to make his living from acting on both stage and screen, he has increasingly done so in order to support his playwriting, from which he has developed a reputation as a provocative social satirist.

Norris's first play was *The Actor Retires* (1992), which was produced by Chicago's now defunct Remains Theatre. The play is a comedy about an actor who decides to change careers and become a furniture maker. Norris wrote it as a vehicle for himself. Another early play was *The Vanishing Twin* (1996); produced at Chicago's Lookingglass Theatre, it was billed as a "rock 'n' roll gothic burlesque."

Norris's association with Steppenwolf, which commissioned and produced his next five plays, allowed him to develop more substantial work. In *The Infidel* (2000), the reasons for a once respected judge's incarceration are gradually revealed through flashbacks and court documents. We come to understand that the violent offense that landed him in jail was provoked by an obsessive love affair. The play contains hilarious satire concerning a human being's capacity to bring about his own ruin. In *Purple Heart* (2002), just a few months after being hospitalized for depression in the wake of her abusive husband's death in the Vietnam War, Carla, an alcoholic, is visited by a maimed veteran who is apparently a complete stranger. We eventually learn—against the backdrop of Carla's difficult family relationships with her teenage son and her judgmental mother-in-law—that this man raped Carla at the hospital when she was sedated. As in *The Infidel,* Norris here contrasts appearance with underlying—often desperate, sometimes vile—human motivation and action. His next play, *We All Went Down to Amsterdam* (2003), is set in a home for the aged where one resident, Mr. Wood, is consumed with regret over an incident in his past involving his family. When a stranger comes to visit him, the details of Mr. Wood's transgression become clear.

The play that brought Norris to national attention as a playwright was *The Pain and the Itch* (2005), a social satire set in flashbacks over a Thanksgiving holiday at the home of a middle-class family. The play takes aim at, among other targets, hypocritical liberals and political intolerance and—as is characteristic of Norris—raises uncomfortable subjects, in this case the possibility of child abuse. Over the course of the play, a household's unpleasant secrets are gradually revealed. Despite the controversy during the Chicago production surrounding putting child actresses into a role onstage that should, many believed, be beyond their level of understanding, the play won Chicago theater's Jefferson Award for the Best New Work of the 2004–2005 season. By this time—as a profile on Norris in *Chicago Magazine* put it at the time—Norris had developed "a reputation for bloodletting with a smile and a classical sense of dramatic structure" (Adler).

Next came *The Unmentionables* (2006), set in an unspecified West African country. It takes aim at all the players in the politics of the Third World: self-righteous missionaries, self-aggrandizing media stars, obliviously exploitative industrialists, corrupt local government officials, and those in any camp who make use of brutality as it suits their purposes. Norris has explained, "Either [the American characters] have decided to go there to make money but are telling themselves it's for the good of the community, or they've gone there to do good for the community but in fact are trying to gratify their own egos, so it's all about what people intend and what they say they intend" (Adler). Remarkably, again, Norris manages to make this both hilarious and disturbing. In an interview during the Washington, D.C., production, Norris commented, "It's very much like *The Pain and the Itch,* which also concerns a particular brand of American hypocrisy." When asked about audience reaction, he said to those who feel "indicted" and "resentful": "I'd like to point out that who I'm indicting is *myself* first and foremost, as an American who is prone to the same self-justifying delusions as they are."

The Pain and the Itch and *The Unmentionables* have gone on to productions in New York and elsewhere. Since *The Unmentionables,* Norris has been working on two, as yet undisclosed, new works.

BIBLIOGRAPHY

Adler, Tony. "Everybody Loves Bruce Norris." *Chicago Magazine* (July 2006). Available online. URL: http://www.chicagomag.com/Chicago-Magazine/July-2006/Everybody-Loves-Bruce-Norris. Accessed Sept. 15, 2008.

Norris, Bruce. Interview with Elissa Goetschius. 2007. Woolly Mammoth Theatre Company. Available online. URL: http://www.woolymammoth.net/performances/bruce_norris_interview. Accessed Sept. 20, 2008.

———. *The Pain and the Itch.* Evanston, Ill.: Northwestern University Press, 2008.

———. *"Purple Heart" and "The Infidel": Two Plays.* Evanston, Ill.: Northwestern University Press, 2004.

NOTTAGE, LYNN (1964–)

Born in Brooklyn, New York, and educated at Brown University (B.A. 1986) and Yale School of Drama (M.F.A. 1989), playwright Lynn Nottage writes about African Americans and Africans. She is particularly interested in—though her work is certainly not limited to—giving a voice to African-American women of her own and previous generations.

Temporarily putting aside full-time playwriting after graduate school, Nottage worked for Amnesty International as a national press officer. In 1993, she wrote the 10-minute dark comedy *Poof!,* which addresses the issue of domestic violence, and submitted it to the HUMANA FESTIVAL at the Actors Theatre of Louisville. The play won the festival's Heideman Award. Thus encouraged, Nottage returned to writing for the theater. Nottage's other *very* short plays include *Becoming American* (2002), part of the multiplaywright anthology of brief plays entitled *Snapshot,* which was also written for the Humana Festival, and *A Stone's Throw* (2004), one of five short plays commissioned by the Women's Project (dedicated to developing plays by women) as part of the "Antigone Project" (for which five female playwrights were asked to create 10–15-minute dramas inspired by Sophocles' heroine Antigone).

Nottage's first produced full-length play was commissioned by New York's Second Stage for a program geared to adolescent audiences. *Crumbs from the Table of Joy* (1995) is a coming-of-age play set in the 1950s. The two teenage daughters of a widowed African-American father move with him from the South to New York. The father's conflicts with his late wife's radical sister and his abrupt remarriage to a white German immigrant force the daughters to deal with sociopolitical and personal challenges.

Nottage's most critically acclaimed play, INTIMATE APPAREL (2003), is set in 1905 in lower Manhattan and imagines the life of an African-American seamstress specializing in intimate apparel. Esther Mills's great talent is most appreciated by a man she can never have, an orthodox Jewish fabric merchant whose religion forbids him from even the most casual touch of her hand. The love she eventually finds through letter writing with a Barbadian laborer proves to be illusion and leads to a disastrous marriage that ends in desertion after he gambles away her life savings. Finally, Esther returns to the boardinghouse of her spinsterhood and begins again. The play won the New York Drama Critics' Circle Award.

Imagined by Nottage as a companion piece to *Intimate Apparel,* the modern-day *Fabulation; or, The Re-Education of Undine* (2004) is a stinging social satire in which a woman, Undine (formerly Sharona Watkins), whose husband embezzles her money, must swallow her haughty pride—which is substantial—and readapt

to life in the Brooklyn projects where she grew up. Nottage has said of the play, "I tried to imagine Esther 100 years later, after she's enjoyed the benefits of the women's rights and civil rights movements and become a fully empowered African-American woman. . . . Esther's journey is about *becoming* empowered, whereas Undine feels completely empowered, so I imagined the opposite journey for her. She falls on hard times, goes through this downward spiral, goes back to her roots. In the end, they both achieve the same thing, which is finding self" (Gener 144). For *Fabulation,* Nottage won an OBIE AWARD for Playwriting.

Nottage certainly does not limit her characters to a single socioeconomic or philosophical group. *Mud, River, Stone* (1997) is about a middle-class African-American couple who set out on a romantic trip to Africa only to be taken hostage in Mozambique. This play that begins as a comedy turns serious as the couple is immersed in the complicated politics of Africa. In *Por'knockers* (2002), a group of mostly African-American activists blow up a government building and then, in their reluctance to claim responsibility, find themselves reexamining their lives and philosophy.

Nottage's wide range of interests and settings is evident in her costume play *Las Meninas* (2002). Set in 1695 and 1664, this historical play is about the queen of France and her servant, an African dwarf, and their illicit affair. When Nottage came across a passing reference to this surprising relationship, she decided to research the pair. This proved difficult because history texts had been sanitized; however, the closer in time she came to the actual events the more accessible information became. The daughter of the union of the white queen and her dwarfed black servant was born in the court of Louis XIV and then immediately removed; she was eventually put in a Benedictine convent, where she subsequently became a nun. Still, little is known of the personal relationship between her parents, and it is that which Nottage imagines in her play. Structurally, the play develops from the point of view of the couple's child as she pieces together their story. Nottage sees Nabo and Queen Marie-Thérèse as a pair of displaced persons: a slave, stolen away from Africa, and a queen given in marriage to settle a dispute between two countries.

Nottage's longstanding interest in human rights and the long-term effects of colonialism is evident in some of her recent work. *Give Again?* (2006) was part of *How Long Is Never? A Response to Darfur,* an evening of short plays; Nottage's one-act contribution comments with humor on Western attitudes toward charity. Nottage's latest play was commissioned by and developed at Chicago's Goodman Theatre. *RUINED* (2008), set in a brothel in the civil war–torn Democratic Republic of the Congo, won the PULITZER PRIZE for drama. Its central character is Mama Nadi, the businesswoman who profits from the bodies of the prostitutes she protects.

Nottage's other works include the screenplay *Side Streets* (1999), the children's musical *A Walk Through Time* (2001), and the vaudeville-style review *Point of Revue* (2006), which features songs and scenes that explore many and varied facets of present-day African-American experience.

BIBLIOGRAPHY

Gener, Randy. "Conjurer of Words." *American Theatre* (Oct. 2005): 22–24, 144–145.

Nottage, Lynn. *"Crumbs from the Table of Joy" and Other Plays.* New York: Theatre Communications Group, 2004.

———. *Intimate Apparel/Fabulation.* New York: Theatre Communications Group, 2004.

———. *"Las Meninas"* [full play text]. *American Theatre* (July 2001): 50+.

O

OBIE (OFF-BROADWAY) AWARDS The Obie Awards were created by New York's *Village Voice* newspaper soon after that publication was established in 1955. The Obies recognize excellence in OFF-BROADWAY theater. Off-Broadway is not so much a location as a set of restrictions: To qualify, a theater must have under 300 seats and be outside the borders of the Times Square theater district. In 1964, the Obie Awards began to include OFF-OFF-BROADWAY plays. Off-Off-Broadway is defined by Actors' Equity as theaters with fewer than 100 seats.

The Obie Awards have less rigid categories than many other theater awards; they include a "Distinguished Performance" category, which honors as many actors, in leading or supporting roles, as have given distinguished performances that year, and a "Special Citation" category, which is very flexible, honoring theaters as well as individuals. In keeping with this desire to recognize excellence whenever (and only if) it appears, there is not always a Best New Play category in the Obies, and more than one play may win. When American plays have been honored, it has been in the categories of "Best New Play," "Best New American Play," "Distinguished Play," or "Playwriting." For a complete list of the American plays and playwrights that have received Obie Awards, see Appendix I.

OCTOROON, THE; OR, LIFE IN LOUISI-ANA DION BOUCICAULT (1859)

The play is based on a novel, *The Quadroon* by Mayne Reid; and like Harriet Beecher Stowe's novel, *Uncle Tom's Cabin,* published just seven years earlier, BOUCICAULT's play contains many racial stereotypes: the cruel Yankee overseer, the "happy" slaves, the kind paternal masters. However, like Stowe's novel, it also raised emotional awareness of the injustices of slavery, an awareness that was necessary for that institution's abolition. Boucicault neither condemns the South nor overtly endorses the abolition of slavery, but he focuses instead on human relationships. The play was generally well received by the public, perhaps *because of* its ambivalence on this controversial issue.

As the play begins, George Peyton has returned from Paris to his aunt's Louisiana plantation, having inherited the property from his late uncle, Judge Peyton. The unscrupulous overseer, McClosky, has largely diminished the family fortune for his own gain; his honest replacement, Scudder, an inventor and not a good businessman, diminishes it further through mismanagement. The light of everyone's life is the beautiful "octoroon" Zoe, the Judge's child by a "quadroon" slave. The Judge freed his daughter from slavery in childhood, and his childless wife has accepted Zoe as a member of the family all her life.

A letter from Liverpool could bring word of a solution to the family's financial crisis. Unless that solution comes, McClosky will own the plantation and, through a legal loophole, will own Zoe as well. McClosky lusts after Zoe and will stop at nothing to have her. He kills a young boy in order to steal the redemptive letter from Liverpool; however, he is caught in the commission of the crime—unbeknownst to anyone, including himself, until the last act—by Scudder's camera. (Boucicault's use as a plot device of this "modern" invention, which was first introduced to America only about 20 years earlier, was quite innovative for its time.)

Meanwhile, George Peyton has declared his love for Zoe. George knows she is illegitimate, but he does not know, until Zoe tells him, that she is an "octoroon." His ardor undiminished, George, the world traveler, suggests that they simply move to another country. It is Zoe who finds their union unacceptable, steeped as she is in the southern mentality of her time: "Of the blood that feeds my heart, one drop in eight is black; . . . that one drop poisons all the flood; . . . I'm an unclean thing—forbidden by laws—I'm an Octoroon!" Zoe entreats George to think of his aunt, who has been a mother to them both and who "would revolt from" their marriage. George's reply would certainly have appealed to the abolitionists in the audience: "Zoe, must we immolate our lives on her prejudice[?]" In a later scene, the evil of slavery is illustrated again when Zoe is auctioned for $25,000.

Once McClosky's crime is revealed by the photographic evidence, the letter is recovered and the plantation saved for the family; it is too late for Zoe, however, who has already committed suicide to avoid becoming the slave and mistress of McClosky.

ODD COUPLE, THE NEIL SIMON (1965) Set in a Manhattan apartment, *The Odd Couple* is a comedy about a pair of men, one neurotically tidy and the other a slob, who share the apartment and get on each other's nerves.

When Felix Unger separates from his wife, his friend Oscar Madison, a divorced sportswriter, invites him to share his apartment. Oscar is accustomed to living in his own mess—and loves it. Clothes and dirty dishes clutter the living room, ashtrays are never emptied, and empty bottles are never removed. When Felix arrives, he brings with him his need for and willingness to provide spotless rooms, home-cooked meals served on time, air freshener, and furniture polish. Oscar's minimal tolerance of Felix's wifelike (in

the conventional, stereotypical sense) habits wears particularly thin when they begin to interfere with his love life. When Felix ruins Oscar's amorous chances with either one of the Pigeon sisters from upstairs by retiring early instead of accepting their invitation to dinner, Oscar cannot forgive him. The next day he confronts Felix by emptying ashtrays on the recently vacuumed floor and spraying air freshener on Felix's plate of food, and as the argument accelerates, finally throwing a plate of linguine at the wall. Oscar throws Felix out, but Felix lands in the apartment of the Pigeon sisters, where he will stay for a few days, until he finds a place of his own. When he returns to collect his things, the two men make up, and Felix promises to return for the poker game next week. At the curtain, Oscar tells his poker buddies to be careful with their ashes because his apartment is "not a pigsty."

In 1991, SIMON said of the play, "[I]t's the most universal play I've written. They do it in Japan as often as they do it here now. It's done all over the world constantly because it is such a universal situation. Two people living together cannot get along all of the time, and it made it unique that it was two men. . . . It was the idea or concept that made it so popular" (Kolin and Kullman 64). In 1985, Simon wrote an adaptation of the play for a predominantly female cast.

BIBLIOGRAPHY
Kolin, Philip C., and Colby H. Kullman, eds. *Speaking on Stage: Interviews with Contemporary American Playwrights.* Tuscaloosa: University of Alabama Press, 1996.

ODETS, CLIFFORD (1906–1963) At the time of his death in the summer of 1963, obituaries uniformly characterized Clifford Odets as the militant young dramatist of the 1930s. In fact, throughout much of his creative life, this handy but superficial label was attached to the writer of AWAKE AND SING! (1935) and WAITING FOR LEFTY (1935). It was the sort of shorthand that the playwright himself understandably resented.

Although Odets's initial successes in the theater helped establish his reputation as an angry champion of the proletariat, there was little in his background to suggest either anger or proletarianism. Clifford Odets was the first child of a middle-class Jewish family in

Philadelphia. His father was a relatively prosperous printer. The family moved to New York, where Odets grew up in predominantly Jewish neighborhoods in the Bronx. Dropping out of high school in the 11th grade, he found small acting jobs on the radio until, at age 20, he broke into theater as a juvenile in a small stock company.

Odets was making little progress in his acting career when in 1930 he became involved with the GROUP THEATRE, a new and dynamic organization just beginning to emerge as a major influence on the New York scene. Throughout his life, even after the bitter animosities and recriminations surrounding the last days of the Group Theatre at the end of the thirties, Odets referred to the Group as the principal influence on his career. While still acting in minor roles with this company, Odets learned of a contest for one-act plays sponsored by the New Theatre League of New York. With encouragement from his mentor HAROLD CLURMAN, Odets retreated to his hotel room and wrote *Waiting for Lefty* in three days.

Waiting for Lefty premiered before an enthusiastic audience at a small theater in Lower Manhattan. The one-act, multiscene drama makes use of a number of theatrical devices to create the illusion of a raucous strike meeting, with actors sometimes shouting their lines from seats in the auditorium. A "strike committee" occupies the stage, and at times the audience is directly harangued. More important than the doctrinaire message is the emotional heat that Odets conveyed. Because it is an openly propagandistic play and because it requires no elaborate stage or scenery, within a few months it was being produced all over the country. The reception was predictably enthusiastic almost everywhere. Even when the play was condemned as more diatribe than drama, it managed to create enough of a stir to enhance the young playwright's reputation. Odets's timing was perfect; the turbulent mood of the depression was in itself a major contributing factor to his instant fame.

Thus, the Group Theatre and the Great Depression were the two formative factors in Odets's career as dramatist. It is hard to imagine his successes with these early plays coming at a time other than the 1930s. To left-oriented, often militant American writ-

ers like Odets, "the theater is a weapon" was a rallying cry; however, the author of *Waiting for Lefty* went on to become a well-paid film writer, to marry a glamorous Hollywood movie queen (Luise Rainer), to live comfortably in Beverly Hills, to enjoy Las Vegas night life, and to speak out freely about Communist infiltration of the arts when he testified in 1952 before the notorious House Committee on Un-American Activities. These are only a few of the contradictions and incongruities apparent in Odets's life.

Concurrently with *Waiting for Lefty* in early 1935, the Group opened Odets's first full-length play on Broadway, a thoroughly revised and renamed work, *Awake and Sing!* This play—today considered by many critics to be Odets's best—showed a less strident side of the playwright. The focus is on the necessity of the two youngest members of the Berger family to escape their stifling environment. Even the dramatist's reliance on some fairly obvious plot devices (an inheritance, a timely suicide) fails to damage this touching and vibrant picture of the struggles of a Bronx family.

Among Odets's less successful plays, several demonstrate his characteristic qualities, such as sympathy for the underdog or the oppressed. *Till the Day I Die* (1935), a short anti-Nazi piece, is the least credible of all. It is violent, as befits its subject matter, but it is also Odets's slightest drama. *Paradise Lost* (1935) presents characters who are unaware that their individual problems are merely manifestations of the general decay of society or their own outmoded values. *Rocket to the Moon* (1938) concerns a middle-class dentist in a midlife crisis. *Night Music* (1940), Odets's first play outside the Group Theatre tent, is a more engaging, sometimes lyrical play about homelessness. It is pleasant, almost whimsical in tone, a major departure from his earlier works.

Odets's big commercial successes came with GOLDEN BOY (1937) and The COUNTRY GIRL (1950). *Golden Boy* is the story of Joe Bonaparte, who puts aside the violin and takes up boxing gloves. Like the earlier *Awake and Sing!*, Odets's raw material in this work is a war within a family. *The Country Girl* concerns an alcoholic actor. This time, the war does not involve a family but is instead a battle over Frank Elgin. His director and his wife tug at Frank from two directions, but in truth both share a single goal: saving Frank from himself. These two plays demonstrate mature craftsmanship and a broad audience appeal; both were eventually turned into popular films.

Clifford Odets's last play, *The Flowering Peach* (1954), based on the biblical Noah story, shows a calmer mood, which was somewhat unexpected from the firebrand who wrote the 1935 works. However, Odets's reputation rests heavily on his rich, colloquial family drama, *Awake and Sing!*, and the angry, experimental *Waiting for Lefty*, his first two produced plays.

If Odets's sudden death from cancer at age 57 prevented him from reaching the full measure of fulfillment that any artist seeks, he did earn his niche in the history of American drama; in 1935, he had four plays running simultaneously in New York. At their weakest, Odets's plays lack subtlety. At their best, they are filled with sharp colloquial language and powerful conflicts. His direct influence on playwrights like ARTHUR MILLER, WILLIAM GIBSON, and PADDY CHAYEFSKY is evident not only in the phrasing and rhythms of the dialogue but also in the focus on middle-class family relationships. Always more an idealist than a doctrinaire leftist, Odets is best characterized not by the "Stormbirds of the Working Class" speech at the conclusion of *Waiting for Lefty* but by the line he directed to the younger generation in *Awake and Sing!*: "Go out and fight so life shouldn't be printed on dollar bills."

BIBLIOGRAPHY

Brenman-Gibson, Margaret. *Clifford Odets, American Playwright: The Years from 1906–1940.* New York: Atheneum, 1981.

Cantor, Harold. *Clifford Odets.* 2d ed. Lanham, Md.: Scarecrow Press, 2000.

Herr, Christopher J. *Clifford Odets and American Political Theatre.* New York: Praeger, 2003.

Mendelsohn, Michael. *Clifford Odets: Humane Dramatist.* DeLand, Fla.: Everett/Edwards, 1969.

Miller, Gabriel. *Clifford Odets.* New York: Continuum, 1989.

———, ed. *Critical Essays on Clifford Odets.* Boston: G. K. Hall, 1991.

Murray, Edward. *Clifford Odets: The Thirties and After.* New York: Frederick Ungar, 1968.

Odets, Clifford. *The Big Knife.* New York: Random House, 1949.

———. *Clash by Night.* New York: Random House, 1942.

———. *The Country Girl.* New York: Viking, 1951.

———. *The Flowering Peach.* New York: Dramatists Play Service, 1954.

———. *Night Music.* New York: Random House, 1940.

———. *Six Plays.* New York: Random House, 1939.

———. *The Time Is Ripe: The 1940 Journals of Clifford Odets.* Edited by William Gibson. New York: Grove Press, 1988.

Weales, Gerald. *Clifford Odets, Playwright.* New York: Pegasus, 1971.

Michael J. Mendelsohn
University of Tampa

OFF-BROADWAY   Off-Broadway developed as an alternative to Broadway, one that would free the creative possibilities of the stage from commercialism. It came into its own in the 1960s and 1970s, with important productions and serious attention from drama critics and the public alike. As early as 1961, the *New Yorker* magazine appointed Edith Oliver its Off-Broadway reviewer. Composed of a loose configuration of theaters scattered throughout Manhattan, the houses, many of them well appointed, seat between 100 and 299 viewers. They now offer a middle range of ticket prices and talent that may at other times be found on Broadway or in films. Among Off-Broadway's major contributions have been audience development, new financial paradigms, a second chance for failed plays, and the freedom for talent to develop.

Off-Broadway has its roots in the art theater movement. Two theaters served as important pioneers. The PROVINCETOWN PLAYERS, born in a shack on a wharf in Cape Cod, settled in Greenwich Village in 1916, where it remained until its demise in 1929. Devoted to American playwriting, it was amateur by design, as a remedy for what was perceived as stagnant, mannered playwriting and acting; but it could boast some of the most interesting minds of the decade—among others, its founders GEORGE CRAM COOK, a classicist, and his wife, SUSAN GLASPELL, feminist and novelist turned playwright; EUGENE O'NEILL, who later won the Nobel Prize in literature; poet EDNA ST. VINCENT MILLAY; designer ROBERT EDMOND JONES; and journalists John Reed and Edmund Wilson. The other pioneering group, the WASHINGTON SQUARE PLAYERS, established in 1915, grew out of a reading group at the Liberal Club in Greenwich Village. Determined to produce the best plays, European and American, it championed modern playwrights like Anton Chekhov, George Bernard Shaw, and Maurice Maeterlinck. Some of the members regrouped after World War I and named themselves the THEATRE GUILD. Under the direction of Lawrence Langner, a lawyer; Maurice Wertheim, a banker; Lee Simonson, a set designer; and Theresa Helburn, its executive director, the Guild dedicated itself to raising the artistic standards of the nation by fostering talent and producing serious European and America plays.

Off-Broadway officially began in 1950 with two exciting new ventures: The Circle in the Square Theatre, like the Provincetown, originated within a community of theater people living communally—in Woodstock, New York. Upon moving to Greenwich Village, they shared apartments in adjacent brownstones off Sheridan Square. Cofounders José Quintero and Theodore Mann believed in a new, intuitive approach to American drama. TENNESSEE WILLIAMS's SUMMER AND SMOKE had failed on Broadway in 1948; their 1952 revival became Off-Broadway's first hit. It demonstrated the value of the more intimate arena-type stage, and Quintero claimed that poverty had freed the theater from a reliance on solid sets and realistic props, and that the bare stage challenged the imagination of the audience. Their second success, a 1956 revival of Eugene O'Neill's The ICEMAN COMETH, which had received mixed reviews at its premiere in 1946, initiated an O'Neill revival and introduced actor Jason Robards Jr. The Circle in the Square was the first American theater to produce Jean Genet's The Balcony, an absurdist comedy about working-class men acting out their ambitions in a brothel and then assuming these roles—as Bishop, Executioner, and General—in real life. It was typical of the new experimental European dramas that would influence generations of American playwrights. In 1969, the success of JULES FEIFFER's LITTLE MURDERS, which had failed on Broadway a year earlier, proved that more than luck was involved. The Circle in the Square had a knack for attracting talent: Colleen Dewhurst, George C. Scott, James Earl Jones, Dustin Hoffman, Geraldine Page, and George Segal were all Circle actors. It was this sort of theatrical intelligence that made the Circle in the Square one of the most important companies in America.

Joseph Papp, who founded the New York Shakespeare Festival and the New York Public Theatre, was another great Off-Broadway innovator. In 1956, he initiated a truck tour of free Shakespeare plays through New York neighborhoods and thus changed the face of theater. His mission was twofold: to bring Shakespeare to the disenfranchised and those priced out of the big houses and to create a new American style of Shakespearean acting, which would combine classical acting and the Stanislavsky Method (see ACTORS STUDIO). Clowning, unusual casting choices, and a mixture of the contemporary with the historical would become its trademarks—soldiers in armor might be watching television in camp. Papp championed colorblind casting and ethnic perspectives, encouraging inner-city actors to find their distinctive voices. He also welcomed big-name actors, who had moved from the stage to film—once a one-way route—back to Off-Broadway. In 1962, he moved his free summer Shakespeare productions into the new Delacorte Theatre in Central Park. In 1967, he rented the Astor Place Library from New York City for $1 and opened five theater spaces. Successful shows, like Michael Bennett's musical A Chorus Line (originally an Off-Broadway workshop production based on anecdotes shared by dancers), which transferred to Broadway in 1975 and ran for almost 15 years, were used to fund experiments, new playwrights, and other fiscal gambles. Two Public Theatre productions, NO PLACE TO BE SOMEBODY by CHARLES GORDONE, an African-American playwright, and PAUL ZINDEL's The EFFECT OF GAMMA RAYS ON MAN-IN-THE-MOON MARIGOLDS, won PULITZER PRIZES in consecutive years, 1970 and 1971. Two years later, another Public Theatre play, Jason Miller's THAT CHAMPIONSHIP SEASON, won the TONY, Pulitzer, and New York Drama Critics' Circle Awards after it relocated to Broadway. An early version of Hair, a rock musical about the hippie generation and the Vietnam draft written by Galt MacDermot, Gerome Ragni, and James Rado and directed by Tom O'Horgan, was staged by the Public in 1967 before it moved to the Biltmore Theatre on Broadway, where it played for four years.

The Roundabout Theatre, which now has a Broadway house, is another Off-Broadway success story. Founded in 1965 by Gene Feist in the basement of a Chelsea supermarket, it garnered praise as a first-rate revival house. As it changed locations and its subscription base grew to become the second largest in the country, it added contemporary drama to its season. In 1991, it moved into the Criterion Center on Broadway and is currently housed in the new American Airlines Theater on 42nd Street. In the early 21st century, it had plays running at four different locations and a new American play program.

A major contribution of the Off-Broadway movement was the growth of audience-specific theater. YIDDISH DRAMA was an early-20th-century forerunner of this movement, a tradition continued by the Folksbeine (with headset translations) and English-language groups like the Jewish Repertory Theatre, Jewish Theatre of New York, and the American Jewish Theatre. During the 1960s, a new wave of audience-specific theaters was born. Although they began OFF-OFF-BROADWAY, they were envisioned as alternatives to commercial theater and, for the most part, quickly moved to larger houses, thanks in part to an increase in government and corporate funding. They were established not only to speak for a targeted community but also to develop the talent pool. They have been a catalyst in nontraditional casting in the commercial worlds of stage and screen.

The Latin community, separated from the theater mainstream by language, established three theaters that have become New York institutions (see HISPANIC DRAMA). Like the Public Theatre, the Puerto Rican Traveling Company, formed in 1967 by actor Miriam Colon and her husband, George P. Edgar, began by touring the city. It still tours but makes its permanent home in the theater district. Repertorio Español was founded by Gilberto Zaldivar and René Buch in 1968, and Intar Hispanic American Arts Center, whose projects include sophisticated funding collaborations between playwrights and composers, began in 1966 under the guidance of Max Ferra. These theaters are important not just for audience development and as a venue for new bilingual voices but also because they are links to Spanish-language theater around the world. Other ethnic Off-Broadway theater includes the Irish Arts Center, the Irish Repertory Theatre, and the Pan Asian Repertory Theatre, founded by Tisa Chang in 1973, which presents new works as well as new perspectives on classic works.

AFRICAN-AMERICAN DRAMA has existed since the 19th century, but it was long limited by segregation to African-American venues. In the early 20th century, African-American actors were typecast in plays written by whites when the roles were not played by whites in blackface, but the production of *The Blacks* by Jean Genet at St. Marks Playhouse in 1961 initiated a new movement. The play is a trial after the rape and murder of a white woman. All the actors were African Americans. Many wore bizarre white masks. The court was presided over by a queen, a judge, a missionary, and other officials. There were confrontations with the audience (who were usually white) about racist attitudes. It was visceral ritualistic drama, an emotional purging. Running for a record 1,408 performances and employing hundred of actors, *The Blacks* provided the impetus for the formation of African-American theater troupes, like the Negro Ensemble Company. Founded in 1967 by African-American actor Robert Hooks, African-American playwright/director DOUGLAS TURNER WARD, and white businessman Gerald S. Krone, it produced important plays, such as Joseph A. Walker's *The RIVER NIGER* (1973) and CHARLES FULLER's *A SOLDIER'S PLAY* (1981). The short-lived New Lafayette Players (1967–73) were based in Harlem. Woodie King Jr.'s New Federal Theatre, established in 1970, has experienced some rocky years and many relocations but is still producing.

Although the rise of Off-Broadway coincided with the women's movement, it is still surprising that there are more than two dozen women's theater groups in New York. One of the earliest was the Interart Theatre, founded by Margo Lewin in 1969 at the Women's Interart Center. The most visible is the Women's Project and Production, founded by Julia Miles in 1978 in a spare room of the American Playhouse. The WOW (Women's One World) Café, a women-only collective, was founded in 1980 by Peggy Shaw and Lois Weaver.

The Women's Shakespeare Company offers all-female casting, while Judith Shakespeare Company follows nontraditional casting. The Looking Glass Theatre revives neglected masterpieces written by women. Because of budget and size, some of these are contractually Off-Off-Broadway houses.

Off-Broadway has proven itself indispensable. By the early 1970s, it was creating the most exciting theater in New York, and the shows were enjoying commercial success. *The Threepenny Opera,* a musical written by Bertolt Brecht and Kurt Weill, opened at the Theatre de Lys in 1955 and ran for more than six years. *The Fantasticks,* the first Off-Broadway musical hit, which opened in 1960, ran for more than 40 years. Off-Broadway companies were the first to produce avant-garde plays, especially those by Genet and the absurdists (see THEATRE OF THE ABSURD), who inspired new generations of American playwrights, such as EDWARD ALBEE, ARTHUR KOPIT, MARIA IRENE FORNÉS, and TINA HOWE. There were also other homegrown Off-Broadway playwrights: WENDY WASSERSTEIN, TERRENCE MCNALLY, A. R. GURNEY, CRAIG LUCAS, DAVID HENRY HWANG, JOHN GUARE, and ADRIENNE KENNEDY. Actors Frank Langella, Faye Dunaway, Al Pacino, Christopher Reeve, Meryl Streep, Sigourney Weaver, Hal Holbrook, Kevin Kline, William Hurt, Holly Hunter, Joel Grey, and Glenn Close were among the many talents who first appeared Off-Broadway. The Drama Desk, the Outer Critics Circle, and Pulitzer Prize committees include Off-Broadway in their awards, and in 1955 the *Village Voice* created its own Off-Broadway awards, the OBIES.

As Broadway presents fewer and fewer plays (as opposed to costly and lucrative musicals) and relatively few *new* plays, Off-Broadway has increasingly become the place where serious drama can be seen in New York. Producers and critics pay serious attention to Playwrights Horizons, the Manhattan Theatre Club, the Atlantic Theatre Company (founded by playwright/director DAVID MAMET and actor William H. Macy in 1983), and Lincoln Center (one of whose stages is now eligible for TONY AWARDS as a Broadway house). The Signature Theatre Company often has dedicated a full season to a contemporary playwright. The Pearl Theatre Company has loyal audiences and

is affiliated with educational programs to train the next generation. Many of these theaters have stayed true to their mission, but the New York Public Theater, now under the direction of Oskar Eustis remains the leader in bridging the gap between Broadway and Off-Broadway, by creating some productions that move uptown while remaining committed to cutting-edge theater.

BIBLIOGRAPHY
Little, Stuart W. *Off-Broadway: The Prophetic Theater.* New York: Coward, McCann, & Geoghegan, 1972.
Price, Julia S. *The Off-Broadway Theater.* New York: Scarecrow Press, 1962.

Glenda Frank
New York, New York

OFF-OFF-BROADWAY
Off-Off-Broadway is the experimental edge of New York theater. If Broadway is about commercial runs, and OFF-BROADWAY today is about new voices and revivals, then Off-Off-Broadway is about theater as performance, an affective experience. Jerry Talmer, writing for the *Village Voice,* coined the phrase "Off-Off-Broadway" in 1960 to identify the new creative approach. Although centralized in the adjacent neighborhoods of the East Village and SoHo, the theaters may also be found in other outlying areas. The venues are professional performance spaces, converted storefronts, old school buildings, basements, or rooms adjoining bars or restaurants. Actors' Equity defines an Off-Off-Broadway theater contractually as any house with fewer than 100 seats. Budgets are low, and the quality of the work is uneven. Off-Off-Broadway is where the hopeful and the talented learn their craft. Audiences are mostly young and adventurous, and ticket prices are sometimes little more than the cost of a movie.

The movement was born in the late 1950s in the East Village, an area where artists had clustered because of the low rents, the colorful ethnic neighborhood, and the easy accessibility to the cultural spots of Manhattan. Although still evolving, Off-Broadway was becoming an institution where making theater required planning and financing. Almost spontaneously, small venues began welcoming impromptu performances, and from this a new audience emerged.

The challenge was putting it all together on a shoe-string; perhaps because of that, Off-Off-Broadway offered an intoxicating freedom to those who had been denied admission to their creative fields. Soon there were dedicated playwrights and performers at places like Caffé Cino, a coffeehouse that was founded in 1958 by Joe Cino, an ex-dancer with a taste for the flamboyant. He invited his customers to use the space to display their art. Performing artists were paid by passing the hat. For the next 10 years, the Cino would produce a new play every other week. Most of the playwrights have vanished, but LANFORD WILSON and SAM SHEPARD went on to Broadway. Ellen Stewart, a West Indian clothing designer, was another seminal figure. She founded what eventually became known as the La MaMa Experimental Theatre Club in a basement in 1961 because a friend could not get his play produced. Stewart used her own funds to keep the theater alive and allowed poor artists to camp out in her apartment. La MaMa had to keep relocating because of fire code violations, but it eventually found a permanent home containing several performance spaces in the East Village.

Churches were critical to the early success of the movement. Ministers saw drama as a way to unite or build a community. The Judson Memorial Church in Greenwich Village dedicated a room to poetry readings. In 1961, the participants formed the Judson Poets' Theatre, which became known for its musicals. Reverend Al Carmines, an assistant minister and composer, became well known for his Off-Off-Broadway chamber musicals, a genre he created. Recognizing that theater could be an integral part of the everyday life of the East Village community, Ralph Cook formed Theatre Genesis in St. Mark's in the Bowery. The American Place Theatre, devoted to new plays about rarely broached social problems, began in St. Clement's Church in the Clinton area of Manhattan. It, in turn, offered a room to a small venture, the Women's Project and Production Company under the direction of Julia Miles, which has grown into an Off-Broadway company (now simply called the Women's Project) dedicated to developing the careers of women in theater. Robert Kalfin's now defunct Chelsea Theatre Center (CTC) found homes in several churches before moving to the Brooklyn Academy of Music (BAM). The CTC was dedicated to new American voices, like that of AMIRI BARAKA in *SLAVE SHIP* (1969), a wrenching drama about the Middle Passage, and to modern European dramas by authors like Federico García Lorca and Edward Bond, whose *Saved* takes a hard look at the British working class. To their credit, none of these churches censored any of the plays, although as the Off-Off-Broadway impetus grew, the subject matter became more daring.

Off-Off-Broadway theaters fall roughly into three categories: the coffeehouses and cafes where impromptu or no-budget presentations are staged, especially during a work's early phase; performance-based groups, which adopt the text as inspiration for multimedia or social consciousness-raising work; and companies that are shoestring miniatures of Off-Broadway, often committed to either revivals or new American plays. Representative of the latter is the Circle Repertory Theatre, located off Sheridan Square and founded by playwright Lanford Wilson, director Marshall W. Mason, and actors Rob Thirkield and Tanya Berezin in 1969 to serve the new American dramatist. The emphasis was on lyrical realism and ensemble acting. Wilson's HOT L BALTIMORE (1973), 5TH OF JULY (1978), and TALLEY'S FOLLY (1979), as well as ALBERT INNAURATO's GEMINI (1977) and JULES FEIFFER's *Knock, Knock* (1976), enjoyed highly successful runs (Circle Rep closed in 1996). The Circle Stage Company, devoted to updated productions of classical dramas, is now known as CSC (Classical Stage Company). It has flourished and seen its artistic directors, like Sharon Ott and David Esbjornson, move on to other successes. In this category, the distinction between Off- and Off-Off-Broadway is budgetary. Manhattan Theatre Club (founded 1970), Playwrights Horizons, WPA, and Hudson Guild Theatre, similar companies dedicated to new American and contemporary drama, are considered Off-Broadway companies. However, the Mint Theatre Company, as an example, has produced admirable revivals of underappreciated American plays, works on smaller budgets, and has retained the Off-Off-Broadway label.

The irreverent spirit of Off-Off-Broadway—the consciousness that continues to define the category—

originated with the LIVING THEATRE and was expanded upon by companies like the Performance Group and the Open Theater. These troupes insisted on new freedoms with the text: the right to interpose or omit scenes, to rewrite dialogue and reshape characters. They—and their modern representatives—adapted novels, letters, and biographies in order to comment on a time period or a contemporary theme. Often the creators were inspired by obscure pieces. The text became secondary to the actors and directors, even to dancers and designers. Many of the presentations were multimedia, open collaborations of creative minds. Dance, theater games, improvisation, and innovative visual and sound effects were all welcome.

Although Judith Malina and Julian Beck created the Living Theatre in 1946, well before Off-Off-Broadway was a movement, it was more a forerunner of the 1960s Off-Off-Broadway movement than a component of the Off-Broadway movement. Malina and Beck wanted to investigate and extend the boundaries of theatrical expression. Their first productions were with nontraditional scripts, a Japanese Noh play and GERTRUDE STEIN's *Dr. Faustus Lights the Lights*. In 1959, they staged JACK GELBER's *The CONNECTION*, about heroin addicts waiting for their supplier. Blurring the border between reality and drama, cast members mingled with the spectators before and after the performance, some demanding handouts or staging confrontations. After touring Europe from 1963–68, they returned with a new style. *FrankenStein*, based loosely on Mary Shelley's novel, was an allegory about primal forces set loose in a repressed world. The actors hung on a grid, forming the outline of the creature with their bodies, and acted out aspects of his appetites and experiences. After performances of *Paradise Now* (1968), in which the cast and spectators mingled in the acting space, audiences were encouraged to continue the sensory as well as political revolution—an overthrow of repressive social and political systems—in the streets.

Richard Schechner, a professor at New York University and editor of *The Drama Review* (formerly, the *Tulane Drama Review*), maintains that in his "environmental" theater, there is no artificial demarcation between audience space and stage; instead, all the space is for both the performers and the audience. The pieces were staged in "found" (nontraditional) venues, often with the audience participating. The first production of his Performance Group was *Dionysus in 69* (1968), an adaptation of *The Bacchae,* with some text from *Antigone* and *Hippolytus* mixed in. It was performed as a series of rituals, including a reenactment of birth in which the actors were nude. In 1970, *Commune* incorporated the violence of Vietnam and Charles Manson into a textual mix of elements from the Bible, 16th-century English drama, and 19th-century American literature. Schechner's production of Sam Shepard's *The TOOTH OF CRIME* (1973) illustrates the conflicting visions of the Off-Off-Broadway community. Schechner felt free, as a theater innovator, to modify the script about an aging rock star who has to confront a younger challenger for his territory, but Shepard was distressed to find his work altered and reinterpreted without his consent.

Joseph Chaikin, an alumnus of the Living Theatre and founder of the Open Theater, experimented with theater games and the collaborative creation of a performance piece. The early work of Mabou Mines, a 1969 collective directed by LEE BREUER, relied primarily on visual images and movement, although they have since produced work inspired by literature. The Ontological-Hysteric Theatre, founded in 1968 by RICHARD FOREMAN, has adapted theoretical scientific texts as well as American classics for precisely organized visuals and movements. The emphasis is on process, invention, and audience reactions, not on plot, character, or logic. The Ridiculous Theatrical Company, founded in 1967 by CHARLES LUDLAM, was technically an Off-Broadway house, but its campy versions of science fiction and classical literature were designed to alter perceptions of reality and gender—as well as to entertain.

The early years of Off-Off-Broadway introduced an explicitness about sexuality, politics, ethnicity, feminism, and alternative lifestyles. Off-Off-Broadway also nurtured many fine performers: Al Pacino, Judd Hirsch, Nick Nolte, Bernadette Peters, Robert De Niro, and Raul Julia. Playwrights obsessed with national themes emerged: Sam Shepard, whose plays reworked American myths, and DAVID RABE, who took a hard look at the generation that had returned from Vietnam.

Today, Off-Off-Broadway is thriving, thanks in part to the many academic drama departments and acting schools that have created a new generation of practitioners. It is best represented by the Fringe Theatre Festival, a 12-day celebration in late August offering more than 200 activities in 20 downtown spaces all within 15 blocks. Tens of thousands of people attend, attracted by low ticket prices; almost round-the-clock shows, representing 17 states and 12 countries; and side attractions, like Fringe Jr. for children, parking-lot Shakespeare, a life-size chess game, workshops, readings, and art exhibits. In the true spirit of Off-Off-Broadway, proposals are judged for their vibrancy, innovation, and diversity. The goal of the festival is to unite the next generation of theater artists and to increase public awareness and support.

BIBLIOGRAPHY

Bottoms, Stephen. *Playing Underground: A Critical History of the 1960s Off-Off Broadway Movement.* Ann Arbor: University of Michigan Press, 2004.

Crespy, David A. *Off-Off Broadway Explosion: How Provocative Playwrights of the 1960s Ignited a New American Theatre.* New York: Back Stage Books, 2003.

Little, Stuart W. *Off-Broadway: The Prophetic Theater.* New York: Coward, McCann, & Geoghegan, 1972.

Rodriguez, Eve, ed. *New York on Stage.* New York: Theatre Development Fund, 1991.

Stone, Wendell C. *Caffe Cino: The Birthplace of Off-Off Broadway.* Carbondale: Southern Illinois University Press, 2005.

Glenda Frank
New York, New York

OF MICE AND MEN John Steinbeck (1937)

A close adaptation of Steinbeck's novel with the same title, *Of Mice and Men* is set in California in the depression era and is the poignant story of loneliness and companionship among migrant workers. Collaborating on the stage adaptation with Steinbeck was the play's director George S. Kaufman, who encouraged Steinbeck to expand the role of Curley's wife as a motivating force. The play won the New York Drama Critics' Circle Award.

Friends since childhood, George Milton and Lennie Small are itinerant farm laborers who travel together. Lennie is huge and exceptionally strong but has the mental capacity of a very young child. As the play begins, the two men are running away from a town in which Lennie has scared a woman by touching her dress; her protests caused him to tighten his hold on the material in panic, and the woman "tells the law she's been raped." Having eluded the authorities, George and Lennie camp for the night under the stars. George becomes exasperated when he discovers that Lennie is keeping a dead mouse in his pocket; Lennie has unintentionally broken the neck of the mouse as he stroked its soft fur, foreshadowing the climax of the play. George complains that he would be better off on his own, without Lennie to cause trouble; this is a refrain that Lennie has heard often, but in truth George is as dependent upon Lennie for human companionship as Lennie is upon George.

When they reach their destination, the bunkhouse for itinerant workers at a large farm, George instructs Lennie to keep his mouth shut and stay out of trouble. George and Lennie hope to keep this job and make enough money to buy a small farm of their own. This is the dream that sustains them, but into George's hope of steering clear of trouble this time come Curley, the boss's son—a small man with a chip on his shoulder—and Curley's flirtatious, sexy, and dissatisfied wife. When Curley picks a fight with Lennie, Lennie crushes Curley's hand. Much later, when Curley's wife comes across Lennie in the barn, where he is hiding from George with a puppy he has accidentally killed, she invites him to stroke her soft hair; when he becomes too rough, she protests and tries to pull away. Lennie panics, and in his attempt to quiet her, he accidentally breaks her neck. With her death comes the death of their dream. George knows that only imprisonment or death awaits Lennie; in order to save him from fear and pain, George tells Lennie the story of their farm that he has told so many times before: "We'll have a cow. And we'll have maybe a pig and chickens . . . and a little piece of alfalfa . . . for the rabbits," which Lennie will be allowed to tend. When Lennie is lost in the dream, his face turned toward the horizon, George shoots him in the back of the head.

Steinbeck elaborates on his theme about the need for human companionship and the high cost of loneliness in the characters Candy and Crooks. Both Candy and Crooks are crippled, and both are isolated, the first because of his age, the other because of his race. Both hope to attach themselves to George and Lennie's dream. In the bunkhouse, just after Candy's old dog has been put out of its misery (an act that foreshadows Lennie's death), George describes to Lennie the piece of land they hope to purchase. Candy overhears him and asks to be a part of the plan. He tells George: "You seen what they done to my dog. They says he wasn't no good to himself nor nobody else. But when I'm that way nobody'll shoot me. I wish somebody would. . . . They won't do nothing like that. I won't have no place to go. . . ." Candy has saved a few hundred dollars, and together with what Lennie and George will make in a month, the three of them can realize their dream much sooner than George had hoped. Old Candy is rejuvenated by the plan. Later, when Lennie wanders into Crooks's room in the barn, Crooks, resentful at first since he, an African American, is not welcome in the bunkhouse, eventually speaks to the simple-minded Lennie of his own loneliness: "You got George. You know he's comin' back. . . . A guy needs somebody . . . to be near him (*his tone whines*). A guy goes nuts if he ain't got nobody. Don't make no difference who it is as long as he's with you." Indeed, Steinbeck asserts, this is our most compelling need as humans, and despite George's complaints about the trouble Lennie causes, the two men find in each other the fulfillment of that need. Steinbeck's characterizations serve his theme so believably that in the final heart-wrenching moment of the play, the audience can fully appreciate the simultaneous love and loss that George is feeling.

John Steinbeck, who won the Nobel Prize in literature in 1962, wrote only three plays, adapting each from one of his own novels. In addition to *Of Mice and Men*, which is certainly the most famous and most often revived, are *The Moon Is Down* (1942) and *Burning Bright* (1950). Others, too, have adapted Steinbeck's novels for the stage, including a celebrated 1990 production of *The Grapes of Wrath*, adapted by Frank Galati.

OH DAD, POOR DAD, MAMMA'S HUNG YOU IN THE CLOSET AND I'M FEELIN' SO SAD Arthur Kopit (1962)

An absurdist (see THEATRE OF THE ABSURD) dark comedy, *Oh Dad, Poor Dad* portrays an overprotective, controlling, and possessive mother's effect on her emotionally damaged son. The play was first produced in Cambridge, Massachusetts, in 1960; the following year, it was produced in London, and it became an OFF-BROADWAY success in 1962.

Madame Rosepettle travels with her two "Venus'-flytraps," her piranha (for which she tries to procure meals of Siamese kittens), the stuffed corpse of her late husband, and, not least—that bewildered case of arrested development—her son, Jonathan. This sheltered, stammering, pathetic 17-year-old (dressed like a 10-year-old) passes much of his time alone with his collections of stamps and coins.

Jonathan, who has been made strange by his mother's twisted philosophy, meets a young woman of 19 who baby-sits for the children of a rich couple. The self-absorbed parents never appear but send Rosalie money and instructions to "keep the children's names straight." Jonathan has been watching Rosalie and her charges through his homemade telescope. Unbeknownst to Jonathan, his mother has invited Rosalie to their hotel suite to visit him while she is out, hoping he will see "what [she] is really like." We soon learn why Madame Rosepettle keeps her son locked indoors: he is, she tells Rosalie, *"susceptible"* to "sunstroke," to "sluts," indeed, to life. Madame contends that just when one is seduced by nature's beauty into sitting under a tree, a bird "lets go his droppings" on one's head.

Later, Madame Rosepettle brings back to her suite the old and rich Commodore Roseabove. She rejects his offer of love and wealth, reveals to him that her dead husband is in the bedroom, and tells him her story in an extraordinary and absurd monologue: Fearful of the motives of men, she married Albert, "ugly and fat." She had sex with him once, conceived their son, who was born after 12 or 13 months "already teething." Albert became a rich man and hired an unsightly secretary, Rosalinda (who was run through a "mangler" at her mother's laundromat as a child).

Albert developed a passion for Rosalinda, stopped sleeping, and died. Madame Rosepettle, in an act of consummate possessiveness, had him stuffed by a taxidermist ("even in death . . . *he was mine!*"). She explains that she keeps her son in isolation in an effort to "save" him from "a world waiting to devour those who trust it; those who love. A world vicious under the hypocrisy of kindness, ruthless under the falseness of a smile."

Jonathan, having witnessed this confession from behind the "Venus'-flytraps," takes the axe from the compartment marked "In Case of Emergency, Break," and kills his mother's carnivorous plants and carnivorous fish. Rosalie arrives, dressed as a child, and begins to seduce him on his mother's bed in the company of his father's corpse. The panic-stricken Jonathan smothers Rosalie. When Mother returns from her nighttime foray to the beach where she has gleefully "annoyed twenty-three" sets of lovers, the desperate Jonathan tries to flag down a passing airplane.

Written while KOPIT was still an undergraduate at Harvard, the play lacks the powerful social commentary of his later INDIANS. Martin Esslin writes in his book *The Theatre of the Absurd*, "[T]he author merely underlines the painful Freudian aspects of his fantasy. In seeming to say, 'Don't take this seriously, I am only piling on the horror for the sake of fun!' Kopit spoils his opportunity to transmute his material into a grotesque poetic image" (271). Though Esslin may be correct that Kopit's play lacks metaphor, its great popularity was a testament to its hilarious parodying of bad child-rearing.

BIBLIOGRAPHY

Esslin, Martin. *The Theatre of the Absurd*. Rev. ed. Garden City, N.Y.: Doubleday, 1969.

OLD MAID, THE ZOË AKINS (1935) This dramatization of Edith Wharton's 1924 novella is most famous for having motivated New York theater critics to start giving their own award when, over the objections of many of them, AKINS's adaptation won the PULITZER PRIZE. These dissenting critics, who preferred the year's other finer contenders (LILLIAN HELLMAN's *The CHILDREN'S HOUR*, CLIFFORD ODETS's *AWAKE AND SING!*, and ROBERT SHERWOOD's *The PETRIFIED FOR-*

EST), resurrected the by then defunct Drama Critics' Circle; the New York Drama Critics' Circle Award has been given for best American play of the year since 1936 (see Appendix I).

Set in New York City among the upper class and covering 21 years (1833–1854), *The Old Maid* opens minutes before Delia Lovell is to be married to a wealthy man of high social standing. We discover that she is still in love with a former beau, Clem Spender, an artist with no prospect of ever earning any money, for whom she waited nearly two years hoping he would come to his senses and go "into his uncle's bank." She is calm in her practical decision, but her cousin Charlotte, also in love with Spender (unbeknownst to Delia), declares she would rather be an old maid than marry for practical reasons. Moments before the ceremony Charlotte brings greetings for the bride from Clem along with a token of his feelings, which she will wear for most of the rest of her life.

Six years later, we find that Charlotte has set up what would today be called a day care center for the children of poor working mothers; among these children is a girl named Clementine, who, we eventually find out, is Charlotte's illegitimate child by none other than Clem Spender, who found comfort in her arms after his true love's wedding. The child is known to have been left on a doorstep as an infant shortly after Charlotte recovered from an "illness" that took her out of town for an extended period; only Charlotte's doctor and Charlotte know the connection. Charlotte is now engaged to marry Delia's brother-in-law, but he disapproves of her keeping the charitable "nursery" after they are married. She confides all to Delia in the hope of both marrying her fiancé and maintaining contact with her child, but when Delia finds out the truth she secretly sabotages (out of both conventional morality and jealousy) the marriage and arranges to support both Charlotte and "Tina."

In the final two "episodes" of the play, we find that since the death of Delia's husband many years before, Charlotte and Tina have lived with Delia and her daughter. The girls have been raised as sisters with Delia playing the part of mother. Charlotte has become the gray and severe old maid aunt. Tina is now old enough to marry and spoiled by Delia enough to expect to get whatever she wants—even an upper-class husband, but she is naïvely unaware that no "respectable" family will accept a "foundling" as a daughter-in-law. Fearing that Tina will, at the hands of her young admirer, come to the same fate as she did, Charlotte wants to take her away where no one knows her history. Delia is intent on legally adopting Tina and soon convinces Charlotte to agree; this will give Tina a socially acceptable name and a fortune. At the end of this conventional melodrama and on the eve of Tina's wedding, Charlotte sacrifices her own emotional needs for the good of her child as she once sacrificed her marital happiness. *The Old Maid* is a portrait of mid-19th-century morality and respectability.

OLEANNA David Mamet (1992)

MAMET's provocative play presents an event—a professor and his student meeting in his office—followed by the two participants' interpretations of that meeting. This discussion of the first meeting occurs because the female student has brought charges of sexual harassment against the male professor based on their first meeting. Since the audience has witnessed the first meeting, it is left to decide whether this is a case of misunderstanding on the part of the student or an act of sabotage. The professor is the more sympathetic character, which is why some feminists object to the play, seeing it as a distortion or, at best, a missed opportunity to examine sexual harassment; many argued that by depicting a man victimized by a woman claiming harassment in an ambiguous situation, Mamet minimized the real problem of sexual harassment against women.

Carol comes to John's office to discuss the grade he has given her on a paper. She is evidently failing his class. She tells him that she does what she is told: She takes notes, and she has bought his book, but she does not understand it. She says the class is *"difficult"* for her. He suggests she drop the course, but she replies, "I *have* to pass." When he asks what she wants him to do, she responds, "Teach me." John begins to feel sympathy for her and speaks to her of his own childhood, during which he was told he was stupid when he could not understand something. John goes

on at some length about his personal feelings about his job and pending promotion; he assumes she is interested because she too has feelings of inferiority and will want to hear about someone who overcame such feelings. But she is waiting to remind him that she wants to know about her "grade." At one point in their discussion, she shouts that she does not understand him, that she does not understand what he is talking about, and he puts his arm around her shoulder for a moment to calm her. At the end of the act, he is called away, by phone, to his surprise party, in the house he and his wife are about to buy, to celebrate the tenure that he almost has.

When act 2 begins, John and Carol are again in his office; it quickly becomes clear that she has reported him to the tenure committee for sexual harassment. Sure that this misunderstanding can be cleared up, John has asked her there to discuss her accusations. Her accusations are certainly distortions of what happened, but there is some truth to what Carol says about education: He has the power; therefore, when he mocks the institution, he mocks the students. When she gets up to leave—nothing yet accomplished from John's point of view—*"he restrains her from leaving,"* and she screams for help.

The third act is their third meeting. Carol has all of the power now. John will lose his job, his house, his reputation. She asks why he "hates" her, but she answers her own question: "It is the power that you hate. So deeply that, that any atmosphere of free discussion is impossible." She goes on to say that she and her "group" feel the powerlessness he is now feeling every day in the educational system. They are "in danger of being deprived" at "any moment" by teachers, by *him*, of their "dream of security"—"by, say, one low grade. . . . Now you *know*. . . . [w]hat it is to be subject to that power." This meeting ends when a phone call informs John that Carol has brought rape charges against him as a result of their second meeting. Stunned and outraged, he tells her to "get out," as he continues to speak on the telephone to his wife, whom he calls "Baby." When the departing Carol says, "and don't call your wife 'baby,'" John "grabs her and begins to beat her," stopping himself before he hits her with a chair.

Mamet's point is that this is what happens when one side has all the power: Those in power take advantage. Those without power lash out in their helplessness. Initially, John has all the power: He understands his own book; he understands what he means. Carol does not understand his point of view, so he will give her a failing grade. When she turns the tables on him and takes all the power, he in his powerlessness lashes out at her physically. Mamet's play raises the issue of power inequity—between teachers and students, between men and women, and by extension between other groups with unequal power—but he does not give us any easy answers.

BIBLIOGRAPHY

Sauer, David K. *David Mamet's "Oleanna."* London and New York: Continuum, 2009.

O'NEILL, EUGENE (GLADSTONE) (1888–1953)

That Eugene O'Neill became the playwright who transformed American drama from an entertainment to a serious literary form is directly traceable to his family background. He was the son of James O'Neill, one of the leading American actors of his day, who in 1883 gave up a promising career as a classical actor to star in Charles Fechter's adaptation of Alexandre Dumas's *The Count of Monte Cristo*. Twenty-nine years and more than 6,000 performances later, he had become forever enshrined in the hearts and minds of American theatergoers, many of whom saw the play every year as it toured throughout the country.

Eugene was the second surviving son (a third, Edmund, had died in infancy) of James and the former Ella Quinlan, a cultured, pious Catholic from Cleveland who had once thought of becoming a nun. James Jr. was born in 1878, and Eugene 10 years later at Barrett House, a New York hotel at 43rd Street and Broadway. His earliest years were spent on tour with his parents and in New London, Connecticut, where the family had a summer cottage. That O'Neill was literally nursed backstage had two antithetical effects on his career. He had an almost instinctual understanding of the theatrical—his third wife, Carlotta, once remarked that he saw life in terms of scenes. But his early exposure to the theater of his father also left him determined not to replicate the melodramatic unliter-

ary *Count of Monte Cristo* and with a desire to move American drama out of what he called "the show shop." The irony of course is that even his best plays—and many of his most innovative—were to contain melodramatic moments, because the word *melodrama* is often simply a description of what is theatrical, of what works onstage.

At the very early age of seven, O'Neill was sent to boarding school at the Academy of Mount St. Vincent in Riverdale, New York; five years later, he was transferred to De La Salle Academy in Manhattan and subsequently to Betts Academy in Stamford, Connecticut, where he completed high school. In 1906, he enrolled at Princeton University, but he dropped out before finishing his freshman year. During these formative years, he saw his parents infrequently, became very close to his high-living older brother, learned of his mother's addiction to morphine, and was, not surprisingly, a loner who found refuge in reading, especially such "shocking" writers of his day as Oscar Wilde, George Bernard Shaw, and Norwegian playwright Henrik Ibsen. The latter two were to become lifelong influences.

After leaving Princeton, O'Neill worked for a brief time in a New York mail-order business, but he spent most of his time in Greenwich Village and Hell's Kitchen and going to the theater. In the spring of 1909, he met Kathleen Jenkins, a well-bred young woman with whom he apparently had little in common; before he could end the relationship, however, she became pregnant, and they married in October 1909, two weeks before he left for Honduras on a mining expedition partially financed by his father. At the end of six months, he returned home, sick with malaria and without any gold. He then became assistant manager of a touring stage company in which his father was starring; thus, he was not present in May 1910, when Kathleen gave birth to Eugene Jr. In June, O'Neill embarked on the first of the several sea voyages that were to prove so important to his career, in this case, 65 days as a working passenger on a Norwegian windjammer between Boston and Buenos Aires. After drifting through a series of temporary jobs in Buenos Aires and hanging out and drinking with sailors and stevedores on the docks, he returned to New York on a British tramp steamer.

Back in New York, he and Kathleen were divorced, and he took up residence at Jimmy-the-Priest's, a bar and flophouse in Lower Manhattan that was to serve as a setting for two of his plays, *"ANNA CHRISTIE"* (1921) and *The ICEMAN COMETH* (1946). In July 1911, he sailed to Southampton, England, as an able seaman on the American liner *New York,* returning one month later on the *Philadelphia* and resuming his dissolute existence at Jimmy-the-Priest's. During this time, he attempted suicide but was revived by some of the bar's other lodgers. After 15 weeks of performing a small role in his father's touring vaudeville version of *Monte Cristo,* he returned to New London for the summer and got a job as a cub reporter on the local newspaper. In the fall of 1912, he became ill with what was eventually diagnosed as a mild case of tuberculosis, a development that precipitated a major conflict between Eugene and his father over whether he would be sent to a public or private sanitorium for treatment; this episode became the basis for *LONG DAY'S JOURNEY INTO NIGHT* (1956).

After spending two days at a public institution, Eugene transferred to the private (but not very expensive) Gaylord Farm Sanitorium in Wallingford, Connecticut, where he remained for what in many ways must be regarded as the most important six months of his life. While at Gaylord, he read voraciously, especially the plays of Swedish dramatist August Strindberg, German playwright Gerhart Hauptmann, and Irish dramatists W. B. Yeats, J. M. Synge, and Lady Gregory, and he decided to become a playwright. He discovered that he had amassed a great deal of material in his life to date, but, more importantly, as his biographer Barrett H. Clark has observed, "In the course of his wanderings he learned something about men, not their hypocritical manners and the masks they wear, but their minds and hearts, their ways of speaking and behaving. He was not an intruder in the underworld, but in some ways a part of it" (22).

The 26-year-old who returned to New London in 1913 to become a playwright had read widely in and seen productions of many of the foreign plays that had revolutionized modern drama. He began by writing 11 realistic melodramatic one-act plays, with titles like *Thirst, Abortion, Fog, Recklessness, Servitude, Warn-*

ings, and *A Wife for a Life;* five of them were published as *"Thirst" and Other Plays* in August 1914, underwritten by his father. Shortly thereafter, O'Neill was accepted into GEORGE PIERCE BAKER's playwriting course at Harvard, where in six months he wrote three more one-acts and his first longer play ("The Personal Equation") and learned the technique he was to follow thereafter in writing his plays—first prepare a scenario and then fill in the dialogue.

He lacked the funds to return to Baker's class for a second year, so he went to New York, where he tried unsuccessfully to interest small theaters in his plays and where he met many of the artists and writers who were to remain important in his life—among them, John Reed, Louise Bryant, GEORGE CRAM COOK, SUSAN GLASPELL, EDNA ST. VINCENT MILLAY, and DJUNA BARNES. In the spring of 1916, he joined several of his New York friends in Provincetown, Massachusetts, on Cape Cod, where the group, dissatisfied with the current commercial American theater, had decided in 1915 to write and put on their own plays, first on the veranda of a private home and then in an abandoned wharf building. On July 28, 1916, O'Neill's one-act *Bound East for Cardiff,* based on his experiences at sea, became his first performed play; *Thirst,* performed later that summer, was his second.

Calling themselves the PROVINCETOWN PLAYERS and pleased by their success, the group decided to continue putting on plays when they returned to New York that fall; they rented a building in Greenwich Village, where they performed only for a subscription audience and forbade critics from attending. During its first season, the Provincetown presented four O'Neill one-acts, *Bound East for Cardiff, Before Breakfast, Fog,* and *The Sniper,* and he developed enough of a following that in October 1917 the WASHINGTON SQUARE PLAYERS, who two years earlier had rejected his plays, produced *In the Zone,* another one-act. Buoyed by his success, he wrote four more one-acts, three of which—*The Long Voyage Home, Ile,* and *The Rope*—were produced by the Provincetown in their 1917–18 season. During this period, he met Agnes Boulton, a writer who became his wife in April 1918. *The Dreamy Kid,* a one-act melodrama and his first attempt to depict blacks; *Where the Cross Is Made,* another one-act sea play; *The Moon of the Caribbees,* a one-act destined to become O'Neill's favorite among his plays; and *Exorcism,* a suicide play that was later destroyed, were all produced by the Provincetown during their 1918–19 and 1919–20 seasons.

By the end of 1919, O'Neill had had professional productions of at least nine of his plays in New York. Because they were presented to a subscription audience and without critics to review them, he was able to develop his craft in a sympathetic, nonthreatening environment—and to do so by writing only one-act plays, which never would have been suitable for the commercial theater. As a consequence, when his first full-length play, BEYOND THE HORIZON, about two brothers and the woman they both love who ultimately causes both of them to pursue lives for which they are unsuited, opened on Broadway on February 3, 1920, O'Neill already had a reputation and an audience ready to welcome his uptown debut. Even the critics, some of whom had managed to sneak into the Provincetown, were enthusiastic, and the play won its author the first of his four PULITZER PRIZES.

James O'Neill died of cancer during the summer of 1920; although Eugene O'Neill was deeply affected by the loss, his productivity was unabated. Two full-length plays, the expressionistic *The* EMPEROR JONES, in which a black Pullman porter posing as the ruler of a West Indian island kingdom is destroyed by his inability to escape his personal and racial past, and *Diff'rent,* a searing portrait of an unhappy couple—with overtones of Freudian psychology—were both produced by the Provincetown in the fall of 1920. His Broadway success also continued with the November 1921 production of *"Anna Christie,"* the story of a prostitute who tries to reform her life through her love for a sailor, only to have him go off to sea after he agrees to marry her, which won him his second Pulitzer Prize. *The Straw,* based on his experiences at Gaylord Farm, also opened in November 1921, at the Greenwich Village Theatre, but it was not successful. His next play, the experimental *The* HAIRY APE, the story of a stoker on a transatlantic liner who tries to fit into a society that constantly rejects him, opened at the Provincetown in March 1922 and did well enough that, like *The Emperor Jones* two years earlier, it was

moved uptown to a Broadway theater. Days before its opening, Ella Quinlan O'Neill died while on a visit to Los Angeles, and James Jr. went on an alcoholic binge from which he essentially never recovered, dying in November 1923. Within a span of three years, O'Neill had lost his entire family, but, as he always did during adversity, he wrote on.

Although *Welded,* a semiautobiographical play about an unhappy marriage—with evident debts to Strindberg—and ALL GOD'S CHILLUN GOT WINGS, a controversial play about an interracial marriage, were both box-office failures in the spring of 1924, DESIRE UNDER THE ELMS, a realistic play about Oedipal struggle and incest in a New England family, was a hit in November 1924. In late 1924, the O'Neills, who had lived in New England during most of their marriage, decided to move to Bermuda for the warmer climate. There, in May 1925, their daughter Oona was born; a son, Shane, had been born in 1919. At this time, O'Neill began to write more completely experimental plays, becoming especially interested in developing theatrical devices that would show the hidden psychology of his characters. The first of these devices was masks, which he used extensively in *The Great God Brown* (1926) to portray his two principal contrasting characters, an artist and a businessman, each of whom envies the other, but the play largely baffled the reviewers who criticized it for its overuse of the device. In STRANGE INTERLUDE (1928), he introduced the similarly intentioned technique of asides to the audience to convey the inner thoughts of his characters. Critics were much kinder to this experiment: The published version became a best-seller, and the play won O'Neill his third Pulitzer Prize. *Marco Millions,* a more realistic play that indicted Western materialism through the figure of Marco Polo, opened three weeks before *Strange Interlude* and was only a modest success. Both of these plays were produced by the prestigious THEATRE GUILD, who were to present all of O'Neill's future plays until the end of his life.

While in rehearsal for these two productions, O'Neill's personal life underwent yet another crisis. His marriage to Agnes, which had long been strained, was seriously jeopardized when he became involved with Carlotta Monterey, an elegant, albeit somewhat self-invented, actress, who pledged her total devotion to him and to his career. After an agonizing several months, during which he proclaimed his love for Agnes in letters from New York, where he was spending time with Carlotta, in February 1928, O'Neill and Carlotta sailed for Europe, settling eventually in France, where they married in July 1929—after an acrimonious divorce battle with Agnes was settled. While life with Carlotta was not always tranquil, she did provide O'Neill with an environment in which he could work undisturbed by family and even friends—whose visits she kept to a minimum. His next play, *Dynamo* (1929), which attacked American society's emphasis on repressive organized religion, failed, but MOURNING BECOMES ELECTRA (1931), a version of the Greek myth of the House of Atreus set in post–Civil War New England, opened to enthusiastic reviews.

The O'Neills returned to the United States for the opening of *Mourning Becomes Electra* and settled in Sea Island, Georgia, where they built a house, and the playwright finished two new works. *Days without End* (1934), which took him eight drafts and seven years to complete and used masks and two actors to symbolize the conflicting sides of a single character, closed after only 57 performances, but AH, WILDERNESS! (1933), his only comedy, which he wrote in a month, depicted the growing pains of a New England teenager and was a big hit. The heat and humidity in Georgia caused the O'Neills to move again, first to Seattle and then to the San Francisco area, where they built another house. In 1936, O'Neill was awarded the Nobel Prize in literature, the second American to be so honored—and then, as now, the only American playwright to receive the award.

It was at their new home, Tao House, that O'Neill wrote what are generally considered his greatest plays. In them, he largely jettisoned his experimental techniques and composed the sort of realistic character-based dramas he had written at the beginning of his career, but he brought to these works an increased understanding of the complexities of human beings, a complexity that his experimental plays had helped him fathom. In *The Iceman Cometh* (written, 1939; produced, 1946), he reached back to his days at Jimmy-the-Priest's and other New York bars and flop-houses to portray a group of men down on their luck who cherish their illusions, their "pipe dreams." *Long Day's Journey into Night* (written, 1941; produced, 1956) is an undoubtedly embellished account of the day in late 1912 when O'Neill and his family learned that he had tuberculosis, with the resultant aggravation of long-simmering family tensions; it is generally acknowledged to be one of the two or three greatest American plays, and it won its author a fourth (albeit posthumous) Pulitzer Prize. A MOON FOR THE MISBEGOTTEN (written, 1943; produced, 1947) is the playwright's homage to the memory of his brother, and HUGHIE (written, 1941; produced, 1958) is essentially a one-act monologue delivered by a type O'Neill knew well, a small-time gambler who is a Broadway sport.

Beginning probably around 1935, O'Neill also began work on a multiplay cycle, "A Tale of Possessors, Self-Dispossessed." Originally conceived as four plays, the project eventually grew to 11 that purported to depict American society from 1775 to 1932 through the saga of a family, who would illustrate his belief that the United States had destroyed itself through its acquisitiveness. Weakened by a series of debilitating illnesses, the last of which was a tremor in his hand that prevented him from writing, he was able to complete only one of the plays, A TOUCH OF THE POET (written, 1942; produced, 1957); a second, *More Stately Mansions* (written, 1938; produced, 1967), survives only in draft form. A scenario of a third, *The Calms of Capricorn,* exists, but the O'Neills destroyed the rest of the material.

The last years of O'Neill's life were unhappy ones. Depressed by the onset of World War II and never entirely healthy after 1940 (when he was only 52 years old, the prime years for many writers), he refused to release his new plays for production until 1946, when *The Iceman Cometh* opened on Broadway, receiving mostly admiring reviews but achieving only a modest run. *A Moon for the Misbegotten* never reached Broadway, closing out of town. It was the last new O'Neill play produced during his lifetime. In 1945, he gave the manuscript of *Long Day's Journey* to his longtime publisher, Bennett Cerf of Random House, with instructions that it not be published or produced until 25 years after the playwright's death in order to protect the surviving members of his family.

Also marring the last decade of O'Neill's life were the 1943 marriage of his daughter Oona to Charlie Chaplin, who was 36 years her senior, and the suicide in 1950 of Eugene Jr., who had become a successful professor of classics at Yale. Tensions in his marriage increased, as the O'Neills moved again, back to San Francisco, to New York, and finally to the Boston area, where on November 27, 1953, he died at the Hotel Shelton. Among his last recorded words were: "Born in a hotel room—and God damn it—died in a hotel room."

At his death, O'Neill's reputation was at its lowest point in three decades, but, under his widow's careful stewardship, that began to change almost immediately. In 1956, Carlotta authorized a revival of *The Iceman Cometh* at a small OFF-BROADWAY theater, the Circle in the Square; this production established Jason Robards Jr. as the quintessential O'Neill actor and José Quintero as the preeminent O'Neill director and began the O'Neill revival in the United States. She then released *A Touch of the Poet, Hughie, More Stately Mansions,* and, ignoring her husband's wishes, *Long Day's Journey into Night* to Sweden's Royal Dramatic Theatre, which produced the world premieres of all of them. Later American productions of these plays, many of which involved Robards and/or Quintero, were instrumental in keeping O'Neill's works before the public. Today, a half-century after his death, his plays are staples of the American regional theater; they are known and performed throughout the world; and hardly a year goes by without a major New York revival of one of them.

Indisputably America's most important playwright, O'Neill nonetheless wrote several plays that were failures and are largely unproduced—and unproduceable—today. But he also wrote perhaps our greatest play and a number of others now regarded as classics of our theater. Furthermore, O'Neill never repeated himself; he was always striving to take American dramatic literature into new territory. With such ambitious aims, he was bound to fail more than those with less lofty goals, but he succeeded enough times to leave an indelible mark.

BIBLIOGRAPHY

Alexander, Doris. *Eugene O'Neill's Creative Struggle: The Decisive Decade, 1924–1933.* University Park: Pennsylvania State University Press, 1992.

———. *Eugene O'Neill's Last Plays: Separating Art from Autobiography.* Athens: University of Georgia Press, 2005.

———. *The Tempering of Eugene O'Neill.* New York: Harcourt, Brace and World, 1962.

Atkinson, Jennifer McCabe. *Eugene O'Neill: A Descriptive Bibliography.* Pittsburgh: University of Pittsburgh Press, 1974.

Barlow, Judith E. *Final Acts: The Creation of Three Late O'Neill Plays.* Athens: University of Georgia Press, 1985.

Bigsby, C. W. E. "Eugene O'Neill." *A Critical Introduction to Twentieth-Century American Drama: Volume One—1900–1940.* Cambridge, England: Cambridge University Press, 1982. 36–119.

Black, Stephen A. *Eugene O'Neill: Beyond Mourning and Tragedy.* New Haven, Conn.: Yale University Press, 1999.

Bogard, Travis. *Contour in Time: The Plays of Eugene O'Neill.* Rev. ed. New York: Oxford University Press, 1988.

———, and Jackson R. Bryer, eds. *Selected Letters of Eugene O'Neill.* New Haven, Conn.: Yale University Press, 1988.

Boulton, Agnes. *Part of a Long Story.* Garden City, N.Y.: Doubleday, 1958.

Bowen, Croswell, with the assistance of Shane O'Neill. *The Curse of the Misbegotten: A Tale of the House of O'Neill.* New York: McGraw-Hill, 1959.

Bryer, Jackson R., ed. *"The Theatre We Worked For": The Letters of Eugene O'Neill to Kenneth Macgowan.* New Haven, Conn.: Yale University Press, 1982.

Cargill, Oscar, N. Bryllion Fagan, and William J. Fisher, eds. *O'Neill and His Plays: Four Decades of Criticism.* New York: New York University Press, 1961.

Chothia, Jean. *Forging a Language: A Study of the Plays of Eugene O'Neill.* Cambridge, England: Cambridge University Press, 1979.

Clark, Barrett H. *Eugene O'Neill: The Man and His Plays.* New York: Dover, 1947.

Commins, Dorothy, ed. *"Love and Admiration and Respect": The O'Neill-Commins Correspondence.* Durham, N.C.: Duke University Press, 1986.

Diggins, John Patrick. *Eugene O'Neill's America: Desire Under Democracy.* Chicago: University of Chicago Press, 2007.

Estrin, Mark W., ed. *Conversations with Eugene O'Neill.* Jackson: University Press of Mississippi, 1990.

Falk, Doris V. *Eugene O'Neill and the Tragic Tension.* New Brunswick, N.J.: Rutgers University Press, 1958.

Floyd, Virginia, ed. *Eugene O'Neill at Work: Newly Released Ideas for Plays.* New York: Frederick Ungar, 1981.

———, ed. *Eugene O'Neill: A World View.* New York: Frederick Ungar, 1979.

Gallup, Donald C. *Eugene O'Neill and His Eleven-Play Cycle: A Tale of Possessors Self-Dispossessed.* New Haven, Conn.: Yale University Press, 1998.

Gassner, John, ed. *O'Neill: A Collection of Critical Essays.* Englewood Cliffs, N.J.: Prentice-Hall, 1964.

Gelb, Arthur, and Barbara Gelb. *O'Neill.* Rev. ed. New York: Harper, 1973.

———. *O'Neill: Life with Monte Cristo.* New York: Applause Theatre Books, 2000.

Houchin, John H., ed. *The Critical Response to Eugene O'Neill.* Westport, Conn.: Greenwood Press, 1993.

King, William Davies, ed. *"A Wind Is Rising": The Correspondence of Agnes Boulton and Eugene O'Neill.* Rutherford, N.J.: Fairleigh Dickinson University Press, 2000.

Manheim, Michael. *Eugene O'Neill's New Language of Kinship.* Syracuse, N.Y.: Syracuse University Press, 1982.

———, ed. *The Cambridge Companion to Eugene O'Neill.* Cambridge, England: Cambridge University Press, 1998.

Martine, James J., ed. *Critical Essays on Eugene O'Neill.* Boston: G. K. Hall, 1984.

Miller, Jordan Y. *Eugene O'Neill and the American Critic: A Summary and Bibliographical Checklist.* 2d ed. Hamden, Conn.: Archon, 1973.

———, ed. *Playwright's Progress: O'Neill and the Critics.* Chicago: Scott, Foresman, 1965.

O'Neill, Eugene. *Complete Plays.* 3 vols. Edited by Travis Bogard. New York: Library of America, 1988.

———. *The Unfinished Plays.* Edited by Virginia Floyd. New York: Frederick Ungar, 1988.

———. *The Unknown O'Neill: Unpublished or Unfamiliar Writings of Eugene O'Neill.* Edited by Travis Bogard. New Haven, Conn.: Yale University Press, 1988.

Raleigh, John Henry. *The Plays of Eugene O'Neill.* Carbondale: Southern Illinois University Press, 1965.

Ranald, Margaret Loftus. *The Eugene O'Neill Companion.* Westport, Conn.: Greenwood Press, 1984.

Roberts, Nancy L., and Arthur W. Roberts, ed. *"As Ever, Gene": The Letters of Eugene O'Neill to George Jean Nathan.* Rutherford, N.J.: Fairleigh Dickinson University Press, 1987.

Sheaffer, Louis. *O'Neill: Son and Artist.* Boston: Little, Brown, 1973.

———. *O'Neill: Son and Playwright.* Boston: Little, Brown, 1968.

Smith, Madeline C., and Richard Eaton. *Eugene O'Neill: An Annotated International Bibliography, 1973–1999.* Jefferson, N.C.: McFarland, 2001.

Tornqvist, Egil. *Eugene O'Neill: A Playwright's Theatre.* Jefferson, N.C.: McFarland, 2004.

Wainscott, Ronald H. *Staging O'Neill: The Experimental Years, 1920–1934.* New Haven, Conn.: Yale University Press, 1988.

ON THE VERGE; OR, THE GEOGRAPHY OF YEARNING Eric Overmyer (1985)

Overmyer's satiric comedy premiered at Baltimore's Center Stage and has since been performed frequently throughout the English-speaking world. Providing three strong roles for women, as well as a tour-de-force role for a single actor playing the other eight wildly eccentric characters (including a yeti, or "abominable snowman," a female fortuneteller, and Mr. Coffee), the play remains popular with directors and actors for the freedom of interpretation allowed within its imaginative conceit. The freewheeling play details in 22 short scenes the adventures of three American Victorian-era lady adventurers as they time-travel from 1888 to the present. At the end of each scene, one of the women addresses the audience directly in a "journal entry," revealing her inner thoughts. The title comes from André Breton, who wrote: "Perhaps the imagination is on the verge of recovering its rights."

The play begins as the experienced travelers—Mary, Fanny, and Alex(andra)—prepare to trek off into "Terra Incognita." As they try to impress each other with tales of their previous exploits, each woman reveals herself: Alex is unconventional, with a penchant for men's trousers and malapropisms; Fanny is stodgy, constantly deferring to her husband, Grover; and Mary is a practical scientist, with an unbridled ambition for fame.

Throughout their adventures, the women discover artifacts inappropriate to their time in history (including an "I Like Ike" button, rusty eggbeaters, and cream cheese). The ladies are disconcerted when words they do not recognize issue from their mouths. (In the play's most famous line, Fanny says, "I have seen the future. And it is slang.") They encounter a man dressed in a German uniform, who is revealed to be a cannibal who has inexplicably appropriated his latest meal's habits and accent. Fanny has a dream in which Grover warns her: "Don't speculate on the future." Their travels take them from a frightening jungle to a frozen ice wall where they have a snowball fight with an abominable snowman. As the first act ends, they are accosted by a motorcycle-riding, rap-spouting "Gorge Troll" and find a 1972 newspaper clipping about Richard Nixon. Mary correctly intuits that they are traversing time as well as space and are therefore absorbing knowledge of the future as they progress.

In the second act, the ladies become increasingly accustomed to the future and its vulgarities, developing a particular fondness for Cool Whip and Jacuzzis. Fanny learns that Grover declared her dead after she had been absent for seven years and then committed suicide himself after the 1929 stock market crash; this knowledge frees her to investigate her options as a newly emancipated woman. The women eventually arrive in 1955, where Fanny and Alex—finding it sufficiently dazzling—decide to stay, while Mary prefers to trek on into the unknown future.

Critics applauded the playwright's wild imagination, clever use of language, and caustic barbs aimed at contemporary culture. Mel Gussow of the *New York Times* wrote of the play: "A frolicsome jaunt through a continuum of space, time, history, geography, feminism and fashion, Mr. Overmyer's cavalcade is on the verge of becoming a thoroughly serendipitous journey" (February 10, 1985).

Douglas W. Gordy
Walnut Creek, California

ORPHANS' HOME CYCLE, THE HORTON FOOTE (1978–1989)

This cycle of nine plays is set in early 20th-century coastal Texas and is based on the story of FOOTE's parents' courtship and marriage. Each play stands alone yet also functions as part of a larger narrative. The first three to be produced, numbers five, six, and seven in the cycle, appeared at the HB Playwrights Foundation Theater in New York in the late 1970s (*Courtship* [1978], *1918* [1979], and *Valentine's Day* [1980]); others followed in the 1980s in New York and throughout the country. Grove Press brought out a three-volume edition of the entire cycle in 1987–89, collecting all the plays for the first time in a single set. (At this writing, five of the nine have also been made into films.) With the exception of EUGENE O'NEILL, whose 11-play historical cycle was never completed, no other American playwright has attempted a sus-

tained-plot cycle of this magnitude and complexity. (Although AUGUST WILSON created a 10-play cycle, one play for each decade of the 20th century, on the African-American experience, his is not a sustained-plot cycle.) Thus, *The Orphans' Home Cycle,* which most critics regard as Foote's masterpiece, occupies a unique position in American dramatic literature.

Foote's plays emerge largely from stories he heard during his childhood in the small coastal town of Wharton, Texas. *The Orphans' Home Cycle* (its title taken from "In Distrust of Merits," a Marianne Moore poem) is set in Harrison, Texas, the fictitious counterpart of Wharton, which functions like William Faulkner's Yoknapatawpha County, and serves as the locale for most of Foote's dramas. The plays cover a period of 26 years, beginning in 1902 with *Roots in the Parched Ground,* which tells of the orphaning of 12-year-old Horace Robedaux, the fictional counterpart of Foote's father, and ending with *The Death of Papa,* set in 1928, in which Horace Jr., Foote's counterpart, appears as a 10-year-old boy. As we follow Horace's journey from child to adult, son to father, we come to know two extended families, his own and that of Elizabeth Vaughn, his wife, across three generations, as well as numerous other townsfolk who weave in and out of Horace's life in a highly complex construct of interconnected stories.

In the opening play, *Roots in a Parched Ground,* Horace's father dies, and his mother Corella remarries. Her new husband, Pete Davenport, rejects Horace, and the couple moves to Houston with his sister Lily Dale, leaving Horace behind with relatives. The remaining plays trace Horace's attempt to create a family of his own. We see Horace at 14, living on an isolated plantation worked by desperate African-American convicts (*Convicts*); at 20, visiting Houston in a vain attempt to become part of Corella and Lily Dale's new family (*Lily Dale*); and at 22, courting a young widow with two children the ages he and his sister were at the time of their father's death (*The Widow Claire*). Plays five, six, and seven tell the story of Horace and Elizabeth's courtship (*Courtship*) and early marriage (*Valentine's Day*) and the loss of their first child to influenza (*1918*), with the final two (*Cousins* and *The Death of Papa*) portraying their later marriage and ending with the death of Elizabeth's father, Henry Vaughn, and the emergence of the next generation in the person of Horace Jr. The cycle comes full circle with *The Death of Papa,* as the death of Mr. Vaughn recalls the death of Horace's father in *Roots in a Parched Ground* and as Horace moves from margin to center, from orphan son to husband and father.

In the course of these nine plays, Foote raises complex questions of identity formation, specifically the ways in which one's social context (family, community, and past history) both contribute to and limit selfhood. Given those patterns of thought and habits of seeing into which we are born, the plays ask, to what extent can we control who we are and whom we choose to become? Other important themes are time, the intricate relationship of past to present, and the importance of place—motifs that situate Foote squarely in the southern literary tradition. Unlike other southern writers, however, Foote's emphasis is not so much on returning home as on leaving it, and home is not so much a specific locale as it is a network of relationships. Often called the "Texas Chekhov," he interrogates these matters in a distinctive style, with understated language limited to the everyday speech of ordinary people and flat, seemingly uneventful plots. To say that nothing happens in these plays, however, is to miss the point. The action in the cycle plays, as in virtually all of Foote's work, is interior. The cycle is also innovative in its use of dramatic form, employing strategies to integrate the nine plays that are more typical of the novel than drama—parallel characters and episodes, inverted situations, unifying motifs, and even paired plays. In its recasting of traditional modes of dialogue, characterization, and structure and its complex network of narratives and themes, *The Orphans' Home Cycle* stands as a remarkable achievement in the American dramatic canon.

BIBLIOGRAPHY

Foote, Horton. *The Orphans' Home Cycle.* New York: Grove Press/Stage & Screen, 2000.

Porter, Laurin. *Orphans' Home: The Voice and Vision of Horton Foote.* Baton Rouge: Louisiana State University Press, 2003.

Laurin R. Porter
University of Texas-Arlington

OSBORN, PAUL **(1901–1988)** Born in Evansville, Indiana, Osborn was educated at the University of Michigan, where he earned a bachelor's degree in 1923 and a master's degree in 1924. After teaching at the University of Michigan for a year, he studied playwriting at Yale with GEORGE PIERCE BAKER. Perhaps not surprisingly, his first play, *Hotbed* (1928), is set on a college campus.

Osborn's first real success was *The Vinegar Tree* in 1930. He is best remembered for *On Borrowed Time* (1938), an adaptation of Lawrence Edward Watkins's novel about an old man who tries to cheat death, and MORNING'S AT SEVEN (1939), an original comedy about a group of elderly siblings and their spouses in midwestern America who contemplate change in the autumn of their lives.

Many of Osborn's stage successes were adaptations. In addition to *On Borrowed Time* (1938), these include *A Bell for Adano* (1944), adapted from John Hersey's novel; *Point of No Return* (1951), based on the novel by John P. Marquand; and *The World of Suzie Wong* (1958), adapted from the novel by Richard Mason.

BIBLIOGRAPHY

Osborn, Paul. *Morning's at Seven.* 1939. Garden City, N.Y.: Doubleday, 1967.

———. *On Borrowed Time.* 1938. New York: Dramatists Play Service, 1969.

———. *Point of No Return.* 1951. New York: Samuel French, 1954.

OUR TOWN THORNTON WILDER (1938) *Our Town* is a seminal work by WILDER in which he dispensed with theatrical conventions, using no scenery or curtain, minimal props, and created a character, the Stage Manager, who directly addresses the audience, to portray an American town and its inhabitants as they live out the joys and sorrows of ordinary life.

The action of the play takes place between 1901 and 1913 (though events beyond 1913 are referred to by the omniscient Stage Manager) in Grover's Corners, New Hampshire, a typical New England town. Act 1 ("Daily Life") covers a day in the life of the town at the turn of the century, centering on the Gibbses and the Webbs, neighboring families. The milkman, the paperboy, and the constable go about their routines, as do

Doc Gibbs, the general practitioner, and Mr. Webb, editor of the town newspaper, and their wives and children. Emily Webb and George Gibbs are growing up next door to each other. Included in this portrait of the town is its history, both geological and human, reported by a professor from the State University and by Mr. Webb. In act 2 ("Love and Marriage"), George and Emily fall in love and get married. In act 3 ("Death"), we learn that Emily has died in childbirth, and we see her join the dead, among whom are her mother-in-law and various townspeople we have met earlier in the play. Emily begs to be allowed to revisit just one day from her lifetime—her 12th birthday—but finds the visit too poignant to bear, every moment in life being far more precious than the living will ever realize. Emily asks the Stage Manager if "any human beings ever realize life while they live it." To which he *"quietly"* replies, "No—Saints and poets maybe—they do some." When she returns to her grave beside Mrs. Gibbs and observes her widowed husband George weeping there, the two women comment on how little the living understand. Simon Stimson, who in life was the troubled, alcoholic choirmaster and who hanged himself, is the least serene of the dead; he tells Emily *"[w]ith mounting violence"* that to be alive is "[t]o move about in a cloud of ignorance. . . . To spend and waste time as though you had millions of years. To be always at the mercy of one self-centered passion, or another. . . . that's the 'happy' existence you wanted to go back to. Ignorance and blindness!" But Mrs. Gibbs admonishes him: "That ain't the whole truth and you know it, Simon Stimson"—not the whole truth but part of the truth, along with Emily's lament that the earth is "too wonderful" to realize.

The Stage Manager, a device with which Wilder first experimented in PULLMAN CAR HIAWATHA (1931), functions here in several ways: He provides the detached point of view from which Wilder intends the members of the audience to view themselves as reflected in the inhabitants of Grover's Corners; he comments on the action as would the chorus in a Greek tragedy; and, more practically, he bridges gaps in time with narrative and suggests props and scenes that must be imagined by the audience. Not bound by the conventions of time, the Stage Manager speaks of the future: Joe, the paperboy, will graduate at the top of his class from MIT; destined to be a great engineer, he will instead die in France during World War I. Not bound by the conventions of the stage, the Stage Manager may dismiss actors and move the action along: "Thank you very much, Ladies. (*To the audience*) Now we'll skip a few hours." The Stage Manager also plays some minor roles.

As he does in some of his other plays—telescoping human time in *The* LONG CHRISTMAS DINNER and geological time in *The* SKIN OF OUR TEETH—in *Our Town,* Wilder goes beyond ordinary time to comment not just on a specific era but also on human existence. Winner of the PULITZER PRIZE, *Our Town* is one of the most often revived plays—in America and abroad—in the history of American drama, and one of the most revered.

BIBLIOGRAPHY
Haberman, Donald. *"Our Town": An American Play.* Boston: Twayne, 1989.

OUTDOOR HISTORICAL DRAMA   Outdoor theater in America, a flourishing enterprise, includes many Shakespeare festivals and a number of religious pageants. Plays focused on the past of the region where they are performed are the most numerous, however, and are the works usually associated with outdoor drama. These history plays are also the dramatic form developed through the outdoor drama movement.

The oldest of the history plays still running is *The Ramona Pageant,* which opened near Hemet, California, in 1923. A dramatization by Garnet Holme of Helen Hunt Jackson's novel, *Ramona* (1884), *The Ramona Pageant* is set in the 1850s; through the love story of an Indian boy and a part-Indian girl, it depicts the plight of the Mission Indians of southern California, whose way of life is destroyed by encroaching Americans.

The play that pioneered the new dramatic form associated with outdoor historical drama and caught the eye of the nation was *The Lost Colony.* Written by PAUL GREEN in 1937 and staged that summer on Roanoke Island, off the coast of North Carolina, *The Lost Colony* is very important historically. A play rather than a pageant, it has suitably developed characters who carry forward a plot made coherent and significant by its theme—the founding of an egalitarian society in the New World with people conditioned by the hierarchical social structures of Europe. At the same time, *The Lost Colony* is intended for performance before a large audience outdoors, so it lacks the tight focus and reliance on small gestures characteristic of plays meant for an indoor theater. Structurally, *The Lost Colony* is episodic, with units of action clearly developed in each scene. The spoken word is important, with dialogue ranging from colloquial to intensely poetic, but other presentational arts are prominent as well: songs and dances, special lighting and sound effects, pantomime and tableaulike staging, a narrator and other nonrepresentational features. Except for four years during World War II, *The Lost Colony* has played every summer on Roanoke Island since its opening.

The Lost Colony attracted national attention. In the wake of its success, Green was besieged with requests from people all over the country wanting him to dramatize something from the history of *their* region. During his lifetime, he staged 16 additional outdoor plays from Washington, D.C., to Southern California, notable among them *The Common Glory* (1947–74) at Williamsburg, Virginia; *Wilderness Road* (1955–74, with interruptions) at Berea, Kentucky; *The Stephen Foster Story* (1959–   ) at Bardstown, Kentucky; *Cross and Sword* (1965–94) at St. Augustine, Florida; *Texas* (1966–   ) at Palo Duro Canyon, Texas; and *Trumpet in the Land* (1970–   ) at New Philadelphia, Ohio.

In 1963, the Institute of Outdoor Drama was established at the University of North Carolina at Chapel Hill. Green's experience had demonstrated the widespread interest in outdoor historical drama and also the need for guidance on the part of communities interested in launching a play. Over the years, the institute has provided such guidance, along with support services for established plays, and has been instrumental in developing new playwrights for the outdoor theater.

Kermit Hunter was the first writer to follow in Green's steps, with *Unto These Hills,* which opened in the summer of 1950 at Cherokee in the North Caro-

lina mountains. *Unto These Hills* deals with the Cherokee Indian Nation and its tragic interaction with white civilization during the 1830s. Hunter wrote several other outdoor historical plays, two of which, like *Unto These Hills,* are still running: *Horn in the West* (1951–   ) at Boone, North Carolina, and *Honey in the Rock* (1961–   ) at Beckley, West Virginia.

Since the emergence of the Institute of Outdoor Drama, with its ability to publicize opportunities and facilitate contacts, a growing number of writers have worked in the outdoor theater. Two of the most successful are Allan W. Eckert and Mark Sumner. Eckert's *Tecumseh!* dramatizes the struggle for the American Midwest in the late 18th and early 19th centuries between the Shawnee Nation and the young American republic. *Tecumseh!* opened in 1973 near Chillicothe, Ohio, the site of a major Shawnee stronghold, and features a haunting Indian suite by the Native American composer Carl T. Fischer.

The appeal of outdoor historical plays can be traced to a natural fascination with local history. The best of the plays go on to provide a moving theatrical experience that enlarges an audience's sense of the national experience—its diversity and what the growth of America cost in outright treachery, ambiguous motives and morals, sacrifice, desperation and courage, self-renouncing nobility, and even outright heroism. Mark Sumner's plays exemplify these possibilities for the outdoor theater. In 1994, his *Pathway to Freedom* opened at Snow Camp, North Carolina, the heart of the Quaker community in the South since the 1700s. The play depicts the Quakers' principled opposition to slavery before the Civil War and tells a story of the underground railroad. In 1998, Sumner's *Black River Traders* opened at Farmington, New Mexico, and focuses on the mingling of cultures (British, Navajo, Anglo-American, and Mexican-American) in the Four Corners region. Opening in 2001, also at Farmington, was Sumner's latest play, *Dreams and Drill Bits,* which follows a family of the region from the farm economy of the 1920s to the oil and gas boom of the 1950s.

The Institute of Outdoor Drama at UNC-Chapel Hill maintains an online directory of outdoor theaters and productions in the United States (www.unc.edu/depts/outdoor/dir/index.html). There are currently

103 such theaters in 39 states and the District of Columbia.

BIBLIOGRAPHY

Brigandi, Phil. *Garnet Holme: California's Pageant Master.* Hemet, Calif.: Ramona Pageant Association, 1991.

Green, Paul. *Dramatic Heritage.* New York: Samuel French, 1953.

Kammen, Michael. *A Season of Youth: The American Revolution and the Historical Imagination.* New York: Knopf, 1978.

McCalmon, George, and Christian Moe. *Creating Historical Drama.* Carbondale: Southern Illinois University Press, 1965.

Selden, Samuel, et al. *Producing America's Outdoor Dramas. UNC Extension Bulletin* 38 (March 1954).

Laurence G. Avery
University of North Carolina–Chapel Hill

OVERMYER, ERIC (1951–)

Playwright Eric Overmyer, whose works have been favorably compared to those of Tom Stoppard, Samuel Beckett, and Harold Pinter, was born in Boulder, Colorado, and grew up in Seattle. He graduated from Reed College in Portland, Oregon, where fellow playwright LEE BLESSING was his roommate. Overmyer subsequently did graduate work at Asolo Conservatory at Florida State University, Brooklyn College, and the City University of New York. He began his career as the literary manager at New York's Playwrights Horizons (1982–84). His first professionally produced play, *Native Speech,* premiered at the Los Angeles Actors Theatre in 1984 and was subsequently produced by Baltimore's Center Stage, where Overmyer was an associate artist from 1984 through 1991. *Native Speech,* about an underground radio disk jockey, introduced the elaborate linguistics and the non-naturalistic vision of a skewed America that would become Overmyer's hallmarks.

Of his work, Overmyer has written: "I want to be surprised in the theatre. I want theatricality in the theatre. I want charged, shaped and heightened language. . . . I want ideas as well as feelings. I want ambiguity and complexity and imagination. I don't want literalness, preaching to the choir, sentiment, political correctness or polemic, easily explainable motivations or naturalistic dialogue or cliché characters" (xii).

His most popular play, ON THE VERGE; OR, THE GEOGRAPHY OF YEARNING, premiered at Center Stage in 1985 and has since become one of the most frequently produced plays nationally, as well as in Canada, Great Britain, and Australia. Providing strong roles for three actresses, the play concerns the time-tripping journey of Victorian lady explorers through the detritus of society from 1888 to the present. *In a Pig's Valise* (1986), a metaphysical detective story with music by composer August Darnell, originated at Center Stage and was later produced at New York's Second Stage in a production starring Nathan Lane. *In Perpetuity throughout the Universe,* a comedy about ghostwriters of right-wing hate manuals, premiered at Center Stage in 1988, and was translated into Quebecois for a Montreal production.

During the 1991–92 academic year, Overmyer was a visiting associate professor of playwriting at Yale, and he has continued to work there occasionally. His plays from that era include *The Heliotrope Bouquet by Scott Joplin and Louis Chauvin* (1991), about the ephemeral nature of art and fame; *Mi Vida Loca* (1991), a family drama about a father's treatment for drug addiction; and *Dark Rapture* (1992), a dark parody commissioned by Seattle's Empty Space Theatre. Later plays have been largely adaptations, including *Alki* (1997), a version of Henrik Ibsen's *Peer Gynt,* set in the Pacific Northwest; *Amphitryon* (1996), subtitled *After Kleist by Way of Molière with a Little Bit of Giraudoux Thrown In,* a modern retelling of the myth of Jupiter's cuckolding of Amphitryon; *Figaro/Figaro* (1996), a conflation of Beaumarchais's original classic with Odon von Horvath's 1936 revisionist sequel; and *Don Quixote de La Jolla* (1993), wherein Cervantes's mad knight is transplanted to modern southern California.

Overmyer virtually abandoned playwriting by the late 1990s, concentrating exclusively on writing for, and eventually producing, television series. These series include *Homicide: Life on the Streets; Law and Order; Close to Home; The Wire;* and *New Amsterdam.* In 2008, he began collaboration on a new series about jazz musicians, to be set in his current part-time home of New Orleans; the program has not yet premiered.

BIBLIOGRAPHY
Overmyer, Eric. *Plays by Eric Overmyer.* New York: Broadway Play Publishing, 1994.

Douglas W. Gordy
Walnut Creek, California

OWENS (BASS), ROCHELLE (1936–)

Poet, playwright, and pioneer in avant-garde American theater, Rochelle Owens is best known for her OBIE AWARD–winning play *Futz* (1967).

Rochelle Bass grew up in Brooklyn and after high school had little formal education (having dropped out of Manhattan's New School). In 1955 she met David Owens, a sculptor and part of the Greenwich Village scene that esteemed art and those who create it and had only contempt for the bourgeoisie. Through her relationship with Owens, she met and was influenced by many artists and writers, including seminal figures in the OFF-OFF BROADWAY movement, in particular Judith Malina and Julian Beck, founders of the iconoclastic LIVING THEATRE, as well as playwright JACK GELBER, whose play *THE CONNECTION* (1959) was a landmark Living Theatre production. Bass, herself, started to write experimental poetry and give readings in the Village. At 20, she began her brief first marriage to David Owens and moved to the Upper West Side.

Rochelle Owens became acquainted with black poet LeRoi Jones, in whose magazine, *Yugen,* some of her poems were published. (Jones, who later took the name AMIRI BARAKA, would write the breakthrough African-American play *DUTCHMAN* [1964].) The year that Owens wrote her first play was also the year she and her first husband separated, 1959, but the play was not produced until years later. In 1967, the La Mama Experimental Theatre Club production of *Futz,* a play about a man who is having a love affair with a pig named Amanda and whose nonconformity costs him his life, was a phenomenal success. The play stirred controversy in some quarters, but, as Clive Barnes archly observed in the *New York Times,* there is a "strong possibility that Miss Owens is not in actual fact recommending bestiality as a way of life—any more than Jonathan Swift in his pamphlet 'A Modest Proposal' was really in favor of cooking and eating tiny babies" (June 14, 1968). Instead, hers was a parable about societal pressures to conform. *Futz* was translated into several languages and was made into a 1969 film, for which Owens wrote the screenplay.

Owens's one-act plays include *Homo* (1966), *The String Game* (1965), *The Queen of Greece* (1969), and *The Karl Marx Play* (1973), a musical comedy, with music by Galt MacDermot. *Who Do You Want, Piere Vidal?* (1982) is a long one-act, descriptively subtitled "A Confrontation Between a Terrorist, a Troubadour and a Japanese-American University Professor."

In the full-length *Beclch* (1968), a white ruler in Africa abuses her power with sexuality and violence. In *He Wants Shih* (1971), a Chinese emperor is a disembodied, speaking head. Dramatic literature scholar Christopher Bigsby has observed that Owens "deals in a surreal, gothic universe. Her plays offer bizarre images, dreamlike structures with an associative logic" which "is not always easy to follow" (308–309). Her deliberately feminist play, *Chucky's Hunch* (1982), concerns an unsuccessful artist whose hostile relationships with his mother and his ex-wife provide an arena for an examination of power and victimization. Other plays include *Kontraption* (1974), *Emma Instigated Me* (1976), and *The Widow and Me Colonel* (1977). Owens has taught at Brown University and the University of Oklahoma and has often lectured and given readings in the United States and abroad; she is also the author of more than a dozen books of poetry.

BIBLIOGRAPHY
Bigsby, C. W. E. *Modern American Drama: 1945–1990.* Cambridge, England: Cambridge University Press, 1992.
Owens, Rochelle. *"Futz" and What Came After.* New York: Random House, 1968.
———. *"The Karl Marx Play" and Others.* New York: Dutton, 1974.
———. *Plays by Rochelle Owens.* New York: Broadway Play Publishing, 2000.

OYAMO (CHARLES F. GORDON) (1943–)

Son of an Ohio steelworker, Charles F. Gordon attended Miami University at Oxford, Ohio, beginning in 1963, for two and a half years before becoming involved with the Black Theatre Workshop in Harlem. Gordon's name is so similar to another

African-American playwright, CHARLES GORDONE, that he took the pen name OyamO (based on a nickname derived by others from his University of Miami–Ohio T-shirt). The first play by OyamO to receive recognition was *Breakout* (1969), which was published in 1971 in the *Black Drama Anthology,* edited by Woodie King Jr. and RON MILNER.

OyamO returned to college in the late 1960s and finished his B.A. at the College of New Rochelle in 1970. In the late 1970s, he was accepted to the graduate playwriting program at Yale University, from which he earned his M.F.A. in 1981. That same year, *The Resurrection of Lady Lester,* a play based on the life of jazz saxophonist Lester Young, premiered at the Yale Repertory Theatre.

OyamO has written more than 30 plays. Perhaps best known among these is *I Am a Man* (1992), based on the events surrounding the strike in 1968 by Memphis sanitation workers that immediately preceded the assassination of Martin Luther King. Other notable works include *Pink and Say* (1996), which was commissioned by the Seattle Children's Theatre and is from a children's book by Patricia Polacco about a white boy and a black boy during the Civil War, and *Let Me Live* (1998), which is set in a Georgia prison in 1932 and examines the injustice of the African-American experience as reflected in the lives of eight inmates. OyamO's plays have been produced at regional theaters around the country, as well as in New York.

In recent years, OyamO has been commissioned by various institutions to write adaptations and histories. *The Sorcerer's Apprentice* (2006), a musical, was commissioned by the Seattle Children's Theatre. *City in a Strait* (2007), about the Civil Rights movement in Detroit, was commissioned by the Mosaic Youth Theatre of Detroit, which also commissioned *Sing Jubilee* (2008), about Fisk University's Jubilee Singers. He is currently working on an adaptation of *I Tituba, Black Witch of Salem,* a novel by Maryse Condé; this commission came from the University of Chigaco's Court Theatre.

During the 1980s, OyamO taught at the College of New Rochelle and at Princeton University, among other institutions; he joined the faculty of the University of Michigan in 1989.

BIBLIOGRAPHY

OyamO. *I Am a Man.* New York: Applause Theatre Books, 1995.
———. *The Resurrection of Lady Lester.* Los Angeles, Calif.: Green Integer Books, 2000.

P

PAINTING CHURCHES TINA HOWE (1983)

Under the Church family's façade of upper-middle-class gentility and literary prowess lies the sad reality of past neuroses and present senility, yet HOWE's *Painting Churches* is also about finding joy where one can, as life enters its final stages.

When Margaret ("Mags") Church comes to Boston to help her elderly parents move from their home on Beacon Hill to their small cottage on Cape Cod, she finds them changed since her last visit. Her father, Gardner Church, a famous New England poet, unable to produce poetry of his own any longer, "writes" instead a book of criticism, which is little more than loose sheets on which are typed fragments of the poems of others. His greatest recent accomplishment has been to teach his parakeet to recite Thomas Gray's "Elegy in a Country Churchyard." Mags's stay gradually reveals her father's incontinence and profound forgetfulness. Her mother's behavior—the mocking tone she often adopts with her husband—seems cruel to Mags; Fanny resents Mags's judgmental attitude since it is she, Fanny, who must daily cope with the reality of an aging spouse. Fanny is at times all frustration and anger: Their income has dried up now that Gardner can no longer write or give public readings, and, worse, Gardner's advancing senility puts all the pressure on Fanny to manage their lives and care for the man who was once her partner. The move to the cottage and the smaller community is prompted by their reduced finances, as well as by the need to keep a close eye on Gardner, whom Fanny fears will get lost in the city.

During her visit, Mags intends to paint her parents' portrait, a long-standing desire of hers. Ironically, it is during this attempt to pose them as she perceives them that she is forced to see them as they are. Mags also confronts some of her own early unhappiness. She speaks—apparently for the first time—to her parents about her childhood eating disorder, which she now realizes stemmed from her mother's perfectionism. Though Mags may realize these things, her mother accepts no responsibility; she merely remembers the six-month period as bizarre, when she remembers it at all.

Mags cannot judge her parents, nor can she really enter the private world of their marriage. Despite their difficulties, they manage to find happy moments together: remembering a favorite painting or poem or shared experience, taking pleasure in a cocktail together (indeed, Fanny is palpably relieved when cocktail hour arrives), or enjoying their daughter's rare visits. Fanny particularly enjoys Mags when she is catty about the upper-class Bostonians with whom she grew up.

Like the enchanting swim Mags recalls taking with her father in phosphorescent waters one summer, what is glorious in life is fleeting: "I remember wishing the moment would hold forever; that we could just be fixed there, laughing and iridescent," but "it was passing already."

PARKS, SUZAN-LORI (1964–)

Suzan-Lori Parks was born in Kentucky into a military family; as a result, she moved around a great deal as a child. She went to high school in Germany but attended college in the United States at Mount Holyoke, where she studied English and German, earning her bachelor's degree in 1985. It was at Mount Holyoke that Parks began to write plays, encouraged to do so by JAMES BALDWIN, from whom she took a creative writing class at nearby Hampshire College. She later studied at Yale University's School of Drama. In 1989, Mel Gussow of the *New York Times* named Parks "the year's most promising new playwright."

Parks's plays consider race relations, gender, and identity, sometimes using allegory and American myth to create social satire. Her works include *Imperceptible Mutabilities in the Third Kingdom* (1989), which has been called both absurdist and allegorical; *The Death of the Last Black Man in the Whole Entire World* (1990), in which characters speak in comic exaggerations of Black English; *Devotees in the Garden of Love* (1992), in which a mother and daughter await the outcome of the war being fought for the daughter's hand; *The America Play* (1993), which addresses the role played by African Americans in the history of this country (and is an early working of some of the aspects of TOPDOG/UNDERDOG [2001]); *Venus* (1996), based on the historical figure Sartje Baartman, an amply proportioned black woman taken to England as a sideshow attraction in the 1880s; *In the Blood* (1999), about a streetwise and homeless mother of five; *Fucking A* (2000), set in a future where the rich and the poor no longer speak the same language; and *Topdog/Underdog,* which examines the bleak existence faced by the African-American male. Parks received OBIE AWARDS for *Imperceptible Mutabilities in the Third Kingdom* (Best New American Play) and *Venus* (Playwriting).

The day after *Topdog/Underdog* opened on Broadway, Parks won the 2002 PULITZER PRIZE for the play. (It had premiered in July of 2001 at the OFF-BROADWAY Public Theatre.) Parks is the first African-American woman to win a Pulitzer Prize for drama and is one of only four African-American women playwrights (the others are LORRAINE HANSBERRY, NTOZAKE SHANGE, and ANNA DEAVERE SMITH) to have a play produced on Broadway.

Parks completed her yearlong project *365 Days/365 Plays* in November of 2003; for a year, she wrote a daily play about whatever came to mind. The project finally reached the stage—many stages, actually, around the country and elsewhere in the English-speaking world—in 2007, when 700 theater groups participated in producing these short dramatic works.

Parks has taught playwriting at various institutions, including Yale and the California Institute of the Arts. In autumn 2008, New York's Public Theatre announced that Parks would become their first "Master Writer," a three-year residency during which she will also be a visiting professor of dramatic writing at New York University's Tisch School of the Arts. Parks has also written screenplays (*Anemone Me* [1990], *Girl 6* [1996]), and *Their Eyes Were Watching God* [2005], based on Zora Neale Hurston's novel), radio plays (*Pickling* [1990], *The Third Kingdom* [1990], and *Locomotive* [1991]), and a novel (*Getting Mother's Body* [2003]).

BIBLIOGRAPHY

Geis, Deborah R. *Suzan-Lori Parks*. Ann Arbor: University of Michigan Press, 2008.

Parks, Suzan-Lori. *"The American Play" and Other Works.* New York: Theatre Communications Group, 1995.

———. *The Red-Letter Plays*. New York: Theatre Communications Group, 2001.

———. *Topdog/Underdog*. New York: Theatre Communications Group, 2001.

———. *365 Days/365 Plays*. New York: Theatre Communications Group, 2006.

———. *Venus*. New York: Theatre Communications Group, 2001.

Wetmore, Kevin J., Jr., and Alycia Smith-Howard, eds. *Suzan-Lori Parks: A Casebook*. New York: Routledge, 2007.

PARNELL, PETER (1953–)

Peter Parnell was born in New York and received his B.A. from Dartmouth College in 1974. After being awarded the Reynolds Traveling Fellowship in Playwriting from Dartmouth (1975–76), he came to the attention of Joseph Papp, producer of the New York Shakespeare Festival/Public Theatre, where his play *Sorrows of Stephen* (1979) first appeared. It tells the story of a young man obsessed by romantic love, fueled by a shelf of 19th-century romantic novels, including the one from which Parnell takes his title, Wolfgang von Goethe's

The Sorrows of Young Werther. The main character, Stephen Hurt, is, in the words of Mel Gussow, theater critic of the *New York Times,* "in love with love. He longs to be smitten and finds grand passion in everyday life." Stephen himself summarizes his problem with women: "I love them. They leave me." After the departure of his latest love, Stephen, like Goethe's callow hero, halfheartedly considers suicide but, in the end, blithely decides he'll just find someone new with whom to be in love. *Sorrows of Stephen,* in Gussow's view, "is a real romantic comedy, sophisticated and sentimental, with an ageless attitude toward the power of positive love" (December 17, 1982). In *The Rise and Rise of Daniel Rocket* (1982), Parnell tells the story of a 12-year-old boy's need to believe in illusions. While considered somewhat simplistic in its approach, most critics appreciated Parnell's accurate portrayal of the quick and violent emotions of children and their urgent need for illusion.

Romance Language (1984) again displays Parnell's love of 19th-century romantic literature, as well as his taste for fantasy. But where his earlier plays focus on the dreams and illusions of youth, this one explores the more adult themes of sexuality, responsibility, and freedom. Among the many characters here are Walt Whitman, Emily Dickinson, Henry David Thoreau, Ralph Waldo Emerson, and Louisa May Alcott, who pit their own egalitarian ideals against a 20th-century perception of freedom. Parnell feels that Walt Whitman's belief that expressing oneself and being free sexually goes hand in hand with being free in every other way. In the course of the play, Emily Dickinson is seduced by an actress, and Louisa May Alcott falls in love with General George Custer, whose nephew suffers an obsession with a transvestite. All the characters in the play are trying to connect with each other and something always seems to be in the way. Frank Rich, writing in the *New York Times,* expressed admiration for the breadth of Parnell's vision, observing that, at the end, "everyone babbles at once in a language as varied as the land they inhabit. It's the soul of Whitman's America singing of course [and Parnell leaves] us with an inspiring sense of how beautiful both its cacophonies and harmonies were meant to be" (November 21, 1984).

Peter Parnell was playwright-in-residence at the Denver Center Theatre Company (1983–84). He is a member of the artistic board at New York's Playwrights Horizons, which has produced many of his plays, including *Hyde in Hollywood* (1989), *Flaubert's Latest* (1992), and *An Imaginary Life* (1993). Parnell's two-part stage adaptation of John Irving's novel *The Cider House Rules* was published in 2001. *QED* (2001), a play inspired by the writings of physicist Richard Feynman, premiered in Los Angeles before moving to New York's Lincoln Center. Parnell's most recent play, *Trumpery* (2007), finds another scientist, Charles Darwin, in personal and professional crisis.

BIBLIOGRAPHY

Parnell, Peter. *The Cider House Rules, Part One: Here in St. Cloud's.* New York: Dramatists Play Service, 2001.

———. *The Cider House Rules, Part Two: In Other Parts of the World.* New York: Dramatists Play Service, 2001.

———. *QED.* New York: Applause Theatre Books, 2002.

———. *The Rise and Rise of Daniel Rocket.* New York: Dramatists Play Service, 1984.

———. *Romance Language.* New York: Samuel French, 1985.

———. *Sorrows of Stephen.* New York: Samuel French, 1980.

Philip M. Isaacs
New York, New York

PATRICK, JOHN (1907–1995) Born in Carmel, California, John Patrick was educated at Columbia and Harvard Universities. During World War II, he served as an ambulance driver with the American Field Service (1942–44). Over the course of his writing career, Patrick produced more than 60 plays and screenplays; some were adaptations and collaborations, but a great many more were original solo works.

Patrick's first successful play, *The HASTY HEART* (1945), was based in part on his wartime experiences. It takes place in a field hospital where wounded allies from several nations show comradeship and decency to each other and to a bitter, dying soldier who comes among them. *The Curious Savage* (1950), which is often revived by amateur groups, takes place in an asylum filled with charming, harmless mental patients; Mrs. Savage's grandchildren place her there because she is giving away their inheritance to help others. John Patrick is best remembered for his award-winning hit *The Teahouse of the August Moon* (1953). The play won the PULITZER PRIZE, the New York Drama Critics' Circle Award, and the TONY AWARD. It tells the story of a young American officer who helps the Okinawans, whom he is charged with teaching "the meaning of Democracy," build the geisha teahouse of their dreams. Other plays include *Good as Gold* (1957), *Everybody Loves Opal* (1961), and *Love Is a Time of Day* (1969). Patrick continued to write for regional theaters well into his seventies and wrote poetry until his death, apparently a suicide, at the age of 90.

BIBLIOGRAPHY
Patrick, John. *The Hasty Heart.* New York: Random House, 1945.
———. *The Teahouse of the August Moon.* New York: Putnam's, 1952.

PAYNE, JOHN HOWARD (1791–1852)

Born in New York City, John Howard Payne began writing reviews for newspapers at the age of 11; at 14, he edited the *Thespian Mirror,* a weekly review of New York theater that was widely read. When he was 15, his first play, *Julia; or, The Wanderer,* a comedy, was produced in New York—for one performance. He was trained in elocution by his father, William Payne, who taught at the Clinton Academy in East Hampton, New York. Payne attended Union College starting in 1806 but remained for only two years, until the bankruptcy and poor health of his father made it necessary for him to go to work.

In 1809, Payne made his acting debut, for which he received high praise. However, his success in New York as an actor was short-lived, prompting him to sail in 1813 to England, where he remained for 20 years. Soon after his arrival in England, he turned his talents to writing for the theater, rather than acting in it. He wrote, translated, or adapted more than 60 plays. Payne's blank verse tragedy, *Brutus; or, the Fall of Tarquin* (1818), a Roman history play, was adapted from several sources, including Voltaire's *Brutus* (Payne was, in fact, charged with plagiarism). The play was very successful and made the actor Edmund Kean a star. The Payne work that is most often found in antholo-

gies of early American drama is another adaptation, *CHARLES THE SECOND; OR, THE MERRY MONARCH* (1824). This comedy was written with American writer Washington Irving (1783–1859), who was responsible for its most memorable character, Captain Copp.

Payne is known as the first American of the theater to gain attention in England. Unfortunately, he was plagued with financial problems throughout his career. After one unsuccessful season in London, he spent time in debtors' prison, yet while in Paris in 1822, he lived at the elegant Palais Royal Hotel.

Payne was also a sometime librettist. He is probably most remembered, along with composer Sir Henry Rowley Bishop, for the song "Home, Sweet Home" ("Be it ever so humble, there's no place like home") from his operetta, *Clari; or, The Maid of Milan,* which was performed at London's Covent Garden in 1823. The operetta was a great success, but Payne was paid a flat 100 pounds for his contribution. The sheet music for "Home, Sweet Home" reportedly sold 100,000 copies in the first year alone; Payne received not a penny of the profits. The song was very popular on both sides during the Civil War.

Payne managed to raise enough money to return to America in 1832. The plays Payne had written in Europe were continually produced in America, but he received no compensation for them (he was an outspoken proponent of copyright protection for American playwrights, but no such laws were enacted until after his death). In 1839, he wrote a play, which was neither produced nor published, called "Romulus, the Shepherd King." He was appointed American consul to Tunis in 1842 under President Tyler; he served there from 1842 to 1845 and again from 1851 until his death in 1852.

BIBLIOGRAPHY
Overmyer, Grace. *America's First Hamlet.* New York: New York University Press, 1957.

PERFORMANCE ART

Performance art is a term that can describe a wide array of activities, from people dressing in period costume acting out scripted and improvised events that memorialize the past, to individuals fasting for days in the enclosed space of an art gallery. The term came into wide usage in the

1970s to describe activities in the art world that had begun flourishing in the early 1960s, events and exhibitions that were not quite theater and not quite visual art. Performance art began to emerge when mainly visual artists, often sculptors influenced by the minimalist aesthetic of the 1960s, started involving their own bodies and their audiences in the event of art-viewing. Minimalist objects, such as Robert Morris's cubes and Carl Andre's metal floor pieces, challenged conventional definitions of art, bringing attention to the role of the spectator and of the site of exhibition as active and necessary parts of the art-making process. Furthermore, many visual artists working with sculpture at the time also began staging events that would later be called performance, at first, mainly centered in New York City. Robert Morris stood inside a hollow wooden column as part of an exhibit and later collaborated with dancers of the Judson Church Group, such as Yvonne Rainer, on dance performances that involved minimal theatricality, emphasizing mundane movements alongside everyday objects like mattresses and stairs. In 1963, Morris staged a performance called *Site* in which he wore a mask that was the exact replica of his own face as he moved large wooden slats to reveal the performance artist Carolee Schneemann in a pose replicating Edouard Manet's painting *Olympia*. Interarts innovations and collaborations such as these influenced a growing number of artists who wanted to de-emphasize the art object per se, bringing more attention to the event of art spectatorship.

Some of these artists, such as Adrian Piper, Vito Acconci, and Chris Burden, worked individually and became identified sometimes as conceptual artists and sometimes as performance artists: What was integral to their art was not the objects they produced but the concepts they brought forth and situations they eventuated. Acconci, Burden, Schneemann, and others were also later called body artists, because they used their bodies like canvases, that is, as the medium with which to make art, sometimes inviting audience members to do things to their bodies as part of the performance, as in the work of Marina Abramovi and Yoko Ono.

During this period of the 1960s and 1970s, performance art also manifested itself in groups. Allan Kaprow and Michael Kirby staged a series of events

they called "Happenings," sometimes for an intimate, invited audience, sometimes for an unsuspecting public. Happenings were not centered around individual artists' bodies; rather, they involved several "actors" who would perform simple acts, such as serving food, in carefully constructed spaces. One of the ideas behind Happenings was to take everyday objects and actions out of their familiar contexts and restage them as art events. Performances such as Richard Schechner's *Dionysus in 69,* performed in 1969, were sometimes also closely related to theater. *Dionysus in 69* was inspired by the Greek tragedy *The Bacchae,* but rather than retell the Dionysus myth, it sought to bring actors and audience into orgiastic, cathartic, Dionysian contact; it was an attempt at creating a mythical temporary community, rather than simply reporting on one. Schechner founded the Performance Group, whose space eventually became the home of the Wooster Group (see ELIZABETH LeCOMPTE), a theater collective that is still well known today for its theatrical innovations and restagings of familiar plays.

In the later 1970s and 1980s, performance art turned increasingly to language and storytelling, as it was taken up by feminist, queer, and antiracist projects to give voice to many suppressed and untold stories. Often autobiographical, storytelling performances could sometimes be scripted, sometimes improvised, and were performed in an array of places, from nightclubs and art galleries to theaters. Robbie McCauley staged a number of plays dealing with the heritage of slavery in the United States, notably *Sally's Rape* (1989), which tells the story of her enslaved great-great-grandmother interspersed with solicitations of audience response.

Today, performance art ranges from spectacles using technological innovations, such as LAURIE ANDERSON's multimedia work, to solo performances featuring a single actor and a few well-worn props. Despite the many possible variations, all performance art tends to emphasize the event of performance, including the audience in the show by being based in real time (as opposed to many plays, which collapse time to depict its passage in a few hours), by using direct address, and often by incorporating an improvisational element. Many performances are not repeatable and do not exist in any other form but as a performance. Ultimately, performance art continues to challenge conventional understandings of art and theater precisely by refusing stable definition, drawing from many disparate forms and conventions in unexpected ways.

BIBLIOGRAPHY

Aronson, Arnold. *American Avant-Garde Theatre: A History.* New York: Routledge, 2000.

Carlson, Marvin. *Performance: A Critical Introduction.* New York: Routledge, 1996.

Goldberg, RoseLee. *Performance Art from Futurism to the Present.* New York: Thames and Hudson, 2001.

———. *Performance: Live Art since 1960.* New York: Harry N. Abrams Publishers, 1998.

Maria Ghira Renu Cappelli
University of California–Berkeley

PETRIFIED FOREST, THE ROBERT E. SHERWOOD (1935)

Set and written in the midst of the depression, *The Petrified Forest* takes place at the Black Mesa Filling Station and Bar BQ on an Arizona desert road that leads to the petrified remnants of a prehistoric forest (known at the time of the play as the Petrified Forest National Monument). These offstage trees-turned-to-stone provide a metaphor for the static lives of the characters and the barrenness of modern life.

Sherwood comments almost immediately on the socioeconomic inequality of the depression and on the alternative to failed capitalism—socialism. The play opens with a conversation between two telegraph linemen who sit in the diner and discuss Russian socialism, which they conclude is for the "benefit of all" and is better for the working man than the current economic system in the United States. As they are leaving, Jason Maple, the proprietor, representing the conservative view, tells them that "preaching . . . red propaganda . . . isn't a very healthy occupation."

Jason is an unhappy man who longs to sell the family business, move to Los Angeles, and open a mechanic's shop there. Jason's father, Gramp Maple, lives in the past (he was once shot at by Billy the Kid—his claim to fame) and controls his son's life by refusing to sell the Black Mesa, through which they eke out a meager living on an isolated desert road. Like her

father, Jason's daughter Gabby is trapped at the Black Mesa against her will. Gabby's mother left her husband and child along with their stark surroundings years ago in order to return to her native France, a country Gabby idealizes and dreams of visiting. While her grandfather and father firmly represent the past and reactionary politics, Gabby is an artist who represents hope for the future. Working at the Black Mesa is also Boze, a young gas attendant who could "have been [an] All-American" football player and who hopes to conquer the fair Gabby. Into the diner come various characters, some of whom are equally victimized by thwarted dreams and two of whom cause change in this static place.

First is Alan Squier, an American who has been living in the south of France off of his wife's money. Alan is a failed novelist, but he is articulate and intelligent, and Gabby is drawn to him. He notices that she reads poetry, and she brings out her paintings to show him—as she has shown no one else. It soon becomes clear that Squier has no money to pay for his meal; Boze is about to throw him out when a wealthy couple from Ohio and their chauffeur arrive. These characters represent two extremes of the depression era, the rich capitalists and their African-American servants. The Chisholms agree—at Gabby's suggestion—to give Alan a lift as far as they are going. Once they have left, Boze resumes his seduction of Gabby, but he is interrupted when Duke Mantee and his gang arrive with weapons drawn. They are on the run from Oklahoma City, where they have killed six people. The gangsters have commandeered the Chisholms' car at gunpoint and put its four occupants, who eventually make their way back to the Black Mesa, out on the road.

Meanwhile, Mantee and his men order food and settle in to wait for Mantee's girlfriend, who his men think is not worth the wait or the risk. Squier returns on foot to warn the people at the filling station about Mantee, but he is too late. As the group converses, SHERWOOD's ideology emerges. Gramps, by reminiscing about Billy the Kid and Wild Bill Hickok, draws an implicit parallel between them and these modern-day (1930s) outlaws. Squier calls Mantee "the last great apostle of rugged individualism." By drawing these comparisons, after the linemen have praised the benefits of socialism, Sherwood seems to be suggesting that the American capitalist philosophy of individualism leads to the rise of thugs and to the economic tribulations of the common person. He addresses, then, two issues of the 1930s—the benefits of socialism in a collapsed economy and the rise of fascism internationally.

All of the characters want something they cannot seem to have. The gangsters are doomed to die at the hands of the police when they seek freedom and capital. Jason is doomed to stay at the Black Mesa instead of in Los Angeles running his own business. Boze hangs onto the newspaper clipping that suggests he was almost an All-American. Mrs. Chisholm regrets her marriage, which took her away from the stage. Only Gabby may break free from her petrified existence and realize her dreams of art and France, but she does so with the help of Alan's sacrifice: Alan signs his life insurance policy over to her and asks Mantee to shoot him before he flees; Mantee does. In the end, Squier gives meaning to his life—something he had come to believe was impossible—by sacrificing it in order to give Gabby money enough to go to France and develop into an artist.

In neither *The Petrified Forest* nor in his PULITZER PRIZE–winning, antiwar play *IDIOT'S DELIGHT* (1936) does Sherwood shy away from political and social commentary. Even more overt, his 1940 Pulitzer Prize–winning *There Shall Be No Night,* which condemned America's pre–Pearl Harbor isolationism, toured the country and led to his role as speechwriter and Department of War Information officer in the Franklin D. Roosevelt administration.

PHILADELPHIA STORY, THE PHILIP BARRY
(1939) A stylish comedy about a wealthy girl and her fall from goddess to human being, *The Philadelphia Story* is BARRY's most enduring play. The play's witty dialogue, including the sarcastic banter of journalists Liz and Mike as they mock their wealthy hosts, and the portrayals of the appealing—albeit rich—Tracy, Dexter, and Dinah contrasted with that of the stuffy, self-important George Kittredge continue to please American audiences, perhaps because the play appeals to America's love of wealth and its simultaneous resentment of it. Certainly the popularity of the 1940 film version, in which Katharine Hepburn repeated her stage role, has kept the play in front of the public as well.

The Lord family has a problem. *Destiny* magazine is blackmailing them: In exchange for keeping father Seth's affair with a dancer quiet, Seth's son, Sandy, has agreed to let *Destiny* cover the fashionable second wedding of the beautiful Tracy Lord, Seth's daughter. The Lords reluctantly admit reporter Macaulay "Mike" Connor and photographer Elizabeth "Liz" Imbrie into their home for the next day's wedding. Tracy's 13-year-old sister Dinah prefers Tracy's first husband, C. K. Dexter Haven, to her stuffy fiancé, George Kittredge, so Dinah calls Dexter and invites him to lunch in Tracy's name.

The marriage between Tracy and Dexter lasted less than a year. Dexter reminds her of the good times they had together by giving her a framed photo of their sailboat, the *True Love,* but the friction between them reemerges when he chastises her for her "prejudice against weakness" and tells her that she will "never be a first class woman or a first class human being, till [she has] learned to have some regard for human frailty." He hopes that her "own foot" will "slip a little sometime." She is offended when he disparagingly refers to her as a "goddess." George on the other hand *wants* a goddess—"a marvelous, distant . . . queen" with a "kind of beautiful purity." To these overtures, Tracy emphatically responds, "I don't want to be worshipped! I want to be loved!" Even Tracy's father, troubled by her judgmental tone toward him, tells her that she "might just as well be made of bronze" because, for all her beauty, she lacks "an understanding heart." All of this (in Tracy's view, unjust) criticism sets her up for a transformation. The catalyst is champagne.

At the pre-wedding party at her uncle Willie's house, Tracy drinks a great deal of champagne and stays up until dawn, mostly with Mike Connor, who tells her, in contrast to what the other men have told her, that she is "made of flesh and blood" and "full of love and warmth and delight." When George finds out that Mike and Tracy have been together in the wee hours of the morning, he assumes the worst and demands an explanation. Tracy decides, despite being substantially cleared of the charges, to give up the judgmental and priggish George and to remarry Dexter, much to the delight of Dinah.

First produced by the THEATRE GUILD, *The Philadelphia Story* was Philip Barry's most commercially successful play; indeed, its success rescued the Theatre Guild temporarily from financial ruin. Barry wrote the play for Hepburn, who bought the movie rights before the play opened and subsequently sold them to MGM.

PIANO LESSON, THE AUGUST WILSON (1990)

Set in Pittsburgh in 1936 among the descendants of slaves, *The Piano Lesson* poses the question: Is it better to preserve the past or to use whatever comes down from the past to build a better future? WILSON does not answer the question; instead, he gives each position a powerful advocate in the characters of Berniece and her brother, Boy Willie.

When Boy Willie arrives from the South with his friend, Lymon, to sell watermelons, he has an ulterior motive. He plans to convince his sister to sell the valuable antique piano carved with the faces of their ancestors by their great-grandfather and depicting the history of their family. Boy Willie wants to take his half of the money, put it together with the money he earns from selling the watermelons and his other savings, and buy a piece of land from the Sutter family, whose ancestors owned his ancestors. Boy Willie believes that his father—who was killed at age 31 for stealing the piano out of the Sutter home—would have wanted him to build on the one thing he was able to leave his children: "The only thing my daddy had to give me was that piano. And he died over giving me that." Boy Willie believes that if his father had been able to, *he* would have traded the piano for land, and he explains to his sister, "If you got a piece of land you'll find everything else fall right into place. You can stand right up next to the white man and talk about the price of cotton . . . and anything else you want to talk about." But Berniece adamantly disagrees, believing that the piano is a sacred family heirloom; she reminds her brother that their mother "polished this piano with her tears for seventeen years" and that the piano has their family's "blood on it."

Berniece's relationship with the piano goes beyond a wish to preserve and revere it. She has not played the instrument since her mother's death years before. When she played for her mother, the older woman could hear Berniece's daddy talking to her, and Berniece as a child imagined that the "pictures came alive and walked through the house." She does not play the piano now because she does not "want to wake them spirits." However, there is a spirit in the house anyway. Boy Willie brings the news that Sutter, the grandson of the man who owned their great-grandfather, has been killed. It is believed that the ghosts of Boy Willie's father and the four other men who died with him (together known as the "Ghosts of the Yellow Dog") shoved Sutter down his well. Since Sutter's death, his ghost has been in Berniece's house. It is only in the final scene of the play, when Berniece plays the piano and calls to her ancestors carved upon it, that she is able to exorcise the ghost of Sutter. This is, symbolically, Berniece's reconnection to her history. For Wilson, maintaining, or reestablishing, a connection to the history of the race is essential for progress. The redemptive quality of that connection is a theme evident in other Wilson plays, in particular KING HEDLEY II (2001).

A strong supporting cast of male characters represent the choices available to African-American men in the 1930s. Boy Willie and his friend Lymon represent the two choices available to rural southerners: Boy Willie wants to continue to farm, not for a white landowner as he has been, but for himself on his own land; Lymon, who has spent time in jail for vagrancy when he was unemployed, believes he will be treated more fairly in a northern city and plans to stay in Pittsburgh after he sells his watermelons. Of Berniece and Boy Willie's uncles, Wining Boy has been a gambler, charmer, ladies' man, and musician, while the steady Doaker, who shares the house with Berniece and her daughter Maretha, has worked on the railroad for 27 years. Berniece's boyfriend, Avery, has found standing in the community by becoming a preacher.

The Piano Lesson won the PULITZER PRIZE and the New York Drama Critics' Circle Award. Despite these awards, the play was not without detractors. Some critics found it too long, and the ending—involving the exorcism of a ghost—was controversial. Wilson, in fact, has suggested that the exorcism is far more important than who ends up with the piano, because what is being confronted and fought by Boy Willie—Sutter's ghost—is the lingering specter of the white man as master over the fate of African Americans.

PICNIC WILLIAM INGE (1953)

Based on an earlier play INGE had written as a struggling college teacher in St. Louis, *Picnic* is the story of how a lonely and handsome young drifter affects the lives of several women in a small town that closely resembles Inge's native Independence, Kansas.

Hal Carter's arrival stirs the longing in Madge Owens, the local beauty queen, to be appreciated for her character instead of her spectacular good looks; Hal also awakens Millie, Madge's younger tomboy sister, to her own feminine possibilities. He prompts both sexual desire and desperation in the aging spinster schoolteacher, Rosemary Sydney, who rooms in the Owens home. In Helen Potts, a middle-aged neighbor, he creates longing for lost opportunities for love and happiness. And in Flo Owens, Madge and Millie's mother, he sparks fear that the impetuous love between Madge and Hal will destroy her dream that Madge will marry Alan Seymour, a wealthy young man who covets Madge as a prospective "trophy wife." Flo, who was long ago abandoned by her husband, hopes for a better, more financially secure life for her daughters, and Hal Carter is clearly a threat to that hope.

Hal himself is only vaguely aware of the effect of his presence on the women around him; he seeks mostly some warmth and stability in his heretofore hard life, arriving to ask Alan, a former friend, for a job. He covers his own sense of inadequacy with braggadocio. Inge skillfully crafts his plot around the town's Labor Day picnic at which Madge is crowned "Queen of Neewollah" (Halloween spelled backwards). Everyone's frustrations and fears erupt into actions that both liberate and shock, and resolution comes with Madge following Hal out of town after they've spent the night together, Rosemary forcing a reluctant suitor to marry her after they have sex, Millie decid-

ing to leave town for college, and Flo realizing that she must accept that Madge and Millie will claim their own futures.

Indeed, acceptance of and adaptation to life's circumstances are dominant themes in all of Inge's important work. These themes reflect his own experience as he struggled to balance his success and its accompanying glare of public attention with his personal struggles against alcohol and the debilitating effects of his carefully closeted homosexuality during a repressive era in our culture's history. Inge is America's most authentic midwestern playwright, a prairie realist whose best work shows the unrest below the placid and wholesome surface stereotypes of that region. *Picnic* is Inge's best-known work because it won the PULITZER PRIZE and was made into a very successful 1956 film shot on location in Kansas.

Ralph F. Voss
University of Alabama

PIÑERO, MIGUEL (1946–1988)

During his short life, Miguel Piñero had a profound influence on Nuyorican (a term referring to Puerto Rican culture in New York) drama. Born in Guarabo, Puerto Rico, Piñero moved to New York City at the age of four and spent much of his youth helping to support his family by means legal and illegal. Piñero's life "on the street" formed the basis for much of his later artistic output, and the majority of his dramatic characters operate in marginalized spaces: prisons, streets, and tenements. Passing through various correctional facilities, Piñero began his work for the theater as poetry he wrote during a stay at Ossining Correctional Facility (Sing Sing). Working with Marvin Felix Camillo in workshops in prison, and later with The Family, Camillo's theatrical group for ex-inmates, Piñero wrote his first and best-known drama, *SHORT EYES* (1974). The play chronicles the murder of an inmate accused of molestation and the effects of this murder on the prison community responsible for it. Later filmed, *Short Eyes* was celebrated for its unflinching and authentic look at life in prison. This award-winning work led to additional important writing for the theater.

In *The Sun Always Shines for the Cool* (1976), we enter the world of players, men of the street. The play centers on the conflict between two of them, Viejo and Cat Eyes, over the fate of Viejo's daughter, Chile Girl, and concludes with Viejo's self-sacrificial suicide. *Midnight Moon at the Greasy Spoon* (1981), a departure from Piñero's focus on alternative spaces, provides a slice-of-life account of the various employees and customers that wander through a Broadway diner, recording the small tragedies and setbacks and the exhaustion of daily life. *Eulogy for a Small Time Thief* (1977) chronicles a day in the life of David Dancer, whose various con jobs and hustles all come back to haunt him, ending in his death. In addition to setting up a "party" where he accidentally pimps a man's daughter to him, he betrays his girlfriend by sleeping with her younger sister; after he is left to his own devices, he is the victim of a professional hit sent by a man he had been scamming.

Playland Blues (1980) tells the story of young hustlers and the possibility of establishing relationships with caring adults while still dealing with the realities of the streets. Piñero also had several one-act plays produced and collected for publication, including *Cold Beer* (c. 1979) and *Tap Dancing and Bruce Lee Kicks* (probably first performed in Los Angeles in the late 1970s), meditations on the role of the writer and the choice of subject matter; *Paper Toilet* (1979), a comedy dealing with gender, sexuality, and the law in a public restroom; *Irving* (no record of first performance date), about the coming out of a gay Jewish man; *The Guntower* (1979), the ruminations of two prison guards; and *Sideshow* (1975), a shorter version of many of the issues explored in *Playland Blues*.

Created by a man who always considered himself an outlaw and an outsider, Piñero's theatrical works reflect their author's investment in voices outside the mainstream. Although he is the subject of a 2001 feature film directed by Leon Ichaso, there is still no book-length critical or biographical work on Piñero.

BIBLIOGRAPHY

Piñero. Dir. Leon Ichaso. With Benjamin Bratt, Talisa Soto, and Mandy Patinkin. Wider, 2001.

Piñero, Miguel. *Outrageous: One Act Plays.* Houston: Arte Público Press, 1986.

———. *Plays: "The Sun Always Shines for the Cool," "Midnight Moon at the Greasy Spoon," "Eulogy for a Small Time Thief."* Houston: Arte Público Press, 1984.

———. *Short Eyes.* New York: Hill & Wang, 1988.

Jon D. Rossini
University of California—Davis

PORGY DUBOSE AND DOROTHY HEYWARD (1927)

Lavishly produced by the prestigious THEATRE GUILD, *Porgy* was an important event in the American theater because of its interracial cast and its detailed focus on a regional African-American culture—that of Charleston, South Carolina—including even its specific dialect. Although praised by most critics, it was criticized by some African Americans for perpetuating racial stereotypes.

The play is set in Catfish Row, a neighborhood teeming with life. The Honey Man chants his song about the honey he sells. Characters sing and speak in a dialect still so filled with African words that the audience does not understand it. Gradually, the HEYWARDS eliminate the African words, and the actors speak more distinctly, drawing the audience in. There is continual movement, except when white policemen come and all the characters retreat into their shuttered houses or adopt a false, deferential attitude. In the original production, by the time the white men enter, the Heywards had so successfully brought their white audience into the multidimensional and authentic culture of Catfish Row that the white men seemed the alien outsiders; this was quite an accomplishment in 1927 and quite a departure from most earlier two-dimensional depictions of African Americans on the American stage.

The action begins on a quiet evening as a group of men shoot craps and the enormous, sexually attractive Crown appears with his "woman," the prostitute Bess. Sportin' Life, a bootlegger who also sells "happy dust," is present, as is the crippled beggar, Porgy. Crown is drunk and argumentative and kills one of the men in the game. After his escape, Bess seeks a place to hide, but only Porgy will help her. Frightened, she goes into his hut.

As time goes by, Porgy and Bess declare their love for each other. Porgy wants her to go to the picnic on Kittiwah Island even though he cannot. Bess goes alone, and Crown, who has been hiding there, arouses her sexual desire; she remains with him for two days.

She is delirious when she returns, but she recovers and is happy to find that Porgy still loves her.

The routine of Catfish Row is torn asunder when there is a hurricane and the men who have been out fishing are drowned. Crown appears and turns the prayers and hymns to bawdy singing and dancing. He daringly runs out into the hurricane to save Clara, who has gone to seek her husband, leaving her baby with Bess. He is presumed to have been killed, but Porgy suspects otherwise and lies in wait for him. Crown appears, looking for Bess; when he goes into the house, Porgy kills him to protect Bess and Clara's baby. When Porgy—never really a suspect because he is crippled—is taken away by the police for questioning, Sportin' Life convinces Bess that he will be gone for months or years and lures her back to the "happy dust," which she had given up. In the final scene, Porgy returns to learn that Bess has gone to New York with Sportin' Life. After finding out that New York is up "Nort," he turns his goat cart around and drives away to find his Bess.

The play was successful, but it has been largely forgotten because of the fame of George Gershwin's later opera *Porgy and Bess* (1935), with lyrics by DuBose Heyward and Ira Gershwin and libretto by DuBose Heyward. (The opera was initially trimmed and produced by the Theatre Guild; it was not until the full opera was revived with William Warfield and Leontyne Price in the title roles in 1952 that it was fully appreciated as grand opera.) Though the play was very well received by white critics—debate among white critics centered over whether the material was serious enough for the grand opera house— many in the African-American community criticized both works for their depiction of blacks as drug addicts, alcoholics, and illiterates, while the prominent doctors, lawyers, and educators of that period in South Carolina, not to mention the equally upstanding and hardworking butchers and bakers, were not in the picture. Many African Americans felt this was simply further exploitation of blacks by whites. However, the play was an undisputed breakthrough for African Americans in theater professions. It provided opportunities for 53 actors from Harlem to perform on Broadway and created opportunities for future African-American actors and playwrights.

Yvonne Shafer
St. John's University

PRELUDE TO A KISS Craig Lucas (1988)

Lucas's romantic comedy was commissioned by and premiered at California's South Coast Repertory in Costa Mesa, California. Subsequently produced Off-Broadway by the Circle Repertory Theatre Company; that production, directed by Lucas's longtime collaborator Norman René, transferred in May 1990 for a long Broadway run.

Peter, a microfiche engineer, meets unconventional bartender Rita, a socialist who claims she has not slept since age 14. She quickly charms Peter, despite her pessimism, but she refuses even to consider bringing children into such a dangerous world. After a six-week courtship, the two decide to wed. At the ceremony, an old man whom nobody recognizes appears and kisses the bride. Something odd happens as the old man, feeling faint, calls Peter "Honey" and as Rita acts strangely euphoric. The old man runs off, while the newlyweds fly to Jamaica for their honeymoon. Peter begins to suspect something is wrong with Rita; she doesn't remember how to mix drinks, is sleeping soundly, has lost all social conscience, and forgets details about her past. Worse, Rita embraces life, urging Peter to impregnate her.

Returning home, Peter's suspicions increase, though friends tell him that marriage inevitably changes people. When the "old" Rita seems to return, Peter suspects that whoever inhabits Rita's body has read her journals and is "impersonating" her. Peter encounters the old man again, who he discovers is harboring Rita's soul in his decrepit body. The old man tells Peter that their souls switched bodies during the kiss and that he is suffering from multiple ailments with only a few months to live. The two try to force the bodies to switch back, without success. Rita and the old man confess that their uncertainties caused each to envy the other at the moment of the switch, and now that they both realize they must face their own destinies without fear, their personalities switch back effortlessly. The old man accepts the inevitability of his demise, while Peter and Rita rejoice in the miracle of their love and future together.

Although audiences and critics embraced Lucas's play as a humorous, contemporary fairy tale, it has a serious philosophical underpinning, and many recognized it as a metaphor for the changes brought about by AIDS (which Lucas, who has lost numerous friends and partners to the disease, admits was his intent). Unlike many more blatant AIDS plays that have aged poorly, *Prelude to a Kiss* still resonates with audiences and continues to be performed frequently.

Douglas W. Gordy
Walnut Creek, California

PRICE, THE ARTHUR MILLER (1968)

Set in the attic of a Manhattan brownstone, *The Price* is the story of two estranged brothers' unsuccessful attempts to reconcile and put to rest the angry betrayals of the past.

Police sergeant Victor Franz and his wife, Esther, meet in the attic of a building scheduled for demolition. The building houses the remains of the Franz family belongings, stored there since the death of Victor's father 16 years before; these now must be sold. They are joined by 89-year-old furniture dealer Gregory Solomon. The unseen player in this transaction is Walter, Victor's estranged brother, now a successful surgeon.

Behind the rift dividing the two brothers is a family history of lost wealth and shattered dreams. After their father lost a fortune in the stock market crash of 1929 and their mother died, Victor, Walter, and their father lived together in this attic, part of what was once their elegant and spacious Manhattan brownstone. When their father failed to overcome his losses ("Some men just don't bounce, that's all."), Victor took care of him, while Walter left home and finished medical school. Later, financial problems forced Victor to leave college and a promising science career and take a temporary job with the police department. Walter had refused to lend Victor the money to stay in school, telling him to "ask Dad." Victor and Esther have always resented Walter for both his refusal to aid them and for his successful career.

Shortly after Victor agrees to take Solomon's offer of $1,100 for the contents of the attic, Walter arrives unexpectedly. In the 16 years since their father's death, the two brothers have rarely spoken. Victor rebuffs Walter's apparent attempts to make amends with offers of financial aid, even as Esther jumps at them. Walter really came to tell Victor the truth. Their father was not bankrupt; he had saved $4,000, a sum he revealed to Walter but not to Victor. Walter desperately needs Victor to admit that it was his choice to stay with their father. "It's a fantasy, Victor—your father was penniless and your brother a son of a bitch, and you play no part in it all," he tells him. Victor just as desperately does not want to admit he suspected the truth. "I couldn't nail him to the wall, could I? He said he had nothing! . . . Jesus, you can't leave everything out like this. The man was a beaten dog, ashamed to walk in the street, how do you demand his last buck . . .?" The play ends with neither brother able to conquer perceived past injustices; they part unreconciled. Solomon, the survivor of countless misfortunes, extends his career by buying the furniture.

The Price marks a return by MILLER to the conflicts of brother against brother and father against son that marked *ALL MY SONS* (1947) and *DEATH OF A SALESMAN* (1949). The play questions the fabric of the American Dream and explores the effect of the economy on a character's fate. In an essay on the origins of the play, Miller has said it was based partially on his feeling that, in fighting the Vietnam War, "we were fighting in a state of forgetfulness" of past history. *The Price,* he explains, "grew out of a need to reconfirm the power of the past, the seedbed of current reality, and the way to possibly reaffirm cause and effect in an insane world. It seemed to me that if, through the mists of denial, the bow of the ancient ship of reality could emerge, the spectacle might once again hold some beauty for an audience" (298).

BIBLIOGRAPHY
Miller, Arthur. *Echoes down the Corridor: Collected Essays: 1944–2000.* Edited by Steven R. Centola. New York: Viking, 2000.

Richard K. Tharp
University of Maryland

PRIDE'S CROSSING TINA HOWE (1997)

Shifting back and forth in time, *Pride's Crossing* celebrates women's spirit, resolve, and achievement, while also depicting its women compromising with patriarchy, either because of their historical era or because of constraining personal circumstances, sometimes including inner fears. The play won the New York Drama Critics' Circle Award.

Now living (with near-deafness, trenchant arthritis, and omens of cancer) in the building that was once the cottage of her wealthy Massachusetts family's chauffeur, nonagenarian Mabel Tidings Bigelow announces—to her housekeeper Vita Bright, to her old poet friend Chandler Coffin, to her visiting granddaughter Julia, and her great-granddaughter Minty—that she wants to hold an Independence Day croquet party. The women who attend, she proclaims, will wear dresses retrieved from her own grandmother's Victorian-era wardrobe.

Much of Mabel's time is spent recalling the past. Her mind flashes back to when she, as a girl on this same Massachusetts seacoast estate, often felt closer to the attentive O'Neills, her family's house servants, than to her own parents. Many people found her Brahmin father stodgy—although Mabel seems to believe that he at least challenged her to turn into the English Channel–swimmer she became. Her mother, so "wrapped up in [her] own misery," remained cold toward her daughter's feats.

During her youth, a symphony conductor adored Mabel, and she herself loved, but fled, her Channel swimming coach, the British champion David Bloom. David, she believed, would have made her feel too "swept away" by his human intensity (ironically, she later praises granddaughter Julia for marrying just such a "typhoon"-like man—even though that man, a physician as was David, now generally ignores Julia).

Instead of marrying David, Mabel wed the handsome, alcoholic, and abusively jealous ex-Harvard-quarterback Porter Bigelow. He came to incarnate for her the principle that good hearts rarely accompany good looks; to the young Mabel, however, Porter somehow had stood for "the rules"—even though her family did not completely push her toward him or firmly reject the Jewish David as a potential mate for a WASP girl. Near the end of the play, Mabel finally does spurn "the rules," urging her guests to play a fully anarchic sort of croquet game; the play's ultimate

scene, though, features her memory of her own and David's necessarily unified teamwork at the time of her 1928 Channel swim.

The play is an homage to HOWE's feminist cousins and ancestors. Howe's character, the housekeeper Vita, has a son named West; Virginia Woolf's friend Vita Sackville-West, who inspired Woolf's cross-dressing character in her novel *Orlando*, comes clearly into allusion-conscious readers' minds. Howe's play, indeed, includes some deliberate gender-bending—and Mabel's brother Frazier is sketched as being as effeminate as Mabel was tomboyish. Like Woolf, Howe seems to champion a view that all human beings are androgynous.

Jeffrey B. Loomis
Northwest Missouri State University

PRINCE OF PARTHIA, THE THOMAS GODFREY (1767)

Godfrey's play is the first drama written by an American-born playwright to be professionally produced in America. A tragedy in blank verse, it is set in ancient Parthia on the banks of the Tigris River in about 200 B.C.E. Godfrey took only the names from Parthian history, and so, although Parthia existed, the play is fiction, not history.

Godfrey probably saw and was influenced by Lewis Hallam's acting company, which arrived from England in 1752 to produce plays for the American colonial audience. In 1754, the group appeared in Philadelphia, where Godfrey—then 18—lived. Indeed, it was this company (under new management after the death of Lewis Hallam and called THE AMERICAN COMPANY) that produced his play on April 24, 1767, in Philadelphia. Godfrey, who died suddenly in 1763 of a fever at age 27, did not live to see the performance.

The play opens as the heroic Prince Arsaces enters Parthia "like shining Mars" after victorious battle; before his first entrance, Arsaces's military prowess and personal virtues are praised at length by his brother, Gotarzes, and by Phraates, an officer of their father's court. During these speeches, a third brother, Vardanes—"arrogant," "ambitious," "licentious"—is contrasted with the virtuous Arsaces.

Queen Thermusa, the wife of King Artabanus and stepmother to his three sons, seeks revenge against

Arsaces because he killed her own son, Vonones, when the latter proved to be a traitor to the king. Thermusa is joined in her hatred of Arsaces by Vardanes, who resents his older brother's status as heir to the crown: "Ye Gods! Why did ye give me such a soul, / (A soul which ev'ry way is form'd for Empire) / And damn me with a younger brother's right?" The queen is also driven by jealousy of Evanthe, who was kidnapped from Arabia by her son Vonones; everyone loves Evanthe—the queen's own husband, as well as both his sons, Arsaces and Vardanes—but Evanthe loves only the virtuous Arsaces. In short, the bitter, middle-aged queen is jealous of the beautiful, young, and popular Evanthe.

The war that has just ended was fought against Arabia, the land of Evanthe's father. Indeed, her father, Bethas, is among the captives brought into the city by the victorious Arsaces. Even before he knows the captive is the father of his beloved, Arsaces is compassionate toward him. Both men express their awareness that reversals of fortune are swift and unpredictable.

When Evanthe comes to the prison merely to seek news of her father from a countryman, she is overjoyed to find her father himself. Arsaces promises to gain Bethas's freedom from the king, which increases Evanthe's affection for him. This happy scene is witnessed by the villain Vardanes and his henchman Lysias. Vardanes's knowledge that his too-perfect big brother will get both the girl and the throne leaves him racked with agony, and he vows to defeat Arsaces or die trying.

The treacherous Vardanes deceives the king into thinking that Arsaces is plotting against him with Bethas. The king, distraught over his perceived loss of Evanthe to his son, believes Vardanes. Arsaces is imprisoned. Once he is out of the way, the king is murdered. The queen personally comes to Arsaces's cell to stab him, but she is stopped by the appearance of her husband's ghost. Evanthe is kept against her will by Vardanes, who threatens to torture and kill Arsaces in her presence if she does not submit to his lust. She appeals to his better nature, but he has none and starts to take her by force. He is interrupted by Lysias who tells him that the palace is being assaulted by the escaped Arsaces and his army. A battle ensues outside the palace.

Evanthe waits for word of her beloved's fate. Unfortunately, her confidante, Cleone, mistakes some other fallen hero for Arsaces and reports his death to Evanthe, who responds by taking poison. Evanthe dies in the arms of Arsaces, who is in fact alive and victorious; because life without her is meaningless, he stabs himself. In fact, the final scenes are something of a bloodbath: Vardanes, Lysias, the queen, the king, Bethas, the young lovers—all are dead. The third brother, Gotarzes, neither a villain nor a saint, becomes king.

The reader may be reminded of the pile of bodies at the end of Shakespeare's *Hamlet* or the pair of bodies in *Romeo and Juliet*. Indeed, throughout the play there are echoes of several of Shakespeare's plays in plot devices and phrasing; there is even the occasional Shakespearean line left intact. Certainly, Godfrey was very familiar with Shakespeare's plays, and clearly his own play is highly derivative of English drama, as was much of very early American drama. Godfrey's characters are often two-dimensional—villains purely villains, the hero too good to be true.

ARTHUR HOBSON QUINN, in his *A History of the American Drama,* suggests that Godfrey's play should not be summarily dismissed as it so often has been by historians, though neither, he believed, should it be judged by modern standards. Quinn wrote of the play: "The tragedy is based upon real human emotion. The passions of love, jealousy, hatred, and revenge, the sentiments of loyalty, pity, and terror, are fundamental and the main motive of the play shaped from these elements, the love of Arsaces and Evanthe, is naturally interwrought with the motive of self-preservation through the danger to the lives of both. These two motives, love and self-preservation, are the two motives of widest appeal to an audience, and Godfrey, with the instinct of a dramatist, selected them for his play" (22).

BIBLIOGRAPHY

Quinn, Arthur Hobson. *A History of the American Drama: From the Beginning to the Civil War.* 2d ed. 1943. New York: Appleton-Century-Crofts, 1951.

PRIZES See AWARDS.

PROCESSIONAL JOHN HOWARD LAWSON (1925)

LAWSON's second major play, *Processional* is traced to an incomplete script from 1920, written while the playwright was living as an expatriate in Paris. Completed in 1924 and produced by the THEATRE GUILD in 1925, this text stands as one of the most significant examples of modernism in the American theater.

Subtitled *a jazz symphony of American life*, *Processional* is set in West Virginia and tells the story of Jim Flimmins, a miner jailed for fighting with the soldiers brought in to crush a strike against the coal company. The play opens with the residents of the town discussing the Governor's recent edict establishing martial law, with the strikers represented by a band of would-be jazz musicians. Between crudely played jazz numbers, the strikers spar with the soldiers, led by the Sheriff and an abstract figure referred to only as "the Man in the Silk Hat."

As the play continues, Jim breaks out of jail, meets and kills a soldier, and flees to the barn where his mother is living. Hiding in a crawl space, he learns that his mother spent the night with drunken soldiers, selling herself to earn money to leave coal country. Enraged, Jim rushes out to face the men who have defiled his mother; instead, he meets Sadie, the daughter of a local shopkeeper. With the sound of soldiers approaching, Jim takes the young woman into a mine and rapes her. The soldiers, in turn, chase, catch, and blind Jim, who becomes caught on a fence.

Six months later, the soldiers have left, and the Ku Klux Klan has taken over. The Klan, led by the Man in the Silk Hat, tries Sadie, who is carrying Jim's child, and Jim's mother, and prepares to punish them for their moral offenses. Jim, now blind, enters. Chaos ensues and without warning, an announcement is made by the Man in the Silk Hat that the strike is over and that a pact will be signed without recrimination on either side. Nonetheless, in an aside, he confesses that the strike leaders will soon be murdered. The play ends with Sadie marrying Jim in a shotgun "jazz wedding," and the miners' jazz band and others march out into the audience in a noisy procession.

Structurally, *Processional* is a complex composite, including elements drawn from American popular entertainment (vaudeville and jazz music) and the European avant-garde. From vaudeville, Lawson borrows stock plot devices, routines, and situations; stereotypical characters; and the constant intrusion of popular music into the action. His interest in the vaudevillian method was rooted in his conviction, as expressed in the preface to the published play, that it offered a "partial reflection," albeit "distorted," on the state of the common worker, matrimony, class relations, and violence in the United States. Thus, his interest in vaudeville extended beyond mere commodification of that popular entertainment form. By fusing stock plot devices and characters from vaudeville with elements borrowed from other forms of artistic expression, Lawson was, instead, seeking to create a method suitable for expressing his vision of an emerging and dynamic nation. While elements from diverse forms such as EXPRESSIONISM and burlesque occasionally surface and merge with vaudeville, the most significant adjunct form is dadaism. Lawson incorporated into *Processional* the grotesque and the absurd, believing that these dadaist elements would endow his vaudeville vision of United States culture in a new and colorful way.

Jonathan L. Chambers
Bowling Green State University

PROOF DAVID AUBURN (2000)

Winner of the PULITZER PRIZE and the TONY AWARD, *Proof* deals with the at once frightening and hopeful prospect of what we will inherit of our parents' genetic makeup. Catherine is 25 and, having given up her early youth and her own education to care for her father after her mother's death, shows signs of both her late father's mathematical genius and his mental instability.

As the play begins, father Robert and daughter Catherine, both mathematicians, speak of her "depression," of his fame, of her need—as her father sees it—to get back to math to help her out of her depression, and of her fears that she will be as mentally unstable as her father. When a graduate student appears from another room, it soon becomes clear that Robert has recently died and that Catherine has been having either a fantasy or a hallucination. The graduate student, Hal, is a Ph.D. candidate in the math department where Robert once taught. He has been sorting the 103 notebooks Robert left behind, in search of some great mathematical discovery, unconvinced that a mind as brilliant as Robert's could simply "shut down"—this, despite Catherine's assurance that the notebooks contain nothing but gibberish.

When Catherine's sister Claire arrives from New York for her father's funeral, she is suspicious of Catherine's claim that there is a student named Hal; until Hal actually walks in, Claire considers it more likely that Catherine is seeing things—convinced as she is that Catherine shares their father's mental illness. After the funeral, the mourners gather at the house for drinking and music, and Hal and Catherine end up in bed together. Catherine allows Hal to see a notebook she keeps locked in a drawer. He finds there an important proof, "historic" in its significance. When Catherine reveals that it is *her* work, neither Claire nor Hal believes her.

In flashbacks, we see Robert in earlier periods: In remission four years earlier, he seems well enough for Catherine to resume her own education at 21; just six months later, it becomes clear, from the nonsense with which he fills his notebooks, that his remission has ended.

Despite what Catherine says about the proof, Claire makes arrangements for her sister to move with her to New York and undergo psychiatric treatment; on the day of their planned departure, Hal returns. He now believes Catherine, having come to the conclusion that the techniques used in the proof are too new to be Robert's work. Catherine, dissatisfied with her inelegant proof, begins at Hal's suggestion to talk him through it—and by doing so returns to life.

The play is influenced, in part, by the life story of schizophrenic mathematician John Nash, whose biography *A Beautiful Mind,* by Sylvia Nasar, was published in 1998, and who was made more famous by the 2001 film, which was very loosely based on Nasar's book. But while John Nash had sons (one of whom is a schizophrenic mathematician), Auburn's Robert had daughters, and the play focuses on the impact on a daughter of such a man, rather than on the man himself. Auburn has said that he chose to make his protagonist a woman because a man would not be expected to care for an ailing parent. Through this choice of a female protagonist, the play confronts the stereotype that suggests women are less capable of high-level math theory than men.

PROVINCETOWN PLAYERS, THE (1915–1922)

The Provincetown Players was one of the most influential of the small, subscription theater groups that sprang up across America during the first two decades of the 20th century (see LITTLE THEATER MOVEMENT). Founded in Provincetown, Massachusetts, and later transplanted to Greenwich Village, it was the only such organization exclusively devoted to producing American plays. The Players' success in developing new American playwrights, most notably EUGENE O'NEILL and SUSAN GLASPELL, has earned Provincetown its special place in American theater history as the "birthplace of American drama."

The company's singular achievements may be attributed to the visionary zeal of its founders, led by the charismatic GEORGE CRAM "Jig" COOK and including Glaspell, John Reed, Hutchins Hapgood, and Neith Boyce. Cook and company yearned for a communally created drama. They began by staging their personal conflicts (Boyce's *Constancy* [1915], which satirized a love affair between Reed and Mabel Dodge) and current cultural obsessions (Cook and Glaspell's *SUPPRESSED DESIRES* [1915], which lampooned Freudian fanaticism). In the summer of 1916, the group welcomed into their midst an unknown Eugene O'Neill, whose sea plays were ideally suited for their newly converted Wharf Theatre. In September, they organized formally as "The Provincetown Players: The Playwrights' Theatre" and rented a space at 139 Macdougal Street in New York City. They remained in Greenwich Village for the next six years, producing nearly 100 plays by 50 American writers. Besides Boyce, Cook, Reed, Glaspell, and O'Neill, the company's roster of playwrights included DJUNA BARNES, Theodore Dreiser, Wilbur Daniel Steele, Rita Wellman, Wallace Stevens, EDNA ST. VINCENT MILLAY, Alfred Kreymborg, Mike Gold, Lawrence Langner, and EDNA FERBER.

The group encouraged experimentation in their theatrical laboratory, resulting in a richly diverse repertory. Provincetown playwrights, inspired by the new European writers (Henrik Ibsen, George Bernard Shaw, August Strindberg, Maurice Maeterlinck, Anton Chekhov, John Millington Synge) but recognizing no single aesthetic authority, worked in all genres and styles, pioneering structural and stylistic features for which there was not yet a suitable critical vocabulary.

O'Neill and Glaspell, who contributed 15 and 11 plays, respectively, led the way in creativity as well as productivity. O'Neill poured human pain and poetry onto the stage in multifarious forms, from macabre melodrama (*Thirst* [1916]) to gritty naturalism (*The Dreamy Kid* [1919]) to expressionistic nightmare (*The Emperor Jones* [1920] and *The Hairy Ape* [1922]). He composed *Before Breakfast* (1916) in one long scene, *The Hairy Ape* in eight short ones. *The Emperor Jones,* a Jungian journey to racial roots, provoked controversy for its perpetuation of racist stereotypes but became the group's major critical and commercial success; African-American actor Charles Gilpin won tremendous acclaim in the leading role. *The Hairy Ape,* another of the group's outstanding successes, depicts an alienated protagonist's struggle to "belong." Both journeys end in death, and both protagonists achieve, if not nobility of character, an indisputable theatrical stature. Glaspell's notable contributions include *Trifles* (1916), an investigation of sexual oppression and gendered perceptions of justice, and *Bernice* (1919), an exploration of the psychological motivations behind a dying woman's wish to present her death as suicide. In both *Trifles* and *Bernice,* the action revolves around characters that are not represented onstage. In these plays and others, Glaspell introduces symbolic, expressionist, and surrealist undercurrents in otherwise naturalistic works. One of Glaspell's most innovative works, *The Verge* (1921), combined an expressionistic visualization with linguistic inventions that prefigure *écriture féminine.*

Committed to social as well as artistic revolution, Provincetown playwrights typically combined aesthetic innovation with radical social critique. Reed's *The Eternal Quadrangle* (1916), Steele's *Not Smart* (1916), O'Neill's *Before Breakfast,* Kreymborg's *Lima Beans* (1917), Langner's *Matinata* (1920), Floyd Dell's *King Arthur's Socks* (1916), Winthrop Parkhurst's *Getting Unmarried* (1919), and almost all the Provincetown plays by women critique conventional morality, especially as it relates to sexual relations. Glaspell's *Trifles, Woman's Honor* (1918), *Chains of Dew* (1922), and *The Verge* critique conventional gender ideology; her *Inheritors* (1921) attacks compromised democracy in postwar America. Other artistically and ideologically representative offerings include Millay's protoabsurdist antiwar fable, *Aria da Capo* (1919), Reed's postwar political cartoon, *The Peace That Passeth Understanding* (1919), Barnes's genre- and gender-defying *Three from the Earth* (1919), Florence Kiper Frank's satirical examination of feminism, eugenics, and anti-Semitism, *Gee-Rusalem* (1918), and Steele's allegorical indictment of New York's religious establishment, *Contemporaries* (1916).

The Players developed a loyal audience and garnered considerable critical attention. Due largely to the achievements of Glaspell and O'Neill, but also because of the inconsistently satisfying, yet compelling efforts of their colleagues, the company's significant influence on developing American drama was generally recognized. Excepting O'Neill, few Provincetown playwrights enjoyed commercial careers, but most of the plays were published, many became Little Theater staples, and those of O'Neill and Glaspell found international audiences. As Provincetown historian Robert Sarlós has affirmed, the impact of Provincetown playwrights is too pervasive to be conclusively charted.

BIBLIOGRAPHY

Black, Cheryl. *The Women of Provincetown: 1915–1922.* Tuscaloosa: University of Alabama Press, 2001.

Cook, George Cram. *Greek Coins.* New York: George H. Doran, 1925.

———, and Frank Shay, eds. *The Provincetown Plays.* Cincinnati: Stewart Kidd, 1921.

Deutsch, Helen, and Stella Hanau. *The Provincetown: A Story of the Theatre.* New York: Farrar and Rinehart, 1931.

Egan, Leona Rust. *Provincetown as a Stage: Provincetown, The Provincetown Players, and the Discovery of Eugene O'Neill.* Orleans, Mass.: Parnassus, 1994.

Glaspell, Susan. *The Road to the Temple.* New York: Frederick A. Stokes, 1927.

Kenton, Edna. *The Provincetown Players and the Playwrights' Theatre, 1915–1922*. Edited by Travis Bogard and Jackson R. Bryer. Jefferson, N.C.: McFarland, 2004.

Murphy, Brenda. *The Provincetown Players and the Culture of Modernity*. New York: Cambridge University Press, 2005.

Ozieblo, Barbara, ed. *The Provincetown Players: A Choice of the Shorter Works*. Sheffield, England: Sheffield Academic Press, 1994.

Sarlós, Robert Károly. *Jig Cook and the Provincetown Players: Theatre in Ferment*. Amherst: University of Massachusetts Press, 1982.

Cheryl Black
University of Missouri

PULITZER PRIZE

American journalist Joseph Pulitzer (1847–1911) established cash prizes for journalism, fiction, nonfiction, and drama in an effort to raise the standard of excellence in these areas of American letters. Born in Hungary, Pulitzer came to the United States while in his teens as a substitute for a Union army draftee during the Civil War; by age 25, he was a newspaper publisher, and by 31, he was the owner of the *St. Louis Post-Dispatch* and an emerging leader in American journalism. In both the *Post-Dispatch* and the *New York World,* which he purchased in 1883, Pulitzer exposed public and private corruption through investigative reports and editorials. He made some powerful enemies and is even thought to have engaged in some "yellow journalism" (sensational journalism with dubious factual basis) himself, but his contributions outweigh the criticisms that have been brought against him.

Perhaps the most significant and certainly the longest lasting of his contributions is the Pulitzer Prize. Pulitzer left money in his will to provide for these prizes, also stipulating that an advisory board had the power to add to or suspend categories within the spirit of his intent. Under Pulitzer's original plan, implemented in 1917, there were 13 prizes, including drama; as of 2003, there were 21 prizes awarded annually. Additions to Pulitzer's original 13 include categories in poetry, music, and photography.

The drama prize is awarded to "a distinguished play by an American author, preferably original in its source and dealing with American life." This wording was adopted in 1964, changed from "original American play, performed in New York, which shall best represent the educational value and power of the stage"; the latter had been adopted in 1929, when the phrase "in raising the standard for good morals, good taste, and good manners" was dropped.

Columbia University awards the Pulitzer Prize in drama annually on the recommendation of the Pulitzer Prize Board, which receives nominations from a committee of Pulitzer Drama Jurors, made up largely of theater critics (with rare exceptions). There have been more than a dozen years since 1917 when the award for drama was not given because no play was found worthy in the view of the judges. The award is announced each spring. For a complete list of the American plays that have been awarded the Pulitzer Prize for drama, see Appendix 1.

BIBLIOGRAPHY
Adler, Thomas P. *Mirror on the Stage: The Pulitzer Plays as an Approach to American Drama*. West Lafayette, Ind.: Purdue University Press, 1987.

Barrett, James Wyman. *Joseph Pulitzer and His World*. New York: Vanguard Press, 1941.

Bates, Douglas. *The Pulitzer Prize: The Inside Story of America's Most Prestigious Award*. New York: Carol Publishing Group, 1991.

Granberg, Wilbur J. *The World of Joseph Pulitzer*. London, New York: Abelard-Schuman, 1965.

Hohenberg, John. *The Pulitzer Diaries: Inside America's Greatest Prize*. Syracuse, N.Y.: Syracuse University Press, 1997.

Toohey, John. *A History of the Pulitzer Prize Plays*. New York: Citadel Press, 1967.

PULLMAN CAR HIAWATHA THORNTON WILDER (1931)

This one-act play, in which WILDER experimented with stage technique, takes place in a Pullman train car, represented on the stage only by chalk marks and plain wooden chairs. The play introduces the device of the Stage Manager, who directs the actions of the other characters as well as participates in the action himself, later used in Wilder's most famous play, OUR TOWN (1938). In *Pullman Car Hiawatha*, passengers in a sleeping car live out and comment on their lives. At one point, the Stage Manager directs them to think aloud, and the audience is then privy to their thoughts. Occasionally, the characters become demanding of the Stage Manager, who must then quiet these small rebellions. One passenger dies during the journey, and angels descend to collect her. Wilder also creates abstract characters representing the weather, the planets, and time, as well as portrays the very real hobo riding under the train. Wilder had seen the premiere of Luigi Pirandello's avant-garde *Six Characters in Search of an Author* in 1920, and it certainly influenced him to use the artificiality of theater as an effective way to get at authentic human experience.

QUINN, ARTHUR HOBSON (1875–1960)

Born in Philadelphia, Arthur Hobson Quinn became a prominent educator, scholar, and historian of American literature, including American dramatic literature. Quinn was educated primarily at the University of Pennsylvania, where he later taught and served as dean. At a time when American literature was not considered sufficiently serious to be a field of study at American universities, Quinn pioneered the first American Literature course at the University of Pennsylvania in 1905 and the first American Drama course in 1918. His works on drama, *A History of American Drama from the Beginning to the Civil War* (1923; revised 1943) and *A History of American Drama from the Civil War to the Present Day* (2 vols., 1927; revised 1936), remain useful sources on the early dramatic literature of the United States. His anthology, *Representative American Plays* (1917; revised 1953), was the first to make some now classic early American dramas available to the general reading public.

Quinn also wrote *Edgar Allan Poe: A Critical Biography* (1941) and was the general editor of *The Literature of the American People: An Historical and Critical Survey* (1951). Quinn's own attempt at creative writing was published in 1899, a collection of short fiction about undergraduate life, entitled *Pennsylvania Stories*.

BIBLIOGRAPHY

Quinn, Arthur Hobson. *A History of the American Drama: From the Beginning to the Civil War.* 2d ed. 1943. New York: Appleton-Century-Crofts, 1951.

———. *A History of the American Drama: From the Civil War to the Present Day.* Rev. ed. 1936. New York: Appleton-Century-Crofts, 1955.

———, ed. *Representative American Plays: From 1767 to the Present Day.* Rev. ed. 1917 New York: Appleton-Century-Crofts, 1953.

R

RABBIT HOLE David Lindsay-Abaire (2006)

This Pulitzer Prize–winning play represents a departure for David Lindsay-Abaire, who came to national attention for his wildly comic, often absurdist pieces, most notably *Fuddy Meers* (1999) and *Kimberly Akimbo* (2001). In contrast, *Rabbit Hole* is a completely realistic—more filmic than theatrical—portrait of grief. Consistent with his other plays, though, is the fact that Lindsay-Abaire has once again placed a woman in a personal world that has been upended and of which she must make sense.

Becca and Howie, a couple around age 40, have lost a son. Their only child, Danny, at age four, just eight months before the play begins, was struck by a car. Becca takes refuge in isolation and obsessive orderliness, seeking to control that which she *can* control, including getting rid of reminders of Danny. Unlike his wife, Howie finds some comfort in a support group and in experiencing all the reminders (Danny's clothes and possessions, his dog, videotapes of him, their house) that his wife would rather not see. Their very different ways of grieving strain their marriage and nearly push Howie into the arms of one of the mothers in his support group.

Becca's sister Izzy's unplanned pregnancy and her mother Nat's tactless—albeit well-intentioned—suggestions about what Becca *ought* to be doing to assuage her grief irritate Becca. She tried the support group for parents of dead children for a while and resented their platitudes about "God's plan," though

she admits she is a little jealous, too, of these people who are able to find comfort in their faith. Nat is in a position to empathize with her daughter, having lost a son herself, but Becca rejects her mother's empathy since she sees no similarity between a four-year-old innocent struck by a car and a 30-year-old heroin addict who hanged himself. However, it is Nat who is able eventually to articulate what Becca is feeling now and what both mothers will feel for the rest of their lives: "At some point it becomes bearable. . . . something you can crawl out from under. And carry around—like a brick in your pocket" and "forget . . . every once in a while," somehow not minding that you will never let go of it because "it's what you have instead of your son."

Jason, the teenage driver of the car that killed Danny, wants to meet with the child's parents. Howie finds this too difficult, but Becca finally sees Jason. He has written a story about a son looking for his dead father in holes (the "rabbit holes" of the title) in other galaxies that lead to parallel universes. Jason's view that such other worlds are "probable" in an infinite universe consoles Becca more than any religion can. He assures her there must be many versions of all of us elsewhere. She is comforted by the possibility that "this [grief-stricken Becca] is just the sad version" of her, and that "somewhere out there [she's] having a good time." The combination of her mother's reality and Jason's description of a scientific possibility bring Becca to the point where she can *begin* with Howie to "crawl out from under" crippling grief and begin to "carry" it.

In his author's note following the published play, Lindsay-Abaire cautions those who will produce the play to get the tone right: The characters are not "morose or inconsolable" but "highly functional, unsentimental, spirited and, often, funny people who are trying to maneuver their way through their grief." Any production of the play, he warns, must "avoid sentimentality and histrionics at all costs" (159). He is wise to caution directors and actors because on the printed page, it is the sadness, far more than the humor, that comes across. The self-preserving human tendency to laugh in the midst of protracted pain is as central to Lindsay-Abaire's portrait of grief in this play as are the human tendencies to assign blame, to feel guilt, and to seek *reasons* when there may be nothing but chance at work.

BIBLIOGRAPHY
Lindsay-Abaire, David. *Rabbit Hole*. New York: Theatre Communications Group, 2006.

RABE, DAVID (1940–)

David Rabe was born and raised in Dubuque, Iowa, where he won school awards for both poetry and fiction. His first play, *Chameleon,* was performed at Loras College in 1959. After graduating from Loras in 1962, he headed to Villanova University for graduate work, establishing a long-term relationship with the theater program where many of his plays were subsequently done in workshops or premiered. In 1965, he was drafted to go to Vietnam; he saw no direct combat but did collect indelible impressions that would later mark his work.

Following his return from Vietnam, Rabe burst onto the American theater scene in a cataclysmic way with productions of both The BASIC TRAINING OF PAVLO HUMMEL and STICKS AND BONES in 1971 at Joseph Papp's Public Theatre. Both plays won numerous prizes, and *Sticks and Bones* went on to Broadway and won the TONY AWARD for Best Play of the 1971–72 season.

Basic Training and *Sticks and Bones* form two parts of what has become known as Rabe's Vietnam trilogy (the third play is STREAMERS [1976]), providing a rich dramatic enactment of this turbulent period of American history. Act 1 of *Basic Training* is set in boot camp prior to departing for Vietnam. The playwright's evocation of this crucible of masculinity exhibits an intense blend of convincing realism heightened by surreal language and a flair for staged ritual. In act 2, the action moves to Vietnam, where Pavlo ends up dying ignominiously in a brothel.

Sticks and Bones became even more controversial. Set in the quintessential middle-American home of Ozzie and Harriet Nelson, of 1950s television fame, the play directs its satire at smug American clichés about family, war, and morality. David, the older Nelson son, has returned from service in Vietnam, not only blind but also suffering from frightening nightmares and profound alienation from an American society oblivious to his suffering and pain. He also laments the separation from his Vietnamese girlfriend, Zung, whom Ozzie denounces as a "yellow whore."

In *In the Boom Boom Room* (1973) and *The Orphan* (1974), Rabe branched out in more experimental directions. Unlike his other plays, *Boom Boom Room* features a female protagonist and for the first time explores issues of sexual identity and commodification. The play ends with a striking ritual of dance, masking, and imprisonment. In *The Orphan,* Rabe combines three stories from ancient Greek sources—the killing of Iphigenia, the return of Agamemnon, and the revenge of Orestes. The characters wear contemporary clothing and speak a diction of mixed classic and contemporary idioms.

In *Streamers* (1976), Rabe returns to the Vietnam War theme in what has since become an American classic. Again set in army boot camp, the play examines masculinity under the pressures of race, homosexuality, and a desire for self-definition and control. The characterization is richer and more convincing than in the earlier plays, and *Streamers* achieves the perfect form for the searing emotional confusion that has become Rabe's trademark. The play won multiple honors, including the New York Drama Critics' Circle Award for Best American Play of 1976.

HURLYBURLY (1984) likewise portrays masculinity under duress, centering on four aging males in the decadent shadow of Hollywood, divorced or estranged from their wives and girlfriends. The stakes are now higher, and addictions of various kinds threaten and derail them. Yet *Hurlyburly* is also wonderfully funny—Rabe's finest effort in the comedic mode—managing to achieve a powerful blend of both humor and tragedy.

Rabe's other plays include *Goose and Tomtom* (1982), a not-very-funny gangster comedy in the mode of Harold Pinter and DAVID MAMET, and *Those the River Keeps* (1991), a companion piece to *Hurlyburly*. *A Question of Mercy* (1997) focuses on a gay couple struggling to deal with impending death from AIDS. The central, affecting dilemma involves the right to choose one's own death and the obligations of the narrator, a doctor, to help or prevent assisted suicide. In May 2003, *The Black Monk,* his adaptation of Anton Chekhov's story of the same name, premiered at the Yale Repertory Theater in New Haven, Connecticut.

Rabe's most recent original play, *The Dog Problem* (2001), synthesizes elements evident in the playwright's earlier work. Act 1 features the clipped, mysterious, gangster-inflected absurdist argot of David Mamet, focused on an alleged sexual ménage-à-trois with a dog. Act 2 spins off into more psychic territory, as a passing priest is dragooned into hearing confession, and the climax turns on questions of sin and retribution in a darkly comic world reminiscent of *Hurlyburly*. (A 2006 feature film of the same name bears no clear relation to Rabe's play.)

In addition to writing plays, Rabe has worked as a journalist at the *New Haven Register* and has written successful screenplays for *I'm Dancing As Fast As I Can* (1981) and *Casualties of War* (1989) and novels, such as *The Crossing Guard* (1994) and *Recital of the Dog* (2000). In recent years Rabe has withdrawn from the world of theater and writes primarily fiction. His latest novel, *Dinosaurs on the Roof,* was published in 2008.

David Rabe's Vietnam trilogy remains the most profound stage treatment of this deeply conflicted period of American history. *Streamers* and *Hurlyburly* are most likely to endure as masterpieces that enact masculine confusion in a time of profound social change. Rabe's plays embody the intense drive to understand and articulate pain and to achieve some kind of viable selfhood, a quest searingly theatrical and deeply tied to rituals of initiation. His emotion-ally dense blend of realism and surrealism, poetry and pop-rock has energized American theater and ensured his place as an important dramatist of the period.

BIBLIOGRAPHY

Kolin, Philip C. *David Rabe: A Stage History and A Primary and Secondary Bibliography.* New York: Garland, 1988.
Rabe, David. *The Dog Problem.* New York: Samuel French, 2002.
———. *Goose and Tomtom.* New York: Grove Press, 1986.
———. *"Hurlyburly" and "Those the River Keeps": Two Plays by David Rabe.* New York: Grove Press, 1995.
———. *In the Boom Boom Room.* Rev. ed. New York: Grove Press, 1986.
———. *A Question of Mercy.* New York: Grove Press, 1998.
———. *Recital of the Dog.* New York: Grove Atlantic, 2000.
———. *Those the River Keeps.* New York: Grove Weidenfeld, 1991.
———. *The Vietnam Plays.* 2 vols. New York: Grove Press, 1993.
Zinman, Toby Silverman, ed. *David Rabe: A Casebook.* New York: Garland, 1991.

David Radavich
Eastern Illinois University

RACHEL ANGELINA WELD GRIMKÉ (1916)   The only completed play by Grimké, *Rachel* focuses on the social problem of racism, but it offers no solution. In it, a young African-American woman rejects marriage and maternity because she is unwilling to bring more children into a world that will persecute them.

Angelina Weld Grimké—not to be confused with her great-aunt, the abolitionist and women's rights advocate, Angelina Grimké Weld, after whom she was named—was a teacher, poet, and playwright; she is associated with key figures from the Harlem Renaissance, and her poetry is included in anthologies compiled by LANGSTON HUGHES and Countee Cullen. Grimké was educated at Cushing Academy in Ashburnham, Massachusetts, and Girls' Latin School in Boston, and in 1902 she graduated from the Boston Normal School of Gymnastics. She immediately began teaching physical education at Armstrong Manual Training School in Washington, D.C., but in 1907, she transferred to the more academic M Street High School (later Dunbar High School), where she had a career as an English teacher until 1926. She published short stories, poems, and essays in journals throughout the 1920s. An ardent advocate of women's rights, Grimké also worked with Margaret Sanger on Sanger's journal, *Birth Control Review.* Though the preferred theme of her poetry was love, a good deal of Grimké's other writing deals with race; this is true of *Rachel* and of her one other play, "Mara," which, like *Rachel,* touches on the subject of lynching. "Mara" was never produced or published.

Rachel, a three-act play, which was commissioned by the NAACP (of which Grimké's father was an executive officer), was first produced in 1916 by the NAACP Drama Committee at the Myrtill Miner Normal School in Washington, D.C. The committee was interested in commissioning a work to counter the view presented in the film *The Birth of a Nation* (1915), in which—among other distortions—the lynch mobs of the post–Civil War Ku Klux Klan are portrayed as heroic. Alain Locke, African-American educator and intellectual, wrote in *Plays of Negro Life* (an anthology edited by Locke and Montgomery Gregory and published in 1927) that *Rachel* was "apparently the first successful drama written by a Negro and interpreted by Negro actors."

At the center of the play is Rachel Loving, who lives with her mother and brother in a New York City tenement. In act 1, when Rachel is a teenager, Mrs. Loving, a seamstress, reveals to Rachel and her brother Tom that their half-brother and their father, a newspaper editor who had spoken out against the lynching of an innocent man, were lynched by a mob 10 years earlier. While Tom responds with anger, Rachel considers the misery that lies ahead for African-American children who face a life of racism and violent persecution: "[I]t would be more merciful to strangle the little things at birth," she laments. Rachel has a particular love for children and has befriended a child, Jimmy, on the stairs of the tenement on that very day. Act 2 begins four years later. Both Tom and Rachel Loving have earned college degrees, but neither is able to find a job "because [their] skins are dark," while white men whose "hands . . . are red with blood" are destined to "succeed." Rachel has adopted Jimmy, whose parents have died. Jimmy returns from school to tell Rachel

that boys threw stones at him and called him "nigger"; Rachel is tormented by her inability to protect him from racism and cries out, "I swear that no child of mine shall ever lie upon my breast, for I will not have it rise up, in the terrible days that are to be, and call me cursed." In act 3, one week later, she rejects the marriage proposal of John Strong, vowing never to marry and bring more African-American children into the world to suffer; instead, she will take care of children—like Jimmy—who are already in the world.

BIBLIOGRAPHY

Grimké, Angelina Weld. *Selected Works of Angelina Weld Grimké.* Edited by Carolivia Herron. New York: Oxford University Press, 1991.

Hull, Gloria T. *Color, Sex and Poetry: Three Women Writers of the Harlem Renaissance.* Bloomington: Indiana University Press, 1987.

Locke, Alain, and Montgomery Gregory, eds. *Plays of Negro Life.* 1927. New York: Negro University Press, 1968.

RADIO GOLF Augustus Wilson (2005)   *Radio Golf* completed August Wilson's 10-play cycle chronicling the African-American experience in the 20th century. Set in 1997, it is the last chronologically; it was also the last Wilson wrote. The play premiered at Yale Repertory Theatre on April 22, 2005, just five months before Wilson's death from liver cancer on October 2 of that year.

As the play begins, Harmond Wilks is moving into his new real estate development office in the Hill District of Pittsburgh with the help of his wife, Mame, who is in public relations. They discuss his upcoming run for mayor. Both are in their late 40s; both are successful, middle-class African Americans. Unlike Mame, Harmond feels an affinity with the Hill District, which he and his partner (and college roommate) Roosevelt Hicks, are on the brink of developing into a gentrified urban site that will include Whole Foods and Starbucks and high-end apartments. Harmond would like his campaign office to be located here, but practical Mame argues that the current population is small and that the low-income residents do not often vote. Soon Roosevelt arrives, complaining about parking his car in this neighborhood, where he may lose its radio and wheels to thieves.

The partners need federal funding to fully realize their redevelopment project. To get these funds the city has to declare the area "blighted"; the two men await that designation with some confidence, but they have already invested significant personal assets getting the project through its preconstruction stages, so they are past the point of rescinding the deal. Into this situation comes an old man who starts to paint one of the condemned houses within the section slated for demolition.

The house is 1839 Wylie, which those familiar with Wilson's work will recognize as Aunt Ester's address. Aunt Ester is the more than 300-year-old offstage wise woman in *Two Trains Running* (1990), set in the 1960s, and in *King Hedley II* (2001), set in the 1980s, and the slightly younger onstage character in *Gem of the Ocean* (2003), set in 1904. In *Gem,* we learn that there has been more than one Aunt Ester, custodian of the African-American collective memory. *Radio Golf* is in a sense a sequel to *Gem of the Ocean* (in *Gem* we come to understand that Black Mary will take on the role and name of Aunt Ester when the older woman dies). The old man in *Radio Golf* who arrives and begins to paint 1839 Wylie is in fact the son of Black Mary/Aunt Ester and Citizen Barlow (also a character in *Gem*); the old man's name is Elder Joe Barlow, and eventually he and Harmond Wilks realize that they are related: Caesar Wilks (see *Gem of the Ocean*) was Harmond Wilks's grandfather and Joe Barlow's uncle. This realization does not take place until well into the play. In the meantime "Old Joe" keeps turning up like a guilty conscience.

Joe is a comical character who seems like a dithery old man, but he has a simple approach to life that is wise in its way—and exasperating to the college-educated set. One character who understands him is Sterling, whom Joe hires to help him paint the house. Sterling is an important character from *Two Trains Running*; it is Sterling who in that play breaks into the butcher shop, in defiance of the law but in the name of what is right, and takes the ham that is owed to Hambone (see *Two Trains Running*). Sterling is now a carpenter because nearly 30 years ago Aunt Ester told him to put down "feeling sorry for [him]self" and "carry some tools" instead. People think he is simple,

but, like Joe, he merely sees things in terms of his own experience ("They handed me a test and I turned it in blank. If you had seventeen dollars and you bought a parrot for twelve dollars how many dollars would you have left? Who the hell gonna spend twelve dollars on a parrot? What you gonna do with it? Do you know how many chickens you can buy for twelve dollars? They thought I didn't know the answer."). Sterling is outraged that Harmond and Roosevelt plan to tear down the house of the legendary Aunt Ester. He is ready to do battle over it if necessary.

Old Joe maintains that the house belongs to him. It has been empty for the 12 years since his mother died, but he never sold it. Harmond explains that the city took it for back taxes and that he bought it from the city. He tells Joe it would have been posted in the paper before it went to auction. This means nothing to Joe, who simply wants to paint his house so his daughter can live in it. Eventually, Harmond finds out that the auction notification never did appear in the paper because he bought the house through a back—and not-quite-legal—channel. He tries to give Joe $10,000 for his house, but the old man, having no intention of vacating, refuses it.

Harmond takes Sterling's advice and goes inside the house himself. He is awestruck by the craftsmanship of the interior; the woodwork has carvings of "faces" and "[a]n old language." Already more inclined than his partner and his wife to respect the Hill District, Harmond gets an injunction to stop the demolition and reimagines the development with the old house as its centerpiece. As he does in *The Piano Lesson* (1990), Wilson here sets up a conflict between honoring the past through preservation and progressing into the future at the expense of history. Mame and Roosevelt think Harmond has lost his mind, but Harmond wants to do "right" ("I'm afraid you look away from what's right too long you won't turn back."). Because Harmond has notified the press of the real estate "backroom dealings over the years" that he has been a party to, his run for mayor is probably a dead issue, and Mame has lost a promised job doing PR for the governor's office. Angry and disappointed, she deserts her husband's campaign and will have nothing to do with the fight over the house. Furthermore,

Roosevelt, with the backing of Bernie Smith, a wealthy white entrepreneur, decides to buy Harmond out of their company because the charter allows him to do so if his partner jeopardizes the business. Incensed when he hears that the white Smith will be brought in to reap the benefits of their work, Harmond calls Roosevelt the "shuffling grinning nigger in the woodpile."

At the end of this scene, which is also the end of the play, Harmond leaves his office with a can of paint that Sterling has left, ready to do battle for Aunt Ester's house and all that it symbolizes. Harmond has lost a great deal, but he is the typical Wilson hero—he gets "right" with himself and he also reestablishes his connection to the past—to his newly found cousin Joe and to the history-laden house whose value he now recognizes. At the end he goes off to fight for what is right—fairness to Joe and preservation of the past; these are Wilsonian principles.

The conflict between Harmond and Roosevelt is the conflict between two very different ways of relating to the white world. Earlier in the play Roosevelt is invited by Bernie Smith, who needs a black face for a radio deal so that he can get a "Minority Tax Certificate" to buy into a radio station. (Roosevelt will later have a golf show on this radio station; golf is both Roosevelt's obsession and his entree into the white business world.) Harmond is upset that his friend would allow himself to be thus used. Roosevelt argues that there was a time when black men were not even "at the table" in such a deal. Instead they "opened the door. . . . shined the shoes. . . . served the drinks." Now he is doing business "the way it's done in America" so that next time he can be "at the head of the table." However, neither Harmond nor Sterling accept this line of reasoning. They represent the opposite—indeed, Wilson's—view. They believe that Roosevelt's behavior perpetuates the inequity between the races. Sterling calls Roosevelt a "Negro"; he tells him, that "a Negro . . . thinks he's a white man. It's Negroes like you who hold us back. . . . You go around kissing the white man's ass then when they see me they think I'm supposed to kiss it too."

Wilson looks at the state of race in America at the end of the 20th century and concludes that, as in the beginning of the century, racism persists, but, in Wilson's view, because of tokenism in business and entertainment, whites can claim they are not "prejudiced." Harmond addresses this with vehement sarcasm in the final scene: "We got a black CEO. The head of our department is black. We couldn't possibly be prejudiced. . . . We got a black guy works in management. Twenty-four million blacks living in poverty but it's their fault. Look, we got a black astronaut. I just love Oprah."

In an interview with fellow PULITZER PRIZE–winning playwright SUZAN-LORI PARKS, Wilson commented on his intentions in writing *Radio Golf*:

> One of the things with *Radio Golf* is that I realized I had to in some way deal with the black middle class, which for the most part is not in the other nine plays. My idea was that the black middle class seems to be divorcing themselves from [the larger black] community, making their fortune on their own without recognizing or acknowledging their connection to the larger community. And I thought: We have gained a lot of sophistication and expertise and resources, and we should be helping that community, which is completely devastated by drugs and crime and the social practices of the past hundred years of the country.

Radio Golf won the New York Drama Critics' Circle Award.

BIBLIOGRAPHY
Wilson, August. Interview with Suzan-Lori Parks. *American Theatre* (Nov. 2005). Available online. URL: http://www.tcg.org/publications/at/Nov05/wilson.cfm. Accessed Sept. 4, 2008.

RAINMAKER, THE N. RICHARD NASH (1954)

A romantic comedy set in a *"western state on a summer day in a time of drought,"* The Rainmaker is the story of a capable but "plain" woman of 27 who discovers her own beauty in the eyes of a traveling con man who promises to bring rain.

Lizzie Curry is a spirited young woman, who lives with and keeps house for her father and brothers. Her father, H. C., has tried to find her a husband, but *"no man outside the family has loved"* her or *"found [her] beautiful."* H. C. and his sons, Noah and Jim, try to invite the sheriff's deputy, File, a divorced man, for dinner, but File—though he likes Lizzie—senses a matrimonial trap and refuses their invitation. Meanwhile, Lizzie has fixed herself up and made a prize-winning dinner. Chance brings another man to take File's seat at the table when Bill Starbuck comes to the Currys' door. Starbuck is a charmer and a charlatan; the family pragmatists, Lizzie and Noah, see through him instantly. When Starbuck claims he can bring rain, H. C. decides to take a chance on him and pays him $100 to try. The simpleminded Jim is enthusiastic and readily accepts the job of beating Starbuck's drum as part of the rainmaking ritual. It later becomes clear that H. C.'s motivation has less to do with rain than with his daughter: He thinks Starbuck might be Lizzie's last chance.

When Starbuck directs H. C. to paint white arrows on the ground outside the house, Lizzie tells her father that she is ashamed of him for letting a man make a fool of him. His response is as much a comment on her life as it is an answer to her question: "I gotta take a chance on him—the whole chance—without fear of gettin' hurt or gettin' cheated or gettin' laughed at—As far as he'll take me." Lizzie's fierce independence and guarded stance when it comes to men prevent her—in her father's view—from getting what she wants, which is love and a family of her own. File too is guarded and independent; having been deserted by his wife, he has lost his faith in all women and guards against being made a fool of a second time.

When Lizzie later takes Starbuck some bedding for the night, he kisses her and convinces her that she *is* beautiful. Soon File and the sheriff come to the Curry ranch to arrest Starbuck, who is wanted in two states. The Currys talk them into letting Starbuck go. As he is leaving, he asks Lizzie to join him, but File finally says to Lizzie the words he was too proud to say to his ex-wife: *"Don't go!!!"* Lizzie chooses File with whom she can be herself rather than a dream of Starbuck's, and it begins to rain.

The Rainmaker was Nash's most successful play. He also wrote the book for the musical adaptation, *110 in the Shade* (1963), music by Harvey Schmidt and lyrics by Tom Jones. His other plays of note are *The Second Best Bed* (1946), a comedy about Anne Hathaway and William Shakespeare, and *Young and Fair* (1948), set in a Boston girls' school.

RAISIN IN THE SUN, A Lorraine Hansberry (1959)

The first play by an African-American woman to be produced on Broadway, Lorraine Hansberry's groundbreaking drama was also among the very first widely seen plays to put a human face on the victims of racism in pre–Civil Rights movement America. *A Raisin in the Sun* won the New York Drama Critics' Circle Award for best play of its season—the first by an African American (of either gender) to do so.

Lena Younger, a widow, lives in a Chicago tenement with her daughter Beneatha, a college student; her son, Walter Lee, a chauffeur; and Walter Lee's wife, Ruth, and son, Travis. Ruth is pregnant and is making secret plans to have an abortion rather than bring another child into their overcrowded apartment. Big Walter's death has left the family with an insurance payment, with which Lena plans to buy a house and rescue her family from the stifling environment of urban poverty. Her revelation to the family that she has put a down payment on a house in suburban Clybourne Park destroys Walter Lee's hope of investing in a liquor store (a plan that Lena already opposes on moral grounds). Walter Lee is at first angry and then, increasingly, depressed, failing to report to work and spending his time in a bar or on the street. Fearing that she is "doing to [Walter] what the rest of the world been doing to" him, Lena asks him to put aside $3,000 of the remaining insurance money in an account for Beneatha's medical school tuition, then to take charge of the rest.

On moving day, Mr. Lindner, a representative of Clybourne Park, comes to dissuade the Youngers from moving into his white neighborhood; he attempts to pay them off, and when an indignant Walter Lee tells him to "get out," Lindner asks why they want to live where they "just aren't wanted," and implies that it might be dangerous to do so. (Hansberry's own family had been the first African-American family in a white suburb and had met a similar reaction. In 1940,

Hansberry's father, a Chicago real estate broker, successfully fought this type of discrimination all the way to the United States Supreme Court [*Hansberry vs. Lee*]; however, the outlawing of racially restrictive covenants did not stop the practice for years to come.)

Later that same day Bobo, Walter Lee's friend, comes to the apartment to break the news to Walter Lee that their associate, Willie, has disappeared with the money they hoped to invest in the liquor store. Distraught, Walter Lee confesses to his family that he has lost all the money, even Beneatha's tuition, which he never deposited in the bank. Mama begins to *"beat him senselessly in the face,"* recalling that her husband worked all his life "like somebody's old horse . . . killing himself" and Walter gave "it all away in a day."

Walter arranges for Mr. Lindner to return, intending to accept Lindner's payoff for staying out of the white neighborhood. To Mama, such an act is undertaken only by one who is "dead inside": It is accepting money that is "a way of telling us we wasn't fit to walk the earth." When Lindner arrives, Mama makes Travis stay near his father, and she instructs Walter to teach his son well, as Willie has taught him. Ultimately, Walter declines Lindner's offer a second time, explaining that theirs is a "proud" family. At that moment, his mother remarks to Ruth, "He finally come into his manhood, today, didn't he? Kind of like the rainbow after the rain."

A central metaphor in the play is the plant that barely survives on the kitchen windowsill, but that Lena lovingly tends and to which she compares her children: "They got spirit," she tells Ruth, "[l]ike this little old plant that ain't never had enough sunshine or nothing," hanging on with the help of Lena's constant nurturing. In the final moment of the play, Lena returns to the apartment, *"grabs her plant,"* and exits.

Two characters in the play represent positions in African-American culture at the time. They are Beneatha's boyfriends. George Murchison, "rich" and "snobbish," aspires to white middle-class values and style (he is Walter Lee's choice for his sister). Joseph Asagai, an African exchange student, teaches Beneatha to love her ethnic beauty, giving her a Nigerian dress and inspiring her to stop straightening her hair. For Beneatha, the most important distinction between the two men is that George is amused by her plan to become a doctor, while Joseph embraces her dream.

The title, a phrase from Langston Hughes's poem, "A Dream Deferred," suggests the potentially devastating despair Walter Lee experiences when his dream of investing in the liquor store dies ("What happens to a dream deferred? / Does it dry up / Like A Raisin in the Sun? / Or fester like a sore"). The allusion also suggests the hope inherent in Walter Lee's act of expelling Mr. Lindner and thereby securing—rather than deferring—the family's dream of a decent home.

BIBLIOGRAPHY

Domina, Lynn, ed. *Understanding "A Raisin in the Sun": A Student Casebook to Issues, Sources, and Historical Documents.* Westport, Conn.: Greenwood Press, 1998.
Kappel, Lawrence, ed. *Readings on "A Raisin in the Sun."* New York: Greenhaven Press, 2000.

REBECK, THERESA (1959?–   ) Raised in Ohio, playwright Theresa Rebeck was educated at Notre Dame (B.A., 1980) and at Brandeis University, where she earned an M.F.A. in Playwriting and a Ph.D. focusing on Victorian melodrama. A prolific writer in several genres, including television, film, and fiction, as well as drama, Rebeck has written more than 25 plays.

One of her earliest, *Sunday on the Rocks,* was first presented at the International Women in Theatre Conference in 1987, but it was the 1994 Boston production that started to bring Rebeck to the attention of audiences and critics. In the play, four women housemates, on an autumn morning, drink and discuss the difficulty of arriving at moral certainty in the modern world. A film version, its screenplay by the playwright, was released in 2004.

Other early full-length plays include *Spike Heels* (1990), a comedy about gender and power, featuring a secretary, her mild-mannered neighbor, and her sleazy boss; *Loose Knit* (1993), a satire in which a knitting circle of five New Yorkers make sweaters as their relationships with men knit together and unravel; *The Family of Mann* (1994), an acerbic look at the manufacture of television shows; *View of the Dome* (1996), about a naïve young attorney and her law school mentor who runs for office in Washington, where, inevitably, power corrupts; *Abstract Expression* (1998), in which an artist, who is a vile human being to everyone including the daughter who cares for him and the son who loathes him, dies and thereby increases the value of his abstract paintings; *The Butterfly Collection* (2000), which takes place over a weekend at the country house of a famous writer, where the conflict between this self-important novelist and his equally self-important actor son is endured by the rest of the family, a guest, and the novelist's new young assistant, to whom both men are attracted; and *DollHouse* (2001), Rebeck's contemporary reworking of Ibsen's *A Doll's House*.

Rebeck has also written many short plays, including these one-acts from the 1990s: *Sex with a Censor, What We're Up Against, Katie and Frank, The Contract,* and *Great to See You.* Her 10-minute plays, most of them written for the annual Boston Theater Marathon, include *Late Arrival* (1999), *The First Day* (2000), *Josephina* (2001), *Art Appreciation* (2002), and *The Actress* (2003).

In 2003 Rebeck won the WILLIAM INGE Festival New Voices Playwriting Award. Since that honor, her output has continued to be substantial. *Omnium Gatherum* (2003), written with Alexandra Gersten-Vassilaros for the HUMANA FESTIVAL of New American Plays at the Actors Theatre of Louisville, is both a comedy of manners and a darker satire of the post–9/11 political climate. At a fashionable New York dinner party, discussion of terrorism and American foreign policy along with pretentious talk of the food and wine seethe and ebb while just outside lurks an apocalyptic vision. *Bad Dates* (2004) is a one-woman comedy about a single mother who, after happening into a successful career in the restaurant business, returns to the trials of dating. *The Bells* (2005), a murder mystery set in the Yukon Territory during the Gold Rush, is an adaptation of the 19th-century melodrama *The Bells* (1871) by Leopold Lewis, who in turn closely adapted it from a French play, *Le Juif Polonais* (*The Polish Jew*) by Erckmann-Chatrian. Rebeck's aim with *The Bells* was to raise melodrama to the level of metaphor as she considers humans in the literal and figurative wilderness.

In 2006, Rebeck had three plays premiering in three cities. *The Water's Edge* (2006) premiered OFF-BROADWAY in New York; it is a tragedy in which, almost two decades after his young daughter has drowned while in his care, a man returns to his wife and adult children (along with his new young girlfriend) and faces the brunt of their bitterness and devastation. *Mauritius* (2006) premiered in Boston; in it, two sisters fight over their inheritance—a valuable stamp collection. As one wants to sell and the other to preserve it, unscrupulous dealers and a long-suffering stamp expert complicate matters. The title refers to the two most valuable stamps in the collection which are from the island of Mauritius. The play's dominant metaphor is the stamps themselves: It is their flaws that give them value. *The Scene* (2006) premiered in Louisville at the Humana Festival; it is a sharply funny play in which a sexy party girl and opportunist from Ohio seduces men on the Manhattan party circuit and wreaks havoc in the life of a married actor. Theater critic John Simon praised Rebeck's use of language in his review of the 2007 New York production: "[I]t is the writing that triumphs in the all important details. There are frantic sentence fragments, stammering reiterations, dragged-out burbles, and every current noncommunicative cliché sovereignly ridiculed."

While many of her plays are in production around the country, her most recent new work includes a comedy about theater, *The Understudy* (2008), as well as her first novel, *Three Girls and Their Brother* (2008), which skewers America's celebrity culture.

Rebeck resents the assumptions that are often made about "women playwrights" and their allegedly limited worldview. She writes in the introduction to her *Complete Plays: 1989–1998,* "I am a feminist in that I believe that women are as fully human as men and that their experiences are as worthy of representation, as universally significant, as men's. I believe that the hero's journey is both male and female. I believe that, as a rule, women are as deeply flawed as men are. I'm interested in writing about the way both genders make mistakes and the ways we grow, or don't grow" (2).

Like many contemporary playwrights, Rebeck earns a good living writing for television (and, in her case, also acting as executive producer for some of the television shows for which she writes, e.g., *Law and Order: Criminal Intent* and *Canterbury's Law*) but prefers to write for the stage, where, among other advantages, a writer has more control over his or her work.

BIBLIOGRAPHY

Rebeck, Theresa. *Complete Plays: 1989–1998*. New York: Smith and Kraus, 1999.

———. *The Complete Plays Volume II: 1999–2007*. New York: Smith and Kraus, 2007.

———. *Complete Plays Volume III: Short Plays 1989–2005*. New York: Smith and Kraus, 2007.

———. *Free Fire Zone: A Playwright's Adventures on the Creative Battlefields of Film, TV, and Theater*. New York: Smith and Kraus, 2007.

Simon, John. "Heaton, Shalhoub Fire Up Caustic Domestic Comedy." Available online. URL: http://www.bloomberg.com. Accessed June 11, 2008.

RIBMAN, RONALD (1932–)

Poet and playwright Ronald Ribman was born in New York City and educated at Brooklyn College and the University of Pittsburgh, where he earned a Ph.D. in English in 1962. Starting out as a poet, Ribman became involved in theater later in his career. His plays are both serious and experimental, often emerging as engaging tragicomedies. Influenced by American poet Wallace Stevens, Ribman is frequently thought to exhibit both Beckettian and absurdist tendencies in his plays, whose settings range from a hospice to a penitentiary, from England during the Middle Ages to Germany in the late 1950s.

In most of Ribman's dramatic works, human cruelty and heartlessness fill the stage. Ribman's works include grotesque characters and images of loss, anguish, and death portrayed in a decaying world. His first play, *Harry, Noon and Night* (1965), produced OFF-BROADWAY, deals with the altercation between Harry, an American Jew, and Immanuel, a German Jew. The argument between these two characters ends with Harry's arrest for murder. The play's provocative opening scene involving a prostitute being kissed and fondled by two men caused some controversy at the time. Ribman's next play is an adaptation of Ivan Turgenev's short story, "The Diary of a Superfluous Man,"

entitled *The Journey of the Fifth Horse* (1966), and portrays the life of Zoditch, a lonely publishing-house reader who becomes progressively obsessed with a dream world through reading a diary. He comes to believe that he is the reflection of the diarist even though they have lived in different epochs. Stuart W. Little, in his history of Off-Broadway theater, maintains that these "two plays established the young Ribman as literarily the most exciting new dramatist at work in the theater, more imaginative, more skillful, and more poetic in his writing than any of his contemporaries" (237).

Considered one of Ribman's best one-act plays, *The Burial of Esposito* (1969) is a melodrama about an Italian barber mourning the death of his son who was killed in Vietnam. The play was performed with two other one-acts: *The Son Who Hunted Tigers in Jakarta*, about the encounter between a couple and the burglar who enters their bedroom at night, and *Sunstroke*, about an eager Peace Corps volunteer whose assignment is not what he expected. The three one-acts appeared under the collective title *Passing Through from Exotic Places*.

A sense of loss pervades Ribman's plays. *The Ceremony of Innocence* (1967) takes place in medieval England and follows King Ethelred's refusal to fight the Danes, his long-time foes. Although his family and his lords advise him to fight, he does not, and, consequently, the Danes kill Ethelred's son and the king is left alone. *The Poison Tree* (1976) is set in an American prison where a black convict chokes a white guard to death. Resentful of the convict, the dead guard's companion, Di Santis, manages to provoke the black prisoner's suicide. Di Santis is finally murdered while the prisoners watch and do nothing to prevent his death.

Cold Storage (1977) portrays a conversation in a hospital roof garden between two men who suffer from cancer. During their confrontation, Richard Landau, a secretive investment adviser who escaped the Holocaust when he was a child, and Parmigian, a stormy complainer, talk about their existence, their pasts, and their illness and imminent death. Even though these characters try to ascertain the cause of their suffering and, indeed, the meaning of their lives, the play ends without hope.

In *Buck* (1983), Ribman depicts his views about television violence through Buck Halloran, a television producer, director, and writer who makes cheap sensational cable movies about crime and violence using real prostitutes and pimps off the streets. He becomes obsessed with watching television murders and imagines how he would kill his wife and her lover. In *The Rug Merchants of Chaos* (1991) Ribman attempts to show that the way to achieve internal peace is by accepting that life is erratic and uncertain. His most recent work, *Dream of the Red Spider* (1993), premiered at the American Repertory Theatre in Cambridge, Massachusetts (a theater at which Ribman's *Sweet Talk at the Richelieu* [1987] and *The Cannibal Masque* and *A Serpent's Egg* [1987] also had their world premieres). The plays of Ronald Ribman are still performed occasionally around the country.

BIBLIOGRAPHY

Little, Stuart W. *Off-Broadway: The Prophetic Theater.* New York: Coward, McCann, and Geoghegan, 1972.

Ribman, Ronald. *Five Plays by Ronald Ribman.* New York: Avon, 1978.

———. *Passing Through From Exotic Places.* New York: Dramatists Play Service, 1970.

———. *"The Rug Merchants of Chaos" and Other Plays.* New York: Theatre Communications Group, 1992.

Estefania Olid-Peña
Georgia State University

RICE, ELMER (1892–1967)

Elmer Rice (born Elmer Reizenstein) was an important playwright and man of the theater for nearly five decades. Born to a poor Jewish family in New York, he left high school for a job after two years. He earned a high school diploma by passing equivalency exams and attended the New York Law School at night; he graduated cum laude in 1912, with admittance to the New York State bar in 1913, but decided he did not want to practice law.

With a friend, Frank W. Harris, Reizenstein had written two unproduced plays, but his first great success was *On Trial* (1914). Reizenstein simply left copies at two producers' offices, and both asked him to come in within 48 hours. The play was innovative with respect to form because of its use of flashbacks and reverse narrative. On opening night, Reizenstein was offered $30,000 for the rights, which he wisely turned down; he went on to make more than $100,000 from the play.

Already theatrically successful, Reizenstein then studied drama at Columbia University with Hatcher Hughes, with whom he collaborated on the play *Wake Up, Jonathan* (1921); by this time, he had changed his name to Rice. He also collaborated with Dorothy Parker (*Close Harmony* [1924]) and PHILIP BARRY (*Cock Robin* [1927]). He was the solo author of the frequently anthologized *The ADDING MACHINE* (1923), an expressionistic satire on the dehumanization of "Mr. Zero" by technology. (A brilliant musical version premiered in Chicago in 2007 with music by Joshua Schmidt and libretto by Jason Loewith and Schmidt.) Less well known but regarded more highly by some critics, *The Subway* (1929) mingles EXPRESSIONISM and naturalism in the dramatization of the seduction and suicide of the working-class Sophie.

Also in 1929, Rice premiered his best play, *STREET SCENE,* for which he received the PULITZER PRIZE. One of the finest examples of naturalism in American drama, *Street Scene* focuses on the lives of inhabitants in a New York City tenement. Despite the melodramatic plot involving Frank Maurrant's murder of his adulterous wife Anna, the play's portrayal of ethnic tension, poverty, ignorance, and the violence attendant on them made it both a critical and commercial success. A musical version, with music by Kurt Weill and lyrics by LANGSTON HUGHES, premiered in 1946.

Rice's versatility as a writer is demonstrated by *See Naples and Die,* a good-humored farce, produced in the same year as *The Subway* and *Street Scene.* His increasing importance to the theater in general is shown by his move into the roles of producer and director. Rice directed *Street Scene* and went on to direct plays by other important writers such as ROBERT E. SHERWOOD (*ABE LINCOLN IN ILLINOIS* [1938]). He produced and directed his own plays *Counsellor-at-Law* and *The Left Bank* in 1931. In 1934, he bought New York's Belasco Theatre, but his critical popularity was waning. Rice had always had leftist sympathies, and his plays *Judgment Day* and *Between Two Worlds* (both 1934) were not well received as some critics wrongly regarded them as close to Marxist propaganda. Unhappy with the "commercialism" of the American theater, he very publicly resigned from it.

He remained active, however, providing backing for the GROUP THEATRE, and playing an important role in the establishment of the FEDERAL THEATRE PROJECT, from which he eventually resigned over issues of censorship. In 1937, he returned to Broadway as one of the founders of the Playwrights' Company, along with MAXWELL ANDERSON, Robert E. Sherwood, SIDNEY HOWARD, and S. N. BEHRMAN. Rice's own plays of this period, *American Landscape* (1938), *Two on an Island* (1940), and *Flight to the West* (1940), were at best moderately successful. His last great hit was *Dream Girl* (1945), which starred his second wife, Betty Field. An imaginatively conceived comedy about one day in the life of Georgina Allerton, who begins the day waking alone and ends it going to bed with her new husband, the play's chief attribute was the seamless integration of Georgina's dream life and reality.

Rice continued to write, but *Love among the Ruins* (1963) is the only play after *Dream Girl* that merits any critical interest. In many ways as experimental in form as EUGENE O'NEILL's, Rice's work differs from O'Neill's in its optimism and fundamental confidence in American democracy.

BIBLIOGRAPHY

Durham, Frank. *Elmer Rice.* New York: Twayne, 1970.

Hogan, Robert Goode. *The Independence of Elmer Rice.* Carbondale: Southern Illinois University Press, 1965.

Palmieri, Anthony F. R. *Elmer Rice, a Playwright's Vision of America.* Rutherford, N.J.: Fairleigh Dickinson University Press, 1980.

Rice, Elmer. *The Living Theatre.* New York: Harper, 1959.

———. *Minority Report: An Autobiography.* New York: Simon and Schuster, 1963.

———. *Seven Plays By Elmer Rice.* New York: Viking Press, 1950.

Vanden Heuvel, Michael. *Elmer Rice: A Research and Production Sourcebook.* Westport, Conn.: Greenwood Press, 1996.

Christopher J. Wheatley
The Catholic University of America

RICHARDSON, JACK (1935–   )

Jack Richardson came of age with EDWARD ALBEE, ARTHUR KOPIT, and JACK GELBER during the 1962–63 season at the Playwrights' Unit of the ACTORS STUDIO in New York. By this time, Richardson had already produced his two most successful plays OFF-BROADWAY, *The Prodigal* (1960) and *Gallows Humor* (1961).

Jack Carter Richardson was born in New York City. After high school, he tried acting in summer stock in New Jersey. He served in the United States Army from 1951–54 and returned to take his degree in philosophy from Columbia University. Richardson soon began to devote his time to writing for the theater. His plays pit the human desire to embrace the imaginative risk and the chaos of individuality against the realistic and deterministic conformity of modern life. For Richardson, modern life can lead only to death, both literal and figurative, because it is so ordered and scripted. He has often been grouped with existential playwrights, such as Jean-Paul Sartre and Samuel Beckett, but Richardson denies his role in any theoretical school. Ironically, it is the overemphasis on theory at the expense of character development and dramatic conflict for which Richardson has been most severely criticized.

The Prodigal was Richardson's first and most successful play. In it, he tells the stories of Orestes, Agamemnon, and Electra by dramatizing Orestes's choice as an existential one, wherein he must choose between his historical destiny to kill his mother Clytemnestra and avenge his father's death and his own personal desire to remain separate from these events. Richardson tackles his complex existential theme with balance, never allowing the philosophical concerns to subsume the dramatic concerns of the characters. *Gallows Humor* was produced the following year to some negative criticism, but again this play was generally successful, praised primarily for its comedic elements. In it, Richardson hopes to force the audience to confront its own ideas about what it means to be truly alive by doubling the roles of a condemned man who attempts to achieve self-awareness on death row and an executioner who questions his marriage, his job, and his own life. Both *The Prodigal* and *Gallows Humor* did much to suggest that Richardson would become a permanent figure in American theater.

However, with the production of *Lorenzo* (1963) on Broadway, Richardson's star began to wane. Set in Italy during the Renaissance, *Lorenzo* is a history play that deals with questions of whether art can exist independent of politics. The play suffers from badly developed secondary characters and an intellectual conflict that is given far more treatment than the dramatic conflict. Richardson's final Broadway play, *Xmas in Las Vegas* (1965), was an even bigger failure than *Lorenzo*. It is the story of Edward Wellspot, a compulsive gambler who drags his family to Las Vegas every Christmas to tempt fate. Richardson turns the American Dream of success by hard work into a dream of success won by chance to comment on the uses and abuses of risk and determinism. The play has comic and insightful moments, but the critics considered its characters to be merely types, the action weak and undeveloped, and the ending implausible. The play was almost unanimously panned.

After 1965, with the exception of an unprofessionally produced play, *As Happy As Kings* (1968), and a short screenplay, *Juan Feldman* (1967), Richardson stopped writing drama. He has since reviewed theater for *Commentary* and other publications and published a novel and a memoir. Richardson's contribution to American theater is marked by his willingness to experiment with form and a desire to challenge his audience intellectually, often at the expense of dramatic action.

BIBLIOGRAPHY

Richardson, Jack. *Gallows Humor.* New York: Dutton, 1961.
———. *Memoir of a Gambler.* New York: Simon and Schuster, 1979.
———. *The Prison Life of Harris Filmore.* Greenwich, Conn.: New York Graphic Society, 1963.
———. *The Prodigal.* New York: Dutton, 1960.
———. *Xmas in Las Vegas.* New York: Dramatists Play Service, 1966.

Paul N. Calvert
Georgia State University

RICHARDSON, WILLIS (1889–1977)   Perhaps the most prolific African-American playwright of the 20th century, with 46 plays, Willis Richardson

was the first African American to have a play produced on Broadway. Although he revealed little about his personal life, he is believed to have been born in Wilmington, North Carolina. After the 1899 race riots in Wilmington, his family moved to Washington, D.C., where he graduated from the M Street High School (later Dunbar High School) in 1910. For the next 44 years, Richardson worked in the Wetting Division of the Bureau of Engraving and Printing. In the 1970s, Richardson was diagnosed with Paget's disease (osteitis deformans), a progressive deterioration of the bone, which led to his death.

In 1915, Richardson began writing through a correspondence course entitled "Poetry and Versification." On seeing Angelina Grimké's play RACHEL (1916), however, he changed the course of his writing. Grimké and other African-American playwrights of that decade and the next used racial conflict as the theme of their plays; Richardson, instead, believed that plays written for African Americans should focus on problems within the African-American community. To this end, he shifted his attention to writing for the stage on that topic. In this manner, Richardson's plays differed from most of the plays written by African Americans prior to 1930.

The Crisis magazine was important in Richardson's career as a dramatist. The editor of *The Crisis,* W. E. B. DuBois, published Richardson's essay, "The Hope of a Negro Drama" (1919), the first of his six published articles on African-American theater. In December 1920, *The King's Dilemma,* Richardson's first play for children, was published in *The Brownies' Book,* a magazine published by *The Crisis* and intended for African-American children. Over the next three years, Richardson contributed five other plays to *The Crisis: The Deacon's Awakening* (1920), *The Gypsy's Finger-Ring* (1921), *The Children's Treasure* (1921), *The Dragon's Tooth* (1921), and *The Chip Woman's Fortune* (1922). *The Deacon's Awakening* was his first play for adults. DuBois arranged for *The Chip Woman's Fortune* to be produced by the Ethiopian Art Theater in Chicago, where it opened in January 1923; it was produced in May 1923 at the Frazee Theater in New York.

Richardson was a pioneer in American theater in several ways. *The Chip Woman's Fortune* is the first play by an African American to be produced on Broadway. Aside from student productions, his play *Mortgaged* (1924) was the first work by an African American to be staged at the theater of Howard University, in Washington, D.C. During the next several years, *The House of Sham, Compromise,* and *The Chip Woman's Fortune,* among other plays by Richardson, were produced at Howard. In literary contests sponsored by *The Crisis,* Richardson was awarded first-place prizes for *The Broken Banjo* (1925) and *The Bootblack Lover* (1926). In 1926, the Gilpin Players of Cleveland produced Richardson's play *Compromise,* marking it as the first play written by an African American to be performed by this theater group. In 1928, Richardson won the Edith Schwab Cup for *The Broken Banjo;* this award was given annually by Yale University to a promising new playwright.

In addition to his support from DuBois, Richardson's career was helped by Carter G. Woodson, editor of Associated Publishers, an African-American publishing house in Washington, D.C. Richardson edited two collections of plays for Woodson. The first, *Plays and Pageants from the Life of the Negro* (1930), included Richardson's introduction and four of his plays. In 1935, Richardson edited a second collection, *Negro History in Thirteen Plays,* and in 1956, Associated Publishers issued a collection of Richardson's plays for children, *The King's Dilemma.*

Although during the 1920s Richardson was acknowledged as a promising new playwright, in subsequent decades, family responsibilities and changing tastes among theater audiences dimmed his hopes for recognition. His attempts to have later plays produced were unsuccessful. Ironically, two weeks before his death he learned that he was receiving the award for "Outstanding Pioneer in Black Theater" by AUDELCO, the Audience Development Committee, an organization in New York City promoting AFRICAN-AMERICAN DRAMA.

BIBLIOGRAPHY

Gray, Christine Rauchfuss. *Willis Richardson: Forgotten Pioneer of African-American Drama.* Westport, Conn.: Greenwood Press, 1999.

Locke, Alain, ed. *Plays of Negro Life.* 1927. New York: Negro University Press, 1968.

Richardson, Willis. *Plays and Pageants from the Life of the Negro.* Washington, D.C.: Associated Publishers, 1930.

Christine R. Gray
Community College of Baltimore County

RIGGS, (ROLLA) LYNN (1899–1954)

RIGGS, (ROLLA) LYNN (1899–1954) Poet and playwright Lynn Riggs is best known for his play *Green Grow the Lilacs* (1931), from which was adapted the Richard Rodgers and Oscar Hammerstein musical *Oklahoma!* (1943). Born in the Cherokee Nation of Indian Territory near what is now Claremore, Oklahoma, Riggs was educated at Claremore's Eastern University Preparatory School and the University of Oklahoma. He served in the United States Army during World War II in the Office of War Information. Riggs—who worked as a reporter, a sales clerk, a singer, and a film extra, as well as a writer—wrote more than 20 plays and a great deal of poetry.

During the fall of 1923, Riggs went to Santa Fe, New Mexico, to recover from apparent tuberculosis. It was in Santa Fe (to which he often returned throughout his life from his New York City apartment) that he began to write poetry and drama. His first play to be produced, *Knives from Syria,* was performed by the Santa Fe Players in 1925. Riggs's first New York production, in 1927, was of his play *Big Lake,* about a teenaged couple who are abused by an older couple from whom they seek help. Considered Riggs's best play, *Green Grow the Lilacs* was produced by the THEATRE GUILD in 1931; this nostalgic drama is set shortly before statehood in an Oklahoma inhabited by cowboys and farmers, as in the time of Riggs's childhood. Riggs's father was an Oklahoma cattleman (and later a bank president). His mother, who died when Riggs was a child, was part Cherokee. It was from her heritage that he drew for *The Cherokee Night* (1932), which looks at the identity problems of people of mixed race—in this case, Cherokee and white.

Riggs's other plays—many of which are also set in Oklahoma—include *The Domino Parlor* (1928; revised as *Hang on to Love* [1948]), *Rancor* (1928), *Roadside* (1930), *A Lantern to See By* (published 1928; produced 1930), *Sump'n Like Wings* (published 1928; produced 1931), *The Lonesome West* (1932), *More Sky* (1934), *Russet Mantle* (1936), *A World Elsewhere* (1940), *The Cream in* the Well (1941), *Laughter from a Cloud* (1947), *All the Way Home* (1948), *Out of Dust* (1949), and—with Nathan Kroll—*Toward the Western Sky* (1951). All of these plays were produced, some in New York, but most at regional and university theaters. At his best, Riggs made poetic drama and comedy out of ordinary life and regional dialect. Riggs also wrote for film and television.

BIBLIOGRAPHY

Braunlich, Phyllis Cole. *Haunted by Home: The Life and Letters of Lynn Riggs.* Norman: University of Oklahoma Press, 1988.

Erhard, Thomas. *Lynn Riggs.* Austin, Tex.: Steck-Vaughn, 1970.

Riggs, Lynn. *Big Lake: A Tragedy in Two Parts.* New York: Samuel French, 1927.

———. *Four Plays.* New York: Samuel French, 1947.

———. *Green Grow the Lilacs: A Play.* New York: Samuel French, 1931.

———. *"Russet Mantle" and "The Cherokee Night": Two Plays.* New York: Samuel French, 1936.

———. *"Sump'n Like Wings" and "A Lantern to See By": Two Oklahoma Plays.* New York: Samuel French, 1928.

RIVERA, JOSÉ (1955–)

José Rivera was born in Puerto Rico in 1955 and moved with his family to Long Island, New York, in 1959. His early interest in the theater was stimulated by a performance of *Rumpelstiltskin* he witnessed at 12; it showed him the potential power of theater. While studying English and theater as an undergraduate at Denison University, he not only wrote but also directed and produced four plays, honing his craft by working in all aspects of the production process. After college, he went to New York and was involved in a number of other occupations, including editing, before finally having the success with his first critically acclaimed play, *The House of Ramón Iglesia* (1983), that enabled him to become a full-time writer.

The House of Ramón Iglesia deals with the fragmentation of a family as the young men come of age and the older generation attempts to return to a life in Puerto Rico they have transformed through nostalgia. Though filmed by PBS, some critics objected to the play's relatively critical representation of Puerto Ricans. His themes constantly return to questions of identity and its relationship to home, the transcendence of love, and the difficulties of negotiating contemporary life. These themes can be understood at least in part as a gesture toward the transformations that Puerto Ricans undergo in their migrations between the mainland United States and the island.

From his beginning in psychological realism, Rivera has expanded his aesthetic to include surrealism and magical realism, creating plays in which the operative logic of the dramatic world is distanced from everyday conceptions of life. The first example of his developing style, *The Promise* (1988), a story of transcendental love very much in the style of Federico Garcia Lorca, narrates the attempts of Guzman to use magic to keep his daughter Lilia from her predestined husband Carmelo. *The Promise* was the first of Rivera's works to be considered magical realist, an aesthetic he has continued to shape and refine after studying with the Colombian novelist Gabriel García Márquez at the Sundance Film Festival. Though this term is a useful description of Rivera's work, he has also expressed concern about its limiting possibilities as a label attached to Latino theater.

Moving to *Marisol* (1992), set in an apocalyptic New York and addressing many of the same concerns as its contemporary ANGELS IN AMERICA, Rivera began working to create more expansive plays of ideas. Combining issues of homelessness, identity, and the structural violence of Reaganomics, *Marisol* delineates the trials and tribulations of a Puerto Rican yuppie dealing with the massive geographic and cultural transformation of a New York City emerging from an angelic war against God. Critically respected, *Marisol* has generated a number of productions following its premiere at the HUMANA FESTIVAL at the Actors Theatre of Louisville.

Cloud Tectonics (1995), whose title emerged from Rivera's conceptual musings on the geology of cloud formations, continues the intersection of complex concepts with alternative forms of realism in exploring the ideas of love, time, and memory conflated in the character Celestina, a woman who lives outside of time. This theme of love and its surreal transformation also haunts Rivera's work in pieces like *Each Day Dies with Sleep* (1990), where the protagonist Nelly attempts to negotiate and escape from the dehumanizing effects of her father and husband. Rivera's play

References to Salvador Dali Make Me Hot (2000) acknowledges the importance of dream logic to surrealism and incorporates this logic into the form of the play. Here, two of the four acts may be interpreted as dreams peopled by Cat, Coyote, and Moon, all of whom carry on conversations with the protagonist Gabriela. However, the distance between dreams and reality is very close in this play, which also references Dali's painting *Two Pieces of Bread Expressing the Sentiment of Love.* Throughout these plays, Rivera's focus on strong women characters is a crucial element.

Other important works by Rivera include his collection of short plays, *Giants Have Us In Their Books* (1993), a series of dark fantasies that Rivera subtitled *Six Children's Plays for Adults,* and *Sueño* (1998), his adaptation of Calderon de la Barca's *La Vida es Sueño* (Life is a Dream). Other works include *The Street of the Sun* (1997), set in Los Angeles and exploring stereotypes and ethnic divisions; *Maricela de la Luz Lights the World* (1998), a piece of children's theater that offers parallels to *Marisol; Sonnets for an Old Century* (2000), a series of monologues spoken by a 23 characters in some kind of limbo space that may in fact be a form of the afterlife; and *Adoration of the Old Woman* (2002), which explores generational shifts and the changing status of Puerto Rico.

Rivera was nominated for an Oscar for his screenplay for the movie *The Motorcyle Diaries* (2004) based on the diaries of Che Guevara; and his play *School of the Americas* (2007) continues his interest in that revolutionary figure, imagining the last days of Guevara's life held captive in a Bolivian schoolhouse. Other important recent works for the stage include *Massacre (Sing to Your Children)* (2007), *Brainpeople* (2008), and *Boleros for the Disenchanted* (2008), about a young couple moving from Puerto Rico to the U.S. mainland.

BIBLIOGRAPHY

Rivera, José. *Giants Have Us In Their Books.* New York: Broadway Play Publishing, 1997.

———. *José Rivera Anthology.* New York: Theatre Communications Group, 2002.

———. *"Marisol" and Other Plays.* New York: Theatre Communications Group, 1997.

———. *Massacre (Sing to Your Children).* New York: Broadway Play Publishing, 2007.

———. *The Promise.* New York: Broadway Play Publishing, 1989.

———. *"References to Salvador Dali Make Me Hot" and Other Plays.* New York: Theatre Communications Group, 2003.

———. *School of the Americas.* New York: Broadway Play Publishing, 2007.

Jon D. Rossini
University of California—Davis

RIVER NIGER, THE Joseph Walker (1973)

Based on Walker's childhood memories, *The River Niger* is about how personal and political struggles bring together and pull apart a black family.

Johnny Williams, a housepainter whose passion is poetry, returns home every day exhausted from work. On paydays, he stops by the local bar and purchases a drink or two before surrendering his paycheck to his wife Mattie. Johnny's best friend and neighbor Dr. Dudley Stanton, a cynical Jamaican, visits often, loans money to Johnny when his has been misspent, and gladly shares a drink with him at the kitchen table. Johnny's mother-in-law, Grandma Wilhemina Brown, a widow and alcoholic herself, lives with the Williamses. Mattie, the long-suffering wife, has cancer. Collectively, their hopes rest in Johnny's son, Jeff, a naval aviator whose return they are expecting.

Jeff arrives only after a series of unexpected guests have entered the Williams household. Ann Vanderguild, Jeff's fiancée, comes with plenty of luggage at the start of the play, meets the Williamses for the first time, and then moves in with them. Mo, Jeff's childhood friend, a black militant and the local gang leader, seeks to convince Jeff to rejoin the gang that they cofounded. The gang consists of four people: Gail, Mo's girlfriend; Skeeter, a drug addict; Al, a gay man and an undercover cop; and Chips, a sexual predator who attempts to rape Ann (offstage) and admits to having had sex with both a corpse and Al.

Jeff, who arrives at night, first encounters Ann; the following day, he sees his family. Mattie is instantly delighted. Grandma Wilhemina repeatedly praises the young man and compares him to the now mythic Ben Brown, her deceased husband. Johnny Williams, drunk, refuses to acknowledge his son until he puts on his uniform. Jeff confesses that he quit the navy several months earlier because he could no longer handle living other people's dreams. Rather than be a naval aviator, he wants to become a lawyer.

Mo dismisses Jeff's career ambitions. Believing that one cannot work from within an oppressive system, he advocates takeovers and bombings to spur social change. In fact, Mo has devised a strike in which he wants Jeff to participate, but the aspiring lawyer refuses. A few scenes later, Mo enacts his plan, and it fails. The gang regroups at the Williams's house. Seconds later, the police surround them. Al identifies himself as an undercover agent. He exchanges gunshots with Johnny, who, with his dying breath, tells everyone to lay the blame for the botched strike and Al's death on him. In death, Johnny gains nobility.

The River Niger is largely based upon the life of Joseph Walker. He, like Jeff, was a naval aviator who quit the navy. His father, a talented man, wasted his talent as a housepainter and drowned it in alcohol. Immensely popular among critics and audiences, *The River Niger* established the reputation of the upstart NEGRO ENSEMBLE COMPANY. With audience demand far exceeding the number of available seats, the play moved to increasingly larger Broadway theaters and won the TONY AWARD.

Harvey Young Jr.
Northwestern University

ROMANCE DAVID MAMET (2005)

Romance is a broad farce in which a chiropractor on trial—for a crime left unstated until it becomes a final-scene punch line—asks for a continuance so that he can attend a nearby Middle East peace conference and bring peace through spinal adjustments that would "restore mental balance to the leaders and, through them, to the populace of the Middle East." The courtroom scenes, which feature an easily distracted judge hopped up on hay-fever medication and lawyers who hurl cultural and religious slurs at one another, has the silliness and pacing of a Marx Brothers movie. As the defense attorney attempts repeatedly to explain why his client wants a continuance, the unfocused judge and his court go off on various tangents, including an argument about whether Shakespeare may have been a gay Jew; the judge's own admission of child molestation; and plenty of flagrant intolerance of sexual orientation, religion, and race.

A subplot involves the gay prosecutor's domestic problems with his lover Bernard, or "Bunny." By the final scene, Bunny has barged into the courtroom with his anger and his suitcase since his boyfriend will not discuss their situation with him on his cell phone, which has already interrupted the proceedings several times. The judge commiserates with Bunny's complaints about his mate. Finally, when the judge decides to let the chiropractor solve the Middle East crisis through spinal manipulation if he will only say "I'm sorry" for his as yet unnamed crime, Bunny recognizes the defendant's voice as that of a man whom he met in Hawaii for an assignation—and a cryptic note in the defendant's day book, mentioned in scene one, becomes suddenly clear. General pandemonium breaks out as a doctor, summoned by the bailiff to attend to the judge, gets into an argument with the chiropractor/defendant about the relative merits of being a medical doctor as opposed to being a chiropractor. After the chiropractor attempts to strangle the doctor, we find out that his unnamed crime was that he "attacked a chiropodist." Bunny calls the chaotic courtroom to attention by banging a frying pan on the table and announces that the Middle East leaders (as he has just learned from his lover's mother by phone) have quit the peace conference because one of them called another an offensive name.

Critics seemed to agree that part of what MAMET is up to here is parodying his own style of overlapping, rapid-fire dialogue. He is also looking for laughs by flying in the face of political correctness. Ben Brantley, in his *New York Times* review, suggested that Mamet's "insult-driven dialogue" is reminiscent of 1960s comedian "Lenny Bruce['s] . . . shock tactics" (March 2, 2005). If there is a theme in all this silliness, it may be that when we Americans, often sanctimoniously, demand that the parties in the Middle East just get along, we should bear in mind that we have our own intolerance and general bad behavior to answer for.

ROSE TATTOO, THE Tennessee Williams (1951)

The Rose Tattoo was written, Williams later recalled, during a period "when [he] was very happy in [his] life" (Devlin 117). He had just returned from a trip to Italy, declaring, "I have never felt more hopeful about human nature as a result of being exposed to the Italians" (Kolin 215), and he was contentedly ensconced in a long-term romantic relationship with Frank Merlo, a tempestuous Italian American to whom the play is dedicated.

It begins with Serafina delle Rose, a seamstress in a Gulf Coast town *"populated mostly by Sicilians,"* anxiously awaiting the return of her beloved husband, Rosario. He is a truck driver, who, having apparently made a lot of money transporting illegal goods underneath the bananas in his 10-ton rig, is on his last trip before he can buy the truck and work for himself. They have a 12-year-old daughter, Rosa, and Serafina is pregnant. She tells a friend that the night this second child was conceived she saw on her breast a rose tattoo like the one on Rosario's chest. While she waits, a local woman, Estelle Hohengarten, comes by and offers her the exorbitant sum of $25 to sew a pink silk shirt in a day for a man she loves who is "wild like a Gypsy."

In a brief second scene, several women and the village priest arrive to tell Serafina that Rosario is dead, shot at the wheel of his truck. Later that same day, a doctor reveals that Serafina, prostrate with grief, has lost her baby; the priest tells him that she has asked to have her husband cremated, even though it is against Catholic Church law, so that she can keep his ashes in an urn in her house. Estelle enters to view the body but is shooed away by the women, who scream at her, "*We* know about you!"

Three years later, Serafina has not left the house since Rosario's death, nor has she gotten dressed, choosing instead to wear a dirty pink slip. Rosa is about to graduate from high school, but her mother has confined her to the house by locking up her clothes because she has fallen in love with a sailor she met at a high school dance. When Rosa's teacher arrives and insists that Serafina permit Rosa to go to her graduation, Serafina rails at the teacher and the school for "ruining the girls" by sponsoring the dance. Still clad in her slip, she chases the teacher and Rosa into the street, embarrassing Rosa, who calls her mother "disgusting" as she leaves.

Shaken by Rosa's epithet, Serafina puts on a dress to go to the graduation, but she is interrupted by two man-crazy floozies who show up to get a blouse Serafina has made for one of them. When Serafina criticizes them for their loose morals and extols the memory of Rosario, the girls tell her that everyone in town knew that he was having an affair with Estelle Hohengarten, a blackjack dealer at a local club, and that Estelle had had a rose tattooed on her chest to match his. Enraged, Serafina refuses to believe them and chases them away with a broom, but she recalls the shirt Estelle asked her to make, and she prays for guidance to the statue of the Madonna that she has placed in her living room, along with the urn and a votive candle.

When Rosa and her boyfriend Jack return from the graduation—which Serafina did not attend—they find Serafina back in her slip and muttering. Soon she interrogates Jack about his intentions toward her daughter; when he tells her that, like Rosa, he is a virgin, she gets him to swear before the Holy Mother that he will "respect" her "innocence." It is clear, however, that Rosa, who inherited her father's passionate nature, is more intent on sex than Jack as they leave for a postgraduation picnic.

Serafina remains troubled by what she has heard about Rosario, shunning the village women, begging the priest to tell her whether her husband ever mentioned another woman during confession, and hysterically attacking him when he refuses. At that moment, Alvaro Mangiacavallo enters. Although he is very good-looking, *"his face and manner are clownish."* He tells her that he drives trunks of bananas—and only bananas—for the Southern Fruit Company and is the sole support of "three dependents"—his "old-maid" sister, his "feeble-minded" grandmother, and his father, who's a "lush." Attracted to him, she tells him about having seen the rose tattoo on her breast; equally drawn to her, he says that his dream is to meet "some sensible older lady" who will be "understanding" and will have "a well-furnished house and a profitable business of some kind." When she asks him what would such a woman want with a man like him, he replies—in words that echo those of so many other

Williams characters—"Love and affection!—in a world that is lonely—and cold!"

Later that evening, Serafina awaits Alvaro's return with a rose in her hair. He shows her that he has a rose tattooed on his chest, but he admits that he got it earlier in the evening because "I wanted to be—close to you . . . to make you happy. . . ." Furious with him, she tells him of the rumors concerning Estelle and Rosario. He picks up the phone and calls Estelle, whom he knows; when Serafina grabs the receiver, Estelle tells her it's true. Serafina smashes the urn, blows out the votive candle, and tells Alvaro to pretend to leave and then return:—"Now I show you how wild and strong like a man a woman can be!"

Early the next morning, Jack and Rosa return, having almost had sex—much to Jack's chagrin (because of his vow to Serafina) and to Rosa's regret (because they did not). They hear Serafina moaning and speaking Rosario's name and assume she's dreaming about him, as she frequently does. Rosa tells Jack that she will meet him later that day so that they can make love before he goes back to sea. Three hours later, Rosa is asleep on the couch, and Alvaro stumbles in, possibly drunk, and goes to her side, muttering *"Che bella!"* Rosa awakens screaming, which rouses Serafina, who is horrified. Alvaro claims he was dreaming and didn't know where he was, but she kicks him out of the house. Rosa appears, wearing a white slip her mother has put aside for her daughter's wedding; after a harsh argument, Serafina sends her off to meet Jack with her blessing. Alvaro returns and calls to Serafina from the street. She reveals to one of the women, "Just now I felt on my breast the burning again of the rose. . . . It means that I have conceived," and she goes to meet Alvaro.

The Rose Tattoo is among the most comic of Williams's plays. Alvaro is an awkward, antiromantic suitor, reminiscent of the clownish bumbling lovers in the plays of Russian dramatist Anton Chekhov, whom Williams much admired; and there is considerable slapstick in the various chases and fights that take place. The play also, typically of Williams's drama, has an abundance of symbols: the rose tattoos, the rose in Serafina's hair, the roses that Jack gives Rosa for graduation—all of which represent sexual passion;

the gossiping women who function as a sort of Greek chorus; and an ominous goat-tending woman with wild hair and hairy legs called the Strega (witch or sorceress), who hovers over the action as a symbol of doom. But the overriding theme of the play is what critic C. W. E. Bigsby calls "the resilience of the human spirit, the undeniable power of the will to live and the primacy of the sexual impulse" (73).

BIBLIOGRAPHY

Bigsby, C. W. E. *A Critical Introduction to Twentieth-Century American Drama: Volume Two—Williams/Albee/Miller.* Cambridge, England: Cambridge University Press, 1984.

Devlin, Albert J., ed. *Conversations with Tennessee Williams.* Jackson: University Press of Mississippi, 1986.

Kolin, Philip C. "'Sentiment and humor in equal measure': Comic Forms in *The Rose Tattoo.*" In *Tennessee Williams: A Tribute,* edited by Jac Tharpe. Jackson: University Press of Mississippi, 1977. 214—231.

ROYAL FAMILY, THE George S. Kaufman and Edna Ferber (1927)   Based on the Drew-Barrymore clan, *The Royal Family* is a romantic comedy about an extended family of actors. At times drawn to the conventional life outside the theater, the Cavendishes invariably choose the life to which they were born.

Fanny Cavendish is the 72-year-old widow of Aubry Cavendish, mother of Julie and Tony Cavendish, grandmother of Gwen, and sister of Herbert "Bertie" Dean (married to the mediocre actress Kitty Dean). All are actors, and so far all have married—and sometimes divorced—actors. Tony has defected from the stage to Hollywood, but he has gotten into trouble with the police there and is bound for New York, the tabloid press at his heels. Julie, currently in a hit play and soon to begin rehearsal in another, anticipates with nostalgia the return from South America of her old flame, Gil Marshall, a wealthy businessman. Julie's daughter, Gwen, is in love with stockbroker Perry Stewart; when she must break an important date with Perry to meet with a playwright, the couple discuss the incompatibility of their schedules and the implications for an unhappy future between a working stage actress and a conventional businessman. (Indeed, there is much evidence throughout the play of irregular meals and hours among the Deans and

Cavendishes.) Perry leaves angry, and Gwen, vowing to quit the stage, disconsolately takes to her room.

Meanwhile, Tony, having arrived from Hollywood, hopes to leave on the next ship for Europe. He has not only slugged his director and walked out on the film, but he has also been named in a "breach of promise suit" by the director's girlfriend. Tony's fans and the press surround the apartment building. Julie has been charged with getting him a passport between her matinee and evening performances, but even with the help of the family's long-time producer, Oscar Wolfe, she is unable to do so. Julie is also concerned about her heartbroken daughter, and she and Fanny extol the joys of a life on the stage to Gwen, trying to convince her to keep her profession *and* marry Perry—but never to sacrifice one for the other. The weekend's excitement is too much for grandmother Fanny, who alarms everyone by fainting. When Gil arrives, he easily uses his wealth and influence to arrange for Tony's passport, and the frazzled Julie, suddenly craving a less manic existence, decides to marry Gil and proclaims that she will "never . . . act again," until she sees the time and realizes she must run or be late for her evening performance. Before leaving, she encourages her daughter to do likewise: marry Perry and give up the theater.

Act 3 takes place one year later. Gwen and Perry are married and have an infant son. Julie has nearly finished her theatrical commitments in preparation for marriage to Gil, who is due back from South America, where he has been for six months. Bert and Kitty have just signed on to play scenes in vaudeville, and Fanny, at 73, is about to take an old play on tour. When Gil arrives and speaks fondly to Julie of the pleasures of living on an isolated plantation in South America and, alternatively, in the English countryside, Julie begins to get cold feet. Her discomfort increases when Gwen reveals that the THEATRE GUILD has asked her to do a play and that she has accepted—since the baby is young and in the constant care of his nurse anyway. Tony returns from his world travels with an experimental play in which he plans to star. (True to form, Tony has also returned because he is dodging an Albanian princess who has taken his attentions more seriously than he intended them.) When Wolfe tells

Julie that he has an innovative new play he would like to produce, she agrees to read it, and a dull marriage to Gil becomes less and less likely. In the final scene, Fanny shows two-month-old Aubrey Cavendish Stewart the portrait on the wall of his great-grandfather and namesake, proclaiming the baby a Cavendish and "the future greatest actor of his day." Fanny, having passed the torch, sinks to her chair and quietly dies.

The colorful Cavendishes and Deans—like their real-life counterparts, the Barrymores and the Drews—fascinated and entertained audiences for a year in the play's original production. Their lively antics and the witty dialogue by KAUFMAN and FERBER have remained fresh: The play was successfully revived on Broadway in 1975 and again in 2009.

RUDNICK, PAUL (1957–)   Satirical playwright, novelist, screenwriter, and essayist Paul Rudnick was born in Piscataway, New Jersey, where his parents' love of theater was a great influence on him as a child. He studied playwriting at Yale University, from which he graduated in 1977.

Rudnick's first play, *Poor Little Lambs* (1982), is set at Yale and is a comedy about the exploits of Yale's all-male a capella singing group; it met with moderate success. (Other early plays include *Cosmetic Surgery* [1983], *Arts and Leisure* [1983], and *Raving* [1984]—all comic one-acts). Rudnick came to the attention of critics with his comedy *I Hate Hamlet* (1991), about a television actor inspired to play Hamlet by the ghost of legendary actor John Barrymore, whose apartment the young actor has rented. *Jeffrey* (1993), while certainly not the first play about AIDS, was the first successful comedy dealing with love in the time of AIDS; the play won an OBIE AWARD. *The Most Fabulous Story Ever Told* (1998) is a comic satire in which a gay couple (Adam and Steve) and a lesbian couple (Jane and Mabel) in the Garden of Eden in act 1 become late-20th-century New Yorkers in act 2—pondering questions of religion and sex throughout.

An evening of plays on gay themes, *Rude Entertainment* (2001) includes three one-acts: *Mr. Charles, Currently of Palm Beach; Very Special Needs;* and *On the Fence. Mr. Charles*, which had a successful solo production in 1998, is about a flamboyantly gay cable-television talk-show host; *Very Special Needs* is about gay adoption; and *On the Fence* is a somewhat sentimental piece—unlike Rudnick's usual, decidedly unsentimental, often "politically incorrect" work—in which Eleanor Roosevelt, the late gay actor Paul Lynde, and Matthew Shepard, the gay college student who was tied to a fence and beaten to death in Wyoming in 1998, converse.

Rudnick's most recent plays include *Regrets Only* (2006), a comedy of manners set in a Manhattan penthouse, and *The New Century* (2008). The latter is the collective title of four short comic plays about "gay men and the women who love them," as Ben Brantley characterized them in his *New York Times* review (April 15, 2008). One of the four was a reprise of *Mr. Charles*.

Rudnick has also written screenplays, notably *Addams Family Values* (1993), *In & Out* (1997) and *The Stepford Wives* (2004); two novels, *Social Disease* (1986) and *I'll Take It* (1989); and a collection of reviews, which first appeared under the pen name Libby Gelman-Waxner in *Premiere* magazine in the late 1980s and early 1990s, entitled *If You Ask Me: The Collected Columns of America's Most Beloved and Irresponsible Critic* (1994). He continues to write for stage and screen and for various periodicals.

BIBLIOGRAPHY
Rudnick, Paul [Libby Gelman-Waxner, pseud.]. *If You Ask Me: The Collected Columns of America's Most Beloved and Irresponsible Critic*. New York: St. Martin's Press, 1994.
———. *I Hate Hamlet*. Garden City, N.Y.: Fireside Theatre, 1991.
———. *Jeffrey*. New York: Dramatists Play Service, 1995.
———. *"The Most Fabulous Story Ever Told" and "Mr. Charles, Currently of Palm Beach": Two Plays*. Woodstock, N.Y.: Overlook Press, 2000.
———. *Regrets Only*. New York: Dramatists Play Service, 2007.

RUHL, SARAH (1974–)

Raised in Wilmette, Illinois, Sarah Ruhl found her early literary influences in her father, who loved language and the origins of words, and her mother, an English teacher, actress, and director. Ruhl was educated at Brown University (B.A., 1997; M.F.A., 2001) where, even as an under-

graduate she impressed her writing teacher, the playwright PAULA VOGEL, with the depth of emotion in her first student play, the 10-minute *Dog Play* (1995). At that time, however, Ruhl was intent on becoming a poet; indeed, when she was 20 she published a collection of her poems, *Death in Another Country*. Ultimately, though, after returning from a study-abroad program and under the influence of Vogel, she did turn to playwriting. She later explained her rationale: "Plays provided a way to open up content and have many voices. . . . [O]nstage one could speak lyrically and with emotion, and . . . the actor was longing for that kind of speech, whereas in poetic discourse, emotion was in some circles becoming embarrassing" (Lahr).

Ruhl's first professionally produced play (at Trinity Repertory Company in Providence, Rhode Island) was the original 1997 version of her *Passion Play*. Inspired by the playwright's reading about the centuries-old Oberammergau tradition, the piece involves the interplay between the lives enacted in a Passion Play put on by the people of an Elizabethan town and the real lives of those townspeople. Between the time Ruhl finished college and started graduate school a few years later, she completed a second play, in which a Passion Play is staged by a Nazi-era town in Germany. And finally, after receiving a commission from Arena Stage in Washington, D.C., she wrote the third and final play of this cycle, which is set in contemporary America; she then condensed the three plays into a single three-and-a-half hour evening in the theater, which premiered under the title *Passion Play* at Arena Stage in 2004. An important overarching theme of the evening is intolerance.

Though *Melancholy Play* (2002), a comedy, comes out of a contemporary American culture of psychopharmacology and of perhaps an overtreatment of even garden-variety sadness as depression, Ruhl does not write a broad satire of that culture; instead, she approaches her subject obliquely. The play is about a woman, Tilly, whose melancholy is so appealing that neither gender can resist falling in love with her. Her multiple affairs—with her psychiatrist, her tailor, and her hairdresser—fall apart in the second act when she becomes happy. In a loony development late in act 2, melancholy people begin to turn into almonds; this is a reference, as Ruhl explains in the published play, to the amygdala, the almond-shaped part of the brain that is the seat of emotion (*"The Clean House" and Other Plays* 231). Ultimately, Tilly and her ex-lovers and the hairdresser's partner, in order to join the now tiny almond-bodied hairdresser, who is bereft at the loss of Tilly, become almonds as well—in other words, embrace, rather than cure, their emotions.

Set in "a version of Pittsburgh," *Late: A Cowboy Song* (2003) is about a young woman, Mary, who marries her childhood sweetheart after she becomes pregnant. The baby is neither wholly male nor wholly female, but after surgery is labeled a girl. Mary wants to name the baby "Blue" because she has a friend named Red, a manly cowgirl or a lady cowboy, whose individuality she admires; she hopes her "daughter," too, will be unfettered by gender labels. Mary's husband is threatened by his wife's relationship with Red (whom he has disliked since grade school), and indeed, Mary's growing love for Red eventually ends the marriage. Despite its potentially melodramatic subject, the play is light and matter-of-fact in tone. *Late* may well have been influenced by Ruhl's work on *Orlando* (2002), an adaptation, for the Piven Theatre Workshop in Evanston, Illinois, of Virginia Woolf's 1928 novel, *Orlando,* which covers the centuries-long adventures of a person of inconsistent gender—as it comments on gender and power.

Eurydice (2003), set in a vaguely suggested 1950s, is a retelling of the Orpheus myth. Ruhl's version focuses on the experience of the dead Eurydice, rather than on Orpheus's rescue mission. Eurydice, a lover of books, and Orpheus, a lover of music, fall in love and marry. Eurydice's dead father, rare among the dead in that he has retained the ability to read and write, writes his daughter a letter on her wedding day. Through the mysterious intercession of "a nasty interesting man," she receives the letter but also dies trying to get away from this man. Entering the underworld, she must pass through the mythic river of forgetfulness, which causes her to forget everyone she has known and all human emotion. Her father, who was not dipped very thoroughly upon *his* arrival, manages to reconnect with his daughter and teaches her a great deal. Just as in the original myth, Orpheus is allowed to descend to Hades and retrieve his wife on the condition that he not look back at her, but alas he does and in so doing loses her again to death. Ruhl dedicated this play to her late father and models Eurydice's father after her own. Part of the play's poignancy comes from the theme that it is memory that makes us who we are.

Ruhl's most-often-produced play, the full-length version of *The Clean House* (2004), premiered at Yale Repertory Theatre; for it, Ruhl won the Susan Smith Blackburn Prize. The inspiration for the play came from a remark Ruhl heard at a party: a woman said almost verbatim what the playwright would later put in the mouth of her character, Lane, at the opening of the play: "It has been a hard month. My cleaning lady—from Brazil—decided that she was depressed one day and stopped cleaning my house. . . . We took her to the hospital and had her medicated and She Still Wouldn't Clean. And—in the meantime—*I've* been cleaning my house! I'm sorry but I did not go to medical school to clean my own house." Ruhl said in an interview in *American Theatre* magazine in 2004 that she "was fascinated and horrified by the political and cultural implications . . . but also by how transparently the woman laid out her case." However, as she wrote the play, it became less political than psychological and metaphorical: What might cleanliness and attitudes toward cleaning symbolize about one's approaches to life and death, for instance? As Lane's need for sterility breaks down, her embrace of life intensifies. Lane's surgeon husband falls in love with Ana, an older Argentinean woman, whose life-affirming attitude in the face of her own terminal cancer influences both Lane and Charles. The cleaning lady, meanwhile, is interested only in joke-telling, her inherited calling in life, and comes up with the perfect joke, one that eventually helps Ana end her life by laughing.

Ruhl's originality gained recognition in 2006 when she received a prestigious MacArthur Fellowship (the so-called genius grant), which is given to artists who have shown exceptional creativity, significant accomplishment, and great promise for the future. Since that time, her plays have included *Dead Man's Cell*

Phone (2007), a satire of how we lionize the dead, in which a woman answers a man's unanswered cell phone in a restaurant only to realize that he is dead. By pretending to be his employee, she hangs on to the phone, continues to answer his calls, and insinuates herself into the lives of his circle, creating stories about the man as she anticipates the emotional needs of those who knew him. *In the Next Room (or the vibrator play)* (2009) is a comedy set in the late Victorian period and is about six lonely people who look for emotional release in a new technology, but finally find it instead in human intimacy.

Ruhl's plays have been given readings and productions around the country—for many of them the development period was protracted and involved various versions in both readings and productions (the dates given above are to the greatest extent possible the premieres of the "final" versions). In fact, Ruhl is one of several playwrights who have become dissatisfied with what for some of them seems an endless development process. In 2003, they formed 13P, a Brooklyn-based group of 13 playwrights whose motto is "We don't develop plays. (We do them.)."

BIBLIOGRAPHY

Lahr, John. "Surreal Life." *New Yorker* (March 17, 2008): 78.
Ruhl, Sarah. *"The Clean House" and Other Plays.* New York: Theatre Communications Group, 2006.

RUINED LYNN NOTTAGE (2008)   Set in a brothel in the civil war–torn Democratic Republic of the Congo, the PULITZER PRIZE–winning *Ruined* is based on interviews that LYNN NOTTAGE conducted in Uganda with 15 Congolese refugees, women who survived rape and torture while caught in the conflict between rebel and government forces. Men on both sides engaged in unspeakable brutality in the name of a supposed higher cause—on one side "liberation," on the other "protection"—devastating the lives of countless women and children. In addition to the interviews, the play, as Nottage has acknowledged, is also inspired by Bertolt Brecht's *Mother Courage*.

As the play begins, Mama Nadi, the proprietress of a bar and brothel, is genially negotiating for some goods with traveling salesman Christian, whom she calls "Professor" because of the poetry he recites.

Clearly her admirer, Christian delights Mama Nadi by remembering the lipstick she has asked for and then mentions that he has another surprise in his truck. Surprising indeed is the additional cargo: three young women; Mama objects that she has enough working girls, but Christian, bribing her with chocolates, finally convinces her to take two for the price of one. Sophie and Salima have been savagely abused by the rebel soldiers who captured them. Now cut loose by their torturers, they face limited options. Christian reveals that Sophie is his niece and that she is "ruined," having been raped with a knife. Mama is irritated that she has been manipulated into taking on another mouth to feed, one incapable of turning tricks. But Christian assures her that the beautiful Sophie can sing to earn her keep and will work hard.

The next scene finds the bar raucous with rebel soldiers playing pool, drinking, bragging about their murderous exploits, and crudely pursuing the prostitutes. Sophie sings and manages to avoid their brutal advances, but Salima must give them what they came for. Salima, who soon becomes pregnant, speaks to Sophie of her husband, Fortune, and of their child. We eventually learn that Salima spent five months in the bush "chained like a goat" to a tree, the sex slave of the rebel soldiers. The day they captured her, one of them stomped on her crying baby's head. When the rebels finally released her, she was rejected by her village, her family, and her husband "for dishonoring" them. Now she is pregnant with the child "of a monster." "Oh, God," she laments to Sophie, "please give me back that morning."

Mama Nadi trades in whatever she can—other women's bodies, diamonds, alcohol—with whomever she can; either side is welcome as long as they leave their bullets at the bar. Mama's place is a neutral zone, but her customers—a gem merchant, miners, the rebels and the government soldiers, as well as Christian—bring news of the brutality, perpetrated by both sides, outside the bar: among these bits of news is word that a pastor has been "butchered"—literally, cut up—by government soldiers for aiding injured rebels, while the staff of the hospital has suffered the same fate at the hands of the rebels. Both sides are ruining the country; Nottage deliberately makes them virtually indistinguishable through double casting and through their equally reprehensible acts on and off stage.

Some of the women still have dreams of a better future: Mama dreams of one day buying a piece of land, like that her family once owned before it was taken by force for the wealth that lay beneath its soil. Sophie is skimming money from Mama's profits so she can pay for an operation to repair her mutilated genitals. (Eventually Mama will give up her valuable raw diamond to the gem merchant, Aziz Harari, so he can arrange for Sophie to have an operation. But Sophie is left behind when Harari must run after his driver or be left behind himself as the fighting converges perilously near the bar.) Josephine, one of Mama's other girls, dreams of Harari's promise of setting her up in an apartment in the city, but to him this is just a game they play; Harari, while not a brutal man, is above all else motivated by self-preservation.

When Salima's husband, a government soldier, comes for her, Mama keeps him from his wife and advises Salima to accept that the woman she once was is dead. She tells her that if she goes back to the village she will always be treated as damaged goods, that the life she remembers is gone, and that the brothel is now her home. In the end we learn that Mama is not speaking from mere self-interest here but that she has reason to know firsthand what these women have been through. She reveals in the play's final scene, after her business has been shut down and Christian asks her to marry him, that she herself is "ruined." This knowledge puts all of her previous actions and words in a new light: What has seemed like exploitation now contains elements of kindness, and what seemed coldness, a mechanism to cope with her own pain.

Ruined premiered at Chicago's Goodman Theatre in the fall of 2008; in 2009, the production moved to New York, where it won the New York Drama Critics' Circle Award and an OBIE AWARD for Best Play. With its entirely non-American setting and characters, the play was a surprise recipient of the Pulitzer Prize, which is traditionally awarded to an American play "dealing with American life."

Speaking about the decades-long strife in Africa about which few Americans even know the grim statistics, Nottage explained her motivation for delving into this subject matter to Jeffrey Brown on PBS's *Newshour* a few weeks after winning the Pulitzer Prize: "I wanted to hear the narratives of the women. . . . Who are they? What is it like to be a woman who hasn't started this war, but finds herself trapped in the middle of [it]. Nearly five million people have died in the Congo . . . and about half of them are women and children, yet we don't know their names. . . . We don't know what their stories are" (June 15, 2009). In *Ruined,* Nottage has given these anonymous slaughtered and abused innocents a voice.

S

SACKLER, HOWARD See *GREAT WHITE HOPE, The.*

SALVATION NELL EDWARD SHELDON **(1908)**
A redemption play that takes place among the poor and wretched of early 20th-century New York, *Salvation Nell* is the story of Nell, a woman who finds God through a Salvation Army mission in the slum where she lives, and her abusive and alcoholic boyfriend, Jim.

The play opens on Christmas Eve at Sid J. McGovern's Empire Bar, a dive full of poor and unemployed drunks. To get a sense of the priorities of these men, we need only meet the father who has stolen a dime from the Christmas stocking given to his child by the mission. Nell Sanders works for Sid, cleaning floors and tables, and sleeps in the cellar. She has had a miserable life, sewing pants as a child in a sweatshop; more recently she worked in a "hash-house" until she was fired for being pregnant. Nell loves Jim, the father of her child and a homeless, unemployed drunk who seems at best indifferent and at worst abusive to her. When one of the other drunks at Sid's grabs Nell and kisses her, Jim nearly beats him to death, gets arrested, and eventually is sent to prison. As Jim is being taken away by the police, he threatens Nell. Nell's boss blames her for this trouble in his bar and fires her. Homeless and alone, she accepts the help and comfort of Ensign Maggie O'Sullivan of the Salvation Army and rejects a life of prostitution.

Act 2 begins eight years later. Nell has been "saved" and is a valued officer in the Salvation Army. She and her son Jimmy, now eight, live in a tenement flat. Salvation Army major Williams, who has had a wretched, misspent youth of his own, has grown fond of Nell and Jimmy, and they of him. Major Williams, we learn, is from a rich family. One of SHELDON's themes is this equality between rich and poor, that is, the idea that both face the possibility of spiritual misery through alcoholism and other poor choices.

When Nell's childhood friend Myrtle reports that Jim has been released from prison, Nell fears he will find her and hurt her. Indeed, Jim does find her, and he is still tough and sinister. He roughly insists that she come west with him the next day. The scene shows that there is a real—though unhealthy—love between them. When he reveals that he will commit a robbery that evening, she tries everything to stop him, even offering him her body. Stricken with guilt, she cannot go through with it, and he hits her, knocking her out before fleeing through the window.

In the final scene of the play, Salvation Nell preaches a simple heartfelt sermon on a street corner outside Sid's bar about redemption for sinners like herself. Her talk reaches Jim, who is in the audience. He did not commit the robbery; instead, he came back to make sure he had not killed Nell. In the final moments, Jim asks for Nell's help, and so it seems that even Jim is redeemable.

Edward Sheldon was an early practitioner of social realism in American drama, yet the ending of *Salvation*

Nell is highly romanticized. The redemption of Jim seems, in view of what has come before, very unlikely. Indeed, to the modern reader, it seems inevitable that Nell will soon be disillusioned once more. The play is in other ways realistic, however. Sheldon's depiction of the poor of New York is convincing and authentic, particularly the natural and fast-moving dialogue in the dialects of early 20th-century New York. The story of Nell and Jim is played out against a backdrop of squalor, abuse, drunkenness, and crime.

In 1926, EUGENE O'NEILL wrote to Sheldon: "Your *Salvation Nell,* along with the work of the Irish Players . . . , was what first opened my eyes to the existence of a real theatre," as opposed to the stagey melodrama typical of turn-of-the-century American drama (199). The act 1 bar scene of *Salvation Nell* is similar in cadence to O'Neill's *The ICEMAN COMETH* (1946), which would be written decades later. Both Sheldon and O'Neill had been influenced by GEORGE PIERCE BAKER, each having taken his playwriting course at Harvard.

Salvation Nell also raises the question of environmental determinism. If Nell and Jim have been raised in squalor and ignorance, can they be blamed for their deplorable existence? Nell says to Jim, "You an' me didn't have no chance did we, Jim? An' it ain't our fault if we didn't come quite up ter the mark." Sheldon offsets the pessimism of determinism, however, by redeeming both characters in the end.

BIBLIOGRAPHY
Bogard, Travis, and Jackson R. Bryer, eds. *The Selected Letters of Eugene O'Neill.* New Haven, Conn.: Yale University Press, 1988.

SAROYAN, WILLIAM (1908–1981)

A novelist and short-story writer as well as a dramatist, William Saroyan often depicted those living in poverty, yet his emphasis was on the joy they found in life despite their conditions. His themes frequently highlighted the essential good to be found in humankind, as well as the kindness and compassion necessary to recognize the good in others.

Born the son of an Armenian immigrant in California, Saroyan spent some of his childhood in an orphanage after the death of his father. At 15, he left school and decided to become a writer, continuing his education by reading on his own. He began his career by publishing articles and short stories in periodicals. His first substantial success came in 1934 when *Story* magazine printed his short story "The Daring Young Man on the Flying Trapeze," which is about a young writer living in poverty during the depression. This success was quickly followed by the publication of three collections of short stories within the next two years. For the rest of his life, Saroyan continued to write, producing numerous works, including novels, essays, plays, and stories. In his later years, he published several memoirs.

For the stage, Saroyan dealt with many of the same themes he explored in his fiction. His first play, MY HEART'S IN THE HIGHLANDS (1939), was produced in connection with both the GROUP THEATRE and the THEATRE GUILD and established his reputation as an avant-garde playwright. The play is about the importance of art and the difficulty impoverished artists have surviving in the American social and economic system. Saroyan's best-known play—also produced by the Group Theatre—is *The TIME OF YOUR LIFE* (1939), in which he presents the ideal of human kindness and compassion and takes the position that humans are essentially good. For the play, Saroyan won the New York Drama Critics' Circle Award and the PULITZER PRIZE, which he refused (his oft-quoted reasons: "Commerce should not patronize art," and "it is no more great or good than anything else I have written."). Though Saroyan continued to write plays through the 1950s, none again achieved the commercial or critical success of his first two. Of his other plays, only *Hello Out There* (1942), *The Beautiful People* (1941), and *The Cave Dwellers* (1957) are occasionally revived.

American writer Richard Rodriguez has said of Saroyan that he "belongs with JOHN STEINBECK, a fellow small town Californian, and of the same generation; he belongs with THORNTON WILDER—with those writers whose aching love of America was formed by the depression and the shadow of war" (*The Newshour,* PBS, May 26, 1997). Days before he died, Saroyan quipped to the press, "Everybody has got to die, but I have always believed an exception would be made in my case. Now what?"

BIBLIOGRAPHY

Floan, Howard Russell. *William Saroyan*. New York: Twayne, 1966.

Foard, Elisabeth C. *William Saroyan: A Reference Guide*. Boston, Mass.: G. K. Hall, 1988.

Foster, Edward Halsey. *William Saroyan*. Boise, Idaho: Boise State University, 1984.

Gifford, Barry, and Lawrence Lee. *Saroyan: A Biography*. New York: Harper & Row, 1984.

Keridian, David. *A Bibliography of William Saroyan, 1934–1964*. San Francisco: Beacham, 1965.

Leggett, John. *A Daring Young Man: A Biography of William Saroyan*. New York: Knopf, 2002.

Rodriguez, Richard. "Time of Our Lives," *The Newshour*. PBS, 26 May 1997.

Saroyan, Aram. *William Saroyan*. San Diego: Harcourt Brace Jovanovich, 1983.

Saroyan, William. *"The Beautiful People" and Two Other Plays*. New York: Harcourt, Brace, 1941.

———. *The New Saroyan Reader: A Connoisseur's Anthology of the Writings of William Saroyan*. Berkeley, Calif.: Creative Arts, 1984.

———. *Three Plays: "My Heart's in the Highlands," "The Time of Your Life," "Love's Old Sweet Song."* New York: Harcourt, Brace, 1940.

Whitmore, Jon. *William Saroyan: A Research and Production Sourcebook*. Westport, Conn.: Greenwood Press, 1994.

SCARECROW; OR, THE GLASS OF TRUTH, THE Percy MacKaye (1910)

Based loosely on the 1852 Nathaniel Hawthorne short story "Feathertop," this four-act play traces the single day's existence of a manufactured man whose emerging humanity casts into relief the folly and vice of the people he engages and the evil embodied by the demon who serves as his sardonic mentor.

The play opens in late-17th-century Massachusetts with the witch Goody Rickby working diligently at her forge fashioning a scarecrow to protect her corn from marauding crows. Her work is interrupted by the appearance of Rachel, a niece of Justice Merton, Rickby's paramour in their youth. Rachel purchases an enchanted mirror from Rickby, who says it reveals people's true natures. As Rachel is about to leave, she encounters Richard Talbot, her fiancé, who castigates the witch for selling charmed items to young girls and threatens to incite a Salem-style examination of Rickby.

After the couple's departure, Rickby confers with Dickon, *"a Yankee improvisation of the Prince of Darkness,"* and together they convert the previously half-finished scarecrow into "Lord Ravensbane." The only telltale sign of Ravensbane's bewitched origin is the pipe that he must constantly smoke in order to remain animate.

The play's middle two acts anatomize early 20th-century American society and culture in the guise of colonial Massachusetts. Although Rachel's infatuation with Ravensbane is excused as the effects of a spell, others come under sharp criticism. The hypocrisy of the social elite is rendered in the figure of Justice Merton, whose depravity compels him to allow his niece to marry the scarecrow, thus preserving his reputation. Merton's sister, Cynthia, and a host of local notables who arrive for a hastily called party represent an American upper class all too ready to fawn over titled foreigners. Two masters of Harvard College provide ready targets for commentary on superficial education, and the governor's secretary, Captain Bugby, embodies foppish slavery to fashion as he enters puffing on a pipe in imitation of Ravensbane. Ravensbane's satiric purpose ends, however, when Talbot uses the mirror to reveal the scarecrow's true nature both to the guests and Ravensbane himself.

The short concluding act centers on Ravensbane's attempts to understand himself and on a series of confrontations with Rickby, Dickon, and, most importantly, Rachel. Discovering his origins, Ravensbane laments the impossibility of uniting with Rachel. Dickon promises that Ravensbane shall have the girl if he is quiet about what he knows, but the scarecrow chooses to preserve Rachel from Dickon's satanic machinations. His unselfish love secures for him a soul and true humanity, a reality reflected in the mirror as Ravensbane dies.

Deemed "a tragedy of the ludicrous" by its author, *The Scarecrow* is Percy MacKaye's best-known play. One of the most intriguing plays in an era dominated by action-packed melodramas and emerging efforts at psychological and social realism, *The Scarecrow*'s effective fantasy suggests its importance as a glimpse into an alternative direction that American drama might have taken.

Gary A. Richardson
Mercer University

SCHENKKAN, ROBERT (FREDERIC, JR.)
(1953–) Robert Schenkkan, best known for his seven-hour epic drama of life in Appalachia, *The KENTUCKY CYCLE* (1991), has managed to juggle the competing demands of being an actor, a screenwriter, and a playwright. Schenkkan was born in Chapel Hill, North Carolina, and grew up in Austin, Texas. His mother and father (a public television executive) fostered his early interests in acting and writing. He received his B.A. from the University of Texas at Austin and an M.F.A. in theater arts from Cornell in 1977. As a member of Ensemble Studio Theatre and an alumnus of New Dramatists, he has been actively involved in performing, starting with appearances in regional theater and leading to several film roles, most visibly in *Star Trek: The Next Generation*. His screenwriting credits include *The Quiet American* (2002), written with Christopher Hampton, and a TV miniseries of *The Andromeda Strain* (2008), written with Michael Crichton.

Schenkkan is the author of 10 full-length plays. After winning regional awards for *The Survivalist* (1982), *Final Passages* (1982), and *Heaven on Earth* (1989), Schenkkan garnered national acclaim for *The Kentucky Cycle*, winning the Los Angeles Drama Critics Circle Award and then the PULITZER PRIZE in 1992. The cycle, in which nine one-act plays chronicle two centuries of exploitation and revenge, was a tremendous hit with audiences and critics alike at its debut in Seattle in 1991, although it met with less success in New York two years later. Individual plays from the work are sometimes performed by community and regional theaters, but the cycle's length makes a complete performance a rarity. The most significant critique of *The Kentucky Cycle* to date is a collection of essays, *Confronting Appalachian Stereotypes: Back Talk from an American Region* (1999), written to counter the way the play presents Appalachian people and their history.

Schenkkan, however, is not a writer of strict historical drama. His work sometimes uses an historical incident as its seed, serving only to introduce themes of history's influence on contemporary America (and how we in turn reinvent our history). Schenkkan often focuses on issues of the American frontier, from the Texas setting of *Heaven on Earth* to *The Kentucky Cycle*'s depiction of avarice in what was once America's western territory; this setting allows for characters with great and often tragic passions, people who believe that they are independent of a civilized commitment to others, free to be whatever they want and to use whatever they can. In 2006, *Lewis and Clark Reach the Euphrates* premiered at the Mark Taper Forum, continuing Schenkkan's interest in using the frontier as the setting for a uniquely American morality play.

By the Waters of Babylon, which premiered at the Oregon Shakespeare Festival in 2005, represents a more personal trend in Schenkkan's work; in it, a family moves from crisis to new possibilities. *The Dream Thief,* written for the Milwaukee Children's Theater in 1998, explores this same theme through two children who are convinced that their father's mysterious illness results from his dreams being stolen.

While Schenkkan's work does not advocate conventional religious belief, it frequently deals with faith and reverence in a more universal sense. *Handler* (2000) raises issues of religious conviction among a community of Pentecostal snake handlers. *Final Passages,* in which a cabin boy poisons all the passengers on a ship, and *Heaven on Earth* both feature characters who question the existence of God and lack any moral compass. The tragedy of *The Kentucky Cycle* lies in its characters' inability to be guided by concerns beyond their own welfare. Schenkkan's plays suggest the need for people to grow beyond their disassociation with each other and with the world around them.

BIBLIOGRAPHY

Billings, Dwight W., Gurney Norman, and Katherine Ledford, eds. *Confronting Appalachian Stereotypes: Back Talk from an American Region.* Lexington: University Press of Kentucky, 1999.
Schenkkan, Robert. *The Kentucky Cycle.* New York: Plume, 1993.

John Paul Middlesworth
University of North Carolina–Chapel Hill

SCHISGAL, MURRAY (1926–)
Murray Schisgal grew up in Brooklyn, New York, the son of eastern European immigrant parents. Before his first one-act plays, *The Typist, The Postman,* and *A Simple*

Kind of Love Story, premiered in London in 1960, Schisgal had a varied career as a naval serviceman, a musician, a teacher, and an attorney. He is particularly well known for his original screenplay for the 1982 film *Tootsie,* coauthored with Larry Gelbart and starring Dustin Hoffman, for which he won an Academy Award. In the theater, his greatest commercial success came with the three-character ironic urban comedy *Luv* (1964), an exploration of "modern" marriage. *Luv* ran for 901 performances in its original New York production and remains in the repertoire of regional, community, and dinner theaters nationwide. In *Luv,* Schisgal explores a theme found in his other works as well: one person's struggle to make something more out of daily existence. The comic background is most often marriage, but, as in *Tootsie,* work, relationships, and sexual attraction are also involved. Made into a movie in 1967 starring Jack Lemmon, Elaine May, and Peter Falk, *Luv* was later revised, to mixed reviews, as a musical, *What about Luv?,* in 1984.

Schisgal's other works include the one-act *The Tiger* (1963, a revised version of *The Postman*), a tale of abduction and love that begins with the kidnapping of a young woman by a disaffected postal worker and ends in their romantic involvement; *The Pushcart Peddlers* (1979), a comedy that revolves around two Eastern European immigrants, cultural assimilation, and the complexities of identity construction; *Closet Madness* (1984), an exploration of homosexuality, misogyny, and friendship by two reacquainted high school friends; *Old Wine in a New Bottle* (1987), a story about a married couple's tumultuous and circuitous journey back to each other; *The Cowboy, the Indian, and the Fervent Feminist* (1993), an antifeminist play in which a woman's therapist and husband escape her political leanings through insanity; and *Sexaholics* (1994), a comic look at sexual addiction. More recently, expanding his contributions to behind-the-scenes work, Schisgal has collaborated as producer with longtime associate Dustin Hoffman for Punch Productions in New York City.

BIBLIOGRAPHY

Schisgal, Murray. *"Closet Madness" and Other Plays by Murray Schisgal.* New York: Samuel French, 1984.
———. *Five One-Act Plays.* New York: Dramatists Play Service, 1968.
———. *Luv.* New York: Coward-McCann, 1965.
———. *"The Pushcart Peddlers," "The Flatulist," and Other Plays.* New York: Dramatists Play Service, 1980.
———. *"Sexaholics" and Other Plays.* New York: Dramatists Play Service, 1995.

Brenda Foley
Marlboro College

SEASCAPE Edward Albee (1975) The play that won Albee his second Pulitzer Prize, *Seascape* depicts the encounter of two superficially very different but actually not all that dissimilar couples on a deserted ocean beach. The first act introduces us to Nancy and Charlie, middle-aged with grown children, who have come to the beach for a picnic and so that she can paint. As they discuss where they are in their lives and where they want to go, it becomes apparent that their viewpoints are very different. Charlie is passive, afraid of change, and unwilling to take risks, while Nancy seeks and welcomes new adventures and challenges. He says, "I don't want to do . . . anything," and insists, "We've earned a little rest." He thinks nostalgically of how, as a child, he used to sink to the bottom of the sea and observe the fish: "[O]ne stops being an intruder, finally—just one more object come to the bottom, or living thing, part of the undulation and the silence." Nancy claims, "We've earned a little *life,*" and fantasizes about going from beach to beach around the world, moving "from one hot sandstrip to another: all the birds and fish and seaside flowers, and all the wondrous people that we'd meet."

Nancy has hardly finished her plea that they ought to try something different, when two large green sea creatures, Leslie and Sarah, appear from behind a dune. After considerable fear and wariness on both sides—not surprisingly, Charlie finds the creatures "terrifying" and Nancy calls them "beautiful"—the two couples introduce themselves. In the course of becoming acquainted, Nancy and Charlie must explain such human matters as shaking hands, what frightens them (Charlie says "deep space," "mortality," and "great . . . green creatures, coming up from the sea"—to which Leslie replies, "You're pretty odd yourselves, though you've probably never looked at it that way."), and why they wear clothes—to cover their private parts (Charlie objects vehemently when, in all innocence, Leslie wants to see Nancy's breasts). In turn, Sarah reveals that she has laid 7,000 eggs and had "hundreds" of children, which either "just float away" or "get eaten by folk passing by." When Nancy explains that humans keep their children with them because they love them, Sarah and Leslie want to know what love is, but Charlie finds it difficult to articulate the idea of "emotions," finally exclaiming about his frustration at dealing with "someone who has no grasp of conceptual matters" and noting that he "might as well be talking to a fish." Sarah and Leslie take great umbrage at this, because they see fish as too numerous, "dirty," and "stupid," whereupon Charlie labels them as bigots, "somebody who thinks he's better than somebody else because they're different." Leslie denies the accusation, asserting, "Being different is interesting; there's nothing implicitly inferior or superior about it"—and Nancy says, "[S]o much for conceptual matters."

When birds and then an airplane appear, the sea creatures, especially Leslie, are afraid of them; clearly, Sarah is braver than her mate, just as Nancy is. When Charlie asks them why they came up out of the sea, Sarah replies that they had "a sense of not belonging," of "having changed," perceiving that everything down there no longer had anything to do with them. Charlie tells them that "there was a time when we *all* were down there" and that, at one time, Leslie didn't even have a tail—to which Leslie responds very defensively because, as Sarah explains, he's "extremely proud of his tail; it's very large and sturdy." Charlie gets caught up in describing what he calls "flux" to a very skeptical Sarah and Leslie; when they ask, "Is it for the better?" he answers, "I don't *know*. Progress is a set of assumptions. It's very beautiful down there." He urges them to stay on land, where "tools," "art," and "mortality" are what separate humans from "the brute beasts."

Leslie is certain that Charlie is referring to them with the "brute beasts" comparison and gets very angry, leading Charlie to point out to him that now he is experiencing emotions: "I want you to know about *all* of it; I'm impatient for you. I want you to experience the whole thing!" In order to bring this about, he deliberately causes Sarah to cry by asking her what she would do if Leslie disappeared forever. Leslie and Sarah indicate that they want to go back into the sea, noting, "It's . . . rather dangerous . . . up here"—to which Charlie adds, "Everywhere." As Leslie and Sarah prepare to leave, Nancy tells them, "You'll have to come back . . . sooner or later. You don't have any choice"—and she offers to help them. When Leslie asks, "How?" Charlie—"*sad, shy*"—says, "*Take* you by the hand?" and Leslie responds, "All right. Begin."

On one level, *Seascape* is about the inevitability of the evolutionary process. As Albee has explained, Leslie and Sarah "have come to the point of no return. They have learned about mortality and love and therefore they can't be what they were" (Bigsby 217). But, like many other Albee plays, it is also about the difficulties inherent in human relationships, about what he describes as "people closing down, how people get along with one another, how they make a marriage" (Gussow 289). Thus, these two couples have more in common than first meets the eye. Charlie, tired of life, yearns to return to his idyllic childhood habit of sitting on the bottom of the sea, while Sarah and Leslie, who have come from that bottom where they found Charlie's beloved fish merely pests and where they no longer "belong," cannot go back there any more than he can. And both couples find themselves in similar predicaments—whether to accept a known and familiar existence or to forge a new one full of uncertainty and peril. The fears expressed by both couples at the end of the play echo those of couples in such earlier Albee works as WHO'S AFRAID OF VIRGINIA WOOLF? (1962) and A DELICATE BALANCE (1966), but Charlie's reaching out to Sarah and Leslie and their acceptance of that gesture represent the sort of communal act that is the hope that sustains the human race on its perilous journey.

BIBLIOGRAPHY

Bigsby, C. W. E. *A Critical Introduction to Twentieth-Century Drama: Volume Two—Williams/Miller/Albee.* Cambridge, England: Cambridge University Press, 1984.

Gussow, Mel. *Edward Albee: A Singular Journey.* New York: Simon and Schuster, 1999.

SECRET SERVICE William Gillette (1896)

Set in Richmond, Virginia, this Civil War drama centers on a Southern family's encounter with a Northern spy, a member of the United States Secret Service. Not to be confused with the modern Secret Service agents who guard the president and his family, the Secret Service of the play is a branch of the military, existing in both the Union and the Confederate armies, involved in spying on and infiltrating the enemy.

The Varney family has given much to the war: A son lies upstairs (and always offstage) wounded, perhaps mortally; the father, a Confederate general, serves at the front; and now 16-year-old Wilfred is anxious to enlist. Indeed, early in act 2, Wilfred receives his father's permission to join him at the front, news that is met with great apprehension by his mother and great excitement and renewed romantic interest by his frivolous and fickle girlfriend, Caroline.

A Northern spy named Dumont, posing as the Confederate captain Thorne, has infiltrated the Varney family and gained the affection of Edith Varney. Edith, in an effort to keep Thorne in Richmond, secures a commission from Confederate president Jefferson Davis himself, which puts Thorne in charge of the Confederate telegraph lines. Edith has thus unwittingly given him the position in which he can do the most damage to the Confederacy. One of the Varneys' slaves, Jonas, is found to be working for Thorne: He delivers to Thorne an encoded message from Thorne's brother, Henry Dumont, who is also a Union spy. By the end of the first act, Thorne's true identity and Jonas's activity are revealed to the shocked Mrs. Varney and her daughter.

A trap is set by Thorne's Confederate counterpart and rival for Edith's affection, Benton Arrelsford, to reveal Thorne as Lewis Dumont of the United States Secret Service. When Thorne and his brother are thrown together at the Varney house and know they are being watched, they pretend to struggle and inflict a leg wound on Henry to "prove" Thorne's loyalty to the South. He is allowed to return to the telegraph office, where he attempts to send a forged order to the Confederate front lines, which will benefit the North. He is detected and stopped by Arrelsford, who has never doubted Thorne's allegiance to the North. Edith

has also witnessed his actions and now believes he is a Yankee spy. When Arrelsford calls for help, Thorne cleverly names Arrelsford the traitor, and Edith supports him. Moments later, Edith sees that he will continue to send the dispatch when what she meant was only to save his life, and she runs from the telegraph office in tears; her father and brother could be killed because of her action. Unable to betray Edith Varney, Thorne revokes the order.

Returning to the Varney house, he is apprehended by young Wilfred, who has returned from battle slightly wounded. Though very young and naive, Wilfred represents the American ideal that will be restored after the war is over. When Arrelsford—who is disliked by all—tells the soldiers to take Thorne out and shoot him, it is Wilfred who objects: "Whatever he is—whatever he's done—he has a right to a trial!" The offstage "trial" turns out to be a brief formality, a mere prelude to an execution. Just as Thorne is led away, the last-minute testimony of the telegraph dispatcher, who revoked the order at Thorne's command, saves him from death. He is led away to prison as he and Edith declare their love until they meet again.

The play is in part simply a thriller about the dangers and the heroism of the life of a spy during the Civil War. Thorne's speech to Edith in act 4 about the nature of his service makes the case clearly: "We can't all die a soldier's death. . . . Some of us have orders for another kind of work—desperate—dare-devil work—the hazardous schemes of the Secret Service. . . . If we win we escape with our lives—if we lose—dragged out and butchered like dogs. . . . These are my orders, Miss Varney . . . and I don't want you to think for one minute that I'm ashamed of it." However, in the end, Thorne would sooner betray his country than his sweetheart. Like Bronson Howard's *SHENANDOAH*, this, too, is a Civil War love story, also written more than two decades after the war's end, in which love transcends political loyalties. The "enemies" of the play are, by the time of its writing and performance, viewed by a reunited country. Our sympathies lie with the Southern Varney family, whom we come to know, as well as with the man, on the winning side, who has tricked them—because he ultimately cannot bring himself to betray Edith.

WILLIAM GILLETTE was a pioneer of realism in American drama; this is evidenced in his lengthy and specific stage directions in *Secret Service,* which are very elaborate, describing gestures, intonation, movement, motivation, as well as detailed set design and costuming.

SERPENT, THE JEAN-CLAUDE VAN ITALLIE (1968)

On May 2, 1968, *The Serpent* premiered at Rome's Teatro delle Arti. During the next three months, the play was performed all over Europe by Joseph Chaikin's Open Theater. When the Open Theater returned to the United States, *The Serpent* was staged at Vassar College and Harvard University before the Open Theater took it on a college tour in March and April 1969; the first public performances in the United States were held from May 29 to June 14, 1970, at Washington Square Methodist Church in New York City.

The Serpent begins with the actors warming up in order for them to become in tune with their bodies before they can effectively communicate with the audience. A ceremonial musical procession then introduces elements that contrapuntally reinforce the play's musical structure. A doctor is seen performing an autopsy on an apparent gunshot victim. The scene transforms into a ritualistic reenactment of the John F. Kennedy assassination as depicted in the Abraham Zapruder film, indelibly stamped on the minds of Americans. The next image is one of Martin Luther King Jr., looking to what he calls the promised land in which a spirit of shared communion will be the norm, replacing the current lack of both commitment and responsibility. The four women of the chorus, dressed in black, address the audience; their role is to keep the play fixed in the audience's collective consciousness. The actors then create the story of the Garden of Eden, presented as a communal rite that is to be intuitively shared by the audience. The Cain-Abel myth is staged next, presumably to imbue subliminally the notion of violence as endemic to humanity throughout history. The Cain-Abel parable becomes linked with original sin and with the Kennedy and King assassinations; the consequences of original sin led to the first murder, which is a prelude to the modern violence personified by the Kennedy and King disasters. *The*

Serpent terminates with a litany of "begatting," suggesting copulation and birth. The play thus ends on a positive note, portraying humanity's discovery of sex in contrast to its use of violence and murder, the subject of previous segments of the play.

The Serpent, which consists of myths, rites, and ceremonies, is subtitled *a ceremony.* It conveys to the audience myths that have been intuitively shared. The dialogue is subordinate to the ceremonial staging effects, and words are used primarily for their incantatory effects. It is a carefully choreographed play, calculated into a series of sounds, noises, incantations, and breathing rhythms. Through months of rigorous rehearsals and preparation, the Open Theater contributed to the work's great success worldwide.

Intimating that the present can learn from the past, *The Serpent* intersperses biblical and modern "scenes." On the surface, it appears to be permeated with a sense of defeatism, guilt, and determinism, defined by our fate, which is "cursed" from our past behaviors. Humanity has lost its chance for Paradise—the idyllic world is gone forever. The result of original sin is a legacy of violence, a curse that is self-inflicted. The correspondence between biblical and modern times is made through myths, which are conveyed through the play's ritualistic structure. It suggests that society, in need of a critical examination, or "autopsy," can be restored through communal sharing. The presentation of the rite leads to an understanding of a sense of shared responsibility, much like the communion of priests and celebrants during Mass. Thus, *The Serpent* provides humanity with a strong sense of purpose in the midst of a society inundated with a history of violence, poor choices, defeatism, and unmitigated guilt.

Gene A. Plunka
University of Memphis

SEVEN GUITARS AUGUST WILSON (1995)

Set in 1948 in the yard of a house in Pittsburgh's Hill District, *Seven Guitars* is part of WILSON's cycle of 10 plays depicting the African-American experience in the 20th century.

As the play begins, a group of friends have gathered after the funeral of Floyd "Schoolboy" Barton, a local blues musician whose lone hit record plays in the background. The recording serves as a bridge to events of the recent past—one week before—in this same yard, where Floyd, having returned from Chicago and from an 18-month affair with another woman, dances with Vera to his own music and tries to win her back. Vera is skeptical, but she lets him spend the night with her in her apartment on the ground floor of the house. Upstairs live Louise and Hedley, in separate quarters. Canewell and Red Carter are also musicians, both of whom collaborated on Floyd's hit record. Neither feels he was well treated by the white Chicago record company, and they are not anxious to repeat the experience, as Floyd hopes they will. Canewell and Red—and Floyd himself—voice the same complaints as Ma Rainey and her musicians do in Wilson's MA RAINEY'S BLACK BOTTOM (1984), namely that although theirs is the talent that is being recorded and sold, they do not receive fair compensation from the white record-company executives who exploit them.

Louise's niece, Ruby—"with her little fast behind," as Louise says—is coming to stay with her aunt because she is in some trouble: One of her boyfriends is dead, and the other—who killed the first out of jealousy—is in prison. Ruby is pregnant by one of them but does not immediately reveal this to her aunt. Louise doesn't have much use for men. Her man "used [her] up" and left her 12 years ago. She advises Vera not to fall for Floyd's line twice. In fact, as soon as Ruby arrives, all of the men, including Floyd, have eyes for her. Eventually, Ruby satisfies the lust of Hedley, a middle-aged man with tuberculosis who kills chickens and turkeys and makes sandwiches to sell; Ruby plans to tell him that her baby is his. Hedley is something of a loose cannon: He stuns the rest of the group by killing a neighbor's rooster suddenly, and he tells Ruby about killing a man who refused to call him, a black man, "King," which is the name his father gave him. (After the incident, he went by the name Hedley.)

Floyd's manager arranges for Floyd, Canewell, and Red to play at a local club and promises to get their instruments out of the pawn shop. When he fails to show up at the pawn shop to meet Floyd, the frustrated Floyd commits a robbery to fund his dreams—

that night's gig, a dress for Vera, and tickets for both of them to Chicago, where he plans to make another record. When Floyd is concealing the cash from the robbery in the garden, Hedley, seeing him in a shaft of light, mistakes him for a mystical figure bringing him his "father's money." When Floyd tells him to go back in the house, Hedley gets his machete from the cellar and kills Floyd. The final scene is back at the funeral gathering, where we learn that the authorities do not know that Hedley is guilty and that his friends are not going to tell.

In Wilson's KING HEDLEY II (2001), set in the same location but in the 1980s, the playwright revisits some of these characters. The title character is Ruby's son—the baby she carries in Seven Guitars, whom she tells Hedley is his. King lives most of his life believing Hedley was his father. He is raised by Louise, whom he calls "Mama Louise" and who has died two months before King Hedley II begins. Canewell is in the play as Stool Pigeon, and Ruby reunites with the imprisoned boyfriend who killed King's real father. In both plays, Wilson examines the limited choices available to African-American men, their consequent frustration, and the violence that results.

SEVEN YEAR ITCH, THE George Axelrod (1952)

Set in a New York City apartment in the heat of summer, The Seven Year Itch takes a comic—and very 1950s—look at temptation and guilt in a married man with a vivid imagination.

Richard Sherman is left alone for the summer when his wife, Helen, and young son head for the beach to avoid the summer heat. Upstairs, a sexy—and friendly—young model is subletting. Richard meets her when she accidentally sends a heavy iron flowerpot over the edge of her terrace onto his, barely missing him. A shaken Richard invites her down for a drink, this brush with death having caused him to resume drinking and smoking, despite his promise to his wife that he would give them up for the sake of his "nervous indigestion." When "The Girl" (never named) comes down, conversation quickly reveals that she has posed nude in a prize-winning photo published in U.S. Camera, which just happens to be on Richard's shelf.

Richard takes fantastic flights into his imagination throughout the play. He first imagines a stenographer at work and then a friend of Helen's, both unable to resist him, overpowered by his unintended animal magnetism; he immediately afterward imagines his wife's laughter at the idea of his being attractive to other women. Once The Girl enters his life, he begins to imagine scenes between the two of them: First, he—"very suave, very Noël Coward"—sweeps her off her feet with his charm and skill at the piano; needless to say, this is far from reality. When she goes upstairs to get some champagne she bought for her birthday, Richard and his conscience discuss his intentions toward her. He also has fantasies about Helen's activities at the beach, imagining that she is being seduced by Tom MacKenzie, an attractive writer of their acquaintance. In another fantasy, Helen has tea with The Girl, the stenographer, and the *"unidentified YOUNG LADY in brassiere and panties,"* whom Richard often watches through her window; they discuss Richard's shortcomings.

When The Girl returns to his apartment with the champagne, Richard drinks most of it and makes a pass at her. She quickly goes home but soon drops another pot on his terrace, and they will see each other tomorrow. The next evening, Richard has an appointment with a psychiatrist whose book is being published by Richard's employer, a 25-cent book publisher. The psychiatrist's book, *Of Man and the Unconscious,* has been retitled—against the author's wishes—*Of Sex and Violence* (Richard's boss also plans to publish an edition of *The Scarlet Letter* retitled *I Was an Adulteress*). Richard discusses his "criminal assault" of the previous evening. He shows the doctor The Girl's photo, at which point Dr. Brubaker "congratulate[s]" him on his "taste" and advises him not to do it again, at least not "precariously balanced on a piano bench."

The following morning, Richard awakens after spending the night with The Girl. While she sleeps, he fantasizes that she is desperately in love with him and he, *"very tough,"* rejects her. His imagination then turns to Helen: He *tells* Helen, who shoots him and herself. His dying gasps are interrupted by a real-world knock on the door. Dr Brubaker has forgotten his briefcase; he deduces that The Girl is in Richard's

bedroom and advises Richard to engage in "vigorous denial" if questioned by Helen. He also suggests that Richard refer The Girl to *him* if she "appears to be in need of psychiatric aid." When The Girl emerges from the bedroom, it is clear that though she likes Richard, she has *not* fallen in love and is quite happy to say good morning and good-bye. While before she had avoided nice guys who fell "desperately in love" with her, now she looks forward to finding "someone who's sweet and intelligent and married—to [her]." As for Richard, he's decided to go to the beach and make sure his wife has eyes only for him.

Axelrod's satiric treatment of marriage, male guilt, and, to a lesser extent, the publishing industry was extremely popular; the comedy ran for more than two years. In 1955, a somewhat sanitized (Richard and The Girl do not have sex) but otherwise fairly faithful version of the play became a film, starring Marilyn Monroe and original cast member Tom Ewell.

SHADOW BOX, THE MICHAEL CRISTOFER (1977)

Winner of the PULITZER PRIZE and the only drama of note by actor-turned-playwright Michael Cristofer, *The Shadow Box* might be seen as, in part, an AIDS play before the age of AIDS. Set on the grounds of a hospice and focusing on three terminally ill patients and the individuals who will be their survivors, the work gives dramatic form to the ideas popularized by Elisabeth Kübler-Ross's influential book *On Death and Dying* (1969). In her book, Kübler-Ross delineated the stages in the process of dying: denial, anger, bargaining, depression or preparatory grief, and, finally, acceptance.

Through a deft handling of stage space, including a downstage interview area, where the characters can talk in an almost stream-of-consciousness fashion with the voice of an unseen, disembodied caregiver (perhaps a doctor, clergy member, or therapist), and a cottage with three playing areas (the porch for Joe, the living room for Brian, and the kitchen for Felicity), Cristofer created an almost cinematic fluidity and, at times, an antiphonal effect through simultaneous dialogue.

Joe, a disillusioned, middle-aged father of a guitar-playing teenage boy, broods over those things he always wanted but has never had, such as a farm in the country and more children, and ponders how little his life has added up to now that he nears the end of it. Although he has moved beyond the denial of approaching death, his wife Maggie has not, and neither has yet been able to tell their son Steve. Maggie at first even refuses to enter the cottage where death awaits, since all she has ever known is marriage, and so she fears that if denied her familiar role of nagging wife, nothing will remain to define her existence. Finally, however, she answers Joe's plea that he not be left to face death alone.

Felicity, a crotchety, older woman given to crude language and to tyrannizing her spinster daughter, is still at the bargaining stage, refusing to go gently and holding on to life until the favorite daughter she had banished can return and be forgiven. But that daughter has long been dead, and her frequent letters have actually been written by the unappreciated Agnes out of duty to a mother whom she no longer loves but to whom she continues to provide hope. For, ironically, Agnes herself has become dependent upon these letters as well, since the only role remaining for her—an emotionally starved woman—is that of martyr.

Brian, a gay writer formerly married to a boozy and sexually adventurous woman and now in a homosexual relationship with Mark, has, near the point of death, discovered anew—in his writing and in his savoring of all experience—much of the energy and magic that had gone out of his life. Although aware of death as life's only certainty, he is still terribly afraid of that final second when one must face—without choice—the absolute unknown. It is left to the flamboyant ex-wife Beverly to goad the unaccepting and defiant Mark, who like most survivors thinks first of himself, into an awareness of Brian's need for him to be there in his last days.

In the play's stylized, lyrical coda, Cristofer eschews a realistic use of language for a more poetic, overlapping one as the characters echo isolated lines of dialogue from earlier in the play and chant their affirmation of life: If they are dying, then they are still alive and so can savor the moment that remains.

Thomas P. Adler
Purdue University

SHANGE,   NTOZAKE (1948–   ) Ntozake Shange was raised in a well-to-do, intellectual environment in Trenton, New Jersey. At birth, she was named Paulette Williams, after her father, Paul Williams, a surgeon, but she rejected this designation as emblematic of patriarchal dominance and for its ties to the African-American history of slavery. Taking the Zulu name *Ntozake* (She who comes with her own things) *Shange* (Who walks like a lion) to celebrate her sense of selfhood and Afrocentrism, in 1972 she moved to New York, without financial support from her parents, and experienced being a poor African-American woman in Harlem.

While in the women's studies program at Sonoma State College in California, Shange began reading her poetry at women's bars. Out of this evolved her first performance piece, FOR COLORED GIRLS WHO HAVE CONSIDERED SUICIDE/WHEN THE RAINBOW IS ENUF (1976); its Broadway production ran for two years and won New York Drama Critics' and Outer Critics Circle Awards. In it, seven African-American women relate individual stories of fear, pain, loss, and joy to create a collective African-American, female voice, which emerges triumphantly with independence and self-knowledge. She followed this with the less idealistic *a photograph: lovers in motion* (1977), originally subtitled "a study of cruelty," which uses photography as a metaphor for life, following the relationship of an abusive male photographer with three women.

Using masks and an elaborate set, *spell #7* (1979) explores the racism faced by African-American artists. Shange's expressionistic dream play, *boogie woogie landscapes* (1979), is even more theatrically complex as it dissects the psyche of an "all-American colored girl." In *From Okra to Greens/A Different Kinda Love Story* (1985), Shange takes a number of her earlier poems and divides them into two voices, creating a metaphoric love story that engages political and gender issues. *The Love Space Demands: A Continuing Saga* (1992) again depicts the plight of African-American women in a series of troubled relationships, but was not a critical success. Parts of the 1994 poetry collection *Liliane: Resurrection of a Daughter,* which contained dialogues between a woman, her psychiatrist, and several past lovers, were also adapted for the stage that same year. In 1995, Steppenwolf produced a musical by Ntozake Shange, Eric Simonson, and Ladysmith Black Mambazo's leader, Joseph Shabalala, called *Nomathemba.* The title means "hope" in Zulu, and is the name of its young female protagonist, who leaves her village, but is sought by her fiancé. *Hydraulics Phat Like Mean* was Shange's contribution to an evening of short plays, each inspired by a Shakespearean sonnet and collectively titled *Love's Fire,* that played at the Public Theater in 1998.

Shange has also written cabaret material, produced readings, and done revisionist adaptations of plays, including Bertolt Brecht's *Mother Courage* (1980), which won an OBIE AWARD for Best Adaptation, Willy Russell's *Educating Rita* (1983), and a musical based on her own novel about an African-American girl experiencing a white environment, *Betsey Brown* (1986). All are marked by her feminism and her commitment to exposing racial and gender stereotypes.

In 2003, Shange wrote and oversaw the production of *Lavender Lizards and Lilac Landmines: Layla's Dream* while serving as artist-in-residence at the University of Florida, Gainesville. This piece, which depicts how the poet Layla surmounts a bad relationship and arrives at self-awareness, has received several productions since. Shange suffered a stroke in 2004, which has slowed down her recent output, but she is still writing verse. In 2007, the New York–based New Federal Theatre organized a monthlong retrospective of events that included a revised version of an earlier short piece by Shange about pre–urban renewal African-American life, *It Hasn't Always Been This Way.* Also in 2007, Shange's daughter Savannah worked with Campo Santo to create the provocative *A Place to Stand;* based on poetry by Shange and Jimmy Santiago, the piece explores the effects of prison on those both inside and out.

Shange calls herself a "race poet-playwright" and tries to create new rituals and mythologies for African Americans through her stylized "choreopoems," which accounts for her refusal to be contained by traditional theatrical boundaries. These "choreopoems" form the bulk of her theatrical work; they are a unique and important contribution to American drama. In them, she mixes poetry, prose, music, and dance to create a theatrical expression she relates to an African-American heritage; it is a type of theater expected to rouse strong emotional responses from its audience. The improvisational feel of her work is intentional, meant to reflect African forms of storytelling, rhythm, movement, and emotional catharsis. This sense of improvisation, along with Shange's mixing of genres, separates her work from more traditional Western verse drama.

Though unconventional, her work is highly emotive and offers a poetic, living picture of African-American culture—"the good and the bad." She refuses to shy away from presenting terrible characters or from confronting controversial topics, such as masturbation, rape, or abortion. For the sake of authenticity and as a rejection of what she sees as limiting patriarchal forms, Shange usually eschews Standard English in favor of African-American vernacular and her own grammatical rules.

BIBLIOGRAPHY

Effiong, Philip Uko. *In Search of a Model for African-American Drama: A Study of Selected Plays by Lorraine Hansberry, Amiri Baraka, and Ntozake Shange.* Lanham, Md.: University Press of America, 2000.

Lester, Neal A. *Ntozake Shange: A Critical Study of the Plays.* New York: Garland, 1995.

Shange, Ntozake. *From Okra to Greens/A Different Kinda Love Story.* New York: Samuel French, 1985.

———. *Liliane: Resurrection of the Daughter.* New York: St. Martin's Press, 1994.

———. *The Love Space Demands: A Continuing Saga.* New York: St. Martin's Press, 1991.

———. *Plays, one.* London: Methuen, 1992.

———. *Three Pieces.* New York: St. Martin's Press, 1981.

Susan C. W. Abbotson
Rhode Island College

SHANLEY, JOHN PATRICK (1950–)

John Patrick Shanley was born and raised in the Bronx, New York. The youngest child in a working-class Irish Catholic family, he grew up among the types of rough and wary people that would later inhabit his plays. Though an avid reader who began writing poetry at age 11, Shanley was expelled from school several times before being sent to a private academy in New Hampshire. After two years in the United States Marine Corps, he discovered playwriting while enrolled in the educational theater program at New York University; he graduated at the top of his class.

Shanley is most often praised for capturing the authentic tone of Irish and Italian working-class people and simultaneously elevating their expression into a kind of operatic poetry. Love—finding it, keeping it, overcoming the pain of losing it—is the central theme of his more than 20 plays and screenplays. His characters are typically people of limited social and economic options, damaged by infidelity, physical and emotional abuse, and loneliness, who struggle to find intimacy through faith in the redeeming power of love.

Shanley's earliest efforts were not particularly successful. *Rockaway* (1982)—the story of a woman who embarks on a spending spree around the world after being misdiagnosed with a terminal illness, declares war on the doctor, and then falls in love with him—was dismissed as a situation comedy full of unlikely and unmotivated actions. Much later, similar criticisms were leveled at his screenplay *Joe Versus the Volcano* (1990), which he also directed. In another plot hinged on misdiagnosed terminal illness, Joe, on his way to throwing himself into a volcano to win mineral rights from the native people for his wealthy benefactor, falls in love and is rescued in an improbable fairy-tale ending.

Shanley's first stage success was *Danny and the Deep Blue Sea* (1984), in which a street brawler who is afraid he may have killed someone and a woman haunted by an incestuous incident with her father spend the night groping toward mutual healing through awkward but determined attempts at emotional intimacy. His next play, *Savage in Limbo* (1985), explores similar struggles among five denizens of a Bronx bar, desperate to change their lives, finding the courage to forge connections with one another. *Italian American Reconciliation* (1988), set in New York's Little Italy, is among his best-known plays and is also one of the most gentle, following the story of a man who discovers he must heal his emotionally violent past with his ex-wife before he can love again. Shanley, dubbed by *New York Times* critic Ben Brantley "a specialist in the combat zone where love and hate blur" (March 5, 2003), also

wrote *Psychopathia Sexualis* (1997), *Where's My Money?* (2001), and *Dirty Story* (2003).

Shanley first achieved national recognition with his screenplay, *Moonstruck* (1987), a whimsical romance about a woman who falls in love with her fiancé's brother, which won the Academy Award for screenwriting. Along with occasional forays into acting and directing, Shanley continues to write for stage, film, and television. He was nominated for an Emmy for his work on HBO's *Live from Baghdad* (2003).

Shanley's 2005 Broadway debut, DOUBT, swept the major awards for Best New Play, including TONY, OBIE NY Drama Critics' Circle, and Drama Desk awards, and won the PULITZER PRIZE. Shanley adapted and directed this drama about suspected sexual misconduct in the priesthood for the 2008 film of the same name. In 2006, Shanley's *Defiance* premiered OFF-BROADWAY; the play is an examination of racism and morality among Vietnam-era Marines and is intended as the second play in a trilogy begun with *Doubt*. He also wrote the book and lyrics for *Romantic Poetry* (2008), a musical valentine to the joys and pangs of love.

BIBLIOGRAPHY

Shanley, John Patrick. *Cellini.* New York: Dramatists Play Service, 2002.

———. *Defiance.* New York: Theatre Communications Group, 2008.

———. *"Dirty Story" and Other Plays.* New York: Theatre Communications Group, 2006.

———. *Doubt.* New York: Theatre Communications Group, 2005.

———. *Missing/Kissing: Missing Marisa, Kissing Christine.* New York: Dramatists Play Service, 1997.

———. *Psychopathia Sexualis.* New York: Dramatists Play Service, 1997.

———. *Sailor's Song.* New York: Dramatists Play Service, 2006.

———. *Thirteen by Shanley.* New York: Applause Theatre Books, 1998.

Roxane Rix
Kutztown University of Pennsylvania

SHAW, IRWIN (1913–1984)   Born in New York, Shaw earned a B.A. from Brooklyn College in 1934 and served as a private first class and a signal corps warrant officer in World War II. Best known for his

screenplay for the 1958 film version of EUGENE O'NEILL'S *DESIRE UNDER THE ELMS* (1924), his 1948 novel *The Young Lions* (critically praised as one of the most significant fictional explorations of World War II), and the highly successful 1976 television miniseries adaptation of his novel *Rich Man, Poor Man,* Shaw actually began his career writing radio scripts for popular programs in the 1930s.

He turned to writing for the stage with *BURY THE DEAD* (1936), a critically successful antiwar one-act play in which six dead soldiers refuse to be buried because they believe they have died in vain; between the two world wars, Shaw's play raised such issues as the public's right to information (even in wartime) and the exploitation of the common soldier for the profit of those with financial and political power. Collaborating with the experimental GROUP THEATRE and continuing his propensity for work interrogating socially conscious themes, Shaw wrote *The Gentle People* (1939), an antifascist fable in which two fishermen murder a gangster who tries to extort money from them. Another Group Theatre endeavor was *Quiet City* (1939), about an upper-middle-class Jewish department store owner who changes his name, converts to Christianity, and exploits his workers until he sees the error of his ways and returns to Judaism determined to improve working conditions. Shaw's *Retreat to Pleasure* (1940), about a young man who seeks pleasure, knowing that war is imminent, was the Group Theatre's final production; by then, few of its members remained.

Shaw's other plays include *Siege* (1937), about Spanish Loyalists during the Spanish civil war; *The Commandos Strike at Dawn* (1943), based on a story by C. S. Forester detailing military resistance to the Nazis by Norwegian soldiers; *Sons and Soldiers* (1944), about a woman who contemplates having children and envisions the life they will face; and *The Assassin* (1946), about the assassination of a traitorous French admiral. The negative critical reaction to *The Assassin,* coupled with the success of his screenplay for *Talk of the Town* (1942), led to a shift in focus toward writing more screenplays, short stories, and novels. After the week-long run of *The Survivors* (1948), a melodrama about Civil War veterans who return home to a family feud, it would be many years before the production of

another Shaw play; the next, *Children from Their Games* (1963), based on his novel of the same title, ran in New York for only four performances.

Notwithstanding his playwriting output, it is as a fiction writer that Shaw gained renown, producing 12 novels (including *The Troubled Air* in 1951, which explored the social phenomenon of McCarthyism, and the popular *Lucy Crown* in 1956) and 84 short stories. Shaw spent much of his life in Europe and died in Switzerland.

BIBLIOGRAPHY

Giles, James R. *Irwin Shaw.* Boston: Twayne, 1983.

Shaw, Irwin. *Bury the Dead.* New York: Dramatists Play Service, 1975.

Shnayarson, Michael. *Irwin Shaw.* New York: Putnam, 1989.

Brenda Foley
Marlboro College

SHELDON, EDWARD (1886–1946)

Born in Chicago, Edward Sheldon was an avid playgoer even in his youth. In 1904, he entered Harvard University, where he took GEORGE PIERCE BAKER's playwriting course. Sheldon graduated from Harvard in 1907 and earned his master's degree the following year. When he was only 22, he had the first of many successes with *SALVATION NELL* (1908), a play in which a young pregnant woman living in squalor finds help and redemption at a Salvation Army mission and eventually brings her drunken, abusive boyfriend to salvation too. Despite its highly romanticized ending, the play's strength is its social realism: It is characterized by realistic immigrant dialect and scenes depicting the squalor, crime, and alcoholism that were prevalent among the poorest classes in New York's slums in the earliest part of the 20th century. Social realism also characterized Sheldon's other early plays, *The NIGGER* (1909), in which he takes on the problem of racism, and *The BOSS* (1911), in which he addresses the problems stemming from the conflict between laborer and capitalist. Sheldon was influenced by Norwegian playwright Henrik Ibsen, whose realistic plays about social problems were being introduced to America at that time.

Sheldon's subsequent plays are not considered as significant as his first three, though several were commercial successes. Among these were *The High Road* (1912), *Romance* (1913), *The Garden of Paradise* (1914), *The Song of Songs* (1914), *Jest* (1919), and *The Lonely Heart* (1921). Fairly early in his career, Sheldon was stricken with severe arthritis, which eventually confined him to bed and robbed him of his eyesight. From 1921 until 1930, he collaborated with other playwrights; for the final 16 years of his life, as his health deteriorated, he remained a force in American theater by helping others with their work. His biographer, Eric Wollencott Barnes, maintained that between 1930 and his death in 1946, Edward Sheldon had a creative hand in at least one play, sometimes more, each season.

BIBLIOGRAPHY

Barnes, Eric Wollencott. *The Man Who Lived Twice: A Biography of Edward Sheldon.* New York: Scribners, 1956.

Ruff, Loren K. *Edward Sheldon.* New York: Twayne, 1982.

SHENANDOAH Bronson Howard (1888)

Though a Civil War play, *Shenandoah* deals more with the love interests of the characters than with the issues of the war. Indeed, Howard entirely avoided the issue of slavery. Thematically, *Shenandoah* asserts the importance of family ties and human love above all else and—having been written about 20 years after the war's end—the inevitability of the preservation of the Union of the United States. In the first moments of the play, the latter theme is articulated by the character Kerchival West when he says, speaking of Fort Sumter, "If [our Southern friends] do fire upon it, the echo of that first shot will be heard above their graves, and Heaven knows how many of our own also; but the flag will still float!—over the graves of both sides." The play begins and ends with a unified country: It opens as the South is about to fire on Fort Sumter, and it closes after the surrender is completed and all fighting has ceased. The war takes place during acts 2 and 3.

As the play opens, two military men, Robert Ellingham and Kerchival West—classmates at West Point, friends who have served together in the West—discuss the possibility of meeting on opposite sides of a battlefield. Each of these men has a sister; each sister loves and is loved in return by her brother's friend. The stage is set, then, for sweethearts to find them-

selves enemies. Again, it is Kerchival West (a Yankee) who articulates a theme of the play as he speaks to his sister about the emotions she feels when her beloved Robert Ellingham (now a Confederate) is in mortal danger in a battle against her own side: "My poor girl! Every woman's heart, the world over, belongs not to any country or any flag, but to her husband—and her lover. Pray for the man you love, sister—it would be treason not to." During the course of the play, both men are presumed dead, but at the end of the war both couples—along with North and South—are reunited.

In a subplot involving Kerchival West and his commanding officer, a lady's honor is defended; a villain is finally defeated; a son redeems himself in his father's eyes for an unnamed youthful indiscretion by volunteering for a suicide mission—and, of course, dies on that mission; and a husband realizes that he has wrongly accused his wife and begs her forgiveness, which she readily gives.

For an example of the play's convoluted (and corny) plot, one need only consider the plotline involving Gertrude's horse: Gertrude Ellingham (Kerchival's beloved), a Southerner, has had a favorite horse since childhood. The Northern army presses that horse into service for the Union. Gertrude is reunited with her horse briefly when the Union army takes possession of her home, but the Yankees will not give him back because he is now General Sheridan's mount. Soon this team of Confederate horse and Yankee general is cheered on by the Confederate girl whose Yankee beloved rides with that general. After the battle—this part is reported late in the play—she sees the horse, grabs his bridle, mounts him, and goes in search of her beloved Kerchival.

The play was justifiably attacked by critics, but it was so loved by audiences that it brought great fortune to its author. The play's historical importance lies in its reflection of the feelings of the country just 23 years after a divisive civil conflict.

SHEPARD, SAM (1943–)

Born Sam Shepard Rogers Jr. in Fort Sheridan, Illinois, Sam Shepard lived on army bases in South Dakota, Utah, Florida, and Guam until he was 12 years old and his family settled in California. By the time he was 20, he had graduated from high school and had dropped out of junior college after a year, immigrating to New York where he worked as a waiter, ersatz musician, would-be actor, and sometime playwright. In 1964, two of his plays, *Cowboys* and *The Rock Garden,* were produced OFF-OFF-BROADWAY, and he began to believe that writing for the theater might be his ideal métier. With more than 40 plays since then, Shepard is one of this country's most inventive and prolific playwrights.

Television, old movies, and romantic American myths provide him with characters and settings. He has a fine ear for 1960s vernacular, especially apparent in the conversations of characters who belong to the drug or rock music cultures, and his outrageously funny protagonists deliver monologues of absurd but entertaining complexity. Frequently, the playwright hints that he is nostalgic for an age when simple heroes could be praised for honest values, and he laments the dissolution of the nuclear family. Anachronisms of time and setting, such as his linking of Mae West and Marlene Dietrich with Paul Bunyan and Jesse James in *Mad Dog Blues* (1971), allow him to mix fantasy and folklore with social commentary. Other plays combine pop music and biography to produce a media event like *Seduced* (1978), which presents the haunting story of a man who resembles Howard Hughes. Winner of an OBIE AWARD for Sustained Achievement in the theater, he also received a PULITZER PRIZE for *BURIED CHILD* (1978).

At the same time as he was gaining recognition as a playwright, Shepard was also cast as a film star in several popular movies; he chose nevertheless to continue writing for the stage. His originality of mind, his unerring ear for speech rhythms, and his wildly imaginative characterizations were possibly less relevant to many theatergoers than his celebrity status. Always distrusting Hollywood's artificiality and distortion of what the playwright considers honest values, he also realizes that success in this area of his life enhanced his reputation in other areas. As his celebrity status increased, the appearance of a new Shepard play became a major cultural event.

Shepard is partly the product of the rise of American pop culture in the late 1950s, when he was a teen-ager, and partly the product of the western literary tradition. As an alienated youth in the Vietnam era, he rebelled against highbrow, intellectual culture and America's growing involvement in foreign policy. Numerous genres of music, including jazz, blues, country and western, and folk, influenced the verbal rhythms and plot contingencies of his written work. His celebration of the working class and its needs is often traced to Walt Whitman. His elliptical stage dialogue and nonlinear story lines recall the THEATRE OF THE ABSURD. His residency in London in the early 1970s and his contacts with the Royal Court Theatre and the Angry Young Men of British theater (playwrights whose works criticized social and economic conditions of the day) and their successors also lent a shape and discipline to his work. In particular, the natural language and subtext of contemporary British playwright Harold Pinter's works (even the plot of Pinter's *Homecoming* [1967]) are to some extent reconfigured in Shepard's *Buried Child.*

Although Shepard's themes and techniques have remained constant throughout his career, one can fairly divide his achievements into decade-long categories. The 1960s featured plays both published and unpublished that were largely one-act dramas with frequently enigmatic, volatile characters in improbable situations: *Cowboys* (1964), *Icarus's Mother* (1965), *Red Cross* (1966), *La Turista* (1967), and *Forensic and the Navigators* (1967) all seemed deliberately obscure and inchoate. The 1970s produced a series of longer, more confident works: *Cowboy Mouth* (1971), *The* TOOTH OF CRIME (1972), and *Geography of a Horse Dreamer* (1974) provided theater audiences with an original American voice. *Angel City* (1976) is a bitter attack on the false values of Los Angeles, which the playwright feels appears to have betrayed its more "wholesome" western origins. In the very late 1970s and early 1980s, Shepard reached the peak of his powers artistically. He wrote his critically acclaimed trilogy: CURSE OF THE STARVING CLASS (1977), *Buried Child,* and TRUE WEST (1980). Each of these three plays focuses on families who have literally abandoned their geographical roots and are betrayed by alcoholic, detached fathers, adulterous mothers, and siblings whose rivalries have developed into a murderous intensity.

The trilogy and the plays that followed, including *FOOL FOR LOVE* (1983) and *A LIE OF THE MIND* (1985), established Shepard as a keen analyst of American family life, innately dysfunctional and beleaguered by a hostile commercialism. In the final decades of the 20th century, Shepard's interests turned more to producing films, but plays like *Simpatico* (1996), *Eyes for Consuela* (1998), and *The Late Henry Moss* (2000) reveal a more sustained and intense analysis of individual characters than he had previously rendered.

Opening OFF-BROADWAY immediately prior to the 2004 presidential election, *The God of Hell* is, as Shepard described it at the time, "a takeoff on Republican fascism." In 2005, Shepard wrote and appeared in the film *Don't Come Knocking* with his longtime partner Jessica Lange. The movie laments America's loss of an heroic western past. The film's protagonist, Howard Spence, played by Shepard, is a thoroughly disillusioned cowboy film star, drowning himself in alcohol, holding on to failed dreams, fearful of aging. *Kicking a Dead Horse* (2008) opens with a dead horse onstage, and beside it, an open grave and the grave-digger, a man who had traveled west in search of some real America; here again Shepard mourns America's loss of authenticity. In all of these recent works, Shepard continues to explore the themes found in his earlier plays.

BIBLIOGRAPHY

Bottoms, Stephen J. *The Theatre of Sam Shepard: States of Crisis*. Cambridge, England: Cambridge University Press, 1998.

Callens, Johan. *Dis/Figuring Sam Shepard*. Brussels and New York: Peter Lang, 2007.

Daniels, Barry, ed. *Joseph Chaikin & Sam Shepard: Letters and Texts, 1972–1984*. New York: New American Library, 1989.

DeRose, David J. *Sam Shepard*. New York: Twayne, 1992.

Hart, Lynda. *Sam Shepard's Metaphorical Stages*. Westport, Conn.: Greenwood, 1987.

King, Kimball, ed. *Sam Shepard: A Casebook*. New York: Garland, 1988.

Marranca, Bonnie, ed. *American Dreams: The Imagination of Sam Shepard*. New York: Performing Arts Journal, 1981.

Mottram, Ron. *Inner Landscapes: The Theatre of Sam Shepard*. Columbia: University of Missouri Press, 1984.

Oumano, Ellen. *Sam Shepard: The Life and Work of an American Dreamer*. New York: St. Martin's Press, 1986.

Rosen, Carol. *Sam Shepard: A 'Poetic Rodeo.'* New York: Palgrave Macmillan, 2005.

Roudané, Matthew, ed. *The Cambridge Companion to Sam Shepard*. Cambridge, England: Cambridge University Press, 2002.

Shepard, Sam. *"Angel City" and Other Plays*. New York: Urizen, 1976.

———. *"Buried Child," "Seduced" and "Suicide in Flat B."* New York: Urizen, 1979.

———. *"Fool for Love" and Other Plays*. New York: Bantam, 1984.

———. *Four Two-Act Plays*. New York: Urizen, 1980.

———. *Kicking a Dead Horse*. New York: Vintage, 2008.

———. *A Lie of the Mind*. New York: Plume, 1987.

———. *Seven Plays*. New York: Bantam, 1984.

———. *Simpatico*. New York: Dramatists Play Service, 1955.

———. *Three Plays: "The Late Henry Moss," "Eyes for Consuela," "When the World Was Green."* New York: Vintage, 2002.

———. *"The Unseen Hand" and Other Plays*. New York: Urizen, 1981.

Shewey, Don. *Sam Shepard*. New York: Da Capo, 1997.

Tucker, Martin. *Sam Shepard*. New York: Continuum, 1992.

Wade, Leslie A. *Sam Shepard and the American Theatre*. New York: Greenwood, 1997.

Wilcox, Leonard, ed. *Rereading Shepard: Contemporary Critical Essays on the Plays of Sam Shepard*. New York: St. Martin's Press, 1993.

Kimball King
University of North Carolina–Chapel Hill

SHERWOOD, ROBERT E. (1896–1955)   Robert E. Sherwood was one of the most admired American playwrights to emerge in the period between the world wars, winning the PULITZER PRIZE three times for drama (as well as once for nonfiction) and enjoying a wide following through the Broadway productions and subsequent film versions of his witty, philosophical comedy-dramas. Despite this success, his work has thus far shown little influence on the generations of post–World War II playwrights.

Robert Emmet Sherwood was born into a wealthy family in New Rochelle, New York. The fourth of five children, he was educated in a series of expensive boarding schools before attending Harvard University. At Harvard, Sherwood wrote a comedy—*Barnum*

Was Right—for the Hasty Pudding Dramatic Club and served as editor of the *Harvard Lampoon*. He left college to enlist in the military in 1917. After being gassed and wounded in France that year, he was hospitalized until near the end of the war. He suffered for the rest of his life from a neuralgic disorder that caused him intense pain in his face and neck. Sherwood's experiences in the war affected him deeply, turning him for a time into a pacifist who struggled mightily with historical events and the necessity of armed defense in the coming decades.

After the armistice, Sherwood found a job at *Vanity Fair* magazine but left for a position at *Life*, initially as a film reviewer and then as editor between 1924 and 1928. Sherwood married Mary Brandon in 1922, and they had a daughter in 1923. In the 1920s, Sherwood's brooding intellect and dark wit earned him a position at the Round Table at the Algonquin Hotel in Manhattan, where he traded barbs with regulars such as Dorothy Parker, Harpo Marx, EDNA FERBER, and GEORGE S. KAUFMAN. Encouraged by this circle of acquaintances, Sherwood wrote a successful comedy about Hannibal's attempt to conquer Rome—*The Road to Rome* (1927). Critics compared the play to those of George Bernard Shaw, the dramatic master of the ideological comedy in the 1920s. Sherwood rejected this comparison in his preface to the play. Like Shaw, Sherwood published intellectually probing prefaces to his plays, explaining in poetic and abstract terms the wider social context for the play and attempting to direct the interpretation of his readers.

Encouraged by his success, Sherwood resigned his journalistic position. He saw productions of four more plays in quick succession: *The Love Nest* (1927), *The Queen's Husband* (1928), *Waterloo Bridge* (1930), and *This Is New York* (1931). None of these were well received by audiences or critics. That trend changed in November 1931, when Sherwood's *Reunion in Vienna* opened in a THEATRE GUILD production starring Alfred Lunt and Lynn Fontanne. This story of a deposed prince-turned-taxi driver who convinces an old flame to have a sexual fling was dismissed by some as a skillfully composed but meaningless comedy. A key comic scene concerns the pathetic reunion of a group of ailing and pompous former aristocrats.

His preface to the play describes it as "a defense mechanism" against the "spirit of moral defeatism" that dominated the West (vii). Sherwood analyzes his present moment as "the limbo-like interlude between one age and another," with neither tradition nor science offering a clear direction and so opening the door for nationalistic aggression (viii). His next plays would confront this crisis directly, using metaphor and in the entertaining format of melodrama.

Sherwood's preface points to the themes of what are now considered his three major plays: *The PETRIFIED FOREST* (1935), *IDIOT'S DELIGHT* (1936), and *ABE LINCOLN IN ILLINOIS* (1938). In *The Petrified Forest*, an escaped murderer and his gang take hostage a representative group of Americans in a restaurant on the edge of the desert. A wan poet, voluntarily captive, asks that the gangster kill him. The poet sees this act as the perfect playing out of the present state of the world—the triumph of the "man of action" over the dreamer.

Idiot's Delight is Sherwood's most complex work, combining comedy, drama, and music in a prescient story about travelers of representative nationalities and social classes who are trapped in an alpine ski lodge at the outbreak of a new world war. Contrasted with the war plot is a comic love story about an American vaudevillian and a former fellow vaudevillian, now a pretended countess. The play won the Pulitzer Prize.

Sherwood's pessimism bottomed out with *Idiot's Delight* and thereafter his playwriting took on the responsibility of promoting positive models for action. *Abe Lincoln in Illinois* wove together Lincoln's actual words and biographical material with fictionalized scenes. Sherwood hoped to show a model of what he called "the solidification of Lincoln" into a powerful democratic leader who would stand up to injustice. *There Shall Be No Night* (1940) turned to a more direct call for military action in the face of totalitarian aggression (in the form of the Russian invasion of Finland). Both *Abe Lincoln in Illinois* and *There Shall Be No Night* were awarded Pulitzer Prizes. Attracted by his obvious abilities and political commitment, Harry Hopkins recruited Sherwood as a speechwriter for President Franklin D. Roosevelt. Sherwood spent the war years as an administrator in the Office of War Information.

After World War II, Sherwood made attempts to return to playwriting, but none of his works met with popular or critical success. *The Rugged Path* (1945) and the posthumously produced *Small War on Murray Hill* (1957) seemed stilted and old-fashioned to many. His attempt at a musical collaboration, *Miss Liberty* (1949), was unpopular, despite the songs of Irving Berlin. Sherwood spent less time writing plays in these later years but saw some of his greatest rewards. His screenplay for *The Best Years of Our Lives* (1946) contributed to the film's winning nine Academy Awards, and his history of the inner workings of the White House, *Roosevelt and Hopkins* (1948), won Sherwood his fourth Pulitzer Prize.

BIBLIOGRAPHY

Alonso, Harriet Hyman. *Robert E. Sherwood: The Playwright in Peace and War.* Amherst: University of Massachusetts Press, 2007.

Brown, John Mason. *The Ordeal of a Playwright: Robert E. Sherwood and the Challenge of War.* New York: Harper & Row, 1970.

———. *The Worlds of Robert E. Sherwood, Mirror to His Times, 1896–1939.* New York: Harper & Row, 1962.

Meserve, Walter. *Robert E. Sherwood: Reluctant Moralist.* New York: Pegasus, 1970.

Sherwood, Robert E. *Abe Lincoln in Illinois.* New York: Scribners, 1939.

———. *Idiot's Delight.* New York: Scribners, 1936.

———. *The Petrified Forest.* New York: Scribners, 1935.

———. *Reunion in Vienna.* New York: Scribners, 1932.

———. *There Shall Be No Night.* New York: Scribners, 1940.

Shuman, R. Baird. *Robert E. Sherwood.* New York: Twayne, 1964.

Mark Fearnow
Hanover College

SHINN, CHRISTOPHER (1975–)

Born in Hartford, Connecticut, Christopher Shinn earned his B.F.A. in dramatic writing at New York University, where he studied with MARÍA IRENE FORNÉS and TONY KUSHNER, among others. Shinn has been commissioned to write plays by both American and British theaters, including Los Angeles's Mark Taper Forum and London's Soho and Royal Court Theatres. His longstanding relationship with the Royal Court Theatre began when, as he once said in an interview, he sent them his first play "on a whim and they said, 'Yes'" (Shinn). Many of Shinn's plays premiered in London before they were produced in the United States.

Shinn's early plays include *Four* (1998, London), in which two sex-starved teenagers in Hartford on the Fourth of July try to connect with their spectacularly unappealing dates, whose vulnerabilities are as profound as their own; *Other People* (2000, London), in which three artists in New York's East Village at Christmastime demonstrate that what is said is often at odds with what is left unsaid; *The Coming World* (2001, London), a play about love and truth and loss in which a young woman on a beach talks with first her bad-boy ex-boyfriend and then his twin brother, both played by a single actor. Shinn uses the device of temperamentally dissimilar identical twin brothers played by a single actor again in his critically acclaimed *DYING CITY* (2006, London), in which a therapist's husband, a reservist, dies in Iraq, leaving his wife and his gay twin to come to terms with his death and all three of their lives. The ambiguities of what at first seem valid assumptions are the focus of the play.

For *Where Do We Live* (2002), which also premiered in London, Shinn won a 2005 Playwriting OBIE after its New York production. The play deals with New York's and America's social and political divisions before and after 9/11. A gay, white, liberal writer and his heterosexual, black drug-dealer neighbor provide the point of intersection for two divergent groups of New Yorkers. In an interview with *American Theatre* magazine in September 2002, Shinn discussed the origins and themes of the play. It grew out of his own 9/11 experience; he was sitting down to write at his desk which looked out on the World Trade Center when he saw the first plane hit the tower. He began what he calls a "personal and political" play a few days later: "I saw that no matter how strong people's feelings about the event were, we hadn't developed a common perspective or vocabulary to discuss it." Shinn first noticed this "fractured" nature of the city when he "saw how hard it was during the Giuliani era for people . . . to wrap their minds around the idea of 'the other'—black, gay, or whatever. . . . New York was still incredibly divided racially and politically." It was these divisions still present after the terrorist attacks that Shinn examines in *Where Do We Live*. In the same interview Shinn went on to discuss his approach to writing plays generally:

> I'm always interested in this as a playwright: How do we get an audience not to watch just one person's story? When we're taught playwriting we're told to focus on the protagonist. To me that's really boring. I was more interested in how do you watch two people, how do you watch four people? Can you write a play where you watch 16 people and you're able to enter each character's subjectivity? They might not have equal weight in the drama, but at any given moment, you are able to say, "Oh, yes, I understand why that person behaves that way."

This intent to bring multiple perspectives to the audience can be seen in all of Shinn's plays.

What Didn't Happen (2002) is set against the Clinton 1990s when a group of friends and colleagues spend time in an upstate New York cottage six years after having been there before. In the "present" day and in flashbacks, they reveal their struggles and unrealized hopes and the poignant inadequacy of human communication. *New York Times* critic Ben Brantley in his review of *What Didn't Happen* called Shinn "a playwright to cherish" (December 11, 2002).

More recent plays include *The Sleepers* (2003), a one-act about two masturbators who meet in a bar; *On the Mountain* (2005), about the opportunistic fan of a dead Seattle rock star, who tries to insinuate himself into the life of the rocker's former girlfriend and her teenage daughter and finds himself attracted to both; and *Now or Later* (2008, London), which takes place on election night in the United States.

Shinn often sets his characters against iconic American dates and images: the Fourth of July, September 11, 2001, the summer cookout and summer cottage among them. His themes frequently touch on the human inability truly to communicate and often explore the disconnect between reality and pretense.

Shinn has taught master classes in playwriting at NYU and in Washington, D.C., and is currently on the playwriting faculty of New York's New School for Drama.

BIBLIOGRAPHY

Shinn, Christopher. *Dying City*. New York: Theatre Communications Group, 2008.

———. Interview. *American Theatre* (Sept. 2002): 60.

———. *On the Mountain*. New York: Dramatists Play Service, 2006.

———. *"Where Do We Live" and Other Plays*. New York: Theatre Communications Group, 2005.

SHORE ACRES James A. Herne (1892)

Shore Acres, a domestic drama dealing with generational conflict within a New England family, was one of the most successful dramas of the 1890s, both critically and commercially. Following an extensive run in New York, the play toured for more than five years, with Herne and his wife—realizing more than one million dollars in the process—in leading roles. The realistic details of writing and staging, the forceful but unstrident espousal of women's rights and the legitimacy of the younger generation's new ideas, the condemnation of crass commercialism, and, not least, the celebration of a family reconciled after conflict made it a work of wide popular appeal.

The play unfolds in a coastal farmhouse in Maine and tells the story of two middle-aged brothers, Martin and Nat Berry, whose different temperaments fuel much of the play's conflict. The gentle "Uncle Nat" is a sympathetic friend to his niece Helen and the young man of advanced ideas, Sam, with whom she is in love. In his youth, Nat was enamored of Ann Berry, Martin's wife, but he stepped aside in favor of his brother, deeding his half of the inherited farm to the young couple as a wedding gift. When the play opens, land speculation has swept over the community, and Martin is intent on subdividing the farm to create vacation properties. Promoting this scheme is Blake, whom Martin wants Helen to marry. She refuses and, with Uncle Nat's blessing, elopes with Sam in a "sensation scene" that sees the boat in which they are escaping nearly dashed on the rocks. In the play's last act, it is Christmas Eve and 15 months have passed. Blake comes to the Berry farmhouse to tell Martin that the Shore Acres subdivision has failed and the considerable money Martin invested in surveying the land, obtained by mortgaging the property, is lost. Shortly thereafter, Helen and husband Sam appear; they are returning to the family from the West with their new baby. They are reconciled with Martin, and when an unopened letter is produced, Uncle Nat discovers that his government pension has been awarded, allowing him to redeem the mortgaged property. In the scene made famous by Herne's acting, Uncle Nat, with the rest of the family having retired, goes about the business of closing up the house for the night. This five-minute pantomime, with the wind howling outside, the snow *"tinkling rhythmically"* on the windowpanes, and the stage darkening with Uncle Nat's exit, beautifully recreated the details of everyday life, providing an emotionally powerful finale.

With its emphasis on true-to-life characters and avoidance of the dominant clichés of melodrama, *Shore Acres* proved a major step forward in American playwriting. The realism of the production, achieved both in acting and design, the play's plea for harmony between traditional and more advanced ways of thinking, and the deeply satisfying resolution place *Shore Acres* in the forefront of an American drama aspiring to realism, truthfulness, and social relevancy.

Craig Clinton
Reed College

SHORT EYES MIGUEL PIÑERO (1974) The

seminal play by a New York Puerto Rican dramatist writing in English, *Short Eyes* emerged out of PIÑERO'S experiences in prison and his work with Felix Marvin Camillo's troupe of ex-inmates, The Family. Recipient of the New York Drama Critics' Circle Award as well as an OBIE AWARD, *Short Eyes* was also made into a film. The play recounts events of one day in "the House of Detention." Juan, the Puerto Rican protagonist, is placed in the awkward position of father-confessor to Clark Davis, a white, middle-class pederast. Davis's crime is looked on with disgust and given its own particular prison label in addition to providing the title of the play (it has also been said that the title comes from a Puerto Rican mispronunciation of the phrase *short heist,* prison slang for pornography).

Davis's presence and the nature of his crime heighten existing sexual and ethnic tensions among the inmates. Verbal and physical conflicts ensue, and following a series of ethical compromises, Davis is killed by his fellow inmates. After his violent death, which is condoned by a prison establishment that finds his crime repulsive, the members of the prison community are informed that Davis was in fact innocent. Juan is left with the uncomfortable reality of knowing that Davis has been guilty in the past, even if he is innocent this time.

Many critics value the authenticity of the work's portrayal of prison life, but the play goes beyond a mere slice-of-life story to explore interpersonal dynamics within a prison, and, in a more general sense, the daily struggle to preserve one's sense of self. In dealing with the prisoners' conflict over the fate of Davis (and themselves), the play raises many of the social issues present in American urban culture in the early 1970s, including race and class issues. This group of male prisoners, already divided along racial and ethnic lines, has its tenuous equilibrium shattered by the entrance of a relatively wealthy new inmate (Davis) who will not ally himself with any of the established prison groups.

The central and most crucial theme is the preservation of one's masculinity and sense of self. Cupcakes, an attractive young Puerto Rican, is encouraged to turn "stuff" (submit to sexual advances) by some of the older inmates, and Juan protects him from these attempts. However, after Davis becomes the target of sexual attention and violence, Cupcakes does not back Juan up in protecting him. Although Cupcakes is not directly involved in the violence that results in Davis's death, Juan assures him of his culpability by insisting that it was his responsibility to stop it. The problem, as Juan tells him, is that "you placed yourself above understanding." Rather than trying to see everyone as potentially worthy of help and respect, Cupcakes has succumbed to the violence and dehumanization of the prison environment. As Juan so powerfully intones in the final line of the play, "your fear of this place stole your spirit. . . . And this ain't no pawnshop."

Jon D. Rossini
University of California—Davis

SHRIKE, THE Joseph Kramm (1952)

Winner of the PULITZER PRIZE and Kramm's only notable work for the stage, *The Shrike* reflects both the renewed interest during the 1950s in the work of Sigmund Freud and psychotherapy and the paranoia unleashed by the McCarthy era, when people found themselves constantly observed, under surveillance and suspicion.

Set in a Kafkaesque mental ward of a big-city hospital, this intensely naturalistic play follows the fate of Jim Downs, who had one great success as a theater director before the war interrupted his career. Separated from his wife Ann and reduced to near penury, he has been having an affair while eking out a living as a part-time teacher. Disillusioned by a society that worships youth and where few chances seem open to him and suffering from a depressive angst, he attempted suicide with an overdose of pills and is now confined and treated as a criminal, because trying to kill oneself and failing is against the law. Although Jim does not believe he has violated any moral sanction, others condemn his act as a blatant disregard for social stability.

Kramm presents the insane asylum as a microcosm of the world; the patients display a mix of nationalities and ethnicities—Jewish, Greek, Hispanic, and Irish among them—and are both black and white, though the former are treated with a patronizing sentimentality. The mental ward, which demands a kind of abnormal perpetual calm from its patients, is equated with the army, with its rules and regimentation; with a prison, where rights and freedoms are denied; and, finally, with the theater itself, a place of pretense, where everyone is being watched and continually made to play a role. Only if these inmates conform to society's desires will they ever appear normal and be deemed sane enough for release.

The true source of Jim's destruction is Ann. Jealous and lonely because of her husband's affair, she harbors even deeper resentment over having sacrificed her own career as an actress when she married (though it is never made clear why she thought a two-career marriage was not feasible). The intervening years have turned her into a possessive vampire bent on emasculating and infantilizing her husband; she even connives with the doctors to achieve the power and control that she covets. Faced with the choice of continued, even permanent incarceration or release into his wife's custody, Jim capitulates and decides to submit to her. Freedom from the hospital only to come under the absolute exercise of Ann's will means, ironically, being trapped in an even more insidious dependency than imprisonment in any ward for the insane.

Kramm implies, in fact, that the sanity of a society that fears and stigmatizes the mentally ill should itself be laid open to question. More generally, the play stands as an indictment of society's need to normalize all behavior.

Thomas P. Adler
Purdue University

SHUE, LARRY (1946–1985)

When Larry Shue died in a commuter plane crash in 1985, the American theater lost one of its brightest comic playwrights. Though he was also a talented actor, Shue is best remembered as the author of several fine contemporary comedies that display his wit and skillful manipulation of plotlines. Years after his death, Shue's plays are frequently revived in regional playhouses, academic institutions, and community theaters throughout the United States.

Throughout his childhood, Shue composed and participated in theater. During his grade school years in Eureka, Kansas, he began writing plays, many of which he staged in his family's garage for a collection of relatives and school friends. When the family moved to Chicago, Shue's comic talents gained local fame when he played Nick Bottom in Shakespeare's *A Midsummer Night's Dream*. Shortly after graduating from Illinois Wesleyan University's School of Theatre Arts in 1968, Shue entered the army during the Vietnam era. Posted to Fort Lee, Virginia, he never saw combat; instead, he became active in the post's Entertainment Division. Released from the army in 1972, he began his professional theater career with the Harlequin Dinner Theatre of Washington, D.C., and Atlanta.

In 1977, Shue joined the Milwaukee Repertory Theatre, an institution that nurtured both his acting and playwriting careers. At the Rep, Shue performed in a broad range of plays; more importantly, the institution made Shue its playwright-in-residence and produced the three fine comedies upon which his reputation is based: *The Nerd* (1981), *Wenceslas Square* (1982), and *The* FOREIGNER (1983).

When it was produced in London's West End in 1984, *The Nerd* became the all-time top-grossing American play in England. It dramatizes the life of a well-to-do architect named Willum. Years earlier, while he was serving in Vietnam, Willum's life was saved by a soldier whom he never met. Willum's home and career are turned upside-down when that soldier, Rick, pays him a visit. In a plot device borrowed from GEORGE S. KAUFMAN and MOSS HART's *The* MAN WHO CAME TO DINNER (1939), the nerdy and annoying Rick overstays his welcome, forcing Willum to concoct a polite way to evict the unwelcome guest.

Although it contains traces of his characteristic farce, *Wenceslas Square* is a more sober work than Shue's previous dramatic output. The play involves an American college professor and his student, who return to Czechoslovakia years after the country has fallen under the domination of the Soviet Union. The two are confronted by questions of prosperity and its artistic implications, as they ready a scholarly tome for publication.

A masterful reinterpretation of a plot-driven French farce, *The Foreigner* remains Shue's best-known and most-often-produced work. Charlie, a hapless, cuckolded Englishman, comes to stay in a remote Georgia guest house while a friend attends to some business. Rather than interact with the local denizens, Charlie feigns that he is from a non-English-speaking country. Gradually, he realizes the nefarious shenanigans of two racist southerners. By the end of the play, the pair have been outwitted by Charlie. The plays satirizes xenophobia, regionalism, and white supremacy.

BIBLIOGRAPHY

Shue, Larry. *The Foreigner.* New York: Dramatists Play Service, 1998.
———. *The Nerd.* New York: Dramatists Play Service, 1998.
———. *Wenceslas Square.* New York: Dramatists Play Service, 1998.

Mark Cosdon
Allegheny College

SIDE MAN WARREN LEIGHT (1998)   *Side Man,* Leight's TONY AWARD–winning play, reaffirms that the American theater's century-long fascination with the decay of the American family was still at the century's end a viable, powerful theatrical theme. Leight's play connects the disintegration of a family with the waning importance of side men in the music business.

Like TENNESSEE WILLIAMS's *The* GLASS MENAGERIE, *Side Man* is presented as a memory play. Narrating and eventually participating as a character in his own family's story is Clifford, the son of Gene and Terry; he relates the story of his parents' courtship, early married years, and eventual breakup, while also playing stage manager for all the action. Clifford's story is prompted by a return visit to New York in 1985, where he finds his father reduced to playing music for an unappreciative and almost nonexistent audience.

Clifford's narration initially takes him back to 1953, the year his mother and father first met, and their optimism about their futures, Gene as a trumpeter and Terry as an artist. Gene actually has a chance at stardom, but the moment eludes him when a recorded performance is miscredited, and another trumpet player receives accolades for Gene's work. Facing even greater disappointment than Gene is Terry, who is at first an idealistic, naive, and foul-mouthed want-to-be artist but later becomes an angry, suicidal alcoholic. She marries Gene amid promises of success and riches but soon finds herself working two shifts at a local diner to support her family as the gigs Gene and his colleagues play become less and less frequent.

Leight's play shows how side men no longer play a vital part of the music culture by including three other side men, Al, Ziggy and Jonesy; the latter ends up going to jail because of his heroin addiction. Gene and Terry's home becomes the center of these men's lives, and as their marriages and professional aspirations vaporize, the apartment fills up with the refuse of those lost opportunities. By the time Clifford (at the age of 10) appears as a character in the narrative, the apartment is completely cluttered with these characters' castoffs.

While *Side Man* follows closely in the tradition of similar domestic dramas like ARTHUR MILLER's *DEATH OF A SALESMAN,* EUGENE O'NEILL's *LONG DAY'S JOURNEY*

INTO NIGHT, and DONALD MARGULIES's *The LOMAN FAM-ILY PICNIC,* Leight has added a new component—music. The focal point of the play occurs as Al, Ziggy, and Gene sit quietly and listen to the last recording Clifford Brown, Clifford's namesake and Gene's idol, made of "A Night in Tunisia." The use of this song is far more effective than any dialogue in conveying the true spirit of Gene as we watch him transformed from his usual introverted and stoic self into a man filled with wonder and amazement at Brown's performance. Leight's reliance on the transformative power of music as well as the changing direction of American music and its impact on the lives of these characters makes *Side Man* a hauntingly powerful play.

William C. Boles
Rollins College

SIGHT UNSEEN DONALD MARGULIES (1992)

A nonlinear play about a celebrity painter, *Sight Unseen* delves into the layers of truth that lie beneath the veneer of a person's life.

American painter Jonathan Waxman, in England for a retrospective of his work, makes an overnight visit to his former lover and her English husband (whom, we eventually learn, she has married primarily in order to gain permanent-resident status in England). Patricia still resents Jonathan for breaking off their relationship 15 years before. Above Patricia and Nick's fireplace is a youthful portrait of a nude Patricia painted by Jonathan. As the scenes jump back and forth in time, it becomes clear that Jonathan's motives for visiting are suspect: He seems to be there only to reclaim the painting, with which he attempts to sneak off at three o'clock in the morning. When Nick and Patricia hear him and come downstairs to investigate, Nick persuades Patricia to let Jonathan buy the painting for an "obscene amount," thereby freeing their lives of its shadow as well as bringing them some much needed cash.

It also becomes clear that Jonathan's work may be as overrated as Nick (an admirer of Renaissance painters) suggests. When pressed by Nick and Patricia, Jonathan admits that his most controversial painting, that of an interracial couple having sex in a desecrated Jewish cemetery, may be more ambiguous than he has

ever before admitted—maybe the woman's hands *do* look like fists, justifying the frequent interpretation that the painting is racist, an interpretation he has always rejected. In another scene, a German art critic who interviews him confronts him with the knowledge that he hired a publicist two years before he became famous, suggesting that his rise to fame may have had more to do with public relations than with talent. Even the implication that the painting of Patricia is an artifact from their love affair turns out not to be true: In the final scene (17 years earlier), she is the live model—and a stranger—in the class in which he painted it; he is reluctant to accept her sexual advances because she is not Jewish, but he is finally seduced. Two years later (in a scene depicted much earlier in the play), on the occasion of his mother's funeral, he tells her he does not love her, and they break up.

The title is a reference to wealthy art collectors buying Waxman paintings "sight unseen": They will take whatever "Waxman" becomes available—at exorbitant prices. Nick finds this practice ludicrous. Jonathan Waxman, himself, indicts the "American" tendency to go see art because one "should" or because Hollywood has familiarized one with an artist's story. He decries this cultural failing to the German critic, but, of course, the reality is that many of his patrons are buying his work merely because it is in fashion.

Jonathan's need to have the painting from his youth may suggest that he yearns for the greater sincerity and truth that were within him at that time—before Patricia, before fame. It is ironic then that he attempts to obtain the painting dishonestly. MARGULIES reveals the truth about Jonathan and his art and his former lover and her husband out of sequence: moving from what is apparent to the reality that lies beneath it. Since the play digs up the truth, in layers, it is no coincidence that Margulies chooses to make Nick and Patricia archaeologists.

Sight Unseen won an OBIE AWARD for Best New American Play (along with two other plays that season, *The BALTIMORE WALTZ* by PAULA VOGEL and *Sally's Rape* by Robbie McCauley).

SILVER, NICKY (1960–)

Playwright Nicky Silver is known for his absurdist comic farces about contemporary—often New York, both gay and straight—life. Born in Philadelphia and raised in Wynnewood, Pennsylvania, Silver graduated from New York University's theater program. His plays, despite their serious undertones, are mostly hilarious.

Some of Silver's earliest work, *Fat Men in Skirts* (1992) and *Free Will and Wanton Lust* (1994), premiered in Washington, D.C., at the Woolly Mammoth Theatre Company. He made his New York debut OFF-OFF-BROADWAY with the absurdist *Pterodactyls* (1993), about the extinction of a WASP family in Philadelphia. In the play, Emma, whose memory loss stems from her desire to forget her childhood, brings home her fiancé Tommy, an orphan, to meet her upper-middle-class Philadelphia parents. At the same time, her brother, Todd, comes home to announce to them that he has AIDS. Emma's fiancé falls in love with her brother and contracts AIDS from him. When Emma shoots herself, Todd rejects Tommy. Todd eventually dies; his mother drinks as usual, and his father begins to lose *his* memory. During the course of the play, Todd digs up a prehistoric animal skeleton from the yard and reconstructs it in the house, symbolizing the outmoded lifestyle and attitudes of the parents.

In *Raised in Captivity* (1995), twins Sebastian and Bernadette Bliss get together for their mother's funeral (she was killed by a showerhead). The play suggests that people are looking for ways out of their personal prisons—professions, marriages, obsessions. Bernadette's husband quits dentistry to become an artist, and eventually Bernadette quits him. Sebastian, still mourning the loss of his longtime lover after 11 years, is obsessed with the convicted murderer with whom he corresponds. Eventually, Sebastian finds comfort in staying with Bernadette to help raise her baby.

Considered his best play by many, *Food Chain* (1995) is a comedy about a group of obsessives: a nearly anorexic poet and the sexually confused—and currently missing—husband her newly thin body has won; an obese junkfood eater—who used to be thin—and his former lover, a narcissistic gay model; and a crisis hotline operator who thinks mostly of herself. Their lives converge when the thin young wife discovers that her husband has become the lover of the gay model. The title comes from the notion that the thin and beautiful are at the top of the sexual food chain in America, while those who are considered grotesque in some way—like the obese Otto—are excluded from happiness.

Silver's plays of the late 1990s received mixed reviews from critics. In *Fit to Be Tied* (1996), a man afraid to open the results of his AIDS test meets the man of his dreams, ties him up, and puts him in his closet. When his tough, boozy mother comes to visit, she convinces the captive young man to love her son. *The Maiden's Prayer* (1998) is about a man who has loved his best friend—who is about to marry a woman—since they were children; he drowns his sorrows in mindless sexual encounters. The bride's sister, a recovering alcoholic, also loves the groom. In *The Eros Trilogy* (1999), a housewife and her gay son reveal themselves through letters; it reminded critics of A. R. GURNEY's *LOVE LETTERS* (1989).

The Altruists (2000) is a farce about a set of self-consciously socially conscious New Yorkers who prove to be superficial, self-absorbed, and unethical. Silver also rewrote the book for a 2002 revival of the 1938 Richard Rodgers and Lorenz Hart musical *The Boys from Syracuse*.

In *Beautiful Child* (2004), a gay son in his mid-thirties returns to visit his unhappily married parents. He has come, as it turns out, after leaving his job as an elementary school art teacher because of charges against him of pedophilia; indeed, the charges are true, but the man sees nothing wrong with his "affair" with an eight-year-old child. As Ben Brantley wrote in his *New York Times* review, "Silver isn't just being sensational. He is using [the son's] confession to explore the boundaries of parental acceptance"—though Brantley found the attempt less than successful despite Silver's often "finely wrought dialogue and monologues" (February 25, 2004). Nor did Silver's most recent play, *Three Changes* (2008), about estranged brothers who reunite and reveal themselves to one another with fatal results, seem to critics to reach the level of brilliance and originality they had come to expect based on the playwright's earlier works.

BIBLIOGRAPHY

Silver, Nicky. *The Altruists*. New York: Dramatists Play Service, 2001.

———. *Beautiful Child.* New York: Dramatists Play Service, 2004.

———. *Eros Trilogy.* New York: Dramatists Play Service, 1999.

———. *Etiquette and Vitriol: "The Food Chain" and Other Plays by Nicky Silver.* New York: Theatre Communications Group, 1996.

———. *Fit to Be Tied.* New York: Dramatists Play Service, 1997.

———. *Maiden's Prayer.* New York: Dramatists Play Service, 1999.

———. *Raised in Captivity.* New York: Theatre Communications Group, 1997.

SIMON, (MARVIN) NEIL (1927–)

Born in the Bronx, New York, Neil Simon grew up in Manhattan. He attended New York University (1944–45) and the University of Denver (1945–46) before serving in the army. After the army, Simon returned to New York where, with his brother, Danny, he soon began to write for radio and eventually for television; Simon's early television credits include *The Phil Silvers Show* and Sid Caesar's *Your Show of Shows.* In writing for the latter, he collaborated with such comedy legends as Mel Brooks, Woody Allen, and Carl Reiner.

It was not until he was 30 that Neil Simon started writing his first play, *Come Blow Your Horn* (1961), and by the time it finally reached the stage, he was 33. The success of this play freed him financially to write the next, a musical called *Little Me* (1962), which in turn subsidized the writing of *Barefoot in the Park* (1963), a tale of newlyweds adjusting to their differences, by which time he was a commercial success. In the 1960s and 1970s, Simon's other hits included the comedies *The ODD COUPLE* (1965), about two divorced men sharing an apartment—which brought him his first TONY AWARD; *The Star Spangled Girl* (1966), about two impoverished young men who publish a protest magazine—writing every article and performing every job on the staff themselves, under pseudonyms—and their pretty, patriotic neighbor; *Plaza Suite* (1968), three one-act plays, each set in New York's Plaza Hotel, dealing with human relationships; *Last of the Red Hot Lovers* (1969), in which a man addresses his midlife crisis by attempting—disastrously—extramarital affairs; *The Prisoner of Second Avenue* (1971), in which

a couple has trouble coping with the stresses of urban life; *The SUNSHINE BOYS* (1972), about a pair of old vaudevillians who are asked to reunite for a television show, years after their acrimonious split; and *California Suite* (1977), four one-acts, each set in a Beverly Hills hotel. The musical comedies *Sweet Charity* (1966), *Promises, Promises* (1968), and *They're Playing Our Song* (1979), for which he wrote the books, were also popular. Despite phenomenal commercial success and often happy critics, serious critical acclaim did not come until later.

Following the death of his first wife in 1973, Simon moved to California and eventually remarried. The play he wrote based on his experience of remarriage, *Chapter Two* (1977), enjoyed a more serious reception by critics, perhaps because it was not pure comedy. However, it was his autobiographical trilogy, which combined comedy and pathos, that finally brought one of America's most prolific and successful playwrights the praise of critics. The trilogy—*BRIGHTON BEACH MEMOIRS* (1983), *BILOXI BLUES* (1985) for which he won another Tony Award, and *BROADWAY BOUND* (1986)—chronicle Simon's childhood, his time in the army, and his start as a television writer, respectively. In 1991, Neil Simon won the PULITZER PRIZE and the Tony Award for *LOST IN YONKERS,* the story of two young brothers placed temporarily in the custody of their embittered German grandmother and their simpleminded and affectionate Aunt Bella.

The tremendous critical acclaim of *Lost in Yonkers* was followed by the much less successful *Jake's Women* (1992), about a writer whose real life has a hard time living up to his imaginary one. Next came the more successful *Laughter on the 23rd Floor* (1993), based on Simon's experiences as a writer for Sid Caesar's *Your Show of Shows. Proposals* (1997), set in a summer cottage in the country rather than in Simon's usual urban setting, moves at a more leisurely pace as it focuses on the relationships of several couples. *The Dinner Party* (2000) enjoyed a respectable Broadway run, despite mixed reviews. More like Simon's early comedies was *45 Seconds from Broadway* (2001), set in the coffee shop of a two-and-a-half-star hotel in New York's theater district and filled with Broadway types and comic one-liners. Simon has described his latest play, *Rose* and Walsh (2003)—later titled *Rose's Dilemma*—as "a love story with such major problems between people that it becomes a drama" (Hirschhorn 11).

Certainly one of the most prolific playwrights in the history of American theater, Neil Simon has also written many film scripts, both screen adaptations of his own plays and original screenplays, and two books of autobiography. His work, always hilarious and frequently moving, is often revived and continues to delight audiences.

BIBLIOGRAPHY
Hirschhorn, Joel. "In Conversation with . . . Neil Simon." *Dramatist* 5, no. 3 (2003): 4–11.
Johnson, Robert K. *Neil Simon.* Boston: Twayne, 1983.
Konas, Gary, ed. *Neil Simon: A Casebook.* New York: Garland, 1997.
Koprince, Susan. *Understanding Neil Simon.* Columbia: University of South Carolina Press, 2002.
McGovern, Edythe M. *Neil Simon: A Critical Study.* New York: Frederick Ungar, 1979.
Simon, Neil. *The Collected Plays of Neil Simon.* Vol. 2. New York: Random House, 1991.
———. *The Collected Plays of Neil Simon.* Vol. 3. New York: Random House, 1991.
———. *The Collected Plays of Neil Simon.* Vol. 4. New York: Touchstone/Simon and Schuster, 1998
———. *The Comedy of Neil Simon.* New York: Random House, 1971.
———. The *Dinner Party.* New York: Samuel French, 2002.
———. *45 Seconds from Broadway.* New York: Samuel French, 2003.
———. *Oscar and Felix: A New Look at "The Odd Couple."* New York: Samuel French, 2004.
———. *The Play Goes On: A Memoir.* New York: Simon and Schuster, 1999.
———. *Proposals.* New York: Samuel French, 1998.
———. *Rewrites: A Memoir.* New York: Simon and Schuster, 1996.
———. *Rose's Dilemma.* New York: Samuel French, 2004.

SISTER MARY IGNATIUS EXPLAINS IT ALL FOR YOU CHRISTOPHER DURANG (1979)

In this one-act comic satire, DURANG indicts Catholic education and Catholicism itself, as defined by the dogmatic and sadistic Sister Mary Ignatius. Sister Mary teaches seven-year-olds about God (He answers all our prayers, but "sometimes the answer to our prayer is 'no'"), heaven, hell, purgatory ("you can expect to be in purgatory for anywhere from 300 years to 700 billion years"), and the difference between mortal and venial sins. She is pleased when Thomas, the representative seven-year-old in the play, gives his rote catechism answers, and she dismisses questions—usually those that suggest the complexity of the human condition—of which she does not approve.

Sister Mary Ignatius and Thomas are visited by a group of her former pupils, from 15 years before: One is gay; one is an unwed mother; another has had two abortions; and a fourth—the least offensive to Sister Mary—is an alcoholic wife-beater. They all reveal to her that they feel she abused them psychologically when she was their teacher. (During Sister Mary Ignatius's monologues, she hints at a psychologically abusive childhood of her own.) One of these former pupils, Diane, is the spokesperson for the antithesis of Sister's dogma. She speaks of her experiences in a random and godless universe that allowed her mother to suffer an excruciating and protracted death from cancer and allowed Diane to be raped by one man and later seduced and impregnated by her psychiatrist. She threatens to kill Sister Mary Ignatius, who kills *her* instead and then promptly explains the Catholic doctrine on self-defense. Then, when her gay former student, Gary, admits that he is still confused enough about the morality of his homosexuality to ask forgiveness for it in confession, she kills him, thereby "send[ing] him to heaven," since he has just that morning gone to confession. Sister Mary then tells the terrified Philomena to "go home before [she] decide[s] [Philomena's] little girl would be better off in a Catholic orphanage." The play ends with Sister Mary continuing to terrorize the remaining former student, Aloysius, making him raise his hand to ask permission to go to the lavatory, and then not letting him—a metaphor for the emotional damage he cannot escape. Worse, she teaches seven-year-old Thomas to terrorize him too.

SISTERS ROSENSWEIG, THE WENDY WASSERSTEIN (1992)

A comedy set in 1991 in a London town house, *The Sisters Rosensweig* centers around three Brooklyn-born sisters facing middle age and its attendant adjustments to identity.

The occasion that brings the women together is the eldest sister Sara's 54th birthday. Sara, a single mother of a nearly adult daughter, is a "brilliant" international banker and an Anglophile. Arriving from a far corner of the Earth is youngest sister Pfeni (changed from Penny), a former foreign correspondent, now a travel writer, and ever the compulsive traveler, whose long-standing—and mostly long-distance—relationship with bisexual British theater director Geoffrey brings her intermittently to London. The third sister, Gorgeous Teitelbaum, is a housewife and mother-turned-radio-personality ("Dr. Gorgeous") from suburban Boston; Gorgeous is married to "a very prominent attorney" and is in London leading women of "the Newton Temple Beth El sisterhood" on a tour.

Each sister is at a crossroads: Sara, who rejected America and her own Jewishness years ago, encounters both again in Geoffrey's associate Mervyn Kant. Merv, Sara's contemporary—they even had acquaintances in common in their youth—is a furrier (fake fur) who embraces both his country and his Jewish heritage. Sara is faced with a choice between Merv and all he represents and her English friend Nick Pym, the perfectly pressed and poised classy accessory. Pfeni feels compelled to return to real journalism and to give a voice to the suffering women of Tajikistan; she must also face the reality of her boyfriend's sexuality when he leaves her because he "misses men." Gorgeous, who has seemed so sure of the correctness of her path, reveals that her husband, Henry, has been out of work for two years and lives in the basement, where he attempts to write detective novels.

In the penultimate scene, Gorgeous's wish for herself and her sisters is "that each of us can say at some point that we had a moment of pure, unadulterated happiness." In the final scene, it seems that each will keep striving for such a moment: Sara chooses Merv, with whom she has had a lively night of sex and conversation, over her sexless but tasteful relationship with Pym. Pfeni is off to Tajikistan. Gorgeous, given a "genuine Chanel suit" by the sisterhood in thanks for her hard work, enjoys it only briefly, having decided

to return it because "somebody's got to pay tuition this fall." For Gorgeous, her children's happiness is inextricably tied to her own.

The three sisters represent different avenues for women of their generation: Sara, the woman who becomes a powerful player in a man's world; the free-spirited, rootless Pfeni; and the more traditional Gorgeous, who nevertheless is forced to tap inner resources when her middle-class American Dream begins to crack. Inheritor of all this is Sara's daughter, Tess, who takes in the life choices of her aunts and her mother but tries to find her own way. As is true of Wasserstein's *The Heidi Chronicles* (1988), a daughter is the beneficiary of the women's movement of her mother's generation—or so her mother's generation fervently hopes. The play also shares a theme with Beth Henley's *Crimes of the Heart* (1979) in its idea that appreciated moments of happiness can make life worth living.

SIX DEGREES OF SEPARATION John Guare (1990)

Basing his play on an incident in New York in the mid-1980s, Guare uses as his central figure a brilliant con artist who takes advantage of wealthy New Yorkers. Guare satirizes modern urban existence and modern American families, especially among the wealthy liberal set.

In a Fifth Avenue apartment, a wealthy art dealer and his wife, Flanders "Flan" and Louisa "Ouisa" Kittredge, are entertaining an old friend and potential art buyer when an unexpected visitor arrives. The young man reports that he has been mugged, says he is a friend of their children, students at Harvard, and claims to be the son of actor Sidney Poitier. He seems to know all about them and to enjoy their company. They are charmed by him, as is their old friend, who more willingly invests in a work by Paul Cézanne because of his evening spent with the charmer, "Paul Poitier." Paul cooks for them, speaks confidentially to them of "Dad," and explains his theories on J. D. Salinger's novel *The Catcher in the Rye*, the topic of his "thesis." He spends the night at the Kittredges' insistence, since his "father" will not arrive in town until the morning. They give him $50 for the morning in case his father's plane is late and send him to bed in their son's room. In the morning, they find him with a male prostitute to whom he has paid the $50. They kick them both out of their home. They know they have been conned to some extent, but they realize how fully only when another couple tells of their nearly identical experience with the same young man.

The two couples go to the police, who have had a similar story from a third source. The common denominator is that all three families once had children at the same boarding school. The sons and daughters are enlisted to help track down Paul. During discussions among the families, it is clear that the Kittredges and their children have an impoverished relationship. Clearly, one of the reasons the parents were so charmed by Paul was that he showed them a respectful affection that was missing from their relationship with their own children.

The Kittredges' daughter solves the mystery of Paul through an old school friend, Trent Conway, who met Paul on the street and gave him information about all the families in his address book in exchange for sexual favors. Trent also taught Paul how to speak and act around the rich. Paul's transformation took just three months. This fact amazes Ouisa; when she learns it, she exclaims, "Trent Conway! The Henry Higgins of our time!"

Ouisa begins to marvel at how this young man could have found them of all the people in the world because of a brief connection her daughter had to a boy in high school. It is here that the title of the play becomes clear: Ouisa read once that "everybody on this planet is separated by only six other people. Six degrees of separation. Between us and everybody else on this planet. The president of the United States. A gondolier in Venice. Fill in the names. I find that A) tremendously comforting that we're so close, and B) like Chinese water torture that we're so close. Because you have to find the right six people to make the connection. . . . It's a profound thought. How Paul found us. . . . How every person is a new door opening up into other worlds."

Once we realize that Paul is a brilliant con artist, a quick study who is utterly believable, his words about *The Catcher in the Rye* take on new resonance in retrospect. When he says of Holden Caulfield, "The boy wants to do so much and can't do anything. Hates all phoniness and only lies to others. Wants everyone to like him . . . and is completely self-involved," he might be speaking of himself. When he says, "one of the great tragedies of our times [is] the death of the imagination" and "the imagination [is] God's gift to make the act of self-examination bearable," he might be talking of himself, the Kittredges, or, as Guare might suggest, all modern human beings.

Meanwhile, Paul has taken on a new disguise. He tells his new friends, Rick and Elizabeth, a naive young couple from Utah, that Flan Kittredge is his father and that Flan abandoned him and his mother years ago. The couple, completely taken in, bring him into their tiny apartment above a roller rink. Paul convinces Rick, over the objections of Elizabeth, to "lend" him their $200 savings. Paul then seduces Rick and disappears. Rick commits suicide, landing on the pavement moments before the Kittredges' friends exit the roller rink in that same building.

When the distraught Elizabeth goes to the police and the police contact the Kittredges, Flan gets a story into the *New York Times* about the brilliant young con artist who manages to take in even sophisticated New Yorkers. Having seen the story, Paul calls Ouisa. He did not know about the suicide, he says. His call interrupts a telephone conversation Ouisa is having with her daughter, who tells her mother that she is getting married. Her mother puts her on hold in order to help Paul in his time of need. Once again, she is able to connect emotionally with Paul, while she can be little more than dismissive with her own daughter. Paul agrees to turn himself in if Ouisa will come with him to the police and be his friend and mentor when he gets out of jail, but the police get to their meeting place first, and she never sees him again.

Drama critic Frank Rich wrote in the *New York Times* that *Six Degrees of Separation* is "an extraordinary high comedy in which broken connections, mistaken identities, and tragic social, familial, and cultural schisms . . . create a . . . searing panorama of urban America in precisely our time" (June 15, 1990).

SKIN OF OUR TEETH, THE THORNTON WILDER (1942)

Set simultaneously in contemporary "Excelsior, New Jersey," and at times of biblical disasters, *The Skin of Our Teeth* disrupts the illusion that the audience is watching a realistic slice of life: An actress complains of her lines, a scene is stopped because an actor identifies with it too closely and becomes violent, and dressers, maids, and ushers are pressed into service when cast members are taken ill. Farcical in tone but serious in intent, the play reassured American audiences that civilization had survived disasters in the past and would endure World War II as well. Winner of the PULITZER PRIZE in 1943, it was also the subject of controversy when Joseph Campbell and Henry Morton Robinson accused Wilder of plagiarizing it from James Joyce's novel *Finnegans Wake* (1939). Despite the refutation of the charge by Edmund Wilson, the controversy may have prevented the play from winning the New York Drama Critics' Circle Award. Thornton Wilder refuted the accusation in a letter he never mailed to the *Saturday Review of Literature*; that letter was recently published in *The Selected Letters of Thornton Wilder* (Wilder and Bryer 412–415).

The play begins with Sabina (Lilith, the embodiment of feminine beauty), servant to the Antrobuses, worrying about the oncoming ice age until she breaks character to snarl that she hates the play and does not understand a word of it. Mrs. Antrobus (Eve, the eternal mother) preserves her children Gladys and Henry (previously named Cain) and home. Mr. Antrobus enters, having invented the wheel and the alphabet. With him come the muses, Homer, Moses, and other figures. Over Mrs. Antrobus's objections, they are given places by the fire, while the pet mammoth and dinosaur are excluded. As the house runs out of fuel, chairs are broken up at the back of the auditorium of the theater to be burned to "save the human race," while Gladys recites the beginning of Genesis to her father.

In act 2, Antrobus has just been elected "President of the Ancient and Honorable Order of Mammals" in Atlantic City and announces his slogan: "Enjoy Yourselves." He is also tempted to an affair with Sabina, despite Mrs. Antrobus's watchword, "Save the Family." A gypsy assures the audience that only charlatans can tell you the past, but nothing is easier than telling the future. As the flood begins, Antrobus saves his family and Sabina, and the fortune-teller reminds him that he must remake the world.

Act 3 takes place after an apocalyptic war: Gladys has a baby and no husband, and Henry, unrepentantly evil, has fought against his father. Mr. Antrobus returns depressed, and Mrs. Antrobus has to talk him into rebuilding the world. Meanwhile, when some of the "actors" become ill, the "management" brings out "splendid volunteers who have kindly consented to help . . . out" by taking the roles of the hours of the night: "[E]ach of the hours of the night is a philosopher, or a great thinker," such as Plato, Aristotle, and Spinoza. The hours cross the stage quoting the philosophers, as Mr. Antrobus determines to start over yet again, and even Henry, with his propensity to violence, is not excluded from the family. The play ends with Sabina speaking the lines with which the play began and promising that the Antrobuses (humanity) will always optimistically begin again.

BIBLIOGRAPHY

Campbell, Joseph, and Henry Morton Robinson. "The Skin of Whose Teeth." *Saturday Review*, 19 December 1942, 3–4.

Wilder, Robin G., and Jackson R. Bryer, eds. *The Selected Letters of Thornton Wilder*. New York: HarperCollins, 2008.

Wilson, Edmund. "The Antrobuses and the Earwickers." *Nation*, 30 January 1943, 167–68.

Christopher J. Wheatley
The Catholic University of America

SLAVE SHIP: AN HISTORICAL PAGEANT
AMIRI BARAKA (LEROI JONES) (1967)   One of the most powerful examples of 1960s environmental theater, *Slave Ship* dramatizes the captivity of African Americans from the Middle Passage through slavery to the contemporary Civil Rights movement.

Most critics agree that *Slave Ship* is BARAKA's most ambitious play from the BLACK ARTS MOVEMENT of the late 1960s. With no significant characters or plot, the play is a depiction of the cyclic chain of black oppression—the suffering of the Middle Passage, the humiliation of the slave markets and quarters, the hopelessness of the contemporary black ghetto. More than half of the text is comprised of author's notes, which direct the music, sounds, silence, and movement of the one-act play. Without individualization and set against a backdrop of constant, yet disruptive motion, the play conveys the experience of history and its effects on African-American lives.

An integral aspect of environmental theater is the use of space to involve the watcher in the play. In the original production, the audience sat on the wooden boards of the slave ship, with mini-stages placed throughout for the actors. Bombardment of the senses involves the audience in the emotion of the play, while it simultaneously destabilizes their ability to make sense of this historical pageant.

The play begins with the sounds of the Middle Passage—drums, whips, chains, and moaning. The first dialogue comes with the white slave traders boasting of their "Black gold," but this quickly is supplanted by the tortured experiences of their cargo: children crying, adults praying to God for help, a distraught African mother committing suicide and infanticide. These visions soon dissipate into the humiliation of the slave markets, and the white traders are now the cruel slave owners coddling favors from Old Tom Slave. As the other slaves are incited by Reverend Turner (Nat Turner) to revolt, Old Tom sells out their plans for a pork chop, and the slave masters exact their revenge. The survivors now begin to refer to each other by Christian names, and the Yoruba language and warrior motifs disappear into degradation and a paralyzing fear of separation. Finally, we see Old Tom turn into New Tom Reverend, a parody of Martin Luther King Jr., who preaches nonviolent resistance. However, this New Tom's inability to deal with his people's suffering, stemming from his desire to be dignified and integrated with the whites, leads to his own murder. As his killers move with murderous intentions toward the disdainful voice of White Jesus, the voice begins to plead. Triumphant dancing to jazz music overtakes the theater, and the actors engage the audience in celebration. The lights cut out at the moment when the dancing audience is relaxed, and the disembodied head of the slain preacher is thrown into the center of the floor, symbolizing violent political action.

Though theater critics at the time questioned the quality of the play's dramatic structure, the audiences who were drawn to it were enthralled by the event. Baraka's intent was to effect change in his black audience, to incite them to outrage and then to action.

Matthew J. Caballero
University of California–Davis

SLOW DANCE ON THE KILLING GROUND William Hanley (1964)

The only play by Hanley to premiere on Broadway, *Slow Dance on the Killing Ground* is a sharply confrontational study of moral relativism and personal responsibility. It is in the form of a continuing conversation among three characters from vastly different backgrounds: Glas, a stoic German shopkeeper; Randall, a mercurial young African American; and Rosie, a Jewish college student.

The action takes place on a single summer evening in 1961, in Glas's rundown convenience store in an industrial district of Brooklyn, New York. Glas, who lives alone in an adjoining apartment, is beginning a desultory inventory when Randall enters, apparently on the run from something. Their ensuing conversation, which touches on subjects as diverse as racism, Franz Kafka's *Metamorphosis,* and the recent execution of Adolf Eichmann, establishes Glas's claim to be a Holocaust survivor and reveals Randall as a highly intelligent young man with a photographic memory whose use of hip street patois (early 1960s style) is entirely affected.

At the end of act 1, Rosie appears. She is looking for the office of an illegal abortionist, where she plans to end an unwanted pregnancy. The remaining two acts of the play consist largely of an impassioned three-way debate about the moral implications of each character's situation. Eventually, each must account for the actions that have brought them together on this particular night. Rosie, a disaffected would-be writer, bitterly denounces the war that killed her father, the empty naïveté of American popular culture, and the loveless union that produced her pregnancy. Glas, who is not a Jew, eventually admits he is not a camp survivor either; rather, he is a Communist who abandoned his Jewish wife and child to the Nazis for the sake of his beliefs. Randall, whose keen intelligence and wide-ranging literacy have done nothing to shield him from a life of crime, confesses to the brutal murder of his mother, a prostitute, in the moments before the play began. For these acts, Glas must atone by continuing to live, and Randall must atone through death, whether at his own hands or those of the state. Only Rosie, whose supposed moral transgression (the abortion) has not yet been committed, remains free, however ambivalently, to control her fate.

Slow Dance on the Killing Ground is one of a number of postwar realist dramas that examine matters of conscience and morality in urban/industrial American society. As such, it bears structural and thematic resemblances to plays like ARTHUR MILLER's ALL MY SONS (1947), ISRAEL HOROVITZ's *The Indian Wants the Bronx* (1967), and the Sidney Lumet/Rod Steiger film *The Pawnbroker* (1965). Although its Broadway run was a relatively short one, the play appeared regularly in the repertories of professional and university theaters for many years after its debut.

Brenda Foley
Marlboro College

SMALL TRAGEDY CRAIG LUCAS (2003)

Set during the mid to late-1990s primarily during the rehearsal period of an amateur production of *Oedipus Rex,* LUCAS's play asks: Should we seek the truth no matter how painful and suffer for knowing it—as Oedipus and Jocasta do; or are we justified in turning a blind eye to the truth so that we may "choose happiness" for ourselves and perhaps our loved ones? Furthermore, Lucas asks if an ability to ignore painful truths is particularly American. *Small Tragedy,* which premiered in Minneapolis in 2003, was produced in 2004 by Playwrights Horizons in New York, where it won a 2004 OBIE AWARD for Best New American Play.

Nathaniel, a Harvard instructor and a director, has written a new adaptation of Sophocles' play, which his wife and codirector, Paola, sometimes finds inconsistent in tone and even inaccurate in places. Paola's criticism is a device that allows the playwright to inform the audience about the historic and linguistic context of *Oedipus Rex:* Paola gives members of the cast literal Greek meanings (*hubris,* for example, is not really "pride," but is "to treat the less powerful, the weak unfairly, to bully them"), and she tells them what was

"common knowledge in ancient Greece" (any unwanted child had its feet "pinned" and was left to die, so why, she asks, wasn't Oedipus curious about that malady of his before the events of the play? Could it have been denial?); these bits of information become important thematically.

We eventually find out that shortly after Paola and Nathaniel were married and when Nathaniel was on the verge of becoming a successful director in Hollywood, Paola (herself an actress about to star in her husband's next film) tested positive for HIV and their careers took a nosedive. He turned to drugs and alcohol for a while, but the couple is coming back by way of Nathaniel's teaching and, now, this amateur production of his adaptation. In addition to Paola and Nathaniel, the cast consists of Jen, an Equity actor trying to get back into acting after having given it all up for an opportunistic ex-lover; her younger and more outspoken roommate, Fanny; and two students, a Bosnian economics major called Hakija and an earnest young gay man named Christmas.

Lucas's play is characterized by a great deal of simultaneous dialogue. In an early scene in a bar after the first *Oedipus* rehearsal, three pairs of characters are engaged in three arguments that gradually work toward agreement: Jen and Fanny both finally decide to stay in the troubled production; Nathaniel and Paola agree to try to work together better as partners, to ratchet down their mutual criticism, and to love each other. Christmas and Hajika agree to leave their sexual orientations a mystery—at least for the time being. In this scene, Lucas seems to be aiming for something akin to the operatic sextet. An example of this technique of overlapping conversation, used to undeniably good effect, is when a speech from *Oedipus* about the doomed couple Oedipus and Jocasta is spoken concurrently with Paola's speech revealing that her HIV diagnosis ended Nathaniel's Hollywood directing career. During her revelation, out of the ancient play come the words "I AM THE PLAGUE. I AM THE PLAGUE. I AM THE PLAGUE."

In his interactions with the Americans in the cast, the outsider Hakija, who is from war-torn, atrocity-filled Bosnia, frequently comments on Americans: "Your movies and books all purport to explain human beings. . . . you can't explain human beings." And in a comment that is central to the play's themes, he remarks, "More than you think . . . like our Oedipus. . . . [Americans are] blind to your own tragedy [and] everyone else's." He reminds us that the slaughter of "two hundred thousand" Bosnian Muslims by their middle-class, professional "Christian neighbors" took place "in full view of the world." Hakija tells two different members of the cast that he is a Muslim who has seen his family tortured, raped, and slaughtered. Christmas hears the story in greatest detail and months later, moved by it, goes to Bosnia in connection with his church (this we are told in the play's penultimate scene) and discovers that Hakija was indeed the name of a Muslim whose family was slaughtered by the Serbs, but that man himself was also killed; the person that the *Oedipus* cast knows as Hakija is the slaughterer, the rapist, the torturer of Muslims, no victim at all, but himself guilty of unspeakable horrors. He, then, is guilty with his fellow Serbs of hubris as Paola defined it, that is, of taking advantage of those who are less powerful.

The other parallel to Sophocles' play is the human capacity for denial. Midway through the play, Paola points out that "the most modern thing about [*Oedipus Rex*]" is this idea: "What human beings don't want to know they just literally allow themselves to not know." Oedipus refuses to tell Jocasta what is going on even after he has figured it out but has not yet verified it. He says he "won't call it by a name till it stands there naked and exposed . . . otherwise, it does not exist." Just as Oedipus had indications which he—and those around him—ignored that he was not what he seemed, so do we and the *Oedipus* cast have reason to doubt Hakija. There are hints that Hakija is not what he says he is, but they are ignored—his explanations believed because everyone wants to believe him; he, like Oedipus, is charismatic and talented.

In the play's finale, which takes place in New York many months after the Boston production, we find that "Hakija"—a born actor, which is why he's so convincing in his charade as a victim—has left economics and has embarked on a promising film career; he lives with and has a child with Jen. Paola and Fanny, now a couple, come with Christmas to expose Hakija to Jen with videotaped evidence of atrocities. But Jen—unlike Oedipus and Jocasta, who upon hearing the truth make themselves suffer—"choose[s] to be happy," though she does first teach him a lesson by making him think something has happened to their baby. (He, as a rapist, torturer, and murderer, has made other parents feel this way and she wants him to feel it, if only briefly.) In her final speech to the audience, she confronts us: "To me Oedipus is a fool. I don't cry for him, I cringe. . . . Hak still always says that Americans don't understand tragedy, and I hope that could always be true. Don't you?" Lucas would like us to look at ourselves and be appalled at what we are willing to ignore as long as we ourselves are comfortable. He means us to look at the human—perhaps specifically, the American—capacity to rationalize our way out of dealing with inconvenient realities.

SMITH, ANNA DEAVERE (1950–)

Born in Baltimore, Maryland, to upper-middle-class working parents, Anna Deavere Smith earned a degree in linguistics from Beaver College and attended the American Conservatory Theater in San Francisco, where she received an M.F.A. and gained experience in acting and directing. Moving to New York, she found work on the stage and screen and taught theater and acting at a series of universities, including Carnegie-Mellon, New York, and Stanford. She was also a visiting artist at Yale for 1982. During this time, Smith developed a unique style of performance, which blends documentary, journalism, and photography to produce a memorable theater experience.

Presented as a series of monologues, Smith plays all of the characters in her dramatic presentations, regardless of gender or ethnicity. With a strong focus on issues of gender, sexuality, and ethnicity, aside from *Aye, Aye, Aye. I'm Integrated* (1984), her work has been part of an ongoing series she titles *On the Road: A Search for American Character,* which began in 1982, and has taken her from coast-to-coast interviewing ordinary people for her material. This series includes *Aunt Julia's Shoes* (1983), *Voices of the Bay Area Women* (1988), and *On Black Identity and Black Theatre* (1990).

Smith gained national recognition with *Fires in the Mirror* (1992), which won a Special Citation OBIE

AWARD, as well as a Drama Desk Award, among others. The play explores the violence that erupted in Crown Heights, Brooklyn, between Jews and blacks after the death of a black boy in an orthodox rabbi's motorcade and the subsequent retaliatory murder of a Jewish student. Smith presents 26 characters taken from all perspectives to examine black-Jewish relations, without bias or prejudice. The play's success led to the commission of *Twilight: Los Angeles, 1992* (1993), which won Obie and TONY AWARDS—among others—but its PULITZER nomination was withdrawn as it was deemed a documentary piece rather than a drama. The play covers the riots following the trial verdict of the police officers who beat Rodney King. Smith conducted hundreds of interviews with Los Angeles residents from every ethnicity and class, many of whose words she repeats verbatim in her performance. Smith sees *House Arrest* (1997), which explores the mythic role of the presidency in American history from the Thomas Jefferson–Sally Hemings controversy to the Monica Lewinsky scandal, as a companion piece. Although originally workshopped and produced in Washington, D.C., with a full company, Smith performed this work solo in 2000.

Smith's 1996 MacArthur Foundation Award, known as a "genius" grant, was given for her invention of a new theatrical genre. She has been praised for her thought-provoking, singlehanded depictions of complex communities and the frank realism with which she presents the social and psychological effects of violence and prejudice. The three years she directed Harvard's Institute on the Arts and Civic Dialogue, further exploring the relationship of art to the local community, culminated in *Piano* (2000), a play for several actors. *Piano* is a fictional, dramatic depiction of gender and racial tension in an affluent Cuban household prior to the Spanish-American War. The year 2000 also saw publication of Smith's book, *Talk to Me,* based on her observations of the time she spent in Washington, D.C., and on the 1996 campaign trail.

Since the 1990s, Smith has appeared in numerous films and television shows; however, she remains committed to the theater. In 2000 for Yale School of Medicine, she performed *Rounding It Out,* based on interviews with doctors and patients at Yale New Haven Hospital. It explores how doctors and patients view and communicate with each other. This was developed into *Let Me Down Easy,* first performed at Stanford in 2006, then at Long Wharf in 2007, and at American Repertory Theater in 2008. It is a one-woman show on health care and how we view the human body.

In 2006, Smith produced another book, *Letters to a Young Artist,* and she is currently working on the screenplay of Edward P. Jones's 2004 Pulitzer Prize–winning novel, *The Known World,* about free black Americans who owned slaves, which she plans to coproduce with John Wells for HBO. She teaches at both Tisch School of the Arts and New York University School of Law.

BIBLIOGRAPHY
Smith, Anna Deavere. *Fires in the Mirror.* New York: Anchor, 1993.
———. *House Arrest/Piano.* New York: Vintage, 2004.
———. *Letters to a Young Artist.* New York: Vintage, 2006.
———. *Plays in Progress.* New York: Theatre Communications Group, 1989.
———. *Talk to Me: Listening Between the Lines.* New York: Random House, 2000.
———. *Twilight: Los Angeles, 1992.* New York: Anchor, 1994.

Susan C. W. Abbotson
Rhode Island College

SOLDIER'S PLAY, A CHARLES FULLER (1981)

First produced by the NEGRO ENSEMBLE COMPANY in 1981, *A Soldier's Play* won the 1982 PULITZER PRIZE. The play centers on the murder of an African-American sergeant at a segregated southern army base during World War II and on the fracturing effect of racism within the African-American community.

Set in 1944 in Louisiana, the play begins with the shooting of Sergeant Waters by an unseen murderer. An African-American officer, Captain Davenport, a lawyer who has been assigned to serve in the military police, is sent in to investigate the case. The army high command has no real interest in solving the murder and cynically sends Davenport because they know the locals will not "charge a white man . . . on the strength of an investigation conducted by a Negro."

The structure of the play is a series of interviews conducted by Davenport of the men who were connected with Waters. Sergeant Waters's all-black platoon does the dirty work and menial labor of the base during the week and on Sundays plays baseball (many of the men having played in the "Negro League"). Sergeant Waters was both the men's sergeant and their coach. As each man testifies, his words lead to a flashback of his interactions related to Waters. We quickly learn that Waters was not a popular man; he was all "spit and polish" and was often hard on the men of his platoon, especially the southerners, who he believed perpetuated the racial stereotypes that kept his race down.

Several of the men have reason to dislike Waters. Private Wilke tells Davenport that Waters stripped him of his rank as punishment for drunkenness. Private First Class Peterson, a southerner, dislikes Waters for his contempt for and abuse of southern blacks; Peterson himself was once badly beaten by Waters. Captain Taylor, Waters's white commanding officer, reveals to Davenport that he believes that two white officers killed Waters since he knows that they had a confrontation with a drunken and disorderly Waters on the night of his death. The two white officers admit to the confrontation and do not conceal their racism, but they deny killing Waters. Private Henson tells of another shooting for which Waters framed one of the southerners in the platoon—Private C. J. Memphis, a mild-mannered, country-bred young man who played guitar and sang the blues at the white officers' club. Wilke backs up Henson's report and tells Davenport of Waters's "crazy hate" for C. J. In a flashback showing C. J. in jail, Waters talks about his mission to rid the world of southern "Niggahs" who play the stereotypical "fool." He reveals that he has gotten rid of three others at other bases, including an "ignorant colored soldier" whom "the white boys . . . [p]aid to tie a tail to his ass and parade around naked making monkey sounds." This occurred in France during World War I; Waters says, "When we slit his throat, you know what that fool asked us, what he had done wrong. . . . [W]e got to turn our backs on his kind." C. J. later hangs himself in his jail cell. Finally, a witness to the Waters shooting, Private Smalls, reveals that it was Peterson who shot Waters (whose last words—referring to the

whites he has tried to emulate—are "They still hate you"). Peterson did it "[f]or C. J.! [For] Everybody!"

In Davenport's final speech, he reports that the white colonel "characterized the events surrounding Waters's murder as, 'the usual, common violence any Commander faces in Negro Military Units.'" Davenport himself characterizes the actions and words of the dead and the guilty as "not worth a life to men with larger hearts—men less split by the madness of race in America."

In his *New York Times* review of the original production of FULLER's play, Frank Rich wrote, "Much as [Waters has] tried to bury his black roots and as far as he's gone in the Army, [he] just can't escape the demon of racism—that sinking feeling that, for all his achievements, *they still hate you.* And in Waters' distorted personality, his men see a magnified, mirror image of what they most fear and hate in themselves—the fear of being destroyed by allowing white racism to define the ambitions of one's life. . . . Mr. Fuller demands that his black characters find the courage to break out of their suicidal, fratricidal cycle—just as he demands that whites end the injustices that have locked his black characters into the nightmare" (November 27, 1981).

SPEED-THE-PLOW DAVID MAMET (1988)

A comedy set in Hollywood, *Speed-the-Plow* satirizes the movie business's ethic of profit over substance (or the appearance of substance) and self-interest over all.

When Charlie Fox brings Bobby Gould a movie proposal, both men see the moneymaking certainty of the project. Doug Brown, a major box-office star, is interested in a script Fox has shown him: a "buddy film, a prison film" with "action, blood, [and] some girl." Fox and Gould are old friends, and Gould is the new "Head of Production" at a Hollywood studio. Fox is quick to point out the "loyalty" he has shown by bringing this deal to Gould rather than to another studio; of course, he is really motivated by his own self-interest. He needs an immediate answer since Brown has given him just one day to seal a deal and is disappointed when Gould finds out that the head of the studio, Mr. Ross, will not be available to meet with them until the next morning.

Meanwhile, Gould is reading a novel he has been asked to give a "courtesy read" by the studio head. The novel has been submitted by an "artsy," well-known, East Coast writer, who is, Gould tells Fox, "crazy as a . . . June bug." The book is about the effects of radiation and suggests that "all radiation has been sent by God. To change us." Gould cynically passes the novel on to his attractive temporary secretary, Karen, flattering the young woman into thinking he values her opinion when he really just wants to get her to his apartment and into his bed, having bet Fox $500 that he could do so.

That night in Gould's apartment, Karen is powerfully moved by the offbeat novel and advises Gould to make it into a film. She contends that the public does not want the kind of film Fox has brought him, since such a film is "degrading to the human spirit." People, she says, do not want "the sex, the titillation, [the] violence"; Gould disagrees, answering that these are in fact what the people "require" and that when he submits the deal to his boss, Ross will "fall upon [his] neck and *kiss* [him]." Karen surprises him by revealing that she knows that he asked her there for sex and that she does not mind. She then speaks to him like an evangelist, suggesting that love and redemption lie in making films of "stories people need to see."

By the next morning, Gould has decided to make the radiation-novel film. When Fox arrives, he is stunned and tries to convince Gould that he is committing professional suicide for an ambitious girl who simply slept with him to get a movie made. When Karen arrives at the office, it soon becomes clear to Gould that Fox's assessment of Karen is correct. She is told to get out, and the two men proceed to their meeting with Ross.

Since neither movie has merit—one is pretentious nonsense and the other is pure sensationalism—MAMET deftly avoids any real depth on the part of his characters. As C. W. E. Bigsby writes, "This is not . . . a question of art versus the market, integrity betrayed by venality. *Speed-the-Plow* is a comic play whose humour is generated by characters who switch from self-serving cant to arrogant honesty with breathless speed" (227–228).

BIBLIOGRAPHY
Bigsby, C. W. E. *Modern American Drama: 1945–1990*. Cambridge, England: Cambridge University Press, 1992.

STALLINGS, LAURENCE TUCKER (1894–1968)   See *WHAT PRICE GLORY?*

STANISLAVSKY, CONSTANTIN (1863–1938)   See ACTORS STUDIO and GROUP THEATRE, The.

STATE OF THE UNION HOWARD LINDSAY AND RUSSEL CROUSE (1945)

Set during the Truman administration, *State of the Union* is a comedy about the attempt of a group of politicians to woo and retain a promising presidential candidate in the period leading up to their national party convention. The play's topical political jokes date it, but the portrayal of career politicians as calculating and cynical is as current as ever.

A politician, Jim Conover; a newspaper publisher, Kay Thorndyke; and Thorndyke's best reporter, Spike MacManus, hope to promote Grant Matthews as a viable candidate for the presidency, but Grant—though flattered—is reluctant. He made a name for himself in the airplane industry during World War II, and he has come to be known as a man of integrity. The Republican Party hopes to capitalize on his reputation and charisma, but Conover, Thorndyke, and MacManus do not want Grant actually to speak his mind for fear he will alienate one block of voters or another. They urge him to compose his speeches in as general terms as possible during the tour they have arranged for him. They also insist that his wife, Mary, go with him so that the couple will give the appearance of happy matrimony, even though Grant is estranged from his wife and having an affair with Kay Thorndyke.

Mary reluctantly agrees to help, and during the course of their trip influences Grant toward his best self. By the time he makes a speech in Wichita, it is from the heart. His sincere candor endears him to the common people—and to his wife—but angers the labor bosses. Conover, made nervous by this new development (since they cannot get the nomination without the labor bosses), comes to Detroit to attempt to influence Grant to be more politic in his approach. Behind Mary's back, Conover arranges for the politically savvy Kay Thorndyke to speak to Grant, and under her influence he tempers his Detroit speech so that it offends no one and says nothing.

The final act takes place at a dinner party in the Matthews's New York apartment. Mary has too many cocktails and tells the politicians exactly what she thinks of their cynical view of the voters and the candidate (most of this happens offstage and is described after the fact). In a final onstage outburst, she accuses them of planning to trade away justice and the peace of the world for the sake of votes. This snaps Grant out of his inclination to seek the presidency. Instead, he tells Mary, he will be politically active for the good of "the people": "I'm going to be in there asking questions, and I'm going to see that the people get the answers." Spike MacManus is left thinking that Grant might just get the nomination despite what the politicians think, and Mary and Grant fall for each other all over again as the curtain falls.

This satire on American party politics won the PULITZER PRIZE. Other memorable works by Howard Lindsay and Russel Crouse include LIFE WITH FATHER (1939), as well as the books for the musicals *Anything Goes* (1934), *Call Me Madam* (1950), and *The Sound of Music* (1959).

STAVIS, BARRIE (1906–2007)

Born into the Stavisky family in New York in 1906 (he legally changed his name to Stavis in 1934), Barrie Stavis was educated at Columbia University by night while holding a day job at a textile house. He worked as a freelance journalist before World War II in Europe and after the war in New York. During the war, he served in the United States Army Signal Corps.

Stavis was involved with the theater group New Stages at its inception; in the winter of 1947, its first production was of his play *Lamp at Midnight*. The founding of New Stages, which was committed to producing plays not likely to be seen on Broadway, marks the beginning of the postwar revival of the OFF-BROADWAY theater.

Stavis is best known for his plays about historical figures and the ideas central to their stories. *The Sun and I* (1937), written with Leona Stavis and produced by the FEDERAL THEATRE PROJECT, focuses on the biblical Joseph in Egypt and looks at the folly of absolute rule. *Lamp at Midnight* (1947) is about the scientist Galileo and his revolutionary scientific theories, which challenged the religious dogma of his day. *The Man Who Never Died* (1955) portrays Joe Hill, the legendary labor organizer and songwriter whose controversial conviction for murder led to his execution by the state of Utah in 1915. *Coat of Many Colors* (1966) is a second treatment of the story of Joseph in Egypt. *Harpers Ferry* (1967) is about the abolitionist John Brown. Stavis also wrote about George Washington and his leadership during the War for Independence in his play *The Raw Edge of Victory* (1986).

Barrie Stavis taught playwriting seminars at various universities around the country. He continued to live and write in New York City until his death at 100.

BIBLIOGRAPHY
Stavis, Barrie. *Coat of Many Colors: A Play about Joseph in Egypt.* New York: A. S. Barnes, 1968.
———. *Harpers Ferry.* New York: A. S. Barnes, 1967.
———. *Lamp at Midnight.* New York: A. S. Barnes, 1966.
———. *The Man Who Never Died.* New York: A. S. Barnes, 1972.
———, and Frank Harmon, eds. *The Songs of Joe Hill.* New York: People's Artists, 1955.

STEIN, GERTRUDE (1874–1946)

Although rarely acknowledged as such, Gertrude Stein is perhaps America's first avant-garde playwright. Stein began writing plays in 1913 and continued until her death in 1946. Born and educated in the United States, Stein spent most of her adult life in France, especially Paris, where she lived first with her brother Leo and later with her partner, Alice B. Toklas. Stein became famous both for her collection of modern paintings and for her connections to the burgeoning artistic avant-garde, most notably, Pablo Picasso, André Breton, and Man Ray. Stein's salons and those who attended them had a profound impact on her drama. Her plays frequently reflect the multiple perspectives found in cubist painting and the juxtaposition of seemingly unrelated images found in avant-garde film. In fact, early critics of Stein accused her of merely imitating her famous friends.

Stein's drama, however, is unique among the artists of the avant-garde and among other American playwrights of the early 20th century. Her first experiments in drama began with *What Happened. A Play* (1913), which contains no characters, no action, no dialogue, and few stage directions. Throughout the 1910s, Stein continued to experiment with such unconventional structure, but it was not until 1927 that she began writing seriously for the stage with her first full-length play, *Four Saints in Three Acts. An Opera to Be Sung.* Written as the libretto for her collaboration with composer Virgil Thomson, *Four Saints* would also become Stein's first and only Broadway success in 1934. Loosely based on the lives of Saint Theresa of Avignon and Saint Ignatius, the libretto explores what would become the major themes in Stein's drama: identity, religion, and life in a modern fragmented world.

While *Four Saints* is most significant as one of only two of her plays performed during her lifetime, Stein's dramatic work improved after this libretto. She would write three other major plays, each one confronting the changing role of the individual in the modern world. *They Must. Be. Wedded. To Their Wife.* (1931)— the only other play produced during Stein's lifetime— focuses on the isolation of individuals from each other, while *Listen to Me* (1936) goes even further and reduces its characters to total anonymity. Stein's best play, *Doctor Faustus Lights the Lights* (1938), incorporates this fragmentation and isolation of humanity into a retelling of the Faust myth. Stein's version begins after Faust has sold his soul to the devil in exchange for electric light and is forced to live under its oppressive glare.

After World War II, Stein wrote two more major works before her death: *Yes Is for a Very Young Man* (1944–46) and *The Mother of Us All* (1944–45). Although written simultaneously, these two final plays could hardly be more different. In *Yes,* Stein writes her most representational work: It is a rather simple and, arguably, overromanticized play about the occupation and liberation of France during World War II, while *Mother* is a modernist opera based on the suffragette Susan B. Anthony and the difficulties of her struggle for equality.

Stein's plays—more than 75 in number—were published in the collections *Geography and Plays, Operas and Plays,* and *Last Operas and Plays.* Since her death in 1946, there have been a surprising number of productions of her plays. *Four Saints* has been professionally produced 15 times; *Doctor Faustus Lights the Lights,* 13; *Yes Is for a Very Young Man,* 11; and *The Mother of Us All,* 17. Many more lesser dramas and numerous dramatic adaptations, both of her drama and prose writings, have been produced as well.

BIBLIOGRAPHY

Bay-Cheng, Sarah. *Mama Dada: Gertrude Stein's Avant-Garde Theater.* New York: Routledge, 2005.

Bowers, Jane Palatini. *"They Watch Me as They Watch This": Gertrude Stein's Metadrama.* Philadelphia: University of Pennsylvania Press, 1991.

Durham, Leslie Atkins. *Staging Gertrude Stein: Absence, Culture, and the Landscape of the American Alternative Theatre.* New York: Palgrave Macmillan, 2005.

Simon, Linda. *Gertrude Stein Remembered.* Lincoln: University of Nebraska Press, 1994.

Stein, Gertrude. *Geography and Plays.* 1922. Madison: University of Wisconsin Press, 1993.

———. *Last Operas and Plays.* 1949. New York: Vintage, 1975.

———. *Operas and Plays.* 1932. Barrytown, N.Y.: Station Hill Arts, 1987.

Wagner-Martin, Linda. *"Favored Strangers": Gertrude Stein and Her Family.* New Brunswick, N.J.: Rutgers University Press, 1995.

White, Ray Lewis. *Gertrude Stein and Alice B. Toklas: A Reference Guide.* Boston, Mass.: G. K. Hall, 1984.

Sarah Bay-Cheng
Colgate University

STEINBECK, JOHN (1902–1968) See *OF MICE AND MEN.*

STICKS AND BONES DAVID RABE (1971)

Part of RABE's Vietnam trilogy (along with *The BASIC TRAINING OF PAVLO HUMMEL* [1971] and *STREAMERS* [1976]), *Sticks and Bones* won the TONY AWARD. It is a searing satire of American commercialism, ethnocentrism, and racism in the Vietnam era using as characters American television icons Ozzie and Harriet Nelson and their sons David and Ricky. When older brother David returns from Vietnam, his reentry into the family proves impossible.

In the world of the television Nelsons (*Ozzie and Harriet* aired from 1952 to 1966), there were no problems that could not be solved by smiling parents in half an hour. Into this idyll Rabe introduces Vietnam. Not only does the family have the problem of a son returning blind and troubled from an ambiguous war, but also their own repressed problems emerge under duress; it becomes clear that the Nelsons were never as flawless as they appeared—and America was never as perfect as we had been led to believe.

David is brought to the house in a dress uniform by a sergeant major, who is delivering damaged boys by the truckload all over the country. When David arrives, the place "feels wrong" to him, and he does not want the sergeant major to abandon him there. His parents try to feed him and to give him a sleeping pill, but he is haunted by and speaks aloud to Zung, his Vietnamese girlfriend, and is haunted by atrocities he witnessed and perhaps participated in. Harriet is concerned about him—wanting to bring in a priest—but Ozzie is more concerned about getting the television repaired. Ricky breezes in with his guitar, and Harriet feeds him a steady stream of junk food, symbolic of the ill-nourishment of his mind and spirit in this household. When they speak, it is in bright greetings or in non sequiturs that indicate they do not really communicate.

Vietnam did not spoil perfection (though it certainly made matters worse); rather, it exposed what lay beneath a façade. It seems as if part of the problem is Ozzie's individuality—and by extension, that of many men in the late 1950s and early 1960s—being subsumed into the roles of husband and father and the attendant expectations of others (before he married he was "nobody's goddamn father [or] husband! I was myself"). He speaks with longing of his youth, when he ran races and won them, taking kickbacks from farmers who arranged the races and bet on him. It becomes clear that he regrets his marriage.

When David tries to tell his parents about Zung, they guess she was a "yellow whore" and self-consciously "understand" ("You were lonely . . . no white

girls around"). In the second act, David whispers to his father, who is sleeping on the couch, that he hates him, and he tells Rick that he lives to "see [him] die." His father awakens and yells at David for sleeping with Zung and raising the possibility they would have "LITTLE BITTY CHINKY YELLOW KIDS! . . . FOR OUR GRANDCHILDREN!" He goes on to say spiteful things to Harriet because she gave birth to such a son. He calls Rick a "PIECE OF SHIT." As this speech ends, David has a vision of Zung. He apologizes to her for letting "the old voices inside" him that he "had trusted all [his] life"—his parents' and the parish priest's—convince him to abandon her.

Of course, the spiritually barren home he returns to is not the only problem. David himself has become part of the violent culture of the Vietnam War. He tells his father, "now sometimes I miss them, all those screaming people." When Father Donald comes to the house at Harriet's request to speak to David, David keeps him at bay with his cane, striking him repeatedly until the priest leaves. Ozzie finds razors sewn into David's cap, making it into a concealed weapon. Ozzie laments to his wife, "We've got somebody living in this house who's killed people." The smell coming from David's room suggests ruin or death.

Under the stress of the situation, the self-absorbed Ozzie has a personal crisis; he questions whether he has any value. His worst fear is that his family "will abandon" him when he is no longer of any use to them. His solution is to make an inventory of all his possessions. This materialistic measure of worth is in sharp contrast to the psychological and spiritual help that David needs. What is brought out in Harriet is her blind faith in her church.

When David tells them that a convoy of trucks is out delivering the war dead and suggests they bring them all into the house and "stack them along the walls," his parents finally put aside any inclination they have had to get involved with this son and revert instead to cleaning up the room as Ricky suggests to his brother that David kill himself. Ozzie and Harriet join Rick in encouraging him to do so. Rick helps him make the cuts in his wrists after Harriet has brought towels and a bowl to catch the blood tidily. They look forward to life getting back to "normal."

Unlike *Pavlo Hummel* and *Streamers*, which focus on army life, *Sticks and Bones* focuses on the alienation of the returning Vietnam soldier, whose reintegration into family and country is made difficult by the chaos and violence he has become used to and by the fresh eyes (David's blindness is an ironic symbol, like the blindness of Sophocles' Tieresias) with which he looks at the empty values of home.

STONE, JOHN AUGUSTUS (1800–1834)

Born in Concord, Massachusetts, in the same year as Thomas Jefferson's election to the presidency, John Augustus Stone is best remembered for his connection to American stage star Edwin Forrest; it was for him that Stone wrote METAMORA; OR, THE LAST OF THE WAMPANOAGS in 1829. Set in late 17th-century America, *Metamora* tells the story of a brave Indian chief's efforts to defend his land against white invaders. Stone based the play on accounts of Indian resistance to early white settlement, including King Philip's War (1675). Despite its historical setting and its Native American characters, the play is a paean to the pioneering spirit of the "common man." Perhaps it is not surprising that a young man born in the first year of Jefferson's presidency, who grew to adulthood during the War of 1812 and the rise of Jacksonian democracy, should have absorbed the political rhetoric of the period.

Stone was only 28 when he won Edwin Forrest's playwriting competition with *Metamora*, yet he had already made a minor name for himself as an actor and author. He had begun performing in his native Massachusetts, but he quickly moved from the Boston theaters to the lively and lucrative New York and Philadelphia playhouses.

His first two plays, *Restoration; or, The Diamond Cross* (1824) and *Tancred; or, the Siege of Antioch* (1827), conform to the prevailing style of the period: heroic tragedies set in exotic locales that hark back to a classical or more "noble" past. While *Metamora* continued in this vein of the heroic tragedy, it was Stone's first play set on American shores and drawing on American history. It captured the attention of the nation, as audiences embraced the character of Metamora as a uniquely American tragic hero. Indeed, the role became the most successful of Forrest's career.

Though *Metamora* continued to dominate the stage for the next 40 years, its author suffered a fate similar to those of many early American playwrights. Americans were wary of "native" authors, still relying largely on Britain, France, and Germany for their dramatic literature. Stone wrote at least eight more plays, including *Tancred, King of Sicily; or, The Archives of Palermo* (1831); *The Demoniac; or, The Prophet's Bride* (1831); *The Lion of the West* (1832)—a revision of a play by James Kirk Paulding that featured the popular frontier character Nimrod Wildfire; *The Ancient Briton* (1833)—also a winner of Forrest's annual playwriting contest; and *The Knight of the Golden West; or, The Yankee in Spain* (1834). Historians note that three other plays credited to Stone—*Fauntleroy; or, The Fatal Forgery; La Rogue, the Regicide;* and *Touretoun*—cannot be accurately dated. None of these plays rivaled *Metamora*.

Little has been written of Stone's life. Much of what *has* been written focuses on his connection with Forrest and *Metamora*. Stone committed suicide on May 29, 1834. Friends suggested that the act had been one of temporary insanity. Yet even in his death, his individuality as a playwright was eclipsed by the star he had helped to create. Forrest erected a memorial to his former colleague—but it is Forrest's own infinitely more famous name that supersedes Stone's on the monument.

BIBLIOGRAPHY

McConachie, Bruce A. "The Theatre of Edwin Forrest and Jacksonian Hero Worship." In *When They Weren't Doing Shakespeare: Essays on Nineteenth-Century British and American Theatre*, edited by Judith L. Fisher and Stephen Watt. Athens: University of Georgia Press, 1989. 3–18.

Rees, James. *The Life of Edwin Forrest.* Philadelphia: T. B. Peterson Brothers, 1874.

Heather Nathans
University of Maryland

STRANGE INTERLUDE EUGENE O'NEILL (1928)

Winner of O'NEILL'S third PULITZER PRIZE, this play in nine acts (approximately four and a half hours in length) was originally performed with a break for dinner. (*Strange Interlude* was successfully revived in a mid-1980s production, which originated in London and also ran in New York.) The play's innovation was an extended use of the dramatic "aside," through which, together with soliloquies, O'Neill was trying to bring to the stage the complexity of a novel by revealing to the audience the characters' innermost thoughts. During the play, its central character, Nina Leeds, along with the men in her orbit, moves from youth to middle age. Her men are Charlie Marsden, the father figure (a writer); Sam Evans, the husband (a businessman); and Ned Darrell, the lover (a scientist). Throughout their complex and interwoven relationships, Nina and these men express themselves not only in dialogue but also in their spoken thoughts, which the audience, but not the other characters, can hear. The device, though sometimes cumbersome, nevertheless allows the psychology of the characters to be revealed. O'Neill once described *Strange Interlude* as "an attempt at the new masked psychological drama . . . without masks" (119); the play depicts the conflict between the inner and the public selves of the characters.

As the play opens, less than a year after the end of World War I, we learn that Nina Leeds's fiancé, Gordon Shaw, was killed in action two days before the armistice. Nina, whose father had convinced Gordon not to marry her until after the war, resents her father and regrets having withheld sex from Gordon. Nina believes that her father gloats over the death of his—to him, inadequate—future son-in-law. Nina "silently" (that is, in asides) expresses the loathing she feels for her father even as she looks him in the face and he "silently" suspects her feelings. Present at this meeting between father and daughter is Charlie, an old family friend who loves Nina in a sexually ambiguous way and who becomes a father figure for her after the death of Professor Leeds. Nina and her father finally express their true feelings aloud, and Nina leaves home to become a nurse in a hospital for veterans.

Only when her father dies, about a year later, does Nina come back to his house. With her come Dr. Ned Darrell and the simpleminded Sam Evans, whom Darrell hopes Nina will marry. Dr. Darrell reveals to the audience, though not to Charlie or Sam, that Nina has been sexually promiscuous at the veterans' hospital in an effort to make up for having withheld sex from

Gordon. Nina is in a precarious mental state, unable to shed a tear for her father and believing that all words—words like "love" and "father"—are lies. She tells Charlie, "I want to believe in something! . . . [S]o I can feel!" Wanting to forgive herself, she tearfully confesses her promiscuity to Charlie, whom she sometimes calls "Father," and asks him to punish her. Charlie advises her to marry the "clean and boyish" Sam Evans, whom she does not love, and be his helpmate and the mother of his children. Nina agrees.

Six months after her marriage to Sam, Sam's mother reveals to Nina that madness runs in Sam's family. This information has been kept from Sam; his mother's hope is that if he never knows and avoids the stress of having a child who is doomed to mental illness, he will be able to avoid madness himself. She convinces Nina to abort the baby she is carrying and gives her permission to get pregnant by another man and have a healthy baby for herself and for Sam. Later, Ned comes to visit Nina and Sam, who now live in Nina's father's house. Alone with Ned, Nina confesses all. Ned encourages her to divorce Sam; she will not. They talk themselves into having a child together and pretending it is Sam's—all for Sam's sake. Nina becomes pregnant and falls in love with Ned. Meanwhile, Sam has lost his job, Nina has been forced to sell her father's house, and they are living in a rented bungalow. Sam contemplates suicide and—at the very least—is willing to give Nina a divorce, convinced as he is that she must hate him for not being able to give her a child. When Ned comes again to visit, he and Nina declare their love for one another; Nina wants to divorce Sam and marry Ned, but Ned is not interested in marriage. He has his career; besides, he "knows her past." (In an example of the convenience of the asides, O'Neill can reveal Ned's true feelings without having to create a character to become Ned's confidant.) Ned, assuming the role of doctor, tells Sam about the baby as if the baby is Sam's. Then, Ned escapes to Europe.

By the time the baby, whom she names Gordon, is in his first year, Nina has come to think of him as hers exclusively, neither Ned's nor Sam's. The infant Gordon is thriving and so is Sam, who is now full of confidence and has become successful in business. Charlie is still a permanent fixture in their lives; he reports to them that he has seen Ned, drinking and womanizing, in Europe. Indeed, Ned has tried to forget Nina; unable to do so, he returns to her, and, as soon as Charlie and Sam have gone out for a walk, Ned and Nina declare their love again. Ned threatens to tell Sam everything, but Nina is quite satisfied with having three men: a husband, a lover, and a father.

Many years pass, and Gordon is a schoolboy of 11, living with his parents, Nina and Sam, on Park Avenue. Sam is now "happy, wealthy, and healthy," and Charlie and Ned, who have backed him in his business ventures, are wealthy as well. Ned is in and out of their lives, returning to America every couple of years to resume his love affair with Nina for months at a time. Nina is less and less interested in the three men, who she claims "make [her] sick," and even more focused on Gordon, who increasingly sides with his "father," Sam. Young Gordon witnesses a kiss between Nina and Ned and is appalled on his father's behalf.

Years pass, and Gordon is finishing college; he is engaged, and the occasion on which Charlie, Ned, Sam and Nina, and his fiancée, Madeline, gather is to watch Gordon win the final boat race of his college career. Nina is so jealous of Madeline that she decides to tell Sam that Ned is Gordon's father and to threaten to tell Gordon the same if Sam does not break up the young couple. She knows Sam will not believe her unless Ned backs her up; Ned refuses to meddle. Nina decides then to tell Madeline about the insanity in the Evans family as her mother-in-law told her, forcing the girl to flee from the engagement, but Ned again stops her.

In the excitement of Gordon's victory, Sam suffers a stroke and some time later dies. In the end, Gordon, secure in the knowledge that he was Sam's son, gives his blessing to the union of Ned and Nina (blind to their years-long affair and simply believing that they sacrificed their love for the sake of his father, Sam—which, of course, is true in a way Gordon has never imagined). However, Ned and Nina, having outlived passion, are no longer in love, and Ned returns to science, while Nina and Charlie, her comforter, agree to marry.

Thematically ambitious, O'Neill's play addresses large questions: What is happiness? What is good-ness, honor, or morality? What is life? Sam's mother says, "Being happy, that's the nearest we can ever come to knowing what's good! Being happy, that's good! The rest is just talk! . . . Whatever you can do to make [Sam] happy is good." She then advises Nina to make Sam and herself happy by doing something that their society considers immoral: having a baby by a man other than her husband. She and Ned do this, believing they are doing it for Sam, but Ned does not anticipate that this bit of "Science"—fertilizing an egg for Sam—will cause him to fall in love. Later, when they are, all of them, "passed beyond desire," they can rest. Sam is dead. Ned returns to his research station in the tropics, to the "unicellular life that floats in the sea and has never learned the cry for happiness"— never again to return to Nina. Charlie and Nina sit and consider how "extravagant and fantastic" all that has happened is since Nina first met Gordon Shaw. Charlie suggests that they "forget the whole distressing episode, regard it as an interlude, of trial and preparation . . . in which our souls have been scraped clean of impure flesh and made worthy to bleach in peace." Nina agrees, "Yes, our lives are merely strange dark interludes in the electrical display of God the Father."

BIBLIOGRAPHY

O'Neill, Eugene. "Memoranda on Masks." In *O'Neill and His Plays,* edited by Oscar Cargill, N. Bryllion Fagin, and William J. Fisher. New York: New York University Press, 1961. 116–122.

STRASBERG, LEE (1901–1982)   See Actors Studio and Group Theatre, The.

STREAMERS David Rabe (1976)   Provocative and violent, *Streamers* is the third in Rabe's trilogy of plays about the Vietnam era, along with *The Basic Training of Pavlo Hummel* (1971) and *Sticks And Bones* (1972). The irrational violence of the play's climax represents the similarly chaotic war that awaits the characters who have completed basic training. *Streamers* won the New York Drama Critics' Circle Award.

The play is set in a room within an army barracks in 1965. The room's tenants are three Specialists,

Fourth Class, just out of basic training and probably headed for Vietnam, the site of an escalating war they were barely aware of when they enlisted: Richie is from Manhattan, has always had money, is openly gay, and has a crush on Billy; an earnest midwesterner, Billy is a college graduate who believes the war is justified and believes Richie must not be—could not possibly be—homosexual; and Roger, one of the few African-Americans on the base, has seen urban violence firsthand. Roger and Billy are close friends and share a disapproval of homosexuality; both hope that Richie is joking when he implies a preference for men, and if he is not joking, then they hope he will abandon homosexuality. Despite their differences, the three men live together in a friendly—even kindhearted—atmosphere.

The first intrusion into their ordered lives is the attempted suicide of a young man who wants to get out of the army at any cost. The second is Carlyle, who has sought out their room because he has been told another African-American soldier lives there. Carlyle is tightly wound and erratic in his behavior. He wants Roger to come to town with him, but Roger prefers to stay and clean up the room with Billy.

While the four young men are likely to go to war, two older sergeants, Rooney and Cokes, represent those who have experienced war already. Cokes is just back from Vietnam and has been diagnosed with leukemia, and Rooney is about to go to Vietnam; both men served in Korea. They come into the younger men's room, drunk and cheerful, singing "Beautiful Streamer" (to the tune of "Beautiful Dreamer"). A streamer is a parachute that has failed to open, and "Beautiful Streamer" is the song that is sung by those who are doomed to die. The title, then, refers to those who are about to die—all of the characters in the play.

Carlyle—menacing and unpredictable—again comes to the room. This time Roger decides to go into town with him and even convinces Billy to come with them for a night of drinking and carousing. When the three return late to join Richie, the drunken Carlyle gradually makes it clear that he wants to have sex with Richie; though Roger is willing to turn the other way and pretend to sleep, Billy is not. An angry Carlyle pulls a switchblade on him and cuts his hand. Billy is

nearly incited to violence himself in response, but he rejects that choice, throwing down his razor and calling Carlyle an animal. Carlyle stabs him in the stomach, and when Sergeant Rooney comes in, Carlyle stabs Rooney to death too. Carlyle represents both the senseless violence of the war and the soldier engaged in it, who is wondering, as Carlyle says at this point, "Ohhhhhh, how'm I gonna get back to the world now." The Military Police come in to take away the bodies and arrest Carlyle.

The play ends when a drunken Sergeant Cokes, looking for his friend Rooney with whom he has been in several traffic accidents that night, dozes off near the bunks of Roger and Richie. The younger men have kept the news of Rooney's death from him, and before he falls asleep Cokes reminisces about a man he killed in combat, telling Roger that the doomed man sang "Beautiful Streamer."

The metaphor of the "streamer" is more extensive than simply the looming prospect of death in Vietnam. It is "an image of a certain determinism. Not only are all the characters victims of their own circumstances, ineffectually reaching out for something to save them, but, like everyone else, they are in free fall without a parachute. They are the products of and subject to chance, but, beyond that, they are all, of course, under an ultimate sentence of death, an inescapable irony. Thus, the returned Vietnam vet is now suffering from leukemia, while his colleague escapes a traffic accident unscathed only to return to the barracks in time to be knifed to death" (Bigsby 276).

BIBLIOGRAPHY
Bigsby, Christopher. "David Rabe." In *Contemporary American Playwrights*. Cambridge, England: Cambridge University Press, 1999. 252–288.

STREETCAR NAMED DESIRE, A TENNESSEE WILLIAMS (1947)

A Streetcar Named Desire is an icon of American and world theater. It was voted the most important American play of the 20th century by the American Theatre Critics Association. Premiering in 1947, *Streetcar,* as directed by ELIA KAZAN and expressionistically designed by JO MIELZINER, was the first play to win three major drama awards in a single year: the PULITZER PRIZE, the New York Drama Critics'

Circle Award, and the Donaldson Award; WILLIAMS was 36. *Streetcar* is quintessential Williams, written in his lyrical prose, set in the gothic southern landscape of New Orleans (Williams's "spiritual home"), and containing his most haunting characters, symbols, and themes.

The *Streetcar* plot is deceptively simple; it is filled, however, with narratives within narratives bridging the temporal and psychic worlds of its characters. Blanche, a dismissed English teacher with a shady and promiscuous past, from Laurel, Mississippi, seeks refuge with her sister Stella in New Orleans. A neurotic personality with the sensibilities of a 19th-century romantic heroine, Blanche mourns both her dead husband (the young homosexual poet Allan Grey) and her lost ancestral southern plantation (Belle Reve, "Beautiful Dream"). She finds her sister's two-room apartment scandalously squalid and Stella's uncouth husband Stanley a beast who is good only for sexual romps. During the "Poker Night" (scene 3), Stanley beats his pregnant wife, who then, with Blanche, seeks sanctuary with the upstairs neighbor Eunice. At the "Poker Night," Blanche meets Mitch, one of Stanley's friends and a mama's boy. She sees in him the protection she yearns for; he sees in her his chance to redeem a life devoid of love. Their ill-fated courtship is juxtaposed against Stanley's extravagant antics with his wife and their rowdy French Quarter friends.

During the long summer, Stanley becomes increasingly angry about Blanche's airs, her daily hot baths, her liquor consumption, and her encampment in his home, and at her birthday party he presents her with a one-way ticket back to Laurel. He also tells Mitch about her sordid past, undercutting her projected image as a demure and proper lady. On the night Stanley takes Stella to the hospital, a betrayed and angry Mitch attempts to rape Blanche (scene 9) but is frightened away by an increasingly unbalanced Blanche, who is ominously visited by an old Mexican woman selling flowers for the dead. Returning home to await the birth of his son, Stanley taunts and then rapes his sister-in-law, pushing her completely over the edge into insanity. In the last scene, the men play poker again as Blanche, dressed in a Della Robbia blue dress, is being readied for her trip to the madhouse, which she fanta-

sizes will be a sea cruise or a reunion with her former beau, Shep Huntley. Stanley has successfully lied to Stella about the rape, and the play ends with Blanche's departure on the arm of a kind stranger, the doctor, as Stanley is reunited with Stella.

Within these narratives of desperation and desire, Williams weaves a complicated pattern of symbols reflecting the conflicts at the heart of *Streetcar*. Blanche arrives at Stanley's apartment with a trunk of papers on the loss of Belle Reve and of clothes broadcasting her reduced condition. The trunk is both a wardrobe closet for Blanche's various performances—from a flirtatious sex kitten in scene 2 to a faded Cleopatra in Mardi Gras rags in scene 10—and a portable sarcophagus for her memories. Perhaps the most famous symbol in the Williams canon, excepting Laura Wingfield's glass menagerie, is the Chinese paper lantern Blanche puts over a naked light bulb to cover the harsh truth of reality and to transform the ugly into the romantic. "I don't want realism," she says. "I want Magic. . . . I don't tell truth, I tell what ought to be the truth." Blanche lives in a fantasy world of antebellum balls and beaux; it is a life of refinement, but the enchantment and tragedy of such a world is ironically encoded in her encounter with a young paperboy whom she gently kisses on the lips and whose paper—the *Evening Star*—she incorporates into the mythology of her desire.

Stella has wholeheartedly accepted Stanley's world—the pulsating sex of the blues piano and hot trumpet and the gamesmanship at the Four Deuces bar—and is transformed into, as Williams describes her, a *"narcotized . . . eastern idol,"* adoring her husband's sexual potency. The symbols associated with Stanley's physicality—liquor bottles, food, animals, loud noises, and his red silk pajamas worn for special occasions like the birth of his son and the rape of Blanche—may separate him from her but ironically also identify him as a dreamer, another investor in illusions. The melody Blanche hears in her head, the Varsouviana, calls her back to an earlier time of romance and is contrapuntally set against the sleazy jazz of Stanley's New Orleans. Blanche and Stanley are, ultimately, both seekers after and victims of desire.

A highly allusive play, *Streetcar* has elicited a variety of interpretations, in some measure a reflection of the tastes of individual decades in which it has been read and produced. Williams has been praised for defining desire. The meaning of *Streetcar* historically has been articulated through its polarities—the Old South of beauty and culture (Blanche) is defeated by the new age of industrialism and brutal materialism (Stanley); the world of light (the name *Blanche DuBois* means white wood) and grace is destroyed by the dark, corrupted world of sex and violence (Stanley Kowalski). But the dichotomies do not hold absolutely. Recent feminist readings see Blanche and Stella as victims of domestic abuse, denied a voice in the heterosexual battle for empowerment. Other current interpretations, however, paint Blanche as a diseased intruder in Stanley and Stella's healthy, fruitful household. For still other critics, *Streetcar* is Williams's plea for the recognition of his own homosexuality, which had to be concealed through the absent character of Allan Grey, who kills himself after Blanche discovers him with another man. Ultimately, *Streetcar* is about one of Williams's most powerful themes—the enemy time and the inescapable vulnerability of those who pursue love on the streetcar named "Desire," which must cross cemeteries to get to Elysian Fields, the land of the happy dead.

BIBLIOGRAPHY

Adler, Thomas P. *"A Streetcar Named Desire": The Moth and the Lantern.* Boston: Twayne, 1990.

Bloom, Harold, ed. *Modern Critical Interpretations: Tennessee Williams's "A Streetcar Named Desire."* New York: Chelsea House, 1988.

Kolin, Philip C., ed. *Confronting Tennessee Williams's "A Streetcar Named Desire": Essays in Critical Pluralism.* Westport, Conn.: Greenwood, 1993.

———. *Williams's "A Streetcar Named Desire."* Cambridge, England: Cambridge University Press, 2000.

Miller, Jordan Y., ed. *Twentieth-Century Interpretation of "A Streetcar Named Desire": A Collection of Critical Essays.* Englewood Cliffs, N.J.: Prentice-Hall, 1971.

Philip C. Kolin
University of Southern Mississippi

STREET SCENE ELMER RICE (1929) This PULITZER PRIZE–winning portrait of a diverse, working-class, immigrant neighborhood in New York City during the 1920s has more than 40 characters. RICE attempted to capture the reality of life in a tenement, including urban noise and passersby. The set, designed by JO MIELZINER, faithfully replicated the exterior of a typical brownstone apartment house. Rice's play explores the relationship of humans to each other, to their environment, and to themselves.

The play is the life that teems in and around the tenement, but within that life of many small, intersecting stories and incidents is a centerpiece, the conflict within the Maurrant family. Mrs. Maurrant, starved for affection and gentleness, is having an affair, which is the talk of the neighborhood. By making the adulterous Mrs. Maurrant a kind and sympathetic character, Rice suggests that the need for an authentic human connection is more important than conventional morality. Mrs. Maurrant's daughter, Rose, a girl of 20, is aware of the gossip and is upset by it. She is a pretty girl who has attracted the advances of her married boss as well as the sincere affection of her neighbor, Sam Kaplan.

Mr. Maurrant suspects his wife's infidelity and returns to the apartment unexpectedly to surprise the lovers; he fatally shoots them both and is himself taken to jail, leaving Rose to care for her young brother, Willie. She rejects the help of others, including Sam, who loves her, because she believes that she and Sam should learn to rely on themselves first—not on each other—and thereby perhaps avoid the mistakes of her parents. She suggests that someday they may be together, but not before they have developed their individual selves.

In addition to the realistic set, there are many details that contribute to the realism of the play, including street vendors, pedestrians, and offstage sounds of children playing, dogs barking, trains, trucks, music, and so on. The difficulties of life are portrayed without gloss: Mrs. Buchanan's difficult childbirth, Mrs. Hildebrand's eviction, following her husband's desertion of her and her two young children, the unkind attitude of the worker from the "Charities" toward the Hildebrands.

Rice's condemnation of anti-Semitism in the play is not subtle. Many of the neighbors look down on the Kaplans. Mr. Kaplan, an elderly socialist, is the object of much derision in the apartment house. The most vocal anti-Semite is Mrs. Jones who, when she notices Sam's interest in Rose, advises Mrs. Maurrant, "I'd think twice before I'd let any child o' mine bring a Jew into the family." The condescending Mrs. Jones has a thug for a son and a tart for a daughter, while the Kaplans, the only Jews in the building, are an educated family. Shirley is a teacher, and Sam is about to start law school, having graduated from college with honors.

Brenda Murphy, in *American Realism and American Drama, 1880–1940*, writes, "Rice was aware that he was attempting a tour de force in trying to make a realistic play out of the staples of melodrama [husband murders his wife and her lover] and comedy [scenes of innocent young love], but his point was precisely that life is made up of melodrama and comedy *as well as* its more commonplace incidents" (186).

BIBLIOGRAPHY
Murphy, Brenda. *American Realism and American Drama, 1880–1940.* Cambridge, England: Cambridge University Press, 1987.

SUBJECT WAS ROSES, THE FRANK GILROY (1964)
When their son returns home from his World War II military service, an estranged couple has a chance to become closer, but years of bitterness have irreparably damaged their relationship. The play won the PULITZER PRIZE, the TONY AWARD, and the New York Drama Critics' Circle Award.

When Timmy Cleary returns home in 1946 after serving in the army, his parents, John and Nettie, are grateful he is alive and physically intact; some of their neighbors' sons were not so lucky. Timmy, now 21, has matured; while in the past he and his mother always formed an "alliance" against his father, he and his father now seem closer—drinking together, talking of the war, going to a ballgame. When the two men return to the house after an outing, Timmy brings roses for his mother but tells her they are from her husband. Nettie is surprised and touched. The roses move her in a way she thought impossible, and she readily agrees to dinner out with her husband and son. When they return home late, John tries to become intimate with his wife; Nettie rejects him, asking him not to "spoil everything," reminding him of his "hotel lobby whores," and finally smashing the rose vase on the floor. He tells her he "had nothing to do with the roses."

The next morning the tension between husband and wife destroys the short-lived affinity between father and son. Gradually, the story of the Cleary marriage is told (in speeches, rather than in dramatic action). Timmy accuses his mother of failing to support her husband: She objected to the lake house he bought; she forbade him to take a lucrative job in Brazil. Timmy criticizes his mother for her devotion to her own mother and especially to her "cripple[d]" and dim-witted nephew. Living with the bitter couple, Timmy himself was made sick with anxiety as a child: waiting for his father's late-night key in the door, "praying" his father would "come home safe" but also "dreading the sound of that key" because of the inevitable fight to follow.

Nettie walks out of the house and is gone for 12 hours. When she returns, she tells her husband and son that these hours were the "only real freedom [she's] ever known" and that she came back because she is "a coward." Nettie tells Timmy about meeting and choosing John over other suitors: He was charming, handsome, sociable, and destined to be "a millionaire by the time he was forty," but the stock market crash of "nineteen twenty-nine took care of that." She chose him—"magnificent. . . . as long as the situation was impersonal"—over the "baker from Paterson" who was "tongue-tied outside, but in the home he would have been beautiful." It is at this point that Timmy admits to her that before he left home three years before, he had "blamed [his father] for everything that was wrong"; when he returned, he blamed his mother. Now he "suspect[s] that no one's to blame."

In the end, John first expresses anger at his son's decision to move out, but after he and his son express their love for one another, John *insists* that Timmy leave, telling his son that he has already hired painters to redo his bedroom. All three know that this is a lie, but it is one that enables them to agree that Timmy must leave this fractured home for his own good.

SUBSTANCE OF FIRE, THE JON ROBIN BAITZ (1991)
Set in New York City in 1987 and 1990, *The Substance of Fire* deals with two generations

of a Jewish publishing family coping with their failing business. The father's ties to the Holocaust influence his decisions to the detriment of the bottom line, which puts him at odds with his children.

Isaac Geldhart's venerable old publishing house is facing bankruptcy, unless a best-selling title can keep the company afloat. Isaac's son, Aaron, whom Isaac brought into the company and who has an M.B.A., wants to publish a trashy, comic novel; he has brought his siblings to town to back him up. Sarah is a California actress who works in children's television; Martin, who survived cancer as a teenager, teaches landscape architecture at Vassar. All of the Geldhart children are in their twenties, and all inherited stock in the company from their mother. Isaac wants to publish "serious work" like "six volumes on the Nazi medical experiments." Last year's titles included *An Atlas of the Holocaust*. As he gets older, Isaac is drawn back to the Holocaust, in which his family perished and during which he lived in hiding. In addition to his desire to publish books related to Nazi horror, he has recently purchased at auction a postcard on which is a little painting of a church, done by Hitler in 1916. When questioned by his children about this purchase, he says that it fascinates him and that he is "out of step with [himself] lately, here in New York."

Isaac is something of a tyrant. He likes to be in control, and to that end, he belittles his children, calling Aaron "an accountant," Martin "a gardener," and telling Sarah that actresses are not "all that bright, really. Are you?" Despite his criticism, Sarah has a self-described "father fixation," as evidenced, she admits, by her affair with an older, somewhat indifferent, married man. Martin—who has stopped accompanying his father to restaurants because Isaac makes such scenes over his dissatisfaction with the food—is tired of his father's "endless posturing, position-taking, ranting, [and] judging." He is also tired of the book culture in which he grew up. Fed up, Martin turns his shares over to Aaron; Sarah's shares soon follow, and Aaron, now in control of the company, is free to publish what he wants.

As act 2 begins three and a half years later, the company is bankrupt, and Isaac vainly hopes to buy the company back by auctioning off some of his rare

book collection. Aaron, who has not seen his father in those three and a half years, is having Isaac's competence assessed by a psychiatric social worker. Years before, the social worker, Marge Hackett, came to a reading at Isaac's apartment with her husband—a notorious embezzler. She and Isaac flirted in the kitchen; recognizing Isaac's name, she has taken his case out of curiosity. During the course of their conversation, Isaac reveals his belief that publishing books on the Nazis will help him somehow to atone for his own survival. Isaac asks Marge to dinner, and she declines, saying that he need not dine alone as he claims: He still has family, not those who died in Europe, but his children. She encourages him, then, to embrace the present. Isaac burns the Hitler postcard, the mythical value of which Marge diminishes by telling Isaac that she did not save her husband's "post-its," suggesting that all criminals leave behind rubbish of no great significance. After burning the postcard, Isaac takes a walk with his son, Martin—finally attempting a reconnection with his living family. JON ROBIN BAITZ has written of his character, Isaac Geldhart: "No matter how hard he toils at re-inventing himself as a Manhattan bon vivant, his past insists on being heard" (Schiff 337).

BIBLIOGRAPHY

Schiff, Ellen, ed. *Fruitful and Multiplying: 9 Contemporary Plays from the American Jewish Repertoire.* New York: Mentor, 1996.

SUMMER AND SMOKE TENNESSEE WILLIAMS (1948)

During the summer of 1946, on the Massachusetts island of Nantucket, WILLIAMS shared a house with novelist and playwright Carson McCullers. While she sat at one end of a long table and adapted her novel *The Member of the Wedding* for the stage, he wrote *Summer and Smoke* at the other end. His play was first produced a year later by Margo Jones at her Theatre '47 in Dallas and opened on Broadway in October 1948.

The play's theme, the incompatibility of body and soul, is symbolized by its split set. On one side is the Episcopal rectory of Glorious Hill, Mississippi, home of Alma Winemiller; her father, the town's minister; and her mother, addled by a breakdown when Alma was a teenager. On the other side is the home next door of Dr. John Buchanan, the town doctor and a widower, and his son, John Jr. In between is the town park, over which looms the stone statue and fountain of an angel named "Eternity." The time is the first 16 years of the 20th century.

In the play's prologue, we see 10-year-olds John and Alma (Spanish for "soul") in the park. She has surreptitiously put a box of handkerchiefs on his desk at school because she's noticed he's had a cold. She explains that because his mother has recently died, he needs someone to take care of him. He tries to give her back the handkerchiefs and confides in her that his father wants him to be a doctor, but he "wouldn't be a doctor for the world" and would rather "go to South America on a boat" and be "a devil." At his urging, she reluctantly allows him to give her *a quick rough kiss.*

The rest of the play is divided into two parts, each subdivided into six scenes. Part 1, "A Summer," begins about 15 years later at the same spot as the prologue. Alma, a talented amateur vocalist and singing teacher, who has nervously been performing at a Fourth of July celebration, and John, who has become a doctor but is testing his father's tolerance with his drinking and womanizing, are watching the fireworks together. Rosa Gonzales, the sexy daughter of the owner of the Moon Lake gambling casino, walks by, and there is clearly a mutual attraction between her and John. Also at the park is Nellie Ewell, whom Alma has accepted as a pupil despite the town's disapproval of her mother's habit of picking up traveling salesmen at the town depot. John tells Alma that she has a reputation in town for "putting on airs a little" and for speaking affectedly; she responds that people don't understand that, since her mother's breakdown, she has had to assume the duties of the minister's wife—which may make her seem strange and has deprived her of her youth. In turn, she tells John that he ought to stop being "an overgrown schoolboy, who wants to be known as the wildest fellow in town," calling it a "desecration" for a "gifted young doctor" to act that way. He asks her to go driving with him, and she agrees, if he will obey the speed limit.

John does not follow through on this planned outing, and when Alma calls to chide him, he agrees to attend a meeting of her group of young people with "artistic and intellectual interests," if she will save him "a seat by the punchbowl." Nellie comes by for a singing lesson and tells Alma that she has a crush on young "Dr. John." John comes to the meeting of the group but leaves abruptly "to call on a patient"; one of the members says that the "patient" is Rosa, whose father carries two guns, and John could get in trouble if he continues to see her. That prediction seems accurate as the next scene begins with Rosa bandaging a wound on John's arm at 2 A.M. that night. Alma comes in to see John's father because she is having one of her frequent heart palpitations during which she can't breathe. John gives her a sedative and examines her heart with his stethoscope; when she asks what he hears, he replies, "Just a little voice saying—Miss Alma is lonesome!" and he says he will take her out that Saturday night.

Despite her father's strenuous objections, Alma goes with John on Saturday night to Moon Lake casino. He tells her he's thinking of leaving medicine and going to South America; she tries to discourage him from this plan by urging him to have loftier goals. When he asks her to stay for a cock-fight and then to go to a room upstairs with him, she refuses, calls a cab, and leaves, saying, *You're not a gentleman!*

Part 2, "A Winter," opens with Alma entertaining her boring, mama's-boy friend Roger Doremus while a loud party with Mexican music is taking place next door, at the Buchanans' (John's father is out of town treating victims of a fever epidemic). When a friend comes by to tell Alma that John and Rosa Gonzales are to be married the next day because of the huge gambling debt John owes Rosa's father, Alma calls John's father. In the midst of the party, John, disgusted by his own behavior and depressed at the prospect of marrying Rosa, goes to Alma's house and asks her to put her cool hands on his flushed face. Back at the Buchanan house, the elder Dr. John returns to find the party in full swing; attempting to evict everyone, he is fatally shot by Rosa's father.

Alma comes to visit John's dying father, and John shows her the anatomy chart in the office, pointing out that she is ignoring her appetites for love and the truth. She responds that there is something "not shown" on the chart, the soul, and "it is *that* that I loved you with," not the anatomical part shown on the chart. He admits that he wouldn't have made love to her the night at the casino because "I'm more afraid of your soul than you're afraid of my body."

Later in the fall, John is welcomed home as a hero for finishing the work his father started by stamping out the fever epidemic. Alma has become a recluse, wearing a dressing gown all day and leaving the house only occasionally very late at night. On her first daytime outing, she encounters Nellie, home from college and looking very grown up, who reports that she's been taking diction classes so that she can speak like Alma and has also been seeing John. She gives Alma a Christmas gift of a handkerchief from the two of them, explaining that John feels that Alma was his "angel of mercy" because their talks "were responsible for his pulling himself together."

In the play's climactic scene, Alma goes to John's office to tell him that she's swallowed her pride and is offering herself to him. He responds that she's won the argument between them; he's come around to her "way of thinking" and realized that there can be a spiritual bond not on the anatomy chart. "The tables have turned with a vengeance," she exclaims and explains, in the play's most telling lines, that it's "like two people exchanging a call on each other at the same time, and each one finding the other gone out, the door locked against him and no one to answer the bell!" Alma has guessed correctly: John and Nellie are to be married. In the play's final scene, Alma picks up a young traveling salesman by the fountain and takes him to Moon Lake casino.

This last scene is described by some critics—and even by Williams himself in a 1972 interview—as evidence of Alma's "complete profligacy" (Devlin 216), while others see it as her "initiation into integrated personhood" (Adler 147). The play is best viewed, however, along with its two immediate predecessors in Williams's canon—*The GLASS MENAGERIE* (1945) and *A STREETCAR NAMED DESIRE* (1947)—as a depiction of the difficulties human beings experience in making an intimate human connection. Whether it is Laura and Jim of the first play, Blanche and Mitch of the second, or Alma and John here, true intimacy eludes Williams's characters. John and Alma's incompatibility, while it may be couched in terms of body and soul in *Summer and Smoke,* really stands more universally for what Williams once described as the "positive message" of his plays, "The crying, almost screaming need of a great worldwide effort to know ourselves and each other a great deal better" (*Where I Live* 90).

BIBLIOGRAPHY

Adler, Thomas P. *American Drama, 1940–1960: A Critical History.* New York: Twayne, 1994.

Devlin, Albert J., ed. *Conversations with Tennessee Williams.* Jackson: University Press of Mississippi, 1986.

Williams, Tennessee. *Where I Live: Selected Essays.* Edited by Christine R. Day and Bob Woods. New York: New Directions, 1978.

SUNSHINE BOYS, THE NEIL SIMON (1972)

One of the first SIMON plays to blend poignancy with comedy, *The Sunshine Boys* is about a pair of aging vaudevillians, one of whom is a curmudgeon who clings to his life as an entertainer, even after he can no longer remember lines or keep his hands steady.

The old vaudeville comedy team, Willie Clark and Al Lewis, are in their seventies now and have not worked together since Al Lewis quit the team, retiring in his sixties, to live quite contentedly with his married daughter. The two were known as "The Sunshine Boys," and now a television network wants them to reunite for a "variety show" featuring "some of the biggest names in the history of show business." Willie's agent, his nephew Ben, proposes the reunion. Willie resents Al for retiring after 43 years of partnership, and he complains to his nephew that Al Lewis had a bad habit of poking him in the chest for emphasis and spitting in his face whenever he said the letter *t*. Despite his reservations, Willie agrees to a meeting. The encounter in Willie's shabby and chilly hotel apartment is itself like a vaudeville skit as the two old men mix up the names of people they have known and theaters at which they have played. Finally, they begin rehearsing "the doctor sketch"; Willie insists that the rehearsal be done *his* way—moving a chair a fraction of an inch, changing a line of the ancient dialogue—so antagonizing Al that he leaves in disgust, proclaiming that Willie is a "LUNATIC BASTARD!"

Later at the television studio for a dress rehearsal, Lewis and Clark have caused so many delays that the show's producers are running out of patience. The dress rehearsal finally begins (the sketch is typical vaudeville fare, including a shapely nurse whom the doctor tricks into bending over repeatedly and other such moments of broad humor); the rehearsal eventually deteriorates into an argument brought on by Al's moist pronunciation of the sentence, "It's *time to* pay your *taxes to the* Treasury," followed by his "*poking Willie in the chest with his finger.*" Willie becomes enraged. Al walks out, and Willie has a heart attack. The producers use a version of the sketch taped years earlier on the *Ed Sullivan Show*.

Post–heart attack, Willie is much the same as ever, except that now his straight man is the registered nurse hired to care for him. Ben arrives to offer his uncle the choice of moving in with his family or into the Actors' Home, a retirement residence; Uncle Willie chooses the latter. Ben has also arranged for a visit from Al Lewis, who brings the news that with the arrival of a new grandchild, he will be moving from his daughter's home to a nice place in New Jersey, the Actors' Home. The curtain falls on the two men arguing about people and places they have known; presumably, the arguments will continue at the Actors' Home until one of them dies.

Simon deals with some serious issues in this comedy: the powerlessness of the elderly, as well as the fight (embodied by Willie) against losing control over one's own life. Simon also addresses a theme that he would later address in the darker character of the grandmother in *LOST IN YONKERS*: The price of persistent unpleasantness or, worse, an obsessive need for control is isolation.

SUPPRESSED DESIRES Susan Glaspell (1915)

Written in collaboration with GLASPELL's husband GEORGE CRAM COOK, the one-act *Suppressed Desires* satirizes the faddish interest in Freudian psychology among Greenwich Village intellectuals of the day.

Henrietta Brewster is obsessed with psychoanalysis, so much so that she awakens her husband Stephen at night to find out what he is dreaming. When Henrietta's married sister Mabel comes to visit, Henrietta finds underlying significance in Mabel's every move and utterance and convinces Mabel that she must have "suppressed desires." Two weeks later, independent of one another and unbeknownst to Henrietta, Stephen and Mabel have both been seeing Dr. Russell, a psychoanalyst who interprets their dreams. The doctor's conclusion: Stephen's suppressed desire is to leave Henrietta, and Mabel's is to leave her husband for Stephen. The outraged Henrietta quickly becomes less enamoured of psychoanalytic theory. Stephen promises not to separate from Henrietta if Henrietta will "separate from psychoanalysis."

A performance of the play in the summer of 1915, along with Neith Boyce's one-act play, *Constancy,* in the home of Boyce and husband Hutchins Hapgood, marked the birth of the PROVINCETOWN PLAYERS; the WASHINGTON SQUARE PLAYERS had rejected Glaspell's comedy.

SUSAN AND GOD Rachel Crothers (1937)

A satirical play, *Susan and God* is about a woman who has a pseudoreligious conversion. She eventually learns to look for God within her own heart, not within a religious movement—but not before meddling in the lives of her friends.

The play begins with a group of sophisticated, idle, rich friends at a country house awaiting the arrival of their friend Susan Trexel. Mike O'Hara and Irene Burroughs, whose house it is, live together, though she is not yet divorced from her second husband. Hutchins "Stubbie" Stubbs and his new wife, a former actress, Leonora, come in from tennis with Clyde Rochester, an actor, and Charlotte Marley. Clyde loves Leonora, who is beginning to wish she had not given up the stage, and Charlotte loves the husband of the absent Susan. We get a sense of Susan and her husband, Barrie, from their friends' gossip before we meet them. He is a very "sweet," very wealthy alcoholic. Susan, we hear, has too much "charm." Irene comments on their tendency to fight: "I *adore* them—but not when they're *together.*" Susan has been in Europe for months, and their 15-year-old daughter, Blossom, has been at boarding school. Now that the school year has ended, she will soon be shipped off to camp for the summer.

When Susan arrives directly from her transatlantic voyage, she is bursting with news: She was introduced to "Lady Wiggam's movement" while in England, and she has found God. It soon becomes clear that she has embraced a fad that calls for universal love and complete honesty—and the use of first names ("Lord Ramsdale's chauffeur called him *Tom*. It was too sweet"). CROTHERS satirizes the frivolousness of women such as Susan: Her manner as she approaches this supposedly weighty subject—"It's the only thing in the world that will stop war. Oh Irene, I've brought you the most ravishing panties."—brings out raucous laughter in her friends.

Meanwhile, Barrie has gone to Blossom's school to pick her up; the four hours they spend getting from the school to Irene's is the longest they have ever been together. Kept from Susan by Irene, Barrie and Blossom retreat to their nearby summer house, which has been closed for years. Blossom, who hates camp, begs her father to let them all three stay there together this summer, like other families. That evening at Irene's, Susan applies her new-found philosophy to her friends, generally butting in and causing problems: Clyde should declare to Stubbie his love for Stubbie's wife; it would be "brave and beautiful." As she tries to reform Irene for living unmarried with Mike, Irene questions her treatment of Barrie: "Your own life is a mess. Clean it up before you begin preaching to other people." Mike decides to teach Susan a lesson. He pretends he is about to confess some unforgivable crime under her influence, as the others, suppressing their laughter, play along. Susan, all sympathy and encouragement, tells him he is not beyond God's help; a drunken Barrie enters and, witnessing the scene, seriously "ask[s] Him" for help too.

In the sober light of the next morning, Barrie makes a deal with Susan. If she will stay in the summer house with him (platonically) and Blossom all summer, he will stop drinking, and if he fails even once he will give her the divorce she has long sought. In the presence of Barrie, Susan, with sarcastic enthusiasm, tells Blossom of their plans. Susan's irony is lost only on the innocent Blossom, not on Barrie and certainly not on the audience. Poor Blossom is overwhelmed, thinking that her parents might actually love her, but

Susan confides to Irene as she departs for her own house, "I don't know *why I'm doing it*. . . . I wish I'd never *heard* of God."

By act 3, nearly three months have passed. Blossom is now happy and healthy, Barrie has not had a drink, and Susan has found that her family is not so bad, though she did nearly run away in the beginning. Susan has also been busy planning a meeting of Lady Wiggam's followers at the end of the summer. When it comes to her attention that the meeting and Blossom's birthday are on the same day, she and Barrie have a discussion that reveals that she will be a key speaker at the meeting and her topic will be his reformation at her hands. She also tells him she hopes he will marry Charlotte, with whom he has played much golf this summer. He is angry and offended and tells her that he stayed away from alcohol only to get her (Susan) back. With that he goes out and gets drunk. His long absence and her worry cause her to realize that she does love him. When he returns sober because Charlotte has helped him through his drunk and his recovery, he is willing to give Susan her freedom. But Susan has had another conversion; she now believes that "God is [not] something out there—to pray to" but "He's *here*—in us." Her life has been given meaning this summer by a real connection to and involvement in the lives of her child and her husband. She finally realizes that it is this, not a religious fad, that will fill the emptiness of her idle, superficial life.

Rachel Crothers's last and most successful play, *Susan and God,* like many of the other plays she wrote in the 1920s and 1930s, satirizes middle-class customs and values connected to marriage, divorce, and family, without actually condemning middle-class institutions. By keeping her satire light and within a range acceptable to her middle-class audience, she kept them happy and maintained her commercial success. One of the follies of the middle class and idle rich that Crothers satirizes here is the adoption of a religious or philosophical fad without real understanding, simply because it was fashionable. "Lady Wiggam's movement" is Buchmanism, also known after 1938 as Moral Re-Armament, which was started by an American evangelist named Frank Buchman, who, in the early 1920s, lectured in England and established a following there. His philosophy involved changing the world by changing one's own life. The irony of Susan's conversion is that it is only when she lets go of Lady Wiggam's movement that she finally begins to achieve its principles.

SWEET BIRD OF YOUTH TENNESSEE WILLIAMS (1959)

Set in a small town somewhere on the Gulf Coast, *Sweet Bird of Youth* looks at flawed and vulnerable characters victimized by bullies and by the passage of time.

Chance Wayne, still attractive, though no longer in the flower of youth, and "The Princess Kosmonopolis" awaken in an *"old-Fashioned but still Fashionable hotel"* in Chance's hometown of St. Cloud. The Princess is really Alexandra Del Lago, a middle-aged film star, whose career was based on youth and beauty and who—now that they have faded—has gone into a tailspin of drugs, alcohol, panic, and younger lovers—like Chance, whom she picked up days before in a Florida resort, where he was working as a beach boy. Miss Del Lago retired from the cinema when she was still young enough to hang on to stardom, but she has recently made a comeback. At the premiere of her new film, when she heard people gasp at her first close-up, she ran from the theater, not looking back until she landed in St. Cloud. Through pills and hash and booze and the oxygen she carries with her, she has kept consciousness and despair at bay.

The two are in St. Cloud this Easter Sunday (significantly, the day of resurrection) morning because Chance hopes to see his true love, Heavenly Finley, again. Chance clings to the hope of a life with Heavenly, one in which they erase the years since their first pure love at 15 and 17, and one in which they become movie stars through the intercession of Miss Del Lago.

But Heavenly is now engaged to Dr. George Scudder, who performed an operation on her to remove the reproductive organs devastated by a venereal disease she caught from Chance during his last visit. Heavenly's father, Boss Finley, a corrupt and racist politician who stopped the young lovers from making a life together when they were still—as Heavenly puts it—"clean," wants Chance out of town or dead. Heavenly

resents her father, who himself married for love but forbade her to do so, and who later also took a mistress for love. She tries to resist him, but he has all the power, and she has none. Tom Finley, Boss's son and henchman, vows to castrate Chance if he finds him; a young black man was recently castrated by some of Boss Finley's men, so the threat is not an empty one.

The "Heckler" comes to every speech of Finley's and calls out questions about Heavenly's operation when Finley tries to "hold her up as the fair white virgin exposed to black lust in the South" as he "lead[s] into his voice of God speech." When the Heckler speaks to Finley's mistress, Miss Lucy, Williams conveys one of the play's ideas: It is the "absolute speechlessness" of God that allows the brutality of men like Finley to persist.

Eventually, Miss Del Lago finds out that her movie was well received by the audience and by critics, who wrote that her talent had "grown" and her acting had achieved "more depth" and "power." Despite this reprieve from oblivion, she remains similar to Chance; both have "despaired-of ambitions," and as Williams writes in his stage directions, they are *equally doomed,* since neither can *"turn back the clock."* She sees the danger that Chance is in and begs him to leave town with her, but Chance goes to his fate as to the inevitable, asking only that the men who come for him at least recognize him in themselves and recognize "the enemy, time, in all of us."

SYLVIA A. R. GURNEY (1996)

A comedy in two acts, *Sylvia* is set in Manhattan. Kate and Greg—their children now grown—move to the city from the suburbs. Greg falls in love with the title character, a stray dog. Can Greg persuade Kate to let him keep Sylvia?

Kate has a new career as an English teacher. Her idealism characterizes many of GURNEY's privileged American women: "I'm trying to put Shakespeare into the junior high curriculum. . . . These kids are fascinated by words. They rap, they rhyme, they invent these exciting phrases and metaphors just the way Shakespeare did." Kate dislikes Sylvia instantly and intensely.

Greg hates his job and may lose it. His career mirrors American economic trends of the late 20th century. An engineer pushed into sales, then bond trading, he now trades currencies. He complains, "I liked manufacturing. . . . I could see what we were making, I could touch it, I could tinker. . . . What's behind currencies? Other currencies. What's behind them? Who knows? Nothing to touch, to see." After a fight with his boss, Greg leaves work early and finds Sylvia in Central Park. She is a Labrador-poodle mix, played by a human.

Scenes in Central Park satirize the behavior of dog-owners, characterized by trendy environmental thinking and pop-psychology obsessions like "male menopause." Scenes in Kate and Greg's apartment and a marriage counselor's office put a 1990s spin on the venerable comic tropes of marital disharmony. Drama lovers will recognize Gurney's debt to English playwrights William Congreve, Oscar Wilde, George Bernard Shaw, and Noël Coward.

Additional fun comes from the writing of three characters for a single male actor—Tom, Greg's mentor in dog psychology; Phyllis, Kate's friend; and Leslie, the marriage counselor. In Sylvia, however, Gurney has created a role full of comic canine business for an actress with superb physical and verbal dexterity. Sylvia, Greg, and Kate talk to each other. Gurney renders Sylvia's bark as a vernacular "Hey! Hey! Hey!" but also gives her the prose style of a *New York Times* columnist: "You had me *spayed,* Greg! You destroyed my womanhood . . . when I still decide that the sun rises and sets only in your direction, then suddenly you're packing me off to some boring nuclear family in Westchester County."

Sylvia can be read as a companion piece to Gurney's *The Perfect Party* (1986) and *The Fourth Wall* (1992; revised version, 2002), which explore a similar theme: couples changing their homes and careers after their child-raising years have ended. In each play, a spouse having a midlife crisis behaves in ways that threaten the marriage.

Arvid F. Sponberg
Valparaiso University

T

TAKE A GIANT STEP LOUIS PETERSON (1953)

Set during a two-week period in a New England town of 1953, *Take a Giant Step* centers around the 17-year-old high-school student Spencer Scott and his experiences as a black youth growing up in a middle-class white neighborhood.

Spencer is expelled from school for a week after protesting against a white teacher's ridiculous history lesson about African Americans in the Civil War and after smoking a cigar in the boys' room. Spencer's father, Lem, a bank employee, regards his son's behavior as a serious offense. His mother, May, stresses that her son has "no business talking back to white women"; her advice is "to try to remember your place." But Spencer's sickly grandmother, May's mother, maintains that the boy should be proud. She is aware of the fact that her grandson has become isolated among the white boys in the neighborhood and that he has been rejected by a white girl.

In the end, after the death of his grandmother and after having his first sexual encounter—with a housemaid—Spencer is on the threshold of becoming a man: Having reconciled with his parents and having regained his health after an illness, he is determined to continue studying music and his academic subjects in order to go to college.

The play is important because it starts where LORRAINE HANSBERRY's frequently praised play, *A RAISIN IN THE SUN* (1959), ends; while the latter tells the story of a black family finally moving into a white neighborhood, *Giant Step* demonstrates the psychological consequences of such a move. The themes of loneliness, isolation, and mistrust dominate the scenes depicted in connection with the main character but also with minor figures like prostitutes. On the other hand, personal independence, self-confidence, and trust are shown as possible effects of the great inner and outer conflicts based on racial tensions. Together with *A Raisin in the Sun,* Ossie Davis's *Purlie Victorious* (1961), and LONNIE ELDER III's *CEREMONIES IN DARK OLD MEN* (1965), *Take a Giant Step* belongs to a group of relatively conservative mainstream African-American dramas that was followed by the more militant work of AMIRI BARAKA and ED BULLINS. In that sense, Peterson captures the mood before the storm. The play was one of the earliest by an African American to reach Broadway.

Thomas Leuchtenmüller
München, Germany

TAKE ME OUT RICHARD GREENBERG (2002)

This delightfully witty play about a baseball star who "comes out" as a homosexual won both a TONY AWARD and the New York Drama Critics' Circle Award in 2003. Surprisingly, it premiered in London (imagine a play featuring cricket premiering in New York), where it was enthusiastically received; the *Daily Telegraph* declared: "*Take Me Out* looks like an American epic, a big three-act drama that takes the pulse of the nation through the medium of baseball" (Spencer). Structur-

522

ally, the play is a series of nonchronological flashbacks orchestrated by two narrators, Kippy Sunderstrom, an articulate philosophical humanist and heterosexual shortstop, and Mason Marzac, an eloquent and (at first) baseball-innocent gay money manager, newly assigned the client Darren Lemming, a baseball star.

Kippy's opening monologue is both exposition and GREENBERG's fond mocking of theatrical exposition. By the end of it, we know that there was "a mess" that started when Darren, the handsome biracial, golden boy of baseball's winningest team, came out unexpectedly at a news conference. Never had there been so much as a hint that he might be gay. The responses among his teammates varied from outright homophobia (some of these players were convinced he would find them irresistible) to wariness to too-familiar encouragement to genuine support. Suddenly he was the darling of the gay community, a role he had no interest in. In fact Darren, secure in his own magnificence as a ballplayer and in its centrality to his life, could not even figure out what all the fuss was about. When Kippy wonders to the audience *why* Darren came out—there was not even "a boyfriend"—or, at least "why *now*," he can only suppose it had something to do with the last time Darren had seen his best friend Davey Battle, who played for another team. Davey had put pressure on Darren to get married and have children, as Davey himself had done; Davey urged him to "love somebody" so that he could "know [his] true nature."

After the flashback of Darren and Davey, we meet Mason for the first time. Until Mason was given the assignment to handle Darren's money, he "would have barely recognized his name." However, after Darren's announcement, which Mason calls "that incredible act of elective heroism," he is all admiration for the man. He tells Darren that his act was "brave," but Darren—in a bit of foreshadowing—objects that it is "only brave if ya think somethin' *bad*'s gonna happen." Over the course of events Darren and Mason become unlikely friends—as the baseball phenom serves as the agent for Mason's introduction to the game. And Mason falls in love with that game. His funny and insightful speech in act 1 about baseball as "a perfect metaphor for hope in a Democratic society" and other observations on the game are among the play's delights.

As the narrators address the audience, directing its collective gaze to one flashback then another, the story of the aftermath of Darren's declaration emerges: The team starts to lose, so Shane Mungitt, a relief pitcher, is called up from the minors. He snaps the losing streak, but he is "a racist, homophobe, hillbilly" as well as the warped product of a homicidal father and a series of orphanages. Given the opportunity to speak on television, he makes racial slurs and complains about having to shower with "a faggot," and is suspended. After a letter ostensibly written by Shane is published, a letter in which he claims he didn't understand the words he said, he is reinstated—in time to save the season. (We find out later that Kippy in a misguided bit of social work actually wrote the letter.) Just before the game of Shane's return, Shane and Darren are in the showers together, where Shane says that Darren was not the "faggot" he was talking about. Darren, in a nonsexual, but decidedly not playful act, hugs him from behind and kisses him. Shane leaves the shower in a murderous rage. When he is put in to relieve the starting pitcher in the ninth inning, he faces Darren's friend Davey and hits him with the first pitch; Davey dies from massive head trauma. Since there is some question about whether the deadly pitch was intentional or not, Shane is briefly held by police and then released, but he is banned from baseball for life.

So who is to blame? Kippy?—for writing the letter that brought Shane back? Darren?—for the fake assault that enraged Shane? Or Darren, again, for fighting with Davey (who calls him a pervert) just before the game and telling him to "drop dead" (this last being overheard from the shower by the demented Shane)? Even the starting pitcher considers and rejects culpability (if only he had finished the game, might the death have been avoided?). Or does the blame fall squarely and solely on the racist (Davey Battle is black), homophobic, and deeply troubled relief pitcher? Greenberg believes that Kippy's belief—which he articulates at the end of act 1—that the ignorant Shane's problem was simply that he did not "have words to name the world with" is misguided;

Greenberg said in an interview that Kippy "operates from the generous, dangerous belief that evil is nothing more than the inability of good to express itself. Which is a lovely notion, but probably not true" (Spencer).

Kippy also philosophizes about the effects of homophobia on a group of men. Why does the team start losing after the announcement? He believes the team goes into "mourning." They lose a "kind of paradise," and like Adam and Eve after their fall from grace, they "see that [they] are naked" (as does the audience, by the way; the full male nudity was quite the talk of the season). There can be no more "pat[ting] fannies" or "snap[ping] towels"; instead, they begin self-consciously to try to prove their masculinity.

Mason is in many ways the voice of the playwright, who like Mason was an adult convert to baseball and who like Mason fell in love with the game. Greenberg admitted as much in an interview in *American Theatre* magazine in October 2002. He said in that same interview that the play—apart from being about "the crisis of masculinity" and the intersection of homosexuality and baseball—is a "love story . . . love for baseball" (Drukman 27).

BIBLIOGRAPHY

Drukman, Steven. "Greenberg's Got Game." *American Theatre* (Oct. 2002): 24–28.
Spencer, Richard. "American Theatre's New Big Hitter." *Daily Telegraph* 18 June 2002.

TAKING OF MISS JANIE, THE ED BULLINS

(1975) Perhaps BULLINS's best-known play, certainly his most honored, *The Taking of Miss Janie* is a metaphor for the misunderstanding and antagonism that went on between races, even among the most seemingly liberal groups of the 1960s. The play won the New York Drama Critics' Circle Award and an OBIE AWARD for Playwriting.

A group of acquaintances—some are friends and some even lovers—move from college through the 1960s. Much of the action is reported in monologues, connected by brief scenes. The play begins and ends with Monty's rape of Janie; in the first scene, he has just finished raping her after years of friendship, and in the final scene, the same rape is just beginning.

Between these two scenes are their first meeting, Janie's experience of Monty's friends at a party, and the monologues that reveal the role each partygoer eventually played in the volatile 1960s.

Janie is an "all-American looking" white liberal from California, and Monty is a writer of "Black Poetry." They meet in a creative-writing class in college at the beginning of the 1960s. When Monty calls her "Miss Janie"—as in "Sho nuf, Miss Janie"—she fails to understand his ironic tone; an admirer of his poetry, she just wants to be his friend. He invites her to a party, where his roommate Rick, a Black Nationalist, objects to her presence and calls her a "devil lady": "The Blackman has slaved in this devil's land for four hundred years." The party is integrated and includes Monty's African-American girlfriends—Peggy, the one he will later marry, and Flossie, the one with whom he will cheat on his wife throughout his marriage. Peggy, after she divorces Monty and then marries and divorces a white husband, finally rejects men altogether and becomes Flossie's lesbian lover. Also present at the party is Janie's racist boyfriend, Lonnie, a jazz musician, who views African-American men as inferior but lucky with women; Lonnie eventually embraces the Baha'i World Faith. Monty's other roommate, Len, invites his white, middle-class, Jewish girlfriend Sharon, whom he later marries. Len and Sharon stay married, but not without difficulty. By the end of the 1960s, Len has moved from Marxism to capitalism, and the two have a growing son. Finally, there is Mort Silberstein, a kind of Jack Kerouac figure. Mort is a Beat poet, "[a] postbeatnik mythic figure," who becomes pathetic in his attempts to get drug money as he reminds others of his former fame.

In a 1997 interview with Kim Pearson, Bullins explained the theme of the play: The relationship between "Monty and Janie, the two antagonistic characters" who are in "a loving, friendly relationship up to a point—is actually a metaphor for race relations, group antagonism, conditions that happen[ed] between people and groups during the 1960s civil rights integrationists/black power era." The two characters are not meant to be precisely realistic. Janie uses Monty as "a symbol of—for her liberalness," while Monty "wanted to complete the relationship sexually, and never made any bones about that: he wanted into the system. And Janie withheld that from him until he took the opportunity some decade or so into their relationship where he took advantage of her by force, physically." Monty's penetration of the "system" by force is symbolic of the change in tactics, during the Civil Rights movement, espoused by the Black Power movement, which became impatient with nonviolent resistance as a means to achieve racial equality. Bullins concluded, "[T]he false pretenses of the liberal whites and the . . . false desires and expectations of integrationist minded—misinformed—liberals [are personified in] those two characters."

BIBLIOGRAPHY

Bullins, Ed. "Interview with Ed Bullins—2/17/97." *College of New Jersey.* Available online. URL: http://kpearson.faculty. tcnj. edu/Articles. 2001.

TALLEY'S FOLLY LANFORD WILSON (1979)

Talley's Folly is the second of three plays that explores the fictional Talley family of Lebanon, Missouri. Following less than a year after 5TH OF JULY, *Talley's Folly* is a two-character play that tells the story of the courtship between Sally Talley, the youngest daughter of the Talley family, and Matt Friedman, an accountant from St. Louis.

Set in an old, elaborate boathouse on the river near the Talley farmhouse, the play takes place on the evening of July 4, 1944. The boathouse is in a state of decay, and locals have dubbed this monstrosity "Talley's Folly." When the play begins, the audience is made aware of the fact that this is a stage set—the lighting is a *"blank white work light: the artificiality of the theatrical set quite apparent. The house lights are up."* When Matt Friedman enters, he addresses the audience directly, much as the Stage Manager does in THORNTON WILDER's OUR TOWN. He sets the scene, telling us how long the play will last ("ninety-seven minutes . . . without intermission") and what the play is about: "this is a waltz . . . a no-holds-barred romantic story." As Matt describes the time and the set, the lights dim, the sound and light effects take over, Sally enters, and the "waltz" begins.

Both Matt and Sally are lonely people, considered outcasts by society: Sally because she is a 31-year-old spinster, the black sheep of the family, and Matt because he is a Jew. During this evening, as Matt tries to woo Sally, bits and pieces of their worlds are revealed. Sally tells of her sheltered and stifling life in the small town, and Matt tells how his family suffered and was driven out of anti-Semitic Europe. In spite of their vast differences in culture and background, they discover that they may have something in common. In the end, with a final nod and wink to the audience, Matt brings down the curtain on this romance, and the audience familiar with *5th of July* knows that they will have a love that lasts a lifetime.

Talley's Folly was awarded the PULITZER PRIZE. Its success led to the rewriting and restaging of *5th of July* (as *Fifth of July*) in 1980 and laid the groundwork for the completion of the Talley trilogy in *A Tale Told* (1981), later revised as *Talley & Son* (1985). *Talley & Son* takes place at the same time as *Talley's Folly*—the action occurs up at the house while Matt and Sally are down in the boathouse. In this play, all the complicated relationships between the family and the town that are talked about in *Fifth of July* and *Talley's Folly* are shown. Indeed, Sally is seen briefly in *Talley & Son* as she leaves the house to go down to the boathouse to meet Matt and at the end when she returns to pack for her departure with him.

Talley's Folly marks LANFORD WILSON's progression from his early plays, written for the coffeehouse theaters in the 1960s, such as *Balm in Gilead* (1965) and *The Rimers of Eldritch* (1966). It demonstrates that he can build characters over a sustained period of time and maintain them without gimmicks, interruptions, or jumping from one set of characters to another. It shows his thorough understanding of the needs of the actors and the audience, and he does this in a deceptively simple play. But *Talley's Folly* is anything but simplistic. While it does have the outward flavor of Wilder's *Our Town,* Wilson takes another tack. *Our Town* points out the stereotypes, frailties, and trivialities that measure our lives; *Talley's Folly* accomplishes this by showing us two people who do not fit neatly into stereotypes and thus find happiness together.

Philip Middleton Williams
Miami, Florida

TALLY, TED (1952–) Ted Tally has earned his literary reputation writing inventive plays for the theater, both dramas and comedies, and remarkable original screenplays and adaptations for the movies. Among the most well-known works are his award-winning play, *Terra Nova* (1977), and his Academy Award–winning screenplay, *The Silence of the Lambs* (1991).

Born in Winston-Salem, North Carolina, and raised by parents who were educators, Tally found encouragement as a young actor in the camaraderie of his high-school theater group. Before graduating from high school, he had written a couple of plays, produced at the prestigious North Carolina Governor's School and at the annual North Carolina High School Drama Festival. Early playwriting success convinced Tally to apply to Yale University, from which he earned a B.A. in 1974 and an M.F.A. in 1977.

Tally's education at Yale afforded him opportunities to observe first-rate productions and to associate with inspired theater students and notable theater artists, including TERRENCE MCNALLY, DAVID MAMET, and ARTHUR KOPIT. At Yale, Tally wrote his first significant play, *Terra Nova*, a tragic story of Robert Falcon Scott's fatal expedition, along with four other men, to the South Pole in 1911. Based on historical accounts and shaped by Scott's personal journals and letters, *Terra Nova* transports the reader/viewer to the harsh Antarctic landscape, where Scott and his rival, Norwegian explorer Roald Amundsen, race over the frozen tundra to claim conquest of the South Pole. While Tally's play is grounded in the hardships and the extreme athleticism of these explorers, the play also examines the limits of heroism and Scott's ultimate defeat.

Following graduate school, Tally wrote several plays revealing a range of dramatic expression extending well beyond tragedy. *Hooters* (1978), praised for its verbal wit and physical comedy, explores the mating rituals of two college-age males. *Coming Attractions* (1980), a comedy with music, offers a satiric glimpse of an American society inclined to make celebrities of disreputable characters. *Silver Linings* (1983) combines Tally's talent for sketch comedy into a series of brilliant scenes capturing the spirit of youth culture. In his introduction to *Silver Linings,* Tally writes, "Revue sketches, after all, are a delightfully useless form of theater. A thousand of them, stacked on top of one another, wouldn't knock the shine off a single MX missile. But they startle, they coax a smile, and they pass the time pleasantly. Perhaps, in the end, that isn't nothing" (5). *Little Footsteps* (1986), a serious comedy, coaxes more than a smile as upwardly mobile parents-to-be face their anxieties.

At present, Tally's work as a playwright is eclipsed by his stunning list of successful film credits, including *Red Dragon* (2002), a prequel to *The Silence of the Lambs,* along with other skillful film adaptations of award-winning novels, including *All the Pretty Horses* (2001) and *Alexander the Great* (2003). In 2008, Tally had no fewer than seven screenplays in various stages of production and preproduction.

BIBLIOGRAPHY

Tally, Ted. *Coming Attractions.* New York: Samuel French, 1982.

———. *Hooters.* New York: Dramatists Play Service, 1978.

———. *Little Footsteps.* New York: Dramatists Play Service, 1986.

———. *Silver Linings.* New York: Dramatists Play Service, 1983.

———. *Terra Nova.* New York: Dramatists Play Service, 1981.

Dwight E. Watson
Wabash College

TARKINGTON, BOOTH (1869–1946) Born to a middle-class family in Indianapolis, Booth Tarkington began his career as a writer of fiction, publishing his first novel, *The Gentleman from Indiana,* in 1898. Tarkington quickly developed a more cosmopolitan outlook than many of his peers, aided in part by a long sojourn in Paris during the first decade of the 20th century. It was, in part, this time abroad that gave him such an interesting perspective on his native land. Certainly his first successful play, *The Man from Home* (1908), seemed to draw on his foreign experiences through the character of Daniel Vorhees Pike, who is so resolutely American that he refuses to believe Europe has anything to offer him.

Tarkington's subsequent works, including the novels *The Magnificent Ambersons* (1918) and the PULITZER PRIZE–winning *Alice Adams* (1921), reveal some of his growing concerns about the development of American culture. He felt that a crass materialism had begun to subsume the nobler aspirations of the American middle class. Indeed, many of his works probe the problem of American provincialism and the threat it posed to the nation's ability either to compete with its more worldly European neighbors or to develop its greatest potential.

It was this combination of provincialism and materialism that seems to have frustrated Tarkington's efforts in the theater. Though he wrote some 22 plays during his career, he struggled against the perception that theater was a less effective medium for conveying a social message than the novel or even the short story. He was frustrated by anti-intellectual audiences and by powerful producers who valued profit over artistic quality. Critics were also unkind about his plays, suggesting that his talents were wasted in this medium. Indeed, Tarkington's most successful plays, *Monsieur Beaucaire* (1901), *The Man from Home* (1908), *The Country Cousin* (1917), and *Clarence* (1921), which launched the career of American actor Alfred Lunt, never garnered the high praise lavished on his novels.

One of Tarkington's most intriguing, though least-known plays, *Poldekin* (1919), offers insight into his efforts to use theater to reshape the society around him. It is an anticommunist manifesto that opened on Broadway in 1920. Though it closed after only 44 performances, it is nevertheless an interesting example of Tarkington's patriotic effort to alert his fellow Americans to what he perceived as the danger of the Communist wave then sweeping Russia.

BIBLIOGRAPHY
Downer, Alan S., ed. *On Plays, Playwrights, and Playgoers: Selections from the Letters of Booth Tarkington to George C. Tyler and John Peter Toohey, 1918–1925.* Princeton, N.J.: Princeton University Library, 1959.

Tarkington, Booth. *Clarence: A Comedy in Four Acts.* New York: Samuel French, 1921.

———. *The Country Cousin: A Comedy in Four Acts.* New York: Samuel French, 1921.

———. *Monsieur Beaucaire.* New York: McClure, Phillips, 1901.

———, and Harry Leon Wilson. *The Man from Home.* New York: Harper, 1908.

Woodress, James. *Booth Tarkington: Gentleman from Indiana.* Philadelphia: J. B. Lippincott, 1955.

Heather Nathans
University of Maryland

TEA AND SYMPATHY ROBERT ANDERSON **(1953)** As ANDERSON wrote this best-known and most-read of his plays, he kept in mind Henry David Thoreau's notion of marching to "a different drummer." In focusing on how any deviation from accepted norms of behavior can result in one's being branded and persecuted, he was also aware of the possible application of his work to the then-prevailing atmosphere of the witch hunt unleashed by the House Un-American Activities Committee/McCarthy hearings, which singled out suspected Communists and gays for blacklisting.

The shy and sexually naive 18-year-old Tom Lee, who walks "light," wears his hair long, sings folksongs, and takes female leads in plays at his all-boys New England prep school, is mercilessly taunted by his classmates; their treatment of him worsens after he is discovered innocently sunbathing nude with one of the housemasters whose sexual orientation is also suspect. Even Tom's skill on the school's tennis team cannot placate his father Herb, who demands that his son reflect favorably back on himself by fulfilling the stereotypical pattern of the manly man. Tom's housemaster, Bill Reynolds, a latent homosexual, covers over his own fears by belittling Tom for his apparent deficiencies, while he conveniently escapes his marriage by leading the other boys on backpacking expeditions.

In response to the suspicions of those around him, Tom tries to regain his self-confidence and prove his masculinity by visiting the town prostitute, after being goaded into doing so. Unable to perform sexually, he attempts suicide. It is left to the housemaster's wife, Laura Reynolds, to allay his sense of failure by convincing him that he is more of a man than the others because, for him, sex must involve "tenderness, gentleness, consideration." Laura herself has experienced loneliness in her marriage to Bill, whose infrequent lovemaking is aggressive and vindictive and leaves her starved for affection; she needs to be needed by Bill, to do something for him, and yet she is aware that she has somehow failed to help him. Although she resolves not to fail Tom in the same way, her moral qualms and societal proprieties at first cause her to recoil from his kiss and reject him. Later, however, she enters his room and gives herself to him sexually in order to erase his self-doubt and restore his sense of manhood, going well beyond the tea and sympathy that such surrogate mothers usually provide. Audiences were held in rapt attention by Anderson's incandescent curtain line, in which Laura, opening her blouse, asks, "Years from now . . . when you talk about this . . . and you will . . . be kind."

Tea and Sympathy as a realistic—albeit melodramatic—psychological problem play is very much a work of its time. Yet it also remains eminently playable and exerts a continued resonance, not only because of the dramatist's great skill in moving characters around on a multilevel set but also for its emphasis on the need to exercise nonjudgmental compassion for difference in all of its forms and its examination of the destructive force of narrow definitions of sex and gender roles.

Thomas P. Adler
Purdue University

TEAHOUSE OF THE AUGUST MOON, THE JOHN PATRICK (1953)

Adapted by PATRICK from a novel by Vern Sneider, *The Teahouse of the August Moon* won the New York Drama Critics' Circle Award as well as the PULITZER PRIZE. Set during the American military occupation of Okinawa following World War II, this comedy portrays an amicable relationship between wily Okinawans and bumbling United States military personnel. The play calls into question the wisdom of imposing American ideals on other cultures, but the tone is lighthearted.

Captain Fisby, a former assistant professor of humanities and ill-suited to the army, finds himself in Okinawa as part of the U.S. military occupation force. He is given an assignment by his commanding officer, Colonel Purdy, a comic figure who makes comments like, "As Mrs. Purdy says, 'East is East and West is West, and there can be no Twain.'" A parody of by-the-book military officers, Colonel Purdy sends Captain Fisby to the village of Tobiki "to teach the natives democracy and make them self-supporting." Citing the American government's "Plan B," he orders Fisby to build a "pentagon-shaped schoolhouse" and "organize a Ladies' League for Democratic Action." Purdy sends along his own translator, the wise and endearing Sakini, to help Fisby, who is determined to do well.

The Okinawan Sakini is an important character. Not only does he play a part in the action of the play, but he also serves as a narrator. He addresses the audience and comments on the action and on the American presence and philosophy. In his opening monologue, Sakini lists the "distinguished record of conquerors" of Okinawa, starting with "fourteenth century . . . Chinese pirates" and ending with "twentieth-century . . . American Marines," yet his tone, though satirical, is certainly not hostile. He seems to view Americans with bemused affection, even when following the orders of the silly and inflexible Colonel Purdy.

When Fisby arrives in Tobiki, the villagers give him gifts: a cricket cage, a lacquered cup, a straw hat. He decides the village must go into the souvenir-making business. He sets the village to work making these items as fast as they can, though such mass production goes against the Okinawans' notion of careful craftsmanship. One gift cannot be mass-produced—the geisha girl that Fisby receives from one villager. The geisha, Lotus Blossom, wants to serve him, and nothing he can do or say will make her leave. Furthermore, the villagers want more than anything to build a teahouse now that their village has a geisha. Fisby finally gives in—casting aside "Plan B"—and allows the villagers to use the materials meant for the school to build the teahouse.

When Colonel Purdy receives Fisby's first progress report, he phones him for an explanation and to inform him that what he considers progress is Major McEvoy's work in another village, where the "fourth graders know the alphabet through 'M' and [the] whole village can sing 'God Bless America' in English." By the time Purdy sends a psychiatrist, Captain McLean, to observe him, Fisby has adopted native dress. Before long, however, McLean—a man who loves organic farming—becomes absorbed by Fisby's idea that he take over the agriculture of the village, and instead of reporting back to Purdy, he joins forces with Fisby.

Meanwhile, the villagers discover that there is no market for their handcrafted souvenirs among the occupation forces, but when Fisby finds out that they have been making "brandy" for years from sweet potatoes, he knows he has found a saleable item. The village prospers as the army, navy, and marines imbibe. Purdy's suspicions are raised by the amount of revenue flowing into Tobiki. When he makes a surprise inspection, he orders the teahouse and the stills destroyed.

It is during Captain Fisby's scene with Lotus Blossom after Purdy has ordered the destruction of the "Teahouse of the August Moon" that the play's theme is overtly stated by Fisby: "Democracy is only a method—an ideal system for people to get together. . . . [U]nfortunately . . . the people who get together . . . are not always ideal." He asks Sakini to translate, adding, "it would be wrong. . . . [t]o impose my way of life on her." Captain Fisby continues, "I will remember what was beautiful in my youth and what I was wise enough to leave beautiful," expressing a respect and appreciation for another culture that was not always shared by the U.S. government.

The point made, Patrick provides a happy ending. It turns out that the government in Washington has misunderstood Purdy's report against Captain Fisby. Washington wants to make an example of Tobiki as a model of "American 'get-up-and-go' in the recovery program." Fortunately for Colonel Purdy, the villagers, "used to hiding things after centuries of occupation," have actually destroyed nothing and all is restored.

TERRY, MEGAN (1932–)

Born Marguerite Duffy in Seattle, Washington, Megan Terry is best known as a central figure in the Open Theater in New York City in the 1960s and for her involvement in community, regional, alternative, and feminist theater in the last three decades of the 20th century. After an apprenticeship under Florence Bean James, first at the Seattle Repertory Playhouse and then at the Banff

(Canada) School of the Fine Arts, Terry received a B.Ed. from the University of Washington and moved to New York City in 1956.

With Joseph Chaikin and Peter Feldmann, Terry founded the Open Theater in 1963. Through the cooperative interaction of directors, playwrights, and actors, the Open Theater developed topical scripts through improvisational techniques. The most influential of these techniques, "transformations," undermine the fixed identity of characters, preclude a coherent psychology, and reject a linear, sometimes even an understandable narrative. Terry's *Calm down Mother: A Transformation for Three Women* (produced 1965; published 1966), for example, explores stereotypical and archetypal gender identities in a series of freewheeling sketches.

Terry's best-known and most widely translated play, VIET ROCK (1966), emerged from workshops that sought to distill "the essence of violence" in relationship to the Vietnam War. *Viet Rock* dramatizes an American soldier's experience from his army physical through basic training and into combat. With more than a hundred characters, its transformational dramaturgy created a play that was less AGITPROP than an exploration of stock attitudes both for and against the war. *Viet Rock* is often identified as the first play about the American involvement in Vietnam and as the first rock musical.

In 1970, Terry's *Approaching Simone* abandoned the free-flowing transformations of earlier (and later) plays to celebrate Simone Weil, the French philosopher whose hunger strike led to her death in 1943 at the age of 34. The culmination of Terry's search for a model of female heroism, *Approaching Simone,* one of Terry's most conventional and perhaps least characteristic plays, won a Best American Play OBIE AWARD and is now widely seen as a landmark in American feminist drama.

In 1974, Terry moved to Nebraska as playwright-in-residence at the Omaha Magic Theatre, where for the next 25 years she premiered most of her more than 50 topical, community-oriented plays on subjects as diverse as women in prison, domestic violence, and homelessness. The appeal of these works, such as *Kegger* (1981), which deals with teenage binge drinking, and *Mollie Bailey's Traveling Family Circus: Featuring Scenes from the Life of Mother Jones* (1983), which was cowritten with JoAnne Metcalf, has been to engage community groups, rather than an intellectual or cultural elite. In the first decade of the 21st century, Terry continues her long association with OMT, creating new works as well as managing the theater's archives.

BIBLIOGRAPHY

Terry, Megan. *Plays by Megan Terry.* New York: Broadway Play Publishing, 1999.

———. *"Viet Rock," "Comings and Goings," "Keep Tightly Closed in a Cool Dry Place," "The Gloaming, Oh My Darling": Four Plays.* New York: Simon and Schuster, 1967.

———, Jo Ann Schmidman, and Sora Kimberlain, eds. *Right Brain Vacation Photos: New Plays and Production Photographs, 1972–1992.* Omaha, Nebr.: Omaha Magic Theatre, 1992.

Joan FitzPatrick Dean
University of Missouri–Kansas City

TEXAS TRILOGY, A PRESTON JONES (1976)

Effectively evoking multiple social classes in fictional mid-20th-century West Texas, *A Texas Trilogy* depicts a town's struggles with its loss of economic importance and with the accompanying loss of its previously unchallenged comfortable racism. Jones emphasizes time's attrition of all youthful hopes for power and pleasure. He suggests a resultant human need to establish spiritually deeper values.

"Stained and faded," "warped and splintered," and "patched," the meeting quarters at the Cattleman's Hotel in Bradleyville, Texas, of the Knights of the White Magnolia are as decrepit as the body and mind of Colonel J. C. Kinkaid, the World War I veteran who is the group's central member. It is evident from the outset of the opening play in Jones's trilogy, *The Last Meeting of the Knights of the White Magnolia,* that the Knights are on the brink of extinction. This all-male, small-town society, anxious to outdo Ku Klux Klan racism (despite sporting fezzes instead of white hoods), once had branches all over Texas, but the total membership is now just Colonel Kinkaid and his few Bradleyville cronies: a bar owner, a supermarket manager, a sottish gasoline station attendant, a "mama's boy" feed salesman, and a

constantly scrapping farmer and oil refinery worker duo. The Knights plan to initiate a new young member, who they hope heralds the group's renaissance, yet Colonel Kinkaid (still reliving, within his dazed brain, his long-ago battlefield forays) would just as soon "shoot" this young citizen of a neighboring town—a place that the colonel associates with another of its natives, his reputedly "cowardly" wartime comrade.

As the colonel's control over his brain disintegrates (but also illuminates his community's current spiritual poverty), the Knights' rituals prove more and more ludicrous, their myths and memories more and more hypocritical, and their deeply held racist ideals more and more obviously inane (especially since Colonel Kinkaid evidently has quietly known for decades that his hero, General John Pershing, gained his nickname, Black Jack, from his very *non*racist attitudes).

The booziest of the White Magnolia brotherhood, the failure-prone gas-pumper Skip Hampton, also appears in the trilogy's second play, *Lu Ann Hampton Laverty Oberlander.* Skip is the older brother of the play's protagonist, Lu Ann. In act 1, set in 1953, Skip still thinks himself a Korean War hero and fantasizes about various future business schemes. By act 2, set in 1963, his ambitions have come to nothing—much like the hapless chinchillas that he was raising, which froze to death. His shame has led him to desperate suicide attempts and will (by 1973 in act 3) make him a penniless, sometimes institutionalized ward of his sister Lu Ann. She, meanwhile, has gone from being a *"healthy pretty"* high school cheerleader (in 1953) to being a *"drugstore pretty"* beauty operator and barroom-haunting divorcée (in 1963) to being a coupon-distributing Howdy Wagon hostess, whose *"beauty is placid and matronly"* (in 1973). While Lu Ann giddily meets one future husband, whom she later divorces, in act 1, and is charmed to meet, in act 2, the man whose trucking accident later leaves her his widow, act 3 simply shows her visited by her high school sweetheart, now a preacher: He was a companion toward whom she never fully warmed because his name lacked the "pretty" allure that her taste for illusion had found in other gents' monikers.

The trilogy's third play occurs on the afternoon before and the late evening after the first play's lodge meeting.

Its title, *The Oldest Living Graduate,* declares the honor that has been bestowed on Colonel Kinkaid by his military alma mater—an honor that the colonel's son, Floyd, encourages, because he hopes other military school alumni will invest in his planned Lake Bradleyville resort. The colonel, however, frustrated by the military pomp that regularly forgets soldiers' real suffering and death, now rebukes such hollow ceremony.

The colonel wills his land by the lake to Floyd only when he knows himself to be dying from a stroke; he had longed to hold firmly onto his memory of a youthful romance once experienced on that land. The colonel may thus, we learn, value "love" (albeit a love surrounded by illusion) much more than he reveres the materialism that dazzles his son.

Jeffrey B. Loomis
Northwest Missouri State University

THAT CHAMPIONSHIP SEASON JASON MILLER (1972)

The action of *That Championship Season* centers around the 20-year reunion of a group of men—now in their late thirties—who as a high school basketball team won the state championship. More than once during the evening, they relive their glory days, remembering the final moments of the championship game in detail; but beneath this celebration of winning lie lives steeped in corruption, a corruption based on self-interest and a victory-at-any-cost mentality. Only Tom, now an alcoholic, is the voice of unvarnished truth, remembering early in the play that they raped a retarded girl when they were freshmen, and late in the play insisting that they remember that the championship was unfairly won.

The reunion is at the home of the now retired "Coach" and includes four of the players. George is now the corrupt mayor of the town: He fixes tickets for his friends and takes kickbacks from former teammate Phil, a coal strip miner who is destroying the local environment to sustain his personal wealth. The police department under George's administration is virtually a rental shop for pornographic films. George is a racist running against a Jewish environmentalist and will stop at nothing to win the next election. James is George's campaign manager, and Tom, the alcoholic, is James's brother.

Phil knows that Sharmen, George's political opponent, will put him out of the strip-mining business, and he fears George will lose the election. Indeed, George barely won the last time, when he ran against "an old alcoholic." To complicate matters further, Phil is having an affair with George's wife, Marion, with whom they apparently all had sex in high school. We find out later that she has had many affairs in recent years. Phil is thinking of defecting to Sharmen while James wants Phil to back *him* for mayor. In an ensuing argument, James reveals Phil's affair with Marion, prompting George to point a loaded gun at Phil. Coach acts as mediator; for him, these men and that championship season are everything, and he must keep them together. George and the coach have discovered that Sharmen had "an uncle"—now dead—who was a Communist decades earlier; they believe slinging such mud will decide the election in George's favor, but Phil says that in 1972 nobody cares about Communists anymore. Phil convinces the coach and George to drop James as campaign manager and hire a professional in exchange for his financial backing. James threatens to ruin George by telling all he knows.

There is tremendous unhappiness in these men's lives, which stems in part from their arrested development. George's wife gave birth to a Down syndrome baby, which George—unable to make his own decision—had institutionalized on the coach's advice. Phil, disappointed in all of his life except "that championship season," engages in risky—even suicidal—behavior, driving drunk in fast cars, sleeping with married and underage women. We learn that James cared for his invalid, alcoholic father until his death, but that he never felt loved or respected by him. And, of course, Tom drowns his misery in alcohol. We also learn that the coach—used to the deference of the championship team—was forced into retirement because he broke the jaw of a student who made an obscene gesture at him.

One member of the team who is not present is Martin, a star player; he has never come back for a reunion. In act 1, the others toast him and seem to have genuine affection for him. However, in act 2, Tom reminds them why Martin never comes to the reunions: Martin broke an unstoppable opposing player's ribs—on the

Coach's suggestion—to get him out of the game; thus, the "championship season is a lie." Now the same teammates—George, Phil, James—who praised Martin and missed him earlier in the play condemn him as a stupid "sonofabitch." This is to preserve their one achievement—the myth on which they have built their pitiful lives. The coach gives a speech. He plays a record of the final seconds of the game. All are sorry; all is forgiven. Only Tom remains cynical.

The play won the New York Drama Critics' Circle Award, the TONY AWARD, and the PULITZER PRIZE. In it, Jason Miller comments on the American myth of success and suggests that winning without integrity is hollow victory. *That Championship Season* is similar in theme to the postwar plays of ARTHUR MILLER, whose *ALL MY SONS* also suggests that success without ethics is valueless and corrupt. Though Jason Miller wrote other plays, he is best known for this award-winning drama; he was also an actor and director.

THEATRE GUILD, THE   For almost 40 years, the Theatre Guild, which proclaimed the desire to advance theater as an art, as opposed to pursuing commercial reward at the box office, was among the most influential producing organizations in America.

The Guild arose in 1919 from the ashes of the earlier, experimentally inclined WASHINGTON SQUARE PLAYERS. The Guild's two prime movers, Lawrence Langner and Theresa Helburn, had been key figures in the earlier organization; with the formation of the Guild, they assumed the roles they would maintain throughout their careers: Langner was in charge of the business end of the organization, and Helburn was chiefly responsible for casting and script selection.

The Guild moved into the Garrick Theatre on West 35th Street, which earlier had been revamped to suit the minimalist tastes of French director Jacques Copeau, sojourning in New York during World War I. Restoring, as best their limited funds would allow, the theater to its earlier, more traditional configuration, they opened in 1919 with Spanish playwright Jacinto Benavente's *The Bonds of Interest* (*Los intereses creados* [1907]), which featured EDNA ST. VINCENT MILLAY in the role of Columbine. Undaunted when the play failed to draw an audience, the Guild persisted, and their second production, St. John Ervine's tragic *John Ferguson* (1919), proved to be a major success. The play, set in northern Ireland, concerns a young girl's seduction by an unscrupulous landowner and the man's subsequent murder by the girl's brother.

The success of the play came about through events of an extraordinary nature: Broadway actors, seeking to improve their lot through unionization, went on strike in August of 1919, closing every play in New York City. Because the Guild was organized as a cooperative, with actors receiving a percentage of the box office, the fledgling union, Actors Equity, left the group alone. Thus, for a period of time, the Guild's *John Ferguson* was the only professional production in town, virtually guaranteeing an audience.

Ervine was to become the liaison between the Guild and George Bernard Shaw, who raised the artistic profile of the organization by granting them the rights to premiere his play *Heartbreak House* (1920). The Guild was eager to undertake the project, and the play was staged amid a great deal of fanfare. Their next Shaw production was *Back to Methuselah* (1922), a gargantuan drama requiring three evenings to be staged in its entirety. Although the production lost money, the Guild claimed that they were willing to sacrifice profit for art and then went on to produce Shaw's *St. Joan* more successfully in 1923.

During its early years, the Guild was faulted for producing the work of European dramatists exclusively. This trend was reversed with the 1923 production of ELMER RICE's expressionistic *The ADDING MACHINE* and SIDNEY HOWARD's *THEY KNEW WHAT THEY WANTED* the following year. In 1927, they added to their prestige by becoming the exclusive producers of EUGENE O'NEILL, staging that season two major works, *Marco Millions* and the enormously successful *STRANGE INTERLUDE*. Other O'Neill productions included *MOURNING BECOMES ELECTRA* (1931) and *The ICEMAN COMETH* (1946).

At the outset of their professional existence, the Guild established a business mechanism that was to serve them well over the years: They initiated a "subscription season," thereby generating, through advance ticket sales, a financial cushion that somewhat reduced the uncertainties of the box office. So successful were they in developing a list of subscribers that in 1925 they had sufficient backing to open their own 1,100-seat Guild Theatre on 52nd Street.

Two years later, the Guild took to the road, offering a repertory "season" of plays in Chicago and Baltimore. The circumstances behind this expansion were as follows: A "Guild School of the Theatre," established in 1926 and soon abandoned, left adrift their acting teacher, Rouben Mamoulian, who was then recruited to direct an all-black cast in DuBois and Dorothy Heyward's play Porgy. The popularity of the drama meant that, during the fall of 1927, time would weigh heavily on the hands of the Guild's regular acting company, and it was determined that they would travel to Chicago and Baltimore with several of their plays where short repertory "seasons" would be presented.

Buoyed by the success of this venture, in 1928, the Guild extended their reach, adding subscription series in Cleveland, Pittsburgh, Boston, and Philadelphia. With subscribers now numbering some 60,000 and advance sales of $600,000, the Guild had become a hugely successful enterprise, but they were still vulnerable to the criticism that they were indistinguishable from any other large-scale commercial producing organization. Critics complained that they selected scripts that would showcase their most popular stars while hypocritically cloaking box office ambitions in the rhetoric of art.

Within the organization itself there was discord. In 1931, two Guild employees, Cheryl Crawford and Harold Clurman, rejecting what they regarded as conservatism and timidity in production decisions, left the Guild to form their own Group Theatre, which proved to be the most innovative production company of the 1930s. In 1938, a group of Guild playwrights that included Robert E. Sherwood (Reunion in Vienna [1931] and Idiot's Delight [1936]) and Maxwell Anderson (Elizabeth the Queen [1930] and Winterset [1935]), provoked by what they regarded as the organization's high-handed treatment of their work, withdrew to form their own Playwright's Production Company.

Despite high-water marks during the 1930s (the George Gershwin Porgy and Bess of 1935, culled from the Heywards' 1927 play, to name one of the most financially successful and artistically enduring, as well as the Pulitzer Prize–winning The Time of Your Life [1939] by William Saroyan), the Guild was confronting a $60,000 debt and imminent demise in 1939. The play that bailed them out was their production that year of The Philadelphia Story with Katharine Hepburn, but the real turnabout came several years later with Oklahoma!, based on Lynn Riggs's Green Grow the Lilacs, a Guild production from 1931. The show, which teamed Rodgers and Hammerstein for the first time, opened in 1943 under Rouben Mamoulian's direction with choreography by Agnes de Mille. Transforming a straight play into a musical had paid off once more. The show ran for more than five years on Broadway, making millions for the Guild and for its investors. (Sales of the recording were also highly lucrative: Oklahoma! pioneered the now standard practice of recording—and selling—Broadway musicals with the original cast.) In 1945, Mamoulian, de Mille, and Rodgers and Hammerstein were again teamed in the production of Carousel, adapted from Ferenc Molnár's Liliom, which the Guild had produced in 1921. Recycling played a major role in the Guild's continuing operation.

The enormous success of Oklahoma! provided the cash infusion the Guild needed to expand their dominion in the early postwar years. The first new market to be developed was radio, with the premiere of "The Theatre Guild on the Air" in September 1945. The program, produced in conjunction with ABC radio, featured one-hour truncations of Theatre Guild favorites, among them Thornton Wilder's Our Town, Henrik Ibsen's A Doll's House, and Shakespeare's Macbeth. The move to television was made in 1947, in collaboration with the developing NBC Television Network. The first play to be televised was the drama responsible for the Guild's initial success, St. John Ervine's John Ferguson. This initial project was to lead, in 1953, to the Guild-produced dramatic program, The United States Steel Hour, which existed for a decade, ceasing production in 1963. On Broadway, the 1950s also saw the Theatre Guild's career-launching production of William Inge's melancholy Come Back, Little Sheba (1950).

By the late 1940s, the Guild was at its peak, with 31 subscription cities and a reputed 150,000 subscribers. Increasingly, however, the organization was coming under fire for announcing shows and then not delivering, using in their promotional material phrases such as "among the prospects" in selling a season's shows. At mid-century, the Guild was reputed to be the richest producing organization in America; it was also generally regarded as no different from any other production company. Indeed, the organization was decried for not financing its own productions; for its failure to produce a permanent acting company, a school, or a studio; and its apparent inability to advance the careers of new American dramatists. Disturbingly, in the view of its critics, the Guild was not investing in its institutional future.

With the deaths of founding members Helburn in 1959 and Langner in 1962, Guild productions severely declined and in 1964, for the first time in its 45-year history, there were no Guild productions whatsoever. Management of the Guild fell to Langner's son, and the company produced an occasional play or film in the late 1960s and 1970s. In the 1980s, the Guild's newsworthy activities were reported, not in the theater columns of the press, but in the travel section: The organization was promoting cruise line holidays featuring evening entertainments—plays, songs, and sketches—performed by "distinguished actors."

BIBLIOGRAPHY

Eaton, Walter Prichard. *The Theatre Guild; the First Ten Years.* Freeport, N.Y.: Books for Libraries Press, 1970.

Helburn, Theresa. *A Wayward Quest.* Boston: Little, Brown, 1960.

Langner, Lawrence. *The Magic Curtain.* New York: E. P. Dutton, 1951.

Nadel, Norman. *A Pictorial History of the Theatre Guild.* New York: Crown, 1969.

Craig Clinton
Reed College

THEATRE OF THE ABSURD Describing the philosophical school of existentialism, French novelist and playwright Albert Camus in *The Myth of Sisyphus* (1942) wrote, "[I]n a universe suddenly divested of illusions and of light, man feels an alien, a stranger. . . . This divorce between man and his life, the actor and his setting, is properly the feeling of absurdity" (6). A few years later, a number of European playwrights, all writing independently and all witnesses to the atrocities of World War II, transformed Camus's existentialist philosophy about the purposelessness of human existence into one of the most influential theatrical movements: the Theatre of the Absurd. The main playwrights and plays associated with absurdism are French: Eugene Ionesco's *The Bald Soprano* (1950), Samuel Beckett's *Waiting for Godot* (1953), and Jean Genet's *The Balcony* (1957). Other playwrights and plays associated with the Theatre of the Absurd are Englishman Harold Pinter's *The Birthday Party* (1958), Spaniard Fernando Arrabal's *Picnic on the Battlefield* (1959), Russian-born Frenchman Arthur Adamov's *Ping Pong* (1955), and American EDWARD ALBEE's *The ZOO STORY* (world premiere in Berlin 1959; American premiere 1960) and *The AMERICAN DREAM* (1961).

Camus and World War II were not the absurdists' only spark. The plays of Euripides and Aristophanes and the Italian theatrical tradition of *commedia dell'arte* are some of the Theatre of the Absurd's earliest antecedents. Modern influences include French playwright Alfred Jarry's *Ubu Roi* (1896), dadaism, surrealism, Italian Luigi Pirandello's plays, and the theatrical theorizings of Frenchman Antonin Artaud and German Bertolt Brecht, as well as circus, vaudeville, and early film comedians, particularly the Marx Brothers.

The absurdists confronted the question of existence in a post-Hiroshima world through an ironic depiction of humanity's role in the universe. Featuring clownlike, alienated, and aimless antiheroes, these playwrights' seriocomic works depicted the helplessness and apparent purposelessness of the individual's existence in a world bereft of Providence. At the same time, they challenged the conventions of the theater by relying on circular plots, abstract characters, metatheatrical references, and dialogue steeped in wordplay.

In American theater, absurdist plays were not as numerous or significant as in Europe. Martin Esslin, who coined the phrase "Theatre of the Absurd," notes that absurdist theater hinges on disillusionment as well as on an uncertainty about the purposefulness of life; both characteristics were experienced by many Europeans after the war. Having escaped the physical and economic devastation of World War II, the United States experienced a period of remarkable economic growth; many of its citizens were living the American Dream. Hence, the social, economic, and cultural struggles that encouraged the themes of absurdism in the plays of Beckett and others were not present in America. It would not be until the end of the 1950s—a full decade after Ionesco and Beckett wrote their first absurdist plays—that absurdism would appear in American plays. However, the absurdism that did arrive in American theaters was more of a response to the materialistic and progressive streak that defined the United States in the 1950s than an outgrowth of Camus's existential philosophy.

Two important events helped bring the absurdist influence to American playwrights. First, the publication of *The Drama Review,* a theatrical journal, introduced the European movement to American theatrical practitioners. Second, Alan Schneider's American production in 1956 of *Waiting for Godot,* the most representative work of the Theatre of the Absurd, thumbed its nose at American realistic drama through its circular structure—where nothing happens, twice: the failure of Godot to arrive; the linguistic games between Didi and Gogo; the metatheatrical blurring of the artificial world of the play and the real world of the audience; and the fact that two characters just sit and wait. Its production made manifest the essential tenets of absurdist drama, and within a few years of its American premiere, the first absurdist American plays appeared.

Many critics have noted the influence of *Waiting for Godot* on JACK GELBER's *The CONNECTION* (1959), one of the first and most successful American absurdist plays. The piece depicts a group of heroin addicts waiting, much like Beckett's characters, for their supplier to arrive. Similar to Beckett, Gelber also blurs the dimensions of reality and the artifice of theater by having the characters seek handouts from the audience during the intermission.

However, the clearest link between Beckett and American absurdism came with Edward Albee, whose first play, the one-act *The Zoo Story,* was at both its German and American premieres paired with Beckett's *Krapp's Last Tape* (1958). In fact, of all the American dramatists to dabble in absurdism, Albee would become the figure most linked to the movement. In *The Zoo Story,* Albee explores the question of our relationship with and obligation to others as well as our role in the world through a seemingly meandering exchange between Jerry and Peter in a park until Jerry's shocking suicide. Albee's more marked absurdist piece is *The American Dream,* which is considered by many to be the most pure representation of American absurdist theater. Through the characters of Mommy, Daddy, and Grandma, Albee skewers the language, image, and nature of the American family and dream, both of which had become idealized during the 1950s. (*The Sandbox* [1960] is an earlier, shorter version of the play featuring the same characters.) With WHO'S AFRAID OF VIRGINIA WOOLF? (1962), Albee captured the same sense of language games found in the European absurdists as he harrowingly depicts an evening's entertainment between two academic couples and the vituperative, alcohol-fueled linguistic battle between its two main characters, George and Martha, although the play's psychological thrust also demonstrates its realist influences. In the 1960s, Albee continued to write plays that included some absurdist elements, including *Tiny Alice* (1964), *Box* (1968), and *Quotations from Chairman Mao Tse-Tung* (1968). However, these plays were further removed from the absurdist tendencies of his earlier works.

Other American playwrights and works associated with the Theatre of the Absurd are ARTHUR KOPIT's *OH DAD, POOR DAD, MAMMA'S HUNG YOU IN THE CLOSET AND I'M FEELIN' SO SAD* (1960) and *The Day the Whores Came out to Play Tennis* (1965); Kenneth Koch's *Bertha* (1959) and *George Washington Crossing the Delaware* (1962); JACK RICHARDSON's *Gallows Humor* (1961); and Arnold Weinstein's *Red Eye of Love* (1958).

While the Theatre of the Absurd was a short-lived movement in American theater, it has had a remarkable influence on subsequent writers. The early plays of SAM SHEPARD, including *Cowboys* (1964) and *The Rock Garden* (1964), are heavily influenced by Beckett's absurdist plays, and throughout Shepard's canon the influence of the Theatre of the Absurd resonates. Numerous other playwrights have acknowledged their influence by the absurdists, including ED BULLINS, ISRAEL HOROVITZ, TINA HOWE, TONY KUSHNER, DAVID MAMET, and DAVID RABE. One contemporary playwright still exhibiting absurdist tendencies is MARIA IRENE FORNÉS, who has cited Schneider's production of *Waiting for Godot* as one of the most significant influences on her writing.

Ultimately, the romance between the Theatre of the Absurd and American playwrights was fleeting. In fact, critics have noted that American absurdist theater reached its peak in 1962, only three years after *The Connection* premiered. In the process, only one major playwright and a handful of important plays emerged from the movement. However, more significant is that while the Theatre of the Absurd movement quickly ended in the United States, its influence on American contemporary playwrights continues.

BIBLIOGRAPHY

Brater, Enoch, and Ruby Cohn, eds. *Around the Absurd: Essays on Modern and Postmodern Drama.* Ann Arbor: University of Michigan Press, 1990.

Camus, Albert. *The Myth of Sisyphus and Other Essays.* Trans. Justin O'Brien. New York: Knopf, 1958.

Esslin, Martin. *The Theatre of the Absurd.* Rev. ed. Garden City, N.Y.: Anchor Books, 1969.

Mayberry, Bob. *Theatre of Discord: Dissonance in Beckett, Albee, and Pinter.* Rutherford, N.J.: Fairleigh Dickinson University Press, 1989.

William Boles
Rollins College

THEY KNEW WHAT THEY WANTED

SIDNEY HOWARD (1924)   Though considered at the time an expression of the "new morality," HOWARD described his play as a retelling of the story of Paolo and Francesca (an episode in Dante's *Inferno,* which was retold by another American playwright, GEORGE HENRY BOKER, in his play *FRANCESCA DA RIMINI* [1855]). Howard's PULITZER PRIZE–winning play was made into the 1956 musical *The Most Happy Fella.*

Italian immigrant and California vintner Tony Patucci—"stout," 60, "jovial, simple"—has grown rich because of Prohibition. He is ready now to marry and have children so that he may leave his wealth and property to them. Tony is about to marry 22-year-old Amy, whom he has seen once from a distance, but with whom he has corresponded and exchanged photographs. Tony's foreman, Joe, who is as handsome and young as Tony is not, has written the letters for Tony. Unbeknownst to Joe, Tony has also sent Amy Joe's photograph as his own. When the bride is due at the station, Tony sets off to meet her train, but having had too much to drink, he drives his car off a bridge. Meanwhile, the angry bride gets a ride from the postman to Tony's farmhouse, and finding Joe there, she decides to forgive him for his tardiness. She confides her life story to Joe before she discovers that he is not the groom. When Tony arrives with two broken legs, Amy is at first inclined to head for the train station; however, since she has nothing to return to, she decides to go through with the wedding.

The wedding feast takes place outside while Tony lies in the house in two casts and in pain, but he is happy: He has his Amy. The bride, meanwhile, is making the best of the situation, though she is openly hostile to Joe. Always a rambler and a ladies' man, but above all, loyal to Tony, Joe plans to leave the next day, against Tony's wishes. When all the guests have gone and Tony has been sedated, Joe and Amy find themselves alone and are passionately drawn to each other.

Three months later, Tony has improved more quickly than the doctor expected, thanks in large part to Amy's presence and to her nursing skills. Amy has made a happy home for Tony and for herself, but when she discovers that she is pregnant from her one sexual encounter with Joe, she agrees with him that the two of them should leave immediately. Despite Joe's wish to do so, Amy cannot leave Tony, whom she loves, without explaining. After Tony's initial fury, he convinces her to stay since she wants a home, he wants a baby, and Joe wants his freedom. They knew what they wanted and decided to follow their desires rather than convention.

Though Howard's characters touch upon such conflicts as religion (Father McKee) versus science (the doctor) and labor (Joe is a union organizer) versus management (Tony), these themes are never explored very fully. Howard's theme is instead the purely human one that suggests happiness is sometimes found when conventional mores are set aside and others are not judged too harshly. In the same year, 1924, EUGENE O'NEILL's drama *DESIRE UNDER THE ELMS* dealt with a similar plot line, that of the young bride of an old man becoming sexually involved with the man's son, with far greater complexity.

THIRD WENDY WASSERSTEIN (2005) This full-length play was originally a one-act play produced in Washington, D.C., in 2004. *Third* was inspired by an encounter WENDY WASSERSTEIN had with a student-athlete waiter in New Hampshire; the young man said in answer to Wasserstein's question about how he liked his college that he had been accused of plagiarism three times. "'And were you guilty?'" she asked. "And he said, 'No it's kind of because of who I am. I went to Andover and I'm a jock.'" Wasserstein turned to her dinner companion and said, "'That's a play. I know that's a play'" (Bryer 8). In the play that she subsequently wrote, a midwestern student athlete at a liberal New England college prompts a feminist scholar and English professor who accuses him of plagiarism to examine her own biases and to realize that *she* has become the establishment—certain and immutable, not so very unlike the one she overthrew at this same college decades earlier.

The play opens as Professor Laurie Jameson gives a somewhat jargon-filled preamble to her English literature class on the first day of the fall semester. She instructs them to set aside any preconceived ideas of canonical texts they may have acquired in high school; they will start with *King Lear*. Professor Jameson's is a feminist reading of the classic; she objects to the traditional reading which regarded Cordelia as the heroine—"vilified the girls with guts, like Goneril and Regan, and lauded the whimpering weaklings." Her prejudice against prep school–educated wrestler Woodson Bull III, whose nickname is "Third," is evident from the beginning. She assumes he comes from money, is Republican, and is not as intelligent as her nonathlete students. It is late 2002 and Jamison's view of Third is influenced by her rage against the Bush-Cheney administration as they build a case for the Iraq War. When Third writes a paper on *King Lear*, one that does not subscribe to his professor's feminist perspective but is eloquent in its quite Freudian interpretation, she assumes he has plagiarized it at least in part, though she can find no hard evidence of this. The case goes to a hearing, where Third successfully defends his paper, though the damage done to his semester is substantial.

Meanwhile, Laurie Jamison's personal life includes an aging, increasingly feebleminded and dependent father for whom she is the favorite daughter, who, like Cordelia, cares for him with kindness and patience and without sentimentality; a husband whom we never see but whose midlife crisis involving weight-lifting and motorcycling we hear about; and two daughters. Emily is a freshman at Swarthmore, and Zooey is an organic cheese–making Vermont lesbian.

As act 2 begins, daughter Emily, home on spring break, happens to meet Third as he tends bar at a local student hangout on a quiet night. Not knowing that he is talking to Jameson's daughter, he tells her about the "bitch professor" who nearly got him thrown out of school. We also learn that Third is "not really" Republican but politically undecided, that his father is a small claims lawyer in Ohio, and that his family is not wealthy (though there was once a grandfather who had money). Emily never reveals her identity to Third, but in some of the most important speeches of the play she later confronts her mother: "You categorized him and got it totally wrong." She tells her mother that though she preaches an "open perspective," she actually has a "limited view." Emily accuses her mother of being as guilty of having "an agenda" as the Bush administration: Jameson needed Third to be guilty of plagiarism (because he and his paper represented to her the patriarchy she had fought against her entire career) just as the Bush administration needed there to be "weapons of mass destruction" to justify going to war. Emily goes on to say, "If he were a gay, Native American playwright you wouldn't have touched him." In a further indictment of Jameson's tendency to bend over backward to be politically correct, Emily points out that her mother is far less critical of her lesbian daughter Zooey's poet partner, though the poet *cheats* on Zooey, than she is of Emily's boyfriend, a bank teller with no higher ambition and no academic credentials. After this confrontation, Emily informs her mother that she will be leaving college to move in with that boyfriend and to waitress while she decides what she wants to do with her life. She does know that she utterly rejects her mother's world, where people are judged by "their schools, their influence, or the success of their latest essay in the *New York Review of Books*."

At the end of the academic year, Laurie Jameson comes to apologize to Woodson Bull III. He has gotten a scholarship to Ohio State University—not for wrestling, as she immediately assumes, but an academic one. He tells her that during the spring semester he stayed away from "courses like [hers] . . . and stuck to economics, statistics and Ancient Greek. [He] got straight A's [and] got into Stanford, too"—again thwarting her preconceived notions about him. She admits to him that to a large extent her ideas were "crystallized" when she was Third's age in 1969. Her "thinking," she admits, "has become as staid as the point of view [she] fought to overrule." Both her experience with this student and the death of her father ("Let me tell you a secret," she says to Third in the final scene. "All it takes is your father dying to know that Goneril and Regan are not the heroines.") shake Laurie Jameson's worldview substantially enough to cause her to take a long leave of absence from the college.

In an interview in 2004, Wasserstein commented on the work she was then doing on expanding *Third* to a full-length play: The audience "need[s] to know why [Jameson] goes back and apologizes to that kid, and that's not clear in the [one-act version]. It was a fun thing to write about because in some ways it goes against the grain. That play in some ways is politically incorrect; and I like the idea of the reverse discrimination. I think that that's very interesting—this woman breaking down—so when I think about that play I also want to know more about her" (Bryer 9). This character development did ultimately constitute the greatest change to the play. The full-length version of *Third* premiered less than four months before Wasserstein's death on January 30, 2006, at age 55; it was included in *The Best Plays* volume for 2005–2006.

BIBLIOGRAPHY
Bryer, Jackson R. "An Uncommon Woman: An Interview with Wendy Wasserstein." *Theatre History Studies* 29 (2009): 1–17.

THOMAS, AUGUSTUS (1857–1934)

Born in St. Louis, Missouri, before the Civil War, Augustus Thomas worked for the railroad and in journalism before becoming a successful playwright. Over the course of his career, Thomas displayed great variety in his plays and adaptations. The dramatic realism prevalent in the 1890s was characterized by minutely realistic sets; audiences were fascinated by real water, real trees, and the like onstage. "Local color plays" were in this tradition, with characters and stories specific to their settings. Augustus Thomas contributed to this genre with his dramas *In Mizzoura* (1893) and *Arizona* (1899). Thomas's interest in psychic phenomena was evident in *The WITCHING HOUR* (1907), in which telepathy and hypnosis are used to solve a murder, and in *As a Man Thinks* (1911), which features hypnosis and infidelity. His works include farces, *The Earl of Pawtucket* (1903) and *Mrs. Leffingwell's Boots* (1905), as well as the costume play *Oliver Goldsmith* (1900). He dramatized a series of cartoons, *The Education of Mr. Pipp* (1905), and adapted popular novels, Hopkinson Smith's *Colonel Carter of Cartersville* (1892) and Richard Harding Davis's *Soldiers of Fortune* (1902), for the stage. *The Copperhead* (1918), a Civil War drama in which a Northerner pretends to have Southern sympathies, made actor Lionel Barrymore a star.

Thomas was for many years president of the American Society of Dramatists, an organization founded in 1890 by BRONSON HOWARD and others; the Society was instrumental in getting copyright laws passed, which protected the work of playwrights from piracy. In 1922, Thomas published his autobiography, *The Print of My Remembrance*.

BIBLIOGRAPHY
Davis, Ronald J. *Augustus Thomas*. Boston: Twayne, 1984.
Quinn, Arthur Hobson. "Augustus Thomas and the Picture of American Life." *A History of the American Drama from the Civil War to the Present Day*. Rev. ed. 1936. New York: Appleton-Century-Crofts, 1955. 239–264.

Thomas, Augustus. *The Print of My Remembrance*. New York: Scribners, 1922.

———. *The Witching Hour*. New York: Harper, 1908.

THOUSAND CLOWNS, A HERB GARDNER (1962)

HERB GARDNER's first play, *A Thousand Clowns*, is a comedy about a free-spirited television writer, who is forced to deal with "the available world" when his unconventional lifestyle threatens his custody of his nephew.

Nick Burns, now 12, was abandoned by his mother seven years ago when she left her brother Murray's apartment for a pack of cigarettes and did not return. Murray, a comedy writer, has been unemployed for six months. As the relationship between uncle and nephew is revealed, it is clear that Nick often acts more like the adult than Murray. When the "genius" school Nick attends finds out that Murray, who is not legally Nick's guardian, is out of work, the Child Welfare Board is informed. Mr. Albert Amanson and Dr. Sandra Markowitz arrive to assess the child's environment; when Murray fails to take their visit as seriously as they do, Amanson leaves for his next case. Sandra remains, feeling compelled to help the Burnses, and quickly falls for the free-spirited Murray. Amanson returns the next morning to inform Murray that the Welfare Board has decided that he is an unfit guardian, but that there will be a hearing in two days where he can offer some proof of a change in his situation.

Murray explains to Sandra what he wants for Nick: "I want him to get to know exactly the special thing he is or else he won't notice it when it starts to go. I want him to stay awake and know who the phonies are. . . . I want to be sure he sees all the wild possibilities. . . . And I want him to know the subtle, sneaky, important reason why he was born a human being and not a chair." She advises him to show the Welfare Board that he wants to be "reliable." He calls his brother, Arnold, who is also his agent, asking him to find him a job that afternoon; but he is so put off by phony television personalities and their idiotic ideas that he returns to Sandy empty-handed and—though apologetic—unwilling to compromise his standards. Disappointed in him, she leaves.

Eventually, he agrees to go back to work for his old boss, the foolish Leo "Chuckles the Chipmunk" Herman, for whom Murray has only contempt. When Leo comes to the apartment, he is anxious to have Murray—who was good for ratings—back on the show; but when Nick does not laugh at Leo's chipmunk routines (because they are not funny), Leo begins to insult him and Murray, saying that Murray has brought Nick up in a "grotesque atmosphere, *unhealthy*" and "freakish." An offended Nick wants to "get rid of" Leo, but Murray must be the grown-up this time, and he tells Nick that they cannot afford to do that since he needs the job. For love of Nick, then, Murray reenters the rat race he loathes.

Herb Gardner said in an interview in 1991, "We all have our way of getting people to listen to us. . . . [S]o I tell jokes, and somewhere in amongst them someone will hear what else I have to say." *A Thousand Clowns* is very funny, but Gardner's theme is a serious one. The world often is the rat race full of compromise and phoniness that Murray Burns sees, but we must deal with this "available world," compromising in some areas in order to maintain in others some of our ideals—or our ties to the people we love. The play is autobiographical only to the extent that in his mid-twenties, Gardner wrote a wildly successful comic strip (*The Nebbishes*), which seemed to be taking over his life; the comic strip and the products on which it was printed (napkins and so on—everything, Gardner said, "but surgical masks") were everywhere, and the people he worked for did not want him to draw anything else. He found himself surrounded by "accountants," and like Murray Burns, he quit. That experience was the impetus for the play: "I wanted to write a play, so I wrote a play about a guy who quit what he was doing." The play was followed by the very successful 1965 screen adaptation, which Gardner wrote, and in which many of the original cast members reprised their roles.

BIBLIOGRAPHY

Gardner, Herb. Interview by Hap Erstein. Conversations with Leading American Playwrights series. Smithsonian Institution, Washington, D.C., November 29, 1991.

THREE MEN ON A HORSE JOHN CECIL HOLM AND GEORGE ABBOTT (1935)

This slight

three-act farce centers on Erwin Trowbridge, a milquetoast greeting-card poet from Ozone Heights, New York, who has an uncanny gift as a racetrack tout. Improbably one of the most popular comedies between the two world wars, *Three Men on a Horse* lightheartedly captures the distressing economic realities of the Great Depression at its height, as well as shows the need for the fearful populace of the United States to regain confidence in the future.

Erwin Trowbridge is secretly aware of his magical ability to forecast winners at the racetrack, but his conscience will not allow him to exploit his talent despite the fact that his lack of monetary success—and his more general lack of confidence—may cost him the love of his wife, Audrey. Erwin's depression over his wife's annoyance sends him to the local bar for a few drinks, leading to a gang of small-time hoods becoming aware of Erwin's predictive abilities, which they decide to exploit. However, Erwin is able to predict winners only while riding on a bus, so the hoods are compelled to take him for frequent rides and otherwise attempt to satisfy his every whim as the innocuous Erwin begins to enjoy his newfound importance. Despite the romantic machinations of an ex-Follies showgirl whose gangster boyfriend is head of the mob, Erwin retains his fundamental childlike innocence. When the showgirl's affections become too obvious, the hood threatens bodily harm to Erwin, and when the hoods doubt one of Erwin's predictions, he loses the ability to predict winners. Having stood up to the jealous hood, the newly confident Erwin returns to Ozone Heights and wins back the affections of his wife.

Directed by coauthor ABBOTT, an expert farceur, *Three Men on a Horse* opened in New York to almost unanimous critical praise. Innumerable revivals on both the professional and amateur stages have made the play a minor classic. In late 1941, *Three Men on a Horse* was adapted to the musical comedy stage as *Banjo Eyes,* a loosely constructed vehicle for stage legend Eddie Cantor, who made his final Broadway appearance as Erwin, singing the popular "We're Having a Baby," and including some patriotic interpolations as America's involvement in World War II began. Another musical adaptation, *Let It Ride!* (1961), was

only a modest success. Abbott's remarkably long career (he died at the age of 107 while still busy with theater work) resulted in numerous Broadway successes, while his coauthor, Holm, had only one other noteworthy theatrical endeavor—when he wrote the libretto for the musical comedy, *Best Foot Forward* (1941).

James Fisher
University of North Carolina at Greensboro

THREE TALL WOMEN EDWARD ALBEE (1994)

After almost 20 years of critically and commercially unsuccessful New York productions of his plays, EDWARD ALBEE won his third PULITZER PRIZE and the New York Drama Critics' Circle Award for *Three Tall Women*. It premiered in English at Vienna's English Theatre in June 1991 and opened in New York in January 1994. The subject is the playwright's adoptive mother who died in 1989; as he explained in the introduction to the published text, he wanted to "write as objective a play as I could about a fictional character who resembled in every way, in every event, someone I had known very, very well."

The play begins with three tall women, designated only as A, B, and C onstage. A is 92 years old, "thin, autocratic, proud"; B, who is A's secretary, "looks rather as A would have at 52"; and C, a young lawyer who has come to get A to attend to some neglected checks and documents, "looks rather as B would have at 26." A is apparently waiting for a visit from her son; while she waits, she reminisces in an occasionally incoherent and often fragmentary fashion about her life. Throughout, B is obviously more tolerant of A's infirmities and eccentricities than C, who is impatient. Most of A's memories have to do with her family. She recalls her mother, who prepared her and her sister "for going out in the world, for men, for making our own way" and who closely critiqued the weekly letters she insisted her daughters send her after they moved to the city. She remembers her husband, who was shorter than she, who had lost one eye in a golfing accident, who had been married twice before she met him, who was from a rich family, and with whom she loved to ride the prizewinning horses they owned. And she thinks of her sister, "smarter" than she, with "more beaux," "prim" (she "didn't like sex"), and a heavy drinker, who didn't marry until she was 40, when the family found "a wop" for her. C is appalled by A's racial epithets, but B explains, "It's the way she learned things." Weeping at her recollections, A asks to be put in bed, where she has a stroke, and the act ends.

The second act begins with A apparently in bed with a "breathing mask" over her nose and mouth and B and C standing over her. But when, shortly thereafter, A enters, it is clear that the figure in the bed is a dummy and that B is now A at age 52, C is A at age 26, and A is herself at 92 and is now "perfectly rational." A and B begin by enlightening C as to what will happen to her later in her life, especially with respect to men. C has recently lost her virginity and imagines that, after "a few others," she will meet "the man of her dreams" and be "very happy." B says she'll meet "a man you'll *dream about*," and A adds, "For a long, long time," but, as to being "very happy," B simply says, grudgingly, "Well. . . ." A comments, "We'll talk about happy sometime." They also tell C about "the little one-eyed man" who looks like "a penguin" that she will marry and then cheat on while he cheats on her; she will marry him partly because, after her father dies, "there *is* the future to look out for . . . and he is rich."

At the moment they tell C that she will have a son, the latter enters. At his appearance, B shouts, "Get out of my house!"; C says, "Stop it!"; and A says, "Let him alone; he's come to see me" (he cannot hear them). When B explains, "I'll never forgive him" and "I never want to see him again" and asks A how she could let him return, A replies that, after 20 years—during which time he missed his father's funeral—he came back when she had a heart attack. She never forgives him, they never reminisce, and "there are no apologies, no recriminations, no tears," she tells B. She continues, If you wait 20 years until you're alone except for your sister "upstairs passed out on the floor," "you *do* want to see him again," even though "[W]e're strangers; we're curious about each other; we leave it at that."

When C asks B how she, romantic optimistic C, turns into cynical realistic B, the latter tells her of her affair with a groom in the stable, of taking care of her

alcoholic sister and aging mother, and of raising her son—who "gets himself thrown out of every school he can find, even one or two we haven't sent him to," whom she catches "doing it with your niece-in-law *and* your nephew-in-law the same week," and who packs a bag one day and leaves without saying a word to his parents. A then tells B about the agonizing death of her husband from cancer and having to sell her beloved jewelry piece by piece to support her lifestyle. At this point, C swears, "I'll never become you—either of you" and asks when will she have some happy times. B responds that the "happiest time" is "now . . . always," that "[S]tanding up here right on top of the middle of it *has* to be the happiest time" because "it's the only time you get a three-hundred-and-sixty-degree view." But A disagrees, concluding the play by asserting that the "happiest moment" is "coming to the end of it" when "you can think about yourself in the third person." "There's a difference," she explains, "between knowing you're going to *die* and *knowing* you're going to die. The second is better; it moves away from the theoretical."

Albee's biographer Mel Gussow has observed that *Three Tall Women* is "not only about dying and death but also about the changes that cumulatively define a life. Why do we become what we are?" (371). He calls it "a wise and prophetic play about the tragic mistakes of life" (371). Albee, in his introduction to the published text, remarks that "very few people who met my adoptive mother in the last twenty years of her life could abide her, while many people who have seen my play find her fascinating." Perhaps the reason for this can be found in the method of the play: By segmenting his mother's life and showing her at different stages, Albee was able to show how she got to be the person she became. When dramatic literature (and fiction, for that matter) shows us the reasons for a character's behavior, no matter how seemingly evil or bizarre it may be, our response to the character becomes more complicated; we may not sympathize, but we understand. Someone who met Frances Albee at the end of her life probably would not have known—or cared to know—how she had become the impossibly difficult, embittered old lady she was, but her son, in choosing to tell her story in the way he did, obviously—if perhaps subconsciously—did want us to see her objectively as a complex and, ultimately, quite fascinating woman.

BIBLIOGRAPHY
Albee, Edward. *Three Tall Women*. New York: Dutton, 1995.
Gussow, Mel. *Edward Albee: A Singular Journey*. New York: Simon and Schuster, 1999.

TIME OF THE CUCKOO, THE ARTHUR LAURENTS (1952)

The bittersweet story of Leona Samish, a thirtyish spinster who travels to Venice seeking romance, *The Time of the Cuckoo* remains LAURENTS's best-remembered play—largely perhaps because of its perennially popular movie adaptation *Summertime* (1955), starring Katharine Hepburn (there was also a less successful musical comedy version, Richard Rodgers and Stephen Sondheim's *Do I Hear a Waltz?* [1965]). Leona and her fellow Americans abroad bring with them a whole trunk full of entrenched attitudes, which allows Laurents to contrast the new world with the old, as ignorance and acquisitiveness confront culture and charm and as puritanical guilt and repression come up against an instinctual Mediterranean lust for living.

Leona, who hides behind a cheery manner (she delights in addressing others as "Cookie") and assuages her loneliness in drink, is desperate for her time of love. She thinks she might find it with the attractive older shopkeeper, Renato Di Rossi, from whom she buys wine-colored goblets that hint at her pent-up passion, yet their sexual mores diverge wildly. Di Rossi, who thinks that Americans obsess too much about sex and abstract considerations of right and wrong, is without moral qualms, espousing a philosophy that advocates seizing the moment. Signora Fioria, the proprietor of the pensione who has had an adulterous affair and is involved in another now, echoes Di Rossi's views, decrying as impractical any code of conduct except discretion and urging her guests into guiltless relationships that leave life a little sweeter. Against these values, Laurents shows up the shortcomings of the more limiting notions held by the younger, beautiful, and blond Yaegers. Eddie Yaeger, an artist experiencing painter's block after a hugely successful first exhibition, returns to an uncompromising belief in absolute fidelity after a brief liaison with the signora in a gondola; his wife June, every bit as romantic as Leona, suffers from the delusory ideal that a wife must be her husband's complete life.

What prevents Leona and Di Rossi from achieving a permanent relationship, however, is not just her inability to accommodate to shifting sexual mores but also a failure within herself; though priding herself on her independence, she doubts her attractiveness to Di Rossi. His gift of a garnet necklace, a present so overwhelming that she—and the audience—literally hear a waltz—temporarily melts her. When it appears, however, that he has made money off of her by exchanging her dollars for counterfeit on the black market, she rejects him and, in her own hurt, strikes out at others by revealing Eddie's unfaithfulness. That Leona insists on keeping the necklace as something material to take back home indicates her insecurity and her need for things as a proof of feelings. Like the older McIlhennys who have money but little sensitivity, Leona can be sure only of things that are tangible, and so the very real affection that Di Rossi felt for her—and without which he believes there can be no pleasure—dissolves. Although it is left unclear whether Leona will return to America any the wiser psychologically and emotionally for her brief encounter, at least she continues her vacation in Venice rather than fleeing from further experiences that might test her traditional morality.

Thomas P. Adler
Purdue University

TIME OF YOUR LIFE, THE WILLIAM SAROYAN (1939)

Set in Nick's Pacific Street Saloon in San Francisco in October of 1939 (the month and year of the play's opening), *The Time of Your Life* juxtaposes good-hearted characters against a bully just weeks after Adolf Hitler's army invaded Poland, setting off World War II. SAROYAN's play won the PULITZER PRIZE, which the playwright refused because he objected to such judgments of art.

Set near the end of the depression, the play depicts a group of unsuccessful people trying to survive. Each character has a dream (in this way it is similar to—though certainly more lighthearted than—another great American barroom play, *The ICEMAN COMETH* [written in 1939, but not produced until 1946]): Willy, a young pinball player, dreams of beating the machine; Kitty, "a two-dollar whore," dreams of a life on the stage interrupted pleasantly by marriage to a young and altruistic doctor who will fall in love with her from the audience; Dudley Bostwick dreams of getting his girl back; Harry wants to be a comedian, but since his jokes are more poignant than funny, Nick hires him to dance instead; young Wesley, who nearly collapses from hunger, just wants s job (Nick gives him one as a piano player, which is where his talent lies); the newsboy dreams of becoming a "great lyric tenor"; Joe, the well-dressed, well-off resident philosopher, wants "to live a civilized life. . . . a life that can't hurt any other life"; and Tom, Joe's simpleminded 30-year-old errand boy, wants to marry the prostitute Kitty. Nick, the softhearted barkeep, employs as many people as he can. Into this mix comes the old man, Murphy, also called "Kit Carson" for his resemblance to a figure from the mythic West, and the villain Blick—a police vice squad detective—who harasses the prostitutes.

In this dive full of society's outcasts, Joe, who feels guilt about having wealth while others suffer, observes life. He explains to Tom that he is a "student . . . of all things. And when my study reveals something of beauty in a place or in a person where by all rights only ugliness or death should be . . . then I know how full of goodness this life is." Saroyan's play is an affirmation of the good that is in most human beings. Joe shows tremendous kindness to Kitty and Tom, helping Tom rescue Kitty from her life of prostitution by getting him a job so that they can marry. The one character who has no redeeming qualities is Blick, the brutal vice squad detective whose cruelty to those who are most vulnerable—Wesley, Murphy, and Kitty—leads to his own murder, to which even the other policemen turn a blind eye.

Kit Carson Murphy is one of the great comic characters of American drama. He comes to the bar and proceeds to tell such extravagantly tall tales—"I don't suppose you ever fell in love with a midget weighing thirty-nine pounds?"; "Ever try to herd cattle on a bicycle?"; "[T]here was a hurricane in Toledo. I remember sitting on the roof of a two-story house, floating northwest."—that most of his listeners do not believe him. Only Joe encourages him, saying "*Very seriously, energetically and sharply* . . . Of course I believe you. Living is an art. It's not bookkeeping." In the end, it is Murphy who shoots Blick offstage and then recounts the incident in the same tone as his other tales, lending credibility to all that he has said before—but probably also making it impossible for the authorities to know whether he is telling the truth.

Saroyan wrote a statement at the beginning of the play, the first lines of which are often quoted: "In the time of your life, live—so that in that good time there shall be no ugliness or death for yourself or for any life that your life touches"; equally important to understanding his theme is another line, also from the opening statement: "Encourage virtue in whatever heart it may have been driven into secrecy and sorrow by the shame and terror of the world." Saroyan's theme, then, is not just about recognizing goodness, but about excavating beneath the surface for the good that harsh circumstances have buried.

TOBACCO ROAD Jack Kirkland (1933)

Based on the best-selling 1932 novel of the same name by Erskine Caldwell, *Tobacco Road* is the story of the Lester family, a poverty-stricken, uneducated group of Georgia sharecroppers. The only conviction any of the family members displays is that of their right to the land, and it is that conviction that drives off many of the members and leaves those who stay to starve.

The play takes place in three acts, all of which are set in or on the front porch of the Lester shack, built alongside Tobacco Road, a dirt road in the depths of Georgia's cotton land. The lack of movement emphasizes the Lester family's shiftlessness as well as their stubborn attachment to a land that refuses to yield, even to those who work hard—and the Lesters do not. Jeeter, the father, is degenerate, adulterous, and unwilling to change. He and his wife, Ada, have produced 15 children. Three remain on the farm: 18-year-old Ellie May, who has a harelip; 16-year-old Dude; and 14-year-old Pearl, who is married to Lov. There is also Jeeter's mother, Grandma Lester.

The action centers on these characters as they lounge around on the porch of the shack. When Lov arrives, he complains about Pearl's lack of expertise in sexual matters. He begins to flirt with Ellie May, who flirts back. A second visitor arrives, the lustful 40-year-old woman preacher, Sister Bessie, who wants to marry Dude. Pearl runs away, and when Ellie May wants to take Pearl's place in the marriage, Jeeter agrees to make the exchange, setting the price at seven dollars, some quilts, and some motor oil. Dude agrees to marry Sister Bessie so that he can drive her automobile. When Ada tries to resist the exchange of Pearl for Ellie Mae, Dude runs her over with Sister Bessie's car, and Jeeter must bury her in the back of the shack. Grandma Lester has wandered into the woods and is probably dead, but Jeeter is by this point too tired to dig a grave. He is left alone on the front porch where he sits and watches the continuing deterioration of his land.

Tobacco Road's initial run was long—from December 4, 1933, to May 31, 1941—a total of 3,182 performances, but the play was often criticized heavily. However, the story is not a simple caricature of white trash. It insists that social conditions, in the case of *Tobacco Road,* the sharecropping system, contribute to the hopelessness and suffering that lead to the degeneracy of families like the Lesters. While far less nobly drawn than the Joad family of John Steinbeck's *The Grapes of Wrath,* the Lesters serve a similar function in illustrating the effects of social oppression. However, unlike the Joads, the Lester family belongs to the genre of southern grotesque. Jeeter has more in common with William Faulkner's Snopes clan than with Tom Joad, but even Faulkner's Snopeses ultimately display morality. The Lester family is unremittingly degenerate; because of *Tobacco Road*'s unsympathetic characters and its humor, audiences have long had a hard time seeing the serious social themes it displays.

Jan Goggans
University of California–Davis

TONY (ANTOINETTE PERRY) AWARD

Given annually for "distinguished achievement" in Broadway theater, the Tony Awards are administered by the League of New York Theatres and Producers and the American Theatre Wing. The awards were established in honor of Antoinette Perry (1888–1946), an actress, director, and philanthropist.

In 1939, Antoinette Perry, playwright RACHEL CROTHERS, and other theater women established the American Theatre Wing War Service, a reconstitution of the Stage Women's War Relief, which Crothers had cofounded in 1917 to help devastated Europeans during World War I. Under the chairmanship of Perry throughout World War II, the Wing's activities included raising money for the war effort, initiating and operating Stage Door Canteens in 10 cities for American servicemen, and, with the USO, touring shows in war zones. When the war ended, the Theatre Wing's focus shifted from war relief to peacetime service, especially in the areas of education and encouragement of young talent. When Perry died in 1946, her friends in theater decided to honor her by naming an award after her, and the Antoinette Perry Awards were established. The first presentations in 1947 were held at a dinner dance. Gradually, the awards presentation evolved into the televised stage show with live audience and entertainment with which we are now familiar.

Unlike the PULITZER PRIZE for drama, which is by definition given to an American play (preferably on an American theme), the Tony Awards include non-American dramas. In 63 years of Tony Awards, from 1947 through 2009, the outstanding play Tony went 21 times to a non-American play. Apart from that, the plays that win tend to be serious rather than comic. The comedies that do win usually have serious undertones—though there are exceptions (TEAHOUSE OF THE AUGUST MOON [Tony, 1954] and BILOXI BLUES [Tony, 1985], for instance). In recent years, there has been some controversy about the relevancy of the Tony Awards because so few dramas are done in Broadway theaters anymore; therefore, the number of plays that are eligible is small, and some very interesting plays are never done on Broadway, making them ineligible. In the last 10 years, some of the Pulitzer Prize–winning plays never came to Broadway (PAULA VOGEL's HOW I LEARNED TO DRIVE [Pulitzer, 1998], DONALD MARGULIES's DINNER WITH FRIENDS [Pulitzer, 2000]). Thus far, the officials of the Tony Awards have resisted efforts to expand the number of eligible theaters to include some of the larger OFF-BROADWAY venues.

For a complete list of the American plays that have won Tony Awards, see Appendix I.

BIBLIOGRAPHY

Jewell, James C., ed. *Broadway and the Tony Awards.* Washington, D.C.: University Press of America, 1977.

Morrow, Lee Alan. *The Tony Award Book: Four Decades of Great American Theater.* New York: Abbeville Press, 1987.

TOOTH OF CRIME, THE Sam Shepard (1972)

Sam Shepard's Obie Award–winning play, *The Tooth of Crime,* is a tour de force of American theater. A futuristic piece rooted in popular culture from the past as well as myths of the American West, *The Tooth of Crime* features rock songs, a linguistic gunfight overseen by an NBA-like referee, cheerleaders, a gangland-like music industry, rich monologues, stunning visual techniques, and achingly violent heartbreak.

The play's main character is Hoss, who is, at the play's start, an established rock star. As the play progresses, his national reputation and personal self-esteem falter and fade. Shepard reinvents the music business by incorporating rumbles and gunfights as crucial components to one's ascension up the charts. Musical and cultural success are not measured merely through talent but by "Star Power." The play's first act quickly establishes that events are spiraling out of control for Hoss as his Star Power begins to wane. Caught off-guard in the rapidly shifting music world, Hoss finds himself a prisoner in his own compound. Surrounding Hoss is his entourage, including Galactic Jack, his supplier of weapons and drugs; Star Man, his zodiac adviser; Becky, his manager; and Cheyenne, his driver. Each one reconfirms Hoss's precarious position in the game. Adding to Hoss's increasing paranoia is the appearance of Crow, a young gypsy, the embodiment of an American rebel, who has emerged out of the desert to challenge Hoss to a one-on-one battle, winner take all.

The play's second act focuses on this battle between Hoss and Crow. They compete not only for dominance in the music arena but also for the essence of Hoss's identity and self. Part of Crow's strength is his talent for mimicry, and in their first meeting Crow perfectly copies Hoss, from his walk to his talk. This loss of identity and the easy emulation of his self by another strongly disturb Hoss, as Crow's ability only reconfirms his own slipping status. Hoss and Crow then engage in a linguistic battle for supremacy that is set up like a combination gun fight/boxing match. While Hoss successfully fends off one of Crow's attacks by calling up the language of the blues, something Crow knows nothing about since he is immersed in the present, Crow still comfortably unseats Hoss through a linguistic virtuosity heavily reliant on the façade of image. Unable to strike a deal with the youngster after his defeat, Hoss enacts the ultimate individualistic act by killing himself, leaving Crow to take possession of his compound, entourage, and place in the game.

Shepard wrote *The Tooth of Crime* while living in London, which allowed him to reassess his perception of America. His play shows his critical assessment of the United States as it aggressively depicts the deterioration of the American West and the American Dream, the difficult challenges facing the will of the individual, the destruction of myths about national identity, and the bankruptcy of a culture reliant on image rather than experience and history.

William C. Boles
Rollins College

TOPDOG/UNDERDOG Suzan-Lori Parks (2001)

After winning the Pulitzer Prize for the play, Parks commented, "*Topdog/Underdog* has a lot to do with the artifice of everyday life, with the performative aspect of life, with the masks we wear, with characters who are between a rock and a hard place."

Lincoln and Booth are African-American brothers, whose father named them after the president and his assassin because—as Lincoln comments to his younger brother—"it was his idea of a joke." Both men are in their thirties and share a seedy furnished room, where they drink and argue and remember the past. Booth is unemployed and obsessed with learning the "3-card monte scam," at which his brother was once a master. Lincoln gave up this con game when a friend and fellow con artist was shot. He now works in an arcade, where, dressed as Abe Lincoln and in "whiteface," he is "shot" in the head by paying customers several times a day. Booth wants his brother to quit the arcade job and go back to 3-card monte (a kind of shell game with cards); Booth wants them to be partners, but Lincoln refuses, though he is willing to teach his brother. At present, Booth lives off shoplifting and his brother's paycheck. We learn much about the lives of the brothers through their conversation: After Lincoln's wife—who slept with Booth and to whom he was unfaithful—left him, he drank heavily and still does. Booth's girlfriend, Grace, is ultimately not interested in a man with no means (we wonder if the good times Booth describes with Grace, whom he eventually kills, are fabrications). As children, the brothers literally witnessed the infidelities of their parents—their father had many women, their mother had "her Thursday man." They were deserted by their mother and, two years later, at 13 and 16, by their father. Each parent left $500 with one of their sons. They refer to this money as their "inheritance," but they have inherited more than cash from their parents; they have inherited doomed lives, as symbolized by the names their father gave them. In the end, their destiny is as violent as that of their namesakes.

As Parks's comment makes clear, there is much pretense in the lives of these men. Booth is always putting on a front for someone—he shoplifts enough goods to make himself and his room appear prosperous enough for Grace, and when she fails to show up, he pretends to his brother that she is on her way when, in fact, she is six hours late and will never arrive. Reminiscing about their youth, Lincoln recalls lemonade stands and tree houses until his brother calls him on this fantasy, forcing him to admit that the "good times" consisted of puncturing their father's car tires and letting him believe that "thuh white man done sabotaged him again." And, of course, there is the artifice of whiteface and costume that Lincoln willingly dons each day to assume his passive role as doomed man waiting for his assassin—foreshadowing his real death at the hands of a brother. The card scam, itself, is a form of acting—and through it Lincoln deftly cons his brother in the final minutes of the play out of the $500 he has saved all these years. For this, Booth shoots him.

In 2002, when *Topdog/Underdog* opened on Broadway (having had an OFF-BROADWAY production in 2001), Parks became the first African-American woman to win a Pulitzer Prize for drama. She is one of only four African-American women playwrights, along with LORRAINE HANSBERRY, NTOZAKE SHANGE, and ANNA DEAVERE SMITH, whose plays have seen Broadway productions.

BIBLIOGRAPHY
"Historic Pulitzer Victory." BBC News. April 9, 2002. Available online. URL: http://news.bbc.co.uk. Downloaded September 17, 2002.

TORCH SONG TRILOGY HARVEY FIERSTEIN (1981)

FIERSTEIN's *Torch Song Trilogy* is composed of three interrelated one-acts: *The International Stud, Fugue in a Nursery,* and *Widows and Children First!* Performed individually OFF-OFF-BROADWAY at La MaMa Experimental Theatre Club in 1979, the three were first combined at the Richard Allen Center in 1981. The four-and-a-half-hour production transferred to Broadway in 1982, where it won Best Play and Actor TONY AWARDS for Fierstein, who reprised his role as Arnold in a 1988 truncated film version.

International Stud is essentially an extended monologue, interrupted by brief two-character scenes and songs. Arnold Becker, flamboyant drag artiste, directly addresses the audience to relate his problems with men. Searching for his ideal fantasy, someone who will accept the real Arnold, he thinks he's found him in naive teacher Ed. Arnold learns too late that Ed is bisexual and terrified of the domestic bliss Arnold envisions. Following the play's most infamous scene, in which Arnold hilariously mimes sodomy in a bar, the two reach a tentative agreement to try to work things out.

Fugue takes place a year later, the entire action staged on a huge bed. Arnold has acquired a new lover, 18-year-old model Alan, after Ed deserted him for a girlfriend named Laurel. She invites them both to spend a weekend at Ed's farm, fueling everyone's jealousies. After Ed's advances to Arnold are rebuffed, he seduces Alan. Following the weekend, Laurel blurts out the indiscretion to the unaware Arnold in explaining why she has left Ed. The two couples eventually reconcile, with Alan and Arnold planning a commitment ceremony and Ed proposing to Laurel.

The last one-act occurs five years later. Arnold is still grieving the loss of Alan, senselessly murdered by gay-bashers, and is in the process of adopting David, a 15-year-old gay youth. Ed has also returned after his failed marriage. They are visited by Arnold's quintessentially Jewish mother who is appalled, originally mistaking David for Arnold's new lover. Following numerous arguments over Arnold's right to his chosen lifestyle, Ma reluctantly accepts him, and Ed and Arnold agree to give their relationship yet another try.

The play remains the most commercially successful gay-themed production ever, a worldwide sensation. Lauded by the straight press, the play divided gay audiences, the more radical element objecting to its parody of heterosexual marriage as the pinnacle of gay achievement. Others saw it as a major step forward precisely because of its portrayal of gays as "normal." The impending AIDS crisis rendered the play's domestic concerns somewhat obsolete in light of the more pressing problems facing the gay community, yet it remains an impressive milestone in contemporary GAY AND LESBIAN THEATER.

Douglas W. Gordy
Walnut Creek, California

TORRENCE, RIDGELY (1875–1950) White

playwright Ridgely Torrence is notable in American theater for his *Three Plays for a Negro Theatre* (1917), an evening of one-act plays. Born in Xenia, Ohio, Torrence graduated from Princeton University in 1897. He was an editor for several magazines: *The Critic* (1903–04), *Cosmopolitan* (1905–07), and the *New Republic* (1920–33). Torrence's literary focus was on poetry. A member of the National Institute of Arts and Letters and a chancellor of the American Society of Poetry, he published several volumes of verse; despite his accomplishments as a poet, it is for his three simple one-act plays that he has earned a place in the history of American drama.

Three Plays for a Negro Theatre is significant in American drama as the first entry of African-American actors in a Broadway production that was neither a musical nor drawn from the minstrel tradition. Opening in April 1917 at the Garden Theatre in New York, it was the first dramatic production on Broadway to feature an all-black cast in serious roles. Emilie Hapgood provided financial backing for the production and funded the Hapgood Players, an African-American theater group. The plays were well received. Newspaper reviews praised the cast, crew, and playwright. According to Alain Locke, an architect of the New Negro Renaissance and the editor of *Plays of Negro Life* (1927), *Three Plays for a Negro Theatre* marked the beginning of AFRICAN-AMERICAN DRAMA. Despite such acclaim, however, it ran for only 10 performances because the United States had declared war on Germany. Afterward, Torrence's plays received minimal attention.

Set in the rural South, *Granny Maumee,* the most significant of the three plays, concerns an elderly African-American woman who, for 50 years, has grieved the loss of Sam, her son, to a white mob. Blinded by fire as she tried to save him, she briefly regains her sight to see her infant grandson for the first time. To her horror, she sees that the child is white and learns that its father is the man who killed Sam. Through spiritual contact with Sam, she forgives the child's father and then dies. Although the plot does rely on voodoo, it rises above stereotypes of African Americans and presents a poignant story with realistic characters. In *The Rider of Dreams,* a husband steals his wife's savings in order to pursue his dream of playing a guitar. *Simon the Cyrenian,* a biblical drama, centers on a black man who helps Jesus carry the cross and wears the crown of thorns as a tribute to his condemned savior.

BIBLIOGRAPHY
Clum, John. *Ridgely Torrence*. Boston: Twayne, 1970.
Locke, Alain, and Montgomery Gregory, eds. *Plays of Negro Life*. 1927. New York: Negro University Press, 1968.

Christine R. Gray
The Community College of Baltimore County

TOUCH OF THE POET, A EUGENE O'NEILL

(1958) Started in 1935 but not completed until 1942 and designed as part of O'NEILL's multiplay cycle "A Tale of Possessors, Self-Dispossessed," in which the consequences of American acquisitiveness were to be shown through successive generations of the Harford family, *A Touch of the Poet* is the only finished play of the cycle that the playwright did not destroy. After the failure of *A MOON FOR THE MISBEGOTTEN* in 1947, O'Neill refused to release *A Touch of the Poet* for production; it was not produced until March 1957, when it premiered in Swedish at Stockholm's Royal Dramatic Theatre. It opened on Broadway in October 1958.

The play takes place on July 27, 1828, in Cornelius Melody's tavern in a village a few miles from Boston. The year is significant because in 1828 an aristocratic Yankee president, John Quincy Adams, was defeated for reelection by Andrew Jackson, the son of a poor Irish immigrant and the hero of the riffraff who frequent Melody's tavern. Con, as he is called by everyone—and surely the nickname has significance in describing his behavior—was born in Ireland, where his father rose from "a thieving shebeen keeper" to live on an estate as a gentleman through moneylending and squeezing his tenants. In revenge against the surrounding gentry who refused to accept him, he raised his son as a gentleman, sending him to school in Dublin. Despite young Con's good looks and success with women and his meritorious service in the British Army, he did not find acceptance either and developed a proclivity for fighting. Con's seductions ceased when he made pregnant and was forced to marry Nora, a pretty girl of peasant origins. When their child, Sara, was born, he brought them all to America and bought the tavern, which he was deceived into believing was going to be on a new coach line. The coach line never materialized, and the tavern has fallen on hard times.

Since coming to America, Con has adopted the habits and attitudes of the Yankee gentry: He favors Adams over Jackson; he keeps a thoroughbred mare whom he feeds with money his family needs for groceries; he speaks formally and properly and dresses in the well-tailored clothes of the English aristocracy; and he is fond of reciting Byron's poem "Childe Harold" to his reflection in the mirror. His attitude toward Nora vacillates between affection and scorn: He treats her like his servant, insults her for her ignorance, and taunts her for her heavy Irish brogue, but in the next breath he apologizes and kisses her warmly. Despite this confusing treatment, Nora loves him unconditionally.

Sara Melody is very critical of her father, although he has tried to raise her as gentry by sending her to a good school—which she insisted on leaving. She is intent on marrying Simon Harford, Harvard graduate and son of wealthy parents, whom she has been nursing back to health in a room above the tavern. Simon has left his father's business, built a cabin in the woods, and is writing a book "about how the world can be changed so people won't be greedy," although lately he has mostly been composing love poems to Sara (she says he has "a touch of the poet in him"). Sara explains to her mother that she will marry Simon because "it's my chance to rise in the world and nothing will keep me from it."

Realizing that it is July 27, the anniversary of the Battle of Talavera, when the Duke of Wellington personally commended Major Cornelius Melody for his bravery, Con will do as he does every year on this day: He will dress up in his uniform, and Nora will prepare and Sara will serve a dinner in his honor. He infuriates Sara by informing her that he must interview Simon to determine if his intentions are honorable and to arrange the dowry—although, of course, the Melodys have no money. For her part, Sara has just been kissed by Simon at her insistence; he was about to propose marriage, but she was too shy to stay in the room until he could do so.

As Con awaits his dinner guests, Deborah Harford enters to see her son. She is 41 but looks 30, and because Con does not know who she is and she does not identify herself, he acts the gallant gentleman with her and tries to kiss her—until she smells the whisky on his breath. Sara enters and is appalled; Con feels Deborah enjoyed his flirtation with her. Sara overhears Deborah telling Simon that his father has been to see his lawyer about preventing the marriage, but when Sara and Deborah talk, Deborah tells her that the greedy Harfords, whom she sees for what they are and who have not ensnared her, would like Sara: "They would see that you are strong and ambitious and determined to take what you want." After Deborah leaves, Con enters in his uniform, and Sara reluctantly admits that he looks impressive, asking sadly—in one of the play's most telling lines—"[W]hy can't you ever be the thing you seem to be?"

After the dinner, Con tells Sara that he has spoken with Simon, whose mother has suggested he wait a year before marrying, an arrangement Con favors because he feels that it will give Mr. Harford time to decide how much money he will give the couple. But then he accuses Sara of marrying only for money and tells her he would consent to it if she could "trick" Simon into getting her pregnant. At this point, Mr. Harford's lawyer, Nicholas Gadsby, arrives to offer the Melodys $3,000 to leave the area. Outraged, Con kicks Gadsby out of the tavern and leaves with one of his cronies to challenge Harford to a duel. Appalled by her father's behavior, Sara decides to seduce Simon—which she does. Her dream of money and position has become secondary to her love, and she can now even understand Nora's love for Con.

Con enters, having been kicked off the Harford property and beaten both physically and psychologically. He calls his behavior that of "a drunken foul-mouthed son of a thieving shebeen keeper who sprang from the filth of a peasant hovel." He goes to the barn and kills his mare, the final symbol of his former self, but refrains from turning the gun on himself, he explains, because he is already a "corpse." The Major is dead, and Con reverts to the brogue he had previously despised, congratulates Sara when she tells him she has seduced Simon—"Leave it to her to get what she wants by hook or by crook."—and tells Nora that he loves her. Sara mourns the loss of the Major— "Won't you be yourself again?"—but Con goes to join his friends in the bar, declaring that he now supports Jackson for president.

Speaking of the Harford men to Sara, Deborah says, "[T]hey never part with their dreams even when they deny them." She could also be describing Con, whose peasant persona is no more authentic than that of the Major. Like so many O'Neill protagonists, from Brutus Jones (The EMPEROR JONES [1920]) to the customers in Harry Hope's bar (The ICEMAN COMETH [1946]), he needs a mask, an illusion, a "life-lie," in a world that offers him no comfortable haven or place to "belong." Ironically, the very qualities that Sara most criticizes in her father are those she struggles with in herself. Like Con, she will use any means to rise above her peasant heritage, although, ultimately, it is love, not greed, that causes her to make love to Simon. Con and Sara also share with James Tyrone Sr. of LONG DAY'S JOURNEY INTO NIGHT (1956), the dream of all immigrants in the land of great opportunity—to make something of themselves—but also face an equally challenging immigrant dilemma—how to do so while also preserving their dignity and identity in an alien new world.

BIBLIOGRAPHY
Josephson, Lennart. *A Role: O'Neill's Cornelius Melody.* Atlantic Highlands, N.J.: Humanities Press, 1978.

TOYS IN THE ATTIC LILLIAN HELLMAN (1960)

Set in New Orleans, *Toys in the Attic* is about a pair of middle-aged spinster sisters and their much younger brother, whom they have raised. The sisters have always claimed to want success for their baby brother, but when he actually achieves some financial success—and, concurrently, some independence—they, especially one sister in particular, sabotage him. The play won the New York Drama Critics' Circle Award.

Carrie and Anna live for news of their charming, ne'er-do-well, recently married brother, Julian. When Julian and his wife, Lily, arrive for an unexpected visit, Julian bears extravagant gifts for his sisters— dresses, furs, ocean-liner tickets for a long-wished-for European vacation, and a paid-off mortgage. Moving men soon arrive with a piano for Carrie and a refrigerator for Anna. Julian also presents his young wife with a diamond ring, insisting that she replace her more modest wedding band with it. Julian's reticence about where he got the money—his vague reference to a real estate deal—arouses the suspicions of his sisters, who know him to be a gambler and a failure at business. Furthermore, the ladies do not like their gifts. The clothes are, Carrie tells him, "whore's" clothes. Lily— who seems in the midst of an emotional breakdown— finds her new ring vulgar and wants her own wedding ring back.

Gradually, Lily's story is revealed. She is 21 and has a history of emotional frailty. Her eccentric and wealthy mother, Albertine Prine, has essentially paid Julian to take the girl in marriage so that she and Henry, an African-American man who lives with her (and who is apparently her lover but poses as her chauffeur), can have some peace. Julian used the money he received from his mother-in-law to pay for an expensive operation that Anna needed, at the time telling his sisters that he has won the money gambling. The present abundance does not spring from that source, however; Henry and Albertine surmise in a private conversation that Julian's former lover, now the wife of a rich man, conspired with Julian to get this money out of her husband, Cy Warkins. Mrs. Warkins knew her husband was working on a land deal—swamp land that would eventually be sold to the railroad at a large profit—and arranged for Julian to buy some of that land first and sell it to Warkins, knowing how valuable it was to him. Also mentioned in this conversation between Henry and Albertine is the fact that Mrs. Warkins, unbeknownst to her husband, is Henry's cousin. Carrie overhears all of this and tells it to the simpleminded and emotionally unstable Lily, who is desperate to keep Julian, because she fears he may return to his former love. Lily phones Warkins and reveals not only his wife's financial betrayal but also the secret of her mixed race. Warkins sends thugs to beat and cut up, but not kill, Julian and Mrs. Warkins.

Meanwhile, Anna accuses Carrie of having always wanted to sleep with Julian. Carrie denies it, but it is Carrie who, perhaps motivated in part by jealousy, gives the private information she overhears to Lily—surely knowing, as Lily may not, that it will ruin some lives. Carrie gets what she wants: the return of the unsuccessful Julian, who belongs more certainly to her—to them—than he did when he was successful. LILLIAN HELLMAN, in a 1966 interview, said of the play: "[T]hree ladies loved one man just as long as he was unsuccessful. The minute he dared to do as they had always told him they wanted him to do—to strike out for himself—they all pounced on him to break him in some fashion" (Murray and Waldhorn 78).

BIBLIOGRAPHY

Murray, Robert, and Gary Waldhorn. "A Playwright Looks at the Theater Today." In *Conversations with Lillian Hellman,* edited by Jackson R. Bryer. Jackson: University Press of Mississippi, 1986. 73–83.

TREADWELL, SOPHIE (1885–1970) Sophie

Anita Treadwell was a playwright, journalist, novelist, and producer, and sometime actor and director. Born and raised in California, she began writing plays as a child and continued this pursuit at the University of California at Berkeley, from which she graduated in 1906. Treadwell hoped to be a performer, but her onstage career was limited to a brief stint in vaudeville and occasional dramatic roles, usually in her own works. In her early years as a reporter, she covered everything from theatrical premieres to baseball games for the *San Francisco Bulletin*. Treadwell soon became a respected journalist whose accomplishments included an "undercover" series on homeless women, an exclusive interview with Mexican revolutionary Pancho Villa, and a European tour as a war correspondent during World War I.

Among Treadwell's early works are *Gringo* (1922), based on her experiences in Mexico, and *O Nightin-Gale* (1925), a comedy about a stage-struck young woman. By far her greatest success was MACHINAL (1928), based on a sensational murder trial. Although most of Treadwell's plays are realistic, *Machinal* is written in the expressionist style (see EXPRESSIONISM), which features flat, symbolic characters as well as repetitive dialogue and action. It tells the story of a sensitive young woman who desperately tries to find happiness in a mechanized, male-dominated world.

Treadwell never had another success comparable to *Machinal,* although she continued writing for many years. Closest in theme and style to *Machinal* is *For Saxophone* (c. 1934), which relies heavily on music, dance, and the voices of unseen characters to tell the story of another young woman trapped in a marriage of convenience; *For Saxophone* was revised many times but never performed. Her works also include *Plumes in the Dust* (1936), based on the life of writer Edgar Allan Poe; *Rights* (c. 1921), an unproduced drama about 18th-century feminist Mary Wollstonecraft; and *Ladies Leave* (1929), a seriocomic look at a young woman's attempt to enliven her marriage by taking a lover. One of Treadwell's best plays, *Hope for a Harvest* (1941), exposes prejudice and environmental destruction in her native California. Embittered by the lukewarm reception of *Harvest,* Treadwell presented no more plays in New York.

Sophie Treadwell was an indefatigable traveler; her journeys throughout the world often inspired her plays, whose settings range from Moscow to Mexico.

She was also an active feminist who marched in favor of women's suffrage. The majority of her plays have female protagonists, and her most common subject is a woman's difficulty in achieving financial and personal independence without sacrificing love. In the course of her career, Treadwell wrote some 40 plays, including seven that appeared on New York stages. In addition, three dramatic works—*Machinal, Highway* (1944), and *Hope for a Harvest*—were adapted for television in the 1950s. Scholars have only recently begun to study her extensive collection of unpublished manuscripts, but her place in the American dramatic canon is already guaranteed by *Machinal,* one of the most important expressionist dramas written in the United States.

BIBLIOGRAPHY

Dickey, Jerry. *Sophie Treadwell: A Research and Production Sourcebook.* Westport, Conn.: Greenwood Press, 1997.

———, and Miriam López-Rodriguez, eds. *Broadway's Bravest Woman: Selected Writings of Sophie Treadwell.* Carbondale: Southern Illinois University Press, 2006.

Ozieblo, Barbara, and Jerry Dickey. *Susan Glaspell and Sophie Treadwell.* New York: Routledge, 2008.

Treadwell, Sophie. *Hope for a Harvest.* New York: Samuel French, 1942.

———. *Machinal.* London: Nick Hern Books, 1993.

Judith E. Barlow
State University of New York–Albany

TRIFLES Susan Glaspell (1916) Based on a murder case that Glaspell covered while a reporter for the *Des Moines Daily News, Trifles* subtly examines the differences between male and female perceptions and attitudes when a farm wife is accused of murdering her husband.

In the *"gloomy kitchen"* of an *"abandoned farmhouse,"* a pair of officials seek evidence against Mrs. Wright for the murder of her husband, who was found dead by his neighbor, Mr. Hale. Mr. and Mrs. Hale accompany to the crime scene the county attorney, the sheriff, and the sheriff's wife (who has come along to get some of Mrs. Wright's personal belongings for her). Mr. Hale recounts finding Mrs. Wright and her dead husband, a rope around his neck. The men are mystified as to what could have motivated Mrs. Wright, but the women notice small things—the unkept house, the chaotic stitching on an otherwise evenly sewn quilt—and believe these provide clues to her mental state and the state of her marriage. To the men, the state of the house is nothing more than evidence of poor housekeeping; they are amused that women worry over mere "trifles."

Mrs. Hale remembers Minnie Foster, before she became Mrs. Wright, as a "sweet and pretty" young woman with a good singing voice, and she remembers Mr. Wright as a "hard man," like "a raw wind that gets to the bone." She regrets that she "stayed away [from the Wrights' home] because it weren't cheerful." She thinks now she might have been a comfort to the isolated and childless Minnie.

The women find an empty birdcage with a broken hinge and then, enshrined in a sewing box, the bird—its neck "wrung." They surmise that Mr. Wright cruelly killed the one thing that gave his wife pleasure and that this was her motivation for breaking his neck with a rope as he slept. When the men, who have been searching the house and grounds, return to the kitchen, they condescend to the women and lament their own failure to find a motive with which to convince a jury of Minnie Wright's guilt. The women conceal the dead bird from their husbands and from the county attorney, perhaps saving Minnie from conviction.

Critics have found the economy of this one-act play masterful: "[J]ust as the women create their instinctive theories out of trifles, so the playwright builds her play out of small gestures (a broken hinge on a birdcage which reflects the broken neck of the bird, the broken neck of the man, but also the broken spirit of the woman, who had bought the cage). The man imprisons the woman, the woman imprisons the bird. And yet they are all imprisoned in a system equally implacable. . . . It is a play which works by understatement" (Bigsby 25–26). First produced by the Provincetown Players, *Trifles* is considered—along with the early plays of Eugene O'Neill—among the best that the group offered in its history.

BIBLIOGRAPHY

Bigsby, C. W. E. *A Critical Introduction to Twentieth Century American Drama: Volume One—1900–1940.* Cambridge, England: Cambridge University Press, 1982.

TRIP TO BOUNTIFUL, THE HORTON FOOTE

(1953) *The Trip to Bountiful* was first produced on television by NBC on March 1, 1953, on the *Goodyear Television Playhouse*. Within a year, the teleplay was staged at New York's Henry Miller's Theatre. Often staged over the following decades, *The Trip to Bountiful* was also released as a highly regarded film in 1985.

In all three versions, Carrie Watts, an aging woman with a heart condition, flees Houston, where she has been living with her struggling son Ludie and his gossipy, meddling wife Jessie Mae, to return to Bountiful, the town of her girlhood. On the bus she befriends a newlywed, Thelma. They share the young woman's happiness in marriage and Carrie's frustrated love for Ray John Murray. Although Ludie and Jessie Mae discover Carrie's flight before she reaches Bountiful, a local sheriff agrees to take her to the home place, now abandoned and decayed. Along the way, it is also revealed that Callie Davis, Carrie's childhood friend, has died, but Mrs. Watts takes courage from her reattachment to the land: "The fields. The trees. The smell of the Gulf. I always got my strength from that. Not from houses, not from people." When her son and daughter-in-law arrive, all three seek reconciliation, in the words of Ludie, to "stop this wrangling once and for all."

Carrie's trip to Bountiful is both sweet and painful. She overcomes physical and legal constraints, ill health, aging, and death, and she shares her life in a deep and moving way with Thelma. But she also must face a past of failed love, the deaths of two children, and a life of compromise. Typical of HORTON FOOTE's strongest characters, she learns to accept the mutability and loss in her history, but she also frees herself from the past, even as she embraces and clarifies it. In *The Trip to Bountiful*, Foote uses Ludie to explore the emotional trials faced by southern men as they moved from traditional small-town ways to the urbanization and corporate life of post–World War II America. Through Jessie Mae and her obsession with beauty parlors, Hollywood, and Coca-Colas, Foote warns of the superficialities in a new popular and material culture. In *Bountiful,* the playwright studies a willful narcissism that threatens love and the family.

BIBLIOGRAPHY
Moore, Barbara, and David G. Yellin, eds. *Horton Foote's Three Trips to Bountiful*. Dallas, Tex.: Southern Methodist University Press, 1993.

Gerald C. Wood
Carson–Newman College

TRUE WEST SAM SHEPARD (1980)

A dark comedy, *True West* is about two brothers who reunite in their mother's house and, in a period of excessive sibling rivalry, first attempt to assume each other's identities and finally engage in mortal combat. SHEPARD explores the concept of a human being's dual nature, and he also touches on ideas about family that he explores more deeply in earlier plays.

Austin, a screenwriter, is borrowing his mother's house in southern California (she is in Alaska) while he works on a movie deal. His brother, Lee, a shiftless, petty criminal who usually lives a drifter's existence in the desert, shows up looking for a way to take advantage. As the play begins, Austin, tidy and clean, is at his typewriter working on a script outline; Lee, filthy and disheveled, leans against the kitchen counter drinking beer. Lee has been casing their mother's neighborhood for possible robbery sites, and he is anxious to borrow his brother's car, which Austin reluctantly loans him in order to get him out of the house while he meets with Hollywood producer Saul Kimmer.

Saul has shown definite interest in Austin's movie idea when Lee returns, a stolen television in his arms, and begins relentlessly telling Saul about his own idea for a movie; Saul finally agrees to consider Lee's idea if Austin will write up an outline. Lee also manages to streamroll Saul—despite the older man's apparent reluctance—into agreeing to play golf with him the next day. Despite objecting to the "contrived" plot and "idiotic" characters in Lee's "Western," Austin writes the outline. Lee, in fact, holds Austin's car hostage until he does so. As the tension mounts between them, Lee points out that any policeman will say that family members "kill each other the most"; these turn out to be prophetic words.

The next day Lee comes back from his golf date. He is such an unlikely looking golfer that he has managed to hustle Saul, letting Saul get ahead "goin' into the back nine" in order to bet his movie deal on the outcome and win. He reports to his brother that part of the deal is that Austin will write Lee's screenplay and Austin's own idea will be dropped. Austin is outraged. When Saul comes by, he confirms that what Lee has said is true.

By the beginning of scene 7 of the nine-scene play, the brothers' roles are reversed. Lee is at the typewriter—albeit composing with little success and typing with one finger—while Austin watches and consumes liquor. Austin threatens to go out and steal, but Lee sneers that he couldn't even steal a toaster. As the next scene begins, we find the drunken brothers: Lee is smashing the typewriter with a golf club and burning his manuscript while Austin polishes the many toasters he has stolen. Empty bottles and cans are on the floor. Lee, in frustration with a telephone operator, rips the phone from the wall. Austin has decided he wants to go live in the desert with Lee. Lee makes another "deal": If Austin will write his screenplay exactly as Lee wants it and give Lee all the credit and all the money, then he'll take him back to the desert with him. Austin agrees.

In the final scene, amid the debris left from the night before, Austin writes longhand as Lee dictates. As they argue about a line, their mother walks in, having returned early from her vacation. Lee suddenly decides to leave, making Austin angry that he is reneging on his deal to take him to the desert. Austin wraps the phone cord around Lee's neck and keeps the pressure on, vigorously choking Lee, until Lee returns his car keys. He is reluctant to let go because Lee "will kill" him if he lets him loose. He asks his brother to let him have a head start; when he finally lets go, Lee is apparently dead. In fact, Lee is only pretending to be dead; catching his brother off guard, he leaps up and blocks his path. The sound of a coyote offstage reminds us of what Austin said earlier: Coyotes of southern California "lure innocent pets away from their homes" and kill them. We suspect that the domesticated Austin is doomed to die at the hands of the animalistic Lee.

At the beginning of Shepard's play, Austin is an educated, married man with children and a profes-

sion. Once in contact with the outlaw and in other ways outsider Lee, this identity begins to crumble. Lee's identity as outsider and menace is ultimately maintained because he cannot really become Austin without Austin's language skills. The play, then, is more about Austin's transformation than Lee's. Austin—seemingly well-adjusted, a societal insider, a professional, and a family man—has the other side of his dual nature exposed through contact with his fairly psychotic brother. Shepard has said of this play that he "wanted to write a play about double nature. . . . I just wanted to give a taste of what it feels like to be two-sided. . . . I think we're split in a much more devastating way than psychology can ever reveal. It's not so cute. Not some little thing we can get over. It's something we've got to live with" (Coe 56). He suggests that, like Austin, we all have another side to us, and it is not so far beneath the surface that circumstances cannot expose it.

Shepard also touches on a theme, often present in his plays, about sons becoming their fathers. When Austin is drunk, Lee tells him he sounds "just like the old man now." Austin replies, "Yeah, well, we all sound alike when we're sloshed. We just sort of echo each other." Austin is completely fed up with his alcoholic father, who lives in the desert; yet in the end, having consumed a great deal of alcohol, he wants only to go live in the desert himself.

Shepard creates a dysfunctional American family: the absent father, an alcoholic loner, lives in the desert; the mother returning early from an unsatisfactory trip to Alaska finds her changed sons in a trashed house and expresses only mild concern—saying *"calmly"* to Austin as he chokes Lee, "You're not killing him are you?"; Lee is a hustler and a drifter, an unstable alcoholic; and the one son who seems to have escaped cannot really escape the side of his nature that was indelibly marked by his family. This family of American grotesques is in keeping with others Shepard has created in CURSE OF THE STARVING CLASS (1977) and BURIED CHILD (1978), the other two plays in his trilogy about families doomed to repeat the past.

BIBLIOGRAPHY

Coe, Robert. "The Saga of Sam Shepard." *New York Times Magazine,* 23 November 1980, 56–58, 118, 120, 122, 124.

TRUTH, THE CLYDE FITCH (1907)

TRUTH, THE CLYDE FITCH (1907) This comedy of manners is considered to be the best of FITCH'S plays, many of which were very popular in their day. It concerns the trouble a young wife gets into by lying to her husband and her husband's willingness to forgive her imperfections because of their love for each other.

Becky Warder tells "fibs," "white lies," which, she is sure, do no harm. As another character says of her, if she takes the "ferry to Jersey City," she claims she has "been abroad." Her trouble begins when she tells her friend, Eve Lindon, and her own husband, Tom Warder, that she has not seen Eve's estranged husband lately; in fact, she has been seeing Fred Lindon daily for some time. She is caught in this lie because Eve is having her husband followed by a detective. Eve reveals Becky's duplicity to Becky's husband, Tom, who refuses to believe Eve and finds her tactics distasteful: He sees her as "one of those dangerous 'well-meaning' persons who do more harm than the people who are purposely malicious." Despite Becky's habitual lying, Fitch creates in her a far more sympathetic character than in the spying and tactless Eve Lindon, even though Eve is truthful while Becky is not. Tom Warder is a decent, mild-mannered, affectionate man, who loves and trusts his wife. Eventually, though, the evidence thrust before him is too convincing to ignore, and he must acknowledge that his wife has lied to him. In fact, she has lied so often that he cannot believe the truth, which is that she has no romantic interest whatever in Fred Lindon and has merely been hoping to effect a reconciliation between the Lindons. Matters become murkier still because Fred has been interpreting the flirtatious Becky's interest as romantic—as indeed is his interest in her.

In a subplot, Becky's father, Mr. Roland, a gambler, a moocher, and a liar himself, is involved in a comic relationship with his landlady, who finances his gambling and fancies he will marry her. Much of the humor in their scenes is derived from Mrs. Crespigny's working-class way of speaking and acting, even as she has pretensions of being of the upper class. The play culminates in the shabby rented rooms of Becky's father, where the heartbroken Becky has fled after Tom decides they must separate. When Roland's freedom from conventional restraints is jeopardized by the invasion of a daughter, he sends word to Tom that Becky is dying, implying she has attempted suicide. Roland enlists Becky's participation in this charade, but when Tom arrives, she cannot go through with deceiving him. Tom is so impressed by her truthfulness, he forgives all, declaring, "We don't love people because they are perfect. . . . [but] because they are themselves."

The Truth is remembered for its vivid depiction, through dialogue more than action, of real people. Fitch portrayed in this play the characters' complicated motives with apparent simplicity, which gave the play greater realism. It was received more enthusiastically in Europe than in New York, where melodrama was in vogue at the time.

TWO TRAINS RUNNING AUGUST WILSON (1990)

TWO TRAINS RUNNING AUGUST WILSON (1990) Set in 1969 in a Pittsburgh diner, *Two Trains Running* is one of WILSON's cycle of 10 plays, each set in a different decade of the 20th century and depicting the African-American experience. Wilson looks at a time in history when African Americans began to take action, on an individual level as well as collectively, against inequality and injustice.

The diner is owned by Memphis, characterized by his logic, honesty, and strong work ethic. We learn that in 1931 Memphis was run off his land by the white man who sold it to him; the man, Stovall, only sold it because he thought it had no water. When Memphis dug a deep well and found water, Stovall claimed the deed was "null and void," set fire to his crops, and killed his beloved mule. Memphis still has the deed to his land, and some day he wants to go and get back his land and kill Stovall if he can. Memphis bought the diner years ago so that he could stop carrying a gun. He saw it as a "way to live out the rest of his life." Now, the city is buying up a 12-block area and tearing down everything. They want to give him less than the property and business are worth, but he maintains he will not take less than $25,000. Others who could afford insurance are setting fires and collecting the insurance money, which far exceeds what the city will pay, but Memphis has never carried insurance because it is too expensive.

Holloway is a daily customer in the diner, which used to do a lively business but is now nearly empty because the surrounding area has become an urban wasteland. Holloway is as superstitious as Memphis is impatient with superstition. He firmly believes that a visit to "Aunt Ester," who is "three hundred and twenty-two years old," will "straighten" anything out. Aunt Ester requires her followers to throw $20 in the river; if they do not, their problems will remain (Aunt Ester is a character that Wilson revisits in KING HEDLEY II [2001], where, Wilson has said, she represents the connection to the past, to the history of black people in America starting with the Middle Passage; she is also in GEM OF THE OCEAN [2003], set in the century's first decade, where she appears onstage; and her house is a powerful symbol in RADIO GOLF [2005], set in 1997 after her death). Besides a firm *"belief in the supernatural,"* the other important aspect of Holloway's character is his *"outrage at injustice."*

Another of the diner's regular visitors is Wolf, a numbers runner. Memphis gets angry when Wolf receives calls there. He does not want the police to raid his place of business, but he plays the numbers himself. They all feel it is the only kind of investment plan available to them. In fact, it wasn't until Memphis hit a number "eight or nine years ago" that he "got to the point where [he] could change [his] clothes every day."

Across the street from the diner is a funeral home, owned and run by West. During most of the play, West is holding a wake and funeral for Prophet Samuel, a charlatan preacher whose many followers made him a wealthy man. West complains that the people lined up around the block to see him in his open casket will not stop rubbing the head of the corpse for "good luck." West is even wealthier than Prophet Samuel because, according to the gossip in the diner, he is not above such practices as reselling coffins and burial suits; furthermore, as Holloway points out, "More people dying than getting saved." The one thing that the people in this depressed neighborhood *can* control is the send-off they give a loved one; therefore, funerals are elaborate, and business for West is steady.

Also across the street is Lutz's butcher shop. Lutz, a white man, hired a black man to paint his fence nine

and a half years before. He said if the job was good he would pay him with a ham. When the job was finished, it was not deemed good enough for the ham. The painter, a mentally unstable man now known as Hambone, visits Lutz every day to demand his ham. Indeed, he says only two lines, and these he repeats during every appearance on stage: "He gonna give me my ham" and "I want my ham." Hambone's insistence on getting the ham he is owed comes to represent the ideal of never settling for just what "the white man throws at you."

The waitress in Memphis's place is Risa, an otherwise attractive woman whose numerous and ugly scars on her legs come from a self-inflicted *"attempt to define herself in terms other than her genitalia."* Despite this, Risa has received much attention from men, which she has resisted; with the arrival of Sterling, a simpleminded young man who was a friend of her brother's when she was still a girl at home, she begins gradually to relent. Sterling has just been released from prison, where he was sent for a bank robbery (the money from which he began to spend "ten minutes later"); Memphis is sure he will be dead or back in prison within "two weeks." Sterling is hoping his luck will improve: He joins the line across the street so that he can rub Prophet Samuel's head, and he visits Aunt Ester. He plays a number Risa gives him and wins, but the white men behind the numbers racket decide to halve the winnings because too many people picked the winning number. Memphis disapproves of Sterling's superstition and of his interest in attending a Black Power rally; Memphis believes what Sterling *needs* to do is to work hard, as Memphis has done. (Sterling is an important character in *Radio Golf.*)

Despite Memphis's ridicule of others for their superstitious behavior, he decides to go see Aunt Ester when the government persists in offering him only $15,000. After seeing her, he and his new lawyer go to court, and he is told he will get $35,000. When he returns to the diner, a little drunk and very happy, he tells his companions about his victory and about his plan. Aunt Ester told him—not "in them words but that's what she meant"—"If you drop the ball, you got to go back and pick it up." Memphis decides to go back to Mississippi and settle the dispute over his land with Stovall—or Stovall's son—once and for all: "I'm going back to Jackson. . . . and pick up the ball." If Aunt Ester is seen as the symbol of the connection to the past, as Wilson has explained, then Memphis's visit to her seems less glaringly out of character.

News comes that Hambone has died in his bed. Memphis asks Risa to get some flowers and to say that they are from "everybody who ever dropped the ball and went back to pick it up." The play ends when Sterling, having broken into Lutz's shop, brings in a ham and gives it to West to be buried with Hambone—finally taking, in Hambone's place, what the latter is owed by the white man after all these years. The play captures the mood of the late 1960s when many African Americans, fed up with the persistent injustice they faced, began to take action.

TYLER, ROYALL (1757–1826)   Born in Boston before the American Revolution, Tyler was not a professional writer, but a lawyer. He graduated from Harvard in 1776 and studied law in Cambridge, Massachusetts. After his military service during the American Revolution, Tyler practiced law first in Maine and then in Boston, during which time he courted, but did not marry, the daughter of John and Abigail Adams. In 1787, Tyler, holding the rank of major, took part in the suppression of Shays's Rebellion. It was on official business consequent to Shays's Rebellion that Tyler went to New York in 1787. Five weeks after his arrival there, he had written and seen staged his comedy, *The CONTRAST;* about a month later, his comic opera *May Day in Town* was produced. Despite his overnight theatrical success in New York, Tyler returned to Boston and the practice of law. During this period, he was a boarder in the home of Mr. and Mrs. Joseph Pearse Palmer, whose daughter, Mary, he later married. In 1790, he moved to Vermont, where he eventually became chief justice of that state's supreme court, as well as a law professor at the University of Vermont. He died in Vermont in 1826.

His play, *The Contrast,* was the first American comedy to be professionally produced. Though sometimes criticized as merely imitative of the English comedy of manners, Tyler's play is significant for its introduction of Jonathan, the Yankee character—the honest, country bumpkin—who became a standard in American drama for the next 50 years. Though he is best remembered for *The Contrast,* Tyler wrote other plays—not all of them produced—as well as essays, poetry, a novel, and his comic opera.

BIBLIOGRAPHY
Tanselle, G. Thomas. *Royall Tyler.* Cambridge, Mass.: Harvard University Press, 1967.

U

UHRY, ALFRED (1936–)

Playwright, lyricist, and educator, Alfred Uhry was born in Atlanta, Georgia, and graduated from Brown University in 1958. He taught high school English and drama for 18 years in New York City until 1980 and later taught at New York University.

Uhry's best known play is DRIVING MISS DAISY (1987), for which he won the PULITZER PRIZE. Miss Daisy Werthan, an aging, well-to-do, southern, Jewish widow is forced by her son to employ a chauffeur when she can no longer safely drive herself. Thus begins a 25-year relationship between Miss Daisy and Hoke Coleburn, her African-American chauffeur. In the affectionate portrayal of these two determined individuals, Uhry subtly deals with the issues of racial and religious bigotry, aging, and human rights.

Uhry's next play also met with great success. *The* LAST NIGHT OF BALLYHOO (1997), set in a Jewish community in the South, won the TONY AWARD. Set in 1939, as Adolf Hitler marched on Poland and the film *Gone with the Wind* premiered in Atlanta, the play deals with pre–World War II anti-Semitism among assimilated, upper-middle-class Jews against those who practiced traditional Judaism. The action centers around a formal dance at the end of a festival called Ballyhoo.

Alfred Uhry has collaborated on several musicals. The most successful of these were *The Robber Bridegroom* (1974), adapted from a Eudora Welty novella, with music by Robert Waldman and book and lyrics by Uhry; and *Parade* (1999), for which he won a Tony Award for best book (*Parade*'s music and lyrics are by Jason Robert Brown). More recently, Uhry wrote the book for *LoveMusic* (2007), a musical about Kurt Weill and his wife and professional partner; Lotte Lenya, with music by Kurt Weill.

Uhry's most recent nonmusical play, *Edgardo Mine* (2006), is set in 1858 in Italy. It is based on a true story about a six-year-old Jew taken from his parents by the Catholic Church because a Catholic servant had secretly baptized the child; the boy is adopted by the pope and raised to become a priest. The play raises questions about both identity and freedom of religion.

BIBLIOGRAPHY
Uhry, Alfred. *Driving Miss Daisy.* New York: Theatre Communications Group, 1988.
———. *The Last Night of Ballyhoo.* New York: Theatre Communications Group, 1997.

UNDER THE GASLIGHT; OR, LIFE AND LOVE IN THESE TIMES AUGUSTIN DALY (1867)

Under the Gaslight received poor reviews when it was first produced, but audiences loved this sensational melodrama. The play contains scenes reminiscent of many popular plays from the 1840s and 1850s about life in New York among the lower classes; unlike these plays, performed only for the classes they portrayed, *Under the Gaslight*, with its depiction of young women of different classes who had been switched in their cradles, also appealed to middle-class audiences.

The pleasant upper-class existence of "cousins" Laura and Pearl Courtland and Laura's fiancé, Ray Trafford, is shattered by the intrusion of a drunken blackmailer, Byke, from whom Pearl's parents, it is revealed, rescued a six-year-old Laura—then a pickpocket—many years before. Ray at first thinks to desert Laura and writes her a letter to that effect; he promptly decides against it, but he fails to destroy the letter, which falls into the hands of a society matron who spreads the news and leads her class in shunning Laura.

Laura moves to a basement apartment and earns money by painting color onto the photographs of the rich. The plot thickens as the villains, Byke and his wife Judas, plan to blackmail the Courtlands and the Traffords with the real secret of the girls' births. This secret is revealed at the end of the play, but it is hinted at earlier: Laura and Pearl were switched in their cribs by a villainous nurse. The little girl adopted by the Courtlands was actually their own daughter, and Pearl is the unwitting impostor, not Laura.

Among the interesting details in DALY's play is a statement made by Snorkey, a Civil War veteran and amputee (the war, of course, had ended just two years before the play was produced): When Laura Courtland, the wronged but always kind heroine, rescues Snorkey just in the nick of time from the railroad tracks—to which he has been tied by the villain Byke—a grateful Snorkey exclaims in disbelief, "And these are the women who ain't to have a vote!" Daly's character makes the remark 53 years before women's suffrage. Snorkey also makes many references to what he and others sacrificed for the country during the Civil War; Snorkey speaks of giving his arm, leaving him since the war with an "empty sleeve," and he remembers his friend "hit by a shell, and knocked into so many pieces [he] didn't know which to call [his] old friend." Drama historian ARTHUR HOBSON QUINN observes that Daly used this character to criticize the United States government's failure to take care of its wounded veterans (12).

Daly depicts many of the harsh realities of the poor. In act 2, there is a scene in a police station through which many of the poor of New York pass, bullied by the justice system. The same police court awards the villain Byke custody of the 19-year-old Laura, whom he falsely claims is his daughter. The homeless veteran, Snorkey, finds a home with other poverty-stricken New Yorkers in a hole under a pier.

In the end, the upper-class girls—she that is one by birth and she that is one by rearing only—find happiness in the upper class. Daly's play seems to suggest that birth is important since Laura, the most genteel of the characters, turns out to be indeed a daughter of the upper class; this would have been reassuring to Daly's middle-class audience. However, he also seems to suggest that character comes from within, not from the external trappings of property and money, a very American ideal.

BIBLIOGRAPHY

Quinn, Arthur Hobson. *A History of the American Drama: From the Civil War to the Present Day.* Rev. ed. 1936. New York: Appleton-Century-Crofts, 1955.

V

VALDÉZ, LUIS (1940–) Luis Valdéz was born in Delano, California, a location that figures prominently in his early theatrical work. His parents were migrant farm workers, and their experiences helped shape the political themes of his early work, which would eventually make him the most recognized Chicano playwright. While attending San Jose State College, he had his first full-length play produced: *The Shrunken Head of Pancho Villa* (1964), a five-act piece that charts questions of assimilation and the economic survival of a Chicano family. After a brief stint with the San Francisco Mime Troupe upon graduation, Valdéz returned to Delano where, in 1965, he helped found El Teatro Campesino (The Farmworker's Theater). This group worked the picket lines of the grape strikes and, with the workers themselves, began performing *actos*—collaboratively produced, short, hyper-stylized, and broadly comedic political sketches with a social vision. These *actos* included *Quinta Temporada* (1966), about the importance of unions, and *Las Dos Caras del Patroncito* (1965), about the two-faced natures of the growers.

After a few years of working with the Farm Workers Organizing Committee, Valdéz and El Teatro decided to broaden the artistic scope of the troupe to deal with other social issues facing Chicanos, including Vietnam (*Vietnam Campesino* [1970] and *Soldado Razo* [1971]), problems with the educational system (*No Saco Nada de la Escuela* [1969]), cultural and political roles (*Los Vendidos* [1967], *Las Huelgistas* [1970], and *The Militants*

[1969]), and other political pieces (*La Conquista de México* [1968]). *Los Vendidos,* the most often anthologized of the *actos,* satirically presents a series of stereotypes to expose the cultural expectations placed on Chicanos. The highly collaborative nature of the *actos* allowed participants to bring their own cultural performance experience into the creative mix; they were designed to be by Chicanos, for Chicanos, and about Chicanos, and were presented in a *mestizaje,* a mixture of English, Spanish, and Caló—a dialect that blends linguistic elements of English and Spanish. Around this time, Valdéz also began work on a new form of drama, the *mito,* which shows "the Chicano through the eyes of God." Examples of the *mito* include *The Dark Root of a Scream* (1967), which explores the psychological experiences of a Chicano soldier in Vietnam, and *Bernabé* (1970), which explores the Chicano's relationship to the land through myth and archetype. Other forms Valdéz worked with include the *corrido,* based on traditional ballads. Valdéz's more recent work centers on issue of masculinity and criminality within the Chicano community.

ZOOT SUIT (1978) explores the *pachuco,* a controversial figure of Chicano culture, through an historical account of the Sleepy Lagoon murder trial in Los Angeles during World War II. The first Chicano play produced on Broadway, *Zoot Suit* marks a transition into professionalized Chicano theater. *I Don't Have to Show You No Stinking Badges!* (1986) charts the return home of Sonny Villa, a Harvard undergraduate and the son of bit-part actors, disturbed by his distance from reality. The entire play is framed as a situation comedy and addresses the realities of middle-class Chicano life. *Bandido!* (1982) explores the genre of melodrama in its account of the life of Tiburcio Vasquez, a historical *bandido* figure also considered to be a potential revolutionary. *Mummified Deer* (2000), set in 1969, was inspired by an article about a 60-year-old mummified fetus and centers on family matriarch Mama Chu and the unraveling of family secrets influenced by Valdéz's own Yaqui heritage. *Earthquake Sun* (2004) is a combination of science fiction and Mayan history, combining myth and virtual reality to explore issues of genetics and lineage.

Corridos!! (2006) expanded and updated the original *Corridos* as a retelling of immigrant tales in song and drama. With El Teatro Campesino, Valdez continues to produce *La Virgen del Tepeyac* and *La Pastorela* during alternating years in San Juan Bautista, and there have been several recent revivals of earlier works, continuing the engaged political and cultural traditions of his work.

BIBLIOGRAPHY

Elam, Harry J., Jr. *Taking It to the Streets: The Social Protest Theater of Amiri Baraka and Luis Valdéz.* Ann Arbor: University of Michigan Press, 1997.

Rossini, Jon D. *Contemporary Latina/o Theater: Wrighting Ethnicity.* Carbondale: Southern Illinois University Press, 2008.

Valdéz, Luis. *Luis Valdéz—Early Works: Actos, Bernabé and Pensamiento Serpentino.* Houston, Tex.: Arte Público Press, 1990.

———. *"Mummified Deer" and Other Plays.* Houston, Tex.: Arte Público Press, 2005.

———. *"Zoot Suit" and Other Plays.* Houston, Tex.: Arte Público Press, 1992.

Jon D. Rossini
University of California—Davis

VAN DRUTEN, JOHN (WILLIAM) (1901–1957)

John van Druten was born in London, England, to a Dutch banker and a Londoner of Dutch parentage. Although he was attracted early to a career in writing, his father insisted on a practical profession. He chose the law, receiving an LL.B. from the University of London in 1923, and later became a special lecturer at the University College of Wales from 1923 to 1926. All the while, though, he persevered in writing; his second play, *Young Woodley* (1925), which established him as a professional playwright, was brought to New York, where it had a successful Broadway run in 1925. Banned by a British censor on the grounds that it disparaged the English public school system, *Young Woodley* was not produced in London until 1928. Van Druten turned this play into his first novel, under the same title, in 1929, and then wrote the screenplay for the 1930 film adaptation. Following this success, he embarked on a lecture tour of the United States and was to make many more visits there before settling in California. He became a naturalized United States citizen in 1944.

John van Druten was a prolific and effective writer of light comedies of manners. With *The Voice of the Turtle* (1943), a romantic comedy set in New York City about a worldly, down-to-earth soldier on leave and his fast-blooming weekend love affair with a young, breathless, somewhat naive actress, he had a major critical and popular success. Here his ability to write charmingly and straightforwardly about his characters brought a singularly genuine quality to what could easily have been a contrived and unbelievable situation. We are made to care for these people because they are real.

That van Druten possessed the inclination and ability to look at all humanity with understanding served him well in *I Remember Mama* (1944), which was based on stories by Kathryn Forbes about a Norwegian-American family. This play, about simple people, caught the depth and humor of their lives in a direct and touching way. It was a hit. He continued to write successful plays through the 1940s and remained in top form when he produced the popular comic fantasy *Bell, Book and Candle* (1950) and a skillful and moving dramatization of Christopher Isherwood's *Berlin Stories*, entitled *I Am a Camera* (1951). In it, he was able to capture the disorientation of rootless people. Each of the many characters was sharply etched, particularly the mercurial central figure of Sally Bowles. *I Am a Camera* received the New York Drama Critics' Circle Award for Best Play in 1952. It was later adapted as the enormously successful musical *Cabaret* (1966).

After *Young Woodley,* van Druten wrote three more novels, but none of them added much to his stature. His Hollywood career included the scenarios for *Night Must Fall* (1937), a thriller based on a play by Emlyn Williams, *Parnell* (1937), *Raffles* (1939), *Johnny Come Lately* (1943), and (with others) *Gaslight* (1944). A number of his own plays were also filmed. Van Druten directed most of his later work for the stage, as well as the classic Richard Rodgers and Oscar Hammerstein musical *The King and I* (1950). In his last years, he devoted himself to the study of religion, which he described in a final volume of reminiscence, *The Widening Circle* (1957).

BIBLIOGRAPHY

Van Druten, John. *Bell, Book and Candle.* New York: Dramatists Play Service, 1951.

———. *I Am a Camera.* 1951. Westport, Conn.: Greenwood Publishing Group, 1971.

———. *I Remember Mama.* 1945. New York: Dramatists Play Service, 1998.

———. *The Playwright at Work.* New York: Harper, 1953.

———. *The Voice of the Turtle.* 1945. New York: Dramatists Play Service, 1998.

———. *The Widening Circle.* New York: Scribners, 1957.

Philip M. Isaacs
New York, New York

VAN ITALLIE, JEAN-CLAUDE (1936–)

With a legacy of approximately 33 plays and eight adaptations that have been presented in experimental and repertory theaters worldwide, Jean-Claude van Itallie has expanded the range of dramatic structure. Born in Brussels, Belgium, van Itallie, his aunt, and his parents fled to the United States when the Nazis entered Brussels in 1940. After a brief sojourn in Forest Hills, New York, the family finally settled in Great Neck, Long Island. In 1958, van Itallie graduated from Harvard University, where he majored in the history and literature of Russia, France, and England. While at Harvard, he wrote his first one-act play, *Hotel: Restricted* (1955), acted in several productions, directed several others, and wrote two three-act plays, *Chet Wilde* (1957) and *Being Born of Earth* (1958).

War (1963), van Itallie's first major play to be produced, premiered at the Barr-Albee-Wilder Playwrights Unit of OFF-BROADWAY's Vandam Theatre. *War* is van Itallie's most autobiographical play. The father-son conflict, represented by the "war" between the Elder Actor and his younger counterpart, is interrupted only temporarily by the Lady, van Itallie's idyllic conception of his mother, who strolls through the park in Brussels with her parasol.

In September 1963, van Itallie was introduced to director Joseph Chaikin, the founder of the Open Theater, an experimental theater group. Chaikin, who was experimenting with improvised acting exercises, asked van Itallie to turn some of the improvisations into plays. This began a decades-long collaboration between van Itallie and Chaikin—one that was to initiate some of the most innovative experiments of the OFF-OFF-BROADWAY theater. During 10 days in July 1964, van Itallie wrote *The Hunter and the Bird,* which continued the Open Theater's experiments with the concept of the Fool, who, in this play, is depicted as the Bird, and the two "Doris plays"—*Almost Like Being* and *I'm Really Here,* which represent van Itallie's concern about the influence of the media on our daily lives. Both *Almost like Being* and *I'm Really Here* are one-act satires on the ersatz quality of the Doris Day movies of the late 1950s and 1960s.

AMERICA HURRAH, which consists of three plays—*TV, Interview,* and *Motel*—opened Off-Broadway in 1966. *TV* deals with the concept of media control over our social perceptions; *Interview* presents images of humanity's alienation and isolation; and *Motel* tries to shock and surprise bourgeois audiences, much like French dramatic theorist Antonin Artaud's Theatre of Cruelty. In 1967, *America Hurrah* won the Outer Critics Circle Award. Van Itallie's other major success of the 1960s was The SERPENT, which premiered at Rome's Teatro delle Arti in May of 1968. During the next three months, the Open Theater performed the play all over Europe. After its initial performances in the United States, the Open Theater won the Off-Broadway OBIE AWARD in 1969, for its production of the play.

During the 1960s, van Itallie also experimented with dramatic form on his own while he was working closely with the Open Theater. *Dream*, written in 1965 and revised in 1966 as *Where Is de Queen?*, was the first of these one-act experimental dramas. Written as a dream's random juxtaposition of images, it is concerned with the quest for the security of childhood (an idyllic world, represented by Queen Victoria), which has been lost in the brutal realities of contemporary society. Other experimental one-act plays of the period between 1965 and 1971 included *The Girl and the Soldier* (1965), *Thoughts on the Instant of Greeting a Friend in the Street* (1967), *Take a Deep Breath* (1968), *Photographs: Mary and Howard* (1969), and *Eat Cake* (1971).

In *The King of the United States* (1972)—later revised as *Mystery Play* (1973)—the performers create an image of a king's face that is a photographic composite of the cast members. Throughout the play, each piece of the composite puzzle is flown into place until the king's image is finally revealed to be representative of our collective consciousness. The play depicts American society as one based upon image rather than spiritual substance.

In 1975, van Itallie and Chaikin created the idea for a new play, *A Fable*. Inspired by Joseph Campbell's *The Mythic Image* and written in a poetic form much like the plays of T. S. Eliot, *A Fable* concerns a mythical quest to kill the Beast. The Journeyor ultimately realizes that the Beast is within; to terminate the eternal quest, we must transcend the Beast within ourselves. Meanwhile, in the early 1970s, van Itallie had become a practicing Buddhist. *Naropa*, written in 1977 (and not yet produced), is based upon Tibetan texts. The play depicts a quest to unlock the secrets of the soul; as was true in *A Fable*, van Itallie indicates that the Beast lies within ourselves.

Bag Lady (1979) is a one-woman monologue that van Itallie originally wrote as a television project. Throughout the play, Clara, the bag lady, rambles on incessantly as she observes life in New York City and becomes a seer with a unique ability to perceive and intuitively understand the consumerism that is destroying modern society. When *Bag Lady* was revived during the "Early Warnings" program at the Manhattan Theatre Club in 1983, van Itallie wrote two new plays for the occasion: *Sunset Freeway* and

Final Orders. *Sunset Freeway* is a long monologue delivered by former waitress and aspiring actress Judy Jensen, who is careening down Los Angeles's freeways en route to a 6:30 P.M. audition that could mean her big break into show business. As she zooms in and out of rush-hour traffic, Judy merges with the radio and billboard advertisements that inundate her consciousness. The play warns us about the dangerous decline of imagination at the hands of external voices from the electronic age. In *Final Orders*, two military men monitor a U.S. nuclear weapons system triggered by a computer. The play examines how individual will can be subsumed by a more powerful external voice, potentially leading to an apocalyptic nightmare.

In 1982, van Itallie completed *The Tibetan Book of the Dead, or How Not to Do It Again*, an adaptation of the Bardo Thödol, a sacred text of Buddhism. The play, which opened at the La MaMa Experimental Theatre Club Annex in 1983, explores the intermediate period of 49 days from one's death to rebirth, known as the Bardo, in which the dead person must make difficult choices at each stage of the journey. *Paradise Ghetto* (1983), van Itallie's most ambitious drama, with 27 scenes in two acts, is set in the Nazi detention camp at Theresienstadt, where Czechoslovakian artists and wealthy German Jews survived by performing cabaret sketches. It is a poignant drama that raises questions about God's role in the Holocaust, about the responsibilities of the artist, and about the limits of collaborating with an unjust government.

The Traveller (1987), based on Joseph Chaikin's similar experience, traces the long recovery process for a successful composer (the Traveller) who undergoes open-heart surgery and then suffers from aphasia. While living in Santa Monica during rehearsals for the Los Angeles production of *The Traveller*, van Itallie wrote *Struck Dumb* (1988), a one-act monologue that the recovering aphasiac Chaikin could perform while touring with SAM SHEPARD's *The War in Heaven* to make a full evening's entertainment. *Struck Dumb* traces one day in the life of Adnan, an aphasiac recovering from a stroke.

The 1990s began with *Ancient Boys* (1990), a one-act play, which consists essentially of flashbacks of the life of AIDS-afflicted Reuben, who, after his suicide, is remembered by his friends. In the early 1990s, van Itallie adapted Russian dramatist Mikhail Bulgakov's *Master i Margarita,* which was produced in New York in 1993. His adaptations of Anton Chekhov's major plays were published as a collection in 1995. Also in the 1990s, he wrote and published a playwriting textbook, *The Playwright's Workbook* (1997), and published his adaptation, *The Tibetan Book of the Dead for Reading Aloud* (1998).

In May 1998, van Itallie opened his one-person autobiographical show, *War, Sex, and Dreams,* in Shelburne Falls, Massachusetts, and has since performed the play in Santa Monica, California, and at La MaMa Experimental Theatre Club in New York City. In 2002, he received the New England Theatre Conference Award for Oustanding Achievement in American Theatre. Van Itallie's *Light* (2004) had its world premiere in Pasadena, California, at the Theatre at Boston Court. The play portrays a witty love triangle among a king, a beautiful scientist marquise, and Voltaire during the Age of Enlightenment. His latest play, *Fear Itself, Secrets of the White House* (2005), premiered in New York and depicts how a cruelly dysfunctional U.S. president's family leads to an inept national policy that results in war. Van Itallie has also kept busy running Shantigar, an educational foundation that brings theater artists, meditation masters, and healers together through workshops that are taught on his farm in western Massachusetts.

BIBLIOGRAPHY

Blumenthal, Eileen. *Joseph Chaikin: Exploring at the Boundaries of Theater.* Cambridge, England: Cambridge University Press, 1984.
Plunka, Gene A. *Jean-Claude van Itallie and the Off-Broadway Theater.* Newark: University of Delaware Press, 1999.
Van Itallie, Jean-Claude. *"America Hurrah" and Other Plays.* New York: Grove Press, 2001.
———. *Chekhov: The Major Plays.* New York: Applause Theatre Books, 1995.
———. *Early Warnings.* New York: Dramatists Play Service, 1983.
———. *The King of the United States.* New York: Dramatists Play Service, 1975.
———. *Mikhail Bulgakov's "Master i Margarita."* New York: Dramatists Play Service, 1994.
———. *Seven Short and Very Short Plays.* New York: Dramatists Play Service, 1967.
———. *"War" and Four Other Plays.* New York: Dramatists Play Service, 1967.

Gene A. Plunka
University of Memphis

VIET ROCK Megan Terry (1966)   In creating one of the earliest "rock musicals," Terry used her own and Joseph Chaikin's "transformational theatre" techniques to make *Viet Rock: A Folk War Movie* (1966) demonstrate the self's "multiple and shifting" personas (Schlueter 61) and the "warring world [as] bereft of stability" (Cohn 290).

The jolting song "The Viet Rock" opens the show: "When the bombs fall / The Viets rock and rock. / When the napalm burns / Then the Viets roll." Soon a *"circle of bodies"* on the stage bursts into improvised *"humming or gurgling,"* and a series of *"joyous, aggressive"* childlike noises evoke human beings' primitive *"imaginative striving to succeed in a frightening situation."* Next, male performers begin to enact the roles of infants, with the women playing their mothers, but their moments of nurturing end abruptly when a Sergeant shouts "Ten-hut!" and declares all the boys ready for the battlefield.

The next scene depicts the Sergeant harassing the recruits. He mocks the very idea of war protesters and also corrects the error that landed his group, albeit only briefly, in dovish Shangri-La instead of in hawkish Vietnam. A major transformation, with a transitional "frug," or polka, acting as link, next turns all the actors into "senators and witnesses" at a military policy investigation in Washington, D.C. Among those who speak are a relatively pacifist *"grand old American Woman Statesman,"* a rhymester "prize fighter," *"a curly-headed writer"* scornful of the media and prophetic of "the fire next time!," the silent Madonna, and a *"serene-faced, beautiful man,"* preaching love. This latter fellow is shouted down by a *"vigorous, contemporary patriot,"* citing past American wars as evidence to defend the concept "Kill for freedom!"

In act 2's opening minutes, stateside mothers and girlfriends yearn for their menfolk, while the Sergeant, off in Vietnam, tries to enforce a fighting mentality among an often oafish, generally lethargic platoon. An American mother is invited to Vietnam to console her dying son, a boy now maimed beyond recognition; then, the same actress, immediately afterward, transforms herself into the Buddhist mother of a dead Vietnamese guerrilla.

Similarly quick theatrical transformations and contrasts dominate Terry's play until its final curtain. A generalized lament against war is at one point aroused among all the females onstage, but it is also simultaneously made ironic by one female's, Hanoi Hannah's, propagandistic berating of the American battle squadrons. Likewise, it seems that nightclub entertainer Saigon Sally summarizes the play's mood with her tune "Antihero baby." Not long afterward, Terry provides alternative endings to the piece: In one, American soldiers deride Lyndon Baines Johnson, their commander-in-chief, and in the other, by contrast, Viet Cong soldiers express deep scorn for the American fighting boys themselves.

BIBLIOGRAPHY

Cohn, Ruby. "Camp, Cruelty, Colloquialism." In *Comic Relief: Humor in Contemporary American Literature,* edited by Sarah Blacher Cohen. Urbana: University of Illinois Press, 1978. 288–289.

Schlueter, June. *"Keep Tightly Closed in a Cool Dry Place:* Megan Terry's Transformational Drama and the Possibilities of Self." *Studies in American Drama 1945–Present* 2 (1987): 59–69.

Jeffrey B. Loomis
Northwest Missouri State University

VIEW FROM THE BRIDGE, A ARTHUR MILLER (1955)

Set in a section of Brooklyn underneath the Brooklyn Bridge, A View from the Bridge is the story of a man's self-destructive, obsessive love for his niece.

Eddie Carbone is a longshoreman who lives with his wife, his two young children (always offstage), and his wife's 17-year-old niece, Catherine. Eddie is protective of Catherine and becomes increasingly resentful of attention paid to her by other men. When his wife's Italian cousins enter the country illegally in order to work on the docks, they stay with the Carbones. Their arrival brings with it tension, since the younger, unmarried cousin, Rodolpho, is as attracted to Catherine as she is to him. Eddie distrusts Rodolpho and is unnaturally jealous of his romance with Catherine. Seeking the advice of a lawyer, Alfieri, Eddie hopes to stop a marriage on legal grounds; he suggests to the lawyer that Rodolpho is only interested in gaining American citizenship and implies that Rodolpho—who sings well and can sew and cook—is homosexual. Alfieri understands that Eddie has "too much love for [his] niece" and advises him to "[l]et her go." Alfieri knows even then "where [Eddie] is going to end."

Alfieri narrates and comments on Eddie's actions and behavior; like the chorus in a Greek tragedy (his speeches are in verse), he also reflects the morals of the society. The second time Eddie consults Alfieri in search of legal advice, Alfieri counsels him to give up his "unnatural" love or suffer the inevitable consequences: "The law is nature. / The law is only a word for what has a right to happen. / When the law is wrong it's because it's unnatural, / But in this case it is natural, / And a river will drown you / If you buck it now. Let her go. And bless her."

Eddie threatens Rodolpho; in turn, Rodolpho's brother, Marco, threatens Eddie. Catherine grows to fear Eddie as she and Rodolpho make definite plans to marry. When the drunken Eddie virtually catches the young couple in bed, he orders Rodolpho out of his home. He kisses Catherine on the mouth and then does the same to Rodolpho, believing that the young man's inability to pull away—Eddie being the stronger of the two—will prove his homosexuality to Catherine. When the lovers remain undeterred, Eddie anonymously reports the Italian brothers to immigration officials, who come and arrest them. When the brothers are released on bail, Marco and Eddie fight; Eddie draws a knife but is himself killed by it.

Eddie's obvious—though unacknowledged—obsessive love (he begs and kisses Catherine like a lover, despite her revulsion) alternates with his attempts to rationalize his actions: He "brought up" the girl. Rodolpho is trying "to turn [her] into a tramp," after he "took the blankets off [his own] bed for" Rodolpho and his brother. And now Marco accuses him of calling the immigration officials, which is making Eddie's "name like a dirty rag" in the community. Finally, inevitably, Eddie, who is equally unwilling to give up Catherine or to admit to the illicit nature of his love, is destroyed. ARTHUR MILLER wrote of the character, "What kills Eddie Carbone is . . . the built-in conscience of the community whose existence he has menaced by betraying it" (Martin 260).

BIBLIOGRAPHY

Martin, Robert, ed. *The Theatre Essays of Arthur Miller.* London: Methuen, 1994.

VOGEL, PAULA (1951–)   Feminist and lesbian playwright Paula Anne Vogel was born in Washington, D.C., the child of a working-class family. Educated at Catholic University, Vogel spent three years in the doctoral program at Cornell University before beginning her work as a dramatist in OFF-BROADWAY and OFF-OFF-BROADWAY theaters. Vogel's earliest works offer a strong feminist perspective and a style inspired by German playwright Bertolt Brecht, as in *Meg* (1977), in the one-act *Apple-Brown Betty* (1977), and especially in *Desdemona: A Play about a Handkerchief* (1977), which had its first staged reading at Cornell in 1977.

It was more than 15 years before *Desdemona* had its first professional productions in 1993 at New York's Bay Street Theatre Festival and New York's Circle Repertory Theatre. The play features the three central female characters of *Othello* in a feminist rethinking (and debunking) of Shakespeare's themes and depictions of women, as the play is skewed to reveal its plot through Desdemona's eyes (English playwright Tom Stoppard's *Rosencrantz and Guildenstern Are Dead* [1967] likewise retells *Hamlet* from the perspective of two peripheral characters).

Vogel's next important play, *The Oldest Profession* (1981), a satire about sexuality and old age dealing with five elderly women who work as prostitutes, was given a first reading at New York's Hudson Guild, followed by two Canadian productions in 1988, a reading at Brown University in 1990, and a staging at Company One in Hartford, Connecticut, in 1991 (in 2004, it would make its New York premiere as part of a Signature Theatre season-long tribute to Vogel). The play's long gestation period reflects the process Vogel

and other contemporary playwrights have embraced, allowing them opportunities to revise and rethink plays through numerous readings, workshops, and productions, often over a long period of time.

And Baby Makes Seven (1984), first produced at the Theatre with Teeth Company at New York's 18th Street Playhouse, had later productions at San Francisco's Theatre Rhinoceros in 1986 and New York's Lucille Lortel Theatre in 1993 in a Circle Repertory Theatre production. It is an episodic work in 14 scenes and an epilogue, somewhat inspired by EDWARD ALBEE's WHO'S AFRAID OF VIRGINIA WOOLF? (1962) in its exploration of what conservative clergy and politicians of the era referred to as "family values." Vogel's other early plays include *Bertha in Blue* (1981) and *The Last Pat Epstein Show before the Reruns* (1982), both written and produced prior to her first widely acclaimed play, *The BALTIMORE WALTZ* (1992), a drama with satiric overtones inspired, in part, by the death of Vogel's brother, Carl, from AIDS. Produced at New York's Circle Repertory Theatre in 1992, following workshops in 1990 at the Perseverance Theatre in Douglas, Alaska, *The Baltimore Waltz* won an OBIE AWARD for Playwriting and has since had numerous productions, including more than 40 international stagings.

Vogel's *The Mineola Twins,* "a comedy in six scenes, four dreams and six wigs," had its original production in 1996, also at the Perseverance Theatre, following developmental workshops and readings at the New York Theatre Workshop. It was subsequently performed in March 1997 at the Trinity Repertory Theatre in Providence, Rhode Island. A broad political satire set on Long Island, *The Mineola Twins* is about twin sisters who lead parallel lives through the 1960s, 1970s, and 1980s. One is a "good-girl" conservative housewife and right-wing radio talk-show host while her sister is a sexually liberated, activist lesbian. The play was well received, but its success was modest in comparison to the critical acclaim that greeted Vogel's HOW I LEARNED TO DRIVE (1997), a controversial comedy-drama dealing with incest and pedophilia and the complex relationship of the abused and the abuser. Depicting pedophilic Uncle Peck and his niece, Li'l Bit, at various stages of their lives, the play, which opened at New York's Vineyard Theatre in 1997, was awarded the PULITZER PRIZE, as well as an Obie Award and the New York Drama Critics' Circle Award. Critics rhapsodized about the play's unique balance of humor and the disturbing subject matter, as well as Vogel's novel approach, which was a boldly theatrical one using a three-person Greek chorus to comment on the action and to portray secondary characters, while also mining considerable and improbable comedy from a devastating circumstance.

Vogel's other 1990s dramas include *Hot 'n' Throbbing* (1993), a play she began writing in 1985 but put aside until after her brother's 1990 death. Inspired by an incident of domestic abuse Vogel overheard on a nearby street one night, *Hot 'n' Throbbing* explores the violent potential in male/female relationships in explicit terms. Partially funded by a National Endowment for the Arts fellowship, *Hot 'n' Throbbing* tested the boundaries of censorship in America. Vogel agreed to sign an obscenity pledge in order to accept the NEA funds but decided to make the play a test of contemporary definitions of obscenity (and the boundaries of the pledge itself), particularly in the censorious mid-1990s. Vogel shares with many contemporary dramatists the need to confront the more challenging and unsettling issues of the day, which leads, inevitably, to controversy. For her, the theater is a communal forum in which to explore the dark corners of human experience. Critics have applauded her ability to imbue her plays with a balanced approach to sensitive topics in the theater's communal setting, while also providing scathing commentary on significant and often disturbing contemporary subjects.

Vogel's plays are designed to probe the inequities of the gender spectrum and issues as diverse as the effects of pornography, violence, nontraditional views of family, and AIDS on millennial life. Vogel's most recent work includes several screenplays, a new libretto for a revival of the 1960s musical *On a Clear Day You Can See Forever,* a novel called *Travels without Charley,* and a new five-act play about Italian castrati.

In 2003, the John F. Kennedy Center for the Performing Arts established the Paula Vogel Award in Playwriting to be given to artists creating works emphasizing tolerance and diversity for disenfranchised voices in American life. In late 2003, Vogel's *The Long Christmas Ride Home,* an experimental work featuring puppetry and Japanese theater technique, was produced by the Trinity Repertory Company. The following year, Vogel received the Award for Literature from the American Academy of Arts and Letters. As a devoted teacher on the faculty of Brown University, Vogel mentored such American dramatists as SARAH RUHL and Pulitzer Prize–winner NILO CRUZ. In 2008, Vogel accepted a five-year appointment as chair of the playwriting department at the Yale School of Drama.

BIBLIOGRAPHY

Vogel, Paula. *And Baby Makes Seven.* New York: Dramatists Play Service, 2006.

———. *"The Baltimore Waltz" and Other Plays.* New York: Theatre Communications Group, 1996.

———. *Desdemona.* New York: Dramatists Play Service, 1995.

———. *Hot 'n' Throbbing.* New York: Dramatists Play Service, 2000.

———. *The Long Christmas Ride Home: A Puppet Play with Actors.* New York: Dramatists Play Service, 2004.

———. *The Mammary Plays: "How I Learned to Drive," "The Mineola Twins."* New York: Theatre Communications Group, 1998.

———. *The Oldest Profession.* New York: Dramatists Play Service, 2005.

James Fisher
University of North Carolina at Greensboro

VOLLMER, LULA (LULU) (1895–1955)

A folk dramatist who used strong, righteous mountain women from her native North Carolina as protagonists, Lula Vollmer has been neglected by theater historians. Her vivid regional language and melodramatic plots were popular in their day, and several of them were adapted as screenplays for leading female film actors.

Her most well known drama, *Sun-Up* (1923), originated at the North Carolina Playmakers Repertory and ran for two years on Broadway and in Chicago. It received praise for its portrayal of Ma Cagle, caught between the law and her own beliefs. A mountain woman of the Carolinas, she has lost both her father and her husband to lawmen. She waits for her young son, Rufe, to reach maturity so he can exact revenge. Before he can do so, World War I breaks out, and Rufe goes to France to fight. When he returns, he has been fundamentally changed and no longer believes in killing for revenge. Ma Cagle has to look elsewhere. The play proved to be so popular with audiences that it was made into a silent movie in 1925 starring Lucille La Verne (the original Ma Cagle on Broadway) and Conrad Nagel. Vollmer followed *Sun-Up* with *The Shame Woman* (1923) and *The Dunce Boy* (1925).

Her 1927 play, *Trigger,* was adapted into the 1934 movie, *Spitfire,* starring Katharine Hepburn. The plot concerns a young faith healer living in the Ozarks, Trigger Hicks, who believes she is being accused of witchcraft. Other plays produced with similar themes include *The Hill Between* (1938), *Sentinels* (1931), *In A Nutshell* (1937), and *Moonshine & Honeysuckle* (1933).

In the 1930s, Vollmer started writing not only screenplays but also short stories and radio plays. Her radio plays, *Grits and Gravy* (1934) and *Widow's Sons* (1937), as well as her short stories written for serials, such as the *Saturday Evening Post,* feature female-centered stories and situations.

BIBLIOGRAPHY

Vollmer, Lula. *"Sun-Up."* In *Best Plays of 1923–24,* edited by Burns Mantle. Boston: Small, Maynard, 1920. 213–234.
———. *The Hill Between: A Folk Play in 3 Acts.* New York: Longmans, Green, 1939.
———. *In a Nutshell.* New York: Hart Stenographic Bureau, 1936.

Helen Huff
City University of New York—
Borough of Manhattan Community College

W

WAITING FOR LEFTY Clifford Odets
(1935) A depression-era AGITPROP drama, *Waiting for Lefty* portrays the plight of the working class and recommends socialism as the redemptive political system and the labor strike as the means to achieve that system. This short, seven-scene play opens on a bare stage where six workers—cab drivers—sit in a semicircle. A corrupt union secretary, Harry Fatt, who is, according to ODETS, an "ugly menace" who "represents the capitalist system" (Brenman-Gibson 304), discourages the men from striking. Depicted in the five short scenes that follow are the difficulties the workers face now or faced before they became cab drivers. In "Joe and Edna," a cab driver and his wife have trouble surviving on the little money he makes: The rent is due, the furniture has been repossessed, the kids are hungry, the union is corrupt, and only the cab company bosses make money. Edna threatens to leave Joe for a man who makes a decent wage and finally convinces him to strike. He is inspired to go out to "look up Lefty Costello."

In "Lab Assistant Episode," an assistant in a medical lab is offered a raise by an industrialist, but there is a catch: In his higher paying position, the assistant will be making "poison gas for modern warfare"; furthermore, he is asked to spy on the chemist he will be assisting. The lab assistant refuses on principle, is fired, and punches the industrialist in the mouth. In "The Young Hack and His Girl," a young engaged couple cannot marry for lack of money. Their families need what little income they bring in, and though the

girl insists she does not care how hard their life together will be as long as they are together, he knows she will come to resent it. In "Labor Spy Episode," a man, claiming to be a worker from another city, speaks out to discourage a strike but turns out to be a paid strikebreaker. In "Interne Episode," a young and qualified surgeon is replaced on a "charity case" by a "Senator's nephew," an "incompetent" who causes the patient to die. The young doctor is outraged that the poor are considered expendable; it is the poor he most wishes to help. When he finds out that he has been fired because he is a Jew, he thinks about going to Russia to do "good work in their socialized medicine," but he finally insists, "Our work's here—America!" He becomes a cab driver. In the final scene, "Strike Episode," word comes to the assembled workers that Lefty is dead, "a bullet in his head." Lefty, for whom they have been waiting for leadership, is never to come, and they—their voices joined by those of the audience—vow to take action themselves and "STRIKE, STRIKE, STRIKE!!!"

Waiting for Lefty was the first left-wing political drama that appealed to a general audience and enjoyed broad commercial success. First produced by the GROUP THEATRE in New York City, the play was soon presented in cities around the country.

BIBLIOGRAPHY
Brenman-Gibson, Margaret. *Clifford Odets, American Playwright: The Years from 1906–1940.* New York: Atheneum, 1981.

WARD, DOUGLAS TURNER (1930–)

Born in Louisiana, Douglas Turner Ward became an actor, playwright, producer, and director, as well as the cofounder of the Negro Ensemble Company. He attended Ohio's Wilberforce College and the University of Michigan but did not complete a formal education before moving to New York at age 19. He worked as a journalist and studied playwriting at the Paul Mann Workshop in New York City. In 1956, Ward made his acting debut in an OFF-BROADWAY production of EUGENE O'NEILL'S *The ICEMAN COMETH,* and in 1959 he had a small role in LORRAINE HANSBERRY'S *A RAISIN IN THE SUN.*

Working with actor Robert Hooks, who had been a fellow member of the touring company of *A Raisin in the Sun,* and with theater manager Gerald Krone, Ward produced two one-act plays of his own, *Happy Ending* and *Day of Absence* (1965), on a double bill. *Happy Ending* is a satirical comedy about race relations; the play examines relationships between white employers and African-American employees, while attacking American materialism. *Day of Absence*—"a reverse minstrel show"—is an expressionistic social satire in which the African-American cast, in white-face and blond wigs, plays the roles of whites in a small southern town on a day when all the African Americans have disappeared.

Some months after the premiere of these two plays, Ward described himself in a *New York Times* article entitled "American Theatre: For Whites Only?" as "a Negro playwright committed to examining the contours, context, and depth of his experiences from an unfettered, imaginative Negro angle of vision" (August 14, 1966). In order to facilitate this commitment, in 1967, Ward, Hooks, and Krone cofounded the Negro Ensemble Company, of which Ward was artistic director until 1987, when he became consulting director. Though the NEC met with some hostility—heckled in London for an anticolonialist play, criticized at home by African Americans who resented its connection to white administrators, playwrights, and backers—there can be no doubt about its positive impact on AFRICAN-AMERICAN DRAMA. The NEC provided many African-American actors an opportunity to play complex characters rather than the stereotypical servants to which they had for so long been limited; for African-American playwrights, the NEC provided a home in which to express the voice of the African-American experience in America. Among the NEC's most notable productions were LONNE ELDER'S *CEREMONIES IN DARK OLD MEN* (1969), Joseph Walker's *The RIVER NIGER* (1972), and CHARLES FULLER'S *Zooman and the Sign* (1980). The success of *The River Niger* enabled the NEC, which had been facing crippling financial problems, to remain viable. In 1981, Ward mounted the company's most successful production, Charles Fuller's *A SOLDIER'S PLAY,* which won the New York Drama Critics' Circle Award and the PULITZER PRIZE. Douglas Turner Ward has directed and played leading roles in many NEC productions; he has also written other plays, including *The Reckoning* (1969) and *Brotherhood* (1970). Ward has also acted on many television shows throughout his career.

In 2008, as NEC celebrated its 40th anniversary season, New York's Signature Theatre announced that it would devote its entire 2008–2009 season to plays from the NEC's repertoire. The Negro Ensemble Company, itself, is still producing plays and conducting workshops, under the current leadership of artistic director Charles Weldon and associate artistic director Oz Scott. Ward, now in his late 70s and retired, in 2004 published a book, with Gus Edwards, of advice for black actors, *Advice to a Young Black Actor: Conversations with Douglas Turner Ward.*

BIBLIOGRAPHY

Edwards, Gus, and Douglas Turner Ward. *Advice to a Young Black Actor: Conversations with Douglas Turner Ward.* Portsmouth, N.H.: Heinemann Drama, 2004.

Ward, Douglas Turner. *Brotherhood: Short One-Act Play.* New York: Dramatists Play Service, 1970.

———. *"Happy Ending" and "Day of Absence."* New York: Dramatists Play Service, 1966.

———. *The Reckoning: A Surreal Southern Fable.* New York: Dramatists Play Service, 1970.

WASHINGTON SQUARE PLAYERS

A short-lived theater company in New York, the Washington Square Players was founded in 1915 by a group of young actors and writers, including Lawrence Langner, Edward Goodman, Philip Moeller, Ida Rauh, and Helen Westley. The Players' mission was to improve the quality of theater in New York by producing intellectual and experimental drama. Originally located in a 40-seat house called the Bandbox Theatre, the group relocated in 1916 to the 600-seat Comedy Theatre.

The Players primarily produced one-act plays by European playwrights, though they also produced a few by Americans. The Washington Square Players folded in 1918, but several members were involved in the 1919 founding of the THEATRE GUILD, which was similarly devoted to cutting-edge theater, but differed in its commitment to giving full-length dramas completely professional productions.

WASSERSTEIN, WENDY (1950–2006)

Wendy Wasserstein was born in Brooklyn, New York, graduated from Mount Holyoke College in 1971 with a degree in history, and went on to earn two master's degrees: a master of arts in 1973 from the City University of New York (CUNY) and a master of fine arts from Yale Drama School three years later. Although she wrote several produced plays before *The HEIDI CHRONICLES* (1988), including *Any Woman Can't* (1973), *Uncommon Women and Others* (1975), *Isn't It Romantic* (1981), and *Tender Offer* (1983), Wasserstein did not become well known until *The Heidi Chronicles* won a series of honors, including the New York Drama Critics' Circle Award, the TONY AWARD, and the PULITZER PRIZE. After *Heidi*, she wrote *Bachelor Girls* (1990) and *Shiksa Goddess* (2001), compilations of previously published satiric essays and short stories about growing up and being female and Jewish in New York, and the plays *The SISTERS ROSENSWEIG* (1992), *An American Daughter* (1997), *Old Money* (2001), and *THIRD* (2005), as well as screenplays and countless articles and reviews.

Wasserstein's importance in the contemporary American dramatic tradition centers on the fact that she was a woman writing about women's issues in a male-dominated art. In fact, because her plays explore women's roles (both public and private) and the effects (both positive and negative) of the feminist movement, Wasserstein has been labeled by many critics as a "feminist playwright." Though she admitted that she thought of herself as a woman writer, she resisted the label of feminist and asked instead that her plays be thought of as exploring the choices of individual women.

Uncommon Women and Others, Wasserstein's first successful play, charts the progress of five women since their graduation from Mount Holyoke College. The play's shift from the past to the present highlights the contrast between the women they were and the choices they believed they would make in 1972 with the women they are and the choices they ended up making in 1978. Wasserstein asserted that this work reveals a "spectrum of women" and thus, the play suggests that these women naturally make a spectrum of different choices for their uncertain futures. Similarly, *Isn't It Romantic* presents its audience with differing choices for women, though it centers less on career options and more overtly on its characters' decisions about marriage. The play follows a brief segment of the lives of Janie Blumberg and Harriet Cornwall, two longtime friends who struggle with the tensions of their romantic involvements.

The Heidi Chronicles, her most critically acclaimed work, also received the most lambasting by feminist scholars. Composed of 11 scenes, the play begins and ends in the historical present, 1989, for Heidi Holland, a successful art historian at Columbia University remorseful about being a single woman in the postfeminist era. The body of the play covers 25 years of Heidi's development from an adolescent feminist activist of the 1960s to her current status as a yuppie of the 1980s. It is Heidi's relationship to traditionalism that troubles many feminist scholars, for she seeks the attention of two men throughout the play and finally chooses to adopt a daughter at the play's close as a means of filling the void in her life. It is through Heidi's lament that the women's movement has failed her by idealizing the concept of the "Superwoman" that Wasserstein exposes the limitations of feminist ideology.

While Wasserstein's earlier works detail the choices made by young women, many of her later plays center on female protagonists who are notably older. *The Sisters Rosensweig* invites Sara, the eldest of the three sisters at 54, to decide whether she will remain alone or become romantically involved with a man her age. This potential relationship takes a backseat, however, to Sara's process of becoming a fully realized self, a woman coming to terms with her Jewish heritage and her identity with respect to her two sisters. *An American Daughter,* set in Washington, D.C., during the Clinton administration and based on the Zoe Baird case, centers on Lyssa Dent Hughes, the 42-year-old daughter of a distinguished senator, a descendant of Ulysses S. Grant, and, most importantly, a physician who has been nominated as Surgeon General of the United States. Perhaps more than any other of Wasserstein's works, this play grapples with a woman's public persona and with the consequences of choosing a life in which one's private choices can be publicly scrutinized. When word gets out that Lyssa has neglected to respond to a notice for jury duty, her integrity is questioned and her nomination challenged. Like Heidi Holland, Lyssa feels betrayed by the feminist movement and by the American public, which seems unwilling to accept an imperfect, yet strong career woman.

In *Old Money,* Wasserstein departed somewhat from her usual exploration of women's roles and instead centered the work on contemporary American society's obsession with glamour and wealth. Set in a 19th-century Upper East Side mansion, the play is a complicated mixture of the past and the present, of "old" and "new" money. It juxtaposes Jeffrey Bernstein's current-day party of moviemaking moguls and investment bankers with Tobias Pfeiffer's turn-of-the (19th to 20th) century relationship to his own wealth. Both Bernstein and Pfeiffer must also relate to their teenage sons, who have idealistic, conflicted notions about money; neither son, it seems, wishes to follow in his father's footsteps. Ultimately, *Old Money* overtly criticizes our new money culture, which purports that wealth can buy happiness and that cash can supersede class. The play includes a troubling subtext of vacuous and gold-digging women, who, like the vampiric Flinty McGee, look for rich men as the means by which they may be propelled into the upper echelons of society. For this, *Old Money* seemed to mark an ominous turn in Wasserstein's work, implicitly arguing that women have regressed, that their roles have come full circle. In *Third,* Wasserstein's final play, a feminist college professor is forced to reexamine her own biases and the actions that stem from them when she unfairly accuses a male athlete of plagiarism; she comes to realize that she has become the stubborn "establishment," not so unlike the one she overthrew in her own youth.

Regardless of where the criticism falls, Wasserstein's dramas succeed in capturing the difficulties some women face in their quests—and desires—to "have it all." Wasserstein's ability to bring together the sadness and humor of experience was her greatest talent; one of her primary contributions to the American stage is a keen sense of wit that nonetheless embraces the seriousness of contemporary life. Her astute dialogue, in which characters' conversations reveal as much as they conceal, is testament to her skill in observing and mirroring human behavior. Furthermore, in creating purposefully realistic dramas, Wasserstein seemed to be suggesting that even in the early 21st century the real work of feminism was far from over.

BIBLIOGRAPHY

Barnett, Claudia, ed. *Wendy Wasserstein: A Casebook.* New York: Garland, 1999.

Ciociola, Gail. *Wendy Wasserstein: Dramatizing Women, Their Choices, Their Boundaries.* Jefferson, N.C.: McFarland, 1998.

Wasserstein, Wendy. *An American Daughter.* New York: Harcourt Brace, 1998.

———. *Bachelor Girls.* New York: Knopf, 1990.

———. *"The Heidi Chronicles" and Other Plays: "The Heidi Chronicles," "Uncommon Women and Others," and "Isn't It Romantic."* New York: Vintage, 1991.

———. *Old Money.* New York: Harcourt, 2002.

———. *Seven One-Act Plays.* New York: Dramatists Play Service, 2000.

———. *Shiksa Goddess; or, How I Spent My Forties.* New York: Knopf, 2001.

———. *The Sisters Rosensweig.* New York: Harcourt Brace, 1993.

———. *Third.* New York: Dramatists Play Service, 2008.

Dina L. Longhitano
University of Maryland

WEDDING BAND: A LOVE/HATE STORY IN BLACK AND WHITE Alice Childress (1966)   Based on a true story told by Childress's grandmother, *Wedding Band* chronicles the common-law marriage of Julia Augustine, a black seamstress, and Herman, a working-class white baker.

The play begins in 1918 in a poor, segregated section of South Carolina. Julia has just moved into her home, where she has three black female neighbors, Mattie, Lula, and Fanny. Initially mysterious, Julia soon confides in the women, explaining that she and Herman have been involved for 10 years: They wish to marry, but state laws forbid interracial marriage. The other women cannot understand how a black woman could desire a white man; reminding Julia of the exploitative sexual relations prevalent between slave masters and their female slaves, they suggest that Julie either terminate the relationship or exploit Herman.

Herman's arrival reveals that he is the provider for his sister and mother, a responsibility that prevents him from leaving South Carolina with Julia. Despite his mother's disapproval, Herman remains attached to Julia and, on their 10th anniversary, brings her an elaborate wedding cake and a wedding band that she can wear on a necklace until they may legally marry. They make plans to move to New York, where antimiscegenation laws do not exist. Herman rises, as if to set their plans into motion, then collapses, a victim of the influenza epidemic that is sweeping the city.

The second act consists of attempts to circumvent the antimiscegenation laws to save Herman's life. Desperate, Julia sends for Herman's sister and mother, hoping that they can arrange a doctor's visit. The women arrive and, unwilling to sacrifice the family reputation to save Herman's life, agree to transport Herman only under the cover of darkness. Finally, Julia, unable to watch silently as the racism of Herman's mother destroys Herman and their relationship, exclaims, "If I wasn't black with all-a Carolina 'gainst me I'd be mistress of your house! . . . Out! And take the last ten years-a my life with you and . . . when he gets better . . . keep him home."

The next day, Julia maintains her decision to respect her black, southern heritage. Herman returns bearing tickets to New York, but Julia is no longer willing to leave. They fight bitterly over race and gender roles, but eventually they come to terms with one another. Though she cares for Herman, Julia symbolically renounces her link to white society while reestablishing her communal and racial ties: She gives the tickets and wedding band to Mattie. As the play ends,

Julia sits alone with Herman as he dies, a death that frees her to return to a people from whom she has been ostracized for the 10 long years of the relationship.

Written during the Civil Rights movement, *Wedding Band* offers both a realistic portrayal of the consequences of an interracial relationship at that time, and an indictment of "anti-woman" laws that forbade divorce and certain marriages in an effort to control women. Most major productions drew criticism from both white and black critics.

Elizabeth A. Osborne
Florida State University

WELLER, MICHAEL (1942–)

Michael Weller, born in New York City and educated at Brandeis University and Britain's Manchester University, has been praised in the *New York Times* by drama critic Frank Rich as the "most sensitive and knowing dramatist of the big-chill generation" (November 13, 1984). From his earliest undergraduate efforts in the mid-1960s, Weller's chief interest has been portraying his peer group as they negotiate the landscape of changing social and personal relationships, from the idealism of the American counterculture movement that erupted in the Vietnam era, through the "me decade" of the 1970s, and into the resurgent materialist impulses of the 1980s. His most well-known plays attempt, through skillful, witty dialogue and realistic characterizations both sympathetic and critical, to plumb the meaning of the American experience and its impact on personal commitment, expectations, and family relations in his generation.

Weller first achieved professional recognition with *Cancer* (1970) at London's Royal Court Theatre. Renamed *Moonchildren* for its American premiere at Washington's Arena Stage, it later won a 1971 Drama Desk Award and an OFF-OFF BROADWAY Review Award before moving to Broadway. Its depiction of college students embroiled in the turbulence of war protests amid the twin spirits of "free love" and "don't trust anyone over thirty" is still praised as a landmark encapsulation of the times. Although his next efforts, *Grant's Movie* (1972), about a violent confrontation between police and war protesters, and a rock musical about Vietnam, *More Than You Deserve* (1973), failed to find audiences, Weller enjoyed success again with *Fishing* (1975). This story of a group of hippies scraping out a living in a dilapidated house on the ocean in the Pacific Northwest was praised for capturing the fear and alienation underlying the seemingly carefree "tune in, turn on, drop out" philosophy of the times.

Fishing later came to be seen as the second in a trilogy of plays that many critics believe reached its pinnacle in *Loose Ends* (1979), winner of the American Theatre Critics/Steinberg New Play Award. This play, like his shorter work, *Split* (1978), examines the breakup of an idealistic young couple through the changes in their relationship brought on by marriage, careers, and adulthood. Its panoramic series of scenes delineate the couple's progression from their meeting on the road to enlightenment in the 1960s to their rueful reunion after diverging views of career, family, and partnership have led to divorce.

Weller began screenwriting with adaptations of the hippie rock musical *Hair* (1979) and E. L. Doctorow's kaleidoscopic romance of early 20th-century America, *Ragtime* (1980), which received nominations for the Academy Award and the Writer's Guild of America Award. Weller again won praise for locating the resonance of society and politics with intimate family relations in his play *Spoils of War* (1988), an "emotional autobiography" of a teenager in the 1950s desperately trying to reunite his divorced parents; it was later filmed for Hallmark Television.

Along with continuing to write for the stage, television, and film, Weller is active in New York City's Cherry Lane Theatre mentoring program for emerging playwrights.

What the Night Is For, the first of a planned trilogy about the reunion of two former lovers, was staged in London's West End in 2002. Two plays by Weller premiered OFF-BROADWAY in 2008: *Fifty Words,* the second play in the trilogy, and a political satire about two injured veterans' journey home from the war in Iraq, *Beast.*

A faculty member at New York's New School for Drama, the playwright was honored in 2005 by the Broken Watch Theatre Company, which christened its New York performance space the Michael Weller Theatre.

BIBLIOGRAPHY

Weller, Michael. *Dogbrain: A Play for Children.* New York: Dramatists Play Service, 1997.
———. *Five Plays.* New York: Theatre Communications Group, 1998.
———. *Ghosts on Fire.* New York: Grove/Atlantic, 1987.
———. *Split.* New York: Samuel French, 2005.
———. *Spoils of War.* New York: Samuel French, 1989.
———. *What the Night Is For.* London: Oberon Books, 2003.

Roxane Rix
Kutztown University of Pennsylvania

WELLMAN, MAC (1945–)

An avant-garde dramatist who describes himself as a "language-poet-playwright," Mac Wellman was born in Cleveland, Ohio. He received a master's degree in literature from the University of Wisconsin at Madison in 1968, following completion of a bachelor's degree from American University a year earlier. After teaching English at Montgomery College in Rockville, Maryland, from 1969 to 1972, Wellman moved to New York City, where he worked as a magazine editor before pursuing a writing career that has included plays, poetry, and novels.

Wellman describes himself as a "linguistic inventor." His plays are on the cutting edge of late 20th-century drama, often fiercely political works focusing on such issues as urban violence, the postmodern isolation of the individual, environmental concerns, and the shallowness of present-day values. Wellman won an OBIE AWARD for three of his plays collectively in 1990: *Bad Penny,* a site-specific work calling on the actors to deliver their lines to each other across a lake in New York's Central Park; *Crowbar,* another site-specific work tracing both the celebrated and tragic history of New York's Victory Theatre and the neighborhood surrounding it; and *Terminal Hip,* a monologue of real slang and made-up expressions suggesting the absurdity of colloquial language. Wellman produced many plays while continuing to teach, holding playwright-in-residence positions at New York University (1981–82), the University of New Mexico (1991), Yale School of Drama (1992), and Princeton University (1992–93), among others.

Wellman's *Sincerity Forever* (1990), for which he received an Obie Award for Playwriting, caused considerable controversy for its harsh attack on "the eloquent ignoramuses of America" who attempt to censor challenging art. *7 Blowjobs* (1991) was a follow-up to *Sincerity Forever* and involved a furor surrounding seven "obscene" photographs delivered to the office of a United States senator. Inspired in part by the controversy over Robert Mapplethorpe's explicit photographs and the reaction of Jesse Helms, a conservative senator from North Carolina, Wellman has been an angry voice against arts censorship in the post–Reagan era. More recent Wellman plays, which feature his characteristic poetic experimentation with language, include *Swoop* (1994), *London (In Ten Cities)* (1996), *The Lesser Magoo* (1997), *The Porcupine Man* (1998), *The Difficulty of Crossing a Field* (1998), *Infrared* (1999), *Jennie Richie* (2001), *Antigone* (2002), *Bitter Bierce* (2003), and the one-act *Before the Before and Before That* (2006). His *Two September* (2006) surprised critics with its depiction of the Vietnam era and somewhat more traditional use of language than is typical in Wellman's most characteristic work.

Critical response to Wellman's work has been decidedly mixed, but his playwriting peers frequently refer to him as a leader in moving late 20th-century American drama away from the conventions of naturalism, which had dominated its stages since the 19th century, toward a poetic, visually inspiring, language-based theatricalism. To some extent, his importance may rest on playwrights he has inspired, including 2001 PULITZER PRIZE–winning dramatist SUZAN-LORI PARKS. Wellman has frequently pointed out that he is interested in what is lost between experience and the ways in which experience can be described by language. He posits that the deepest spiritual yearnings of humanity are shallow; in his theater, he strives for "an exploration of the consequences of this perplexing and disquieting truth." Wellman, who has written in excess of 60 plays (both full-length and one-act works), is compared to James Joyce, Lewis Carroll, and GERTRUDE STEIN by critics who admire his linguistic acrobatics and absurd humor. He has generally chosen to produce his work in OFF-BROADWAY and university theaters, where his experimental style tends to find more appreciative audiences. In 2003, Wellman received an Obie Award for Lifetime Achievement.

Wellman is a professor of playwriting and coordinator of the playwriting program at Brooklyn College. Ever the experimenter, he published his first collection of short stories, *A Chronicle of the Madness of Small Worlds,* in 2008.

BIBLIOGRAPHY

Wellman, Mac. *The Bad Infinity: Eight Plays by Mac Wellman.* Baltimore, Md.: Johns Hopkins University Press, 1994.

———. *Cellophane: Plays.* Baltimore, Md.: Johns Hopkins University Press, 2001.

———. *The Fortuneteller.* Los Angeles, Calif.: Sun & Moon Press, 1991.

———. *Harm's Way.* New York: Broadway Play Publishing, 2008.

———. *The Land beyond the Forest: "Dracula" and "Swoop."* Los Angeles, Calif.: Sun & Moon Press, 1995.

———. *Two Plays: "A Murder of Crows" and "The Hyacinth Macaw."* Los Angeles, Calif.: Sun & Moon Press, 1994.

———. *Whirligig.* New York: Theatre Communications Group, 1989.

James Fisher
University of North Carolina at Greensboro

WHAT PRICE GLORY? LAURENCE STALLINGS AND MAXWELL ANDERSON (1924) Set in France during World War I, this comedy-drama presents a realistic, unromanticized view of war and of soldiers. Stallings wrote from experience, having fought and lost a leg in France during World War I. His contemporary, and eventual colleague, ANDERSON, on the other hand, was a pacifist, a philosophy that cost him a teaching job and an editorial post before he found work at the *New York World,* where he met Stallings.

Sergeant Quirt and his nemesis Captain Flagg have served together before; they have a history of antagonism—over discipline and over women—that has previously played itself out in Cuba and in China. Now they find themselves together again in the chaos and terror that is World War I. They are hard-drinking, fist-fighting, womanizing men; part of the play centers on their rivalry over Charmaine, the promiscuous daughter of a French innkeeper. However, the greater impact of the play comes from its point of view on the war as articulated mostly by Captain Flagg, who has gruff sympathy for his own men but only contempt for the military's high command.

The playwrights' realistic view of war and their irreverence for the military command are evident throughout *What Price Glory?* Early in the play, Flagg complains, "[H]alf our men are green replacements" and "God knows most of 'em haven't got long to live." After receiving a message from headquarters, he declares, "Damn headquarters! It's some more of that world-safe-for-democracy slush. . . . I'd like to rub their noses in a few of the latrines I've slept in, keeping up army morale and losing men because some screaming fool back in the New Jersey sector thinks he's playing with paper dolls." After Flagg's company returns to the frontlines, one of Flagg's corporals describes Flagg's ultimately futile attempt to save a wounded man: The dying man is "holding half his guts with his bare hands and hollering for somebody to turn him loose so he could shoot himself." Minutes later, after Flagg attempts to comfort one of his lieutenants who is having an emotional breakdown ("Why in God's name can't we all go home? Who gives a damn for this lousy, stinking little town but the poor French bastards who live here? . . . *sobbing*"), two inexperienced lieutenants arrive. Flagg tells them he has no sergeants to "spare . . . to teach little boys how to adjust their diapers" and sardonically comments that he and his men "propose to die in order that corps headquarters may be decorated."

In the final scene of the play, Quirt and Flagg, drunk and exhausted, fight over the opportunistic Charmaine, but before either can rest in her arms, they are ordered to return to the frontlines. As he joins Flagg, Quirt sums up the play's theme: "What a lot of God damn fools it takes to make a war!"

Critics praised the play's authenticity and its decidedly unromantic view of war and the waste left in its wake. Disillusioned post–World War I audiences welcomed its honesty and realism.

WHO'S AFRAID OF VIRGINIA WOOLF?

EDWARD ALBEE (1962) Set at a small college in the home of a history professor and his wife, *Who's Afraid of Virginia Woolf?* is a funny and serious four-character play in which a childless, middle-aged couple expose their caustic relationship and their secrets to a younger couple, new to the campus. ALBEE's drama won the TONY AWARD and the New York Drama Critics' Circle Award and established his reputation as a major American dramatist. It was also selected for the PULITZER PRIZE by the Pulitzer drama jury, but their recommendation was rejected by the advisory board at Columbia University.

George has been married to Martha, the college president's daughter, for more than 20 years. As the play begins, they are arriving home at 2 A.M. from a party at "Daddy's" house. Martha, already inebriated, has invited a young couple to join them: Nick is the new biology professor, fit and attractive; his wife, Honey, is "mousy," sweet, and dull. Far into the night, the two couples drink to excess as George and Martha spar with one another. Their exchanges are caustic, even vicious at times, yet each has evident appreciation of the other's capacities for wit and cruelty. Martha speaks of George's professional shortcomings in a "game" he calls "Humiliate the Host": George has failed to succeed Martha's father as head of the college—as both Martha and her father had hoped; indeed, he is not even chairman of his department. These failures, which make Martha contemptuous, are always evident in the intimate world of a small-college faculty. George, his shortcomings thus revealed to the younger man, next plays "Get the Guests" by repeating personal details that Nick has told him about his marriage to Honey. When George tells a story about a young couple and the hysterical pregnancy that precipitated their wedding, Honey recognizes it as her own story and runs to the bathroom to vomit—not for the first time tonight. Later, Nick and Martha disappear for a while to play—or attempt to play—"Hump the Hostess," as George calls it, a "game" Martha apparently engages in frequently.

An ongoing source of tension between George and Martha is any mention of their "son." Martha mentions him early in the play in violation of some rule she and George alone understand. The son is ammunition in their perpetual battle. Each accuses the other of being the boy's tormentor. At the end of act 2, George decides—while Martha and Nick are out of the room together—to tell Martha that word has come that their son is dead. In act 3, after Martha is fully engaged, at George's insistence, in telling the story of her son's birth and early life, George tells her he has been killed in an accident. Her curious objection, "YOU CAN'T HAVE HIM DIE," brings Nick to the realization that the "son" is the invention of this childless couple. After Honey and Nick depart, we see in a final scene of loss and tenderness, as they face a future without the "son" who is at once a comfort and a weapon they use against each other, that beneath the contempt and bitterness, there is a real connection between them. Whether that connection will endure is unclear. The stripping away of the illusion of the son is an "exorcism," as the title ("The Exorcism") of act 3 makes clear; what follows will be the couple's choice of how to live without their illusions.

Edward Albee in an interview in the 1980s with Jackson R. Bryer, said that "*Virginia Woolf* . . . was pretty much about the corrupting influence of false illusions, a response to O'NEILL's play *The* ICEMAN COMETH, which postulates that you've got to have false illusions. *Virginia Woolf* says that you don't have to have them. It's a lot better if you can get along without them."

As for the choice of the names George and Martha (as in "Washington"), Albee said in the same interview, "I thought, why not have a little fun, I mean, after all, they *do* represent some of the failed principles of the American Revolution, perhaps [smiling wryly, Albee continued], but that was just kidding around. And I named Nick after Nikita Krushchev, who was running the Soviet Union, but then again I had all sorts of fun things in that play. I had several quotes from *Streetcar* [*A* STREETCAR NAMED DESIRE (1947)] so that when TENNESSEE WILLIAMS came to see the play he'd get a kick out of it. I named the old Western Union messenger after a close friend of mine. . . . I stud my plays with things that [are] fun for me and fun for my friends. . . . What's more fun is when the scholars get at it—the humorless scholars—and something that you've done for fun, they find all sorts of hidden, wonderful meaning in."

BIBLIOGRAPHY

Albee, Edward. Interview by Jackson R. Bryer. *United States Information Service.* Video. Title No.: AZ99999410.

Bottoms, Stephen J. *Albee: "Who's Afraid of Virginia Woolf?"* Cambridge, England: Cambridge University Press, 2000.

WHY MARRY? JESSE LYNCH WILLIAMS (1917)

This social comedy and discussion play won the first PULITZER PRIZE given for drama. Influenced by the style and sensibility of George Bernard Shaw, whose plays raise serious social issues through witty dialogue and irony, the play contains at least 10 different discussion scenes and was well received by the reading public when it was published under the title *And So They Were Married* in 1914 (it was not produced until 1917). Quite different from the sober, melodramatic social problem plays that precede it, *Why Marry?* found a receptive American audience. Through the relationships of five couples, Williams's play addresses divorce, women's roles and options, and the double standard, among other provocative issues.

The wealthy John is married to Lucy, whom he considers his possession; Lucy accepts her situation—though not always without complaint—because she has no training to earn money of her own. John's sister Jean is seducing a rich playboy, Rex, whom she does not love, knowing that marriage to him will be a form of prostitution. Judge Everett, an uncle, and his wife have been married for four years, but having decided that they are happier separated, they are filing for divorce; they are pleased with themselves for their lack of hypocrisy. Cousin Theodore, a member of the clergy, has a fatalistic view of life—sex and other unpleasantries are "necessary evil[s]"; his wife, having had a great many children, is now in a sanatorium. John's other sister Helen is financially independent and intellectually able to hold her own with the brilliant scientist Ernest Hamilton, with whom she works. They are in love and are lovers, but they have no interest in marrying because they see—in John and Lucy, for instance—that such a "legal union" is too often a "spiritual separation." Though Theodore—speaking for society—disapproves of the arrangement of Helen and Ernest, he is willing to bless the union of Rex and Jean, despite the fact that the first is an equal partnership based on love, while the latter is an exchange of money for sex and subservience.

Respectability triumphs in the end, however; the Judge and his wife do not, after all, divorce, and Helen and Ernest do, after all, marry. (Having gotten them to admit that they are married in the sight of God, the sly Judge Everett quickly, "by the authority vested in" him, pronounces them "man and wife.") It is as if Williams could not quite sustain his criticism of convention, or perhaps he doubted his audience's willingness to accept fully such criticism.

WILDER, THORNTON NIVEN (1897–1975)

Thornton Wilder once remarked that when the rest of his generation went to Paris, he went to Rome, referring to a year spent studying archaeology and Latin at the American Academy in 1920–21. While Wilder's importance to American theater stems from his rejection of the dramatic realism that dominated the American stage through much of the 20th century, he saw himself as "a rediscoverer of forgotten goods," the dramatic techniques of the classical Greek and Renaissance theaters. Among the most cosmopolitan of American playwrights (he was fluent in Italian, Spanish, French, and German), he nevertheless celebrated small-town American life and stressed the centrality of the family to society.

Wilder was born in Madison, Wisconsin, where his father was editor of the *Wisconsin State Journal*. He subsequently lived in China, when his father was consul general in Hong Kong and Shanghai, and in Berkeley, California. At Oberlin College, where he began his undergraduate work, and subsequently at Yale University, he began writing "three-minute" plays, 16 of which were collected in *"The Angel That Troubled the Waters" and Other Plays* (1928). Somewhat influenced by Theodore Dreiser's *Plays of the Natural and Supernatural,* they reveal Wilder's interest in religious themes and his indifference to naturalistic staging. While at Yale, Wilder also wrote *The Trumpet Shall Sound,* an allegorical treatment of Ben Jonson's *The Alchemist* transplanted to New York in 1871, which was published in the *Yale Literary Magazine* in four installments in 1919–20.

After returning from Rome, Wilder taught at the Lawrenceville School in New Jersey and completed a master's in French literature at Princeton University. During this period he wrote two novels: *The Cabala* (1926), which shows the influence of Marcel Proust, and *The Bridge of San Luis Rey* (1927), which won the Pulitzer Prize and became a best seller that enabled Wilder to spend the rest of his life as a writer. Wilder's third novel, *The Woman of Andros* (1930), earned him a venomous attack from Marxist critic Michael Gold, who claimed that Wilder was the purveyor of bloodless good taste to the bourgeoisie.

While teaching at the University of Chicago, Wilder published *"The Long Christmas Dinner" and Other Plays* (1931). Three of the plays, *Queens of France, Love and How to Cure It,* and *Such Things Only Happen in Books,* are subtle satires on the assumptions of realism, presented in realistic form. But *The Long Christmas Dinner, Pullman Car Hiawatha,* and *The Happy Journey to Trenton and Camden,* all among the most frequently performed American one-act plays, anticipate Wilder's later work through such devices as telescoping time and dispensing with scenery. His plays, Wilder asserts in his preface to *Three Plays,* try "to capture not verisimilitude but reality" (*American Characteristics* 108).

Wilder's translation of André Obey's *Le Viol de Lucrèce* played on Broadway in 1932 and his adaptation of Henrik Ibsen's *A Doll's House* was produced there in 1937. A fourth novel, *Heaven's My Destination,* came out in 1934. *Our Town,* probably the most produced American play, opened in 1938 and won Wilder his second Pulitzer Prize (Wilder is the only author to have won the prize for both fiction and drama). The first act shows daily life in a New England town, the second examines love and marriage, and the third, following Dante, takes place amongst the dead. Throughout, Wilder tries, as he has written, to dramatize "a value above all price for the smallest events" and "to record a village's life on the stage, with realism and generality" (*American Characteristics* 109, 101).

Wilder's next play, *The Merchant of Yonkers* (1938), a lighthearted parody of well-made farces, was unsuccessful; slightly revised in 1954 as *The Matchmaker,* it was popular on both sides of the Atlantic. When turned into the 1964 musical *Hello, Dolly!,* it provided substantial income for Wilder for the rest of his life.

In 1942, *The Skin of Our Teeth* won Wilder his third Pulitzer Prize, but not without controversy. Joseph Campbell and Henry Robinson, in two celebrated *Saturday Review of Literature* articles, claimed Wilder had plagiarized James Joyce's *Finnegans Wake,* a charge based on confusion between indebtedness and theft, since the play was almost equally inspired by Ole Olsen and Chic Johnson's *Hellzapoppin.* Act 1 takes place simultaneously during the Ice Age and in contemporary New Jersey, act 2 during the biblical Flood, and act 3 after some cataclysmic war. Staged during World War II, the play optimistically asserts that civilization will always be rebuilt. After the war, the play was widely praised in Europe in general and Germany in particular. In 1942, Wilder also wrote the screenplay for what Alfred Hitchcock came to describe as his favorite among his movies, *Shadow of a Doubt.* During World War II, Wilder enlisted in the U.S. Army Air Corps, serving in intelligence in Algeria and Italy, and rose from captain to lieutenant colonel.

A brief skit, *Our Century,* was written for the Century Club in 1947, and Wilder's novel, *The Ides of March,* about the last days of *Julius Caesar,* was published in 1948 to limited success. His play *The Alcestiad* (also known as *A Life in the Sun*) premiered at the Edinburgh Festival in 1955. Modeled on Greek drama and showing the influence of Søren Kierkegaard's Christian existentialism, the first act shows Alcestis receiving a sign from Apollo that she should marry Admetus; the second act dramatizes her decision to give up her life for him and her rescue from Hades by Hercules; and the third act shows her dissuading her son from killing the usurper Agis. A satyr play (a grotesquely comic treatment of serious mythological events), *The Drunken Sisters,* first produced in Zurich in 1957, provides an addendum to *The Alcestiad,* with a comic version of Apollo tricking the Fates into giving him the life of Alcestis. Although not well received, Wilder subsequently wrote a German-language libretto for Louise Talma's operatic version of *The Alcestiad* in 1962 (Wilder also wrote a German-language libretto for Paul Hindemith's operatic *The Long Christmas Dinner* in 1961).

Wilder worked sporadically on two seven-act play cycles, *The Seven Deadly Sins* and *The Seven Ages of Man,* for many years. *Bernice* (Pride) and *The Wreck of the 5:25* (Sloth) were produced in Germany in 1957, and *Someone from Assisi* (Lust), *Infancy,* and *Childhood* in New York in 1962. More of the plays have been performed posthumously, particularly at the Actors Theatre of Louisville in 1997: *A Ringing of Doorbells* (Envy), *In Shakespeare and the Bible* (Wrath), *Youth,* and *The Rivers under the Earth* (possibly meant to represent Middle Age). His last two completed works were novels: *The Eighth Day,* which won the National Book Award in 1968, and *Theophilus North* (1973).

While Wilder's critical reputation appeared to be in decline in the 1970s and 1980s, a resurgence of interest has begun to reestablish him as a major American dramatist.

BIBLIOGRAPHY
Blank, Martin, ed. *Critical Essays on Thornton Wilder.* New York: G. K. Hall, 1996.
———, Dalma Hunyadi Brunauer, and David Garrett Izzo, eds. *Thornton Wilder: New Essays.* West Cornwall, Conn.: Locust Hill Press, 1999.
Bryer, Jackson R., ed. *Conversations with Thornton Wilder.* Jackson: University Press of Mississippi, 1992.
Burbank, Rex. *Thornton Wilder.* Rev. ed. New York: Twayne, 1978.
Burns, Edward M., and Ulla E. Dydo, with William Rice, eds. *The Letters of Gertrude Stein & Thornton Wilder.* New Haven, Conn.: Yale University Press, 1996.
Goldstein, Malcolm. *The Art of Thornton Wilder.* Lincoln: University of Nebraska Press, 1965.
Goldstone, Richard H. *Thornton Wilder: An Intimate Portrait.* New York: Saturday Review Press/Dutton, 1975.
———, and Gary Anderson. *Thornton Wilder: An Annotated Bibliography of Works by and about Thornton Wilder.* New York: AMS Press, 1982.
Haberman, Donald. *The Plays of Thornton Wilder: A Critical Study.* Middletown, Conn.: Wesleyan University Press, 1967.
Harrison, Gilbert A. *The Enthusiast: A Life of Thornton Wilder.* New Haven, Conn.: Ticknor & Fields, 1983.
Konkle, Lincoln. *Thornton Wilder and the Puritan Narrative Tradition.* Columbia: University of Missouri Press, 2006.
Lifton, Paul. *Vast Encyclopedia: The Theatre of Thornton Wilder.* Westport, Conn.: Greenwood Press, 1995.
Walsh, Claudette. *Thornton Wilder: A Reference Guide, 1926–1990.* New York: G. K. Hall, 1993.
Wilder, Amos Niven. *Thornton Wilder and His Public.* Philadelphia: Fortress Press, 1980.

Wilder, Robin G., and Jackson R. Bryer, eds. *The Selected Letters of Thornton Wilder.* New York: HarperCollins, 2008.

Wilder, Thornton. *American Characteristics and Other Essays.* Edited by Donald Gallup. New York: Harper & Row, 1979.

———. *Collected Plays and Writings on Theatre.* Edited by J. D. McClatchy. New York: Library of America, 2007.

———. *The Collected Short Plays of Thornton Wilder.* 2 vols. New York: Theatre Communications Group, 1997 and 1998.

———. *The Journals of Thornton Wilder: 1939–1961.* Edited by Donald Gallup. New Haven, Conn.: Yale University Press, 1985.

Christopher J. Wheatley
The Catholic University of America

WILLIAMS, JESSE LYNCH (1871–1929)

Born in Sterling, Illinois, Jesse Lynch Williams received his bachelor's degree from Princeton in 1892 and his master's in 1895. At Princeton, Williams was a cofounder, with BOOTH TARKINGTON and others, of the Triangle Club, a theatrical group that still flourishes there. While a graduate student, Williams wrote *Princeton Stories* (1895), which portrays the campus life of an American undergraduate. After Princeton, he became a reporter for the *New York Sun* and wrote fiction on the side. From 1904 to 1929, he wrote six novels and four plays.

He is remembered for his play *WHY MARRY?* (1917), which questions the conventions of marriage, but ends conventionally, and which won the first PULITZER PRIZE for drama. His other plays are *The Stolen Story* (1906), based on his experiences as a newspaper reporter; *Why Not?* (1922), which deals with the problems faced by divorced people at a time when divorce was still considered somewhat scandalous; and *Lovely Lady* (1925), an unsuccessful play about a woman who sets her trap for a successful attorney—or his handsome son (both men send her packing).

BIBLIOGRAPHY
Williams, Jesse Lynch. *Why Marry?* New York: Scribners, 1918.

WILLIAMS, SAMM-ART (SAMUEL ARTHUR) (1946–)

Playwright Samm-Art Williams differs from many African-American play-wrights of his generation in that his plays do not present a dichotomy between the black middle class—whom the more militant playwrights characterized as Uncle Toms—and civil rights activists. Williams believes that many of the playwrights in the 1960s and early 1970s did not show a balanced picture, namely that there were principled people in both groups—just as there were some without principles in both.

Williams was born and raised in the small town of Burgaw, North Carolina, which was the model for the town of Cross Roads in his most famous play, *Home* (1979). Though his parents separated when he was very young, he and his mother were surrounded by a loving extended family. His mother, who was a high school English and drama teacher, encouraged his interests in writing and acting. In particular, she familiarized him with the plays of Shakespeare and the works of LANGSTON HUGHES and James Weldon Johnson, among many other writers. She also directed him in school plays. When he left home to attend Morgan State College in Baltimore, these interests had to be substantially set aside (though he did continue to write poetry) because the college had no drama department and only two creative writing classes. Williams majored in political science.

After graduating in 1968, he moved to Philadelphia and became involved in the Freedom Theater there. In 1973, he moved to New York, where he worked in various odd jobs and as an actor. His first part in a play in New York was in Ken Eulo's *Black Jesus* (1973). Acting in a production at the Negro Ensemble Company put Williams in contact with DOUGLAS TURNER WARD. Williams then finished one of the three plays he had been working on; *Welcome to Black River* (1975), produced by the Negro Ensemble Company's Play-wrights Workshop, is set in a rural community not unlike that in which Williams grew up. It involves a black family and a white family with a shared history. His early plays, produced either by the Negro Ensemble Company or by Williams himself, were *The Coming* and *Do Unto Others* (1976); *A Love Play* (1976); *The Last Caravan* (1977), a musical comedy about a man who looks for an elixir to restore his virility in old age; and *Brass Birds Don't Sing* (1978), the story of two sisters who, after they are rescued from Lebensborn, the

Nazi breeding camp, suffer further persecution in America.

With the Negro Ensemble Company's production of his comedy *Home* (1979), Williams achieved critical and commercial success. Set in the Vietnam era, the play is the story of a young African-American man, Cephus Miles, who loses his land in rural North Carolina to back taxes while serving a prison term for refusing to go to war. When he is released, he is forced to try his luck in the North. Hard times there turn him toward drugs and alcohol, but in the end he is able to reclaim his land. Driven by his love of the land and his longing for home, he finds that he *can* go home again. The structure of the play has Cephus telling the tale, remembering events from his front porch, with wit and warmth. *New York Times* critic Mel Gussow wrote after the Negro Ensemble Company production transferred to Broadway, "If Twain were black and from North Carolina, he might have written like Samm-Art Williams" (May 8, 1980). The overwhelming success of the play brought Williams into the glare of instant fame; he was expected to turn out more hits, but his subsequent plays did not enjoy the success of *Home*.

Williams continued his acting career as he continued to write. In the 1980s, several of his plays were produced. *The Sixteenth Round* (1980) is about an aging boxer who expects to be killed by the mob for throwing a fight; physically and mentally debilitated by his sport, he waits for his executioner. In *Friends* (1983), two blind men share an apartment and eventually discover that they have loved the same woman. *Bojangles* (1985) is a musical based on the career of the legendary tap dancer, Bill "Bojangles" Robinson; and *Eyes of the American* (1985) is a political drama set in a Caribbean nation. Williams contributed to an anthology program entitled *Orchids* (1986), which consisted of one-act adaptations of Anton Chekhov's short stories; other contributors were WENDY WASSERSTEIN, JOHN GUARE, DAVID MAMET, MARIE IRENE FORNÉS, MICHAEL WELLER, and Spalding Gray. Williams's most recent new play, *The Waiting Room* (2007), was produced by the Negro Ensemble Company; a comedy set in a hospital waiting room, the play concerns secrets and the generation gap in an African-American family.

Williams has had a long and prosperous acting career onstage, in television, and in film since the early 1970s, and he has never stopped writing. After living in Los Angeles for almost two decades, Williams returned to his native North Carolina in the late 1990s. He is at present artist-in-residence at North Carolina Central University. As part of the 2008–2009 Signature Theatre season devoted to classic plays from the repertoire of the Negro Ensemble Company, Williams's *Home* was given a fine revival in 2008.

BIBLIOGRAPHY

Williams, Samm-Art. *Eyes of the American.* New York: Samuel French, 1986.
———. *Home.* New York: Dramatists Play Service, 1980.
———. *Woman from the Town.* New York: Samuel French, 1990.

WILLIAMS, TENNESSEE (1911–1983) "Tennessee Williams's voice is the most distinctively poetic, the most idiosyncratically moving, at the same time the most firmly dramatic to have come the American Theater's way—ever. He is our best playwright"; this was the assessment of *New York Times* critic Walter Kerr (May 22, 1977). Williams is indisputably among the most important playwrights, along with EUGENE O'NEILL, ARTHUR MILLER, EDWARD ALBEE, and AUGUST WILSON, in the history of American drama. He was born Thomas Lanier Williams III in Columbus, Mississippi. As a young boy, he suffered from a severe case of diphtheria and later from Bright's disease. Also in childhood, Williams began a lifelong bond with his older sister Rose, a bond that would transcend his alcoholic bouts with depression and Rose's schizophrenia (followed by a 1943 prefrontal lobotomy).

When America entered World War I, Williams's father, Cornelius, who had been a traveling salesman for most of his marriage, began to manage the sales force at the International Shoe Company in St. Louis. His wife, Edwina, and the children soon joined him in the North. In 1919, Edwina gave birth to a third child, Walter Dakin Williams, whom Cornelius believed was not his, but to whom he nevertheless acted in a supportive and appreciative way. On the other hand, there was something about Tom—his shy, hesitant way, as well as his bookish, reclusive tendencies—that aroused feelings of contempt in Cornelius, to the point where he would scornfully call him "Aunt Nancy." Under the strain of living in a new northern urban environment with a hostile and difficult husband, Edwina weakened and became sick, and the unhappy Tom was allowed to return in 1920 to Mississippi—specifically, Clarksdale—to live with his mother's parents for a full semester, where his intelligence would shine in the classroom and his southern drawl was not an open invitation for ridicule.

Williams's career as a professional writer began at the age of 16 in 1927, when he earned $5 for taking third place in a contest sponsored by a true confession magazine. A year later, he received $35 from *Weird Tales* for his story, "The Vengeance of Nitocris," based on an episode found in Herodotus. In 1929, he entered the school of journalism at the University of Missouri in Columbia, and in 1930 wrote his first play, "Beauty is the Word," which took sixth place in a play contest. Entering another play contest the following fall, Williams wrote *Hot Milk at Three in the Morning,* a far more visceral play than his earlier entry—this one about an angry young man trapped in a marriage with an infant child and a sick wife. Some years later, he would rewrite it as *Moony's Kid Don't Cry* (1936).

In 1932, after Williams completed his third year at the University of Missouri, he returned to St. Louis to find that his father, enraged that Tom had flunked R. O.T.C., refused to pay his tuition for his senior year. Cornelius got his son a job at the International Shoe Company, where Williams worked for three years, writing poems and short stories at night. An eventual breakdown, which the doctors termed "total exhaustion," resulted in a release from the monotonous rigors of the warehouse. This and a summer spent in Memphis with his grandparents (next door to whom lived the director of a small informal summer theater group with which Williams became involved) began to move Williams slowly but surely toward a life obsessively devoted to writing plays for theaters that wanted them.

In the spring of 1936, Williams entered a one-act play contest; he wrote "The Magic Tower" in a week's time to meet the contest deadline. The play, which is about a young couple who decide to live in splendid isolation in order to preserve the romantic quality of their marriage only to discover after a year that the thrill is gone, won the contest. It also caught the eye of Willard Holland, the charismatic director of a local theater company called the Mummers. In March of 1937, the Mummers premiered Williams's first full-length play, *Candles to the Sun,* a powerful Marxist melodrama set in the Alabama coal fields and featuring strong female characters, the wives and widows of the miners. Williams's second full-length play, *Fugitive Kind* (not to be confused with *The Fugitive Kind,* the 1960 film version of Williams's *Orpheus Descending* [1957]), was produced by the Mummers in the fall of 1937 and was a critical failure. Set in a St. Louis flophouse, the play depicted the social ills of the depression.

While attending a semester course in playwriting at the University of Iowa in 1938, Williams finished *Spring Storm,* which portrays four unmarried young people in their twenties, living in a Mississippi Delta town in 1937; their romantic lives intertwine, crossing over class boundaries and cultural taboos. *Spring Storm* is the first play in which one can hear the authentic voice of Tennessee Williams. And in retrospect, it is a long farewell to a segregated agrarian South, as well as to the legal system and lifestyle that supported it, the South that would disappear forever a decade or so after World War II. Despite its quality, *Spring Storm* received a negative response from faculty and students alike, perhaps because the head of the Iowa theater department, E. C. Mabie, was one of the ideological architects of the FEDERAL THEATRE PROJECT and ran a program designed to train writers of AGIT-PROP plays and LIVING NEWSPAPERS.

Williams's next full-length play, *Not about Nightingales,* was inspired by a sensational 1938 news story, describing an incident in a Pennsylvania prison in which striking inmates were killed. It depicts the misery of men caged like animals and determined to escape (and was produced for the first time in London in 1998). In this play, Williams announced his own newfound, hard-boiled artistic credo, a determination to turn away from seemingly sentimental plays, like *Spring Storm,* in the midst of the continuing social upheaval of the depression. It was not until 1939 and 1940 that Williams would return to his true calling, first announced by *Spring Storm*: the writing of full-length plays that mark him as the poet-playwright of the dispossessed. But instead of concentrating on groups—miners, hobos, prisoners—his plays would concentrate on individuals, forlorn characters who deliver long, poignant, poetic arias, often looking back over their lives.

At the end of 1938, Williams entered three full-length plays and three one-acts collected under the title "American Blues," in a GROUP THEATRE play contest, which, the following March, awarded "American Blues" a $100 prize; for the first time, Williams signed his name as Tennessee Williams. As a result of the subsequent publicity, he was contacted by Audrey Wood, who became his agent for the next 30 years. In September of 1939, Williams finally went to New York, where he saw Broadway plays, was introduced to the members of the Group Theatre, and began work on a new full-length play titled *Battle of Angels* (1940), which never reached Broadway but closed in Boston in 1941 after 12 performances; Williams would later rewrite it as *Orpheus Descending*.

With his first Broadway play, *The GLASS MENAGERIE* (1945), now an acclaimed and enduring masterpiece, Williams enlarged the form and scope of the realistic tradition by inventing the memory play, permitting the character Tom to be both narrator of the recollected action and a chief participant in it—to look back in sadness and poignant regret at the depression and his impoverished family (mother, sister, and vanished father). It is Tom's wrenching guilt and continuing attachment to Laura that drive him to tell her story, long after he himself has escaped from their coffinlike apartment. Because *The Glass Menagerie* takes place inside of Tom's head, it is finally poetic in both language and form. Therefore, it represents the beginning of a new post–World War II strategy and style, alternately called poetic realism and psychological realism.

The opening of *The Glass Menagerie* to great acclaim marked the beginning of a 17-year period in which 11 new full-length Tennessee Williams plays were produced in New York, all but one on Broadway. Most of them received laudatory reviews and had successful runs. *A STREETCAR NAMED DESIRE* (1947) and *CAT ON A HOT TIN ROOF* (1955) each received the PULITZER PRIZE. This string of notable dramatic work ends with *The NIGHT OF THE IGUANA* (1961). Even some of those works regarded as "failures" in their initial Broadway productions—*SUMMER AND SMOKE* (1948), *CAMINO REAL* (1953), and *Orpheus Descending*—were revived years later and received more sympathetic reviews that established their worth.

When the final curtain came down on opening night of Williams's second Broadway play, *A Streetcar Named Desire,* the audience cheered for half an hour. In *Streetcar,* Williams boldly depicts Blanche DuBois as an alcoholic who has recklessly and obsessively pursued sexual partners in an effort to numb her own suffering; the playwright succeeds, however, in making her a sympathetic and heroic character by giving her the power of poetic speech. Blanche is also a defiant character who refuses to submit to the brutal world—until, when her brother-in-law Stanley rapes her, it breaks her.

The next play, *Summer and Smoke,* opened while *Streetcar* was still running and suffered by comparison. After the explosive urgency of *Streetcar,* the brooding languid pace of *Summer and Smoke* seemed to disappoint audiences and most critics. The play is about a southern spinster—a minister's daughter—and her repressed love for a young doctor. Eventually, the doctor falls in love with a younger woman, and Alma, in the final scene, initiates what we assume will be the first in a future of assignations with strangers. It was not until 1952, when the OFF-BROADWAY Circle in the Square Theatre revived the play with Geraldine Page as Alma, that it received the attention it deserved (*Summer and Smoke* was later revised as *Eccentricities of a NightinGale* [1964]).

The ROSE TATTOO (1951) is a comedy about love, betrayal, and grief, heavy with melodramatic overtones, set in a Sicilian community along the Gulf Coast west of New Orleans. In it, a woman comes to terms with her late husband's infidelity and embraces life in the arms of a new man. *Camino Real* is a free-flowing, fantasmagoric, poetic, occasionally plotless play that pits the humanistic tradition of reason and art against the punishing power of a fascist police state. The play was in part an angry protest against the political climate of the 1950s, an age of political witchhunts. Among the play's great lines are Byron's last words as he ventures out into the "Terra Incognita"; they could be the legend that perfectly describes Williams's life and artistic career: "Attempt voyages! Make them! There's nothing else."

Sexuality and cruelty are frequent themes in Williams's plays, and both are featured in three other plays of this period. Each work touches on the unspeakable cruelty human beings are capable of inflicting on one another. In *Orpheus Descending,* an itinerant young man awakens the passion in an older woman trapped in a loveless marriage to the man who killed her father. When they are found out, they are killed by the husband and his cronies, and the young man is burned to death by a lynch mob. *Suddenly Last Summer* (1958) is a short play in which an aging woman tries to force her niece to have a lobotomy in order to keep her from telling the truth about the woman's homosexual son who was killed and eaten by youths. In *Sweet Bird of Youth* (1959), an aging film star tries to drown her desperation in drugs, alcohol, and sex with the beautiful young man, Chance Wayne, she has picked up. Chance hopes to return to his high school sweetheart and true love—and thereby turn back the hands of time—but the young woman's father, a powerful man who loathes Chance for leaving his daughter, Heavenly, infected with venereal disease, vows to have him castrated.

Finally, *The Night of the Iguana* is one of Williams's most highly regarded plays. In it, two strangers meet and talk and come to terms with their own demons. One is a former clergyman whose spiritual needs and sexual appetites are forever in conflict; the other, a female artist traveling with her dying poet grandfather, is emotionally isolated and fears intimacy.

After *The Night of the Iguana,* Williams continued to write, but further critical success eluded him. This was certainly in part because of his increasing abuse of drugs and alcohol, which, sadly, left him unfocused at best and, on one occasion in 1969, briefly institutionalized; among the considerable output of this period—*The Milk Train Doesn't Stop Here Anymore* (1963), *Slapstick Tragedy* (1966), *The Two Character Play* (1967; revised as *Out Cry* [1973]), *The Seven Descents of Myrtle* (1968; revised as *Kingdom of Earth* [1975]), *In the Bar of a Tokyo Hotel* (1969), *Small Craft Warnings* (1972), *The Red Devil Battery Sign* (1975), *Vieux Carré* (1977), *Creve Coeur* (1978; revised as *A Lovely Sunday for Creve Coeur* [1979]), *Clothes for a Summer Hotel* (1980), *Something Cloudy, Something Clear* (1981), and *A House Not Meant to Stand* (1982)— one finds passages that contain the unmistakable poetry of Tennessee Williams. In any case, the body of work from Williams's most fertile period, between the mid-1940s and the early 1960s, secured his reputation as one of America's greatest playwrights. At his best, he was a master builder of plots and the heroic poet of the defeated. As Maggie cries out plaintively to her alcoholic husband Brick in *Cat on a Hot Tin Roof,* "[L]ife has got to be allowed to continue even after the dream of life is—all—over." Williams biographer Lyle Leverich says it best: "Tennessee Williams was, first to last, our foremost poet-playwright. He gave up only when death intervened" (xxviii).

BIBLIOGRAPHY

Bigsby, C. W. E. "Tennessee Williams." In *A Critical Introduction to Twentieth-Century American Drama.* Vol. 2, *Williams/Miller/Albee.* Cambridge, England: Cambridge University Press, 1984. 15–134.

Bray, Robert, ed. *Tennessee Williams and His Contemporaries.* Newcastle, England: Cambridge Scholars Publishing, 2007.

Crandell, George W. *Tennessee Williams: A Descriptive Bibliography.* Pittsburgh: University of Pittsburgh Press, 1995.

Devlin, Albert J., ed. *Conversations with Tennessee Williams.* Jackson: University Press of Mississippi, 1986.

———, and Nancy M. Tischler, eds. *The Selected Letters of Tennessee Williams—Volume I: 1920–1945.* New York: New Directions, 2000.

———, eds. *The Selected Letters of Tennessee Williams—Volume 2: 1945–1957.* New York: New Directions, 2004.

Griffin, Alice. *Understanding Tennessee Williams.* Columbia: University of South Carolina Press, 1995.

Hayman, Ronald. *Tennessee Williams: Everyone Else Is an Audience.* New Haven, Conn.: Yale University Press, 1993.

Jackson, Esther Merle. *The Broken World of Tennessee Williams.* Madison: University of Wisconsin Press, 1966.

Kolin, Philip C., ed. *Tennessee Williams: A Guide to Research and Performance.* Westport, Conn.: Greenwood Press, 1998.

————, ed. *The Tennessee Williams Encyclopedia.* Westport, Conn.: Greenwood Press, 2004.

————, ed. *The Undiscovered Country: The Later Plays of Tennessee Williams.* New York: Peter Lang, 2002.

Leverich, Lyle. *Tom: The Unknown Tennessee Williams.* New York: Crown, 1995.

Martin, Robert A., ed. *Critical Essays on Tennessee Williams.* New York: G. K. Hall, 1997.

McCann, John S. *The Critical Reputation of Tennessee Williams: A Reference Guide.* Boston: G. K. Hall, 1983.

Murphy, Brenda. *Tennessee Williams and Elia Kazan: A Collaboration in the Theatre.* Cambridge, England: Cambridge University Press, 1992.

Paller, Michael. *Gentleman Callers: Tennessee Williams, Homosexuality, and Mid-Twentieth-Century Drama.* New York: Palgrave Macmillan, 2005.

Roudané, Matthew C., ed. *The Cambridge Companion to Tennessee Williams.* Cambridge, England: Cambridge University Press, 1997.

Spoto, Donald. *The Kindness of Strangers: The Life of Tennessee Williams.* Boston: Little, Brown, 1985.

Tharpe, Jac, ed. *Tennessee Williams: A Tribute.* Jackson: University Press of Mississippi, 1977.

Voss, Ralph F., ed. *Magical Muse: Millennial Essays on Tennessee Williams.* Tuscaloosa: University of Alabama Press, 2002.

Williams, Tennessee. *Five O'Clock Angel: Letters of Tennessee Williams to Maria St. Just—1948–1982.* New York: Knopf, 1990.

————. *Fugitive Kind.* Edited by Allean Hale. New York: New Directions, 2001.

————. *A House Not Meant to Stand.* Edited by Thomas Keith. New York: New Directions, 2008.

————. *Memoirs.* Garden City, N.Y.: Doubleday, 1975.

————. *"Mister Paradise" and Other One-Act Plays by Tennessee Williams.* Edited by Nicholas Moschovakis and David Roessel. New York: New Directions, 2005.

————. *Notebooks.* Edited by Margaret Bradham Thornton. New Haven, Conn.: Yale University Press, 2006.

————. *Plays.* 2 vols. Edited by Mel Gussow and Kenneth Holditch. New York: Library of America, 2000.

————. *Stairs to the Roof.* Edited by Allean Hale. New York: New Directions, 2000.

————. *"The Traveling Companion" and Other Plays.* Edited by Annette J. Saddik. New York: New Directions, 2008.

————. *Where I Live: Selected Essays.* Edited by Christine R. Day and Bob Woods. New York: New Directions, 1978.

Windham, Donald, ed. *Tennessee Williams's Letters to Donald Windham, 1940–1965.* New York: Holt, Rinehart and Winston, 1976.

Dan Isaac
New York, New York

WILLIS, NATHANIEL PARKER (1806–1867)

Best remembered for his career as an essayist and for his romantic comedy, *Tortesa, the Usurer* (1839), Nathaniel Parker Willis personified the gentleman of letters in early 19th-century America. Born in Portland, Maine, and educated at Yale, Willis became, as Edwin Forrest later described, "the head" of a "literary coterie by the fiat of whom every man must fall" (McConachie 73). Forrest's accusation sprang from an incident in which he believed Willis had used the power he wielded in the popular press to destroy Forrest's marriage. Willis had described Forrest as being of a "different class" from his wife, implying that the rugged Jacksonian stage star lacked sufficient intellect to keep pace with his wife's circle of friends. Forrest retaliated in 1851 by attacking Willis on the street, knocking him to the ground, and beating him with a cane.

Though the episode with Forrest was an extreme example, in many ways, it exemplified Willis's perception of the growing class rift in American culture. Willis's suggestion that Forrest (the embodiment of Jacksonian manliness) lacked the social refinement necessary to pass in "polite" society is a problem echoed in his play *Tortesa, the Usurer.* The central character is a social climber who hopes to push his way into good society by marrying a woman with a higher social status. As Tortesa says, "What need have I of forty generations / To build my name up? I have bought with money / The fairest daughter of their haughtiest line!"

Tortesa was created for the National Theatre's actor-manager, James William Wallack, who adopted the role as one of his favorites. Willis had won a dramatic contest two years before he wrote *Tortesa,* when he created *Bianca Visconti* (1837) for the actress Josephine Clifton. His subsequent play for Clifton, *The Kentucky Heiress* (1837), was not as popular. Willis was writing verse plays at a period in American history when "native" authors were still treated with less respect than European imports, and he received strong criticism for his work, which was described as "imperfectly constructed," with the "parts not well harmonized." Yet critics acknowledged that despite the flaws in his plays, "we think highly of the drama as a whole" (Moses 259).

At the time Willis wrote *Tortesa* and *Bianca,* the United States had not yet established copyright laws that protected dramatic authors, and it was ultimately more profitable for him to return to a career in journalism. In 1843, he became the editor of the *New Mirror* (he had been one of the editors of the *New York Mirror* in 1831, before moving to Europe, where he spent five years traveling and where he wrote *Pencillings by the Way* [1835]). Aside from his dramas and his essays, Willis is remembered for his ardent defense of colleague Edgar Allan Poe, who was viciously attacked by literary critic Rufus Wilmont Griswold. His defense of Poe can also be read as a defense of America's rising literary sphere, something he strove all his life to establish as an equal to any in Europe.

BIBLIOGRAPHY
Auser, Cortland P. *Nathaniel P. Willis.* New York: Twayne, 1970.
Baker, Thomas Nelson. *Sentiment and Celebrity: Nathaniel Parker Willis and the Trials of Literary Fame.* New York: Oxford University Press, 1999.
Beers, Henry A. *Nathaniel Parker Willis.* Boston: Houghton Mifflin, 1885.
McConachie, Bruce A. *Melodramatic Formations: American Theatre and Society, 1820–1870.* Iowa City: University of Iowa Press, 1992.
Moses, Montrose J. *Representative Plays by American Dramatists.* 1918. New York: Benjamin Blom, 1964.

Heather Nathans
University of Maryland

WILSON, AUGUST (1945–2005) The plays
of the African-American dramatist August Wilson won two PULITZER PRIZES, a TONY AWARD (of his 10 cycle plays, only one, the revised JITNEY [2000], was not nominated), and innumerable critics' awards. These honors acknowledge a body of work that made Wilson, by any standard, one of the foremost playwrights in the history of the American stage. Wilson's intense and lyrical dramas feature well-defined characters, themes drawn from the lives of 20th-century African Americans, and a stage language in the style of American poetic realism. Most of Wilson's plays are part of his ambitious cycle of 10 plays—one set in each decade of the 20th century—depicting the African-American experience.

Born Frederick August Kittel, son of Frederick August and Daisy (Wilson) Kittel, in Pittsburgh, Pennsylvania, Wilson grew up in the Hill district of that city, an economically depressed African-American community in which he set many of his plays. His white father, a baker by profession, left when Wilson was 11, and the family's tenuous economic situation worsened as his mother, a cleaning woman, struggled to raise Wilson and his five siblings. (In the early 1970s, he legally adopted his mother's maiden name.) When his mother remarried, Wilson's family moved to a predominantly white suburb. After he was falsely accused of plagiarism, Wilson dropped out of his high school, where he was the only black student. Interested in art and literature, he educated himself at the local library before enlisting in the United States Army in 1962.

Calling himself a "black nationalist," Wilson became involved in the Civil Rights movement in the mid-1960s and began writing poetry. In 1968, he cofounded with writer and teacher Rob Penny the Black Horizon Theatre in Pittsburgh, where the two produced current black drama. Penny and Wilson also established the Kuntu Writers Workshop in 1976. Wilson's first play came out of a series of poems he wrote about a character named Black Bart: *Black Bart and the Sacred Hills,* a musical satire, was done as a staged reading at the Inner City Theatre in Los Angeles in 1978.

In 1978, Wilson moved to St. Paul, Minnesota, where he began writing dramatic sketches for the Science Museum of Minnesota, a job he held until 1981. In 1981, *Black Bart and the Sacred Hills* was produced at the Penumbra Theatre in St. Paul. It was in Minnesota that Wilson's playwriting, which he continued to develop, began to reflect the dialects and unique rhythms of speech he had heard in his early years in Pittsburgh. He wrote the first version of *Jitney,* a play set in a gypsy cab station in the Hill District of Pittsburgh, and submitted it and *Black Bart* to the Eugene O'Neill Theatre Center's National Playwrights' Conference; both plays were rejected. However, the Playwrights' Center in Minneapolis gave *Jitney* and Wilson's next play, *Fullerton Street,* staged readings in 1981. *Jitney* was produced by Pittsburgh's Allegheny Repertory Theatre in 1982. In 2000, a revised *Jitney* opened on Broadway, where it won Wilson his seventh New York Drama Critics' Circle Award.

Wilson was significantly inspired by music—especially jazz and the blues—and he employed music in his plays, both to underscore his language and to set mood and period. His first critical and commercial success was MA RAINEY'S BLACK BOTTOM (1984). Featuring real-life 1920s blues singer Ma Rainey and her musicians, this drama explores the ways in which Rainey was exploited by her record producers, and how she used her prowess before the microphone to attain some measure of power within a profoundly racist society. The play was accepted for a workshop production at the 1982 Eugene O'Neill Center's Playwrights' Conference—where Wilson first worked with director Lloyd Richards—and produced at Yale Repertory Theatre under Richards's direction in April 1984. *Ma Rainey's Black Bottom* was the first Wilson play to reach Broadway, where it opened at the Cort Theatre in October 1984. It was proclaimed a work of art by appreciative critics and won the New York Drama Critics' Circle Award. In 2003, a revival starring Whoopi Goldberg opened on Broadway but was not successful.

The next play in Wilson's cycle, JOE TURNER'S COME AND GONE, opened, again at Yale under Richards's direction, in April 1986. This was followed by a production at Arena Stage in Washington, D.C., in October 1987 and at New York's Ethel Barrymore Theatre in 1988. The play won the New York Drama Critics' Circle Award and was praised by critics as Wilson's most ambitious play to date. *Joe Turner* is set in 1911 in a Pittsburgh boarding house accommodating southern blacks migrating north and deals specifically with a man attempting to reconnect his family, torn apart by his sudden disappearance when he was forced to seven years of labor in a chain gang.

Joe Turner was followed by FENCES, which opened in April 1985 at Yale under Richards's direction. After runs at Chicago's Goodman Theatre and in San Francisco, *Fences* opened in March 1987 at New York's Forty-Sixth Street Theatre. Wilson's most critically acclaimed and commercially successful drama, *Fences* was awarded the Pulitzer Prize, the Tony Award, and the New York Drama Critics' Circle Award. The play's protagonist is Troy Maxson, a former Negro League baseball player, now middle-aged and working as a garbage man in the grim poverty of the black ghetto in the 1950s. Embittered by his own experiences, Troy tries to prevent his son, Cory, from accepting a football scholarship to attend college, a perverse response that even he must know will keep Cory from any hope of improving his chances of success. Troy's bitterness also leads to womanizing, which produces an illegitimate child that he expects his wife, Rose, to raise. Through the character of Troy, Wilson explores his recurring theme of the tragic effects of the frustrated ambitions of those excluded from society's opportunities because of race, though the play ends on a somewhat hopeful note as Cory, now in the military, returns home to reckon with his father's spirit after Troy's death. Cory's return underscores another recurring theme in Wilson's plays: the need for African Americans both to honor the past and move boldly into the future, without the baggage of the past.

The PIANO LESSON (1987), Wilson's next play, deals centrally with just that subject. It was given a first public reading in 1987 at the Eugene O'Neill Theatre Center's National Playwrights' Conference prior to a Yale production, again under Richards's direction, which opened in November 1987 (followed by a run at Boston's Huntington Theatre in 1988). Opening in New York in 1990, *The Piano Lesson* brought Wilson his second Pulitzer Prize and the New York Drama Critics' Circle Award. Set in the home of Berniece Charles and her family in Pittsburgh, the play centers on an ornate 137-year-old upright piano that, over the course of this evocative drama, becomes a source of contention within the family; it represents differing views of the Charles family's history and future. Berniece sees the piano as a significant family heirloom to be cherished, but for Boy Willie, her brother, selling the piano means the possibility of a return to the family's roots in Mississippi through the purchase of the very land on which their forebears had been held in slavery. In this play, many recurring Wilson themes coalesce—the "lost" past of oppressed African Americans, here symbolized by the piano (and its "lesson" for the play's characters, as well as for the audience), and the difficulty for blacks to find opportunity in the America of the present and the future. Establishing himself through the opportunity presented by the piano's worth is Boy Willie's goal. The piano is something of a family album of ghosts for Berniece, as she recalls its meaning to various family members, especially her mother, who talked to the spirits of the family dead through the piano. Critical acclaim was virtually unanimous, with particular praise for the lyricism of Wilson's writing and for his skills as a theatrical storyteller. *The Piano Lesson,* with much of its original cast, was filmed for CBS-TV's *Hallmark Hall of Fame* series in 1995; once again, it met with critical approval.

The next play in Wilson's cycle, TWO TRAINS RUNNING, written in 1990 and first produced at Yale, again under Richards's direction, was followed by a 1992 Broadway production, which won the New York Drama Critics' Circle Award. In a Pittsburgh diner on a block slated for urban renewal in 1969, a group of men anticipate the funeral of a local preacher and a rally in response to the assassination of Malcolm X. The play's only woman, the waitress Risa, has purposely scarred her legs as a way of avoiding contact with men and, more important, as a means of forcing those around her to look at her in more substantive ways. Despite respectful reviews, the play had a disappointingly short run. In January and February 1995, Chicago's Goodman Theatre premiered Wilson's SEVEN GUITARS (originally entitled *Moon Going Down*), a drama set in the 1940s and dealing with the lives of black blues musicians and the frustration that often drives their choices. It moved to Broadway for a moderately successful run later in 1995, winning Wilson another New York Drama Critics' Circle Award. The next installment in Wilson's cycle, KING HEDLEY II (2001), is set in 1985 in Pittsburgh's Hill District in the midst of Ronald Reagan's presidency. "Trickle down" economics seem to have missed the Hill, where drugs, gangs, failed businesses, and drive-by shootings dominate the lives of those in this devastated black community. Hedley, the central character, tries to rise above these overwhelming circumstances, but the sheer weight of the social problems and his own limitations make it impossible.

In 1997, Wilson inspired a theatrical controversy when he argued for a separatist black American culture on the grounds that white cultural institutions would never enthusiastically or effectively nurture black artists. After exchanging opposing views in print, Wilson publicly debated director and scholar Robert Brustein on the subject.

Early in the new millennium, Wilson was at work on a screenplay for an as-yet unproduced film version of *Fences* and completed the plays in his cycle of dramas on the black experience in America. In early 2003, GEM OF THE OCEAN, set in the 1900s, opened at Chicago's Goodman Theatre. Two years later, in April 2005, RADIO GOLF, the final cycle play, premiered at the Yale Repertory Theatre. Wilson also wrote a one-man autobiographical play, *How I Learned What I Learned* (2003); Lawrence Van Gelder wrote in the *New York Times* that it "meditates on [Wilson's] struggles as an artist at the crossroads of black and white culture" (May 21, 2003). It opened for a limited run in May 2003 at the Seattle Repertory Theater.

Two months after the last of the 10 cycle plays opened, Wilson was diagnosed with liver cancer, leading to his death on October 2, 2005, a devastating loss to the American theater. Two years after his death, a boxed set of the cycle plays called *The August Wilson Century Cyle* was published, with introductions to each play by leading American artists and writers, including SUZAN-LORI PARKS, TONY KUSHNER, Toni Morrison, Frank Rich, Ishmael Reed, Samuel J. Freedman, and others. Wilson's unique career provided significant inspiration to aspiring dramatists in the areas of artistic and thematic ambition, and his 10-play cycle stands as both a classic of American dramatic literature and a document of the experience of African Americans.

BIBLIOGRAPHY

Bigsby, Christopher, ed. *The Cambridge Companion to August Wilson.* Cambridge and New York: Cambridge University Press, 2007.

Bloom, Harold, ed. *August Wilson.* New York: Chelsea House Publishers, 2001.

Bogumil, Mary L. *Understanding August Wilson.* Columbia: University of South Carolina Press, 1998.

Bryer, Jackson R., and Mary C. Hartig, eds. *Conversations with August Wilson.* Jackson: University Press of Mississippi, 2006.

Clark, Keith. *Black Manhood in James Baldwin, Ernest J. Gaines, and August Wilson.* Urbana: University of Illinois Press, 2002.

Elam, Harry J., Jr. *The Past as Present in the Drama of August Wilson.* Ann Arbor: University of Michigan Press, 2004.

Elkins, Marilyn, ed. *August Wilson: A Casebook.* New York: Routledge, 2000.

Herrington, Joan. *I Ain't Sorry for Nothin' I Done: August Wilson's Process of Playwriting.* New York: Limelight, 1998.

Nadel, Alan, ed. *May All Your Fences Have Gates: Essays on the Drama of August Wilson.* Iowa City: University of Iowa Press, 1994.

Pereira, Kim. *August Wilson and the African-American Odyssey.* Urbana: University of Illinois Press, 1995.

Shafer, Yvonne. *August Wilson: A Research and Production Sourcebook.* Westport, Conn.: Greenwood Press, 1998.

Shannon, Sandra G. *The Dramatic Vision of August Wilson.* Washington, D.C.: Howard University Press, 1995.

Wang, Qun. *An In-Depth Study of the Major Plays of African-American Playwright August Wilson: Vernacularizing the Blues on Stage.* Lewiston, N.Y.: Edwin Mellen Press, 1999.

Williams, Dana A., and Sandra G. Shannon, eds. *August Wilson and Black Aesthetics.* New York: Palgrave Macmillan, 2004.

Wilson, August. *The August Wilson Century Cycle.* New York: Theatre Communications Group, 2007.

————. *Cultivating the Ground on Which We Stand.* New York: St. Martin's, 2002.

————. *The Ground on Which I Stand.* New York: Theatre Communications Group, 2001.

Wolfe, Peter. *August Wilson.* Boston: Twayne, 1999.

James Fisher
University of North Carolina at Greensboro

WILSON, LANFORD (1937–)

Lanford Wilson emerged as one of America's leading playwrights in the last third of the 20th century. His works demonstrate a voice and a clarity of character that is unique in the annals of the American stage. Using what he calls "lyric realism," a technique that combines characters, stories, gentle humor, and harsh reality, Wilson has created a memorable body of work.

Like many post–World War II playwrights, Wilson uses characters and experiences from his own life in his plays. He was born in Lebanon, Missouri. His parents were divorced when he was five; his father moved to San Diego, remarried, and went to work in an aircraft factory. Wilson and his mother moved to Springfield, Missouri, where she worked in a garment factory and later married a dairy inspector. When Wilson was 18, he went to California to visit his father and stayed there, working at the same factory as his father. This reunion was not a happy one, and after a year or so, he moved to Chicago, where he worked for an advertising agency and took some playwriting courses at the University of Chicago. In 1962, he moved to New York City and soon became involved with the "café theater" work being done at such OFF-OFF-BROADWAY venues as the Caffe Cino and La MaMa Experimental Theatre Club.

It was at these coffeehouse theaters in 1963 that his first plays—one-acts such as *So Long at the Fair* (1963), *Home Free* (1964), and *The Madness of Lady Bright* (1964)—were produced and where he first worked with director Marshall W. Mason. Their meeting in 1964 was the beginning of one of the most successful collaborations between a playwright and a director in American theater history. Beginning with *The Sand Castle* (1965), Wilson had 13 plays produced OFF-BROADWAY between 1965 and 1969. Most of them were directed by Mason, with many of the same actors, forming an informal company that included Tanya Berezin, Michael Powell, and Rob Thirkield.

Wilson's work Off-Broadway attracted the attention of producers on Broadway. Two of his plays, *The Gingham Dog* (1969) and *Lemon Sky* (1970), moved to Broadway after regional productions. But the success of Wilson's work relies on intimate contact with the audience, something unattainable in the comparatively large theaters of Broadway, and both plays, while critically lauded, closed after very short runs. It was clear to both Wilson and Mason that Wilson's plays were not meant to be staged in such large venues. In 1969, Wilson and Mason, along with Berezin and Thirkield, formed the Circle Repertory Theatre

Company, dedicated to performing new plays by new writers with a strong and largely permanent company of actors. This gave Wilson a home in which to write his plays and a family for whom to write. First working in a walk-up warehouse, then moving to the Sheridan Square Playhouse in Greenwich Village, Circle Rep quickly established a reputation for excellence. With the consistent support of Circle Rep's actors and directors, Wilson was able to try out his plays and work through them long before having to present them as fully staged productions.

A good deal of Wilson's life found its way onto the stage. The Talley series—FIFTH OF JULY (1977; revised 1980), TALLEY'S FOLLY (1979), and Talley & Son (1985)—takes place in Lebanon, Missouri. The Talley family depicted in these plays is well-off; they are partners in the town bank and run a garment factory (Wilson's family was not rich, but he observed with a keen eye those who were). Lemon Sky (1970) is the story of his reunion with his father and stepfamily in San Diego. Balm in Gilead (1964) is about life in a New York all-night diner with a collection of street people and strangers. The HOT L BALTIMORE (1973) is based on Wilson's brief career as a hotel night clerk. Throughout each of these plays, there is a strong sense of character and of each person's search for a place to belong.

The first play of Wilson's to receive significant public notice was The Hot l Baltimore. Set in the lobby of a run-down railroad hotel in Baltimore (the title's missing "e" indicates the burned-out neon sign over the entrance), it brings together a diverse collection of characters—hookers, slightly addled old people, young hustlers, an out-of-place rich boy searching for his father, and the all-seeing, all-knowing, worldly-wise desk clerk. In structure, it was similar to previous plays by Wilson, using an ensemble cast and overlapping dialogue, as in Balm in Gilead and The Rimers of Eldritch, but The Hot l Baltimore had a well-defined plotline and a great deal of comedy.

The success of The Hot l Baltimore made life comfortable for Circle Rep and Wilson. After the failures of his Broadway plays, he had been writing short plays and scenes for the resident company, but with the success of The Hot l Baltimore, he turned his attention to writing full-length plays that attracted a wider audience. The next major work that attracted critical praise was The Mound Builders (1975). It tells the story of an archaeologist working in southern Illinois and his personal family struggles, as well as shows the pressures of working against a deadline—the site he was digging was due to be flooded by the construction of a new dam. This theme of personal struggle in the shadow of impending outside forces, already an element in many of his plays, comes to the fore in The Mound Builders.

5th of July opened at the Circle Rep in 1978. It takes place in the Talley family home in Lebanon, Missouri, and tells the story of a Fourth of July weekend reunion of friends, family, and lovers. On its surface, the play appears to have many melodramatic elements—gay lovers, out-of-wedlock children—but Wilson's subtle characterizations and understated exploration of relationships are effective. There are no dramatic outbursts, no threats of violence or intimidation, no ultimatums, and his use of humor as both a weapon and a shield defines the people portrayed in microscopic detail. (Two years later, Wilson rewrote parts of 5th of July and changed the title to Fifth of July.)

5th of July was succeeded by Talley's Folly (1979). It tells the story of the courtship of Matt Friedman and Sally Talley and takes place on July 4, 1944, in a run-down Victorian boathouse on the river down the hill from the Talley house. It is a two-character play, and Wilson uses a technique borrowed from THORNTON WILDER'S OUR TOWN: Matt talks to the audience and makes comments throughout the play, much like the Stage Manager in Wilder's play. Talley's Folly won the PULITZER PRIZE. The last play in the Talley series was A Tale Told (1981). It introduces the rest of the Talley family and also takes place on the night of July 4, 1944. (Sally appears in the beginning of A Tale Told as she leaves the house to go down to the boathouse to meet Matt Friedman and again at the end.) Wilson combines several of his storytelling devices in this play—including direct address to the audience and the collage of several stories going on at once—as the family patriarch manipulates people to do his dirty work. In 1985, Wilson rewrote the play and retitled it Talley & Son.

Wilson's next play, *BURN THIS* (1987), featured a cast of four and is the story of the aftermath of the death of Robbie and the impact it has on his friends, Larry, Anna, and Burton, and on Pale, Robbie's brother, to whom Anna has an instant attraction. *Burn This* was also the last play produced by the Circle Rep with Marshall Mason as the artistic director. In July 1987, he resigned his post to go to California to try his hand at film direction. Mason's departure from the day-to-day operation of Circle Rep did not halt his collaboration with Wilson. They joined forces again on *Redwood Curtain* (1992), a play about a traumatized Vietnam veteran living an isolated existence in the redwood forest of northern California, and on *Sympathetic Magic* (1997), which ponders life and the universe and was not well received by critics.

Although Circle Rep folded in 1996 for financial reasons, Wilson kept writing, working with regional theaters or as an artist-in-residence at universities, often with former colleagues and friends. In 1999, he taught playwriting at Arizona State University in Tempe, where Mason had joined the faculty, and he wrote two plays on commission for the Purple Rose Theatre in Chelsea, Michigan, founded by former Circle Rep actor Jeff Daniels: *Book of Days* (1998) and *Rain Dance* (2001). New York's Off-Broadway Signature Theatre devoted its 2002–03 season to Wilson's plays, with productions of *Burn This, Book of Days, Fifth of July,* and *Rain Dance.*

In addition to the numerous awards Wilson received for his work while at Circle Rep, he was awarded the WILLIAM INGE Distinguished Achievement in the American Theatre Award in 2001, and in 2004 he was inducted into the American Academy of Arts and Letters.

BIBLIOGRAPHY

Barnett, Gene A. *Lanford Wilson.* Boston: G. K. Hall, 1987.

Bryer, Jackson R., ed. *Lanford Wilson: A Casebook.* New York: Garland, 1994.

Busby, Mark. *Lanford Wilson.* Boise, Idaho: Boise State University, 1987.

Williams, Philip Middleton. *A Comfortable House: Lanford Wilson, Marshall W. Mason, and the Circle Repertory Theatre.* Jefferson, N.C.: McFarland, 1993.

Wilson, Lanford. *Book of Days.* New York: Grove Press, 2000.

———. *Collected Works, Volume I: 1965–1970.* Lyme, N.H.: Smith and Kraus, 1996.

———. *Collected Works, Volume II: 1970–1983.* Lyme, N.H.: Smith and Kraus, 1998.

———. *Collected Works, Volume III: The Talley Trilogy.* Lyme, N.H.: Smith and Kraus, 1999.

———. *Rain Dance.* New York: Dramatists Play Service, 2005.

———. *A Sense of Place or Virgil Is Still the Frogboy.* New York: Dramatists Play Service, 1999.

Philip Middleton Williams
Miami, Florida

WINGS ARTHUR KOPIT **(1978)**   As KOPIT explains in his preface to the published play, *Wings* was first commissioned in 1976 as a radio play by Earplay, a drama project of National Public Radio. Free to choose any subject, Kopit decided to tackle one close to him at that time: the devastating effects of stroke, which had left his father trapped inside a body and mind that would no longer cooperate. Since his father's case was too severe to serve Kopit's artistic purpose, he based his play on two women with varying degrees of aphasia whom he encountered at his father's rehabilitation center. After Kopit adapted his radio play for the stage, it was produced by Yale Repertory Theatre, whose production was brought to New York. In *Wings,* Kopit portrays the mystery and frustration of aphasia from the point of view of the patient.

Mrs. Stilson—a former aviatrix who once climbed out on the wings of biplanes for the entertainment of crowds below—experiences a catastrophic stroke. Her cognitive abilities are shattered; she no longer recognizes something as simple as a comb or people as significant as her own children. Gradually, the shards of her memory begin to assemble, though never completely. The process of this partial recovery is intensely difficult, and Mrs. Stilson, a woman in her seventies, finally succumbs to death, which in the last scene takes the form of acceptance of flight into the unknown dark. The play is divided into four sections: In the first brief section, "Prelude," Mrs. Stilson sits reading comfortably in the moments before her stroke. In "Catastrophe," using visual and sound effects, Kopit portrays the immediate aftermath of a stroke from the patient's point of view; in this section, Mrs. Stilson is taken to the hospital and initially treated by the emergency staff there. In "Awakening," she struggles to make sense of what is around her and to make herself understood, finding—frustratingly—that her language ability is inoperative. And, in the final section, "Explorations," she makes laborious progress toward coherence with the affectionate help of her speech therapist.

The play, a departure for Kopit from his usual absurdist works, won the TONY AWARD. It was made into a 1993 musical of the same name, with music by Jeffrey Lunden and book and lyrics by Arthur Perlman.

BIBLIOGRAPHY
Kopit, Arthur. *Wings.* New York: Hill & Wang, 1978.

WINTERSET MAXWELL ANDERSON (1935) One of ANDERSON's most celebrated plays, this blank-verse drama is based on the Sacco and Vanzetti case of 1921, in which two Italian anarchists were convicted of murder. It was widely believed that they were innocent and were convicted because of their radical political beliefs. Anderson's play is set 12 years after an innocent man, the anarchist Romagna, is tried and executed for murder; his son, Mio, whose mother died of grief shortly after his father's execution, has returned to the scene of the events, hoping to clear his father's name and avenge his death.

Converging on the scene—a squalid basement tenement at the base of a bridge—are Mio; Trock, the man actually guilty of the murder for which Romagna was executed; Judge Gaunt, who presided over Romagna's trial and sentenced him to the electric chair; and Garth, a former member of Trock's gang who lives with his sister, Miriamne, and his father, Rabbi Esdras. Trock has just been released from prison and plans to silence anyone who might reveal his guilt. Garth, who witnessed the murder Trock committed, has kept silent to save himself, and Judge Gaunt has just returned from a period of wandering during which he was out of his mind. Both of these men are in danger from Trock. Ironically, Trock, so desperate to save himself that he will resort to murder, has only six months to live—a victim of disease. (By the end of the play, as Esdras makes his final speech about the nature of human existence, it seems probable that the playwright means Trock's limited lifespan to be symbolic of the brevity of all human life.)

The treatment of guilt in the play is particularly interesting. Garth feels great guilt for not speaking up during Romagna's trial, yet if he speaks now he will die either at the hands of the state or at the hands of Trock. When he speaks to his father, the rabbi, about what he should do, his father advises him to remain silent and live. When 15-year-old Miriamne objects, saying, "If I had to do it—/ I think I'd die," her father replies, "Yes, child. Because you are young." Esdras justifies his advice to his son by taking the position that we are all guilty—"We are none of us free of regret"—and by taking an historic view: "The ground we walk on is . . . hard with blood and bones of those who died unjustly. There's not one title to land or life . . . but was built on rape and murder." Judge Gaunt takes two positions: When he is out of his mind (and, therefore, inhabiting his emotions), he feels guilt; he tells a policeman who is harassing a crowd, "Make not yourself an instrument of death lest you sleep to wake sobbing." However, when he becomes lucid again, he takes the position that to reverse a verdict that was arrived at through due process of the law—no matter what the evidence—undermines the law and is, therefore, against the "common good." (Mio argues: When "the jury comes in loaded to soak an anarchist and a foreigner, it may be due process of law but it's also murder!") Both religion (the rabbi) and the justice system (the judge), then, rationalize the injustice done to Romagna.

Mio, who seeks truth and vindication for love of his father, and Miriamne, who prefers truth but remains silent for love of her brother, are drawn to one another and fall in love. Mio ultimately decides not to avenge his father's death if it will make Miriamne suffer—as her brother's death surely will. He asks her to "teach" him "how to live and forget to hate." But Trock and his men wait outside the tenement for Mio so that they can kill him. Miriamne suggests a path that "they can't watch." Mio goes that way and is shot. A distraught Miriamne, in order to prove to the dying Mio that she did not send him to his death on purpose, provokes the murderers to kill her too. Mio is already dead when she crawls back, saying, "You can believe I wouldn't hurt you, because I'm dying." Garth and Esdras are left to bury the dead. Esdras has the final monologue, in which he speaks of inexplicable human existence, particularly how it finds its meaning in the attempts to understand it: "On this star, / in this hard star-adventure, knowing not / what the fires mean to right and left, nor whether / a meaning was intended or presumed, / man can stand up, and look out blind, and say: / in all these turning lights I find no clue, / only a masterless night, and in my blood / no certain answer, yet is my mind my own, / yet is my heart a cry toward something dim / in distance, which is higher than I am / and makes me emperor of the endless dark / even in seeking!"

Unusual for its mixture of blank verse and modern events, *Winterset* is considered one of Anderson's finest achievements. The 1935 production of the play, which won the first New York Drama Critics' Circle Award, was enhanced by the stunning set design of Jo Mielziner, featuring a soaring Brooklyn Bridge receding into fog.

WIT (ACTUAL TITLE: W;T) Margaret Edson (1999)

This Pulitzer Prize–winning drama depicts the final months of an English literature scholar as she dies of ovarian cancer. The individuality and humanity—and the wit—of Vivian Bearing are revealed in a series of monologues and scenes against the backdrop of a dehumanizing clinical setting.

Vivian Bearing, once an uncompromising scholar and "professor of seventeenth-century poetry, specializing in the Holy Sonnets of John Donne," is now at the mercy of doctors in a research hospital. When she was teaching—we see this in a series of flashbacks, and Edson clearly states it in her stage directions— Vivian *"ruthlessly denied her simpering students the touch of human kindness she now seeks."* Very early in the play in a single flashback, we see who taught Vivian to be thus uncompromising: Professor E. M. Ashford, a woman who was about the age then that Vivian is now, when Vivian herself was a 22-year-old student, *"eager and intimidated."* In the flashback, Professor Ashford chastises Vivian for having chosen an edition

of Donne's poems that contains "hysterical punctuation." The scene is significant not only for its revelations about Vivian but also because it establishes Donne's poetry as a thematic device in the play. The "hysterical punctuation" is the use of a semicolon where Donne's choice had been a comma: The correct edition, Professor Ashford tells her student, "reads: 'And death shall be no more, *comma,* death thou shalt die.' (*As she recites this line, she makes a little gesture at the comma.*) Nothing but a breath—a comma—separates life from life everlasting." Ironically, it is Professor Ashford—now 80—who shows Vivian the most humanity she encounters in her final days. (Vivian's parents are dead, she has no siblings, and she has never married.) In a profoundly touching, yet unsentimental scene, the old scholar climbs up on the bed and puts her arms around the suffering and nearly unconscious Vivian. Ashford suggests she recite "something by Donne," but Vivian moans in protest, so Ashford reads the only book that is handy, a children's book she has purchased for her great-grandson's fifth birthday, *The Runaway Bunny,* musing quietly to herself as she does so that it is "a little allegory of the soul." By the time she finishes the short book, Vivian has fallen asleep, and Ashford quietly departs, having brought some comfort.

Throughout the play, the research doctors seem more concerned with gathering data than with allowing Vivian Bearing a dignified death. In a final insult, young Dr. Posner calls the resuscitation team to Vivian's bedside though her chart is marked DNR (do not resuscitate). The sympathetic nurse, Susie, manages to stop the team, after much shouting and struggling, before they have succeeded in shocking Vivian's heart into beating again. As the team, annoyed at Dr. Posner for his mistake, stops working and consults the chart, the deceased Vivian slips from the bed toward *"a little light. She is now attentive and eager."* She slips off the trappings of the hospital. *"The instant she is naked and beautiful, reaching for the light—"* the stage lights go out. She is released from her pain, and we recall Donne's lines on death as well as Ashford's comments about them.

In writing this—her only—play, Margaret Edson (who holds degrees in literature and history and is an elementary school teacher) drew on her experiences working in the cancer and AIDS unit of a research hospital. The fact that the audiences came at all surprised Edson, who assumed that the apparently bleak topics of cancer and death would keep them away. In fact, both the popular and critical response to Edson's play were overwhelmingly positive. In 2001, Mike Nichols directed and produced an HBO film adaptation of the play starring British actress Emma Thompson. Edson admires the film, but she believes that Vivian's experience is confided to the audience with greater personal immediacy from a stage than on film.

WITCHING HOUR, THE AUGUSTUS THOMAS (1907)   Considered THOMAS's best play, this sensational drama accepts the premise that telepathy and instant hypnosis are real. Thomas's knowledge of telepathy came from his association with Washington Irving Bishop, a St. Louis "mind reader" for whom he worked as a publicist 20 years before he wrote *The Witching Hour*. The play combines parapsychology with murder and romance and was very popular in its day.

Jack Brookfield is a very successful professional gambler. He supports his sister, Alice, and his niece, Viola, who is his particular favorite. When Viola's young fiancé, Clay, accidentally murders a man who has been taunting him, Jack and the U.S. Supreme Court justice who teaches Jack about telepathy and hypnosis work together to save the young man from a death sentence. They achieve this in part by sending mental messages to the jury and by exposing to the press the prosecutor's own guilt in a separate murder, thereby focusing against the prosecution the minds of all newspaper readers; they believe all that thinking will get to the isolated, deliberating jury. At one point in the play, when the prosecutor tries to shoot him, Jack hypnotizes him, rendering him instantly harmless before he can pull the trigger.

At the center of the murder trial, which is never depicted on stage, is the jealousy the prosecutor, Frank Hardmuth, feels toward Clay Whipple, Viola's fiancé. Frank wanted to marry Viola himself and was discouraged from doing so by Uncle Jack, who knew of Frank's crime. Another love story involves Jack and

Clay's widowed mother, Helen; their old flame is rekindled, but Helen has never approved of Jack's gambling, which is why she rejected him when they were young. In the end, Jack rejects gambling, enabling Helen to accept him at long last, because he realizes that his good luck all these years was attributable to his unrecognized skill at mind reading. To continue would not be fair to the other gamblers, and Jack is a fair fellow. So fair is he, in fact, that when he realizes that he probably put the murder plot into the mind of Frank Hardmuth, he drives Frank across the border.

Aside from the presence of a popular leading man, John Mason, the secret to the success of what now seems a hopelessly contrived play was the early-20th-century public's faddish interest in telepathy and hypnosis, on which Thomas capitalized. The play's successful run in New York was followed by a lengthy tour of the country.

WOLFE, GEORGE C. (1954–)   Prominent African-American playwright and director George C. Wolfe was born in Frankfort, Kentucky, the son of a government worker and a school principal. He attended predominately black elementary and secondary schools prior to enrolling at Pomona College in Claremont, California. As a theater (directing) major, Wolfe was twice named a regional winner for playwriting at the American College Theatre Festival (ACTF). He later enrolled in the dramatic writing/musical theater M.F.A. program at New York University and following graduation in 1983 pursued a career as a librettist and playwright.

The success that Wolfe enjoyed as a student in the 1970s continued into the 1980s and 1990s. In 1985, *Paradise,* his full-length musical, which originally was staged in Cincinnati, Ohio, opened OFF-OFF-BROADWAY. The following year, Wolfe's musical, *Queenie Pie,* about the fantasy world of an aging beauty queen, premiered at the Kennedy Center in Washington, D.C. The same year, Wolfe's *The Colored Museum,* his postmodern play depicting the experience of the black body both onstage and offstage, was first produced by the Crossroads Theatre in New Brunswick, New Jersey.

In 1989, Crossroads also premiered *Spunk,* Wolfe's adaptation of three stories by ZORA NEALE HURSTON—*Sweat,* about a woman terrorized by her husband; *Story in Harlem Slang,* about gigolos who stage a street corner brawl; and *The Gilded Six Bit,* about a couple whose materialistic lust for gold is redeemed by the birth of a child.

Wolfe's play *Jelly's Last Jam,* about legendary jazz musician Jelly Roll Morton, opened on Broadway in 1992 featuring actor/dancer Gregory Hines. The following year, he was named the artistic director of the prestigious New York Shakespeare Festival/Public Theatre (NYSF). The same year he directed TONY KUSHNER'S *ANGELS IN AMERICA: The Millennium Approaches* and received the TONY AWARD for direction. Three years later, he would win the Tony Award for best direction again for his musical *Bring in da Noise/ Bring in da Funk.*

Since the mid-1990s, Wolfe has remained active. He directed *The Tempest* starring Patrick Stewart for the NYSF. The production proved so popular that following its free run in Central Park, it moved to Broadway. Wolfe has used his influence at the Public Theatre to nurture the talents of new playwrights. One of his protégés, SUZAN-LORI PARKS, whose plays have been staged at the Public since the beginning of Wolfe's directorship, was awarded the 2002 PULITZER PRIZE for her play *TOPDOG/UNDERDOG.* Wolfe directed the original production of *Topdog/Underdog* and received an OBIE AWARD for his efforts. While mentoring the next generation of theater practitioners, the playwright/director has worked to preserve the history and heritage of AFRICAN-AMERICAN DRAMA. In 2002, he wrote and directed *Harlem Song,* a musical based on 20th-century black culture in Harlem, and staged it in the Apollo Theatre, Harlem's most revered performance space.

Wolfe has worked with some of the brightest stars on the theatrical stage. He directed Elaine Stritch's one-woman show, *Elaine Stritch at Liberty* (2001), ANNA DEVEARE SMITH's performance piece on the L.A. riots, *Twilight: Los Angeles, 1992* (1993), and, at the Chicago Lyric Opera, the opera *Amistad* (1997), music by Anthony Davis and libretto by Thulani Davis.

In his last years at the Public Theatre, Wolfe was involved in the productions of such award-winning

works as RICHARD GREENBERG's *TAKE ME OUT* (2003), as producer, and Tony Kushner's autobiographical musical about changing race relations in the South during the civil rights era, *Caroline, or Change* (2004), as director. In the fall of 2004, Wolfe stepped down as head of the Public Theatre in order to have the time to write screenplays and plays, as well as pursue other creative projects. Since leaving the Public, Wolfe has directed the award-winning television film *Lackawanna Blues* (2005) and the feature film *Nights in Rodanthe* (2008).

BIBLIOGRAPHY
Wolfe, George C. *The Colored Museum.* New York: Broadway Play Publishing, 1987.
———. *Jelly's Last Jam.* New York: Theatre Communications Group, 1993.
———. *Spunk: Three Tales by Zora Neal Hurston.* New York: Theatre Communications Group, 1993.

Harvey Young Jr.
Northwestern University

WOMEN, THE CLARE BOOTHE (1936)

This comedy satirizes gossip and infidelity among wealthy husbands and wives in New York's upper class. Though the husbands never appear in the play, they are seldom far from the conversation and motivation of the women.

The play begins in the Park Avenue living room of Mary Haines, where a group of friends have gathered to play bridge one afternoon. We learn, largely because the catty Sylvia Fowler gossips about the others when they leave the room, that some of the husbands, including Mary's, are having affairs. Mary believes that she has an ideal marriage and a faithful husband until Sylvia's indiscreet manicurist reveals to her that her husband is having an affair with shopgirl Crystal Allen. Mary's mother advises her to take a trip and do nothing about Stephen's infidelity, explaining to her daughter that such action on the part of men is motivated by the same impulse that causes women to buy new clothes or redecorate their houses. Mary follows her mother's advice, but when she returns from Bermuda she finds that her husband has not only continued his affair but has also introduced their young children to his mistress. When Mary finds herself in a dress shop with Crystal, who is charging her new clothes to Mr. Stephen Haines, Mary confronts her; when the affair reaches the newspaper gossip columns—because of Sylvia's inclination to gossip—Mary confronts Stephen. Soon Mary is in Reno, Nevada, seeking a divorce, and Stephen marries Crystal. Two years pass between acts 2 and 3, by which time Crystal is having an affair with the fifth husband of a "countess"—by marriage. Mary learns of it from her young daughter who has overhead her stepmother on the telephone with her lover. Mary vows to reclaim her husband, whom she still loves; she goes to a nightclub, where all interested parties are assembled, and exposes the faithless Crystal.

In this cast of 35 women are represented upper-class women and the working-class women who cater to and sometimes resent them. BOOTHE has the opportunity here to express many of the views of the women of her time. Several minor characters speak for the less fortunate lower classes: A nurse chastises Edith (one of Mary's bridge buddies) when—having just given birth—she complains about childbirth; the nurse says to Edith, "try having a baby in a cold filthy kitchen, without ether, without a change of linen . . . without a cent to bring it up." Later, in a Reno, Nevada, hotel room, a hotel maid explains to Peggy (another of the bridge players) that she once had saved enough money to leave her abusive husband, but she was forced to stay with him when she found out she was pregnant. In the final act's expensive nightclub, a "cigarette girl" comments bitterly to the coat check attendant, "It isn't fair! Why [Mike and I] could get married and have a family on that [fur] coat." Meanwhile, the women of the leisure class gossip and swap husbands. Though that leisure class does not speak in a single voice, there does seem to be some agreement that hanging onto one's marriage and the financial security that comes with it—even in the face of a husband's infidelity—is preferable to the more precarious life of a divorcee. Certainly this view dates the play. (In fact, there is only one woman in Mary Haines's class with a job and no husband: Nancy, a writer of bad novels.) Though the play seems outmoded now, in its day, it humorously exposed some of the hypocrisy and social irresponsibility of the wealthy.

WRIGHT, CRAIG (1965?–) Born in San Juan, Puerto Rico, Craig Wright moved around a great deal because of his father's job until at 14 he settled in Minneapolis, where he lived until he was 36. Wright wrote his first play at 21 while working as an actor in a children's theater; he won a Jerome Fellowship of $5,000 for it and turned from acting to writing. Like the work of many playwrights of his generation, Wright's plays have premiered at regional theaters and theater festivals around the country, rather than in New York.

As a teenager, Wright converted to Christianity, having been raised until his mother's death when he was nine as an observant Jew. He eventually earned a master of divinity degree from United Theological Seminary, but about the time he graduated, he had success with his play *The Pavilion* (2000) and was never ordained. Asked in an interview in 2006 if he considers himself a religious playwright, Wright responded, "No. I see myself as a writer who tells stories about normal people with really big questions. Sometimes they are religious, sometimes they are romantic, sometimes they are both—like in *Grace*." *Grace* (2004) premiered at Woolly Mammoth in Washington, D.C., and is about an evangelical Christian couple involved in Christian-themed real estate development schemes and in the life of a troubled neighbor; Wright here examines the concept of grace in its various meanings.

Molly's Delicious (1997), which premiered at Philadelphia's Arden Theatre, and *Orange Flower Water* (2002), which premiered at the Contemporary American Theater Festival in Shepardstown, West Virginia, are both set in a fictional Pine City, Minnesota. The first is about a love triangle and idealism among the young—a pregnant girl, her boyfriend in the service in Vietnam, and a junior undertaker—in 1965 amid Minnesota's apple orchards. *Orange Flower Water* is about the disintegration of two marriages because of an adulterous affair.

The Pavilion, which premiered at City Theatre Company in Pittsburgh, also takes place in "Pine City." In it, a high school couple, who split up when she became pregnant, meet again at their 20th high school reunion; featuring a philosophical narrator who also plays some supporting roles, the play has been seen as a tribute to THORNTON WILDER's American classic OUR TOWN. *Recent Tragic Events* (2002), which premiered at Washington's Woolly Mammoth, is Wright's September 11 play in which a young woman on a blind date in Minnesota awaits word of her twin sister who is in New York City on September 11; the play's most bizarre and comic character is Joyce Carol Oates as a sock puppet.

Main Street (2003), an adaptation of Sinclair Lewis's novel, was written for the Great American History Theatre of St. Paul, Minnesota. *Melissa Arctic* (2004), an adaptation of Shakespeare's *The Winter's Tale,* was produced at the Folger Shakespeare Theatre in Washington, D.C., and won for Wright the 2005 Charles MacArthur Award for Outstanding New Play (part of Washington's Helen Hayes Awards).

Lady (2007) premiered at Chicago's Steppenwolf Theatre and involves three hunting buddies whose lifetime of shared experiences cannot counterbalance their increasingly divergent political views. *The Unseen* (2007) premiered at the HUMANA FESTIVAL of New American Plays at the Actors Theatre of Louisville. The play takes place in a prison in an unspecified location where two prisoners are tortured daily for years by a brutal, masked—and conflicted—guard. Eventually the tapping of an unseen third prisoner brings hope to one and skepticism to the other. The effect of torture on the humanity of the torturer and the responses of human beings to dire circumstances are among the play's themes.

More recently, *Better Late* (2008), written with LARRY GELBART, premiered at suburban Chicago's Northlight Theatre and is a domestic comedy in which a woman and her current and former husbands share a home. *Mistakes Were Made* premiered at Chicago's Red Orchid Theatre in the fall of 2009.

Short plays—three- to 10-minute plays—written for the Humana Festival at Louisville include *A Quick Tour of the Monument* and *Bomb Squad,* both part of the multi-playwright anthology *Snapshot* (2002).

Wright, who now lives in Los Angeles, regularly writes for television, notably for *Six Feet Under* and *Lost;* he is also the creator and executive producer of *Dirty Sexy Money.* He has said that his income from television and film writing gives him the freedom to write whatever he likes for the theater without having to worry about appealing to a commercial audience.

BIBLIOGRAPHY

Wright, Craig. Interview with Ina Rometsch. *Furious Theatre Blog.* 25 Sept. 2006. Furious Theatre Company. Available online. URL: http://furioustheatre.blogspot.com/2006/09/interview-with-playwright-craig-wright.html. Accessed June 11, 2008.
———. *Orange Flower Water.* New York: Dramatists Play Service, 2004.
———. *The Pavilion.* New York: Dramatists Play Service, 2003.
———. *Recent Tragic Events.* New York: Dramatists Play Service, 2004.

WRIGHT, DOUG (1963?–)

Playwright Doug Wright was born in Dallas, Texas, and educated at Yale University (B.A. in art history, 1985) and New York University's Tisch School of the Arts (M.F.A. in playwriting, 1987). He is perhaps best known for his PULITZER PRIZE–winning play *I AM MY OWN WIFE* (2003).

Wright's first play, *The Stonewater Rapture* (1987), is set in his home state of Texas. In it, a high school couple grapple with their sexual urges in a conservative Christian community and later try to reconcile their fundamentalist worldview with the violent reality of a sexual assault experienced by the girl. The play was included in *The Best Short Plays of 1987.* Other early works include *Interrogating the Nude* (1989), a satire involving seminal 20th-century artist Marcel Duchamp; *Dinosaurs* (1990), which concerns a country singer, an evangelist, and a dinosaur park; and the musical *Buzzsaw Berkeley* (1989), with songs by Michael John LaChiusa, which is a satirical mix of slasher film and Judy Garland/Mickey Rooney let's-put-on-a-show musical.

In *Watbanaland* (1995), a nursery school teacher desperately wants a child, but her Wall Street husband is reluctant since—unbeknownst to his wife—he has already fathered a brain-damaged infant with his mistress; the mistress meanwhile finds a new boyfriend, while the wife adopts Third World info-commercial children, has visions, and develops a hysterical pregnancy. Scenes are at times comic, at times poignant. This mixture of the serious and the humorous is typical of Wright's work.

Wright's breakthrough play was *Quills* (1995), which won him an OBIE AWARD for Playwriting. (He also wrote the critically acclaimed screenplay for the 2000 film version.) The play is about the imprisoned Marquis de Sade and in particular about the suppression of what he wrote while imprisoned. *Quills* makes a powerful statement about freedom of expression and the public's right to decide what it will read or view in a free society.

Unwrap Your Candy (2001) is an evening of four short plays: the title piece, *Unwrap Your Candy,* in which members of an audience assemble in theater seats and think aloud; *Lot 13: The Bone Violin,* in which the parents of a violin prodigy and others involved in the child's life talk about the absent child at an auction (*Lot 13* is included in *The Best American Short Plays 1994–1995*); *Wildwood Park,* in which the house where a famous crime was committed is offered to a client by an increasingly unhinged real estate agent as we gradually learn the grisly details of the crime; and *Baby Talk,* in which a pregnant woman's fetus speaks to her from the womb—not always pleasantly. (*Not Suitable for Children* was the collective title of an earlier version of three of the plays in *Unwrap Your Candy.*)

Wright began his research for *I Am My Own Wife* (2003) before writing *Quills* but experienced some difficulties with the piece, as his subject, the East German antique collector and transvestite Charlotte von Mahlsdorf (born Lothar Berfelde), proved to be more complicated than he had initially believed. Wright first thought of "her" as a purely heroic figure who had maintained her singular identity living openly under an oppressive regime, about whom he planned to write an objective biographical play; however, when Charlotte's Stasi (East German secret police) file revealed that she was to some extent a collaborator, he decided to change the concept to a piece in which she spoke in her own words—illusions and all—and in which the playwright himself would appear as a character. Once he arrived at this concept, he was able to shape the play, which won both the Pulitzer Prize and the TONY AWARD for Best Play.

Wright wrote the book for *Grey Gardens* (2006), a musical based in part on the grim documentary of the same name about Big Edie and Little Edie Beale. Relatives of Jacqueline Bouvier Kennedy Onassis, the Beales by the 1970s had descended from high society into disheveled eccentricity in a squalid, cat-filled ruin of a mansion. The first act, based loosely on the diary of Little Edie, shows the mother and daughter as they had been years before, among family and friends in their intact East Hampton home, where even in affluence and health they reveal the seeds of what is to become of them by act 2 and the 1970s. Other musical credits include the book for the stage adaptation of *The Little Mermaid* (2008).

BIBLIOGRAPHY

Wright, Doug. *I Am My Own Wife.* New York: Faber and Faber, 2004.
———. *"Quills" and Other Plays.* New York: Faber and Faber, 2005.
———. *The Stonewater Rapture.* New York: Dramatists Play Service, 1998.
———. *Unwrap Your Candy: An Evening of One-Act Plays.* New York: Dramatists Play Service, 2002.
———, and Michael Korie. *Grey Gardens.* New York: Applause Theatre and Cinema Books, 2007.

Y

YANKOWITZ, SUSAN (1941–) Most noted for her playwriting, Susan Yankowitz is also a novelist, poet, and lyricist in the modern American avant-garde theater. Inspired by German playwright Bertolt Brecht and French dramatic theorist Antonin Artaud, her plays often confront their audiences with collective responsibility and social problems, depart from traditional linear storylines, and make use of imagery, symbols, rhythm, and language.

A graduate of Sarah Lawrence College, Yankowitz began writing prose as a child. After a trip to India, she became interested in writing for the theater and attended the Yale School of Drama. Her first professional experience was as resident playwright for Joseph Chaikin's Open Theater, an OFF-OFF-BROAD-WAY, experimental ensemble that presented politically engaged works during the 1960s. While there, Yankowitz wrote *Terminal* (1969), a memorable piece about death that has since been revised and revived multiple times by members of the now defunct Open Theater. Yankowitz has also written a number of other plays, many of which illustrate the influence of the Open Theater's style, including *A Knife in the Heart* (1983). Written in the aftermath of John Hinckley's assassination attempt on President Ronald Reagan, *Knife* reflects the possible motivations behind an otherwise respectable young man killing several people, including a state governor, for little reason. In addition to showing Yankowitz's interest in addressing societal questions, *Knife* demonstrates her approach to

drama: "It raises central questions about how we view women and how we view men, questions about individuality and masculinity and strength of character and how do you distinguish yourself in American society" (Welsh).

After three years with the Open Theater Company, Yankowitz left to pursue other literary genres. She wrote a novel, *Silent Witness* (1976), in which she explored the mind of a deaf-mute (she later rewrote it as a screenplay), as well as poems, essays, short stories, and experimental theater pieces. In the early 1980s, disturbed by trends in professional, progressive theaters, Yankowitz withdrew entirely from writing for the stage. Only after Chaikin, her early mentor, suffered a stroke that resulted in aphasia (an acquired communication disorder, usually brought on by stroke or brain injury), did she return to theater. Chaikin, struggling to regain a place in the performing arts, asked Yankowitz to write a piece that would eventually become one of her most popular plays, *Night Sky* (1991). In *Night Sky*, aphasia is seen through the eyes of a brilliant astronomer who suffers brain damage in an auto accident, leaving her struggling to overcome her injury and reclaim her life. (Another play that deals with the aftermath of a stroke resulting in aphasia is ARTHUR KOPIT's *WINGS* [1978].)

In addition to many plays, including *Slaughterhouse Play* (1969), *Baby* (1984), *Alarms* (1986), *Slain in the Spirit: The Promise of Jim Jones* (1995), *Phaedra in Delirium* (1998), and *The Revenge* (2002), Yankowitz writes for the musical stage as well. *Cheri* (2002) combines musical theater with opera.

Recent projects include *Foreign Bodies* (2007) and *Seven* (2008). The latter is a collaborative docudrama created with six other award-winning playwrights and is a testament to the contributions and humanity of seven extraordinary women in their own diverse cultures around the world. Yankowitz began developing her mixed-media puppet play, *The Ludicrous Trial of Mr. P* (in progress), while a resident artist at HERE Arts Center in New York City in 2007. Her plays have been translated into 10 foreign languages, including French, Hebrew, Japanese, Catalan, Dutch, and German, and have been published and performed widely.

BIBLIOGRAPHY

Welsh, Anne Marie. "Susan Yankowitz Cuts to the Moral Quick with 'Knife.'" *San Diego Union-Tribune,* 27 Oct. 2002, F1.

Yankowitz, Susan. "Night Sky." In *Playwriting Women: Seven Plays from the Women's Project,* edited by Julia Miles. Portsmouth, N.H.: Heinemann, 1993. 169–214.

———. "Phaedra in Delirium." In *Divine Fire: Eight Contemporary Plays Inspired by the Greeks,* edited by Caridad Svich. New York: Back Stage Books, 2005. 375–408.

———. "Slaughterhouse Play." In *New American Plays.* Vol. 4, edited by Robert W. Corrigan. New York: Hill & Wang, 1965. 2–70.

Elizabeth A. Osborne
Florida State University

YELLOWMAN Dael Orlandersmith (2002)

In her play about two African Americans of different hues, Dael Orlandersmith takes on the tricky subject of intraracial prejudice and its potentially lethal destructiveness. The play examines how the bigotry and damaged self-images of adults confuse and shape children. Remarkably, Orlandersmith's memory play calls for only two actors and two chairs, yet the story covers more than 12 years and has many characters, all conveyed—no matter the accent, age, or gender—by Alma and Eugene as they tell their own story and act out their own lives from early grammar school to young adulthood. They provide the voices of relatives and friends who figure in their story, which is, necessarily, told from *their* perspectives as it is based on their memories of events. The play reads more like a short story than a play; however, seeing it performed by two well-cast, excellent actors is to experience it as the playwright intended.

Alma is a large black women, "medium to dark brown-skinned" and Eugene is a "*very* fair skinned" black man; both are in their late 30s or early 40s. Alma begins the play with a litany of observations about her mother and "women like her mother"; her soliloquy is a long free-verse poem about the harsh lives of these large, dark women, who were not considered attractive. They were abused by men, and they felt—in their darkness and bigness—they deserved that abuse. These women "believed had they been born 'rich and high yella' they wouldn't have suffered" and "they thanked God that [Alma] wasn't born dark." Much lighter still is Eugene; he is what, in the Gullah dialect of South Carolina, is called "high yella." His father is very dark-skinned and handsome, but when he is well into his bourbon, he thinks himself ugly and becomes abusive; he tells his son, "Your best bet high yella is to get outta my face before I hurt you."

The chronological narrative begins when Alma and Eugene begin to tell and act out their grammar school days in the 1960s, beginning when she was seven and he nine. Eugene and Alma and another boy, Alton, meet and become inseparable friends, having glorious fun together. Other dark children feel slighted when Alma and Alton seem to prefer the company of "dat ole yella boy from St. Stephen." Similarly, a light-skinned boy, Wyce, is appalled that Eugene plays with Alton and Alma. The three innocent children simply want to enjoy their games inspired by comic books and television shows, but the parents' problem with shades of color causes Alma to contemplate leaving life if God cannot make her "light and small," and causes Eugene and Alton confusion and fear and finally a lost friendship.

Alma's gin-soaked mother Odelia's self-loathing is evident as she batters away at Alma's self-worth. She chides Alma for running—at seven—in the sun with the boys because "ya don't wanna git black"; she advises her to marry someone light like Eugene, "dat purdy yella boy," not dark like Alton—"dat boy is BLACK—BLACK and UGLY." Odelia (who is Alton's color) blames her daughter for having "run John [Alma's light-skinned father] off" when he returned to Odelia for a drunken visit years after impregnating and abandoning her; John abuses Odelia and, despite that—as Alma tells it—she pleads and pants after him "like a dog." A drunken Odelia then abuses her child and forces her to eat a root Odelia believes will make Alma light: "EAT it—If ya was light, John woulda been heah."

In a parallel situation in Eugene's family, his mother's father, light-skinned as his daughter, disowned her when she married Eugene's dark-skinned father. When Eugene is in high school, Thelma sends her father a picture of Eugene, knowing his appearance alone will convince the grandfather to acknowledge the boy. Not only does his grandfather agree to see Eugene—and upon seeing him, exclaims "Thank God!"—but he eventually leaves his considerable property to him. The older man tells his grandson, "the world can be hard on us/ people like us. . . . The white man hates us/ dark skinned niggers hate us." When he goes on to insult Eugene's own father, Eugene wants nothing more to do with him.

As a young teenager, Eugene hangs out with the light-skinned and quite evil Wyce (who brutally kills Alton's puppy to intimidate Alton when he calls Wyce a "punk"). Under Wyce's influence, Eugene dates light-skinned girls, but he soon realizes that he loves only Alma, and she only him. By the time they graduate from high school, Alma has begun to see glimpses of Odelia in herself (she laments that though she can adopt Eugene's accent and diction, she "cannot change THE BODY"). Determined to make a better life for herself than her mother has, determined never to "pant" after a man "like a dog," she accepts a full scholarship to Hunter College in New York.

Meanwhile, Eugene's father gets him a job at Georgia Pacific, where the older man is a foreman. Eugene is loathed by the darker workers and ridiculed by them—including his own father. In contrast, Alma flourishes in New York; feeling confident and adventurous, she "never knew how full life could be." Eugene visits her, and it takes a while and a few visits before she can get Odelia's voice ("ole ugly black fat ting") to retreat from her head in Eugene's presence. Over time they manage to shed the distorted perceptions of their parents; Eugene plans to move up to New York when they eventually marry and find his own life as Alma is finding hers. But when Eugene's grandfather dies and they must go back to South Carolina for the funeral, Eugene and his father, fueled by rage and alcohol, exchange racial epithets and get into a brutal fight that ends in death. A pregnant Alma forces herself to miscarry, and Eugene goes to prison for the murder of his father.

Discussing the play's multiple themes in an interview for Kentucky Educational Television, Orlandersmith said that in *Yellowman* she looks at "internal racism— the rift between light-skinned and dark-skinned [African-American] people, which has its roots in slavery. . . . how it affects black folks. And beyond that . . . *Yellowman* is about the sins of the father . . . and . . . mother. It's about alcoholism. It's about how children are not seen as people." Furthermore, as she told a London interviewer when *Yellowman* opened there in 2004, it is about the fact that "people who oppress are also victims," and asks the question, "Can we escape our destiny? Are we a product of social conditioning, even if we are aware" of it? Finally, the issues of race addressed in the play are complicated because they are mixed with issues of gender bias and socioeconomic status.

A New Yorker, Dael Orlandersmith, actor, poet, and playwright, is best known for *Yellowman,* in which the playwright played Alma in the New York and Seattle productions (indeed, she first began to write for the stage to create parts for herself). Her other theater pieces include her one-woman shows *Beauty's Daughter* (1994), *Monster* (1996), *The Gimmick* (1998), and, since *Yellowman,* the three-actor play about a pair of Irish brothers and a Puerto Rican girl from New York, *Raw Boys* (2005), as well as a one-woman show entitled *Stoop Stories* (2009).

BIBLIOGRAPHY

Orlandersmith, Dael. Interview. "Black Women Playwrights: Interviews: Dael Orlandersmith." *American Shorts.* [© 2008. Kentucky Educational Television]. Available online. URL: http://www.ket.org/american shorts/poof/orlandersmith.htm. Accessed July 5, 2008.
———. Interview with Dominick Cavandish. 7 May 2004. "Let's Talk About Theatre" [podcast] *Theatre Voice* [London]. Available online. URL: http://www.theatrevoice.com/ listennow/player/?audioID=153. Accessed July 5, 2008.

YIDDISH DRAMA Professional Yiddish theater developed in Europe in the mid-19th century, and in the late 19th century first came to America, where it became a part of the Eastern European Jewish immigrant community in New York City and other urban centers. Yiddish theater groups performed plays in the Yiddish language for an immigrant audience; the fare offered by these theaters ranged from music hall revues to operettas, family melodramas to intellectual avant-garde theater.

Written in Hebrew characters, Yiddish is based upon medieval German and includes Hebrew, Russian, and Polish words. Yiddish was the home language for most of the Eastern European Jews who came to America during the great migration of the late 19th and early 20th centuries.

Frequently, the themes of Yiddish plays set in America centered around immigration, assimilation, and the conflict between old and new world ways of life. Young Jews were often portrayed as dangerously close to rejecting their cultural traditions by falling in love with gentiles or by engaging in other scandalous behaviors. While American ways were often portrayed as inexplicable and even immoral, Jewish life in Europe had been so plagued by poverty and persecution that the plays often reflected some ambivalence about which way of life was superior.

Most notable of the Yiddish playwrights were Russian-born Jacob Gordin (1853–1909), whose themes included women's rights, socialism, and the importance of education for the masses; Polish-born Sholem Asch (1880–1957), many of whose plays dealt with the conflict between Orthodox and non-Orthodox Jews; Polish-born David Pinsky (1872–1959), whose themes included Jewish history and domestic love and jealousy; and Russian-born Peretz Hirshbein (1880–1948), who wrote about Jewish life in rural Russia.

Yiddish theater groups were among the first in America to experiment with Constantin Stanislavsky's "Method" (see ACTORS STUDIO) acting and with EXPRESSIONISM. The Yiddish Art Theatre and the Jewish Art Theatre, both in New York, were among these avant-garde groups. Of the several Yiddish theaters begun in the early part of the 20th century, one has been continuously active: Established in the 1920s by a group of Yiddish actors in New York, Folksbiene ("People's Stage") Yiddish Theatre produced socially conscious works by the likes of Henrik Ibsen, Maxim Gorky, and Upton Sinclair, in Yiddish, as well as works by Yiddish authors. Folksbiene is still active in New York City.

As the number of Yiddish speakers declined after World War II, so too did the demand for Yiddish theater. Some Yiddish theater groups remain around the country; most are nonprofessional groups connected with universities or Jewish community centers.

BIBLIOGRAPHY
Lifson, David S. *The Yiddish Theatre in America*. New York: Thomas Yoseloff, 1965.
———. *Vagabond Stars: A World History of Yiddish Theater.* 1977. Syracuse, N.Y.: Syracuse University Press, 1995.

YOU CAN'T TAKE IT WITH YOU MOSS HART AND GEORGE S. KAUFMAN (1936)

This delightful comedy about the eccentric family of Martin "Grandpa" Vanderhof won the PULITZER PRIZE. Martin Vanderhof's home in New York City is *"a house where you do as you like and no questions asked."* Vanderhof's daughter Penny Sycamore has been writing bad plays ever since a typewriter was delivered by mistake eight years earlier. Her married daughter Essie, never out of her ballet slippers, wants to be a dancer, despite her lack of talent, and makes candy, which her husband, Ed, delivers. Ed's interests are his xylophone and his printing press, both of which reside in the living room. Paul Sycamore, Penny's husband and Essie's father, is busy with Mr. de Pinna (who came to the house to deliver ice eight years ago and stayed) making fireworks in the basement to sell on the upcoming Fourth of July. For dinner, Rheba the maid mildly informs them, they will have "cornflakes, watermelon, some of those candies Miss Essie made, and some kind of meat." Ed, delighted to have something to print, promptly prints up a menu. Supporting all of these eccentrics is Grandpa, who quit the world of business 35 years ago when he realized he "wasn't having any fun" and has "been a happy man ever since."

Alice Sycamore is the 22-year-old daughter of Paul and Penny; she is *"in daily contact with the world"* and has *"escaped the tinge of mild insanity that pervades the rest of them."* It is through Alice that the outside world comes into the Vanderhof home. She works for a Wall Street firm and is in love with the boss's son, Tony Kirby. When Tony proposes marriage, she is at first reluctant because, though she loves her family, she fears they will not mix with the conventional Kirbys. When she finally agrees, a dinner party at her home is planned for the introductions.

Meanwhile, an Internal Revenue agent comes to the house to inform Grandpa that, according to IRS records, he has paid no income tax since it was instituted in 1914. Grandpa says it is true and that he "doesn't believe in" income tax because he gets nothing tangible or worthwhile for the money he pays. This subplot is resolved at the end of the play when the IRS writes a letter of apology for not understanding that Martin Vanderhof died eight years before (a milkman, who had come to the house and stayed for five years, died there; Mr. Martin Vanderhof, never having learned the man's name, gave him his own for the death certificate).

The Kirbys come to dinner the night before they are expected and find Alice's family in all its glorious eccentricity. The evening is a disaster. "G-men" come in search of Ed, who has been printing socialist slogans, just for the fun of running his printing press, and delivering them with boxes of Essie's candy. Explosives are found in the basement, accidentally ignite, and everyone spends the night in jail. Alice's engagement to Tony is off until Grandpa convinces Mr. Kirby that his chronic indigestion stems from the fact that he is not suited to Wall Street and that he should not force his son into the Wall Street life against his will. He reminds Kirby that he had dreams similar to his son's at age 25: "How many of us would be willing to settle when we're young for what we eventually get? . . . It's only a handful of the lucky ones that can look back and say that they even came close." Money isn't everything, and anyway "you can't take it with you." That is the theme of this lighthearted play, which ends with a converted Mr. Kirby sitting around the dinner table with the happy young couple and the offbeat Vanderhof household.

You Can't Take It with You is similar in tone and concept to *HARVEY* (1944) and *ARSENIC AND OLD LACE* (1941), in as much as the naive, slightly crazy charac-

ters have a wisdom that they bring to the outside world when the plot forces them into contact with it. The play enjoyed a long Broadway run, was made into an Academy Award-winning film (1938), and has been revived often by both professional and amateur groups.

YOU KNOW I CAN'T HEAR YOU WHEN THE WATER'S RUNNING ROBERT ANDERSON (1967)

This evening of four one-act plays became ANDERSON's longest-running Broadway success (at 756 performances, putting it ahead of the 1953 classic *TEA AND SYMPATHY*'s 712). As their collective title suggests, each of these short works concerns the inability to communicate, in one form or another. In "The Shock of Recognition," Jack Barnstable has written a play whose lead character is to enter naked, uttering the evening's overall title. Barnstable extravagantly imagines that having nudity onstage in order to assert every person's vulnerability and mortality will somehow go down in the annals of modern theater as equivalent to Nora's slamming the door in Henrik Ibsen's *A Doll's House*. A none-too-attractive actor, Richard Pawling, is only too anxious to get the part, but Barnstable and his producer's queasiness prevent him from stripping down any further than to his boxer shorts in this sharply written play, in which Anderson intends to undercut the stereotypical image of the beefy macho male idealized by popular culture.

In "The Footsteps of Doves," a shopping expedition to buy twin beds to replace a double, signifies a couple's separation over the question of continued physical relations in a middle-aged marriage. George fears that infrequent sex squeezed together in a coffin-sized twin might send him into the arms of another, while Harriet mistakenly believes that the changes accompanying menopause necessitate a dulling of her affectionate side that a bed for one will nicely accommodate. Harriet wins the shopping battle, but she may have mortally wounded the marriage, since the more romantic George, who depends on sex for comfort amidst the depersonalization of contemporary life, will charitably deliver their old double bed to the recently divorced Jill—and very likely snuggle up in it with her.

"I'll Be Home for Christmas," Anderson's only play to feature blue-collar characters, finds Edith and Chuck Berringer at odds over sex education and birth control advice to their teenage children. While Edith urges a utilitarian approach to physical gratification and pleasure, Chuck wants sex to mean something more; feeling lonely and disillusioned, yet fully committed to fidelity, he regards love as a beauty and a blessing. But for all his sensitivity and insight, he has been unable to communicate his love to his children, as a letter from his oldest son reveals. Only in the final moments does the audience understand the allusive resonance of the playlet's title: The dreams of those who fought in the war—and the values they defended—have, in reality, crumbled.

In "I'm Herbert," which is somewhat akin to a vaudeville skit, Anderson focuses on how memory, dulled and confused by the passage of time, still provides humankind with a sense of continuity. The memories of the crotchety and somewhat senile Herbert and Muriel, each of whom has been married two and possibly three times before, ricochet off one another in an often hilarious series of contradictions. Yet, finally, the subjective truth of blissful love created by faulty memory to which Herbert and Muriel assent may prove infinitely more satisfying than the contested reality of youth and middle-age faced by the characters in the evening's other plays.

Thomas P. Adler
Purdue University

YOUNG MAN FROM ATLANTA, THE

HORTON FOOTE (1995) *The Young Man from Atlanta* was first produced by the OFF-BROADWAY Signature Theatre Company in its 1994–95 series of four FOOTE plays. It was later produced at the Alley Theatre in Houston, in 1996, and, in early 1997, at both Chicago's Goodman Theatre and Broadway's Longacre Theatre. It won the PULITZER PRIZE.

The Young Man from Atlanta reconsiders the lives and perspectives of characters who appear in other Foote plays. In this case the focus is on Will Kidder, Lily Dale Kidder, and Pete Davenport, who are in *The* ORPHANS' HOME CYCLE, most centrally in *Lily Dale*. As Foote

explains in his introduction to the Dutton edition of the play, in *The Young Man from Atlanta,* he explores Will's "dilemma" that his "optimistic, hardworking, confident" world view does not jibe with present realities. Lily Dale, despite the vanity and selfishness she exhibited in earlier plays, is revealed as "more complex," more human, and more vulnerable (xi).

The play opens with Will Kidder, a salesman, asserting the excellence of his country, city, and family life. As he loses his job and subsequently becomes ill from the transition and stress, the audience is introduced to an even deeper sadness and concern: His son, Bill Kidder, has drowned in a Florida lake. During the course of the play, Will and his wife, Lily Dale, adjust to less ambitious financial and personal horizons as they remember the ways they failed to love and nurture their son. It is also revealed that Randy Carter, the son's roommate, has arrived from Atlanta, wanting to visit with Bill's family. This is another source of conflict between Will and Lily Dale; he wants to avoid the young man from Atlanta, while she has seen him and wants to continue to do so. Eventually, Will learns that Bill gave Randy more than $100,000, probably committed suicide, and may have been romantically involved with Randy. But before the whole truth is revealed, Lily Dale and Will decide to cut short their investigation and live in mystery, asserting, as Will says to his wife: "There was a Bill I knew and a Bill you knew and that's the only Bill I care to know about."

Through the usual Foote dedramatization and complex subtext, *The Young Man from Atlanta* asks for humility and compassion in the face of the mutability and mystery at the heart of human experience. As Etta Doris, the former cook for the Kidders, declares, "Everything changes. The Lord giveth and he taketh away. . . . We're here today and gone tomorrow. Blessed be the name of the Lord."

BIBLIOGRAPHY

Foote, Horton. *The Young Man from Atlanta.* New York: Dutton, 1995.

Gerald C. Wood
Carson-Newman College

Z

ZINDEL, PAUL (1936–2003) Paul Zindel's parents separated when he was young, and his domineering, abusive mother raised him and his sister, moving them around as she pursued a variety of failed schemes. Early on, Zindel found the world of his imagination an escape from a life he found unbearable. At 15 he contracted tuberculosis, and during his lengthy recuperation, his interest in the arts increased. While majoring in chemistry and education at Wagner College, he attended a conference at which EDWARD ALBEE spoke. While taking a creative writing course with Albee in his final year at Wagner, he became hooked on theater. During that year, Zindel wrote *Dimensions of Peacocks* (1959), a play about a troubled youth and his demented mother, and *Euthanasia and the Endless Hearts* (1960), which had a successful coffeehouse production in New York. His next play, *A Dream of Swallows* (1964), about a nasty drunk who tortures the inmates at an asylum she visits, closed after only one performance.

After college, Zindel worked briefly as a technical writer, then for 10 years balanced teaching high school chemistry with writing for the theater, before turning to writing full-time. In 1967, he took a break from school to become playwright-in-residence at Houston's Alley Theatre, which was where his most successful play, *The EFFECT OF GAMMA RAYS ON MAN-IN-THE-MOON MARIGOLDS* (1964), had first been produced. Its central character, an embittered mother whose unrealistic dreams have been shattered and

who vents her frustration on her two daughters, is based on Zindel's mother. The title concept suggests that even in harsh conditions, beautiful flowers can grow, and we see this in one daughter's unrelenting enthusiasm for science. Its New York production in 1970 won OBIE and New York Drama Critics' Circle Awards for Best Play, a Drama Desk Award for most promising playwright, as well as the PULITZER PRIZE the following year. It marked the pinnacle of Zindel's dramatic success.

In the meantime, Zindel had begun writing for television with *Let Me Hear You Whisper* (1966), a drama about a lonely lady trying to save a dolphin from vivisection. His next theater piece was *And Miss Reardon Drinks a Little* (1967), about three sisters who have been psychologically scarred by their mother and each other. *The Secret Affairs of Mildred Wild* (1972) is stylistically more experimental with its dream sequences, but it has a similar tone, setting, and array of characters. The Wilds are eccentric misfits trying, through cookery and movies, to survive in a hostile world. *Ladies at the Alamo* (1975) portrays five women in a struggle for control over a Texas theater complex; it closed after only 20 performances. Dismayed by the increasingly short runs of his plays, Zindel removed himself to Hollywood, where he worked on screenplays and television. In 1986, he returned to New York and produced *Amulets against the Dragon Forces* (1989), about young boys hustling in 1950s Staten Island, returning to the familiar, autobiographical territory of his first plays, with a young male protagonist whose active imagination helps him survive a bitter and neurotic mother. After *Amulets,* he declared an intention to explore new dramatic territory. His next play, *Every Seventeen Minutes the Crowd Goes Crazy* (1996), was about gambling and follows the fortunes of a family of teenage children who try to survive after their parents run away.

After viewing an early television production of *Gamma Rays,* Harper & Row editor Charlotte Zolotow asked Zindel to write a young adult novel, and the result was *The Pigman* (1968). His theater experience led him naturally into the first-person narratives of his fiction. Zindel became well known for his young adult fiction, but he still considered himself primarily a playwright, using his fiction to work out storylines for his plays in the fashion of TENNESSEE WILLIAMS. Like Williams, Zindel produced a number of memorable women—alcoholics, who are psychologically unbalanced and incapable of facing reality—and he explored the family and relationship dynamics resulting from such dysfunctional characters. Zindel's strength lay in his ability to empathize with the monsters he created, and he invited his audience to do so along with him; the humor his characters generated assists in this. He depicted ultimately fragile characters, seeking shelter from an unfair, hostile, and often crazy outer world. Much of his material was semiautobiographical, as he explored elements of his own past with dark humor and an underlying sensitivity.

BIBLIOGRAPHY

Zindel, Paul. *Amulets against the Dragon Forces.* New York: Dramatists Play Service, 1989.

———. *And Miss Reardon Drinks a Little.* New York: Dramatists Play Service, 1971.

———. *The Effect of Gamma Rays on Man-in-the-Moon Marigolds.* New York: Harper & Row, 1970.

———. *Every Seventeen Minutes the Crowd Goes Crazy.* New York: Dramatists Play Service, 2000.

———. *Ladies at the Alamo.* New York: Dramatists Play Service, 1977.

———. *The Secret Affairs of Mildred Wild.* New York: Dramatists Play Service, 1973.

Susan C. W. Abbotson
Rhode Island College

ZOO STORY, THE EDWARD ALBEE (1960)

First produced in Berlin in 1959 at the Schiller Theater Workstatt, then, in 1960, as one of a double bill with Samuel Beckett's *Krapp's Last Tape* at the Provincetown Playhouse in New York City, *The Zoo Story* established ALBEE as a major voice in contemporary American theater. Controversial from the start, Albee was considered by some critics as the enfant terrible playwright of the 1960s and by others as a posturing manqué absurdist, recycling, in an American idiom, the worn clichés of late modernist European EXPRESSIONISM. Critical feuds aside, the play is a powerful indictment of middle-class mediocrity, cultural alienation, and social anomie couched in a weird neorealistic, tragicomic parody of classical naturalism. It also presages the political and cultural upheaval that would define the 1960s as the counterculture challenged the old, established social order of the 1950s.

On its surface, the action of the play is deceptively simple: Peter, a man *"in his early forties"* wearing *"tweeds,"* carrying *"horn-rimmed glasses,"* and sitting alone in a park reading a book, is approached by Jerry, a *"man in his late thirties"* who dresses *"carelessly"* as if to indicate *"a great weariness."* Jerry leads Peter through a series of what seem to be innocuous stories about himself but which turn into more pointedly aggressive and accusatory recollections designed to question the validity of Peter's life, his marriage, his values—the very reasons for his existence and all he has ever believed in. Jerry claims to have been to the zoo, where he made a decision to do something that Peter will "read about in the papers tomorrow." He finally pulls a knife and tosses it to Peter. Provoked and frightened, Peter wields the knife defensively as Jerry impales himself on it. What starts out for Peter as an ordinary, uneventful day turns into an extraordinary, life-altering encounter.

Peter, a textbook publisher, is the quintessential average Everyman. A paragon of predictability, he lives a mundane life of normalcy, representing all that is expected and comfortable in the contrived world of the American bourgeoisie. He is a family man with a wife, two daughters, two cats, and two parakeets, anesthetized by his firm belief in the "old pigeonhole bit." Jerry, on the other hand, describes himself as a "permanent transient," living in a "laughably small room" separated from the other occupants by beaverboard. He is disenfranchised, one of the dispossessed so desperate "to talk to somebody, really *talk*," that he confuses love and companionship with sadomasochistic violence. In one of the stories Jerry tells Peter, he describes an encounter with his landlady's dog. Whenever Jerry would enter the rooming house, the dog would attack him, so Jerry decided that he would first try to "kill the dog with kindness, and if that doesn't work . . . just kill him." The story of the dog suggests Jerry's frustration with other people: his parents, for instance, represented by "two empty picture frames," and his landlady, a lecherous lush. He views relationships as exploitative, manipulative strategies designed to protect people from emotional engagement. In a sense, Jerry's episode with the dog is practice for his attempt to reach out to Peter, to expose him to the emptiness of his insular world. Because he cannot communicate intimately with people, Jerry has first tried to establish relationships with animals, attempting to reconnect with his primitive self, stripped of all the perfunctory habits of social conditioning, and hoping to escape the "bars" of convention that separate people from each other. He has gone to the zoo in a last ditch effort "to find out more about the way people exist with animals, and . . . with each other." Just talking to Peter will not work, since doing so has created more resistance. So Jerry tries tickling him, then punching him, until he finally forces Peter to kill him. The murder, however, is ironically redemptive, as Jerry shocks Peter out of his "vegetable" life and returns him to the truth of his atavistic, instinctual, animal self.

In 2004, a prequel to *The Zoo Story,* titled *Homelife,* premiered; under the collective title *Peter and Jerry,* it was paired with *The Zoo Story.* In 2007, the collective title was changed to *At Home at the Zoo.*

Jeff Johnson
Brevard Community College

ZOOT SUIT Luis Valdéz (1978)

The leading light of Chicano theater, Valdéz is best known for his documentary play *Zoot Suit*. The first Chicano play to appear on Broadway, *Zoot Suit* places Mexican Americans into an American historical context as American citizens. His characters are cross-cultural in everything they do and say, from dancing swing and mambo, to speaking a mix of English, Spanish, and "hip." In addition to the influences of German playwright Bertolt Brecht and the Living Newspaper theater of the 1930s, the play incorporates traditional elements of Mexican theater, including aspects of the political *acto,* with its exposure of social ills, the mythic *mito,* with references to Aztec mythology, and the ballad style *corrido,* with dance and a musical narrative. In the 1940s, Chicano renegades were marked by their zoot suits, and the play relates the aesthetic behind this, as well as the resulting problems. The play's narrator, El Pachuco, a spiritual alter ego of its central protagonist, Henry Reyna, offers a powerful commentary on the difficulties of being Chicano in a racist American society.

Pachuco, in his zoot suit, is the embodiment of the macho *pachuco* stereotype. He sets the scene and offers commentary throughout. At a typical *barrio* dance, two gangs face off before being violently attacked by the police, who arrest almost the entire 38th Street gang. The gang and its leader, Henry Reyna, are indicted for the murder of the son of a Chicano rancher. While police and press talk of a "Mexican crime wave" and gang wars, it becomes apparent that these are largely fantasies born of wartime hysteria and media hype. As Henry and Pachuco talk in jail, Pachuco bolsters Henry's spirit, and we witness flashbacks, most involving Henry's home life, which humanize the "criminals." A story of racism, mistaken identity, and defeated hope evolves. The police beat the suspects, the court case is a mockery of justice, and everyone, although patently innocent, gets sentenced to life imprisonment. After a lengthy appeal, a series of riots, and the tireless efforts of a committee of activists, they are finally released.

Based on historical fact, *Zoot Suit* relates the story of the 1942 Sleepy Lagoon murder trial and the resulting riots. But it is told with sympathy and understanding for the Mexican Americans involved, rather than from the dominant culture's viewpoint. Valdéz reveals previously ignored truths about police brutality toward Chicanos and a racist wartime paranoia, which,

Pachuco insists, are not just problems of the past. Pachuco illustrates Henry's inner attitude of defiance against an unfair system, but Henry is not always in agreement with his alter ego. Henry refuses to give up hope that he may one day beat the system, a hope Pachuco denies but Valdéz appears to validate. Rather than the violent thug created by the press, Henry is a hard worker, loves his family and girlfriend, and stops more fights than he starts. The play ends with a choice of possible endings for Henry's story, illustrating various options available for Chicanos: a life of crime and early death from drugs, enlistment and heroic death in battle, or a peaceful family life with wife and children.

Susan C. W. Abbotson
Rhode Island College

APPENDIX I

WINNERS OF MAJOR DRAMA PRIZES

PULITZER PRIZE WINNERS

What follows is a list of the plays that have been awarded the Pulitzer Prize in drama. Years when no award was given are indicated. (See also PULITZER PRIZE.)

1917 (No Award)

1918 *Why Marry?,* Jesse Lynch Williams

1919 (No Award)

1920 *Beyond the Horizon,* Eugene O'Neill

1921 *Miss Lulu Bett,* Zona Gale

1922 *"Anna Christie,"* Eugene O'Neill

1923 *Icebound,* Owen Davis

1924 *Hell-Bent fer Heaven,* Hatcher Hughes

1925 *They Knew What They Wanted,* Sidney Howard

1926 *Craig's Wife,* George Kelly

1927 *In Abraham's Bosom,* Paul Green

1928 *Strange Interlude,* Eugene O'Neill

1929 *Street Scene,* Elmer Rice

1930 *The Green Pastures,* Marc Connelly

1931 *Alison's House,* Susan Glaspell

1932 *Of Thee I Sing* [musical], George S. Kaufman, Morrie Ryskind, and Ira Gershwin

1933 *Both Your Houses,* Maxwell Anderson

1934 *Men in White,* Sidney Kingsley

1935 *The Old Maid,* Zoë Akins

1936 *Idiot's Delight,* Robert E. Sherwood

1937 *You Can't Take It with You,* Moss Hart and George S. Kaufman

1938 *Our Town,* Thornton Wilder

1939 *Abe Lincoln in Illinois,* Robert E. Sherwood

1940 *The Time of Your Life,* William Saroyan

1941 *There Shall Be No Night,* Robert E. Sherwood

1942 (No Award)

1943 *The Skin of Our Teeth,* Thornton Wilder

1944 (No Award)

1945 *Harvey,* Mary Chase

1946 *State of the Union,* Russel Crouse and Howard Lindsay

1947 (No Award)

1948 *A Streetcar Named Desire,* Tennessee Williams

1949 *Death of a Salesman,* Arthur Miller

1950 *South Pacific* [musical], Richard Rodgers, Oscar Hammerstein II, and Joshua Logan

1951 (No Award)

1952 *The Shrike,* Joseph Kramm

1953 *Picnic,* William Inge

1954 *The Teahouse of the August Moon,* John Patrick

1955 *Cat on a Hot Tin Roof,* Tennessee Williams

1956 *The Diary of Anne Frank,* Albert Hackett and Frances Goodrich

1957 *Long Day's Journey into Night,* Eugene O'Neill

1958 *Look Homeward, Angel,* Ketti Frings

1959 *J. B.,* Archibald MacLeish

1960 *Fiorello!* [musical], Jerome Weidman, George Abbott, Jerry Bock, and Sheldon Harnick

1961 *All The Way Home,* Tad Mosel

1962 *How to Succeed in Business without Really Trying* [musical], Frank Loesser and Abe Burrows

1963 (No Award)

1964 (No Award)

1965 *The Subject Was Roses,* Frank D. Gilroy

1966 (No Award)

1967 *A Delicate Balance,* Edward Albee

1968 (No Award)

1969 *The Great White Hope,* Howard Sackler

1970 *No Place to Be Somebody,* Charles Gordone

1971 *The Effect of Gamma Rays on Man-in-the-Moon Marigolds,* Paul Zindel

1972 (No Award)

1973 *That Championship Season,* Jason Miller

1974 (No Award)

1975 *Seascape,* Edward Albee

1976 *A Chorus Line* [musical], Michael Bennett, James Kirkwood, Nicholas Dante, Marvin Hamlisch, and Edward Kleban

1977 *The Shadow Box,* Michael Cristofer

1978 *The Gin Game,* Donald L. Coburn

1979 *Buried Child,* Sam Shepard

1980 *Talley's Folly,* Lanford Wilson

1981 *Crimes of the Heart,* Beth Henley

1982 *A Soldier's Play,* Charles Fuller

1983 *'night, Mother,* Marsha Norman

1984 *Glengarry Glen Ross,* David Mamet

1985 *Sunday in the Park with George* [musical], Stephen Sondheim and James Lapine

1986 (No Award)

1987 *Fences,* August Wilson

1988 *Driving Miss Daisy,* Alfred Uhry

1989 *The Heidi Chronicles,* Wendy Wasserstein

1990 *The Piano Lesson,* August Wilson

1991 *Lost in Yonkers,* Neil Simon

1992 *The Kentucky Cycle,* Robert Schenkkan

1993 *Angels in America: Millennium Approaches,* Tony Kushner

1994 *Three Tall Women,* Edward Albee

1995 *The Young Man from Atlanta,* Horton Foote

1996 *Rent* [musical], Jonathan Larson

1997 (No Award)

1998 *How I Learned to Drive,* Paula Vogel

1999 *Wit,* Margaret Edson

2000 *Dinner with Friends,* Donald Margulies

2001 *Proof,* David Auburn

2002 *Topdog/Underdog,* Suzan-Lori Parks

2003 *Anna in the Tropics,* Nilo Cruz

2004 *I Am My Own Wife,* Doug Wright

2005 *Doubt,* John Patrick Shanley

2006 (No Award)

2007 *Rabbit Hole,* David Lindsay-Abaire

2008 *August: Osage County,* Tracy Letts

2009 *Ruined,* Lynn Nottage

www.pulitzer.org

NEW YORK DRAMA CRITICS' CIRCLE AWARD WINNERS

What follows is the list of American plays that have been recipients of the New York Drama Critics' Circle Award. The NYDCCA is usually given to one foreign and one American play each year; years when no award was given to an American play are indicated. (There is a category for best musical as well, but those winners are not included here.) (See also AWARDS.)

1936 *Winterset,* Maxwell Anderson

1937 *High Tor,* Maxwell Anderson

1938 *Of Mice and Men,* John Steinbeck

1939 (No award given to an American play)

1940 *The Time of Your Life,* William Saroyan

1941 *Watch on the Rhine*, Lillian Hellman

1942 (No award given to an American play)

1943 *The Patriots*, Sidney Kingsley

1944 (No award given to an American play)

1945 *The Glass Menagerie*, Tennessee Williams

1946 (No award given to a play, foreign or American)

1947 *All My Sons*, Arthur Miller

1948 *A Streetcar Named Desire*, Tennessee Williams

1949 *Death of a Salesman*, Arthur Miller

1950 *The Member of the Wedding*, Carson McCullers

1951 *Darkness at Noon*, Sidney Kingsley

1952 *I Am a Camera*, John van Druten

1953 *Picnic*, William Inge

1954 *The Teahouse of the August Moon*, John Patrick

1955 *Cat on a Hot Tin Roof*, Tennessee Williams

1956 *The Diary of Anne Frank*, Frances Goodrich and Albert Hackett

1957 *Long Day's Journey into Night*, Eugene O'Neill

1958 *Look Homeward, Angel*, Ketti Frings

1959 *A Raisin in the Sun*, Lorraine Hansberry

1960 *Toys in the Attic*, Lillian Hellman

1961 *All the Way Home*, Tad Mosel

1962 *The Night of the Iguana*, Tennessee Williams

1963 *Who's Afraid of Virginia Woolf?*, Edward Albee

1964 (No award given to an American play)

1965 *The Subject Was Roses*, Frank D. Gilroy

1966 (No award given to an American play)

1967 (No award given to an American play)

1968 (No award given to an American play)

1969 *The Great White Hope*, Howard Sackler

1970 *The Effect of Gamma Rays on Man-in-the-Moon Marigolds*, Paul Zindel

1971 *The House of Blue Leaves*, John Guare

1972 *That Championship Season*, Jason Miller

1973 *The Hot l Baltimore*, Lanford Wilson

1974 *Short Eyes*, Miguel Piñero

1975 *The Taking of Miss Janie*, Ed Bullins

1976 *Streamers*, David Rabe

1977 *American Buffalo*, David Mamet

1978 (No award given to an American play)

1979 *The Elephant Man*, Bernard Pomerance

1980 *Talley's Folly*, Lanford Wilson

1981 *Crimes of the Heart*, Beth Henley

1982 *A Soldier's Play*, Charles Fuller

1983 *Brighton Beach Memoirs*, Neil Simon

1984 *Glengarry Glen Ross*, David Mamet

1985 *Ma Rainey's Black Bottom*, August Wilson

1986 *A Lie of the Mind*, Sam Shepard

1987 *Fences*, August Wilson

1988 *Joe Turner's Come and Gone*, August Wilson

1989 *The Heidi Chronicles*, Wendy Wasserstein

1990 *The Piano Lesson*, August Wilson

1991 *Six Degrees of Separation*, John Guare

1992 *Two Trains Running*, August Wilson

1993 *Angels in America: Millennium Approaches*, Tony Kushner

1994 *Three Tall Women*, Edward Albee (*Twilight: Los Angeles, 1992*, Anna Deavere Smith, received an award "for unique contribution to theatrical form.")

1995 *Love! Valour! Compassion!*, Terrence McNally

1996 *Seven Guitars*, August Wilson

1997 *How I Learned to Drive*, Paula Vogel

1998 *Pride's Crossing*, Tina Howe

1999 *Wit*, Margaret Edson

2000 *Jitney*, August Wilson

2001 *Proof*, David Auburn

2002 *The Goat, or Who Is Sylvia?*, Edward Albee

2003 *Take Me Out*, Richard Greenberg

2004 *Intimate Apparel*, Lynn Nottage

2005 *Doubt*, John Patrick Shanley

2006 (No award given to an American play)

2007 *Radio Golf*, August Wilson

2008 *August: Osage County*, Tracy Letts

2009 *Ruined*, Lynn Nottage

www.dramacritics.org.

THE AMERICAN THEATRE WING'S ANTOINETTE PERRY "TONY" AWARD WINNERS

What follows is the list of those years when the Best Play Award was given to an American play. (See also TONY AWARD.)

1947 Author (Dramatic) Arthur Miller (*All My Sons*)*

1948 *Mister Roberts*, Thomas Heggen and Joshua Logan

1949 *Death of a Salesman*, Arthur Miller

1951 *The Rose Tattoo*, Tennessee Williams

1953 *The Crucible*, Arthur Miller

1954 *The Teahouse of the August Moon*, John Patrick

1955 *The Desperate Hours*, Joseph Hayes

1956 *The Diary of Anne Frank*, Frances Goodrich and Albert Hackett

1957 *Long Day's Journey into Night*, Eugene O'Neill

1958 *Sunrise at Campobello*, Dore Schary

1959 *J. B.*, Archibald MacLeish

1960 *The Miracle Worker*, William Gibson

1963 *Who's Afraid of Virginia Woolf?*, Edward Albee

1965 *The Subject Was Roses*, Frank Gilroy
Author (Dramatic) Neil Simon (*The Odd Couple*)*

1969 *The Great White Hope*, Howard Sackler

1972 *Sticks and Bones*, David Rabe

1973 *That Championship Season*, Jason Miller

1974 *The River Niger*, Joseph A. Walker

1977 *The Shadow Box*, Michael Cristofer

1979 *The Elephant Man*, Bernard Pomerance

1980 *Children of a Lesser God*, Mark Medoff

1983 *Torch Song Trilogy*, Harvey Fierstein

1985 *Biloxi Blues*, Neil Simon

1986 *I'm Not Rappaport*, Herb Gardner

*Here the award was designated to the "author" for a specific play; in all other instances, the award was designated to the "play."

1987 *Fences*, August Wilson

1988 *M. Butterfly*, David Henry Hwang

1989 *The Heidi Chronicles*, Wendy Wasserstein

1990 *The Grapes of Wrath*, Frank Galati

1991 *Lost in Yonkers*, Neil Simon

1993 *Angels in America: Millennium Approaches*, Tony Kushner

1994 *Angels in America: Perestroika*, Tony Kushner

1995 *Love! Valour! Compassion!*, Terrence McNally

1996 *Master Class*, Terrence McNally

1997 *The Last Night of Ballyhoo*, Alfred Uhry

1999 *Side Man*, Warren Leight

2001 *Proof*, David Auburn

2002 *The Goat, or Who Is Sylvia?*, Edward Albee

2003 *Take Me Out*, Richard Greenberg

2004 *I Am My Own Wife*, Doug Wright

2005 *Doubt*, John Patrick Shanley

2008 *August: Osage County*, Tracy Letts

www.tonyawards.com

THE VILLAGE VOICE OFF-BROADWAY "OBIE" AWARD WINNERS

The Obie Award categories are not constant, and as many plays or playwrights as are worthy of recognition are awarded. Listed below are American plays and playwrights. (See also OBIE AWARDS.)

1956   **Best New Play**
Absolom, Lionel Abel

1957   **Best New Play**
A House Remembered, Louis Lippa

1960   **Best New Play**
The Connection, Jack Gelber

Distinguished Play
The Zoo Story, Edward Albee
The Prodigal, Jack Richardson

1962   **Best American Play**
Who'll Save the Plowboy, Frank D. Gilroy

1964   **Best American Play**
Dutchman, LeRoi Jones (Amiri Baraka)

Distinguished Play
Home Movies, Rosalyn Drexler
Funnyhouse of the Negro, Adrienne Kennedy

1965   **Best American Play**
The Old Glory, Robert Lowell

Distinguished Play
Promenade and *The Successful Life of Three*,
Maria Irene Fornés

1966   **Best American Play**
The Journey of the Fifth Horse, Ronald
Ribman

Distinguished Play
Chicago, Icarus's Mother, and *Red Cross*,
Sam Shepard

1967   **Distinguished Play**
Futz, Rochelle Owens
La Turista, Sam Shepard

1968   **Distinguished Play**
Muzeeka, John Guare
The Indian Wants the Bronx, Israel Horovitz
Forensic and the Navigator and *Melodrama
Play*, Sam Shepard

1969   **Best American Play**
Little Murders, Jules Feiffer

1970   **Best American Play (tie)**
Approaching Simone, Megan Terry
*The Effect of Gamma Rays on Man-in-the-
Moon Marigolds*, Paul Zindel

Distinguished Play
The Deer Kill, Murray Mednick

1971   **Best American Play**
The House of Blue Leaves, John Guare

Distinguished Play
The Fabulous Miss Marie and *In New
England Winter*, Ed Bullins
The Basic Training of Pavlo Hummel, David
Rabe

1973   **Best American Play (tie)**
The Hot l Baltimore, Lanford Wilson
The River Niger, Joseph A. Walker

Distinguished Play
What If It Had Turned Up Heads?, J. E.
Gaines
The Tooth of Crime, Sam Shepard
Bigfoot, Ronald Tavel

1974   **Best American Play**
Short Eyes, Miguel Piñero

Distinguished Play
The Great MacDaddy, Paul Carter Harrison
Bad Habits, Terrence McNally
When You Comin' Back, Red Ryder?, Mark
Medoff

1975   **Best New American Play**
The First Breeze of Summer, Leslie Lee

Playwriting
Ed Bullins, *The Taking of Miss Janie*
Wallace Shawn, *Our Late Night*
Sam Shepard, *Action*
Lanford Wilson, *The Mound Builders*

1976   **Best New American Play**
American Buffalo and *Sexual Perversity in
Chicago*, David Mamet

1977   **Best New American Play**
Curse of the Starving Class, Sam Shepard

Playwriting
David Berry, *G. R. Point*
Maria Irene Fornés, *Fefu and Her Friends*
William Hauptmann, *Domino Courts*
Albert Innaurato, *Gemini* and *The
Transfiguration of Benno Blimpie*

1978   **Best New American Play**
Shaggy Dog Animation, Lee Breuer

1979   **Best New American Play**
Josephine, Michael McClure

Playwriting
Rosalyn Drexler, *The Writer's Opera*
Susan Miller, *Nasty Rumors* and *Final Remarks*

Richard Nelson, *Vienna Notes*
Bernard Pomerance, *The Elephant Man*
Sam Shepard, *Buried Child*

1980   *Playwriting*
Lee Breuer, *A Prelude to Death in Venice*
Christopher Durang, *Sister Mary Ignatius Explains It All for You*
Romulus Linney, *Tennessee*
Jeff Weiss, *That's How the Rent Gets Paid (Part Three)*

Sustained Achievement
Sam Shepard

1981   **Best New American Play**
FOB, David Henry Hwang

Playwriting
Charles Fuller, *Zooman and the Sign*
Amlin Gray, *How I Got That Story*
Len Jenkin, *Limbo Tales*

1982   **Best New American Play (tie)**
Metamorphosis in Miniature, Noa Ain
Mr. Dead and Mrs. Free, Squat Theatre

Playwriting
Robert Auletta, *Stops* and *Virgins*

Sustained Achievement
Maria Irene Fornés

1983   *Playwriting*
David Mamet, *Edmond*

Distinguished Playwriting
Tina Howe, *Painting Churches*

Most Promising Young Playwright
Harry Kondoleon

1984   **Best New American Play**
Fool for Love, Sam Shepard

Playwriting
Maria Irene Fornés, *The Danube, Sarita, and Mud*
Len Jenkin, *Five of Us*
Ted Tally, *Terra Nova*

1985   **Best New American Play**
The Conduct of Life, Maria Irene Fornés

Playwriting
Rosalyn Drexler, *Transients Welcome*
Christopher Durang, *The Marriage of Bette and Boo*
William M. Hoffman, *As Is*

1986   *Playwriting*
Eric Bogosian, *Drinking in America*
Martha Clarke, Charles L. Mee, Richard Peaslee, *Vienna: Lusthaus*
John Jesurun, *Deep Sleep*
Lee Nagrin, *Bird/Bear*

1987   **Best New American Play**
The Cure and *Film Is Evil, Radio Is Good,* Richard Foreman

1988   **Best New American Play**
Abingdon Square, Maria Irene Fornés

Sustained Achievement
Richard Foreman

1990   **Best New American Play (tie)**
Prelude to a Kiss, Craig Lucas
Bad Penny, Crowbar, and *Terminal Hip,* Mac Wellman
Imperceptible Mutabilities in the Third Kingdom, Suzan-Lori Parks

1991   **Best New American Play**
The Fever, Wallace Shawn

Playwriting
John Guare, *Six Degrees of Separation*
Mac Wellman, *Sincerity Forever*

1992   **Best New American Play (tie)**
Sight Unseen, Donald Margulies
Sally's Rape, Robbie McCauley
The Baltimore Waltz, Paula Vogel

Sustained Excellence in Playwriting
Neal Bell
Romulus Linney

1993   *Playwriting*
Harry Kondoleon, *The Houseguests*
Larry Kramer, *The Destiny of Me*
José Rivera, *Marisol*
Paul Rudnick, *Jeffrey*

1994   **Best Play**
Twilight: Los Angeles, 1992, Anna Deavere Smith

Playwriting
Eric Bogosian, Pounding Nails in the Floor with My Forehead
Howard Korder, The Lights

Sustained Achievement
Edward Albee

1995   **Best Play**
Cryptogram, David Mamet

Playwriting
David Hancock, The Convention of Cartography
Tony Kushner, Slavs!
Terrence McNally, Love! Valor! Compassion!
Susan Miller, My Left Breast

1996   **Best New American Play**
June and Jean in Concert, Adrienne Kennedy
Sleep Deprivation Chamber, Adam P. Kennedy and Adrienne Kennedy

Playwriting
Ain Gordon, Wally's Ghost
Donald Margulies, The Model Apartment
Suzan-Lori Parks, Venus
Doug Wright, Quills

1997   **Best Play**
One Flea Spare, Naomi Wallace

Playwriting
Eve Ensler, The Vagina Monologues
David Henry Hwang, Golden Child
Paula Vogel, How I Learned to Drive
Lanford Wilson, Sympathetic Magic

1998   **Best Play**
Pearls for Pigs and Benita Canova, Richard Foreman

1999   **Playwriting**
Christopher Durang, Betty's Summer Vacation
David Hancock, The Race of the Ark Tattoo

2001   **Playwriting**
José Rivera, References to Salvador Dali Make Me Hot

2002   **Playwriting**
Melissa James Gibson, [sic]
Tony Kushner, Homebody/Kabul

2003   **Lifetime Achievement**
Mac Wellman

2004   **Best New American Play**
Small Tragedy, Craig Lucas

2005   **Playwriting**
Christopher Shinn, Where Do We Live
John Patrick Shanley, Doubt
Lynn Nottage, Fabulation

2006   **Playwriting**
Rolin Jones, The Intelligent Design of Jenny Chow

2008   **Playwriting**
Horton Foote, Dividing the Estate
David Henry Hwang, Yellow Face

Lifetime Achievement
Adrienne Kennedy

2009   **Best New American Play**
Ruined, Lynn Nottage

www.villagevoice.com/obies

APPENDIX II

SELECTED BIBLIOGRAPHY

Ackerman, Alan L., Jr. *American Literature and the Nineteenth-Century Stage*. Baltimore: Johns Hopkins University Press, 1999.

Adler, Thomas P. *American Drama, 1940–1960: A Critical History*. New York: Twayne, 1994.

———. *Mirror on the Stage: The Pulitzer Plays as an Approach to American Drama*. West Lafayette, Ind.: Purdue University Press, 1987.

Anderson, John. *The American Theatre. An Interpretive History*. New York: Dial Press, 1938.

Atkinson, Brooks. *Broadway*. New York: Macmillan, 1970.

Bank, Rosemarie K. *Theatre Culture in America, 1825–1860*. Cambridge, England: Cambridge University Press, 1997.

Bentley, Eric. *The Dramatic Event: An American Chronicle*. New York: Horizon Press, 1954.

Berkowitz, Gerald M. *American Drama of the Twentieth Century*. New York: Longman, 1992.

———. *New Broadways: Theatre across America, 1950–1980*. Totowa, N.J.: Rowan and Littlefield, 1982.

Bernheim, Alfred. *The Business of the American Theatre: An Economic History of the American Theatre, 1750–1932*. 1932. New York: Benjamin Blom, 1964.

Bernstein, Samuel J. *The Strands Entwined: A New Direction in American Drama*. Boston: Northeastern University Press, 1980.

Besko, Kathleen, and Rachel Koenig, eds. *Interviews with Contemporary Women Playwrights*. New York: Beech Tree Books, 1987.

Bigsby C. W. E. *A Critical Introduction to Twentieth-Century American Drama*. Vol. 1, *1900–1940*. Cambridge, England: Cambridge University Press, 1982.

———. *A Critical Introduction to Twentieth-Century American Drama*. Vol. 2, *Williams/Miller/Albee*. Cambridge, England: Cambridge University Press, 1984.

———. *A Critical Introduction to Twentieth-Century American Drama*. Vol. 3, *Beyond Broadway*. Cambridge, England: Cambridge University Press, 1985.

———. *Modern American Drama: 1945–1990*. Cambridge, England: Cambridge University Press, 1992.

———. *Modern American Drama: 1945–2000*. Cambridge, England: Cambridge University Press, 2000.

Bigsby, Christopher. *Contemporary American Playwrights*. Cambridge, England: Cambridge University Press, 1999.

Blatanis, Konstantinos. *Popular Culture Icons in Contemporary American Drama*. Teaneck, N.J.: Fairleigh Dickinson University Press, 2003.

Bloom, Clive, ed. *American Drama*. New York: St. Martin's Press, 1995.

Bogard, Travis, Richard Moody, and Walter Meserve. *The Revels History of Drama in English—Volume VIII: American Drama*. New York: Barnes and Noble, 1977.

Bordman, Gerald. *American Theatre: A Chronicle of Comedy and Drama: 1869–1914*. New York: Oxford University Press, 1994.

———. *American Theatre: A Chronicle of Comedy and Drama: 1914–1930*. New York: Oxford University Press, 1995.

———. *American Theatre: A Chronicle of Comedy and Drama: 1930–1969*. New York: Oxford University Press, 1996.

Brater, Enoch, ed. *Feminine Focus: The New Women Playwrights*. New York: Oxford University Press, 1989.

Brietzke, Zander. *American Drama in the Age of Film*. Tuscaloosa: University of Alabama Press, 2007.

Broussard, Louis. *American Drama: Contemporary Allegory from Eugene O'Neill to Tennessee Williams*. Norman: University of Oklahoma Press, 1962.

Brown, Janet. *Taking Center Stage: Feminism in Contemporary U.S. Drama*. Metuchen, N.J.: Scarecrow Press, 1991.

Brown, Jared. *The Theatre in America during the Revolution*. Cambridge, England: Cambridge University Press, 1995.

Brustein, Robert. *Reimagining American Theatre*. New York: Hill & Wang, 1991.

Bryer, Jackson R., ed. *The Playwright's Art: Conversations with Contemporary American Dramatists*. New Brunswick, N.J.: Rutgers University Press, 1995.

Burke, Sally. *American Feminist Playwrights: A Critical History*. New York: Twayne, 1997.

Carpenter, Charles A. *Dramatists and the Bomb: American and British Playwrights Confront the Nuclear Age, 1945–1964*. Westport, Conn.: Greenwood Press, 1999.

Case, Sue-Ellen. *Feminism and Theatre*. New York: Methuen, 1988.

———. *Performing Feminisms: Feminist Critical Theory and Theatre*. Baltimore: Johns Hopkins University Press, 1990.

Chinoy, Helen Frich, and Linda Walsh Jenkins, eds. *Women in American Theatre*. Rev. ed. New York: Theatre Communications Group, 1987.

Clurman, Harold. *The Fervent Years*. New York: Knopf, 1945.

Cohn, Ruby. *Anglo-American Interplay in Recent Drama*. Cambridge, England: Cambridge University Press, 1995.

———. *Dialogue in American Drama*. Bloomington: Indiana University Press, 1971.

———. *New American Dramatists: 1960–1980*. New York: Grove Press, 1982.

Cole, Susan Letzler. *Playwrights in Rehearsal: The Seduction of Company*. New York: Routledge, 2001.

Davis, Walter A. *Get the Guests: Psychoanalysis, Modern American Drama, and the Audience*. Madison: University of Wisconsin Press, 1994.

Dawson, Gary Fisher. *Documentary Theatre in the United States: An Historical Survey and Analysis of Its Content, Form, and Stagecraft*. Westport, Conn.: Greenwood Press, 1999.

Debusscher, Gilbert, and Henry I. Schvey, eds. *New Essays on American Drama*. Amsterdam: Rodopi, 1989.

Demastes, William W., ed. *American Playwrights, 1880–1945: A Research and Production Sourcebook*. Westport, Conn.: Greenwood Press, 1995.

———. *Beyond Naturalism: A New Realism in American Theatre*. Westport, Conn.: Greenwood, 1988.

———, ed. *Realism and the American Dramatic Tradition*. Tuscaloosa: University of Alabama Press, 1996.

———, and Iris Smith Fischer, eds. *Interrogating America through Theatre and Performance*. New York: Palgrave Macmillan, 2007.

Dickinson, Thomas H. *Playwrights of the New American Theater*. New York: Macmillan, 1925.

DiGaetani, John L., ed. *A Search for a Postmodern Theater: Interviews with Contemporary Playwrights*. New York: Greenwood Press, 1991.

Dolan, Jill. *Feminist Spectator As Critic*. Ann Arbor: University of Michigan Press, 1988.

Dorman, James H. *Theatre in the Antebellum South, 1815–1861*. Chapel Hill: University of North Carolina Press, 1967.

Downer, Alan S., ed. *American Drama and Its Critics: A Collection of Critical Essays*. Chicago: University of Chicago Press, 1965.

———, ed. *The American Theater Today*. New York: Basic Books, 1967.

———. *Fifty Years of American Drama: 1900–1950*. Chicago: Henry Regnery, 1951.

Dukore, Bernard F., ed. *American Dramatists, 1918–1940*. New York: Grove/Atlantic, 1984.

Dunlap, William. *A History of the American Theatre*. 1832. Reprint, New York: Burt Franklin, 1963.

Dusenbury, Winifred. *The Theme of Loneliness in Modern American Drama*. Gainesville: University of Florida Press, 1960.

Eddleman, Floyd Eugene. *American Drama Criticism: Supplement II to the Second Edition*. Hamden, Conn.: Shoe String Press, 1989.

———. *American Drama Criticism: Supplement III to the Second Edition*. Hamden, Conn.: Shoe String Press, 1992.

Engle, Ron, and Tice L. Miller, eds. *The American Stage: Social and Economic Issues from the Colonial*

Period to the Present. Cambridge, England: Cambridge University Press, 1993.

Engle, Sherry D. *New Women Dramatists in America, 1890–1920*. New York: Palgrave Macmillan, 2007.

Erdman, Harley. *Staging the Jew*. New York: Twayne, 1997.

Falb, Lewis W. *American Drama in Paris, 1945–1970*. Chapel Hill: University of North Carolina Press, 1973.

Fearnow, Mark. *The American Stage and the Great Depression: A Cultural History of the Grotesque*. Cambridge, England: Cambridge University Press, 1997.

Fenn, J. W. *Levitating the Pentagon: Evolutions in the American Theatre of the Vietnam Era*. Newark: University of Delaware Press, 1992.

Fisher, James, and Felicia Hardison Londré. *Historical Dictionary of American Theatre: Modernism*. Lanham, Md.: Scarecrow Press, 2007.

Fisher, Judith L., and Stephen Watt, eds. *When They Weren't Doing Shakespeare: Essays on Nineteenth-Century British and American Theatre*. Athens: University of Georgia Press, 1989.

Flexner, Eleanor. *American Playwrights 1918–1938*. New York: Simon and Schuster, 1938.

Freedman, Morris. *American Drama in Social Context*. Carbondale: Southern Illinois University Press, 1971.

Frenz, Horst, ed. *American Playwrights on Drama*. New York: Hill & Wang, 1965.

Frick, John W. *Theatre, Culture and Temperance Reform in Nineteenth-Century America*. New York: Cambridge University Press, 2003.

Gagey, Edmond. *Revolution in American Drama*. New York: Columbia University Press, 1947.

Gardner, Rufus. *The Splintered Stage: The Decline of the American Theatre*. New York: Macmillan, 1965.

Gassner, John. *Theatre at the Crossroads: Plays and Playwrights of the Mid-Century American Stage*. New York: Holt, Rinehart and Winston, 1960.

Gewirtz, Arthur, and James J. Kolb, eds. *Art, Glitter, and Glitz: Mainstream Playwrights and Popular Theatre in 1920s America*. Westport, Conn.: Praeger, 2003.

———, eds. *Experimenters, Rebels, and Disparate Voices: The Theatre of the 1920s Celebrates American Diversity*. Westport, Conn.: Praeger, 2003.

Golden, Joseph. *The Death of Tinker Bell: American Theatre in the Twentieth Century*. Syracuse, N.Y.: Syracuse University Press, 1967.

Goldstein, Malcolm. *The Political Stage: American Drama and Theater of the Great Depression*. New York: Oxford University Press, 1974.

Gottfried, Martin. *A Theatre Divided: The Postwar American Stage*. Boston: Little, Brown, 1967.

Greene, Alexis, ed. *Women Who Write Plays: Interviews with American Dramatists*. Hanover, N.H.: Smith and Kraus, 2001.

Greenfield, Thomas A. *Work and the Work Ethic in American Drama, 1920–1970*. Columbia: University of Missouri Press, 1982.

Grimsted, David. *Melodrama Unveiled: American Theatre and Culture, 1800–1850*. 1968. Berkeley: University of California Press, 1987.

Hall, Roger A. *Performing the American Frontier, 1870–1906*. Cambridge, England: Cambridge University Press, 2001.

Hartman, John Geoffrey. *The Development of American Social Comedy from 1787 to 1936*. Philadelphia: University of Pennsylvania Press, 1939.

Havens, David F. *The Columbian Muse of Comedy*. Carbondale: Southern Illinois University Press, 1973.

Henderson, Mary C. *Theater in America*. New York: Harry N. Abrams, 1986.

Herman, William. *Understanding Contemporary American Drama*. Columbia: University of South Carolina Press, 1987.

Herrington, Joan, ed. *The Playwright's Muse*. New York: Routledge, 2002.

Herron, Ima Honaker. *The Small Town in American Drama*. Dallas, Tex.: Southern Methodist University Press, 1969.

Hewitt, Bernard. *Theatre U.S.A., 1965 to 1957*. New York: McGraw-Hill, 1959.

Himelstein, Morgan Y. *Drama Was a Weapon: The Left-Wing Theatre in New York—1929–1941*. New Brunswick, N.J.: Rutgers University Press, 1963.

Hischak, Thomas S. *American Theatre: A Chronicle of Comedy and Drama, 1969–2000*. New York: Oxford University Press, 2001.

Hodge, Francis. *Yankee Theatre: The Image of America on Stage, 1825–1850*. Austin: University of Texas Press, 1964.

Houchin, John H. *Censorship of the American Theatre in the Twentieth Century*. Cambridge: Cambridge University Press, 2003.

Hughes, Catherine. *Plays, Politics, and Polemics*. New York: Drama Book Specialists, 1973.

Hughes, Glenn. *A History of the American Theatre, 1700–1950.* New York: Samuel French, 1951.

Jenckes, Norma, ed. *New Readings in American Drama: Something's Happening Here.* New York: Peter Lang, 2002.

Jenkins, Ron. *Acrobats of the Soul: Comedy and Virtuosity in Contemporary American Theatre.* New York: Theatre Communications Group, 1998.

Jerz, Dennis G. *Technology in American Drama, 1920–1950: Soul and Society in the Age of the Machine.* Westport, Conn.: Greenwood Press, 2003.

Johnson, Claudia Durst. *Church and Stage: The Theatre as Target of Religious Condemnation in Nineteenth Century America.* Jefferson, N.C.: McFarland, 2008.

Kaye, Nick. *Postmodernism and Performance.* New York: Macmillan, 1994.

Kernan, Alvin B., ed. *Modern American Theatre.* Englewood Cliffs, N.J.: Prentice-Hall, 1967.

Keyssar, Helene, ed. *Feminist Theatre and Theory.* New York: St. Martin's Press, 1996.

King, Bruce, ed. *Contemporary American Theatre.* New York: St. Martin's Press, 1991.

King, Kimball, ed. *Hollywood on Stage: Playwrights Evaluate the Culture Industry.* New York: Garland, 1997.

———, ed. *Modern Dramatists: A Casebook of Major British, Irish, and American Playwrights.* New York: Routledge, 2001.

———, and Tom Fahy, eds. *Peering behind the Curtain: Disability, Illness, and the Extraordinary Body in Contemporary Theatre.* New York: Routledge, 2002.

Kolin, Philip C., ed. *American Playwrights since 1945: A Guide to Scholarship, Criticism, and Performance.* New York: Greenwood Press, 1989.

———, and Colby H. Kullman, eds. *Speaking on Stage: Interviews with Contemporary American Playwrights.* Tuscaloosa: University of Alabama Press, 1996.

Koster, Donald Nelson. *The Theme of Divorce in American Drama, 1871–1939.* Philadelphia: University of Pennsylvania Press, 1942.

Krasner, David. *American Drama 1945–2000: An Introduction.* Malden, Mass.: Blackwell, 2006.

———, ed. *A Companion to Twentieth-Century American Drama.* Malden, Mass.: Blackwell, 2005.

Krutch, Joseph Wood. *The American Drama since 1918.* Rev. ed. New York: George Braziller, 1957.

Kubiak, Anthony. *Agitated States: Performance in the American Theater of Cruelty.* Ann Arbor: University of Michigan Press, 2002.

Leiter, Samuel L. *Ten Seasons: New York Theatre in the Seventies.* New York: Greenwood Press, 1986.

Lewis, Allan. *American Plays and Playwrights of the Contemporary Theatre.* New York: Crown, 1965.

McClain, Noreen Barnes, ed. *Representations of Gender on the Nineteenth-Century American Stage.* Tuscaloosa: University of Alabama Press, 2002.

McConachie, Bruce A. *American Theater in the Culture of the Cold War: Producing and Contesting Containment, 1947–1962.* Iowa City: University of Iowa Press, 2003.

———. *Melodramatic Formations: American Theatre and Society, 1820–1870.* Iowa City: University of Iowa Press, 1992.

MacDonald, Erik. *Theater at the Margins: Text and the Post-Structured Stage.* Ann Arbor: University of Michigan Press, 1993.

McDonald, Robert L., and Linda Rohrer Page, eds. *Southern Women Playwrights: New Essays in Literary History and Criticism.* Tuscaloosa: University of Alabama Press, 2002.

McDonnell, Patricia. *On the Edge of Your Seat: Popular Theater and Film in Early Twentieth-Century American Art.* New Haven, Conn.: Yale University Press, 2002.

Marra, Kim, and Robert A. Schanke, eds. *Staging Desire: Queer Readings of American Theater History.* Ann Arbor: University of Michigan Press, 2002.

Marranca, Bonnie, and Gautam Dasgupta, eds. *Conversations on Art and Performance.* Baltimore: Johns Hopkins University Press, 1999.

Mason, Jeffrey D. *Melodrama and the Myth of America.* Bloomington: Indiana University Press, 1993.

———, and J. Ellen Gainor, eds. *Performing America: Cultural Nationalism in American Theater.* Ann Arbor: University of Michigan Press, 1999.

Maufort, Marc, ed. *Staging Difference: Cultural Pluralism in American Theatre and Drama.* New York: Peter Lang, 1995.

Meserve, Walter J. *American Drama to 1900: A Guide to Information Sources.* Detroit: Gale, 1980.

———. *An Emerging Entertainment: The Drama of the American People to 1828.* Bloomington: Indiana University Press, 1977.

———. *Heralds of Promise: The Drama of the American People in the Age of Jackson, 1829–1849.* New York: Greenwood Press, 1986.

———. *An Outline History of American Drama.* New York: Feedback Theatrebooks & Prospero Press, 1994.

Miller, Jordan Y., and Winifred L. Frazer. *American Drama between the Wars: A Critical History.* Boston: G. K. Hall, 1991.

Miller, Tice L. *Entertaining the Nation: American Drama in the Eighteenth and Nineteenth Centuries.* Carbondale: Southern Illinois University Press, 2007.

Moody, Richard. *America Takes the Stage: Romanticism in American Drama and Theatre.* Bloomington: University of Indiana Press, 1955.

Mordden, Eric. *The American Theatre.* New York: Oxford University Press, 1981.

Moses, Montrose J., and John Mason Brown, eds. *The American Theatre as Seen by Its Critics, 1752–1934.* New York: W. W. Norton, 1934.

Murphy, Brenda. *American Realism and American Drama, 1880–1940.* Cambridge, England: Cambridge University Press, 1987.

———, ed. *The Cambridge Companion to American Women Playwrights.* Cambridge, England: Cambridge University Press, 1999.

———. *Congressional Theatre: Dramatizing McCarthyism on Stage, Film, and Television.* Cambridge, England: Cambridge University Press, 1999.

———, ed. *Twentieth-Century American Drama.* 4 vols. London: Routledge, 2006.

Nathans, Heather S. *Early American Theatre from the Revolution to Thomas Jefferson: Into the Hands of the People.* Cambridge, England: Cambridge University Press, 2003.

———. *Slavery and Sentiment on the American Stage, 1787–1861: Lifting the Veil of Black.* Cambridge and New York: Cambridge University Press, 2009.

Novick, Julius. *Beyond Broadway: The Quest for Permanent Theatres.* New York: Hill & Wang, 1968.

Ozieblo, Barbara, and Maria Dolores Narbona-Carrión, eds. *Codifying the National Self: Spectators, Actors, and the American Dramatic Text.* Brussels: P. I. E.—Peter Lang, 2006.

———, and Miriam López-Rodríguez, eds. *Staging a Cultural Paradigm: The Political and the Personal in American Drama.* New York: Peter Lang, 2002.

Palmer, Helen, and Jane A. Dyson. *American Dramatic Criticism, Interpolations, 1890–1965, Inclusive of American Drama since the First Play Produced in America.* Hamden, Conn.: Shoe String Press, 1967.

———. *American Drama Criticism, Supplement I.* Hamden, Conn.: Shoe String Press, 1970.

Poggi, Jack. *Theatre in America: The Impact of Economic Forces—1870–1967.* Ithaca, N.Y.: Cornell University Press, 1968.

Porter, Thomas E. *Myth and Modern American Drama.* Detroit, Mich.: Wayne State University Press, 1969.

Proehl, Geoffrey S. *Coming Home Again: American Family Drama and the Figure of the Prodigal.* Madison, N.J.: Fairleigh Dickinson University Press, 1997.

Quinn, Arthur Hobson. *A History of the American Drama: From the Beginning to the Civil War.* 2d ed. 1943. New York: Appleton-Century-Crofts, 1951.

———. *A History of the American Drama: From the Civil War to the Present Day.* Rev. ed. 1936. New York: Appleton-Century-Crofts, 1955.

Rabkin, Gerald. *Drama and Commitment: Politics in the American Theatre of the Thirties.* Bloomington: Indiana University Press, 1964.

Rankin, Hugh F. *The Theater in Colonial America.* Chapel Hill: University of North Carolina Press, 1965.

Richards, Jeffrey H. *Theatre Enough: American Culture and the Metaphor of the World Stage, 1607–1789.* Durham, N.C.: Duke University Press, 1991.

Richardson, Gary A. *American Drama from the Colonial Period through World War I: A Critical History.* New York: Twayne, 1993.

Robinson, Marc. *The American Play: 1787–2000.* New Haven, Conn.: Yale University Press, 2009.

———. *The Other American Drama.* Cambridge, England: Cambridge University Press, 1994.

Roudané, Matthew. *American Drama since 1960: A Critical History.* New York: Twayne, 1996.

———, ed. *Public Issues, Private Tensions: Contemporary American Drama.* New York: AMS Press, 1993.

Saal, Ilka. *New Deal Theater: The Vernacular Tradition in American Political Theater.* New York: Palgrave Macmillan, 2007.

Salem, James M. *A Guide to Critical Reviews: Part I: American Drama, 1909–1969.* Metuchen, N.J.: Scarecrow Press, 1973.

Savran, David, ed. *In Their Own Words: Contemporary American Playwrights.* New York: Theatre Communications Group, 1988.

———, ed. *The Playwright's Voice.* New York: Theatre Communications Group, 1999.

———. *A Queer Sort of Materialism: Recontextualizing American Theater.* Ann Arbor: University of Michigan Press, 2003.

Scanlan, Tom. *Family, Drama, and American Dreams.* Westport, Conn.: Greenwood Press, 1978.

Scharine, Richard G. *From Class to Caste in American Drama: Political and Social Themes since the 1930s.* New York: Greenwood Press, 1991.

Schlueter, June, ed. *Modern American Drama: The Female Canon.* Teaneck, N.J.: Fairleigh Dickinson University Press, 1990.

Schroeder, Patricia R. *The Feminist Possibilities of Dramatic Realism.* Teaneck, N.J.: Fairleigh Dickinson University Press, 1996.

———. *The Presence of the Past in Modern American Drama.* Teaneck, N.J.: Fairleigh Dickinson University Press, 1989.

Schulman, Sarah. *Stagestruck: Theater, AIDS, and the Marketing of Gay America.* Durham, N.C.: Duke University Press, 1998.

Seller, Maxine Schwartz, ed. *Ethnic Theatre in the United States.* Westport, Conn.: Greenwood Press, 1983.

Shaffer, Jason. *Performing Patriotism: National Identity in the Colonial and Revolutionary American Theatre.* Philadelphia: University of Pennsylvania Press, 2007.

Shaland, Irene. *American Theater and Drama Research: An Annotated Guide to Information Sources, 1945–1990.* Jefferson, N.C.: McFarland, 1991.

Shank, Theodore. *Beyond the Boundaries: American Alternative Theatre.* Ann Arbor: University of Michigan Press, 2000.

Shatsky, Joel, and Michael Taub, eds. *Contemporary Jewish-American Dramatists and Poets: A Bio-Critical Sourcebook.* Westport, Conn.: Greenwood Press, 1999.

Sievers, W. David. *Freud on Broadway: A History of Psychoanalysis and the American Drama.* New York: Hermitage House, 1955.

Smiley, Sam. *The Drama of Attack: Didactic Plays of the American Depression.* Columbia: University of Missouri Press, 1972.

Smith, Susan Harris. *American Drama: The Bastard Art.* Cambridge, England: Cambridge University Press, 1997.

Stanley, William T. *Broadway in the West End: An Index of Reviews of American Theatre in London, 1950–1975.* Westport, Conn.: Greenwood Press, 1978.

Szilassy, Zoltán. *American Theater of the 1960s.* Carbondale: Southern Illinois University Press, 1986.

Taylor, Karen Malpede. *People's Theatre in Amerika.* New York: Drama Book Specialists, 1972.

Taylor, William E., ed. *Modern American Drama: Essays in Criticism.* DeLand, Fla.: Everett/Edwards, 1968.

Vanden Heuvel, Michael. *Performing Drama/Dramatizing Performance.* Ann Arbor: University of Michigan Press, 1991.

Vaughn, Jack A. *Early American Dramatists from the Beginnings to 1900.* New York: Frederick Ungar, 1981.

Vorlicky, Robert. *Act like a Man: Challenging Masculinities in American Drama.* Ann Arbor: University of Michigan Press, 1995.

Wainscott, Ronald H. *The Emergence of the Modern American Theater, 1914–1929.* New Haven, Conn.: Yale University Press, 1997.

Watson, Charles S. *The History of Southern Drama.* Lexington: University Press of Kentucky, 1997.

Weales, Gerald. *American Drama since World War II.* New York: Harcourt, Brace and World, 1962.

———. *The Jumping Off-Place: American Drama in the 1960s.* New York: Macmillan, 1969.

Wertheim, Albert. *Staging the War: American Drama and World War II.* Bloomington: Indiana University Press, 2004.

Wilmer, S. E. *Theatre, Society and the Nation: Staging American Identities.* Cambridge: Cambridge University Press, 2002.

Wilmeth, Don B., and Christopher Bigsby, eds. *The Cambridge History of American Theatre.* Vol. 1, *Beginnings to 1870.* Cambridge, England: Cambridge University Press, 1998.

———, eds. *The Cambridge History of American Theatre.* Vol. 2, *1870–1945.* Cambridge, England: Cambridge University Press, 1999.

———, eds. *The Cambridge History of American Theatre.* Vol. 3, *Post–World War II to the 1990s.* Cambridge, England: Cambridge University Press, 2000.

Wilson, Garff B. *Three Hundred Years of American Drama and Theatre: From "Ye Bare and Ye Cubb" to "Hair."* Englewood Cliffs, N.J.: Prentice-Hall, 1973.

Witham, Barry B., ed. *Theatre in the United States: A Documentary History.* Vol. 1, *1750–1915, Theatre in the Colonies and the United States.* Cambridge, England: Cambridge University Press, 1996.

Wolter, Jürgen C., ed. *The Dawning of American Drama: American Dramatic Criticism, 1746–1915.* Westport, Conn.: Greenwood Press, 1993.

Zeigler, Joseph Wesley. *Regional Theatre: The Revolutionary Stage.* Minneapolis: University of Minnesota Press, 1973.

LIST OF CONTRIBUTORS

Susan C. W. Abbotson, Rhode Island College

Thomas P. Adler, Purdue University

Laurence G. Avery, University of North Carolina–Chapel Hill

Judith E. Barlow, State University of New York at Albany

Claudia Barnett, Middle Tennessee State University

Sarah Bay-Cheng, Colgate University

Christopher Brooks Bell, Georgia Military College

Robin Seaton Brown, University of North Carolina–Chapel Hill

Cheryl Black, University of Missouri

Karen C. Blansfield, University of North Carolina–Chapel Hill

William C. Boles, Rollins College

Martha Gilman Bower, Indiana University of Pennsylvania

Matthew S. Caballero, University of California–Davis

Paul N. Calvert, Georgia State University

Maria Ghira Renu Cappelli, University of California–Berkeley

Jonathan L. Chambers, Bowling Green State University

Craig Clinton, Reed College

Susan S. Cole, Appalachian State University

Timothy D. Conners, Central Michigan University

Mark Cosdon, Allegheny College

Nena Couch, Ohio State University

Scott T. Cummings, Boston College

Mary L. Cutler, University of North Dakota

Joan FitzPatrick Dean, University of Missouri–Kansas City

Kurt Eisen, Tennessee Tech University

Harry J. Elam Jr., Stanford University

Mark W. Estrin, Rhode Island College

Mark Fearnow, Hanover College

James Fisher, University of North Carolina at Greensboro

Leonard Fleischer, Brooklyn, New York

Brenda Foley, Marlboro College

Glenda Frank, New York, New York

Joseph E. Gawel, Temple University

Luc Gilleman, Smith College

Jan Goggans, University of California–Davis

Douglas W. Gordy, Walnut Creek, California

Kathleen M. Gough, University of California–Berkeley

Christine R. Gray, The Community College of Baltimore County

Robert F. Gross, Hobart and William Smith Colleges

Mary C. Henderson, Congers, New York

Helen Huff, City University of New York—Borough of Manhattan Community College

Dan Isaac, New York, New York

Philip M. Isaacs, New York, New York

Jeff Johnson, Brevard Community College

Elizabeth S. Kim, University of Wisconsin–Whitewater

Kimball King, University of North Carolina–Chapel Hill

Karl Kippola, American University

Philip C. Kolin, University of Southern Mississippi

Gary Konas. University of Wisconsin–La Crosse

Colby H. Kullman, University of Mississippi

Claire Leich-Galland, City University of New York

Thomas Leuchtenmüller, München, Germany

Dina L. Longhitano, University of Maryland

Jeffrey B. Loomis, Northwest Missouri State University

Jennifer Madden, Brown University

Michael J. Mendelsohn, University of Tampa

John Paul Middlesworth, University of North Carolina–Chapel Hill

Brenda Murphy, University of Connecticut

Heather Nathans, University of Maryland

Michael M. O'Hara, Ball State University

Estefania Olid-Peña, Georgia State University

Elizabeth A. Osborne, Florida State University

Gene A. Plunka, University of Memphis

Laurin R. Porter, University of Texas–Arlington

David Radavich, Eastern Illinois University

Sarah Reuning, University of North Carolina–Chapel Hill

Brian Richardson, University of Maryland

Gary A. Richardson, Mercer University

Roxane Rix, Kutztown University of Pennsylvania

Jon D. Rossini, University of California–Davis

Matthew Roudané, Georgia State University

Yvonne Shafer, St. John's University

Robert Lewis Smith, Kutztown University of Pennsylvania

Valerie Rae Smith, Messiah College

Arvid F. Sponberg, Valparaiso University

Tony J. Stafford, University of Texas–El Paso

Jennifer Stiles, Boston College

Richard K. Tharp, University of Maryland

Michael Vanden Heuvel, University of Wisconsin–Madison

Ralph F. Voss, University of Alabama

Dwight Watson, Wabash College

Christopher J. Wheatley, The Catholic University of America

Philip Middleton Williams, Miami, Florida

Evan D. Winet, Cornell University

Gerald C. Wood, Carson–Newman College

Harvey Young Jr., Northwestern University

Philip Zwerling, Ursinus College

INDEX